Introduction to Federal Income Taxation in Canada

39th Edition, 2018-2019

By

Robert E. Beam, FCPA, FCA
Professor Emeritus, University of Waterloo

Stanley N. Laiken, Ph.D., CPA (Honorary)
Professor Emeritus, University of Waterloo

James J. Barnett, FCPA, FCA
University of Waterloo

Nathalie Johnstone, MPAcc, FCPA, FCA
University of Saskatchewan

Devan Mescall, Ph.D., CPA, CA
University of Saskatchewan

Julie Robson, MAcc, CPA, CA, CPA (Illinois)
University of Waterloo

Contributors

Thomas Haddrath, CPA, CMA

Christy MacDonald, Ph.D., CPA, CA
Deloitte, Kitchener

Barbara Rockx, MAcc, CPA, CA
University of Toronto

Wolters Kluwer
300-90 Sheppard Avenue East
Toronto Ontario
M2N 6X1

1 800 268 4522
wolterskluwer.ca

Wolters Kluwer

Published by Wolters Kluwer Canada Limited

Library and Archives Canada has catalogued this publication as follows:

Beam, Robert E.

Introduction to federal income taxation in Canada / by Robert E. Beam, Stanley N. Laiken, James Barnett, Nathalie Johnstone, Devan Mescall, Julie Robson

1980/81 ed.–

ISSN 0821-5340

ISBN 978-1-55496-987-6 (39th edition, 2018/2019)

1. Income tax — Canada. 2. Income tax — Problems, exercises, etc.

I. Laiken, Stanley – II. Barnett, James

III. Wolters Kluwer Canada Limited IV. Title

KE5759.B43 343.7105'2 C83-030860-1

KF6370.B43

ISBN: 978-1-55496-987–6

Typeset by Wolters Kluwer Canada Limited.

Printed in Canada.

¶1,120.40 Flexibility

At the same time, the income tax system must be sufficiently flexible to permit its use as an instrument of economic policy to achieve specified economic objectives. Of course, what might be considered economically desirable may not be politically feasible. For example, the Carter Commission recommendation to achieve horizontal equity by taxing all sources of economic gain equally, because "a buck is a buck", was apparently rejected for political reasons.

¶1,120.50 Certainty

Certainty means that taxpayers know in advance the tax consequences of any transaction so that they may plan their affairs accordingly. The taxpayer must be in a position to understand and determine with some certainty the payer of the tax, the base of the tax, the amount of the tax, the deadline for payment of the tax, and the method of payment. There are many areas of uncertainty in the Canadian tax system, mostly due to the fact that all sources of income are not taxed in the same way. For example, employment income may be subject to a less favourable tax treatment than business income; however, the distinction between an employee and a self-employed person is often difficult to make and creates uncertainty as to the tax treatment that applies in a particular situation. If the tax treatment of employment income and business income were the same, there would be less uncertainty. In order to mitigate the risk of uncertainty, the CRA provides taxpayers with the opportunity to apply for an advance tax ruling on transactions they propose to undertake. However, it is difficult to provide complete certainty when complex transactions are undertaken.

¶1,120.60 Simplicity and Compliance

The Canadian tax system is based on self-assessment, which means that taxpayers are required to assess their income tax and file the appropriate income tax return on an annual basis. The CRA then assesses the return and has the power to investigate and make changes when inaccuracies or omissions are found. In order to ensure compliance by taxpayers and limit the number of investigations and reassessments, the tax system must be simple. Ideally, individuals with simple tax situations should not be compelled to seek professional advice to prepare their returns.

Naturally, a tax system is expected to have some degree of complexity, particularly with regard to business transactions. It should not, however, be so complex that only a limited number of tax professionals can understand how it works. This level of complexity seems to vary. In some areas there appears to be tax simplification, especially as it relates to an individual earning salary income. On the other hand, complexity seems to be the direction that the Act is taking in some areas, such as the rules on forgiveness of debt and foreign investments. When taxpayers and government officials can no longer apply the provisions of the Act without professional assistance, the degree of dissatisfaction towards the system increases and may incite tax avoidance and tax evasion.

As is the case with the certainty objective, it is difficult to provide simplicity when complex transactions are undertaken.

¶1,120.70 Feasibility and Efficiency

Administration of the tax must be feasible and efficient. Thus, the total costs, including those to the taxpayer, of administering and collecting the tax should be as low as possible. The costs of administration and collection of the Canadian income tax are very low when compared with those of other countries.

created by the taxpayer in moving it from one stage of production or distribution to another.

¶1,110.20 Incidence of the Tax

Another method of classifying taxes is by the incidence of the tax, which determines the taxpayer who ultimately bears the tax.

The incidence of a direct tax is likely to be on the initial payer of the tax. For example, the burden of the individual income tax is generally considered to be on the individual who pays the tax. While an income tax may be paid by a corporation, the incidence of the tax may be on customers, suppliers, employees, or shareholders of the corporation, depending on its economic ability to pass the tax on to the others.

The incidence of an indirect tax is usually not on the initial payer of the tax, but is on someone else. A sales tax imposed at the manufacturer's level is an example of such an indirect tax.

¶1,110.30 Nature of the Tax

Finally, taxes can be classified by the nature of the tax levy. A proportional or flat tax is levied at a constant percentage of the income of the payer of the tax. Under certain conditions, the corporate income tax can be considered as such a tax. A progressive tax is levied at an increasing percentage of the income of the payer, as is the case of the personal income tax. Similarly, a regressive tax is levied at a decreasing percentage of the income of the payer. A sales tax is considered to be a regressive tax to the extent that those with higher income may spend a lower proportion of that income on the item subject to the sales tax.

¶1,120 Desirable Characteristics of a Tax

¶1,120.10 Horizontal Equity

One of the most important principles of a tax system is that it be fair. An income tax should be equitable on two dimensions. It should be equitable horizontally so that persons at the same economic level are affected by the tax to the same degree in terms of the amount of tax, irrespective of the form of income generated. A taxpayer who earns $100,000 in salary should pay the same amount of tax as one who earns $100,000 in investment income.

¶1,120.20 Vertical Equity

An income tax should also be equitable vertically so that persons at a higher economic level pay a greater share of the tax based on their greater ability to pay than those at a lower economic level. This implies that persons with income levels of $100,000 should proportionally pay more tax than those who earn $25,000, because they have at their disposal more funds in excess of what is required to satisfy their personal needs.

¶1,120.30 Neutrality

An income tax should be neutral so that the tax does not affect economic decisions. For the tax system to be considered neutral, a decision based on the after-tax results of an economic opportunity should not be any different than it would have been in the absence of taxation. Where a tax system provides incentives that affect business or personal decisions, the tax system becomes less than neutral.

¶1,090 Pause and Reflect — Summary of Learning Goals

After working through this section, ¶1,000, you should be able to:

- Explain the different roles that professional accountants and lawyers may play in providing tax services.

¶1,100 Tax Principles and Concepts

Overview

Although tax often has a negative connotation because it requires a taxpayer to give up some of their wealth, good tax policy is essential to a well-functioning society. Tax in some form is necessary, as it provides a government with the revenue required to operate. There are many different ways to structure a tax. The form a tax takes can have an impact on different taxpayers and the economy in various ways. Therefore, tax policy is important to a society and can create a competitive advantage or disadvantage for the country *vis-à-vis* other tax regimes. As individuals with extensive knowledge of tax policies, it is important that professional accountants understand the impact that tax policies and tax changes may have on taxpayers, and, more broadly, on government revenues and the economy. This allows them not only to provide insights to their clients, but also to participate in the public discourse on policy proposals.

After working through this section, ¶1,100, you will be able to:

- Know the principles that make good tax policy.
- Apply your knowledge of the principles of good tax policy to assess prospective tax policies.

¶1,110 Classification of Taxes

¶1,110.10 Basis of the Tax

Taxes can be classified in a number of different ways. One such method is the basis of the tax, with the name of the tax reflecting to some extent the tax base or what is to be taxed.

Head tax: A tax on the existence of a particular type of taxpayer, such as a tax of $X paid by all individuals over the age of 18.

Income tax: A tax on the income of the taxpayer, as is exemplified by a tax on the income of individuals or corporations.

Wealth tax: A tax on capital gains or succession duties, or a tax on the accumulated capital of a taxpayer.

Commodity tax: A tax on the consumption of the commodity subject to tax, as is the case of a provincial retail sales tax.

User tax: A toll for a bridge or road; a tax on the use of a facility or service.

Tariff: A tax or duty usually imposed on imported goods to increase the price of such goods relative to domestic goods.

Transfer tax: A tax on the value of property transferred from one owner to another, as is the case on the transfer of land under certain conditions.

Business transfer tax: A value-added tax, or a multi-stage sales tax, such as the goods and services tax or harmonized sales tax, is a tax on the increase in value of a commodity

Learning Goals

Know, Understand and Explain

By the end of this chapter you will know, understand and be able to explain:

- The different roles that professional accountants and lawyers may play in providing tax services.
- The principles that make good tax policy.
- How the perspective on income differs among economic analysis, financial reporting, and the *Income Tax Act*.
- How tax policy is created in Canada.
- The appeals process in the Canadian tax system.
- Strategies for interpreting the *Income Tax Act*.
- How to reference the *Income Tax Act*.
- The common sources of tax rules and sources for interpretation in the Canadian tax system.

Exercises

¶1,850 in the Study Guide

Apply

By the end of this chapter you will be able to apply your knowledge and understanding to:

- Assess the attributes of prospective tax policies.

Assignment Problems

¶1,875 in the Study Guide

Overview

This chapter provides an introduction to the essential concepts and skills required to learn and practice tax.

- First, it provides an introduction to the practice of tax for professional accountants and discusses key tax services which a professional accountant may be called on to provide.
- Second, it provides an introduction to the principles and concepts of taxation, specifically *income* taxation.
- Third, it provides a description of the Canadian tax system, including its historical roots as well as the legal and administrative structures on which it is built and operates.
- Fourth is a discussion of the basics of tax research, including both guidance on interpretation of the *Income Tax Act* (the "Act")[1] as well as a description of primary and secondary sources of tax guidance.

---

[1] Unless otherwise stated, all statutory references are to the *Income Tax Act*, R.S.C. 1985, c. 1 (5th Supplement), as amended (referred to as the "Act").

Table of Contents

Acknowledgements

Over the years, many people have participated in the preparation, revision, and improvement of these materials. The authors would like to acknowledge their indebtedness to all who have helped in this undertaking. The Institute of Chartered Accountants of Ontario (as it was then called) funded the initial concept and application of these materials. Students in the School of Accounting and Finance, including the Master of Taxation program of the University of Waterloo, have provided invaluable assistance in revising and polishing the final manuscript for each edition. In addition, a number of our colleagues teaching either full-time or part-time at various universities and colleges have made most helpful comments for the improvement of this book.

Many contributors have provided text materials or problems, which were added to the book and helped with annual revisions and updates. More recently, a special thanks to Barb Rockx, who has updated the integrated case problems, and to Thomas Haddrath, who has updated the sample exam questions.

As a result of the continuous change in materials on taxation, all editions require extensive revisions. A considerable burden was placed, as usual, on the Editorial Department of Wolters Kluwer Limited. The authors would like to acknowledge Shauna Biemann, Kristen Charles-Vardon, Lauren Shorser, Bradley Smith, Kelly Bettencourt, and many others on the Editorial Team, as well as the Production and Quality Control teams, who made the 39th edition of the text a reality. This was a significant undertaking within a short timeframe. We would also like to thank other key members of the Wolters Kluwer team who made significant contributions to the success of the book: Caroline Cobham, Ken Brakel, Tara Isard, and Natasha Menon.

In an undertaking of this nature, our family members have had to bear a burden that is often unrecognized, and certainly unrewarded. We greatly appreciate their contribution of patience and understanding to the preparation of this book because, without them, there would be nothing!

June 2018

Robert E. Beam

Stanley N. Laiken

James J. Barnett

Nathalie Johnstone

Devan Mescall

Julie Robson

Note on Legislation for Thirty-Ninth Edition

The 39th edition of the book has been updated to include proposed and enacted legislation up to and including the March 22, 2018 Notice of Ways and Means Motion (NWMM), which contains selected measures from the February 27, 2018 federal Budget. Although the NWMM is not referred to in this edition, the federal Budget proposals covered by the NWMM motion have been referenced.

need to be able to blend a number of complex provisions into a comprehensive plan to accomplish the goals of your client or employer.

At the beginning of each chapter of this book we will provide you with what you should know, understand and explain, and be able to apply as a result of studying that chapter.

Materials at the introductory level on Canadian income tax legislation are not easy to study. A conscientious effort to do the work and, particularly, to do problems and apply what has been read is essential to a good understanding of this material. The authors have attempted to meet the challenge of presenting the material by setting out the work that must be done and by explaining, as best they can, the major provisions of the legislation. The challenge of learning the material is, of course, left to the student.

June 2018

Robert E. Beam

Stanley N. Laiken

James J. Barnett

Nathalie Johnstone

Devan Mescall

Julie Robson

Review Questions

A set of review questions is provided for each chapter in the Study Guide that accompanies this book. These short-answer questions attempt to review key points made in the text or points that are not integrated into the example problems, multiple choice questions, exercises, or assignment problems in the chapter. Discussion notes on the review questions are provided in the Study Guide.

Multiple Choice Questions

Since multiple choice questions are common in professional examinations and can be very helpful in learning specific provisions of the Act, this textbook provides six or seven such questions covering the material in Chapters 2 to 19 for each of those chapters in the Study Guide, for a total of over 100 questions. Annotated solutions are provided to enhance learning through self-study. These solutions can be found in the Study Guide.

Exercises

Exercises have been provided for each chapter in the Study Guide. These usually consist of short problems to highlight particular areas of the chapter. They are designed to be fairly narrow in scope, to provide the student with an opportunity to apply the material in the chapter to a specific problem situation. Solutions to these exercises have been provided in the Study Guide that accompanies this book.

Assignment Problems

Assignment problems are provided in the Study Guide for each chapter of these materials. These problems are designed to have the student apply the material discussed in each chapter to an actual fact or problem situation. While these problems focus on the key elements of the chapter in much the same way that the solved example problems in the commentary do, the problems are not identical in their coverage or presentation. As a result, it will be necessary for the student to read the assignment problems very carefully in preparing a solution. Solutions to these problems are not available.

Suggested Approach

The authors suggest the following approach to the use of these materials. First, the students should identify the issue in an assignment problem that they need to research, then scan the headings of the particular chapter and use them to look for the topics that relate to that issue. Once the relevant parts of the chapter are identified, they should read the commentary, including any referenced material such as sections of the Act or Regulations and CRA publications. Reviewing any example problems to see how the provisions work will also help develop understanding. The solutions provided for these problems will demonstrate the approach that can be taken for the type of example problem under consideration. The solutions can also be used as a check on the student's understanding as well as a means of providing further interpretation and explanation of the material covered. The exercises at the end of the chapter can be used in a similar manner. Once the parts of a chapter have been completed in this manner, the student should be sufficiently prepared to attempt the assignment problems relevant to a particular part or to the whole chapter. When reviewing material for examination or other purposes, the multiple choice questions and the exercise problems that are similar to assignment problems at the end of each chapter can be attempted. The solutions in the Study Guide can then be checked. Review might also focus on the approaches used to address the various types of problems presented.

Learning Goals

To be a successful tax adviser it is not enough to just know the technical material found in the Act and supporting materials. You need to understand the purpose behind the rules so you can explain to others why your tax plan does not violate either the provision as it is written or purpose behind the provision. You also

designed to present situations which will help students to focus their attention on the reading and understanding of a particular provision or set of provisions with the objective of developing more generalized skills to be used in the interpretation of the Act.

To help the student deal with problems and cases in this way, a note on "Identifying Tax-Related Issues" is provided in the first section of the Study Guide, following the Table of Contents. In addition, to help the student learn how to read and interpret the Act, a note on "Reading the *Income Tax Act*" is provided in that first section of the Study Guide.

References

References are provided in the outer margin of the text beside the paragraphs to which they pertain. These references are to the following sources:

(1) ITA refers to the sections of the *Income Tax Act* to be discussed in the chapter;

(2) ITR refers to the Income Tax Regulations, which are also found in the volume containing the Act;

(3) ETA refers to sections of the *Excise Tax Act*, in which provisions of the Goods and Services Tax (GST)/ Harmonized Sales Tax (HST) can be found;

(4) IT, IC, and ATR refer, respectively, to Interpretation Bulletins, Information Circulars, and Advance Tax Rulings and are available on the CRA's website;

(5) ITTN refers to Income Tax Technical News releases that are published by the CRA intermittently to provide current technical interpretation;

(6) *Folios* refers to *Income Tax Folios* which are being published by the CRA in chapters by topic to update and replace ITs and ITTNs; and

(7) Cda-U.S. TT refers to the *Canada–United States Income Tax Convention (1980)*.

An explanation of these references is provided at the beginning of Chapter 1. References to sections of the Act are provided for exercises and assignment problems. It should also be understood that in the course of their use within the paragraph of the text, all references preceded by such specific terms as "section", "subsection", "paragraph", "subparagraph", etc., without any indication of the pertinent statute, refer to the provisions of the *Income Tax Act*. Similarly, the provisions of the Income Tax Regulations are preceded by the term "Regulation" without specifying the relevant legislation. In the margin, these references are preceded by "ITA" and "ITR", respectively.

References to the *Excise Tax Act* are usually part of Chapter 20 of the text and are specifically indicated as being to that legislation. References in the margin are preceded by "ETA".

Acronyms

An alphabetical list of acronyms used in the book appears in the first section of the Study Guide immediately following the Table of Contents. The list provides the meaning of the acronym and paragraph references where the term is used in the textbook.

Practise What You've Learned

Throughout each chapter the authors have provided a list of review, multiple choice, and exercise questions which students can use to practice the topics they have just reviewed. These have been strategically placed to enable the student to pause and practice their understanding of the materials they have just covered. This will enable students to make more efficient use of the study guide.

About This Book

How the Text Is Organized

The study of Canadian federal income taxation is made more complex if there is a lack of organization in the presentation of these materials for systematic study. While the *Income Tax Act* (the Act), the statute governing the federal taxation of income in Canada, is organized generally by source of income, some interpretive material available to students at the introductory level is often organized by topics which may cover elements of several sources.

Since the authors of these materials feel that it is important to the understanding of the Act that the student generally studies the major provisions of the statute in sequence, the chapters of this book generally follow the organization of the Act. The purpose of these materials is to guide the student in the study at the introductory level of the major provisions of the Act and some of the related provisions in the *Excise Tax Act* (the ETA) pertaining to the Goods and Services Tax/Harmonized Sales Tax. A copy of the Act, whether in paper or electronic format, and access to the Canada Revenue Agency's (CRA's) publications are considered to be important supplemental materials for the course. The purpose is to organize the student's reference to interpretive material in the order of presentation in the Act. This book is designed to encourage students to refer to the Act, case law, and the CRA's publications. CRA publications are available at no charge on the CRA website: www.cra-arc.gc.ca.

The Importance of Problem Material

The commentary presented in this book highlights key areas of the Act. The textbook provides additional interpretation of particularly difficult provisions of the Act or elements of the common law or case law in the area. The basic concepts and principles underlying the rules of the legislation are emphasized throughout these materials. Most important for the study of income taxation, it provides fact situations or example problems which demonstrate the application of the provisions of the Act to realistic situations. In fact, the primary teaching approach used in this book is the presentation of example problems and exercises with solutions. These solutions demonstrate various methods of approaching actual problems in income taxation. The solutions also provide explanatory and interpretive notes, which are an important component of these materials, often expanding a topic beyond the confines of the particular facts under discussion.

Materials that may go beyond what might be expected of an entry-level professional accountant are preceded by an "Advanced" icon (Ⓐ).

The authors must emphasize that these materials are in no way intended to be a substitute for the Act. Students should read the Act not only for the purpose of becoming familiar with a particular provision under study, but also for the purpose of learning how to read and interpret the legislation in general. These materials are

¶1,120.80 How Does the Canadian Income Tax Measure Up?

Familiarity with the specifics of the Canadian income tax legislation will facilitate an evaluation of its characteristics relative to these ideal characteristics.

At the outset of its report on tax simplification,[3] the House of Commons Standing Committee on Finance and Economic Affairs made the following general observations on the current Canadian tax system.

> In addition to raising revenue efficiently, the ideal tax system is equitable and simple, and it assists the promotion of economic growth. Unfortunately, the goals of the ideal tax system often conflict. Changes made to make the system more equitable or to increase economic growth may make the system less simple. In fact since the early 1970s the trade-offs between equity and simplicity and between growth and simplicity have been quite one-sided: if one of the goals had to give, it was always simplicity. The result, of course, is a Tax Act that even experts find confusing and a tax form for the average taxpayer that is daunting in length and complexity.
>
> Any tax system is defined by six characteristics:
>
> 1. who pays the tax,
> 2. the base to be taxed,
> 3. the rates to be applied to the base,
> 4. general exemptions,
> 5. general deductions, and
> 6. other selective measures [including how and when the tax is to be paid].
>
> The nature of the six characteristics determines how much revenue is produced by the tax system, as well as the equity of the system and its ability to promote growth. It is the exemptions, deductions and other selective tax measures that make modern tax systems so complicated. There are in Canada, for example, over one hundred selective tax measures dealing with personal income tax. There are even more measures dealing with corporate tax.
>
> The *Income Tax Act* includes the tax measures, and the tax forms must allow for them. Too often the tax system is changed — the changes rationalized in terms of improved equity or economic growth — with no attention to the possible increased complexity of the Tax Act and tax forms. The Act and forms are treated as matters that can take care of themselves — an attitude that provides no check on the ever-increasing complexity of the Tax Act and tax forms. The Committee believes that the analysis of the tax system must be realigned with attention devoted to simplifying both the Act and the forms.

¶1,190 Pause and Reflect — Summary of Learning Goals

After working through this section, ¶1,100, you should be able to:

---

[3] This report was released on June 19, 1986.

- Know the principles that make good tax policy.
- Apply your knowledge of the principles of good tax policy to assess prospective tax policies.

¶1,200 Introduction to Income Tax

Overview

Although we have a variety of taxes in Canada, the discussion in this book focuses primarily on federal income tax and the GST/HST. An introduction to the concept of income and the provisions of the *Income Tax Act* are discussed below.

After working through this section, ¶1,200, you will be able to:

- Understand how the perspective on income differs among economic analysis, financial reporting, and the *Income Tax Act*.

¶1,210 Approaches to Defining Income

Overview

Surprisingly, there is no formal definition of the word "income" in the Act. Section 3 might be considered the closest to a definition, although it really provides a set of rules for aggregating a taxpayer's income from various sources. Since there is no statutory definition, it is customary in legal practice to refer to prior judicial decisions which may define the term or which may have referred to a standard dictionary to establish the ordinary meaning of the word. The *Concise Oxford English Dictionary* defines "income" as "the money or other assets received, esp. periodically or in a year, from one's business, lands, work, investments, etc.". While income is usually thought of as a monetary receipt or currency, it may take the form of "money's worth", that is, something of commercial value such as gold, shares, wheat, etc.

ITA: 3 Income for taxation year

The Act has a unique purpose in its calculation of income: to provide a basis for taxation. Naturally, it requires application of its own rules in that computation. However, the Act's perspective on income has been influenced by the concept of income from the perspective of the economist as well as the perspective of Generally Accepted Accounting Principles.

¶1,210.10 The Economist's Perspective

Economist Adam Smith considered income to be "net" income, that is, gross revenues less expenses incurred to produce revenues. This is a basic principle of the Canadian income tax system. Adam Smith's concept of income was limited to the three sources of rent, profit, and wages. Excluded from income were capital gains, windfalls, and gifts. In more recent years, the economist's concept of income has been broadened to include all net increases in economic power between two points in time. This would include gains of all kinds and imputed income. To impute means "to assign a value of something by inference from the value of the products or processes to which it contributes".[4] Imputed income requires a calculation of income where value was created or enjoyed by the taxpayer, but a formal receipt of currency may not have taken place or been recorded. An example of imputed income would be the value of a tax professor's labour in preparing his or her own tax return. Obviously, there are considerable valuation and administrative problems in collecting taxes on such imputed income, as value created does not necessarily equate to cashflow to pay taxes. Not surprisingly, this perspective is not the primary perspective on

[4] *Concise Oxford English Dictionary*.

income embraced by the *Income Tax Act*. However, the major review of Canadian tax policy completed by the Carter Commission in 1967 recommended a comprehensive tax base concept that came close to this broader concept of income.

¶1,210.20 The Role of Generally Accepted Accounting Principles

The *Income Tax Act* states that income from a business is the "profit" from that business However, the computation of profit is not completely specified by provisions in the Act. According to common law, profit is the calculation of income on "sound commercial principles", which may include generally accepted accounting principles (GAAP), unless a particular provision of the Act or principle of common law requires otherwise.

Canada requires that public enterprises follow International Financial Reporting Standards (IFRS) and private companies follow Accounting Standards for Private Enterprise (ASPE). As a result, GAAP will be used to refer to both IFRS and ASPE, as appropriate.

Until the early 1990s, the courts were inconsistent in their reference to GAAP as an authoritative source for interpretation of profit under the *Income Tax Act*. The Supreme Court decision in *Symes v. The Queen et al.* appears to have cleared the air by the following statement:

Cases: *Symes v. The Queen*, 94 DTC 6001 (SCC)

> . . . Any reference to G.A.A.P. connotes a degree of control by professional accountants which is inconsistent with a legal test for "profit" under s. 9(1). Further, whereas an accountant questioning the propriety of a deduction may be motivated by a desire to present an appropriately conservative picture of current profitability, the *Income Tax Act* is motivated by a different purpose: the raising of public revenues. For these reasons, it is more appropriate in considering the s. 9(1) business test to speak of "well accepted principles of business (or accounting) practice" or "well accepted principles of commercial trading".

Therefore, GAAP is still to be considered, but should be put into the context of overall business practices and should not stand alone. In the case of *Canderel Limited v. Her Majesty the Queen*, the Supreme Court of Canada stated, as a principle, that well-accepted business principles, which include but are not limited to GAAP, are not rules of law but are interpretative aids. To the extent that they may influence the calculation of income, they will do so only on a case-by-case basis, depending on the facts of the taxpayer's financial situation.

Cases: *Canderel Limited v. The Queen*, 98 DTC 6100 (SCC)

It must be emphasized that the rules within the Act, which are used in the computation of income for tax purposes, result in an income computation that will vary widely from income for financial accounting purposes. An important example of this is the depreciation of capital assets. The Act requires the use of the capital cost allowance system, based primarily on a declining balance method, in lieu of depreciation for financial accounting purposes, which may incorporate a variety of methods. The difference in the rules for calculating income for tax purposes and financial purposes is reasonable, as financial reporting and tax reporting serve two distinct purposes.

¶1,220 Important Concepts within the *Income Tax Act*

Overview

Within the *Income Tax Act*, a great deal of consistency exists across the calculation of amounts and the tax treatment in varying situations. Specific rules discussed in the chapters that follow are based on these important consistencies and the concepts discussed below.

¶1,220.10 The Doctrine of Constructive Receipt

The "constructive receipt" of income involves the inclusion of amounts which may not actually be received but are beneficially received or receivable. For example, there is a provision that deems the taxpayer to have received amounts withheld as tax by his or her employer. Although the taxpayer does not receive these amounts, they are included in his or her income subject to tax. The use of the accrual system is another example of the use of the concept of constructive receipt. While amounts in accounts receivable have not actually been received, they are included in income.

ITA: 153(3) Deemed effect of deduction

In applying the doctrine of constructive receipt, one of the key determinants is that the amounts must be beneficially received or receivable by the taxpayer so that his or her use of the amounts is free and unrestricted. The test was set out in the early Canadian case of *Kenneth B.S. Robertson Ltd. v. M.N.R.* in the form of the following questions:

Cases: *Kenneth B. S. Robertson Ltd. v. Minister of National Revenue*, 2 DTC 655 (EC)

> Is his right to it (the amount) absolute and under no restriction, contractual or otherwise, as to its disposition, use or enjoyment? To put it another way, can an amount in a taxpayer's hands be regarded as an item of profit or gain from his business as long as he holds it subject to specific and unfulfilled conditions and his right to retain it and apply it to his own use has not yet accrued and may never accrue?

As an example of an amount that is not constructively or beneficially received, consider retail sales taxes collected by retailers and passed on to the provincial government. In this case, the retailer simply acts as a conduit or transmitter of the amount and, therefore, is not taxed on it.[5]

¶1,220.20 Income Versus Capital

Receipts can be classified as either income or capital. A common analogy used by the courts likens a capital asset to a tree which produces income during the period of ownership in the form of fruit. Sale of the tree results in a receipt of capital and capital gains treatment, whereas sale of the fruit results in a receipt of income. As long as taxation has existed in Canada, receipts of capital have received more favourable tax consequences than receipts of income. This situation continues to exist, since only half of capital gains are included in income.

The problem of determining whether a given receipt is one of capital or one of income has been the subject of countless court cases. In subsequent chapters, the major factors used by the courts in their determination will be examined, and a number of cases will be used to illustrate these factors. One factor is the nature of the asset, which is determined from its use or intended use. The classic capital asset is one which produces income from holding it or using it.

This topic is covered in greater detail in Chapters 4 and 8, where we look at business income and capital gains, respectively.

---

[5] For two Canadian cases which illustrate situations in which constructive receipt was at issue, see *Cliffe v. M.N.R.*, 57 DTC 305 (T.A.B.), dealing with unpaid salaries left in a corporation and *Green v. M.N.R.*, 50 DTC 320 (T.A.B.), dealing with unpaid interest left in a corporation. For an application of the concept of constructive receipt to a third-party payment in a marital breakdown situation, see the case of *The Queen v. Arsenault*, 96 DTC 6131 (F.C.A.), in which the "free and unrestricted use" test was at issue. For an example of a fact situation in which it was concluded that the test that an amount must have been received by someone for the benefit of the payee was not met, see *Markman v. M.N.R.*, 89 DTC 253 (T.C.C.).

¶1,220.30 Aggregation Formula

For Canadian taxpayers, both income and capital receipts, resulting in income subject to tax, are aggregated by the rules of section 3, irrespective of geographic source. The computation of income for tax purposes is illustrated by Exhibit 1-1. We will return to these aggregation rules in a subsequent chapter after all of the sources of income have been considered so that the terminology used in section 3 is more meaningful. Until then, a cursory examination of the section will provide an overview of the coverage of subsequent chapters.

Exhibit 1-1 Simplified Computation of Income Under Division B, Section 3

ITA Par.	Type of income	ITA Subdivision	Chapter(s)
3(*a*)	Worldwide income (positive amounts only after subtracting deductible expenses) from non-capital sources including:		
	• Office or employment	a	3
	• Business	b	4 and 5
	• Property	b	5 and 6
	• Other non-capital sources	d	9
Plus			
3(*b*)	Net taxable capital gains (not negative)[1]	c	7 and 8
Less			
3(*c*)	General deductions not attributable to any specific source	e	9
Less			
3(*d*)	Negative amounts or losses from non-capital sources including:		
	• Office or employment[2]	a	3
	• Business[2]	b	4 and 5
	• Property[2]	b	5 and 6

ITA Par.	Type of income	ITA Subdivision	Chapter(s)
Equals			
3(*e*), (*f*)	Division B income or "income for tax purposes"		

[1] If allowable capital losses exceed taxable capital gains then this net capital loss is deductible in a carryover year (i.e., the previous three years or any future year) under Division C (see Chapter 10 for individuals and Chapter 11 for corporations).

[2] If the losses from an office, employment, business, and property exceed the income from other sources, then it will be necessary to calculate the non-capital loss that can be carried back to previous years or forward to future years under Division C (see Chapter 10 for individuals and Chapter 11 for corporations).

Helpful Tip for Using the *Income Tax Act*

Note how section 3 represents the expression of a complex formula in words contained in one very long sentence. For example, paragraph 3(*a*) requires the taxpayer to "determine the total of all amounts" of income from all of the non-capital sources, e.g., employment income, business income, and sundry receipts. In fact, this aggregate includes only positive amounts, i.e., an excess of inclusions over deductions, from these sources. However, it is only evident that these amounts must be positive when paragraph 3(d), referring to losses from the same non-capital sources, is read.

Paragraph 3(*b*) requires the taxpayer to "determine the amount, if any, by which the total of" two amounts exceeds a third amount which, itself, requires a sub-calculation. In the language of the Act, the use of the words "if any", when referring to the calculation of an excess, means that if the calculated amount is negative, the amount is set at nil. That is, if the calculated amount is negative, there is no excess of the sum required in subparagraph 3(*b*)(i) over the amount calculated in subparagraph 3(*b*)(ii). In interpreting a provision of this nature, it is often helpful to determine the underlying computational formula and to substitute numbers from a particular fact situation into the formula. This procedure will be demonstrated in a subsequent example.

¶1,220.40 Sourcing or Tracing of Income

A taxpayer must compute his or her income or loss from each source independently by allocating deductions in amounts that can be applied reasonably to each revenue source. For example, a taxpayer who is employed and also carries on a business must compute the income from business and income from employment separately. His employment expenses cannot be deducted from his business income. Similarly, in the allocation of business

ITA: 4 Income or loss from a source or from sources in a place

income among various provinces only the deductions that can be traced to or allowed by that particular jurisdiction can be deducted in arriving at income for tax purposes.

Generally, the Act does not require an amount to be included in or deducted from income more than once unless a provision is so worded to specifically do so.[6]

Although income is not defined in the Act, once it has been determined that there is income, then this income must be attached to a particular source. For example, income from employment found in Subdivision a of Division B gathers together all of the employment income inclusions as specifically determined in sections 5, 6, and 7 minus all of the permitted deductions found in section 8. This sourcing of income and deductions would be continued for:

Subdivision b — Business or Property Income

Subdivision c — Taxable Capital Gains and Allowable Capital Losses

Subdivision d — Other Income

Once the sourcing of income has been completed, then the ordering rules for Division B, which are found in section 3 of the Act, can be applied.

¶1,230 Determination of Net Income for Tax Purposes, Taxable Income, and Federal Income Tax for Individuals

The calculation of a taxpayer's tax liability is accomplished by completing three distinct computations as described below.

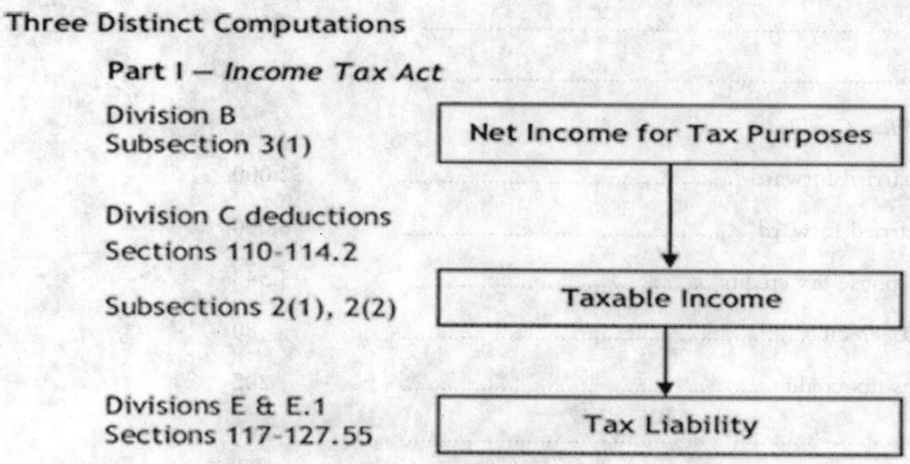

As various rules are discussed in the upcoming chapters, it is important to recognize how individual issues fit into the three computations of either net income for tax purposes, taxable income, or tax liability.

- Chapter 3 to Chapter 9 deal primarily with the calculation of the first computation, net income for tax purposes.
- Chapter 10 presents the details required to calculate taxable income and the tax liability for an individual.

[6] For example, see *Joel Attis v M.N.R.*, 92 DTC 1128 (T.C.C.), involving the repayment of shareholder loans.

- Chapter 11 and Chapter 12 present the details required to calculate taxable income and the tax liability for a corporation.

A large number of issues and details will be discussed throughout the chapters of this book. Keeping this computation structure in mind will help you to maintain a perspective of how the details fit into the overall calculation of a taxpayer's tax liability.

Example

The following list of income, losses, deductions, and tax credits has been determined correctly by a junior staff accountant prior to the preparation of the tax return for Ms. Beth Kelly.

Income (net)	
Employment	$60,000
Property (interest and dividends)	1,200
Taxable capital gains (net of allowable capital losses)	7,500
Pension income	5,000
Deductions and Losses	
Moving expenses	$600
Business loss	3,100
Carry Forward Losses and Tax Credits	
Non-capital losses carried forward	$2,000
Net capital losses carried forward	6,000
Basic personal and spouse tax credits	3,543
Medical expenses tax credit	80
Charitable donations tax credit	202
Pension tax credit	300
Canada Pension Plan contributions tax credit	389
Employment Insurance premiums tax credit	129
Dividend tax credit	100
Canada employment credit	179

A calculation of Beth Kelly's Tax Liability would result as follows:

Division B — Section 3

Par. 3(*a*)	*Subdivision a*			
	Sec. 5, 6, 7, 8	Employment		$60,000
	Subdivision b			
	Business income (net losses)		Nil	
	Property			
	Par. 12(1)(*c*), (*j*)	Interest and dividends	1,200	1,200
	Subdivision d			
	Ssec. 56(1)	Pension income		5,000
				$66,200
Par. 3(*b*)	*Subdivision c*			
	Sec. 38	Taxable capital gains net of allowable capital losses (not negative)		$7,500
				$73,700
Par. 3(*c*)	*Subdivision e*			
	Sec. 62	Moving expenses		(600)
				$73,100
Par. 3(*d*)	Sec. 9	Business loss		(3,100)
		Division B income		$70,000

Division C — Section 111.1

Par. 111(1)(*a*)	Non-capital losses carried over	$(2,000)	
Par. 111(1)(*b*)	Net capital losses carried over	(6,000)	(8,000)
Taxable income			$62,000

Division E — Section 118.92

Federal tax before credits			$10,184
Less tax credits:			
Sec. 118	Personal tax credits	$3,542	
Sec. 118.7	CPP tax credit	389	
Sec. 118.7	EI premium tax credit	129	
Ssec. 118(3)	Pension tax credit	300	
Ssec. 118(10)	Canada employment credit	179	
Sec. 118.2	Medical expense credit	80	
Sec. 118.1	Donation tax credit	202	
Sec. 121	Dividend tax credit	100	(4,921)
Basic federal tax			$5,263

¶1,290 Pause and Reflect — Summary of Learning Goals

After working through this section, ¶1,200, you should be able to:

- Understand how the perspective on income differs among economic analysis, financial reporting, and the *Income Tax Act*.

¶1,300 The Canadian Tax System

Overview

Before moving on to the detailed rules required for the calculation of a taxpayer's income tax liability, which will be covered in the upcoming chapters, it is important to have an understanding of the Canadian tax system. The Canadian tax system includes legislation, administrative practices, and enforcement mechanisms. This section will introduce these important aspects of income taxation in Canada.

After working through this section, ¶1,300, you will be able to:

- Know how tax policy becomes law.
- Know how the *Income Tax Act* came to be in Canada.

¶1,310 Brief History of the *Income Tax Act*

Income tax was first imposed federally in 1917 as a temporary measure to help finance World War I under the *Income War Tax Act*, a simple and short document of about 11 pages in length. (See the front matter of the Wolters Kluwer 100th Edition of the *Canadian*

Income Tax Act and Regulations, pp. ix to xix.) It generated revenue to supplement the revenues from the more traditional custom and excise taxes. In 1948, Parliament passed the *Income Tax Act*. The *Income War Tax Act* was merged into this new legislation, and although the new Act involved a rewording and codification of the old law, there were few changes in policy. Essentially, income tax introduced in 1917 as a temporary measure persists today.

A major reform of federal income tax legislation began in 1962 with the setting up of the Royal Commission on Taxation under the chairmanship of the late Kenneth Carter. The Carter Commission presented its seven-volume report in 1967 recommending fundamental changes in tax legislation that would use a comprehensive tax base including capital gains, which were previously tax-free.

This report led to the issuing of the November 1969 White Paper on Tax Reform followed by the Budget address on June 18, 1971 and Bill C-259 to amend the *Income Tax Act*. This bill was given Royal Assent on December 23, 1971, and became effective January 1, 1972. Since then, every Budget address has presented a considerable number of amendments to the tax legislation to both "fine-tune" the existing legislation and introduce new fiscal policy.

Sixteen years later, on June 18, 1987, the government released a White Paper on Tax Reform which was to be implemented in two phases. Phase One, implemented in 1988, included changes to the personal and corporate income tax systems and interim changes to the existing federal sales tax. Phase Two replaced the existing federal sales tax with a broad-based multi-stage sales tax referred to as the goods and services tax (GST), effective January 1, 1991. In provinces which have agreed to harmonize their provincial sales tax (PST) with the GST, this tax has become the harmonized sales tax (HST).

The fact that income tax, introduced in 1917 as a temporary measure, is still in existence, albeit in a substantially expanded form, is easily explained. In order to finance public expenditures and implement its economic and social policy, the government has had to collect revenues in various forms. Taxing the income of individuals and corporations has provided it with a reliable and increasing source of revenue.

Currently, based on 2017–2018 projections, income taxes comprise about 66% of total federal government revenues, with personal income taxes raising almost three and a half times the amount of revenue as corporate income taxes. Sales and excise taxes, including the GST, represent about 17% of total federal government revenues. Exhibit 1-2 gives some indication of the relative importance of various taxes.

Exhibit 1-2 Government of Canada Budgetary Revenues (2017–2018 Projection)

Revenue item	Billions of dollars[1]	Percentage
Personal income tax	161.4	49.9
Corporate income taxes	47.3	14.6

Revenue item	Billions of dollars[1]	Percentage
Non-Resident income tax	8.3	2.6
Employment insurance contributions	21.7	6.7
Goods and services tax	37.7	11.7
Customs import duties	5.5	1.7
Other tax revenue	12.1	3.7
Non-tax revenue	29.4	9.1
Total budgetary revenues	323.4	100.0

[1] Source: Table A 2.7, "The Revenue Outlook", Annex 2, "Details of Economic and Fiscal Projections", *Equality Growth: A Strong Middle Class*, Budget 2018, Department of Finance Canada, February 27, 2018.

¶1,320 Constitutional Basis for Income Taxation

The *British North America Act, 1867*, renamed the *Constitution Act, 1867* in the process of the repatriation of the Constitution, grants authority for all taxation in Canada, separating federal and provincial powers to impose income taxes. Subsection 91(3) of the *Constitution Act, 1867* provides the federal government with unlimited powers of taxation by permitting the "raising of money by any mode or system of taxation". On the other hand, subsection 92(2) of the same act limits provincial powers to direct taxation of income earned in the province and of income of persons resident in the province. Even with a fairly liberal interpretation of the provincial powers of direct taxation, in order to meet increasing provincial requirements over the years, there has been a constant trading of tax points through federal-provincial taxation agreements. Nevertheless, intergovernmental problems of raising revenues through taxation persist.

¶1,330 The Federal Budgetary Process

Overview

There are special procedures for adopting fiscal legislation and several levels of government are involved in the passage of new or amended tax law. (See Figure 1-1.)

All proposals for change originate in the Department of Finance. A bill to amend the Act cannot be tabled before a "Notice of Ways and Motion to Amend the *Income Tax Act*" has been presented to the House of Commons. The Minister of Finance will clear major proposals with the Prime Minister and Cabinet before presenting a Notice of Ways and Means Motion to Amend the *Income Tax Act* to the House of Commons. Once permission is granted in the House of Commons, a bill is introduced. Before the bill receives Royal Assent by the Governor General, it is reviewed and discussed in detail by the Standing Committee on Finance and Economic Affairs and a total of three readings take place in both the House of Commons and the Senate. A discussion of this process follows.

Figure 1-1

Budgetary Process

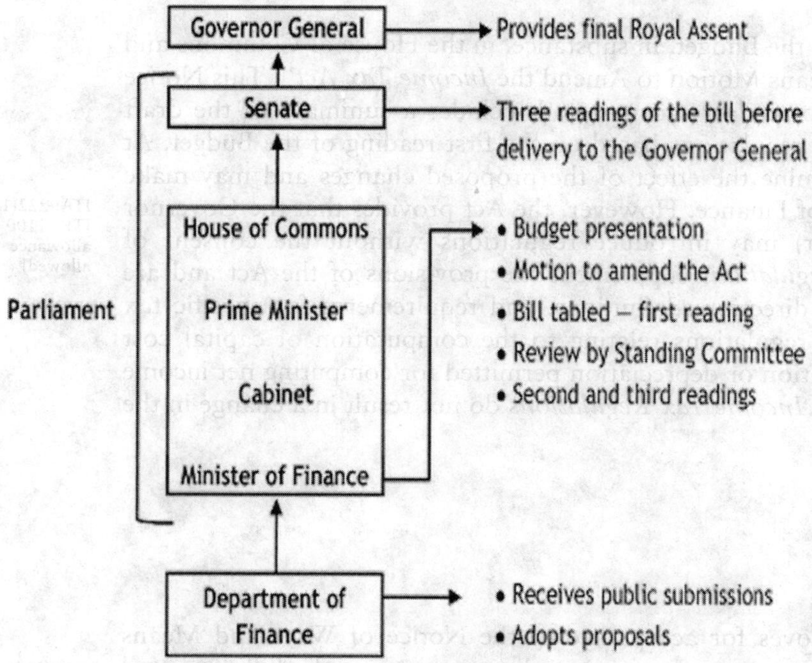

¶1,330.10 Public Submissions for Change or Amendment

On an ongoing basis, and before initiating detailed work on the Budget, the Minister of Finance accepts and reviews "submissions for change" to the income tax system. The Minister also encourages submissions from politicians, economists, tax advisers, academics, and other interested parties, including taxpayers.

¶1,330.20 Adoption of Specific Proposals

The Minister considers and adopts specific proposals for the Budget. Secrecy is critical during this stage to prevent arbitrage in the marketplace. There is absolutely no public involvement at this point — no formal way to publicly debate the proposals considered. Tax professionals and economists criticize this approach because the Minister does not call upon them for professional advice or comments. To ensure that taxpayers do not have an unfair advantage in planning their transactions, the proposed legislation has an "effective date", generally the Budget date, not the date on which the bill is adopted. The department also introduces many proposed tax law changes in the form of Department of Finance News Releases. These are often released without prior announcement and generally take effect immediately upon release of the proposal. For example, changes to the tax benefits of charitable donations made under tax shelter arrangements were announced and effective the same day. While the intent of these releases is often to counter tax avoidance schemes, they can also address relatively minor tax changes.

¶1,330.30 Federal Budget Presentation to the House of Commons

The Minister of Finance presents the Budget, in substance, in the House of Commons and tables a "Notice of Ways and Means Motion to Amend the *Income Tax Act*". This Notice is then available to the public in readable format and includes a summary of the draft income tax changes to rules and regulations based on the first reading of the Budget. At this point, taxpayers may determine the effect of the proposed changes and may make submissions to the Department of Finance. However, the Act provides that the Governor in Council (the federal cabinet) may introduce regulations without the consent of Parliament. The *Income Tax Regulations* supplement the provisions of the Act and are specifically intended to provide direction, definitions, and requirements for specific tax rules. An example includes the regulations relating to the computation of capital cost allowance, which is the amortization or depreciation permitted for computing net income for tax purposes. Changes to the *Income Tax Regulations* do not result in a change in the Act itself.

ITA: 222(1) Definitions; ITR: 1100 [Capital cost allowance – deductions allowed]

¶1,330.40 Passage of Law

At a later date, the Minister moves for acceptance of the Notice of Ways and Means Motion and then the House of Commons passes a resolution to accept the bill to amend the *Income Tax Act*. The bill contains detailed measures to repeal, amend, or add to provisions of the Act. A second reading of the bill, clause by clause, and a third reading in the House of Commons, as well as a similar process of three readings in the Senate, take place prior to Royal Assent. The Notice of Ways and Means Motion to Amend the *Income Tax Act* must receive Royal Assent before the proposed changes become statute law. This process will often take several months — sometimes more than a year.

Not all Budget proposals become law immediately. For example, in 1984, the Minister of Finance proposed significant changes to registered retirement plans and other deferred pension plans with most of the legislation delayed until 1990. Delay in tax legislation can create uncertainties for taxpayers, particularly at the time of tax filing. Most proposed changes are retroactive to the date of announcement of the proposed rule.

Parliament passes the statutory laws of Canada, and the CRA enforces and administers the tax laws. Tax rules are becoming increasingly complex because many of the tax provisions are mathematical formulas in legal format. The Act also contains many phrases that reference other sections or subsections of the Act. For many years, the government did not release any interpretations or explanations with the draft legislation. This created significant confusion until 1982, when the Department of Finance began publishing Technical Notes (Explanatory Notes) with draft legislation. While these notes do not represent official or statutory interpretations, they are useful in helping to determine the underlying legislative intent and promoting understanding of the tax rule.

¶1,390 Pause and Reflect — Summary of Learning Goals

After working through this section, ¶1,300, you should be able to:

- Know how tax policy becomes law.
- Know how the *Income Tax Act* came to be in Canada.

¶1,400 Administration and Enforcement of the Act

Overview

The purpose of this section of the chapter is to provide a broad overview of how the tax legislation is administered and enforced. A discussion of the specific details of provisions dealing with these aspects of the law is deferred until Chapter 14, where it can be related more meaningfully to material covered in the intervening chapters.

After working through this section, ¶1,400, you will be able to:

- Know how the burden of proof is weighed in tax cases.
- Understand the appeals process in the Canadian tax system.

¶1,410 Onus of Proof

In tax matters, it has been established by the Supreme Court of Canada in the case of *Johnston v. M.N.R.* that the taxpayer always has the burden of proving that an assessment is incorrect. Placing the burden of proof on the taxpayer is often referred to as a "reverse onus", because the usual burden of proof is on the Crown. In tax matters, the reverse onus is justified, since it is assumed that under our self-assessment system the taxpayer has all of the basic data under his or her own control.[7] Because of this, keeping appropriate tax records is especially important.

ITA: 163(3) Burden of proof in respect of penalties; Cases: *Roderick W. S. Johnston v. Minister of National Revenue*, 3 DTC 1182 (SCC)

In the case of *M.N.R. v. Taylor*, it was established that the standard of proof in cases dealing with the Act need only be that of the "balance of probabilities" used in civil cases rather than the more rigorous standard of "beyond reasonable doubt" used in criminal proceedings. Where penalties are assessed, the burden of proof of the facts justifying the assessment of the penalties is transferred to the Minister. The standard of proof that the Minister must demonstrate is that of the "balance of probabilities".

Cases: *Minister of National Revenue v. Maurice Taylor*, 61 DTC 1139 (EC)

¶1,420 Appeals

Overview

Interpretation of many tax rules requires judgement and, as a result, can lead to situations where the tax treatment is not certain. How the rules apply to a set of facts may be interpreted differently between the taxpayer and the CRA. If a taxpayer does not agree with the CRA's position, they may appeal the outcome. This section discusses appeal options available to a taxpayer.

---

[7] This onus of proof was applied in the case of *Violi v. M.N.R.*, 80 DTC 1191 (T.R.B.).

¶1,420.10 Initial Steps

Prior to taking any formal steps in the appeal procedure, the taxpayer may consult with CRA officials responsible for his or her file in the appropriate Tax Services Office. Many differences can be resolved in this less formal manner. If, however, they cannot be resolved at this stage to the taxpayer's satisfaction, a notice of objection may be filed as the first formal step. There is no prescribed form at the present time. The notice of objection simply contains a statement of the facts and the reasons for objection.

In the case of corporations or certain trusts, the notice of objection must be received by the CRA on or before the 90th day subsequent to the date of mailing of the notice of assessment.

In the case of individuals or testamentary trusts, the deadline is the later of

- one year after the day the taxpayer is required to pay the balance of tax due for a year (i.e., April 30), and
- 90 days after the mailing of the notice of assessment for the year.

¶1,420.20 Tax Court of Canada

If the taxpayer is not satisfied with the CRA's decision on the Notice of Objection, he or she has 90 days after the final decision rendered by the CRA on the Notice of Objection to appeal to the Tax Court of Canada (T.C.C.). It is highly accessible, meeting in cities across Canada.

The Tax Court of Canada now has exclusive jurisdiction to hear appeals under the Act and certain other federal statutes. On appeal to the Tax Court, the taxpayer is given the option of an "informal procedure" or a "general procedure".

¶1,420.30 Informal Procedure

The informal procedure may be elected when the amount of federal tax and penalties in issue for one taxation year is $25,000 or less or when the amount of the losses is $50,000 or less. The only requirement of the informal procedure is that the appeal is submitted in writing. Court rules of evidence are flexible, so the taxpayer can represent himself or herself or be represented by an agent (i.e., any individual) who may or may not be a lawyer. However, the taxpayer cannot appeal on questions of fact from a Tax Court decision reached through the informal procedure and the decision cannot be used as a precedent in subsequent cases. Judicial review of a judgment under the informal procedure lies with the Federal Court of Appeal (F.C.A.) on errors of law or erroneous findings of fact made in a perverse or capricious manner.

¶1,420.40 General Procedure

Where the general procedure is chosen in the Tax Court of Canada, the Court will be bound by strict rules of evidence. The taxpayer can represent himself or herself or be represented by legal counsel.

¶1,420.50 Federal Court of Appeal

From the general procedure, either the taxpayer or the CRA can appeal the decision of the Tax Court to the Federal Court of Appeal and the Tax Court decision can be used as a precedent in other cases. This appeal must be made within 30 days from the date of the Tax Court decision.

¶1,420.60 Supreme Court of Canada

The ultimate court of appeal for tax cases in Canada is the Supreme Court of Canada (S.C.C.). At this level, questions of legal interpretation are raised rather than questions of fact alone. Not many cases on tax matters are given leave to appeal to the Supreme Court of Canada.

¶1,430 Administration and Enforcement

While the Department of Finance formulates tax policy, the CRA controls, regulates, manages, and supervises the income tax system. Direct contact between the taxpayer and the CRA is generally made through one of the more than 50 Tax Services Offices. Trained assessors and special investigators who conduct desk audits of an individual's return or field audits of business returns are located in these offices.

The Head Office in Ottawa serves to maintain efficiency and uniformity of treatment across Canada, by supervising and directing the activities of the Tax Services Offices. In addition, a number of regional Taxation Centres are maintained to do routine operations and the initial processing of all individual income tax returns, among other things.

¶1,440 Tax Evasion, Avoidance, and Planning

It is important to distinguish the terms "tax evasion", "tax avoidance", and "tax planning". Generally, tax evasion involves knowingly reporting tax that is less than the tax payable under the law with an attempt to deceive by omitting revenue, fraudulently claiming deductions (such as claiming personal expenses in calculating income), or failing to use all of the true facts of a situation. This is clearly illegal and can be prosecuted as such. Tax evasion is enforced under both criminal law (the imposition of a fine and possibly imprisonment) and civil law (payment of the tax, applicable interest, and penalties imposed by the Act). An Information Circular provides a description of the consequences of tax evasion.

Information Circulars: IC 73-10R3 Tax Evasion

Tax avoidance is generally considered to arise in cases in which the taxpayer has legally circumvented the law resulting in the reduction or elimination of tax through a scheme or series of transactions which do not truly reflect the real facts. Although such tax avoidance is not illegal, the CRA will challenge it by various available means. Tax avoidance transactions do not have a *bona fide* business purpose and usually involve a misuse of the provisions of the Act read as a whole.

Finally, the CRA suggests that tax planning involves cases of tax reduction or elimination that are clearly provided for or not specifically prohibited in the law in a manner that is genuine and open within the framework of the law. For example, certain corporate reorganizations to shield business assets from liability are specifically allowed and can favourably reduce taxes payable. It is not only legal to undertake tax planning for clients, it is a proper and ethical use of the professional accountant's skills.

Despite these statements which attempt to distinguish the terms, there are undoubtedly judgements that must be made in distinguishing between cases of tax evasion and tax avoidance and between cases of tax avoidance and tax planning.

Exhibit 1-3 Legal and Illegal Methods of Reducing Tax

	Tax Planning	Tax Avoidance	Tax Evasion
Taxpayer goal	To favourably reduce taxes payable within the object and spirit of the law	Deliberate planning of events and transactions to circumvent the law and avoid paying taxes	To avoid taxes by failing to disclose complete and accurate information
Legality	Legal	Not illegal; Transactions can be ignored if successfully challenged	Illegal; Criminal offence; Civil wrongdoing
Penalty	None	Arrears and interest plus taxes owing and possible penalties owing	Fine, possible imprisonment, arrears, interest plus taxes, and civil penalties

The Act contains a general anti-avoidance rule (GAAR). In the words of the explanatory notes accompanying Bill C-139, which were issued on June 30, 1988 and introduced the GAAR, the rule is: ITA: 245 [General anti-avoidance rule]

> intended to prevent abusive tax avoidance transactions or arrangements, but at the same time is not intended to interfere with legitimate commercial and family transactions. Consequently, the new rule seeks to distinguish between legitimate tax planning and abusive tax avoidance and to establish a reasonable balance between the protection of the tax base and the need for certainty for taxpayers in planning their affairs.[8]

¶1,490 Pause and Reflect — Summary of Learning Goals

After working through this section, ¶1,400, you should be able to:

- Know how the burden of proof is weighed in tax cases.
- Understand the appeals process in the Canadian tax system.

[8] Reproduced in *Technical Notes to Bill C-139*, Special Report No. 851, Extra Edition, Wolters Kluwer Limited, June 30, 1988, p. 313.

¶1,500 Tax Practice — Interpretation of the *Income Tax Act*

Overview

The ability to read and understand the *Income Tax Act* is essential to being a tax practitioner. It is important to be able to interpret the Act in order to advise clients of the tax consequences of their transactions and to deal with the CRA on assessments and rulings. Knowing the principles and rules used by the courts in their interpretation of the Act is important, since their interpretations are an essential part of the law. Although these skills are common for those approaching tax from a legal background, they are skills unique to the practice of tax for a professional accountant. Learning to read and understand legal text is a skill that takes patience and practice. Using the Act is no different. This section provides an introduction to strategies for reading and interpreting the Act.

After working through this section, ¶1,500, you will be able to:

- Understand strategies for interpreting the *Income Tax Act*.

¶1,510 Precision

The development of tax legislation over the years has included the acceptance of rules of interpretation or construction (from the verb "to construe") of the income tax law. Every attempt is made to achieve precision in the language of tax legislation so that it is clearly understood and provides the taxpayer with some degree of certainty about his or her tax liability. The following quote is from a famous British decision heard in 1891 on the question of the drafting of legislation:

> It is not enough to attain a degree of precision which a person reading in good faith can understand, but it is necessary to attain if possible to a degree of precision which a person reading in bad faith cannot misunderstand (and) it is all the better if he cannot pretend to misunderstand it.[9]

It is important to read every word of a provision very carefully to determine the following components:

(1) to whom the provision applies, i.e., an individual, a corporation, a partnership or a trust and, if more than one, their relationship;

(2) the transactions to which the provision applies and the conditions that must exist for the provision to apply (e.g., a receipt of salary, the carrying on of a business, or the payment of interest);

(3) the consequences of the provision, if it applies (e.g., a tax must be paid); and

(4) the time frame over which the provision applies, such as a particular year or a part of a year (e.g., a particular year for an inclusion or a period of time for filing a return).

¶1,515 Plain and Obvious Meaning

It has long been held that the words used in a taxing statute must be given their plain and obvious meaning, unless there is a specific definition contained in the statute or unless another meaning is required in the context of the remainder of the Act. This has become

[9] *In re Castioni* (1891), 1 Q.B. 149 at 167.

known as the "Golden Rule" of interpretation or construction, and it was expressed by Lord Atkinson of the British House of Lords as follows:

> In the construction of statutes their words must be interpreted in their ordinary grammatical sense, unless there be something in the context, or in the object of the statute in which they occur, or in the circumstances with reference to which they are used, to show that they were used in a special sense different from their ordinary grammatical sense.[10]

In an elaboration of this principle, Lord Wensleydale stated:

> . . . the grammatical and ordinary sense of the word is to be adhered to, unless that would lead to some absurdity or some repugnance or inconsistency with the rest of the [statute], in which case the grammatical and ordinary sense of the words may be modified so as to avoid that absurdity and inconsistency but no farther.[11]

This principle is intended to increase the taxpayer's certainty of his or her position.

A word may have more than one ordinary meaning, depending on how it is used. For example, the word "rent" can be used as a noun in reference to an amount paid or received. The same word can be used as a verb by either the landlord or the tenant, i.e., to rent to or to rent from a person. In a similar landlord/tenant situation, the word "lease" can be used as a noun in reference to the contract between the two or as a verb in the same way that the verb "rent" can be used. Therefore, it is always important to determine the context in which the word is used and how it is used. The location in the Act or in a provision can affect the meaning to be used for a word or phrase.

The meaning of a provision cannot be extended by an interpretation which is not clear from the words used. Lord Cairns expanded on this point in an 1869 case by stating:

> . . . if the person sought to be taxed comes within the letter of the law he must be taxed, however great the hardship may appear to the judicial mind to be. On the other hand, if the Crown, seeking to recover the tax, cannot bring the subject within the letter of the law, the subject is free, however apparently within the spirit of the law the case might otherwise appear to be. In other words, if there be admissible in statute, what is called an equitable construction, certainly such a construction is not admissible in a taxing statute, where you can simply adhere to the words of the statute.[12]

This point is illustrated in the case of *Witthuhn v. M.N.R.*, in which a taxpayer was denied a deduction for certain medical expenses because the patient was confined to bed or a special type of rocking chair rather than "to a bed or wheelchair" as required at the time of the case and, in fact, until the provision was amended in 1986.

Cases: *Walter Witthuhn v. Minister of National Revenue*, 57 DTC 174 (TAB)

This approach appears to have been softened to some extent in the case of *Overdyck v. M.N.R.*, where the taxpayer used a leg brace to go to work and a chair with castor-like wheels while at work. The same wording was given a much more liberal interpretation on the basis that if the taxpayer had been left completely alone without external aid or assistance, he would have been in bed at all times as a result of paralysis in one leg. In fact, where courts have found wording to be unclear, they have interpreted the words in a manner that is fair in the situation under consideration.

Cases: *Overdyk v. The Minister of National Revenue*, 83 DTC 307 (TRB)

---

[10] *Victoria (City) v. Bishop of Vancouver Island* (1921), 2 A.C. 384 (P.C.) at 387.

[11] *Grey v. Pearson* (1857), 6 H.L.C. 61 at 106.

[12] *Partington v. Attorney General* (1869), L.R. 4 H.L. 100 at 122.

¶1,520 Definitions in the Act

Various provisions of the Act contain lists of defined words or phrases. Subsection 248(1) contains a long list of terms or phrases. The preamble (i.e., opening words) to that provision is very short, but it is very important. It states "in this Act" and means that the definition provided is to be used wherever the word or phrase is used anywhere in the Act.

In some instances, the definitions in subsection 248(1) are assigned the meaning of the term from another section. For example, the definition of "private corporation" in subsection 248(1) has the meaning assigned by subsection 89(1). The preamble to subsection 89(1) states, "in this subdivision", i.e., Subdivision h of Division B of Part I of the Act, meaning that, generally, the definitions covered in subsection 89(1) apply when the words listed in subsection 89(1) are used in Subdivision h. However, in the case of a "private corporation", the definition is used wherever the term is used in the Act, as a result of its listing in subsection 248(1) and the cross-reference there.

Sometimes the definitions listed in a subsection are limited to the section of the Act in which the subsection appears. For example, the term "excluded consideration" is defined in subsection 74.4(1), which has the preamble "in this section", meaning that the definition applies only to the use of the term in subsection 74.4. The "in this section" preamble is important when the same term is defined differently in two different sections. For example, the term "earned income" is defined in subsection 63(3) for use in section 63 pertaining to the child care expense deduction. The same term is defined differently in subsection 146(1) for use in section 146 pertaining to registered retirement savings plans.

¶1,525 Meaning and Distinction in Words Commonly Used in the Act

Often a word or phrase will be defined using the word "means" or "includes". "Means" indicates that the definition of the word being defined is exhaustive or restrictive, at least, for the purposes of its use in the Act. In these cases, the definition stated applies only to the given word or phrase. For example, the definition of "balance-due day" in subsection 248(1) uses "means" to limit the meaning. Other definitions use the word "includes" to indicate that the definition is not exhaustive and that the ordinary meaning of the word or phrase can be used in addition to the included meanings. For example, the term "borrowed money" in subsection 248(1) uses the word "includes", leaving out many common items that would ordinarily be referred to as borrowed money. Note that the definition of "office" in subsection 248(1) uses both "means" and "includes" in the same definition.

Provisions that require or allow someone to do something use the words "may" or "shall". The use of "may" makes the requirement permissive, while the use of "shall" makes the requirement obligatory. Note that in subsection 2(1) "an income tax *shall* be paid". However, specified amounts "*may* be deducted" by an employee under subsection 8(1).

Another important distinction in the use of words is between "and" and "or". For example, in paragraph 256(1)(*c*), there are three conditions and they are all joined by "and". Thus, all three conditions must be met for the rule to apply. On the other hand, in paragraph 256(1)(*b*), there are two conditions stated and they are joined by "or". Therefore, only one of the two conditions needs to be met for the rule to apply. In this case the two conditions are mutually exclusive, so only one can possibly apply in a given fact situation.

The use of the word "except" can be very important in applying a rule. In paragraph 6(1)(*b*), the general rule is stated in about two lines and those words are followed by the word "except". The list of exceptions is long and very detailed and, as a result, the reader can easily forget the general rule.

The Act will often use the phrase "for greater certainty" to expand the application of a rule or definition to include something specific. This occurs, for example, in paragraph 256(1.2)(*b*).

It is common for the Act to use the word "deem". For example, subsection 250(1) deems an individual to be a full-year resident of Canada if certain specified conditions are met. If an individual fits one of the conditions, that person will be deemed to be a full-year resident for tax purposes, even if that individual would not otherwise be treated like a full-year resident because of physical absence for all or a part of the year.

The Act often uses the term "prescribed" in connection with the *Income Tax Regulations* or a form. For example, subparagraph 6(1)(*k*)(v) refers to an "amount prescribed". In the Regulation footnote to paragraph 6(1)(*k*), the reader is referred to Regulation 7305.1 for the prescribed amount. Another use of the word "prescribed" occurs in paragraph 8(6.1)(*a*) of the Act, in reference to a form to be used by an employer to certify for the deduction for an eligible tool of a tradesperson. The prescribed form (T777) is found under the "Form" heading in the related matter for section 8 in the Wolters Kluwer edition of the *Income Tax Act*.

¶1,530 Intention of Parliament

In interpreting or construing a taxing statute, inferences about the intention of Parliament are often made. As indicated previously, the Department of Finance now often publishes detailed explanatory notes to accompany draft legislation. These notes may be helpful in determining intention but are not binding on a court. No interpretation is allowed to defeat the plain intention of the legislation. The courts assume that what is stated in the Act is what was meant by Parliament.[13] Thus, a meaning that is consistent with the intention of Parliament will prevail.

¶1,535 Remission Orders

Taxing statutes were to be interpreted strictly, according to early rules of interpretation. However, where doubt exists, the construction of the statute was to be resolved in favour of the taxpayer in the case of a charging provision and in favour of the Crown in the case of an exemption provision. In addition, if it was not possible for the courts to render what they considered to be an equitable decision in a particular case, relief for the taxpayer could be found under the *Financial Administration Act*. Subsection 17(1) of that Act provides for the remission of taxes and penalties when it is considered in the public interest.[14]

¶1,540 Contextual Approach

The Supreme Court of Canada has suggested that the strict interpretation rule is still applicable where the plain meaning of the words is straightforward. Where the provision

[13] This is illustrated by the case of *M.N.R. v. MacInnes*, 54 DTC 1031 (Ex. Ct.), on the meaning of "property substituted". The intention of Parliament as a means of interpretation was also raised in the case of *Duha Printers (Western) Ltd. v. The Queen*, 98 DTC 6334 (S.C.C.).

[14] For a case which refers a taxpayer to the *Financial Administration Act*, see *Bayraktaroglu v. M.N.R.*, 73 DTC 27 (T.R.B.).

is vague and/or confusing, it is to be interpreted within its context in the Act on a basis consistent with the objective of the Act and the intention of Parliament, which may reflect political, economic, social, or technological objectives. This "object and spirit" test of interpretation was used in the case of *Stubart Investments Ltd. v. The Queen* by the Supreme Court of Canada and, at least to some extent, has been codified in the general anti-avoidance rule ("GAAR") of the Act.[15] The Supreme Court has often quoted the authority on the interpretation of statutes, E.E. Driedger in *Construction of Statutes*,[16] as follows:

ITA: 245(4) Application of subsection (2); Cases: *Stubart Investments Limited v. The Queen*, 84 DTC 6305 (SCC)

> Today, there is only one principle or approach, namely, the words of an Act are to be read in their entire context and in their grammatical and ordinary sense harmoniously with the scheme of the Act, the object of the Act, and the intention of Parliament.

In the case of *Corporation Notre-Dame de Bon-Secours v. Communauté Urbaine de Québec*, the Supreme Court of Canada again rejected the strict rule of interpretation in cases of doubt, as outlined above, and established the following rules of interpretation:

Cases: *Corporation Notre-Dame de Bon-Secours v. Communaute Urbaine de Quebec*, 95 DTC 5017 (SCC)

(1) tax legislation should be interpreted according to ordinary rules of statutory interpretation;

(2) a legislative provision should be given a strict or liberal interpretation depending on the purpose underlying it and that purpose must be identified in the light of the context of the statute, its objective and the legislative intent (i.e., the "teleological" approach);[17]

(3) the teleological approach will favour the taxpayer or the tax department depending solely on the legislative provision in question and not on predetermined presumptions;

(4) substance will prevail over form (see discussion below) where this is consistent with the wording and objective of the statute; and

(5) only a reasonable doubt, not resolved by ordinary rules of interpretation, will be settled by recourse to the residual presumption in favour of the taxpayer.

¶1,545 Form Versus Substance

The issue of form versus substance has long posed a problem in the application of the tax legislation to a taxpayer's situation. It was addressed in the often cited 1935 British case of the *Duke of Westminster*[18] in which a member of the House of Lords, Lord Tomlin, stated that:

> Every man is entitled if he can to order his affairs so that the tax attaching under the appropriate Acts is less than it would otherwise be. If he succeeds in ordering them so as to secure this result, then, however unappreciative the Commissioners of Inland Revenue or his fellow taxpayers may be of his ingenuity, he cannot be compelled to pay an increased tax. This so-called doctrine of "the substance" seems to me to be nothing more than an attempt to make a man pay notwithstanding that he has so ordered his affairs that the amount of tax sought from him is not legally claimable . . .

---

[15] See *Antosko et al. v. The Queen*, 94 DTC 6314 (S.C.C.), and *Friesen v. The Queen*, 95 DTC 5551 (S.C.C.).

[16] E.E. Driedger, *Construction of Statutes*, 2nd ed. (Toronto: Butterworths, 1983), 87.

[17] This approach was applied in the case of *Harvey C. Smith Drugs Limited v. The Queen*, 95 DTC 5026 (F.C.A.).

[18] [1936] A.C. 1 (H.L.), at pp. 19–20.

> . . . There may be, of course, cases where documents are not *bona fide* nor intended to be acted upon but are only used as a cloak to conceal a different transaction.

Thus, the form or legal effect of a transaction must prevail in attempting to determine the tax effects, unless the taxing statute requires that such form be disregarded in cases where form is inconsistent with the wording and objective of the Act, or unless the form is considered to be a "sham" which misrepresents the true form, based on the facts of the case.[19] Another British case[20] has described a "sham" as:

> . . . acts done or documents executed by the parties to the sham which were intended by them to give to third parties and to the Courts the appearance of creating between the parties legal rights and obligations different from the actual legal rights and obligations (if any) which the parties intended to create.
>
> . . . For acts and documents to be a sham, with whatever legal consequence falls from this, all the parties thereto must have a common intention that the acts or documents are not to create the legal rights and obligations which they give the appearance of creating . . .

Furthermore, the courts have even applied what has come to be known as a "repugnancy" or "smell" test in certain situations where substance was at considerable variance with the form of a transaction.

¶1,550 Exceptions Override General

The Act contains a number of statements of general principle followed by an exception or series of exceptions to that rule. An exception or other specific provision of the legislation will override the general provision, but the former must be given a strict interpretation. This rule was followed in a Canadian case,[21] when the judge stated that:

> . . . the subsection must, in my opinion, be regarded as an exception to the general rule, and while it must be given its full effect so far as it goes, it is to be strictly construed and not extended to anything beyond the scope of the natural meaning of the language used, regardless again of how much a particular case may seem to fall within its supposed spirit or intendment.

Thus, a taxpayer cannot obtain an exemption from tax unless the circumstances fall squarely within the wording of the provision.

¶1,555 Specific Words Followed by General

A principle that has been important in the interpretation of the Act over the years is the *ejusdem generis* rule for enumerations of similar items. According to this rule, when a series of specific words in a statute is followed by general words, the general words are confined to the same scope as the specific words. This rule could be involved in the interpretation of the words "other remuneration" as used in subsection 5(1), which states that "... a taxpayer's income for a taxation year from an office or employment is the salary, wages and other remuneration, including gratuities, received by him in the year". The scope of the meaning of the specific words "salary", "wages", and "gratuities" might be used to constrain the meaning of the words "other remuneration".

---

[19] This was confirmed by the Supreme Court of Canada in the case of *Stubart Investments Ltd. v. The Queen*, 84 DTC 6305.

[20] *Snook v. London and West Riding Investments Ltd.*, [1967] 1 All E.R. 518 at 528.

[21] *Dunkelman v. M.N.R.*, 59 DTC 1242 (Ex. Ct.), at 1244.

¶1,560 Precedents

Another principle deals with the role of court decisions as precedents, often referred to as the concept of *stare decisis*. This principle establishes that decisions on similar facts are to be similar. The precedent value of a case is determined by the seniority of the court. A decision of a higher Canadian court is binding on a lower Canadian court in a subsequent decision. Exceptions to the rule are rare, but do occur where, for example, a lower court judge can show that a senior court judge's conclusions are based on incorrect reasons resulting in incorrect conclusions.[22] At a given level of court, consistency in decisions on similar facts is usually attempted. If a decided case is not to apply to a given situation, the facts of the decided case must be distinguished or differentiated sufficiently from the case under consideration to justify a different decision. In the case of *B.B. Fast & Sons Distributors Ltd. v. M.N.R.*, a member of the Tax Review Board, as it was then, invoked the "judicial comity rule" indicating that judgments of courts of equal or co-ordinate jurisdiction should be followed in the absence of strong reasons to the contrary. However, it has been recognized that too rigid adherence to precedent might lead to injustice in a particular case and also unduly restrict the proper development of the law.

Cases: *B. B. Fast & Sons Distributors Ltd. v. The Minister of National Revenue*, 82 DTC 1017 (TRB)

¶1,565 *Interpretation Act*

Finally, the effects of the *Interpretation Act*, which deals with the interpretation of Canadian statutes, should be considered. In subsection 3(3), the *Interpretation Act* recognizes rules of construction to the extent that they are not inconsistent with a provision of this act. In section 14, the *Interpretation Act* sets out some rules of construction of its own regarding the use of definitions and the interpretation of exceptions to rules. Section 27 deals with the interpretation of time limits specified in a statute. For example, if such a deadline falls on a holiday, the deadline is extended to the following day that is not a holiday. Section 32 provides that deviations from a prescribed form which do not affect the substance do not invalidate the form used. Gender is dealt with in subsection 33(1), which states that "words importing female persons include male persons and corporations and words importing male persons include female persons and corporations".

¶1,590 Pause and Reflect — Summary of Learning Goals

After working through this section, ¶1,500, you should be able to:

- Understand strategies for interpreting the *Income Tax Act*.

¶1,600 Tax Research — Sources

Overview

Although the *Income Tax Act* is the primary source of tax policy, a number of sources contribute to makeup the Canadian tax system. This section describes the information that can be found within the Act, its structure, and additional sources beyond the Act where a practitioner may find guidance.

After working through this section, ¶1,600, you will be able to:

- Understand how to reference the *Income Tax Act*.
- Know the common sources of tax rules and sources for interpretation in the Canadian tax system.

---

22 *489599 B.C. Ltd. v. The Queen*, 2008 DTC 4107 (TCC).

¶1,610 The *Income Tax Act*

An overview of the Act can best be obtained from an inspection of the Table of Contents to the Act. A detailed sectional list of the Act is provided at the beginning of Wolters Kluwer's *Canadian Income Tax Act with Regulations*.

The Act is divided into over 40 Parts, most of which represent specific types of tax, other than income tax. Of course, the largest Part deals with income tax and, because of its size, requires further classification into Divisions and Subdivisions. Exhibit 1-4 illustrates this structure of the Act with selected categories of provisions.

Exhibit 1-4 Structure of the *Income Tax Act*

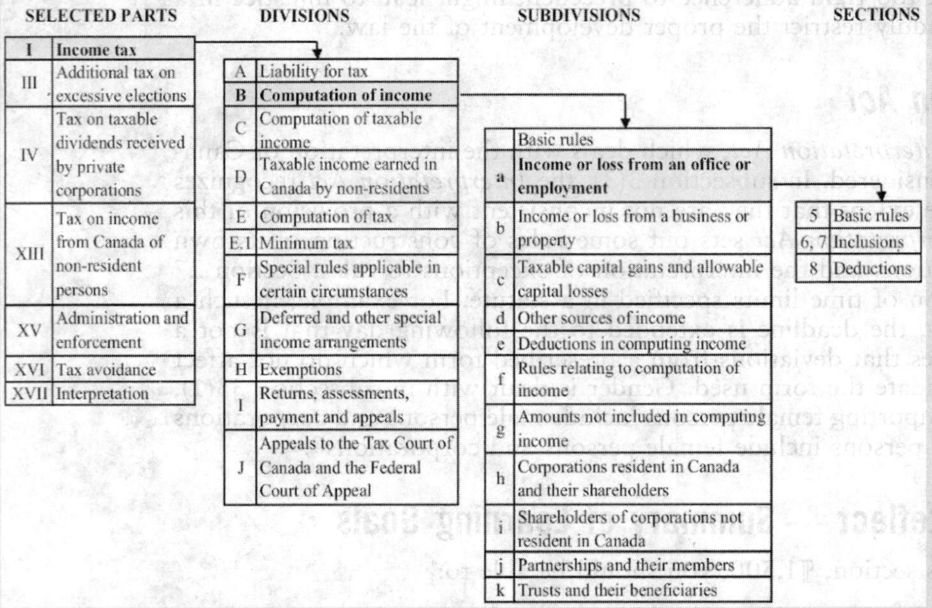
SELECTED PARTS
DIVISIONS
SUBDIVISIONS
SECTIONS
I Income tax
III Additional tax on excessive elections
IV Tax on taxable dividends received by private corporations
XIII Tax on income from Canada of non-resident persons
XV Administration and enforcement
XVI Tax avoidance
XVII Interpretation
A Liability for tax
B Computation of income
C Computation of taxable income
D Taxable income earned in Canada by non-residents
E Computation of tax
E.1 Minimum tax
F Special rules applicable in certain circumstances
G Deferred and other special income arrangements
H Exemptions
I Returns, assessments, payment and appeals
J Appeals to the Tax Court of Canada and the Federal Court of Appeal
Basic rules
a Income or loss from an office or employment
b Income or loss from a business or property
c Taxable capital gains and allowable capital losses
d Other sources of income
e Deductions in computing income
f Rules relating to computation of income
g Amounts not included in computing income
h Corporations resident in Canada and their shareholders
i Shareholders of corporations not resident in Canada
j Partnerships and their members
k Trusts and their beneficiaries
5 Basic rules
6, 7 Inclusions
8 Deductions

A chart of this nature will be presented in each chapter to help the reader become familiar with the location within this structure of the provisions covered by the chapter. The study of income taxation requires a thorough understanding of the organization, structure, and coverage of the Act.

¶1,610.10 How Do I Reference the Act?

For ease of reference, provisions are numbered, separating various elements of the provision. For example, consider the following reference:

6(1)(*b*)(i)(A)

This reference can be broken down as follows:

- 6: section

- (1): subsection
- (*b*): paragraph
- (i): subparagraph
- (A): clause

The above reference would be called "clause 6(1)(*b*)(i)(A)", stating the numerals and letters in order, in normal speech. If necessary, a subclause would be referred to with an upper case Roman numeral (I, II, III, etc.), and a subsubclause would be referred to with an Arabic numeral (1, 2, 3, etc.)

Periodically, amendments are made to the Act and it is necessary to insert new provisions between existing provisions without renumbering the whole Act. For example, a reference such as section 6 subsection (2.1) is entered between subsections 6(2) and 6(3).

Some sections, like section 3, have no subsections. Hence, references skip directly to paragraphs, as is the case in paragraph 3(*a*). As a short-form reference in this book, the following abbreviations may be used with a provision:

Sec. for section	Par. for paragraph
Ssec. for subsection	Spar. for subparagraph

¶1,620 Related References

¶1,620.10 Historical Footnotes

The history footnotes to each provision of the Act determine when the provision is applicable, what statute made the amendment, and what transitional rules, if any, apply in the implementation of new rules. The Wolters Kluwer edition of the Act provides, after each provision, a history of all changes subsequent to the enactment of the 5th Supplement in 1994. (A history of changes prior to 1994 can be found in a separate volume, "Former Income Tax Act, S.C. 1970-71-72, c. 63". In the electronic version, activate the "Former Act" link at the end of the provision and then activate the history link of that version of the Act).

¶1,620.20 Related Matters

After each provision Wolters Kluwer often provides references to a wealth of information that may help you in your research.

- related sections;
- related regulations;
- related Interpretation Bulletins (gradually being replaced by Income Tax Folios) and Information Circulars, divided into primary and secondary references;
- Advance Tax Rulings;
- authorized or "prescribed" forms;
- references to Income Tax Technical News issues (gradually being incorporated gradually into Income Tax Folios);

- related Tax Window Files; and
- related landmark court decisions.

Some of the items listed are described below.

Example

Refer to paragraph 20(1)(*q*), Employer's contributions to RPP or PRPP, in the Act.

- Related sections: Subsection 146(5), Amount of RRSP premiums deductible, subsection 147(8), Amount of employer's contribution deductible
- Regulations: Part XXVII
- Interpretation Bulletins: Primary — IT-105 Administration costs of pensions plans
- Information Circulars: IC 72-13R8 Employees' pension plans
- Forms: T2 SCH 15

¶1,620.30 Draft Legislation: Pending Amendments

A federal Budget may introduce draft legislation to implement new tax policy initiatives. Alternatively, technical amendments may be made to correct anomalies in the law to either close down abuses or to rectify inequalities in the law. Wolters Kluwer's Income Tax Act includes these as "Amendments not yet in force" following the specific provision of the Act which they amend. The source and application date of the amendment is also shown.

¶1,620.40 Income Tax Application Rules

The Income Tax Application Rules, 1971 (ITAR) immediately follow the Act in the print version of the Wolters Kluwer edition of the *Income Tax Act*. These rules provide largely for the transition from the pre-1972 Act and its system of taxation to the current Act and its system of taxation, including the introduction of the taxation of capital gains.

¶1,620.50 International Tax Conventions or Treaties

The Act must be interpreted in light of International Tax Conventions which Canada has negotiated with many countries in order to reduce the impact of potential double taxation and tax avoidance. Both the Canada-United States Tax Convention (1980) and the Canada-U.K. Income Tax Convention (1978) are reproduced in the Wolters Kluwer edition of the Act. Over 80 others have been or are being negotiated. It is important to note that tax conventions override the provisions of the *Income Tax Act* and should be the first reference source when examining the tax implications of cross-border transactions.

¶1,620.60 *Income Tax Regulations*

The *Income Tax Regulations* (Regulations) are set out to handle various specific situations and to carry on the general purposes and provisions of the Act. Unlike the Act itself, these Regulations, which are part of the law, may be passed by Order-in-Council without ratification by Parliament. However, Regulations must be written within the authority of a particular section of the Act and cannot be independent of the Act.

¶1,630 Other Interpretive Sources

Overview

Although not part of the Act itself, a number of sources have important roles in the interpretation of the Act.

¶1,630.10 Judicial Decisions (Common Law)

One of these important interpretive sources is case law.

- Judicial decisions, which form the common law, on income tax matters may be appealed up to the Supreme Court of Canada (S.C.C.).
- The middle-level court hearing tax cases is the Federal Court of Appeal (F.C.A.). Prior to 1990, income tax cases went to the Federal Court, which was divided into two divisions: the Federal Court-Trial Division (F.C.T.D.) and the F.C.A. Cases would first go to the F.C.T.D. and then to the F.C.A. After 1990, only the F.C.A. was used for income tax cases, with the F.C.T.D. hearing some administrative matters pertaining to income tax. In 2003, the *Federal Courts Act*[23] was amended, creating two separate courts: the F.C.A. and the Federal Court (F.C.). The F.C.A. continues to hear income tax cases, while the F.C. hears administrative matters pertaining to income tax.
- The lowest level of court hearing tax cases is now called the Tax Court of Canada (T.C.C.). Prior to 1984, the lowest level court was the Tax Review Board (T.R.B.), which was known as the Tax Appeal Board (T.A.B.) prior to 1972.
- Court decisions, which are almost always based on particular sets of facts, interpret the application of the law to these facts. Most tax cases heard in Canada are published by Wolters Kluwer in the Dominion Tax Cases. These cases are referred to using the name of the taxpayer, a citation such as 83 DTC 5041, and the court level, as follows: *Nowegijick v. The Queen*, 83 DTC 5041 (S.C.C.).

While the courts' decisions represent the law, as interpreted for a specific set of facts, and may be useful as a guide in interpreting the law more generally, it must be remembered that each set of facts differs from the previous cases in some degree and that a slight difference in the facts of a given case may materially affect the outcome.

Often a Canadian court will refer to a decision of a court outside Canada, such as a U.S. court or a court in a country with legislation and common law rooted in the British system. These decisions, at any level, made outside Canada are not binding on a Canadian court, but they may be referred to as persuasive, particularly where principles of taxation or tax legislation are similar.

The part of a decided case that provides a binding precedent is referred to as the *ratio decidendi*, or reasons for judgment. Precedents established in previous cases create a foundation for applying principles of law (or for interpreting the law when a similar fact situation is presented to a court).

[23] R.S., 1985, c. F-7.

Often, a judicial decision will contain comments that are not necessary for the decision in the fact situation under consideration. These comments are known as *obiter dicta*, or comments made in passing. These comments are not part of the precedent established by the case under consideration. Therefore, they are not necessarily binding on other courts, but they may provide insights to the interpretation of the law in different fact situations in subsequent cases.

¶1,630.20 Forms

Forms issued by the Canada Revenue Agency ("CRA") and officially prescribed by the legislation may provide some insights to the interpretation of a provision in the legislation.

All of these forms can be obtained from the district taxation offices, the CRA's website (www.cra-arc.gc.ca), or from commercial publishers.

¶1,630.30 CRA Publications

The CRA releases some explanatory information on the official position in various taxation matters through a series of publications which are available on its website. The series of publications include:

Information Circulars (ICs)

These deal mainly with administrative and procedural matters.

Interpretation Bulletins (ITs)

These outline the CRA's interpretation of specific sections of the tax law. (These are gradually being replaced by Income Tax Folios. See below.)

Advance Tax Rulings (ATRs)

These contain disguised summaries of certain advance income tax rulings given by the CRA and selected for publication. The last published ATR was March 1996. The ATRs have been replaced by published technical interpretations discussed below.

Technical Interpretations

Commercial tax publishers are able to access the CRA's responses to taxpayers' requests for technical interpretations on specific tax issues. For example, Wolters Kluwer publishes in print form and electronically a summary of the more significant interpretations, called Window on Canadian Tax,. In addition, Wolters Kluwer publishes the full text of all technical interpretations, referred to as Tax Window Files, in electronic form.

Information Booklets

In addition, the CRA publishes a number of non-technical information pamphlets for the general public and technical guides on specific topics. These are available at the district taxation offices, the CRA's website, or on the commercial tax publisher websites.

Income Tax Technical News (ITTNs)

The CRA issues this periodic newsletter, which provides timely commentary on recent tax issues and which can be found in the aforementioned sources.

Income Tax Folios

In August 2012, the CRA announced the introduction of a new technical publication, Income Tax Folios, to update Interpretation Bulletins, many of which are out of date. This publication is organized by subject matter and subdivided into topic-specific chapters which contain an updated version of one or more Interpretation Bulletins. The Folios will also gradually incorporate the material currently in ITTNs.

As updated versions of these publications are gradually includedin Income Tax Folios, the ITs and ITTNs are cancelled. This updating process has been underway since March 2013 and is expected to take several years. The CRA website contains Tables of Concordance between converted Interpretation Bulletins and Income Tax Folios (http://www.cra-arc.gc.ca/tx/tchncl/ncmtx/cncrdnc-eng.html) and between ITTNs and Income Tax Folios (http://www.cra-arc.gc.ca/tx/tchncl/ncmtx/cncrdnc-ttn-eng.html).

The above publications, representing what is known as "departmental practice", or "administrative practice", are not the law, although in the case of *Nowegijick v. The Queen* Mr. Justice Dickson of the Supreme Court of Canada stated that "administrative policy and interpretation are not determinative, but are entitled to weight and can be an 'important factor' in case of doubt about the meaning of legislation". In the case of *The Queen v. Royal Trust Corporation of Canada*, it was noted that an Interpretation Bulletin interpreted a provision in a manner which Mr. Justice Urie of the Federal Court of Appeal concluded was correct.

Cases: *Nowegijick v. The Queen*, 83 DTC 5041 (SCC); *Her Majesty The Queen v. Royal Trust Corporation of Canada*, 83 DTC 5172 (FCA)

¶1,630.40 Technical Notes and Explanations

Technical notes are issued by the Department of Finance to explain new legislation when it is introduced. These notes are provided for an understanding of amendments and not as an official interpretation of the provisions they describe. Although the impact of the technical notes on judicial decisions is not always known, they should at least establish the general or broad intention of Parliament in respect of a particular issue.

With respect to these Technical Notes, the Department of Finance generally indicates that:

> These explanatory notes are provided to assist in an understanding of amendments to the *Income Tax Act*, the Income Tax Application Rules and related statutes. These notes are intended for information purposes only and should not be construed as an official interpretation of the provisions they describe.

¶1,630.50 Generally Accepted Accounting Principles (GAAP)

Generally accepted accounting principles have been important guides in the interpretation of the Act where the statutory law was silent on a particular point. Canada requires public enterprises to adopt International Financial Reporting Standards (IFRS) by 2011. References in this text to generally accepted accounting principles (GAAP) will include IFRS for public enterprises and Accounting Standards for Private Enterprises (ASPE) as appropriate.

¶1,690 Pause and Reflect — Summary of Learning Goals

After working through this section, ¶1,600, you should be able to:

- Understand how to reference the *Income Tax Act*.
- Know the common sources of tax rules and sources for interpretation in the Canadian tax system.

¶1,690.99 Practise What You've Learned

Refer to the following sections of the Study Guide to practise what you've learned:

¶1,850 — Exercises

- Exercise 1 — Identify Sections of the Act
- Exercise 2 — Determine income, taxable income and federal tax

¶1,900 Pause and Reflect — Summary of Learning Goals for This Chapter

After working through all the sections of this chapter, you should be able to:

- Explain the different roles that professional accountants and lawyers may play in providing tax services.
- Explain the principles that make good tax policy.
- Explain how tax policy is created in Canada
- Explain the appeals process in the Canadian tax system.
- Apply strategies for interpreting the *Income Tax Act*.
- Understand how to reference the *Income Tax Act*.
- Understand the common sources of tax rules and sources for interpretation in the Canadian tax system.
- Apply your knowledge to assess the attributes of prospective tax policies.

CHAPTER 2

Liability for Tax

Learning Goals

Know, Understand and Explain

By the end of this chapter you will know, understand and be able to explain:

- The definition of person under the Act.
- Factors used to determine the residency status of a person under the Act.
- The tax liability for resident and non-resident persons.
- The effects of an existing international tax treaty on the tax liability of a person.

Apply

By the end of this chapter you will be able to apply your knowledge and understanding to:

- Determine the residency status of an individual, including the status of a part-year resident in a year of transition.
- Determine the residency status of a corporation.
- Advise clients and employers on the tax implications of the determined residency status.

Review Questions
¶2,800 in the Study Guide

Multiple Choice Questions
¶2,825 in the Study Guide

Exercises
¶2,850 in the Study Guide

Assignment Problems
¶2,875 in the Study Guide

Overview

This chapter focuses on the question of who is liable to pay Canadian income tax. The Canadian tax system is based on the residency status of a taxpayer. We will discuss how to determine who is liable to pay Canadian income and what income sources are subject to tax. We will also work through whether it is to the taxpayer's advantage or disadvantage to be a resident or non-resident depending upon the tax laws of each jurisdiction in which the taxpayer's income is earned, the interaction of these laws and any relevant tax treaty. Many non-tax factors may also impact the choice.

The following chart provides an overview of the provisions of the *Income Tax Act* covered by this chapter.

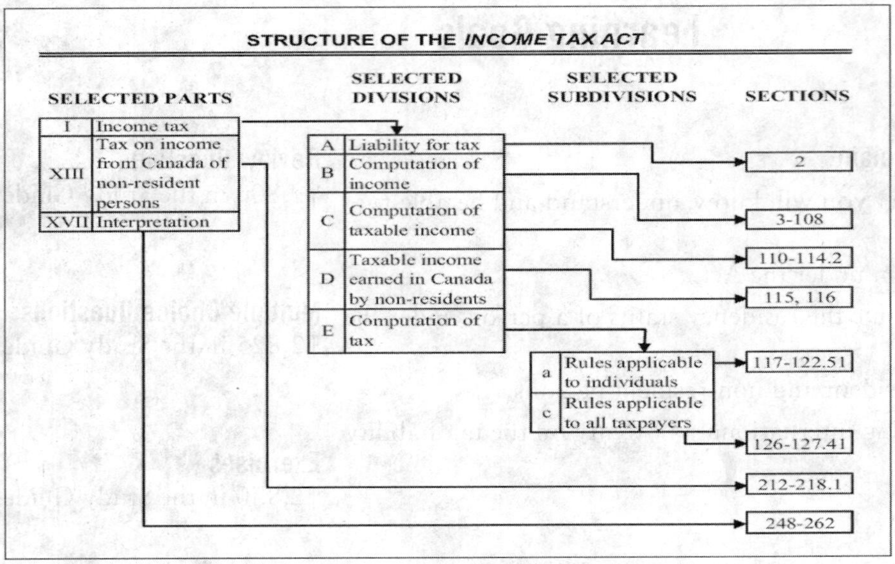

There are several criteria that can be used to establish income tax liability in a country, including citizenship, domicile and residence. In Canada, the major criterion used is residence.

The Act contains the charging provision for residents of Canada in respect of income under Part I. The provision charges taxpayers with responsibility for paying the tax by use of the words "an income tax shall be paid". Read the following provision carefully and consider some of the key terms used in that subsection:

ITA: 2(1) Tax payable by persons resident in Canada

> An *income* tax shall be paid as required by this Act on the *taxable income* for Each *taxation year* of every *person resident* in *Canada* at any time in the year.

Let's review the important components of the charging provision:

- Income: as indicated in Chapter 1, the word income is not defined in the Act.
- Taxable Income: this is a technical phrase with a limited and special meaning.

ITA: 2(2) Taxable income, 248(1) Definitions

- Taxation year: taxation year is defined in the Act.

ITA: 249(1) Definition of "taxation year"

- Person: this word is defined to include both an individual and a corporation. A trust is also considered to be a person under the definition, which will be discussed in Chapter 18.

ITA: 248(1) person

- Resident: this word is not fully defined in the Act, and is the subject of discussion in much of this chapter.

The charging provision indicates that a person (corporation, individual or trust) resident in Canada is taxed on their worldwide income. The taxable income of a resident of Canada is subject to Canadian income tax regardless of the country in which the income is earned or generated. Depending on the tax regulations of the foreign country where the income was earned or generated, this could create a situation where a person resident in Canada is subject to both foreign and Canadian tax on foreign source income. To avoid potential double taxation, Canada has negotiated a number of international reciprocal tax agreements that will be discussed in more detail later in this chapter. A key principle followed by these agreements is that the country in which the income is earned has priority

ITA: 2(1) Tax payable by persons resident in Canada

in taxing that income and the country in which the taxpayer is a resident allows all or some part of the foreign tax paid as a credit against the domestic tax. So while a Canadian resident may be required to include the foreign source income in taxable income, the tax payable may be reduced by the foreign tax paid in the other country.

After working through all the sections of this chapter, you will be able to:

- Explain the factors to consider when determining the residency status of an individual and a corporation.
- Analyze the situational facts to conclude on the residency status of an individual and a corporation.
- Explain the tax implications of an individual or a corporation's residency status.
- Explain how international tax treaties are used to determine the residency status of an individual or a corporation.
- Determine the circumstances in which a person that is an individual and a corporation will be liable for tax in Canada.
- Discuss the tax implication of residency status on an individual or a corporation's tax liability.

¶2,000 Liability of Individuals for Canadian Income Tax

Overview

Individuals resident in Canada are subject to tax on their worldwide income. The major issue in this area is whether the individual is resident in Canada. Residency has become more and more important in recent years as taxpayers with increased mobility attempt to establish residence or non-residence status to reduce their income tax liability. In order to determine an individual's liability to the Canadian tax system, we must first determine their residency status.

The Act also imposes an income tax on individuals who are not resident in Canada, but only if they are:

- employed in Canada,
- carry on business in Canada, or
- dispose of taxable Canadian property.

See the example below for "degrees" of residency.

Example

Degrees of Canadian Residency

Resident	Pays tax in Canada on worldwide income
Part-year resident	Year in which residency status changes Either became a resident or became a non-resident of Canada during the year For period of residency, pays tax in Canada on worldwide income For period of residency, pays tax in Canada on worldwide income For period of non-residency, pays tax in Canada on income earned in Canada from employment, carrying on business and disposal of taxable Canadian property
Non-resident	Pays tax in Canada on income earned in Canada from employment, carrying on business and disposal of taxable Canadian property

Example

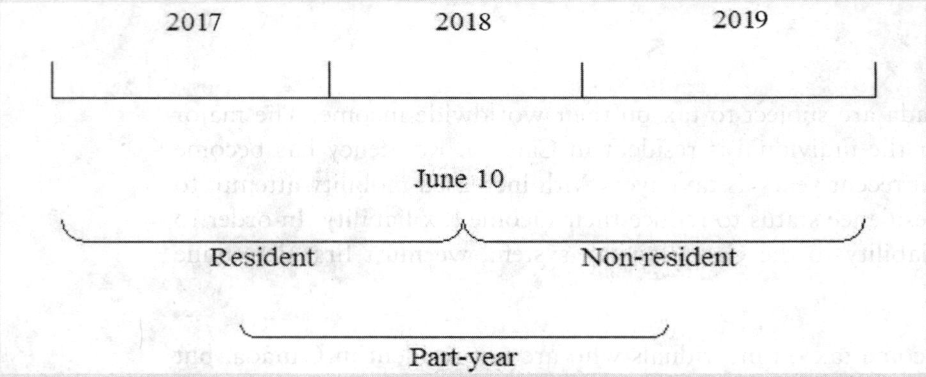

In this example an individual is resident of Canada, and then, on June 10, 2018, the individual makes a clean break and becomes a non-resident. Up until the date of the clean break on June 10, they will pay tax in Canada on their worldwide income as a resident. After June 10, the individual will pay tax in Canada only as a non-resident. As a result, in 2018, they are considered a part-year resident, since they are a resident for only part of the year.

¶2,005 Liability for Tax — Canadian Resident

There are three residency statuses for individuals:

(1) Resident, including a deemed resident under the "sojourner" rules

(2) Part-Year Resident

(3) Non-Resident

A Canadian resident is taxed on their worldwide income for the full taxation year. The concept of residency is not fully defined in the Act; therefore we must look at principles and factors developed by the courts over the years. When considering the residency status of an individual note two main concepts:

- Residency must be established somewhere; that is, an individual must have residential ties to a country and

- When leaving Canada, the facts of the situation are reviewed to determine the taxpayer's *intention* to permanently sever ties.

Intention is an important concept, but it is difficult to determine, which has led to several key court cases on this issue. An argument for continuing residential ties can be made after a physical absence, in particular, when the return could have been foreseen because of the existence of, for example, a contract of employment on return. No particular length of absence results in an individual becoming a non-resident.

¶2,010 Common Law Concept of Canadian Resident

A Canadian resident is taxed on their worldwide income for the full year. An individual may be an actual resident in Canada or may be deemed a resident ("sojourner" – see ¶2,010.20). It is possible for a person to be considered a Canadian resident by virtue of principles of common law or case law that have evolved over the years. Residence is determined by the application of these general principles to the facts of each case.

A key statement describing the residence of an individual under common law principles was made in a 1921 British decision,[1] which described residence as "a continuing state of relationship between a person and a place which arises from the durable concurrence of a number of circumstances". Facts must be found to establish the continuing state of relationship, that is, ties to the country. The landmark Canadian case in this area is *Thomson v. M.N.R.*, and another often-cited case is that of *Meldrum v. M.N.R.* Both cases involved individuals who stayed in Canada for short periods of time on a regular basis. The courts considered facts relevant to establishing the "continuing state of relationship".

Cases: *Thomson v. M.N.R.*, 2 DTC 812 (SCC); *John William Meldrum v. M.N.R.*, 50 DTC 232 (TAB)

[1] *Weymys v. Weymys*, [1921] Sess. Cas. 30, at p. 40.

Case Decision — British Court

Consider the following situation presented to a British court.[2] The taxpayer had lived in England throughout her lifetime. For the year in question she stored her furniture, travelled on the Continent with no permanent abode in any one place, stayed in England only a short time, maintained a bank account in England and held no salaried position anywhere. The court held that she was resident in England. The court considered the relationship between a person's life and the place in which the taxpayer spent at least part of their time. A person's ties to a country need not manifest in a permanent home.

This case supports the fact that a taxpayer does not have to have a permanent home to be considered a resident. All facts are considered when determining the "continuing state of relationship."

Case Decision — British Court

In another British case,[3] the following facts were presented. A British subject gave up a leased house in England. He lived on the Continent in an apartment. He made visits of four or five months to London to obtain medical advice, to visit relatives or the graves of his parents, and to take part in certain religious observances. Again, the court held that he was resident in England.

An important fact in this case was that he returned to the proximity of relatives and friends. It should be noted that the courts have determined that an individual can be resident in more than one country and that an individual must be resident in at least one country at any moment in time.

Case Decision — Canadian Courts

In the *Thomson* case, the taxpayer lived in Canada until 1923, when he decided to establish his home outside of Canada. From 1925 to 1931, he lived mainly in the United States, paying few visits to Canada. From 1932 to 1941, inclusive, the taxpayer spent the summers in Canada occupying a large home with a staff

[2] *Reid v. C.I.R.*, [1926] 10 T.C. 673.

[3] *Levene v. C.I.R.*, [1928] A.C. 217.

of servants in Riverside, New Brunswick. During this time, he did not file Canadian tax returns. In 1941, the Department of National Revenue (now the Canada Revenue Agency) requested that he file a return for 1940, which he refused to do. The Department then assessed him for income tax. An appeal to the Exchequer Court of Canada was dismissed and the taxpayer then appealed to the Supreme Court of Canada. There his appeal was dismissed on the basis that there was nothing of a casual or non-permanent character about his residence in New Brunswick, even though he lived there for slightly less than 183 days in each year. Hence, he was "ordinarily resident" in Canada and not a mere "sojourner".

Cases: *Thomson v. M.N.R.*, 2 DTC 812 (SCC)

Case Decision — Canadian Courts

In the *Meldrum* case, the individual, a sea-captain living in New York and sailing between ports in the United States and Canada, bought a property in Nova Scotia near his Canadian port-of-call. The house was furnished and occupied by his married daughter, but the captain and his wife stayed there during the captain's annual two weeks of vacation, and the two best rooms in the house were regarded as theirs whenever they might choose to visit.

Cases: *John William Meldrum v. M.N.R.*, 50 DTC 232 (TAB)

The Tax Appeal Board allowed the captain's appeal. They found that a degree of permanence and substance had to be present to create the status of "resident". Such elements were not present in sufficient degree in the appellant's case to make him resident or ordinarily resident. On the facts, the captain was more properly described as a visitor and not a resident.

Several inferences or conclusions can be made from the court cases presented above. The term "continuing state of relationship" and "ordinary resident" are based on specific case facts and no two cases are exactly the same. To determine residency status, we must review all the facts to determine where an individual conducts their normal everyday life, and to what degree the factors indicate a permanent tie to the country.

¶2,010.10 Administrative Practice

As a result of the many court cases, the CRA has developed factors to be considered when determining an individual's residency status. An Income Tax Folio categorizes the type of facts that can be used for an individual to establish residential ties for a "continuing state of relationship". Many of these facts would appear to have held some importance in previous court decisions. However, it must be remembered that statements on administrative practice in any CRA publication represent the opinion of the CRA and not the law.

Income Tax Folio: S5-F1-C1 Determining an Individual's Residence Status

(1) Maintaining a dwelling,

(2) Immediate family members remaining in Canada, and

(3) Secondary ties.

Maintaining a Dwelling

Maintaining a dwelling, whether owned or leased, suitable for year-round occupancy and available for occupation would establish an important residential tie to Canada. It is important to note that the property simply needs to be available for occupation by the taxpayer. The taxpayer does not have to sell their dwelling to cease this residential tie. Rather, they may be able to rent or lease the property to an arm's length individual. The key term is that it is not available for the taxpayer's occupation. If it is rented to a non-arm's length person or to an arm's length person on terms and conditions that are not arm's length, then it may be considered to be available for the taxpayer's use.

Immediate Family

A spouse or common-law partner and other dependent members of the immediate family remaining in Canada when an individual leaves is regarded by the CRA as an important residential tie. A separation due to the breakdown of a relationship would, of course, reduce the significance of this factor if the individual, in leaving, severs other residential ties.

Secondary Ties

Maintaining personal property and social ties in Canada indicates a "continuing state of relationship" through secondary residential ties. It should be emphasized that none of the ties in this third category taken alone would be enough to determine Canadian residence. However, one or more of these ties in combination with others, particularly in the first two categories, would make a strong package of ties indicating residence. When determining residence, it becomes important to give each fact an appropriate weight according to its importance. Secondary factors may include:

- Furniture,
- Clothing,
- Cars and recreational vehicles,
- Provincial or territorial hospitalization and medical insurance coverage,
- Seasonal residences, such as a cottage,
- Active investment in a Canadian business,
- Employment with a Canadian employer,
- Canadian bank accounts, retirement savings plans, credit cards and security accounts,
- Canadian landed immigrant status or appropriate work permits,
- Canadian passport, Canadian driver's license and vehicle registration, and membership in Canadian unions or professional organization,
- Recreational and religious organization memberships in Canada.

In order to establish that an individual is not a Canadian resident, the severance of residential ties with Canada <u>and</u> the establishment of residential ties elsewhere is important for determining residency in Canada. Although an individual can be a resident of more than one country, establishing residential ties elsewhere provides an indication of the intention of a taxpayer in terms of residency. Occasional, but not regular, return visits for personal or business reasons would not likely jeopardize the severance of Canadian residence.

¶2,010.20 Deemed Resident — Sojourning

A deemed resident is treated like a resident and is taxed on their worldwide income for a full year. While the Act does not define resident or residence, it does deem an individual to be a resident if one of the conditions of a deeming rule is met.

It is important to note the use of the word "deemed" in provisions of the Act. The effect is to establish a set of conditions and treat a taxpayer, or an action that meets those conditions, in a manner desired by the legislation. In this case, a deemed resident will be treated like a resident and taxed on worldwide income. Were it not for this deeming provision, the individual may not be considered to be a resident and might be considered a non-resident.

ITA: 250(1) Person deemed resident

This provision states, among other conditions, that a person is deemed to be resident in Canada throughout the taxation year if they "sojourned" in Canada in the year for an aggregate of 183 days or more. The Canada Revenue Agency's practice is to count any part of a day as a "day" for this purpose. The word "sojourn" has the connotation of a temporary visit rather than a permanent stay.

Example

Traci resides in southern California from November 1 to April 30 of each year, with the exception of 21 days during that period, which are spent in the Canadian Rockies marketing new product lines. From May 1 to October 31 of each year, Traci travels extensively in and out of Canada, marketing her ski apparel.

During this year, Traci spent a total of 190 days in Canada and 15 days in Europe. In this case, Traci could be deemed to be a resident of Canada, because she sojourned in Canada for an aggregate of 183 days or more. As a result, she would be liable for tax in Canada on her worldwide income for the whole year.

It should be noted that spending less than 183 days in Canada does not necessarily make an individual non-resident, if he or she is not merely visiting, but has more substantial residential ties.

¶2,015 Part-Year Resident

At any particular point in time, an individual is either a resident of Canada, with the income tax consequences discussed above, or a non-resident, with possible income tax consequences to be discussed. This status of a part-year resident can only occur in the year an individual ceases residency or establishes residency in Canada.

"Part-year residence" describes the position of an individual in the year they either became or ceased to be a Canadian resident. Part-year residence can occur when an individual, having had full residential ties, leaves Canada during a year. Similarly, when an individual who did not have such ties for a prior period comes to Canada during a year and establishes full residential ties, they would be considered to be a part-year resident for that year. The year of exit or entry is the year of part-year residence status.

A part-year resident is taxed in Canada on their worldwide income earned during the part of the year in which they are considered resident in Canada. If applicable, deductions in the computation of taxable income are allocated to the period of part-year residence. A similar allocation of amounts deductible as non-refundable tax credits may be made.

ITA: 114 Individual resident in Canada for only part of year; 118.91 Part-year residents

These provisions require that during some other part of the year the taxpayer was not resident in Canada. This means that an individual will be taxed in Canada on their worldwide income for the period in a year during which they were a resident. This period constitutes the taxpayer's taxation year for the computation of income taxable in Canada during that year. Were it not for these rules, an individual might be regarded as a resident for the full year and taxable on worldwide income for the whole year.

Thus, the part-year residence rules provide an *exception* to the more general residence rules. An individual who ceases residency later in the year, but who spent more than 183 days in Canada, would still have the status of part-year resident for the period they are considered resident in Canada. In the year an individual ceases or establishes residency, the sojourner rules would not apply. For example, a non-resident enters Canada on March 1 of the current year and establishes residential ties. This individual would be a part-year resident from March 1 to December 31, which is approximately 306 days (ignoring a leap year). The sojourner rules would not apply to deem this individual a resident for the full year.

¶2,015.10 Clean Break or Fresh Start: The Concept

To break residential ties or establish residence, facts must be found to show that the person made either a "clean break" from Canada or a "fresh start" in Canada during the year.

Example

Clean Break

An example of a "clean break" might involve a person who has resided in Canada and leaves Canada to start a new job in Seattle, Washington. The person sells their home, packs up their personal belongings and drives to Seattle with their family on August 31. The person severs all ties, which indicates an intention not to return.

This individual would be considered a part-year resident for the period of January 1 to August 31 in the year they ceased residency and would be taxed on their worldwide income in Canada during that timeframe. For the period of September 1 to December 31, the individual would be a non-resident and would only be taxed on specific sources of income, to be discussed later in the chapter. Even though the individual was resident in Canada for more than 183 days, they would not be considered a "sojourner" as their stay in Canada is not considered temporary, as required by the deeming rules.

ITA: 250(1)(a)

Example

Fresh Start

An example of a "fresh start" might involve a non-resident person who moves to Canada to take up residence on April 1 of the year. In this case, the person would be in Canada for more than 183 days, but their stay in the country for the period in question would not be temporary, as required by the rule to deem an individual to be a resident. This individual would be a part-year resident for the year they established residency in Canada.[4]

ITA: 250(1)(a)

Income Tax Folio: S5-F1-C1 Determining an Individual's Residence Status

If a "clean break" or severing of ties can be established by the facts, then the individual becomes a non-resident after the "clean break". The CRA considers a "clean break" to have been made on the latest of the date on which:

(1) the individual leaves Canada,

(2) the individual's spouse or common-law partner and/or dependants leave Canada, or

(3) the individual becomes a resident of the country to which he or she is immigrating.

If the existing ties are not considered by the facts to be severed, then the individual remains a Canadian resident. The third point indicates the importance of establishing residency elsewhere. Until residency is established in another country, the individual may remain a resident in Canada and be taxed on their worldwide income.

Example

The following fact situation is an example of the contrast between a resident with continuing ties and a resident who has severed ties and become a non-resident.

On October 15 of this year, Jeremy began his new career managing a foreign manufacturing business in Thailand. He left Canada on October 10 and worked on a temporary basis for two months, while still maintaining his home, car and other personal belongings in Canada. On December 20 of this year, Jeremy returned home for two weeks to visit his relatives during the holiday season. Jeremy kept his provincial health care insurance and transferred his club membership to non-resident status. In this case, Jeremy would be considered to be a resident of Canada for the entire taxation year.

[4] The cases of *Schujahn v. M.N.R.*, 62 DTC 1225 (Ex. Ct.), and *Truchon v. M.N.R.*, 70 DTC 1277 (T.A.B.) illustrate the differences between deemed full-time and part-year resident.

To become a non-resident next year, Jeremy should sever most of his residential ties with Canada and establish resident status in Thailand. He may be required to cancel his provincial health care insurance plan, sell (or rent on a long-term basis) his home and car and sell or move other personal belongings. By doing this he would demonstrate that he does not have a continuing state of relationship, i.e., continuing significant ties, with Canada and indicate that he does not intend to return to Canada on a permanent basis.

Once Jeremy becomes a non-resident, he should limit the length of his visits in Canada to reduce the possibility that he be deemed a resident under the "sojourner" rules.

¶2,020 Liability of Non-Residents

A non-resident individual, subject to the provisions of an international tax agreement, is required to pay tax on certain Canadian source income. A non-resident individual who

ITA: 2(3) Tax payable by non-resident persons

(1) was employed in Canada,

(2) carried on business in Canada, or

(3) disposed of taxable Canadian property

at any time in the year or a previous year is liable to pay income tax.

The addition of the phrase "or a previous year" means that income earned in Canada by a non-resident but not received until a later year will be taxed in that later year when the non- resident might not be employed or carrying on business in Canada. Tax cannot be avoided by deferring salaries or business income until a year when no income is earned in Canada.

ITA: 115 Non-resident's taxable income in Canada

It should be emphasized that a person who is a non-resident for the entire year cannot be a part-year resident. To be a part-year resident, there must be a period in which the person was resident and a period in which the person was a non-resident.

ITA: 114 Individual resident in Canada for only part of year, 118.91 Part-year residents

A non-resident who earns income in Canada, other than from sources listed above, may still be subject to withholding tax. For example, a non-resident earning interest or dividends in Canada will have a 25% tax withheld at source under Part XIII of the Act. The withholding tax can be modified, usually in an effort to reduce the withholding tax, by an income tax treaty, if any, between Canada and the taxpayer's country of residence.

ITA: 212(1) Tax

¶2,020.10 The Meaning of Carrying on Business in Canada

The phrase "carrying on business" is not specifically defined in the Act. The courts have tended to interpret the phrase as implying a continuous business activity.[5] A "business", on the other hand, is not required to involve a continuous business activity by virtue of its definition, which includes an "adventure or concern in the nature of trade". An adventure in the nature of trade can be simply described as a scheme to make a profit in the same manner as a person who is in that line of business.[6] The definition of "extended meaning

ITA: 248(1) Definitions; 253 Extended meaning of "carrying on business"

[5] See *Tara Explorations & Development Co. Ltd. v M.N.R.*, 72 DTC 6288 (S.C.C.), affirming 70 DTC 6370 (Ex. Ct.).

[6] See *M.N.R. v. Taylor*, 56 DTC 1125 (Ex. Ct.), and IT-459.

of carrying on business" describes activities that, if engaged in by a non-resident person, result in the non-resident being deemed to have been carrying on business.

Generally speaking, soliciting orders makes a non-resident person liable to be deemed to be carrying on business. The main determinant of carrying on business in a place is the location in which the contract in a transaction is made, not the location of the offering of an item for sale. ITA: 253 Extended meaning of "carrying on business"

The courts have also looked beyond the place where the contract was concluded to the place where the operations occur from which profits arise in substance. These factors indicate the place of performance of the contract: where payment is made, where work is done or where goods are delivered. The specific activities listed in the definition of "carrying on business" override the common law principle of place of performance.

Example

A non-resident offering something for sale in Canada through an employee who is a salesperson is carrying on business in Canada.

On the other hand, a non-resident selling to an independent contractor, like a Canadian-based retailer or wholesaler who resells the item in Canada, is not carrying on business in Canada.

The distinction between an employee and an independent contractor is important and will be explained more fully in Chapter 3. The distinction must be made on the facts of each case. These facts must establish the degree of responsibility enjoyed by the person who is soliciting orders or offering goods for sale. The courts have considered the following factors in this distinction:

(1) whether the parties describe or refer to their relationship as one of an independent contractor and a supplier;

(2) whether the alleged independent contractor carries on business in the name of the supplier or in his or her own name; and

(3) whether the independent contractor acts for other suppliers.

The greater the independence from the supplier and the greater the degree of responsibility, the greater the likelihood that the situation involves a non-resident supplier selling to an independent contractor. The supplier is not carrying on business in Canada and is not taxable in Canada on business income earned in Canada.

Note that the use of words "carried on" or "carrying on", "solicited", and "offered" implies a continuity of activity over a period of time. The courts have indicated that an isolated transaction, even one that is described in the definition of "carrying on business", does not fit the concept of continuity over time. Continuity of activity may, depending on the facts, be necessary to establish a "carrying on" of business, unless the isolated transaction in Canada is part of the normal international business activities of the non-resident. ITA: 2(3)(b), 253 Extended meaning of "carrying on business"

On the other hand, the CRA has expressed the view, in a memorandum obtained under Access to Information legislation, that the activity could be carried on in Canada for only a short duration and still be considered to be carrying on business.

¶2,025 International Tax Treaties and Individuals

Canada has negotiated many reciprocal tax treaties with other countries with the objective of preventing incidences of double taxation and tax avoidance. These situations may result from the overlapping of tax provisions applicable to persons subject to tax in the two jurisdictions that are parties in the treaty. The treaty of greatest significance is probably the Canada–U.S. Tax Convention[7] because of the considerable interrelationship of the two countries. The major provisions are described very briefly below.

¶2,025.10 Services

The provision regarding employees in the Canada–U.S. Tax Convention is typical of many treaties that Canada has negotiated with other countries. The provision deals with the taxation of income from employment and exempts a resident of Canada from U.S. taxation on salaries, wages and other similar remuneration derived from an employment in the United States under certain conditions. The conditions are:

Tax Treaties: XV Income from Employment

(1) that the remuneration does not exceed US$10,000, or

(2) that the employee is present in the United States for a period not exceeding an aggregate of 183 days in any 12-month period starting or ending in the year and the remuneration is not borne by an employer who is a resident of the United States or by a "permanent establishment" or a "fixed base" which the employer has in the United States.

Note, however, that as a resident of Canada, the individual would be taxable in Canada on worldwide income, including that earned in the United States and exempt from taxation in the United States.

Another provision deals with income from independent personal services, i.e., from self-employment. For example, an individual who is resident in Canada would only be taxed in the United States if the individual has or had a "permanent establishment", regularly available to them in the United States. The tax in the United States would be limited to that on income attributable to the permanent establishment in the United States. The provision is reciprocal in relation to residents of the United States performing personal services in Canada under the same conditions.

Tax Treaties: VIII Transportation

A Canadian individual earning self-employed income in the United States will be taxed in the United States if they have a permanent establishment in the United States or one of the following two conditions is met:

Tax Treaties: VII Business Profits, V Permanent Establishment

(1) Those services are performed in the U.S. by an individual who is present in the U.S. for a period or periods aggregating 183 days or more in any twelve-month period, and, during that period or periods, more than 50 percent of the gross active business revenues of the enterprise consists of income derived from the services performed in the U.S. by that individual; or

(2) The services are provided in the U.S. for an aggregate of 183 days or more in any twelve-month period with respect to the same or connected project for customers who are either residents of the U.S. or who maintain a permanent establishment

[7] *Canada–United States Income Tax Convention* (1980), S.C. 1984, c. 20.

in the U.S. and the services are provided in respect of that permanent establishment.

¶2,025.20 Resident and "Tie-Breaker" Rules

For the purposes of the Convention, the term "resident" is defined as: Tax Treaties: IV Residence

> any person that, under the laws of [one country], is liable to tax therein by reason of his domicile, residence, citizenship, place of management, place of incorporation or any other criterion of a similar nature. . . .

Paragraph 2 provides "tie-breaker" rules where an individual can be considered by paragraph 1 to be a resident of both countries. In this case, the individual's residence is determined as follows:

(1) they are deemed to be a resident of the country in which they have a permanent home available; if they have a permanent home available in both countries or in neither country, they are deemed to be a resident of the country with which their personal and economic relations are closer (i.e., centre of vital interests);

(2) if the country in which the individual has their centre of vital interests cannot be determined, the individual is deemed to be a resident of the country in which they have an habitual abode, (i.e., the country the individual spends the most time in);

(3) if the individual has an habitual abode in both countries or in neither country, they are deemed to be a resident of the country of which they are a citizen; and

(4) if the individual is a citizen of both countries, or neither country, the "competent authorities" of the countries will settle the question by mutual agreement.

When these "tie-breaker rules" contained in a treaty apply, and it is determined that an individual is a resident of another country, then the Act deems the individual to be a non-resident of Canada. ITA: 250(5) Deemed non-resident

The term "competent authority" is defined in Article III, paragraph 1(g) to mean the Minister of National Revenue in Canada and the Secretary of the Treasury in the United States, or their designates.

¶2,025.30 Permanent Establishment

The term "permanent establishment" is defined in Article V to mean "a fixed place of business through which the business of a resident of a [country] is wholly or partly carried on". The term specifically includes:

(1) a place of management, a branch, an office and a factory, among others; and

(2) a person, other than an independent contractor, who has and habitually exercises an authority to conclude contracts in, say, Canada in the name of the resident of the U.S.

However, the term "permanent establishment" does not include a fixed place of business in one country used solely in one or more of the following activities of the resident of the other country: Tax Treaties: V Permanent Establishment

(1) the use of facilities for the purpose of storage, display, or delivery of goods or merchandise belonging to the resident of the other country;

(2) the maintenance of a stock of goods or merchandise belonging to the resident of the other country for the purpose of storage, display, or delivery;

(3) the maintenance of a stock of goods or merchandise belonging to the resident of the other country for the purpose of processing by another person;

(4) the purchase of goods or merchandise, or the collection of information, for the resident of the other country; and

(5) advertising, the supply of information, scientific research, or similar activities which have a preparatory or auxiliary character for the resident of the other country.

¶2,030 Summary of the Residence Issue for an Individual

An individual will be either a resident of Canada or a non-resident. A resident of Canada is taxable in Canada on worldwide income. A non-resident is taxable in Canada, generally, only on Canadian-source income. If, in a particular year, an individual leaves Canada and severs ties to Canada, after having been a resident, or enters Canada and establishes ties to Canada, after having been a non-resident, the individual will be a part-year resident for the part of that year while fully resident in Canada and a non-resident for the other part of the year. Part-year residence is a transitional status. A part-year resident is taxable in Canada on worldwide income only for the part of the year while fully resident. An individual who is a non-resident of Canada can be deemed to be a resident of Canada.

ITA: 250(1) Person deemed resident

The approach below provides a series of steps you can take to help you address the issue of an individual's residency status.

Approach

Steps to Addressing Residency Issue

(1) Assess the Situation and Identify the Issue: Gather all the facts leading up to, during and after the move. The facts should be organized into:

(a) Significant residential ties: dwelling place, spouse (including common-law), and dependants

(b) Secondary residential ties in Canada: such as personal property, social and economic ties, hospitalization and medical insurance, landed immigrant status, etc. For a more complete list, refer to the checklist below.

(2) Analyze the Issue based on the information gathered.

(a) Develop your best arguments for both resident and non-resident status. Be balanced in your analysis.

(b) Analyze the strengths and weaknesses of your arguments by evaluating the facts rather than by simply classifying the facts.

(3) Advise and Recommend:

(a) Arrive at a conclusion of resident, non-resident, or deemed resident consistent with your analysis.

(b) If there is a change in residency status, then determine the date on which that change most likely took place. In the year of change the individual will be a part-year resident, i.e., resident for part of the year and non-resident for part of the year.

(c) If your conclusion is non-resident, then did the individual sojourn in Canada for 183 days or more while a non-resident?

(d) If there is a change in residency status, then determine how the individual will pay tax:

(i) Before the date on which their residency changed,

(ii) After the date on which their residency changed, and

(iii) For the year in which their residency changed.

Checklist of Factors to Consider When Determining an Individual's Residency Status

Factor	Resident	Non-resident
Significant residential ties		
(a) dwelling place		
(b) spouse or common-law partner		
(c) dependants		
Secondary residential ties		
(a) personal property in Canada		
(b) social ties with Canada		
(c) economic ties with Canada		
(d) landed immigrant status or appropriate work permits		
(e) hospitalization and medical insurance coverage from Canada		
(f) driver's license from Canada		
(g) vehicle registration in Canada		
(h) seasonal dwelling place in Canada		
(i) Canadian passport		
(j) Memberships in Canadian union or professional organization		

Factor	Resident	Non-resident
Other residential ties of limited importance		
(a) retention of Canadian mailing address		
(b) Canadian post office box		
(c) Canadian safety deposit box		
(d) personal stationery or business cards showing Canadian address		
(e) telephone listing in Canada		
(f) Canadian newspaper and magazine subscriptions		
Nature of absence from Canada		
(a) evidence of intention to permanently sever ties with Canada		
(b) regularity and length of visits to Canada		
(c) residence ties outside of Canada		

The checklist provides a helpful checklist of facts to consider when evaluating a case in which there has been a change in the residence status of an individual. It elaborates on the common law principle of "a continuing state of relationship" by establishing the existence of either continuing ties to Canada or ties elsewhere.

In a transitional year, when an individual leaves Canada, having been a resident, the ties to Canada may be severed (i.e., a "clean break" was made). Alternatively, when an individual moves into Canada, having been a non-resident, the ties to Canada may be established (i.e., a "fresh start" was made) and ties elsewhere may be severed.

Note that resident status and non-resident status are mutually exclusive. An individual cannot be a resident of Canada and a non-resident at the same time. The facts that support one status can usually be used to refute the other, although it is possible for an individual to be a resident of more than one country at the same time.

Using the steps approach and applying the checklist presented above should not be part of a general and mechanistic process. These tools should provide a basis for evaluating a specific case with specific facts. The process should not end with a mere classification of the facts but must provide a thoughtful evaluation of the facts in terms of strengths and weaknesses to support one or more residence options. There can be two opposite perspectives on any given fact in a particular case. No matter which side you evaluate, you will have to be aware of how the other side will regard any particular fact used to support your position.

Example Problem 2-1

Eighteen years ago, Mr. Harv DeHaan, a U.S. citizen, moved to Vancouver with his parents. He went to high school in Vancouver and upon completion of his program he was employed in construction work in the Vancouver area. In time he became a construction supervisor. He married a Canadian five years ago. The couple subsequently purchased a home in Vancouver where they lived and raised two children. He never became a Canadian citizen.

During the year in question, the state of the construction industry in Vancouver was such that he could not be employed on a regular basis, although he did work on several jobs during the year. Effective August 1 of that year, he accepted an offer of employment with a construction company operating in the State of Washington, and during the remainder of the year, and the entire following year, he worked on construction jobs in the State of Washington and in Alaska. He rented an apartment in Seattle, Washington but maintained his home in Vancouver where his wife and children made their regular home. The household telephone listing in the Vancouver telephone directory was in his name. He visited his family when he was able to take time to go to Vancouver. He always returned to the Vancouver address when his duties permitted.

During the year in question, he worked a total of 800 hours on the new job, earning substantially more than US$10,000.

REQUIRED

Prepare a memo for the tax person in your firm who will advise Mr. DeHaan on his income tax liability for the year in question. Evaluate in detail the alternatives in the residence issue as they relate to this fact situation for the year in question. Discuss each possible degree of residence and its tax consequences. State your conclusion on the case after considering the relevant international tax agreement and appropriately weighing the significance of the facts in the case.

SOLUTION

(1) Assess the Situation and Identify the Issues: Gather all the facts and identify the issues raised by those facts

Cases: *Lawrence C. Gillis v. M.N.R.*, 69 DTC 488 (TAB)

(a) Significant residential ties: owned a house in Canada; employed in Canada on a full-time basis for 18 years; educated and married in Canada; wife and children lived in Canada; recently took a job in Washington, at which he worked 800 hours; rented an apartment in Seattle, Washington.

(b) Secondary residential ties in Canada: telephone listed in his name, visited his family whenever possible, but did not become a Canadian citizen

(2) Analyze the Issue based on the information gathered. Look at the facts that support each of the following options: Resident, deemed resident, part-year resident, and non-resident.

(a) Resident Option:

- He lived in Canada on a full-time basis for 18 years in which time he was educated, employed and married in Canada;
- He owned a house in Canada and had a household telephone listed in his name;
- His wife and children live in Canada; and
- He visited his family whenever possible.

The fact that he rented an apartment in the United States does not make him a non-resident of Canada because an individual can have more than one residence.

If the taxpayer is found to be a resident of Canada under the common law, he will be taxed in Canada on his worldwide income for the year. For this degree of residence to be found, "a continuing state of relationship between the person and a place" must be established. Citizenship is irrelevant to the question of residence.

ITA: 2(1) Tax payable by persons resident in Canada

(b) Deemed resident option

An individual is deemed to be resident in Canada if he or she sojourns in Canada for 183 days or more in a year. In this case, the taxpayer was in Canada more than 183 days during the year in question. He was not on a sojourn or temporary stay in Canada during the period of the year in question to August 1, given his previous ties to Canada. The deeming rule is not applicable to deem him to be a resident.

ITA: 250(1)(a)

If the taxpayer is deemed to be resident, he will be taxed in Canada on worldwide income for the year.

ITA: 2(1) Tax payable by persons resident in Canada

(c) Part-year resident option

The taxpayer can be found to be a part-year resident of Canada only in a year in which he became, or ceased to be, a resident of Canada. In this case there was no "clean break" from Canada since the taxpayer maintained most of his ties with Canada. The only change was that his job took him away from Canada, and he needed an apartment in the United States. This action is not indicative of a "clean break". Note that facts that support an argument for a "clean break" contradict an argument for "a continuing state of relationship" and vice versa. It is only necessary to discuss these facts that support one degree of residence or the other.

ITA: 2(1) Tax payable by persons resident in Canada, 118.91 Part-year residents

If there has been a clean break/fresh start, then he will be taxed in Canada on his worldwide income for the part of the year that he was resident in Canada. Personal credits taken in the computation of tax must be prorated. To establish this degree of residence, a "clean break" from Canada must have been made.

(d) Non-resident option

The final possible option that could result in taxation in Canada in the year is that of the non-resident who is employed in Canada or carries on business in Canada. In this case, employment in Canada must be established. During the first part of the year in question, the taxpayer was employed in Canada from time to time.

A possible exemption under the Canada–U.S. Tax Convention applicable in the year must be checked to establish an exemption from tax in either Canada or the U.S. To be exempt from tax in the United States, a resident of Canada must establish that they were either present in the United States for a total of less than 184 days and employed by a Canadian business in the United States or earned less than US$10,000 there.

In this case, the taxpayer was in the United States less than 184 days in the year in question, but he was not employed by a Canadian business, and he did not earn less than US$10,000. To be exempt from tax in Canada, a resident of the United States must establish that they were either present in Canada for less than 184 days and employed by a U.S. business or earned less than C$10,000. He was in Canada more than183 days in the year, so he could not be exempt from Canadian tax.

Under the Canada–U.S. Tax Convention, income from independent personal services, i.e., non-employment related services, earned by an individual who is resident in one country may be taxed in the other country if the individual has or had a "fixed base" regularly available to them in the other country. The income is subject to tax in the other country only to the extent that it is attributable to the fixed base in that country. The term "fixed base" is not defined.

If he is determined to be a non-resident, the taxpayer is taxed in Canada only on his employment or business income earned in Canada in the year or a previous year. ITA: 2(3)(a), 2(3)(b)

(3) Advise and Recommend:

The taxpayer is most likely a resident of Canada. He has not severed his ties to indicate a "clean break" based on the facts of this case. If a "clean break" is not established in the year, the non-resident category is not possible in that year. Deemed residence is not a possibility in this case. The taxpayer will be required to file a tax return as a full-year resident of Canada and will be liable for tax on his worldwide income. In order to remove the possibility of double tax, he will likely receive a foreign tax credit (discussed in Chapter 10) for any tax liability in the United States.

¶2,035 Non-Tax Factors Affecting Planning for the Residence of an Individual

Establishing that an individual is taxable as a full-time resident or a non-resident, or not taxable in Canada at all, is not the same as determining the best form of residency. Being a resident of Canada and taxed on worldwide income, is not always worse than being a non-resident who is not taxable in Canada and taxed in full elsewhere. The best form of residency for an individual in a particular situation depends on many factors, some of which involve tax liability and some of which do not.

Newspaper and other articles frequently appear presenting comparisons of the net tax burden of a particular individual taxed in Canada and in another jurisdiction. As a result of different income tax rates and allowable deductions in different jurisdictions, the net income tax differences can be considerable. The implication is often that the resident of Canada is better off or worse off on an after-tax basis in the other jurisdiction. These comparisons can be misleading if they do not consider a number of non-tax factors that might have an impact on the situation. For example, differences in the cost of health care and how an individual finances it can offset differences in net tax. A Canadian Minister of Finance, commenting on relatively higher levels of taxation in Canada, was reported to have stated: "if taxes were the only reason [to leave Canada], the Cayman Islands would be the most populated area in the world".

While employment opportunities at the forefront of a particular field of interest or training and higher remuneration levels may be an attraction in a particular jurisdiction, quality-of-life factors should also be considered. Differences in the cost and quality of healthcare in another jurisdiction should be considered. Different climatic conditions may solve certain health problems such as asthma or allergies. Differences in both the standard of living and the cost of living should be assessed. Cultural differences may require adjustments that may be made more difficult by geographic separation from family and social ties. Some countries may be less socially or politically stable, resulting in less personal safety and more crime. Economic differences, such as less availability of credit, may exist. Also, financial exchange risks may be encountered and exchange controls may make it difficult to remove capital from some jurisdictions.

¶2,100 Comprehensive Consideration of the Residence of an Individual

For any taxation areas not resolved by a provision of the Act, there are several stages where a tax advisor may become involved:

(1) Planning: At the planning stage, the facts of the situation have not been completed. The issue here is how the fact situation will be regarded for taxation purposes and whether steps can be taken to achieve the desired outcome.

(2) Filing: At the filing stage, the facts represent completed transactions, but the client has not yet filed the return that will report the transactions. The issue here is to determine the best way to report the transaction when filing the return, given a fixed set of facts.

(3) Appeal: At the appeal stage, the facts of the case represent completed transactions that have been reported for income tax purposes and have been reassessed by the CRA. At this stage, the question is whether there is a sufficient basis to pursue the issue with the CRA further or to accept the reassessment as issued.

¶2,105 Consider Both Sides

Regardless of the stage, appeal, filing or planning, in which the advisor becomes involved, the type of analysis of the facts that should be done is essentially the same. When analyzing the situation, a tax advisor must review all the facts systematically to arrive at a logical conclusion. No matter how strongly the advisor may feel about a particular conclusion, it is important to consider both sides of the issue. A case for one particular side can be strengthened by considering the arguments for the opposing side and developing arguments against that opposing position. If this can be anticipated before actual discussions with the other side, fewer surprises will result.

¶2,110 Advise and Recommend

The third step is to advise and recommend. While the method of analysis may be essentially the same at all stages of a tax situation, the form of the advice offered may differ, depending on the stage.

(1) Planning: The planning stage provides the greatest opportunity to help the client structure the situation to achieve the best tax result. At this stage, it is possible to modify the situation and its facts to achieve the desired outcome, because the originally planned facts have not been undertaken at this stage. However, even this stage requires a thorough evaluation of the situation and its potential tax consequences.

(2) Filing: At the initial compliance stage of filing the return, an indication of the alternatives and their tax consequences are needed to help the client decide on a filing position.

(3) Appeal: At the reassessment stage, advice on whether there is a reasonably strong basis to pursue the client's position should be presented.

Below is a decision tree specific to step 3, conclude and advise, on the implications of a specific residency status.

EXHIBIT 2-1
Residency Tests
Framework for Analysis of Residence Fact Situation

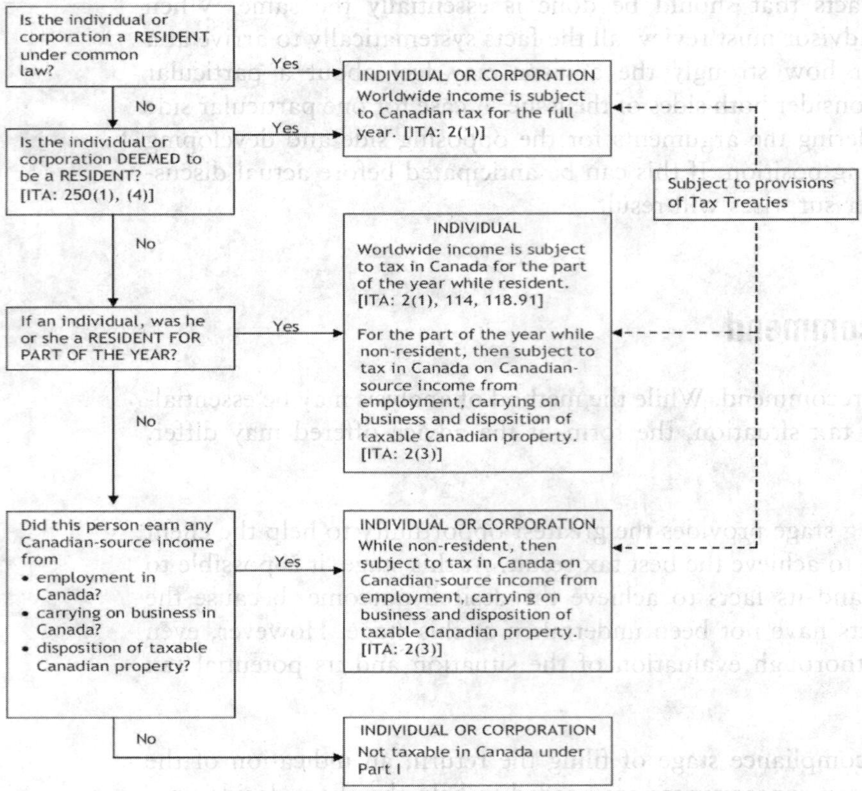

¶2,200 Liability of Corporations for Income Tax

The liability of a corporation for income tax in Canada depends on whether the corporation is a resident or a non-resident. The existence of a deeming rule to establish corporate residence, based on incorporation in Canada, means that contentious issues pertaining to corporate residence in Canada are limited. In recent years, there has been little litigation on the residence of corporations.

¶2,205 Charging Provision

The word "person" includes a corporation; therefore, the charging provision for corporations is the same as that for individuals. One major difference between individuals and corporations relates to the concept of a part-year resident. Since the taxation year of a corporation need not coincide with the calendar year and need not be a full 12 months, there is no need for a concept of part-year residence pertaining to a corporation. When, at any time, a corporation is incorporated in Canada and commences operations, a taxation year begins. When a corporation terminates its incorporation in Canada, a taxation year ends. The appropriate rules pertaining to resident corporations are applied for those taxation years, and the concept of part-year residence is not required for corporations.

ITA: 2 [Tax payable], 249 Definition of "taxation year"

¶2,210 Residence of Corporations

Since a corporation is an artificial legal entity, it does not "reside" anywhere in same sense of an individual. We must review the both the deeming provisions and the common law concepts of corporate residency to determine the status of a corporation.

ITA: 250(4)(a) Corporation Deemed Resident

¶2,210.10 Deemed Residence

A corporation incorporated in Canada after April 26, 1965, is deemed to be resident in Canada throughout a taxation year. This deeming rule clearly settles the issue of corporate residence for corporations incorporated in Canada in recent years. A corporation incorporated in Canada before April 27, 1965 is deemed to be resident in Canada if it was resident by the common law principle discussed below or it carried on business in Canada during any taxation year ending after April 26, 1965.[8] A corporation that is not incorporated in Canada may still be a Canadian resident under the common law principle that its central management and control are in Canada.

¶2,210.20 Common Law Concept of Corporate Residence

The courts have established a "central management and control rule" to help determine the residency status of a corporation. Usually central management and control exists where the board of directors meets to make decisions on company policy.

ITA: 250(4)(c) Corporation Deemed Resident

Case Summary — British Court

A 1906 British case, *DeBeers Consolidated Mines Ltd. v. Howe*,[9] established the "central management and control rule", based on the following facts. The company was incorporated in South Africa and had its head office there. The board of directors regularly met in London, and the real control was exercised in London, although no business was carried on in the United Kingdom. The corporation was held to be resident in the United Kingdom because "a corporation resides where the real business is being carried on and the real business is carried on where the central management and control actually abide".

Case Summary — British Court

In another British case, *Unit Construction Co. Ltd. v. Bullock*,[10] the following facts were presented. The appellant company was a wholly owned subsidiary of a British company and so were three companies registered in Kenya. The appellant had made some payments to these companies that would be tax

[8] For the purposes of this chapter, paragraph 250(4)(*b*) can be ignored.

[9] *DeBeers Consolidated Mines Ltd. v. Howe*, [1906] A.C. 455.

[10] *Unit Construction Co. Ltd. v. Bullock*, [1959] 3 W.W.R. 1022.

deductible only if the companies were resident in the United Kingdom for the year in question.

In addition to being registered in Kenya, the companies carried on business entirely outside the United Kingdom, and their articles of association expressly provided that their directors' meetings be held anywhere except in the United Kingdom. At a certain point in time, the situation of the companies had become so serious that it was unwise to allow them to be managed in Africa any longer, and it was decided that management be taken over by the parent.

From that time, any decision of importance that concerned the running of the companies was made in London by the directors of the parent.

The House of Lords of the United Kingdom held the following in this case:

> . . . on these facts the seat of the "central management and control" of the subsidiaries passed from Africa to the United Kingdom. This is a straightforward case of de facto control being actively exercised in the United Kingdom while the local directors stood aside from their directorial duties. . . .

This case has been used as an authority for the principle that central management and control and, therefore, residence of a company is not necessarily in the country where the board of directors meets even if they have de jure or legal control.

The case of *The King v. British Columbia Electric Railway Company Ltd.* established the principle that the place of incorporation of a company is not relevant by itself. Deemed residence of a corporation requires incorporation in Canada. *Bedford Overseas Freighters Ltd. v. M.N.R.* illustrates the application of the "central management and control" rule to a Canadian fact situation. If a corporation is considered to be a resident in Canada at any time in the year, it is taxed on its worldwide income for the year as if it had been resident throughout the year. There is no concept of part-year residence for corporations.

Cases: *The King v. British Columbia Electric Railway Co. Ltd*, 2 DTC 824 (SCC); *Bedford Overseas Freighters Limited v. Minister of National Revenue*, 70 DTC 6072 (EC)

Example

Consider the following fact situation as an example of the application of the common law concept of corporate residence. Offshore Co. was incorporated in Sri Lanka in 1984 and is 100% owned by a company incorporated in Canada. The Board of Directors meets and makes most decisions in Sri Lanka. Although one-third of the directors live in Canada, all operating decisions of Offshore Co. are made by the management team in Sri Lanka.

Since central management and control does not appear to be exercised in Canada, in this case the corporation could be considered to be a non-resident. Offshore Co. would only be liable for tax in Canada on its Canadian source income.

¶2,215 Liability of Non-Resident Corporations

To be considered a non-resident, a corporation cannot be incorporated in Canada after April 26, 1965, subject to certain specific exceptions. A non-resident corporation may be taxable in Canada on its Canadian-source income. While a corporation cannot be "employed", it is possible for a corporation that is not incorporated in Canada to carry on business in Canada andbe taxable on its Canadian-source business income. The consideration of what constitutes a carrying on of business by a corporation in Canada is generally the same as that for an individual.

ITA: 250(4) Corporation deemed resident; 2(3) Tax payable by non-resident persons

One perspective on carrying on business involving a corporation may not exist for an individual. A corporation may be formed for a single business purpose, which, if implemented in a single transaction, would involve no continuity of activity in the carrying on of business. In the case of *Placrefid Ltd. v. M.N.R.*, the court held that a single transaction of this type of corporate situation constituted a carrying on of business. The provisions of a tax treaty may eliminate the liability for tax in Canada of a non-resident corporation carrying on business in Canada.

Cases: *Placrefid Limited v. Her Majesty the Queen*, 92 DTC 6480 (FCTD)

¶2,220 International Tax Treaties and Corporations

Most of the major treaties carry a provision similar to that in Article VII of the *Canada–U.S. Income Tax Convention* in which a U.S. enterprise is not subject to taxation by Canada on its "business profits" unless the enterprise carries on business in Canada through a "permanent establishment" located in Canada. If it has such a permanent establishment, it is subject to tax in Canada only on the income attributable to the permanent establishment. The key determinants of a permanent establishment are a fixed place of business or a person who habitually exercises authority to contract for their principal. Note that an independent agent is not considered such a person. A list of activities that do not constitute a fixed place of business is provided in the discussion of international tax treaties and individuals, above.[11]

Tax Treaties: VII Business Profits; V Permanent Establishment

The definition of the term "resident" quoted above from Article IV applies to a corporation as well as to an individual. Where that definition would determine that a corporation is a resident of both countries, then paragraph 3 of Article IV would deem the corporation to be resident in the country of its incorporation.

¶2,225 Comprehensive Consideration of the Residence of a Corporation

Example Problem 2-2

Niagara Corporation was incorporated in the State of New York on March 1, 1981. The head office of the corporation was established in Buffalo, New York,

[11] The cases of *American Wheelabrator & Equipment Corporation v. M.N.R.*, 51 DTC 285 (T.A.B.), and *Tara Explorations and Development Company Limited v. M.N.R.*, 70 DTC 6370 (Ex. Ct.), consider the concept of a permanent establishment.

along with production and warehouse facilities. The directors of the company, the president, and the general manager were all U.S. citizens resident in Buffalo. Meetings necessary to maintain the corporate charter and major business meetings to discuss corporate strategy were held in Buffalo. The main corporation books and records were maintained at the company's head office.

One of the main reasons for locating the company facilities in Buffalo was to exploit the Canadian market for the company's product. As a result, immediately upon incorporation, a sales office was set up in rented premises in Toronto from which orders for its product could be solicited from Canadian customers. A head salesperson was hired to manage the sales effort conducted through the Toronto office by himself and two subordinate salespersons. In addition, an office secretary reporting to the head salesperson was hired. All of these personnel were Canadian citizens resident in Canada.

The Toronto office was identified by the company name on the door. The office telephone was listed in the company's name. The salespersons solicited orders in the Canadian market, but they had to be approved by the head office in Buffalo. Once authorized by head office, the merchandise was shipped from the warehouses there. However, the Toronto office invoiced its Canadian customers, and payments were made to the Toronto office and deposited to a bank account in the company's name in Toronto. The Toronto office operating expenses, including the salaries of all Toronto personnel and the commissions of the salespersons, were paid from the Toronto bank account by cheques signed by the head salesperson in Toronto. Records of these receipts and disbursements were kept in a set of books at the Toronto office. At the end of each month, the Toronto office would remit all but a nominal amount of the balance remaining in the bank account to head office.

By the end of the last year, the Canadian market for its product was such that the expense of maintaining an office in downtown Toronto was not warranted. Effective January 1 of the current year, the head salesperson was instructed to carry out all of his duties from a room built to accommodate the work in the basement of his home. The two subordinate salespersons reported to him there. The home telephone with a listing in the head salesperson's name was used for the business. All salespersons carried business cards printed with the company name and the number of this residence's phone. It was felt that the services of the secretary were unnecessary at this location since the head salesperson's spouse could be paid to do the secretarial work on a part-time basis. A telephone answering service was hired to take messages when no one was home.

REQUIRED

Prepare a memo for the tax person in your firm who will advise Niagara Corporation on the income tax consequences of these facts for the current year. Evaluate in detail the residence issue alternatives related to this fact situation for the current year. Discuss each possible option of residence and its tax consequences. State your conclusions on the case after considering the relevant international tax agreement and weighing the significance of the facts in the case.

SOLUTION

(1) Assess the Situation and Identify the Issues: Gather all the facts summarized in the above statement of facts and "required".

Cases: *American Wheelabrator & Equipment Corporation v. M.N.R.*, 51 DTC 285 (TAB); *Tara Exploration and Development Company Limited v. Minister of National Revenue*, 70 DTC 6370 (EC)

(2) Analyze the Issue based on the information gathered. Our analysis will look at the facts that support each of the following options: Resident, deemed resident, and non-resident.

(a) Canadian resident option

Since residence is not fully defined in the Act, it is necessary to make a determination based on the specific facts of each case. A corporation can be found to be resident by common law principle. If this is the case, the corporation will be taxed in Canada on its worldwide income. The common law principle that must be in evidence is that "central management and control" are in Canada. In this case, the directors, president and general manager managed from head office in the United States. Corporate business and strategy meetings were held in the United States. Corporate books and records, with the exception of the Toronto records, were kept in the United States. The Toronto records are probably not sufficient to establish central management and control since they are subsidiary documents. Also, the management function undertaken by the head salesperson would probably not be major enough to indicate central management and control of the company.

ITA: 2(1) Tax payable by persons resident in Canada

(b) Deemed resident option

A corporation can be deemed resident by meeting the conditions of subsection 250(4), and, as a result, it would be taxed in Canada on its worldwide income. To be deemed resident, the corporation must be incorporated in Canada. In this case, since the company was not incorporated in Canada, the date of incorporation is irrelevant and the questions raised in the deeming rule of residence (by common law principle) or of carrying on business in Canada need not be addressed.

ITA: 2(1) Tax payable by persons resident in Canada; 250(4) Corporation deemed resident

(c) Non-resident option

Under the third option of residence, the corporation can be considered a non-resident carrying on business in Canada. It can then be taxed in Canada on profits from its business in Canada. Carrying on business in Canada must be established by the facts of the case. Soliciting orders in Canada is enough to establish carrying on business in Canada. This raises the question as to whether the salesperson was an employee of the corporation or an independent contractor. If he is an employee, then the corporation could be considered to be carrying on a business in Canada. The following facts indicate that he is an employee rather than an independent contractor operating his own business in Canada:

ITA: 2(3)(b), 253 Extended meaning of "carrying on business"

(i) he carried on business in the name of the company;

(ii) he acted only for the company and no one else;

(iii) he had no stock of merchandise of his own; and

(iv) the books and records kept in Canada were not those of an independent business, but were only enough to maintain an office in Canada.

The Canada–U.S. Tax Convention must be consulted to determine if the corporation can be exempted from tax in Canada on its profits from carrying on business in Canada. In order to be exempt, the corporation must establish that it is not operating from a "permanent establishment" in Canada. During the current year, the corporation did not have a fixed place of business in Canada. Other facts that can be used to show no permanent establishment in Canada include:

(i) the salesperson did not have authority to contract, because acceptance was given only in New York;

(ii) there was no stock of merchandise in Canada (note that under Article V paragraph 6(b) of the Canada–U.S. Tax Convention, a fixed place of business used to maintain a stock of merchandise for the purpose of storage, display or delivery will not constitute a permanent establishment);

(iii) the only office used was in the house that had no company identification; and

(iv) the bank account and records were not sufficient to establish a permanent establishment in Canada.

(3) Advise and Recommend:

In conclusion, the corporation would not likely be taxable in Canada. The tax treaty would exempt the company from tax as a non-resident on its profits since they were not earned from a permanent establishment in Canada. Also, the facts do not warrant finding either full-time residence or deemed residence.

¶2,290 Pause and Reflect — Summary of Learning Goals

After working through sections ¶2,000 to ¶2,200, you should be able to:

- Explain the factors to consider when determining the residency status of an individual and a corporation.
- Analyze the situational facts to conclude on the residency status of an individual and a corporation.
- Explain the tax implications of an individual or a corporation's residency status.
- Explain how international tax treaties are used to determine the residency status of an individual or a corporation.

- Determine the circumstances in which a person that is an individual and a corporation will be liable for tax in Canada.
- Discuss the tax implication of their residency status on an individual or a corporation's tax liability.

¶2,290.99 Practise What You've Learned

Refer to the following sections of the Study Guide to practise what you've learned:

¶2,800 — Review Questions

- Question 1 — Individual Residency
- Question 2 — Individual Residency
- Question 3 — Individual Residency
- Question 7 — Corporate Residency
- Question 8 — Corporate Residency

¶2,825 — Multiple Choice Questions

- Question 2 — Individual residency
- Question 3 — Canadian income of non-resident
- Question 4 — Canadian income of part-year resident

¶2,850 — Exercises

- Exercise 2 — Individual Residency
- Exercise 3 — Individual Residency
- Exercise 4 — Individual Residency
- Exercise 7 — Corporate Residency
- Exercise 8 — Corporate Residency
- Exercise 9 — Corporate Residency

CHAPTER 3

Employment Income

ADVANCED CONTENT IN THIS CHAPTER

Ⓐ Stock Option Cash Outs

Ⓐ Cost for Leased Passenger Vehicle

Learning Goals

Know, Understand and Explain

By the end of this chapter you will know, understand and be able to explain:

- The basic provisions of the *Income Tax Act* (the Act) that relate to employment income.
- The factors that distinguish an employee from a self-employed individual.
- What amounts must be included in employment income.
- How employment deductions are calculated.
- The special rules relating to the expenses of a commission sales person.

Apply

By the end of this chapter you will be able to apply:

- Your knowledge and understanding to calculate net employment income to real-life situations.

Review Questions
¶3,800 in the Study Guide

Multiple Choice Questions
¶3,825 in the Study Guide

Exercises
¶3,850 in the Study Guide

Assignment Problems
¶3,875 in the Study Guide

Overview

The first source of income mentioned in the Act is employment income. A taxpayer will include in their net income for tax purposes taxable employment income less any allowable deductions. The calculation of net employment income can be found in Division B, Part I, Subdivision a of the Act. The following list indicates the relevant sections that outline the calculation of net employment income:

Inclusions

- Salary, wages, and gratuities received (ITA: Sec 5)
- Other income inclusions arising from employment (ITA: Sec 6)
- Stock option benefits (ITA: Sec 7)

Deductions

- Only those deductions listed in the Act and that relate to the earning of employment income may be deducted. (ITA: Sec 8)

The chart below highlights where a taxpayer can find the major provisions that outline the calculation of employment income.

PART I — DIVISION B, SUBDIVISION a

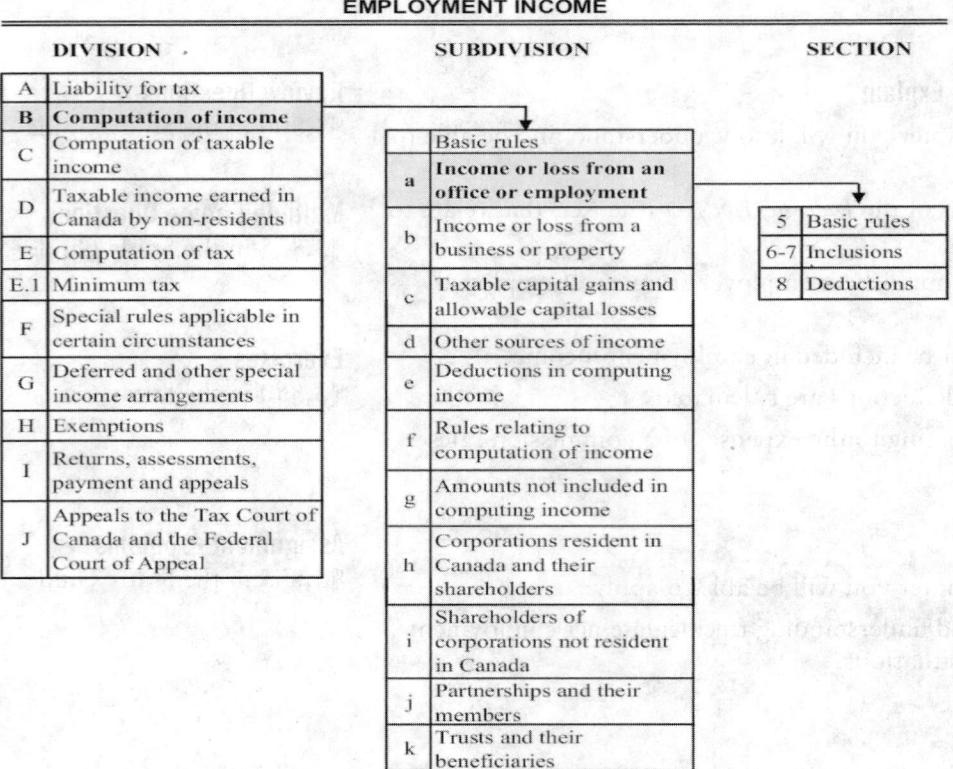

EMPLOYMENT INCOME

DIVISION

A	Liability for tax
B	**Computation of income**
C	Computation of taxable income
D	Taxable income earned in Canada by non-residents
E	Computation of tax
E.1	Minimum tax
F	Special rules applicable in certain circumstances
G	Deferred and other special income arrangements
H	Exemptions
I	Returns, assessments, payment and appeals
J	Appeals to the Tax Court of Canada and the Federal Court of Appeal

SUBDIVISION

	Basic rules
a	**Income or loss from an office or employment**
b	Income or loss from a business or property
c	Taxable capital gains and allowable capital losses
d	Other sources of income
e	Deductions in computing income
f	Rules relating to computation of income
g	Amounts not included in computing income
h	Corporations resident in Canada and their shareholders
i	Shareholders of corporations not resident in Canada
j	Partnerships and their members
k	Trusts and their beneficiaries

SECTION

5	Basic rules
6-7	Inclusions
8	Deductions

This chapter will consider, first, whether a person is an employee or self-employed. Next, the major inclusions and deductions from employment income are considered. Finally, the income tax implications of the GST/HST rebate on employee expenditures are discussed.

After working through all the sections of this chapter, you will be able to:

- Identify and explain the basic provisions of the Act that relate to employment income.
- Explain the factors that distinguish an employee from a self-employed individual.
- Analyze specific case facts to determine the if an individual is considered an employee or self-employed.
- Explain whether the amounts received or receivable from an employer are include in employment income for tax purposes.
- Explain the eligible expenses for an employee given the specific circumstances.
- Apply your knowledge to correctly calculate the net employment income of an individual.

¶3,000 Basic Rules

In this section we will review the basic rules that related to all employees, such as the determination of an employment relationship, the definition of a taxation year for an employee and the definition of remuneration.

After working through this section, ¶3,000, you will be able to:

- Explain the factors that distinguish an employee from a self-employed individual.
- Conclude on the status, employed or self-employed, of an individual as it relates to the work performed for a business.
- Discuss the tax implications of amounts received, receivable, or enjoyed by an employee, including salary, wages, and other remuneration.
- Explain the taxation year for an employed individual.

¶3,005 Employed Versus Self-Employed or Independent Contractors

Overview

Prior to determining a taxpayer's net income from employment, we must first determine whether a person is an employee or a self-employed contractor. For income tax purposes, there are benefits and drawbacks to each status, as shown below.

	Employee status	Self-employed/independent contractor status
Expense deductions	Limited to those deductions specifically listed in section 8.	Treated as businesses and are allowed to deduct all reasonable expenses incurred for the purpose of gaining or producing income from business (excluding capital outlays such as the cost of land and other fixed assets).[1]
Income tax, CPP, EI	Employer withholds from pay and remits to the CRA on employee's behalf. Employer pays additional "employer" CPP and EI amounts.	Required to pay the "employer" portion of CPP. Ineligible for general EI benefits. No withholding is required on payment received.[2]
Labour law purposes	Protection for severance, pension, and injury compensation rights[1]	May be required to pay their own liability insurance and wouldn't have job protection

[1] This option provides more benefit to the individual.

[2] This option provides more benefit to the employer.

ITA: 67 General limitation re expenses, 18(1)(a) General limitation, 18(1)(b) Capital outlay or loss

The definition of an employee is not provided in the Act. For the determination of employment status, we must look to the principles outlined by the courts which were made clear by the Supreme Court in *671122 Ontario Ltd. v. Sagaz Industries Inc.* In this case, the Court considered all facts that reflected the relationship between the parties. The following tests have evolved in the courts:

Cases: *671122 Ontario Ltd. v. Sagaz Industries Inc.*, 2001 SCC 59

- Economic Reality test,
- Integration test, and
- Specific Result test.

No one test or factor is decisive in determining whether an individual is an employee or a self-employed (independent) contractor. The case of *Wiebe Door Services Ltd. v. M.N.R.* emphasizes the need to examine all of the facts in the situation, in order to make a determination of employment status.

Cases: *Wiebe Door Services Ltd. v. The Minister of National Revenue*, 87 DTC 5025 (FCA)

Case Summary

Conclusion No One Test

The Supreme Court, in *671122 Ontario Ltd. v. Sagaz Industries Inc.*, made it clear, at paragraph 46, that no one test can be used to determine whether someone is an employee or is self-employed:

> 46 In my opinion, there is no one conclusive test which can be universally applied to determine whether a person is an employee or an independent contractor. Lord Denning stated in *Stevenson Jordan* [(1952) 1 The Times L.R. 101 (C.A.)], supra, that it may be impossible to give a precise definition of the distinction (p. 111) and, similarly, Fleming observed that "no one single test seems to yield an invariably clear and acceptable answer to the many variables of ever changing employment relations . . ." (p. 146). Further, I agree with MacGuigan J.A. in *Wiebe Door* [87 DTC 5025 (FCA)], at p. 563, citing *Atiyah* [Professor P.S. Atiyah Vicarious Liability in the Law of Torts, London, Butterworths, 1967, p. 41], supra, at p. 38, that what must always occur is a search for the total relationship of the parties:
>
>> [I]t is exceedingly doubtful whether the search for a formula in the nature of a single test for identifying a contract of service any longer serves a useful purpose . . . The most that can profitably be done is to examine all the possible factors which have been referred to in these cases as bearing on the nature of the relationship between the parties concerned. Clearly not all of these factors will be relevant in all cases, or have the same weight in all cases. Equally clearly no magic formula can be propounded for determining which factors should, in any given case, be treated as the determining ones.

¶3,005.10 The Economic Reality Test

The economic reality test examines several economic facts to help understand the nature of the relationship between the payer and the worker. This test can be broken up into three dimensions to aid in the determination of the relationship. These subtests are:

Cases: *671122 Ontario Ltd. v. Sagaz Industries Inc.*, 2001 SCC 59

- The control test: determines whether the individual is directed by someone who is in a position to order or require not only what is to be done but how it is to be done.
- The ownership of tools test: determines who bears the cost of the tools necessary to perform the services and/or work.
- The profit/loss test: determines which party in the relationship bears the risk of loss or has the possibility of making profit.

The Control Test

The control test reviews:

- who has the right to give orders and instructions to a worker on the manner in which the work is to be carried out;
- who controls how the work is to be performed; and
- when it will be performed.

In the view of the CRA, control "exists if the person for whom services are performed has the right to control the amount, the nature, and the management of the work to be done and the manner of doing it".

Interpretation Bulletins: IT-525R (Consolidated) Performing Artists (Consolidated)

The shortcomings of the control test reveal themselves in circumstances where it is difficult, because of the nature of the work, to exercise any control over the manner in which the work is performed. In particular, the courts have found the test to be too inflexible in determining the issue in respect of professionals and highly skilled tradespeople who are hired for their knowledge and expertise; that is, they do not need to be told how to do a job.

Case Summary

The Royal Winnipeg Ballet v. M.N.R

At issue was whether the dancers of the Royal Winnipeg Ballet ("RWB") were employees or self-employed independent contractors. Justice Sharlow, in finding that the dancers were independent contractors, made the following statement, at paragraph 66 of the decision:

> The control factor in this case, as in most cases, requires particular attention. It seems to me that while the degree of control exercised by the RWB over the work of the dancers is extensive, it is no more than is needed to stage a series of ballets over a well planned season of performances. If the RWB were to stage a ballet using guest artists in all principal roles, the

> RWB's control over the guest artists would be the same as if each role were performed by a dancer engaged for the season. If it is accepted (as it must be), that a guest artist may accept a role with the RWB without becoming its employee, then the element of control must be consistent with the guest artist being an independent contractor. Therefore, the elements of control in this case cannot reasonably be considered to be inconsistent with the parties' understanding that the dancers were independent contractors.

The Federal Court of Appeal considered the relevance of the intention of the parties. Justice Sharlow, at paragraph 62, indicated that

Cases: *The Royal Winnipeg Ballet v. M.N.R.*, 2006 DTC 6323 (FCA)

> "a stipulation in a contract as to the legal nature of the relationship created by the contract cannot be determinative". However, she went on to state, at paragraph 64, " . . . it seems to me wrong in principle to set aside, as worthy of no weight, the uncontradicted evidence of the parties as to their common understanding of their legal relationship, even if that evidence cannot be conclusive". She concluded, at paragraph 67, " . . . this is a case where the common understanding of the parties as to the nature of their legal relationship is borne out by the contractual terms and the other relevant facts".

As a result, the dancers were considered to be self-employed.

The Ownership of Tools Test

In the case where the taxpayer doing the work supplies the funds or equipment necessary to perform the work and takes on financial risk or responsibility, the ownership of tools test would determine the taxpayer to be an independent contractor. The requirement to provide their own tools and resources implies that the taxpayer is taking on an economic risk associated with performing the service required.

This test becomes less conclusive in scenarios where the taxpayer providing the work is a professional whose main tool is knowledge or expertise.

The Profit/Loss Test

Where the taxpayer doing the work

- has a chance of making a profit;
- risks incurring a loss from bad debts, damages to assets, or delivery delays; and
- must cover operating costs,

there is evidence of an independent contractor or self-employed status. On the other hand, in an employer–employee relationship, the employee typically receives payment for services from the business regardless of whether the business collects the costs from the client or customer.

¶3,005.20 Integration Test

The integration test examines whether the individual doing the work is economically dependent on the organization. In this test, it is important to review the facts from the point of view of the individual, not the payer (i.e., the business). The more dependent the individual is on the organization, the more likely he or she will appear to be an employee. Consideration can be given, for example, to the proportion of the individual's income derived from the organization and the availability to the individual of benefits available to employees of the organization.

¶3,005.30 Specific Result Test

The specific result test is the third test in determining the status of the relationship. In an employer–employee relationship, the employee puts his or her personal services at the disposal of the employer during a given period of time without reference to a specified result. Generally, the accomplishment of work is on an ongoing basis.

On the other hand, where a worker and payer agree that certain specified work will be done with assistance provided by the worker, it may be inferred that an independent contractor relationship exists. In the CRA's view, this test is satisfied where the facts suggest that "a person is engaged to achieve a defined objective and is given all the freedom to obtain the desired result". The facts used in the application of the integration or organization test may also be useful in the specific result test since the tests appear to be closely related.

Interpretation Bulletins: IT-525R (Consolidated) Performing Artists (Consolidated)

¶3,005.40 Other Considerations

CRA Administrative Policy

The CRA does not have a specific Interpretation Bulletin dealing with the differences between employees and self-employed individuals. However, there is a brief description of the general principles involved in determining the employment status of an individual worker in RC 4110 "Employee or Self-employed?" The CRA guide outlines the steps determined by the courts: first determine the intent of the working arrangement, then determine the specific facts to verify if the facts reflect the intent of the two parties. A more detailed application of the tests or factors used in the case of performing artists is provided in another Interpretation Bulletin, entitled "Performing Artists".

Interpretation Bulletins: IT-525R (Consolidated) Performing Artists (Consolidated)

The approach below outlines the steps that should be taken in the analysis of this issue.

Approach

Steps to Addressing Employed Versus Self-Employed Issue

(1) Assess the Situation and Identify the Issues:

(a) Gather all the facts relating to the person's position and activities.

(b) Organize your thoughts around the following tests:

Step 1 Determine the intent of the two parties

Step 2

(i) Economic reality or entrepreneur test

- Control,
- Ownership of tools, and
- Chance of profit/risk of loss;

(ii) Integration or organization test; and

(iii) Specific result test.

(2) Analyze the Issues:

(a) Based on the tests above, develop your best arguments for both employed and self-employed. Be balanced in your analysis.

(b) Analyze the strengths and weaknesses of your arguments.

(3) Conclude and Advise:

(a) Arrive at a conclusion of employed or self-employed consistent with your analysis.

(b) Assess the impact of your decision and advise on the implications.

(i) Expenses deductible for tax purposes,

(ii) Tax rates applicable to the income, and

(iii) Non-tax factors such as employee and government benefits.

Example Problem 3-1

The taxpayer, a professional pathologist, was appointed Director of the Clinical Chemistry Laboratory of a hospital for a period of five years. He reported to the hospital's Director of Laboratories who advised the taxpayer what his work involved and decided the amount to be paid to the taxpayer. The hospital supplied all the necessary laboratory facilities and equipment. The laboratory conducted tests exclusively for the patients of the hospital, although some tests were referred out by the hospital to private laboratories.

The taxpayer's main responsibility was to ensure that the output and quality of the work done in the laboratory by 15 technologists who were employees of the hospital was acceptable. He did not have the authority to hire or fire any of the technologists who worked under him, but could, if necessary, request additional help from the hospital's administration. The taxpayer did not have to arrange for or pay his replacement if he was absent from the laboratory for vacations or other lengthy periods of time. Substitute pathologists were paid directly by the hospital.

The normal deductions from employees' salaries were made by the hospital in respect of the taxpayer's remuneration. The taxpayer also participated in the group insurance plan toward which the hospital made substantial contributions. The taxpayer also deducted expenses for professional dues, property taxes, business fees, liability insurance, books and journals, telephone, accounting fees, and travel and conventions.

REQUIRED

Is the taxpayer in this case an employee or an independent contractor? In presenting your answer, discuss the tests that are applied by the courts in this type of situation and consider how the facts relate to these tests. What are the general tax consequences of your findings?

SOLUTION

Step 1: Assess the Situation and Identify the Issues

The following is based on the decision of the Chairman of the Tax Review Board in the case of *Hauser v. M.N.R.* Based on the information above, the intention of the two parties appears to reflect an employment relationship. The hospital took the responsibility to provide replacements during longer periods of time such as vacations. The hospital withholds normal deductions and contributes to the group insurance plan, similar to other employees.

Cases: *Wolfgang Hauser v. M.N.R.*, 78 DTC 1532 (TRB)

Step 2: Analyze the Issues

Next, we must analyze the facts based on the three tests to determine if the facts are consistent with the intent of the parties involved.

(i) The Economic Reality or Entrepreneur Test:

Control Test: The control test was found by the courts to be too inflexible in determining the issue, particularly in respect of professionals and highly trained, skilled trades people. Key factors considered by the courts are:

- Director of Laboratories could not or would not interfere in the taxpayer's exercise of his professional skills. This indicates self-employed contractor.
- There are usual strict controls of an employer over the employee's work that are not found in this instance, which indicates self-employed contractor.
- The taxpayer, as a staff member, was under the hospital's control for the general assignment and reporting of his work and for the amount of remuneration that would be allocated to him. Indicates an employee–employer relationship.

Although these factors would not be present if the appellant were in fact a private practitioner, the application of the control test is not, in the circumstances of this appeal, a wholly satisfactory or conclusive one.

Ownership of tools test: This aspect of the economic reality test is more revealing of the nature of the relationship. We should compare the taxpayer's professional activities in the hospital's chemistry laboratory with that of a private practitioner operating his own private laboratory. The factors considered by the courts are the following:

- All equipment and supplies are provided by the hospital.
- The taxpayer can request additional support staff from hospital administration, and all support staff are hired and paid directly by the hospital. This indicates an employee/employer relationship.
- Unlike a self-employed contractor, the taxpayer was not required to seek out new clients; the patients were those of the hospital. This indicates an employee/employer relationship.
- The knowledge and expertise required to perform his duties are inconclusive since these skills can be used in his capacity as an employee or self-employed individual.
- Substitute pathologists are paid directly by the hospital, which indicates an employee relationship.

Based on the Economic Reality test, there are more factors that indicate the taxpayer was under a contract for services to the hospital as an employer rather than that of a self-employed contractor.

(ii) The Integration Test:

The facts suggest an economic dependence on the organization. In such circumstances the courts have held that the taxpayer was an employee. Factors considered in this analysis:

- The taxpayer was appointed for a period of five years by the hospital under a contract of service. By this agreement, his knowledge and skills in pathology or in any other related field in which the taxpayer may have been qualified was employed in the hospital's general organization in the treatment of patients.
- The payer deducted normal payroll deductions, such as income tax, EI, and CPP, in respect of the taxpayer's salary, and the taxpayer participated in the hospital's group insurance plan. This indicates the payer's intent of employment relationship. Since the worker accepted that arrangement for a number of years, this indicates the objective intent of the worker to be treated like an employee.

(iii) The Specific Result Test:

According to the Specific Result test, the courts can reasonably conclude that the taxpayer was an employee of the hospital.

- The taxpayer was appointed as Director of the Clinical Chemistry Laboratory of the hospital for a five-year period on a full-time basis. This indicates an employee/employer relationship.
- His income from the hospital, though paid periodically, was calculated on a yearly basis. This indicates an employee–employer relationship.
- The taxpayer's personal professional services were at the disposition of the hospital. This indicates an employee–employer relationship.
- The taxpayer's work was done on a continuous day-to-day basis without there being any limited or specified amount of work that the taxpayer had, by contract, to accomplish. This indicates an employee–employer relationship.
- The taxpayer had to do the work personally and did not employ or pay substitute part-time pathologists to do his work in his absence. This indicates an employee/employer relationship.

Step 3 Conclude and Advise

As a result of reviewing the intent of the two parties and applying all three tests to the facts of this case, there is nothing that supports the contention that the taxpayer was under a contract for services or was an independent contractor. All the evidence clearly indicates that the taxpayer was under a contract of service and was an employee.

The consequence of this finding is that the taxpayer's income would be taxed as employment income with the resultant restricted deductions.

¶3,010 Defining the Taxation Year

Employment income is reported on a calendar-year basis; therefore the taxation year of an individual always ends December 31. ITA: 249(1)(b)

Likewise, current legislation requires the self-employed to have a December 31 year end or to use a more complicated method of reporting business income.

An employee attempting to circumvent the mandatory calendar year reporting by incorporating his or her "business" would be known as a personal services business ("PSB"). This is often referred as an "incorporated employee". The primary goal of incorporating their employment services is to gain access to less restrictive expense deductions of a self-employed contractor and the beneficial tax rates of a corporation. The special rules governing a PSB effectively eliminate the advantages in this type of situation. Refer to ¶12,155 for a full discussion of PSBs.

ITA: 18(1)(p) Limitation re personal services business expenses, 125(7) Definitions

¶3,015 Salary, Wages, and Other Remuneration Including Gratuities

"Salary" and "wages" are terms commonly used in practice, but the term "remuneration" has a more general all-encompassing meaning. Remuneration includes all items received as a result of the individual's employment. It includes such items as bonuses, tips, honoraria, and commissions paid to employees. The term remuneration includes amounts or benefits received directly (i.e., the payment of a salary) or indirectly (i.e., an employer pays an employee's rent by sending a monthly cheque directly to the landlord).

ITA: 5 [Income or loss from office or employment]

The key phrase to remember is that if the amount was received, either directly or indirectly, as a result of employment, it is part of the employee's remuneration. Examples of remuneration are:

- the payment of a hockey player's agent fee by a hockey club;
- a tax equalization payment made to an employee to compensate for the higher Canadian taxes; and
- a trip incentive paid to a sales person by the employer's supplier.

Note:

Gratuities are specifically listed as a part of an employee's remuneration inclusion. While gratuities are amounts received from an employer's customers, they are indirectly a result of an individual's capacity as an employee and therefore must be included in employment income.

¶3,020 Amounts Received

Employment income is determined on a cash basis. Only amounts received in the year will be included in employment income, regardless of when they are earned. For example, providing an employee with an advance on their pay will result in that amount being included in employment income in the year the advance is received. Deferring the payment of a bonus until a later time will affect the level of income of an individual in the year received, not earned. Given the ability to defer income by paying a bonus at a later date, the Act has outlined situations where the deferral of payment of tax will not be accepted. A voluntary deferment of remuneration that the employee had an unconditional right to receive will be included in the employee's income in the year the remuneration became receivable.

Example

An employee who was legally entitled to receive a bonus in December asks her employer to defer the payment until January. She would be deemed to have received the bonus in December under the principle of constructive receipt, as established in common-law court decisions. She would be required to include the bonus in the year it became receivable to her.

¶3,090 Pause and Reflect — Summary of Learning Goals

After working through this section, ¶3,000, you should be able to:

- Explain the factors that distinguish an employee from a self-employed individual.
- Conclude on the status, employed or self-employed, of an individual as it relates to the work performed for a business.
- Discuss the tax implications of amounts received, receivable or enjoyed by an employee, including salary, wages, and other remuneration.
- Explain the taxation year for an employed individual.

¶3,090.99 Practise What You've Learned

Refer to the following sections of the Study Guide to practise what you've learned:

¶3,800 — Review Questions

- Question 2 — Employed vs Self-Employed
- Question 3 — Employed vs Self-Employed
- Question 4 — Employed vs Self-Employed
- Question 5 — Employed vs Self-Employed
- Question 6 — Employed vs Self-Employed
- Question 7 — Amount Received
- Question 8 — Amount Received

¶3,850 — Exercises

- Exercise 1 — Employed vs Self-Employed
- Exercise 2 — Employed vs Self-Employed
- Exercise 14 — Employed vs Self-Employed

¶3,100 Employment Benefit Inclusions

Overview

Employment benefits that must be included in income from employment are outlined in section 6 and 7 of the Act. Subsections 6(1.1) to (23) provide details relating to exceptions, formulas, and limits for the benefits contained in subsection 6(1). When attempting to determine if a particular benefit is taxable, scanning the list of paragraph headings is the first step.

In reading the subsections relating to the list of inclusions in subsection 6(1), it is important to read the preamble which provides that amounts established to be taxable in subsections are to be "included in computing the income of a taxpayer for a taxation year as income from an office or employment."

ITA: 6(1) Amounts to be included as income from office or employment

After working through this section, ¶3,100, you will be able to:

- Explain the general concept of a direct and indirect benefit.
- Explain what a benefit is and how to value that benefit.
- Explain which benefits are exempt from income inclusion.
- Explain the taxation of specific employee benefits including, employee loans, employer stock options and employer provided automobiles.
- Explain the taxation of allowances including when an allowance is required to be included in employment income.
- Explain the specific rules related to employee loans, including the interest benefit, special rules related to home purchase loans and loan forgiveness.
- Apply your knowledge to calculate the specific amounts to be included in employment income under a comprehensive "real-life" scenarios.

¶3,105 General Rules

¶3,105.10 Concept of a Benefit

Paragraph 6(1)(*a*) itself begins with a preamble which states the general rule for including benefits that arise in the course of or by virtue of an office or employment. The general wording in the preamble indicates that all benefits received and enjoyed by virtue of an individual's employment will be included as part of the employee's remuneration and will be taxable.

ITA: 6(1)(a) Value of benefits

Case Summary

"in respect of" defined

The preamble in paragraph 6(1)(*a*) is very broadly worded, as emphasized by the Supreme Court of Canada in the case of *The Queen v. Savage*, so that it would seem to catch any possible benefit which arises from employment. The Court went on to quote from its decision in *Nowegijick v. The Queen*, where it stated that:

Cases: *Her Majesty The Queen v. Elizabeth Joan Savage*, 83 DTC 5409 (SCC); *Nowegijick v. The Queen*, 83 DTC 5041 (SCC)

> The words "in respect of" are . . . words of the widest possible scope. They impart such meaning as "in relation to", "with reference to" or "in connection with". The phrases "in respect of" is probably the widest of any expression intended to convey some connection between two related subject matters.

"benefit" defined

In the case of *The Queen v. Poynton*, Evans, J.A. stated, on the issue of determining whether a benefit is received or enjoyed:

> . . . [a benefit] is a material acquisition which confers an *economic benefit on the taxpayer* [emphasis added] and does not constitute an exemption, e.g., loan or gift. . . .

This concept of a benefit was cited with approval by Justice Dickson in *The Queen v. Savage*. In the case of *A.G. v. Hoefele*, Linden, J.A. elaborated on that concept:

> According to the Supreme Court of Canada, then, to be taxable as a "benefit", a receipt must confer an economic benefit. In other words, a receipt must increase the recipient's net worth to be taxable. Conversely, a receipt which does not increase net worth is not a benefit and is not taxable.

Cases: *The Queen v. Fred E. Poynton*, 72 DTC 6329 (ONCA)

Cases: *Her Majesty The Queen v. Elizabeth Joan Savage*, 83 DTC 5409 (SCC); *Attorney General of Canada v. Enrique Hoefele, Thomas D. Zaugg, Peter Mikkelsen and Dan Krall*, 95 DTC 5602 (FCA)

A good starting point is to assume that all benefits received or enjoyed that fit the definition above will result in a taxable benefit to the employee. Once we make that assumption, we would review the paragraphs in subsection 6(1) for any exceptions.

¶3,105.20 Indirect Benefits

The preamble to 6(1)(*a*) discusses that benefits that arise by virtue of an office or employment must be included in employment income. This includes all benefits received directly or indirectly, as a result of the individual's employment. This indicates that an individual can include the value of a benefit in employment income regardless of who provides the benefit. It would also indicate that if a related person receives a benefit as a result of the individual's employment, an amount will be included in the employee's employment income for the year.

Consider the following three independent situations.

Situation 1

An employee receives a cash reward from a supplier of his employer for reaching a record sales quota.

The cash reward is received from a supplier rather than from the employer. However, the benefit was "received by virtue of employment". Paragraph 6(1)(a) is broad in its inclusion of benefits and does not specifically state that remuneration be from the employer. This indicates that all awards should be included as a taxable benefit. The supplier will be able to deduct the cost of the reward since it was incurred as an incentive for salespersons to increase sales. In terms of taxable benefits, it should not matter who provided the reward, since the reward was received by virtue of employment.

Situation 2

A salesperson was rewarded with an all-expense-paid trip for the employee and her spouse to the Annual Conference in San Francisco. As part of the trip, the salesperson would be involved in meetings and demonstrations for the majority of the time in San Francisco.

Since the employee would be learning about many of the new products and also meeting prospective customers, it is clear that the trip would be for employment purposes, and therefore not taxable to the employee. However, it is unnecessary for the employee's spouse to be present and the value of the trip (airfare and meals) relating to the spouse will be considered a taxable benefit to the employee.

Situation 3

ABC Corporation's CEO owns a condominium in Hawaii where top executives and their spouses stay, from time to time, for personal leisure only. The CEO pays all upkeep and other incidental expenses of the condo.

The condominium is owned and maintained by the CEO. The purpose of providing the condominium to employees is to reward senior employees with an annual trip. Over the past several years this has created longer-term employer–employee relationships and improved employee morale and effective team leadership. The company does not fund the trip and none of the expenses are deducted from the CEO's personal income. It is important to note that the CEO does not use any of the corporate funds to maintain the condominium.

Since the condominium is the personal-use property of the CEO, and the employer does not pay or contribute to the costs, the benefit provided to top executives would not be taxable.

If, however, the corporation owned the condominium or reimbursed the CEO for maintenance costs, then a taxable benefit would be imputed to each employee who used the condominium. If the employer owns a condominium in the Bahamas and it allows the employee to use it for two weeks while on vacation, there would be a taxable benefit to the employee. The value of the benefit is not the cost of maintaining the condominium for the employer but the rent that the employee would have paid to an unrelated third party for the use of similar accommodation.

Compare and Contrast

Situation	Summary of Tax Implications
1. Employee receives cash from supplier	• Cash is received by virtue of employment — Taxable Benefit.
2. Salesperson — conference trip with spouse.	• Salesperson — primary beneficiary is employer — non-taxable benefit. • Salesperson's spouse – personal benefit – taxable benefit.
3. Use of condo by senior employees — condo owned and maintained by CEO.	• CEO pays all the costs associated with condo and is not deducting the costs — non-taxable benefit.
3. Use of condo by senior employees — condo costs covered by the corporation	• Costs are covered by the corporation and deducted as an expense — taxable benefit for senior employees.

¶3,110 Definition and Valuation of the Benefits

Paragraph 6(1)(*a*) outlines that all benefits must be included in employment income at a specific value. This creates two issues, one of valuation and one relating to the definition of a benefit. The word "benefit" is not defined in the Act. According to the Supreme Court of Canada, to be taxable as a "benefit", a receipt must confer an economic benefit. In other words, a receipt must increase the recipient's net worth to be taxable. Conversely, a receipt which does not increase net worth is not a benefit and is not taxable.

Cases: *Her Majesty The Queen v. Elizabeth Joan Savage*, 83 DTC 5409 (SCC); *Attorney General of Canada v. Enrique Hoefele, Thomas D. Zaugg, Peter Mikkelsen and Dan Krall*, 95 DTC 5602 (FCA)

The Act does not define the valuation methods for benefits, which may pose a problem. The CRA's Income Tax Folio entitled "Benefits and Allowances Received from Employment" indicates that the employer must determine the value or make a reasonable estimation of the value. This would indicate that the value of the benefit could be equal to the cost the employer pays for the benefit or a reasonable estimation of the value.

Income Tax Folio: S2-F3-C2 Benefits and Allowances Received from Employment

¶3,115 Exceptions to Income Inclusion

The general statement of the rule in paragraph 6(1)(*a*) is followed by specific statutory exceptions to the rule, outlined as follows:

(i) employer's contributions to:

(a) A registered pension plan or pooled registered pension plan,

(b) A group sickness or accident insurance plan which includes all types of income protection plans,

(c) Private health services plan premiums and provincial health tax levies, but not provincial health plan premiums,

(d) A supplementary unemployment benefit plan, including both public and private plans,

(e) A deferred profit sharing plan,

(f) A group term life insurance policy (except for the plans referred to in ITA 6(4));

(ii) benefits under a retirement compensation arrangement, an employee benefit plan or an employee trust, already included in income under other provisions;

(iii) benefits in respect of the use of an automobile, already included in income under another provision. The calculation of which will be discussed later in the chapter;

ITA: 6(1)(e) Standby charge for automobile, 6(1)(k) Automobile operating expense benefit, 6(1)(l) Where standby charge does not apply

(iv) benefits from counselling service in respect of mental or physical health and reemployment or retirement of the employee;

(v) benefits under a salary deferral arrangement already included in income by reason of subsection 6(11); and

(vi) education assistance that is received by an individual other than the employee under a program, provided by the employer, that is designed to assist individuals further their education if:

(a) the employee deals with the employer at arm's length, and

(b) it is reasonable to conclude that the benefit is not a substitute for salary, wages, or other remuneration of the taxpayer.

Benefits relating to retirement compensation arrangements listed in part (ii) above pose an issue with the timing difference between an employer's ability to deduct the costs and the employee's income inclusion. To address these concerns several restrictions were introduced for non-registered income deferral plans:

ITA: 56(1)(x) Retirement compensation arrangement, 56(1)(z) Idem

- retirement compensation arrangements;

ITA: 6(1)(g) Employee benefit plan benefits

- employee benefit plans; and

ITA: 6(1)(h) Employee trust

- employee trusts.

¶3,115.10 Group Term Life Insurance

Contrast the treatment of group term life insurance premiums paid by the employer and group sickness or accident insurance premiums paid by the employer. These are two separate forms of insurance. Although, subparagraph 6(1)(*a*)(i) identifies employer-paid group term life insurance plan premiums as an exception to the general statement of income inclusion in paragraph 6(1)(*a*), subsection 6(4) clarifies that the full employer-paid premium should be included in an employee's income.

The reason for this odd treatment for the life insurance premiums is that, originally, subsection 6(4) put a dollar limit on the amount of life insurance for which the premium would be exempt under subparagraph 6(1)(*a*)(i). When the government changed its policy on this exemption to make the premiums a fully taxable benefit, it amended subsection 6(4) to remove that dollar limit to the exemption, rather than removing the exemption in subparagraph 6(1)(*a*)(i) and subsection 6(4) altogether. Perhaps the government treated the situation in this way to preserve the option of reinstating a dollar limit to the exemption in subsection 6(4) at some point in the future.

¶3,120 Employee Loans

Overview

Employment income includes an imputed interest benefit on an interest-free or low-interest loan made by an employer and received by an employee in his or her capacity as an employee. The benefit is defined as the difference between the interest calculated at the prescribed interest rate and the actual interest charged by the employer in respect of the calendar year.

ITA: 6(9) Amount in respect of interest on employee debt; 80.4(1) Loans

Since the prescribed rate, provided by the CRA, may change for each quarter, the interest benefit included in employment income for each quarter may fluctuate. It is important to note that only the interest actually paid to the employer can be deducted from the imputed interest benefit. Interest is considered paid, in respect of a particular year, if paid in the year or by January 30 of the following year.

ITR: 4300 [Interpretation], 4301 Prescribed Rate of Interest

As we will see in Chapter 6, interest cost incurred (paid) to earn business or property income may be deducted against the income earned. For example, if an employee borrowed money from a bank to purchase an automobile to use in the performance of their job, that employee would be able to deduct the interest paid to the bank, within the prescribed limits.

To maintain an element of fairness, the Act permits the employee, who has included an employee loan imputed interest benefit in employment income, to treat the amount included in employment income as interest paid. The effect of this rule is to meet the interest paid condition for various deductions, such as interest paid on funds borrowed to purchase a car for use in employment or to purchase shares of a corporate employer.

ITA: 8(1)(j) Motor vehicle and aircraft costs; 20(1)(c) Interest

As we will see in later chapters, interest paid on funds borrowed to purchase certain income-producing assets may be deducted if all conditions are met. One such condition is that the interest be paid. By deeming the imputed interest benefit to be paid interest, all or a part of the imputed interest benefit may be deductible under the right circumstances. It must be emphasized that the imputed interest is only deductible if the amount qualifies under all of the specific conditions of these provisions.

¶3,120.10 Specific Rules for Home Purchase Loans

The imputed interest benefit for home purchase loans and home relocation loans have some beneficial rules associated with the calculation. The calculation for these loans are still calculated for each quarter the loan is outstanding, but the interest rate used to determine the benefit is limited to the lesser of:

(a) the prescribed rate for the quarter while the loan is outstanding; and

(b) the prescribed rate in effect at the time of the loan, often referred to as the "ceiling rate"

ITA: 80.4(4) Interest on loans for home purchase or relocation

Part (b) of this calculation is set for five years, to be reset to the prescribed rate every five years on the anniversary date. This is similar to signing into a five year mortgage term with a bank or mortgage broker.

ITA: 80.4(6) Deemed new home purchase loans

This is beneficial to the employees as this means the maximum imputed interest benefit that will be included in employee's income, in respect of a home loan, will be the balance of the loan × the ceiling rate. This maximum allows the employee to plan for the cash flows related to the tax implications.

The "ceiling rate" is only available to home purchase loans and home relocation loans. A home relocation loan is defined as loan received by virtue of their employment:

- for relocation for employment purposes to another location in Canada, and,
- if the move brings the taxpayer or his or her spouse at least 40 kilometres closer to a new employment location, when compared to the old residence.

¶3,120.20 Partial Exemption Related to Home Relocation Loans

The Act contains a partial exemption for the imputed interest income inclusion, as described above, for the first $25,000 of a "home relocation loan". The exemption is calculated as the lesser of:

- $25,000 or
- the amount of the home relocation loan × the prescribed rate used to calculate the employment income inclusion.

This exemption is deducted in the calculation of taxable income, under Division C, rather than a deduction against employment income. This means that the full benefit of the home relocation loan, as calculated above in ¶3,120.10, is included in net income for tax purposes. It is deductible during the first five years of the loan to the extent of the imputed interest net of qualified interest payments. This topic will be discussed in further detail in Chapter 10.

Note that the CRA computes interest on a daily basis. Following normal commercial practice, the CRA calculates interest commencing with the first day that a debt is incurred and excluding the day on which the debt is repaid, unless a provision of the Act specifies another method of calculation.

Approach

Steps to addressing an employee loan calculation

(1) Assess the Situation and Identify the Issues — Gather all the facts relating to the individual's employee loan.

(2) Analyze the Issues — Based on the information gathered determine:

(a) The amount of interest benefit to be included in employment income. If the loan is used for several different types of purchases, separate out the components of the imputed interest.

(b) The total amount, if any, of the loan that must be included in income.

(3) Conclude and Advise: Assess the impact of your calculation and advise on the implications, such as:

(a) the amount that may be deductible under specific circumstances; and

(b) tax rates applicable to the income.

Example Problem 3-2

On May 1 of this year, Mr. Roberts borrowed from his employer, Stanley Inc., $35,000 evidenced by a 1% promissory note with principal repayable in five equal instalments on the anniversary date and interest payable monthly. Mr. Roberts spent the $35,000 on the following acquisitions:

(1) $10,000 for a second-hand car which he needs to carry out his duties of employment (Approximately 60% of the time);

(2) $5,000 for acquiring dividend-paying common shares in his brother's corporation; and

(3) $20,000 as a down payment on a new condominium which he moved into immediately.

Assume that the prescribed interest rates for this year are the following:

1st quarter: 2%	2nd quarter: 1%	3rd quarter: 3%	4th quarter: 2%

REQUIRED

Discuss the tax consequences of the above transactions, supporting them with all necessary computations. Ignore the effects of any leap year.

SOLUTION

(1) Assess the Situation and Identify the Issues:

Mr. Roberts has been provided with an employee loan to purchase a second-hand vehicle, a personal condominium and shares that earn dividend income. The interest on the loan is 1%, while the prescribed rate varies in each quarter (2%, 1%, 3%, and 2%).

(2) Analyze the Issues:

Mr. Roberts will have an imputed employment income inclusion for the accrued interest from May 1 to December 31 of this year under subsection 6(9) by virtue of subsection 80.4(1). The calculation of the imputed interest benefit is below:

Car and share portion of the loan:

2nd quarter (May 1 to June 30)	
61/365 × 1% × $15,000 =	$ 25
3rd quarter (July 1 to September 30)	
92/365 × 3% × $15,000 =	113

4th quarter (October 1 to December 31)		
92/365 × 2% × $15,000 =	76	$214
Condominium portion of the loan:[1]		
May 1 to December 31 inclusive		
245/365 × 1% × $20,000 =		134
Total		$348
Less the interest paid for year on all loans:		
245/365 × 1% × ($15,000 + $20,000) =		(235)
Imputed interest benefit inclusion		$ 113

[1] The condominium portion of the loan should qualify as a home purchase loan. The interest benefit is calculated based on the lower of the prescribed rate on the date the loan was provided by the employer and the prescribe rate for the quarter. In this case, the loan was entered into on May 1 when the prescribed rate was 1%. Since that 1% prescribed rate is less than the subsequent quarter rates of 2% and 3%, the 1% prescribed rate will be used for all 3 quarters.

(3) Conclude and Advise:

Mr. Roberts will be required to include an imputed interest benefit in his employment income. Since the condominium is for personal use, the imputed interest benefit relating to the condominium cannot be deducted.

Deductions:

Although deductions are not discussed until the latter part of this chapter and subsequent chapters, a conceptual discussion of the possible deductions may be helpful in understanding the complete effects of employee loans. The imputed interest benefit for the car and shares may be deduct as follows:

Portion of loan used to acquire the car and shares ($15,000):

Under section 80.5, the imputed interest income related to the car and shares is deemed to be paid and may be eligible for deduction. Both of these amounts must meet further income earning tests in paragraphs 8(1)(j) and 20(1)(c), in order to qualify for deductions.

Portion of loan used to acquire the condominium ($20,000):

There is no available deduction in connection with the home purchase loan except in Division C, if the loan is considered a home relocation loan. As there is no indication that the employee has relocated, the deduction would not be available. The conditions for the deduction are described above and in Chapter 10.

¶3,120.30 Forgiveness of Employee Loans

The Act determines the value of an employment benefit arising on the forgiveness of an employee loan. The effect of this provision is to include in employment income the amount of the employer loan or other indebtedness net of any payments made by the employee (i.e., the forgiven amount). This treatment is logical since the principal amount of the loan is not taxed when received. If a repayment with after-tax funds is not required because the loan was forgiven, the employee receives an economic benefit.

ITA: 6(1)(a) Value of benefits, 6(15) Forgiveness of employee debt

¶3,120.90 Pause and Reflect — Summary of Learning Goals

After working through this section, ¶3,120, you will be able to:

- Explain the tax implications of employee loans, including the interest benefit, special rules related to home purchase loans.
- Explain the tax implication to an individual in the year the employee forgives an employee debt.
- Apply your knowledge to determine the imputed interest benefit that must be included in the individual's employment income in a specific taxation year.

¶3,125 Stock Options

Overview

Employee stock options are an incentive that may be offered to employees as part of their compensation package. Under these options, the employee has the right to purchase shares of the corporation at an option price, often the corporation's current value per share, agreed to at the time the option is granted. This form of compensation attempts to align the employee's interests with those of the shareholders. If the value of the company's stock rises, holders of options experience a direct financial benefit since they will be able to purchase the shares at a price lower than current market value. This gives employees an incentive to behave in ways that will increase the company's stock price. At some point in the future, the employee may elect to exercise the option and purchase the shares at the option price. Then the employee can decide to either sell the shares or hold them for future price appreciation.

Two income tax issues arise, at this stage, from an employee's perspective:

- The nature of the income inclusion: is it employment income or capital gain, or both?
- The timing of the inclusion.

Conceptually, the stock options will create both employment income and a capital gain (loss) for the employee. In general:

- **Employment income:** is the difference between the fair market value of the shares at the time the option is exercised and the option price the employee paid for the shares.
- **Capital gain or loss:** is the difference between the proceeds of disposition on the sale of the shares and the fair market value of the shares at the time the options are exercised.

Exercising a stock option will result in employment income if the option price paid is less than the fair market value of the shares at the time the employee exercises the option. However, the timing of the inclusion and the ultimate effect on taxable income will depend upon a number of factors:

- the type of corporation issuing the options (i.e., public corporation or Canadian controlled private corporation),

- whether the employee and the corporation are dealing at arm's length (i.e., the employee and the corporation are not related);

- the relationship of option price to the fair market value of the shares when the option is granted. This refers to whether or not the option is "in the money" at the time of grant date. Options are "in the money" if the fair market value of the shares is greater than option price at grant date.

It is important to note that these rules relate to stock options received by virtue of an individual's employment. Any stock options received for other reasons, for example, by virtue of an individual's shareholdings, would not fall under these provisions.

After reviewing this section, ¶3,125, you should be able to:

- Explain the circumstances in which stock options must be included in employment income.

- Determine the taxation year in which amounts related to stock options employment benefit should be included in employment income.

- Explain the tax implications of employee stock options as they relate to public company and CCPC shares, including the amounts used to determine the employment income inclusion and adjusted cost base of the shares once exercised.

- Explain the circumstances in which an employee can claim the Division C deduction in arriving at taxable income.

- Calculate the specific amounts to be included employment for stock options under various scenarios.

¶3,125.10 Rules Applicable to Public Corporations

There are three important dates related to stock options received from a public corporation. The option grant date, the exercise date and the selling date. The tax implications of each date will be discussed below:

(1) Option Grant date: the employee is granted the option to purchase a certain number of shares at a specified price, known as the option price. The options typically have an exercise time frame to allow the employees to hold the options without exercising. Most stock options will have an expiry date. There are no tax implications to an employee at the time the options are granted.

(2) Exercise date: the employee has exercised the option to purchase the shares at the option price. An employee of a public company will include an employee benefit equal to:

$$\text{Number of Options Exercised} \times \left[\text{Fair Market Value (FMV) of shares when options exercised} - \text{Option Price} \right]$$

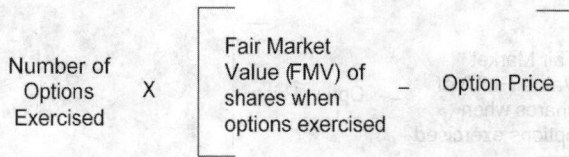

(3) Selling date: the employee will include in their net income for tax purposes, a capital gain or loss equal to:

$$\text{Number of Options Exercised} \times \left[\text{Proceeds of disposition} - \text{FMV of shares at exercise date} \right]$$

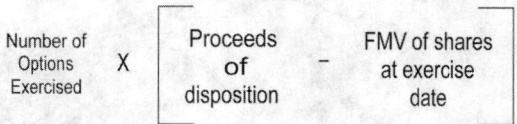

The capital gain or loss that occurs at the selling date would be included in the calculation of net income for tax purposes at the current capital gains (loss) inclusion rate (currently 50%). Further discussion relating the capital gains (losses) can be found in Chapter 7.

The amounts calculated at exercise and sale date are included in the individual's net income for tax purposes.

Division C Deduction

If an employee is granted options that were not in the money at grant date, there is an available Division C partial deduction available to employees in the calculation of taxable income, equal to one-half of the employment income inclusion. ITA: 110(1)(d) Employee options

¶3,125.20 Rules Applicable to Canadian-Controlled Private Corporations

An exception to the general rules described above is provided for stock options granted by Canadian-controlled private corporations (CCPC). There is still an employment income inclusion, equal to the excess of the fair market value at the date the option is exercised and the option price. However, the inclusion of that benefit occurs at the time that the shares are disposed of, thereby deferring the inclusion of the benefit. The tax treatment for employees from CCPC would be as follows:

(1) Option Grant date: the employee is granted the option to purchase a certain number of shares at a specified price, known as the option price.

(2) Exercise date: the employee has exercised the option to purchase the shares at the option price. No amount will be included in employment income until the shares are sold.

(3) Selling date: the employee will include two sources of income, the employment income inclusion and a capital gain or loss equal to:

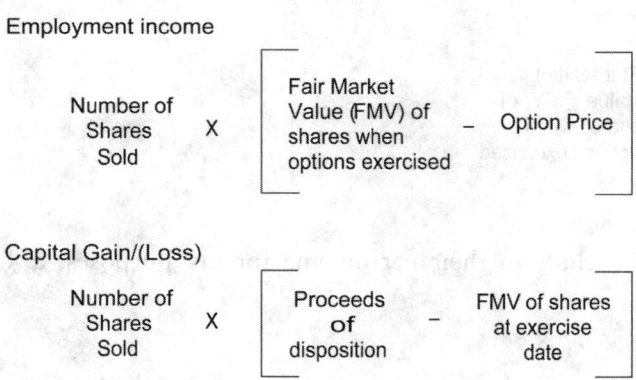

Employment income

$$\text{Number of Shares Sold} \times \left[\text{Fair Market Value (FMV) of shares when options exercised} - \text{Option Price}\right]$$

Capital Gain/(Loss)

$$\text{Number of Shares Sold} \times \left[\text{Proceeds of disposition} - \text{FMV of shares at exercise date}\right]$$

Division C Deduction

As with the public corporation stock options, there may be a deduction in the calculation of taxable income, under Division C, if one of two criteria is met:

(1) if the options are not in the money at grant date, there will be a deduction equal to one-half of the employment income inclusion under ITA 110(1)(*d*), or

(2) if the options were in the money at grant date but the employee held the shares for at least 24 months (e.g., they are not sold before the second anniversary date), there will be a deduction available equal to one-half of the employment income inclusion under ITA 110(1)(*d.1*).

There are two important points to remember when discussing stock option benefits.

(1) The deduction of one-half of the employment income inclusion would be taken in the same taxation year as the employment income inclusion.

(2) The employment income inclusion will be the same regardless of whether the employee works for a public corporation or a CCPC. It is the timing of the inclusion that is different between the two types of corporations. For employees of public corporations, the employment income inclusion occurs in the year the employee exercises their options. It is the timing of the employment income inclusion that will differ between public corporation stock options and CCPC. For employees of a CCPC, the employment income inclusion can occur over several years since it is included only in the year the shares are sold.

¶3,125.30 Summary

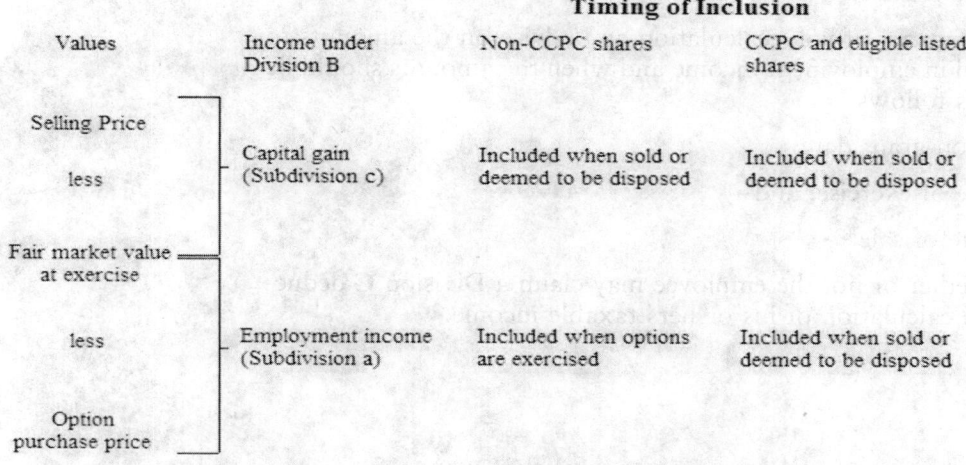

		Timing of Inclusion	
Values	Income under Division B	Non-CCPC shares	CCPC and eligible listed shares
Selling Price			
less	Capital gain (Subdivision c)	Included when sold or deemed to be disposed	Included when sold or deemed to be disposed
Fair market value at exercise			
less	Employment income (Subdivision a)	Included when options are exercised	Included when sold or deemed to be disposed
Option purchase price			

Approach

Steps to addressing an employee stock option benefit

(1) Assess the Situation and Identify the Issues — Gather all the facts relating to the individual's stock options including:

(a) The type of corporation that has granted the stock options: private or public;

(b) The option price, the fair value at exercise date and the proceeds of disposition per share; and

(c) The fair market value of the shares at grant date.

(2) Analyze the Issues — Based on the information gathered determine:

(a) The timing of the employment income inclusion;

(b) The employment income inclusion amount based on the fair value at exercise price less the option price; and

(c) The capital gain or loss on the sale of the stock options.

(3) Conclude and Advise:

(a) Assess the impact of your calculation and advise on the amounts to be included in employment income and when the amounts should be included as follows:

(i) The option grant date;

(ii) The date of exercise; and

(iii) The date of sale

(b) Assess whether or not the employee may claim a Division C deduction in the calculation of his or hers taxable income.

Example Problem 3-3

Scenario 1

Mr. Dietrich, who is employed by Public Co. Ltd., was granted an option in year one to purchase up to 5,000 common shares at $10 after completion of his fifth year of employment. The fair market value of the common shares at the time of granting the right was $12. He does not have any other shares.

During Mr. Dietrich's seventh year of employment he decided to exercise part of his right and purchased 1,000 shares with a fair market value of $15 at that date.

Three years later, Mr. Dietrich sold the shares at $25 per share.

REQUIRED

Discuss the tax implications of each of the above transactions.

SOLUTION

(1) Assess the Situation and Identify the Issues — Gather the facts related to the employee's stock option:

- The granting corporation is a public company.
- Exercise price is $10 per share.
- Fair market value on exercise date is $15 per share.
- Fair market value when the share options were granted is $12.
- Proceeds of disposition for is $25 per share.

(2) Analyze the Situation:

(a) The timing of the employment income inclusion is bases on the type of corporation that has granted the options. These options have been granted by a public company therefore the employment income inclusion will occur in the year the option is exercised.

(b) The employment income inclusion would be calculated as the difference between the fair market value and the option price:

1,000 shares × ($15 – $10) = $5,000

(c) The Capital gain or loss would be calculated in the year of sale. The capital gain or loss is based on the proceeds of disposition received less the fair market value of the shares on exercise date. The capital gain would be calculated as follows:

1,000 shares × ($25 – $15[1]) = $10,000

(3) Conclude and Advise:

(a) The amounts to be included in income are as follows:

(i) When option is granted: There is no tax effect when Mr. Dietrich is granted the right to purchase shares through the stock option plan. Since no tangible benefit has been received, there will be no income inclusion.

(ii) When option is exercised: Mr. Dietrich must take into employment income the amount calculated based on the fair market value at exercise date less the option price paid. This amount is $5,000 (as calculated above). Note that there has been no disposition at this point, he will have to find the funds to pay the tax from other sources.

(iii) When the shares are sold: Mr. Dietrich must include a capital gain in his net income for tax purposes. The taxable capital gain is $5,000, ½ of the capital gain of $10,000 (as calculated above), and is included in Subdivision c of Division B.

(b) Division C deduction: There will be no deduction of one-half, since the option price ($10) is less than the fair market value ($12) at the date the option was granted. Since the options were in the money at grant date, the employee does not qualify for the Division C deduction.

NOTE TO SOLUTION

[1] His cost is determined as the exercise price ($10) plus an addition to his cost base of the amount per share ($5) included in employment income under section 7. Both of these amounts represent tax-paid dollars that will not be taxed further on disposition.

Example Problem 3-4

Scenario 2

Mr. Dietrich, who is employed by Public Co. Ltd., was granted an option in year one to purchase up to 5,000 common shares at $13 after completion of his fifth year of employment. The fair market value of the common shares at the time of granting the right was $12. He does not have any other shares.

During Mr. Dietrich's seventh year of employment he decided to exercise part of his right and purchased 1,000 shares with a fair market value of $15 at that date.

Three years later, Mr. Dietrich sold all the shares at $25 per share.

REQUIRED

Discuss the tax implications of each of the above transactions now that the option price is $13 per share (instead of the $10 in the first scenario).

SOLUTION

(1) Assess the Situation and Identify the Issues — Gather the facts related to the employee's stock option:

- The granting corporation is a public company (the same as Scenario 1).
- Exercise price is $13 per share (different than in Scenario 1).
- Fair market value on exercise date is $15 per share (the same as Scenario 1).
- Fair market value when the share options were granted is $12 (the same as Scenario 1).
- Proceeds of disposition for is $25 per share(the same as Scenario 1).

(2) Analyze the situation:

(a) The timing of the employment income inclusion is bases on the type of corporation that has granted the options. These options have been granted by a public company therefore the employment income inclusion will occur in the year the option is exercised.

(b) The employment income inclusion would be calculated as the difference between the fair market value and the option price:

$$1{,}000 \text{ shares} \times (\$15 - \$13) = \$2{,}000$$

(c) The Capital gain or loss would be calculated in the year of sale. The capital gain or loss is based on the proceeds of disposition received less the fair market value of the shares on exercise date. The capital gain would be calculated as follows:

$$1{,}000 \text{ shares} \times (\$25 - \$15^{(1)}) = \$10{,}000$$

(3) Conclude and Advise:

(a) The amounts to be included in income are as follows:

(i) When option is granted: There is no tax effect when Mr. Dietrich is granted the right to purchase shares through the stock option plan. Since no tangible benefit has been received, there will be no income inclusion.

(ii) When option is exercised: Mr. Dietrich must take into employment income the amount calculated based on the fair market value at exercise date less the option price paid. This amount is $2,000 (as calculated above). Note that there has been no disposition at this point, he will have to find the funds to pay the tax from other sources.

(iii) When the shares are sold: Mr. Dietrich must include the taxable capital gain in his net income for tax purposes. The taxable capital gain is $5,000, ½ of the capital gain of $10,000 (as calculated above), and is included in Subdivision c of Division B.

(b) Division C deduction: In this case, he will be entitled to the one-half deduction, since the exercise price was greater than the fair market value at the date the option was granted. The deduction is equal to ½ of the employment income inclusion in the year. Mr. Dietrich could deduct $1,000 (½ × $2,000).

NOTE TO SOLUTION

(1) His cost is determined as the exercise price ($10) plus an addition to his cost base of the amount per share ($2) included in employment income under section 7. Both of these amounts represent tax-paid dollars that will not be taxed further on disposition.

Example Problem 3-5

Scenario 3

Mr. Dietrich, who is employed by Canadian Controlled Private Corporation (CCPC), was granted an option in year one to purchase up to 5,000 common shares at $10 after completion of his fifth year of employment. The fair market value of the common shares at the time of granting the right was $12. He does not have any other shares.

During Mr. Dietrich's seventh year of employment he decided to exercise part of his right and purchased 1,000 shares with a fair market value of $15 at that date.

Three years later, Mr. Dietrich sold all the shares at $25 per share.

REQUIRED

Discuss the tax implications of each of the above transactions.

SOLUTION

(1) Assess the Situation and Identify the Issues — Gather the facts related to the employee's stock option:

- The granting corporation is a CCPC (different than in Scenario 1).
- Exercise price is $10 per share (the same as Scenario 1).
- Fair market value on exercise date is $15 per share (the same as Scenario 1).
- Fair market value when the share options were granted is $12 (the same as Scenario 1).
- Proceeds of disposition for is $25 per share(the same as Scenario 1).

(2) Analyze the situation:

(a) The timing of the employment income inclusion is based on the type of corporation that has granted the options. These options have been granted by a CCPC therefore the employment income inclusion will occur in the year the shares are sold.

(b) The employment income inclusion would be calculated as the difference between the fair market value and the option price:

$$1{,}000 \text{ shares} \times (\$15 - \$10) = \$5{,}000$$

(c) The Capital gain or loss would be calculated in the year of sale. The capital gain or loss is based on the proceeds of disposition received less the fair market value of the shares on exercise date. The capital gain would be calculated as follows:

$$1{,}000 \text{ shares} \times (\$25 - \$15^{(1)}) = \$10{,}000$$

(3) Conclude and Advise:

(a) The amounts to be included in income are as follows:

(i) When option is granted: There is no tax effect when Mr. Dietrich is granted the right to purchase shares through the stock option plan. Since no tangible benefit has been received, there will be no income inclusion.

(ii) When option is exercised: Mr. Dietrich has exercised options granted from a CCPC. No amount will be include in his employment income until the shares are sold.

(iii) When the shares are sold: Mr. Dietrich must include both an employment income inclusion and a capital gain. The employment income inclusion will be $5,000 (as calculated above). The capital gain is included in his net income for tax purposes at the current inclusion rate of ½. The taxable capital gain is ½ of $10,000 (as calculated above) and is included in Subdivision c of Division B.

(b) Division C deduction: In this case, he will be entitled to the one-half deduction, since he retained the shares for more than two years. Mr. Dietrich could deduct $2,500 (½ × $5,000).

SUMMARY OF SOLUTION

	Part A *Public Corporation Option Price < FMV at Grant and Exercise Dates*	Part B *Public Corporation Option Price > FMV at Grant*	Part C *Canadian-Controlled Private Corporation (CCPC)*
Year 1 (Option granted)	No tax effects in the year the option is granted.	No tax effects in the year the option is granted.	No tax effects in the year the option is granted.
Year 7 (Option exercised)	Recognize employment income benefit.	Recognize employment income benefit and deduct one-half of the benefit in Division C.	No tax effects until the shares are sold.
Year 10 (Shares sold)	Recognize capital gain only.	Recognize capital gain only.	Recognize employment income benefit, Division C deduction and capital gain.

Both stock option rules required an employment inclusion of $5,000; the difference was the timing of the inclusion. Where the stock option was offered by a Canadian-controlled private corporation, then the employment inclusion is at the time of disposition of the shares. For stock options from all other corporate employers, the employment inclusion is at the date the option is exercised.

The Division C deductions were designed to give the same net effect as a capital gain at the appropriate net inclusion rate without permitting these amounts to qualify for the capital gains deduction. Both of these deductions will be discussed in further detail in Chapter 10.

NOTE TO SOLUTION

(1) His cost is determined as the exercise price ($10) plus an addition to his cost base of the amount per share ($5) included in employment income under section 7. Both of these amounts represent tax-paid dollars that will not be taxed further on disposition.

¶3,125.40 Additional Considerations Relating to Stock Options

Valuation of Shares

The valuation of shares relating to a public corporation is relatively simple if the shares are actively traded. However, establishing the value of shares where there is no listing or open market is more difficult. In recent years, comprehensive methods of determining the value of such shares have been used. The CRA's approach to valuations of this nature is contained in Information Circular 89-3.

Stock Options — Withholding Tax

Tax is required to be withheld at source on a stock option benefit, as if it were a bonus. The tax is withheld in the year the option is exercised, not in the year the option is granted. However, this withholding requirement does not apply to:

- the portion of the benefit that is deductible under Division C; or
- benefits arising from rights granted before 2011 that included a written condition prohibiting the taxpayer from disposing of the securities acquired under the agreement for a period of time after exercise.

Risk Factors

Over the years, stock options have proven to be a fairly successful compensation scheme for many executives and other employees. There are, however, risk factors common to all equity investments. Public share prices fluctuate constantly depending on industry trends, interest and exchange rates, government policies, and various other global factors. Exercising stock options and simultaneously disposing of the shares minimizes the risk of a taxable benefit in employment income and an economic loss on the disposition of the shares. This is possible if an employee exercises the option to acquire shares at a time when the market price is high and subsequently disposes of the shares when the market price is down.

Ⓐ Stock Option Cash Outs

Where an employee has been granted a stock option, he or she may have the right to sell that option back to his or her employer in exchange for cash. If this is done, then the employee will recognize employment income equal to the amount received and the employer will receive a tax deduction for the same amount. To prevent the possibility of both a Division C deduction for the employee and an income deduction for the employer, the tax deduction is limited. Please refer to Chapter 10 for more details on the Division C deduction.

¶3,125.90 Pause and Reflect — Summary of Learning Goals

After working through this section, ¶3,125, you will be able to:

- Explain the circumstances in which stock options must be included in employment income.
- Determine the taxation year in which amounts related to stock options employment benefit should be included in employment income.

- Explain the tax implications of employee stock options as they relate to public company and CCPC shares, including the amounts used to determine the employment income inclusion and adjusted cost base of the shares once exercised.
- Explain the circumstances in which an employee can claim the Division C deduction in arriving at taxable income.
- Calculate the specific amounts to be included employment for stock options under various scenarios.

¶3,130 Automobile Benefits

Overview

Where an automobile is provided by an employer to an employee, the employee receives the benefit of not having to invest tens of thousands of his or her own dollars to purchase an automobile for use that would include both personal and employment. As a result, the *Income Tax Act* specifies how the quantity of the benefit will be calculated. These rules consider two primary benefits:

(1) the standby charge: this is the benefit that the employee receives from having the use of a capital asset; and

(2) the operating benefit: this is the benefit received as a result of the employer paying for the cost of operating the vehicle provided.

To begin, we must understand the terminology. Several definitions in respect of cars are briefly summarized below:

(1) Motor vehicle — an automotive vehicle (undefined) designed to be used on highways and streets but not trolley buses or vehicles on rails.

(2) Automobile — a motor vehicle designed to carry up to nine individuals plus baggage, including vans, certain pick-up trucks and station wagons but excluding ambulances, taxis, hearses, vehicle inventory and clearly marked fire department, police [or Emergency Medical Services ("EMS")] vehicles.

(3) Passenger vehicle — an automobile acquired or leased.

It is important to determine which of the above definitions is being referred to. For example, paragraph 6(1)(*b*) on allowances refers to a motor vehicle, subsection 6(2) on the standby charge refers to an automobile, and section 67.2 on the limitation of deductions (discussed below) refers to a passenger vehicle.

After reviewing this section, ¶3,130, you should be able to:

- Explain the circumstances in which an automobile benefit must be included in employment income.
- Explain the purpose of the standby charge, reduce standby charge and operating benefit.
- Apply your knowledge to calculate the amount of standby charge and operating benefit that must be included in employment income.
- Apply your knowledge to provide recommendations planning techniques to reduce the amount of the standby charge to be included in income.

¶3,130.10 Calculation of the Standby Charge Benefit

A standby charge represents a benefit conferred upon an employee through the availability of a company-owned or leased automobile for any use, whether for employment or personal. Since the employee has a company automobile made available for his or her use of any kind, i.e., personal or employment, and does not have to spend after-tax dollars on either purchasing or leasing an automobile, the government reasoned that this benefit should be taxed somehow on the principle of equity.

The concept is not unreasonable. Since availability rather than actual use of the company automobile is the basis for this calculation, some unsuspecting employee could have an income inclusion of the rather high minimum standby charge.

The Act provides the following formula to establish a reasonable standby charge:

Where

A is the lesser of:[1]

a) total personal-use kilometres driven during the available time period, and

b) the value determined for B (as defined below) during the days available

B is 1,667 km × (total days available/30);[2]

C is the full original cost of an employer-owned automobile, including HST;

D is (the total days in the period the automobile is available/30);[3]

E is the lease payments, including HST, made by the employer;

F is the portion of the lease payments that relates to insurance for loss damages and liability in using the automobile.

The formula can be broken down into two portions:

Employer-owned vehicles

$$A/B \times [2\% \times (C \times D)]$$

Employer-leased vehicles

$$A/B \times [2/3(E - F)]$$

The separate A/B ratio represents a reduction of the standby charge. This ratio can only be applied to reduce the normal standby charge in situations where the employee uses the vehicle primarily (more than 50%) for employment related purposes.

ITA: 6(1)(a) Value of benefits, 248(1) Definitions; Interpretation Bulletins: IT-63R5 Benefits, Including Standby Charge for a Automobile, from the Personal Use of a Motor Vehicle Supplied by an Employer — after 1992

The standby charge and operating benefits apply only to automobiles. An "automobile" is defined in the Act as a "motor vehicle . . . designed or adapted primarily to carry individuals on highways and streets and that has a seating capacity for not more than the driver and 8 passengers". The definition then provides for some exceptions.

---

[1] Note that amount A, above, is deemed to be equal to amount B unless:

(i) the taxpayer is required by the employer to use the automobile in respect of his or her duties of employment, and

(ii) the automobile is used primarily (more than 50%) in his or her duties of employment.

[2] Rounded according to the rule in the definition (i.e., to the nearest whole number, unless the fractional part is .5, in which case round the fraction down).

[3] The capital cost limitations in paragraph 13(7)(g) and Regulation 7307, as subsequently described, do not apply.

Where an employee is provided with one of these "excepted" vehicles, or some other vehicle, this does not mean there is no taxable benefit associated with that employer-provided vehicle. The value of the benefit is taxable. While any reasonable approach to determining the benefit is acceptable, the Act indicates that it should reflect what an arm's length cost for substitute/similar transportation would be. In some circumstances, a per-kilometre rate would be acceptable.

¶3,130.20 Calculation of the Operating Benefit

A taxable benefit arises when an employer pays for the operating expenses related to an employer-provided vehicle and not reimbursed by the employee. Automobile operating expenses include gasoline, insurance, and maintenance costs, but not parking costs. Any benefit related to personal parking is included in income separately unless the advantage from it accrues primarily to the employer, rather than the employee.

ITA: (6)(1)(a)(iii)

The default method for calculating the operating benefit is:

the number of personal kilometres driven in a year × the prescribed rate.

The prescribed rate is 26 cents per kilometre for 2018.

An alternative method is available for computing the operating cost benefit where the employee uses the employer provided vehicle primarily for work (more than 50%). The alternative method is to calculate the operating benefit as 50% of the reduced standby charge. The employee must inform their employer in writing before the end of the taxation year that they intend to use this alternative method.

Any reimbursement made to the employer during the year or within 45 days of the end of the year relates to the personal use of the vehicle will reduce the employment income inclusion related to that vehicle.

¶3,130.30 Summary of Employer-Provided Automobile Benefits

The illustration below provides a graphical summary of benefits derived from an employer providing an automobile and/or paying for operating costs.

Figure 3-1
Automobile Benefits

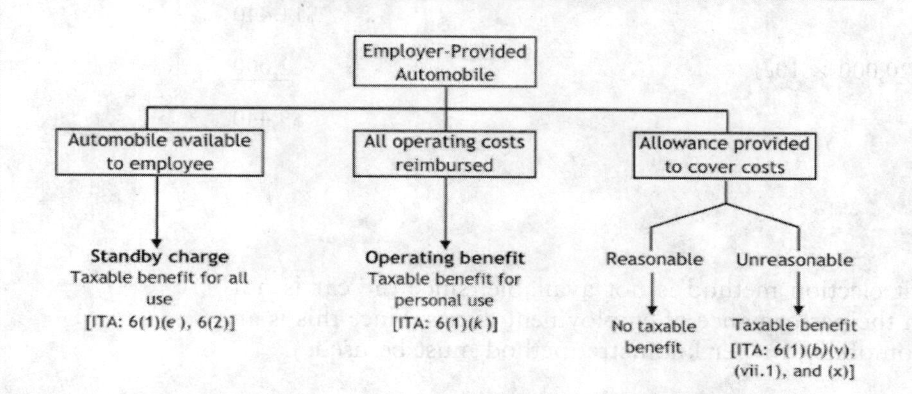

Example Problem 3-6

Automobile owned by employer

Original cost of automobile including HST	$26,000
Operating cost for the year paid by employer, including HST	$ 3,000[1]
Employment-use kilometres	10,000
Total kilometres driven for the year	30,000
Number of months available	12
Reimbursement to employer for personal use at 10¢ per kilometre	$ 2,000

[1] Includes insurance of $600, but excludes parking.

REQUIRED

Compute the standby charge and operating benefit for the use of the automobile.

SOLUTION

Standby charge — we cannot reduce the standby charge since the vehicle is not used more than 50% in the performance of their employment duties. Therefore, in this situation, the value of A in the formula (i.e., 20,004 kilometres) is deemed to be equal to the value of B in the formula (i.e., 1,667 × 12 rounded). The formula for the standby charge is

20,004/20,004 × 2% × $26,000 × 12 months =	$6,240
Operating benefit (20,000 km × $0.26)[(1)]	5,200
	$11,440
Less: amount reimbursed (20,000 × 10¢)	2,000
Total car benefits	$9,440

NOTE TO SOLUTION

[(1)] The operating benefit election method is not available, since the car is not used more than 50% in the performance of employment duties. Since this is an employer-provided automobile, the per kilometre method must be used.

Example Problem 3-7

Automobile owned by employer — same facts as Example Problem 3-6, except the employment-use kilometres are 24,000.

REQUIRED

Compute the standby charge and operating benefit for the use of the automobile.

SOLUTION

Standby charge — The formula for the standby charge is

6,000[(1)]/20,004 × 2% × $26,000 × 12 months =	$1,872
Operating benefit[(2)]	936
	$ 2,808
Less: amount reimbursed (6,000 × 10¢)	600
Total car benefits	$2,208

NOTES TO SOLUTION

(1) Lesser of (a) 6,000 kilometres and (b) 1,667 kilometres × 12 months. In this situation the employee qualifies for the standby charge reduction since the car is used primarily (i.e., more than 50%) in the performance of employment duties.

(2) The operating benefit election method is available to the employee since the car is used more than 50%. This method would result in a lower income inclusion ($936 (i.e., 50% of $1,872) versus $1,560 (i.e., 6,000 kilometres × $0.26)).

Example Problem 3-8

Automobile leased by employer

Yearly lease cost including $500 of insurance and HST	$5,000
Operating cost for the year paid by employer, including HST	$3,000[1]
Employment-use kilometres	4,000
Total kilometres driven for the year	16,000

Number of months available	12
Reimbursement to employer for personal use at 5¢ per kilometre	$600

[1] Excludes parking.

REQUIRED

Compute the standby charge and operating benefit for the use of the automobile.

SOLUTION

Standby charge — we cannot reduce the standby charge since the vehicle is not use more than 50% in the performance of their employment duties. Therefore, in this situation, the value of A in the formula (i.e., 20,004 kilometres) is deemed to be equal to the value of B in the formula (i.e., 1,667 × 12 rounded). The formula for the standby charge is

20,004/20,004 × 2/3 × ($5,000 – 500) =	$3,000
Operating benefit (12,000 km × $0.26)[(1)]	3,120
	$6,120
Less: amount reimbursed	600
Total car benefits	$5,520

NOTE TO SOLUTION

(1) In this situation, the employee does not qualify for the standby charge reduction or the operating benefit alternative, because he or she did not use the car more than 50% in the performance of the employment duties.

Example Problem 3-9

Automobile leased by employer — same facts as Example Problem 3-8, except the employment-use kilometres are 12,000.

REQUIRED

Compute the standby charge and operating benefit for the use of the automobile.

SOLUTION

Standby charge — The formula for the standby charge is

4,000[(1)]/20,004 × 2/3 × ($5,000 − 500) =	$600
Operating benefit[(2)]	300
	$ 900
Less: amount reimbursed (4,000 × 5¢)	200
Total car benefits	$700

NOTES TO SOLUTION

(1) The employee qualifies for the standby charge reduction, since he or she used the car more than 50% (i.e., 75%) in the performance of his or her duties. In this case the numerator would be the lesser of: (a) 4,000, and (b) 1,667 × 12 months.

(2) The employee does qualify for the operating benefit alternative method of computing the operating cost benefits, since the car was used more than 50% in the performance of his or her duties. In this situation, the election would give a lower gross income inclusion of $300 (i.e., 50% of $600) versus $1,040 (4,000 kilometres × $0.26).

¶3,130.40 Employee-Owned Automobile Operating Expense Benefit

A separate rule applies in cases where the automobile is provided by the employee and where an employer pays for automobile operating costs, including costs for personal use of the automobile. For example, an employee may use his or her own automobile for employment purposes, but the employer pays, through a business credit card, for all operating costs of the automobile, including costs of driving to and from work which are personal costs.

ITA: 6(1)(l) Where standby charge does not apply, 6(1)(k) Automobile operating expense benefit

The value of any benefit received by an employee for automobile operating expenses attributable to personal use must be included in income. To arrive at the value of this benefit, the total costs paid by the employer should be prorated by the ratio of personal-use kilometres to total kilometres driven by the employee. Amounts paid by the employee to the employer can be deducted from the benefit. Of course, this method requires record-keeping of employment and personal kilometres in a log, but there is no simpler, alternative method allowed for an employee-provided automobile. Note that the value of this benefit is determined using GST-included operating expenses.

ITA: 6(1)(l) Where standby charge does not apply

¶3,130.90 Pause and Reflect — Summary of Learning Goals

After working through this section, ¶3,130, you will be able to:

- Explain the circumstances in which an automobile benefit must be included in employment income.
- Explain the purpose of the standby charge, reduce standby charge and operating benefit.
- Apply your knowledge to calculate the amount of standby charge and operating benefit that must be included in employment income.
- Apply your knowledge to provide recommendations planning techniques to reduce the amount of the standby charge to be included in income.

¶3,135 Allowances

Overview

First, the differences between an allowance and a reimbursement must be identified. Typically, a reimbursement involves the payment by an employee of an expense of his or her employer and the recovery from the employer of the amount paid as substantiated by vouchers or receipts. Generally, a reimbursement is not a taxable benefit to the employee.

On the other hand, an allowance is a fixed amount which is paid to an employee in excess of his or her salary without the requirement that the employee substantiate the amounts expended. An Interpretation Bulletin, "Vehicle, Travel and Sales Expenses of Employees", adopts these meanings for the terms "allowance" and "reimbursement", respectively.

Interpretation Bulletins: IT-522R Vehicle, Travel and Sales Expenses of Employees

Case Summary

Two precedent-setting judicial decisions on this issue are presented in *Ransom v. M.N.R.* and *Splane v. The Queen*. Both cases established a two-stage test for determining if a payment to an employee is employment income. First, a determination must be made as to whether the payment is an allowance or a reimbursement. If the payment is an allowance, then the rules in paragraph 6(1)(*b*) apply. If the payment is a reimbursement, then a further determination must be made as to whether the employee has received an "economic benefit". Normally, there is no benefit if the employee is in the same economic position as he or she was in prior to the employer-driven transaction which gave rise to payment.

Cases: *Cyril John Ransom v. Minister of National Revenue*, 67 DTC 5235 (EC); : *Her Majesty the Queen v. R. Orrin J. Splane*, 92 DTC 6021 (FCA)

The courts have established a two-stage test for determining if a payment to an employee is employment income:

(1) Is the payment an allowance or reimbursement?

- An allowance — paragraph 6(1)(*b*) applies
- A reimbursement — requires further review

(2) If it is a reimbursement, did the employee receive an economic benefit?

When an allowance received from the employer is excluded from employment income then the related expenses cannot be deducted by the employee.

The preamble in paragraph 6(1)(*b*) establishes the general rule that all allowances received must be included in employment income, unless specifically listed as an exception. There are many exceptions listed in paragraph 6(1)(*b*), but only the more common exceptions will be discussed below.

¶3,135.10 Allowance for Travelling Expense of Sales Person

Allowances received by an employee who sells property or negotiates contracts will not be taxable providing the following conditions are met:

ITA: 6(1)(b)(v)

(1) the allowance must be reasonable;

(2) the allowance must be only for travelling expenses, including motor vehicle expenses; and

(3) the recipient (hereinafter referred to as a "sales/negotiating person") must be involved in the selling of property or the negotiating of contracts for his or her employer.

The word "reasonable" is not defined in the Act and, therefore, must be applied to the particular facts of the situation. For example, a reasonable daily allowance for the travelling expense of the president of a large public corporation (a person who negotiates contracts) would be entirely different than a reasonable daily allowance for a salesperson for the same organization.

Where a sales/negotiating person receives an allowance for the use of a motor vehicle, the allowance must be reasonable and based solely on kilometres used to conduct employment duties in order to be tax-free.

Case Summary

In the case of *Hudema v. The Queen*, the taxpayer claimed that a car allowance was not reasonable because the allowance did not cover all of his expenses of operating the car. This was not sufficient evidence to prove that the allowance was not reasonable because the court was not convinced that the taxpayer was making a reasonable use of his vehicle. Since the taxpayer made very little personal use of the car, averaging about 15% per year over five years, he attributed most of the costs of operating his car to his work. The court indicated that the taxpayer did not establish that it was sensible to make such little personal use of the car that he used for work. The court further indicated that the employer's allowance should only be expected to pay for such reasonable use of his car as his work required. To be reasonable, the allowance should cover virtually all the costs of his car as relates to work use, both capital and operating. The court suggested that the taxpayer should have provided evidence of the number of hours per week for which he had to use the car for work.

Cases: *William Hudema v. Her Majesty the Queen*, 94 DTC 6287 (FCTD)

¶3,135.20 Allowance for Travelling Expenses of Other Employees

Another common exception concerns an allowance for travelling expenses of other employees and has the following conditions:

(1) the employee (hereinafter referred to as "ordinary employee") does not sell property or negotiate contracts;

(2) the allowance must be reasonable in the circumstances;

(3) the allowance must be for travelling expenses, but not for the use of a motor vehicle (which is discussed separately below); and

(4) the recipient must travel away from the municipality and metropolitan area of the employer's establishment at which the employee ordinarily worked.

Note the difference between the conditions for sales/negotiating persons and ordinary employees. There is no geographical limitation placed on an allowance for sales/negotiating employees.

¶3,135.30 Allowance for Motor Vehicles — Ordinary Employees

The Act sets out the conditions for exempting a motor vehicle allowance received by an ordinary employee (e.g., those employees not negotiating contracts). Motor vehicle allowances received by ordinary employees are not restricted to travelling away from the municipality or metropolitan area. This distinction is important and the reason motor vehicle allowances for ordinary employees are listed separate from other travel allowances above.

In order for a motor vehicle allowance to be received tax-free (e.g., not included in employment income) the following conditions must be met:

(1) the allowance must be reasonable in the circumstances, and

(2) the allowance must relate to motor vehicle expenses related to travelling in the performance of employment duties.

A reasonable allowance is defined in Interpretation Bulletin "Vehicle and other travelling expenses Employees" as one that is based solely on employment based kilometres. The CRA will, as a general rule, consider the kilometre allowances permitted by regulation as deductions for employers as reasonable allowances. These amounts (for 2018), generally, are 55¢ on the first 5,000 kilometres and 49¢ on the remaining kilometres. However, at the same time, the CRA acknowledges that reasonableness of an allowance is normally decided based on the particular facts of the situation.

Interpretation Bulletins: IT-522R Vehicle, Travel and Sales Expenses of Employees

The Interpretation Bulletin further discusses that where an employee receives a set periodic amount (i.e., a monthly allowance of $250), the allowance may be tax-free if:

(1) there is a beginning of the year agreement between the employer and employee that the employee will receive a stated amount per kilometre for business-related travel;

(2) there is a year end accounting for any difference between the advances and the actual business-related kilometres; and

(3) the amounts received are reasonable.

The CRA has indicated that, if the employer pays an employee both a flat-rate allowance and a per-kilometre allowance for the same use of the automobile, the whole amount is deemed to be one allowance that is taxable, since it is not based solely on the number of kilometres driven. They have indicated that the two allowances can be separated, if the employer pays a reasonable per-kilometre rate for travel outside the employment area and a flat monthly rate for travel inside the employment area. In this case, the two amounts are not for the same use and the per-kilometre allowance, in this case, would not be taxable, but the flat-rate allowance would be.

¶3,135.90 Pause and Reflect — Summary of Learning Goals

After working through this section, ¶3,135, you should be able to:

- Identify the difference between an allowance and reimbursement.
- Identify the different types of allowances.
- Discuss the tax implications of various allowances.
- Calculate the specific amounts to be included in employment for taxable allowances.

¶3,140 Other Benefits

Overview

There are many benefits that may be provided to an employee as part of their remuneration package. The CRA Income Tax Folio S2-F3-C2, "Benefits and Allowances Received from Employment" provides the CRA's interpretation on how many of these items may be treated for tax purposes. While the list of taxable benefits is significant, the more common employee benefits, on top of those discussed earlier, are:

- flexible benefit programs;
- boarding and lodging, including rent-free and low-rent housing;
- employer paid educational costs and memberships;
- loyalty programs, such as frequent flyer points;
- financial counselling;
- business trips with spouse
- non-cash gifts and awards; and
- overtime meals.

This list is far from all-inclusive, as there are many different ways to provide a benefit to an employee. The general wording in the Act indicates that all benefits received and enjoyed by virtue of an individual's employment will be included as part of the employee's remuneration and will be taxable. From there we review the Act for any exceptions to this rule. We will discuss the more common benefits below.

¶3,140.10 Board and Lodging

All board and lodging supplied by an employer will be considered a taxable benefit in the year, unless specifically excluded as an exception. The CRA Interpretation Bulletin outlines that if a "reasonable amount" is recovered from the employee, then board and subsidized meals will not be considered a taxable benefit. The CRA indicates that a "reasonable amount" is one which covers costs, including food preparation and service costs. Where a lesser amount is recovered, the difference between that amount and the above total costs will be a taxable benefit.

ITA: 6(1)(a) Value of benefits; Income Tax Folio: S2-F3-C2 Benefits and Allowances Received from Employment

Subsection 6(6) outlines specific exceptions to the inclusion of board and lodging in employment income. The Act excludes the value of board and lodging at a special work site or remote location. The conditions that must be met for the exception to apply may be summarized as follows:

(1) the special work site must be a distance away from the employee's ordinary residence such that he or she cannot reasonably be expected to travel daily, and the temporary nature of the duties or the remoteness of the work site must be such that it is not reasonable to establish and maintain a self-contained domestic establishment as his or her principal place of residence; and

(2) the board and lodging is necessary for not less than 36 hours and, if an allowance in respect of the board and lodging is paid by the employer, the allowance is not in excess of a reasonable amount.

This topic is covered in more detail in the CRA Interpretation Bulletin entitled "Employment at Special Work Sites or Remote Work Locations".

Interpretation Bulletins: IT-91R4 Employment at Special Work Sites or Remote Work Locations

¶3,140.20 Flexible Benefit Programs

Flexible benefit programs enable employees to select from a menu of available benefits, some of which are taxable and some of which are not. There is no specific provision within the Act that governs flexible benefit programs. The taxation of each component is determined by its characteristics. For example, if an employee chooses health benefits as part of their flexible benefit program, the health benefits would not be taxable, as outlined earlier.

¶3,140.30 The CRA Administrative Practice

The CRA often outlines their administrative practices regarding the tax treatment of specific items. These administrative policies do not necessarily enforce the tax statutes because it is often not practical to do so.

Income Tax Folio S2-F3-C2, "Benefits and Allowances Received from Employment" is an important reference for employment benefit planning. It contains (i) a list of items which, if received or enjoyed by an employee, must be included in employment income, and (ii) a second list of items which need not be included, despite the general wording of the preamble in paragraph 6(1)(*a*), if the CRA's conditions outlined in the Folio are met. It is important to note that the CRA's administrative policies do not apply to performance-related rewards (e.g., awards based on sales targets) or cash or near-cash gifts (e.g., gift certificates).

Income Tax Folio: S2-F3-C2 Benefits and Allowances Received from Employment

Clearly, it may be worthwhile on an after-tax basis for an employee to trade taxable salary or fringe benefits for an equivalent amount of non-taxable benefits that are desired by the employee. The more common benefits outlined in Income Tax Folio S2-F3-C2 are outlined below:

Income Tax Folio: S2-F3-C2 Benefits and Allowances Received from Employment

- **Employee membership:** membership in a social club paid by an employer will not be considered a taxable benefit if the employer is the primary beneficiary of the membership. If an employer pays professional membership dues and the professional dues are a condition of employment, the employer would be considered the primary beneficiary and the professional dues would not be a taxable benefits.

- **Loyalty programs (e.g., frequent flyer points)** on a personal credit card when travelling on employer reimbursed business trips or incurring other business related expenses: Effective for 2009, the CRA will no longer require these employment benefits to be included in employment income providing that:

  Guides: T4130 Employer's Guide — Taxable Benefits and Allowances

  (1) the points cannot be converted to cash,

  (2) the plan is not an alternate form of remuneration, or

  (3) the plan is not for tax avoidance purposes.

  It should be noted that where an employer controls the points (e.g., a company credit card), the employer will continue to be required to report the fair market value of any benefits received by the employee on the employee's T4 slip when the points are redeemed.

- **Financial counselling and tax return preparation:** these are considered taxable whether provided directly or indirectly by an employer. Financial counselling in respect of re-employment or retirement are considered to be a non-taxable benefit.

- **Business trips where the employee's spouse travels with the employee:** The CRA's position in respect of business trips for spouses of employees indicates that there is no employment benefit to the employee if the spouse was, in fact, engaged primarily in the business activities on behalf of the employer as opposed to engaged primarily in personal activities.

- **Non-cash gifts and awards:** non-cash gifts provided to arm's length employees (e.g., an employee who is not related to the employer) will not be taxable if:

  Income Tax Folio: S2-F3-C2 Benefits and Allowances Received from Employment

  (1) the total aggregate value of all non-cash gifts and awards to that employee is less than $500 annually; or

  (2) it is a separate non-cash long service/anniversary award with a total value of $500 or less. In order to qualify:

  - the anniversary award cannot be for less than five years of service, or
  - for five years since the last long service award had been provided to the employee.

  Any value in excess of $500 for each will be taxable. For the purposes of applying the $500 thresholds, the annual gifts and awards threshold and the long service/anniversary awards threshold are separate. In other words, a shortfall in value under one policy cannot be used to offset an excess value of the other.

- **Immaterial or Nominal amounts:** items of an immaterial or nominal value, such as coffee, tea, T-shirts with employer logos, mugs, plaques, trophies, etc., will not be considered a taxable benefit to employees. There is no defined monetary threshold that determines an immaterial amount. Factors that may be taken into account include the value, frequency, and administrative practicability of accounting for nominal benefits.

- **Computers supplied by employer:** home computers supplied by an employer are not considered to be a taxable benefit providing the computer use is primarily for the benefit of the employer.
- **Overtime Meals and Allowances:** if an employee receives a meal or meal allowance related to working overtime, the CRA will consider the benefit to be non-taxable if:

  (1) the value of the meal or meal allowance is reasonable (defined as a value of up to $17);

  (2) the employee works two or more hours of overtime before or after his or her scheduled hours of work; and

  (3) the overtime is infrequent or occasional. This is defined as less than three times a week. This condition may also be met where the meal or allowance is provided three or more times per week on an occasional basis to meet workload demands such as major repairs or periodic financial reporting.

¶3,140.40 Housing Loss and Housing Cost Benefits

The Act addresses the income tax consequences of employer-provided compensation in respect of losses on a disposition of the employee's residence and other housing-related payments such as financing subsidies.

ITA: 6(19) Benefit re housing loss, 6(23) Employer-provided housing subsidies

An amount received by an individual from an employer to compensate for a loss on the sale of a home, may result in a taxable benefit in the year received. The Act outlines that one-half of any amount in excess of $15,000 must be included in net employment income.

Example

An employee is relocated and realizes a loss of $30,000 on the sale of their home. The employer reimburses the employee for $25,000 of the loss.

- The first $15,000 is tax free.
- The employee will have an income inclusion of $5,000 [(25,000 – 15,000) × 50%] in the year received.

In order to qualify for this treatment the loss must be an "eligible housing loss" which is defined as:

- In general terms, a "housing loss" is the cost of the residence minus the proceeds of disposition,

  ITA: 6(21) Housing loss

- An "eligible housing loss" is defined as the taxpayer's housing loss that is in respect of an eligible relocation of the taxpayer or non-arm's length person; and

  ITA: 6(22) Eligible housing loss

- An "eligible relocation" is defined as a relocation where there is a 40-kilometre minimum on the difference in the distance between the old residence and the new work location, and the distance between the new residence and the new work location.

  ITA: 6(19) Benefit re housing loss, 6(23) Employer-provided housing subsidies, 62 Moving expenses, 248(1) Definitions

Example

If the distance between an employee's old residence and the new work location is 100 kilometres, and the distance between the new residence and the new work location is 20 kilometres, the difference in the two distances is 80 kilometres. The move from the old residence to the new residence would qualify as an eligible relocation.

Finally, the Act contains a catch-all provision, "for greater certainty", that includes in the income of the employee all other employer-provided payments or any other type of assistance by anyone in respect of housing.

ITA: 6(23) Employer-provided housing subsidies

¶3,140.50 Director's and Other Fees

A corporate director holds an "office", as defined in the Act. As a result, fees received by a director are received by virtue of an office and, hence, must be included as employment income. The effect of including such fees in employment income is to limit the deductions to those allowed against employment income.

¶3,140.60 Volunteer Services Exemption

Volunteer emergency workers often receive an allowance to help cover any costs associated with their volunteer position (i.e., additional insurance). The first $1,000 can be considered tax-free if the individual:

- is not employed by the public authority for a same or similar business; and
- did not receive a salary for the emergency work in addition to the allowance.

Payments that qualify are those received for the same or similar duties as:

- volunteer firefighters: a 15% non-refundable tax credit based on an amount of $3,000 is provided for eligible volunteer firefighters. An individual who claims this credit is not eligible to claim the $1,000 exemption;
- volunteer ambulance technicians; and
- emergency service volunteers assisting in the search and rescue of individuals or in other emergency situations and disasters.

¶3,140.70 Benefits From Employer-Paid GST/HST

Where an employee receives a taxable benefit from his or her employer, the employer is liable for and must remit the relevant GST/HST. The employee in turn is deemed to receive a taxable benefit which generally includes the employer-paid GST/HST. This employment income inclusion of GST/HST places the employee in the same economic position as if he or she acquired the goods or services on the open market. In essence, the Act includes an employer-paid GST/HST in employment income.

Note that the inclusion of the full GST/HST paid by the employer in providing the benefit ignores any reimbursement by the employee for the taxable benefit/taxable supply. This is logical if the objective is to place the employee in the same position as if he or she acquired the supply on the open market and, therefore, would pay GST/HST on the full amount rather than a partial net payment.

The general rule is that any benefit included in income under either the general benefits inclusion rule or the standby charge is subject to the GST/HST. However, two significant exceptions are:

(a) zero-rated supplies found in Schedule VI of the ETA (e.g., gift food baskets where 90% or more of the value of the supply is zero-rated); and

(b) exempt supplies found in Schedule V of the ETA (e.g., daycare services, low-rent and rent-free housing, low-interest and interest-free loans, premiums for government health services and tuition fees for exempt education services).

The practical application of including GST/HST paid by the employer in income is fairly limited. The most common applications would be:

(a) personal use of an employer's automobile by way of the standby charge; and

(b) other payments by the employer that would be considered taxable benefits such as automobile operating and parking costs for personal purposes, travelling expenses relating to vacations, spouse's non-business-related travelling costs, and gifts valued in excess of $500 annually on which the employer would have paid GST/HST in providing the item to the employee.

Common taxable benefits and the GST/HST treatment are listed below.

Taxable Benefit	GST/HST Included	GST/HST Excluded
Automobile — standby charge	√	
Employee counselling services	√	
Group term life insurance		√
Gift: in cash		√
Gift: not in cash	√	
Holiday trips	√	
Housing, board, and lodging	depends on the accommodations	
Subsidized meals	√	
Interest-free and low-interest loans		√
Provincial hospitalization and medical insurance plans		√
Stock options		√
Recreational facilities	√	
Moving expenses allowance	√	

¶3,140.80 Group Sickness and Accident Insurance Plans

Section 6 excepts the inclusion in employment income of premiums paid by an employer on behalf of an employee to a group sickness or accident insurance plan. However, amounts received as a result of a disability claim by an employee in respect of a sickness or accident, disability or income maintenance plan, if the employer has made any contribution, must be taken into employment income. Hence, such plans become tainted if the employer pays all or any portion of the premium.

ITA: 6(1)(a) Value of benefits, 6(1)(f) Employment insurance benefits

In terms of employee benefit planning, there is a basic trade-off in the tax treatment of these plans. On the one hand, all employees can receive a relatively small tax-free benefit by having the employer pay the premium. However, those relatively few employees who become disabled and receive insurance payments will be taxed on those payments. On the other hand, all employees can incur a relatively small cost by paying the premium. In this case, the relatively few employees who become disabled and receive insurance payments will receive those payments tax free.

Where an employee has paid any amount of the premiums, these amounts are deductible from the disability benefits received in arriving at the benefit.

ITA: 6(1)(f) Employment insurance benefits

Non-group plans are treated in exactly the opposite manner. The premiums paid by the employer are treated as employment income. However, payments received in respect of these plans are not considered as income.

Sickness or Accident Insurance Plan

	Group		Non-Group	
Summary	**Premium**	**Disability Benefit**	**Premium**	**Disability Benefit**
Employer pays all or part of premium	Not included in income	Included in income	Included in income	Not included in income
Employee pays all of premium	Not deducted in income	Not included in income	Not deducted in income	Not included in income

¶3,140.90 Pause and Reflect — Summary of Learning Goals

After working through this section, ¶3,140, you should be able to:

- Explain the tax implications of receiving an employment benefit.
- Explain the CRA administrative policies as they relate to specific employee benefits.
- Apply your knowledge to calculate the income inclusions of various employee benefits based on the CRA administrative policies.
- Apply your knowledge to calculate the tax implications of various employment income inclusions such as housing losses, volunteer services, and director fees.

¶3,140.99 Practise What You've Learned

Refer to the following sections of the Study Guide to practise what you've learned:

¶3,800 — Review Questions

- Question 10 — Group Sickness and Accident Insurance Plans
- Question 11 — Employee Loans
- Question 12 — Allowances
- Question 13 — Automobile Benefits

¶3,825 — Multiple Choice Questions

- Question 1 — Automobile Benefits
- Question 2 — Automobile Benefits
- Question 4 — Employee Loans
- Question 5 — Stock Options

¶3,850 — Exercises

- Exercise 3 — Employee Benefits
- Exercise 5 — Employee Benefits
- Exercise 6 — Allowances
- Exercise 7 — Group Sickness and Accident Insurance Plans
- Exercise 8 — Stock Options
- Exercise 9 — Employee Benefits
- Exercise 13 — Employee Benefits

¶3,200 Deductions From Employment Income

Overview

Subsection 8(1) lists all of the deductions that may be claimed in computing income from an office or employment. Only those items listed in subsection 8(1) are allowed deduction, which means if it isn't listed in the subsection 8(1), the expense cannot be deducted in computing employment income. The preamble to subsection 8(1) restricts these deductions to expenses which relate in some manner to the earning of employment income.

The Act imposes a general limitation on the deductibility of expenses. To be deductible, the amount of the expenditure must be "reasonable in the circumstances". What is reasonable in the circumstances depends on the particular facts of a situation and may be determined by reference to a standard, such as an industry average or a previously accepted historical average, among others. Another general limitation denies the deduction of an expense incurred to commit an offence under specified sections of the Criminal

Code. For example, a pizza delivery driver who incurs a speeding ticket while delivering a pizza to a customer would not be able to deduct the ticket, regardless of the fact that it was incurred while performing employment duties.

Common expenses specifically allowed in the Act available for deduction against employment income are:

(1) Expenses incurred by employees who earn commission income from selling or negotiating contracts for the employer, referred to as "sales/negotiating persons" in this textbook. ITA: 8(1)(f) Sales expenses

(2) Travelling expenses, for "ordinary" employees, other than motor vehicle expenses. ITA: 8(1)(h) Travel expenses

(3) Motor vehicle expenses, for "ordinary" employees. ITA: 8(1)(h.1) Motor vehicle travel expenses

(4) Professional membership dues and annual union dues required to perform employment duties. ITA: 8(1)(i) Dues and other expenses of performing duties

(5) Office rent or workspace-in-home, under specific circumstances.

(6) Legal expenses paid to collect or establish a right to salary/wages owed to the employee by the employer or former employer. ITA: 8(1)(b) Legal expenses of employee

(7) Contributions to an employer's registered pension plan. ITA: 8(1)(m) Employee's registered pension plan contributions

After working through this section, ¶3,200, you will be able to:

- Explain which employment expenses may be deducted in the Act.
- Explain the factors that determine the deductibility of expenses against employment income.
- Apply you knowledge to specific circumstances to determine the deductibility of eligible employment expenses.
- Apply your knowledge to specific circumstances to calculate the specific amount eligible for deduction.

¶3,205 Sales/Negotiating Person's Expenses

An individual who earns their living selling goods or services in return for commission income often has to spend money on travel, meals, and promotional material in order to earn this commission income. Because of this, the Act provides these types of employees options for deducting these additional expenses.

Unlike other employees whose deductions are restricted to only those specifically listed in the act, employees who sell property or negotiate contracts (i.e., sales persons) are allowed to deduct any type of expense as long as that expense was incurred for the purpose of earning income from employment. However, these additional types of deductions that are allowed for sales persons and not other employees are limited in terms of dollar value to the amount of commission income. ITA: 8(1)(f) Sales expenses

Common expenses that may be deducted but that are limited to commission income, providing the conditions below are met, are:

- Advertising and promotional expense (i.e., meals with clients, promotional gifts).
- Travel expenses, including airfare, accommodations, and 50% of meals.

- Telephone expenses, used exclusively to earn employment income.
- Insurance and property taxes as they relate to a home office, discussed later in the chapter.
- Certain automobile expenses as they relate to the earning of employment income: gas, vehicle insurance, license, and repairs, as well as parking.

Other expenses may also be deducted, but are not limited to commission income. These expenses include:

- certain home office expenses such as utilities, maintenance and repairs, office supplies, long distance phone calls, dedicated phone line or cellular phone airtime;
- capital cost allowance or leasing costs on a vehicle; and
- interest paid to purchase a vehicle.

ITA: 8(1)(i) Dues and other expenses of performing duties, 8(1)(j) Motor vehicle and aircraft costs

Providing the expenses are incurred for the purposes of earning employment income, they may be deducted. Personal expenses cannot be deducted in computing employment income. Refer to ¶4,610 in chapter 4, which provides a comparison chart of the available deductions for sales/negotiating persons, ordinary employees and sole proprietors.

Of course, these expenditures are subject to the general restrictions, just discussed, and a number of specific restrictions and/or exceptions. For example, expenditures in respect of the use of a yacht, camp, lodge, or golf course, and membership fees in private clubs are not deductible.

ITA: 8(1)(f)(vi), 18(1)(l) Use of recreational facilities and club dues

Note the conditions in the provision that must be met for the expenses to be deductible.

- The employee must be required to pay his or her own expenses as stipulated in the contract of employment.[4] ITA: 8(1)(f)(i)
- The employee must be ordinarily required to carry on the duties of employment away from the employer's place of business. ITA: 8(1)(f)(ii)
- The remuneration must be dependent on volume of sales or contracts. ITA: 8(1)(f)(iii)
- A non-taxable travel allowance cannot be received. Note, a travel allowance does not include an automobile allowance. ITA: 8(1)(f)(i.v)

If the travel allowance is not reasonable, then the sales/negotiating person must include the allowance in income. An unreasonable allowance is one that is less than a reasonable amount, greater than a reasonable amount, or deemed not to be reasonable. He or she may then deduct the expenses, since the employee would not be in receipt of an excluded allowance in such circumstances.

It is important to note that a sales/negotiating person may deduct under 8(1)(*f*) or 8(1)(*h*) and (*h*.1), but not both. Deductions under paragraphs 8(1)(*i*) and (*j*) are available to all employees. Where travel expenses, alone, exceed the amount of commissions or similar income, it is advantageous to use the deduction under paragraphs 8(1)(*h*) and (*h*.1), instead of paragraph 8(1)(*f*). Where a deduction is possible for an amount either under paragraph 8(1)(*f*) or paragraph 8(1)(*i*), it is better to deduct under paragraph 8(1)(*i*), which is not limited by commissions or similar income, to preserve deduction room under paragraph 8(1)(*f*).

---

[4] See two Federal Court of Appeal cases: *The Queen v. Moore*, 90 DTC 6200 (F.C.A.), and *The Queen v. Betz*, 90 DTC 6201 (F.C.A.). In these decisions, the Court expanded the concept of a contractual obligation to include unwritten conditions which would result in an unfavourable performance assessment.

¶3,210 Ordinary Employee's Travel Expenses Including Motor Vehicle Expenses

The travelling expenses of employees who are not involved in the selling of property or negotiating of contracts are deductible under one of two provisions:

- paragraph 8(1)(*h*) — Travelling expenses other than motor vehicle expenses
- paragraph 8(1)(*h*.1) — Motor vehicle expenses

Deductible travelling expenses include all transportation costs, such as vehicle costs and airfare, accommodations and 50% of meals, providing the following three conditions are met:

- The employee must ordinarily be required to carry out his or her duties away from his or her employer's place of business. The CRA's interpretation of "ordinarily" is habitually or customarily and should be done with some degree of regularity.
- The employee must be required to pay for the travelling expenses as part of their employment contract.
- The employee cannot be in receipt of a tax-exempt allowance for travelling expenses.

Employees who have received an allowance that is greater or less than a reasonable amount can include the allowance in income and can deduct the related expenses, because they would not be in receipt of an excluded (reasonable) allowance in such circumstances. Whether an allowance is reasonable depends upon all the facts in a particular circumstance.

Employees who make deductions under paragraph 8(1)(*f*), (*h*), or (*h*.1) and subparagraph 8(1)(*i*)(ii) or (iii) must file a prescribed form (T2200) signed by their employers certifying that the conditions set out in these provisions were met in the year. It is important to note that travel between home and work is considered to be personal in nature and therefore the related expenses are not deductible.

¶3,210.10 Limitations

The Act limits the deduction of specific costs, regardless of whether incurred for the purposes of earning employment income:

- The cost of meals consumed while travelling for an employer is limited to 50% of the lesser of the amount paid and a reasonable amount. ITA: 67.1 Expenses for food, etc.
- Meal costs under 8(1)(*f*) and (*h*) are only deductible where the meal is consumed when the taxpayer is away, for 12 hours or more, from the municipality or metropolitan area where the employee usually reports for work. ITA: 8(4) Meals

Expenditures in respect of the use of a yacht, camp, lodge, or golf course, and membership fees in private clubs are not deductible. ITA: 18(1)(l) Use of recreational facilities and club dues

Exhibit 3-1 summarizes and compares all employee deductions under paragraphs 8(1)(*f*), (*h*), and (*h*.1).

Exhibit 3-1 Employee Deduction Provisions

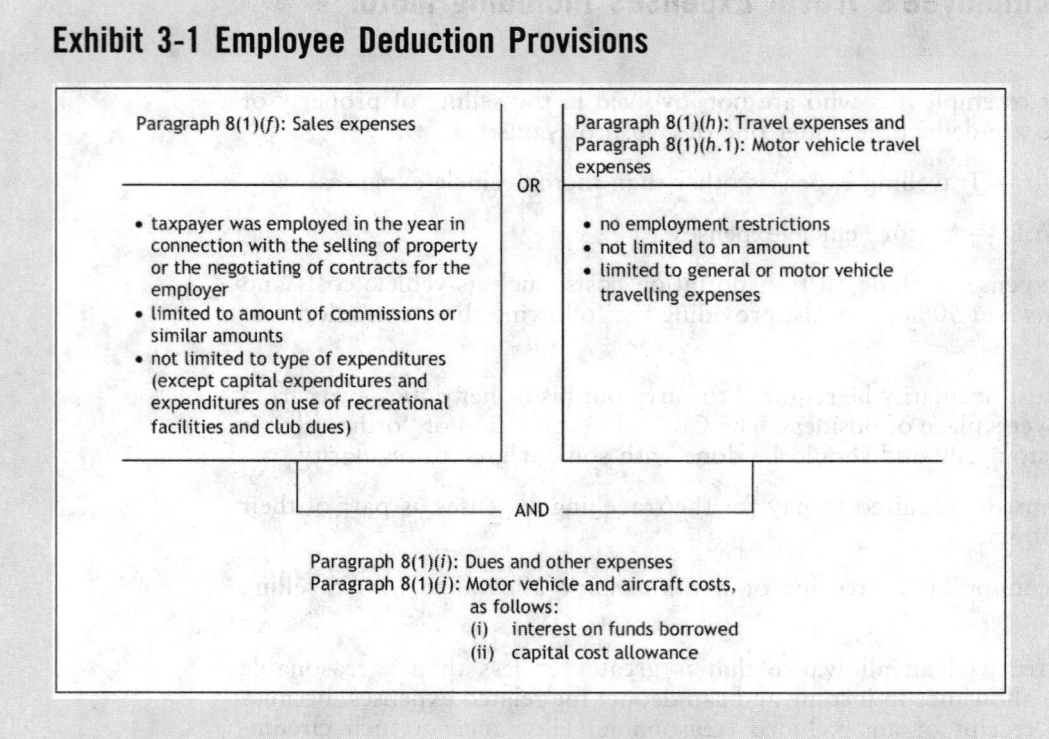

Paragraph 8(1)(*f*): Sales expenses	OR	Paragraph 8(1)(*h*): Travel expenses and Paragraph 8(1)(*h*.1): Motor vehicle travel expenses
• taxpayer was employed in the year in connection with the selling of property or the negotiating of contracts for the employer • limited to amount of commissions or similar amounts • not limited to type of expenditures (except capital expenditures and expenditures on use of recreational facilities and club dues)		• no employment restrictions • not limited to an amount • limited to general or motor vehicle travelling expenses

AND

Paragraph 8(1)(*i*): Dues and other expenses
Paragraph 8(1)(*j*): Motor vehicle and aircraft costs, as follows:
(i) interest on funds borrowed
(ii) capital cost allowance

¶3,215 Motor Vehicle Capital Cost — Interest and CCA

Overview

A deduction is available for capital costs related to motor vehicles and aircraft, such as interest paid on loans to purchase the vehicle and depreciation for tax purposes (known as capital cost allowance or CCA). These items are only deductible if an employee may deduct other expenditures under paragraph 8(1)(*f*), (*h*) or (*h*.1) as a result of meeting the conditions for deduction. This means that an employee who receives a tax-exempt allowance could not deduct capital costs related to a motor vehicle or aircraft. ITA: (8)(1)(j)

Capital cost allowance will be discussed in more detail in Chapter 5. However, at this stage, all that has to be understood is that accounting depreciation and capital cost allowance (CCA) are quite similar. The major exception is that in respect of depreciable capital properties that are motor vehicles and aircraft the maximum deduction must be based on the declining balance method (30% for motor vehicles and 40% for aircraft) and that in the year of acquisition the rates are one-half of the normal rate.

Note that in the case of an aircraft, the use thereof *must be required* for employment purposes (e.g., a pilot for courier is required to provide his or her own aircraft to perform their duties). In addition, the deduction in respect of an aircraft is limited to the amount that is reasonable in the circumstances in relation to the availability of other modes of transportation. A motor vehicle need only be used for employment purposes to qualify for a deduction. ITA: 8(9) Presumption

Example

An employee is required to use her personal automobile in performing her employment duties. The employee qualifies for other deductions under ITA 8(1)(*f*). The employee purchases a vehicle costing $25,000 in 2017 and uses the vehicle to perform their duties. The allowed CCA deduction would be:

2017:	$25,000 × 30% × ½	=	$3,750
2018:	($25,000 – 3,750) × 30%	=	$6,375

While the maximum amounts of CCA are calculated above, these would be further restricted to the portion used to earn employment income. For example, the employee above drove a total of 15,000 kilometres in 2017, 9,000 of which were related to earning employment income. The total deduction available against employment income in 2017 would be:

2017:	$3,750 × 9,000/15,000	=	$2,250

¶3,215.10 Imputed Interest Deemed Paid

There is an employment income inclusion, under subsection 6(9), for a benefit obtained through a low-interest loan to an employee. The computation of the benefit was previously discussed under employee loans in this chapter. This interest income inclusion is deemed to be interest paid. Hence, this deemed interest payment is eligible for a deduction along with interest actually paid. As with the CCA shown above, the interest deduction must be prorated for employment kilometres driven or hours flown to arrive at the allowable deduction.

ITA: 80.5 Deemed interest, 8(1)(j) Motor vehicle and aircraft costs

¶3,215.20 Limitations

Interest on Money Borrowed For Passenger Vehicle

The Act limits the amount deductible in respect of interest on funds borrowed or debt incurred on the acquisition of a passenger vehicle to the lesser of:

ITA: 67.2 Interest on money borrowed for passenger vehicle

(1) the actual amount payable (or paid); and

(2) $300 for each 30-day period that the automobile loan or debt was outstanding in the year.

Note that there is no rounding of the number of periods to a number of full months as there is in the standby charge rules. The resulting lesser amount is further prorated by the portion of employment use to the total use based on kilometres driven.

Capital Cost for Passenger Vehicle

The Act and Regulations place limits on the capital cost of a passenger vehicle. The capital cost of the vehicle is limited to $30,000 plus the HST on the $30,000.

ITA: 13(7)(g); ITR: 7307(1)

Where the passenger vehicle is acquired from a person with whom the purchaser does not deal at arm's length (usually a related person), the capital cost is deemed to be the least of:

(1) the fair market value;

(2) the undepreciated capital cost of the seller; and

(3) the dollar maximum found in the above summary, currently $30,000.

Cost for Leased Passenger Vehicle

Passenger vehicle leasing costs are limited in a manner equivalent to the $30,000 capital cost restriction as described above. The deductible portion of the leasing costs is calculated as the lesser of (1) and (2) calculated as:

ITA: 67.3 Limitation re cost of leasing passenger vehicle

(1) $[(A \times B)/30] - C - D - E$,

where

A is a dollar monthly maximum, as prescribed, currently $800 a month plus HST;

B is the aggregate of the number of days the vehicle was leased for all years to the end of the present year;

C is the aggregate of the lease costs deducted in all preceding years;

D is imputed interest, at the prescribed rate, on refundable amounts, (e.g., deposits) over $1,000;

E is total reimbursement receivable in respect of the lease in the year;

and

(2) $[(F \times G)/0.85H] - D - E$

where

F is the total lease charges payable (including HST) for the year;

G is the dollar maximum capital cost prescribed, currently $30,000[5];

H is the greater of:

a) a dollar maximum prescribed amount[6], and

b) the manufacturer's list price.

Monthly lease payments can be managed so as to reduce the monthly lease payments to an amount below the prescribed amount (currently $800). For example, an individual may place a large down payment on a lease in order to reduce the monthly payment to $800. This formula is intended to limit the lease payments to an equivalent of the limit on the capital cost of a vehicle and the interest paid on a purchased vehicle.

---

[5] Regulation 7303(1) definition of formula term B.

[6] Regulation 7307(4) calculates the appropriate number for years after 1997 by multiplying the capital cost maximum amount (see above) by 100/85, i.e., 100/85 × [$30,000 × (1 + 0.13)] = $39,882, assuming an HST rate of 13%.

The formula is intended to ensure that the monthly lease payments do not exceed the maximum prescribed amount. This formula may further reduce the lease payment to an amount lower than the prescribed amount, currently $800. Part (b) of the formula allows a fraction of the total lease charges as a maximum deduction. The fraction is based on the maximum prescribed capital cost for capital cost allowance (currently $30,000), relative to 85% of the manufacturer's list price of the car. The higher the list price in the denominator of the fraction, the lower the value of the fraction and the lower the amount of lease payments that can be deducted.

¶3,215.30 Application of the Automobile Allowances and Expense Rules

Example Problem 3-10

Mr. Alex Otto acquired an automobile on July 1, 2018, to be used in connection with his duties of employment. Alex is required by contract to use his own car and to pay directly all the expenses. Alex does not have any commission income. The following information, some of which is estimated, relates to the newly acquired car:

Cost of car (including HST)	$37,290
Total kilometres driven in the ownership period	25,000
Total kilometres in respect of his employer's business	15,000
Capital cost allowance rate (½ × 30%)	
15% Interest paid on bank loan in respect of the car	$1,950
Gas and oil	1,800
Maintenance	300
Insurance	1,400
Licences	100

Alex lives in a province which has an HST rate of 13%.

REQUIRED

Determine the amount deductible in the taxation year in respect of the car expenditures in the following situations, on the assumption that the above expenses were reasonable and ignoring the effects of any leap year:

(1) no kilometre allowance was received;

(2) a reasonable allowance of 38¢ per kilometre in respect of employment driving was received;

(3) an unreasonable allowance of 5¢ per kilometre in respect of employment driving was received;

(4) a reasonable allowance of 25¢ per kilometre in respect of employment driving plus a yearly allowance of $2,000 was received;

(5) an unreasonable allowance of $1 per kilometre in respect of employment driving was received.

SOLUTION

Potentially deductible expenses (before prorating for employment use):

Capital cost allowance limit:		
(½ × 30%) × ($30,000 × 1.13)		$5,085
Interest expense — lesser of:		
a) $1,950 (actual)		
b) $300 × (184/30)		1,840
Gas and oil	1,800	
Maintenance	300	
Insurance	1,400	
Licences	100	
Total vehicle expenses		3,600
Total expenses before prorating		$10,525
Portion relating to employment use:		
15,000 km/25,000 km × $10,525 =		$6,315

Alternative Fact Situations

(1) All of the $6,315 automobile expenses would be deductible, since all the conditions of these provisions have been met as follows:

(a) the automobile is used in connection with his employment duties;

(b) there is a contractual obligation to use his own car and to pay directly all of the automobile expenses;

(c) a reasonable allowance had not been received; and

(d) he was not eligible for a deduction as a sales/negotiating person in respect of the automobile expenses.

(2) None of the $6,315 would be deductible, since subparagraph 6(1)(*b*)(vii.1) exempts reasonable allowances. No amount was included in employment income. Therefore, no deductions related to the expenses are available.

(3) Since the 5¢ per kilometre allowance is not a reasonable amount, Mr. Otto must include the allowance in income and would be permitted the $6,315 deduction that relates to earning his employment income.

(4) Although the combined package of the two allowances may be reasonable in the circumstances, the Act deems the two allowances not to be a reasonable amount and, hence, taxable, since one of the motor vehicle allowances received was not based solely on kilometres. Since these allowances are taxable and therefore included in employment income, the $6,315 would be deductible.

(5) An unreasonable allowance of $1 per kilometre would be taxable, since the amount is in excess of a reasonable amount. Hence, the restricted expenses of $6,315 would be deductible.

Example Problem 3-11

Mr. Jonathan is required by his contract of employment to use his own car in the performance of his employment duties and to pay for all expenses. Mr. Jonathan leased a BMW from Expensive Cars Unlimited. The following facts relate to the leased car:

Lease period	Jan. 1, 2018 to Dec. 31, 2019
Lease cost per month including HST	$900
Manufacturer's list price, excluding HST	$50,000

Mr. Jonathan was not reimbursed for any portion of the lease cost. Mr. Jonathan lives in a province which has an HST rate of 13%.

REQUIRED

Determine the allowable lease cost which qualifies for a deduction under section 67.3 in 2018 before prorating for employment use. Ignore the effects of the leap year.

SOLUTION

The allowable lease cost before prorating for employment use would be calculated as the lessor of:

(1) ($900 × 1.13) × (365/30) = $12,374

(2) ($800 × 12) × ($30,000 × 1.13)/(0.85 × 50,000[1]) = $7,657

Therefore the allowable least cost is $7,657.

NOTES TO SOLUTION

[1] The greater of: i) 100/85 × ($30,000 × 1.13) = $39,882 and ii) $50,000.

Example Problem 3-12

Ms. Elana is required by her contract of employment to use her own car in the performance of her employment duties and to pay for all expenses. Ms. Elana leased a Mercedes from Sky's-The-Limit Leasing. The following facts relate to the leased Mercedes:

Lease period	Oct. 1, 2016 to Sept. 30, 2019
Lease cost per month, including HST	$1,600
Manufacturer's list price, excluding HST	$60,000
Total kilometres	30,000
Total employment kilometres	20,000
Gas and oil	$ 1,500
Maintenance	700
Insurance	2,000
Licences	100

REQUIRED

Determine the amount deductible in respect of the car for the year 2018 on the assumption that a total of $13,893 of leasing costs had been deducted prior to 2018. Assume an HST rate of 14%. Ignore the effects of the leap year.

SOLUTION

Gas and oil	$ 1,500	
Maintenance	700	
Insurance	2,000	
Licences	100	
Leasing costs — lesser of:		
a) ($800 × 1.14) × 822 days[(1)]/30	– $13,893	= $11,096
b) ($1,600 × 12) × ($30,000 × 1.14)/ (0.85 × 60,000[(2)])		= $ 12,875

The deductible amount for the car in 2018 before prorating would be $11,096.

NOTES TO SOLUTION

(1) 92 days in 2016 + 365 days in 2017 + 365 in 2018.

(2) The greater of: i) 100/85 × ($30,000 × 1.14) = $40,235 and ii) $60,000.

¶3,220 Dues and Other Expenses

An employee who is required to pay expenses related to their employment duties may also deduct the following:

- annual professional membership dues paid to maintain standing in a profession recognized by statute;
- office rent paid;
- salary paid to an assistant (including the CPP and EI premiums payable in respect of the assistant);
- the cost of supplies paid; and
- annual union membership dues paid.

In order for an amount to be deductible, it must either be paid by the employee or, if the employer paid the amount, it must be included in the employee's income as a taxable benefit. There are a number of restrictions that are placed on the expenses above:

(1) Membership dues must be directly related to your employment duties. For example, a professional accountant who teaches English literature in the secondary school system cannot deduct his or her accounting association dues, but can deduct his or her teaching association dues. ITA: 8(1)(i)(i), 8(1)(i)(iv)

(2) A limitation is placed on dues which prohibits the deduction of amounts that are not directly attributable to the ordinary operating expenses of the organization which is levying the dues. ITA: 8(5) Dues not deductible

(3) The employment contract requires the employee to pay rent for an office, the salary to an assistant and/or the cost of supplies. ITA: 8(1)(i)(ii), 8(1)(i)(iii)

¶3,225 Workspace in Home

There are restrictions on the deductibility of expenses related to workspace in the home for employees. The provision only applies to individuals who are entitled to deductions for sales expenses and/or for rent or supplies related to a workspace in a home. A deduction for a home office is only permitted if:

(1) the workspace in the home is the place where the individual principally (more than 50% of the time) performs the employment duties; or

(2) if the condition of a) above is not met, the following two conditions must be met:

(a) the work space must be used exclusively for the purpose of earning employment income during the period, and

(b) the work space must be used on a regular and continuous basis for meeting customers or other persons in the ordinary course of performing the employment duties.

As long as more than 50% of the employment duties are performed in the home workspace, then test (a), above, has been met and test (b) above can be ignored. Where test (a) is not met, then the exclusive condition in tests in (b)(i) and (ii) above, must be met. The word "exclusively" is not defined in the Act. Merriam-Webster Online 8 defines "exclusive", used in this context, as "single, sole . . . whole, undivided", which is a much more onerous test.

Once one of the conditions in (a) or (b), above, has been met in the year of the expenditure, then the workspace deduction is restricted to employment-source income. However, there is an indefinite carryforward provision as long as the employee can meet either test (a) or (b), above, in the future year of deduction.

Supplies related to a workspace in the home include expenses paid for the maintenance of the home such as the cost of fuel, electricity, light bulbs, cleaning materials and minor repairs. For an individual earning commission income, property taxes and insurance paid on a home owned by the individual are deductible. All of these expenses must be allocated between the workspace and the personal space of the home on a reasonable basis such as floor space.

Note that no provision in section 8 allows the deduction of interest on funds borrowed in any manner for the purchase of a home for any use by the employee.

Exhibit 3-2 lists some common home office expenses and their treatment by employees earning commission income and other employees.

Exhibit 3-2 Home Office Expenses

Expenses	Commission employees	Other employees
Rent	√	√
Repairs and maintenance	√	√
Supplies	√	√
Telephone (long-distance charges)	√	√
Utilities	√	√
Home insurance	√	X
Property taxes	√	X
Mortgage interest	X	X

¶3,230 Other Expenses

¶3,230.10 Legal Expenses

Certain legal expenses incurred by employees are deductible. The expenses are limited to those incurred to collect or establish a right to remuneration owed to the employee by an employer or former employer. This deduction is extended to amounts not owed to the employee directly by the employer, if the amounts, when received, would be taxable as employment income. For example, legal fees incurred by an employee to collect insurance benefits under a sickness or accident insurance policy provided through an employer are deductible.

¶3,230.20 Tradesperson's Tool Expenses

A deduction is allowed from employment income earned as a tradesperson in a taxation year to a maximum of $500 for eligible new tools. This deduction is computed as the excess, if any, of the total cost to the individual of one or more eligible tools over $1,161 to a maximum excess of $500.

ITA: 8(1)(s) Deduction — tradesperson's tools, 8(6.1) Eligible tool of tradesperson

An "eligible tool" is defined to be a tool (including ancillary equipment) that:

- was new and, hence, not used for any purpose whatsoever before it is acquired by the individual;
- is certified by the individual's employer in prescribed form to be required as a condition of, and for use in, the individual's employment as a tradesperson in the year; and
- is, unless the device or equipment can be used only for the purpose of measuring, locating, or calculating, not an electronic communication device or electronic data processing equipment.

The cost of the tools used for computing tax depreciation (i.e., capital cost allowance) or for capital gains purposes is reduced by the amount of this deduction. ITA: 8(7) Cost of tool

¶3,230.30 Registered Pension Plans

There are two different types of registered pension plans (RPPs): defined benefit and money purchase (defined contribution). Defined benefit plans guarantee a predetermined amount of retirement income based on a flat amount per year of service or a percentage of the employee's earnings over a defined period. The defined benefit RPPs are funded by actuarially-determined contributions by the employee and/or employer.

Money purchase RPPs provide whatever pension income that the contributed funds in the plan can purchase through the acquisition of an annuity. No predetermined amount of pension income is guaranteed under a money purchase plan. Benefits will depend upon the actual contributions, the investment return of the plan and annuity rates at the date of purchase.

The Act imposes a limit of 18% of employee earnings and a prescribed dollar limit for all contributions (employee and/or employer portions) to registered pension plans (RPPs), registered retirement savings plans (RRSPs) and deferred profit sharing plans (DPSPs). The mechanics of this limit will be discussed further in Chapter 9.

Total annual comprehensive dollar limits for money purchase RPPs for employer and/or employee contributions are set at the following amounts:

2015	2016	2017	2018	2019
$25,370	$26,010	$26,230	$26,500	indexed

Paragraph 8(1)(*m*) allows the deduction of employee contributions to a registered pension plan but only as determined by subsection 147.2(4) found under Division G, "Deferred and Other Special Income Arrangements".

¶3,290 Pause and Reflect — Summary of Learning Goals

After working through this section, ¶3,200, you should be able to:

- Explain which employment expenses may be deducted in the Act.
- Explain the factors that determine the deductibility of expenses against employment income.
- Apply you knowledge to specific circumstances to determine the deductibility of eligible employment expenses.
- Apply your knowledge to specific circumstances to calculate the specific amount eligible for deduction.

¶3,290.99 Practise What You've Learned

Refer to the following sections of the Study Guide to practise what you've learned:

¶3,800 — Review Questions

- Question 14 — Sales/Negotiating Person's Expenses
- Question 15 — Sales/Negotiating Person's Expenses

¶3,825 — Multiple Choice Questions

- Question 3 — Home Office
- Question 6 — Sales/Negotiating Person's Expenses

¶3,850 — Exercises

- Exercise 10 — Home Office
- Exercise 11 — Sales/Negotiating Person's Expenses
- Exercise 12 — Employee Benefits and Expenses
- Exercise 15 — Sales/Negotiating Person's Expenses

¶3,300 Comprehensive Employment Income Example

The following illustration is a comprehensive example of how "employment income" is determined under Subdivision a of Division B. The solution is cross-referenced to the appropriate section in the Act. Read carefully these cross-references and the supporting notes which highlight the key points in each related paragraph. However, note that the assignment problems may contain additional points not covered in this illustration.

Example Problem 3-13

Ms. Elliott, who lives and works in Ontario, is employed as an internal auditor by MCS Ltd., a public corporation, for the calendar year 2017. She provides you with the following information concerning her receipts, taxable benefits, and expenditures:

Gross salary		$60,000
Income taxes withheld	$15,900	
CPP Contributions	2,594	
EI contributions (max. amount)	858	
RPP contributions (money purchase)	3,000	
United Way donation	100	
Reimbursement paid to employer for use of company car and its operating costs	300	(22,752)
Net salary		$37,248

MCS Ltd. pays the following amounts on behalf of Ms. Elliott:

(1) Premiums for the following medical plans:

(i) Drug plan — Sun Life	$275
(ii) Extended health care — Liberty Mutual	$350

The company paid a provincial employer health tax (not a premium).

(2) MCS Ltd. provides Ms. Elliott with a car to be used in connection with the duties of her employment and 20% for pleasure based on total kilometres for 2018 of 25,000.

The company paid the following automobile expenses:

(i) Operating costs (including HST)	$3,200
(ii) Lease costs (including HST)	4,500

(3) Ms. Elliott, who must travel regularly away from her employer's place of business, receives a monthly allowance of $400 to cover her accommodation and meals while travelling. She is, however, required by contract to pay for those expenses directly. Her actual expenses for

meals and entertainment were $3,000 including HST, and $4,000, including HST, for accommodation, all of which were reasonable under the circumstances.

Ms. Elliott also supplies you with the following selected expenditures:

(i) Registered retirement savings plan contributions	$1,500
(ii) Legal fees paid in collecting back pay from a former employer (including HST)	200
(iii) Professional accounting dues (including HST)	300

REQUIRED

Calculate Ms. Elliott's employment income for tax purposes for 2018 (as determined by Subdivision a of Division B of the Act). Ignore the GST/HST rebate on employee deductions.

SOLUTION

(A) Employment income

Reference				
Ssec. 5(1)	Salary[(1)]			$60,000
Par. 6(1)(*e*)	Standby charge[(2)]	$750		
Par. 6(1)(*k*)	Operating cost — car[(3)]	375	$1,125	
	Less: payments to company		300	825
Spar. 6(1)(*b*)(vii)	Travel allowance[(4)]			4,800
				$65,625
	Less:			
Par. 8(1)(*b*)	Legal fees[(5)]		$200	
Par. 8(1)(*h*)	Travel expenses[(6)]		5,500	
Par. 8(1)(*i*)	Professional dues[(7)]		300	
Par. 8(1)(*m*)	RPP contributions[(8)]		3,000	(9,000)
	Employment income — Subdivision a[(9)]			$56,625

NOTES TO SOLUTION

(1) The Act refers to remuneration received in the calendar year only, but this does not mean that the net salary is the amount included in employment income. The Act deems that taxes withheld have been received at the time remuneration etc. was paid.

(2) The standby charge will be computed as

$$5{,}000 \text{ km}/20{,}004 \text{ km} \times 2/3 \times (\$4{,}500) = \$750$$

Ms. Elliott is entitled to the standby charge reduction, since she uses the car for business more than 50% of the total kilometres.

(3) Ms. Elliott qualifies for the election method of determining a benefit derived from employer-paid automobile operating costs, since her employment-use is in excess of 50% of the total use. The operating costs under this election method would result in a reduced income inclusion of $375 [20% × 25,000 kilometres × $0.26 = $1,300 under the kilometre alternative versus (50% × $750) = $375].

(4) Allowances are dealt with in paragraph 6(1)(*b*), which includes all allowances in income with 10 specific exceptions. One such exception, which is applicable in this situation, applies to most employees, but not salespersons or persons who negotiate contracts, since there is a special provision for them. There are two specific conditions that must be met in order for the allowance to be non-taxable. The first condition is that the allowance must be a reasonable amount. The second condition is that the employee must be travelling outside the metropolitan area where his or her employer is located.

On the assumption that Ms. Elliott's travelling expenses were reasonable in the circumstances, the monthly allowance of $400 ($4,800 annually) was not a reasonable amount since the actual expenses were $7,000.

Therefore, the allowance is a taxable allowance and she can claim her actual travel expenses.

(5) Legal fees are deductible only if they are paid:

- in the year
- to collect, or establish a right to, an amount that, if received, would be included in the employee's employment income.

[(6)] Ms. Elliott can deduct her travelling expenses because she meets all the conditions of the relevant provision. First, she must travel regularly away from her employer's place of a business. Second, she is required by contract to pay for these expenses. Finally, she is not in receipt of an exempt allowance since the allowance that she receives is less than a reasonable amount and, as a result, has been included in income.

The deductible expenses are composed of:

Accommodation	$4,000
Meals and entertainment expenses (50% × $3,000)	$1,500
	$5,500

Note how the determination of the reasonableness of the allowance was based on the full expenditures, which were considered reasonable. The results was that the allowance was not reasonable and, hence, it was included in employment income. However, the meals expenditures were only 50% deductible.

[(7)] Professional dues are deductible only if the dues are for a profession recognized by statute and if the dues related to the employment income as per the preamble to section 8.

[(8)] Registered pension plan: an employee is permitted to deduct, for tax purposes, his or her contributions to a money purchase registered pension plan to a maximum of $26,500 in 2018, but this amount is the maximum amount for the combined employee-employer contributions.

[(9)] Items excluded from computation:

(1) Employers' contributions to a private health plan, such as the drug and extended health care plans and provincial health service tax levies, are not taxable benefits.

(2) The Act includes all benefits received or enjoyed through employment with certain specific exemptions that do not include public medical plan premiums paid by an employer. However, in Ontario, as in several other provinces, provincial medical plan premiums have been replaced by a health services tax based on total payroll; hence, there is no taxable benefit for individual employees.

(3) Registered retirement savings plan contributions are deducted under Subdivision e, not Subdivision a.

(4) Income tax is not deductible.

(5) United Way, a charitable donation, is not deductible under Division B. (A charitable donation made by an individual is eligible for a non-refundable tax credit under Division E.)

(6) CPP contributions and EI premiums are not deductible under Division B, but they are eligible for non-refundable tax credits under Division E.

¶3,900 Pause and Reflect — Summary of Learning Goals for This Chapter

After working through all the sections of the chapter, you should be able to:

- Identify the basic provisions of the Act that relate to employment income.
- Identify and discuss the factors that distinguish an employee from a self-employed individual. Apply case facts to conclude on an individual's employment status.
- Understand and explain what amounts must be included in employment income, and how deductions from employment income are determined and calculated.
- Identify and discuss the special rules relating to the expenses of a commission sales person.
- Apply your knowledge to calculate the net employment income in specific real-life circumstances.

CHAPTER 4

Income From Business: General Concepts and Rules

ADVANCED CONTENT IN THIS CHAPTER

Ⓐ Deferral Anti-Avoidance ¶4,210.20

Ⓐ Adjustment for Amortization Allocation to Inventory: Absorption Accounting ¶4,320.50

Ⓐ Employer's Contribution Under a Deferred Profit Sharing Plan ¶4,560.50

Learning Goals

Know, Understand and Explain

By the end of this chapter you will know, understand and be able to explain:

- The basic provisions of the *Income Tax Act* (the Act) that relate to the calculation of business income.
- The criteria for determining whether a gain is one of capital or business income.
- The underlying distinction between business income and property income.
- The rules outlining amounts to be deducted from business income for tax purposes.

Apply

By the end of this chapter you will be able to apply your knowledge and understanding to:

- Start with accounting income and make the necessary adjustments to arrive at business income for tax purposes.

Analyze

By the end of this chapter you will be able to analyze:

- Different sources of income and determine whether it should be treated as capital or business income.
- A situation and determine whether reasonable expectation of profit exists.

Review Questions

¶4,800 in the Study Guide

Multiple Choice Questions

¶4,825 in the Study Guide

Exercises

¶4,850 in the Study Guide

Assignment Problems

¶4,875 in the Study Guide

Overview

The focus of this chapter is the calculation of income from business for tax purposes. This includes the calculation of both inclusions to business income (i.e., revenues) and deductions from business income (i.e., expenses). The following chart will help to locate in the Act the key provisions discussed in this chapter.

PART I — DIVISION B, SUBDIVISION b

BUSINESS OR PROPERTY

DIVISION

A	Liability for tax
B	**Computation of income**
C	Computation of taxable income
D	Taxable income earned in Canada by non-residents
E	Computation of tax
E.1	Minimum tax
F	Special rules applicable in certain circumstances
G	Deferred and other special income arrangements
H	Exemptions
I	Returns, assessments, payment and appeals
J	Appeals to the Tax Court of Canada and the Federal Court of Appeal

SUBDIVISION

	Basic rules
a	Income or loss from an office or employment
b	**Income or loss from a business or property**
c	Taxable capital gains and allowable capital losses
d	Other sources of income
e	Deductions in computing income
f	Rules relating to computation of income
g	Amounts not included in computing income
h	Corporations resident in Canada and their shareholders
i	Shareholders of corporations not resident in Canada
j	Partnerships and their members
k	Trusts and their beneficiaries

SECTION

9-11	Basic rules
12-17	Inclusions
18-21	Deductions
22-25	Ceasing to carry on business
26-37	Special cases

For tax purposes, income from a business is added to total income. Recall that the taxpayer is required to determine income from each source and to include income from employment, business, and property. For tax purposes, "source" generally refers to the cause giving rise to the activity and each business must be recognized as a "distinct source" of income, separate from employment income, income from property, and taxable capital gains.

ITA: 3(a), 3(d)

Section 4 provides the general rule for determining a taxpayer's income or loss from a particular source. The general rule requires that only deductions applicable to a specific source may be claimed against income from that source. Taxpayers who carry on a business in more than one place should also apportion business income by territorial place. The Act provides little guidance, yet apportionment by geographic location becomes significant when operations are scattered internationally and among provinces. Regulations provide some guidance for income earned from a business in a province by corporations and individuals, respectively.

ITA: 4(1) Income or loss from a source or from sources in a place, 4(1)(b)

Subdivision b of Division B of Part I of the Act contains the primary rules for the computation of income from business. Most of what will be covered will be found in sections 9 through 21. Some of the more important provisions are as follows:

ITR: 400 Interpretation, 2603 Income from Business

Inclusions

- Sec. 9 — A taxpayer's income (loss) for a taxation year from a business is their profit (loss) from that business for the year
- Sec. 10 — Rules related to inventory
- Sec. 12 — Income inclusions
- Sec. 13 — Rules related to capital cost allowance
- Sec. 14 — Rules related to eligible capital property

Deductions

- Sec. 18 — Limitations on the deductibility of expenses
- Sec. 19 — Limitation on advertising expenses
- Sec. 20 — Deductions permitted

Hint For Reading These Deduction Sections Of The Act

The interaction between section 18 and section 20 requires careful attention. For example, paragraph 18(1)(*b*) does not allow any deduction that is on account of capital, including amortization. However, paragraph 20(1)(*a*) allows a deduction for capital cost allowance and paragraph 20(1)(*l*) allows a deduction for doubtful debts. Both of these items are capital in nature. So, just because you find a provision in section 18 that would disallow, generally, a particular expense, don't give up. Look in section 20 to see if there is another provision that will allow the expense in question under specified conditions. Notice that the preamble to subsection 20(1) states: "notwithstanding paragraphs 18(1)(*a*), (*b*) and (*h*) . . .". Hence, subsection 20(1) provides for exceptions to the general prohibitions rules in subsection 18(1).

¶4,000 Basic Rules

Overview

The word "business" is very broadly defined in the Act, although the definition specifically excludes an office or employment. It must be understood that the word "income" when used in the Act, while not defined in the Act, means income after the deduction of expenses currently incurred to produce it. Subdivision b contains numerous specific rules regarding amounts to be included in income and amounts which may or may not be deducted for income tax purposes. Income from a business for a tax year is the "profit" business source for the year.

ITA: 9(1) Income, 248(1) Definitions

¶4,010 What is Profit?

According to common law, as discussed below, profit is the calculation of income, on "sound commercial principles", which may include generally accepted accounting principles ("GAAP"), unless a particular provision of the Act or principle of common law requires otherwise.

Canada requires that public enterprises follow International Financial Reporting Standards ("IFRS") and private companies follow Accounting Standards for Private Enterprise ("ASPE"). As a result, the term "GAAP" will be used to refer to both IFRS and ASPE, as appropriate.

GAAP are often considered to reflect ordinary commercial principles, the legal concept, held by the courts to be a key determinant of profits. Nevertheless, it should be noted that the word "profit" is not required by the legislation to be interpreted in conformity with GAAP, even where the Act is silent on the treatment of a particular transaction.

Where GAAP envisage more than one method of determining income, the courts have adopted the "truer picture" approach, choosing the method that provides the truer picture of income as in the case of *West Kootenay Power and Light Co. Ltd. v. The Queen*. In this case, considerable emphasis was placed on the matching of expenses to the income that was generated by the expenditure.

Specific provisions of the Act can create considerable differences between income for tax purposes and income for accounting purposes. One of the major causes of such differences results from the write-off of capital expenditures over a period of years. However, tax treatment in certain areas of the Act, including the valuation of inventory and the deductibility of prepaid expenses, has moved closer to GAAP.

While the Canada Revenue Agency ("CRA") has often taken the position that profit computed under GAAP most accurately reflects income in these situations, the courts have, on occasion, rejected conformity between income for accounting and tax purposes, particularly in cases where GAAP were at variance with the court's legal concept of ordinary commercial trading and business principles and practices or with a legal concept of income.[1] The case of *The Queen v. Metropolitan Properties Co. Ltd.*, on the measurement of business profit, clearly indicates "the desirability of applying generally accepted commercial and business practice as reflected in the generally accepted accounting principles".

Cases: *Her Majesty the Queen v. Metropolitan Properties Co. Limited*, 85 DTC 5128 (FCTD)

Thus, according to the reasoning of the court in the *Metropolitan Properties* case, in the absence of a specific provision, a legal principle, or recognized commercial practice to deal with the tax treatment of a particular transaction, GAAP are applied to meet the objectives of the income tax system.

On the other hand, in the case of *Symes v. The Queen*, the Supreme Court of Canada expressed the view that to rely on GAAP for a determination of profit would suggest a degree of control by professional accountants that was inconsistent with a legal test for profit. The Supreme Court suggested the use of "well accepted principles of business (or accounting) practice" or "well accepted principles of commercial trading", but did not suggest how to determine these principles or how to differentiate them from GAAP. Again, in the absence of a specific provision of the Act or a clearly stated legal principle, reliance on GAAP may provide a reasonable guideline.[2]

Cases: *Symes v. The Queen*, 94 DTC 6001 (SCC)

[1] There have been many cases in this area, including *M.N.R. v. Publishers Guild of Canada Limited*, 57 DTC 1017 (Ex. Ct.).

[2] For further discussion of the role of GAAP in interpreting profit for tax purposes, see Joanne E. Magee, "The Profit GAAP", *CA Magazine*, April 1995, pp. 32–35.

Framework for Analysis in Determining Profit

Cases: *Canderel Limited v. The Queen*, 98 DTC 6100 (SCC)

The Supreme Court of Canada case of *Canderel Limited v. The Queen*, provided the following framework for analysis in the determination of profit.

(1) The determination of profit is a question of law.

(2) The profit of a business for a taxation year is to be determined by setting against the revenues from the business for that year the expenses incurred in earning that income.[3]

(3) In seeking to determine profit, the goal is to obtain an accurate picture of the taxpayer's profit for the given year.

(4) In calculating profit, the taxpayer is free to use any method which is not inconsistent with:

(a) the provisions of the *Income Tax Act*;

(b) established case law principles or "rules of law"; and

(c) well-accepted business principles.

(5) Well-accepted business principles, which include but are not limited to the formal codification found in GAAP, are not rules of law but interpretive aids. To the extent that they may influence the calculation of income, they will do so only on a case-by-case basis, depending upon the facts of the taxpayer's financial situation.

(6) On reassessment, once the taxpayer has shown that he has provided an accurate picture of income for the year, which is consistent with the Act, the case law, and well-accepted business principles, the onus shifts to the Minister to show either that the figure provided does *not* represent an accurate picture, or that another method of computation would provide a *more* accurate picture.

¶4,100 Distinguishing Types of Income

Overview

Individuals and corporations may hold property for a variety of reasons. For example, Joan, an individual, may purchase land to build a personal residence, whereas another taxpayer, Zed Rent Co., may purchase an adjacent piece of land with the intention of earning rental income. Realtor Co. may purchase the parcel of land down the road as a piece of inventory for speculation.

When a taxpayer disposes of property, the proceeds minus the cost will result in either:

- a capital gain or loss; or
- income or loss from a business or from a property.

[3] *M.N.R. v. Irwin*, 64 DTC 5227 (S.C.C.); *Associated Investors of Canada Ltd. v. M.N.R.*, [No. 2], 67 DTC 5096 (Ex. Ct.).

Alternatively, when a taxpayer purchases and holds property to earn income, the income earned while the property is held is reported as either:

- income or loss from a business; or
- income or loss from property.

Therefore, two separate types of transactions exist:

- the income or loss produced from the disposition of property; and
- the income or loss produced during the ownership of property.

Distinguishing the types of income produced by these separate transactions will be discussed in this section beginning with income versus capital receipts on the disposition of property followed by a discussion of business versus property transactions during ownership.

¶4,110 Business Income Versus Capital Receipt[4]

Overview

The argument over whether a particular receipt is business income in nature or capital in nature has given rise to thousands of court cases over the years. This is primarily due to the taxation treatment of these two items; business income receipts are fully taxed and capital receipts are only partially taxed as capital gains. Historically, the inclusion rate for capital gains has ranged from 0% to 75%, with the current inclusion rate being 50%.

The courts have at times applied the analogy of a fruit-bearing tree to cases in which the determination of a capital or income transaction was at issue. The analogy attempts to focus the determination on how an asset has been used. A capital asset is likened to the tree which produces income in the form of fruit. Sale of the fruit would be equivalent to income whereas a sale of the tree would be regarded as a capital transaction. However, the analogy breaks down under the facts of certain cases.

Exhibit 4-1 outlines the steps that should be taken to analyze the issue.

Exhibit 4-1 Steps to Addressing Income Versus Capital Gain Issue

(1) Gather all the facts leading up to, during, and after the transaction, and identify the issues.

(2) Develop your best arguments for both income treatment and capital gain treatment. Be balanced in your analysis. Consider the "badges of trade" in Exhibit 4-2.

(3) Analyze the strengths and weaknesses of your arguments, by evaluating the facts, rather than simply classifying or listing the facts.

[4] For a more detailed discussion of this topic, see Robert E. Beam and Stanley N. Laiken, "Adventure or Concern in the Nature of Trade: The Key to Taxpayer Intention", (1996) vol. 44, no. 3 *Canadian Tax Journal*, pp. 888–913.

(4) Arrive at a conclusion of income or capital gain consistent with your analysis.

(5) Determine how the transaction will be taxed if the taxpayer is:

(a) An individual, or

(b) A corporation.

¶4,110.10 Objective of the Analysis

To make the distinction between an income and a capital transaction, the courts attempt to assess the intention of the taxpayer in the transaction and to answer the question: did the taxpayer deliberately seek a profit of an income rather than a capital gain nature? At the time of a court hearing, the courts can view in perspective the taxpayer's whole course of conduct for the period before, during and after the transaction in question. An attempt is made to substantiate this by facts which establish the taxpayer's general course of conduct.

Secondary intention is established by looking at whether the taxpayer has built into a transaction, at the time of purchase, a profitable alternative in the event that the primary intention is frustrated. For example, if land is acquired to develop a new retail outlet for a business, but appropriate zoning changes are not approved and subsequently the land is sold at a profit, that profit may be considered to be the result of the alternative business intention and may be regarded as business income if the purchaser acquired the land with the intention to make a profit if the zoning approval was not received. It should be noted that in order for the secondary intention to result in the transaction being considered business income, the secondary objective to sell the asset for profit must have been a significant motivation in making the original purchase of the asset.[5]

How to Interpret Secondary Intention

Cases: *Paul Racine, Amédée Demers and François Nolin v. Minister of National Revenue*, 65 DTC 5098 (EC)

The concept of secondary intention was clarified in the case of *Racine et al. v. M.N.R.* as follows:

> To give a transaction which involves the acquisition of capital the double character of also being at the same time an adventure in the nature of trade, the purchaser must have in his mind, at *the moment of the purchase*, the possibility of reselling *as an operating motivation* for the acquisition; that is to say that he must have had in mind that upon a certain type of circumstances arising he had hopes of being able to resell it at a profit instead of using the thing purchased for purposes of capital. (Italics added.)

[5] Two good examples of this situation are given by the cases of *Regal Heights Ltd. v. M.N.R.*, 60 DTC 1270 (S.C.C.), and *Fraser v. M.N.R.*, 64 DTC 5224 (S.C.C.).

In the case of *Armstrong v. The Queen*, the Court stated further "that circumstances which force the sale of property or make such a sale attractive do not have the effect of *retroactively converting* a property held to produce income and as a capital property into something of a trading nature". [Italics added.]

Cases: *Gerald Armstrong v. Her Majesty The Queen*, 85 DTC 5396 (FCTD)

¶4,110.20 Observable Behavioural Factors or "Badges of Trade"

While the courts have indicated that taxpayer intention is the objective in a determination of whether a transaction results in a receipt of business income or capital, it should be recognized that intention is a state of mind. Intention must be inferred from an observation of a taxpayer's behaviour or a taxpayer's whole course of conduct. Based on the observable behaviour of a taxpayer, courts have developed a set of indicators, often referred to as "badges of trade", to determine whether an adventure or concern in the nature of trade was present in a transaction and, hence, whether business income resulted.

To determine whether a gain on the disposition of property is business income or a capital gain, it is useful to apply an analytical framework to a fact situation. The objective of applying such a framework is to systematically evaluate the facts to determine whether a transaction or series of transactions bear the "badges of trade" or behavioural fact pattern consistent with an intention to generate business income. A list of behavioural factors ("badges of trade") that can be used as a reference might comprise the following:

(1) *Relation of the transaction to the taxpayer's business*: A transaction may be regarded as a business income transaction if it is very similar to one in which the taxpayer would be involved in his or her normal business or profession. If a taxpayer undertakes a transaction in association with others, then the relationship of the transaction to the normal business or profession of these associates can be considered. This factor is helpful in determining whether a taxpayer had a secondary intention to make a profit on the sale of an asset. If a taxpayer has special knowledge or expertise or had direct access to these, it might be inferred that in a particular transaction a profitable "escape hatch" was known and a motivation at the time of the purchase.

(2) *Activity or organization normally associated with trade*: The nature of the activity surrounding a transaction (volume etc.) or the level of organization of the transaction may be such that it is very similar to one which would be undertaken by a business person normally engaged in such transactions, and therefore the transaction can be considered "an adventure in the nature of trade". Two classic cases of this involved British taxpayers one of whom purchased a carload of toilet paper and resold it at a profit[6] and the other of whom purchased a carload of whisky and sold it at a profit.[7] Transacting in such commodities by the carload is an indication of an intention to trade which would result in the gains being assessed as business income. To apply this factor, it is necessary to determine how the transaction in question was organized. If a transaction was handled in the same way as a normal business transaction was handled, in terms of quantities of a commodity purchased, method of promotion and sale, etc., there may be

Interpretation Bulletins: IT-459 Adventure or concern in the nature of trade

[6] *Rutledge v. C.I.R.*, [1929] 14 T.C. 490.

[7] *C.I.R. v. Fraser*, [1942] 24 T.C. 498.

evidence of an adventure in the nature of trade. The Interpretation Bulletin entitled "Adventure or concern in the nature of trade" deals with the concept in more detail, in particular, under the heading "Taxpayer's Conduct".

(3) *Nature of the assets involved:* The courts distinguish between fixed assets, which if sold result in a capital transaction, and "circulating" or working capital assets, which if sold result in an income transaction. Hence, the particular use of an asset by a taxpayer may determine its nature for that taxpayer. Some assets, by their nature, can only be regarded as inventory. For example, whisky or toilet paper cannot produce income in such forms as interest, dividends, rents, etc. Income from these commodities can only be earned when they are sold, as inventory, for a price higher than their cost. The Interpretation Bulletin entitled "Adventure or concern in the nature of trade" deals with this factor under the heading "Nature of the Property".

Interpretation Bulletins: IT-459 Adventure or concern in the nature of trade

(4) *Number and frequency of transactions by the same taxpayer in a given period of time:* A relatively large number of transactions in a given period of time may indicate that the taxpayer is involved in a business activity which will result in income transactions. Hence, extensive involvement in a particular type of transaction may be indicative of business activity. It should be emphasized, however, that an isolated transaction may still be considered an "adventure in the nature of trade", that is, of a business nature.

(5) *Length of the period of ownership of the asset:* The length of the holding period for an asset may be used to determine whether the asset is being treated as inventory or as a capital asset. The shorter the period of ownership, the more likely is the gain to be regarded as business income from an adventure in the nature of trade.

(6) *Supplemental work on or in connection with the property disposed of in the transaction:* Work done on a property to enhance its value or to make it more marketable may indicate an adventure in the nature of trade resulting in business income on the disposition. Intensive advertising and promotion of the property for sale would be a similar indicator.

(7) *Circumstances that caused the disposition:* An unsolicited offer that results in the sale or a sale motivated by an unforeseen need for funds may argue against the existence of an adventure in the nature of trade, because of the evidence of the lack of a plan to turn a profit on a sale.

(8) *Corporate objects or partnership agreement:* Articles of incorporation may suggest that the corporation was engaged in a business which it had been created to carry on. Some judicial decisions, in the past, have held that a transaction, although unrelated to the taxpayer's usual business, fell within the objects of a corporation as represented by its charter and, as a result, was a transaction of a business nature. This can occur when the objects of a corporation are set out in a very broad manner in its charter to provide for future flexibility. On the other hand, in the case of *Sutton Lumber & Trading Company Ltd. v. M.N.R.*, the Supreme Court of Canada ignored a corporation's objects on the basis that what is relevant is not what a corporation can do under its objects, but what, in fact, it did do. Furthermore, it should be noted that, although some provincial corporation legislation provides for corporations having objects, the *Canada Business Corporations Act* and the Ontario *Business Corporations Act* do not provide for stated corporate objects. Thus, the relevance of this factor may be

Cases: *Sutton Lumber & Trading Company Limited v. Minister of National Revenue*, 53 DTC 1158 (SCC)

diminished. It should be noted that the stated objectives of a partnership organization, as outlined in a partnership agreement or other document, might be regarded in the same way.

This is not an exhaustive list of behavioural factors that can be observed. The factors used to determine whether a receipt is one of income or capital may depend on the type of property involved. The CRA has developed lists of specific factors for certain types of assets. Some examples are provided below:

CRA List of Behavioural Factors for Real Estate Property

Interpretation Bulletins: IT-218R Profit, capital gains and losses from the sale of real estate, including farmland and inherited land and conversion of real estate from capital property to inventory and vice versa

The CRA has developed a list of about 12 factors which the courts have considered and lists them in the Interpretation Bulletin entitled "Profit, capital gains and losses from the sale of real estate".

Factors or badges of trade pertaining specifically to real estate transactions not already indicated in the foregoing list include:

(1) feasibility of the taxpayer's stated intention;

(2) geographical location and zoned use of the real estate;

(3) extent to which stated intention was carried out by the taxpayer;

(4) evidence of a change in stated intention after the purchase (care must be taken to establish the intention at the time of purchase because it has been regarded as more important by the courts);

(5) the extent to which borrowed money was used to finance the acquisition and the terms of the financing; and

(6) factors that motivated the sale.

CRA List of Behavioural Factors for Securities

Interpretation Bulletins: IT-479R Transactions in securities

The Interpretation Bulletin entitled "Transactions in securities" lists some of the factors or badges of trade that are used in distinguishing between a receipt of income and a receipt of capital on the disposition of securities. Some of the factors listed in paragraph 11 of the bulletin and not listed among the factors already discussed include:

(1) knowledge of or experience in securities markets;

(2) time spent studying the securities markets and investigating potential purchases;

(3) financing primarily by margin or other forms of debt; and

(4) advertising or otherwise making it known that the taxpayer is willing to purchase securities.

¶4,110.40 Summary

Exhibit 4-2 diagrams the analytical strategy discussed above for distinguishing capital income from business income. Note how an assessment of the existence of badges of trade from the facts is used to infer intention of the taxpayer at the time of the purchase of the property in question. Evidence of the existence of significant badges of trade suggests an intention to engage in a profit-making scheme or an adventure in the nature of trade and therefore indicates business income. The lack of that evidence may suggest an investment intention resulting in capital gains treatment.

EXHIBIT 4-2

Analytical Framework for Capital Versus Income Issue

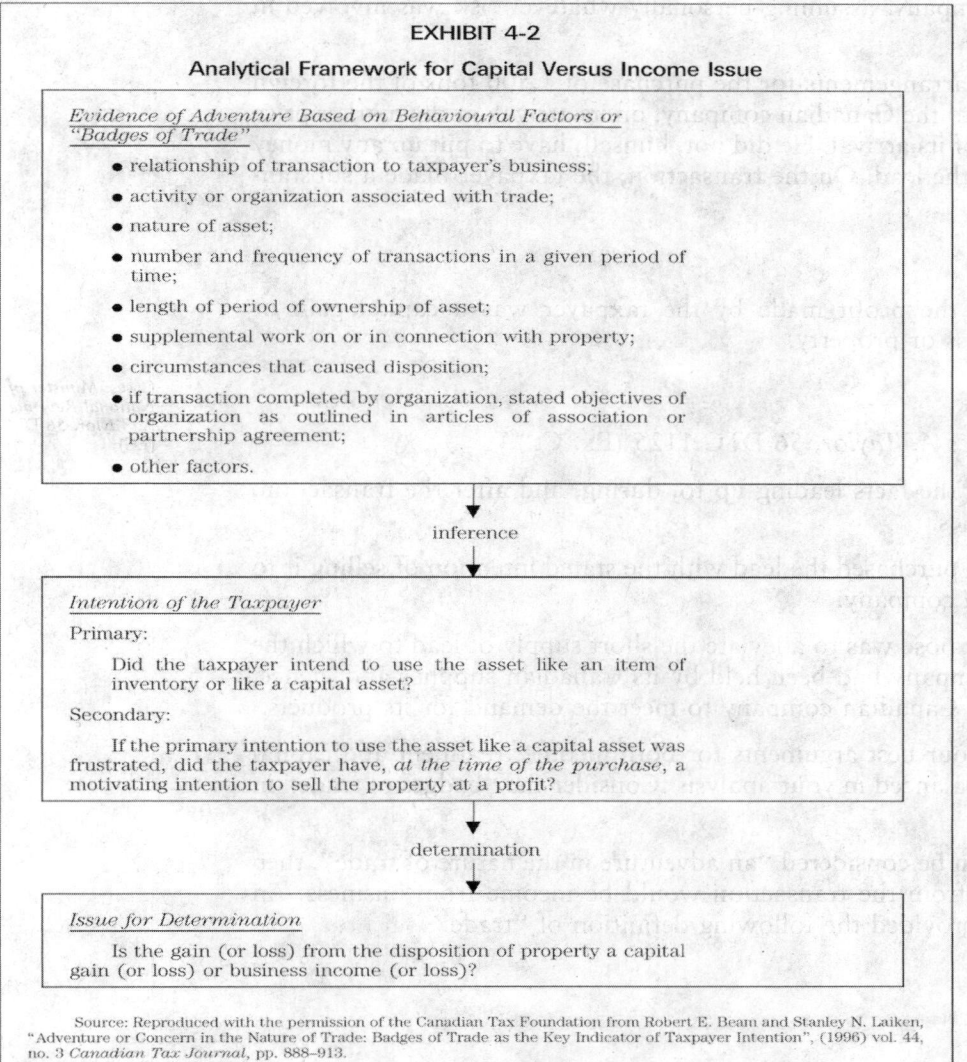

Evidence of Adventure Based on Behavioural Factors or "Badges of Trade"

- relationship of transaction to taxpayer's business;
- activity or organization associated with trade;
- nature of asset;
- number and frequency of transactions in a given period of time;
- length of period of ownership of asset;
- supplemental work on or in connection with property;
- circumstances that caused disposition;
- if transaction completed by organization, stated objectives of organization as outlined in articles of association or partnership agreement;
- other factors.

↓ inference ↓

Intention of the Taxpayer

Primary:

Did the taxpayer intend to use the asset like an item of inventory or like a capital asset?

Secondary:

If the primary intention to use the asset like a capital asset was frustrated, did the taxpayer have, *at the time of the purchase*, a motivating intention to sell the property at a profit?

↓ determination ↓

Issue for Determination

Is the gain (or loss) from the disposition of property a capital gain (or loss) or business income (or loss)?

Source: Reproduced with the permission of the Canadian Tax Foundation from Robert E. Beam and Stanley N. Laiken, "Adventure or Concern in the Nature of Trade: Badges of Trade as the Key Indicator of Taxpayer Intention", (1996) vol. 44, no. 3 *Canadian Tax Journal*, pp. 888–913.

Example Problem 4-1

The taxpayer was the president and general manager of a Canadian company involved in the fabrication of various products of non-ferrous metals, including lead. The company purchased all of its lead requirements from a Canadian supplier which was the only producer of lead in Canada. However, the Canadian supplier held the company to a quota and, as a result, the company lost considerable business.

In these circumstances, the Canadian company requested the permission of its U.S. parent to import foreign lead. This meant buying it for future delivery in about three months. The risk of importing lead for future delivery was contrary to the business policy set for the Canadian company by the U.S. parent. However, the taxpayer was granted permission to purchase the lead himself and sell it to the Canadian company, assuming personally whatever risk was involved in the transaction.

The taxpayer made arrangements for the purchase of 1,500 tons of the foreign lead and for its sale to the Canadian company, on its arrival, at the market price of lead on the date of its arrival. He did not, himself, have to put up any money for the purchase of the lead. On the transaction, the taxpayer made a substantial profit.

REQUIRED

Determine whether the profit made by the taxpayer was a capital gain or income from business or property.

SOLUTION

[See *M.N.R. v. James A. Taylor*, 56 DTC 1125 (Ex. Ct.).]

Cases: *Minister of National Revenue v. James A. Taylor*, 56 DTC 1125 (EC)

Step 1 — Gather all the facts leading up to, during, and after the transaction, and identify the issues.

- The taxpayer purchased the lead with the stated intention of selling it to the Canadian company.
- His stated purpose was to alleviate the short supply of lead to which the Canadian company had been held by its Canadian supplier and, hence, to enable the Canadian company to meet the demand for its products.

Step 2 — Develop your best arguments for both income treatment and capital gain treatment. Be balanced in your analysis. Consider the "badges of trade" in Exhibit 4-2.

If the transaction can be considered "an adventure in the nature of trade", then the profit resulting from the transaction would be income from business. An 1896 British case[8] provided the following definition of "trade":

[8] *Grainger and Son v. Gough* (1896), 3 R.T.C. 462.

> . . . Trade in its largest sense is the business of selling, with a view to profit, goods which the trader has either manufactured or himself purchased.

A 1904 British case[9] set out a test for determining whether the gain from a transaction was capital or income as follows:

> . . . Is the sum of gain that has been made a mere enhancement of value by realizing a security, or is it a gain made in an operation of business in carrying out a scheme for profit-making?

Case Facts That May Suggest Business Income Treatment

- The element of speculation is a characteristic consistent with a badge of trade.
- The nature and quantity of the lead is suggestive of an intent for resale as it does not appear likely to be used in a capital nature.

Case Facts That May Suggest Capital Gains Treatment

- The fact that this was an isolated transaction makes it appear more characteristically as a capital transaction.
- The transaction is totally different in nature from any of the other activities of the taxpayer and that he has never entered into a transaction of the kind before or since. This suggests characteristics of a capital transaction.
- It might be argued that since the taxpayer, as president and general manager of the Canadian company, was an employee, he was not carrying on a business of his own. Hence, the transaction in question was not related to a business that he was carrying on personally, as might be the case of a commodity dealer.

Step 3 — Analyze the strengths and weaknesses of your arguments, by evaluating the facts, rather than simply classifying or listing the facts.

- The element of speculation may determine that a transaction is characteristic of what a trader would do. It can be said that the transaction has the "badges of trade". Thus, if the transaction is of the same kind and is carried on in the same way as a transaction of an ordinary trader or dealer in the same kind of property, it may be called an adventure in the nature of trade.
- The nature and quantity of the subject matter of the transaction may be such as to exclude the possibility that its sale was the realization of an investment of a capital nature. This would lead to the conclusion that the taxpayer's purchase and sale of 1,500 tons of lead was an adventure in the nature of trade. He could not do anything with the lead except sell it. In fact, he dealt with the lead in the same manner as any dealer in imported lead would have done.

---

[9] *Californian Copper Syndicate Ltd. v. Harris*, [1904] 5 T.C. 159.

- The fact that this was an isolated transaction cannot preclude it from being an adventure in the nature of trade. The word "adventure" implies a single or isolated transaction. Furthermore, it is not essential to a transaction being an adventure in the nature of trade that an organization be set up to carry it into effect.
- Finally, the fact that a transaction is totally different in nature from any of the other activities of the taxpayer and that he has never entered into a transaction of the kind before does not, by itself, preclude it from being an adventure in the nature of trade.

Step 4 — Arrive at a conclusion of income or capital gain consistent with your analysis.

The Exchequer Court of Canada, the predecessor of the Federal Court of Canada, concluded in this case that the taxpayer's transaction was an adventure in the nature of trade.

Step 5 — Determine how the transaction will be taxed.

The profit was taxable as income from business carried on by the taxpayer, Taylor.

Note: While the *Taylor* case is regarded as a landmark case in this area, it was a relatively early case and, hence, not all of the behavioural factors that are known today had been developed by the courts at the time of that decision.

¶4,110.50 Examples of Capital Versus Business Income in Practice

There are many issues that can arise where the treatment of receipt as capital or business income are dependent on the treatment of the related asset or nature of the receipt. Some examples are as follows:

Non-Performance of Business Contracts

Damages received for non-performance of business contracts are usually intended to place the recipient in the same position as he or she would have been had the contract been performed. Since the performance of a business contract usually results in business income, damages for non-performance are generally regarded as business income.

Cancellation of Agency Agreements

While the cancellation of an agency agreement has been held to be business income, if such an agreement is of sufficient importance to constitute part of the company's total business structure, the compensation paid on the termination of such a contract may be treated as capital. This was the situation in a U.K. decision.[10] In that case an English company

[10] *Van den Berghs, Ltd. v. Clark*, [1935] A.C. 431

entered into an agreement with a competing Dutch company to co-operate in the manufacture and sale of margarine and to share in the resulting profits and losses. The agreement was to last for about 30 years, but it had to be terminated earlier and the Dutch company paid the English company a large sum of money to terminate the agreement. The British House of Lords held that the rights of the English company under the agreement constituted a capital asset and the sum paid for its cancellation was a capital receipt. For a Canadian case in this area see *Parsons-Steiner Limited v. M.N.R.*, which dealt with the cancellation of an agency agreement of 22 years standing accounting for 80% of the appellant's business. In *Pepsi-Cola Canada Ltd. v. The Queen*, a payment made on the termination of a bottling and distributorship agreement was held to be for goodwill and, hence, a capital receipt. On the other hand, compensation for cancelling a contract entered into in the course of the appellant's regular business was held to be taxable as income in *The Great Lakes Paper Company, Limited v. M.N.R.*

Cases: *Parsons-Steiner Limited v. Minister of National Revenue*, 62 DTC 1148 (EC); *Pepsi-Cola Canada Ltd. v. Her Majesty the Queen*, 79 DTC 5387 (FCA); *The Great Lakes Paper Company, Limited v. M.N.R.*, 61 DTC 564 (TAB)

Loss of Property

Damages for loss of property may be regarded as a receipt of capital if the property involved was fixed capital, and a receipt of business income if the property was an asset such as inventory whose sale would have resulted in business income.

Subsidies

The question of whether a government or any other subsidy is capital or business income will depend on the purpose of the subsidy. A business income receipt may result from a subsidy to:

- supplement the taxpayer's income or enable him or her to operate at a profit; or
- ensure a reasonable return to the taxpayer on capital invested.

On the other hand, a capital receipt may result from a subsidy to:

- reimburse or assist the taxpayer in respect of a capital purchase; or
- encourage an activity in the public interest such as the prevention of unemployment.

The case of *Saint John Drydock & Shipbuilding Co. Ltd. v. M.N.R.* is a leading Canadian decision on the question of whether a subsidy should be regarded as a receipt of income or capital. The general principles followed by the CRA in making this distinction are set out in the Interpretation Bulletin entitled "Government Assistance — General Comments".

Cases: *Saint John Dry Dock & Shipbuilding Company, Limited v. Minister of National Revenue*, 2 DTC 663 (EC); Interpretation Bulletins: IT-273R2 Government Assistance — General Comments

Ⓐ Forgiveness of Debt Rules

When a debt is settled or forgiven by the creditor for less than its principal amount and the debt was incurred for the purpose of earning income from a business or property, the debt forgiveness rules will apply. Note that personal debt would normally be excluded from these rules.

The debt forgiveness rules laid out in the Act are complex rules that reduce certain tax-loss carryovers or tax accounts by the amount of debt forgiven.

ITA: 80 [Debt forgiveness rules]

The following is a summary of the tax values that are reduced where a taxpayer has had some debt forgiven. The forgiven amount of the debt reduces tax values in this sequence or order.

ITA: 80(3) Reductions of non-capital losses, 80(12) Capital gain where current year capital loss

(1) Non-capital losses

(2) Net capital losses

(3) Depreciable property

(4) Cumulative eligible capital

(5) Non-depreciable capital property

To the extent there is still some forgiven debt that has not been applied, the balance will be treated as follows:

(1) Capital gain, or

(2) 50% included in income (100% if a partnership).

The effect of this is to increase income either now or in the future.

Where the debt was incurred in a business activity, the income inclusion is considered to be income from the business. The effect of this provision is to fully offset the benefit of not having to repay all or part of a debt with after-tax funds. The specific rules on debt forgiveness are beyond the scope of this text.

¶4,110.90 Pause and Reflect — Summary of Learning Goals

After working through this section, ¶4,110, you should be able to:

- Determine whether a source of income should be treated as capital in nature or as business income.
- Explain why distinguishing business income from income that is capital in nature is important.

¶4,120 Business Income Versus Property Income

Overview

Over a taxation period, income or losses generally arise from holding or using property. Whether this income is income from property or income from a business is not always easily determined. The basic test is whether the income earned is active or passive income. If the income requires little or no activity by the taxpayer (or his or her employees), the income is usually considered passive and is income from property. Examples would include dividends on shares, interest on bank savings, and similar investments such as bonds, royalties, and rental income. It does not result from the same degree of time and effort as does business income, which may be described as active income. The passive *versus* active test has proven to not always be easy to apply or administer as there is always the question of the "degree" of required activity. Consequently, the Act contains specific directives for many cases. For example, "property", which consequently produces property income, is defined to specifically include:

ITA: 248(1) Definitions

- a right of any kind, a share or a *chose*[11] in action;

[11] "*Chose*" is defined in *Irwin Law's Canadian Legal Dictionary* as, "A personal right incapable of possession but enforceable through legal action, such as a contractual right."

- unless a contrary intention is evident, money;[12]
- a timber resource property; and
- work in progress of a business that is a profession.

¶4,120.10 Reasons for Distinction Between Business and Property Income

Although the Act groups income from a business with income from property, the distinction between the two sources is still important for the following reasons.

- Property income earned by an individual is considered a return on equity, or passive income, and, except for rental income, is excluded from the earned income calculation in the determination of the maximum RRSP contribution limit, whereas self-employed business income is included in the earned income calculation.[13]
- The definition of "earned income" for eligibility for a deduction for child care expenses includes business income but excludes all income from property.
- Property income derived from rental properties is subject to separate rules. For example, capital cost allowance claimed against rental income may not create or increase a loss from rental properties.
- Business income earned by a corporation has special rules, such as the small business deduction for active business income, and the manufacturing and processing deduction for profits derived from manufacturing. Alternatively, corporations holding properties and investments are taxed at a much higher rate.
- The income attribution rules (discussed in Chapter 8) generally apply only to the non-arm's length transfer of property income and not to the transfer of business income.
- Non-resident taxpayers are taxed on income from a business carried on in Canada, while income from property is subject to withholding tax under a different part of the Act.

¶4,120.20 Determination by Corporations

Corporations, like individuals, are affected by the distinction between business income and income from property. Where a corporation has a business, the principal purpose of which is to earn income from property (defined as interest, dividends, rents, and royalties, but excluding leasing income from other than real property), that income is considered inactive or passive (hence, income from property) unless the corporation employs more than five full-time employees. The subjective test of activity has been replaced by the objective test of the number of full-time employees. It is also possible for a corporation to earn income from property as well as business income. The difference between business income and other income is very important for corporations, as it affects the rate of tax used. This will be reviewed in Chapters 11 and 12.

ITA: 125(7) Definitions

---

[12] "Money" is perhaps an arbitrary word choice; however, the intent is to indicate that property includes gold, silver, copper, nickel, coins, and any paper notes, such as bank notes and cheques, and extends to property, possessions, and wealth. Although inflationary and deflationary gains are not recognized, the disposition of foreign currency can lead to foreign exchange gains and losses

[13] Subsection 146(1) defines "earned income" for the purpose of computing the maximum RRSP contribution limit. It is important to note that earned income carries a different definition for the purpose of computing earned income for the childcare deduction.

Investment income earned by a corporation is generally considered income from property. However, the Act excludes income from property that is "incident to or pertains to an active business carried on by [the corporation], or that is used or held principally for the purpose of gaining or producing income from an active business". Examples of active business income are, interest charged on accounts receivable, interest on monies held in short-term investments, and rents received from renting an (otherwise) unused portion of a manufacturer's premises. Where any short-term investment becomes more or less permanent — that is, it is never depleted in the course of carrying on the business — the interest earned is income from property. ITA: 129(4) Definitions

¶4,120.30 Determination by Partnership

Where a person is a limited partner or a person not actively engaged in the partnership business on a regular, continuous, or substantial basis, his or her partnership income is deemed to be income from property and not income from a business. While the latter portion of this provision relies on the activity test, it at least provides some guidance on the degree of required activity.

¶4,120.90 Pause and Reflect — Summary of Learning Goals

After working through this section, ¶4,120, you should be able to:

- Determine whether a source of income should be treated as business income or property income.
- Explain why distinguishing business income from other sources of income (such as capital, investment income, etc.) is important.

¶4,120.99 Practise What You've Learned

Refer to the following sections of the Study Guide to practise what you've learned:

¶4,800 — Review Questions

- Question 1 — Distinguishing Types of Income

¶4,825 — Multiple Choice Questions

- Question 5 — Business Income Versus Capital Receipt

¶4,850 — Exercises

- Exercise 2 — Business Income Versus Capital Receipt
- Exercise 5 — Distinguishing Types of Income
- Exercise 13 — Business Income Versus Capital Receipt

¶4,200 Reporting of Business Income

Overview

The period for which business income is reported can vary by taxpayer. This section summarizes some of the specific rules surrounding reporting periods for business income, as well as specific rules concerning specific receipts that may or may not be included as business income.

¶4,210 Reporting Periods

Overview

Corporations will report business income based on their fiscal period. However, the reporting period for an individual has specific rules discussed as follows.

¶4,210.10 Sole Proprietorship

Individuals who report business income, including professional income, generally must report that income on a calendar year basis, according to the definition of "fiscal period". This requirement applies to a sole proprietorship and a professional corporation, which is any corporation that carries on the professional practice of an accountant, dentist, lawyer, medical doctor, veterinarian, or chiropractor. The requirement also applies to partnerships in which at least one member is an individual, a professional corporation or another affected partnership.

ITA: 249.1(1) Definition of "fiscal period", 248(1) Definitions

However, there is a provision for an alternative fiscal period for a business carried on by an individual. A change in the end of a fiscal period can only be made with ministerial concurrence. An off-calendar fiscal year end for an unincorporated business is possible, if an individual files an election in prescribed form by the date on which the individual must file a tax return for the year. The election can be revoked in a future period, in which case the calendar-year fiscal period must be used.

ITA: 249.1(4) Alternative method, 249.1(6) Revocation of election, 249.1(7) Change of fiscal period

Ⓐ ¶4,210.20 Deferral Anti-Avoidance

To prevent a deferral in the reporting of income on an off-calendar fiscal period, additional rules for the reporting of business income must be followed. A formula is provided that effectively computes income from an unincorporated business with an off-calendar year end on a calendar year basis by the use of an estimating procedure.

ITA: 249.1(4) Alternative method, 34.1 Additional business income

For example, the system applies to a January 31 business year end as follows. First, the taxpayer includes income from the unincorporated business for the fiscal period ended, say, January 31, 2018. To this amount, the taxpayer must add an estimate of business income for the "stub period" from February 1, 2018 to December 31, 2018. The estimate is based on a proration of 11/12 or 11 months of income in the fiscal period ended January 31, 2018. From the sum, the taxpayer can subtract the stub period addition made in the 2017 tax return. This alternative method recognizes that there are valid non-tax business reasons for using an off-calendar year end and allows such a year end to be maintained.

The following illustrates this adjustment for a January 31 year end in 2018 and 2019, with no expected change in income over the two years:

		2018	2019
Income for the year ended January 31, 2018 and 2019		$120,000	$120,000
Add:	estimate of income for the period February 1, 2018 and 2019 to December 31, 2018 and 2019 = 11/12 × income for the 12 months ended January 31, 2018 and 2019	110,000	110,000
Deduct:	last year's estimate (2017 estimate assumed)	(105,000)	(110,000)
Income for tax purposes for 2018 and 2019		$125,000	$120,000

Note how the 2018 income reflects the increase in income from 2017 to 2018 that would otherwise be deferred a year, while the 2019 income reflects the steady-state income of $120,000 over 2018 and 2019.

When an off-calendar year end reflects less than 12 months of business operations, due to the commencement of business, the stub-period income addition is adjusted so that an appropriate amount not exceeding 12 months of income is reported in a calendar-year period.

ITA: 34.1(1) Additional business income, 34.1(2) Additional income election

¶4,220 Reporting of Specific Receipts

Overview

In addition to the rules distinguishing the source of income above, some receipts have additional rules that must be considered when deciding whether they are to be reported as business income. This can include profits from an illegal business, profits from betting and windfall profits.

¶4,220.10 Profits From an Illegal Business

Profits from an illegal business are still taxable. This principle was established in a 1932 U.K. case[14] in which the following statement was made:

> . . . The revenue [authorities], representing the state, are merely looking at an accomplished fact. It is not condoning it, or taking part in it. It merely finds profit made from what appears to be a trade, and the revenue laws say that profits made from a trade are to be taxed.

This was re-established in the Canadian case of *No. 275 v. M.N.R.* Having established the taxation of receipts, the question of deductions arises in terms of substantiating expenses incurred to produce the profits from an illegal business. This was the situation in *M.N.R. v. Eldridge* involving the operator of a call-girl organization who attempted to claim certain cash expenditures. Substantiated, non-capital expenditures incurred to produce income from an illegal business are normally deductible. However, the deduction of specified illegal payments is prohibited. Hence, illegal payments under specified sections of the *Criminal Code* made to:

ITA: 67.5 Non-deductibility of illegal payments; Income Tax Folio: S4-F2-C1 Deductibility of Fines and Penalties; Cases: 55 DTC 439 (TAB); *Minister of National Revenue v. Olva Diana Eldridge*, 64 DTC 5338 (EC)

- government officials in Canada,
- officials engaged in the administration of justice in Canada,

[14] *Mann v. Nash*, [1932] 1 K.B. 752.

- persons under a duty as agents or employees, and
- persons responsible for collecting fares or admission fees

are not deductible where

- the payments are made to induce, or attempt to induce, the recipient to breach his or her duty, and
- the payment is made for doing anything that is an offence under the specified sections of the *Criminal Code*.

Refer to Income Tax Folio, "Lottery Winnings, Miscellaneous Receipts, and Income (and Losses) from Crime", for the CRA's position in this area.

Income Tax Folio: S3-F9-C1 Lottery Winnings, Miscellaneous Receipts, and Income (and Losses) from Crime

¶4,220.20 Profits From Betting, Gambling, and Windfalls

The proceeds of private betting or gambling for mere pleasure have generally been regarded as not taxable as long as the activity is not organized and of a business nature. This will be the case even if the bets, perhaps even made with borrowed funds, are high and the gains substantial. However, someone like a bookmaker will be taxable on his or her profits because he or she will be regarded as carrying on a business. The existence of a system for the minimization or management of risk may indicate a professional gambler. In this case, the winnings would be taxable and, conceivably, the losses would be deductible.

A non-taxable windfall can be distinguished from income if the recipient has no expectation of receiving the payment. Perhaps a more widely recognized form of windfall is a lottery winning, which is not taxable.

Income Tax Folio: S3-F9-C1 Lottery Winnings, Miscellaneous Receipts, and Income (and Losses) from Crime

¶4,300 Calculation of Business Income

Overview

Once it has been determined that a receipt of income is to be reported as business income, the amount of income must be calculated by following the general rules laid out in the Act. This generally involves beginning with net income for accounting purposes and then making appropriate adjustments to the receipts also referred to as inclusions (amounts included as business income) and to the expenses also referred to as deductions (amounts deducted from business income).

¶4,310 Conversion of Accounting Income to Net Business Income for Tax Purposes

Overview

All taxpayers (individuals, corporations, trusts, etc.) follow the same general rules in calculating business income. The calculation of business income for tax purposes begins with accounting net income. Accounting net income is adjusted or reconciled to net business income for tax purposes by:

- the subtraction of income that is not taxable, but was included for accounting purposes;
- the addition of taxable income that was not included in accounting income;

- the addition (reversal) of expenses not allowed for tax purposes (non-deductible) that have been deducted for accounting purposes; and
- the subtraction of expenditures deductible for tax purposes, but were not deductible for accounting purposes.

¶4,310.10 Summary of Sections to Consider During the Conversion

The Act contains broad provisions governing the conversion of accounting income from a specific source to income for tax purposes. Most of the differences between accounting income and income for tax purposes from a business are dealt with in subdivision b, sections 9 to 37.

- Section 9, Profit from business.
- Section 10, Inventory valuation.
- Section 11, Proprietorships.
- Sections 12 to 17, Income inclusions, i.e., all amounts receivable.
- Sections 18, 19, 19.1, Non-deductible expenses.
- Section 20, Deductions specifically permitted.
- Sections 22 to 25, Rules that apply if the business ceases to exist.
- Sections 26 to 37, Special situations that may apply.

The four principal sections relating to the determination of business income are sections 9, 12, 18, and 20. The other sections of subdivision b refine the principal rules and should not be ignored. There is an important relationship between those four sections of the Act when determining business income. These sections form the pillars on which the entire structure for the taxation of business income stands.

Each section will be reviewed in more detail later, but the following is a brief summary:

- Section 9 sets out the basic rules of general application for determining the taxpayer's income from a business.
- Section 12 states when income should be taxed, according to the amounts, received or receivable, that have not been included in the profit established under section 9. However, even if certain amounts are to be included in income under section 12, some reserves may be allowed under section 20 to reduce the business income. For example, a business deducts $4,000 as a doubtful debt reserve in 2017. In 2018, the $4,000 doubtful debt reserve from 2017 must be included in income and the business would deduct a new doubtful debt reserve for 2018.

ITA: 12(1)(d) Reserve for doubtful debts, 20(1)(l) Doubtful or impaired debts

- Section 18 includes the general rule that no deduction of an outlay or expense may be claimed against income unless it was made or incurred by the taxpayer for the purpose of gaining or producing income from a particular business or property. Section 18 itemizes certain deductions that are disallowed in computing a taxpayer's income from business. It is one of the key sections to refer to in order to establish if an amount is deductible or not, or included or not when computing business income.
- Section 20 is another key section that contains deductions that are specifically permitted by the statute in computing income from business or property. As a general rule, section 20 deals with deductions of certain items that were either

included in income in compliance with section 12 or did not qualify as deductions because of the section 18 limitations. For example, paragraph 18(1)(*b*) disallows a deduction on account of capital, while paragraph 20(1)(*a*) allows the deduction for capital cost allowance for part of the capital cost of a property in accordance with income tax regulations. This is an example of how a specific provision, such as paragraph 20(1)(*a*), overrides a general limiting provision, such as paragraph 18(1)(*b*). While section 20 also sets out rules for the deductibility of certain other items such as interest expense, finance charges, and various other items, section 18 specifically prohibits the deduction of certain outlays in the computation of net income from business or property.

- Section 67 needs particular attention, being a general limitation provision regarding expenses. To restrict taxpayers from deducting unreasonable expenses, section 67 was added to ensure that all expenses deducted are reasonable in the circumstances. This section essentially gives the CRA the right to reduce a deductible expense to a reasonable amount. Items that are deductible for accounting purposes may not always be reasonable in the circumstances. For example, section 67.1 requires that 50% of meals and entertainment expense be added to accounting net income in the computation of net income for tax purposes.

Also, note the existence of other differences, such as the fact that consolidated and equity statements are not allowed for tax purposes. Consolidated financial statements represent multiple legal entities bound as a single economic unit. By reason of the definition of a "taxpayer", each legal entity is required to report separately for tax purposes. Because of these variances, it is necessary to reconcile the differences by adjusting net income for accounting purposes to net business income for tax purposes. The basic formula in arriving at business income for tax purposes may be simplified[15] as follows.

ITA: 248(24) Accounting methods

Income from a business for tax purposes is equal to:

Starting Point:	Subsection 9(1)	"Profit", or accounting net income
plus	sections 12 to 17	Income inclusions not included in "profit"
plus	sections 18(1), 19	Disallowed expenses and reserves
plus	section 67	Unreasonable amounts
minus	subsection 20(1)	Expenses and reserves specifically allowed but not deducted in "profit"
plus		Capital losses — book losses on the disposal of capital property
minus		Capital gains — book gains on the disposal of capital property
Finishing Point:		Income from a business for tax purposes

[15] The objective in this basic formula is to show the underlying flow of the calculation. Many other sections may apply, depending on the taxable entity, type of business, type of transactions, legal reorganizations, etc., that require the inclusion of other sections of the Act.

Capital gains and losses are not recognized as a source of business income; therefore, any gain or loss from the disposition of capital property is backed out of income from a business and accounted for separately. ITA: 3(b)

¶4,320 Inventory Valuation

Overview

For many businesses, the cost of goods sold is an important expense that is deducted in the calculation of net income. This is true for the calculation of business income for tax purposes as well. However the Act lays out specific provisions to govern the valuation of inventory and, therefore, the cost of goods sold.

¶4,320.10 Market or Lower of Cost or Market

The Act permits the valuation of each item in an inventory at the lower of cost or market. A degree of variation is permitted by an income tax regulation which allows all of the items in the inventory to be valued at fair market value. This regulation might be used, where the fair market value of all items is lower than the valuation provided by the lower of cost or market for each item, to maximize cost of goods sold, and, thereby, minimize tax. However, there could be situations where the higher value would be desirable, for example, to reduce a loss that might expire. Again, the choice permitted between the Act and the regulation could be used to provide the higher valuation as necessary, but the effect may be minimal, given the choices permitted. Furthermore, as will be seen from a subsequent discussion, the choice may be permanent, such that the long-term effects of the alternate choice should be considered.

ITA: 10(1) Valuation of inventory, 10(2.1) Methods of valuation to be the same; ITR: 1801 Valuation

¶4,320.20 Specific Identification

Where the cost of items in an inventory can be identified, it is the actual laid down cost that must be used. This would include invoice cost plus duties, freight and insurance. In the case of goods in process and finished goods in the inventory of a manufacturing concern, cost will also include the cost of direct labour and in some cases the applicable share of overhead expenses. According to an Interpretation Bulletin, the cost of manufactured goods must include overhead allocated on a direct costing or absorption costing basis. The Act requires the inclusion in cost any non-deductible interest and property taxes on vacant land held as inventory of a business.

Interpretation Bulletins: IT-473R Inventory Valuation; ITA: 10(1.1) Certain expenses included in cost

¶4,320.30 First In, First Out

Where individual items cannot be identified for costing, a convention or assumption, usually "first in, first out" ("FIFO"), must be applied for the purpose of determining cost of inventory on hand.

The use of "last in, first out" ("LIFO") as an assumption about cost has long been fought by the CRA as illustrated by the case of *M.N.R. v. Anaconda American Brass Ltd.* In that case it was held by the Judicial Committee of the Privy Council of the House of Lords of the United Kingdom (to which decisions of the Supreme Court of Canada could be appealed until the mid-1950s), first, that an assumption of any kind in determining inventory value could only be made to the extent that the facts about actual cost were not ascertainable. Furthermore, in the particular case of *Anaconda*, the LIFO assumption disregarded the actual flow of inventory through the business. As a result, LIFO is only

Cases: *M.N.R. v. Anaconda American Brass Ltd*, 55 DTC 1220 (Privy Council)

acceptable if it reflects the physical flow of inventory, otherwise it is prohibited. In addition, LIFO is not acceptable under IFRS and Canadian GAAP.

¶4,320.40 Meaning of "Cost" and "Market"

For the meaning of the word "market" in the valuation of inventory, refer to the *CPA ["Chartered Professional Accountants"] Canada Handbook*. Market price within the handbook is referred to as net realizable value and defined in IAS paragraph 6 for publicly accountable entities, and Section 3031.07 for entities that are not publicly accountable, as "the estimated selling price in the ordinary course of business less the estimated cost of completion and the estimated costs necessary to make the sale".

The meaning of the terms "cost" and "market" are further considered in the Interpretation Bulletin entitled "Inventory Valuation".

Interpretation Bulletins: IT-473R Inventory Valuation

It is interesting to note that the Act specifies that replacement cost must be used for the fair market value of certain property that is advertising or packaging material, parts, supplies or other property of this nature which is considered to be inventory. Note, also, that work in progress of a business that is a profession is considered to be inventory with a fair market value equal to the amount that can reasonably be expected to become receivable after the end of the year. However, for greater certainty, these types of property are considered to be inventory and, hence, subject to the Act's valuation rules for inventory.

ITA: 10(1) Valuation of inventory, 10(4)(a), 10(4)(b), 10(5) Inventory

The Act requires that the value attributed to the opening inventory be the same as that attributed to the closing inventory of the year before. This ensures that no profits escape tax by a break in the continuity of the inventory figures between the end of one year and the beginning of the next.

ITA: 10(2) Continuation of valuation

A taxpayer must value inventory at the end of a year using the same method as that used at the end of the preceding year. A taxpayer is permitted to change the valuation method used for inventory of a business where permission is obtained from the CRA. The result is to restrict the flexibility in the choice of inventory valuation method from one year to another. However, there may be some flexibility within a particular inventory valuation method. For example, a business that is required to value its inventory at the lower of cost or market at the end of a year because that method was used at the end of the preceding year, may still have a choice in determining cost for the purposes of this valuation method. This provision appears to codify accounting principles requiring that the opening and closing inventories of a given year be valued on the same basis and correct the value of opening inventory where it has not been valued as required by the Act. As a result, corrected opening inventory may differ from closing inventory of the preceding year, thereby forcing the effects of the change on the income of the year of the correction only.

ITA: 10(1) Valuation of inventory, 10(2.1) Methods of valuation to be the same, 10(3) Incorrect valuation

Example Problem 4-2

Sam Brown builds houses in various parts of the city. At the end of his fiscal year he has four homes left in his inventory. Sam's records show the following information on each house:

	Actual total cost	Cost to rebuild house	Market list price
1. Happy Valley Road	$40,000	$50,000	$75,000
2. Thruway Drive	25,000	20,000	18,000
3. Creekside Place	40,000	45,000	42,000
4. Briar Lane	25,000	22,000	24,000

From past experience Sam knows that he can sell each house for its market list price less 10% for commissions and bargaining.

REQUIRED

Using the valuation alternatives available to him, determine the value of Sam's closing inventory. Indicate the basis for each valuation and select the one more advantageous to him, assuming he wants to minimize income for tax purposes. (Assume that the method of valuing inventory could change with permission.)

ITA: 10(2.1) Methods of valuation to be the same

SOLUTION

In this case, since the houses are finished, net realizable value would be the appropriate indicator of market value. This would be calculated from the information given by reducing market list price by the 10% direct cost of making the sale. The following would form the basis of the decision:

House	Cost	Market		Lower on each unit
1	$40,000	$67,500	(90% of $75,000)	$40,000
2	25,000	16,200	(90% of $18,000)	16,200
3	40,000	37,800	(90% of $42,000)	37,800
4	25,000	21,600	(90% of $24,000)	21,600
		$143,100		$115,600

Using the rules in the Act, the inventory could be valued at $115,600 which is the lower of cost or market for each item. The Regulations would permit the use of the market value of all items ($143,100). In this case, if the business is profitable, the more advantageous valuation would be based on the lower of cost or market for each item because it would provide the lower valuation, thereby increasing cost of goods sold and decreasing income subject to tax. On the other hand, if the business is in a loss position for the year, some of the losses can be absorbed by choosing the regulation alternative of market value to decrease cost of goods sold, thereby increasing the gross margin available to offset losses for the year. The choice is limited by the provision of the Act that requires that the method chosen for ending inventory in the current year must be the same as the method used for closing inventory at the end of the previous year unless ministerial permission for a change is granted.

ITA: 10(1) Valuation of inventory, 10(2.1) Methods of valuation to be the same; ITR: 1801 Valuation

¶4,320.50 Adjustment for Amortization Allocation to Inventory: Absorption Accounting

To the extent that the cost of closing inventory for financial accounting purposes *includes an allocation* by the use of absorption costing of amortization, obsolescence or depletion write-offs, such an allocation must be added to income for the year. This rule requires the full add-back of amortization in the reconciliation of income for tax purposes with income for financial accounting purposes. The add-back is required despite the fact that any amortization included in the cost of closing inventory is not charged as an expense in the year, because the value of closing inventory reduces the cost of goods sold. Since the same allocation for accounting purposes will be included in the cost of opening inventory of the next year, a deduction of the amount of the allocation added in the current year for tax purposes is made in the subsequent year. These adjustments are unnecessary if the taxpayer has used the direct costing method and, as a result, has not included in the cost of inventory for financial accounting purposes an allowance in respect of amortization, obsolescence, or depletion.

ITA: 12(1)(r) Inventory adjustment, 20(1)(ii) Inventory adjustment

Example Problem 4-3

Absolute Co. recorded total amortization of $5,000 in Year 1 (first year of operations), of which $1,000 is included as part of the cost of its ending inventory. In Year 2 the amounts were $10,250 and $1,250, respectively. For tax purposes Absolute Co. claimed capital cost allowance of $12,000 in each year.

Net income per financial statements, using absorption costing, was computed as follows:

	Year 1	Year 2
Gross revenue	$170,000	$340,000
Opening inventory	$0	$ 20,000
Cost of goods manufactured	100,000	205,000

	Year 1	Year 2
Closing inventory	(20,000)	(25,000)
Cost of goods sold	$80,000	$200,000
General and administration	$40,000	$50,000
Net income per financial statements	$50,000	$90,000

SOLUTION

	Absorption costing	Amortization expense	Direct costing[1]
Year 1			
Gross revenue	$170,000		$170,000
Opening inventory	$0		$0
Cost of goods manufactured	100,000	$5,000	95,000
Closing inventory	(20,000)	(1,000)	(19,000)
Cost of goods sold	$80,000	$4,000	$76,000
General and administration	$40,000		$45,000[2]
Net income per financial statements	$50,000		$49,000
Add back:			
Amortization expense (net)	4,000		5,000
Paragraph 12(1)(*r*) amortization	1,000		0
Deduct:			
Capital cost allowance	(12,000)		(12,000)
Net income for tax purposes	$43,000		$42,000
Year 2			
Gross revenue	$340,000		$340,000
Opening inventory	$20,000	$1,000	$19,000
Cost of goods manufactured	205,000	10,250	194,750
Closing inventory	(25,000)	(1,250)	(23,750)

	Absorption costing	Amortization expense	Direct costing[1]
Cost of goods sold	$200,000	$10,000	$190,000
General and administration	$50,000		$60,250
Net income per financial statements	$90,000		$89,750
Add back:			
Amortization expense	10,000		10,250
Paragraph 12(1)(*r*) amortization	1,250		0
Deduct:			
Paragraph 20(1)(*ii*) inventory adjustment	(1,000)		0
Capital cost allowance	(12,000)		(12,000)
Net income for tax purposes	$88,250		$88,000

NOTES TO SOLUTION

(1) Direct costing is provided for comparative purposes only. Note how the adjustments to net income for tax purposes for absorption costing amortization result in a higher net income amount in comparison with direct costing.

(2) Under direct costing, general and administration expenses include amortization of $5,000 in Year 1 and $10,250 in Year 2.

¶4,390 Pause and Reflect — Summary of Learning Goals

After working through this section, ¶4,300, you should be able to:

- Explain how accounting income is used in the calculation of business income for tax purposes.
- Identify an acceptable method of inventory valuation for tax purposes.
- Calculate the cost of goods sold to be used in the computation of business income for tax purposes.

¶4,390.99 Practise What You've Learned

Refer to the following sections of the Study Guide to practise what you've learned:

¶4,850 — Exercises

- Exercise 6 — Inventory Valuation
- Exercise 12 — Conversion of Accounting Income to Net Business Income for Tax Purposes

¶4,400 Inclusions

Overview

There can often be differences between the calculation of income for accounting purposes and for tax purposes. One of the sources of difference is the receipts that are required to be included in the calculation of business income. This section summarizes the amounts that are required to be included in the calculation of business income for tax purposes and highlights some of the most common differences that arise when comparing these requirements to GAAP.

ITA: 12 Income inclusions, 17 Amount owing by non-resident

¶4,410 Inclusions in Income for Tax Purposes

Many small corporations and self-employed individuals engaged in a business do not prepare financial statements using GAAP. This is often because the sole users of financial statements are owners, managers, and the CRA. If financial statements are not prepared in accordance with GAAP, there is the possibility that the cash basis of accounting, rather than the accrual method of accounting is being used. The Act resolves this possibility by requiring that any amount receivable by the taxpayer (including amounts receivable in future taxation years) for goods or services rendered in the course of business in the taxation year are to be included in income.

ITA: 12(1)(b) Amounts receivable

However, the Act also allows the cash basis of accounting where that method is accepted under the Act. Farmers and fishers are permitted to use the cash basis, and professionals are allowed to exclude work in progress.

ITA: 28(1) Farming or fishing business, 34 Professional business

In accordance with GAAP, many accrued estimates are necessary to satisfy the principles of matching and conservatism, estimates that may conflict with legislative intent. For example, an allowance for doubtful accounts is set up to ensure that the company has matched the potential bad debt expense with current revenues, and to ensure the accounts receivable balance is fairly stated. Generally, the Act does not accept accounting reserves. Instead, reserves are added back to income and the Act then may offer a limited and regulated deduction to offset this income inclusion. Although this may appear unusual and overly administrative, the purpose is to force taxpayers to calculate their reserves on a tax basis every year.

Another intent is to allow for an inclusion of certain items that are generally not recorded as revenue for tax purposes. For example, inducement payments such as amounts received by a tenant from a landlord for leasehold improvements would not be taxable unless a specific provision required it.

ITA: 12(1)(x) Inducement, reimbursement, etc.

It is impossible to commit to memory all of the items required to be included in income and all the deductions disallowed by section 18 or allowed by section 20. Understanding the Act and the underlying intent will assist students and professionals in income tax research, analysis, and preparation. When computing net income from a business for tax purposes, section 12 is first reviewed for amounts to be added to GAAP net income, and expenses are checked against section 18 to ensure they pass the test of deductibility. Finally, section 20 is examined to see if any alternative reserves or limited deductions are available. In this chapter, the intent is to provide users with a logical understanding of the computation of net business income and not all inclusions, deductions, or disallowed deductions will be covered in detail. If additional research is warranted, income tax folios or interpretation bulletins, information circulars, and case law should be considered.

The following table provides a brief summary of items that are usually included in the calculation of income from a business or property.

Calculation of Income From a Business or Property

ITA Reference	Description	Related Reference
12(1)(*a*)	Services to be rendered in future	20(1)(*m*), (*m*.2)
12(1)(*b*)	A/R for services rendered	20(1)(*n*), 68
12(1)(*d*), (*e*)	Reserves — bad debts and warranties	20(1)(*l*), (*m*), (*n*)
12(1)(*f*)	Insurance proceeds — depreciable property	
12(1)(*g*)	Payments based on production or use	
12(1)(*i*)	Bad debts recovered	
12(1)(*c*), (*j*), (*k*)	Interest, dividends	82(1), 84, 89
12(1)(*l*)	Partnership income	96 to 103
12(1)(*x*)	Inducement payments, reimbursements	20(1)(*hh*)

¶4,420 Amounts Received and Receivable

Amounts received for services to be rendered or goods to be delivered are included in income. This represents a divergence from accounting principles which would defer such amounts of income until the year in which they are earned. However, a reasonable reserve for unearned amounts included in income can be taken. The Act's system for reserves will be discussed later in this chapter. The Act would include amounts received such as prepaid rent, payments for the warranty of merchandise, and container deposits. A deduction for refunds of amounts previously included in income under this paragraph is provided to offset the fact that a reserve would not be available for a refunded amount.

ITA: 12(1)(a) Services, etc., to be rendered, 20(1)(m) Reserve in respect of certain goods and services, 20(1)(m.2) Repayment of amount previously included in income

Amounts receivable in respect of services rendered or property sold during the year in the course of business are brought into income. Amounts included because they are receivable must be legally receivable as a result of the taxpayer's having completed the performance of the service contracted for. Holdbacks, common in the construction industry, are not legally receivable until the year in which the architect's or engineer's final certificate accepting and approving work done is issued. The Act provides that these rules are enacted "for greater certainty" and should not be interpreted to imply that any amount not referred to, such as amounts received and earned in the year, are not to be included in income from business.

ITA: 12(1)(b) Amounts receivable, 12(2) Interpretation

A complementary reserve (limited to three years) is available for property sold to recognize the uncertainty of collecting these amounts. An amount will be deemed to have become receivable on the earlier of the day when the account was rendered and the day on which it would have been rendered had there been no undue delay.

ITA: 20(1)(n) Reserve for unpaid amounts, 20(8) No deduction in respect of property in certain circumstances

¶4,420.10 Professional Business

Amounts receivable in respect of services that have been billed are required to be included in income from the business of a professional. Work in progress at the end of a year, representing unbilled services of a business that is a profession, is considered to be inventory.

ITA: 10(5)(a)

An election is available to a taxpayer whose business is the professional practice of an accountant, dentist, lawyer, medical doctor, veterinarian or chiropractor. The election allows the taxpayer to exclude from business income any amount in respect of work in progress at the end of the year. Where the election is made, it must be used in all subsequent taxation years unless the election is revoked with the permission of the CRA. The CRA's interpretation of these rules is contained in the Interpretation Bulletin entitled "Election by professionals to exclude work in progress from income".

ITA: 34(a), 34(b); Interpretation Bulletins: IT-457R Election by Professionals to Exclude Work in Progress from Income

¶4,430 Inducement Payments or Reimbursements

When an asset is acquired or a deductible expense is incurred, any amounts received as a reimbursement or as an inducement must be included in income from business or property unless this amount already has reduced the cost of the property or the amount of the expense. The types of receipts contemplated by this provision include inducements, grants, subsidies, reimbursements, etc., and amounts received indirectly from these sources, perhaps, through a not-for-profit entity. An example of such inducements would be receipts by a commercial tenant who was reimbursed by a landlord for part or all of the cost of making leasehold improvements. As an alternative, the recipient may elect to reduce the capital cost or the cost of the related property or the amount of the related expense. The provision brings the tax treatment of such receipts in line with generally accepted commercial principles. This area has been a source of contentious issues which were not fully resolved by the CRA's Interpretation Bulletin, "Premiums and other amounts with respect to leases". Note that this Interpretation Bulletin also deals with the position of the payer which is not specifically dealt with in the legislation.

ITA: 13(7.4) Deemed capital cost, 53(2.1) Election; Interpretation Bulletins: IT-457R Election by Professionals to Exclude Work in Progress from Income

Government subsidies, inducement payments to tenants, reimbursements, forgivable loans, or allowances received in a form of payment must be included in income of the taxpayer. There are exceptions, for example, if the subsidy or inducement is used to acquire capital property. A taxpayer can elect to offset an inducement payment against the capital cost of property acquired with the payment.

ITA: 12(1)(x) Inducement, reimbursement, etc., 12(2.2) Deemed outlay or expense

¶4,440 Restrictive Covenants

A restrictive covenant is an agreement, whereby a taxpayer agrees to limit the rights he or she would otherwise have. An example of this would be a non-competition agreement that accompanies the sale of a business, where the seller of the business agrees not to undertake a similar business in a specified geographic area after the sale. Payments received for a restrictive covenant must be included in income. To the extent that a taxpayer receives an amount for a restrictive covenant, the amount must be included in income except to the extent that a related person is required to take it into income. For a full discussion on the treatment of payments received for restrictive covenants please refer to Chapter 9, under the heading "¶9,055 Restrictive Covenants".

ITA: 12(1)(x)(v.1), 56.4(1) Definitions, 56.4(2) Income — restrictive covenants

¶4,450 Partnership Income

Partnerships, trusts, and corporations are considered separate legal entities. However, partnerships are not taxable entities within the income tax system in Canada. Partnerships do not file tax returns, though an annual information return must be filed. The intent of this regulation is to provide the CRA with information on the income of the partnership and the partners who share in the sources of income. In addition, each partner must include in his or her tax return the partner's share of partnership income. This requires the preparation of a statement of partnership income that includes an allocation of each partner's share of the income. The income allocated from the partnership to each partner remains the same source of income as it was at the partnership level. For example, income from property at the partnership level is reported as property income by the individual partner; income from business remains income from business; and taxable capital gains remain taxable capital gains. Chapter 18 provides general rules for the computation of partnership income.

ITA: 12(1)(l) Partnership income, 96(1) General rules; ITR: 229 Partnership Return

¶4,460 Barter Transactions

When one taxpayer accepts property (goods or a right to services) in exchange for goods and/or services, a barter transaction exists. If you provide dental services in exchange for dance lessons, you would be entering into a barter transaction. In such a situation, sales revenue equal to the fair market value of the goods or services provided must be recognized in income for tax purposes. It is important to note that payment in kind (non-cash consideration) is not a "gift". A voluntary and gratuitous transfer of property without any expectation of reward or payment from one person to another is a non-taxable gift. This distinction is important because the barter transaction is a reciprocal exchange and is fully taxable. As with any other revenue-earning process, the cost of the goods or services provided in the exchange are deductible. When payment in kind is for personal use, an additional problem exists. For example, the exchange of legal services for a sprinkler system for a personal residence is complex. The law firm has earned revenues equal to the fair market value and a distribution in the form of salary, dividend or draw is made to the lawyer.

ITA: 69(1) Inadequate considerations; Interpretation Bulletins: IT-490 Barter transactions

¶4,490 Pause and Reflect — Summary of Learning Goals

After working through this section, ¶4,400, you should be able to:

- Explain how accounting income is used to determine business income for tax purposes.
- Identify amounts that must be included in business income.

- Explain differences in what would be considered revenue between accounting income and business income for tax purposes.
- Calculate the adjustments required for inclusions to income in the computation of business income for tax purposes.

¶4,490.99 Practise What You've Learned

Refer to the following sections of the Study Guide to practise what you've learned:

¶4,800 — Review Questions

- Question 4 — Inducement Payments and Reimbursements
- Question 6 — Inducement Payments and Reimbursements

¶4,500 Deductions

Overview

To proceed with the calculation of net income for tax purposes, it is necessary to determine which expenses are disallowed or restricted as a deduction for tax purposes. Section 18 is the principal section outlining the amounts that are not deductible in calculating net income from a business. Remember that the Act does not specifically list all of the expenses deductible in the computation of business income and cannot be relied on to test the deductibility of an expense.

¶4,505 Disallowed or Restricted Deductions

In practice, if an expense is not specifically addressed in the Act, it is usually deductible for tax purposes if the expense is:

- deductible using generally accepted accounting principles;
- not a capital expenditure;
- incurred to earn income for tax purposes;
- not a personal expense or expenditure; and
- reasonable in the circumstances.

If the amount in question is material, taxpayers generally consult tax professionals to assist them in interpreting the law and the administrative treatment. It is often necessary to require professional assistance, particularly if case research and further interpretation of the statute are warranted. Difficulty arises with expenses that are deductible for accounting purposes but not for tax purposes.

¶4,505.10 Deductible for Accounting Purposes but Not for Tax Purposes

Many deductions for accounting purposes, such as the write-down of property to fair market value and deductions for amortization, are disallowed for tax purposes. In particular, the Act disallows any deductions for capital expenditures. It is also possible that some expenses properly taken for accounting purposes do not fit into our income tax system at all. An area of concern is the treatment of future costs of environmental clean-up. Accounting standards require that when reasonably determinable, provisions should be made for future removal and site restoration costs. However, the *Income Tax Act* has not specifically addressed how estimated environmental clean-up costs should be treated.

ITA: 18(1)(b) Capital outlay or loss; Other Publications: CPA Handbook 3060.39

An expense taken for tax purposes must be for the purpose of gaining or producing income from the business or property, but the Act disallows a provision for reserves for a contingent liability. Several cases involving the deductibility of estimated future environmental clean-up costs have been tried in the courts. The courts have been reluctant to adopt the new generally accepted accounting principle in the calculation of taxable income, mainly because of the difficulty in estimating the amount of the future liability. In *The Queen v. Nomad Sand & Gravel Ltd.*, the judge cited a precedent decision by Viscount Simonds that "new theories of accountancy, though they may be accepted and put into practice by business men, do not finally determine a trading company's income for tax purposes".[16]

ITA: 18(1)(a) General limitation, 18(1)(e) Reserves, etc; Cases: *Her Majesty the Queen v. Nomad Sand and Gravel Limited*, 91 DTC 5032 (FCA)

¶4,510 Deductibility of Expenditures

Overview

The first test of deductibility is actually contained in the words of subsection 9(1) which state that:

> . . .subject to this Part, a taxpayer's income for a taxation year from a business or property is his profit therefrom for the year.

As previously indicated, the courts have often relied on ordinary commercial practices (generally but not limited to GAAP) to provide the basis of profit, unless the Act specifically requires an alternate treatment. Hence, the deductibility of an expenditure under GAAP, subject to ordinary commercial practices, should be considered where the Act is silent on the treatment of the expenditure. The specific provisions of the Act that may require an alternate treatment are contained, generally, in sections 18, 19, 20, and 67.[17]

Sections 18 and 19, in essence, prohibit the deduction of specified expenditures through the use of the words "no deduction shall be made". However, the rules in sections 18 and 19 actually establish general principles or tests of deductibility under the Act. If an expenditure is not prohibited by a rule in section 18 or 19, that is, if an expenditure passes the set of sequential tests in these provisions, the expenditure is deductible. If an expenditure fails one of the tests in section 18 or 19, then subsection 20(1) should be consulted for the existence of a specific exception which would allow the deduction of the expenditure. Some of the more common tests of deductibility pertaining to income from business are discussed here.

[16] Robin J. MacKnight, "Square Pegs and Round Holes: Environmental Cost Under the Income Tax Act", *1990 Conference Report*, Canadian Tax Foundation, p. 10:5.

[17] This system of testing the deductibility of an expenditure was discussed in the case of *The Queen v. MerBan Capital Corporation Limited*, 89 DTC 5404 (F.C.A.).

¶4,510.10 General Test — To Gain or Produce Income

To pass the general test of deductibility, an expense or outlay must:

ITA: 18(1)(a) General limitation

(1) be made or incurred by the taxpayer for the purpose of gaining, producing, or maintaining income; and

(2) be expected to generate income related to the taxpayer's business or property.

The meaning of "for the purpose of gaining or producing income" has been at issue in many cases. While the club dues at issue in *The Royal Trust Company v. M.N.R.* are now specifically not deductible, the case is important in demonstrating the relative remoteness between the expenditure and its purpose to produce income. That is, while the items listed, including club dues, are not deductible, the principle established in the *Royal Trust* case may still hold for items not specifically prohibited by that paragraph or others.

ITA: 18(1)(l) Use of recreational facilities and club dues; Cases: *The Royal Trust Company v. M.N.R.*, 57 DTC 1055 (Ex. Ct.)

Generally, all that need be demonstrated is that the expenditure was expected to generate income, although no income may have been generated. This was the issue in *Booth v. M.N.R.* involving a poet and painter who claimed certain expenses as deductions. Also, *The Queen v. Lalande and Watelle* (affirmed by the Federal Court of Appeal) dealt with the deduction by doctors of legal fees and payments under loan guarantees in situations which could increase their clientele. In the case of *Speck v. M.N.R.*, the Tax Court of Canada held that a full-time teacher, who incurred losses for three years followed by small profits for two years when he started a part-time business involving the restoration of automobiles, had reasonable expectations of turning a profit and these expectations had been met within the expected five years.

Cases: *Booth v. M.N.R.*, 79 DTC 595 (TRB); *Dr. Eugene Lalande and Dr. Hubert Watelle v. Sa Majestée La Reine*, 89 DTC 5178 (FCA); *Gary John Speck v. The Minister of National Revenue*, 88 DTC 1518 (TCC)

¶4,510.20 Expenditure of a Capital Nature

An expenditure may pass the test of having been made for the purpose of gaining, producing, or maintaining income, but may still be prohibited as a deduction of an outlay of a capital nature. A capital expenditure has been described in a United Kingdom case[18] by the following statement:

ITA: 18(1)(b) Capital outlay or loss

> . . . when an expenditure is made, not only once and for all, but with a view to bringing into existence an asset or advantage for the enduring benefit of a trade, . . . there is very good reason (in the absence of special circumstances leading to an opposite conclusion) for treating such an expenditure as properly attributable not to revenue but to capital.

¶4,510.30 Personal and Living Expenses

One would presume that paragraph 18(1)(*a*) and section 67 would automatically disallow personal and living expenses because they were not incurred to earn income. However, paragraph 18(1)(*h*) confirms that personal or living expenses, other than travel away from home in the course of carrying on business, are not deductible. Subsection 248(1) defines "personal and living expenses" as an expense incurred for:

ITA: 18(1)(h) Personal and living expenses; Interpretation Bulletins: IT-487 General limitation on deduction of outlays or expenses

- properties that are for the benefit of the taxpayer or a person connected by blood relationship, marriage, common-law partnership, or adoption, and that are not maintained in connection with a business carried on with a reasonable expectation of profit;
- premiums for life insurance, annuities, and similar contracts; and

[18] *British Insulated and Helsby Cables Ltd. v. Atherton* [1926], A.C. 205.

- expenses for property maintained for the beneficiary of an estate or trust.

This definition is not exhaustive, so it includes anything that has the ordinary meaning of this expression. For example, a taxpayer who carries on a business may incur travelling expenses to go to Europe to meet clients. If reasonable, these expenses are deductible (subject to the restrictions in subsection 67.1(1) for any meals and entertainment). But if the business trip is extended to provide a vacation, these additional expenses will be considered personal outlays and will be denied by paragraph 18(1)(*h*). The most common personal and living expenses dealt with in court cases are automobile, home office, and entertainment expenses.

¶4,520 Other Prohibited Deductions

Overview

The Act specifically identifies a number of expenses that are not allowed to be deducted in the calculation of business income for tax purposes. The following section discusses some of the most common prohibited deductions below.

¶4,520.10 Reserves

ITA: 18(1)(e) Reserves, etc., 20(1) Deductions permitted in computing income from business or property

The deduction of a reserve, a contingent liability or a sinking fund is prohibited, except as permitted by the Act. Allowable reserves will be discussed later in this chapter.

A contingent liability is one where the existence of the liability depends on an event occurring that may or may not happen, sometimes referred to as a condition precedent. This type of liability only becomes deductible in the year that it becomes an unconditional liability. For example, a product defect is found, so the manufacturer records a liability and expense to recognize that customers may make claims in the future to fix the defect. This liability is contingent on a customer coming forward with an actual claim. Until that event happens and the liability becomes measurable, there is no deduction. In summary, potential liabilities that depend on future events happening to establish them as real liabilities are not deductible until that future event occurs.

A variation of the contingent liability is a liability that is unconditional or "real" today, but that has the possibility of being reduced or eliminated in the future by a subsequent condition. This liability is deductible now, with the possibility of a future event reducing the liability. This possibility has led to the potential for abuse, as evidenced by the case of *Collins v. The Queen*, where the Court allowed the taxpayer to deduct interest expenses as they accrued, even though the taxpayer had a right to reduce the amount payable in respect of the interest expenses. As a result, legislation applies to an otherwise unconditional expenditure in respect of which there is a contingent amount. This anti-avoidance provision applies where it is reasonable to conclude that the taxpayer will exercise their right to trigger an event that would reduce the liability. The result is that an otherwise unconditional liability will become a conditional liability and not be deductible.

Cases: *The Queen v. Proulx* , 2011 DTC 5028 (FCA); ITA: 143.4 Expenditure — Limit for Contingent Amount

¶4,520.15 Payments on Discounted Bonds

When bonds are issued at a discount, usually because the contractual interest rate is lower than the market interest rate, the cost of the discount is incurred on the repayment of the debt at its face value. A deduction is not permitted for the amount paid or payable in

ITA: 18(1)(f) Payments on discounted bonds, 20(1)(f)

respect of the discount except as specifically permitted. This prohibition exists to discourage the issue of debt at a relatively large discount which might provide the holder of the debt with more advantageous capital gains treatment.

Discount on certain obligations

¶4,520.20 Use of Recreational Facilities and Club Dues

The deduction of club and other recreational facilities dues is strictly prohibited no matter how important they may be to the revenue-producing process. In addition, this provision denies the deduction of expenses incurred for the use or maintenance of a yacht, a camp, a lodge, or a golf course, unless these facilities are provided to the general public as in the course of the taxpayer's business.[19] Note, also, that the prohibition applies only to expenditures incurred in respect of a yacht, camp, lodge or golf course. Similar expenditures incurred in respect of a restaurant or hotel would not be prohibited. In its decision, the Supreme Court upheld the intention of Parliament to discriminate in this way, based on the very specific words used in the provision. However, the CRA indicated that it had reconsidered its interpretation of the word "facility" in relation to a golf course. The CRA will consider that "facility" as used in that subparagraph should be interpreted in connection with the words "golf course" as to only include recreational amenities provided by a golf club. Accordingly, a "facility" will not include the dining room, banquet halls, conference rooms, beverage rooms, or lounges of a golf club and thus the deduction of the cost of meals and beverages incurred at a golf club will not be denied. As a result, the tax treatment of meals and beverages at a golf club will parallel that of meals and beverages consumed at an independent restaurant.[20]

ITA: 18(1)(l) Use of recreational facilities and club dues, 18(1)(l)(i)

¶4,520.25 Political Contributions

There is a specific prohibition against the deduction of political contributions. A limited tax credit is provided for individuals. Corporations are precluded from making federal political contributions by the federal *Elections Act*.

ITA: 18(1)(n) Political contributions, 127(3) Contributions to registered parties and candidates

¶4,520.30 Automobile Expenses

The deduction of an allowance paid or payable to an employee for the employment use of an automobile is limited. However, there is no deduction limit if the amount of the allowance must be included in the employee's income. The *Income Tax Regulations* (ITR) prescribe the deductible limit. For 2018, the rates are 55 cents per kilometre for the first 5,000 kilometres driven and 49 cents per kilometre thereafter, with a four cent per kilometre premium for driving in the Yukon Territory, Northwest Territories, or Nunavut.

ITA: 18(1)(r) Certain automobile expenses; ITR: 7306 [Prescribed amount – automobile allowance]

¶4,520.35 Payments Under the Act

Any amount paid or payable under the Act is not deductible. This provision would prohibit, for greater certainty, the deduction of federal income taxes, interest, and penalties, all of which are imposed under the Act. However, a deduction for interest paid on a tax refund that a taxpayer is required to repay because the refund was excessive is allowed.

ITA: 18(1)(t) Payments under different acts, 20(1)(ll) Repayment of interest

---

[19] In the case of *Sie-Mac Pipeline Contractors Ltd. v. The Queen*, 93 DTC 5158 (S.C.C.), the Supreme Court of Canada held that to use a lodge does not require that it be owned or rented or exclusively controlled.

[20] "Entertainment at golf clubs", Tax Window File, Document No. 9803677, February 17, 1998.

¶4,520.40 Prepaid Expenses

In a move to bring the treatment of certain prepaid expenses for tax purposes in line with the treatment for accounting purposes, the deduction of such expenses in the year of outlay is prohibited. These expenses are deductible only in the taxation year to which the expenses relate. Expenditures treated in this manner are the following:

ITA: 18(9) Limitation respecting prepaid expenses

- payments for services to be rendered after the end of the year;
- payments of interest, taxes, rent, or royalties in respect of a period after the end of the year; and
- payments for insurance in respect of a period after the end of the year.

¶4,520.45 Expenses of Investing in Sheltered Plans

While interest and certain financing expenses are usually deductible under several provisions in section 20, section 18 prohibits the deduction of these expenses in respect of indebtedness incurred for the purposes listed therein. Note that the items listed pertain to deductible investments in sheltered retirement plans in which income is not taxed as long as it remains in the plan. Also, the deduction of administration fees and investment counselling fees pertaining to certain plans, as discussed in Chapter 9, are prohibited.

ITA: 18(1)(u) Fees — individual saving plans, 18(11) Limitation

¶4,520.50 Workspace in Home

The deduction of the costs of maintaining a workspace in an individual's home (i.e., "a self-contained domestic establishment in which the individual resides"), are prohibited unless the office meets one of the following two tests:

ITA: 18(12) Work space in home

(1) the workspace is the individual's principal place of business; or

(2) it is used on a regular and continuous basis for meeting clients, customers, or patients of the individual in earning income from business.

In the case of these exceptions, the costs are deductible only to the extent of income from the business. Thus, these home office expenses cannot be used to create a loss from the business, although a carryforward is available for excess expenses. This carryforward may be indefinite, according to an Interpretation Bulletin, "Work space in home expenses", as long as one of the two tests stated above is met. For the CRA's interpretation of the term "principal place of business" and "regular and continuous basis", see the Interpretation Bulletin. The case of *Jenkins et. al. v. The Queen* addressed the meaning of "principle place of business" for a fisher. The Court concluded that the principal place of business is where the "business elements" of the business are engaged in, such as "telephoning customers and suppliers, filling in invoices, doing payroll, maintaining books and records, contacting authorities for licences, preparing tax returns, chasing down receivables, handling complaints, creating business plans, preparing financial statements, talking to accountants and lawyers, etc." The courts stated that "the actual harvesting of fish is the core of a fishing business, but it is not where the business side of fishing occurs."

Income Tax Folio: S4-F2-C2 Business Use of Home Expenses; Cases: *Jenkins et al. v. The Queen*, 2005 DTC 384 (TCC)

¶4,520.55 Limitation on Accrued Expenses

In normal circumstances a deductible expenditure incurred by one taxpayer is matched, within a reasonable period of time, by the income receipt in the hands of the creditor. However, the Act has provisions to thwart contrived situations between persons not dealing at arm's length or between employers and employees where the debtor uses the

ITA: 78 Unpaid amounts

accrual method of accounting and the creditor is on the cash method and where actual payment is unduly deferred.

Related persons are deemed not to deal at arm's length with each other. Chapter 6 deals with related individuals and Chapter 12 deals with related corporations and individuals. For the time being, assume that the normal interpretation of "related" applies. In addition, the provision indicates that it is question of fact whether persons not related to each other were, at a particular time, dealing with each other at arm's length. The Interpretation Bulletin entitled "Meaning of Arm's Length" lists the following criteria that could be used in determining whether a transaction has occurred at arm's length:

ITA: 251(1) Arm's length; Income Tax Folio: S1-F5-C1 Related Persons and Dealing at Arm's Length

- a common mind directs the bargaining for both parties to the transaction;
- the parties to the transaction were acting in concert without separate interests; and
- one party in fact controls the other party.

In order for an expense (e.g., accrued wages) that remains unpaid at the end of the taxation year to be deductible for tax purposes, it must constitute a genuine liability of the taxpayer. For a genuine liability to exist there must be an enforceable claim by the creditor (e.g., the employee) with a reasonable expectation that the debt in fact will be paid. Where there is not a genuine liability, the amount will be treated as contingent liability or reserve and will be denied.

Interpretation Bulletins: IT-109R2 Unpaid Amounts; ITA: 18(1)(e) Reserves, etc.

(i) Unpaid amounts

Unpaid amounts, in non-arm's length circumstances, are subject to specific rules. Such an unpaid amount must be paid within two years of the end of the taxation year in which it was declared payable or accrued. If an amount remains unpaid after that two-year period, it must be brought back into income on the first day of the third taxation year following that in which the payable was declared. Thus, an unpaid amount declared payable in 2016 must be paid by the end of the 2018 taxation year or be included in income at the beginning of the 2019 taxation year.

ITA: 78(1) Unpaid amounts

The two parties can file an election by the date on which the corporation is required to file its tax return for the 2018 taxation year (i.e., by June 30, 2019) that the amount be deemed to have been paid on the first day of the 2019 taxation year and to have been loaned, net of appropriate withholding tax, back to the corporation. Then, the corporation would be liable to remit the amount deemed to have been withheld, by departmental practice, on or before July 15, 2019 in this case, and a repayment of the loan would have no further tax consequences. An Interpretation Bulletin provides further explanation of this provision and a more complete discussion of the interplay of these provisions is contained in Chapter 13, under the heading "Accrued bonuses and other amounts".

ITA: 78(1)(b)

(ii) Unpaid remuneration and other amounts

In the case of items of remuneration, the Act requires that salaries, wages, or other remuneration (other than specified exceptions) must be paid within 179 days of the end of the taxation year in which the expense was incurred. If an amount is unpaid after that day, it will be deemed not to have been incurred as an expense and, therefore, will not be deductible until the year in which it is actually paid. However, by administrative practice, the CRA indicates in the Interpretation Bulletin entitled "Unpaid amounts" that a payment made on the 180th day is considered to have been made within the time limit and the rule that denies the accrual will not apply. Other remuneration includes unfunded

ITA: 78(4) Unpaid remuneration and other amounts; Interpretation Bulletins: IT-109R2 Unpaid Amounts obligations in respect of pension benefits and retiring allowances. The election for deemed repayment, as described above, is not available for unpaid remuneration. An amount of accrued remuneration must be legally paid.

¶4,520.90 Pause and Reflect — Summary of Learning Goals

After working through this section, ¶4,520, you should be able to:

- Identify differences in deductions allowed for accounting income and business income for tax purposes.
- Calculate the adjustments required for deductions from income in the computation of business income for tax purposes.

¶4,530 Source of Income

Overview

Some activities and their related expenditures may be difficult to distinguish between personal and commercial or business in nature. An example would be a taxpayer who enjoys cooking and creates online cooking videos on YouTube. Any revenue generated from the postings would be included in income, but can the taxpayer deduct related expenses such as groceries, kitchen appliances etc., in excess of those revenues?

¶4,530.10 The Supreme Court's Two-Stage Test

The Supreme Court of Canada provided a two-stage approach to determine, first, whether a source of income exists and, then, whether the source of income, if any, is from business or property. Analysis of this source of income issue should address two questions:

Cases: 2002 DTC 6969; ITA: 18(1)(h) Personal and living expenses

(a) Is the activity of the taxpayer undertaken in pursuit of profit, or is it a personal endeavour?

This first question, reflecting the first stage, attempts to determine whether a source of income exists. The Court indicated that this first stage of the test is to distinguish between commercial and personal activities.

(b) If it is not a personal endeavour, is the source of income a business or property?

Where the activities are solely personal, like a hobby or other personal pursuit, no further analysis is necessary. In this situation, there is no pursuit of profit intended. There is not a source of income for the purposes of the Act, and expenses in excess of revenues are not deductible in the current year or in a carry-over year. Where the activities are purely of a commercial nature, i.e., there is an intention to pursue a profit, there is a source of income and the second stage addresses whether that income is from business or from property under the Act. This distinction will be made clearer in Chapter 6. In this situation, there is no need to analyze the taxpayer's business acumen, if losses occur, and there is no need to establish a reasonable expectation of profit ("REOP"), because it is assumed by the purely commercial nature of the activity.

Where a taxpayer's activities contain a personal element, the first stage question will require further analysis. In the *Stewart* case, the Supreme Court indicated, at paragraph 52, that "where the nature of a taxpayer venture contains elements which suggest that it could be considered a hobby or other personal pursuit, but the venture is undertaken in a sufficiently commercial manner, the venture will be considered a source of income for the purposes of the Act.

At paragraph 54 of the Supreme Court decision on the Stewart case, the Court stated that

> . . . in order for an activity to be classified commercial in nature, the taxpayer must have the subjective intention to profit; in addition, . . . this determination should be made by looking at a variety of objective factors. . . . This requires the taxpayer to establish that his or her predominant intention is to make a profit from the activity and that the activity has been carried out in accordance with objective standards of businesslike behaviour.

This is often referred to as the commerciality of an activity that provides objective evidence of an intention to earn a profit.

In the *Stewart* case, the Supreme Court of Canada clarified and limited the application of the REOP test by indicating that the REOP test has no application where there is no personal benefit element to a transaction. In the Court's opinion, where there is a personal benefit element, the test is only one of a number of factors that can be used to assess the commercial nature of an activity, thereby, undertaken in the pursuit of profit.[21] The objective factors cited by the court in the *Stewart* case are:

(1) the profit and loss experience in past years;

(2) the taxpayer's training;

(3) the taxpayer's intended course of action;

(4) the capability of the venture to show a profit; and

(5) any other factors.

Exhibit 4-3 provides an expanded checklist of objective factors that can be used for planning purposes or for fact evaluation purposes to provide evidence of the commerciality of an activity where there is a personal benefit in an activity. The checklist may help to assess the commercial nature of an activity and the businesslike behaviour of the taxpayer in that activity. The factors were derived largely from two U.S. studies of jurisprudence on a similar issue in U.S. tax law. Since the factors are based on U.S. jurisprudence, they have no direct precedent value in Canada. However, they are of more general applicability and may provide a basis or a framework for developing arguments for the existence, or lack thereof, of a predominant intention to make a profit from an activity in a Canadian fact situation.

Exhibit 4-3 Checklist of General Factors Used To Determine the Commerciality of an Activity or of Operating in a Businesslike Manner

(1) Manner in which activity is operated:

(a) activity held out to community as a business

[21] For a more complete discussion of the *Stewart* case and the jurisprudence that led to that decision, see Rayna F. Laiken and Stanley N. Laiken, "Working with the Source Test, the Supreme Court's Replacement for the Reasonable Expectation of Profit Test", (2002) vol. 50, no. 3, *Canadian Tax Journal*, pp. 1147-1177.

- (b) activity operated in a businesslike manner
- (c) activity operated in manner similar to comparable profitable businesses
- (d) unsuccessful methods discontinued and new ones adopted
- (e) formal books and records maintained
- (f) separate bank account maintained
- (g) record-keeping system provides for the determination of segment profits and relevant costs
- (h) detailed non-financial records maintained
- (i) operating methods changed to improve profitability
- (j) level of advertising or promotion undertaken
- (k) development plan formulated, followed and adjusted
- (l) scale of operations sufficient to be profitable

(2) Elements of personal pleasure or recreation:

- (a) taxpayer obtains personal pleasure from the activity
- (b) facilities are utilitarian
- (c) conduct of activity involves social or recreational functions (apart from the activity itself)
- (d) long-time interest in activity as a hobby
- (e) operating methods constrained by personal motives
- (f) personal use separately accounted for

(3) Expertise of the taxpayer or his or her advisers:

- (a) prior experience in the activity
- (b) profit potential determined prior to entry
- (c) pre-entry advice (or prior preparation) sought and followed
- (d) post-entry advice sought and followed
- (e) taxpayer belongs to business-related associations
- (f) new or superior techniques developed

(4) History of income and loss:

- (a) average ratio of receipts to disbursements
- (b) percentage of years where receipts less than 5% of disbursements
- (c) average magnitude of losses
- (d) trend of losses declining

(e) number of years activity was operated
(f) losses due to circumstances beyond taxpayer's control
(g) percentage of years with profits
(h) reasonable start-up period
(i) trend of gross revenues

(5) Time and effort expended:
(a) competent and well-informed manager employed
(b) competent labour employed
(c) average time spent on activity by taxpayer
(d) taxpayer withdrew from another business to devote most of his/her time to the activity
(e) taxpayer did physical labour

(6) Financial status of taxpayer:
(a) taxpayer's average income before activity loss
(b) extent of tax savings from net losses
(c) average ratio of activity losses to other income
(d) taxpayer maintains an extravagant standard of living
(e) majority of taxpayer's other income is from investments
(f) extent of other net assets of taxpayer
(g) amount of capital invested in the operation

(7) Amount of occasional profits:
(a) ratio of average profit to average loss
(b) amount of largest profit earned
(c) ratio of net losses to net assets

(8) Sale or discontinuance of activity:
(a) activity sold or discontinued because no chance for profit
(b) activity sold or discontinued for any reason

(9) Success of taxpayer in other activities:
(a) extent of experience in similar successful business
(b) history of losses in a similar activity

(10) Expected appreciation of asset value:
(a) taxpayer expected property to appreciate in value as the major source of investment return

Sources: Jane O. Burns and S. Michael Groomer, "An Analysis of Tax Court Decisions That Assess the Profit Motive of Farming-Oriented Operations," *The Journal of the American Taxation Association*, Fall 1983, pp. 23-39.

Jack Robison, "Tax Court Classification of Activities Not Engaged in for Profit: Some Empirical Evidence," *The Journal of the American Taxation Association*, Fall 1983, pp. 7-22.

¶4,540 Limitations on Deductible Expenditures

To be deductible, the amount must be "reasonable in the circumstances." This would suggest a comparison of the amount of an expenditure with the amount of similar expenditures made in similar situations by other taxpayers.

ITA: 67 General limitation re expenses

¶4,550 Summary of Prohibited Deductions

Items listed in subsection 18(1) are prohibited from being deducted because of the nature of the expenditure . . .

Summary of Deductions Specifically Not Deductible or Restricted

ITA Reference	Item Not Deductible or Restricted
18(1)(*a*)	Not deductible unless incurred to earn income from business or property
18(1)(*b*)	Capital expenditures including depreciation, obsolescence or depletion except as expressly permitted
18(1)(*c*)	Expense incurred to earn exempt income
18(1)(*e*)	Reserves and contingent liabilities
18(1)(*h*)	Personal or living expenses
18(1)(*l*)	Use of recreational facilities and club dues
18(1)(*n*)	Political contributions
18(1)(*p*)	Personal service business expenses
18(1)(*r*)	Automobile mileage rates
18(1)(*t*)	Interest and penalties under the *Income Tax Act* or interest under the *Excise Tax Act*
18(2)	Interest and property taxes on land
18(3.1)	Costs related to construction of building or ownership of land
18(9)	Prepaid expenses
18(12)	Workspace in the home limitations

ITA Reference	Item Not Deductible or Restricted
18(13)	Superficial loss
67	Outlay or expense must be reasonable in the circumstances
67.1	Expenses for food and entertainment
67.2	Interest on loans to buy a passenger vehicle
67.3	Costs of leasing a passenger vehicle
67.5	Illegal payments
67.6	Fines and penalties

GST/HST is not deductible to a registrant where the GST/HST provides an input tax credit. The input tax credit, in effect, eliminates the GST/HST as a cost and, hence, GST/HST should not be deductible in these cases.

ITA: 248(16) Goods and services tax — input tax credit and rebate

A deduction is prohibited in respect of an expenditure incurred for the purpose of doing anything that is an offence under section 3 of the *Corruption of Foreign Public Officials Act* involving bribery of a foreign public official to obtain a business advantage or any of the following sections of the Criminal Code:

ITA: 67.5(1) Non-deductibility of illegal payments

- section 119 — bribery of judicial officers, etc.
- section 120 — bribery of officers
- section 121 — frauds on the government
- section 123 — municipal corruption
- section 124 — selling or purchasing office
- section 125 — influencing or negotiating appointments or dealing in offices
- section 393 — fraud in relation to fares, etc.
- section 426 — secret commissions

Deductions are also prohibited where the payment is made in a conspiracy to commit an offence under one of the above sections or a conspiracy in Canada to commit a similar offence under the law of another country.

Recent court cases have allowed the deductibility of fines and penalties incurred in the ordinary course of earning income unless the underlying action was so offensive that the fine or penalty could not reasonably be considered to have had an income-earning purpose. To bring certainty to this area of tax law, fines or penalties incurred are not deductible if they are imposed by law — whether by a government, government agency, regulator, court or other tribunal, or any other person with statutory authority to levy fines or penalties. This would include fines and penalties imposed under the laws of a foreign country. This would not include penalties or damages paid under private contracts. Part of this provision includes authority to exempt prescribed fines and penalties from its application, although there are no exemptions at this time.

ITA: 67.6 Non-deductibility of fines and penalties

¶4,560 Deductions Specifically Permitted

Overview

Although the Act specifically prohibits the deduction of certain expenses, it also provides clarification of expenses that are specifically allowed to be deducted from the calculation of business income for tax purposes, despite the general prohibitions in section 18. Therefore, it is important to consult Section 20 when determining the ultimate deductibility of certain expenses.

¶4,560.10 Summary of Deductions Specifically Permitted

Usually, the general principles and rules (e.g., sections 18, 67, etc.) determining the deductibility of an outlay or expenditure are to be applied first. If a particular outlay or expenditure does not pass the tests of deductibility set out in section 18 or 19, then the lists in section 20 of exceptions to the general principles and rules should be consulted. The wording of subsection 20(1) recognizes that some of the deductions listed in the subsection may be prohibited by a general rule in subsection 18(1), and negates that effect by inserting the words "notwithstanding paragraphs 18(1)(*a*), (*b*) and (*h*), . . . there may be deducted.". The following are some of the more common deductions provided in section 20.

Summary of Deductions Specifically Permitted (Section 20)

ITA Reference	Deductions Specifically Allowed	Related References
20(1)(*a*)	Capital cost allowance	18(1)(*b*)
20(1)(*b*)	Incorporation expenses	18(1)(*b*)
20(1)(*c*), (*d*)	Capital amount interest	Folio S3-F6-C1
20(1)(*e*)	Expenses of issuing shares or borrowing money	18(1)(*b*)
20(1)(*e*.2)	Premiums on life insurance used as collateral	18(1)(*c*)
20(1)(*f*)	Discount on debt obligations	18(1)(*f*)
20(1)(*l*)–(*p*)	Reserves	18(1)(*e*)
20(1)(*q*)	Employer's contribution to registered pension plan	147.2
20(1)(*y*)	Employer's contribution under a deferred profit sharing plan	147(8)
20(1)(*z*)	Cancellation of lease	18(1)(*q*)
20(1)(*aa*)	Landscaping of grounds	18(1)(*b*)
20(1)(*cc*)	Expenses of representation	18(1)(*b*)
20(1)(*dd*)	Investigation of site	18(1)(*b*)
20(1)(*ee*)	Utilities service connection	18(1)(*b*)

ITA Reference	Deductions Specifically Allowed	Related References
20(1)(*qq*), (*rr*)	Disability-related modifications and equipment	18(1)(*b*)
20(10)	Convention expenses	

¶4,560.15 Write-Offs of Capital Expenditures

While section 18 prohibits the deduction of a capital nature, section 20 overrides this prohibition and permits the deduction of the capital cost of depreciable capital property and the cost of eligible capital property, respectively, through the capital cost allowance (CCA) system of annual write-offs to be discussed in detail in Chapter 5.

ITA: 18(1)(b) Capital outlay or loss, 20(1)(a) Capital cost of property, 20(1)(b) Incorporation expenses

Incorporation expenses have, generally, been regarded as capital expenditures. However, the first $3,000 of these expenses incurred in a year is deductible from income. Only amounts in excess of $3,000 of incorporation expenses incurred in the year must be capitalized.

¶4,560.20 Interest

Interest paid or payable on funds borrowed to finance the capital expenditures of a business would be considered as payment on account of capital and, therefore, would be prohibited from deduction. However, the Act specifically provides for the deduction of interest on funds borrowed to earn income, i.e., on the purchase of assets or on indebtedness arising from the acquisition of capital assets. Compound interest is deductible if the base interest is deductible.

ITA: 18(1)(b) Capital outlay or loss, 20(1)(c) Interest

An Income Tax Folio is a prime source for the CRA's administrative position on interest deductibility in that it provides commentary on all the key issues and some of the tax planning techniques used to ensure the deductibility of interest.

Income Tax Folio: S3-F6-C1 Interest Deductibility

¶4,560.25 Expenses of Issuing Shares or Borrowing Money

The type of expenses contemplated by paragraph 20(1)(*e*) includes printing and advertising costs, filing fees, legal and accounting fees, registration and transfer fees, and commissions or bonuses on the issue or sale of shares. Also deductible by this provision are similar expenses incurred in the course of becoming indebted on the purchase of capital property acquired to earn income. Similarly, refinancing costs such as rescheduling, restructuring or assumption of debt used for the purpose of earning business income are also deductible under this provision.

Not included in the deduction would be amounts paid or payable on account of the principal amount of the indebtedness. Since the deductible expenditures are still considered to be of a capital nature, the Act requires that the deduction be amortized equally over five years (prorated on a daily basis for short taxation years) to achieve a better matching of expenses and revenues. Any undeducted balance of borrowing costs are deductible for the year in which the debt is fully repaid (otherwise than as a part of a refinancing).[22]

ITA: 20(1)(e) Expenses re financing

[22] Two cases heard under this provision are: *Enterprise Foundry Co. Ltd. v. M.N.R.*, 59 DTC 318 (T.A.B.), on a capital reorganization and *Dominion Electrohome Industries Ltd. v. M.N.R.*, 68 DTC 256 (T.A.B.), on a call premium.

Annual fees payable as a standby charge, guarantee fee, registrar fee, transfer agent fee, filing fee or any similar fee in respect of borrowing money, incurring indebtedness or rescheduling or restructuring a debt obligation are also deductible.

ITA: 20(1)(e.1) Annual fees, etc.

¶4,560.30 Premiums on Life Insurance Used as Collateral

A limited deduction is allowed for life insurance premiums where the policy has been assigned as collateral for a loan. The lender must require the assignment of the policy as collateral for the loan. The principal business of the lender must be the lending of money or the purchase of debt obligations. The interest payable on the funds borrowed must be deductible. The deduction is limited to the portion of the premium that represents the net cost of pure insurance.

ITA: 20(1)(c) Interest, 20(1)(e.2) Premiums on life insurance used as collateral

¶4,560.35 Discount on Debt Obligations

Subsection 18(1) contains several provisions that would deny the deduction of all or any part of a discount from the face value of a debt obligation like a bond, debenture, note, mortgage, etc. Since the discount would be considered to be of a capital nature, its deduction is prohibited. The amortization of the discount, for financial accounting purposes, over the life of the debt instrument would not be deductible for tax purposes, because the annual amortization would be considered to be in the nature of a prohibited reserve. In addition, the deduction of the actual cash outlay on redemption or open market purchase is specifically denied, except to the extent permitted by the Act. The latter provision permits a full deduction of the discount (an actual cash outlay on redemption or maturity) at the earlier of redemption or maturity if:

ITA: 18(1) General limitations, 18(1)(e) Reserves, etc., 20(1)(f) Discount on certain obligations

(1) the debt security is issued at not less than 97% of face value; *and*

(2) the yield to maturity is not more than 4/3 of the nominal or coupon interest rate.

If one, or both, of these conditions is not met, then only 1/2 of the discount is deductible, again at the earlier of redemption or maturity. The 1/2 fraction is intended to reflect the allowable or deductible portion of a capital loss.

This rule discourages the issue of debt securities at a large discount by agreeing to pay a low rate of interest relative to the market. The concern is that only the lower than normal interest rate would be taxable to the debtholder at full rates and the gain from the discounted issue price to the par value would be a fractionally taxed capital gain to the debtholder. On the other hand, an acceptable discount of 3% is sufficient to account for normal market fluctuations in interest rates between the time of setting the rate and the time of issue of the debt.

¶4,560.40 The System for Reserves Under the Act

The deduction of a reserve is prohibited except for those reserves that are specifically permitted in Part I of the Act.

ITA: 18(1)(e) Reserves, etc.

The reserves that may be deducted include:

ITA: 20(1) Deductions permitted in computing income from business or property

- reserve for doubtful debts;

ITA: 20(1)(l) Doubtful or impaired debts

- reserve for goods not delivered and services not rendered or deposits on returnable containers (other than bottles), but limited by another rule;

ITA: 20(1)(m) Reserve in respect of certain goods and services, 20(6) Special reserves

- manufacturer's warranty reserve for amounts paid or payable to an insurer to insure liability under warranty agreement; and
- reserve for an amount not due until a later year under an instalment sales contract limited by another rule.

ITA: 20(1)(m.1) Manufacturer's warranty reserve
ITA: 20(1)(n) Reserve for unpaid amounts, 20(8) No deduction in respect of property in certain circumstances

A reasonable reserve can be claimed for an amount not due until a later year where products or services are provided to a customer but some or all of the payment is not "due" until after the year end of the business. Generally, some of the payment must be due at a time that is two years later than the time of the sale. However, a reserve cannot be claimed in a year if the sale occurred more than 36 months before the end of the year. Thus, a reserve can be deducted for no more than three years, including the year of sale.

ITA: 20(1)(n) Reserve for unpaid amounts, 20(8) No deduction in respect of property in certain circumstances

Any reserve taken in a given year under one of these provisions must be brought back into income in the following year under one of the following provisions in subsection 12(1):

- reserve for doubtful debts; and
- reserve in respect of certain goods and services, deposits, or manufacturer's warranty reserve.

ITA: 12(1)(d) Reserve for doubtful debts

ITA: 12(1)(e) Reserves for certain goods and services, etc.

In that following year, a new reserve can be taken based on the taxpayer's circumstances at that time. The inclusion of last year's reserve in income and the deduction of a new reserve this year forces the taxpayer to re-evaluate the circumstances and to establish a new reserve which can be substantiated by these circumstances.

The Interpretation Bulletin entitled "Bad debts and reserves for doubtful debts" describes the method suggested by the CRA for determining an appropriate reserve for doubtful debts. A deduction for bad or doubtful debts can only be taken to the extent that the amount has already been taken into income.

Interpretation Bulletins: IT-442R Bad Debts and Reserves for Doubtful Debts

Where a debt has been established by the taxpayer to have become a bad debt, rather than merely a debt of doubtful collectability, the amount of the bad debt can be written off as an expense. A bad debt written off in this way need not be included in income in the following year. However, if and when a bad debt is recovered, then the amount of recovery is added to income in the year of receipt. It is a question of fact whether a debt has become a bad debt and, hence, uncollectible, rather than simply of doubtful collectability.

ITA: 12(1)(i) Bad debts recovered, 20(1)(p) Bad debts

Example Problem 4-4

The Greyduck Bus Lines Limited issues books of junior student tickets containing 20 transportation passes for $20 per book. The following information relates to books sold and tickets used:

	Year 1	Year 2	Year 3
Number of books sold	2,000	2,500	4,000
Number of tickets used:			

	Year 1	Year 2	Year 3
from Year 1 sales	25,000	11,000	expired
from Year 2 sales		31,250	13,750
from Year 3 sales			50,000

REQUIRED

Compute the effect of these transactions on the net income from business of this company, assuming 10% of the tickets sold in a year are expected to expire at the beginning of the second year from the end of the year of sale.

SOLUTION

		Applicable provisions
Year 1		
Include amount received in income ($20 × 2,000)	$40,000	par. 12(1)(*a*)
Less: reserve for services not provided[(1)]	11,000	par. 20(1)(*m*)
Income	$29,000	
Year 2		
Include amount received in income ($20 × 2,500)	$50,000	par. 12(1)(*a*)
Add: reserve from previous year	11,000	par. 12(1)(*e*)
	$61,000	
Less: reserve for services not provided[(2)]	13,750	par. 20(1)(*m*)
Income	$47,250	
Year 3		
Include amount received in income ($20 × 4,000)	$80,000	par. 12(1)(*a*)
Add: reserve from previous year	13,750	par. 12(1)(*e*)
	$93,750	

		Applicable provisions
Less: reserve for services not provided[3]	22,000	par. 20(1)(*m*)
Income	$71,750	

NOTES TO SOLUTION

[1] The reserve is limited to a reasonable amount based on services that it is reasonably expected will have to be provided. In this case, no service will have to be provided for 10% of all tickets sold in the year. Of the 40,000 tickets (20 tickets × 2,000 books) sold in Year 1, 25,000 have been used and 4,000 will expire (10% of 40,000) leaving 11,000 for which service will have to be provided. At $1 per ticket ($20 / 20) a reasonable reserve would be $11,000 ($1 × 11,000). Note that subsection 20(6) limits this reserve to the amount included in income for transportation not provided before the end of the year. In this case transportation has not been provided on 15,000 tickets (40,000 – 25,000) providing a limit at $1 per ticket of $15,000.

[2] Using the above process, service will have to be provided for 13,750 tickets since 5,000 (10% of 50,000) will expire and 31,250 have been used. Thus, a reasonable reserve at $1 per ticket is $13,750. The limit on this reserve would be on 18,750 tickets (50,000 – 31,250) at $1 per ticket or $18,750.

[3] Service will have to be provided for 22,000 tickets since 8,000 (10% of 80,000) will expire and 50,000 have been used. The reserve at $1 per ticket would be $22,000 and the subsection 20(6) limit on that reserve would be on 30,000 tickets (80,000 – 50,000) at $1 per ticket or $30,000.

Example Problem 4-5

On July 1, 2015, Delta Company sold some inventory with a value of $100,000 and a cost of $40,000. A cash down payment of $10,000 was made and the balance was payable in four annual instalments of $20,000 and a final payment of $10,000. The purchaser is at arm's length.

REQUIRED

How much of an inventory sales reserve can the company take in each year covered by the instalment sale? Use a December 31 year end.

SOLUTION

The Act limits the inventory sales reserve available to a three-year period. A reserve is not deductible for a year end that is more than 36 months after the sale.

Calculation of reserve:

		Accounts receivable	Profit content
July 1, 2015	— sale price of article	$100,000	$60,000
	— cash down payment	10,000	6,000
Dec. 31, 2015	— balance receivable	$90,000	
	— reserve allowable(1)		$54,000
2016	— instalment due	20,000	12,000
Dec. 31, 2016	— balance receivable	$70,000	
	— reserve allowable(1)		$42,000
2017	— instalment due	20,000	12,000
Dec. 31, 2017	— balance receivable	$50,000	
	— reserve allowable(1)		$30,000
2018	— instalment due	20,000	12,000
Dec. 31, 2018	— balance receivable	$30,000	$18,000
	— reserve allowable (more than 36 months after sale)		Nil

Income effect:

			Net reported income
2015	— Profit on sale [par. 12(1)(*b*)]	$60,000	
	— Reserve [par. 20(1)(*n*)]	(54,000)	$6,000
2016	— Previous year reserve [par. 12(1)(*e*)]	$54,000	
	— Reserve [par. 20(1)(*n*)]	(42,000)	12,000
2017	— Previous year reserve [par. 12(1)(*e*)]	$42,000	
	— Reserve [par. 20(1)(*n*)]	(30,000)	12,000

			Net reported income
2018	— Previous year reserve [par. 12(1)(*e*)]	$30,000	
	— Reserve [par. 20(1)(*n*) and ssec. 20(8)]	—	30,000
	Total income reported over four years		$60,000

NOTE TO SOLUTION

(1) Reserve = gross profit / gross selling price × amount receivable

¶4,560.45 Employer's Contribution to Registered Pension Plan

The deduction of employer contributions to a registered pension plan (RPP) is permitted. Deductible contributions may be made by the employer either in the year to which the deduction is to apply or within 120 days after the end of that taxation year. Contributions made in the 120-day period which are in excess of the deduction limit for the preceding year may be deductible in the year in which they are made if the deduction limit for the year is not exceeded.

ITA: 20(1)(q) Employer's contributions to RPP or PRPP, 147.2 Pension contributions deductible — employer contributions

Two types of RPP are envisaged.

- A defined benefit plan promises a defined retirement benefit which is specified by a formula. In the case of a defined benefit RPP, all contributions are deductible if they are determined by an actuary to be necessary to fund the benefits for which the RPP was registered to provide.
- A money purchase or defined contribution plan specifies a contribution requirement with the retirement benefit dependent on the funds accumulated in the plan at the time of retirement.

In the case of a money purchase RPP, the total of employer and employee contributions are limited to:

ITA: 147.1(8) Pension adjustment limits

the lesser of:

(1) 18% of the employer's compensation defined to be employment income inclusions under sections 5 and 6 for the particular year; and

ITA: 147.1(1) Definitions

(2) a specified dollar limit, defined as the money purchase limit. The limits for money purchase RPPs are as follows:

ITA: 147.1(1) Definitions

- for 2015 $25,370
- for 2016 $26,010
- for 2017 $26,230
- for 2018 $26,500
- for 2019 indexed

A violation of the limits set for either type of plan can lead to the revocation of the RPP registration status. If this occurs, all amounts in the plan become taxable, having lost their sheltered status.

¶4,560.50 Employer's Contribution Under a Deferred Profit Sharing Plan

Employer contributions to a deferred profit sharing plan (DPSP) are deductible within limits. An employer may deduct an amount which is paid in the year or within 120 days after the end of the year to a trustee to the extent that the amount was paid in accordance with the terms of the plan and was not deducted by the employer in a previous year.

ITA: 20(1)(y) Employer's contributions under deferred profit sharing plan, 147(8) Amount of employer's contribution deductible

A formula is provided to determine the amount of an employer's contribution to a DPSP that is deductible. Generally, where there is no RPP, the employer's contribution limit in respect of an employee for a year is the lesser of:

ITA: 147(5.1) Contribution limits, 147(5.1)(a)

(1) one-half of the money purchase dollar limit for the year, as discussed above; and

(2) 18% of the employee's compensation (as defined) for the year.

ITA: 147.1(1) Definitions

Therefore, to be deductible in a year, contributions should not exceed the lesser amount computed.

Where an employer participates in both a DPSP and an RPP for the benefit of an employee, the employer's total contribution to both plans is limited. It is rare for an employer to provide both a DPSP and an RPP together.

ITA: 147(5.1)(c)

¶4,560.55 Cancellation of Lease

Where the owner of a property is required to pay an amount to a lessee for the cancellation of the lease, the costs of cancelling the lease are treated as a type of prepaid expense, as long as the property continues to be owned by the lessor or by a non-arm's length person. As a result, the costs may be deducted over what would have been the remaining term of the lease, including renewal periods, to a maximum of 40 years. The unamortized balance of these costs (½ of the unamortized balance, in the case of capital property) is deductible if the property is sold. An amount that does not meet the conditions of these two paragraphs is not deductible.

ITA: 18(1)(q) Limitation re cancellation of lease, 20(1)(z) Cancellation of lease, 20(1)(z.1) Idem

¶4,560.60 Landscaping of Grounds

A deduction of an amount paid in the year for landscaping of grounds around a building that is used to produce income from business is allowed. Were it not for this provision the expenditure would be considered to be of a capital nature.

ITA: 20(1)(aa) Landscaping of grounds

¶4,560.70 Expenses of Representation

The expenses of representation for the purpose of obtaining a licence, permit, franchise or trademark related to the business of a taxpayer are deductible. Given the capital nature of the assets acquired, these expenditures would otherwise be prohibited. Note that the representations must be made to a government body or agency to be deductible.

ITA: 18(1)(b) Capital outlay or loss, 20(1)(cc) Expenses of representation

Instead of deducting the full amount allowed, a taxpayer may elect to deduct one-tenth of the full amount in the year of expenditure and the nine immediately following taxation years. The Regulations set out the documents that must be filed to implement the election.

ITA: 20(1)(cc) Expenses of representation, 20(9) Application of para. (1)(cc); ITR: 4100 [Election]

¶4,560.75 Investigation of Site

The deduction of an amount paid in the year for investigating the suitability of a site for a building or other structure planned for use in the taxpayer's existing business is permitted.

ITA: 20(1)(dd) Investigation of site

¶4,560.80 Utilities Service Connection

An amount paid in the year to an arm's length person to make connections for the supply of electricity, gas, telephone service, water, or sewers is deductible. Without this provision no deduction would be permitted, since the expenditure is of a capital nature. Furthermore, no capital cost allowance would be permitted, because the taxpayer normally does not own the service connections.

ITA: 20(1)(ee) Utilities service connection

¶4,560.85 Disability-Related Modifications and Equipment

A deduction, in the payment year, of the full cost of prescribed renovations or alterations to a building used primarily in a business is allowed. The expenditures must be made to enable individuals who have a mobility impairment to gain access to the building or be mobile within it. The building need not be owned by the taxpayer making the expenditure.

ITA: 20(1)(qq) Disability-related modifications to buildings

The deduction, in the payment year, of the cost of any prescribed disability-specific device or equipment which assists individuals with a sight, hearing, or mobility impairment is allowed. The type of expenditure envisaged includes installation of elevator car position indicators, visible fire alarm indicators, telephone devices, listening devices for group meetings and disability-specific computer software and hardware.

If it were not for these provisions, the expenditures could be considered of a capital nature and could not be expensed. Clearly, the rules provide an incentive to implement social policy.

¶4,560.90 Convention Expenses

Attendance at a convention may be considered to give rise to expenditures of a capital nature, perhaps, in the form of increased knowledge. However, the Act permits the deduction from a taxpayer's business income of amounts paid in attending up to two conventions per year. Attendance at the convention must be in connection with the business. The location of the convention must be within the territorial scope of the organization holding the convention. Note that an internal business meeting, such as a sales conference within a business, is not considered to be a convention.

ITA: 20(10) Convention expenses

¶4,560.95 Pause and Reflect — Summary of Learning Goals

After working through this section, ¶4,560, you should be able to:

- Identify deductions specifically allowed for business income for tax purposes that may not be allowed for accounting income.
- Calculate the adjustments required to accounting income for these specific deductions in order to compute business income for tax purposes.

¶4,570 Summary of the Deductibility of Expenses

To determine the deductibility of an outlay or expenditure after considering the general principles and rules in section 18, the list of deductions under section 20 should be scanned. This can be done quickly by reference to the table of contents for the Act. In addition, Wolters Kluwer's Canadian Tax Reporter Commentary lists court case decisions for a wide variety of expenditures. This list is based on court decisions made on the question of the deductibility of many types of expenditures for tax purposes. However, it should be noted that because the commentary list is based largely on case law, the deductibility of any particular type of expenditure is heavily dependent on the specific facts of the case and the specific law in force at the time of the case. Care should be taken to determine the facts that resulted in a particular decision and the wording of the Act at the time of the case, since some court decisions may be at variance with current law.

Example Problem 4-6

You are the auditor for Corporate Welfare Limited and you have been given an income statement prepared for financial accounting purposes showing a loss for its fiscal year ended December 31, 2018 of $112,000. Your audit uncovers the following:

(a) appraisal expense contains cost of determining asset values for insurance purposes		$4,000
(b) wages expense contains amounts (matched by employees) relating to money purchase (defined contribution) registered pension plan contributions, made during the first 120 days of 2019 but allocated by the accountant to 2018, in respect of current services on behalf of the following executives (employment compensation for the year shown in brackets):		
President (Mr. C.S. Bloom, 100% owner; $200,000)	$15,710	
Vice-President ($95,000)	6,000	
Accountant ($80,000)	5,000	
Plant Supervisor ($65,000)	4,000	30,600
(c) cost of landscaping written off		10,000
(d) legal expenses for		
(i) defence of a suit, brought by a customer, for failure to deliver merchandise on time	$3,500	
(ii) articles of amendment to revise company's articles of incorporation	2,500	
(iii) cost of disputing income tax	4,000	10,000
(e) revenues included a dividend received from a Canadian subsidiary		80,000

(f) interest expense included amortization of bond discount on bonds maturing in 2018		12,000
(g) miscellaneous expense contained donations for the year to		
(i) duly registered charities	$4,000	
(ii) the Conlibdem political party (a registered party)	7,000	11,000
(h) insurance expense contained whole life insurance premium paid on the life of Mr. C.S. Bloom (proceeds payable to the company; not group life)		10,000
(i) salaries expense contained a dividend payable to Mr. Bloom		8,000
(j) bad debts expense including $4,000 in respect of a loan to a shareholder of a supplier totalled		10,000
(k) extraordinary maintenance arising from conversion of premises including replacement of heating and air-conditioning systems, plumbing, electrical wiring and concrete foundations in respect of a building was written off to repairs and maintenance in the amount of		150,000
(l) salaries expense included a bonus paid to Mr. Bloom		15,000
(m) interest expense included interest in respect of the acquisition of 90% of the shares of another Canadian corporation		115,000
(n) convention expenses over three days of Mr. Bloom and his family ($2,000 thereof represents costs relating to Mrs. Bloom and their two children, who attended for social purposes only; $500 of the remaining amount relates to the cost of meals consumed by Mr. Bloom)		5,000
(o) administration expense contains an embezzlement loss caused by a minor employee of the company		10,000
(p) (i) management bonuses included in wages expense but not paid in 2018		50,000
(ii) bonuses accrued at the end of 2017 which were not, and will not be, paid in 2018		35,000
(q) property taxes paid in 2018 include an amount paid for the company's fishing lodge		1,000

(r) the company as a lessor agreed to pay and expensed $15,000 on June 30, 2018 to cancel a lease that could have been in force until December 31, 2023 with renewal periods, but in 2018 actually paid only	10,000
(s) the company paid damages for failing to deliver goods on time under an action for breach of contract brought by one of its suppliers and the amount was expensed in the financial accounts	12,000
(t) cost of constructing a cement ramp to facilitate wheelchair access to the company's premises, capitalized by the accountant	6,000

REQUIRED

Compute the company's income or loss from business or property for tax purposes, but do not compute tax deductions in respect of depreciable capital or eligible capital property. Indicate the applicable sections of the Act or brief reasons to substantiate your answer. Indicate in a separate list the applicable section of the Act or brief reasons for not considering an item in your computations. Make sure all items are accounted for. Ignore the effects of any leap year.

SOLUTION

			Applicable sections
Loss for financial accounting purposes		$(112,000)	sec. 9
Add items not deductible for tax purposes: Excess allocations to 2018 of contributions[(1)]	$4,920		par. 20(1)(*q*)
Amortization of bond discount[(2)]	12,000		par. 18(1)(*b*)
Donations[(3)]	11,000		par. 18(1)(*a*)
Life insurance premium[(4)]	10,000		par. 18(1)(*a*)
Dividend payable[(5)]	8,000		
Bad debt re: loan to shareholder of supplier[(6)]	4,000		par. 20(1)(*p*)
Extraordinary maintenance[(7)]	150,000		par. 18(1)(*b*)
Convention expenses[(8)]	2,250		par. 18(1)(*h*)
Bonuses accrued and not paid[(9)]	35,000		ssec. 78(4)

			Applicable sections
Non-deductible prepaid lease cancellation amount[10]	13,837	$251,007	par. 20(1)(*z*)
		$139,007	
Deduct items deductible for tax purposes: Wheelchair access ramp		$6,000	par. 20(1)(*qq*)
Income from business or property for tax purposes[10]		$133,007	

NOTES TO SOLUTION

[1] In this case, involving a money purchase RPP, assuming the employee contributions are matched by the employer corporation and that the employee's contributions are fully deductible, the corporation will have a non-deductible contribution in respect of 2018 computed as follows:

	Pres.	V.P.	Acct.	Super.
Least of:				
(a) Employer plus employee RPP contributions	$31,420	$12,000	$10,000	$8,000
(b) Money purchase dollar limit for 2018 (all $26,500)	$26,500	$26,500	$26,500	$26,500
(c) 18% of compensation	$36,000	$17,100	$14,400	$11,700
Least amount	$26,500	$12,000	$10,000	$8,000
Less: employer and employee contributions	31,420	12,000	10,000	8,000
Employer's non-deductible contributions for 2018	$4,920	Nil	Nil	Nil

Total amount to be added back: $4,920

Since the $4,920 non-deductible amount was contributed in the first 120 days of 2019, it can be a part of the deductible contribution for 2019 without danger of a revocation of the registration status of the RPP, as long as contributions in 2019 do not exceed deduction limits for 2019.

[2] The Act specifically prohibits the amortization of an amount that is capital in nature. The Act prohibits all reserves, except as expressly provided for in the Act. The Act specifically denies the deduction of an actual cash outlay on redemption or open market purchases except to the extent permitted.

ITA: 18(1)(b) Capital outlay or loss, 18(1)(e) Reserves, etc., 18(1)(f) Payments on discounted bonds, 20(1)(f) Discount on certain obligations

(3) Donations are not deductible in the computation of income if they were not incurred to earn income. However, charitable donations of a corporation are deductible in Division C dealing with the computation of taxable income, and political contributions are eligible for a tax credit in Division E dealing with the computation of tax.

ITA: 110.1 Deduction for gifts, 127(3) Contributions to registered parties and candidates

(4) Life insurance premiums paid on the lives of officers, employees or shareholders where the policies are payable to the company do not produce income. Hence, the premiums are not deductible unless the policy is required to obtain financing, such as a bank loan. The Act limits the amount of a deductible premium to the net cost of pure insurance, determined by reference to standard mortality assumptions.

ITA: 20(1)(e.2) Premiums on life insurance used as collateral

(5) Dividends are not paid to produce income; they are a distribution of income after it has been earned.

(6) The Act requires that an amount be previously included in income if it is to be written off as a bad debt. On this loan, which was not a trade account receivable, no amount would have been included in sales and, hence, in income. However, a further adjustment may be allowed under section 50 which will be discussed in Chapter 8, under the heading "Debts Established to be Bad Debts".

ITA: 20(1)(p) Bad debts

(7) An expenditure which prolongs the life of an asset is regarded as capital in nature, but an expenditure which restores an asset to its original condition is regarded as an expenditure of an income nature. In this case, the expenditure, as described, appears to be of a capital nature.

ITA: 18(1)(b) Capital outlay or loss

(8) Personal or living expenses are specifically prohibited as a deduction, except, for example, an item such as convention expenses specifically allowed. The Act provides that the deductible cost of meals while attending a convention is 50% of the actual cost, on the assumption that the cost is reasonable. Where the fees for a convention do not specify the cost of meals or entertainment included in those fees, the Act will deem the cost to be $50 per day and that amount will be subject to the 50% limitation. In this case, since the cost is specified, 50% of $500, or $250, is not deductible and must be added in the reconciliation.

ITA: 18(1)(h) Personal and living expenses, 20(10) Convention expenses, 67.1(1) Expenses for food, etc., 67.1(3) Fees for convention, etc.

(9) The bonuses accrued at the end of 2017 are not deductible in 2018, since they were not paid within the time limit. The $35,000 would, therefore, have been added back to 2017 income. These bonuses can only be deducted when they are actually paid.

ITA: 78(4) Unpaid remuneration and other amounts

(10) The costs of cancelling a lease are treated as a prepaid expense, as long as the property continues to be owned by the lessor or a person with whom he or she does not deal at arm's length. As such it may be deducted over the remaining term of the cancelled lease, including renewal periods, subject to a maximum limit of 40 years. In this case, the number of days in the remainder of the lease is 184 in 2018 and six years of 365 days per year (ignoring leap years) for a total of 2,374 days. Thus, the deduction for 2018 is given by 184/2,374 × $15,000 or $1,163. Therefore, the non-deductible amount of the $15,000 payment is $13,837 (i.e., $15,000 - $1,163). Another rule provides a deduction of the unamortized balance if the property is sold.

ITA: 20(1)(z) Cancellation of lease, 20(1)(z.1) Idem

Other items:

(1) The cost of an appraisal made for the purpose of maintaining adequate insurance coverage is regarded as a normal business expense and is deductible.

(2) The Act allows a deduction for an employer contribution to a registered pension plan of the amount calculated in another provision. The amounts calculated in respect of all employees shown other than the President are deductible, as shown in Note (1).

ITA: 20(1)(q) Employer's contributions to RPP or PRPP, 147.2(1) Pension contributions deductible — employer contributions

(3) The deduction of landscaping costs is allowed, even though they might otherwise be considered of a capital nature.

ITA: 20(1)(aa) Landscaping of grounds

(4)

(a) The cost of defending a suit brought by a customer is regarded as a business expense if it pertains to trading transactions.

(b) The cost of disputing an income tax case is deductible. The legal expenses of $4,000 could also be deducted, in which case they should not be added back in the computation of income from business.

ITA: 60(o) Legal expenses

(5) A dividend received is to be included in income from property.

ITA: 12(1)(j) Dividends from resident corporations

(6) Bad debt expenses are deductible as long as the account has previously resulted in an inclusion in income. In the normal course of setting up an account receivable a credit would be made to sales, thereby including the amount in income. The treatment of a bad debt expense for tax purposes is identical to the treatment of the expense for financial accounting purposes. In fact, the tax treatment of both the reserve and the expense parallels the accounting treatment. The previous year's reserve is reversed by including it in current income and a new reserve is set up for the current year by taking a deduction. A debt established to be bad is written off and a recovery of such a debt previously written off is included in income.

ITA: 12(1)(d) Reserve for doubtful debts, 12(1)(i) Bad debts recovered, 20(1)(l) Doubtful or impaired debts, 20(1)(p) Bad debts

(7) A bonus expense is a deductible business expense to the extent that it meets the test of being "reasonable in the circumstances." The $50,000 bonus expensed in 2018 is deductible in 2018 as long as it is paid on or before June 27, 2019.

ITA: 18(1)(a) General limitation, 67 General limitation re expenses

(8) The deduction of interest on funds borrowed to buy shares is permitted since dividend income will be earned.

ITA: 20(1)(c) Interest

(9) The deduction of Mr. Bloom's convention expenses is permitted (except for part of the cost of meals which is limited), as long as the conditions of that provision are met.

ITA: 20(10) Convention expenses, 67.3 Limitation re cost of leasing passenger vehicle, 67.1 Expenses for food, etc.

(10) Losses in cash or misappropriation of merchandise sustained by the criminal action of employees or officers will be allowed as deductions from income as being incidental to carrying on of business. However,

such a loss attributable to a partner or senior officer is not usually regarded as a normal business risk and is not deductible. In the case of *Cassidy's Limited v. M.N.R.*, the Tax Court of Canada disagreed specifically with the previous position of the CRA, which argued that, because a theft was committed by a senior employee, the losses resulting from the theft are not deductible by the employer. The Court held that "the amounts lost due to the defalcation were non-capital losses, the deductions of which are deductible in computing profit in accordance with ordinary commercial principles and are not prohibited by the Act" and, hence, allowed the deduction. The current CRA position is that the deductibility of such theft depends on the circumstances of each case.

Cases: *Cassidy's Limited (formerly Packer Floor Coverings Ltd.) v. The Minister of National Revenue*, 89 DTC 686 (TCC); Income Tax Folio: S3-F9-C1 Lottery Winnings, Miscellaneous Receipts, and Income (and Losses) from Crime

(11) Damages for failure to deliver goods are regarded as normal business expenses.

¶4,580 Summary of Business Income Adjustments

The following chart summarizes some of the various adjustments to accounting income needed to arrive at income for tax purposes. Review the chart to ensure you are familiar with all of these common adjustments.

Add		**Deduct**	
Income received but not earned	12(1)(*a*)	Reserve in respect of future goods and services	20(1)(*m*)
Amounts receivable	12(1)(*b*)	Doubtful debts	20(1)(*l*)
		Bad debts	20(1)(*p*)
Expenses not incurred to earn income	18(1)(*a*)		
Capital outlay or loss	18(1)(*b*)	CCA expenses	20(1)(*a*), (*b*)
		Interest	20(1)(*c*)
		Expenses of financing	20(1)(*e*)
		Terminal loss	20(16)
		Bad debts	20(1)(*p*)
		Landscaping	20(1)(*aa*)
		Investment counsel	20(1)(*bb*)
		Investigation of site	20(1)(*dd*)
		Utility service connection	20(1)(*ee*)
		Disability related modifications to buildings, equipment	20(1)(*qq*), (*rr*)

Add		Deduct	
Incurred to earn exempt income	18(1)(*c*)	Premiums on life insurance used as collateral	20(1)(*e*.2)
Reserves, contingent liabilities, etc.	18(1)(*e*)	Doubtful debts	20(1)(*l*)
		Reserve in respect of future goods and services	20(1)(*m*)
		Reserve for unpaid amounts	20(1)(*n*)
Payment on discounted bonds	18(1)(*f*)	Discount on certain obligations	20(1)(*f*)
Personal or living expenses	18(1)(*h*)	Limit on food and entertainment	67.1
		Limit on interest and lease costs for a passenger vehicle	67.2–67.4
		Capital cost of luxury automobile	13(7)(*g*)
		Convention expenses	20(10)
Use of recreational facilities and club dues	18(1)(*l*)		
Political contributions	18(1)(*n*)		
Limitation re personal service business expenses	18(1)(*p*)		
Limitation re cancellation of lease	18(1)(*q*)	Cancellation of lease	20(1)(*z*)
Limit on certain interest and property tax	18(2)		
Costs related to construction of building or ownership of land	18(3.1)		
Prepaid expenses	18(9)		
Unreasonable expenses	67		
Illegal payments, fines, and penalties	67.5, 67.6		

¶4,590 Pause and Reflect — Summary of Learning Goals

After completing this section, ¶4,500, you should be able to:

- Identify all adjustments that need to be made to convert accounting income to business income.
- Calculate business income for tax purposes by starting with accounting income.
- Explain why accounting income and business income may differ.

¶4,590.99 Practise What You've Learned

Refer to the following sections of the Study Guide to practise what you've learned:

¶4,800 — Review Questions

- Question 7 — Deductions
- Question 8 — Interest
- Question 9 — Disallowed or Restricted Deductions
- Question 10 — Write-offs of Capital Expenditures

¶4,825 — Multiple Choice Questions

- Question 2 — Deductions
- Question 3 — Deductions
- Question 4 — Deductions
- Question 6 — Deductions

¶4,850 — Exercises

- Exercise 1 — Deductions
- Exercise 3 — Automobile Expenses
- Exercise 4 — Inducement Payments or Reimbursements
- Exercise 8 — Deductions
- Exercise 9 — Office in the Home
- Exercise 10 — Deductions
- Exercise 11 — Interest

¶4,600 Additional Issues Concerning Business Income

Overview

Beyond the details discussed above, there are some unique circumstances which can affect the calculation of business income. These include ceasing to carry on a business and scientific research and experimental development expenses, which are discussed in this section.

¶4,610 Sales/Negotiating Person's Expenses Revisited

Overview

One of the topics dealt with in the preceding chapter on employment income was the deductibility of the expenses of sales/negotiating persons (i.e., individuals employed in connection with the selling of property or negotiating of contracts). Unlike other employees, sales/negotiating persons can deduct expenses incurred to produce employment income. However, these allowable expenses are limited to the amount of commission income or other similar amounts, fixed by reference to the volume of sales made or the contracts negotiated, received in the year. It is interesting to compare the limited deductions for expenses available to a sales/negotiating person who is an employee with the broader deductions available to a person performing similar functions as an independent business person. Note how, as the risk of uncertainty of income increases from employee to sales/negotiating person to proprietor, the breadth of expenses allowed increases.

ITA: 8(1)(f) Sales expenses, 8(1)(j) Motor vehicle and aircraft costs

Comparison of Deductions

	Ordinary Employee[1]	Salesperson/Negotiator		Proprietor
	[s. 8(1)(*h*), (*h*.1), (*i*), (*j*)]	[s. 8(1)(*f*)]	[s. 8(1)(*i*), (*j*)]	
Home Office:				
Utilities	√		√	√
Mortgage interest				√
House insurance		√		√
Property taxes		√		√
Maintenance and repairs	√		√	√
Office supplies	√		√	√
CCA on computer				√
Automobile expenses:				
Operating	√	√		√
CCA	√		√	√
Interest on loan	√		√	√
Convention (excl. meals)				√
Promotional expenses		√		√
Limit on expenses	None	Commission Income	None	None

[1] Required to travel for employer, but no sales commission earned.

¶4,610.10 Automobiles

The following are some of the common deductions related to automobiles:

- Interest on money borrowed for passenger vehicles; ITA: 67.2 Interest on money borrowed for passenger vehicle
- Deductible lease payment restriction; ITA: 67.3 Limitation re cost of leasing passenger vehicle
- CCA restriction on passenger vehicles; ITA: 13(7)(g), 13(7)(h)
- Limit on which CCA may be claimed ($30,000 plus GST/HST for 2018); ITR: 7307(b)
- Definition of passenger vehicles. ITA: 248(1) Definitions

¶4,610.15 Automobile Allowances

As discussed previously in this chapter, the Act and the ITR limit the deduction by an employer of allowances paid to employees for the use of an automobile in the course of employment or business to a prescribed amount per kilometre, except where the allowance is required to be included in the employee's income under paragraph 6(1)(*b*). ITA: 18(1)(r) Certain automobile expenses; ITR: 7306 [Prescribed amount – automobile allowance]

¶4,610.20 Office in the Home

Also, as previously discussed, the deductibility of the costs relating to a place of business in the residence of a self-employed individual is restricted. A prorated portion of these "home office" expenses, such as rent, capital cost allowance, property taxes, and mortgage interest or operating costs, including heating, electricity, insurance or maintenance may be deducted only if the space is either: ITA: 18(12) Work space in home

- the individual's principal place of business; or
- used exclusively by the individual on a regular and continuous basis for meeting clients, customers or patients.

The deduction for home office expenses is further restricted to the income for the year from the business for which the office is used. However, any excess of deduction disallowed in a year may be treated as home office expenses incurred in a following year, according to the Income Tax Folio entitled "Business Use of Home Expenses". A parallel provision to restrict the deduction of home office expenses by an employee was presented in Chapter 3. Income Tax Folio: S4-F2-C2; ITA: 8(13) Work space in home

¶4,610.25 Meals and Entertainment

The amount of a deduction by all taxpayers for food, beverage, and entertainment is restricted to the lesser of 50% of the amount paid or payable or a reasonable amount. This limitation applies to all business meals, including food and beverage, as well as to the cost of meals while travelling or attending a seminar, conference, convention or similar function. The restriction also applies to tickets to an entertainment or sporting event, gratuities and cover charges, room rentals to provide entertainment and the cost of private boxes at sports facilities. The limitation applies to the taxpayer incurring the costs in the case where a reimbursement is made. The following are exclusions from the 50% limitation: ITA: 67.1 Expenses for food, etc.

(1) the cost to a restaurant, airline, or hotel of providing meals to customers in the ordinary course of business;

(2) meals or entertainment expenses relating to an event intended primarily to benefit a registered charity;

(3) the cost of meals or entertainment that is included as a taxable benefit to the employee or where the employer is reimbursed for the cost; and

(4) the cost of meals and recreation provided by an employer for the general benefit of all employees at a particular place of business in respect of occasional events not exceeding six events per year.

The Interpretation Bulletin entitled "Food, Beverages and Entertainment Expenses" presents the CRA's interpretation of this provision.

Interpretation Bulletins: IT-518R Food, Beverages and Entertainment Expenses

Example Problem 4-7

Ms. Jo Schmaltz is a salesperson who earned a total of $25,000 in 2018, including $5,000 in commissions. She was required to travel in her job and she was required to pay her own expenses, all of which were reasonable in the circumstances and consisted of the following:

(a) entertainment of clients including golf club membership dues of $500 (incurred in equal monthly amounts)		$3,700
(b) home office expenses (allocated by floor space of office portion of home):		
mortgage interest	$450	
municipal taxes	400	
capital cost allowance	300	
utilities	1,000	
maintenance and repairs	850	3,000
This is the only office space available for her work.		
(c) capital cost allowance on car used 75% for business		3,570
(d) car operating expenses		3,100
(e) convention dues (excluding meals and entertainment)		1,000
(f) travellers' association (a trade union) dues		300
(g) meals while travelling		900

ITA: 8(1)(f) Sales expenses, 8(1)(f)(v), 8(1)(f)(vi), 8(1)(i)(ii), 8(1)(j) Motor vehicle and aircraft costs, 8(13) Work space in home, 8(13)(a)(i), 8(13)(a)(ii); Interpretation Bulletins: IT-352R2 Employee's expenses, including work space in home expenses; Cases: *Richard Felton v. The Minister of National Revenue*, 89 DTC 233 (TCC); *Her Majesty the Queen v. Nick Thompson*, 89 DTC 5439 (FCTD)

REQUIRED

(A) Compute Jo's minimum employment income for 2018.

(B) Compute Jo's minimum business income, assuming she is an independent business person with $25,000 in sales rather than an employee.

SOLUTION

			Applicable provisions
(A) Employment income			
Salary and commissions		$25,000	sec. 5
Deductions:			
Entertainment[1] (50% of $3,200)	$ 1,600		par. 8(1)(*f*) par. 18(1)(*l*) ssec. 67.1(1)
Home office:[2] municipal taxes	400		par. 8(1)(*f*)
Car operating expenses (75% of $3,100)	2,325		par. 8(1)(*f*)
Meal expenses (50% of $900)	450		ssec. 67.1(1)
Total	$ 4,775		
Deductions not in excess of commission[3]		$(4,775)	par. 8(1)(*f*)
		$20,225	
Less: association dues[4]	$ 300		par. 8(1)(*i*)
CCA on car (75% of $3,570)	2,678		par. 8(1)(*j*)
Utilities	1,000		par. 8(1)(*i*)
Maintenance and repairs	850	(4,828)	par. 8(1)(*i*)
Employment income[5], [6]		$15,397	
(B) Business income			
Sales		$25,000	sec. 9
Deductions:			
Entertainment[7] (50% of $3,200)	$ 1,600		par. 18(1)(*a*)
CCA on car (75% of $3,570)	2,678		par. 20(1)(*a*)
Car operating expenses (75% of $3,100)	2,325		par. 18(1)(*a*)
Convention expenses	1,000		ssec. 20(10)
Meals (50% of $900)	450		par. 18(1)(*a*)
Association dues	300	(8,353)	par. 18(1)(*a*)
Income from business[8] (before home office expense)		$16,647	par. 18(1)(*a*) par. 20(1)(*a*) par. 20(1)(*c*)
Less: home office expense[9]		(3,000)	
Income from business		$13,647	

Note that the difference between employment income of $15,397 and business income of $13,647 is $1,750. This amount consists of the following expenses that are not deductible from employment income but are deductible from business income:

Interest and CCA on home office ($450 + $300)	$750
Convention expenses	1,000
Total	$1,750

NOTES TO SOLUTION

(1) To be deductible as a salesperson's expenses, an expenditure must be made to earn employment income. However, the relevant provision specifically denies deductions which fall under paragraph 18(1)(*l*), which lists an outlay for the use of a golf course.

(2) Outlays on account of capital are not deductible except for interest and capital cost allowance on a car used in the course of employment. The interest is on account of the home mortgage and the capital cost allowance is not for a car. Municipal taxes and home insurance are deductible, as confirmed by the decision of the Tax Court of Canada in *Felton v. M.N.R.* In that case, the taxpayer sought to deduct mortgage interest, property taxes, insurance premiums and the cost of utilities for his home as rent. The court held that rent involves only a payment arising out of a landlord and tenant relationship, such that the expenses incurred for an owner-occupied home could not be considered as rent. However, the court did recognize the CRA's assessing practices in respect of maintenance costs and utilities. The Federal Court–Trial Division concurred with the *Felton* decision in *The Queen v. Thompson*.

The Act sets out two tests, one of which must be met, if any amount of home office expense is to be deductible. One requires that the workspace be the place where the individual principally performs the duties of the office or employment. The alternative test requires that both of the following conditions be met:

(1) the workspace is used exclusively for employment during the period in respect of which the deduction relates, and

(2) the workspace is used on a regular and continuous basis for meeting customers or other persons in the ordinary course of employment.

ITA: 8(13)(a)(i), 8(13)(a)(ii), 8(13)(c), 8(1)(f) Sales expenses, 8(2) General limitation, 8(1)(f) Sales expenses, 8(1)(h) Travel expenses, 8(1)(h.1) Motor vehicle travel expenses, 8(1)(h) Travel expenses, 8(1)(i)(iii), 8(1)(i)(iv), 8(1)(j)(ii), 18(1)(l) Use of recreational facilities and club dues; Interpretation Bulletins: IT-352R2 Employee's expenses, including work space in home expenses

If one of the two tests is met, the deductible expenses are limited to the employee's employment income for the year. Therefore, workspace deduction cannot create a loss from employment. However, the provision allows for what amounts to an indefinite carryforward. In this case, where all expenses are limited to the amount of commission income, the limitation on home office expenses will have no effect.

(3) Note that the salesperson's expense deduction requires that expenses, to be deductible, cannot exceed the commission.

(4) Paragraph 8(1)(*f*) does not restrict the deductions under paragraph 8(1)(*i*) or 8(1)(*j*) (i.e., interest and capital cost allowance on car, utilities and maintenance) to commission income.

(5) Convention expenses may not be deducted from employment income since they are not listed in subsection 8(1).

(6) Due to the limitation placed on deductible expenses, i.e., expenses cannot exceed commission income, an alternative set of provisions may be preferable. In this alternative, the employee could make use of the deductions covering travelling expenses and motor vehicle expenses, rather than the salesperson's deduction. Although these alternative rules do not provide for the deduction of entertainment expenses, there is no commission income limitation on the amount of meal expenses deductible (except for the 50% limitation on the cost of meals) or on car operating expenses deductible.

In this particular case, using the paragraphs 8(1)(*h*) and (*h*.1) alternative is not better because expenses deductible under paragraph 8(1)(*f*) do not exceed the commission income limit, as is usually the case. If expenses deductible under paragraph 8(1)(*f*) were expected to exceed commission income on a regular basis, it might be best to negotiate a higher commission, trading that for a lower salary. The employer should be indifferent if the total salary and commission are the same.

(7) Golf club membership dues are not deductible because of the prohibition.

(8) The issue of employment versus self-employment was considered in the previous chapter. The courts have applied the following three tests as discussed in the previous chapter:

(1) the economic reality or entrepreneur test, i.e., control, ownership of the tools, chance of profit and risk of loss;

(2) integration or organization test, i.e., whether the worker is economically dependent on the organization; and

(3) the specific result test, i.e., a contract envisaging the accomplishment of a specific job or task.

(9) All of the home office expenses, including the interest and capital cost allowance, are deductible to the extent incurred to earn income, if the conditions are met. However, she may not want to claim the capital cost allowance because of the principal residence rules which will be discussed in the chapters on capital gains taxation. The deduction of expenses pertaining to work space in a home are allowed where it is either the individual's principal place of business or used exclusively on a regular and continuous basis for meeting clients, customers or patients of the individual. Deductible expenses cannot exceed the individual's income from business before the deduction of these expenses. However, excess expenses of this nature may be carried forward. As a result of this restriction, home office expenses should be separated from other deductible expenses and deducted last, as shown.

¶4,610.90 Pause and Reflect — Summary of Learning Goals

After working through this section, ¶4,610, you should be able to:

- Identify differences in deductions allowed for business income, a commission sales person, and an employee.

¶4,620 Ceasing To Carry on Business

Overview

When a business reaches the end of its life cycle, the sale of certain assets can generate business income. This section discusses the potential for business income for tax purposes that may be generated through the sale of accounts receivable or inventory during the sale of a business.

¶4,620.10 Sale of Accounts Receivable

In order to deduct a reserve for doubtful debts or to write off a bad debt, an amount in respect of the debt must have been included previously in income. This would not be the case, if accounts judged to be doubtful or bad were purchased from someone else. To alleviate the problems that this may cause, where a person has sold all or substantially all of the property used in a business to a purchaser who will continue the business, the Act provides for a joint election (referred to as a Section 22 election) by the vendor and purchaser which permits the purchaser to take the reserve or write-off in respect of accounts receivable.

ITA: 20(1)(l) Doubtful or impaired debts, 20(1)(p) Bad debts; 22 Sale of accounts receivable

To illustrate this election, assume that accounts receivable having a face value of $14,000 with an existing reserve of $3,000 are sold for their assessed fair market value of $10,000. The following represents the procedure that must be followed jointly by the buyer and seller to allow the buyer future reserves and write-offs on the accounts purchased:

ITA: 22 Sale of accounts receivable

SELLER

Accounts receivable		*Reserve*	
$14,000			$3,000
	$10,000(1)		
	4,000(3)	(2) $3,000	
NIL			NIL

BUYER

Accounts receivable		*Reserve*	
(1) $14,000			NIL

(1) Cash	$10,000	
Accounts receivable		$10,000
(2) Reserve	3,000	
Income		3,000
(3) Business loss	4,000	
Accounts receivable		4,000

(1) Accounts receivable	$14,000	
Cash		$10,000
Income		4,000

NOTE: Buyer could then set up an appropriate reserve for doubtful debts and could write off any of these debts should they prove bad.

Note that the loss to the seller under the election is a business loss. If the election were not made, the loss of $4,000 would be a capital loss, only ½ allowable as a deduction and only deductible against taxable capital gains of $2,000.

¶4,620.20 Sale of Inventory

Where a taxpayer disposes of a business or part of a business, any inventory sold is deemed to have been sold in the course of carrying on the business. Thus, the proceeds of the sale result in income for the seller and become the cost of the inventory to the buyer. The purpose of this provision is to ensure that a lump sum sale of inventory on the sale of a business is treated in exactly the same way as the usual sale of inventory in the normal course of carrying on business.

ITA: 23 Sale of inventory

CHAPTER 5

The Capital Cost Allowance System for Depreciable Property Including Intangibles

ADVANCED CONTENT IN THIS CHAPTER

Ⓐ Ownership of Property ¶5,045.20

Ⓐ Separate Class Rule for Electronic Office Equipment ¶5,045.50

Ⓐ Transfer to Another Class — Avoiding Recapture ¶5,045.60

Ⓐ Advanced Rules Related to the Depreciable Property ¶5,065

Ⓐ Change in Use and Part Disposition Rules ¶5,065.10

Ⓐ Change from Income-producing to other Purpose

Ⓐ Change in Non-income-producing to Income-producing Purpose

Ⓐ Property Acquired for Multiple Purposes ¶5,065.20

Ⓐ Franchises and Similar Property ¶5,065.30

Ⓐ Non-Arm's Length Transfer of Depreciable Property ¶5,065.40

Learning Goals

Know, Understand and Explain

By the end of this chapter you will know, understand and be able to explain:

- The basic provisions of the *Income Tax Act* (the Act) that relate to depreciable property, including intangibles.
- The similiarities and differences between the accounting and tax deductions as they relate to depreciable and capital property.
- That capital cost allowance amounts are the tax equivalent of accounting amortization/depreciation for capital, including intangible, property.
- How to classify commonly purchased assets given the information and circumstances.
- The tax implications of asset disposal as it relates to depreciable, including intangible, property.

Review Questions
¶5,800 in the Study Guide

Multiple Choice Questions
¶5,825 in the Study Guide

Exercises
¶5,850 in the Study Guide

Apply

By the end of this chapter you will be able to apply your knowledge and understanding to:

- Correctly calculate capital cost allowance amounts that replace accounting deductions.
- Advise taxpayers on the tax implications of the purchase and sale of these assets.

Assignment Problems
¶5,875 in the Study Guide

Overview

Although the rules pertaining to depreciable property are similar to accounting, there are some key differences. While accounting amortization allows for some professional judgement to determine amortization policies for a particular asset, the Act restricts amortizing the capital cost of depreciable property, including intangibles, based on the asset class. For tax purposes, the rates and methods of write-off of cost reflect economic policy incentives to invest in certain depreciable property. The concept of matching the deduction to the income earned from the asset is still the underlying concept in determining the asset's capital cost allowance rate.

The rules related to deductions for depreciable property are found in Subdivision b (income or loss from a business or property) of Division B of the Act and in the Regulations.

PART I — DIVISION B, SUBDIVISION b

BUSINESS OR PROPERTY

DIVISION

A	Liability for tax
B	**Computation of income**
C	Computation of taxable income
D	Taxable income earned in Canada by non-residents
E	Computation of tax
E.1	Minimum tax
F	Special rules applicable in certain circumstances
G	Deferred and other special income arrangements
H	Exemptions
I	Returns, assessments, payment and appeals
J	Appeals to the Tax Court of Canada and the Federal Court of Appeal

SUBDIVISION

	Basic rules
a	Income or loss from an office or employment
b	**Income or loss from a business or property**
c	Taxable capital gains and allowable capital losses
d	Other sources of income
e	Deductions in computing income
f	Rules relating to computation of income
g	Amounts not included in computing income
h	Corporations resident in Canada and their shareholders
i	Shareholders of corporations not resident in Canada
j	Partnerships and their members
k	Trusts and their beneficiaries

SECTION

9-11	Basic rules
12-17	Inclusions
18-21	**Deductions**
20(1)	**(incl. CCA)**
22-25	Ceasing to carry on business
26-37	Special cases

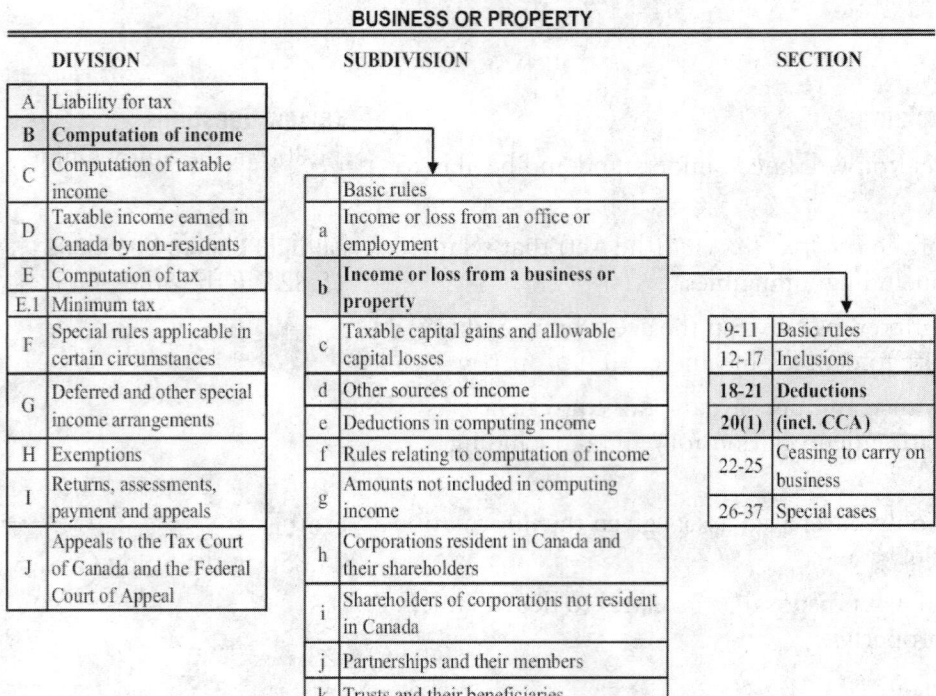

The major rules related to these deductions are found in the following parts of the Act:

Inclusion and Special Rules		**Deduction and special rules**	
Ssec.13(1)	Recaptured CCA	Par. 18(1)(*b*)	No deduction for amortization
Ssec.13(2)	Luxury automobiles	Par. 20(1)(*a*)	
Ssec.13(4)	Replacement property	Ssec.20(16)	Terminal loss
Ssec.13(7)	Special rules	Reg. 1100	CCA rules
Ssec.13(21)	Definitions	Reg. 1100(2)	Half-year rule
Ssec.13(21.1)	Loss on certain transfers within affiliated groups	Reg. 7307(1)	CCA limits on automobiles
Ssec.13(26)	Available for use	Reg. Sch. III-VI	Classes of property

¶5,000 The Capital Cost Allowance System

Overview

In computing net income from a business for tax purposes, an expense is deductible only to the extent it is laid out to earn income for that taxation year. Capital property usually provides a long-term benefit, allowing the business to use the property to earn income over several periods, so the true cost of generating revenues in one taxation period is typically less than the actual cost of the property. The income tax rules related to the deduction of capital property are intended to enforce the matching principle. For this reason, the Act disallows the deduction of the costs for capital expenditures.

Income Tax Folio: S3-F4-C1 General Discussion of Capital Cost Allowance; ITA: 18(1)(a) General limitation, 18(1)(b) Capital outlay or loss

After working through section ¶5,000 of the chapter, you will be able to:

- Explain the similarities and differences between the accounting and tax deductions as they relate to depreciable assets.
- Explain how the capital cost allowance system works to provide a tax deduction along with the flexibilities in the system.
- Apply your knowledge to determine the correct capital cost class in which to place a depreciable asset.
- Explain and calculate the effect a disposition of a depreciable asset will have on the overall business net income, including the calculation of recapture and terminal loss.
- Apply your knowledge to correctly calculate the maximum capital cost allowance a business may claim in a year, based on the specific facts in the case.
- Apply your knowledge to advise the client on the tax implications of asset purchases and disposal and provide recommendations and planning suggestions on how to minimize overall taxes payable.

¶5,005 Introduction

¶5,005.10 Capital Property — Accounting Versus Taxation

For accounting purposes, it is generally acceptable to amortize or deplete the asset and reflect the cost of the asset in the determination of net income over a period of years. The objective of amortization, for financial statement accounting purposes, is to match the cost of producing the revenues to net income. Accounting amortization often requires professional judgement to determine the useful life, residual values, and other components.

For tax purposes, the accounting methods of amortization are replaced by the capital cost allowance (CCA) system. While amortization can incorporate a variety of methods, the CCA system is specific and leaves few choices in the computation of a CCA claim. Another important difference is that accounting amortization is required under generally accepted accounting principles while CCA is an optional or permissive deductions, within limits, under the Act.

¶5,005.20 Types of Capital Property

In the Act, capital property is separated into two general categories:

- non-depreciable capital property; and

- depreciable property (including intangibles).

Non-depreciable capital property is not defined in the Act; it includes receivables and other capital property such as land, investments, personal-use property, and listed personal property. Since this property is not used up or worn out over time in the production of income, non-depreciable capital property is not eligible for capital cost allowance.

Depreciable property is defined as property acquired by the taxpayer where CCA was or will be allowed. Since depreciable property is also treated as capital property, a capital gain may arise. Conversely, a capital loss is disallowed on the disposition of depreciable property because the decline in value is fully deducted through the CCA system. The Act permits a deduction from net income to reflect the wear and tear of depreciable property based on the capital cost allowance system. For the most part, the CCA system is based on the declining balance method. A significant feature of the CCA system is the grouping of assets into prescribed classes, including a class for intangibles such as goodwill, patents, unlimited life franchises, and incorporation costs in excess of $3,000. By prescribing a specific method and specific rates to each prescribed class (depending on the type of the depreciable asset), alternative methods and the range of possible results are minimized. This reduces tax-motivated transactions and enhances neutrality.

ITA: 13(21) depreciable property, 39(1)(b), 20(1)(a) Capital cost of property

¶5,005.30 CCA and Neutrality

The CCA system was designed and implemented not only to narrow the choices of amortization methods to taxpayers but also to provide the government with a means of implementing fiscal policy. Although policy makers do consider the economic life and utility received from an asset, many of the rates and class categories were determined with fiscal policy objectives and budgetary requirements in mind.

Example

Manufacturing Equipment and Computers

Over the years, the class, rate, and computational method for manufacturing equipment have varied to encourage investment in the manufacturing and processing industry, regardless of the equipment's expected or actual useful life.

Modified capital cost allowance rules for computer equipment and certain manufacturing equipment provide a rate that more accurately reflects technological obsolescence.

The CCA system is not tax neutral because the allowance claimed on a depreciable asset affects the after-tax cash flow received on the asset. Tax-neutral amortization would not permit the tax law to govern or influence investment decisions.

¶5,005.40 CCA and Tax Planning

Every capital investment decision should include consideration of the capital cost allowance (CCA) system. For tax purposes, CCA is an optional or permissive deductions. Depending on the profitability of the taxpayer and the availability of losses claimed, a corporation has a certain amount of discretion as to the amount of CCA deducted. This is especially relevant when a corporation has loss carryforward amounts with a high probability of expiration as discussed in Chapter 10. The opportunity to claim capital cost allowance is never lost, as long as the asset is in a tax pool.

Suppose, for instance, that a corporation decided not to claim CCA in a taxation period because of the availability of losses, either from the current year or from carryforwards from prior years. The asset balance of the capital property will be available in the following year. Each year, the taxpayer may claim any amount of CCA from zero to the maximum allowable claim, based on the asset balance and the CCA rate for that pool, regardless of how much CCA was claimed in a prior year. The larger the asset balance in the pool, the larger the CCA that may be claimed in a year. It is important to note that if a business chooses to not claim a CCA deduction in a particular year, they cannot double up on their CCA deduction in the following year.

Management can quantify the net present value of the tax savings that will result from claiming declining-balance capital cost allowance to determine the net-of-tax cost of an asset by applying a relatively simple formula:

$$\frac{\text{Cost} \times \text{Tax rate} \times \text{CCA rate}}{\text{Rate of return} + \text{CCA rate}}$$

Where the asset is subject to the half-year rule (explained later in this chapter), the formula above is adjusted as follows:

$$\frac{[\text{Cost} \times \text{Tax rate} \times \text{CCA rate}}{\text{Rate of return} + \text{CCA Rate}]} \times \frac{[1 + (\text{Rate of Return}/2)}{(1 + \text{Rate of Return})]}$$

This CCA tax shield represents a tax-free recovery of some or all of the tax-paid cost of the depreciable asset. For example, if a depreciable asset is purchased for $10,000, that amount represents a tax-paid cost, since the funds come from after-tax resources. In the case of depreciable property, the CCA deduction shields income from being taxed to the extent of the CCA claim and the income is earned tax free.

Example Problem 5-1

ABC Canada Limited is considering a new piece of equipment that costs $100,000. It is a Class 10 asset (30% CCA rate) and would be subject to the half-year rule. ABC's corporate tax rate is 28% and the company expects at least a 9% return on the investment in the asset.

REQUIRED

What is the cost of the asset after considering the net present value of the tax reductions associated with the capital cost allowance allowed in measuring income for tax purposes?

SOLUTION

Cost of asset	\$ 100,000
Less income tax-paid cost recovery from CCA:	
$\frac{\$100{,}000 \times .28 \times .30}{.09 + .30} \times \left[\frac{1 + .09/2}{1 + .09}\right]$	= \$ 20,649
After tax cost of asset	\$ 79,351

¶5,005.50 CCA as a Permissive Deduction

The rate of capital cost allowance (CCA) applied to each class is specified as a maximum rate. The taxpayer may, therefore, claim any amount of capital cost allowance up to a maximum of the amount given by the capital cost allowance rate multiplied by the balance in the class at the end of the taxation year.

Under certain conditions, it may be advantageous for the taxpayer to take less than the maximum amount of capital cost allowance allowed. Only the amount actually taken is deducted from the balance in the class of assets. The remaining balance is carried forward and is available for future capital cost allowance claims. In an Information Circular, the Canada Revenue Agency (CRA) indicates some conditions under which it will accept a request from a taxpayer to reassess a return for a previous year to adjust a permissive deduction such as capital cost allowance.

Information Circulars: IC 84-1 Revision of capital cost allowance claims and other permissive deductions

¶5,005.60 Available-for-Use Rule

Taxpayers may not start claiming capital cost allowance until the property has become "available for use" by the taxpayer. Very generally, the property is available for use when it is delivered and capable of performing the function for which it was acquired. A building is available for use at the earlier of:

ITA: 13(26) Restriction on deduction before available for use, 13(27) Interpretation — available for use, 13(28) Idem, 13(29) Idem, 13(30) Transfers of property, 13(31) Idem, 13(32) Leased property

(a) when all or substantially all of the building is first used for its intended purpose, and

(b) the second taxation year after the year of acquisition.

These rules must be consulted for their application to a specific asset under the particular conditions of the asset's purchase.

Since an asset is eligible for a capital cost allowance claim in the year in which it becomes available for use, the half-year rule (see ¶5,025) applies to the asset in that year, in most cases.

ITR: 1100(2) Property Acquired in the Year

¶5,005.70 Comparison of Capital Cost Allowance and Accounting Amortization — Main Differences

Although capital cost allowance for depreciable capital assets, including intangibles, is the tax equivalent of amortization there are a number of important differences, which give rise to the need for future income tax accounting.

While financial accounting uses useful life as the basis of the write-off of a capital expenditure, the tax system might be based on useful life, legal life (as in the case of leasehold improvements or patents), or fiscal policy. While accounting amortization must adhere to the principles of consistency, the tax system allows for a deduction of any amount up to the maximum permitted for each class.

For accounting purposes, differences between book value and proceeds of disposition are considered gains or losses on the sale of an asset. However, the tax system provides for the write-off of the actual decline in value of assets during their holding period. The system requires the inclusion in income of recapture (see ¶5,025.20) of capital cost allowance where the capital cost allowance deductions have resulted in an undepreciated capital cost that is less than the proceeds of disposition, and the recognition of a terminal loss (see ¶5,025) where capital cost allowance deductions did not fully reflect the decreased value of the asset pool.

ITA: 18(1)(b) Capital outlay or loss; ITR: 1100 [Capital cost allowance – deductions allowed]

Under appropriate circumstances, the sale of an asset may also result in a capital gain. However, there can never, under any circumstances, be a capital loss on depreciable property. All declines in value are handled through the capital cost allowance deduction and the final adjustment through either recapture or a terminal loss.

¶5,010 Basic Rules

Capital property provides a long-term benefit that allows a business to earn revenues over a period of time. The Act disallows a deduction of the cost of capital property unless specifically allowed in the Act. Over time and use, most capital property decrease in value. Providing the capital property was purchased to provide a long-term benefit and is used to earn income, the Act outlines the method in which capital cost may be deducted. While Par. 20(1)(*a*) provides the ability to deduct capital cost allowance, it is the *Income Tax Regulations* that provide the detailed information, including CCA rates and descriptions of the assets to be included in a particular CCA class.

¶5,015 Eligibility for Capital Cost Allowance

¶5,015.10 Depreciable Property — Important Exclusions

The Act is not very helpful in determining what is "depreciable property" since the definition refers to property in respect of which a taxpayer is entitled to claim a deduction under paragraph 20(1)(*a*). Therefore, property must fit into one of the prescribed classes of CCA or Schedule II to be depreciable. Even if a property fits in a prescribed class, it may not be depreciable property if it is excluded under a Regulation. The following items are the most important exclusions:

ITR: 1102 Property Not Included

- property, the cost of which is deductible in computing income;
- property that is described in inventory;
- property not acquired for the purpose of gaining or producing income;
- property that is a yacht, camp, lodge, golf course, or facility for which expenses are not deductible by reason of paragraph 18(1)(*l*);

- land; and
- property situated outside Canada that is owned by non-residents.

¶5,015.20 Employees and CCA

Employees are generally prohibited from claiming capital cost allowance. Very limited exceptions to this rule are provided for motor vehicle and aircraft costs, and for musical instruments. To qualify for these capital cost allowance claims, the employee must use the automobile, aircraft, or instrument to perform his/her employment duties.

ITA: 8(2) General limitation; 8(1)(j) Motor vehicle and aircraft costs; 8(1)(p) Musical instrument costs

These restrictions on CCA pose problems when an employee must use his or her own computer or home office equipment. Employees are only allowed CCA on the three types of assets noted above. Where applicable, the employee and employer should recognize other alternatives, such as a leasing arrangement, where a deduction may be available under paragraph 8(1)(*f*), or an independent contractor arrangement, where technically feasible under tax law.

¶5,015.30 Businesses and CCA

As a general rule, businesses may deduct CCA for capital assets used in the income-earning process. The Act allows a deduction for such part of the capital cost, as prescribed by the *Income Tax Regulations*.

ITA: 20(1)(a) Capital cost of property

¶5,020 Classes of Assets for Tangible Capital Property

An important feature of the capital cost allowance system is the grouping of depreciable property into prescribed classes that are established by the Regulations (Part XI and Schedule II, primarily). When a taxpayer has a number of properties within a particular class, the properties of that class are treated as one unit for the purposes of capital cost allowance.

ITR: 1100(1)(a.1) Class 1, 1100(5b.1), 1101 Businesses and Properties, 1104(2) eligible nonresidential building

Exhibit 5-1 Common Classes

Class 1 (4%)	Most buildings or other structures, including component parts such as electrical wiring and fixtures, plumbing, heating and central air conditioning
Class 1-MB (10%)	Manufacturing buildings (MB) used at least 90% (measured by square footage) for manufacturing and processing purposes (acquired on or after March 19, 2007 and not used by anyone before March 19, 2007); each building added to this class is put in its own separate class
Class 1-NRB (6%)	Non-residential buildings (NRB) (acquired on or after March 19, 2007 and not used by anyone before March 19, 2007); each building added to this class is put in its own separate class
Class 8 (20%)	Miscellaneous tangible capital property, such as furniture, fixtures, and outdoor advertising signs, and machinery or equipment, such as photocopiers, refrigeration equipment, telephones, and tools costing $500 or more, and property not included in another class (i.e., general default class for tangible capital property)

ITR: 1100(1)(a.1) Class 1, 1100(5b.1), 1101 Businesses and Properties, 1104(2) eligible nonresidential building

ITR: 1101(1af) [Passenger vehicle]

Class 10 (30%)	Automotive equipment, such as automobiles (except taxis and those used in a daily rental business), vans, trucks, tractors, wagons and trailers
Class 10.1 (30%)	A passenger vehicle with a cost in excess of the prescribed limit (i.e., $30,000 if acquired after 2000); each vehicle added to this class is put in its own separate class
Class 12 (100%)	Tools, instruments, and kitchen utensils costing less than $500; linen, uniforms, dies, jigs, or moulds; rental videocassettes; computer application software
Class 13	Lease hold interest
Class 14	Patent,[1] franchise, concession or licence for a limited period
Class 14.1[1] (5%)	Indefinite-term intangibles such as goodwill, incorporation costs in excess of $3,000, customer lists, and franchises, among others purchased after 2016.
Class 17 (8%)	Roads, parking lots, sidewalks, airplane runways, storage areas, or similar surface construction
Class 43 (30%)	Machinery and equipment used in Canada primarily to manufacture and process goods for sale or lease
Class 44[2] (25%)	Patents and rights to use patented information acquired for a limited or unlimited period
Class 50 (55%)	General purpose electronic data processing equipment and systems software for the equipment (acquired after March 18, 2007)
Class 53 (50%)	Manufacturing and processing machinery and equipment (acquired after 2015 but before 2026. Manufacturing equipment purchased after 2025 will be placed in Class 43 (30%))

[1] Class 14.1 was established to amortize the cost, after 2016, of intangibles that were previously treated as eligible capital property. Class 14.1 is a standard declining balance class subject to the half-year, recapture, and terminal loss rules for the other classes of that nature. Where a taxpayer carries on more than one separate business, there must be a separate Class 14.1 for each business. Note that incorporation costs are included in Class 14.1. However, only incorporation costs in excess of $3,000 are added to Class 14.1. The first $3,000 of incorporation costs are deductible.

[2] Regulation 1103(2h) provides that taxpayers may elect not to use Class 44 for such patents, in which case the property will be classified in Class 14.

ITA: 13(7)(g); Interpretation Bulletins: IT-206R Separate businesses

ITA: 20(1)(b) Incorporation expenses

A convenient alphabetical list of many depreciable assets can be found in an "Alphabetical List of Assets" in the preface materials and in the Topical Index to the Wolters Kluwer edition of the *Income Tax Act*, under the heading "capital cost allowance". However, the latter listing contains only property specifically itemized in the class descriptions. Hence, property referred to in more general terms in the class description may not appear in the list.

Approach

Steps to calculating the maximum capital cost allowance for a particular class or year

(1) Assess the Situation and Identify the Issue — Gather the following information:

(a) the opening undepreciated cost of capital for existing classes,

(b) determine if any depreciable assets have been purchased in the year, including:

(i) the type of depreciable asset,

(ii) the purchase price,

(iii) any costs incurred to get the assets available for use, including transportation, modification, etc., and

(iv) any inducement related to the asset purchased;

(c) determine if any depreciable assets have been disposed of in the year, including:

(i) the disposition proceeds, including any disposition costs,

(ii) the original cost of the property that was disposed, and

(iii) the CCA class the asset was included in when purchased.

(2) Analyze the Issue:

(a) Based on the information gathered, determine:

(i) the appropriate CCA class in which to add or remove the asset,

(ii) if there are any special rules related to that CCA class. (i.e., no recapture or terminal loss on Class 10.1 or no half-year rule for Class 14),

(iii) the correct CCA rate to apply to the pool;

(b) Calculate the maximum CCA as shown in Exhibit 5-2.

(3) Advise/Recommend:

(a) Assess your client's needs to determine the amount of CCA to claim. The range that may be claimed is zero to the maximum CCA calculated in Step 2. Consider:

(i) the level of business or property income in the current year, and

(ii) tax rates applicable in the year, versus future tax rates.

(b) Based on the maximum CCA determined in Step 2 and the client's needs, advise on the amount the client should claim for CCA in the year.

¶5,025 Rules for Calculating CCA

The basic rules of the capital cost allowance system are as follows:

Exhibit 5-2 Basic Rules of the Capital Cost Allowance System Applied to a Prescribed Class of Assets

Undepreciated capital cost of the class at the beginning of the year		$xxx
Add: purchases during the year		xxx
		$ xxx
Deduct: dispositions during the year at the lesser of (LOCP):		
(a) capital cost	$ xxx	
(b) proceeds of disposition	$ xxx	(xxx)
Undepreciated capital cost before adjustment		$ xxx
Deduct: ½ net amount[1]		(xxx)
Undepreciated capital cost before CCA		$ xxx
Deduct: capital cost allowance in the class for the year		(xxx)
Add: ½ net amount[1]		xxx
Undepreciated capital cost of the class at the beginning of the following year		$xxx

[1]Purchases during the year	$ xxx
Deduct: lesser of capital cost and proceeds of disposition above	(xxx)
Net amount (positive amounts only)	$ xxx

The calculation shown above in Exhibit 5-2, for many classes, can be restated as follows:

(1) In the year an asset of a particular class is purchased, the full purchase cost (capital cost) is added to the balance known as undepreciated capital cost (UCC) of the class of assets;

ITA: 13(21) undepreciated capital cost

(2) In the year an asset of a particular class is disposed of, the full proceeds of disposition, providing they do not exceed the original cost, are subtracted from the balance in the class of assets. This rule can be restated as the requirement to remove the lesser of capital cost and proceeds (LOCP), meaning the maximum amount removed from the pool is the original cost;[1] and

[1] Note that proceeds in excess of capital cost may give rise to a capital gain on disposition.

(3) At the end of the taxation year,

(a) if the balance in the class of assets (i.e., UCC) is positive and there are still assets in that class,

(i) subtract from the balance in the account ½ of the excess, if any, of purchases minus disposals made in the year (i.e., ½ × (a – b), above) — this is known as the half-year rule,

ITR: 1100(2) Property Acquired in the Year

(ii) deduct up to the maximum capital cost allowance (CCA) at the prescribed rate for the class on the positive balance, and

ITA: 20(1)(a) Capital cost of property

(iii) add back the ½ of the net amount subtracted in (A), above;

(b) if the balance in the class of assets is negative, take the negative balance into income as recaptured capital cost allowance and set the balance in the class at zero; and

ITA: 13(1) Recaptured depreciation

(c) if the balance in the class of assets is positive, but all of the assets in the class have been disposed of so there are no more assets in the class, take the positive balance, known as a terminal loss, as a deduction from income and set the balance in the class at zero.

ITA: 20(16) Terminal loss

¶5,025.10 Additions and the Half-Year Rule

Exhibit 5-3 indicates an adjustment for one-half of the net additions to the class in the year. This is known as the half-year rule and is set out in the Regulations under the heading "Property Acquired in the Year". The half-year rule is an attempt to deal with the deduction that is allowed in the year of acquisition. It was implemented to correct the fact that assets purchased later in the taxation year would otherwise be eligible for the maximum CCA during the year. The Act uses a simple, arbitrary adjustment of one-half of net additions (additions in excess of disposition) as an alternative to adjusting for the actual period of ownership in the year of acquisition or disposal.

Notice that no adjustments other than the half-year rule adjustment are made for the length of time in the year that an asset is owned. An asset purchased near the end of the year will normally increase the balance in the asset class, resulting in a one-half capital cost allowance claim for the year for that asset net of dispositions. On the other hand, an asset sold near the end of the year will normally reduce the balance in the asset class, resulting in a decrease in the amount subject to the capital cost allowance for the year.

The half-year rule applies to all classes except the following:

ITR: 1100(2) Property Acquired in the Year

(1) property described in the Regulations pertaining to certified vessels;

ITR: 1100(1)(v) Canadian vessels

(2) Class 12 paragraphs (*a*) to (*c*), (*e*) to (*i*), (*k*), (*l*) and (*p*) to (*s*) in Schedule II; and

(3) Classes 13, 14, 15, 23, 24, 27, 29, and 34 in Schedule II.

However, there are similar adjustments provided for some classes that have a similar effect to the half-year rule:

(1) property described as certified vessels in the Regulations;

ITR: 1100(1)(v)(iv)

(2) property of Class 13 in Schedule II (leasehold improvements); and

ITR: 1100(1)(b) Class 13 — [Leasehold interest]

(3) property of Classes 24, 27, 29, and 34 (some accelerated write-off classes) in Schedule II.

ITR: 1100(1)(t) Classes 24, 27, 29 and 34, 1100(1)(ta) [Classes 24, 27, 29 and 34]

It would appear that the only property for which some form of adjustment to reflect the half-year rule is not made is the following:

(1) property in Class 12 paragraphs (*a*) to (*c*), (*e*) to (*i*), (*k*), (*l*), and (*p*) to (*s*); and

(2) property in Classes 14 and 15.

Exhibit 5-3 Common Property Not Affected by the Half-Year Rule

Class	Paragraph	Property
12	(a)	a book that is a part of a lending library
	(b)	chinaware, cutlery or other tableware
	(c)	a kitchen utensil costing less than $500
	(e)	a medical or dental instrument costing less than $500
	(g)	linen
	(h)	a tool costing less than $500
	(i)	a uniform
	(k)	rental apparel or costume, including accessories
14		a patent, franchise, concession or licence for a limited period

Example Problem 5-2

Ferguson, a professional landscaper, operates an unincorporated yard maintenance business. He has been in business for five years. At the end of the prior year, the UCC in Class 10, containing two mowing tractors, was $3,000. This year, Ferguson purchased two more mowing tractors for a total cost of $6,800. Ferguson would like to maximize the CCA claimed in the current taxation year as his taxable income is estimated to be greater than $100,000.

REQUIRED

Calculate the maximum CCA claim this year and next year.

SOLUTION

Step 1 — Assess the Situation and Identify the Issue:

Gather all the necessary information related to the asset purchases in the year, the opening UCC and the CCA Rate.

- No disposals in the year
- Additions cost are $6,800 with no costs incurred to make the asset available for use

Step 2 — Analyze the Issue:

- Mowing tractors are included in Class 10 which has a CCA rate of 30%
- Class 10 is subject to the half-year rule for net additions

Calculate CCA:

UCC at the beginning of this year (given)	$3,000
Add: purchases during the year	6,800
	$9,800
Deduct: dispositions(LOCP)	Nil
UCC before adjustment	$9,800
Deduct: ½ ($6,800 – nil) (i.e., ½ (additions – disposals))	(3,400)
UCC before CCA	$6,400
Deduct: CCA @ 30% for Class 10	(1,920)
Add: ½ net amount	3,400
UCC at the beginning of the following year (end of the current year)	$7,880
Purchases net of dispositions @ LOCP in the year	Nil
UCC before CCA	$7,880
Deduct: CCA @ 30%	(2,364)
UCC at the beginning of the following year	$5,516

Step 3 — Advise/Recommend:

The maximum CCA that may be claimed in the current year is $1,920. Since Ferguson wants to minimize the overall taxes paid in the year, we recommend that he take the maximum available deduction of $1,920.

Non-Arm's Length Transactions and the Half Year Rule

The half-year rule does not apply to property acquired from a person not dealing at arm's length (see ¶6,110) with the acquirer if:

(1) the property was depreciable property of the transferor; and

(2) the property was owned continuously by the transferor from a day that was at least 365 days before the end of the taxation year of the acquirer in which the property was acquired.

This exception is very important when corporate reorganizations are undertaken among related corporations, since it allows the transfer of property between such corporations without the impediment of the half-year rule, except for property that was acquired less than 365 days before the end of the taxation year of the acquiring corporation.

¶5,025.20 Recapture and Terminal Loss

The concepts of recapture and terminal loss play an important role in the capital cost allowance system. The rates used for a specific pool of assets are prescribed, leaving little ability to deduct more even though the asset value may be used up over a shorter period of time. Conversely, based on those same rates, it is possible that the asset value may not be declining as quickly as the prescribed rates allow. The role of the recapture and terminal loss concept is to provide a catch-up mechanism for those discrepancies when an asset is sold. When an asset's value has not decreased in value as quickly as the CCA allowance claimed in previous years, an asset will have an overall higher residual value when sold. This will result in recapture of previously claimed CCA.

Example

Recapture

ABC corporation has an asset with the following tax values:

Capital cost	$10,000
Proceeds	8,000
Undepreciated capital cost	7,000

Based on this information, we can see that the corporation has claimed $3,000 ($10,000 – 7,000) in CCA in the previous years (assuming that it is the only asset to ever be included in that class). Since the proceeds of disposition are greater than the undepreciated capital cost of $7,000, we know that the asset has not decreased in value as quickly as allowed for by the prescribed CCA rate. In short, ABC's asset has been overdepreciated. The sale of this asset will trigger the catch-up mechanism in the form of recapture as follows:

Capital cost	$10,000	Reflects CCA claimed
Proceeds	8,000	Excess CCA claimed
Undepreciated capital cost	7,000	becomes recaptured

Overall, the corporation has deducted CCA of $3,000 in prior years. In the year of sale, the excess $1,000 in CCA claimed in the past, based on the value of the asset at sale, will be included in income. This serves to recapture a deduction that was previously claimed.

Conversely, when an asset's value has decreased in value at a greater rate than the prescribed CCA rate, the asset will have a lower residual value than its remaining undepreciated cost of capital. This may result in an additional deduction called a terminal loss. Since similar assets are pooled into one class, it is important to mention that a terminal loss cannot only occur when the last asset in the class is sold.

Example

Terminal loss

ABC corporation has an asset with the following tax values:

Capital cost	$10,000
Undepreciated capital cost	7,000
Proceeds	5,000

Based on this information, we can see that the corporation has claimed $3,000 ($10,000 – 7,000) in CCA in the previous years (assuming that it is the only asset to ever be included in that class). Since the proceeds of disposition are less than the undepreciated capital cost of $7,000, we know that the asset has decreased in value at a greater rate than allowed for by the prescribed CCA rate. In short, ABC's asset has been underdepreciated. Assuming this is the only asset in the pool, the sale of this asset will trigger the catch-up mechanism in the form of terminal as follows:

Capital cost................	$10,000	Reflects CCA claimed
Undepreciated capital cost.....	7,000	
Proceeds..................	5,000	Reflects additional deduction needed

Overall, the corporation has deducted CCA of $3,000 in prior years. In the year of sale, an additional deduction of $2,000 in the form of a terminal loss will be claimed. This brings the total deduction to $5,000 ($3,000 in CCA and $2,000 in terminal loss) which represents the actual decrease in value as a result of using this asset.

The rules for the calculation of recapture and terminal loss are illustrated below.

Figure 5-1

Dispositions of Depreciable Property

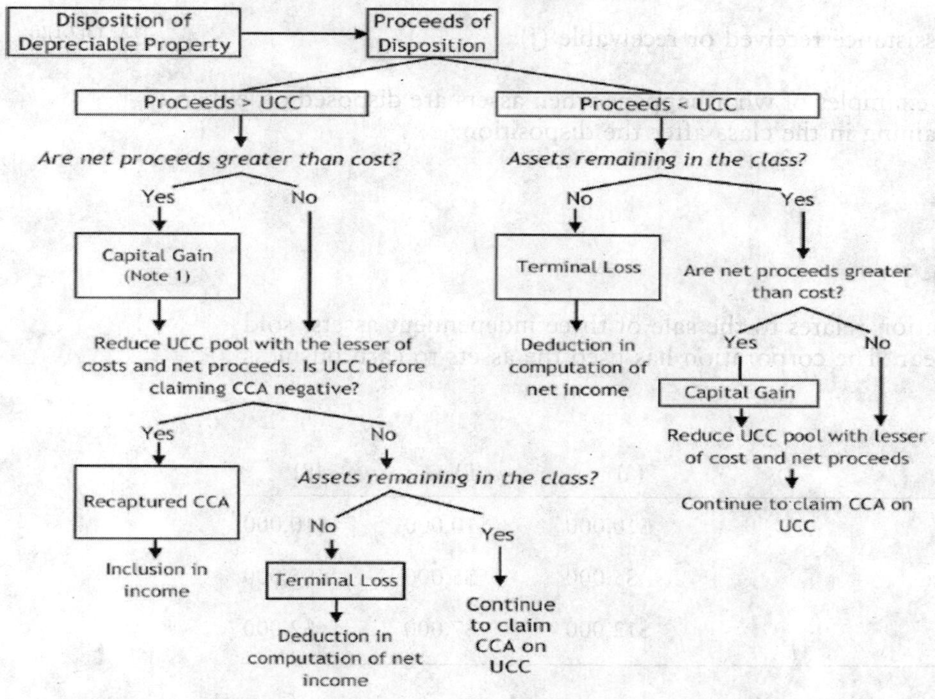

Note 1: The capital gain (net proceeds minus cost) arises only when proceeds exceed the capital cost of the property. The UCC is reduced by the lesser of cost and net proceeds.

The definition below paraphrases the Act's definition of undepreciated capital cost. The capital letters in brackets shown after each item below coincide with the letters in the algebraic formula in the Act definition. Some of the less mainstream items have been omitted.

ITA: 13(21) undepreciated capital cost

The sum of:

(a) the capital cost of depreciable property (A),

(b) all amounts previously included in income as recapture (B), and

(c) all amounts of grants and other assistance deemed to be capital cost that were repaid (C),

ITA: 13(7.1) Deemed capital cost of certain property

less the sum of:

ITA: 20(1)(a) Capital cost of property, 20(16) Terminal loss

(a) the total depreciation previously allowed (E),

(b) for dispositions, the lesser of (i) proceeds of disposition net of expenses of disposition and (ii) capital cost (F),

(c) all amounts of investment tax credit claimed (I) (see Chapters 11 and 12), and

ITA: 127(5) Investment tax credit, 127(6) Investment tax credit of cooperative corporation

(d) grants and other assistance received or receivable (J).

ITA: 13(7.1)(f)

See the problems below for examples of what happens when assets are disposed of, either with or without assets remaining in the class after the disposition.

Example Problem 5-3

The following information relates to the sale of three independent assets, sold by Dante Inc. in the year. The corporation has used the assets to earn business income in the past.

	(A)	(B)	(C)
Original cost	$10,000	$10,000	$10,000
Undepreciated capital cost	$5,000	$5,000	$5,000
Proceeds of disposition	$12,000	$7,000	$2,000

REQUIRED

What are the tax consequences if the asset is sold for its fair market value in each of these situations?

SOLUTION

Asset A

Step 1 — Assess the Situation and Identify the Issue: Gather the information related to the disposal of the asset:

i.	The disposition proceeds, including any disposition costs	$12,000
ii.	The original cost of the property that was disposed	10,000
iii.	The undepreciated capital cost	5,000

Step 2 — Analyze the Issue: Calculate the effects of the sale of the asset using the information gathered.

				CG		Recapture or Terminal Loss
Proceeds	$12	Capital Gain	Proceeds	$12	UCC	$5
Capital Cost	$10		Cost	(10)	LOCP	(10)
		Recapture	Capital Gain	$2	Recapture	($5)
UCC	$5					

Step 3 — Advise/Recommend: Since it is sold for more than its cost, the sale of this asset will result in two sources of income for Dante Inc. Dante will have a taxable capital gain of $1,000 (50% × $2,000) and recapture of $5,000 for a total of $6,000 in net income for tax purposes.

Notes:

The taxation of capital gains is covered in Chapter 7. Capital gains are included in net income for tax purposes at the current inclusion rate of 50%.

Asset B

Step 1 — Assess the Situation and Identify the Issue: Gather the information related to the disposal of the asset:

i.	The disposition proceeds, including any disposition costs	$ 7,000
ii.	The original cost of the property that was disposed	10,000
iii.	The undepreciated capital cost	5,000

Step 2 — Analyze the Issue: Calculate the effects of the sale of the asset using the information gathered.

Capital cost	$10			CG		Recapture or Terminal Loss
Proceeds	$7	Recapture	Proceeds		UCC	$5
UCC	$5		Cost		LOCP	(7)
			Capital Gain	NA	Recapture	($2)

Step 3 — Advise/Recommend: In this case, Dante's proceeds are between the UCC and original cost. Although proceeds are less than the original cost, there is no capital loss since any reduction in value is taken care of through the CCA system (Chapter 7). The lower of cost or proceeds ($7,000) will be credited to the class, resulting in a negative balance of $2,000. This will result in the recapture of the previous CCA claims of $2,000, which will be included in Dante's net income for tax purposes.

Asset C

In this case, we must consider if there are other assets in the pool. We will look at both scenarios.

(1) Assuming there are no other assets in the pool:

Step 1 — Assess the Situation and Identify the Issue: Gather the information related to the disposal of the asset:

i.	The disposition proceeds, including any disposition costs	$ 2,000
ii.	The original cost of the property that was disposed	10,000
iii.	The undepreciated capital cost	5,000
iv.	Additional information: this is the last asset in the pool	

Step 2 — Analyze the Issue: Calculate the effects of the sale of the asset using the information gathered.

Capital Cost	$10			CG		Recapture or Terminal Loss
UCC	$5	Terminal loss	Proceeds		UCC	$5
Proceeds	$2		Cost		LOCP	(2)
			Capital Gain	NA	Terminal loss	$3

Step 3 — Advise/Recommend: In this case, Dante's proceeds are lower than the UCC and are the last assets in the pool. Although proceeds are less than the original cost, there is no capital loss since any reduction in value is taken care of through the CCA system (Chapter 7). The lower of cost or proceeds ($2,000) will be credited to the class, resulting in a remaining balance of $3,000. This results in a terminal loss of $3,000, since not enough CCA was claimed to reflect the true decline in economic value of the asset.

(2) Assuming there are <u>other assets</u> in the pool:

Step 1 — Assess the Situation and Identify the Issue: Gather the information related to the disposal of the asset:

v.	The disposition proceeds, including any disposition costs	$ 2,000
vi.	The original cost of the property that was disposed	10,000
vii.	The undepreciated capital cost	5,000
viii.	Additional information: still at least one other asset in the pool.	

Step 2 — Analyze the Issue: Calculate the effects of the sale of the asset using the information gathered.

			CG			Recapture or Terminal Loss
Capital Cost	$10					
			Proceeds		UCC	$5
UCC	$5	Terminal loss	Cost		LOCP	(2)
			Capital Gain	NA	Remaining Balance	$3
Proceeds	$2					

Step 3 — Advise/Recommend: In this case, Dante's proceeds are lower than the UCC and are the last assets in the pool. Although proceeds are less than original cost, there is no capital loss since any reduction in value is taken care of through the CCA system (Chapter 7). The lower of cost or proceeds ($2,000) will be credited to the class, resulting in a remaining balance of $3,000. This will <u>NOT</u> result in a terminal loss; instead, CCA will be claimed on the remaining balance of $3,000, since there are remaining assets in the class.

¶5,030 Pause and Reflect — Summary of Learning Goals

After working through sections ¶5,010 to ¶5,025, you should be able to:

- explain the similarities and differences between the accounting and tax deductions as they relate to depreciable assets;
- apply your knowledge to determine the correct capital cost class in which to place a depreciable asset;
- explain how the capital cost allowance system works to provide a tax deduction, including that a business:
  - may deduct CCA up to the maximum allowed for a specific class in the year, and
  - must pool similar assets in a specified class, with the exception of a few assets such as luxury automobiles and electronic office equipment;
- explain the tax implications of the disposition of depreciable assets on the taxable income in the year;

- explain the purpose of the recapture of capital cost and terminal loss system for depreciable assets;
- explain the effects of the half-year rule on the calculation of capital cost in the year of acquisition;
- apply your knowledge to correctly calculate the maximum capital cost allowance a business may claim in a year, based on the specific facts in the case. A calculation would include the correct application of the:
  - net additions in the year, which comprises additions less disposals and the half-year rule,
  - removal of the lower of cost or proceeds from the CCA pool when an depreciable asset is disposed of, and
  - CCA rate to the end of year undepreciated cost of capital.

¶5,030.99 Practise What You've Learned

Refer to the following sections of the Study Guide to practise what you've learned:

¶5,800 — Review Questions

- Question 1 — Year of acquisition
- Question 2 — Terminal loss
- Question 3 — Cost amount
- Question 4 — Capital cost amount
- Question 5 — Half year rule
- Question 6 — Half year rule
- Question 7 — Property title
- Question 12 — Patent
- Question 13 — Intangible asset
- Question 14 — Intangible asset sale

¶5,825 — Multiple Choice Questions

- Question 3 — Intangible Assets
- Question 5 — CCA
- Question 6 — Patent options

¶5,850 — Exercises

- Exercise 1 — Choice of CCA Class
- Exercise 4 — CCA schedule

¶5,045 Special Rules

¶5,045.10 Taxation Year Less Than 12 Months

There is no need to prorate capital cost allowance (other than through the half-year rule adjustment) for the period in a taxation year that an asset was owned by the taxpayer. This applies to full 12-month taxation years. However, when a taxation year is less than 12 months, capital cost allowance must be prorated by the proportion of 365 to the number of days in the taxation year. A short taxation year may occur, for example, in the first or last years of the operation of an incorporated business or in a year in which there has been a change in the fiscal year. In this case, this proration of CCA will pertain mostly to corporations for which the taxation year is defined to be the fiscal period. The taxation year of an individual is a calendar year. However, the business income earned by a sole proprietor is still determined by the fiscal year. If the fiscal period of the business income of a sole proprietor is shorter than 12 months, the CCA will need to be prorated.

ITR: 1100(3) Taxation Years Less Than 12 Months

The proration only pertains to a short taxation year. It is completely independent of the half-year rule adjustment that must be made, where applicable, irrespective of the length of the taxation year. It is possible that in a short taxation year, the CCA of a newly acquired asset would be subject to the half-year rule and be prorated for the number of days in the taxation year.

Exceptions to CCA Proration

A common exception to this short-year proration rule is Class 14, which includes limited-life patents, franchises, licences, etc. Class 14 already has a mechanism in the formula to account for a short-taxation year. As will be seen later in this chapter, there is a proration of capital cost allowance for assets in Class 14 based on the number of days the asset is owned in a taxation year. Therefore, the effect is quite similar to the short-year proration rule.

ITA: 249(1) Definition of "taxation year"; ITR: 1100(3) Taxation Years Less Than 12 Months; Interpretation Bulletins: IT-522R Vehicle, Travel and Sales Expenses of Employees

An employee does not have to prorate the capital cost allowance on his or her automobile in the first year of use of an existing car for employment purposes, although the half-year rule applies to the purchase of a new automobile.

Where depreciable capital property is used by an individual to produce income from a source that is property (e.g., rental income), the full calendar year is considered to be the taxation year of the individual and no prorating is necessary, regardless of when the capital property was purchased in the year.

Example Problem 5-4

Nadia began her advertising business, Ads R Us Ltd. on March 1 of this year. The corporation's year end is December 31. In this year, the first year of business, the corporation purchased furniture (Class 8) for $3,000 and a computer and systems software (Class 50) for $4,200.

REQUIRED

Calculate the maximum CCA that Ads R Us Ltd. can claim in the first year of business.

SOLUTION

	Class 8	Class 50
	20%	55%
UCC at the beginning of this year	Nil	Nil
Add: purchases during the year	$3,000	$4,200
	$3,000	$4,200
Deduct: disposition (LOCP)	Nil	Nil
UCC before adjustment	$3,000	$4,200
Deduct: 1/2 (additions – disposals)	(1,500)	(2,100)
UCC before CCA	$1,500	$2,100
Deduct CCA × 306/365 days in the year	(252)	(968)
Add: 1/2 net amount	1,500	2,100
UCC at the beginning of the following year	$2,748	$3,232

¶5,045.20 Ownership of Property

Generally, in order to be eligible for capital cost allowance on depreciable property, the taxpayer must have either the title to the asset or all the incidents of title such as possession, use and risk. An exception is Class 13 leasehold improvements that are made by the tenant, but the owner of the building has title to the improvements.

In some circumstances, a taxpayer does not always have ownership or a leasehold interest (Class 13) in a capital asset for which they have incurred a cost. In this situation, capital cost allowance (CCA) may not be claimed for the expenditure. This was the situation in *Saskatoon Community Broadcasting Co. Ltd. v. M.N.R.*, in which the appellant incurred costs to construct a new broadcasting gondola in an arena and was given the sole right to use the new gondola. The facility was the property of the arena company. The construction costs were held to be a non-deductible capital outlay, and the broadcasting company could not take capital cost allowance because it did not own the property and it did not have a leasehold interest in the facility. Under the tax legislation in force now, this type of expenditure would be added to class 14.1 as an intangible asset with a 5% rate of CCA.

Income Tax Folio: S3-F4-C1 General Discussion of Capital Cost Allowance; Cases: *Saskatoon Community Broadcasting Co. Ltd. v. Minister of National Revenue*, 58 DTC 491 (TAB)

¶5,045.30 Disposition of Property

A disposition of property is defined to include "any transaction or event entitling a taxpayer to proceeds of disposition of the property". The use of the word "include" in the definition does not limit the meaning of disposition of property to a situation where there are proceeds of disposition.

ITA: 248(1) disposition

The CRA gives examples of events it considers to be dispositions without any actual proceeds, including cases of property that are stolen, destroyed, confiscated, or expropriated without any compensation or property that is lost or abandoned without expectation of recovery. In the case of *The Queen v. Compagnie Immobilière BCN Limitée*, the Supreme Court of Canada indicated that a claim for capital cost allowance could not be made in lieu of a terminal loss deduction when a building no longer existed. Capital cost allowance can only be claimed when property in a class continues to exist. This follows from the operation of the system in which no claim can be made for capital cost allowance on an asset in the year of its disposition.

Interpretation Bulletins: IT-460 Dispositions — Absence of Consideration; Cases: *Her Majesty the Queen v. Compagnie Immobilière BCN Limitée*, 79 DTC 5068 (SCC)

Example Problem 5-5

Portable Tools Rental Limited incorporated and commenced business on April 1, 2013 and has a December 31 year end. The company rents portable tools for short terms and the following are its transactions:

		Portable Tools **Class 10: 30%**
2013	100 tools purchased at various times during the year for $950 each	$95,000
2014	20 tools purchased in June for $1,000 each	20,000
2016	30 tools (well-maintained) sold in November for $1,000 each	30,000
2018	50 tools sold in February for $700 each	35,000

REQUIRED

Prepare a schedule showing the effects of these transactions on Class 10 and on the income of the company for the period of years indicated. (Ignore the leap-year effects.)

SOLUTION

Step 1 — Assess the situation: gather the information related to the Class 10 capital asset purchases and disposal for the years 2013, 2014, 2016, and 2018. See above for this.

Step 2 — Identify the Issues: Determine the nature and timing of the income (recapture) or deductions (CCA) arising from the transactions in capital assets.

Step 3 — Analyze the issue: Calculate the effects of the purchase and disposition of the assets on Class 10 using the information gathered above.

		Portable Tools Class 10: 30%
2013	Additions: 100 tools purchased for $950 each	$95,000
	UCC at the end of 2013 before adjustment	$95,000
	Less: ½ of net amount during the year	(47,500)
	UCC before CCA	$47,500
	CCA claimed @ 30%; prorated, because of short first year, for 275 days ($47,500 × 0.3 × 275/365)	(10,736)
	Add: ½ of net amount during the year	47,500
	UCC at the beginning of 2014	$84,264
2014	Additions: 20 tools purchased for $1,000 each	20,000
	UCC at the end of 2014 before adjustment	$104,264
	Less: ½ of net amount during the year	(10,000)
	UCC before CCA	$94,264
	CCA claimed @ 30% ($94,264 × 0.3)	(28,279)
	Add: ½ of net amount during the year	10,000
	UCC at the beginning of 2015	$75,985
2015	No additions or dispositions	
	CCA claimed @ 30% ($75,985 × 0.3)	(22,796)
	UCC at the beginning of 2016	$53,189
2016	Disposals: 30 tools sold for $1,000 each (cost: $950 each; $1,500 total capital gain)	(28,500)
	UCC before CCA	$24,689
	CCA claimed @ 30% ($24,689 × 0.3)	(7,407)
	UCC at the beginning of 2017	$17,282
2017	No additions or dispositions	
	CCA claimed @ 30% ($17,282 × 0.3)	(5,185)

		Portable Tools Class 10: 30%
	UCC at the beginning of 2018	$12,097
2018	Disposals: 50 tools sold for $700 each (cost: $950 each; no capital loss on depreciable property)	(35,000)
	UCC at the end of 2018	$(22,903)
	Recapture of CCA taken into income	22,903
	UCC at the beginning of 2019	Nil

Step 4 — Advise/Recommend: Based on the calculations above Portable Tools Rental Inc. will have the results on their income for the 6 years noted:

	2013	2014	2015	2016	2017	2018
CCA Deduction	(10,736)	(28,279)	(22,796)	(7,407)	(5,185)	Nil
Recapture	—	—	—	—	—	22,903

¶5,045.40 Automobiles Used in Employment or Business

Class 10.1 Automobiles

Recall from Chapter 3 that employees who use their own automobiles to earn employment income and who are entitled to a deduction:

- for sales/negotiating person's expenses, ITA: 8(1)(f) Sales expenses
- for travel expenses (other than motor vehicle expenses), or ITA: 8(1)(h) Travel expenses
- for motor vehicle expenses, ITA: 8(1)(h.1) Motor vehicle travel expenses

are entitled to deduct capital cost allowance (CCA) on the automobiles. ITA: 8(1)(j) Motor vehicle and aircraft costs

Where an automobile is used to earn employment or business income, capital cost allowance on the automobile is deductible up to the prescribed limit, currently $30,000. When an automobile's capital cost is greater than the prescribed limit, it must be placed in Class 10.1, which has special rules related to CCA.

In either case, the capital cost used as the basis for capital cost allowance is limited to the lower of the actual cost paid and a prescribed amount, plus federal sales tax (i.e., GST) and provincial sales tax (PST) or harmonized sales tax (HST). This limitation applies to all taxpayers, whether employed or self-employed, incorporated or unincorporated.

In the case where a taxpayer is an HST registrant, the GST/HST paid on the automobile, up to the prescribed limit, is applied to offset the HST collected. As a result, the HST is excluded from the class since the taxpayer has no effective HST cost to add to capital cost.

ITA: 248(16) Goods and services tax — input tax credit and rebate

There are three additional rules relating to CCA for a Class 10.1 asset that must be considered:

(1) No Recapture or Terminal Loss: No recapture of CCA or terminal loss will apply in the year of disposition.

(2) Separate Class 10.1 for each automobile: Since no recapture or terminal loss will be claimed in the year of disposition, each automobile having a cost in excess of $30,000 plus HST (if applicable) must be placed in a separate Class 10.1 and not pooled.

(3) CCA in year of disposition: Since the terminal loss or recapture rules do not apply to automobiles in Class 10.1, a special capital cost allowance calculation applies in the year of disposition. One-half of the capital cost allowance that would have been allowed in respect of the automobile, had it not been disposed of, may be deducted. To qualify for this special "half-year rule", the taxpayer must have disposed of an automobile that was included in Class 10.1 and was owned by them at the end of the preceding year.

Class 10 Automobiles

For automobiles included in Class 10 because they cost less than the prescribed limit (currently $30,000) we must look at the type of taxpayer, employee, or anyone other than an employee, for the treatment.

Employees would be required to include in their employment income the amount of capital cost allowance claimed subject to recapture for the automobiles they own. On the other hand, a terminal loss on the disposition of the automobile is not a specifically allowed deduction from employment income. There is no provision in Section 8 that allows a deduction of a terminal loss that may occur on the disposition of an employee-owned automobile. Since a terminal loss is not specifically allowed as a deduction from employment income, the Act prohibits its deduction.

When an automobile costs less than the prescribed limit and is owned by a taxpayer other than an employee, the usual rules for deducting capital cost allowance, subject to the half-year rule, including recapture or deducting a terminal loss apply. These usual rules would apply to an automobile used in a business by and owned by, for example, a proprietor, a partner, or a corporation.

¶5,045.50 Separate Class Rule for Electronic Office Equipment

Taxpayers may elect to place one or more specified properties that would ordinarily be classified in Class 8 in a separate class. The specified properties are:

ITR: 1101(5p) Rapidly Depreciating Electronic Equipment

(a) computer software, presumably systems software for electronic process control or monitor equipment and electronic communications control equipment, normally classified in Class 8 (i.e., not classified in another class);

(b) a photocopier, normally included in Class 8 assets; and

(c) office equipment that is electronic communications equipment, such as a facsimile transmission device or telephone equipment, normally included in Class 8 assets.

Property placed in separate classes in this manner must have a capital cost of at least $1,000.

The election allows one or more such properties to be placed in a separate Class 8 asset. The advantage of the separate class would be the availability of a terminal loss deduction when all of the assets in the class are sold for less than the UCC of that class. If assets of this nature decline in value faster than the CCA rates of 20% for Class 8 imply, perhaps due to technological obsolescence, then a terminal loss on disposition is likely if these assets are separated from other Class 8 assets.

A special transfer rule requires the transfer of Class 8 assets of a separate class back to their main Class 8 asset after four taxation years. This means that if the assets in a separate class have not been disposed before the fifth year since their acquisition (i.e., still owned in year five), the remaining UCC must be transfer to a pooled Class 8 asset and the potential terminal loss deduction in the separate class will no longer be available.

ITR: 1103(2g) Transfers to Class 8, Class 10 or Class 43

The separate class election is extended to manufacturing and processing property included in Class 43 assets costing more than $1,000. The election must be filed with the income tax return for the taxation year in which the property is acquired. After five years, any remaining UCC in each separate class must be transferred into the general Class 43 UCC pool.

ITR: 1101(5s) Manufacturing or Processing Property, 1101(5q) Rapidly Depreciating Electronic Equipment, 1103(2g) Transfers to Class 8, Class 10 or Class 43

¶5,045.60 Transfer to Another Class — Avoiding Recapture

The government will often make classification changes to effect a change in the percentage rate of CCA allowed. For example, at one time, frame buildings were a Class 6 asset with a 10% CCA allowed. Then these were reclassified in Class 3 (the class for brick buildings) with only 5% CCA allowed. Later, both brick and frame buildings were included in Class 1, which has a basic 4% CCA rate. However, only newly acquired buildings were put in the reclassified prescribed class. Buildings that were already in Class 3 or 6 stayed in that class.

ITR: 1103(2d) Elections to Make Certain Transfers

Suppose that a business is replacing a building that has been depreciated through Class 3. In this circumstance, it is possible that the business could end up with a recapture of CCA if the disposition proceeds were greater than the UCC. Normally, because similar assets are pooled together, the capital cost of the new building would eliminate any negative UCC, but in this case the new building would go into Class 1, not Class 3. In this situation, the Act provides relief. The UCC of the old property in the existing Class 3 may be transferred to the newly acquired Class 1 immediately before the disposition. This will allow a recapture of CCA in the old Class 3 to be wholly or partially avoided.

ITR: 1103(2d) Elections to Make Certain Transfers

Such a transfer satisfies the principle of fairness, as the taxpayer has no control over the class categorization of assets. The taxpayer should not bear taxes simply because the government has revised the applicable class.

¶5,045.70 Interest Expense

Most profitable businesses are looking to minimize their income for tax purposes and generally prefer to deduct interest expense as it is incured. In some cases, taxpayers may not need deductions, such as where their income is minimal and/or they have losses being carried forward. Non-capital loss carryforwards expire if not used within 20 years. These taxpayers might prefer to defer some deductions.

ITA: 20(1)(c) Interest

The Act allows taxpayers to elect to capitalize certain interest expenses rather than claim them as deductions when incurred. Only interest incurred in respect to the acquisition of depreciable property is eligible for this election. By making the election, the interest is added to the capital cost of the acquired depreciable property instead of being claimed as a current-year deduction. The interest-inclusive capital cost is the amount on which CCA is claimed. A taxpayer may make this election if there is insufficient taxable income to use the interest deduction. This provides a useful way of deferring the deduction to future years as capital cost allowance. If in a taxation year, the taxpayer ceases to add the borrowing costs to the capital cost of the depreciable property, the election will not be available for this depreciable property in subsequent years. A similar election exists for interest incurred in connection with many natural resource exploration and development properties.

ITA: 21(1) Cost of borrowed money, 21(2) Borrowed money used for exploration or development

Where a taxpayer is involved in construction, renovation, or alterations of buildings, interest and other expenditures must be capitalized until the building is completed or "all or substantially all" of the property is used for its intended purpose. Any interest captured by this provision is ineligible for the above discussed election, as it must be capitalized.

ITA: 18(3.1) Costs relating to construction of building or ownership of land

¶5,045.80 Capital Cost Reduction for Cost Assistance

When a grant, subsidy, forgivable loan, deduction from tax, investment allowance, or other assistance is received on the acquisition of property, the amount of the assistance received reduces the capital cost of depreciable property, so that CCA is claimed only on the net cost of the asset.

ITA: 13(7.1) Deemed capital cost of certain property

Investment tax credits (ITCs) (see Chapter 11) are a form of subsidy from the government. An ITC reduces the capital cost of depreciable property. Since these investment tax credits are difficult to compute until tax payable is determined, the credit reduces the UCC in the year following the taxation year in which it is claimed. As well, any GST input tax credit received during the year will reduce the UCC amount before CCA is determined.

¶5,045.90 Inducement Payments

The capital cost of a depreciable capital property may also be reduced when a taxpayer receives an inducement payment, in respect of the cost of the property, that would otherwise be taxable. To be entitled to a capital cost reduction instead of being subject to an inclusion in income, the taxpayer must make an election to this effect no later than the date on which they are required to file an income tax return for the taxation year when the taxpayer received the inducement payment, or for the subsequent year if the property was acquired during that subsequent year.

ITA: 12(1)(x) Inducement, reimbursement, etc., 13(7.4) Deemed capital cost

The amount chosen as a capital cost reduction cannot exceed the least of the following amounts:

- the amount received as an inducement payment;
- the capital cost of the property; or
- zero, if the property was disposed of before the year during which the reduction could be sought.

¶5,045.95 Pause and Reflect — Summary of Learning Goals

After working through this section, ¶5,045, you should be able to:

- Explain the tax implications of a short fiscal year end when calculating the capital cost allowance.

- Explain the special rules related to electronic office equipment and the tax implications of owning the electronic office equipment for a period longer than 4 years.
- Explain the effects of cost assistance on the capital cost of depreciable property.
- Explain the tax choices on the treatment of inducement payments.
- Apply your knowledge of the special tax rules to advise taxpayers on the tax implications of the purchase and sale of depreciable property.

¶5,045.99 Practise What You've Learned

Refer to the following sections of the Study Guide to practise what you've learned:

¶5,800 — Review Questions

- Question 9 — Short fiscal period
- Question 10 — CCA in year of disposal

¶5,825 — Multiple Choice Questions

- Question 1 — Luxury vehicle CCA

¶5,850 — Exercises

- Exercise 2 — Luxury automobile CCA
- Exercise 3 — Sale of luxury automobile
- Exercise 8 — Personal CCA on automobile
- Exercise 9 — Sale of intangible capital property
- Exercise 10 — Purchase and Sale of intangible capital property
- Exercise 11 — Purchase and sale of goodwill

¶5,055 Exceptions to the Declining Balance Method

¶5,055.10 Leasehold Improvements

Not all classes of assets use a declining balance method to compute capital cost allowance. Special treatment is accorded to a leasehold interest. The capital cost allowance that may be claimed for a leasehold interest (Class 13) after the first year of ownership is the lesser of:

ITR: 1100(1)(b) Class 13 — [Leasehold interest], Sch.III

(i) ⅕ of the capital cost of the leasehold interest; and

(ii) the capital cost of the leasehold interest divided by the number of 12-month periods from the beginning of the taxation year in which the cost was incurred to the end of the term of the lease plus the first renewal term (i.e., the number of months in the remainder of the lease term plus one renewal option divided by 12). The divisor is not to exceed a total of 40 such 12-month periods.

The first year write-off would be ½ of the above amount to provide the equivalent of the half-year rule.

Example

A $16,000 leasehold improvement is made on a rented building on which the taxpayer has a lease for five years with two successive options to renew of three years and two years. The CCA for a year other than the first year would be calculated as the lesser of:

(1)	1/5 of the capital cost (1/5 × $16,000)	$ 3,200
(2)	Capital cost divided by the number of 12-month periods from the beginning of the taxation year in which the cost was incurred to the end of the term of the lease plus the first renewal term not to exceed 40 years $16,000 / (5 + 3)	2,000

$1,000 capital cost allowance would be taken in the first year, $2,000 in each of the next seven years and the remaining $1,000 in the ninth year.

By using one renewal option in the formula, it is assumed that at least one renewal option will be exercised. If an option to renew is not exercised, then there may be a terminal loss at the end of the lease, if there are no other leasehold interests being amortized on other leases. All leasehold improvements are included into one Class 13 pool for all of the taxpayer's leasehold interests on all leased properties used in a particular source of income.

The formula for Class 13 implies that leasehold improvements must be written off over a minimum of 5 years, unless the lease is not renewed and the taxpayer does not hold any other leasehold improvements.

¶5,055.20 Class 14 Limited-Life Intangibles

A patent or a right to use patented information for a limited or unlimited period is considered a Class 44 asset, with a 25% declining balance rate. There is an exception that allows a taxpayer to elect that such property not be included in Class 44. Under this election, patents for a limited period would be classified in Class 14. This election might be used when the patent is purchased late in its legal life, such that the straight-line capital cost allowance of Class 14 would exceed the 25% declining balance capital cost allowance of Class 44.

ITR: 1103(2h) Elections Not to Include Properties in Class 44

Straight-line capital cost allowance is also used for items in Class 14, which generally includes limited-life intangibles such as patents, franchises, concessions, or licences. For this class, the capital cost of each property in the class is divided by the remaining legal life, at the acquisition date, of the property to obtain the amount of capital cost allowance for the year. Note that the legal life of a patent is 20 years. An Interpretation Bulletin indicates the CRA's view is that the capital cost should be prorated over the number of days in the remaining life of the Class 14 asset. This is one of the classes not affected by the half-year rule.

Interpretation Bulletins: IT-477 (Consolidated) Capital cost allowance — Patents, franchises, concessions and licences

A taxpayer must classify property that is a patent or a right to use patented information for a limited or unlimited period in Class 44 with a 25% declining balance rate. However, a taxpayer can elect that such property not be included in Class 44. Under this election, patents for a limited period would be classified in Class 14. This election might be used when the patent is purchased late in its legal life, such that the straight-line capital cost allowance of Class 14 would exceed the 25% declining balance capital cost allowance of Class 44.

¶5,055.30 Insurance Proceeds Expended on Damaged Depreciable Property

Any part of insurance proceeds payable for damaged depreciable property that was spent on repairing the damage within the year or within a reasonable time after the damage must be included in income. The amount included will be offset by the amount deducted as an expense of repairing the property so that there will be no net effect on the taxpayer's income. If any part of the insurance proceeds is not expended in this manner, the unused portion will be treated as proceeds of disposition of depreciable property and will be treated according to the basic rules for proceeds.

ITA: 12(1)(f) Insurance proceeds expended, 13(21) proceeds of disposition (f)

Example Problem 5-6

Wally's is a department store operating in the area. In May 2016, a fire virtually destroyed the building. The only asset that was recovered was an F.A.D. computer, and it was substantially damaged. The computer had been purchased by Wally's in December 2015 at a cost of $75,000 and as a Class 50 asset it had been depreciated at a rate of 55% since 2015.

In August 2016, under an insurance policy with the Risk-Averters Insurance Company, Wally's received $25,000 for the damage to the computer. Wally's had the computer repaired to its original condition in 2016 at a cost of $23,000.

REQUIRED

Trace the effects of these events on the balance of the undepreciated capital cost accounts for the computer from 2015 through to the beginning balance for 2018 in the computer account. As you trace the effects, indicate all deductions from and inclusions in income from the business for the years indicated. Assume that the appropriate election is made.

SOLUTION

Computer – Class 50: 55%

2015	Additions: computer	$75,000
	UCC at the end of 2015	$75,000
	Half-year rule adjustment	(37,500)
		37,500

	CCA claimed @ 55%	(20,635)
	Half-year rule adjustment	37,500
	UCC at the beginning of 2016	$54,375
2016[1]	Disposals: proceeds of disposition in the amount of unexpended insurance proceeds	(2,000)
	UCC at the end of 2016	$52,375
	CCA claimed @ 55%	(28,806)
	UCC at the beginning of 2017	$23,569
2017	No additions or disposals	
	CCA claimed at 55%	(12,963)
	UCC at the beginning of 2018	$10,606

[1] In 2016, income would be increased by insurance proceeds received of $25,000, but this amount would be offset by the deduction of repair expense of $23,000. Thus, the net effect on income is nil, which is as it should be. The other $2,000 received is a capital receipt that reduces undepreciated capital cost.

¶5,055.90 Pause and Reflect — Summary of Learning Goals

After working through this section, ¶5,055, you should be able to:

- apply your knowledge to assess which depreciable assets are included in CCA classes that are exceptions to the declining balance rule, such as Classes 13 and 14;
- explain the rules related to the deduction of leasehold improvements, along with the circumstances that may result in the non-deductibility of leasehold improvements;
- apply your knowledge to calculate the tax implications of insurance proceeds expended on damaged depreciable property; and
- apply your knowledge of the special rules relating to the exceptions to declining balance and advise taxpayers on the tax implications of the purchase or disposal of these exceptions.

¶5,055.99 Practise What You've Learned

Refer to the following sections of the Study Guide to practise what you've learned:

¶5,825 — Multiple Choice Questions

- Question 2 — Leasehold improvements
- Question 4 — Leasehold improvements

¶5,850 — Exercises

- Exercise 4 — CCA schedule
- Exercise 5 — Rental property CCA
- Exercise 6 — CCA calculations
- Exercise 7 — CCA schedule
- Exercise 8 — Personal CCA on automobile
- Exercise 12 — CCA calculations

¶5,065 Advanced Rules Related to the Depreciable Property

¶5,065.10 Change in Use and Part Disposition Rules

Rules are set out for the determination of capital cost and proceeds of disposition in the following five situations: ITA: 13(7) Rules applicable

- change from income-producing to other purpose;
- change from non-income-producing to income-producing purpose;
- property acquired for multiple purposes;
- change in proportion of use for producing income and other purposes; and
- non-arm's length transfer of depreciable property.

Change from Income-producing to other Purpose

In this case, property is acquired for producing income, but its use changes to another purpose. Consider the situation where a taxpayer had a house that they rented and later lived in themselves. At the time of the change in use, the taxpayer is deemed to have disposed of a depreciable asset at its fair market value. This deemed disposition may result in either recapture or a terminal loss. The deemed reacquisition at fair market value establishes the cost of the asset for personal use. The problem of determining fair market value without a transaction gives rise to cases in which the value of a house relative to the value of the land on which it is situated is at issue. ITA: 13(7)(a)

Change in Non-income-producing to Income-producing Purpose

In this situation, property is acquired for a non-income producing purpose, but its use then changes to producing income. Consider the case if the first situation were reversed. At the time of the change in use, the taxpayer is deemed to acquire a depreciable asset at its fair market value where that value is less than its cost, representing a decline in value.

But where the fair market value of the asset is greater than its cost, representing an increase in value, the capital cost of the asset for CCA purposes will, generally[2], be limited to the lesser of:

(i) the fair market value of the property at the time of the change in use			xxx
(ii) the total of			
(A) cost at the time of the change in use		xxx	
(B) the fair market value of the property at the time of the change in use	xxx		
less: cost at the time of change in use	xxx		
excess, if any	xxx		
½ of excess	–	xxx	xxx

As a result of this latter rule, the capital cost of the asset for the purposes of computing capital cost allowance is limited to the sum of two components. That sum comprises the actual cost of the asset before the change in use plus the amount, if any, of taxable capital gain resulting from the deemed disposition on the change in use. Therefore, there can be no step-up in the capital cost to fair market value, because the step-up in capital cost is limited to ½ of the gain from actual cost up to fair market value.[3]

The capital cost of the asset for CCA purposes after the change in use and the application of the limited step-up will reflect an amount that has been fully tax paid by the owner. Since the taxpayer will pay tax on only ½ of the capital gain, only ½ of the gain may be added to the original cost. The rationale for this limitation is that the stepped-up capital cost will provide the base for future CCA that is fully deductible from business or property income. A taxpayer should only expect to fully deduct a cost that was fully tax paid.

ITR: 1100(2.2) Property Acquired in the Year, 1100(2.2)(f)

The half-year rule to reduce first-year capital cost allowance would appear to apply because the conditions that provide exceptions to this rule for property of a class in Schedule II are not met. In particular, the condition that the property, subject to the change in use to income-producing purposes, would not have been depreciable property at the time of the change in use if its previous use was non-income-producing is not met. It makes some sense to impose the half-year rule at the change in use to income-producing purposes, because the half-year rule would usually not have been applied on acquisition for the previous non-income-producing purpose. Note that a change in use from income-producing purpose to non-income-producing purpose should not be affected by the half-year rule, because the property would not be depreciable property if its purpose is not income-producing.

---

[2] The actual formula in paragraph 13(7)(*b*) provides for an adjustment in respect of the capital gains deduction. Such a deduction is only available for qualified farm property that might be subject to a change in use. As a result, the adjustment will not be common.

[3] For a more detailed discussion of paragraphs 13(7)(*b*), (*d*), and (*e*), see Robert E. Beam and Stanley N. Laiken, "Changes in Use and Non-Arm's Length Transfer of Depreciable Property", *Canadian Tax Journal*, Vol. 35, No. 2, March–April 1987, p. 453.

ⓐ ¶5,065.20 Property Acquired for Multiple Purposes

In this case, property is acquired both for producing income and for another purpose. For example, consider the situation where a taxpayer buys a duplex and lives in one half, renting the other half. At the time of the purchase, half of the cost of the building is allocated to depreciable assets of the taxpayer. On the sale of the property, half of the proceeds are regarded as proceeds of the depreciable asset. ITA: 13(7)(c)

ⓐ ¶5,065.30 Franchises and Similar Property

Class 14 includes certain property that is a patent, franchise, concession, or licence for a limited period. The cost of such property is expensed under the capital cost allowance system by taking the straight-line capital cost allowance over the remaining legal life of the property. Note in particular that this property must have a limited life. The amounts that can be considered as the capital cost of a patent were at issue in *Weinberger v. M.N.R.* The Court held that not only the amount paid to have the invention patented but also the costs to produce and perfect the invention to the point where the patent can be obtained are considered to be the capital cost of the patent. Cases: *Weinberger v. Minister of National Revenue*, 64 DTC 5060 (EC)

If the cost of a patent is added to Class 14 because the taxpayer has elected that the property not be included in Class 44, it will be eligible for capital cost allowance on a straight-line basis over its remaining legal life of 20 years. However, the CRA suggests that expenditures incurred in making any representation for the purpose of obtaining a franchise or a patent (among others) to a government or public body relating to a business of the taxpayer would be deductible immediately. In lieu of an immediate deduction, the taxpayer may elect in a prescribed manner to deduct one-tenth of the amount otherwise eligible for deduction in each of the 10 consecutive years beginning with the year in which the expenditure is made. Three possibilities for dealing with expenses of representation may be available: ITR: 1103(2h) Elections Not to Include Properties in Class 44; ITA: 20(1)(cc) Expenses of representation; Interpretation Bulletins: IT-99R5 Legal and Accounting Fees

(1) an immediate deduction of the cost; ITA: 20(9) Application of para. (1)(cc), 20(1)(cc) Expenses of representation

(2) a deduction of the cost over a 10-year period; and

(3) capitalization of the cost in the appropriate CCA class (14 or 44) (see below).

Any amount deducted immediately or over 10 years is subject to recapture. ITA: 13(12) Application of para. 20(1)(cc)

Certain property, such as franchises, may have an indefinite life in contrast to a limited life (Class 14). If this is the case, the property is classified in Class 14.1 with its declining balance rate of 5%.

ⓐ ¶5,065.40 Non-Arm's Length Transfer of Depreciable Property

The context for these rules is discussed in more detail in Chapter 7, under the ¶7,210 heading of "Transactions With Non-Arm's Length Individuals", and in Chapter 16, under the ¶16,125 heading of "Depreciable Property". They apply where depreciable property is transferred between persons not dealing at arm's length, which is also discussed in Chapter 6. Income Tax Folio: S1-F5-C1 Related Persons and Dealing at Arm's Length; ITA: 13(7)(e)

These rules prevent the realization of benefits from a transfer when an increase in value over cost is taxable to the transferor as a capital gain (i.e., half taxable), but would be fully depreciable from fair market value at the time of the transfer to the transferee if it were not for these rules. The adjustment to the capital cost of property transferred to the non-arm's length transferee is similar to the calculation presented for a change in use of property, ITA: 13(7)(b), 13(7)(e), 251 Arm's length

where only cost plus the taxable capital gain to the transferor can be depreciated by the transferee.

Were it not for this provision, the individual could obtain an increase in UCC that would be fully deductible in the hands of the child without paying tax on half of the capital gain because capital gains are only half taxable.

Example

Consider the case of an individual who sells a depreciable property with the following tax features to a child:

Fair market value	$10,000
Capital cost	8,000
UCC	3,000

The $8,000 of the original capital cost represents a tax-paid cost that the individual has a right to recover tax free through CCA claims or a possible terminal loss on disposition. CCA claims and a terminal loss are fully deductible. The CCA system allows for the deduction as a proxy for the decline in value of the asset.

Sale to an unrelated person

If the asset were sold to a non-related arm's length party the result would be as follows:

Proceeds of disposition	$10,000	UCC	$3,000
Capital cost	8,000	LOCP	(8,000)
Capital Gain	2,000	UCC	(5,000)
Taxable Capital Gain	1,000	Recapture	5,000

The purchaser would have a cost base of $10,000 on the depreciable property. The seller would have total income of $6,000 ($5,000 in recapture and $1,000 taxable capital gain) on the sale of the property. The parties are unrelated so there was no motivation to increase the tax base for this asset.

Sale to a non-arm's length person – a child

In this case, when the asset is transferred to a non-arm's length person, if it were not for this provision the result above would benefit the related parties as it would allow the increase in value for depreciation purposes without fully taxing the increase in value. The child, a related person, has acquired the depreciable asset from the parent. The results for the parent are the same as the situation where the parent sells to an unrelated person. The parent will have total income of $6,000 ($5,000 in recapture and $1,000 taxable capital gain) on the sale of the property.

Unlike the example above, the capital cost for the child will be adjusted from the actual cost of $10,000. The cost base for capital cost purposes would be equal to

Original capital cost before the transfer	$8,000
Plus ½ of the capital gain	1,000
Capital cost for UCC purposes	$9,000

ITA: 13(7)(e)

Were it not for this provision, the individual could obtain an increase in UCC that would be fully deductible in the hands of the child without paying tax half of the capital gain because capital gains are only half taxable.

¶5,065.90 Pause and Reflect — Summary of Learning Goals

After working through this section, ¶5,065, you should be able to:

- explain the tax implications of a change in use related to a depreciable property, including the determination of the capital cost for UCC purposes;
- apply your knowledge to a change in use circumstance to advise a taxpayer on the tax implications in various scenarios;
- apply your knowledge to advise the client on the tax implications of asset purchases and disposal and provide recommendations and planning suggestions on how to minimize overall taxes payable, including specific circumstances such as:
  - a situation where there is a change in use related to a depreciable property, including the determination of the capital cost for UCC purposes;
- explain the rules related to the transfer of a depreciable asset to a non-arm's length individual, including the tax effects on the transferor as well as the deemed capital cost to the transferee.

CHAPTER 6

Income From Property

ADVANCED CONTENT IN THIS CHAPTER

Learning Goals

Know, Understand and Explain

By the end of this chapter you will know, understand and be able to explain:

- The basic provisions of the *Income Tax Act* (the Act) that relate to property income and attribution rules.
- The rules relating to the inclusion of interest income for corporations, trusts and individuals.
- The difference between eligible and ineligible dividends and its effects on the taxation of an individual.
- The distinction between property and business income.
- The purpose of integration and how it affects the overall tax paid on income earned in a corporation.

Review Questions
¶6,800 in the Study Guide

Multiple Choice Questions
¶6,825 in the Study Guide

Exercises
¶6,850 in the Study Guide

Apply

By the end of this chapter you will be able to apply your knowledge and understanding to:

- Correctly determine the amount of interest and dividends that must be included in income.
- Correctly determine the eligible expenses that may be deducted against property income.
- Advise taxpayers on the tax implications of a non-arm's length transaction as it relates to income splitting.
- Advise taxpayers on tax planning techniques to maximize deductions and minimize overall tax.

Assignment Problems
¶6,875 in the Study Guide

Overview

Income for tax purposes (Division B income) is calculated by determining income from each source separately. We have already dealt with two sources of income before this chapter: employment income and business income. Both business income and property income are determined by Subdivision b of Division B in Part I of the Act. Although most of the rules dealing with these two sources of income are similar, it is important to notice that there are some significant differences. Since some sources of income are treated more generously than others for tax purposes, such as partial inclusion in income (even exemptions from income) for tax purposes, generous deductions, or lower tax rates, taxpayers will naturally try to characterize their income to a source which will give better tax treatments. Various anti-avoidance rules are introduced to prevent abusive planning.

ITA: 3 Income for taxation year

The characterization of property income and business income is a question of fact. In general, investors earn income from property with a relatively passive approach. For example, when an individual invests in bonds, he or she can earn interest income without doing much work. This gives rise to property income. On the other hand, if an individual actively trades bonds in the capital market on a consistent basis (i.e., daily), the interest income may be classified as business income since the individual is working regularly to earn the income. In general, business income requires more activities in a process that combines time, effort, and capital investment.

Note

Income or loss from property does not include capital gains or capital losses. This exclusion is important when considering the deductibility of an expenditure that depends on producing income from property. Capital gains and losses are dealt with in Chapters 7 and 8, as there are special rules related to this type of investment.

The following chart provides an overview of the location of most of these provisions.

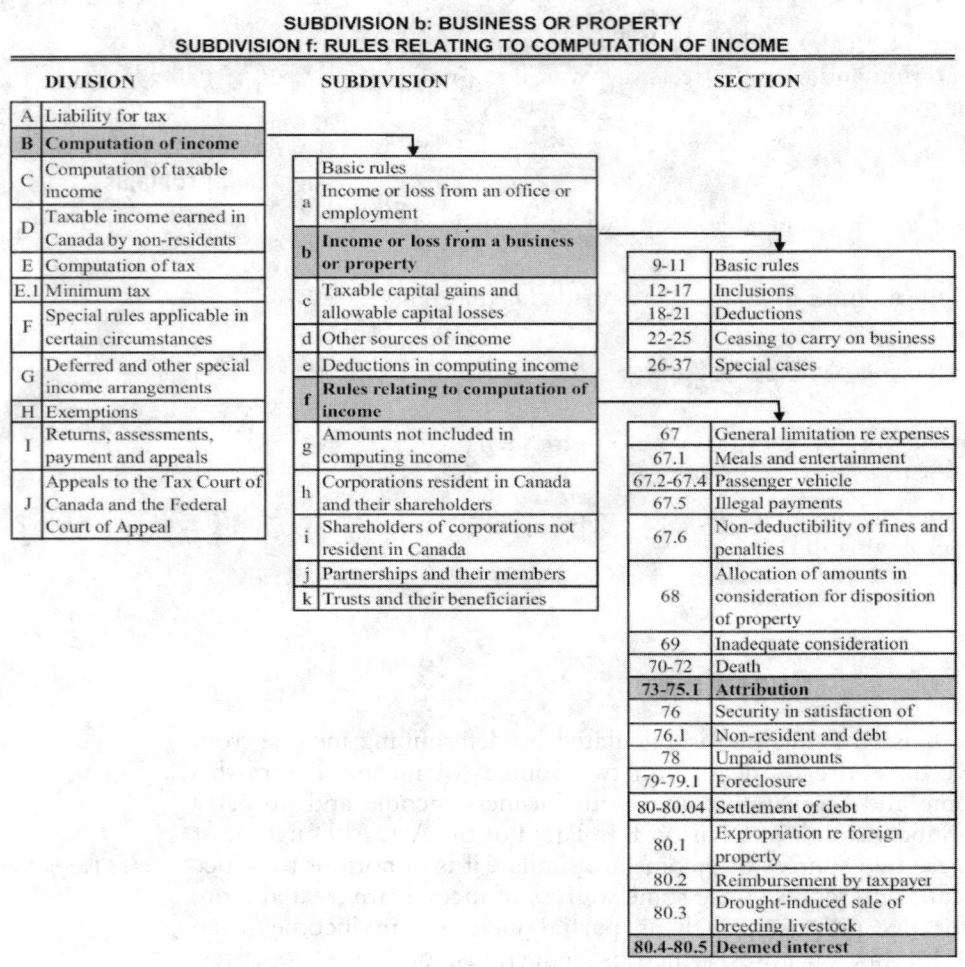

PART I — DIVISION B

SUBDIVISION b: BUSINESS OR PROPERTY
SUBDIVISION f: RULES RELATING TO COMPUTATION OF INCOME

DIVISION

A	Liability for tax
B	**Computation of income**
C	Computation of taxable income
D	Taxable income earned in Canada by non-residents
E	Computation of tax
E.1	Minimum tax
F	Special rules applicable in certain circumstances
G	Deferred and other special income arrangements
H	Exemptions
I	Returns, assessments, payment and appeals
J	Appeals to the Tax Court of Canada and the Federal Court of Appeal

SUBDIVISION

a	Basic rules Income or loss from an office or employment
b	**Income or loss from a business or property**
c	Taxable capital gains and allowable capital losses
d	Other sources of income
e	Deductions in computing income
f	**Rules relating to computation of income**
g	Amounts not included in computing income
h	Corporations resident in Canada and their shareholders
i	Shareholders of corporations not resident in Canada
j	Partnerships and their members
k	Trusts and their beneficiaries

SECTION

9-11	Basic rules
12-17	Inclusions
18-21	Deductions
22-25	Ceasing to carry on business
26-37	Special cases

67	General limitation re expenses
67.1	Meals and entertainment
67.2-67.4	Passenger vehicle
67.5	Illegal payments
67.6	Non-deductibility of fines and penalties
68	Allocation of amounts in consideration for disposition of property
69	Inadequate consideration
70-72	Death
73-75.1	**Attribution**
76	Security in satisfaction of
76.1	Non-resident and debt
78	Unpaid amounts
79-79.1	Foreclosure
80-80.04	Settlement of debt
80.1	Expropriation re foreign property
80.2	Reimbursement by taxpayer
80.3	Drought-induced sale of breeding livestock
80.4-80.5	**Deemed interest**

Subdivision b of Division B of Part I of the Act contains the primary rules for the computation of income from property. Like the rules for business income discussed in Chapter 4, most of what will be covered will be found in sections 9 through 21.

The more common provisions are discussed in this chapter and are as follows:

Inclusions

- Income (loss) for a taxation year from a property is the profit (loss) from that property for the year (ITA: Sec. 9)
- Income inclusions (ITA: Sec. 12)
- Rules related to capital cost allowance (ITA: Sec. 13)
- Rules for shareholder benefits (discussed in Chapter 13) (ITA: Sec. 15)

Deductions

- Limitations on the deductibility of expenses (ITA: Sec. 18)
- Deductions permitted (ITA: Sec. 20)

In addition, Subdivision f of Division B also provides some rules that are relevant to the computation of property income. For example, the attribution rules determine who is to report the property income received by a particular person (discussed later in this chapter). As well, there is a deemed interest benefit to be reported by individuals who received a loan by virtue of their shareholding (discussed in Chapter 13).

ITA: 74.1 [Transfers and loans to spouse or common-law partner or minor], 74.5 Transfers for fair market consideration; 15 Benefit conferred on shareholder, 80.4 Loans

¶6,000 Inclusions

Overview

The Act requires a taxpayer to include the following returns on investments in the calculation of income from a property:

ITA: 12(1) Income inclusions

- interest income from savings, deposits, loans, bonds, and debentures;
- dividends from shares; and
- income based on the production or use of property.

The Act identifies specific property income inclusions to ensure that individuals recognize all sources of property income. Although taxpayers receive information slips (T3s, T5s, T600s) from the investee for some property income, other property income, such as rental income, is reported in an income statement format. Ultimately, it is the taxpayers' responsibility to record all investment income, whether or not an information slip is received.

After working through section ¶6,000 of the chapter, you will be able to:

- explain the meaning of interest and the different methods that must be used to determine the amount of interest income for a particular taxation year;
- explain the timing of the inclusion of interest income as it relates to special circumstances such as discounted bonds, treasury bills, zero coupon bonds and bonds sold with accrued interest;
- apply your knowledge to determine when the receipt of income is based on production or use and the tax implications of the classification;
- explain the purpose of the dividend gross-up and the dividend tax credit system;
- explain the difference in the tax implication of receiving various forms of dividends;
- apply your knowledge to correctly calculate the amount of interest income that a taxpayer must include in a particular taxation year; and

- apply your knowledge to correctly calculate the tax implications of receiving various forms of dividends.

¶6,005 Interest Income

¶6,005.10 The Meaning of Interest

The term "interest" is not defined in the Act. The Supreme Court of Canada has defined interest to be "the return or consideration or compensation for the use or retention by one person of a sum of money, belonging to, in a colloquial sense, or owed to, another." This definition has been adopted by the Canada Revenue Agency ("CRA").

Cases: *Re: Farm Security Act, [1947]S.C.R. 394*, aff'd [1949] A.C. 110; Interpretation Bulletins: IT-396R Interest Income

In many situations it is often unclear whether an amount paid or payable is in the nature of interest or, as in the case of a discount on a bond, is something else. In order to clarify the issue and prevent taxpayers from converting amounts from interest to capital, provisions have been legislated in the Act and the Regulations deeming amounts to be interest and requiring them to be brought into income at specified intervals.

¶6,005.20 Method of Reporting Income

In effect, the primary method for computing interest on a "debt obligation" is an annual accrual method. The Act requires the use of this method for corporations, partnerships, certain trusts, and individuals. The term "debt obligation" is not defined in the Act, although the term is used in the definition of an "investment contract". The CRA indicates that "the term 'debt obligation' is considered to include, for example, bank accounts, term deposits, guaranteed investment certificates, mortgages, corporate bonds and loans".

ITA: 12(1)(c) Interest, 12(3) Interest income, 12(4) Interest from investment contract, 12(11)(a); Interpretation Bulletins: IT-396R Interest Income

The Act uses the words "received" or "receivable". This indicates that the taxpayer has a choice between using at least two bases of accounting for interest income — the cash basis and the receivable basis. However, consideration must be given to the annual accrual rules, which modify the requirements. Under the cash method, interest is recognized as income only when actually received. Under the receivable method, interest is considered income when the amount has become legally due and payment is enforceable.

ITA: 12(1)(c) Interest; 12(3) Interest income, 12(4) Interest from investment contract

Example

Assume a bond had an interest payment scheduled for December 15 but the payment was delayed and not paid/received until January.

Cash Method: The interest would be income in January.

Accrual Method: The interest would be income at December 15.

The Act requires that the method for a particular category of interest-earning instrument be consistently followed.

The annual accrual method appears to be required for most common sources of interest income. However, when interest is received, it must be included in income to the extent that the interest has not been included previously by the accrual method. This indicates that taxpayers are required to use the earlier of the cash method and an annual accrual method. As a result, it is not possible to defer the recognition of compounding interest by

ITA: 12(1)(c) Interest

using the cash method to report that interest only when it is received. Given that the interest may have to be included in income earlier than the actual receipt of the cash, there may be a disadvantage to a compounding-interest debt security. The interest income may create a tax payable in a year when no cash payment of interest is actually received.

Approach

Steps to calculating the interest income for a particular taxation year

(1) Assess the Situation and Identify the Issues — Gather the following information:

(a) What type of taxpayer owns the interest earning instrument (i.e., individual, corporation or trust)?

(b) What are the characteristics of the interest earning instrument (i.e., interest rate, maturity date, cash payment of interest)?

(c) Other information specific to the scenario.

(2) Analyze the Issue:

(a) Based on the information gathered, determine the options available under the current tax legislation to record the interest income (i.e., accrual, cash or annual accrual).

(b) Calculate the interest income to be included in net income for tax purposes in the year(s) specified. Consider the compounding interest that is reinvested in your calculation.

(3) Conclude and Advise:

(a) Advise the client on the implications of including non-cash interest in net income for tax purposes. Consider the cash flow implications of accruing interest.

¶6,005.30 Accrual Rules for Individuals

The Act requires that individual taxpayers holding an interest in an investment contract include in net income for tax purposes any interest accrued up to the anniversary date, to the extent that it has not previously been included in income. While individuals are allowed to use either the cash or receivable basis, this choice is tempered by the Act, which imposes a modified or annual accrual basis on these taxpayers. An individual must include in income any interest accrued up to each annual anniversary date of the investment contract.

ITA: 12(4) Interest from investment contract, 12(11)(b); 12(1)(c) Interest

This indicates that individuals must include interest income in net income for tax purposes the earlier of (a) the date the interest is paid, and (b) the anniversary date of the contract.

- An "investment contract" is defined as any debt obligation, other than a salary deferral arrangement, various types of income-based debt, certain government-sponsored debt for small businesses, or prescribed contracts (of which there are none at the present).

ITA: 12(11)(a)

- An "anniversary day" is defined as the day that is one year after the day before the date of issue and every successive one year interval, unless the contract is disposed of before such a day. For example, if an investment is issued on March 30, 2017, the anniversary day will be March 29, 2018, and every subsequent year until disposed of.

Example Problem 6-1

Kelly purchased a $1,000 face value bond on January 2, 2018, for $1,000. The bond was issued on the same date. Interest is payable at 4% compounded semi-annually on uncashed coupons on each of June 30 and December 31 at the investor's option.

REQUIRED

Assume Kelly does not exercise her option to receive any cash interest before maturity, when would she first have to include an amount in income?

SOLUTION

Step 1 — Assess the Situation and Identify the Issues: Gather the facts for the scenario

(1) What type of taxpayer owns the interest earning instrument? An individual.

(2) What are the characteristics of the interest earning instrument?

- Interest rate: 4%
- Maturity Date: .... 5 years
- Cash payment: .... At option of investor

(3) Other information: Investor has chosen to not exercise their option to receive the interest; therefore, no cash is received until maturity.

Step 2 — Analyze the Issue:

(1) Based on the information gathered, determine the options available under the current tax legislation to record the interest income. As this is an individual, there are two options: the cash or the annual accrual.

(2) Calculate the interest income to be included in net income for tax purposes in the year(s) specified:

2018: As an individual, Kelly must include the interest income on the earlier of the cash received and the annual accrual.

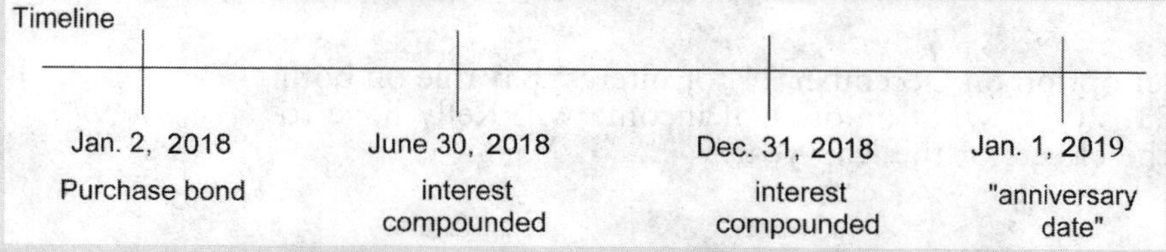

ITA: 12(4) Interest from investment contract, 12(11) Definitions

2018:

1.	Cash received in 2018	zero
2.	Anniversary date in 2018	None

As an individual, Kelly will not include any interest income since there has been no cash received nor has there been an anniversary date.

2019:

1.	Cash received in 2019	zero
2.	Anniversary date in 2019	
	$\$1,000 \times 4\% \times {}^{180}/_{365}$	\$19.73
	$(\$1,000 + 19.73) \times 4\% \times {}^{184}/_{365}$	20.56
	$(\$1,000 + 19.73 + 20.56) \times 4\% \times {}^{1}/_{365}$	0.11
	Total interest	40.40

As an individual, Kelly must include the interest income on the earlier of the cash received and the annual accrual.

Step 3 — Conclude and Advise: Kelly will be required to include interest income of \$40.40 in her 2019 taxation year. Since she has chosen to not receive any cash until maturity, she will have to pay tax on \$40.40 which will create a cash outflow with no offsetting cash inflow.

ITA: 12(1)(c) Interest, 12(4) Interest from investment contract

Example Problem 6-2

Kelly purchased a \$1,000 face value bond on January 2, 2018, for \$1,000. The bond was issued on the same date. Interest is payable at 4% compounded semi-annually on uncashed coupons on each of June 30 and December 31 at the investor's option.

REQUIRED

Assume Kelly exercised her option on December 31 for interest payable on both June 30 and December 31, 2018. What amount of income will Kelly have to include in 2018. Ignore the effects of the leap year.

SOLUTION

Step 1 — Assess the situation and Identify the Issues: Gather the facts for the scenario

(1) What type of taxpayer owns the interest earning instrument? An individual.

(2) What are the characteristics of the interest earning instrument?

- Interest rate: 4%
- Maturity Date: .... 5 years
- Cash payment: .... At option of investor

(3) Other information: Investor has chosen to exercise their option to receive the cash interest for June and December on December 31, 2018.

Step 2 — Analyze the issue:

- Based on the information gathered, determine the options available under the current tax legislation to record the interest income. Since this is an individual, there are two options — the cash or the annual accrual.
- Calculate the interest income to be included in net income for tax purposes in the year(s) specified:

2018: As an individual, Kelly must include the interest income on the earlier of the cash received and the annual accrual.

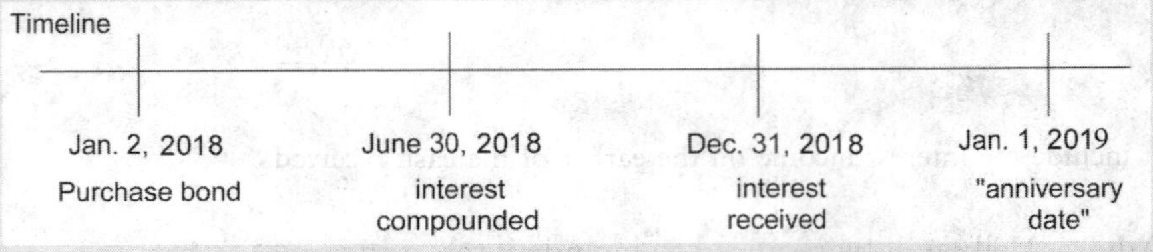

Cash received in 2018:

January 2 to June 30 — \$1000 × 4% × $^{180}/_{365}$	\$19.73
July 1 to December 31 — (\$1,000 + 19.73) × 4% × $^{184}/_{365}$	20.56
Total Cash received in 2018	\$40.29

Step 3 — Conclude and Advise:

Kelly will have to include \$40.29 in interest income even though there is no anniversary date in 2018. Kelly chose to exercise the option to receive cash interest on December 31, 2018 and as a result she must include the income in 2018 rather than in 2019 on the first anniversary date.

¶6,005.40 Accrual Rules for Taxpayers Other Than Individuals

The Act requires that corporations, partnerships and certain trusts use the accrual method of accounting for interest income (excluding interest on some types of debt). The two other bases, cash or annual accrual methods, are not available to these taxpayers.

Example Problem 6-3

Kelsey Corporation purchased a $1,000 face value bond on January 15, 2018, for $1,000. The corporation has a December 31 year end. The bond was issued on the same date, January 15, 2018. Interest is payable at 4% compounded semi-annually on uncashed coupons on each of June 30 and December 31 at the investor's option. The bond matures in five years.

REQUIRED

If Kelsey Corporation does not exercise the option to receive any cash interest until maturity, what amount of interest would the corporation include in its net income for tax purposes for the taxation years 2018 and 2019? Ignore the effects of the leap year.

SOLUTION

Step 1 — Assess the Situation and Identify the Issues: Gather the facts for the scenario

(1) What type of taxpayer owns the interest earning instrument? A corporation.

(2) What are the characteristics of the interest earning instrument?

- Interest rate: 4%
- Maturity Date: .... 5 years
- Cash payment: .... At option of investor

(3) Other information: Investor has chosen to not exercise its option to receive the interest; therefore, no cash is received until Maturity.

Step 2 — Analyze the Issue:

(1) Based on the information gathered, determine the options available under the current tax legislation to record the interest income.

As this is a corporation, the only option is the accrual method.

(2) Calculate the interest income to be included in net income for tax purposes in the year(s) specified:

Taxation year	Interest income	
December 31, 2018	$\$1,000 \times 4\% \times {}^{166}/_{365}$	$18.19
	$(\$1,000 + 18.19) \times 4\% \times {}^{184}/_{365}$	20.53
	Total interest in 2018	$38.72
December 31, 2019	$(\$1,000 + 38.72) \times 4\% \times {}^{181}/_{365}$	$20.60
	$(\$1,038.72 + 20.60) \times 4\% \times {}^{184}/_{365}$	21.36
	Total interest in 2019	$41.96

Step 3 — Conclude and Advise

This taxpayer is a corporation, and therefore must use the accrual method. The corporation will have to include interest income of $38.72 in their 2018 net income for tax purposes and $41.96 in their 2019 net income for tax purposes. Since no cash interest has been received, the corporation will have a cash outflow equal to the taxes owing without any cash inflow from the investment. The corporation should consider exercising the option to receive some cash on June 30 and December 31 to help offset the taxes owing.

¶6,005.50 Other Interest Income Provisions

Interest and principal may be blended by making a loan at a discount but redeemable at par, or made at par but repayable at a premium. When a loan has a blended payment, the question is whether the discount or premium is interest income or capital gain. The treatment of the payment is important because interest income is included in a taxpayer's income at a 100% inclusion rate, while capital gains receive special treatment, currently only including any gain at an inclusion rate of 50%. The treatment of the income results in a different tax liability.

A number of factors must be considered to determine whether the discount or premium is interest or a capital gain. These factors include the amount determined by the terms of the loan agreement and the price at which the property is sold.

It is important to note that there is not necessarily an interest component in all payments of this nature. A taxpayer need not charge interest in such a transaction. If the property is sold at fair market value, no interest component in the payments will be assumed. On the other hand, an interest inclusion provision will apply to the sale of property if the contractual price, in total, exceeds the fair market value of the property.[1]

ITA: 16(1) Income and capital combined

Interest on a scholarship trust fund is not taxable to a parent or grandparent who establishes the fund under the registered education savings plan (RESP) legislation. This provision, which is discussed in more detail in Chapter 9, shelters the accumulated interest such that no tax is paid on it until it is paid out for the benefit of the child. At that time, if it arises, the interest is considered to be the income of the recipient child.

ITA: 146.1 [Registered education savings plans]

[1] This was the situation in the case of *Groulx v. M.N.R.*, 67 DTC 5284 (S.C.C.).

The current rules relating to interest income are summarized as follows:

Summary of Interest Income Reporting

(1) Corporations, partnerships, and trusts ITA: 12(3) Interest income

- Accrual method of accounting

(2) Individuals is the earlier of: ITA: 12(4) Interest from investment contract, 12(11) Definitions

- annual accrual based on the anniversary date of an investment contract; and
- cash interest received.

Note: Remember that the accrual rules applicable to an individual do not apply if the interest was received prior to the anniversary date, since the interest must then be reported under the general rules. Thus, the accrual rules do not apply with respect to investment contracts of a duration of less than one year and investment contracts that provide for the payment of interest at intervals of a year or less. ITA: 12(1)(c) Interest

Example

Claudette purchased a $10,000, 4%, five-year GIC (guaranteed income certificate) from her bank on February 2, 2017. All the interest will be paid to her at the end of the five years. Claudette will not report any interest income from this GIC in 2017. This is because:

- no amount has been received;
- no amount is receivable;
- she is not subject to the accrual method as she is not a corporation, partnership, or trust; and
- the anniversary date did not fall in 2017.

For the 2018 taxation year, Claudette must report the interest that has accrued to the February 1, 2018 anniversary date. That would be $10,000 × 4% = $400.

In the 2019 taxation year, Claudette will report the interest accrued to the second anniversary date of February 1, 2019. That would be $10,400 × 4% = $416. As the above example shows, some deferral is available to individual taxpayers where the interest is paid on an annual or greater period, if the timing of the investment acquisition is early in the year.

¶6,010 Purchasing a Corporate Bond at a Discount

¶6,010.10 Investor's Position

As discussed earlier, we must consider whether the discount is considered interest income or capital in nature. A corporate debenture may be purchased today, at a discount, for $790, but will be repayable at its face value of $1,000. The debenture pays annual interest of 7% of $1,000 or $70 per year. Should the discount be considered interest or a capital item? Is interest income equal to the annual amount received ($70) or should it include the discount of $210 on the purchase of the bond; or should it be the effective interest rate?

From an economic perspective, the discount is usually set by the marketplace to compensate for an investor's desire for a higher rate of interest. The investor may want compensation for the increased inherent risk of the investment, or the prevailing market rate of interest may be higher than the stated interest rate on the bond. In theory, the discount that compensates for the higher market rate of interest should be considered interest income for tax purposes.

The Act requires that, if a payment can be regarded in part as interest and in part as capital, the interest portion should be included in income to the extent the amount is paid or payable. According to the CRA, a blended payment exists when the content of income and capital is not ascertainable. In this situation, it is very difficult to assess which part is interest.

ITA: 16(1)(a), 16(1)(b)

When an interest-bearing bond is purchased at a price that reflects the fair market value, the CRA accepts the view that subsection 16(1) would not apply and any discount or premium represents a capital portion. Therefore, if a bond is sold at a discount to account for a difference between the stated interest rate on the bond and the prevailing market rate of interest, one can argue that the bond was sold at fair market value and the discount will be treated a capital item, rather than as interest income.

¶6,010.20 Issuer's Position

The legislation deals with potentially abusive situations. For example, a corporation could issue a bond at a deep discount to raise the effective interest rate on the bond and, hence, increase the amount of deductible interest to the corporation. The Act addresses this situation by defining and providing separate rules for a "deep" discount versus a "shallow" discount.

ITA: 20(1)(f) Discount on certain obligations

When a deep discount exists, only 50% of the discount can be deducted as if it were interest expense. A deep discount exists when:

(1) the obligation is issued at a discount greater than 3%, or

(2) the yield rate on the debt obligation exceeds the nominal rate by more than one-third.

Example

A taxable corporation issues a bond with a face value of $1,000 and an annual coupon rate of 7% at a price of $970. The bond matures in five years. The nominal rate of interest 7% and the effective rate of interest 7.75%.

Since the yield is not greater than 4/3 of the nominal rate and the original discount did not exceed 3%, this is considered a shallow discount. The entire discount is deductible by the issuing corporation on payment at maturity or when paid, if earlier. It would have taken failure of only one of the two tests to invoke the 50% deduction rule.

Example

Another taxable corporation issues a bond with a face value of $1,000 and a coupon rate of 5% at a price of $920. The bond matures in five years. The nominal rate of interest 5% and the effective rate of interest 6.95%.

Since the yield is greater than 4/3 of the nominal rate and the discount exceeded 3%, this is considered a deep discount. Only 50% of the discount can be deducted by the issuing corporation on payment at maturity or when paid, if earlier. Again, only one of the two tests need have failed to invoke this result.

¶6,015 Treasury Bills

Treasury bills are always purchased at a discount. At maturity, the investor receives the face value of the treasury bill. The amount of the discount represents, in substance, a payment for interest; therefore, the discount is included in income to the extent the amount was received or became receivable.

ITA: 12(1)(c) Interest, 16(1) Income and capital combined

Example

On December 1, Henri Ltd. (December 31 year end) purchased $9,886 worth of 90-day T-bills. The treasury bills mature at $10,000 on March 1. In the year of purchase and year of maturity, Henri Ltd.'s income will include the following:

Ignoring the effects of the leap year and assuming the T-bills are not cashed in early, the difference between the price paid and the maturity value of the T-bill represents interest income. Since the Act requires that interest of a corporation be accrued at year end, interest is computed using the treasury bill rate and prorating the interest based on days outstanding.

ITA: 12(3) Interest income

Year 1 interest income ($10,000-$9,886) × 31/90 = $39.27

Year 2 interest income ($10,000-$9,886) × 59/90 = $74.73

¶6,020 Zero Coupon Bonds

Zero coupon bonds, or strip bonds sold without coupons, are long-term bonds with interest paid as part of the redemption proceeds at the date of maturity. No cash is received prior to maturity date. For tax purposes, the Regulations dealing with prescribed debt obligations indicate that the difference between the cost of the bond and the maturity value represents the present value of the accumulated interest income (compounded on an annual basis for a Type I bond).

ITR: 7000 Prescribed Debt Obligations

Example

Assume that a strip bond is purchased today for $1,500 and will mature at $10,000 in 20 years. In other words, the taxpayer receives $8,500 in compound interest, but the amount is not receivable until year 20. The taxpayer will include the following interest income in Year 1 and Year 2:

For tax purposes, the Regulations require that the accrued interest portion be calculated and recognized in each taxation year. The annual accrued interest should be based on the investment's yields to maturity. Note that the yield (i) is the same each year. However, since the compound interest portion is added to the bond amount, more accrued interest is earned each year.

ITR: 7000(1)(a)

Computation of yield: $\$1{,}500 = \$10{,}000/(1 + i)^{20}$

$i = 9.95\%$

Interest in Year 1	= $1,500 × 9.95%
	= $149.25
Interest in Year 2	= ($1,500 + 149.25) × 9.95%
	= $164.10

This type of investment works well in a self-directed RRSP, or in a deferred-income fund, because the accrued interest is not taxed until the funds are ultimately withdrawn. In contrast, if the strip bonds are held outside a deferred-income fund, tax is payable each year on the calculated accrued interest. This could create a cash-flow burden because no annual cash interest is received to offset the taxes owing on the accrued interest.

Other situations are addressed in the Regulations, such as debt instruments with rates of interest changing depending on some future event (such as early disposition). The legislative intent of this regulation is to remove taxpayer bias towards certain investments and discourage tax-motivated purchases and dispositions of investments. The law is fairly strict and requires that interest be accrued based on the maximum interest potentially payable.

ITR: 7000 Prescribed Debt Obligations

¶6,025 Purchasing an Accrued Interest Bond

Most corporate and other bonds and debentures are traded securities, just like shares, and can be acquired/sold through an investment dealer. When these are traded at a date other than the specified interest date, interest will have accrued on the bond. When a debt obligation is transferred on a date other than the date of payment of interest, the purchaser must reimburse the seller for the accrued interest not yet received from the issuer. The Act stipulates how the interest income is to be divided between the transferor (seller) and transferee (purchaser):

ITA: 20(14) Accrued bond interest

- The transferor must include interest accrued up to the date of the transfer. The amount included in income is excluded from the proceeds of the debt obligation.
- The transferee must include interest from the date of the transfer.

The seller will receive total proceeds equal to the value of the debt obligation plus the accrued interest. In the year received, the seller will include the interest received as part of the sale in net income.

Conversely, the buyer has paid for the accrued interest as part of the purchase price. The cash interest the buyer will receive in the future will include this accrued interest. Since the accrued interest, to the date of the sale, has been included in the seller's net income, the buyer should not be taxed on the same amount. The Act stipulates that the buyer can deduct this accrued interest paid to the seller as an expense in the year against the interest income. This happens because the bond issuer pays all the interest on the next due date to the holder of the bond at that time. This means that the purchaser will include the cash interest received from the bond issuer in net income, but then take a deduction for the interest paid to the seller as part of the purchase.

Example

Softco Ltd. has an outstanding bond issue with a face value of $10,000 on which it pays interest at 4%. The interest is payable semi-annually, on June 15 and December 15. On October 15, Randy sold his Softco Ltd. bonds on the open market and they were acquired by Saleem. Compute the income that each of Randy and Saleem must report in the year from the bond.

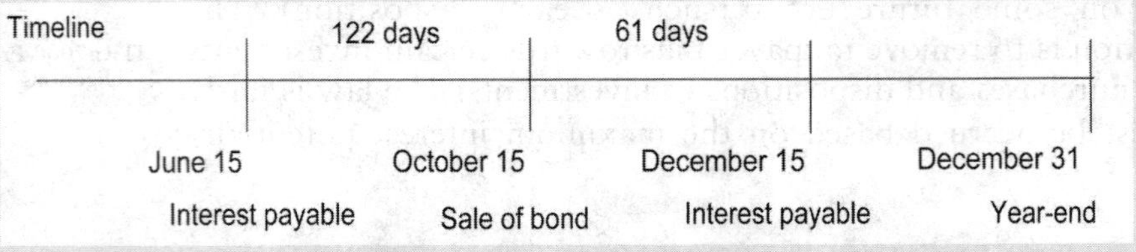

Saleem would pay, and Randy would receive, the following amount (rounded) for the bonds.

Face value of bond	$10,000
Interest from June 16 to October 15 (122 days of 183 × $200)	133
Total Payment	$10,133

In filing their respective personal income tax returns for the year, Saleem and Randy would report the interest as follows:

	Randy		Saleem
	Dec. – June		**June – Dec.**
T5 slip received from Softco Ltd. For interest received from Softco	$200		$200
Add (subtract) interest received/paid on sale/acquisition of the bond	133	June – Oct.	(133)
Interest from Softco Ltd. bond	$333		$67

Net result is that Randy receives interest income from December to October, and Saleem receives income from October to December.

¶6,030 Payments Based on Production or Use

When selling a property, the buyer and the seller can determine the sales price in various ways. For example, the price can be a lump-sum amount of money payable upon closing of the agreement, or as an instalment sale where the sales price can be payable over a period of time. Alternatively, the price may be determined by reference to a formula which is dependent on the use of, or production from, the property.

The concern from a tax perspective is that the buyer and seller may be motivated to convert a property income transaction into a capital transaction. The distinction between a receipt of income and a receipt of capital must be considered in this circumstance. Property income is fully taxable while capital gains are included in income at the current inclusion rate of 50%.

Payments that are expressed as instalments of the sale price of property but are actually payments depending on the use of or production of that property should be taxed as property income, rather than as capital. Property is broadly defined as including not only real and personal property, but also intangible property such as patents, franchises and rights of all kinds, such as oil and gas, timber, gravel and rock, books and manuals, etc.

ITA: 12(1)(g) Payments based on production or use, 248(1) Definitions

Approach

Steps to determining the taxation of a sale of property

(1) Assess the Situation and Identify the Issues:

(a) Gather all the facts relating to the taxpayer's situation.

(2) Analyze the Issues:

(a) Consider whether the receipt is on account of business or property income. See ¶4,110.20 for factors to consider.

(i) Analyze the strengths and weaknesses of your arguments by evaluating the facts rather than simply classifying or listing the facts.

(b) Next, if the receipt is considered property income, consider if the receipt is dependent on production or use.

(i) Analyze the strengths and weaknesses of your arguments, by evaluating the facts, rather than simply classifying or listing the facts.

(3) Conclude and Advise:

(a) Arrive at a conclusion on the treatment of the receipts, consistent with your analysis.

(b) Explain the implications of your conclusion and advise the client on the impact of your conclusion.

The Act provides that any amount received on production or use of property disposed must be included as property income. The purpose of this rule is to prevent taxpayers from characterizing property income as a capital gain (a topic discussed in Chapters 7 and 8), which will attract a lower tax rate through partial inclusion of income for tax purposes. Despite the clarity of the provision, it has been the subject of many appeals because ordinary instalment payments of principal, which are not taxed as income, may not be substantially different from payments based on production or use which are taxed as property income. The case summary below gives more details of such a transaction and its tax treatments.

ITA: 12(1)(g) Payments based on production or use

Example Problem 6-4

The appellant, a farmer, entered into an agreement with the Department of Highways of Alberta under which she granted the Department the right to enter upon her land for the purpose of taking clay for use in the construction of a highway. Employees of the Department removed the crop growing on the land designated in the agreement, removed the topsoil from the area, removed the quantity of clay subsoil required for highway construction, replaced the topsoil and levelled off the area. Pursuant to the agreement, the appellant received compensation of $10,000 in full settlement of "general damages, loss of crop, cost of restoring areas and reduction of yields." The Minister added the $10,000 to the appellant's declared income. The appellant objected.

ITA: 9(1) Income, 12(1)(g) Payments based on production or use

REQUIRED

Decide this case on the basis of whether the receipt of $10,000 can be considered business or property income under either or both of the sections cited by the Minister.

SOLUTION

Cases: *Mary Frances Randle v. M.N.R.*, 65 DTC 507 (TAB)

Step 1 — Assess the Situation and Identify the Issues:

(1) Gather all the facts related to the situation above.

Step 2 — Analyze the Issues:

(1) Consider whether the receipt is on account of business or property income, using the facts gathered.

ITA: 9(1) Income, 248(1) Definitions

Arguments for treating as business income:

- The receipt was not like normal property income (i.e., dividends, interest, rent, or royalties).

Arguments for treating as property income:

- There are no facts that connect the payment to her normal business activities (farming).
- The relation of the transaction to farming is fairly remote except for the compensation for current crops.
- It is unlikely that this was a frequent transaction, indicating a non-business income receipt.
- There was no intention either of a primary or secondary nature to make a profit from a business operation in this situation.
- The receipt was more like a reimbursement for a capital item.

- The nature of the asset involved is more like fixed capital in land than working capital in inventory except, again, for the current crop.
- Damages for loss of earnings capacity, as this seemed to be, are not considered income, but generally regarded as a capital receipt.

(2) Next consider if the property income includes a payment that is dependent on production or use. Based on the discussion in Part A, the receipt would be considered property income.

ITA: 12(1)(g) Payments based on production or use

- No relation between the amount received and the amount of clay taken is indicated.
- There was no continuing activity in the sale of clay which might indicate more clearly a payment dependent on production or use.
- The agreement indicated that the appellant did not sell the clay or the land, but received money in compensation for damages sustained.

Step 3 — Conclude and Advise:

Based on the analysis above, it might be concluded that most of the money was compensation for the loss of a portion of a capital asset and for restoring it to its former state of production. However, the amount paid for the current crop in the designated area as part of the appellant's inventory should be included in income.

¶6,030.99 Practise What You've Learned

Refer to the following sections of the Study Guide to practise what you've learned:

¶6,800 — Review Questions

- Question 1 — Interest Income

¶6,850 — Exercises

- Exercise 1 — Interest Income

¶6,040 Dividends From Corporations Resident in Canada

¶6,040.10 Dividends Defined

When a business is incorporated, we must consider the eventual distribution of profits. Profitable corporations may deal with cash profits by reinvesting in the operations or pay out the after-tax profits to the shareholders. When the corporation distributes after-tax profits to a shareholder, either in cash or in kind, the shareholder is said to have received a dividend.

ITA: 12(1)(j) Dividends from resident corporations, 12(1)(k) Foreign corporations, trusts and investment entities

There are essentially two forms of dividends: cash dividends and dividends-in-kind. The most common form of dividend is a cash dividend. A dividend-in-kind is the distribution of profit through the payment of something other than cash. The cash equivalent (fair market value) of the asset received is the amount of the dividend for tax purposes. Consequently, a dividend-in-kind is no different from a cash dividend. However, where the dividend-in-kind is a stock dividend, special rules apply.

The term dividend is defined in the Act, but not in great detail. However, both the CRA and the courts have agreed that any distribution of income that is divided pro rata among shareholders may properly be described as a dividend, unless the corporation can show that it is another type of payment. Provisions in the Act qualify the meaning of a dividend to include both cash and dividends-in-kind.

ITA: 248(1) Definitions

Dividends (other than capital or qualifying dividends) from resident corporations are labelled "taxable dividends", whereas those from non-resident corporations are simply labelled "dividends". The distinction between a taxable dividend and an ordinary 'dividend' is important and will be discussed further in this chapter and in Chapter 10.

The Act requires that taxpayers include all taxable dividends received from both resident corporations and non-resident corporations in the calculation of net income. A "taxable dividend" is defined as a dividend other than a tax-free capital dividend or a qualifying dividend on tax-deferred preferred shares. There are special rules, outlined in this chapter, as to how taxable dividends are included in income. Taxable dividend should not be interpreted to mean "anything other than a non-taxable dividend".

ITA: 12(1)(j) Dividends from resident corporations, 12(1)(k) Foreign corporations, trusts and investment entities, 90(1) Dividend from non-resident corporation, 82(1) Taxable dividends received, 89(1) Definitions

Further, there are a number of provisions in the Act that address and include in income the withdrawal of money or realization of other benefits by shareholders from corporations. These amounts are often characterized as deemed dividends. The Act will direct whether the deemed dividend is a taxable dividend.

ITA: 84 Deemed dividend

¶6,040.20 Dividends Included in Income

How a dividend is taxed depends on whether:

- the recipient is an individual (including a non-corporate partner and a trust) or a corporation,
- the dividend is from a resident or a non-resident corporation,
- it is a stock dividend, and
- it is an income amount that is just being deemed a dividend.

Each of the possibilities will be looked at separately.

Figure 6-1

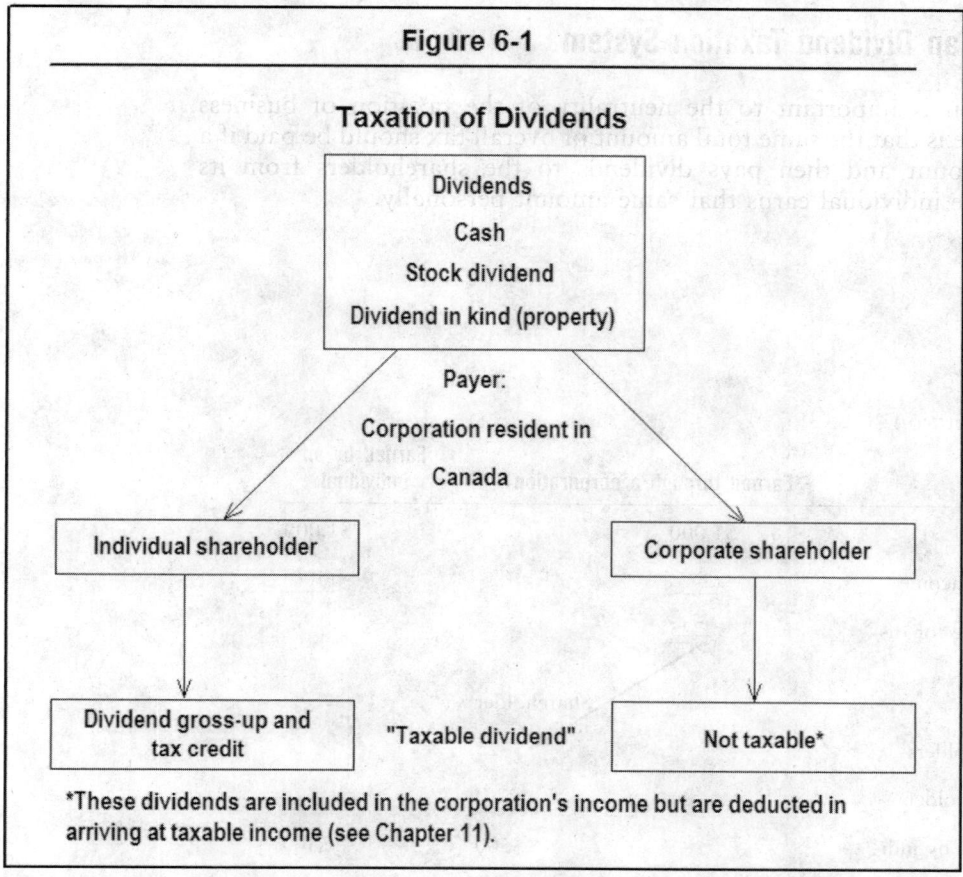

Taxation of Dividends

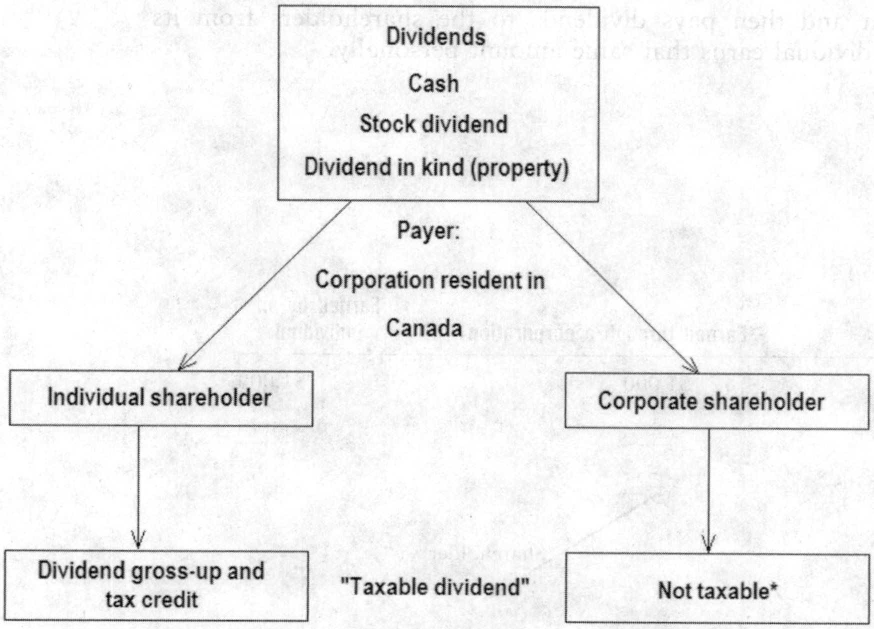

*These dividends are included in the corporation's income but are deducted in arriving at taxable income (see Chapter 11).

The Issue

In Chapter 2, we discussed the question of who is liable for tax in Canada. We learned that there are three taxpayers who are liable for tax: an individual, a corporation, and a trust. Income earned in a corporation has two levels of tax, tax at the corporate level and a second tax on the distribution of profits as dividends to the shareholders of the corporation.

The Canadian tax system attempts to make the form of business ownership neutral, in that it attempts to remove any advantages or disadvantages between one form of organization over another. This is known as integration and attempts to impose the same amount of tax on income earned, regardless of the structure chosen to carry on the economic activity. Without any adjustments in the tax rules, income earned in a corporation would be penalized by double taxation, as compared to a situation where an individual earns the income directly.

The Act contains a number of special rules designed to provide relief from double taxation of income earned through a corporation. In the following section, we will discuss one of the mechanisms introduced into the Canadian tax system to address the double taxation problem.

Overview of the Canadian Dividend Taxation System

The concept of integration is important to the neutrality of the taxation of business income. The basic objective is that the same total amount of overall tax should be paid if a corporation earns an amount and then pays dividends to the shareholders from its after-tax earnings, or if the individual earns that same amount personally.

Example

Illustration of Integration

	Earned through a corporation		Earned by an individual
Business income earned	$1,000		$1,000
Tax paid on business income	(275)		(500)
After-tax cash available for distribution	725		
		Shareholder	
Distribution to shareholders		$725	
Tax paid by the shareholder		(225)	
After-tax cash retained by individual		$500	$500

It is important to note that this illustration highlights a situation where integration works perfectly. This scenario has been simplified to illustrate the overall purpose of the dividend tax system. In this scenario, the corporate tax rate is 27.5% and the individual tax rate is 50%.

Perfect integration relies on two assumptions:

- a perfect theoretical corporate and individual tax, shown above, resulting in the same amount of total tax paid, and
- deferral of payment of the dividend does not occur.

Integration and its imperfections are discussed in further detail in sections ¶12,000 and in ¶13,315.

The following is the tool used in the Act to achieve integration (in theory):

- the individual shareholder must include in income the full pre-tax income earned by the corporation by grossing up the amount of the dividend received and calculating tax on that base, and

- the individual should receive a dividend tax credit for all the income tax paid by the corporation.

The Dividend Gross-up and Dividend Tax Credit System for Individuals

The purpose of grossing up the dividends received from a corporation is to restore the dividends to the pre-tax amount of income that was earned in the corporation. This means that shareholders would include in their income an amount greater than the actual dividend received. This grossed-up amount is intended to reflect pre-tax corporate income that has been distributed to the shareholder.

The combined federal and provincial dividend tax credit is intended to give credit for the corporate tax paid. In a perfect scenario, the dividend tax credit will be equal to the gross-up amount. As we will see in later chapters, the provincial dividend tax credit varies from province to province which results in a discrepancy in integration. We will discuss this issue of imperfections in more detail in Chapter 12.

Note that the dividend gross-up and tax credit procedure applies where:

- individual shareholders receive the dividend (corporate shareholders are discussed in Chapter 11); and
- dividends are received from Canadian resident corporations (dividends received by individuals from non-resident corporations are fully taxed without using the dividend gross-up or the tax credits).

Note:

Corporations are NOT subject to the dividend gross-up and dividend tax credit, only trusts and individuals will include the grossed up dividend in net income for tax purposes. As seen in Figure 6-1, dividends received by corporate shareholders are not taxable.

The corporate tax rates in Canada have changed significantly in the past several years. As a result, the corporate tax rate depends on the type of corporation engaged in the economic activities. For example, a Canadian-controlled private corporation ("CCPC") pays a lower level of tax on the first $500,000 of business profits as compared to a public company. In order for our integration system to work well, the Act must address the possibility of two different levels of taxation paid in a corporation when considering the gross-up and dividend tax credit.

Keeping in mind that the purpose of the gross-up is to restore the actual dividends received back to the pre-tax income earned in the corporation, the Act uses two calculations of the gross-up and the dividend tax credit. The calculation used depends on the type of corporation that issued the dividends and the type of income from which the dividends are issued. Note that different types of corporations (e.g., public versus private) with different types of income (e.g., active business income versus investment income) will be taxed at different tax rates in the corporation. The taxation of corporations will be discussed in greater detail in Chapter 11 and 12.

Type 1 — Dividends — Other Than Eligible Dividends

A CCPC that earns active business income that is taxed at the low corporate rate (i.e., on the first $500,000 in active business income), or a CCPC that earns investment income, will only be able to pay out a non-eligible dividend, i.e., a dividend that is not eligible for the higher gross-up and tax credit rates.

Example

The following shows the effects of receiving a non-eligible dividend:

Cash dividend	$10,000
Dividend gross-up of 16%	1,600
Grossed-up dividend	$11,600
Federal Dividend tax credit of 8/11 of gross-up	1,164
Provincial Dividend tax credit of 3/11[1] of gross-up	436

[1] This assumes that the provincial dividend tax credit is equal to 3/11. It is important to note that the dividend tax credit is different in each province and can vary significantly. The concept of provincial dividend tax credit is discussed in greater detail in Chapter 10.

In this situation, the dividends received plus a 16% gross-up will be included in the individual's income, thus representing the pre-tax income earned in a corporation. The individual shareholder's income would include the grossed-up dividend, which is greater than the actual dividend received.

ITA: 82(1) Taxable dividends received, 12(1)(j) Dividends from resident corporations

This dividend income (116% of the amount received) will be subject to tax in full at the individual's tax rate, which is dependent on his or her income level. We will outline more about the progressive tax rate system in Chapter 10. As discussed above, to mitigate the problem of double taxation, the Act allows for a dividend tax credit, which will reduce the individual's tax paid on dividends. The dividend tax credit is intended to give the individual (or trust) credit for the tax already paid in the corporation.

The federal dividend tax credit can be calculated in one of the following three ways (same amount but different calculations):

ITA: 121 Deduction for taxable dividends

- 11.64% of the actual dividends paid (non-grossed up amount), or
- 8/11 × 16% (gross-up) = 11.64% of dividends paid,

  or
- 10.03% × 116% (grossed-up dividend) = 11.64% of dividends paid.

Example

The Dividend Tax System with Ineligible Dividends

The following example shows the implications of the ineligible dividend treatment for individuals. Consider two individuals, one paying federal tax at a marginal rate of 15% and the other paying federal tax at the top marginal rate of 33%. We will assume that both individuals live in a province with a tax on income rate of 10% and 17%, respectively. Also assume that the combined federal and provincial dividend tax credit is equal to the gross-up.

Each shareholder receives an ineligible dividend of $1,000. Remember that ineligible dividends are created when a CCPC earns either active business income subject to a low tax rate or investment income.

Taxpayer's marginal tax rate (federal and provincial combined)		25%	50%
Dividend	(A)	$ 1,000	$ 1,000
Add: gross-up of 16% of dividend		160	160
Grossed-up dividend subject to tax		$ 1,160	$ 1,160
Tax on grossed-up dividend at marginal tax rate		$ 290	$ 580
Less: federal and provincial dividend tax credit (assume equal to the gross-up)		(160)[2]	(160)[2]
Net tax payable	(B)	$ 130	$ 420
After-tax dividend [(A) – (B)]		$ 870	$ 580

[2] Note that the dividend tax credit is not affected by the individual's marginal tax rate because it represents the income tax paid by the corporation. In this example, we have assumed that the provincial dividend tax credit is 3/11 to provide a combined dividend tax credit that is equal to the gross-up amount. It is important to note that the provincial dividend tax credit may vary.

Type 2 — Eligible Dividends

(1) Eligible Dividends — Dividends from a public corporation resident in Canada taxed at the general corporate rate and a CCPC resident in Canada distributed from business income taxed at the general corporate rate (not the low corporate tax rate)

In this situation, the gross-up rate is 38% and the federal dividend tax credit can be calculated in one of the following three ways (same amount but different calculations):

ITA: 121 Deduction for taxable dividends

- 20.7% of the dividends paid, or
- $6/11 \times 38\%$ (gross-up) = 20.7% of the dividends paid,

  or
- 15% (rounded) × 138% (grossed-up dividends) = 20.7% of the dividends paid.

Example

The Dividend Tax System with Eligible Dividends

The following example show implications of the eligible dividend treatment for individuals, consider two individuals, one paying federal tax at a marginal rate of 15% and the other paying federal tax at the top marginal rate of 33%. We will assume that both individuals live in a province with a tax on income of 10% and 17%, respectively. Also assume that the combined federal and provincial dividend tax credit is equal to the gross-up.

Each shareholder receives an eligible dividend of $1,000.

Taxpayer's marginal tax rate (federal and provincial combined)		25%	50%
Dividend	(A)	$ 1,000	$ 1,000
Add: gross-up of 38% of dividend		380	380
Grossed-up dividend subject to tax		$ 1,380	$ 1,380
Tax on grossed-up dividend at marginal tax rate		$ 345	$ 690
Less: federal and provincial dividend tax credit (equal to the gross-up)		(380)*	(380)*
Net tax payable	(B)	Nil**	$ 310
After-tax dividend [(A) – (B)]		$ 1,000	$ 690

* Note that the dividend tax credit is not affected by the individual's marginal tax rate because it represents the income tax paid by the corporation. In this example, we have assumed that the provincial dividend tax credit is 5/11 to provide a combined dividend tax credit that is equal to the gross-up amount. It is important to note that the provincial dividend tax credit may vary.

** The excess dividend tax credit of $35 ($345-$380) is available to deduct from federal tax on other income.

Example Problem 6-5

Ian Plant faces a 12% provincial tax on income and a federal tax rate of 20.5%. On an investment of $5,000 in the shares of a Canadian-resident public corporation, he receives $362.50 of taxable dividends for a yield of 7.25%. He is considering the alternative of investing his funds in a bond paying 9%. Assume that the combined federal and provincial dividend tax credit is equal to the gross-up.

REQUIRED

Compute the after-tax return from the alternative investments to compare their desirability.

SOLUTION

(A)	Dividend	
	Dividend	$362.50
	Add: gross-up of 38% of dividend	137.75
	Grossed-up dividend subject to tax	$500.25
	Tax on grossed-up dividend @ 32.5% (i.e., 20.5% + 12%)	$162.58
	Less: dividend tax credit (federal and provincial)	(137.75)
	Net tax payable	$ 24.83
	After-tax dividend ($362.50 – $24.83)	$337.67
(B)	Interest	
	Interest income (9% of $5,000)	$450.00
	Tax payable @ 32.5%	$146.25
	After-tax interest ($450.00 – $146.25)	$303.75

NOTE TO SOLUTION

Although the pre-tax dividend yield of 7.25% is lower than the pre-tax interest yield of 9%, the after-tax return from the dividend of $337.67 or 6.75% of the investment is greater than the after-tax return from the interest of $303.75 or 6.08% of the $5,000 invested. Furthermore, it should be remembered that there may be a greater potential for a return from capital gains on the shares compared to the bond. This would influence the decision when the after-tax dividend yield is lower than the after-tax interest yield. Note that investment in shares will normally be riskier than investment in bonds.

¶6,040.30 Dividends Received From Non-Resident Corporations

Dividends received by individuals from non-resident corporations are still taxable but the dividend gross-up rules do not apply as they are not Canadian-sourced. This is justifiable because the government has no reason to try to integrate a foreign tax system or to provide an incentive for individuals to invest in non-resident corporations.

ITA: 12(1)(k) Foreign corporations, trusts and investment entities, 90(1) Dividend from non-resident corporation

The foreign dividend income may have had income tax withheld at the source since it was paid to a non-resident of the country of origin. The taxable amount of the dividend is not reduced by this tax. The taxpayer may be entitled to a foreign tax credit with respect to those taxes. Foreign tax credits are discussed in Chapter 10.

¶6,090 Pause and Reflect — Summary of Learning Goals

After working through this section, ¶6,000, you should be able to:

- explain the meaning of interest and the different methods that must be used to determine the amount of interest income for a particular taxation year;
- explain the timing of the inclusion of interest income as it relates to special circumstances such as discounted bonds, treasury bills, zero coupon bonds, and bonds sold with accrued interest;
- apply your knowledge to determine when the receipt of income is based on production or use and the tax implications of the classification;
- explain the purpose of the dividend gross-up and the dividend tax credit system;
- explain the difference in the tax implication between eligible, ineligible dividends, and foreign dividends;
- apply your knowledge to correctly calculate the amount of interest income that taxpayers must include in a particular taxation year; and
- apply your knowledge to correctly calculate the tax implications of receiving eligible, ineligible, and foreign corporation dividends.

¶6,090.99 Practise What You've Learned

Refer to the following sections of the Study Guide to practise what you've learned:

¶6,825 — Multiple Choice Questions

- Question 1 — Dividends — CCPC
- Question 5 — Dividends — CCPC, public

¶6,100 Income Attribution

Overview — The Reason for Attribution

Under the Canadian income tax system, an individual is a taxpayer who is liable for tax on his or her taxable income. An individual's taxable income is subject to a progressive tax structure. Under such a structure, as an individual earns more income, his or her tax rate increases. For example, if Mom earns $100,000, she will pay more tax than if Mom and Dad each earn $50,000. Thus, the high-income taxpayer will have an incentive to reduce tax by splitting (transferring) income with family members who earn less income and pay tax at a lower rate.

Example

Income splitting

Ms. Abigail, a high-income earner, holds bonds which earn interest income. Her top marginal tax rate is 50%. For every dollar in interest earned, she will pay $50 in tax. To minimize tax, she may transfer the bonds to her 5-year old daughter. Her daughter has no other source of income; therefore her daughter will not have to pay tax on the interest income (due to personal tax credits) or will pay tax at a much lower rate. Overall, the combined tax payable is lower, therefore Ms. Abigail would be motivated to split the income with her daughter.

In order to protect the integrity of the progressive tax system, the Act has introduced various attribution rules to prevent certain forms of income splitting (like the example above) among immediate family members. In general terms, the attribution rules ensure that, regardless of who holds the legal title to the income earning asset, the income earned will be taxed in the transferor's hands (i.e., attribute back to the transferor). The most common forms of income that may be subject to the attribution rules include:

ITA: 74.1 [Transfers and loans to spouse or common-law partner or minor], 74.5 Transfers for fair market consideration, 56(4.1) Interest free or low interest loans, 56(5) Exception for split income

- interest income,
- capital gains (on assets transferred to a spouse),
- dividends (unless subject to "kiddie tax" discussed in ¶6,150 later in the chapter), and
- rental income.

Note

Business income is not subject to attribution. The distinction is made between property and business income for the main reason that business income requires active participation while property income is much less active in nature.

"Income attribution" is a process of allocating income earned on property that was transferred to a non-arm's length individual back to the original owner (the transferor).

Example

Attribution

In the example discussed earlier, although the 5-year-old daughter owns the bonds after the transfer, for tax purposes, the interest income earned on the bonds will be attributed back to Ms. Abigail. Ms. Abigail will include the interest income in her net income for tax purposes and pay tax on that income, even though her daughter received the interest income.

Cases: *George Lackie v. Her Majesty the Queen*, 79 DTC 5309 (FCA)*George E. Lackie v. Her Majesty the Queen*, 78 DTC 6128 (FCTD)

Attribution means that the income or loss earned by the spouse or minor is considered to be the income or loss of the transferor during his or her lifetime as long as he or she is resident in Canada.

The word "transfer" has been used frequently throughout the various attribution rules. It includes a sale, whether or not the proceeds are at fair market value. Financing the sale by a loan does not change the concept of a transfer in this context. Gifting is also a form of transfer.

After working through section ¶6,100 of the chapter, you will be able to:

- explain the meaning of related persons and how that relates to the attribution rules;
- explain the attribution rules and the circumstances in which they apply;
- explain the various anti-avoidance rules relating to attribution;
- explain the purpose of the "kiddie tax" and the circumstances in which "kiddie tax" applies;
- apply your knowledge to calculate the tax implications of splitting income with a non-arm's length individual;
- apply your knowledge to calculate the tax implications of receiving income subject to the "kiddie tax"; and
- apply your knowledge to advise a client on planning methods to avoid income attribution.

¶6,110 Definition of Related Persons

The attribution rules apply to certain non-arm's length individuals. The Act deems related persons <u>not</u> to deal at arm's length with each other and therefore the attribution rules apply.

ITA: 251(1)(a)

Exhibit 6-1 attempts to present schematically all of the provisions defining related individuals, as well as the CRA's interpretations. Related individuals are diagrammed in relation to a taxpayer (i.e., "you"). For tax purposes, you are related to your:

ITA: 251 Arm's length, 252 Extended meaning of "child"; Income Tax Folio: S1-F5-C1 Related Persons and Dealing at Arm's Length

- direct-line antecedents such as your or your spouse's parents, grandparents, great grandparents, and your descendants such as your children, grandchildren great grandchildren, etc.,
- adopted children,

- children's spouses (i.e., son-in-law, daughter-in-law),
- siblings and their spouses (i.e., sister-in-law, brother-in-law), and
- your spouse's siblings (i.e., your husband's sister/brother) and their spouse.

Note that where the word "spouse" is used, it is intended to include the concept of a common-law partner, including a same-sex partner.

Exhibit 6-1 Schematic Diagram of Related Individuals

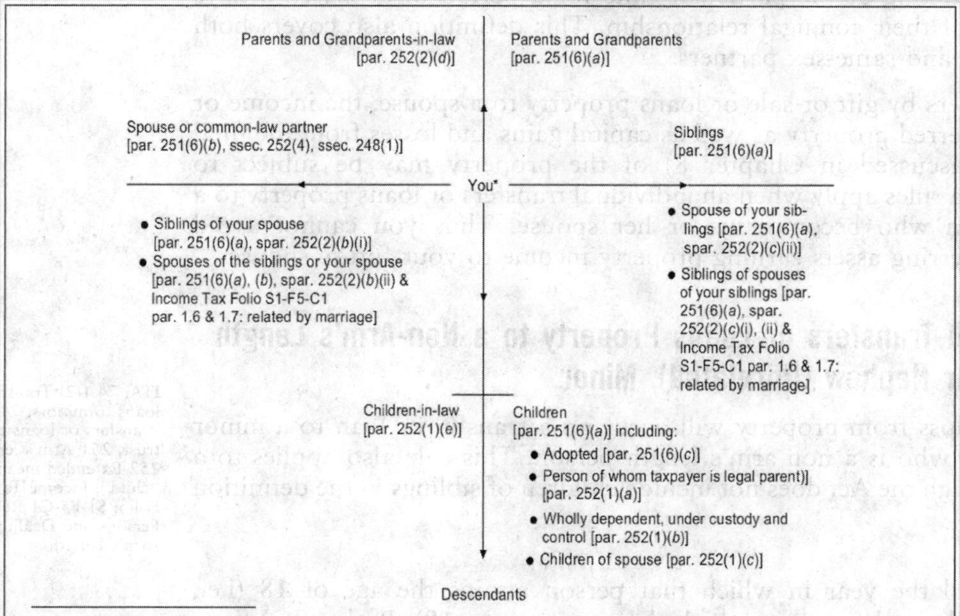

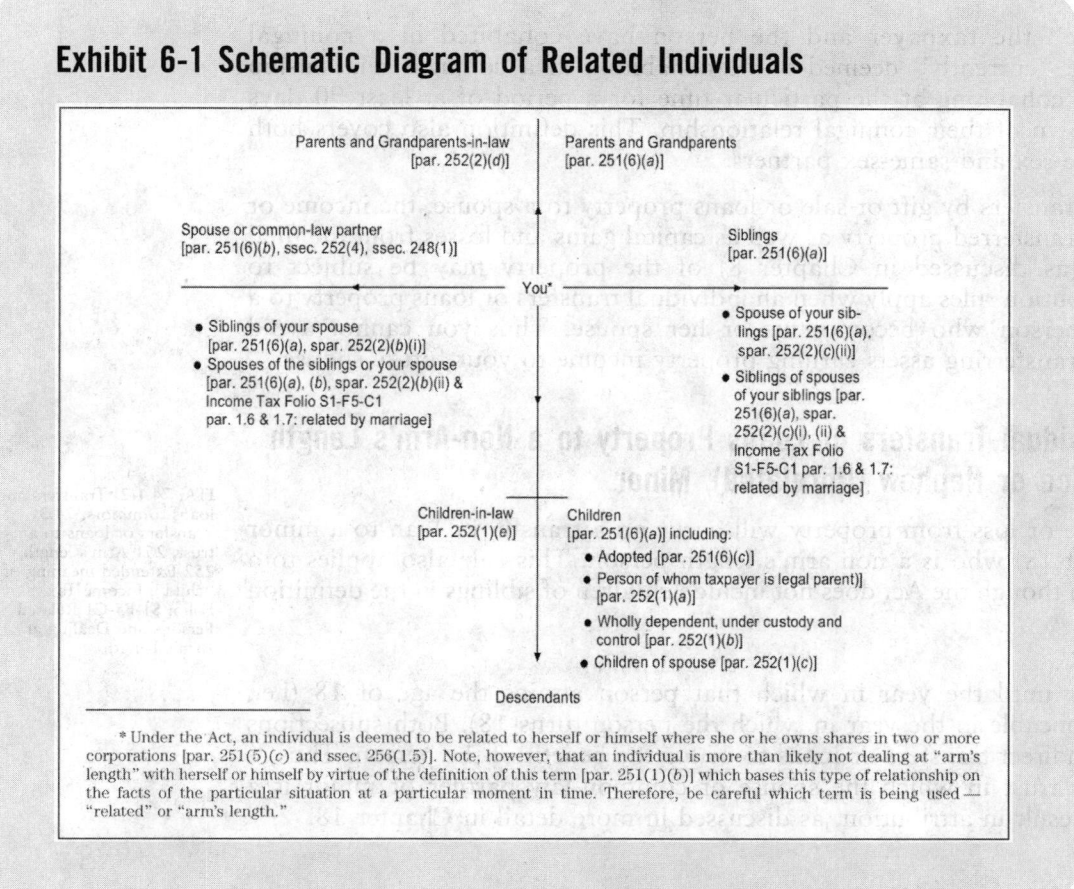

* Under the Act, an individual is deemed to be related to herself or himself where she or he owns shares in two or more corporations [par. 251(5)(c) and ssec. 256(1.5)]. Note, however, that an individual is more than likely not dealing at "arm's length" with herself or himself by virtue of the definition of this term [par. 251(1)(b)] which bases this type of relationship on the facts of the particular situation at a particular moment in time. Therefore, be careful which term is being used — "related" or "arm's length."

¶6,115 Transactions Subject to Income Attribution

Income attribution may occur when an asset earning property income and or capital gains and losses is transferred in the following scenarios:

(1) an individual transfer or loans property to a spouse, or

(2) an individual transfers or loan property to a non-arm's length (related), or a niece or nephew (unrelated), minor.

¶6,115.10 An Individual Transfers or Loans Property to a Spouse

It is important to remember that the term spouse includes common-law opposite-sex and same-sex partners. For purposes of attribution, we will use the term spouse to represent all three of these terms (spouse and common-law partner, including same-sex partner).

ITA: 74.1(1) Transfers and loans to spouse or common-law partner

"Common-law partner" is defined as a person who cohabits at that time in a conjugal relationship with the taxpayer and either

ITA: 248(1) Definitions

(1) has so cohabited with the taxpayer for a continuous period of at least one year, or

(2) would be the parent of a child of whom the taxpayer is a parent.

Where "at any time" the taxpayer and the person have cohabited in a conjugal relationship, they are "currently" deemed to be cohabiting in a conjugal relationship unless they were not cohabiting at the particular time for a period of at least 90 days because of a breakdown of their conjugal relationship. This definition also covers both common-law opposite-sex and same-sex partners.

When an individual transfers by gift or sale or loans property to a spouse, the income or loss incurred on the transferred property as well as capital gains and losses from the final sale or disposition (as discussed in Chapter 8) of the property may be subject to attribution. The attribution rules apply when an individual transfers or loans property to a spouse including a person who becomes his or her spouse. Thus you cannot avoid attribution rules by transferring assets earning property income to your future spouse.

¶6,115.20 An Individual Transfers or Loans Property to a Non-Arm's Length (Related), or a Niece or Nephew (Unrelated), Minor

ITA: 74.1(2) Transfers and loans to minors, 74.3 Transfers or loans to a trust, 251 Arm's length, 252 Extended meaning of "child"; Income Tax Folio: S1-F5-C1 Related Persons and Dealing at Arm's Length

Attribution of income or loss from property will occur on a transfer or loan to a minor (i.e., under the age of 18) who is a non-arm's length person. This rule also applies to a niece or nephew, even though the Act does not include children of siblings in the definition of related parties.

Attribution continues until the year in which that person attains the age of 18 (i.e., attribution is not applicable in the year in which the person turns 18). Both subsections pertain to direct or indirect transfers or loans to or for the benefit of the person. Thus, a transfer or loan to a trust in which the spouse or common-law partner or minor is a beneficiary will still result in attribution, as discussed in more detail in Chapter 18.

¶6,120 Avoiding Income Attributions

While the attributions rules in the Act are meant to discourage the splitting of income, there are various exceptions to the application of these rules provided by the legislation. A number of very specific conditions must be fulfilled before the taxpayer will be exempted from the attribution rules. The purpose of the exception is to allow transfers between non-arm's length parties that are consistent with the terms we would see between arm's length (unrelated) parties. The exceptions are discussed below.

ITA: 74.5 Transfers for fair market consideration

¶6,120.10 Fair Market Value Transfer

When a property is transferred at the fair market value and fair market value consideration is received in return, these attribution rules will not apply. Note the use of the word received. This indicates that in order for attribution not to apply, the transferor must receive payment equal to the fair market value of the asset transferred.

Transfers at any amount other than fair market value (greater or lower) will be subject to attribution, including all gifts of income-earning property. Gifts of income-earning property would be subject to the attribution rules as the property is transferred for consideration of zero, which is less than the fair market value of the property transferred.

¶6,120.20 Interest Charged

It is possible to sell an income-earning property to a non-arm's length individual using debt without applying the attribution rules to future property income received. Several criteria must be met in order for attribution not to apply to future income:

ITA: 74.5 Transfers for fair market consideration

- The interest charges must be at least equal to the lesser of
  - the prescribed rate, or
  - an arm's length rate (to be referred to here as a "commercial" rate).
- If funds are loaned directly then interest at a commercial rate, as determined above, must be charged and paid on the loan or attribution will occur.
- The interest must be paid within 30 days of the end of each and every year in which the debt was outstanding or attribution will occur. This means the transferee cannot miss even one annual interest payment.

The use of a loan to transfer property to a non-arm's length individual reduces or eliminates the income splitting benefits. A loan at a commercial rate creates income to the lender (the transferor), thereby reducing or eliminating any splitting advantage on income from property, but places the borrower in a position to earn a capital gain and property income that will not be attributed to the transferor. The borrower may be able to deduct the interest paid against the property income.

¶6,120.30 Spousal Election

At this point it is important to introduce the concept of a spousal rollover. The Act allows for the transfer of capital property to a spouse without triggering a deemed disposition. Under the spousal rollover, accrued capital gains and recaptured CCA on depreciable capital property and other capital property is automatically deferred on the transfer of such property to a spouse or a common-law partner. This concept is discussed further in ¶7,215.20.

ITA: 73(1) Inter vivos transfers by individuals

This automatic transfer poses a problem in the case of attribution. If the spousal rollover is used to transfer the capital property, all accrued income will be deferred, but any future income will attribute back to the transferring spouse. If the goal is to split income in the future and avoid attribution, the transferor spouse must elect out of the spousal rollover.

If the transferor elects out of the spousal rollover, a disposition will occur at the fair market value, triggering a capital gain or loss and any recaptured CCA. This results in an immediate tax consequence to the transferring spouse. If the asset being transferred is shares of a qualified small business corporation shares or qualified farm property, the capital gains deduction could be used to offset all or part of the income inclusion. The capital gains deduction is discussed further in ¶7,035.

Example

Fred, whose income is taxed in the top bracket, owns a property worth $50,000. The property earns $5,000 of income each year. Barb, Fred's wife, has no income. Therefore, Fred would like to split future income with his wife. Fred sells the property to Barb for $50,000 cash. While fair market value was paid to Fred, the property would still roll over to Barb unless Fred elects out of the automatic rollover.

Assuming Fred receives consideration equal to the fair market value of the property AND Fred elects out of the rollover provisions, the future income of $5,000 each year would be taxed in Barb's hands. The effect is to transfer the future income to Barb. It should be noted that by electing out of the rollover, Fred will be triggering the sale of the property at fair market value which may create some taxable income at the time of transfer.

However, we should consider what Fred does with the $50,000 cash received as a result of the sale. If that $50,000 is reinvested in Fred's hands, the income will attract tax at the top rate and the benefits of income splitting may be reduced, unless the original property transferred generated a large capital gain on its ultimate disposition by Barb. At that time, the capital gain on the original property transferred to Barb would not be subject to attribution because the original transfer took place for fair market value consideration.

To gain the maximum benefit from the transfer and the income splitting opportunity, a better option may be for Fred to use the $50,000 in cash received to reduce debt on personal items, such as a mortgage, personal loan, or credit card.

¶6,120.40 Marital Breakdown

There is an exception to the attribution rules which applies where spouses live separate and apart by reason of a breakdown of their marriage. Any income or loss that relates to the period of separation is exempted from attribution.

ITA: 74.5(3) Spouses or common-law partners living apart

Summary

Avoiding attribution rules

Transfer to a spouse:

ITA: 74.5(1) Transfers for fair market consideration

- **Must** elect out of the automatic spousal rollover in subsection 73(1).
- Acquiring spouse must pay fair market value consideration.
  - If a loan is used as fair market value consideration, two additional rules must be adhered to:

- interest must be charged at the prescribed rate or commercial rate, and
- interest must be paid within 30 days of the calendar year end (i.e., January 30) each year.

- Attribution ceases if the spouses are living separate and apart by reason of the breakdown of their relationship. This exception applies to property income, but not capital gains unless an election has been made.

ITA: 74.5(3) Spouses or common-law partners living apart

Transfer to a non-arm's length minor children and/or nieces and nephews:

ITA: 74.5(1) Transfers for fair market consideration

- Purchaser must pay fair market value consideration.
  - If a loan is used as fair market value consideration, two addition rules must be adhered to:
    - interest must be charged at the prescribed rate or commercial rate, and
    - interest must be paid within 30 days of the calendar year end (i.e., January 30) each year.
- Important to note that attribution ceases in the year the minor turns 18.

Approach

Steps to addressing a non-arm's length sale

(1) Assess the Situation and Identify the Issues:

(a) Gather all the facts relating to the taxpayer's situation including:

(i) the relationship between the seller and purchaser,

(ii) determine the amount of consideration paid, and

(iii) if the consideration is a loan, determine the payment terms including interest to be charged as well as expected payment of interest.

(2) Analyze the Issues:

(a) Based on the information gathered, determine the following if attribution will apply based on the transaction terms.

(3) Conclude and Advise:

(a) Arrive at a conclusion on the treatment of the future income, and

(b) Provide suggestions on how to improve the situation, if possible.

Example Problem 6-6

- Mr. A is taxed in the top bracket (highest personal tax rate) and he owns a bond which is worth $50,000. Mr. A paid $50,000 for the bond. It earns $5,000 of interest income (one type of property income).
- Mrs. A (Mr. A's spouse) has no income.
- Mr. A gifts the bond to Mrs. A.

REQUIRED

(1) What are the tax consequences to Mr. and Mrs. A?

(2) What are the tax consequences to Mr. and Mrs. A, if Mr. A sells the bond to Mrs. A at its fair market value of $50,000 for cash and they jointly elect out of the automatic rollover?

(3) What are the tax consequences to Mr. and Mrs. A if Mr. A makes a loan of $50,000 to Mrs. A instead of gifting the bond to her or taking cash from her? What if Mr. A charges Mrs. A interest on the loan at a rate which is lower than the prescribed interest rate? They do not elect out of the automatic rollover.

SOLUTION

(1) The tax consequences are as follows: when Mr. A gifts the bond to Mrs. A, there will be no gain or loss (fair market value equals cost). After the bond has been gifted to Mrs. A, the $5,000 annual interest income will be subject to the attribution rule, since the transfer of the bond was not at fair market value when it was gifted to Mrs. A. Note that all gifts of income-earning property are subject to the attribution rules as well as any transfers of property not at fair market value. The $5,000 interest income will be included in Mr. A's income instead of Mrs. A's income. If Mrs. A sells the bond to a third party, any gains or losses from selling the bond will also be attributed back to Mr. A (as discussed in Chapter 8).

ITA: 73(1) Inter vivos transfers by individuals, 74.1(1) Transfers and loans to spouse or common-law partner, 74.5(1) Transfers for fair market consideration, 74.2 Gain or loss deemed that of lender or transferor

(2) The tax consequences will change. The immediate tax consequences to Mr. A remain the same. There will be no gain or loss (fair market value equals cost). However, in this case the attribution rule will not apply to the $5,000 of interest income because Mrs. A paid fair market value for the bond and they elected out of the rollover. The $5,000 interest income will be included in Mrs. A's income.

ITA: 73(1) Inter vivos transfers by individuals, 74.5(1) Transfers for fair market consideration

(3) The tax consequences are that the $5,000 annual interest income will be included in Mr. A's income and taxed at his marginal tax rate.

If Mr. A charges interest at the lesser of the prescribed rate or an arm's length commercial rate, the $5,000 annual property income will be included in Mrs. A's income. The interest charged by Mr. A must be paid by Mrs. A within 30 days of the end of each year in which the loan is outstanding. The attribution rule will not apply due to the fair market value consideration paid

ITA: 74.5(2) Loans for value

by Mrs. A in this situation. However, Mrs. A will be able to deduct the interest she pays from her interest income on the bond, leaving little if any income to be taxed at her lower rate.

Example Problem 6-7

- Ms. Brown is taxed in the top bracket and she owns a bond worth $50,000. The original cost to Ms. Brown was $50,000. The bond produces $5,000 of interest income.
- Junior is Ms. Brown's son. He is 15 years old and he has no income.
- Ms. Brown gifted the property to Junior.

REQUIRED

(1) What are the tax consequences to Ms. Brown and Junior?

(2) What are the tax consequences to Ms. Brown and Junior if Ms. Brown sells the property to Junior and takes back a loan?

SOLUTION

(1) The tax consequences are similar to the ones between Ms. Brown and her spouse. However, when Junior sells the property to a third party, the capital gains or losses will not be subject to the attribution rules (as discussed in Chapter 8). Junior will include the capital gains or losses in his income.

(2) The attribution rule will apply unless the loan is for the $50,000 fair market value and Ms. Brown charges interest at the lesser of either the prescribed rate or an arm's length commercial rate. Junior must pay interest to Ms. Brown within 30 days of the end of each year in which the loan is outstanding. Junior will be able to deduct the interest paid, minimizing the income-splitting benefit.

¶6,130 Anti-Avoidance Rules Relating to Attribution

A number of anti-avoidance rules are contained in the attribution provisions.

¶6,130.10 Repayment of Existing Indebtedness

One rule prevents a person from taking out a commercial loan to purchase an income-producing property and then borrowing money interest-free from his or her spouse to repay the commercial debt. If this is done, any property income or capital gains or losses from the income-producing property will be attributed to the spouse who made the interest-free loan.

¶6,130.20 Back-to-Back Loans

An anti-avoidance rule is provided to prevent circumventing the attribution rules by the use of "back-to-back" loans and transfers. The rule envisages a situation where property is deposited with a financial institution paying no interest with an agreement that the same amount be loaned to the depositor's spouse at a nominal rate of interest, say, 2%. In this case, the use of the intermediary would be disregarded. The attribution rules will apply to include in the income of the original transferor the income earned by the property owned by the ultimate transferee. Of course, if such a back-to-back loan is made at a commercial rate or a back-to-back transfer is made for fair market value consideration, then no attribution will take place.

ITA: 74.5(6) Back to back loans and transfers

¶6,130.30 Loan Guarantees

The avoidance of the attribution rules by the use of loan guarantees is proscribed. For example, instead of Spouse A lending income-producing property to Spouse B, Spouse A could guarantee a loan made by another person or a financial institution to Spouse B who would use the proceeds of the loan to buy income-producing property. Unless a commercial rate of interest is charged and paid on the loan to Spouse B, Spouse A will have to include the income from the property.

ITA: 74.5(7) Guarantees

¶6,130.40 Artificial Transactions

A general anti-avoidance rule is provided to prevent "artificial transactions" which would benefit from the application of the attribution rules. In the past, taxpayers have devised transactions or a series of transactions known as "reverse attribution plans" to have income attributed to a low-income taxpayer. Therefore, if one of the main reasons for a loan or transfer is to reduce the amount of tax that would be paid, the attribution rules discussed will not apply. Another example of such artificial attribution is given in a CRA Interpretation Bulletin.

ITA: 74.5(11) Artificial transactions; Interpretation Bulletins: IT-511R Interspousal and certain other transfers and loans of property

¶6,130.50 Compensation

Two CRA Interpretation Bulletins indicate that an individual can remunerate a spouse or a related minor for services provided in a business carried on by the payer as long as certain conditions in the Act are met. These conditions require that the amount paid must be deductible in determining the payer's business income (according to the general rules of deductibility discussed in Chapter 4) and included in the recipient's income. Payments under the child tax benefits program, as discussed in ¶10,530, are not subject to the income attribution rule applicable on transfers or loans to minors. As a result, the income attribution rules do not apply to income arising from child tax benefits transferred or loaned to the child.

ITA: 74.1(2) Transfers and loans to minors, 74.5(12)(b); Interpretation Bulletins: IT-510 Transfers and loans of property made after May 22, 1985 to related minor, IT-511R Interspousal and certain other transfers and loans of property

¶6,130.60 Corporation

Finally, anti-avoidance rules generally prevent income splitting through the use of a corporation. This provision is discussed at greater length in Chapter 13.

ITA: 74.4 [Transfers and loans to corporations]

¶6,135 "Second-Generations" Income From Property

The term "property" is defined in the Act. It includes substituted property, but does not include income earned on attributed income, often referred to as "second-generation" income.

ITA: 248(1) Definitions, 248(5) Substituted property

Example

Second-generation Income

If a $10,000 bond bearing interest at 10% annually is given to a spouse, the $1,000 of interest income received by the recipient of the bond is attributed to the transferor spouse. If the $1,000 is reinvested by the recipient spouse at, say, 10%, the $100 of interest earned on the reinvested interest is not attributed to the transferor spouse. The $100 is income of the recipient spouse earned on income, i.e., the $1,000, that has been attributed. Hence, the $100 is referred to as second-generation income.

¶6,140 Loans or Transfers to Non-Arm's Length Individuals Who Are 18 Years of Age or Older

The attribution rules do not apply to loans or transfers to non-arm's length persons who are 18 years of age or older. However, anti-avoidance rules prevent the avoidance of tax on loans between non-arm's length individuals. Income from property resulting from a low-interest or a no-interest loan by an individual to another non-arm's length individual will be attributed back to the lender. The key condition for the attribution rule to apply is that one of the main reasons for the loan is to reduce or avoid tax on income from the property or substituted property. Therefore, loans between non-arm's length individuals, both of whom are taxed at the same rate, would appear not to be caught by these provisions. Similarly, if the loaned funds are spent on non-income-producing property (e.g., personal-use property, living expenses, etc.), then the "one of the main reasons" test would not be met. Note that the attribution rules apply only to loans, but not to sales or gifts.

ITA: 56(4.1) Interest free or low interest loans, 56(4.3) Repayment of existing indebtedness, 74.1 [Transfers and loans to spouse or common-law partner or minor], 74.5 Transfers for fair market consideration

Loans that bear a commercial or arm's length rate of interest are exempt from the attribution rule. The interest must, in fact, be paid within 30 days of the end of the year in respect of which it was charged for the exemption to apply. Refinancing a loan subject to the above attribution rule with another loan will not circumvent the attribution rule.

ITA: 56(4.1) Interest free or low interest loans, 56(4.2) Exception, 56(4.3) Repayment of existing indebtedness

¶6,145 Summary of Income Attribution Rules

Exhibit 6-2 summarizes the major rules pertaining to the attribution of income from property.

Exhibit 6-2 Attribution of Income[1] From Property[2] Conceptual Summary

	Transaction		
Recipient	**Transfer by gift**	**Transfer by sale**	**Transaction involving a loan**
Spouse or common-law partner[3] [ssec. 74.1(1)]	• Income or loss from property attributed to transferor	• If no fair market value consideration received: Income or loss from property attributed to transferor	• If no interest at a commercial rate paid: Income or loss from property attributed to transferor
		• If fair market value consideration received:[4] No attribution	• If interest at a commercial rate paid:[4] No attribution
Minors who are not at arm's length [secs. 251 and 252] or who are nieces and nephews [ssec. 74.1(2)]	• Income or loss from property attributed to transferor	• Same as for transfer by gift (dependent on whether fair market value consideration received)	• Same as for transfer by gift (dependent on whether fair market value consideration received)
Other non-arm's length individuals not subject to section 74.1 [ssec. 56(4.1)]	• No attribution	• No attribution	• Income only from property attributed to transferor, if one of the main reasons for the loan was to reduce or avoid tax and market rate of interest not paid

[1] Excluding second-generation income.

[2] Including substituted property as defined in subsection 248(5). Income from business is not attributed in any of these transactions. Attribution of capital gains or losses is discussed in Chapter 7.

[3] Attribution of capital gains and losses on transfers or loans to a spouse is discussed in Chapter 7.

[4] To avoid attribution, the taxpayer must elect to waive the deferral of accrued income under subsection 73(1) (discussed in ¶6,120 and ¶7,215.40) and must transfer for fair market value consideration. Where a loan is involved, interest at a commercial rate must be paid within 30 days of the end of every year in which the loan is outstanding.

¶6,150 Tax on Split Income Earned by Persons Under 18 Years of Age — "The Kiddie Tax"

Overview

The income attribution rules discussed above do not apply to income from a business, such as a proprietorship or a partnership, transferred to a minor. Prior to the introduction of the "kiddie tax", it was possible to split income with minor children without attribution applying, as corporate attribution rules do not apply to dividends from certain private corporations that carry on an active business in Canada.

To address this exclusion from attribution rules, a specific anti-avoidance rule was introduced. In general, the "kiddie tax" rules apply to dividends from a private Canadian or foreign corporation. This tax eliminates the incentive to income split through distributions of dividends from private corporations to minor children. The tax rate on these dividends is the top marginal tax rate of an individual, and the amount of tax payable is net of the dividend tax credit and the foreign tax credit. The minor child cannot use any other tax credits (such as the personal tax credit — discussed in Chapter 10) to reduce their overall tax payable.

ITA: 120.4 Tax on split income [Kiddie tax]

¶6,150.10 Split Income

The special tax, introduce in 2000, on split income applies to the following types of income that are earned by persons under 18 years of age:

ITA: 120.4 Tax on split income [Kiddie tax]

- taxable dividends derived from shares that are not listed on a designated Canadian or foreign stock exchange (i.e., essentially, shares of a private corporation) and that are received directly or indirectly through a trust or partnership;
- taxable capital gains derived from shares that are not listed on a designated Canadian or foreign stock exchange (i.e., essentially, shares of a private corporation) and that are received directly or indirectly through a trust or partnership; providing they are:
  (1) included in the income of a minor, and
  (2) from a disposition of shares to a non-arm's length person if taxable dividends on such shares would have been subject to the tax on split income;
- shareholder benefits included in the minor's income under section15; and
- partnership or trust income, including taxable capital gains, derived from the provision of goods and services to a business that is carried on by:
  (1) a person related to the minor,
  (2) a corporation which has a "specified shareholder" who is related to the minor, or
  (3) a professional corporation which has a shareholder who is related to the minor.

ITA: 248(1) Definitions

In the case of taxable capital gains listed above, for the purpose of the "kiddie tax", an amount equal to two times these taxable capital gains will be deemed to be dividends and subject to "kiddie tax" at the top marginal rate. Since capital gains are considered to accrue from reinvested retained earnings, it would be possible to avoid the tax on split income ("kiddie tax") in a non-arm's length situation by retaining income in the

ITA: 120.4(4) Taxable capital gain

corporation rather than paying it out as a dividend. The dividends could be paid out once the minor child reaches the age of 18.

Proposed amendments to the *Income Tax Act* released July 18, 2017, and a later revision to the amendments in draft legislation released December 13, 2017, drastically limits the ability to split income with low-income family members through an extension of the tax on split income (TOSI) rules effective January 1, 2018. Chapter 13 provides a thorough discussion of the new rules.

¶6,150.20 Tax Treatment of Split Income

The split income is:

- subject to tax at the top marginal rate, including applicable surtax, instead of the graduated rates;
- not eligible for any deductions or credits, except for the dividend tax credit and foreign tax credits; and
- eligible for an offsetting deduction from taxable income equal to the specified income, so that this amount would not be taxed again normally under Part I of the Act.

Note that the tax on split income applies to the minor, at the top marginal tax rate, and not to the transferor of the property. This is punitive as there is no ability to reduce the marginal tax rate. This also indicates that attribution does not apply to any income that is subject to the tax on split income (the "kiddie tax").

ITA: 56(5) Exception for split income, 74.5(13) Exception from attribution rules

¶6,150.30 Exceptions to Tax on Split Income (TOSI)

The special income splitting tax does not apply to:

- income from a corporation or a partnership paid to individuals over 18 years of age (i.e., not a "specified individual");
- taxable dividends from shares listed on a designated stock exchange, which may be subject to the attribution rules applicable to minors;
- reasonable remuneration to minors, which is not subject to the attribution rules;
- capital gains on the disposition of the shares of a private Canadian or foreign corporation, which is not subject to the attribution rules;
- income from property inherited from a parent, which would not be subject to the attribution rules;
- minors who have no parent who is resident in Canada at any time in the year; or
- income from property inherited from someone other than a parent if the minor is in full-time attendance at a post-secondary institution or is eligible for the disability tax credit.

Example

Christine has heard that she can save some tax by having her children, ages 14 and 16, own shares in her company and then paying them dividends. Since her children only earn a small amount of income they will pay little, if any, tax and can use the cash to finance their educations. Christine has been advised that she can exchange her common shares for preference shares and have her children purchase new common shares for a nominal price using their own cash, thereby avoiding the attribution rules. Her company only earns active business income.

In this case, the regular attribution rules will not apply, but "kiddie tax" will apply. The shares are private-company shares and the persons receiving the dividends are less than 18 years of age. As a result, the dividends will be taxed at the top marginal tax rate and any income-splitting benefit will be lost.

¶6,155 What Else Can Be "Income Split"?

In general, income splitting is still permissible under certain situations. For example, the spousal RRSP contribution and income splitting on pension income is allowed in the Act. We will discuss this topic more in later chapters.

ITA: 56(1)(a.1) Benefits under CPP/QPP

¶6,190 Pause and Reflect — Summary of Learning Goals

After working through this section, ¶6,100, you should be able to:

- explain the meaning of related persons and how that relates to the attribution rules;
- explain the attribution rules and the circumstances in which they apply;
- explain the various anti-avoidance rules relating to attribution;
- explain the purpose of the "kiddie tax" and the circumstances in which "kiddie tax" applies;
- apply your knowledge to calculate the tax implications of splitting income with a non-arm's length individual;
- apply your knowledge to calculate the tax implications of receiving income subject to the "kiddie tax"; and
- apply your knowledge to advise a client on planning methods to avoid income attribution.

¶6,190.99 Practise What You've Learned

Refer to the following sections of the Study Guide to practise what you've learned:

¶6,800 — Review Questions

- Question 2 — Attribution
- Question 3 — Attribution

¶6,825 — Multiple Choice Questions

- Question 3 — Attribution
- Question 6 — Kiddie Tax

¶6,850 — Exercises

- Exercise 2 — Attribution — Spouse
- Exercise 10 — Non-arm's length transactions

¶6,200 Deductions

Overview

After reviewing the property income inclusion, we can now discuss the income deductions that are available in the current legislation. The rules related to deductions can be found in two main sections:

- Sec. 18 Limitations on the deductibility of expenses
- Sec. 20 Deductions permitted

As with the calculation of business income (reviewed in Chapter 4), the general rules in section 18 of the Act outline some basic concepts for deduction. The most commonly applied rules are:

- Income earning test: no outlay or expense may be deducted unless it was made or incurred for the purposes of earning income. The general starting point for this is generally accepted accounting principles.

ITA: 18(1)a), 18(1)(b)
Capital outlay or loss

- Capital test: no deduction of a capital outlay, unless specifically listed in the Act.
- Reserve test: no deduction of a reserve, unless specifically listed in the Act.
- Personal expense test: no deduction of expenses that relate to personal expenses.
- Reasonableness test: all expenses must be reasonable under the circumstances.

When reviewing the Act to determine the eligibility of the deduction of expenses against property income, the starting point should be to review the rules in section 18. If those rules deny the deduction of an expense, either through the general rules or specific exclusion rules, one must then look at the rules in section 20. Section 20 deals with deductions of certain items that were excluded because of the section 18 limitations. In essence, section 20 overrides the rules listed in section 18.

Example

An individual owns a house that is currently being used to earn rental income. We need to determine if the individual can deduct the cost of purchasing the house against the rental income earned in the year.

Step 1 — Review Section 18 to determine if there are any restrictions on the deduction.

- Income earning test: the cost of the house was incurred to earn property income; therefore, this test is met.
- Capital test: the house is a long-term asset that may be used for many years to earn property income. This test states that no deduction may be taken if it is on account of capital. For this reason, the cost of the house cannot be deducted.

Step 2 — Review Section 20 to determine if there are any exceptions to the restriction in section 18.

- Paragraph 20(1)(a) specifically allows the deduction for capital cost allowance for capital items in accordance with the rules included in the *Income Tax Regulations*.

Step 3 — Conclude on the deductibility of the cost of the house

- Since Section 20 has a specific rule that allows the deduction of capital cost over time, section 20 overrides section 18 and allows the deduction.

After working through section ¶6,200 of the chapter, you will be able to:

- explain the basic rules for determining the deductibility of an expense against property income;
- explain the limitations on the deduction of CCA against rental income;
- explain the various limitations on the deductibility of interest income;
- apply your knowledge to calculate the amount of interest that may be deducted on vacant land and buildings under construction; and
- apply your knowledge to advise a taxpayer on the options available for specific expenses and the overall tax implications of those options.

¶6,205 Limitation on Deduction of Carrying Charges — Vacant Land

Carrying charges, such as interest and property taxes, on vacant land are only deductible to the extent of the taxpayer's net income from the land. These rules apply to property developers whose business is the sale or development of land, or to land that is held but not used in a business. This restriction discourages speculation in real estate (where the intention is not to use the real estate for business purposes but to hold the piece of property for capital gains).

ITA: 18(2) Limit on certain interest and property tax, 18(2)(d), 18(3) Definitions, 53(1)(h) [Adjustments to cost base — Land]

Under these rules, any carrying charges that cannot be deducted will be added to the cost base of the land. An increase in the cost base of the land will reduce the capital gain on the sale of the land. Capital gains are covered in Chapter 7.

Exceptions to This Rule

Land which is used or held primarily for an income-producing purpose is exempted from the above limitation. In a special case where the land is vacant for part of the year and used for business for the remainder, the carrying charges would be deductible, as the Act does not specify a minimum time period in the year. However, the costs during construction on the land would not be deductible (see ¶6,210 below).

Corporations whose principal business is the leasing, rental or sale, and the development for lease, rental or sale of real property are permitted to deduct carrying charges on vacant land, in excess of net income before deducting carrying charges. The limit of this deduction is the corporation's "base level deduction". That limit is interest computed at the prescribed rate (as previously discussed in this Chapter) on a loan of $1 million outstanding throughout the year. ITA: 18(2) Limit on certain interest and property tax, 18(2)(f), 18(3) Definitions

Example Problem 6-8

In 2016, Mr. Walkovia acquired a vacant lot in a downtown area of the city intending to build an office complex. By late 2018, he decided to abandon the project. The property was disposed of just before the end of the year. Because of the unforeseen problems encountered in the development, it was not considered to have been held for speculation.

While the property was owned by Mr. Walkovia, it had been used as a city parking lot with the following results:

	2016	2017	2018
Net income (loss) before interest and property taxes*	$11,000	$ 6,000	$ (3,000)
Interest and property taxes	9,500	10,000	10,500

* This amount is equal to gross revenue in excess of all other expenses.

REQUIRED

(A) Consider the effect of these data on the income of Mr. Walkovia for tax purposes.

(B) If the land had been owned by a corporation whose principal business was the development and sale of land, what would be the effects of these data? Assume a prescribed rate of interest of 8% throughout the period in question.

SOLUTION

(A) Since the land, held for development in this case, is not excluded from the limitation, interest and property taxes will be deductible only to the extent of gross revenues in excess of all other expenses, i.e., net income before interest and property taxes. As a result, the following amounts would be reported as income for the years indicated:

ITA: 18(2) Limit on certain interest and property tax

	2016	2017	2018
Gross revenue less expenses other than interest and property taxes	$11,000	$ 6,000	$(3,000)
Less: interest and property taxes	9,500	10,000	Nil
Income (loss) for the year	$ 1,500	Nil	$(3,000)
Non-deductible interest and property taxes added to adjusted cost base of land	Nil	$ 4,000	$10,500

(B) In this case, a loss created by the deduction of interest and property tax is permitted. However, the excess of interest and property tax that is deductible is limited to an amount of interest computed at the 8% prescribed rate, assumed in this case, on a notional principal amount of $1,000,000. The $80,000 limit in this case is referred to as the base level deduction. The following losses would be reported by a corporation:

ITA: 18(2)(f)

		2016		2017		2018
Gross revenue less expenses other than interest and property taxes		$11,000		$6,000		$(3,000)
Less the lesser of:						
(a) interest and property taxes	$9,500		$10,000		$10,500	
(b) base level deduction	$80,000		$80,000		$80,000	
lesser amount		(9,500)		(10,000)		(10,500)
Income (loss) for the year		$1,500		$(4,000)		$(13,000)

Note that the losses are of value to a corporation if it generates sufficient income from other sources to be absorbed by the deduction of the losses. For that reason, the value of losses is inherent in the ability to shield income from tax.

¶6,210 "Soft Costs" Relating to Construction of Buildings or Ownership of Land

"Soft costs" include interest expenses, legal and accounting fees, mortgage fees, insurance, and property taxes. Soft costs incurred, during the period of construction, renovation, or alternation of a building are not deductible as current expenses, and must be added to the cost of the building. Similarly, such costs in respect of the ownership of the land on which the building is under construction must also be capitalized.

Note that the restriction on the deduction of these expenses only applies to expenses incurred before completion of construction, renovation, or alternation of the building. The Act provides for the determination of the date on which the work is completed. It is also worth noting that the Act specifies that capitalization is required for the costs "attributable" to, and not merely incurred in, the period of construction. For example, a company must capitalize the interest on the bank loan it took out to construct a building for the time during which construction took place. If the company chose to prepay some of the interest before construction commenced, it still would not be able to deduct the interest in the current year.

ITA: 18(3.1) Costs relating to construction of building or ownership of land, 18(3.3) Completion

Costs such as capital cost allowance on the building, the landscaping expenses, and disability-related modifications to buildings are exempted from the above rules. The Act permits a taxpayer to deduct soft costs incurred in the year up to the taxpayer's income earned on the building that's under construction, renovation, or alternation.

ITA: 18(3.1) Costs relating to construction of building or ownership of land

Issuance costs, such as accounting fees and underwriter fees, are one-time costs to acquire financing for the project of acquiring long-term capital assets. While some portion of such costs is inevitably attributable to the period of construction, it is difficult to determine how much. Therefore, the general tax treatment is to amortize these costs over five years (similar to the treatment of other financing fees) instead of through the CCA schedule of the underlying asset.

ITA: 20(1)(e) Expenses re financing

¶6,215 Rental Properties — Limitations Related to CCA

Overview

As seen in Chapter 5, the capital cost of a long-term asset can be deducted through the capital cost allowance ("CCA") system. The CCA is computed on the balance at the end of the year in a pool or class of similar assets. Dispositions throughout the year reduce the balance in a class and may even cause the balance to be negative. However, to the extent that disposals are offset by a purchase of more assets for the class during the year, recapture will be deferred. Thus, the ability to offset a negative balance in a class of assets with purchases of similar assets during the year reduces or eliminates the need to pay tax on income from recapture of capital cost allowances on the sale of an asset in the year. The Act restricts this ability for certain rental property to avoid the deferral of recapture indefinitely.

¶6,215.10 Separate CCA Classes — Rental Property Over $50,000

Each rental property purchased that costs $50,000 or more must be placed in a separate CCA class. This will result in recapture when a building is sold for proceeds in excess of the undepreciated capital cost in the class (i.e., when the UCC balance becomes negative at the end of the taxation year).

The purpose of the rule is to prevent taxpayers from avoiding recapture of CCA when selling a rental property by buying another rental property of the same class. Without this provision, a taxpayer could buy a new rental property at the end of the taxation year to offset the negative balance. The separate class rule intends to force recognition of recapture each time the pool has a negative balance, as a result of a sale.

¶6,215.20 Losses from Rental Property

The aggregation formula reviewed in ¶1,220.30 highlights the fact that property losses can be used to reduce other sources of income. The Act restricts the ability to create or increase a rental loss using CCA. The purpose of this provision is to restrict a taxpayer's ability to shelter other sources of income by offsetting a loss created by capital cost allowances on a rental building or leasing properties against those other sources of income. For example, rental losses from CCA will not be available to shield income from employment or from business.

ITA: 3(d)

As an exception to this rule, losses created by capital cost allowances on rental property will not be deductible from non-rental income. However, rental property is narrowly defined to mean the rental building, thereby excluding furniture and fixtures from this treatment. As a result, the regulations dealing with leasing properties were added to prohibit the deduction of losses from non-rental income created by capital cost allowance on furniture and fixtures leased in a building except for corporations in the business of leasing property. Thus, a taxpayer cannot shelter other sources of income by offsetting a loss created by capital cost allowances on a rental building or leasing properties against those other sources of income, unless the taxpayer is a corporation or a partnership of corporations whose principal business was the property rental or leasing business.

ITR: 1100(11) Rental Properties, 1100(14) Rental Properties, 1100(15) Leasing Properties, 1100(20) Leasing Properties; Interpretation Bulletins: IT-195R4 Rental property — Capital cost allowance restrictions

Example Problem 6-9

Irene owns six rental buildings with the following information pertaining to each:

	Building					
	1	2	3	4	5	6
Cost	$30,000	$132,000	$71,000	$49,000	$350,000	$47,000
UCC, January 1, 2018	22,000	90,000	49,000	40,000	238,000	38,000
Rental revenue in 2018	1,600	17,000	8,000	3,800	45,000	6,000
Cash expenses:						
Interest	Nil	$ 1,200	$1,700	Nil	$ 3,200	$1,400

	Building 1	Building 2	Building 3	Building 4	Building 5	Building 6
Property taxes	$400	3,000	1,500	$ 800	8,000	1,200
Other expenses	800	11,000	7,500	1,600	29,000	5,800

Late in 2018, buildings 1 and 2 were sold for proceeds of $40,000 and $91,000, respectively.

Building 5 was built by Irene in 2012 to be rented as a warehouse. All other buildings were purchased after 1987.

REQUIRED

Prepare a schedule showing the maximum capital cost allowance which may be claimed for tax purposes assuming Irene owns no other rental properties. Assume all buildings are of brick construction.

SOLUTION

	CLASS 1: 4%			CLASS 1 (NRB): 6%
	BUILDINGS 1, 4, 6 UNDER $50,000	BUILDING 2	BUILDING 3	BUILDING 5
UCC, January 1, 2018	$100,000	$90,000	$49,000	$238,000
Dispositions in the year	30,000[(1)]	91,000	-	-
UCC, December 31, 2018	$ 70,000	$(1,000)	$49,000	$238,000
CCA for 2018 (max.: $4,300 see below)	2,800[(2)]	-	1,500[(2)]	Nil
Recapture	-	1,000	-	-
UCC, January 1, 2019	$ 67,200	Nil	$47,500	$238,000

	CLASS 1: 4%			CLASS 1 (NRB): 6%
	BUILDINGS 1, 4, 6 UNDER $50,000	BUILDING 2	BUILDING 3	BUILDING 5
Total Revenue in 2018				$ 81,400
Add: recapture [ssec. 13(1)–(3)]				1,000
Less: total cash expenses				(78,100)
Net income before CCA				$ 4,300
CCA — Amount deductible re: limitation				(4,300)

NOTES TO SOLUTION

(1) The balance is never reduced by more than the original cost on the disposition of an asset; capital gain of $10,000 (i.e., $40,000 – $30,000).

(2) CCA potentially available in 2018:

Buildings with cost under $50,000 (4% of $70,000)	$ 2,800
Building 3 (4% of $49,000)	1,960
Building 5 (6% of $238,000)	14,280
Total	$16,660

Where deducting the maximum allowable CCA is not possible, as in this case, or not desirable, it is usually advisable to take CCA in lower-rate classes first. This preserves a higher balance in the higher-rate classes for the future when it may be possible to deduct relatively higher amounts of CCA in the higher-rate classes.

¶6,220 Interest Deduction

Overview

"Interest" is not a defined term in the Act. The determination of what is interest is a question of law. The definition of interest has been addressed in several court decisions, including *Shell Canada Limited v. The Queen* and *Miller v. The Queen*. As in *Miller*, interest for tax purposes is generally accepted to mean an amount that has met three criteria:

Cases: 99 DTC 5669*Brenda J. Miller v. Her Majesty The Queen*, 85 DTC 5354 (FCTD)

- the amount must be calculated on a day-to-day accrual basis,

- the amount must be calculated on a principal sum (or a right to a principal sum), and
- the amount must be compensation for the use of the principal sum (or the right to the principal sum).

In general, interest represents payment for the use of debt capital. The Act allows a taxpayer to deduct interest on money borrowed to earn income from business or property. ITA: 20(1)(c) Interest

A taxpayer can deduct interest if it:

- is paid or payable in the year,
- arises from a legal obligation,
- is payable on borrowed money that is used for the purpose of earning income (other than exempt income) from a business or property, and
- is reasonable in amount.

¶6,220.10 Interest

There are some statutory limits on the deduction of interest. We have discussed some of them in Chapter 4. The following are a few examples:

- the deduction of interest imposed under the Act is denied; ITA: 18(1)(i) Limitation re employer's contribution under supplementary unemployment benefit plan
- the deduction of interest on funds borrowed to buy vacant land is limited; ITA: 18(2) Limit on certain interest and property tax
- interest that is part of "soft costs" must be capitalized; ITA: 18(3.1) Costs relating to construction of building or ownership of land
- the deduction of interest paid to certain non-residents is limited; and ITA: 18(4)–18(8)
- the deduction for interest on borrowed funds to make a contribution to tax sheltered retirement savings funds, such as RRSPs, is denied. ITA: 18(11) Limitation

Note that the interest on interest is called compound interest. Compound interest is deductible if the original amount borrowed meets the test of interest deductibility. However, compound interest is only deductible when it is paid and not when it is payable.

Example

A parent with two children is preparing a will. One child is active in the parent's business and the other is not. The parent is considering the following two options with respect to the business:

(1) leave the business to the child who will be active in the business on the condition that the child give the other child an amount equal to 50% of the fair market value of the business on the parent's death, and

(2) leave 50% of the business to each of the two children on the condition that the child who will be active in the business buy the 50% left to the other child.

In either case, the active child will have to borrow the funds to pay the other child. We must determine which is the best alternative for the child who will be active in the business.

Based on the use of the borrowed funds, the interest incurred under the second alternative will be deductible, because the funds will be used to buy shares which will produce income. Interest incurred under the first alternative will not be deductible, because the use of the borrowed funds will not produce income.

¶6,220.20 Loss of the Source of Income

From the above section, we know that the general principle of interest deductibility is that the borrowed money must be used for the purpose of earning income from a business or property. However, a problem can arise if an investment financed with debt declines in value and is sold at a loss. The investor reinvests the proceeds but does not pay off the loan. Should interest still be deductible when the source of income is lost?

Example

A taxpayer borrows $10,000 to acquire an income-producing property. During the holding period of that property, the interest has been deducted from income for tax purposes. When the property declines in value to $6,000, the property is sold and the taxpayer invests the $6,000 of proceeds in another income-producing property. The original loan has not been repaid. Determine whether the interest expense on the loan related to the $4,000 realized loss in value will be deductible.

If we use the general principle of interest deductibility, the interest on the remaining debt would no longer be deductible as it is not currently used for the purpose of earning income from a business or property. The Act addresses this issue. A rule applies to deem the $4,000 of borrowed money to continue to be used for the purpose of earning income from the property, as long as the original property was capital property (other than real estate or depreciable property). This allows the interest on the $4,000 to qualify for the deduction.

ITA: 20.1 [Borrowed money used to earn income from business or property]

¶6,220.30 Capitalization of Interest

At the taxpayer's election, the Act permits certain borrowing costs and interest to be treated as non-deductible expenses and added to the cost of depreciable property in respect of which the expenses were incurred. This election might be made, for example, if the deduction of such costs would create a loss that could not be absorbed in the loss carryover period which will be discussed in a later Chapter. The costs eligible for such deferment are amounts otherwise deductible as interest and other expenses of borrowing money. This is particularly advantageous if the interest is in respect of assets in fast write-off classes such as Class 12.

ITA: 21 Cost of borrowed money; 20(1)(c) Interest, 20(1)(d) Compound interest, 20(1)(e) Expenses re financing

¶6,225 Carrying Charges

Individual taxpayers may claim carrying charges as deductions against property income such as interest and dividends. The deductions available to individual taxpayers include: management or safe custody fees, accounting fees, and any other carrying costs normally incurred to earn property income. The deduction of safety deposit box fees is specifically prohibited.

ITA: 18(11)(i.1)

Brokerage fees incurred on the purchase and sale of securities are not deductible as a carrying charge. Commissions charged on the acquisitions of shares become part of the adjusted cost base and commissions charged on disposition reduce the capital gain or loss. These fees represent a capital charge and affect the capital gain or loss on eventual sale of the securities.

ITA: 40 [Calculation of gain, loss or reserve]

¶6,230 Investment Counsel Fees

Taxpayers can also deduct fees paid for the advisability of purchasing or selling a specific security or for the administration or management of shares or securities. These fees must be paid to advisers whose principal business is investment counselling and fund management and must be related to earning income outside of a tax-deferred account or registered retirement savings plan.

ITA: 20(1)(bb) Fees paid to investment counsel; Interpretation Bulletins: IT-124R6 Contributions to Registered Retirement Savings Plans, IT- 238R2

¶6,235 Legal and Accounting Fees

All legal and accounting fees are deductible to the extent that they are incurred for the purpose of gaining or producing business or property income. It is important to note that the purpose of the fees determines whether they are deductible. Generally, fees incurred for preparing financial records, minutes of shareholder meetings, making annual corporate findings, conducting appeals for taxes, and watching legislation that affects the taxpayer's business or property income are deductible. Specifically, the Act allows a deduction for fees paid for advice or assistance in preparing an objection or appeal to the CRA, Tax Court or other government office. Any costs awarded to taxpayers for amounts deducted under this provision must be included in income. Fees for preparation of income tax returns are also deductible if there is a source of property income.

ITA: 20(1)(cc) Expenses of representation, 56(1)(i) Deferred profit sharing plan, 60(o) Legal expenses; Interpretation Bulletins: IT-99R5 Legal and Accounting Fees

Fees incurred for the acquisition/sale of capital property are included as part of the cost of the property or reduce the sale proceeds.

¶6,240 Foreign Non-Business Income Tax

Investors with foreign investments are generally subject to withholding tax in the foreign jurisdiction. Taxpayers resident in Canada must pay tax on their worldwide income. To provide taxpayers with relief, a foreign tax credit is available. This credit is limited to 15% of the foreign income from property. However, the Act permits individuals to claim a deduction from property income equal to the foreign taxes paid in excess of 15%. A foreign tax credit is usually more advantageous than a deduction because the credit is applied directly against income taxes.

ITA: 126 Foreign tax deduction, 20(11) Foreign taxes on income from property exceeding 15%, 20(12) Foreign non-business income tax

This position, taken by the CRA, was confirmed in the case of *The Queen v. Bronfman Trust*, when the Supreme Court of Canada held that what was important was the use of the borrowed funds. In this decision, the Supreme Court, in its examination, was not able to trace the funds borrowed directly to an income-earning source (eligible use source) and,

Cases: *Her Majesty The Queen v. Phyllis Barbara*

hence, denied the deduction of the related interest. It would appear that in these cases, the decision in the *Bronfman Trust* case would stand. Therefore, in order for interest on borrowed funds to be deductible, the taxpayer must still trace the funds borrowed to an income-producing purpose.

Bronfman Trust, 87 DTC 5059 (SCC)

¶6,245 Depreciation-Based or Similar Tax Shelters

Depreciation-based or similar tax shelters such as residential buildings, films, yachts, hotels, recreational vehicles and nursing homes have been available in the past. They have been used as a tool of fiscal policy to encourage investment in certain areas by providing a fast write-off. For example, a high CCA rate, or a large absolute dollar write-off of an amount invested will reduce the after-tax cash outflow of the initial investment. As extensive use of these shelters is perceived as abuse of the system by the Department of Finance, the ability to shelter other income with losses created by capital cost allowances has been either eliminated or reduced in effect.

Assets sold as tax shelters have been very high risk investments, with probably only a small chance that the investment would be profitable. The main advantage of an investment in a sheltered asset has been a tax deferral which was most valuable to those in the higher tax brackets. For example, an investor purchasing a $100,000 interest in an asset may have had to pay only $5,000 in the first year, but was entitled to a $15,000 tax deduction of capital cost allowance at the 30% rate for Class 10, subject to the half-year rule. However, the $95,000 balance will have to be paid, and the investor may be confronted by cash flow problems if he or she receives no income from the asset. These investments are also usually very illiquid.

All investments shelter the cost of the investment from taxation. For example, it will be demonstrated in the next two Chapters how the cost of an investment in stock is "written off" against the proceeds of disposition when the stock is sold. It can be shown that the advantage of the faster write-off of a tax shelter cannot provide a profit for an investment that does not return both its cost and its after-tax carrying charges. Thus, an investment decision should be made primarily on its value as an investment without regard to any accelerated tax write-off that may be available and should not be based solely on the advantage of an early or large write-off of the investment. There is little advantage to making a $100,000 investment that turns out to be almost worthless, in order to write off the $100,000 and save about $50,000 in taxes!

¶6,290 Pause and Reflect — Summary of Learning Goals

After working through this section, ¶6,200, you should be able to:

- Explain the basic rules for determining the deductibility of an expense against property income.
- Explain the limitations to the deduction of CCA against rental income.
- Explain the various limitations on the deductibility of interest income.
- Apply your knowledge to calculate the amount of interest that may be deducted on vacant land and buildings under construction.
- Apply your knowledge to advise a taxpayer on the options available for specific expenses and the overall tax implications of those options.

¶6,290.99 Practise What You've Learned

Refer to the following sections of the Study Guide to practise what you've learned:

¶6,800 — Review Questions

- Question 4 — Interest deductibility
- Question 5 — CCA on rental income
- Question 6 — Interest deductibility
- Question 9 — Interest deductibility

¶6,825 — Multiple Choice Questions

- Question 2 — Rental property CCA
- Question 4 — Deductible expenses

¶6,850 — Exercises

- Exercise 1 — Interest income
- Exercise 3 — Carrying charges on land
- Exercise 4 — Rental property CCA
- Exercise 5 — Rental property disposal
- Exercise 6 — Interest deductibility
- Exercise 7 — Rental property
- Exercise 8 — Rental property during construction
- Exercise 9 — Business or property income expenditure

¶6,300 Personal Loan Planning and Interest Deductibility

Overview

In general, as indicated above, expenditures made or incurred for the purpose of gaining or producing income from property are deductible from that income. The amounts of such expenditures must be reasonable in the circumstances.

¶6,305 Deductibility of Interest Expenses

Under the current concept of interest deductibility, there need only be a reasonable expectation of earning income. The concept of income in this case is general, referring to gross income inclusions for tax purposes, not net income. No income need actually be earned in a year in order to deduct interest paid or payable in that year.

ITA: 20(1)(c) Interest

In the case of preferred shares or fixed income securities producing interest held by an individual, the CRA will allow an interest expense deduction that is not restricted to the income from the investment. Interest at a reasonable rate on funds borrowed to buy common shares will be fully deductible irrespective of the dividend yield, which may even be zero, because of the reasonable expectation of an increase in the dividend rate on common shares.

Income Tax Folio: S3-F6-C1 Interest Deductibility

The deductibility of interest is determined by the use of the borrowed funds. Thus, interest paid on a mortgage, the proceeds of which are used to invest in certain securities, is deductible because the interest is paid in respect of funds used to produce income. On the other hand, interest on funds borrowed to purchase personal property is not deductible because it is not used to produce income.

Loan planning would suggest that the taxpayer borrow funds which will be used to produce income, thereby making the interest tax deductible. This permits the taxpayer to allocate his or her savings to purchases such as assets used for personal purposes, including the family home or a car not used for business, which do not produce income.

Great care must be taken in maintaining the connection between the interest paid and the use of the funds borrowed. In one case, a taxpayer received a loan from his employer and used the proceeds to finance the purchase of securities. He secured the loan with a mortgage on his house. In this situation, the interest on the loan was deductible because the loan could be directly linked to the purchase of the securities. However, when the taxpayer was transferred and he sold his house, he had to pay off the loan from the proceeds of sale. He then purchased another house in his new work location and financed the purchase with a mortgage. He deducted mortgage interest on the new house against his investment income on the same basis as before, but the CRA disallowed that interest deduction. It was argued that the money was not used to produce income, but to acquire the new house. In this case, the taxpayer did not maintain the direct connection between the loan and the use of the funds. Had he not paid off the employer's loan but secured the loan with a new mortgage on the new home, he would have maintained that connection.

Income Tax Folio: S3-F6-C1 Interest Deductibility

Case Summary

The Queen v. Bronfman Trust

The requirement to maintain a direct connection between the loan and the income-earning property was confirmed in the case of *The Queen v. Bronfman Trust*, when the Supreme Court of Canada held that what was important was the use of the borrowed funds.

Cases: *Her Majesty The Queen v. Phyllis Barbara Bronfman Trust*, 87 DTC 5059 (SCC)

In this case, the Supreme Court, in its examination, was not able to trace the funds borrowed directly to an income-earning source (eligible use source) and, hence, denied the deduction of the related interest. Based on this decision we can conclude that if other similar situations occur where the funds borrowed could not be traced to the income-earning source, the courts would deny the deduction of interest. Therefore, in order for interest on borrowed funds to be deductible, the taxpayer must still trace the funds borrowed to an income-producing purpose.

¶6,310 Commentary on *Singleton* and *Ludco*

Case Summary

Singleton

(i) Facts

Singleton involved a lawyer who had a capital account in his law firm with a balance of at least $300,000. Mr. Singleton's firm paid him his $300,000 capital and he used the funds to purchase a new house. On the same day, he borrowed $300,000 and contributed it to his firm as a capital contribution, where it was used by the firm as working capital in its business. The loan was secured on the house. Although the house was purchased in his wife's name, Mr. Singleton was legally obligated to make the mortgage payments, thereby fulfilling the requirement that the interest be paid pursuant to a "legal obligation".

Cases: *The Queen v. John R. Singleton*, 2001 DTC 5533 (SCC)

(ii) Issue

The issue of *Singleton* is whether the borrowed money was used for the purpose of earning income from a business.

(iii) The Supreme Court of Canada Decision

The Supreme Court of Canada held that the interest payments were deductible under the *Income Tax Act*. The court concluded that, given the effect of the legal relationships, the taxpayer borrowed money and used that money to refinance the capital account in the law firm. This was a direct and eligible use of funds within the meaning of the provision which allows the deduction of interest on borrowed funds.

ITA: 20(1)(c) Interest

Case Summary

Ludco

(i) Facts

In *Ludco*, the taxpayer used approximately $7.5 million of borrowed money to purchase shares in two offshore corporations in the Bahamas (known as a tax haven). During the period in which it held the shares, Ludco deducted approximately $6 million of interest and included $600,000 of dividends in its incomes. When the shares were disposed of, it reported a gain of $9,200,000.

Cases: *Ludco et al v. The Queen*, 2001 DTC 5505 (SCC)

The Minister disallowed the deduction of the $6 million interest expense on the grounds that the shares were acquired to earn a capital gain (partially included in income for tax purposes as a different source) instead of for the purpose of earning income from property.

(ii) Issue

The issue in the *Ludco* case is whether the $7.5 million borrowed funds was used by the taxpayers for the purpose of earning income from property when the investment earned only $600,000 of dividend income.

(iii) The Supreme Court of Canada Decision

In its decision, the Supreme Court of Canada held that the word "income" in the provision of the Act which allows deduction of interest on borrowed funds meant gross and not net income. Therefore, the taxpayer only needs to have a reasonable expectation of earning some revenue to support his interest deduction. As a result, the interest was deductible in this case.

¶6,315 Tax Planning

Tax is an important factor affecting investment decisions. The objective of this section is to provide a brief discussion that is useful for thinking about how taxes affect investment decisions.

When an investor has multiple investment opportunities, but limited funds, the rule of thumb is to compare the after-tax return on available funds. If the investor has to borrow to invest, the investment decision may depend on that financing. On the other hand, the interest deductibility depends on the type of investment undertaken. In general, if the funds are borrowed to acquire property that is used to generate property income, then interest paid on the loan is deductible for tax purposes. Interest on a loan used to buy a personal asset such as a home is, generally, not deductible. The following example illustrates the differences in after-tax returns on investments.

From the above analysis, we can see that the general strategy is that you should buy personal assets with your own funds (since interest is not deductible on borrowed funds used to purchase personal assets) and then use these assets as collateral to borrow to invest in assets that will earn property income (since interest is deductible in that situation).

If you already have a mortgage on the personal asset, and it can be prepaid without penalty, you should pay it down using your own cash. However, if the mortgage is not open for such payments in full or in part, it may be worthwhile setting aside savings for the purpose of paying down the mortgage when it is due for renewal. Paying down an old, low-interest mortgage may not be the best investment, but certainly paying down one at a higher interest rate is worth considering.

Example

Ms. Prudent has always considered investing her savings to be a high priority. This year she has saved $5,000; however, Ms. Prudent has just discovered that she will need to purchase a new car which will cost an additional $5,000 with her trade-in. She can borrow the funds for the car from the dealer at a very favourable rate of 2%, while funds borrowed from a stockbroker to invest in corporate shares will cost 3%. She is in a 48% (combined federal and provincial) tax bracket.

How could Ms. Prudent accomplish her goals at a minimum cost in this situation?

Ms. Prudent should buy the car with her accumulated savings of $5,000 and borrow $5,000 from the stockbroker for her investments. While the pre-tax cost of the investment loan will be higher than a car loan, the 3% will be deductible resulting in an after-tax cost of 1.56% (i.e., 3%(1 – 0.48)) compared with the 2% car loan which is not tax deductible. The result is a saving of .44% which, on a loan of $5,000, would amount to about $22 in the first year.

¶6,390 Pause and Reflect — Summary of Learning Goals

After working through this section, ¶6,300, you should be able to:

- Explain the tax planning and support that must be provided in order to maintain the deductibility of interest.
- Apply your knowledge to advise taxpayers on ways to maximize the after-tax value of personal and investment assets through tax planning techniques.

¶6,400 Differences Between Business and Property Income

At this point, it would be worthwhile to isolate the provisions which have been examined so far and identify which apply to either business or property income.

¶6,405 Provisions Applicable to Business Income Only

The following deductions apply only to business income:

- reserves;
- certain specific expenses, such as
  - expenses of representation,
  - site investigation, and
  - utilities services connection;
- convention expenses; and
- short-year proration for capital cost allowance.

ITA: 20(1)(b) Incorporation expenses, 20(1)(m) Reserve in respect of certain goods and services, 20(1)(m.1) Manufacturer's warranty reserve, 20(1)(m.2) Repayment of amount previously included in income, 20(1)(n) Reserve for unpaid amounts, 20(1)(cc) Expenses of representation, 20(1)(dd) Investigation of site, 20(1)(ee) Utilities service connection, 20(10) Convention expenses; ITR: 1100(3) Taxation Years Less Than 12 Months

¶6,410 Provisions Applicable to Property Income Only

The following deductions apply only to property income:

- restriction on capital cost allowance for rental properties;
- attribution rules; and
- foreign taxes on property income in excess of 15% deductible.

CHAPTER 7

Capital Gains: Personal

ADVANCED CONTENT IN THIS CHAPTER

Learning Goals

Know, Understand and Explain

By the end of this chapter you will know, understand and be able to explain:

- The different types of capital gains a taxpayer can incur on the sale of capital property.
- The special provisions for the taxation of capital gains as they relate to the different types of capital property.
- The meaning of a capital gain, taxable capital gain, capital loss, and allowable capital loss.
- The circumstances in which an individual can claim the principal residence exemption.
- The tax implications on the death of a taxpayer.
- The tax implications on ceasing or establishing residency in Canada.

Apply

By the end of this chapter you will be able to apply your knowledge and understanding to:

- Classify capital property into three different categories: personal use, listed personal, and other capital property.
- Correctly determine the tax implications of non-arm's length transfers.
- Correctly determine the adjusted cost base and the proceeds of disposition on the disposition of a capital property under various circumstances.
- Minimize the tax implications of disposing of more than one principal residence.
- Apply your knowledge to advise a client or employer on the tax implications on the death of a taxpayer and plan to meet the client's needs.
- Apply your knowledge to advise a client or employer on the tax implications of ceasing or establishing residency in Canada.

Review Questions

¶7,800 in the Study Guide

Multiple Choice Questions

¶7,825 in the Study Guide

Exercises

¶7,850 in the Study Guide

Assignment Problems

¶7,875 in the Study Guide

Overview

This chapter, along with Chapter 8, will review the more common provisions related to the taxation of capital gains.

The taxation of capital gains began in 1972, when a complete set of rules was introduced to the legislation. Prior to this, it was common for taxpayers to arrange transactions to look like capital dispositions rather than income transactions, to reduce their overall tax payable to nil. The 1972 legislative changes were influenced to some degree by the 1962 Royal Commission on Taxation, led by Mr. Kenneth Carter, which recommended the full taxation of capital gains on the disposition of all property, gifts, and unrealized gains in support of a comprehensive tax base on the grounds that "a buck is a buck". If capital gains are taxed like other sources of income, all taxpayers are in the same position (horizontal equity). Equally important is vertical equity, meaning that taxpayers who can afford to contribute do so, one of the primary principles of our Canadian taxation system.

The capital gains tax rules have evolved over time. Under the current rules, one-half of capital gains are included in income as taxable capital gains and these can be offset by allowable capital losses. Subdivision c of Division B of Part I of the Act contains the primary rules for the computation of taxable capital gains and allowable capital losses. The following chart will help to locate these provisions in the Act.

PART I — DIVISION B, SUBDIVISION c

CAPITAL GAINS & LOSSES

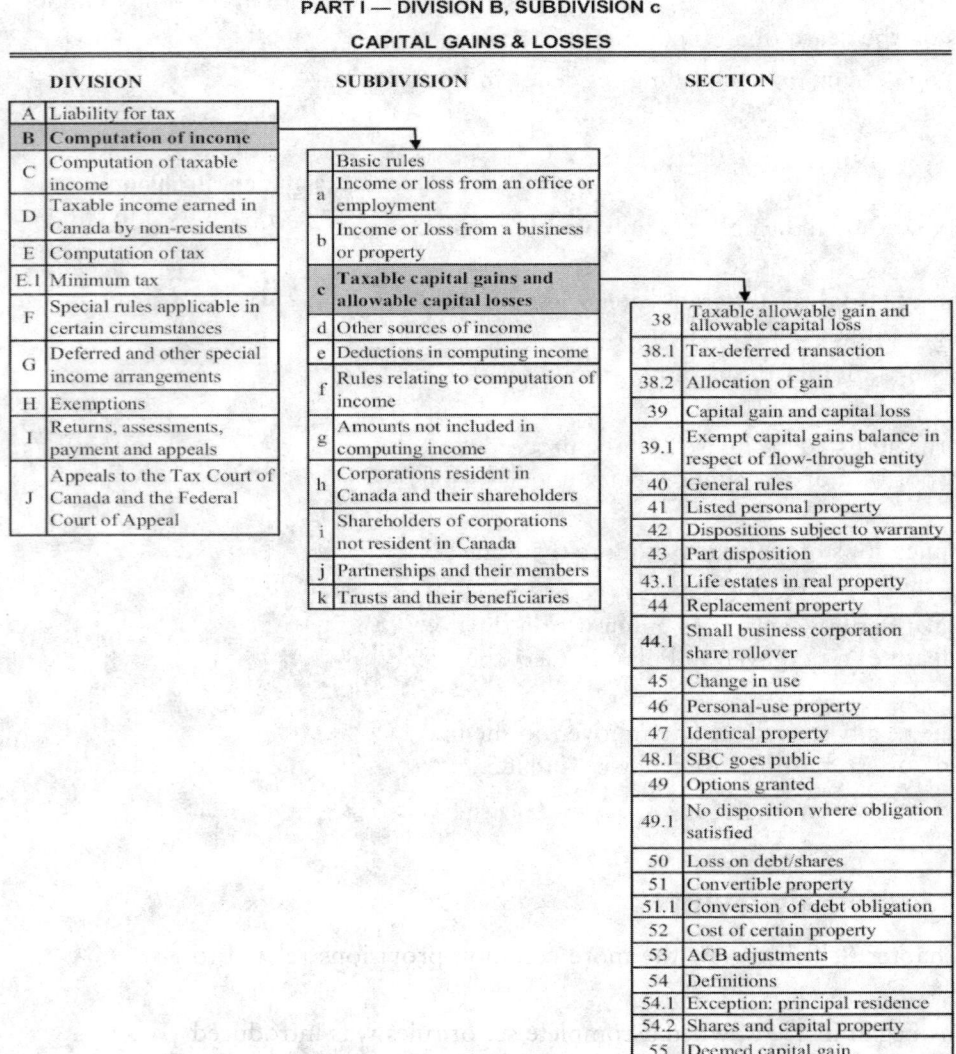

DIVISION

A	Liability for tax
B	**Computation of income**
C	Computation of taxable income
D	Taxable income earned in Canada by non-residents
E	Computation of tax
E.1	Minimum tax
F	Special rules applicable in certain circumstances
G	Deferred and other special income arrangements
H	Exemptions
I	Returns, assessments, payment and appeals
J	Appeals to the Tax Court of Canada and the Federal Court of Appeal

SUBDIVISION

	Basic rules
a	Income or loss from an office or employment
b	Income or loss from a business or property
c	**Taxable capital gains and allowable capital losses**
d	Other sources of income
e	Deductions in computing income
f	Rules relating to computation of income
g	Amounts not included in computing income
h	Corporations resident in Canada and their shareholders
i	Shareholders of corporations not resident in Canada
j	Partnerships and their members
k	Trusts and their beneficiaries

SECTION

38	Taxable allowable gain and allowable capital loss
38.1	Tax-deferred transaction
38.2	Allocation of gain
39	Capital gain and capital loss
39.1	Exempt capital gains balance in respect of flow-through entity
40	General rules
41	Listed personal property
42	Dispositions subject to warranty
43	Part disposition
43.1	Life estates in real property
44	Replacement property
44.1	Small business corporation share rollover
45	Change in use
46	Personal-use property
47	Identical property
48.1	SBC goes public
49	Options granted
49.1	No disposition where obligation satisfied
50	Loss on debt/shares
51	Convertible property
51.1	Conversion of debt obligation
52	Cost of certain property
53	ACB adjustments
54	Definitions
54.1	Exception: principal residence
54.2	Shares and capital property
.55	Deemed capital gain

Some of the more important provisions included in Subdivision C of Division B that cover capital gains are as follows:

- Sec. 39: Meaning of capital gain, capital loss, and business investment loss,
- Sec. 40: General rules including principal residence exemption,
- Sec. 41: Listed personal property,
- Sec. 44.1: Capital gains deferral,
- Sec. 45: Change in use,
- Sec. 46: Personal-use property,
- Sec. 47: Identical properties
- Sec. 49: Options
- Sec. 51: Convertible property
- Sec. 52: Cost
- Sec. 53: Adjustments to cost base
- Sec. 54: Definitions

In addition to the provisions above, Subdivision f of Division B provides some rules that are relevant to the inclusion of capital gains income. For example, the attribution rules determine whether the capital gains or losses received by a particular person should be attributed to someone else. Rules pertaining to the deemed disposition on death are also covered.

ITA: 74.2 Gain or loss deemed that of lender or transferor, 74.3 Transfers or loans to a trust; 70 Death of a taxpayer

Also, Division F deals with the rules for the treatment of capital property when an individual ceases to be or becomes a resident of Canada.

ITA: 128.1 [Immigration and emigration]

After working through all the sections of the chapter, you will be able to:

- Explain the meaning of a capital gain, taxable capital gain, capital loss, and allowable capital loss.
- Explain the three types of capital property: personal-use, listed personal, and other capital property.
- Explain the special provisions for the taxation of capital gains as they relate to:
  - Personal use property,
  - Listed personal property,
  - Other capital property.
- Explain how to determine the adjusted cost base and the proceeds of disposition on the disposition of a capital property under various circumstances.
- Explain the circumstances in which an individual can claim the principal residence exemption.
- Apply your knowledge to determine the tax implications of a disposition of a capital property to a non-arm's length individual.
- Apply your knowledge to minimize tax on the disposition of a principal residence.

- Apply your knowledge to specific circumstances to minimize the tax paid by the taxpayer on the disposition of a capital property.
- Apply your knowledge to advise a client or your employer on the tax implications on the death of a taxpayer and plan to meet the client's or employer's needs.
- Apply your knowledge to advise a client or your employer on the tax implications of ceasing or establishing residency in Canada.

¶7,000 General Rules

Overview

Capital gains receive special tax treatment. They are included in a taxpayer's income based on the inclusion rate for the period in which the capital gain occurred.

After working through this section, ¶7,000, you will be able to:

- Explain capital property, including: personal use property, listed personal property and other property.
- Apply your knowledge to a specific situation to correctly classify a capital property into one of the three main categories of capital property.
- Explain the difference between accounting and income tax terminology for capital property.
- Explain the situations where a deemed disposition of a capital property might occur.
- Explain the components that are used to determine a capital gain or loss (i.e., P of D, ACB, and expenses).
- Explain why capital losses on depreciable property are denied under the Act.
- Explain the election that may be made to ensure that the disposition of Canadian securities is treated as capital in nature.

¶7,005 Inclusion Rates

The inclusion rate is the percentage that is applied to the capital gain to determine the portion of the capital gain that should be subject to tax. The result is included in income as a taxable capital gain. The inclusion rate has changed over the years, as summarized in the chart below:

Time Period	Inclusion Rate
1972 to 1987	50%
1988 and 1989	66⅔%
1990 to February 27, 2000	75%
February 28 to October 17, 2000	66⅔%
After October 17, 2000	50%

¶7,010 Terminology

Prior to reviewing the rules related to capital gains, we should discuss the common terminology used when discussing the taxation of the sale of capital property. The terminology can be looked at in terms of the full value (100%) and in terms of the taxable value (currently at 50%) after the inclusion rate is applied.

100%	50%
Capital gain	Taxable capital gain
Capital loss	Allowable capital loss
Business investment loss	Allowable business investment loss
Capital gains exemption	Capital gains deduction

Example

Jackson Smith would like to know how the sale of his capital property will be treated for tax purposes. He has provided you with the following information:

Property A: Capital Gain	$10,000
Property B: Taxable Capital Gain	$7,500

Jackson will have to include in his net income for tax purposes:

Property A: Capital Gains	$10,000
× the current inclusion rate	50%
Property A: Taxable Capital Gains	$5,000
Property B: Taxable Capital Gains	$7,500
Total Taxable Capital Gains included in income	$12,500

Note that we have applied the current capital gains inclusion rate to the capital gains from Property A but not to Property B. Property A has provided us with the gain since acquisition in terms of the full value. Since capital gains are only taxable at an inclusion rate of 50%, we need to multiply the amount to determine the taxable value. The gain since acquisition in Property B has been provided to us in terms of the taxable value (rather than 100% of the full value), therefore no adjustment needs to be made.

It is also necessary to become acquainted with the basic terminology and abbreviations illustrated below before attempting to read the pertinent sections in Subdivision c.

Accounting terminology			**Income tax terminology**	
Selling price		$xx	Proceeds of disposition (P of D)[1]	Sec. 54
Cost	$xx		Adjusted cost base (ACB)[2]	Sec. 54
Selling costs	xx	(xx)	Expenses of disposition (SC)[2]	Ssec. 40(1)
Profit (loss)		$ xx	Gain (loss)	
		(xx)	Exemption or reserve, if any[3]	Sec. 40
		$xx	Capital gain (CG) or Capital loss (CL)	Sec. 39
		$xx	Taxable capital gain (TCG) or[4] Allowable capital loss (ACL)	Sec. 38

[1] "Proceeds of disposition" is a much broader term than "selling price" because it includes deemed proceeds. ITA: 54 proceeds of disposition

[2] "Adjusted cost base" also encompasses more than the traditional accounting "laid-down cost". There are over 40 specific adjustments to the accounting actual cost. Selling costs are not included in the adjusted cost base and, hence, may in themselves give rise to a capital loss. ITA: 54 adjusted cost base, 53 Adjustments to cost base

[3] "Exemptions" are deducted from the "gain" in order to arrive at the capital gain. There are two major exemptions: one pertains to a principal residence (a permanent exemption from tax) and the other provides a reserve for amounts not due in the year (a tax deferral). These are discussed in detail later in this Chapter (principal residence) and Chapter 8 (reserve).

[4] A taxable capital gain (allowable capital loss) is the portion of the capital gain (capital loss) taken into income. The inclusion rate is currently 50%.

¶7,015 Capital Property — Defined

Overview

A capital gain is the amount by which proceeds of disposition exceed the adjusted cost base and any disposition costs on the sale of capital property. Capital property is defined as: ITA: 54 Definitions

- any depreciable property, and
- any other property that would result in a capital gain or loss upon disposition.

"Property" is defined as "property of any kind . . . and . . . includes . . . a right . . ., a share or a chose in action". Capital property is generally referred to as an asset that provides the owner with a long-term and enduring benefit. Generally, capital gains or losses result from the disposition of a capital property such as shares, investments, real estate, art, a machine, a house, a cottage, or another personal property. ITA: 248(1) Definitions

¶7,015.10 Income vs. Capital

It is not uncommon, however, for these same types of property, such as shares or real estate, to be held as inventory and treated as an item sold to produce business income. The key is the intention the taxpayer had when they originally purchased the property.

Example

The same semi-trailer may be treated differently depending on the owner of the truck.

Truck owner/driver: A semi-trailer purchased by a truck driver for the purpose of earning delivery income would be considered a capital asset. Any gain on the sale of the semi-trailer would be considered capital in nature.

Truck Distributor: The same semi-trailer purchased by a retail company for the purpose of resale would be considered inventory. Any profit from the sale of the semi-trailer, by the retail company, would not be considered a capital asset. The profit on the sale would be considered on account of income.

The reason for the different treatment relates to the intention of the taxpayer that purchased the semi-trailer. The truck driver purchased the semi-trailer with the intention of using the capital asset to earn income over a long period of time (i.e., several years of income-earning potential). Conversely, the retail company purchased the semi-trailer for resale as part of an ongoing business.

It is often necessary to call upon the courts to determine whether the nature of transactions is on account of income rather than capital. In Chapter 4, we reviewed the observable behavioural factors that the courts used to determine the classification of a transaction as capital in nature. The more common factors are outlined below. For a more detailed review please see section ¶4,110.20.

(1) Relationship of the transaction to the taxpayer's business;

(2) Activity or organization normally associated with trade;

(3) Nature of the asset involved;

(4) Number and frequency of the transactions;

(5) Length of the period of ownership of the asset;

(6) Supplemental work on or in connection with the property disposed of in the transaction;

(7) Circumstances that caused the disposition;

(8) Corporate objects or partnership agreement.

The asset that generates business or property income from year to year is quite different from the asset that is used for personal consumption or enjoyment. Paragraph 3(*b*) contains the income inclusion provision that requires "net taxable capital gains" to be included in the calculation of net income.

¶7,015.20 The Aggregation Formula Revisited

Chapter 1, section ¶1,220.30, introduced the aggregation formula that outlines the different sources of income. Subdivision c in Dividend B of Part I of the Act outlines the rules related to capital gains and losses. It is important to note two things within the aggregation formula:

- the total in subdivision c of the aggregation formula cannot be negative; and
- net capital gains are distinguished from net listed personal property gains and allowable capital losses. The Act has different rules for different types of capital property. The rules governing the calculation of the taxable capital gain for these properties will be discussed later in the chapter.

¶7,015.30 Categories of Capital Property

Capital property includes:

- Personal-use property;
- Listed personal property;
- Other capital property

Personal-use property ("PUP")

Personal-use property is property owned by a taxpayer (including a corporation or trust) for the personal use or enjoyment of the taxpayer or for a person or beneficiary related to the taxpayer. Some examples of personal-use property include an individual's furniture, sports equipment, personal residence, cars, and personal effects.

ITA: 40(2)(g)(iii), 54 Definitions

The Act distinguishes these from other property because personal-use property is used for personal consumption rather than for generating income. Since personal-use property is consumed and wears out, capital losses related to most personal-use property may never be offset against any capital gains or other sources of revenue. While losses from personal use property cannot be used to offset other capital gains or revenue, the gains on disposition of this type of capital property must be included in income. Please refer to ¶7,105 for more details.

ITA: 3(b)

Listed personal property ("LPP")

Listed personal property is a subset of personal-use property designed to segregate collectibles that generally do not depreciate. While listed personal property does have a personal-use side, it is often purchased for its investment potential as well. These types of assets can appreciate significantly over the period of investment. Unlike personal-use property, losses on LPP may be claimed, but only against gains on LPP. The other rules applicable to PUP also apply to LPP. The Act is very specific as to what constitutes a listed-personal property asset. Please refer to ¶7,110 for more details.

ITA: 41 Taxable net gain from disposition of listed personal property, 54 Definitions

Other capital property

Other capital property includes property, other than personal-use or listed personal property, acquired for the purpose of earning income. It includes:

- business assets,
- capital investments, such as buildings, rental properties, and machinery, and
- financial instruments that are not inventory.

Assuming the primary intention of purchasing this type of asset was to earn another source of income, the gains and losses on the disposition would be considered capital in nature.

Note that gains and losses on the disposition of inventory are on account of income rather than capital and therefore are not subject to the capital gains rules. Eligible capital property, defined in Chapter 5, is also not a capital property, as any gains are included as business income.

Schematic classification

Figure 7-1 summarizes the categories of capital property.

Figure 7-1

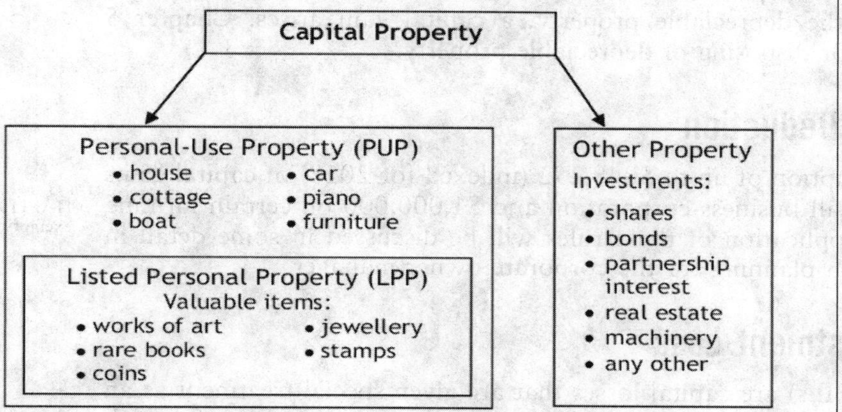

¶7,020 Disposition of Capital Property

Capital gains treatment requires a disposition. The Act contains the definition of "disposition" of property, for both actual and deemed dispositions. In general terms, a disposition includes any transaction entitling a taxpayer to proceeds of disposition. This definition, then, specifies situations that are considered to be dispositions.

ITA: 248(1) Definitions

In some cases, transfers of property do not give rise to actual proceeds, but will be deemed to be dispositions for tax purposes. These will include deemed dispositions, such as dispositions:

ITA: 45(1) Property with more than one use, 70(5) Capital property of a deceased taxpayer, 69(1) Inadequate considerations, 128.1(1) Immigration

- on the change in use of property;
- on the death of a taxpayer;
- by way of gift during the lifetime of a taxpayer; and
- when a taxpayer ceases to be a resident of Canada.

¶7,025 Capital Losses — General

Allowable capital losses can be deducted from taxable capital gains and taxable net gains from listed personal property, to the extent needed to bring those gains to zero. Any excess losses, referred to as "net capital losses", can be carried back three years or forward indefinitely to reduce taxable capital gains in the applicable taxation years. Chapters 10 and 11 discuss the rules for applying net capital loss carryover amounts for individuals and corporations, respectively.

¶7,030 Restrictions on Capital Losses

A capital loss from the disposition of depreciable capital property (any property eligible for CCA) is denied under the Act. CCA rules, explained in Chapter 5, allow the cost associated with the purchase of a depreciable property that earns income to be deducted through the CCA system. When depreciable property is disposed of for proceeds less than the original cost, the result will be either a terminal loss, a recapture, or a reduction of the UCC of the class. Since the decline in value of this type of capital property is already deducted through the CCA write-off, we should not be able to further deduct a capital loss. Therefore a capital loss on depreciable property is denied. If proceeds of disposition exceed the capital cost of the depreciable property, a capital gain arises. Chapter 5 provides the tax treatment for disposing of depreciable property.

ITA: 39(1)(b)(i)

¶7,035 Capital Gains Deduction

There is a capital gains exemption of up to $848,252 (indexed for 2018) of capital gains on qualifying shares of a small business corporation and $1,000,000 on certain farming and fishing property. The application of these rules will be discussed in some detail in Chapter 13, which deals with planning for the corporate owner-manager.

ITA: 110.6 [Capital gains exemption]

¶7,040 Business Investment Loss

Business investment losses (BILs) are capital losses that are given special treatment as an incentive for investing in small business. In general terms, BILs are capital losses which occur on the disposition of either shares or debt of a small business corporation.

ITA: 39(1)(c)

The term "small business corporation" is defined in the Act and discussed in more detail in a Chapter 13. Generally, a small business corporation is a Canadian-controlled private corporation, where all or substantially all of the fair market value of its assets are:

ITA: 248(1) Definitions

(a) used to carry on an active business primarily in Canada;

(b) shares or debt of connected (as discussed in a Chapter 13 small business corporations; or

(c) a combination of (a) and (b).

Note that these BILs are still capital losses and, therefore, only fractionally deductible. The fractional amount deductible, which uses the same inclusion rate as capital losses (i.e., 50% currently), is called an allowable business investment loss (ABIL). The use of ABILs will be discussed later in this chapter at ¶7,510.

¶7,045 Election Re Disposition of Canadian Securities

A taxpayer can elect that the disposition of "Canadian securities" will always be a capital receipt, despite the common law guidelines discussed in ¶7,015. Until the introduction of these rules, the CRA had not consistently assessed taxpayers on trading transactions in which there was an obvious intention to make a quick profit rather than to hold the shares as an income-producing investment. The dilemma is resolved with this election.

ITA: 39(4)-(6); Forms: T123 Election on Disposition of Canadian Securities

Once this election is made, it will remain in force forever, unless the taxpayer, at the time of a disposition, is one of the prescribed taxpayers listed in the provision who is not permitted this election. One of the exclusions is a "dealer in securities" and, of course, it will be a matter of fact whether an individual will be considered to be a "dealer" because of his or her past and present trading activities. The general rules used by the CRA to determine whether securities transactions will be afforded capital or income treatment are outlined in an Interpretation Bulletin entitled "Transactions in securities".

ITA: 39(5) Exception; Interpretation Bulletins: IT-479R Transactions in securities

The CRA's administrative position in respect of commodity transactions, including futures, is quite similar to the statutory provisions in respect of Canadian securities discussed above. The guidelines which must be adhered to are set out in the Interpretation Bulletin entitled "Commodity Futures and Certain Commodities".

Interpretation Bulletins: IT-346R Commodity Futures and Certain Commodities

¶7,050 Computation of Capital Gains and Capital Losses

Overview

A gain on the disposition of property is determined as:

ITA: 40(1)(a)(i), 54 Definitions

(1) proceeds of disposition minus

(2) the aggregate of:

(a) adjusted cost base, and

(b) expenses of the disposition.

A loss is generally a negative amount resulting from the application of the above formula. Restated, a loss could be calculated as the adjusted cost base and expenses of disposition minus proceeds of disposition. A loss on depreciable capital property is denied by the Act, since the total decline in value should have been accounted for through the capital cost allowance system, if applicable.

ITA: 39(1)(b)(i)

¶7,050.10 Proceeds of Disposition

In most cases, proceeds of disposition will be the value of the consideration received or receivable. Where a deemed disposition occurs, the proceeds usually will be deemed to be the fair market value of the property at the time of the disposition.

The definitions of terms for purposes of capital gains and losses are provided in a definition section within Subdivision c. The definition of "proceeds of disposition" found in this section provides some very specific inclusions and exclusions that go beyond our normal idea of proceeds.

ITA: 54 proceeds of disposition

The following is a list of Interpretation Bulletins and Income Tax Folios that give further guidance:

Folio S3-F9-C1	Lottery Winnings, Miscellaneous Receipts, and Income (and Losses) from Crime
Folio S3-F4-C1	General Discussion of Capital Cost Allowance
IT-259R4	Exchanges of property
IT-460	Dispositions — absence of consideration

One of the components of the proceeds of disposition of shares, a partnership interest, or business assets might be an agreement not to compete with the purchaser. This is known as a restrictive covenant. This topic is covered by a comprehensive package of provisions related to payments received by individuals for covenants. For a full discussion on the treatment of payments received for covenants, please refer to Chapter 9.

¶7,050.20 Adjusted Cost Base

Adjusted cost base starts with actual out-of-pocket cost or deemed cost on receipt of a gift or inheritance and is then modified. A provision establishes the cost base as amounts in respect of the value of the property which have been included in the taxpayer's income. For example, the cost of property received as a dividend in kind is the fair market value of the property received.

ITA: 52 [Cost of certain property], 52(2) Cost of property received as dividend in kind, 52(3) Cost of stock dividend

Subsection 53(1) (additions) and subsection 53(2) (reductions) set out a number of adjustments such as:

- the employment income inclusion arising from the acquisition of share through a stock option is added to the cost of the share; and

ITA: 7 [Employee stock options], 53(1)(j) [Adjustments to cost base — Share or fund unit taxed as stock option benefit]

- the cost base of a bond is reduced by the amount of accrued interest paid for on the purchase of the bond and this accrued interest is deducted from interest earned during the holding period of the bond.

ITA: 20(14) Accrued bond interest, 53(2)(i) [Amounts to be deducted — Capital interest in a non-resident trust]

There are a number of adjustments in respect of shares of a corporation, many of which will be described in more detail in later chapters. But a conceptual understanding of these adjustments is necessary in determining the adjusted cost base of a particular class of shares.

- The cost base of shares is increased by deemed dividends that arise in transactions (with some exceptions) where the paid-up capital of the corporation is increased by more than the increase in the fair market value of the net assets of the corporation. Paid-up capital of shares is generally (but not always) the stated or par value for accounting purposes and is discussed in more detail in Chapter 15.

ITA: 53(1)(b) [Adjustments to cost base — Deemed dividend], 54(1)

- The cost base of shares received as consideration for any transfer of property to a corporation is increased by the amount of any capital loss denied by reason of a "stop-loss" rule applied on the transfer.

ITA: 53(1)(f.2) [Adjustments to cost base — Denied loss on transfer of shares to corporation], 40(3.6)(b)

There are also some adjustments to cost where assets are transferred without any consideration:

- An asset transferred by way of gift is normally deemed to be disposed of by the transferor at fair market value and received by the transferee at the same value.

- If an asset is transferred from a corporation to its shareholder, then the corporation is deemed to have disposed of the asset at fair market value and the shareholder is deemed to have received the asset with a cost at the same value. In addition, the shareholder will have received a benefit that will be included in income.

- If an asset is won in a lottery, then it is deemed to be received with a cost base equal to fair market value.

Under certain circumstances it is possible to have a negative adjusted cost base for a capital asset. A negative adjusted cost base results at any time when the sum of the amounts deducted is greater than the cost of the property plus the sum of amounts added to it. In most circumstances, a negative adjusted cost base is deemed to be an immediate capital gain at the time an adjustment causes the adjusted cost base to become negative. At the same time, the adjusted cost base is brought to zero and future adjustments are made from that zero base.

ITA: 40(3) Deemed gain where amounts to be deducted from adjusted cost base exceed cost plus amounts to be added to adjusted cost base, 53(1)(a) [Adjustments to cost base — Deemed gain resulting from negative ACB]

A partnership interest in a general (but not a limited liability) partnership is exempt from the negative adjusted cost base rules. That is to say that a negative adjusted cost base will not result in the partner recognizing a capital gain immediately. Note that a limited partnership is one in which there is one general partner and all other partners are limited partners. This is not the same as a limited liability partnership ("LLP"), which has no general partner, since all partners are involved in the management of the LLP. Please refer to section ¶18,070 for additional discussion on adjusted cost base of partnership units.

¶7,050.30 Expenses of the Disposition

A gain or a loss on the disposition of a capital property includes the deduction of outlays and expenses related to that disposition. These types of expenses cannot reduce your other income, but rather will reduce the overall gain or increase the overall loss on disposition. The Act does not specifically list the types of expenses eligible for deduction.

The more common types of disposition costs are:

- Expenses incurred to fix-up the capital property for sale,
- Finders' fees,
- Brokers' fees,
- Surveyors' fees,
- Legal fees,
- Transfer taxes, and
- Advertising costs.

¶7,055 Mutual Funds and Dividend Reinvestment Plans

It is not unusual for mutual fund investors to reinvest the income received or allocated from their investment into acquiring more units of the fund. Similarly, many corporate shareholders participate in dividend reinvestment plans (DRIPs) where the dividends are used to acquire more shares in the company. In most cases, the investor must pay tax on the income that was received or receivable, regardless of whether the income is reinvested in additional mutual funds.

Example Problem 7-1

Martha sold all the units of some mutual funds that she owned for proceeds of $40,000. She had bought them for $20,000. This amount bought 1,185.319 units in the fund. She has never taken any money out of the fund; any income has been reinvested automatically. Over the years, her information slips have indicated the following:

	Dividend Received	Taxable Dividend	Federal Dividend Tax Credit	Taxable Capital Gain
2018	$2,000	$2,760	$415	$1,500
2017	$1,000	$1,380	$207	$300
	$3,000	$4,140	$ 622	$ 1,800

REQUIRED

Determine Martha's capital gain or loss on the sale of her mutual fund units.

SOLUTION

Proceeds		$40,000
Adjusted Cost Base (ACB):		
Original Cost	$20,000	
Dividend reinvestment	$3,000	
CG reinvestment ($1,800 ÷ ½)	$3,600	$(26,600)
Capital Gain		$13,400
Taxable Capital Gain (½)		$6,700

Since the taxpayer has already paid tax on the investment income that was reinvested, we must add the reinvested amount to the ACB of the mutual fund units or corporate shares, otherwise the ACB will be understated. Adding the reinvested amount to the ACB of the unit or shares ensures that double taxation does not occur when they are eventually sold.

¶7,090 Pause and Reflect — Summary of Learning Goals

After working through this section, ¶7,000, you should be able to:

- Explain the different types of capital property, including: personal use property, listed personal property, and other property.

- Apply your knowledge to a specific situation to correctly classify a capital property into one of the three main categories of capital property.
- Explain the difference between accounting and income tax terminology for capital property.
- Explain the situations where a deemed disposition of a capital property might occur.
- Explain the components that are used to determine a capital gain or loss (i.e., P of D, ACB, and expenses).
- Explain why capital losses on depreciable property are denied under the Act.
- Explain the election that may be made to ensure that the disposition of Canadian securities is treated as capital in nature.

¶7,090.99 Practise What You've Learned

Refer to the following sections of the Study Guide to practise what you've learned:

¶7,800 — Review Questions

- Question 1 — Disposition of Capital Property

¶7,100 Specific Provisions for the Taxation of Capital Gains

Overview

The general rules above outline the basic calculation that should be performed when the disposition of a capital property occurs. This section explains some of the special rules for the taxation of capital gains on specific types of disposition.

After working through this section, ¶7,100, you will be able to:

- Apply your knowledge of the specific provisions relating to personal-use property and listed personal property to correctly calculate the income inclusion in a given period.
- Explain if a property meets the definition of a principal residence and explain the tax implications of disposing of a principal residence.
- Apply your knowledge to correctly determine the taxable portion of the capital gain in a situation where the principal residence exemption is applied to the disposition of more than one principal residence.
- Apply your knowledge of the provisions to calculate the adjusted cost base for identical shares that have been disposed of in the year.
- Explain the purpose of the superficial loss rules and correctly apply the provisions to determine the capital loss that is denied.

- Apply your knowledge of the provisions to determine the tax implications of put and call options, for both the buyer and the seller.
- Apply your knowledge of the provisions to calculate the capital gains deferral on the reinvestment of small business corporation shares.
- Apply your knowledge to advise clients on the tax implications of transferring capital property to non-arm's length persons, specifically to spouse and minor and adult children.

¶7,105 Personal-Use Property

"Personal-use property" ("PUP") is defined as property used primarily for personal use or enjoyment. There are two special rules that must be considered when a personal-use property is disposed of:

(1) No capital loss on the disposition of a PUP may be deducted.

(2) A minimum adjusted cost base and proceeds of disposition are used when calculating the capital gain or loss on the disposition of a PUP.

¶7,105.10 No Capital Loss on PUP

While gains on personal-use property (PUP) are subject to tax, losses on such property are denied and may not be deducted. The loss on any particular item is considered to be a personal or living expense. Personal-use property will typically generate losses on disposal because such property often declines in value over time through use. This means that it is possible to have a capital gain on the sale of a personal-use property in a given year while not being able to offset that capital gain with a PUP capital loss, since the loss would be denied.

ITA: 54 Definitions, 40(2)(g)(iii)

¶7,105.20 Minimum Adjusted Cost Base and Proceeds of Disposition

For the purpose of calculating the capital gain or loss on any disposal of PUP, the taxpayer's cost is deemed to be the greater of the adjusted cost base of the property and $1,000. Similarly, the taxpayer's proceeds of disposition are deemed to be the greater of actual proceeds and $1,000.

ITA: 46(1) Personal-use property

Example

Jacob Johnson sells two personal-use properties in the year. He would like you to comment on the tax implications of the sale. The following is information related to the two PUPs:

	PUP #1	PUP #2
ACB	$800	$1,300
P of D	$1,200	$700

The capital gain or capital loss on the sale of the two properties would be as follows:

	PUP #1		PUP # 2
P of D	$1,200	Deemed P of D	$1,000
Deemed ACB	$(1,000)	ACB	$(1,300)
CG	$200	CL	Nil

The capital loss on PUP #2 is denied and cannot be used to offset the capital gain of PUP #1.

If a taxpayer disposes of any part of a personal-use property, for the purposes of computing the capital gain or loss on the disposal, the $1,000 minimum cost and the $1,000 minimum proceeds must be apportioned on the basis of the proportion of the PUP attributable to the part disposed of.

ITA: 46(2) Where part only of property disposed of

These "part disposition" rules also apply to a disposition of part of a personal-use property that would ordinarily be disposed of as a set. Thus, several dispositions of pieces of the set would be considered to be parts of a single PUP disposition. If all of the pieces of a set are acquired by one person or by a group consisting of persons who are not dealing at arm's length, the taxpayer is deemed to have made a single disposition.

ITA: 46(3) Properties ordinarily disposed of as a set

Losses arising from debts taken on the sale of personal-use property that become uncollectible in the future will be restricted. The loss can only be recognized to the extent that the gain was previously recognized on the disposition of personal-use property in return for the debt.

ITA: 50(2) Where debt a personal-use property

¶7,110 Listed Personal Property

"Listed personal property" (LPP) is a special subset of personal-use property. Hence the rules related to the personal-use property discussed above also apply to the listed personal property, with one exception. Capital losses on listed personal property may be used to offset capital gains on listed personal property.

ITA: 54 Definitions

There are several restrictions related to the capital losses on LPPS that should be highlighted:

(1) Capital losses may only be used against capital gains on LPPs, and

(2) The carryover provisions are more restrictive than those of general capital losses. Any unused capital losses on LPPs can be carried back three years and forward for only seven years.

Unlike all other loss carryover provisions which are found in Division C, the carryovers from LPP capital losses are applied in Division B, using the capital loss (100%) amount rather than the allowable capital loss amount (50%). This approach can be seen in the aggregation formula with the use of the special term, "net gain". A "net gain" is defined as listed personal property capital gains minus:

ITA: 41(2) Determination of net gain

(1) listed personal property capital losses in the year; and

(2) listed personal property capital losses arising from the seven preceding years or the three years immediately following.

One benefit of the specification of the carryover amounts (as 100%) in this way is that there is no need to track the different capital gains inclusion rates in the carryover period for LPPs.

Similar to other capital losses, LPP losses that are carried over can be deducted at the option of the taxpayer, except that the earliest LPP losses must be deducted before any losses of a subsequent year.

ITA: 54 Definitions

Examine carefully the very restrictive list of capital property, which qualifies for the listed personal property rules found in the definition of the term. The list is limited to a taxpayer's personal-use property that is:

(a) a print, etching, drawing, painting, sculpture, or other similar work of art,

(b) jewellery,

(c) a rare folio, rare manuscript, or rare book,

(d) a stamp, or

(e) a coin.

If an item cannot be found in that list, it is not LPP and, therefore, capital losses cannot be applied against capital gains.

Example Problem 7-2

The following capital gains and losses have been computed using the $1,000 rule:

	Year 1	Year 2
Capital gain		
Other property	$1,000	—
Personal Use Property (PUP)	$200	—
Listed Personal Property (LPP)	$100	$160
Capital losses		
Other property	$200	$300
Personal Use Property (PUP)	$120	$1,200
Listed Personal Property (LPP)	$160	—

REQUIRED

Compute net taxable capital gains for taxation years 1 and 2.

SOLUTION

	Year 1		Year 2	
Net Taxable capital gains				
Other property		$500		—
Personal Use Property (PUP)		$100		—
LPP – capital gains	$100		$160	
LPP Capital loss[1]	(100)		—	
LPP carryforward	—		$(60)	
Net × ½	0	0	$100	$50
Total		$600		$50
Allowable capital loss				
Other property[2]		(100)		(50)
Net taxable capital gain		$500		$0

NOTES TO SOLUTION

[1] Taxable net gains from LPP must be greater than or equal to zero. Losses from LPP can be carried back three years or carried forward seven years. The solution carries forward $60 of the loss to the LPP gains in Year 2. Losses from listed personal property are carried over in full amount as capital losses. Thus, $60 of the Year 1 LPP capital losses become net LPP capital losses and are available for carryforward to offset capital gains from listed personal property.

[2] The losses on personal-use property are not deductible. Allowable capital losses from other property are only deductible to the extent that net taxable capital gains are greater than or equal to zero. As a result, for Year 2, of the allowable capital losses of $150, $50 is applied to Year 2 and the $100 balance is available for carryforward indefinitely or may be carried back to Year 1 to reduce taxable income in either case.

¶7,110.99 Practise What You've Learned

Refer to the following sections of the Study Guide to practise what you've learned:

¶7,800 — Review Questions

- Question 4 — Personal use property
- Question 5 — Personal use property

¶7,825 — Multiple Choice Questions

- Question 5 — Personal use and listed personal property

¶7,850 — Exercises

- Exercise 4 — Personal use and listed personal property
- Exercise 7 – Listed personal property

¶7,115 Principal Residence Exemption

While an individual's principal residence is a personal-use property that may result in a capital gain on disposition, the Act offers a special reduction against this type of capital gain. This exemption is known as the principal residence exemption ("PRE"). While in most cases the exemption claimed would offset the entire capital gain that would normally occur on the sale of a personal-use property, it is still possible to have a capital gain on the sale of a principal residence.

A "principal residence" is defined as virtually any housing unit or right to such a unit: ITA: 54 Definitions

- owned by the taxpayer either by himself or herself or jointly; and
- ordinarily inhabited by the taxpayer, the taxpayer's spouse or former spouse, or the taxpayer's child at any time in the year.

Note that the CRA states that a taxpayer may designate any residence as his or her principal residence as long as he or she ordinarily inhabits the home, even for a short period. This may be the case when the residence was disposed of early in the year or acquired late in the year. It is important to note that owning a principal residence in the year, even if owned for less than 365 days in the year, counts as a full year of ownership. Also, a seasonal residence, such as a cottage, can be considered to be ordinarily inhabited. Income Tax Folio: S1-F3-C2 Principal Residence

To be a principal residence, the property must be designated as such in the year of disposal. The exemption applies not only to the building but also up to one-half hectare of subjacent and adjacent land. If all of the land exceeds one-half hectare, the additional land must be shown to be necessary to the taxpayer's use and enjoyment to be eligible for this exemption. There have been a number of court cases dealing with this issue of necessity to use and enjoyment.[1]

[1] For some senior level court decisions on this issue, see *The Queen v. Yates*, 83 DTC 5158 (F.C.T.D.), affirmed by 86 DTC 6296 (F.C.A.), *Haber v. The Queen*, 83 DTC 5004 (F.C.T.D.), *Augart v. The Queen*, 93 DTC 5205 (F.C.A.), and *Carlile v. The Queen*, 95 DTC 5483 (F.C.A.).

The formula for determining the exempt portion of a capital gain on the disposition or deemed disposition of a principal residence is shown in the simplified formula below: ITA: 40(2)(b)

((1 + number of years designated) / Number of years owned) × gain

In using this formula the following points should be noted:

(1) Only one housing unit can be designated as a principal residence per family unit. For purposes of the definition of "principal residence" a family unit is defined to include spouses and their unmarried children.

(2) The years referred to in the numerator and denominator refer to those years after 1971.

(3) Deemed dispositions and the resultant modification to the formula will be discussed later in this chapter (¶7,115.20 and ¶7,115.50).

(4) The taxpayer must be resident in Canada for tax purposes.

(5) An individual who purchased a home before becoming a resident of Canada and, hence, was not resident at the time of acquisition of a property, is not entitled to use the "1 +" for that property. ITA: 40(2)(b)

Since a family unit can only designate one housing unit as a principal residence for any particular year, the "1 +" in the numerator of the fraction was intended to protect one housing unit in a situation where a family sells one house and buys another in the same year. In that situation, the family owns two houses in the year, but can only designate one as the principal residence for that particular year.

The disposition of a principal residence must be reported with the individual's tax return for the year of the disposition, even when the principal residence exemption has fully offset the gain. The principal residence exemption is denied when the disposition is not reported. However, a late-filed report is possible with a penalty of $100 per month late from the individual's filing deadline to a maximum of $8,000. ITA: 152(4)(b.3), 220(3.21) Designations and allocations

Example

In 2018, John and his spouse Karen decided it was time to upgrade their family home. Their family had grown and they felt they needed more space for themselves and their two young children. Due to a seller's market, they sold their home quickly for $375,000. In June of 2018, the family moved to their new home in Warman, a suburb of Saskatoon.

John and Karen had purchased their Saskatoon home in the summer of 2011 for $275,000. They are seeking your advice as to the tax implications of the sale of this home. John informs you that neither he nor Karen has owned another property during this time frame.

In this circumstance, the entire capital gain would be deferred, assuming John and Karen elect the Saskatoon home as their principal residence for enough years to shelter the capital gains.

The calculation would be as follows:

Proceeds of disposition.	$375,000
Adjusted cost base.	(275,000)
Capital Gain on the sale of the principal residence.	$100,000
Less the principal residence exemption (see below)	$(100,000)
Capital gain on the principal residence	Nil

Calculation of the principal residence exemption:

Designate the Saskatoon home for enough years less 1 to reduce the capital gain to nil. In this case, the home is owned for a total of 8 years. In order to shelter the entire gain we would need to designate the Saskatoon home for 7 years as follows:

$$((1 + 7 \text{ years designated}) / 8 \text{ years owned}) \times \$100{,}000 = \$100{,}000.$$

We would designate the home as the principal residence for the 2011 through to 2016 taxation years. This would leave the 2018 taxation year available for the new Warman home to be designated as the principal residence.

Note that to be in the position to use the "1 +" in the numerator, the taxpayer must be willing to designate the housing unit as a principal residence for at least one year. That is, the numerator can never be 1 + 0. The exemption formula containing the "1 +" is not applicable at all if the taxpayer does not designate the housing unit as the principal residence for any year. Therefore, the minimum numerator will be 1 + 1.

¶7,115.10 More than One Principal Residence

A taxpayer owning more than one residence can designate only one of his or her residences for a given year as the principal residence. This is done at the time when an actual or deemed disposition is reported. Although the regulations require that a designation form be filed with the tax return in the year of the disposition, the CRA does not require this form to be filed unless there is a taxable capital gain after applying the exempt portion according to the designation rules.

Forms: T2091; Income Tax Folio: S1-F3-C2 Principal Residence

Approach

Steps to minimizing tax on the disposition of two or more principal residences.

(1) Assess the Situation and Identify the Issues — Gather the following information:

(a) How many properties are being sold in the year,

(b) The year of purchase for each property,

(c) The proceeds of disposition and adjusted cost base for determining the capital gain.

(2) Analyze the Issues:

(a) Based on the information gathered, determine:

(i) The number of years available to allocate amongst the properties,

(ii) The capital gain per year for each principal residence.

(b) Calculate the principal residence exemption by allocating the maximum number of years to the property with the highest capital gain per year to reduce that capital gain to nil.

(i) Allocate the remaining years to the property with the next highest gain per year, until all the available years are used.

(ii) Remember to allocate at least one year to each property to ensure each is allocated using the "1 +" rule.

(c) Deduct the principal residence exemption from the capital gain of each property to determine the total capital gain that must be included in the taxpayer's income.

Example Problem 7-3

Mr. Talbot is in the process of retiring and moving to another city. He decides to sell his two residences and provides you with the following information as at September 30, 2018, the date of sale.

Residence	Date of purchase	Selling price	Cost
City home	2009	$170,000	$100,000
Cottage	2014	$90,000	$40,000

REQUIRED

Calculate the minimum total taxable capital gain on the disposition of the two residences.

SOLUTION

Step 1 — Assess the Situation and Identify the Issue — Gather the information related to each property. This has already been provided.

Step 2 — Analyze the Issues:

Step 2(a) – Based on the information provided, determine:

(i) The number of years during which each property is owned: The city home has been owned during ten years while the cottage has been owned during five years. In the five taxation years, 2009-2013, Mr. Talbot owned only one residence, the city home. He has no option but to designate his city home as his principal residences for those 5 years. The remaining five years, 2014 to 2018, can be allocated to either the cottage or the home. Therefore we must determine the best way to allocate the 5 years. Remember to allocate at least one year to each property to maximize on the "1 +" rule.

(ii) The capital gain per year:

	City home	Cottage
P of D	$170,000	$90,000
ACB	$(100,000)	$(40,000)
Gain	$70,000	$50,000
Gain per year	$70,000 / 10 years = $7,000	$50,000 / 5 years = $10,000

Step 2(b) — Calculate the number of years to allocate to each property to minimize overall tax, keeping in mind that you should always allocate at least one year to each property.

- Mr. Talbot should allocate 6 years to the city home. The first 5 years, 2009 to 2013, must go to the city home since Mr. Talbot only owned the city home during that time. As we need one more year, we can choose any other year to the city home, say 2014 to shelter 6 years of the gain on the city home. Since the cottage has the largest gain per year, we want to ensure to claim enough years to reduce the gain on the cottage to zero.
- Since we are allocating 1 year for the "1 +" rule for each property that we designate as his principal residence, we would only need to designate the cottage as the principal residence for 4 years (5 years of ownership less 1). The remaining years can be allocated to the city home. The years would be allocated as follows:

City home:	6 years in total: 5 years (2009–2013) and 1 additional year (say 2014)
Cottage:	4 years (2015 to 2018)

Step 2 (c) – Calculate the principal residence exemption for each property and deduct it from the capital gain.

		City home		Cottage
Gain as calculated above		$70,000		$50,000
Exemption	(1 + 6)/10	$(49,000)	(1 + 4)/5	$(50,000)
Capital gain		$21,000		Nil
Taxable capital gain (50%)		$10,500		

Poor tax planning — The scenario above revisited

A common mistake is to allocate too many years to the property with the highest capital gain per year. If we allocate 5 years to the cottage (rather than the optimal 4 used above) we will waste one of the years that is designated to the cottage due to the "1 +" rule. Note that the exemption cannot exceed the gain on the property.

Below is the calculation of the taxable capital gain if we allocate the full five years to the cottage, leaving only 5 years to allocate to the city home.

		City home		Cottage
Gain as calculated above		$70,000		$50,000
Exemption	(1 + 5)/10	$(42,000)	(1 + 5)/5	$(50,000)
Capital gain		$28,000		Nil
Taxable capital gain (50%)		$14,000		

As can be seen above, if we allocate 5 full years to the cottage, leaving us only 5 years to allocate to the city home the capital gain increases by $7,000, which represents one year of capital gain on that home.

¶7,115.20 Change in Use of a Principal Residence

Personal-use to income producing

The change-in-use election can be used in connection with a principal residence where the initial change of use is from personal use to income-producing use. For example, this would occur when a taxpayer lives in a home for a period of time and then converts the home into a rental property. As discussed in previous chapters, a change in use of a property will result in the deemed disposition of the property, at fair market value, on the day the change in use occurs.

ITA: 45(2), 45(3)

Paragraph (*d*) of the definition of a "principal residence" permits a taxpayer, who changes the use of his or her home, to designate this home as his or her principal residence for up to four years, as long as he or she has elected not to have changed the use. Filing a subsection 45(2) election will defer the capital gain on the change in use of the principal residence until such a time as the property is sold or the election is rescinded.

ITA: 45(2) Election where change of use, 54 principal residence

This election and the designation as a principal residence are two separate and distinct acts. The CRA normally permits a taxpayer to file a retroactive election in connection with a principal residence only. A further consequence of the election is that the taxpayer cannot claim capital cost allowance against any income from that property. So, in the situation where a taxpayer elects to not have a change in use when the taxpayer converts the home into a rental property, that taxpayer cannot claim CCA as a deduction against the rental income earned.

ITA: 45(2) Election where change of use; ITR: 1102(1)(c); Income Tax Folio: S1-F3-C2 Principal Residence

Income producing to personal-use

The definition of a "principal residence", together with another rule, provides for a similar four-year maximum designation in situations where the property was converted from an initial income-producing purpose to personal use and is designated as a principal residence. This election must be made on the earlier of 90 days after a ministerial demand or the normal filing-due date (see Chapter 14) for the year of the disposition of the property.

ITA: 45(3) Election concerning principal residence, 54 principal residence, 45(4) Where election cannot be made, 45(2) Election where change of use

This provision is not applicable in respect of recapture and this election will be revoked if any capital cost allowance is claimed. The combination of the two change-in-use elections cannot exceed four years.

The principal residence exemption formula must now be modified to take into account a possible change in use as follows:

ITA: 40(2)(b)

$$\frac{\text{1 + the number of years for which the property is designated after the date on which it was last acquired}}{\text{Number of years during which the property was owned after the date on which it was last acquired}} \times \text{gain realized}$$

"The date on which it was last acquired" can, if applicable, refer to a deemed reacquisition for personal use after a change in use.

Example Problem 7-4

Mr. Jacobs owned a home in Calgary which he purchased in 2007. During 2010, he decided to relocate because of business reasons and moved to Vancouver. He rented an apartment in Vancouver and rented out his Calgary home. In

2016, he returned to Calgary to live in his original home. He anticipates selling the Calgary home in 2018 and retiring. The following data relates to his home:

Calgary home:	Cost	2007	$140,000
	FMV	2010	$200,000
	FMV	2016	$320,000
	Proceeds	2018 (estimated)	$415,000

REQUIRED

(A) Compute the minimum capital gain, based on the above information. Assume Mr. Jacobs makes an election on a late-filed basis when he files his 2016 tax return.

ITA: 45(2) Election where change of use; Income Tax Folio: S1-F3-C2 Principal Residence

(B) Re-do Part (A) on the assumption that Mr. Jacobs does not elect.

Part (A) — Election to be deemed not to have changed the use:

ITA: 45(2) Election where change of use

When Mr. Jacobs moves out of the Calgary home and begins to rent it out, there is a deemed disposition on the change in use. However, if he makes an election, then the result is that there is no change in use and the property remains a personal-use property. In addition, paragraph (*d*) of the definition of a "principal residence" provides that it is possible for this property to be designated as his principal residence for up to four additional years even though he is not living there. This would allow him to designate the property as his principal residence for the years 2007–2010 and 2016–2018 based on the years he lived there and for the years 2011–2014 based on the four additional years. The only year missing is 2015 and it is protected with the "1 +" rule.

ITA: 45(2) Election where change of use, 54 principal residence

	Calgary home
Gain	$275,000
Exempt portion	$(275,000)(1)
Capital gain	Nil
Taxable capital gain	Nil

Since an election is made to deem there not to be a change in use of the Calgary home, then there is no need to determine UCC. He will not be able to claim CCA as a deduction against his rental income.

ITA: 13(7) Rules applicable, 45(2) Election where change of use

Part (B) — No election:

ITA: 45(2) Election where change of use

In 2010, when Mr. Jacobs moves out of his Calgary home and begins to rent it to earn income, there is a deemed disposition on the change in use. Since he has been living in the house since he bought it in 2007, he can claim the principal residence exemption on the gain that results from the deemed disposition. By designating the years 2007–2009 he can eliminate the full gain as shown below.

ITA: 45(3) Election concerning principal residence

2010	Calgary Home
P of D, deemed	$200,000
ACB	$(140,000)
Gain	$60,000
Exempt portion	$(60,000)[(2)]
Capital gain	Nil

Since no election was made on the Calgary home, then the UCC in 2010 will be deemed to be $170,000 (cost of $140,000 plus the taxable capital gain equal to 50% of $60,000). (Refer to ¶5,065 for an explanation of this provision.) On the deemed disposition of the Calgary home in 2016, there will be recapture to the extent that any CCA was claimed on the home between 2010 and 2015. Mr. Jacob's decision to claim CCA would be based on a variety of factors. For purposes of this example, we will assume he does not claim CCA and therefore would not have any recapture on the change in use in 2016.

ITA: 13(7)(e)

In 2016, when he returns to Calgary and moves back into the house, there is another change in use and a resulting deemed disposition. In this case the principal residence exemption can be claimed for the years 2010 and 2016, since the house was his principal residence at some point during each of those years.

	Calgary Home
P of D, deemed	$320,000
ACB	$(200,000)
Gain	$120,000
Exempt portion	$(51,429)[(3)]
Capital gain	$68,571
Taxable Capital gain (½)	$34,286

Finally, when the Calgary home is sold in 2018, there would be no capital gain as shown below.

	Calgary home
P of D — estimated	$415,000
ACB — deemed	$(320,000)
Gain	$95,000
Exempt portion	$(95,000)[4]
Capital gain	Nil

In summary, by making no elections, he will report a capital gain of $34,286 in 2016 along with any recaptured CCA that also has to be reported.

If he had made the election in 2016 when the house was changed from income-producing to personal-use property, then the capital gain could be deferred and would not have to be reported until the actual disposition in 2018.

ITA: 45(3) Election concerning principal residence

NOTES TO SOLUTION

ITA: 54 Definitions

(1) ((1 + 11) / 12) × $275,000 = $275,000:

- 2007–2010 — owner-occupied
- 2011–2014 — paragraph (*d*) of the definition of "principal residence", maximum four years
- 2016–2017 — owner-occupied

(2) ((1 + 3) / 4) × $60,000 = $60,000; 2007–2009

(3) ((1 + 2) / 7) × $120,000 = $51,429; 2010 and 2016 — owner-occupied

(4) ((1 + 2) / 3) × $95,000 = $95,000; 2017–2018

¶7,115.30 Section 54.1 — Extended Designation

This relieving provision was added to aid taxpayers and their spouses who are transferred by their employers to another location and keep their home in the original location. In such an event, paragraph (*b*) of the definition of a "principal residence" applies without the four-year limitation, as long as the taxpayer complies with the specific conditions of this subsection. This provides relief for the taxpayer who moves for employment purposes to be able to designate their home as their principal residence for all the years they remain with the employer in another location.

ITA: 54 Definitions

¶7,115.40 Income Tax Folio S1-F3-C2 — Principal Residence

Income Tax Folios (or their predecessor Interpretation Bulletins) provide an excellent example of how administrative practice differs from the actual law. For example, the term "ordinarily inhabited" has been interpreted by the CRA, for purposes of section 54 only, to mean "a short period of time in the year". However, the facts of each particular case

Income Tax Folio: S1-F3-C2 Principal Residence

must be considered. A taxpayer who abuses the application of this CRA interpretation could conceivably be reassessed and potentially taken to court on this issue.

One should note the difference between partial changes in use where there are no structural changes and partial changes where there are structural changes to the residence. In cases where the change in use is "ancillary" or secondary to the main purpose of the residence, the CRA's view is that no change has taken place for the purpose of section 54. Therefore, the taxpayer may still designate the residence as a principal residence as long as he or she does not claim any capital cost allowance. Where the change is more substantial, this option does not exist. In this case, the residence will have more than one use and each must be treated differently for tax purposes.

Income Tax Folio: S1-F3-C2 Principal Residence

¶7,115.50 Principal Residence Exemption — Transfer Between Spouses

Single-ownership situations

This provision enables the transfer of a wholly-owned principal residence from one spouse to another with complete or partial relief from the taxation of the capital gain, depending upon the principal residence designation circumstances. This rule does not apply to the interspousal transfer of a home which was previously jointly owned (discussed later in this part of the chapter). The provision does apply where one spouse owns a residence solely and transfers this residence to the other spouse.

ITA: 73(1) Inter vivos transfers by individuals, 70(6) Where transfer or distribution to spouse or spouse trust; 40(4) Disposal of principal residence to spouse or trust for spouse

A provision determines the period of ownership for the transferee spouse for purposes of the principal residence exempting formula. The result is that the transferee spouse is deemed to have owned the property since the time the transferor spouse originally acquired it. Thus, the recipient spouse will be able to designate the home as a principal residence for the same years that it would have qualified for the transferor spouse.

ITA: 40(2)(b), 40(4)(a)

The years of designation by the transferee spouse for the period of ownership by the transferor spouse are those years which were actually designated by the transferor spouse, plus those years after the transfer for which the transferee spouse ordinarily resided in the transferred residence. The automatic interspousal rollover or deferral rule must be applicable (i.e., no election out of the interspousal rollover in section 73), so no gain would be recognized on the transfer of the home.

ITA: 40(4)(b); 73(1) Inter vivos transfers by individuals, 40(4)(b)(ii)

A designation form should be completed by the transferor spouse, even if it is not filed, so that the recipient spouse can determine the appropriate designation on the ultimate disposition of the property. This would fully protect the capital gain on the residence, if the residence had been the only one owned by the family unit.

If the transfer to the recipient spouse takes place as a result of the death of the transferor spouse, the actual designation requirement by the transferor spouse is removed, but the residence must have been ordinarily inhabited by the transferor spouse for the years before death that the recipient spouse chooses to designate the home.

ITA: 70(6) Where transfer or distribution to spouse or spouse trust, 40(4)(b)(i)

Where two residences are owned by one spouse, the transfer of one of the residences to the other spouse only offers partial relief, because of the limitation of one principal residence per family unit. In this situation, the transferee spouse will be deemed to have owned the property since the time the transferor spouse originally acquired the property. However, the years of designation will be limited to those years in which the transferor actually designates the transferred residence as his or her principal residence plus those years in which the transferee spouse "ordinarily inhabited" the transferred residence.[2] Therefore,

ITA: 54 Definitions

[2] See the CRA Technical Interpretation Document No. 9502557, February 9, 1995.

one of the two properties will be left unsheltered, at least in part, by the designation rules in paragraph (*c*) of the definition of a "principal residence". A disposition by, or the death of, the spouse who owns the two properties would trigger a taxable capital gain on the less-designated property, minus an exemption based on the ever-present extra year of designation ("1 +" rule) and the number of years owned.

Example Problem 7-5

Spouse A owns two residences:

	Residence 1	Residence 2
FMV	$100,000	$200,000
ACB	$50,000	$100,000
Year of acquisition	2005	2005

Both spouses have resided in both homes since 2006. In 2013, Spouse A transferred Residence 2 to Spouse B as a gift. Spouse B sold the transferred residence in 2018 for $300,000. Spouse A has not designated, at any time, Residence 2 as his principal residence.

REQUIRED

(1) Compute the effect of the above transaction as if subsection 40(4) did not exist.

(2) Apply subsection 40(4) to the transaction.

(3) Apply subsection 40(4) to the transaction on the assumption that spouse A had previously designated Residence 2 for two years.

SOLUTION

(1) As if subsection 40(4) did not exist:

2013 — Transfer of residence to Spouse B (rollover automatically applies since the facts do not indicate that Spouse A elected not to have the rollover apply; refer to the discussion of the attribution rules later in this chapter for a more detailed explanation of this provision)

ITA: 73 Inter vivos transfers by individuals

P of D (deemed)	$100,000
ACB	$(100,000)
Gain	Nil

ITA: 73 Inter vivos transfers by individuals

Note that no principal residence designation was required to reduce the gain to nil.

2018 — Spouse B sells home

P of D (deemed)	$300,000
ACB	$(100,000)
Gain	$200,000
Exemption: ((1 + 5 years designated by B) / 6 years owned by B) × $200,000	$(200,000)
Capital Gain	Nil
Years of designation: any five of 2013–2018	

ITA: 73 Inter vivos transfers by individuals

The gain of $200,000 was completely eliminated by Spouse B designating Residence 2 for five years under the principal residence rules, because:

- Spouse B owned the residence for six years (2013–2018, inclusive), and
- Spouse B ordinarily inhabited the residence for those years.

Hence, the entire gain is eliminated and Spouse A has saved the designation of years 2006–2012, plus one year of 2013–2018.

Note that there is no attribution since the capital gain is nil. However, depending upon the use of the $300,000 proceeds by Spouse B, there is potential attribution under the substituted property rule, discussed later in this chapter.

(2) With subsection 40(4):

2018 — Spouse B sells home

P of D	$300,000
ACB	$(100,000)
Gain	$200,000
Exemption [(1 + 12[(1)]) / 13[(2)]] × $200,000 =	$(200,000)
Capital Gain[(3)]	Nil

ITA: 73 Inter vivos transfers by individuals

The application of subsection 40(4) results in the same nil capital gain, but has eliminated all the principal residence designation years for Spouse A for Residence 1, except for one year.

(3) Spouse A had previously designated Residence 2 for two years:

The answer would be the same as Part (2). The years designated would be the two years designated by Spouse A, plus 10 years by Spouse B for a total of 12 years, thereby, eliminating the entire gain.

NOTES TO SOLUTION

(1) Spouse B can designate the transferred residence for the actual years or deemed years that he or she owned and ordinarily inhabited the residence (12 years) plus any other years for which Spouse A made a designation (in this case nil). ITA: 40(4)(a)

(2) The number of years owned includes the ownership years of Spouse A.

(3) The taxable capital gain, if any, will be attributed back to Spouse A, if realized during his or her lifetime.

Additional Notes:

- If this transfer had been as a consequence of Spouse A's death, the years of designation available would be expanded to include the potential designations available to Spouse A (or his or her legal representative). Hence, the entire gain would be exempt, but Residence 1 could not be designated for the years used to designate Residence 2.
- This example was designed to demonstrate how subsection 40(4) is applied and no tax planning was taken into account. Some of the factors which should be considered would be:
  - the relative size of the future gain on the two homes;
  - the tax rates of the respective spouses who own the homes; and
  - the potential application of the attribution rules to the ultimate non-exempt capital gains on the homes.

Joint ownership situations

Where two residences are each jointly owned by spouses, subsection 40(4) does not have any effect, since the definition of a "principal residence" governs years of joint ownership. Hence, each spouse enjoys an unrestricted right to designate either residence as his or her principal residence under the exemption formula. A transfer of ownership so that one residence is wholly owned by one spouse and the other residence is wholly owned by the other spouse will maximize the potential principal residence designation for years owned before 1982, when both spouses could have a principal residence. Therefore, there will be no tax consequences, since both spouses have owned, although only partially, the residence for the entire period. The transferee spouse can designate the entire residence as his or her principal residence. ITA: 54 Definitions; 40(2)(b)

¶7,115.99 Practise What You've Learned

Refer to the following sections of the Study Guide to practise what you've learned:

*¶7,800 — **Review Questions***

- Question 3 — Principal Residence
- Question 11 — Change in use of principal residence

*¶7,825 — **Multiple Choice Questions***

- Question 2 — Principal Residence
- Question 3 — Change in use of principal residence

*¶7,850 — **Exercises***

- Exercise 1 — Principal Residence
- Exercise 2 — Principal Residence
- Exercise 3 — Change in use of principal residence

¶7,120 Pooling of Identical Assets

There are many and varied methods of arriving at a cost base for identical assets for accounting purposes. However, for tax purposes, there is only one method, namely, the "floating weighted average method".

For stock transactions, the floating weighted average cost is calculated by dividing the aggregate of the costs of the identical properties by the number of such identical properties.

For bonds, debentures, notes, etc., the floating weighted average cost is calculated as:

$$\frac{\text{Aggregate of the cost of the identical properties}}{\text{(Principal amounts of all identical properties/Principal amount of the property disposed of)}}$$

Example

Assume an individual purchased three $1,000 bonds of a corporation for $2,880. Later, a $500 bond of the same series of bonds of the corporation was purchased for $490. The weighted average cost of one of the $1,000 bond is:

$\underline{\$2{,}880 + \$490} = \$963$

[(3 × $1,000) + $500]/$1,000

Similarly, the weighted average cost of the $500 bond is:

$$\frac{\$2{,}880 + \$490}{[(3 \times \$1{,}000) + \$500]/\$500} = \$481 \text{ (or one-half the cost of a \$1,000 bond)}$$

Many investors purchase shares or units of mutual funds to hold outside of RRSP investments. Mutual funds allocate their income to their investors, such that the income is taxable to the investors and not to the mutual fund. As a result, investors must include in their income for tax purposes the amount of net investment income, such as interest and dividends and net taxable capital gains paid or payable to them in the year. Often income allocated to the investor is reinvested in additional units in the fund, rather than paid out. Since reinvested income amounts would have been taxed in the hands of the investor, whether or not actually distributed, these amounts can be added to the adjusted cost base (ACB) of the investor's units in the fund. It is important to note that the adjustments made to the ACB, which are listed below, depend on the type of income allocated to the taxpayer.

- Interest income: the full amount of the interest income would increase the ACB of the mutual fund.
- Capital gains: while only 50% of the capital gain is included in the taxpayer's income, the ACB of the mutual funds would be adjusted for the full capital gain (100%).
- Dividends: the adjustment amount would be the actual dividend, not the grossed-up dividend.

After the reinvestment, the ACB of each unit owned in the mutual fund must be averaged by dividing the total ACB of all units in the mutual fund owned by the investor by the total number of units owned.

When an investor redeems or disposes of units in a mutual fund, a capital gain (or loss) is realized. The calculation of the capital gain (or loss) follows the normal formula of proceeds of disposition minus the sum of the investor's ACB and selling costs. This capital gain (or loss) is separate and distinct from the taxable capital gains allocated from the income of the fund which are made annually and taxed as paid or declared payable. Refer to Example Problem 7-2 in ¶7,110, shown earlier in the chapter.

Example Problem 7-6

Consider the following transactions in the shares of Dachshund Airways Ltd:

Date	Type of transaction	Number of shares	Cost per share (selling price)	Total cost (selling price)
April 2006	Purchase	100	$1	$100
March 2008	Purchase	150	$2	$300
Aug. 2011	Sale	(200)	$(3)	$(600)
June 2014	Purchase	100	$4	$400
July 2016	Purchase	300	$5	$1,500
Oct. 2018	Sale	(250)	$(6)	$(1,500)

REQUIRED

Compute the taxable capital gains, if any, on the 2011 and the 2018 sales.

SOLUTION

August 2011 sale:

P of D (200 shares @ $3)	$600
ACB (200 shares @ $1.60[(1)])	$(320)
CG	$280
TCG (½ × $280)	$140

October 2018 sale:

P of D (250 shares @ $6)	$1,500
ACB (250 shares @ $4.40[(2)])	$(1,100)
CG	$400
TCG (½ × $400)	$200

There are 200 shares with a weighted average cost of $4.40 on hand after the 2018 sale.

NOTES TO SOLUTION

(1)	100	shares @ $1 =	$100
	150	shares @ $2 =	$300
	250		$400
		$400 ÷ 250 = $1.60 per share	
(2)	50	shares @ $1.60 =	$80
	100	shares @ $4.00 =	$400
	300	shares @ $5.00 =	$1,500
	450		$1,980
		$1,980 ÷ 450 = $4.40 per share	

¶7,120.10 Identical Properties Exempt From Cost Averaging Rule

The Act requires that the cost of identical properties acquired by a taxpayer be averaged over all such properties. Generally, this results in each of the properties having the same adjusted cost base ("ACB"), ensuring that the capital gain or loss on the disposition of any one of the properties can be determined without having to identify a particular property as the property that has been disposed of.

ITA: 47(1) Identical properties

Certain securities are exempt from the cost-averaging rule by deeming such securities not to be identical to any other securities acquired by the taxpayer for the purposes of this cost-averaging rule. The specific securities to which this exemption applies are as follows:

ITA: 47(1) Identical properties, 47(3) Securities acquired by employee

- Securities (i.e., shares of a corporation and units of a mutual fund trust) acquired under an employee option agreement for which a deferral is provided and securities acquired in exchange for such securities under specified circumstances.
- Securities acquired under an employee option agreement where the securities are designated by the taxpayer and deemed by the Act to be the securities that are the subject of a disposition of identical securities occurring within 30 days after the acquisition.
- Employer shares received by an employee as part of a lump-sum payment on withdrawing from a deferred profit sharing plan (DPSP), where the employee filed an election in respect of those shares. Such an election allows the taxpayer to defer taxation on the growth of the shares while they were held by the plan until such time as the employee disposes of the shares.

ITA: 7(1.1) Employee stock options, 7(8) Deferral in respect of non-CCPC employee options, 7(1.31) Disposition of newly-acquired security, 147(10.1) Single payment on retirement, etc.

The effect of a security being exempted from the cost-averaging rule is that the ACB of the security and, thus, the capital gain or loss on its disposition, is determined without regard to the ACB of any other securities owned by the taxpayer. In other words, each security to which the exemption applies has its own unique ACB.

¶7,125 Disposition of Shares Acquired Under a Stock Option

Under the stock option benefit rules, there is a special provision which applies when a taxpayer disposes of a security that is identical to other securities already owned by the taxpayer. The provision allows the taxpayer to designate the particular security that is being disposed of.

ITA: 7(1.31) Disposition of newly-acquired security

In order for this subsection to apply, certain conditions must be met.

- The particular security must have been acquired under an employee stock option agreement, as described in the Act.

ITA: 7(1) Agreement to issue securities to employees

- The ***disposition must occur no later than 30 days*** after the taxpayer acquires the particular security.
- There ***must be no other acquisitions or dispositions*** of identical securities in the intervening period; that is, after the acquisition of the particular security and before the disposition in respect of which the designation is being made. However, this does not preclude the taxpayer from acquiring other identical securities at the same time as the disposition in respect of which the designation is being made.
- The taxpayer ***must make the designation*** in the tax return that is filed for the year in which the disposition occurs.
- The taxpayer must not have designated the particular security in connection with the disposition of any other security.

Example Problem 7-7

On May 1, 2016, Joseph acquired 750 shares of his corporate employer on the open market. On May 1, 2017, he acquired another 750 shares on the open market. On May 1, 2018, he acquired an additional 1,000 shares under employee stock options. Immediately thereafter, he sold 1,500 shares.

REQUIRED

How should Joseph calculate his cost base on the disposition of his shares?

SOLUTION

In his tax return for 2017, he can designate the 1,000 stock option shares as constituting part of the shares that were sold. The 1,500 shares being sold by Joseph are deemed to comprise the 1,000 stock option shares and 500 of the 1,500 shares that Joseph acquired on the open market. Alternatively, he can use the weighted average cost of all the shares.

Securities to which this provision applies are deemed, for the purpose of the cost-averaging rule, not to be identical to any other securities owned by the taxpayer. Consequently, the ACB of each such security and, thus, the capital gain or loss on the disposition of the security, is determined without regard to the ACB of any other securities owned by the taxpayer.

ITA: 47(3) Securities acquired by employee, 7(1) Agreement to issue securities to employees, 47(1) Identical properties

The Act accommodates the practice of specific identification. The significance of specific identification is that it allows a taxpayer to deduct a portion of the employment benefit that the taxpayer is deemed to have received in respect of the taxpayer's acquisition of a qualifying employee option security, if the taxpayer disposes of the security by donating it to a qualifying charity within 30 days after its acquisition.

ITA: 7(1.31) Disposition of newly-acquired security, 110(1)(d.01) Charitable donation of employee option securities, 7(1) Agreement to issue securities to employees

¶7,130 Adjusted Cost Base of Shares Acquired Under a Stock Option

The Act provides for an addition to the ACB of a share acquired by a taxpayer under an employee option agreement. The amount that is added to the ACB is the amount of the employment benefit that the taxpayer (or a non-arm's length person) is deemed to have received in connection with the acquisition of the security.

ITA: 53(1)(j) [Adjustments to cost base — Share or fund unit taxed as stock option benefit]; 7(1) Agreement to issue securities to employees

The amount added to the ACB of the shares acquired under a stock option is generally equal to the excess of the fair market value of the security at the time the options are exercised over the option price paid to acquire the security. The amount is added to the ACB in the year in which the benefit is deemed to have been received, which is generally the year in which the taxpayer acquires the security.

In effect, the adjusted cost base of the shares acquired under a stock option plan would be equal to the fair market value of the shares at the time the stock option is exercised. This is also the case for options granted by a Canadian-controlled private corporation (CCPC) to an arm's length person, even though there is a rule that applies to defer recognition of the benefit to the year in which the taxpayer disposes of the security (as discussed in Chapter 3). The employment benefit is included in the ACB of the security at the time of acquisition, even if recognition of the employment benefit is deferred, for tax purposes, until the taxpayer disposes of the security.

ITA: 7(1.1) Employee stock options; 53(1)(j) [Adjustments to cost base — Share or fund unit taxed as stock option benefit]

¶7,135 Cost of Certain Properties

¶7,135.10 General Consideration

The cost of property is usually incurred by the acquisition of the property with after-tax funds. Thus, when a capital property is acquired for $100, the funds used in the purchase have usually been subjected to income tax. That is why, on the disposition of the property for, say, $150, the $100 of cost is not taxed; only the $50 of gain above cost is taxed. Thus, cost is recovered tax-free on a disposition, because it represents an amount on which tax was already paid.

Normally the cost of capital property or the capital cost of depreciable capital property is the laid-down cost for accounting purposes. However, a number of provisions deem the cost to be an amount other than laid-down cost. Where a taxpayer has acquired property and an amount in respect of the value of the property is included in the taxpayer's income, that amount is added to the cost of the property.

ITA: 52 [Cost of certain property]

Example

If a shareholder had a benefit in kind (i.e., in property) which was included in his or her income, then the income inclusion would be added to the cost of the property so received. Since the income inclusion in respect of the benefit would be taxed, the amount of the benefit can be considered as a tax-paid cost of the property, according to the concept of cost discussed above.

ITA: 52(1) Cost of certain property the value of which is included in income, 15(1) Benefit conferred on shareholder

There is one notable exception to this rule, namely, an employment income inclusion arising from a stock option benefit, which was discussed in ¶3,125.

ITA: 52(1) Cost of certain property the value of which is included in income, 7 [Employee stock options]

¶7,135.20 Dividends in Kind and Lottery Prizes

Sometimes a company will pay dividends in property other than cash; these are called dividends in kind. Since the shareholder will pay tax on the full fair market value of the property paid as a dividend, the cost to the shareholder of the property received will be the same fair market value.

ITA: 52(2) Cost of property received as dividend in kind

If a lottery prize is received, the cost of this prize to the winner is the fair market value of the prize. Since lottery prizes in Canada are not taxable, adding the fair market value of the prize to the cost base ensure that the lottery winnings will not be taxed when the prize is eventually disposed of.

ITA: 40(2)(f), 52(4) Cost of property acquired as prize

Example

An individual wins a car as a lottery prize and the fair market value of the car is $35,000. The cost of the car to the individual is $35,000 even though the prize is not included in income. Since lottery prizes in Canada are not taxable, this adjustment ensures that the first $35,000 in value is not taxed on disposition.

¶7,135.30 Stock Dividends

A stock dividend is treated in the same manner as any other dividend for purposes of determining income. For tax purposes, a stock dividend that is received by an individual is grossed up and included in net income. The cost base of shares acquired through a stock dividend is deemed to be equal to its paid-up capital which is, generally, the stated capital[3] on the accounting balance sheet. The reason for this treatment will become more apparent when paid-up capital and corporate distributions are discussed in Chapter 15.

ITA: 52(3) Cost of stock dividend

[3] In some provinces, this amount may be the par value.

Example Problem 7-8

Mr. Arnett purchased 1,000 shares of Sure-Fire Limited, a public corporation, at $50 per share in 2013. Mr. Arnett received the following dividends subsequent to that time:

2014	A stock dividend of 10% which resulted in an increase in the paid-up capital of $10 for each share issued.
2015	A stock dividend of 10% which resulted in an increase in the paid-up capital of $10 for each share issued.
2016	Cash dividend of $5 per share.
2017	A stock dividend of 10% which resulted in an increase in the paid-up capital of $10 for each share issued.

REQUIRED

Compute the taxable capital gain or allowable capital loss if Mr. Arnett sold 100 of the above shares in 2018 for $45 per share less brokerage fees of $100.

SOLUTION

2018	P of D (100 shares @ $45)		$4,500
	ACB (100 shares @ $40.05[(1)])	$4,005	
	Selling cost	$100	$(4,105)
	Capital gain		$395
	Taxable capital gain (½ × $395)		$198

NOTE TO SOLUTION

(1)

2013	1,000	shares — purchased @ $50 each	$50,000
2014	100	shares — stock dividend of 10% @ $10 each	$1,000
	1,100		
2015	110	shares — stock dividend of 10% @ $10 each	$1,100
	1,210		

2017	121	shares — stock dividend of 10% @ $10 each	$1,210
	1,331		$53,310

$53,310 ÷ 1,331 = $40.05

¶7,140 Superficial Losses

A "superficial loss" as defined in the Act is usually, but not necessarily, associated with the trading of securities. The provisions are meant to deal with situations where a taxpayer disposes of an asset to trigger a loss but has immediate intentions to repurchase the asset. It is common for a taxpayer to trigger a loss on securities with an accrued capital loss at the end of the year to offset a capital gain previously realized in the year. Then the taxpayer repurchases the same or identical securities, almost immediately, because of their long-term potential. In this case, the taxpayer has converted a "paper" loss into a realized loss, but after the repurchase continues to own essentially the same securities. This is the essence of a superficial loss.

ITA: 54 Definitions

The provisions in the Act deny the use of a "superficial loss" at the time of the disposition. The superficial loss is not completely denied, but rather the provisions permits the superficial loss to be added to the adjusted cost base of the substituted property (the newly acquired shares). The end result is to defer the triggering of the loss until the newly acquired substituted property is disposed of.

ITA: 53(1)(f) [Adjustments to cost base — Substituted property]

There are three conditions necessary in order to establish a superficial loss:

(1) the taxpayer or an "affiliated person" must dispose of the property;

(2) the taxpayer or an affiliated person acquires or re-acquires the same or identical property during the period beginning 30 days before the disposition and ending 30 days after the disposition; and

(3) the taxpayer or an affiliated person, at the end of the period referred to in point (2) above, still owns at least some of the property.

An "affiliated person" is, in essence, the taxpayer's spouse or a corporation controlled by either the taxpayer or the taxpayer's spouse. The conditions above ensure that a taxpayer is not able to circumvent the provisions by having a spouse or corporation that they control repurchase the identical property 30 days before or after the disposition.

ITA: 251.1(1) Definition of "affiliated persons"

Example Problem 7-9

Mr. Sung bought 1,000 shares of Norwood Ltd. at $10 per share on October 1, 2017. On December 15, 2017, Mr. Sung sold 1,000 shares at $5. On January 3, 2018, he bought 1,000 shares at $6. On November 15, 2018, he sold 1,000 shares at $10.

REQUIRED

Compute the taxable capital gain or allowable capital loss on each of the above transactions.

SOLUTION

Dec. 15, 2017	P of D (1,000 shares @ $5)	$ 5,000
	ACB (1,000 shares @ $10)	$(10,000)
	Capital loss	Nil

There is a superficial loss of $5,000, since he purchased the shares within the 30-day time limit and still owns the shares at the end of the period which is 30 days after December 15. In essence, the purchase on January 3, 2018 allows him to maintain his ownership position in the shares after the sale. The superficial loss of $5,000 will be added to the adjusted cost base of the shares acquired on January 3, 2018. This has the effect of delaying, but not denying, the recognition of the loss.

Nov. 15, 2018	P of D (1,000 shares @ $10)	$10,000
	ACB (1,000 shares[1])	$(11,000)
	Capital loss	$(1,000)

Since Mr. Sung has no shares on hand 30 days after the sale on November 15, 2018, there cannot be a superficial loss.

NOTE TO SOLUTION

(1)	1,000 shares @ $6 =	$ 6,000
	Dec. 15 Sup. loss =	$5,000
		$11,000

Example Problem 7-10

Ms. Tabuchi is considering selling all of her remaining shares of Open Mining Ltd., a public corporation. She is uncertain of the adjusted cost base of the shares. The following is the historical data concerning her holdings in Open Mining Ltd.

June 1, 2014	Purchased 500 shares @ $2 per share.
Jan. 15, 2015	Received a stock dividend of 10%. The paid-up capital of the corporation was credited with one dollar for each share issued.
July 1, 2016	Purchased additional 1,000 shares @ $5 per share.
April 15, 2017	Received a stock dividend of 10%. The paid-up capital of the corporation was credited with $6 for each additional share.
June 19, 2018	Purchased an additional 1,000 shares @ $9.
Aug. 1, 2018	Sold 500 shares @ $5 plus commission of $150.

REQUIRED

Determine the adjusted cost base of Ms. Tabuchi's shares in Open Mining Ltd.

SOLUTION

Adjusted Cost Base				Transaction
June 1, 2014	500	shares @ $2 – purchase		$1,000
Jan 15, 2015	50	shares – 10% stock dividend @$1		$50
July 1, 2016	1,000	shares @ $5 – purchase		$5,000
	1,550			
April 15, 2017	155	shares – 10% stock dividend @ $6		$930
June 19, 2018	1,000	shares @ $9		$9,000
	2,705			$15,980
Aug. 1, 2018	(500)	P of D @ $5	$2,500	
		ACB (500 shares × $15,980/2,705) (rounded)	$(2,954)	$(2,954)
			$(454)	
		Selling Costs	$(150)	
		Capital loss	$604	
	2,205	Shares @ $5.91		$13,026

¶7,145 Transfer of Property to an RRSP

Similar to the superficial loss rules discussed above, a loss from the disposition of property to a trust governed by an RRSP to which taxpayers or their spouses are beneficiaries is deemed to be nil. Since the property is still held by the taxpayer, now indirectly through an RRSP, a loss should not be allowed on the transfer. However, this type of transfer is considered a disposition with proceeds equal to the FMV at the time of transfer. If the taxpayer realizes a capital gain, it must be included in computing income.

ITA: 40(2)(g)(iv)

¶7,150 Options

There are two basic types of option:

ITA: 49(1) Granting of options

- an option to buy property (known as a call option); and
- an option to sell property (known as a put option).

As a general rule, when an option is granted, there is a disposition of a property with an adjusted cost base of nil by the grantor or issuer. The result is a capital gain to the grantor in the amount of the proceeds for the option in the year the option is granted. The grantee or holder of the option has acquired a capital property with an adjusted cost base equal to the amount paid for the option.

If the option expires, the grantor retains the property so the grantor's tax position is unchanged. The capital gain on the sale of the option has already been recognized and the grantor's cost base of the property remains unchanged. The grantee (the purchaser of the option) now holds an option that can no longer be exercised. Since the option has expired, the value is nil and the grantee has a capital loss in the year of expiration.

There are two exceptions to the general rule noted above:

- When an option in respect of a principal residence is granted, there is no disposition. As a result, if an option on a principal residence expires, there would have been no inclusion for the grantor and, therefore, no tax effect. The grantee would be denied a loss on expiration, because the option on a principal residence would be regarded as a personal-use property (see ¶7,105.10 above).

ITA: 49(1)(a), 40(2)(g)(iii), 54 Definitions

- The other exception is for an option granted by a corporation to another person to buy securities to be issued by the corporation. In this case, the corporation has no disposition at the time the option is granted. However, if the option expires, the corporation is deemed to have disposed of a capital property with an adjusted cost base of nil. The proceeds are deemed to be equal to the amount, if any, received for granting the option. As a result, when this type of option expires, a capital gain is realized.

ITA: 49(2) Expired option — shares

¶7,150.10 Call Option

If an option to acquire property (i.e., a call option) is exercised, then the granting of the option and its exercise are deemed not to be a disposition to the vendor. When the option is exercised, there is a disposition of the property underlying the option by the vendor and the purchaser acquires the optioned property.

ITA: 49(3) Where option to acquire exercised

On the exercise of the option, the vendor of the optioned property must include the consideration received for the option in proceeds of disposition of the property sold in the year in which the option is exercised. The vendor, who was the grantor of the option, can file an amended return for the year in which the amount received for the option was included in income to remove the amount received for the option from income for that year. This amended return must be filed by the time the return for the year in which the option was exercised must be filed. The purchaser of the property must add the cost of the option held to the cost of the property acquired when the option was exercised.

ITA: 49(4) Reassessment where option exercised in subsequent year

Example

In Year 1, Jim pays $10,000 to Bill for an option to acquire his shares in Opco Inc. for $500,000. Bill's ACB of the Opco Inc. shares is $300,000. In Year 2, Jim exercises the option and pays Bill $500,000 for his shares in Opco Inc. The following would be the result of the transaction in each of the two years:

Year 1 — the option is sold to Jim

(1) Bill would report a capital gain equal to $10,000 which is the proceeds received for the sale of the option less a cost base of nil (since the option has no cost base). The taxable capital gain is $5,000 (50% × $10,000).

(2) Jim's cost base for the option is $10,000.

Year 2 — the option is exercised by Jim

Bill

(1) Bill would amend his Year 1 tax return to remove the taxable capital gain of $5,000 that was reported. He would receive a refund on the tax paid in Year 1.

(2) Next, Bill would have proceeds of disposition of $510,000 ($500,000 + 10,000) on the sale of the shares. His capital gain would be $210,000 ($510,000 – $300,000) on the sale of the shares. The taxable capital gain is $105,000 (50% × $210,000).

Jim

(1) Jim's adjusted cost for the share he purchased from Bill would be equal to $510,000 ($500,000 plus the $10,000 paid for the option).

Note that the total proceeds of disposition to Bill is equal to the adjusted cost base of Jim.

¶7,150.20 Put Option

If an option to sell property (i.e., a put option) is exercised, the rules are similar to those for the exercise of a call option. Note, however, that the grantor of a put option is the purchaser of the property on exercise of the option and will have been paid an amount by the vendor of the underlying property. The granting of the option and its exercise are deemed not to be a disposition of property.

ITA: 49(3) Where option to acquire exercised, 49(3.1) Where option to dispose exercised

The vendor of the optioned property, who paid for the right to "put" or sell the property to the purchaser of the optioned property, must deduct the amount paid for the option from proceeds of disposition of the property sold. The purchaser of the optioned property must deduct the amount received for the put option from the cost of the property acquired. The grantor of the option (i.e., the purchaser of the property in this case) can file an amended return for the year in which the amount received for the option was included in income and to exclude the amount received for the option from income in the year of the grant.

ITA: 49(4) Reassessment where option exercised in subsequent year

Example

In Year 1, Don pays $15,000 to Bruce for the right to sell 1,000 shares of Holdco Inc. to Bruce for $300,000 at any time in the next three years. Don originally paid $120,000 for the 1,000 Holdco Inc. shares. In Year 2, Don exercises the option and Bruce pays Don $300,000 for Don's 1,000 shares of Holdco Inc. The following would be the result of the transaction in each of the two years:

Year 1 — the option is sold by Bruce

(1) Bruce received $15,000 in proceeds of disposition, but since there is no cost base for the option, he will include a capital gain of $15,000.

(2) Don now owns the option with a cost base of $15,000.

Year 2 — the option is exercised by Don

Bruce

(1) Bruce pays Don $300,000 for Don's 1,000 shares in Holdco Inc.

(2) Bruce would amend his Year 1 return to remove the capital gain, $15,000, recorded in Year 1.

(3) Bruce can now reduce the cost base of the shares purchased to reflect the proceeds received from the option. The adjusted cost base of the 1,000 shares Bruce purchased from Don as a result of this put option would be the actual amount Bruce paid, $285,000 ($300,000 less the $15,000 he received for the option).

Don

(1) Don's proceeds of disposition on the sale of the 1,000 shares would be the net amount he received, $285,000 ($300,000 less the $15,000 Don paid to Bruce for the option to sell).

(2) Don's capital gain would be $165,000 (P of D of $285,000 less the ACB of $120,000).

¶7,150.30 Summary

The basic rules for the taxation of options as capital property are summarized below.

Summary

Basic Rules for the Taxation of Options as Capital Property

Event	Call Option (Option to buy a property)		Put Option (Option to sell a property)	
	Grantor (Seller)	Grantee (Buyer)	Grantor (Buyer)	Grantee (Seller)
Option granted	• Amount received for option included as a capital gain	• Amount paid for option is the ACB of the option	• Amount received for option included as a capital gain	• Amount paid for option is the ACB of the option
Option Exercised	• Amount received for option is added to proceeds of underlying property sold • File amended return (if necessary) for the year the option is granted to remove the capital gain from income	• Amount paid for the option is added to the ACB of the underlying property purchased	• Amount received for option deducted from cost of underlying property purchased • File amended return (if necessary) for the year the option is granted to remove the capital gain from income	• Amount paid for option is deducted from proceeds of underlying property sold
Option expired	• No change in tax position	• Amount paid for option is realized as a capital loss	• No change in tax position	• Amount paid for option is realized as a capital loss

Example Problem 7-11

Ms. Smart owned a capital property that had an adjusted cost base of $100,000. In 2016, she granted Mr. Li an option to buy the property from her by the end of 2018 at an option price of $160,000. Mr. Li paid $16,000 to Ms. Smart for the option.

REQUIRED

(1) What are the income tax implications to Ms. Smart and Mr. Li in 2016?

(2) What are the income tax implications to Ms. Smart and Mr. Li in 2018 if:

(a) the call option expires?

(b) the call option is exercised?

SOLUTION

(1) In 2016, Ms. Smart has granted a call option with an adjusted cost base of nil and proceeds of disposition of $16,000. On this disposition, she must report a capital gain of $16,000 in 2016. Mr. Li has acquired a capital property in the option with an adjusted cost base of $16,000.

(2) Tax implications in 2018:

(a) If the option expires at the end of 2018 because Mr. Li chooses not to exercise it and acquire the capital property, then there are no further tax implications to Ms. Smart. She has already included the capital gain in 2016 on granting the option and she retains the capital property with an adjusted cost base of $100,000. In 2018, Mr. Li has a capital loss of $16,000, since the option held at that cost has become worthless on expiration. Of course, that capital loss can only be applied to a capital gain in the current year, 2018, the three preceding years, 2015, 2016, and 2017, or any year subsequent to 2018.

(b) If the call option is exercised in 2018 and Mr. Li acquires the property for $160,000, then Ms. Smart can file an amended return for 2016 to remove the $16,000 capital gain from her income in that year. However, her proceeds of disposition on the sale in 2018 will amount to the $160,000 received as the agreed price under the option plus the $16,000 received for the option in 2016. Thus, she will report in 2018 a capital gain of $76,000 (i.e., $160,000 + $16,000 – $100,000). Mr. Li will have acquired the property which will have an adjusted cost base of $176,000 (i.e., $160,000 + $16,000).

¶7,155 Convertible Properties

Where a taxpayer acquires shares from a corporation on the conversion of a convertible security, referred to as a convertible property, the exchange is deemed not to have been a disposition of property. The cost to the taxpayer of the shares received is deemed to be the adjusted cost base of the convertible property owned immediately before the exchange. There is a further condition in this rollover provision that the taxpayer must not have received any consideration (such as cash) other than shares in exchange for his or her convertible property. ITA: 51 Convertible property

Example

A convertible debenture was acquired at face value of $100. The conversion privilege entitles the holder to five common shares. The taxpayer exercises the conversion privilege at a time when the common shares are trading at $30 per share.

On the date the conversion occurs, the taxpayer is deemed to have acquired the new common shares at $20 each ($100/5). Since the fair market value of the shares is $30 each, the taxpayer has effectively deferred recognition of $50 per bond or a $10 per share capital gain.

¶7,160 Capital Gains Deferral

Overview

An individual is permitted to defer the recognition of a capital gain in respect of certain small business investments. To obtain the deferral, the proceeds from the sale of the small business investment must be used to acquire other small business investments. In order to qualify for the deferral, the taxpayer must have disposed of a qualified disposition. In general terms, if all the proceeds of disposition on the sale of a small business investment are used to acquire another small business investment, the entire capital gain may be deferred. ITA: 44.1 (2)

¶7,160.10 Qualified Disposition Defined

A qualifying disposition by an individual is a disposition of common shares of the capital stock of a corporation owned by the individual where each such share was:

- an eligible small business corporation (defined below) share of the individual,
- a common share of the capital stock of an active business corporation (defined below) throughout the time it was owned by the individual, and
- owned by the individual throughout the 185-day period that ended immediately before the disposition.

The active business of the corporation has to be carried on primarily in Canada at all times in the period that began when the individual last acquired the share and ended when the disposition occurred (the "ownership period"), if that period is less than 730 days. In any other case, that active business has to be carried on primarily in Canada for at least 730 days during the ownership period. ITA: 44.1 (9)

¶7,160.20 Eligible Small Business Corporation Defined

The term "eligible small business corporation" is relevant for the purposes of the term "eligible small business corporation share". An eligible small business corporation, at a particular time, means a Canadian-controlled private corporation all or substantially all of the fair market value of the assets of which is, at that time, attributable to assets of the corporation that are:

- assets used principally in an active business carried on primarily in Canada by the corporation or an eligible small business corporation related to it,
- shares of or debt issued by other eligible small business corporations related to the corporation, or
- a combination of those two types of assets.

An "eligible small business corporation share" of an individual is a common share issued by a corporation to the individual where:

- at the time the share is issued, the corporation was an "eligible small business corporation" (see above) and immediately before, and
- after that time the total carrying value of its assets and the assets of corporations related to it does not exceed $50 million.

¶7,160.30 Calculation of the Deferral Amount

Prior to reviewing the details of the calculation for the "permitted deferral", three points should be highlighted:

(1) The individual may claim a "permitted deferral" that is less than the maximum amount available as calculated by the formula below. This allows for flexibility in planning for future tax implications.

(2) The permitted deferral is the amount of a capital gain from the disposition that can be deferred. It reduces the gain of the individual for the disposition.

(3) The deferred gain on the old investments will reduce the ACB of the new investments, which is similar to the treatment of replacement property discussed in Chapter 8.

The "permitted deferral" of an individual is calculated using the formula:

$$(G/H) \times I$$

where:

G is the lesser of the individual's proceeds of disposition from the old small business investment and the cost to the individual of a replacement share;

H is the individual's proceeds of disposition from the old small business investment; and

I is the individual's capital gain from the old small business investment.

Example Problem 7-12

Jennifer S. Lee disposed of shares of corporation A with an adjusted cost base of $3 million for proceeds of disposition of $4.5 million. Jennifer immediately purchased replacement shares in corporation B with a cost of $2.2 million and in corporation C with a cost of $2.3 million. All shares are eligible small business corporation shares.

REQUIRED

Compute the capital gain, after the deferral, on the disposition of the shares of corporation A and the ACB of the replacement shares in corporations B and C.

SOLUTION

Jennifer's capital gain without the deferral would be calculated as:

Capital gain otherwise determined:	
Proceeds	$4,500,000
ACB	$3,000,000
Capital gain	$1,500,000
Permitted deferral:	
G/H × I = $4,500,000/$4,500,000 × $1,500,000 =	$1,500,000
G = lesser of:	
1. Proceeds of disposition =	$4,500,000
2. Cost of replacement shares =	$4,500,000
H = Proceeds of disposition =	$4,500,000
I = Capital gain =	$1,500,000

Jennifer's capital gain that will be reported is calculated as follows:

Capital gain otherwise determined	$1,500,000
Less: Permitted deferral	$1,500,000
Capital gain	$ Nil

The ACB reduction is determined by the formula D × (E/F) found in the definition of the reduction, and is applied as follows:

Corporation B: $1,500,000 × ($2,200,000/$4,500,000) =	$733,333

Corporation C: $1,500,000 × ($2,300,000/$4,500,000) =	$766,667

Note that the sum of the ACB reductions is $1.5 million, which is equal to the total capital gain deferred.

The adjusted cost base of the replacement shares is, therefore:

Corporation B: $2,2000,000 – $733,333 =	$1,466,667
Corporation C: $2,300,000 – $766,667 =	$1,533,333

Note that the sum of these ACBs is $3 million, which is actual cost net of the permitted deferral.

¶7,190 Pause and Reflect — Summary of Learning Goals

After working through this section, ¶7,100, you should be able to:

- Apply your knowledge of the specific provisions relating to personal-use property and listed-personal property to correctly calculate the income inclusion in a given period.
- Explain if a property meets the definition of a principal residence and explain the tax implications of disposing of a principal residence.
- Apply your knowledge to correctly determine the taxable portion of the capital gain in a situation where the principal residence exemption is applied to the disposition of more than one principal residence.
- Apply your knowledge of the provisions to calculate the adjusted cost base for identical shares that have been disposed of in the year.
- Explain the purpose of the superficial loss rules and correctly apply the provisions to determine the capital loss that is denied.
- Apply your knowledge of the provisions to determine the tax implications of put and call options, for both the buyer and the seller.
- Apply your knowledge of the provisions to calculate the capital gains deferral on the reinvestment of small business corporation shares.
- Apply your knowledge to advise clients on the tax implications of transferring capital property to a non-arm's length person, specifically to a spouse and minor and adult children.

¶7,190.99 Practise What You've Learned

Refer to the following sections of the Study Guide to practise what you've learned:

¶7,800 — Review Questions

- Question 2 — Negative ACB
- Question 4 — Capital loss
- Question 6 — Sale of shares
- Question 7 — Capital losses exceeding capital gains in the year

¶7,825 — Multiple Choice Questions

- Question 4 — Stock dividend

¶7,850 — Exercises

- Exercise 5 — Stock transactions
- Exercise 6 — Stock transactions
- Exercise 8 — Stock dividends
- Exercise 15 — Superficial loss

¶7,200 Non-Arm's Length Transfers and the Attribution Rules Revisited

Overview

Now that we have worked through the materials related to capital gains, we need to revisit transfers between non-arm's length parties, introduced in Chapter 6.

After working through this section, ¶7,200, you will be able to:

- Explain the meaning of related persons and how that relates to the attribution rules.
- Explain the attribution rules and the circumstances in which they apply.
- Apply your knowledge of the non-arm's length rules as they relate to the disposition of a capital property to a non-arm's length individual.
- Apply your knowledge to advise a client on planning methods to avoid income attribution.

¶7,205 Non-Arm's Length Transfers

The non-arm's length transfer rules are designed to prevent tax avoidance in certain transactions between persons not dealing at arm's length. The term "arm's length" is defined by providing that related persons are deemed not to deal with each other at arm's length. A taxpayer (or anyone not dealing at arm's length with the taxpayer) and an *inter*

ITA: 69(1) Inadequate considerations, 251(1)(a), 251(1)(b)

vivos or testamentary trust cannot deal at arm's length, if the taxpayer is an income or capital beneficiary of the trust. (Refer to Chapter 18 for more information on trusts.)

It is a question of fact whether persons not related to each other are dealing with each other at arm's length. The CRA sets out in an Income Tax Folio the following criteria, which have generally been used by the courts to determine whether a transaction has occurred at arm's length:

ITA: 251(1)(c); Income Tax Folio: S1-F5-C1 Related Persons and Dealing at Arm's Length

- Was there a common mind which directs the bargaining for both parties to a transaction?
- Were the parties to a transaction acting in concert without separate interests?

and

- Was there *"de facto"* control?

Refer to paragraphs 1.37 and 1.41 of the Income Tax Folio for more details on these points. These conditions may arise in dealings between business partners or close friends.

Summary

Who Does Not Deal at Arm's Length? Subsection 251(1)

(1) Related persons.

(2) A beneficiary, or anyone not dealing at arm's length with the beneficiary, and the *inter vivos* or testamentary trust.

(3) It is a question of fact.

Related persons are further defined in terms of individuals and corporations:

- Related individuals are those connected by blood, marriage or adoption and these connections are further specified. (A schematic diagram of related individuals under the Act is presented in Chapter 6 as Exhibit 6-1.)

ITA: 251(2) Definition of "related persons", 251(2)(b), 251(6) Blood relationship, etc; Income Tax Folio: S1-F5-C1 Related Persons and Dealing at Arm's Length

- Non-arm's length relationships between persons and corporations require control, either by one person or a group of related persons. Control in this situation means ownership of more than 50% of the voting shares.
- The concept of control is expanded in situations involving related groups and in the case of a person holding certain options.

ITA: 251(5) Control by related groups, options, etc.

- The subsections also indicates that a person is deemed to be related to himself or herself in cases where the person owns shares in two or more corporations.

Since the word "person" is defined to include a corporation, two corporations can be related. Furthermore, two corporations are related if they meet one of six conditions set out in the Act.

ITA: 248(1) Definitions, 251(2)(c)

¶7,210 Transactions With Non-arm's Length Individuals

Normally, the market forces of demand and supply will place the value of a transaction at fair market value. However, non-arm's length transactions may not reflect a normal transaction driven by the market forces. For that reason, the Act deems related persons not to deal at arm's length with each other. In addition, it is a question of fact whether unrelated persons deal with each other at arm's length. ITA: 251(1)(a), 251(1)(c)

When a taxpayer enters into a transaction with a related party (non-arm's length person) or with an unrelated party in which the transaction is considered not to be at arm's length, special rules apply to prevent the elimination or reduction of tax by selling at a price other than the fair market value. In practice, these rules are often referred to as the fair market value (FMV) rules and are intended to be punitive if non-arm's length parties do not sell at FMV. ITA: 69 Inadequate considerations

Example

Assume that Mr. A owns a property with an FMV of $10,000 and that he originally paid $5,000 for that property. He decides to sell the property to his daughter, who is under 18, for $8,000. Note that this price is lower than the (FMV).

Immediate tax consequence to Mr. A of the transaction:

	Sale at $8,000	Sale at $10,000
Proceeds of sales	$10,000	$10,000
Cost base (amount he paid)	$(5,000)	$(5,000)
Gain	$5,000	$5,000

If Mr. A's daughter sells the property immediately at $10,000 (FMV), she will have to recognize a gain of:

	Sale at $8,000	Sale at $10,000
Proceeds of sales	$10,000	$10,000
Cost base (amount he paid)	$(8,000)	$(10,000)
Gain	$2,000	$Nil

Total gain from the transaction:

	Sale at $8,000	Sale at $10,000
Mr.A	$5,000	$5,000
Daughter	$2,000	Nil
Total	$7,000	$5,000

If Mr. A sold the property to his daughter at fair market value, the total gain will be $5,000. This total gain would be consistent with the gain that would be recorded if Mr. A sold the property to an arm's length (unrelated) person. Since the related party did not use fair market value as consideration, a total gain of $7,000 is subject to tax which means that the $2,000 gain is taxed twice. These special anti-avoidance rules in the Act penalize taxpayers who enter into transactions which are not at fair market value.

ITA: 69 Inadequate considerations

A penalty similar to the above also occurs when the selling price is higher than the fair market value.

¶7,210.10 The Technical Rules

Generally, in situations involving the non-arm's length transfer of anything, including both tangible and intangible property, the transferor is deemed to receive proceeds equal to its fair market value at the time of the transfer, if the actual transfer price is less than fair market value. This rule would include gifts for no proceeds. However, no downward adjustment is made to the actual price received if it is more than fair market value.

On the other side, the transferee is deemed to have acquired property at a cost equal to its fair market value at the time of the transfer if he or she paid more than fair market value or if he or she received it as a gift, bequest, or inheritance, but not if he or she paid less than fair market value. In the case of a payment of less than fair market value, no adjustment is made to the actual price paid. There are exceptions to these rules on the transfer of such property to a spouse under certain conditions. The exhibit below summarizes the fair market value rules.

These rules do not apply to the transfer of assets between spouses, as spousal transfers happen automatically between spouses (see ¶7,215.20). These rules would only apply to a spousal transfer if the transferor elects out of the interspousal rollover rules, thereby subjecting the transfer between spouses to the fair market value rules below.

Summary

Consideration in Gifts and Non-Arm's Length Transfers

Transfer Proceeds	P of D to transferor (Seller)	ACB to Transferee (Purchaser)	Double Taxation
P of D greater than FMV	Actual proceeds received	Adjusted to be the FMV [par. 69(1)(*a*)] – even though a greater amount is paid.	Yes Double tax may occur on disposition by purchaser, since we have only adjusted one side of the contract.
P of D less than FMV	Adjusted upwards to equal FMV of the asset at the time of transfer. [par. 69(1)(*b*)]	No adjustment – the actual amount paid is the ACB to the transferee.	Yes Double tax may occur on disposition by purchaser, since we have only adjusted one side of the contract.
Gifting – no P of D Deemed disposition at FMV	Equal to FMV of the asset at the time of transfer. [par. 69(1)(*b*)[1]]	Equal to the FMV of the asset at the time of transfer. [par. 69(1)(c)[1]]	No In this case both sides are adjusted to the FMV.
P of D equal to FMV	Actual proceeds received.	Actual cost paid.	No In this case, FMV is paid and both sides are using the FMV at the time of the transaction.

[1] Note that these fair market value rules apply to gifts even at arm's length.

As can be seen in the summary of the fair market value rules above, when a non-arm's length transaction occurs at an amount greater than or less than fair market value, only one side of the transaction is adjusted, creating a potential for double tax in the future when the transferee sells the asset.

Example

A parent owns 1,000 shares in HIE corporation. The shares have an ACB of $15,000, a fair market value of $45,000 and the value is expected to climb to $90,000 in the next three years. The parent would like to transfer the shares to their adult child. The parent would like to know the tax implications of three scenarios:

(1) Selling the shares for $20,000

(2) Selling the shares for $50,000

(3) Gifting the shares

The chart below summarizes the tax implications of the three scenarios:

(1) Selling the shares for $20,000		Parent	Child
P of D	$45,000		
ACB	$(15,000)		$20,000
Capital Gain		$30,000	

In this scenario, the parent will pay tax based on the increase in fair market value of the shares The double tax will occur when the child sells the shares in the future. As can be seen, the increase in value between the ACB of $15,000 and the Fair Market Value of $45,000 has now been taxed in the parent's return. However, since the child paid less than FMV there is no adjustment to the child's cost base. The amount between $20,000 and $45,000 ($25,000) will be taxed again when the child disposes of the shares for $45,000 or more. This creates a situation where double tax may occur.

(2) Selling the shares for $50,000		Parent	Child
P of D	$50,000		
ACB	$(15,000)		$45,000
Capital Gain		$35,000	

In this scenario, the parent has received $50,000 in proceeds of disposition and therefore will pay tax on the difference between $50,000 and the ACB of $15,000. As can be seen, the child's ACB is reduced to the FMV and will be less than the amount actually paid. This scenario results in the difference between $50,000 and $45,000, ($5,000) being taxed again if the child sells the shares for an amount greater than $50,000.

(3) Gifting the shares for		Parent	Child
P of D	$45,000		
ACB	$(15,000)		$45,000
Capital Gain		$30,000	

In this scenario, the parent has received no proceeds but will have to include a capital gain of $30,000 in income. The child's ACB will be equal to the FMV of $45,000, the same amount of proceeds used to calculate the capital gain for the parent. This scenario does not have the potential of creating double tax.

When we review the example above, we can see that in all three scenarios, the parent cannot avoid the recognition of the accrued capital gain on the property transferred. In the case of a transfer through gifting or with proceeds of disposition less than the FMV, the accrued gain that is recognized is equal to the FMV less the ACB of the parent's shares. In the case where the transfer happens at an amount greater than FMV, the capital gain will be based on the proceeds of disposition, thereby creating a larger capital gain than is actually accrued on the shares.

¶7,215 Attribution Rules

¶7,215.10 Capital Gains on Spousal Transfers or Loans

In Chapter 6, the attribution rules, relating to income from property only, were discussed for transfers and loans. Capital gains and losses are also similarly attributed back, but only to the transferor spouse or common-law partner for all transfers (i.e., gifts and sales) or for loans. Included in capital gains or losses attributed to a spouse or common-law partner are capital gains or losses on reinvested capital gains or losses or other previously attributed income from property.

ITA: 74.2(1) Gain or loss deemed that of lender or transferor

A careful reading of these attribution provisions and the concept of "substituted property" indicates that these gains or losses continue to be subject to attribution. Hence, there is no exemption from attribution for "second-generation" capital gains or losses, unlike the exemption for "second-generation" income from property. This means that the capital gain or loss arising from a "substituted property" will also attribute back to the transferor.

"Common-law partner" is defined as "a person who cohabits . . . in a conjugal relationship with the taxpayer . . . for a continuous period of at least one year".

ITA: 248(1) common-law partner

A series of anti-avoidance provisions apply attribution to transactions such as:

- back-to-back loans and transfers to third parties,

- repayment of loan through additional transfers and loans,
- loan guarantees for all or part of the principal and/or interest, or
- artificial transactions which use the attribution rules to the taxpayer's advantage.

ITA: 74.5(6) Back to back loans and transfers, 74.1(3) Repayment of existing indebtedness, 74.5(7) Guarantees, 74.5(11) Artificial transactions

Capital gains and losses arising from transfers and loans to related and deemed related minors do not result in attribution to the transferor (except for *inter vivos* transfers of farming property which is tax-deferred by a rollover and beyond the scope of this text).

¶7,215.20 Interspousal Rollover

The interspousal rollover rule has the effect of deferring any accrued gains on transfers between spouses or common-law partners. The deferral occurs because the transferor is automatically deemed to have transferred the property at proceeds exactly equal to his or her adjusted cost base immediately prior to the transfer. Note here that the transfer is an actual transaction which must be reported, even though the gain is nil. The transferee spouse or common-law partner will have an adjusted cost base exactly equal to the deemed proceeds of disposition at the time of transfer (i.e., the adjusted cost base of the transferor spouse or common-law partner). This spousal rollover means that the receiving spouse takes over the same tax position that the transferring spouse held.

ITA: 73 Inter vivos transfers by individuals

When the transferee spouse or common-law partner disposes of the property, the gain or loss will be attributed back to the transferor spouse or common-law partner, as long as they are married or in a common-law relationship. If an interspousal rollover occurs, all income, first generation property income and capital gains included, will attribute back to the transferor.

¶7,215.30 Breakdown of Relationship

The provision which pertains to the attribution of capital gains continues to apply to spouses, or common-law partners, living apart by reason of a breakdown of their marriage or common-law relationship. In this situation, however, when both spouses or common-law partners have jointly elected, capital gains attribution will not apply. The election must be filed with the tax return of the transferor spouse or common-law partner in any year ending after the separation occurs. Note that this provision is much harsher than the attribution relieving provision for income from property which does not require that an election be filed. It should be noted that attribution ceases once the couple is divorced.

ITA: 74.5(3)(b), 74.5(3)(a); Interpretation Bulletins: IT-511R Interspousal and certain other transfers and loans of property

¶7,215.40 Elect out of Interspousal Rollover

Alternatively, the transferor spouse or common-law partner can elect not to have interspousal rollover apply. If such an election is made, the normal non-arm's length rules apply under section 69 as previously discussed (see ¶7210.20). Hence, the property will be deemed to be disposed of at the fair market value at the date of transfer and there will be immediate tax consequences to the transferor on the transfer. Simply electing out of the interspousal rollover does not prevent future income attribution. Two things must exist in order for the future income not to attribute back to the transferor. The transferor must:

ITA: 73(1) Inter vivos transfers by individuals

- elect out of the interspousal rollover, and
- receive FMV consideration.

This means that for proper income splitting to occur, the receiving spouse must pay FMV consideration in the form of cash, other property, or an FMV loan. If the consideration received included a loan, then the interest rate must be on a commercial basis (the lesser of the prescribed rate at the time the loan was made and the non-arm's length rate as determined by the marketplace) and the accrued interest must be actually paid no later than 30 days after each and every December 31 that the loan is outstanding.

ITA: 74.5(1)(a), 74.5(1)(c); 74.5(1)(b)

If the property is sold to a spouse or common-law partner at less than the fair market value and the taxpayer elects not to use the interspousal rollover, there would be a double penalty. This would be the worst possible scenario involving a spousal transfer.

- First, the transferor would have immediate tax consequences on the transfer of the shares equal to the FMV at the time of transfer less the ACB of the shares.

ITA: 74.5(1)(a)

- Second, the attribution rules would apply to both income and capital gains, since the fair market value of the property transferred and the consideration received are not equal. Since the transferor elected out of the interspousal rollover, the fair market value rules would apply to adjust the transferor's proceeds of disposition up to the FMV, while leaving the acquiring spouse's ACB equal to the actual price paid. Hence, the avoided capital gain would be taxed twice.

ITA: 69(1)(c)

If, however, the transfer had been a gift, then both the proceeds and the adjusted cost base would be bumped to the fair market value. Again, the attribution of future income and capital gain would not have been avoided, since no consideration was received.

ITA: 69(1)(b)(ii), 69(1)(c)

¶7,215.50 Recapture

In order to prevent the avoidance of recapture on the transfer of depreciable property between spouses, the following additional rules apply. When the undepreciated capital cost is less than the capital cost to the transferor, then for purposes of capital cost allowance computations:

ITA: 73(2) Capital cost and amount deemed allowed to spouse, etc., or trust

(1) the capital cost to the transferee is deemed to be the capital cost to the transferor; and

(2) the difference between the capital cost and the deemed capital cost to the spouse will be treated as a capital cost allowance taken by the transferee.

¶7,220 Summary of Provisions

Approach

Steps to addressing a non-arm's length sale

(1) Assess the Situation and Identify the Issues:

- Gather all the facts relating to the taxpayer's situation including:
  - (a) the relationship between the seller and purchaser,
  - (b) determine the amount of consideration paid, and
  - (c) if the consideration is a loan, determine the payment terms, including interest, to be charged.

(2) Analyze the Issues:

- Based on the information gathered, determine the following:
  - (a) if attribution will apply based on the transaction terms,
  - (b) if it a spousal transfer, discuss the implication of:
    - (i) the automatic rollover and
    - (ii) electing out of the rollover, and
  - (c) calculate the immediate tax implications related to the transaction.

(3) Conclude and Advise:

- (a) arrive at a conclusion on the treatment of the future income.
- (b) provide suggestions on how to improve the situation, if possible.

Below you will find two summaries that expand on the attribution rules introduced in Chapter 6 to include the application of the capital gains attribution rules discussed in this chapter. The first summary deals with transfers between spouses while the second summarizes the rules pertaining to minors and other non-arm's length persons.

Exhibit 7-1 Transfers or Loans of Property to Spouse or Common-Law Partner Conceptual Summary

(A) Proceeds and Cost on Transfer

Transaction		*Transferor's proceeds*	*Transferee's cost*
(1) gift	• no election out of interspousal rollover*	Transferor's ACB/UCC	Transferor's ACB/UCC
	• elect not to have rollover	FMV [par. 69(1)(*b*)]	FMV [par. 69(1)(*c*)]
(2) sale	• no election out of interspousal rollover	Transferor's ACB/UCC	Transferor's ACB/UCC
	• elect not to have rollover	greater of: • actual proceeds • FMV [ssec. 69(1)]	Lesser of: • actual cost • FMV [ssec. 69(1)]

(B) Attribution of Income and Capital Gains

	Business income	*Property income***	*Capital gains****
On transferred or loaned property and substituted property****	n/a	Attributed [ssec. 74.1(1)]	Attributed [sec. 74.2]

However, neither property income nor capital gains are attributed if the following two conditions are met:

(1) fair market consideration is received,***** and

(2) the election out of the interspousal rollover is used.

* The interspousal rollover applies *automatically* on a transfer of property between spouses or common-law partners at the ACB of the property; that is, the transferor spouse or common-law partner is deemed to have received proceeds of disposition equal to ACB and the transferee spouse or common-law partner is deemed to have acquired the property at the same ACB. However, the provision contains an election that allows the spouses or common-law partners not to have the rollover apply, in which case the normal non-arm's length rules apply to the transaction which will be considered to have taken place at fair market value.

** Including losses but excluding second-generation income from property.

*** Including capital losses and including second-generation capital gains (losses) after December 31, 1987.

**** Substituted property is defined in subsection 248(5).

***** To avoid attribution, the taxpayer must elect to waive the deferral of accrued income afforded by the interspousal rollover and must transfer for fair market value consideration. Where a loan is involved, interest must be paid within 30 days of the end of every year in which the loan is outstanding.

Exhibit 7-2 Transfers or Loans of Property to Minors and Other Non-Arm's Length Individuals Conceptual Summary

(A) Proceeds and Cost on Transfer

	Transferor's proceeds	*Transferee's cost*
(1) gift	FMV [par. 69(1)(*b*)]	FMV [par. 69(1)(*c*)]
(2) sale	greater of: • actual proceeds • FMV [ssec. 69(1)]	Lesser of: • actual cost • FMV [ssec. 69(1)]

(B) Attribution of Income and Capital Gains

	Business income	*Property income**	*Capital gains*
Minors** who are not at arm's length (generally, related) or who are nieces and nephews • on transferred*** or loaned property and substituted property****	n/a	Attributed [ssec. 74.1(2)]	n/a
Other non-arm's length individuals not subject to section 74.1 • only on loaned property if one of the main reasons for the loan was to reduce or avoid tax	n/a	Attributed [ssec. 56(4.1)]	n/a

* Including losses but excluding second-generation income from property.

** An income-splitting tax applies at the top marginal tax rate on dividends or shareholder benefits received by minors from private corporations and certain income from a partnership or trust. (See Chapter 6 for a discussion of this provision.) Income that is subject to the income-splitting tax is not be subject to the attribution rules.

*** To avoid attribution the taxpayer must transfer for fair market value consideration. Where a loan is involved, interest must be paid within 30 days of the end of the year in which the loan is outstanding.

**** Substituted property is defined in subsection 248(5).

¶7,290 Pause and Reflect — Summary of Learning Goals

After working through this section, ¶7,200, you should be able to:

- Explain the meaning of related persons and how that relates to the attribution rules.

- Explain the attribution rules and the circumstances in which they apply.
- Apply your knowledge of the non-arm's length rules as they relate to the disposition of a capital property to a non-arm's length individual.
- Apply your knowledge to advise a client on planning methods to avoid income attribution.

¶7,290.99 Practise What You've Learned

Refer to the following sections of the Study Guide to practise what you've learned:

¶7,800 — Review Questions

- Question 19 — Non-arm's length

¶7,825 — Multiple Choice Questions

- Question 6 — Transactions with child
- Question 7 — Transactions with spouse
- Question 8 — Transactions with spouse and child

¶7,850 — Exercises

- Exercise 9 — Arm's length
- Exercise 10 — Non-arm's length transaction
- Exercise 11 — Transactions with spouse
- Exercise 13 — Sale of shares
- Exercise 14 — Non-arm's length transactions
- Exercise 16 — Non-arm's length transactions

¶7,300 Death of a Taxpayer

¶7,305 Deemed Disposition on Death

Overview

Capital gains may be triggered upon the death of a taxpayer depending on the status of the beneficiaries and the type of assets transferred. Death is the final opportunity to tax unrealized gains that have accrued to the taxpayer. Generally, the taxpayer is deemed to have disposed of all his or her capital assets at their fair market value as at the date of his or her death. ITA: 70(5)(a)

¶7,305.10 Non-Depreciable Assets

In respect of non-depreciable capital assets transferred on death to a spouse, the basic rules are similar to those on transfer between living spouses. The deceased is deemed to have disposed of the assets at his or her adjusted cost base and the surviving spouse or common-law partner assumes that cost base. Hence, no capital gain or recapture will be triggered unless the estate elects not to have the interspousal rollover on death apply, or until the surviving spouse or common-law partner disposes of the assets.

ITA: 70(6) Where transfer or distribution to spouse or spouse trust, 73 Inter vivos transfers by individuals; 70(6.2) Election; Interpretation BulletinsIT-305R4 Testamentary Spouse Trusts

Non-depreciable property received by a beneficiary, other than a spouse or common-law partner, is deemed to be disposed at fair market value at the time of death. Any resulting capital gain or loss on the property would be include on the deceased's final return.

¶7,305.20 Depreciable Property

Depreciable property received by a beneficiary, other than a spouse or common-law partner, is deemed to be disposed of at fair market value at the date of death. Any resulting capital gain or recapture would be included on the deceased's final return.

ITA: 70(5)(a)

The beneficiary's deemed cost would be the fair market value of the property received. There is one adjustment that must be made for UCC purposes to the beneficiary's cost in the case where the fair market value is less than the original cost. The beneficiary's cost would be equal to the deceased's original cost and the excess of cost over fair market value would be deemed to have been taken as CCA. The end result is that the beneficiary's UCC is the fair market value.

Where a spouse or common-law partner is the beneficiary of depreciable property and where no election out of the interspousal rollover has been filed, the proceeds of disposition are deemed to be the undepreciated capital cost prorated on a capital cost basis.

ITA: 70(6.2) Election

If a beneficiary inherits property from a deceased person who is not the beneficiary's spouse, then the beneficiary will have a cost base on this inherited property equal to the fair market value at the time of death. This will then be equal to the deemed proceeds to the deceased on his or her final return. Chapter 14 discusses, in some detail, the various filing alternatives available upon death of a taxpayer.

¶7,390 Pause and Reflect — Summary of Learning Goals

After working through this section, ¶7,300, you should be able to:

- Explain the tax treatment of depreciable and non-depreciable capital property on the death of an individual.
- Apply your knowledge to determine the capital gain (or loss) based on the beneficiary receiving the property.
- Apply your knowledge to advise clients on how to plan for the disposition of capital property on death in order to minimize tax.

¶7,390.99 Practise What You've Learned

Refer to the following sections of the Study Guide to practise what you've learned:

¶7,800 — Review Questions

- Question 10 — Death of a taxpayer

¶7,825 — Multiple Choice Questions

- Question 9 — Death of a taxpayer

¶7,400 Leaving and Entering Canada

Tax rules for taxpayers who become or cease to be resident in Canada are provided by the Act. When a taxpayer ceases to be a resident of Canada, all of that person's capital property is deemed to have been disposed of at its fair market value. Examples of capital property include:

ITA: 128.1 [Immigration and emigration], 128.1(4) Emigration

- shares, including shares of private corporations,
- bonds,
- real estate outside Canada, and
- boats, recreational vehicles, and automobiles.

This situation ensures that a taxpayer is subject to tax on any gains accrued during their period of residency in Canada.

Where the taxpayer is an individual, the following properties, generally, those that would be subject to Canadian tax in the hands of a non-resident, are exempted from the deemed disposition:

(1) Property that can be described, conceptually, as:

- Canadian property that is not very movable, such as real property or capital property used in a business carried on through a permanent establishment in Canada, or
- Canadian property that is not very liquid or marketable, such as employment-related stock options.

The taxpayer will continue to be liable for tax on the disposition of such property, but as a non-resident. However, the taxpayer may elect not to have this exemption apply so that capital gains (losses) are triggered to offset other capital losses (gains).

ITA: 2(3) Tax payable by non-resident persons

(2) Property of a business carried on by the individual in Canada. Income from such property, including capital property, eligible capital property and property described in the inventory of the business, will be taxable as business income earned by a non-resident.

ITA: 2(3) Tax payable by non-resident persons

(3) The right to receive certain payments such as pension payments and other retirement benefits, including rights under RRSPs, RPPs and DPSPs, or a right

under a registered education savings plan on which the taxpayer will be liable for withholding tax.

A taxpayer is prevented from triggering only allowable capital losses while protecting potential taxable capital gains through the available elections previously described. In this situation, losses, except listed personal property losses, are restricted to the taxable capital gains actually triggered by the deemed disposition. ITA: 128.1(4) Emigration

The Act provides an exception in the case of a short-term resident of Canada. The tax on departure does not apply to capital property which an individual owned on last becoming a resident of Canada, if he or she resided in Canada for 60 months or less during the 10 years preceding his or her departure. Under these conditions, he or she will be exempt from the deemed disposition on any property, which he or she brought with him or her and took away again. Also exempt is property acquired by inheritance or bequest after the individual last became resident in Canada. However, the taxpayer will still be subject to the rules of this section on other property he or she acquired while he or she was resident in Canada. ITA: 128.1(4) Emigration

To set the cost of property for a person entering Canada such that the taxpayer is taxed only on gains subsequent to his or her entry, the Act provides that where a taxpayer becomes a Canadian resident, he or she is deemed to have acquired all of his or her property, other than taxable Canadian property and inventory or eligible capital property of a business carried on in Canada, at its fair market value at the time the taxpayer became a Canadian resident. ITA: 128.1(1) Immigration

¶7,490 Pause and Reflect — Summary of Learning Goals

After working through this section, ¶7,400, you should be able to:

- Explain the tax implications of ceasing Canadian residency when an individual owns capital property.
- Explain which capital properties are exempt for the deemed disposition rules on ceasing Canadian residency.
- Explain the future tax implications to a non-resident, as they relate to the exempt capital property.
- Apply your knowledge to determine the capital gain (or loss) on ceasing residency.

¶7,490.99 Practise What You've Learned

Refer to the following sections of the Study Guide to practise what you've learned:

¶7,800 — Review Questions

- Question 13 — Ceasing residency

¶7,825 — Multiple Choice Questions

- Question 10 — Becoming non-resident

¶7,850 — Exercises

- Exercise 12 — Becoming a resident

¶7,500 Computational Rules

¶7,505 Section 3 Revisited

In Chapter 1, Exhibit 1-1 showed a picture of how section 3 is organized. At this point, several technical components have been examined in Chapters 2 to 7, so it is a good time to review the formula for determining net income for tax purposes. We will also highlight the carryover rules contained in section 3.

Paragraph 3(*a*) includes the aggregate of all income from each non-capital source: property, business, office and employment, plus the other non-capital sources of income found in Subdivision d of Division B which is examined in Chapter 9. The amount determined for each source must be a positive amount (i.e., losses or an excess of deductions over inclusions from a particular source are not considered here).

Paragraph 3(*b*) deals with taxable capital gains and allowable capital losses, and is composed of the excess of:

(1) all taxable capital gains, excluding those from LPPs

plus

(2) listed personal property taxable net gains discussed previously ITA: 41(2) Determination of net gain

minus

(3) allowable capital losses, except for

(a) LPP losses, and

(b) allowable business investment losses (ABILs).

Paragraph 3(*c*) adds together paragraphs 3(*a*) and (*b*) and subtracts Subdivision e deductions such as moving expenses, alimony, RRSPs, etc. All of these topics will be covered in Chapter 9.

Paragraph 3(*d*) subtracts various types of losses from any excess amount calculated in paragraph 3(*c*). The losses deducted are from the following sources:

(1) office, employment, business and property (i.e., losses from non-capital sources), and

(2) ABILs.

Note the special treatment accorded to ABILs. Normally, allowable capital losses can only be claimed against taxable capital gains. However, ABILs have no such restriction and, hence, are deducted along with other losses from non-capital sources (e.g., losses from business and property). Deducting ABILs, effectively, against all sources of income, rather than only against net taxable capital gains may result in a more rapid deduction of ABILs, which is the intent of the ABIL investment incentive. As a capital loss, however, ABILs are still only ½ deductible. ITA: 3(b), 3(d)

¶7,510 Allowable Business Investment Losses

The definition of a "business investment loss" includes capital losses arising from the disposition of shares and debts of a small business corporation. ITA: 39(1)(c)

¶7,510.10 Small Business Corporation ("SBC") Defined

An SBC is generally defined to be a Canadian-controlled private corporation, where all or substantially all of the fair market value of the assets were, at that time, used principally in an active business carried on primarily in Canada. Assets would include the shares of SBCs which were connected to the holding corporation. (The concept of a "connected" corporation is discussed in Chapter 12.) For the purposes of a business investment loss only, an SBC which ceases to meet the conditions in the definition of an SBC will still be considered as an SBC if at any time in the 12 months preceding the disposition it met the conditions in the definition of an SBC.

ITA: 248(1) Definitions; 186(4) Corporations connected with particular corporation, 39(1)(c)

¶7,510.20 Terminology

Since business investment losses (BILs) are really only a subset of capital losses, allowable business investment losses (ABILs) for a particular year are determined by the same inclusion rates as allowable capital losses as shown in ¶7,000.

100%	50%
Business Investment Loss	Allowable Business Investment Loss

¶7,510.30 Disposition

A business investment loss must arise from a disposition of shares or debt of a small business corporation where:

(1) The disposition of the shares or debt is to an arms-length person,

(2) The debt has become a bad debt in the year, or

(3) For shares not actually disposed of, the company has become bankrupt during the year, is in the process of winding up or is insolvent, has no value, and has ceased to carry on business.

¶7,510.40 Disallowed Portion

A portion of a BIL, equal to an amount of capital gains that has previously benefited from a capital gains deduction, is disallowed. The capital gains deduction referred to is either a past claim for the general capital gains deduction that was eliminated or the continuing capital gains deduction for shares of a qualified small business corporation or qualified farm property. In general terms, this means that using a BIL today may affect the ability to claim a portion of the capital gains deduction in the future. If the capital gains deduction has been claimed in the past, all or a portion of the BIL will be disallowed.

ITA: 39(9) Deduction from business investment loss

This disallowed portion reduces the BIL and resultant ABIL, for purposes of the deduction under paragraph 3(*d*). In effect, an individual cannot obtain a benefit of the capital gains deduction on capital gains that are not offset by capital losses in the form of BILs, at the same time as he or she obtains a benefit from ABILs which offset non-capital sources of income under paragraph 3(*d*).

A fraction (see above chart) of the disallowed BIL reverts to an allowable capital loss for the year realized. This allowable capital loss will possibly offset taxable capital gains which will not be available for the capital gains deduction, as a result.

The portion of a BIL that is disallowed is computed as the lesser of:

ITA: 39(9) Deduction from business investment loss

(a)	the BIL for the year (before deducting the disallowed portion)	$xxxx
(b)	the cumulative capital gains exemption (100% of capital gain) claimed in previous years which is parallel with the full BIL amount).	$xxxx
	minus: the cumulative disallowed portion of BILs in preceding years.	$(xxxx)
		$xxxx

Note that part (a) above uses the full business investment loss (not the fractional allowable business investment loss). However, the capital gains deduction is a fractional amount. Therefore, to make parts (a) and (b) comparable, the capital gains deduction must be adjusted to convert the deduction to a full amount of gain that has been exempted. Hence, multiplying a 1999 capital gains deduction, for example, by $4/3$ adjusts the $3/4$ fractional amount to the required full amount (i.e., $4/3 \times 3/4 = 1$).

¶7,510.50 Non-Capital Loss

Any portion of the ABIL (i.e., an amount that has not been disallowed), which is not deducted under paragraph 3(*d*), is added to the non-capital losses for the year subject to the non-capital loss carryover rules, discussed in Chapter 10 for individuals and Chapter 11 for corporations. However, if the ABIL, which was treated as a non-capital loss, is not used by the end of the 10th carry forward year, it becomes a net capital loss. In essence, this means it reverts to its original character as an allowable capital loss, and is restricted by the net capital loss carryover rules.

ITA: 111(8) non-capital loss

Figure 7-2 attempts to map the treatment of BILs under the provisions described above.

Figure 7-2
Treatment of a Business Investment Loss

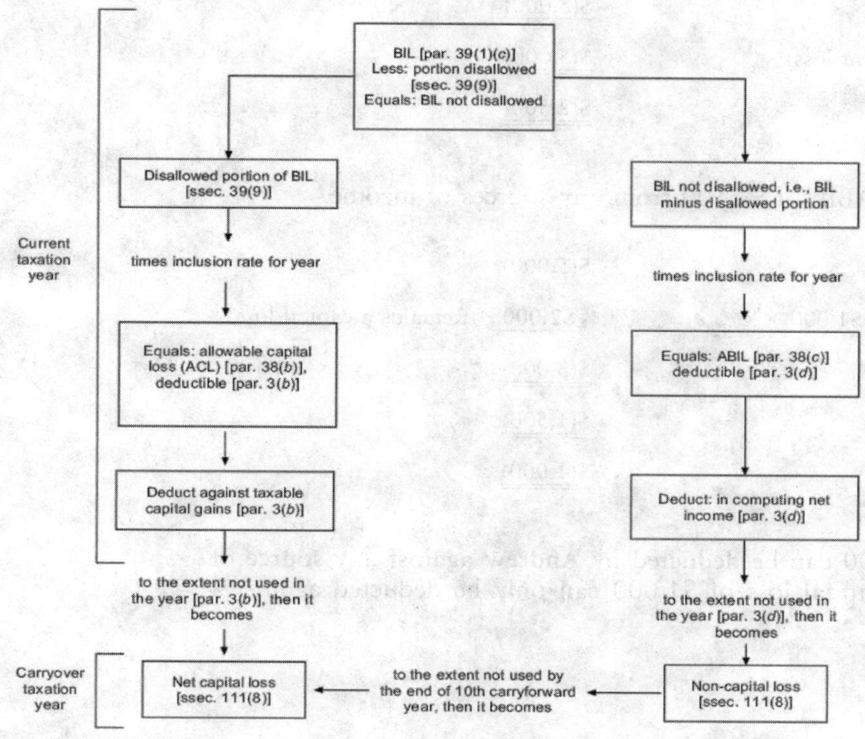

Example Problem 7-13

Andrew invested $5,000 in shares of Balance Corporation Ltd. The corporation is now bankrupt and the shares have a fair market value of nil.

REQUIRED

(1) If Andrew has not claimed a capital gains deduction in previous years, what is Andrew's allowable business investment loss and what can it be deducted against in the year?

(2) If Andrew had claimed a capital gains deduction of $1,000 (inclusion rate already applied) five years ago, what is Andrew's tax position with respect to the loss on the shares this year?

SOLUTION

(1)	P of D	$ Nil	
	ACB	$(5,000)	
	CL (Business investment loss)	$(5,000)	
	ABIL	$(2,500)	

Andrew can deduct the ABIL of $2,500 from any sources of income.

(2)	CL (above)	$(5,000)	
	Less: disallowed BIL ($1,000 × 2)	$2,000	Remains a capital loss
	BIL	$(3,000)	
	ABIL	$(1,500)	
	ACL ($2,000 × ½)	$(1,000)	

While the ABIL of $1,500 can be deducted by Andrew against any source of income, the allowable capital loss of $1,000 can only be deducted against a taxable capital gain.

Example Problem 7-14

	2016	2017	2018
Employment income	$10,000	$12,000	$15,000
Business income (loss)	$(25,000)	$6,000	$10,000
Property income (loss)	$3,000	$(2,000)	$1,000
Capital gains (capital losses)			
LPP	$2,000	$(5,000)	$7,000
PUP	$(4,000)	$8,000	$2,000
Other	$10,000	$(17,000)[1]	$4,000

[1] Includes a business investment loss of $2,000.

REQUIRED

Determine the income under Division B according to section 3, after filing any necessary amended returns for each of the years indicated above. (For the purposes of this type of problem, dealing with each item, line-by-line, across the years, will help keep track of carryovers more easily than dealing with income one year at a time.)

SOLUTION

	2016	2017	2018
Par. 3(*a*) — Sum of income from non-capital sources (non-negative):			
Employment	$10,000	$12,000	$15,000
Business (no losses)	—	$6,000	$10,000
Property (no losses)	$3,000	—	$1,000
	$13,000	$18,000	$26,000
Par. 3(*b*) — Sum of net taxable capital gains (non-negative):			
LPP	Nil[(1)]	Nil	$2,000[(2)]
PUP	Nil[(3)]	$4,000[(4)]	$1,000[(5)]
Other	$5,000[(6)]	$(4,000)[(7)]	$2,000[(8)]
	$5,000	Nil	$5,000
Sum of par. 3(*a*) and par. 3(*b*)	$18,000	$18,000	$31,000
Par. 3(*d*) — Sum of losses from non-capital sources:			
Business loss	$(18,000)[(9)]	—	—
Property loss	—	$(2,000)	—
ABIL	—	$(1,000)[(10)]	—
Income under Division B	Nil	$15,000	$31,000

NOTES TO SOLUTION

[(1)] The $2,000 listed personal property capital gain in 2016 was offset and removed by amending the 2016 return for $2,000 of the 2017 loss, carried back to 2016. Note how LPP losses are carried over in their full amount, not their fractional allowable amount. Therefore, no consideration need be given to changing capital gains inclusion rates, if applicable, in the carryover period for LPPs.

(2) There was still $3,000 of the listed personal property capital loss in 2017 to be applied against the listed personal property gain in 2018, of $7,000 (($7,000 – $3,000) × ½ = $2,000).

(3) No losses are allowed on the personal-use property assets.

(4) ½ × $8,000.

(5) ½ × $2,000.

(6) ½ × $10,000.

(7) Only $4,000 of the allowable capital loss of $7,500 [½ × ($17,000 – $2,000)] was applied to reduce paragraph 3(*b*) amount to nil. The remaining $3,500 will be applied to another year but under Division C, not Division B.

(8) ½ × $4,000.

(9) Only $18,000 of the business loss of $25,000 was applied to bring the income under Division B to nil. The remainder ($7,000) may be carried back three years and forward seven, but these losses are deductible in the carryover year in Division C, not Division B.

(10) The *allowable* business investment loss is $1,000 (½ × $2,000).

¶7,900 Pause and Reflect — Summary of Learning Goals for this Chapter

After working through all the sections of the chapter, you should be able to:

- Explain the meaning of a capital gain, taxable capital gain, capital loss and allowable capital loss.
- Apply your knowledge to a specific situation to correctly classify capital property into three different categories: personal-use, listed personal, and other capital property.
- Explain the special provisions for the taxation of capital gains as they relate to:
  - Personal use property,
  - Listed personal property,
  - Other capital property.
- Apply your knowledge to correctly determine the adjusted cost base and the proceeds of disposition on the disposition of a capital property under various circumstances.

- Explain the circumstances in which an individual can claim the principal residence exemption.
- Apply your knowledge of the non-arm's length rules as they relate to the disposition of a capital property to a non-arm's length individual.
- Apply your knowledge of the rules related to principal residence to minimize tax on the disposition of a principal residence.
- Apply your knowledge to specific circumstances to minimize the tax paid by the taxpayer on the disposition of a capital property.
- Apply your knowledge to advise a client or your employer on the tax implications on the death of a taxpayer and plan to meet the client's or employer's needs.
- Apply your knowledge to advise a client or your employer on the tax implications of ceasing or establishing residency in Canada.

CHAPTER 8

Capital Gains: Business Related

ADVANCED CONTENT IN THIS CHAPTER

Learning Goals

Know, Understand and Explain

By the end of this chapter you will know, understand and be able to explain:

- The tax implications of selling a property through instalment payments and the options available to minimize tax.
- The tax implications of a bad debt as it relates to the disposition of a capital property.
- The deferral available when a property is replaced within the eligible time frame for both involuntary and voluntary disposition.
- The rules related to the disposition of land and building where a terminal loss occurs as a result of the sale.

Apply

By the end of this chapter you will be able to apply your knowledge and understanding to:

- Conclude whether the nature of a transaction is business income or capital gain by applying accepted behavioural factors to case facts.
- Correctly calculate the capital gains reserve that may be claimed in a given period.
- Determine the adjusted cost base of a depreciable asset, including any allowable adjustments and for non-arm's length situations.
- Correctly calculate the deferral amount and the cost base of the new property under the replacement property rules for both capital gains and recapture.
- Correctly calculate the reallocation of proceeds of disposition between the land and building when a terminal loss occurs on the building as a result of the sale.
- Correctly determine the tax implication when a capital property has a deemed disposition as a result of a change in use.
- Apply your knowledge to specific circumstances to minimize the current tax paid by the client on the disposition of a capital property.

Review Questions
¶8,800 in the Study Guide

Multiple Choice Questions
¶8,825 in the Study Guide

Exercises
¶8,850 in the Study Guide

Assignment Problems
¶8,875 in the Study Guide

Overview

As mentioned in Chapter 7, Subdivision c of Division B of Part I of the Act contains the primary rules for the computation of taxable capital gains and allowable capital losses. While the rules discussed in Chapter 7 are applicable to all taxpayers, including corporations, there are particular rules that typically only arise in a business context. This chapter will focus on the taxation of capital gains related to a business transaction.

After working through all the sections of this chapter, you will be able to:

- Apply the behavioural factors in a specific scenario to determine whether the nature of a transaction is business income or capital gain.
- Explain the tax implications of selling a property through instalment payments and the options available to minimize tax.
- Apply your knowledge to calculate the capital gains reserve that may be claimed in a given period.
- Apply your knowledge to determine the adjusted cost base of a depreciable asset, including any allowable adjustments and for non-arm's length situations.
- Explain the tax implications of a bad debt as it relates to the disposition of a capital property.
- Explain the deferral available when a property is replaced within the eligible time frame for both involuntary and voluntary disposition.
- Apply your knowledge to calculate the deferral amount and the cost base of the new property under the replacement property rules for both capital gains and recapture.
- Explain the rules related to the disposition of land and building where a terminal loss occurs as a result of the sale.
- Apply your knowledge to calculate the reallocation of proceeds of disposition between the land and building when a terminal loss occurs on the building as a result of the sale.
- Apply your knowledge to correctly determine the tax implication when a capital property has a deemed disposition as a result of a change in use.
- Apply your knowledge to specific circumstances to minimize the current tax paid by the client on the disposition of a capital property.

The following chart will help to locate in the Act the major provisions dealt with in this chapter.

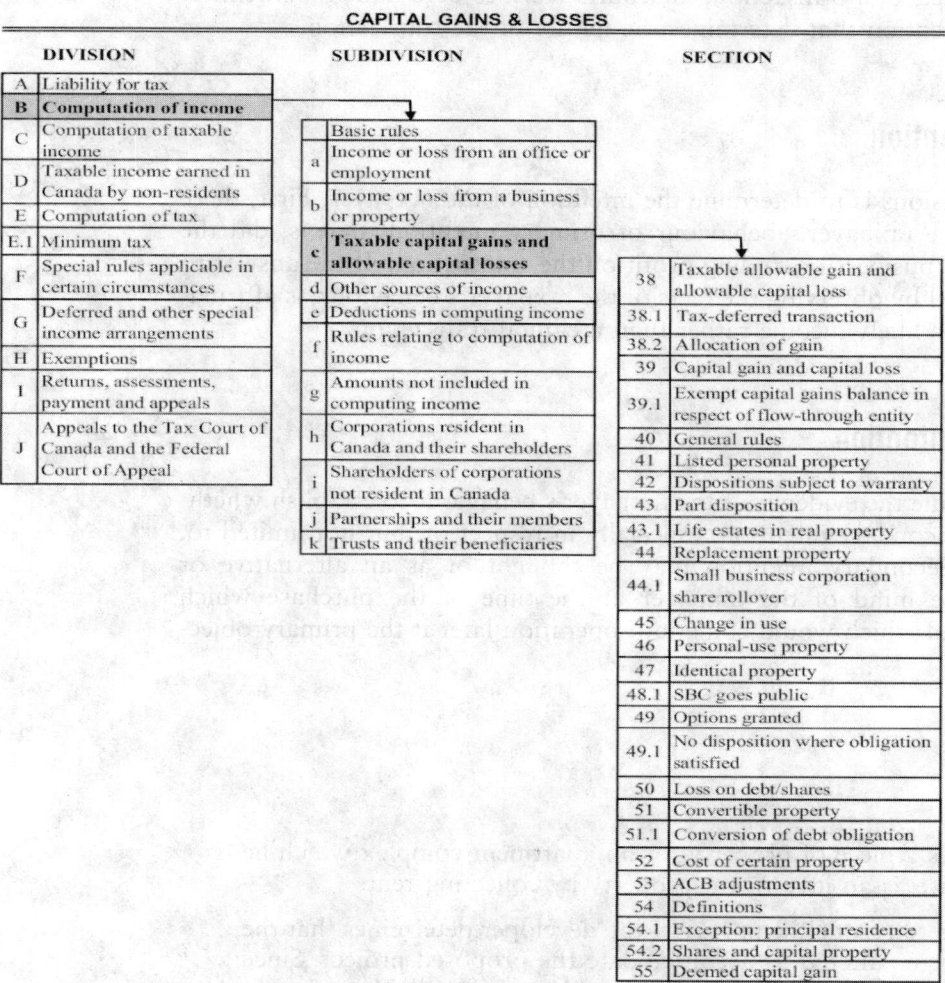

PART I — DIVISION B, SUBDIVISION c
CAPITAL GAINS & LOSSES

DIVISION

A	Liability for tax
B	**Computation of income**
C	Computation of taxable income
D	Taxable income earned in Canada by non-residents
E	Computation of tax
E.1	Minimum tax
F	Special rules applicable in certain circumstances
G	Deferred and other special income arrangements
H	Exemptions
I	Returns, assessments, payment and appeals
J	Appeals to the Tax Court of Canada and the Federal Court of Appeal

SUBDIVISION

	Basic rules
a	Income or loss from an office or employment
b	Income or loss from a business or property
c	**Taxable capital gains and allowable capital losses**
d	Other sources of income
e	Deductions in computing income
f	Rules relating to computation of income
g	Amounts not included in computing income
h	Corporations resident in Canada and their shareholders
i	Shareholders of corporations not resident in Canada
j	Partnerships and their members
k	Trusts and their beneficiaries

SECTION

38	Taxable allowable gain and allowable capital loss
38.1	Tax-deferred transaction
38.2	Allocation of gain
39	Capital gain and capital loss
39.1	Exempt capital gains balance in respect of flow-through entity
40	General rules
41	Listed personal property
42	Dispositions subject to warranty
43	Part disposition
43.1	Life estates in real property
44	Replacement property
44.1	Small business corporation share rollover
45	Change in use
46	Personal-use property
47	Identical property
48.1	SBC goes public
49	Options granted
49.1	No disposition where obligation satisfied
50	Loss on debt/shares
51	Convertible property
51.1	Conversion of debt obligation
52	Cost of certain property
53	ACB adjustments
54	Definitions
54.1	Exception: principal residence
54.2	Shares and capital property
55	Deemed capital gain

¶8,000 Capital Gains in a Business Transaction

¶8,005 Capital Receipt Versus Income Receipt Revisited

Overview

As seen in Chapter 7, the Act does not define a capital gain. The provisions merely set out the technical computations to be made once it has been determined whether a transaction is an income receipt or a capital receipt. Taxpayers must turn to the guidelines which have been laid down by the courts through past judicial decisions. Even then, there is no clear-cut set of rules which will apply in all situations. The result has been one of the most confusing and controversial areas of taxation, giving rise to thousands of court cases since the advent of federal income taxation in Canada.

A set of behavioural factors, which were introduced in Chapter 4 and revisited in Chapter 7, were developed by the courts to help in determining whether the transaction falls into the capital category or the income category. In determining the type of income, based on the facts, we must review the taxpayer's whole course of conduct before, during, and after the transaction.

In reviewing the specific facts of a transaction, the courts work to determine the intention of a taxpayer. It is this intention that determines the nature of the transaction.

¶8,005.10 Primary Intention

The objective of most decisions is to determine the intention of the taxpayer. First, there may be an indicator in the taxpayer's behaviour of primary intention; that is, did the taxpayer intend to make a business or trading profit on the transaction? If the answer to this question, as determined by observing the facts of the taxpayer's behaviour, is affirmative, then the transaction is likely income rather than a capital transaction.

¶8,005.20 Secondary Intention

The courts may also examine the evidence of the taxpayer's behaviour to establish whether the taxpayer had any secondary intention, especially in respect of, but not limited to, real estate transactions. Secondary intention may be thought of as an alternative or secondary objective in the mind of the taxpayer at the time of the purchase which motivated the purchase and which would come into operation later if the primary objective is thwarted.

Example

A developer purchases a piece of property for an apartment complex which he or she plans to operate as an investment property by collecting rent.

After several attempts to rezone the property, the developer determines that the zoning bylaws cannot be altered to accommodate the proposed project. Since the project cannot move forward, the developer subsequently sells the property at a profit.

The courts would likely view this as an income transaction by way of the taxpayer's secondary intention, on the assumption that the taxpayer, as an experienced developer, would probably be confidant, at the time of purchase, that he or she could remove himself or herself from the situation at a profit when the primary objective could not be achieved.

¶8,005.30 Observable Behavioural Factors

Remember that the primary objective is to determine the taxpayer's intention when entering into the transaction. Intention is a state of mind and cannot be observed directly, but has to be inferred or deduced from observable facts from the taxpayer's behaviour. In Chapter 4, we reviewed the observable behavioural factors that the courts used to determine the classification of a transaction as capital in nature. The more common factors are outlined below. For a more detailed review, please see section ¶4,110.

(1) Relationship of the transaction to the taxpayer's business;

(2) Activity or organization normally associated with trade;

(3) Nature of the asset involved;

(4) Number and frequency of the transactions;

(5) Length of the period of ownership of the asset;

(6) Supplemental work on or in connection with the property disposed of in the transaction;

(7) Circumstances that caused the disposition;

(8) Corporate objects or partnership agreement.

Interpretation Bulletins: IT-459 Adventure or concern in the nature of trade

The more complete description of these factors presented in Chapter 4 should be reviewed. Reference should also be made to an Interpretation Bulletin where the CRA lists about 12 factors pertaining to real estate transactions. Where a disposition of securities is at issue, the CRA lists some relevant factors to consider in its Interpretation Bulletin entitled "Transactions in securities".

Interpretation Bulletins: IT-218R Profit, capital gains and losses from the sale of real estate, including farmland and inherited land and conversion of real estate from capital property to inventory and vice versa, IT-479R Transactions in securities

¶8,010 Capital Gain Reserve

It is not uncommon for a taxpayer to receive proceeds of disposition for a property over a period of years. The most common example occurs where the seller provides the purchaser with a first or second mortgage in order to facilitate the purchase of the property. From a policy perspective, to ensure equitable tax treatment and remain consistent with the definition of a "disposition" in the Act, taxpayers should not pay tax on taxable capital gains until they collect the proceeds and they have the cash to pay the tax.

When a taxpayer does not receive the full proceeds in the year of disposition, the Act allows a taxpayer to defer a portion of the gain realized by claiming a reasonable reserve on the gain. A reasonable reserve is not defined in the Act. The CRA has taken the position that a reasonable reserve is based on prorated uncollected proceeds times the capital gain.

ITA: 40(1)(a)(iii); Interpretation Bulletins: IT-236R4 Reserves — Disposition of Capital Property

A reasonable reserve is calculated by a specific formula that accounts for amounts not due until a later date. However, the formula also limits the length of the payment terms, from a tax perspective, so that the tax on taxable capital gains is not postponed unduly. If no limits were imposed, taxpayers could plan transactions to defer the taxation of the gains over a very long period, if not indefinitely.

ITA: 40(1)(a)

Example

A parent could sell property to a child with the payment due in 25 years. If no limit was imposed, the gain would be taxable in 25 years.

Regardless of the term of agreed repayment, the maximum deferral time allowed by the reserve is five years. The reserve is extended to 10 years for certain property (small business corporation shares or farm or fishing property) disposed of to a child.

In order to claim a capital gains reserve, a sale transaction must be on account of capital and all or part of the proceeds of disposition must be payable after the end of the year. The first step would be to determine if the sale of property is on account of capital. If the answer is yes, then a reserve may be claimed if some or all of the proceeds are due in a later period.

The formula for the reserve is calculated as the lesser of:

a) Proceeds not yet due/Total proceeds × Gain = Reasonable reserve (i.e., the fraction of the gain represented by the portion of the total proceeds not due at the end of the year)

and

b) (1/5 of gain) × (4 – number of preceding years ending after disposition)

As can be seen when reviewing the formula, the taxpayer will be required to include, at a minimum, 20% of the capital gain into income in the year of sale. The formula above means that regardless of the terms of sale, the entire capital gain will be included in the seller's income within a five-year time frame, even when the proceeds are not received. The usual maximum period over which the gain can be spread for inclusion in income is five years, including the year of disposition, assuming not all the proceeds are received within that five-year time frame. It should be noted that the first part of the formula deals with the actual proceeds not yet due. If a taxpayer receives a large amount of proceeds in the earlier years, it is possible that a larger capital gain may be required to be included in income. If all the proceeds of disposition are received before the five year maximum, the capital gain will be included in income.

Example

Mr. Tom Rex sold a capital property for $300,000 on December 31, 2018. The adjusted cost base of the property is $140,000 and the selling costs were $20,000. In return for the capital property, Mr. Rex took back the following:

Cash		$ 45,000
Note Receivable:		
	1st payment on December 31, 2019	105,000
	Balance due on July 1, 2020	150,000

The tax implications of the sale for 2018 and 2019 are as follows:

		2018
P of D		$300,000
Adjusted Cost base	$140,000	
Expenses of disposition	20,000	(160,000)
Gain		$140,000
Less reserve – lesser of:		
a) $255,000/$300,000 × $140,000 =	$119,000	
b) (1/5 × $140,000) × (4 – 0) =	112,000	(112,000)
Capital Gain		$ 28,000
Taxable Capital Gain (½)		$14,000
		2019
Inclusion in income — 2018 reserve		$112,000
Less reserve — lesser of:		
a) $150,000/$300,000 × $140,000 =	$70,000	
b) (1/5 × $140,000) × (4 – 1) =	84,000	(70,000)
Capital Gain		$42,000
Taxable Capital Gain (½)		$21,000

Mr. Rex will have to include 20% of the capital gain ($28,000) in 2018 and will pay tax on ½ of that capital gain ($14,000).

In 2019, Mr. Rex receives a large cash payment, bringing his total cash received on the sale to 50% of the sales price. As a result, Mr. Rex is required to include a larger capital gain in 2019.

When we review the total capital gain included in 2018 and 2019, we can see that Mr. Rex will have included a total capital gains of $70,000 ($28,000 in 2018 and $42,000 in 2019). This is equivalent to 50% of the total $140,000 capital gain and relates to the fact that 50% of the proceeds have been received.

The effect of this reserve system is to spread the capital gain realized on a disposition over a maximum of five years, including the year of the disposition. However, if the period of collection of the proceeds is less than five years, the system will spread the capital gain over the period of collection.

The CRA's interpretation of the applicability of the reserve provision has indicated that the reserve is based on amounts that are payable to the taxpayer after the end of the year. Where a demand note is accepted on a disposition, eligibility for a reserve can be improved by adding a condition that the note be payable, say, 10 days after demand. A demand made at the end of the year does not require payment until 10 days later with this condition.

Interpretation Bulletins: IT-236R4 Reserves — Disposition of Capital Property

Consistent with the treatment of other reserves, as discussed in Chapter 4, a reserve must be taken into income in the year following the deduction of a reserve. If eligible, a new reasonable reserve may be claimed.

ITA: 40(1)(a)(ii)

The reserve is only used to defer capital gains. There is no reserve against recaptured depreciation. Also, the reserve cannot be claimed:

ITA: 40(2) Limitations, 72 Reserves, etc., for year of death

- by a non-resident,
- where the purchaser is a controlled or controlling corporation,
- if the purchaser is a partnership, where the vendor is a majority interest partner, or
- in the year of death.

Example Problem 8-1

Ms. Gamma sold a capital property for $200,000 on December 31, 2018. Of that price, $180,000 was not due until December 2019. The adjusted cost base of the property was $130,000 and the selling costs were $20,000.

REQUIRED

Determine the taxable capital gain for 2018 and 2019 using the capital gains reserve provision.

ITA: 40(1)(a)

SOLUTION

		2018
Proceeds of disposition		$200,000
Adjusted Cost Base	$130,000	
Expenses of disposition	20,000	(150,000)
Gain		$50,000
Less 2018 Reserve — lesser of:		
a) $180,000/$200,000 × $50,000 =	$45,000	
b) (1/5 × $50,000) × (4 – 0)	$40,000	(40,000)

Capital Gain included		$10,000
Taxable Capital Gain (½ of capital gain)		$ 5,000
		2019
Inclusion of 2018 reserve		$40,000
Less 2019 Reserve — lesser of:		
a) Nil/$200,000 × $50,000	Nil	
b) (1/5 × $50,000) × (4 – 1)	$30,000	Nil
Capital Gain included		$40,000
Taxable Capital Gain (½ of capital gain)		$20,000

Ms. Gamma will be required to include a taxable capital gain of $5,000 in her 2018 tax return. All of the proceeds of disposition have been received in 2019. As a result, Ms. Gamma will include the remaining taxable capital gain of $20,000 in her 2019 tax return.

¶8,015 Adjusted Cost Base and Capital Cost

The "adjusted cost base" of most capital property, as defined, is usually its cost plus or minus legislated adjustments. Cost is not defined for taxation purposes. The usual starting point is *cost* for accounting purposes which comprises laid-down cost, including the invoice cost, relevant sales, excise, and customs taxes, insurance, freight, and, perhaps, some start-up costs. Where the person is a GST/HST registrant and is eligible for an input tax credit, the GST/HST should be excluded from adjusted cost base, because the GST/HST is not a cost if it is recovered by an input tax credit.

ITA: 54 Definitions, 53 Adjustments to cost base

There is an important exception to the above general rules in respect of depreciable property. In order to preserve the integrity of the capital cost allowance system, the adjusted cost base of depreciable property cannot be allowed to fluctuate as a result of the previously mentioned adjustments. Hence, the "adjusted cost base" of depreciable property is defined to be its capital cost, which in turn takes us back to cost for accounting purposes without adjustments.

ITA: 53 Adjustments to cost base, 54 Definitions

Subsection 53(1) (additions) and subsection 53(2) (reductions) set out a number of adjustments, some of which we have already examined.

- The cost base of land is increased by interest and property taxes denied as an expense.

ITA: 18(2) Limit on certain interest and property tax, 53(1)(h) [Adjustments to cost base — Land]

- Reasonable costs of surveying or valuing property in respect of its acquisition or disposition which are denied are added to the cost of the property.

ITA: 18(1)(b) Capital outlay or loss, 53(1)(n) [Adjustments to cost base — Costs of surveying or valuing property]

- The cost of property is reduced by government assistance for capital property.

ITA: 53(2)(k) [Amounts to be deducted — Government assistance]

¶8,015.99 Practise What You've Learned

¶8,800 — Review Questions

- Question 1 — Income vs. capital
- Question 2 — Income vs. capital
- Question 3 — Income vs. capital
- Question 4 — Income vs. capital

¶8,825 — Multiple Choice Questions

- Question 1 — Capital Gains Reserve
- Question 3 — Income vs. capital

¶8,850 — Exercises

- Exercise 6 — Income vs. capital
- Exercise 8 — Income vs. capital

¶8,020 Non-Arm's Length Transfer of Depreciable Property

If a depreciable property is transferred in a non-arm's length transaction, then this has implications for the operation of the capital cost allowance system. Deeming proceeds of disposition and cost of acquisition to be the fair market value will affect potential recapture of capital cost allowance on disposition and the base on which capital cost allowance is computed on acquisition.

If this type of transaction takes place, then there are special rules to determine what the undepreciated capital cost (UCC) of the property is to the acquirer. The results depend on whether an election is made under the interspousal rollover not to have the automatic rollover apply and whether there is an accrued gain on the property at the time of transfer. ITA: 13(7)(e), 73(1) Inter vivos transfers by individuals

If no election is made on the interspousal transfer, this means the property automatically rolls over at the transferor's UCC. ITA: 73(1) Inter vivos transfers by individuals

If an election is made to not have the spousal rollover occur (i.e., elect out of the rollover provisions), then the property will be disposed of at fair market value and the UCC of the property to the acquirer will be deemed to be equal to: ITA: 13(7)(e)

the cost of the property to the transferor immediately before the transfer

plus

the taxable capital gain realized on the transfer.

The addition of only the taxable capital gain restricts the UCC of the property to the transferee to the amount on which the transferor has paid tax.

¶8,025 Debts Established To Be Bad Debts

Overview

Where a debt taken back from the purchaser of a capital property is established to have become a bad debt, the seller can elect to have disposed of the debt and to have reacquired it immediately at a cost equal to nil. The deemed disposition results in a capital loss to offset any part of the gain on disposition of the property represented in the debt.

ITA: 50(1) Debts established to be bad debts and shares of bankrupt corporation

The deemed reacquisition at a nil cost may result in a further capital gain if any part of the debt is ultimately collected.

¶8,025.10 The Nature of the Bad Debt Reserve

There is no provision for an "allowance for doubtful debts" in computing capital gains. At best, a reserve is provided for the uncollected gain portion of the proceeds, payable after the end of the year. This, of course, does not help the taxpayer when the amount of the debt is payable in the year but not collectible, because the debt has become bad.

ITA: 50(2) Where debt a personal-use property

When a business has accounts receivable from the sale of goods or services and some of those accounts become doubtful, then an allowance for doubtful accounts can be claimed as a deduction against business income (see ¶4,520.10). However, if these accounts receivable are sold to a third party, then any loss on the sale (the difference between the face amount of the receivables and the proceeds) is treated as a capital loss for tax purposes. If the purchaser also buys substantially all (90% or more) of the other assets of the business and continues to carry on the business (see ¶4,620.10), the loss on the sale of accounts receivable is treated as a capital loss, unless an election is made to allow the loss to be claimed as a business loss.

ITA: 22 Sale of accounts receivable

Also, the treatment of a bad debt resulting from the disposition of personal-use property is different. In that case, the Act allows a capital loss only to the extent of the capital gains on the original disposition.

¶8,025.20 Disposition of Shares — Insolvent Corporations

A deemed disposition of the shares of an insolvent corporation occurs to realize the capital loss if:

ITA: 50(1)(b)(iii)

- neither the corporation nor a corporation controlled by it carries on business in the year;
- the fair market value of the shares is nil;
- it is reasonable to expect that the corporation will be dissolved or wound up and will not start to carry on business; and
- the taxpayer elects to have this provision apply.

There will be another deemed disposition for proceeds of disposition equal to the ACB of the shares before the subsection 50(1) deemed disposition if:

ITA: 50(1.1) Idem

- the taxpayer elects a deemed disposition; and

ITA: 50(1)(b)(iii)

- within 24 months of the disposition the corporation or a corporation controlled by it carries on business and the taxpayer or a non-arm's length person owns the shares.

This deemed disposition will result in a capital gain equal to the capital loss realized by the election. The shares are deemed to be reacquired at the adjusted cost base immediately before the disposition.

ITA: 50(1)(b)(iii), 50(1.1) Idem

¶8,030 Part Disposition

If a taxpayer makes a partial disposition of a capital property, he or she must allocate a reasonable portion of the total adjusted cost base of the capital property to the proceeds of partial disposition to determine the capital gain or loss. The portion of this cost allocated to the part sold should be in the ratio of the value of the part sold to the total value of the capital property. A valuation problem is very likely to arise, particularly if the value of the part sold is not, in fact, proportional to total value. This might be the case, for example, where a taxpayer owns land with lake frontage and the half of the property fronting on the lake is sold leaving the other half without such lake access.

ITA: 43 General rule for part dispositions

¶8,035 Replacement Property

Overview

In many situations, a taxpayer disposes of a property only to reacquire a replacement property with the funds received from the sale. For example, a growing corporation may outgrow their current warehouse and need to move to a larger location to meet their business needs. As a result, the corporation will sell the smaller warehouse only to repurchase a larger property needed to earn income. Given that the disposition of the property often creates a tax burden and a resulting cash outflow, this would indicate that less cash is available to purchase the new property. To alleviate some of this immediate tax burden, the Act permits the deferral of some or all of the capital gain on property which is disposed of and which is subsequently replaced.

There are two basic types of disposition which qualify for this deferral (often referred to in practice as a "rollover"):

(1) an involuntary disposition of property which has been lost, stolen, destroyed, or taken by order of statutory authority (e.g., expropriation, bankruptcy); and

(2) a voluntary disposition of real property, referred to as "former business property", that usually occurs on the relocation of a business.

It is possible that the outlay for the replacement property might not be made in the same year as the involuntary disposition. A major asset may take some time to replace even if the taxpayer immediately begins to plan the reconstruction or replacement. As a result, the election to defer may not apply immediately, as the election can only occur when the property has been replaced.

ITA: 13(1) Recaptured depreciation, 13(21) proceeds of disposition

In the year in which proceeds of disposition become receivable, the disposition is handled in the normal manner by reporting the gain. If the replacement property is acquired within the allowed time (discussed below), an amended return would be filed for the year in which the proceeds became receivable to remove the previously recorded gain and implement the rollover.

ITA: 44(2) Time of disposition and of receipt of proceeds

¶8,035.10 Involuntary Disposition

Ordinarily, any insurance recovery for stolen, lost, or destroyed (but not merely damaged) depreciable or capital property or any expropriation proceeds would be considered as "proceeds of disposition". The pooling of properties into the same class may help offset a potential recapture, assuming the property is replaced in the same year. The capital gain on the disposition would normally be required to be included in income. It may not be possible to replace a property in the same year when an involuntary disposition occurs as it is an unplanned disposition. To help alleviate the problem, the ITA allows for a potential deferral.

For involuntary dispositions, the taxpayer may qualify for the election to defer both the capital gain and the recapture if the replacement is made by the later of either:

- 24 months after the initial taxation year, or
- the end of the second taxation year following the year in which proceeds are considered receivable.

The disposition of the old property is deemed to have occurred only when the proceeds are "receivable". In the case of involuntary dispositions, the rules for determining when proceeds are receivable can be summarized as the earliest of:

(1) the day the taxpayer has agreed to the full amount of the compensation;

(2) the day the compensation is finally determined by a court or tribunal;

(3) the day that is two years from the day of loss, destruction, or taking where a claim or suit has not been taken before the courts;

(4) the day the taxpayer dies or ceases to be a resident of Canada; and

(5) the day immediately before the winding-up of a corporation (other than a Canadian subsidiary owned 90% of more) where the taxpayer is a corporation.

Basically, a replacement property is property that is acquired for the "same or similar use" as the original property and used for gaining or producing income from the "same or similar business" by the taxpayer or related persons. Note that replacement property need not be of the same class of depreciable property as the original property. The CRA's interpretation of the term "same or similar use" and of the term "same or similar business" are set out in an Interpretation Bulletin.

ITA: 44(5) Replacement property; Interpretation Bulletins: IT-259R4 Exchanges of Property

Example Problem 8-2

Recapture – Involuntary Disposition

Wally's is a department store operating in the area. Its operations are carried on in a building which is owned by the company. The capital cost of the building to Wally's in September 2014 was $400,000. The company has been taking capital cost allowance on the structure on the basis that it is a Class 1 (NRB) asset with a capital cost allowance rate of 6%. In May 2016, a fire virtually destroyed the building.

In August 2016, under an insurance policy with the Risk-Averters Insurance Company, Wally's received $385,000 for the destruction of the building. In 2018, a new building was constructed for $465,000.

REQUIRED

Trace the effects of these events on the balance of the undepreciated capital cost accounts in the building account for the building from 2014 through to the beginning balance for 2019. As you trace the effects, indicate all deductions from and inclusions in income from the business for the years indicated. Assume that the appropriate election is made.

ITA: 13(4) Exchanges of property

SOLUTION

Building – Separate Class 1 (NRB): 6%

2014	Additions: purchase of building			$400,000
	UCC at the end of 2014			400,000
	CCA claimed @ 6% ((($400,000 – (½ × 400,000)) × 0.06)			(12,000)
	UCC at the beginning of 2015			$388,000
2015	No additions or disposals			
	CCA claimed @ 6% ($388,000 × 0.06)			(23,280)
	UCC at beginning of 2016			$364,720
2016	Disposal: insurance proceeds - lesser of:			
	Original cost	$400,000		
	Proceeds of disposition	$385,000		(385,000)
	UCC at the end of 2016			(20,280)
	Recapture taken into income			20,280
	UCC at beginning of 2017			Nil
2017	No change			
	UCC at beginning of 2018			Nil
2018	Property is replaced — File an amended return for 2016 as follows:			
	UCC at beginning of 2016			$364,720
	Reduction of UCC[1] :			
	- Normal deduction is the lesser of:			
	(i) Proceeds	$385,000		
	(ii) Cost	$400,000	$385,000	
	- Reduced by lesser of:			

ITA: 13(21) proceeds of disposition (c)

ITA: 13(4) Exchanges of property

ITA: 13(4)(c)

ITA: 13(4)(c)

(i) Excess, if any, of $385,000 (as determined in year of disposition) over UCC of $364,720 at the beginning of 2016 (i.e. recapture in 2016)	$20,280			
(ii) Cost of replacement asset	465,000	($20,280)	(364,720)	
UCC at the end of 2016			Nil	

Building – New Separate Class 1 (NRB): 6%

2018	Additions: purchase of new building[2]	$465,000	
	Deemed proceeds of disposition (equal to reduction calculated above)	(20,280)	ITA: 13(4)(d)
	UCC at the end of 2018	$444,720	
	CCA @ 6% ((($444,720 – (½ × $444,720)) × 0.06)	(13,342)	
	UCC at beginning of 2019	$431,378	

NOTES TO SOLUTION

[1] To generalize the proceeds reduction rule, it would appear that as long as the cost of the replacement property exceeds the recapture that would otherwise result on the disposition (i.e., the $20,280, above), there will be no actual recaptured capital cost allowance on the disposition. In effect, part of the proceeds of disposition of the former property is transferred from the year in which the disposition occurred to the year in which the replacement property is acquired. This avoids recapture in the year of disposition and reduces the undepreciated capital cost of whichever class of property the replacement property falls into.

ITA: 13(4)(c)

[2] The rules allow for a replacement with an asset of another class. The old building was in a separate Class 1 (NRB); the new building is in a new separate Class 1 (NRB) and still qualifies as replacement property for the rollover.

ITA: 13(4) Exchanges of property

In the year of the disposition, a taxpayer may choose to either:

(1) recognize the usual capital gain (i.e., P of D minus ACB and selling costs), or

(2) elect to report the capital gain as the lesser of:

(a) the actual capital gain in (1) above, and

(b) the excess, if any, of proceeds for the old property over the cost of replacement (i.e., the amount of the proceeds not spent on the new property).

¶8,035.20 Voluntary Disposition

The same rules permitting an offset of recapture and capital gains caused by proceeds of disposition apply on certain voluntary dispositions of depreciable "former business property". However, in this case, the replacement must be made by the later of either:

ITA: 248(1) former business property

- 12 months after the initial taxation year, or
- the end of the first taxation year following the year of disposition.

The term "former business property" is defined to mean real property (i.e., land and buildings) or an interest therein (i.e., a leasehold interest) that is capital property used primarily for the purpose of earning business income. These rules pertaining to a former business property might be used in a business relocation to avoid recapture and capital gains on the disposition of buildings.

ITA: 44(1)(b), 248(1) former business property; 13(4.2) Election — limited period franchise, concession or license

Normally, a building is the only depreciable property eligible for the replacement property rules for voluntary dispositions. However, a limited-period franchise, concession, or license will also be eligible. The replacement property rules are extended where the transferor and transferee jointly elect to have these rules apply.

ITA: 13(4.2) Election — limited period franchise, concession or license, 13(4.3) Effect of election

¶8,035.30 Adjusted Cost Base of the Replacement Property

The adjusted cost base for the replacement property under the election above will be reduced by the deferred capital gain. This is the essence of a rollover or deferral which, in this case, is accomplished by the reduction of the adjusted cost base of the new property. By reducing the adjusted cost base, a future capital gain (or reduced capital loss) in the amount of the deferred gain will arise on the ultimate disposition of the new property.

ITA: 44(1)(f)

Example Problem 8-3

Quick Growth Stores Ltd. has decided to change the present location of its retail store, now in a suburban area, to the Yonge Street strip in downtown Toronto. The following facts relate to the disposition of the original property in March 2017.

	Land	Cl 1 Building	Cl 8 Equipment
Cost	$30,000	$50,000	$5,000
UCC	-	30,000	1,500
P of D	70,000	100,000	500

Quick Growth Stores Ltd. purchased its Yonge Street property in August 2018 for the following amounts:

Land	$100,000
Building — brick (new and unused)	150,000
Equipment	20,000

The company wishes to elect to defer both the capital gain and the recapture.

ITA: 13(4) Exchanges of property, 44(1) Exchanges of property

REQUIRED

Indicate the tax consequences if Quick Growth Stores Ltd. elects, assuming that its fiscal year end is December 31.

SOLUTION

This situation involves the voluntary disposition of a former business property in respect of the land and building. As a result, the taxpayer corporation must replace the land and building within the later of one taxation year or 12 months from the end of the December 31, 2017 taxation year (i.e., the taxation year of the disposition), in order to obtain the benefits of the rollover. It is often helpful to use a time line to graph the qualifying period of replacement as follows:

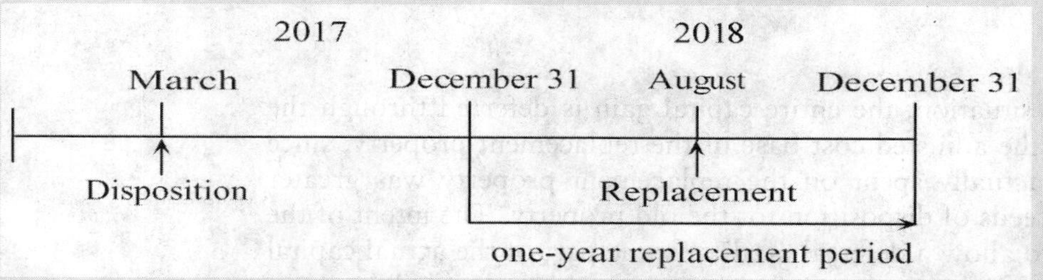

(A) Effect of election to defer capital gains – filed on an amended return for 2017:

Gain to be recognized in year of disposal — 2017

ITA: 44 Exchanges of property, 44(1)(e)

(1) Capital Gain, computed as:

		Land	Building
Lesser of:			
(I)	P of D	$70,000	$100,000
	ACB	(30,000)	(50,000)
	Capital gain	$ 40,000	$50,000
(II)	P of D	$70,000	$100,000

	Land	Building
Replacement cost	(100,000)	(150,000)
Excess, if any	Nil	Nil

The lesser of the actual capital gain and the proceeds not spent on the replacement property is nil in both cases. Therefore, the full amount of the gain can be deferred by reducing the adjusted cost base of the replacement land and building.

Adjusted cost base of replacement land is ITA: 44(1)(f)

$100,000 – $40,000 = $60,000

Adjusted cost base of replacement building is ITA: 44(1)(f)

$150,000 – $50,000 = $100,000

(2) Equipment — Nil

Equipment does not qualify as "former business property". In any case, there is a loss which is not allowed as a capital loss. ITA: 39(1)(b)(i)

Comments:

(1) In the above situation, the entire capital gain is deferred through the reduction of the adjusted cost base of the replacement property, since the amount actually spent on the replacement property was greater than the proceeds of disposition for the old property. The intent of the provision is to allow a deferral of all or some part of the actual capital gain and, hence, the tax on that gain, where the proceeds have been spent to acquire a new property. Conceptually, if the proceeds have been spent in this manner, there would be no funds from the disposition of the old property to pay the taxes, so the taxes are deferred. Note how the reduction in the adjusted cost base of the replacement property implements the deferral. Consider the replacement land which was acquired at a cost of $100,000. Its cost base is $60,000 after the adjustment for the deferred gain. If that land were sold immediately for its indicated value of $100,000 (it was just purchased for that amount), a capital gain of $40,000 (i.e., $100,000 – $60,000) would be realized. That capital gain is exactly the gain on the old land that was deferred.

(2) Since the replacement property was acquired after the filing of the 2017 corporate tax returns (June 30, 2018), the resultant capital gain and any recapture must be reported in the year of disposition. A request for an amended return must be made in the year of acquisition.

Interpretation Bulletins: IT-259R4 Exchanges of Property

Acceptable security may be provided in lieu of the payment of outstanding taxes.

(B) Effect of election to defer the recapture, re building — filed on an amended return for 2017:

2017			Cl. 1: 4%
UCC immediately before disposal			$30,000
Less: deemed disposal reducing UCC:			
- Normal deduction is the lesser of:			
i)	cost ($50,000)		
ii)	P of D ($100,000)	$50,000	
- Reduced by the lesser of:			
(i)	amount determined above ($50,000) less UCC above ($30,000)	(20,000)	
(ii)	cost of replacement	(150,000)	$30,000
UCC, December 31, 2017			Nil

ITA: 13(4)(c)

Comment:

As long as the cost of replacement ($150,000) is greater than the amount of the recapture ($20,000) that would otherwise result on the disposition, there will be full deferral of the recapture.

2018		Cl 1 – NRB:[1] 6%
Add: Capital Cost of Replacement Property		
Cost of Replacement	$150,000	
Less: reduction for deferred gain	50,000	
Deemed capital cost	$100,000	
Less: reduction for deferred recapture	20,000	$80,000
UCC, December 31, 2018		$80,000

ITA: 13(4)(d), 44(1)(f)

CCA, 2018 (6% of ½ × $80,000)		2,400
UCC, January 1, 2019		$77,600

[1] Separate Class 1 for new and unused non-residential buildings.

Comment:

Normally, when depreciable property of a class is sold and replaced with property of the same class in the year of disposition, all or some part of the potential recapture on the disposition is offset by the purchase before the end of the year. For example, if the new building had been purchased for $100,000 in 2017 and if it could have been added to the same class as the old building, the following UCC balance would have resulted:

UCC immediately before disposal		$30,000
Deduct lesser of:		
(i) Cost of building disposed of	$50,000	
(ii) Proceeds of disposition	$100,000	
Lesser amount		(50,000)
Add: capital cost of replacement building		100,000
UCC, December 31, 2017		$80,000

Note that this is the same amount as the UCC balance at December 31, 2018 after the rollover is implemented.

ITA: 13(4) Exchanges of property

In deferring the recapture, the election provides two additional benefits:

(1) it allows for a replacement to take place in a subsequent year, and

(2) it allows for a replacement with a property in a different class.

Example Problem 8-4

Quick Growth Stores Ltd. has decided to change the present location of its retail store, now in a suburban area, to the Yonge Street strip in downtown Toronto. The following facts relate to the disposition of the original property in March 2017.

	Land	Cl 1 Building	Cl 8 Equipment
Cost	$30,000	$50,000	$5,000
UCC	-	30,000	1,500
P of D	70,000	100,000	500

Quick Growth Stores Ltd. purchased its Yonge Street property in August 2018 for the following amounts:

Land	$ 45,000
Building — brick (new and unused)	150,000
Equipment	20,000

Note that the only change in this scenario from the previous example is that the acquisition cost of the new land is less than the proceeds of disposition of the land sold.

REQUIRED

Indicate the tax consequences for the *land only*, if Quick Growth Stores Ltd. elects, under section 44 (assuming that its fiscal year end is December 31.)

SOLUTION

The gain on the land to be recognized in year of disposal (2017) is now $25,000, computed as:

Lesser of: (A)	P of D	$70,000
	ACB	(30,000)
	CG	$40,000
(B)	P of D	$70,000
	Replacement Cost	(45,000)
	Excess, if any	$25,000

Adjusted cost base in 2018 of replacement property is:

Replacement Cost	$45,000
Deferred gain ($40,000 – $25,000)	(15,000)
ACB of replacement property	$30,000

ITA: 44(1)(f)

Comment:

In this scenario, the cost of the new land is lower than the P of D on the sale of the old land. The taxpayer has retained cash on the sale of the land and therefore has the funds to pay the tax on a portion of the capital gain. As a result, only a portion of the tax is deferred.

¶8,035.40 Election for Additional Deferral

This particular election permits the proceeds on the dispositions of former business property (land and buildings) to be reallocated between the two components so that less capital gain or recapture would be triggered. This election appears to recognize the fact that when a property consisting of land and building is sold, it is usually sold for proceeds which represent the fair market value of the total property. In this situation, the land and building are not priced separately. Therefore, the original allocation of proceeds between land and building may have been fairly arbitrary.

ITA: 44(6) Deemed proceeds of disposition

Example Problem 8-5

Quick Growth Stores Ltd. has decided to change the present location of its retail store, now in a suburban area, to the Yonge Street strip in downtown Toronto. The following facts relate to the disposition of the original property in March 2017.

	Land	Cl 1 Building	Cl 8 Equipment
Cost	$30,000	$50,000	$5,000
UCC	-	30,000	1,500
Proceeds	70,000	100,000	500

Quick Growth Stores Ltd. purchased its Yonge Street property in August 2018 for the following amounts:

Land	$ 45,000
Building — brick (new and unused)	150,000
Equipment	20,000

REQUIRED

Indicate the tax consequences of electing an additional deferral in respect of the building.

ITA: 44(6) Deemed proceeds of disposition

SOLUTION

Re-examining the facts above, it would be possible to elect to transfer $25,000 of the land proceeds to the building proceeds, thereby eliminating the capital gain. Note that the trade-off is a reduced capital cost of the building and, hence, a lower capital cost allowance base. Therefore, the cost of deferring tax on $25,000 of capital gain is to reduce the capital cost allowance over the holding period of the building in the future.

(A) Effect of the election

ITA: 44(6) Deemed proceeds of disposition, 44(1)(e)

Gain to be recognized in year of disposal (2017)

(i) Capital gain, computed as:			Land	Building
Lesser of:	(I)	Actual P of D	$ 70,000	$100,000
		Election	(25,000)	25,000
		Deemed P of D	$ 45,000	$125,000
		ACB	(30,000)	(50,000)
		CG	$ 15,000	$ 75,000
	(II)	Deemed P of D above	$ 45,000	$125,000
		Replacement cost	(45,000)	(150,000)
		Excess, if any	Nil	Nil

ITA: 44(6) Deemed proceeds of disposition

Adjusted cost base of replacement land is: ITA: 44(1)(f)

$45,000 – ($15,000 – Nil) = $30,000

Adjusted cost base of replacement building is: ITA: 44(1)(f)

$150,000 – ($75,000 – Nil) = $75,000

Comment:

Note that the key to a reallocation of proceeds that will successfully defer more of the capital gain is a replacement cost of one of the assets (i.e., either land or building) that is sufficiently in excess of original proceeds of disposition, to allow for an increase in proceeds on that asset without triggering a gain. In this case, the replacement cost of the building, at $150,000, exceeds the original proceeds of the old building of $100,000. Therefore, up to $50,000 can be added to the proceeds and still leave the excess of proceeds over replacement cost at nil. In this case, only $25,000 needs to be removed from the proceeds of the land to allow all of the gain to be deferred.

(B) Effect of election to defer recapture on building — Filed on an amended return for 2017.

2017			Cl 1: 4%	
UCC immediately before disposal			$30,000	
Less: deemed disposal reducing UCC				ITA: 13(4)(c)
- Normal deduction is the lesser of:				
(i) Cost ($50,000)				
(ii) P of D ($100,000)[1]		$50,000		
- Reduced by the lesser of:				ITA: 13(4)(c)
(i) amount determined above ($50,000) less UCC above ($30,000) equals ($20,000)				
(ii) Cost of replacement ($150,000)		(20,000)	30,000	
UCC after disposal			Nil	
2017			Cl. 1-NRB:[1] 6%	
Add:	Capital cost of replacement property			ITA: 13(4)(d)
	Cost of replacement	$150,000		
	Less: reduction for deferred gain	75,000		ITA: 44(1)(f)
	Deemed capital cost	$ 75,000		
	Less: reduction for deferred recapture	20,000	$55,000	ITA: 13(4)(d)
	UCC, December 31, 2017		$55,000	
	CCA, 2016 (6% of ½ × $55,000)		1,650	
	UCC, January 1, 2018		$53,350	

[1] Separate Class 1 for new and unused non-residential buildings.

Comment:

The results of using the election for additional deferral can be compared with the original application of the deferral as follows: ITA: 44(6) Deemed proceeds of disposition

	Without election	*With Election*	Difference
Capital gains recognized:			
land	$ 25,000	Nil	$25,000
building	Nil	Nil	Nil

		Without election	*With Election*	**Difference**
ACB of replacement property:				
	land	30,000	$30,000	Nil
	building	100,000	75,000	25,000
UCC (before CCA) of replacement building		80,000	55,000	25,000

The above shows that no capital gain on the land has to be recognized as a result of the election. This is reflected in the adjusted cost base of the building, which is $25,000 lower. This lower ACB will potentially result in a higher capital gain on the ultimate disposition of the building, if it is sold for a capital gain. Also, the UCC of the building is $25,000 lower, resulting in less annual CCA. To evaluate the trade-off the following should be compared:

ITA: 44(6) Deemed proceeds of disposition

(1) the tax that would be paid now on a capital gain of $25,000 or a taxable capital gain of $12,500 (i.e., ½ × $25,000), and

(2) the present value of the CCA tax shield[(2)] from $25,000 of capital cost in Class 1: NRB.

NOTES TO SOLUTION

[(1)] Note that the deemed proceeds arising from the election are not applicable for the purpose of a deferral of recapture, since the election is only applicable to Subdivision c, which deals with taxable capital gains and allowable capital losses.

ITA: 13 Recaptured depreciation, 44(6) Deemed proceeds of disposition

[(2)] The present value of the CCA tax shield, including the effect of the half-year rule, can be computed from the following:

$$PV = [(C \times R \times T)/(R + 1)] \times [(1 + I/2)/(1 + I)]$$

where

PV = present value of the CCA tax shield,

C = capital cost of the asset,

R = rate of CCA for the class,

I = after-tax discount rate,

T = tax rate.

Summary

Replacement Property

Deferral of Capital Gain

Key Question: Did you spend at least the proceeds on the replacement property?

If you spent at least the proceeds from the sale of the former property to buy the replacement property, then the full amount of the gain will be deferred. The deferral is built into the reduction of the cost base of the replacement property.

If you sell both land and building, then this concept applies to the combined proceeds and the combined replacement cost.

Deferral of Recapture

Key Question: Did you spend at least the amount of the recapture on the replacement property?

If you spent at least an amount equal to the potential recapture from the sale of the former property to buy the replacement property, then the full amount of the recapture will be deferred. The deferral is built into the reduction of the undepreciated capital cost of the replacement property.

¶8,035.99 Practise What You've Learned

¶8,800 — Review Questions

- Question 7 — Replacement property
- Question 8 — Replacement property
- Question 9 — Replacement property

¶8,825 — Multiple Choice Questions

- Question 2 — Replacement property
- Question 4 — Replacement property

¶8,850 — Exercises

- Exercise 2 — Sale of accounts receivable
- Exercise 5 — Replacement property
- Exercise 7 — Sale of a business; Replacement property

¶8,040 Reallocation of Proceeds — Special Circumstances

In a situation where land is disposed of in the same taxation year as a building, it is possible that a reallocation of the proceeds of disposition for the building and land will be required.

Case Summary

An interesting situation arose in the case of *The Queen v. Malloney's Studio Limited*, in which the taxpayer agreed to sell land clear of buildings and, therefore, had to demolish an existing building before disposing of the land. The Minister allocated part of the proceeds of disposition for the property to the demolished building, resulting in recapture. The taxpayer argued that the entire price related to the land. The Supreme Court of Canada held that the price related only to the land because the building was not part of the sale. No part of the price was for property "damaged, destroyed, taken or injuriously affected" because the purchase did not cause the damage as envisaged by the definition of "proceeds of disposition". Since none of the proceeds for the property had to be allocated to the building, the taxpayer could deduct a terminal loss on the building, since it was the only building in its class, and, at the same time, all of the proceeds created a capital gain which was only fractionally taxable.

Cases: *Her Majesty The Queen v. Malloney's Studio Limited*, 79 DTC 5124 (SCC); ITA: 13(21) proceeds of disposition

Perhaps as a reaction to the result of the above case, a provision was added to the Act to provide rules to reallocate proceeds of disposition between land and buildings on their sale. If the sale of a building results in a terminal loss, this provision will likely apply if land is sold, creating a capital gain in the same taxation year as the building.

ITA: 13(21.1) Disposition of building

If this provision applies, the original proceeds of disposition for both the land and building will be reallocated in such a way as to reduce or eliminate the terminal loss on the building. The amount of the reallocated proceeds of disposition of the building may be greater than the fair market value of the building.

In the situation where the land is sold in the same taxation year as the building, the amount which is treated as proceeds of disposition of the building may be greater than the fair market value of the building, thereby reducing or eliminating the potential terminal loss. At the same time, the capital gain on the sale of the land will be reduced by the amount of the terminal loss eliminated on the building. Thus, the potential terminal loss on the building will be used to offset the gain on the land. The result is to convert what might have been a terminal loss, which is fully deductible, into a reduction of a capital gain, in essence, one-half deductible.

It is easiest to see and understand the concept of the provision if the building that is disposed is the only building in its class, as is the case in the following example problem. However, it should be realized that the provision applies even if there is no actual terminal loss in the class, because there is at least one other building in the class.

Example Problem 8-6

Alaya Limited owned a real property which it sold during the current taxation year for a total of $200,000. The land had a fair market value of $150,000 and an adjusted cost base of $100,000. The building had a fair market value of $50,000. It was the only building in the class which had an undepreciated capital cost of $75,000 and a capital cost of $90,000.

REQUIRED

(1) Determine the tax consequences of the sale of the building in this transaction.

(2) If the purchaser wanted to buy only the building for $50,000 and remove it at his or her own expense to another location, what would be the tax consequences of the sale of the building?

SOLUTION

(1) If proceeds of disposition of the building are considered to be equal to its fair market value of $50,000, which is less than the undepreciated capital cost of the class and the capital cost, the proceeds of disposition of the building will be deemed to be the following: ITA: 13(21.1)(a)

P of D of building = lesser of:

(i) (I) FMV of land and building		$200,000
minus		
(II) lesser of:		
— ACB of land	$100,000	
— FMV of land	$150,000	100,000
		$100,000
(ii) greater of:		
(I) FMV of building	$50,000	
(II) lesser of capital cost and UCC of building	$75,000	$75,000

= $75,000

Since proceeds of disposition are deemed to be equal to the undepreciated capital cost of the class, there is no terminal loss and no recapture. Note that proceeds of disposition of the land will be deemed to be:

(i) P of D of land and building	$200,000	
minus		
(ii) deemed P of D of building (above)	75,000	$125,000

This will result in a capital gain of $25,000 on the land (i.e., $125,000 – $100,000).

If it were not for the rule being illustrated, there would have been a capital gain on the land of $50,000 (i.e., $150,000 – $100,000) and a terminal loss on the building of $25,000 (i.e., $50,000 – $75,000). The effect of the rule can be seen from the following comparison: ITA: 13(21.1)(a)

Income effect	Without par. 13(21.1)(*a*)	With par. 13(21.1)(*a*)
Taxable capital gain on land:		
½ × $50,000	$ 25,000	
½ × $25,000		$12,500
Terminal loss on building	(25,000)	(Nil)
Effect on net income	Nil	$12,500

The rule has converted the terminal loss on the building, which is normally fully deductible, into an amount that is, in effect, only ½ deductible by reducing the gain on the land (which is only ½ taxable). Note that this conversion of a terminal loss only occurs if there is a capital gain on the land. ITA: 13(21.1)(a)

(2) In this case, proceeds of disposition of the building will be deemed to be the following: ITA: 13(21.1)(b)

P of D of building =	(i) P of D of building (without ssec. 13(21.1))		$ 50,000
	plus		
	(ii) greater of:		
	(I) UCC of building (Class 3) $75,000	$75,000	
	(II) FMV of building $50,000		
	minus P of D of building in (i) above	$50,000	
	excess × ½	$25,000 × ½	$ 12,500
			$ 62,500
UCC of class			75,000
Terminal loss			$(12,500)

Note how the decline in value of $25,000 from undepreciated capital cost to fair market value of the building has been rendered, essentially one-half deductible in this situation. This effect parallels that illustrated in part (A) above.

Summary

Disposal of Land and Building

Subsection 13(21.1)

Key Question: Was there a capital gain on the land and a terminal loss on the building?

If so, an amount equal to the terminal loss (but not greater than the capital gain) will reduce the proceeds on the land and increase the proceeds on the building. This will reduce the capital gain and the terminal loss will be eliminated.

Where the land is not disposed of in the same year, one-half of the apparent terminal loss on the building will be deductible, resulting in what is, in effect, an allowable capital loss on the sale of the building instead of an ordinary loss. However, the deductible amount of the loss will technically be considered a business loss.

¶8,045 Disposition of Depreciable Property

A capital gain will arise on the disposition of depreciable property if the proceeds of disposition exceed the total of the adjusted cost base of the property plus the disposal costs. Recall that capital losses may never be claimed in respect of depreciable property and that the undepreciated capital cost is irrelevant in the determination of a capital gain. As such property depreciates over time, any decline in value is deemed to be normal depreciation and is therefore not considered to be a capital loss. Furthermore, if this type of property is sold for less than its capital cost, the rules on capital cost allowance will apply to recognize a terminal loss, recapture of capital cost allowance, or to reduce the UCC of the class in which the property was included. To claim a capital loss would, in fact, be double counting the decline in value.

The following diagrams may help to show the different possible outcomes on the disposition of depreciable property, where there is only one asset in the class. To determine whether there is recapture or terminal loss, the lower of cost or proceeds (LOCP) is credited to the CCA class in which the asset was found.

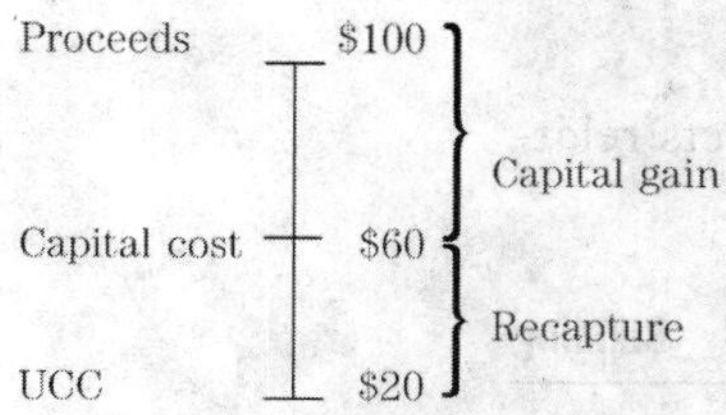

	CG		Recapture/ Terminal Loss
Proceeds	$100	UCC	$ 20
Cost	(60)	LOCP	(60)
Capital gain	$ 40	Recapture	$ 40

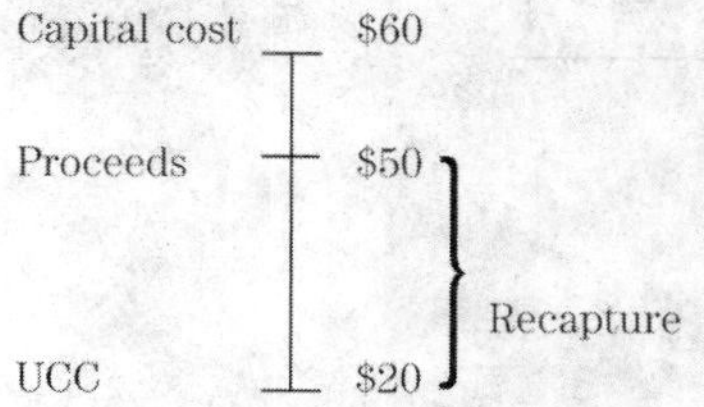

	CG		Recapture/ Terminal Loss
Proceeds		UCC	$ 20
Cost		LOCP	(50)
Capital gain	N/A	Recapture	$ 30

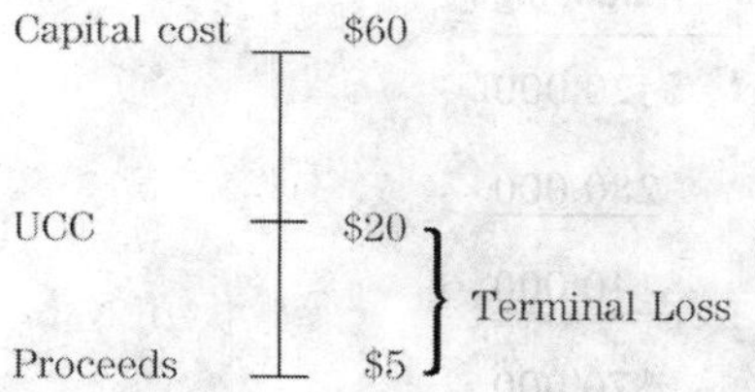

	CG		Recapture/ Terminal Loss
Proceeds		UCC	$ 20
Cost		LOCP	(5)
Capital gain	N/A	Terminal Loss	$ 15

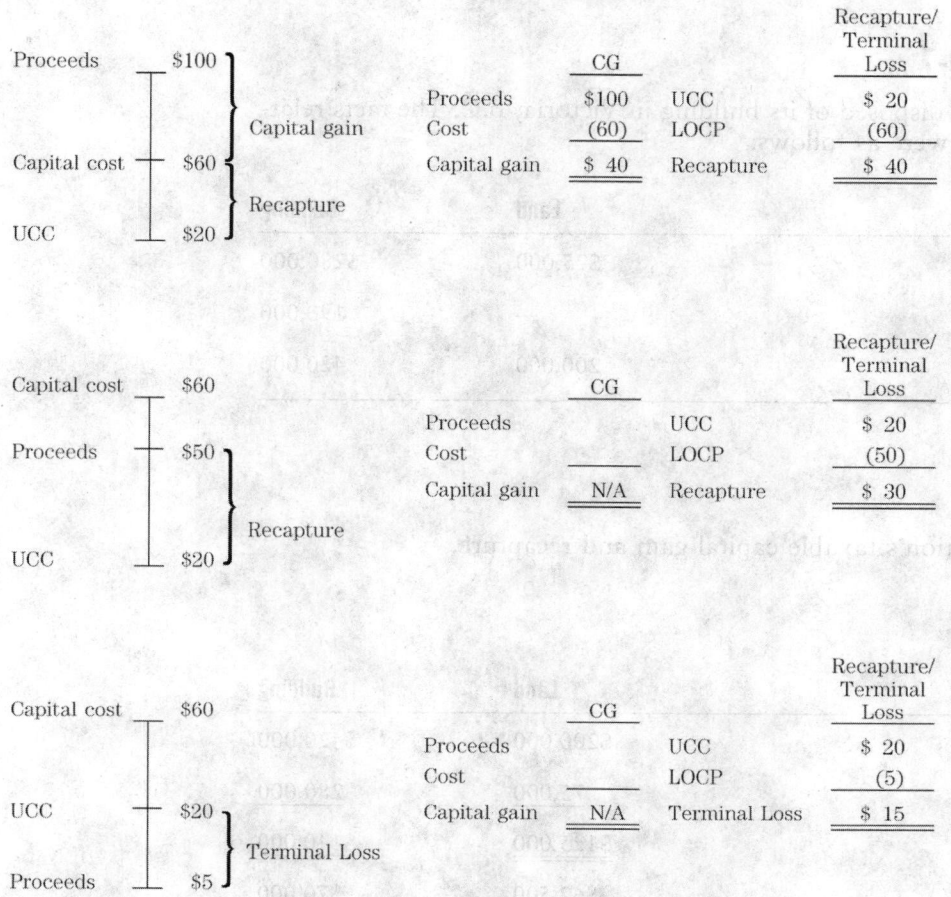

Note: The difference between proceeds and UCC always needs to be accounted for.

If there is more than one asset in the class, then there are two options.

(1) If proceeds are greater than the adjusted cost base of the asset, then there is a capital gain and the lower of cost or proceeds is credited to the CCA class. Since the proceeds are greater than the adjusted cost base, the adjusted cost base would be credited to (i.e., would reduce) the CCA class. If the CCA class then becomes negative, there is recapture. If there is a positive balance, then CCA continues to be claimed on the remaining assets in the pool.

(2) If proceeds are less than the adjusted cost base, then the lower of cost or proceeds is credited to (i.e., reduces) the CCA class. Since the proceeds are less than the adjusted cost base, the proceeds would be credited to the CCA class. If the CCA class then becomes negative, there is recapture. If there is a positive balance, then CCA continues to be claimed. Remember from previous discussions (¶7,030) that a capital loss on depreciable property is denied. ITA: 39(1)(b)(i)

Example Problem 8-7

Lanice J. Corporation disposed of its building in Victoria, B.C. The facts relating to the disposition were as follows:

	Land	Building
Adjusted cost base	$75,000	$280,000
UCC	—	190,000
Proceeds	200,000	420,000

REQUIRED

Compute the corporation's taxable capital gain and recapture.

SOLUTION

	Land	Building
Proceeds	$200,000	$420,000
Adjusted cost base	75,000	280,000
Capital gain	$125,000	$140,000
Taxable capital gain (50%)	$62,500	$70,000

The calculation of the depreciation recapture, if any, is separate as "proceeds" for that purpose cannot exceed capital cost.

UCC	$190,000
Lesser of capital cost and proceeds	(280,000)
Recaptured CCA	$90,000

¶8,050 Election on Change in Use

Overview

When a taxpayer changes the use of property, he or she is deemed to have sold that property at the fair market value and to have reacquired the same property immediately thereafter at the fair market value, which becomes his or her new adjusted cost base.

ITA: 45(1)(a), 45(1)(b), 45(1)(c)

Where property has a dual use, its cost must be apportioned between the uses on a percentage basis and that basis will be used on the disposition of the property. If the percentage for a particular use is changed either up or down, there will be a proportionate deemed disposition and reacquisition at the fair market value at that time. Note that these rules are similar in concept to the rules pertaining to depreciable property with respect to changes of use and the capital cost allowance system.

ITA: 13(7) Rules applicable

The CRA indicates that a change in use does not include a transfer of property from one income-producing use to another such use by the same taxpayer. As examples, the CRA suggests that the change-in-use rules do not apply when real estate used to produce income from a business or property is converted to inventory, because holding the property as inventory is still an income-producing use. Similarly, the rules do not apply where inventory is converted to capital property which is used to produce income from a business or property.

Interpretation Bulletins: IT-218R Profit, capital gains and losses from the sale of real estate, including farmland and inherited land and conversion of real estate from capital property to inventory and vice versa

The Interpretation Bulletin provides numerical examples of how to handle these conversions to separate income gains from capital gains by the use of a "notional disposition". It is only on an actual disposition that income gains alone may be realized in these situations.

Interpretation Bulletins: IT-218R Profit, capital gains and losses from the sale of real estate, including farmland and inherited land and conversion of real estate from capital property to inventory and vice versa

¶8,050.10 Change in Use — Personal-Use Property

For personal-use property only, a taxpayer may elect to defer the capital gain until such time as he or she:

- decides to dispose of the asset;
- is deemed to dispose of the asset; or
- decides to rescind the election.

This election applies only when the property was used originally for personal use and remains in force until one of the above conditions occurs. For example, a taxpayer may have a yacht which is used for personal use. Later, the taxpayer decides to rent out the yacht. He or she may elect to defer the potential gain on the change in use. This election will remain in force even when he or she changes its use back to personal use unless, of course, he or she rescinds the election.

ITA: 45(2) Election where change of use

Note that this election is not available in a situation where the property was first used to produce income and then is changed to personal use.

Example Problem 8-8

A taxpayer purchased a yacht in 2010 at a cost of $24,000. In 2013, the taxpayer changed the use and rented the yacht for the next two years. The fair market value at the time the property became an income-producing asset was $30,000. During 2015, he converted the yacht back to exclusive personal use. The fair market value at this time was $33,000. In 2018, the taxpayer sold the yacht for $60,000.

REQUIRED

Compare the taxable capital gain arising with and without the election to be deemed not to have changed the use.

ITA: 45(2) Election where change of use

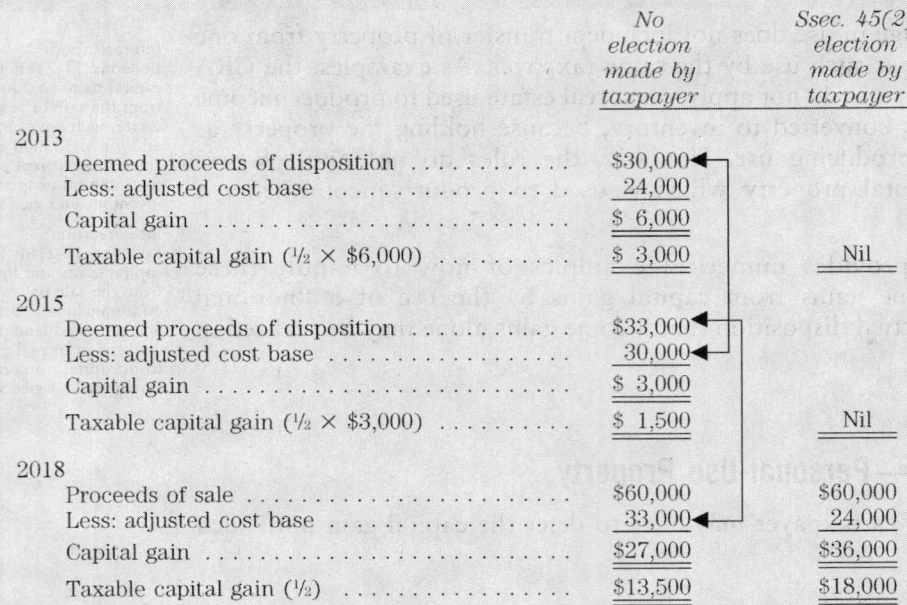

	No election made by taxpayer	*Ssec. 45(2) election made by taxpayer*
2013		
Deemed proceeds of disposition	$30,000	
Less: adjusted cost base	24,000	
Capital gain	$ 6,000	
Taxable capital gain (½ × $6,000)	$ 3,000	Nil
2015		
Deemed proceeds of disposition	$33,000	
Less: adjusted cost base	30,000	
Capital gain	$ 3,000	
Taxable capital gain (½ × $3,000)	$ 1,500	Nil
2018		
Proceeds of sale	$60,000	$60,000
Less: adjusted cost base	33,000	24,000
Capital gain	$27,000	$36,000
Taxable capital gain (½)	$13,500	$18,000

NOTES TO EXAMPLE PROBLEM

Theoretically, there should be no difference in the total taxable capital gain between the two options available, only a timing difference in the payment of the tax. Where the inclusion rate is constant, the election would normally be the preferred treatment, since the change in use has not generated any cash. Hence, there are a number of other factors to be considered:

(1) Does the taxpayer have any capital losses which he or she may wish to trigger?

(2) Will the taxpayer move to a higher tax bracket in the future?

(3) Conversely, does the taxpayer anticipate a decrease in income at some time in the future?

ITA: 45(2) Election where change of use; 45(3) Election concerning principal residence

If the facts in the example problem had been reversed and the taxpayer had acquired the yacht for rental purposes and subsequently converted the yacht to personal use, this election would not be available. However, if the property was a rental building which was converted to personal use and was designated as a principal residence in a subsequent disposition, a rollover or deferral would be provided.

If an election is made not to have a change in use, then there will be no need to determine the UCC of the yacht, since it is deemed to still be personal-use property. If an election is not made, then a UCC must be determined and these rules, as explained in Chapter 5, will result in a UCC in 2013 of $27,000 (cost of $24,000 plus the TCG at 50% of $6,000). On the deemed disposition in 2015, there may be recapture to the extent that any CCA was claimed on the yacht.

ITA: 45(2) Election where change of use, 13(7) Rules applicable

Ⓐ ¶8,060 Foreign Exchange Gains and Losses

Taxpayers must first determine whether the foreign exchange gain or loss arose from an income or a capital receipt, using the common law rules discussed in ¶4,110 and ¶8,005. For income receipts, the full gain or loss will be included in arriving at business or property income under Subdivision b. For capital receipts, the net capital gain or loss is determined in the normal manner. However, for individuals, but not corporations, the net capital gain or loss is reduced by a maximum of $200.

ITA: 39(2) Foreign exchange capital gains and losses; 39(1.1) Foreign currency dispositions by an individual

Example Problem 8-9

Mr. Coates made capital transactions which resulted in the following currency gains and losses during the following years:

	2016	*2017*	*2018*
Total currency gains	$800	$180	$250
Total currency losses	300	40	400

REQUIRED

Compute the capital gains (losses) on foreign currency for each of the years shown.

SOLUTION

	2016	*2017*	*2018*
Net capital gain (loss)	$500	$140	$(150)
Exempt portion of excess	200	140	(150)
Capital gain (loss)	$300	Nil	Nil

A currency gain or loss must be distinct and separate from another transaction that may have given rise to the currency transaction. For example, the sale of an article must be computed in Canadian dollars valued at the time of the sale in order to arrive at a gain or loss on that disposition. A subsequent conversion of foreign funds received would give rise to the currency gain or loss.

¶8,100 Income Reconciliation Revisited

One of the major adjustments to accounting income in its conversion to income for tax purposes is the exclusion of book gains and losses on the disposition of capital property and the inclusion of taxable capital gains and allowable capital losses.

Example Problem 8-10

Capital Hill Ltd. has disposed of the following capital assets during 2018:

	Proceeds disposition	Cost	Book value	Undepreciated capital cost
Securities	$ 500	$ 5,000	n/a	n/a
Land	52,500	30,000	n/a	n/a
Building[1]	76,250	20,000	$ 3,000	$4,500
Equipment[2]	500	10,000	1,000	1,500

[1] Ignore section 44 considerations.
[2] Only asset in class.

REQUIRED

Indicate the adjustments to be made in the reconciliation of accounting income to tax purposes.

SOLUTION

Reference	ADDITIONS	
Sec. 3	Securities — book loss: ($500 – $5,000)	$ 4,500
Sec. 38	Land — taxable capital gain: ($52,500 – $30,000) × ½	11,250
Sec. 38	Building — taxable capital gain: ($76,250 – $20,000) × ½	28,125
Sec. 13	Building — recapture: ($4,500 – $20,000)	15,500
Sec. 3	Equipment — book loss: ($500 – $1,000)	500
	Total additions	$ 59,875

Reference	DEDUCTIONS	
Sec. 38	Securities — allowable capital loss: ($500 - $5,000) × 1/2	$ 2,250[1]
Sec. 3	Land — book gain: ($52,500 - $30,000)	22,500
Sec. 3	Building — book gain: ($76,250 - $3,000)	73,250
Par. 39(1)(*b*)	Equipment — capital loss	Nil
Ssec. 20(16)	— terminal loss ($1,500 - $500)	1,000
	Total deductions	$ 99,000

[1] Can only be deducted to the extent that there are taxable capital gains.

¶8,900 Pause and Reflect — Summary of Learning Goals for This Chapter

After working through all the sections of this chapter, you should be able to:

- Apply the behavioral factors in a specific scenario to determine whether the nature of a transaction is business income or capital gain.
- Explain the tax implications of selling a property through instalment payments and the options available to minimize tax.
- Apply your knowledge to calculate the capital gains reserve that may be claimed in a given period.
- Apply your knowledge to determine the adjusted cost base of a depreciable asset, including any allowable adjustments and for non-arm's length situations.
- Explain the tax implications of a bad debt as it relates to the disposition of a capital property.
- Explain the deferral available when a property is replaced within the eligible time frame for both involuntary and voluntary disposition.
- Apply your knowledge to calculate the deferral amount and the cost base of the new property, under the replacement property rules for both capital gains and recapture.
- Explain the rules related to the disposition of land and building where a terminal loss occurs as a result of the sale.
- Apply your knowledge to calculate the reallocation of proceeds of disposition between the land and building when a terminal loss occurs on the building as a result of the sale.
- Apply your knowledge to correctly determine the tax implication when a capital property has a deemed disposition as a result of a change in use.

- Apply your knowledge to specific circumstances to minimize the current tax paid by the client on the disposition of a capital property.

¶8,900.99 Practise What You've Learned

¶8,800 — Review Questions

- Question 7 — Replacement property
- Question 8 — Replacement property
- Question 9 — Replacement property

¶8,825 — Multiple Choice Questions

- Question 5 — Disposal of building with terminal loss

¶8,850 — Exercises

- Exercise 3 — Sale of building with terminal loss
- Exercise 4 — Inherited property

CHAPTER 9

Other Sources of Income and Deductions in Computing Income

ADVANCED CONTENT IN THIS CHAPTER

Learning Goals

Know, Understand and Explain

By the end of this chapter you will know, understand and be able to explain:

- The basic provisions of the *Income Tax Act* that relate to income and other deductions.
- How pension income is taxed.
- How to calculate the taxable portion of an annuity.
- How contributions and withdrawls from RESP and RDSP programs affect the calculation of net income for tax purposes.
- The benefits of contributing to an RESP or RDSP.
- The difference in tax treatment for spousal support and child support.
- The difference between an RRSP contribution and a contribution to spousal RRSP and when it may benefit a taxpayer.
- The taxation of contributions and withdrawls into Registered Savings Plans.
- The different tax treatments for contributions and withdrawls for TFSAs, RRSPs and RESPs.
- The tax impacts of transitioning RSPs into retirement income.
- When moving expenses are deductible and when they are not.

Review Questions
¶9,800 in the Study Guide

Multiple Choice Questions
¶9,825 in the Study Guide

Exercises
¶9,850 in the Study Guide

Apply

By the end of this chapter you will be able to apply your knowledge and understanding to:

- Calculate deductible moving expenses.
- Calculate deductible child care expenses.
- Calculate disability support deductions.
- Split pension and CPP income to minimize tax payable.
- Calculate the RRSP contribution limit for a taxpayer.

Assignment Problems
¶9,875 in the Study Guide

Overview

The Act includes a number of income inclusions and expense deductions that do not fit within the definitions of employment, income from business, income from property, or capital gains. This collection of miscellaneous but important provisions are grouped together and discussed as Other Income and Deductions. They include income common to many individual Canadian tax returns such as pensions, spousal support and amounts from registered savings plans such as registered education savings plans (RESP) and registered disability savings plan (RDSP). Additionally they include deductions common to individuals for items such as contributions to registered savings plans, childcare expenses and moving expenses.

PART I — DIVISION B

SUBDIVISION d: OTHER SOURCES OF INCOME
SUBDIVISION e: DEDUCTIONS IN COMPUTING INCOME
SUBDIVISION g: AMOUNTS NOT INCLUDED IN COMPUTING INCOME

DIVISION

A	Liability for tax
B	**Computation of income**
C	Computation of taxable income
D	Taxable income earned in Canada by non-residents
E	Computation of tax
E.1	Minimum tax
F	Special rules applicable in certain circumstances
G	**Deferred and other special income**
H	Exemptions
I	Returns, assessments, payment and appeals
J	Appeals to the Tax Court of Canada and the Federal Court of Appeal

SUBDIVISION

	Basic rules
a	Income or loss from an office or employment
b	Income or loss from a business or property
c	Taxable capital gains and allowable capital losses
d	**Other sources of income**
e	**Deductions in computing income**
f	Rules relating to computation of income
g	**Amounts not included in computing income**
h	Corporations resident in Canada and their shareholders
i	Shareholders of corporations not resident in Canada
j	Partnerships and their members
k	Trusts and their beneficiaries

SECTION

56	General
56.1	Support
56.2-56.3	Debt forgiveness
56.4	Restrictive covenants
57	Certain pensions
58	Government annuities
59-59.1	Resource property

60-60.03	Other deductions
60.1	Support
60.2	Refund of AVCs
61-61.1	IAACs
61.2-61.4	Debt forgiveness
62	Moving expenses
63	Child care expenses
64	Attendant care
64.1	Individual absent from Canada
65-66.8	Resource property

81	Amounts not included in income

144	Employees profit sharing plans
144.1	Employee Life and Health Trust
145	Registered supplementary unemployment benefit plans
146	RRSP
146.01	Home Buyers' Plan
146.02	Lifelong Learning Plan
146.1	RESP
146.2	TFSA
146.3	RRIF
146.4	RDSP
147	DPSP
147.1-147.4	RPP
147.5	Pooled Registered Pension Plans
148	Life insurance policies
148.1	Eligible funeral arrangements

149	Miscellaneous exemptions
149.1-149.2	Qualified Donees

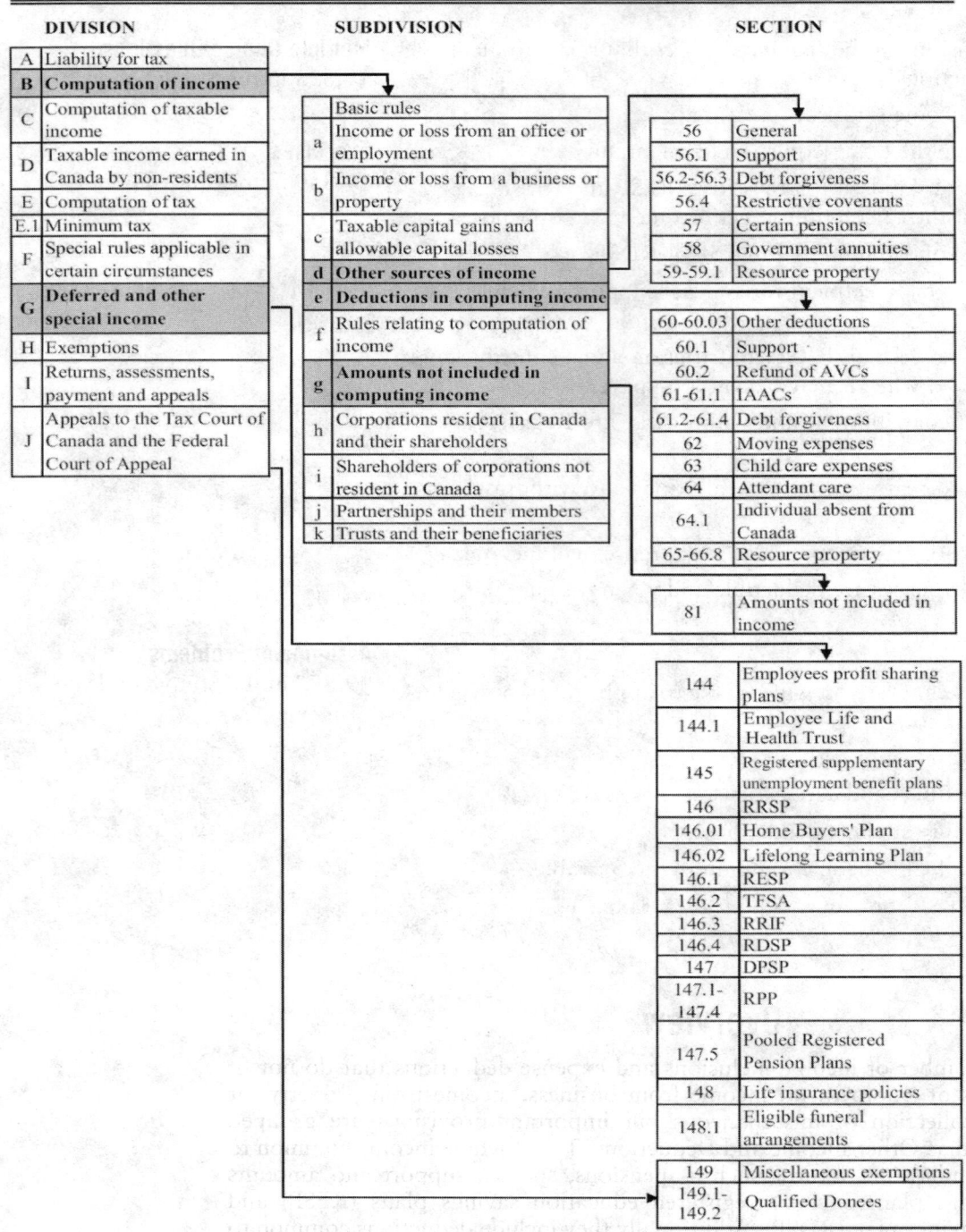

¶9,000 Other Sources of Income

Overview

Section 56 presents a list of miscellaneous types of income, other than employment and business or property that must be included in the calculation of a taxpayer's net income for tax purposes. Section 56.1 extends the rules and specifically discusses income pertaining to marital breakdown situations. Sections 57 to 59.1, which will not be discussed in this text, deal with certain pension plans, government annuities and resource properties in more detail.

Summary of Other Sources of Income

ITA Reference	Other Sources of Income
56(1)(*a*)(i)–(iv)	Benefits in the nature of pensions
56(1)(*a*)(ii)	Retiring allowances and other payments on termination of employment
56(1)(*b*)	Support receipts and payments
56(1)(*d*)	Annuity payments
56(1)(*h*), (*i*), (*q*), (*t*)	Amounts received from deferred income plans
56(1)(*n*)	Education assistance payments
56(1)(*l*)	Legal costs awarded by a court
56(1)(*u*)	Social assistance payments
56(1)(*v*)	Workers' Compensation
56(2)	Indirect payments
56(6)	Child care benefit
56.4	Restrictive covenants

¶9,005 Retiring

Overview

Many benefits received during retirement do not fit into the classifications of employment income, business income, property income, or capital gains and losses. However, many of these receipts are required to be included in net income for tax purposes and are discussed below.

¶9,005.10 Benefits in the Nature of Pensions

This provision includes in income amounts received as pension benefits including those received under the *Old Age Security Act* and the Canada Pension Plan. An Interpretation Bulletin discusses the inclusion of these benefits. "Retiring allowances" are included in the calculation of net income for tax purposes, as discussed further below. "Death benefits" are also defined very precisely for the purposes of the Act and are included in income. Note the exemption of a maximum of $10,000 of death benefit contained in the definition of the term. Any benefits received under the *Employment Insurance Act* are included in income and, therefore, taxable.

ITA: 56(1)(a)(i), 56(1)(a)(iv), 248(1) retiring allowances; Interpretation Bulletins: IT-499R Superannuation or pension benefits; ITA: 248(1) death benefits

¶9,005.20 Income Splitting

Spouses or common-law partners who meet certain conditions can split equally their pension income and Canada Pension Plan income. The term "spouse or common-law partner" is defined as two persons, regardless of sex, who cohabit in a conjugal relationship and have done so for a continuous period of at least 12 months. This income sharing arrangement would be most useful where the individuals have different tax rates and amounts of income.

ITA: 248(1) common-law partner

Income Splitting — Canada Pension Plan

The amount which can be shared is 50% of the combined CPP benefits received but prorated by the length of the time the individuals have been living together in relation to the contributory period. Where one individual was a contributor and the other individual was not, then the non-contributor must be at least 60 years of age at the time of this election. Applications are available from the Income Security Programs Department of Human Resources Development Canada.

Income Splitting — Pension Income

An individual resident in Canada may allocate to their resident spouse or common-law partner up to one-half of their pension income (eligible pension income) that qualifies for the pension income tax credit.

For individuals aged 65 years and over, eligible pension income includes annuity payments under a registered pension plan, a registered retirement savings plan, or a deferred profit sharing plan or payments out of a registered retirement income fund. For individuals less than 65 years of age, eligible pension income includes annuity payments under a registered pension plan and certain other payments received as a result of the death of the individual's spouse or common-law partner.

ITA: 60.03(1) eligible pension income, 118(7) eligible pension income

Since this will reduce one person's income, and probably cause another to pay tax, there is a requirement that both parties agree to the splitting of the income.

ITA: 60.03(2) Effect of pension income split

¶9,010 Allowances and Other Payments on Termination of Employment

In the absence of any express terms as to termination in a contract of employment, which is covered in Chapter 3, the general principle is that all other payments on the termination of employment are taxable as a retiring allowance. The provision provides exceptions for amounts out of an employee benefit plan, a retirement compensation arrangement, or a salary deferral arrangement. All three of these are plans specifically defined and are not particularly common.

ITA: 6(3) Payments by employer to employee, 56(1)(a)(ii), 248(1) employee benefit plan, retirement compensation arrangement, salary deferral arrangement

The definition of a retiring allowance excludes pension income and death benefits, but specifically includes payments in respect of:

ITA: 248(1) retiring allowance

(a) retirement from an office or employment in recognition of long service; or

(b) loss of office including court-awarded damages received by the taxpayer, or as a bequest, by a dependant or relation of the taxpayer or his or her legal representative.

For information on transferring some or all of a retiring allowance to an RRSP, please refer to ¶9,380.20.

¶9,015 Annuity Payments

An "annuity" is defined as "an investment of money entitling [the] investor to [a] series of equal annual sums".[1] This enhances the definition found in the Act. The full amount of an annuity payment that is received is included in income, then the capital portion of the annuity, if any, is deducted.

ITA: 12.2(1) Amount to be included, 248(1) annuity

The capital portion of the annuity payment represents the tax-paid dollars used in the purchase of the investment (purchase price) and hence are removed. This is consistent treatment with the concept of return of capital seen throughout the Act including the calculation of capital gains discussed in the previous two chapters. The method of computing the capital element of an annuity is set out in the Regulations. In essence, the capital element is given by the ratio:

ITR: 300 Capital Element of Annuity Payments

the capital outlay to buy the annuity / the total payments to be received or expected to be received under the contract

This ratio would be multiplied by the annual annuity payment.

The following annuity payments do not qualify for this deduction:

(a) a superannuation or pension benefit;

(b) a payment under a registered retirement savings plan or registered retirement income fund; or

(c) a payment resulting from a deferred profit sharing plan.

These types of annuities are excluded because they are paid out of income which has not been subjected to tax; that is, the cost of these annuities has been allowed as a deduction in computing income. Annuities required to be included under another provision of the Act or any that are subject to income accrual rules are also subject to different treatment.

[1] *The Concise Oxford Dictionary.*

¶9,020 Amounts Received From Deferred Income Plans

The Act allows for the deferral of income through specific savings plans. This means that amounts that generally would be included in the calculation of net income for tax purpose are allowed to be excluded in these circumstances generally while the amounts are left within the savings plans. When dollars are received or removed from these plans, an amount of income is often generated.

The detailed rules governing these plans are found in Division G "Deferred and Other Special Income Arrangements". RESPs, RRSPs, HBPs, LLPs, DPSPs, and RRIFs will be discussed in more detail later in this chapter.

The following paragraphs take into income any amounts received by the taxpayer from the deferred income plans:

Provisions Outlining the Treatment of Amounts Received from Deferred Income Plans

Paragraph 56(1)(*h*)	Registered retirement savings plan (RRSP)
Paragraph 56(1)(*h*.1)	Home buyer's plan (HBP)
Paragraph 56(1)(*h*.2)	Lifelong learning plan (LLP)
Paragraph 56(1)(*i*)	Deferred profit sharing plan (DPSP)
Paragraph 56(1)(*q*)	Registered education savings plan (RESP)
Paragraph 56(1)(*q*.1)	Registered disability savings plan (RDSP)
Paragraph 56(1)(*t*)	Registered retirement income fund (RRIF)

¶9,025 Registered Education Savings Plan (RESP)

Overview

Contributions to an RESP are not deductible, but the investment income accrues tax-free. Contributions are not included in income when paid out, but the investment income is included in the beneficiary's income when it is paid out.

¶9,025.10 Concept and Limits

RESPs, as defined, allow individuals to contribute, without an annual limit, to a plan to fund post-secondary education of a qualified beneficiary. The lifetime contribution limit in respect of a beneficiary is $50,000 over a maximum of 31 years (35 years if the beneficiary is entitled to the disability tax credit). Contributions are not deductible when contributed to the plan and, hence, the contributions are not taxable when they are withdrawn. However the investment income earned on the contributions is taxable upon withdrawal. Neither the trust holding the property of a plan nor the contributor or subscriber is

ITA: 146.1(1) registered education savings plan or RESP; 204.9(1) RESP lifetime limit; 146.1(5) Trust not taxable, 146.1(6) Subscriber not taxable

taxable on the investment income earned while the amounts are held within the plan, so the investment income of the plan is considered sheltered or deferred.

The following summarizes the time limits for a RESP.

ITA: 146.1 specified plan (b), 146.1 specified plan (c), 146.1(2)(h)(i), 146.1(2)(h)(ii), 146.1(2)(i)(i), 146.1(2)(i)(ii)

Time Limit	Type of Plan	Limit
Years of contribution	Regular	31 years
	Disabled	35 years
Termination	Regular	35 years
	Disabled	40 years
Lifetime contribution limit		$50,000

The accumulated investment income is taxable to a beneficiary as he or she receives the funds to pay for education expenses while enrolled as a full-time student in a post-secondary educational institution, called "educational assistance payments". Educational assistance payments can be made in connection with occupational skills programs at educational institutions certified by the Minister of Employment and Social Development.

ITA: 56(1)(q) Education savings plan payments, 146.1(1) educational assistance payment

Eligibility for education assistance payments from an RESP is extended to part-time studies. Students 16 years of age or older may receive up to $2,500 of education assistance payments for each 13-week semester of part-time study. A greater amount may be approved by the Minister of Employment and Social Development on a case-by-case basis.

A family plan RESP can be established for a number of beneficiaries related by blood or adoption. The income from such an RESP can be paid to any one or more of the beneficiaries who pursue higher education. However, the RESP cannot allow an individual to become a beneficiary after he or she turns 21.

¶9,025.20 Canada Education Savings Grant (CESG)

Basic CESG

To increase the attractiveness of saving for education through an RESP, the government provides a CESG of 20% of the first $2,500 of annual contributions to an RESP for the benefit of children up to age 18.[2] This amounts to a maximum grant of $500 per year per child. The CESG is paid directly to the RESP. The maximum CESG that can be *paid* to an RESP in respect of a particular beneficiary is $7,200. In the case of a family plan RESP involving more than one beneficiary, the maximum CESG that can be *received* by a particular beneficiary as educational assistance payments is $7,200. CESG contribution room of $2,500 per year is accumulated for each child under 18 years old. Thus, where less than a $2,500 contribution is made in a year, the 20% grant will be paid in a subsequent year when RESP contributions are made. If a child does not pursue higher education to qualify for educational assistance payments, the CESG must be repaid to the government by the RESP.

[2] *Canada Education Savings Act.*

Additional CESG

The CESG matching rate for contributions made to an RESP by low and middle-income families is determined as follows. Where a child is the beneficiary of the RESP and under the age of 18 throughout the year, the first $500 contributed in the year will attract:

- a 20% CESG matching rate, if the qualifying net income of the child's family is $46,605 or less; or
- a 10% CESG matching rate if the qualifying net income of the child's family is between $46,605 and $93,208.

All income levels are for 2018 and will change annually.

There is no carry forward of the enhanced rate to future years and the income thresholds are indexed to inflation.

Family net income in 2018	up to $46,605	between $46,605 and $93,208
CESG	20% on first $500	10% on first $500

Ⓐ ¶9,025.30 Canada Learning Bond (CLB)

In addition, a CLB provides a source of education savings for children of low-income families. Each child born after December 31, 2004 is eligible for an initial CLB of $500 and subsequent annual CLB's of $100 in each year up to and including the year the child turns 15, provided that the child's family income is below the applicable threshold. The thresholds are based on the number of children in the family. For example, for families with three children or less the threshold is the lowest income tax bracket ($46,605 in 2018). The total amount of the CLB payments cannot exceed $2,000 per child and can be transferred to an RESP at any time before the child reaches 18. The CLB must be applied for. The CLB is payable into an RESP of which the child is a beneficiary.

¶9,025.40 Distribution From an RESP

An RESP is permitted to distribute any part of its accumulated income to the subscriber (the individual that contributed the money, such as a parent), under certain conditions, as follows:

- the subscriber is alive;
- each beneficiary of the RESP is either:
  (1) over 21 years of age and not eligible to receive educational assistance payments, or
  (2) has died; and
- the RESP has been in existence for at least 10 years. ITA: 146.1(2)(d.1)

These distributions are included in the subscriber's income. The Minister may waive the "over 21 years of age" and the "at least 10 years" restrictions where a beneficiary under an RESP is mentally impaired. The distributions may be rolled over to the subscriber's (or his or her spouse's) RRSP, to the extent that the subscriber has contribution room. The limit on this rollover is $50,000. A 20% tax is imposed on the amount of the RESP distribution received in excess of the limited amount transferred to RRSPs.

ITA: 146.1(2.2) Waiver of conditions for accumulated income payments, 204.94 [Tax on accumulated income payments]

¶9,025.90 Pause and Reflect — Summary of Learning Goals

After working through this section, ¶9,025, you should be able to:

- Know the tax implications of contributing to, saving through and removing from a Registered Education Savings Plan.

¶9,030 Registered Disability Savings Plan (RDSP)

Overview

To help parents and others save for the long-term financial security of a child with a severe disability, the Act provides for a registered disability savings plan (RDSP) with a Canada Disability Savings Grant (CDSG) program and Canada Disability Savings Bond (CDSB) program. The RDSP will be based generally on the existing RESP design.

ITA: 146.4 [Registered disability savings plan]

¶9,030.10 Eligibility

Generally, any person eligible for the disability tax credit (DTC) and resident in Canada, or the parent or other legal representative of such a person, is eligible to establish an RDSP. The DTC-eligible individual is the plan beneficiary.

The plan termination is required only if the beneficiary's condition has factually improved to the extent that he or she no longer qualifies for the DTC. This deals with the concern that someone may qualify for the DTC but not claim it.

ITA: 146.4(p)(ii); 146.4(12)(d)

¶9,030.20 Tax Treatment

Contributions to an RDSP are not deductible, but the investment income accrues tax-free. Contributions are not included in income when paid out, but the investment income is included in the beneficiary's income when it is paid out.

¶9,030.30 Contributions

Contributions to an RDSP are limited to a lifetime maximum of $200,000 in respect of the beneficiary, with no annual limit. There is no restriction on who can contribute to the plan. Contributions are permitted until the end of the year in which the beneficiary attains 59 years of age.

The registered retirement savings plan (RRSP) rollover rules allow a rollover of a deceased individual's RRSP proceeds to the RDSP of the child or grandchild who was financially dependent on the deceased individual and who has an impairment in physical or mental functions. These rules also apply to registered retirement income fund (RRIF) proceeds and to certain lump-sum amounts paid from registered pension plans (RPPs).

ITA: 60.011 [Qualifying trust annuity]

In recognition of the fact that families of children with disabilities may not be able to contribute regularly to their plans, a 10-year carryforward of CDSG and CDSB entitlements is available.

¶9,030.40 Canada Disability Savings Grant (CDSG)

To provide additional direct government assistance to help ensure the future financial security of a child with a severe disability, RDSP contributions made in the year qualify for CDSGs at matching rates of 100%, 200%, or 300%, depending on family net income and the amount contributed. The family's second preceding year's income is used to determine the grant and bond payments. Therefore, 2018 payments are based on family income from 2016.

Family net income in 2016	up to $93,208	over $93,208
CDSG	300% on first $500	100% on first $1,000
	200% on next $1,000	

The family net income threshold will be indexed to inflation.

There is an annual limit of $3,500 and a lifetime limit of $70,000 on CDSGs paid in respect of an RDSP beneficiary. An RDSP is eligible to receive CDSGs until the end of the year in which the beneficiary attains 49 years of age.

¶9,030.50 Canada Disability Savings Bond (CDSB)

To ensure that RDSPs help promote the future financial security of children with a severe disability in lower-income families, CDSBs of up to $1,000 are paid annually to the RDSPs of low and modest-income beneficiaries and families. CDSBs are not contingent on contributions to an RDSP.

The maximum $1,000 CDSB is paid to an RDSP where family net income does not exceed $30,450. The CDSB is phased out gradually for those with family net income between $30,450 and $46,605.

There is a lifetime limit of $20,000 on CDSBs paid in respect of an RDSP beneficiary. An RDSP is eligible to receive CDSBs until the end of the year in which the beneficiary turns 49 years of age.

¶9,030.60 Payments

Payments from an RDSP are required to commence by the end of the year in which the beneficiary attains 60 years of age. Payments are subject to a maximum annual limit deter-mined by reference to the life expectancy of the beneficiary and the fair market value of the property in the plan. The beneficiary or their legal representative is permitted to encroach on the capital and income of the plan.

¶9,030.70 Death or Cessation of Disability

Where the beneficiary of an RDSP either ceases to be eligible for the DTC or dies, the funds in the RDSP are required to be paid to the beneficiary or pass to his or her estate. That amount is included in the beneficiary's income

¶9,030.90 Pause and Reflect — Summary of Learning Goals

After working through this section, ¶9,030, you should be able to:

- Know the tax implications of contributing to, saving through, and removing funds from a Registered Disability Savings Plan.

¶9,035 Education Assistance Payments

In general, many scholarships, fellowships and bursaries are not taxable, because they are exempt from income. However, amounts that do not meet the requirements for exemption are required to be included in income.

There is a full exemption for scholarships, fellowships, and bursaries received by a taxpayer in connection with the taxpayer's enrolment in a program at a designated educational institution where the taxpayer may claim the education tax credit. A program at a post-secondary school level only includes a program leading to a college or CEGEP diploma or a bachelor, masters, or doctoral degree. This means that post-doctoral fellowships will be taxable.

ITA: 56(3)(a); 56(3)(b)

The full exemption of scholarships and bursaries is also available to those received for elementary and secondary school programs.

There are certain restrictions on the amounts which qualify as scholarships, bursaries, prizes, etc. Amounts received from a registered education savings plan, amounts received in the course of a business, and amounts received in respect of employment are excluded. Note that the grant portion of provincial or federal education assistance payments is considered to be income under this paragraph. Certain prescribed prizes are excluded from income completely. Generally, these prizes may be described as recognition by the general public for meritorious achievement in the arts, sciences, or public service; thus these amounts do not represent a payment in respect of a contract of service.

ITA: 56(1)(n) Scholarships, bursaries, etc; ITR: 7700 [Prescribed prize]

If the scholarship, fellowship, or bursary amount is approved for a part-time program, the scholarship exemption is normally limited to the amount of tuition paid for the program plus the costs of program-related materials.

In summary, these provisions include in income:

ITA: 56(1)(n) Scholarships, bursaries, etc., 56(3)(c); Income Tax Folio: S1-F2-C3 Scholarships, Research Grants and Other Education Assistance

(1) scholarships, fellowships, bursaries, or prizes for achievement in a field of endeavour of the taxpayer *in excess* of the taxpayer's scholarship exemption for a taxation year, and project grants, received by artists, net of the related, contractual project expenses; and

(2) research grants in excess of expenses which are unreimbursed, non-personal, or living expenses, except for *bona fide* travelling expenses, incurred in carrying on the research.

ITA: 56(1)(o) Research grants

¶9,040 Support Receipts and Payments

Overview

It is important to note that support payments made for the benefit of a spouse (spousal support) upon marital breakdown and support payments made for the benefit of the children (child support) have two very different tax effects.

The spousal support affects the tax outcomes of both the recipient of the payment and the payer and the income inclusions and deductions are mirror images of each other. The recipient of spousal support includes the amount in income to be taxed, while the payer has a deduction of the same amount from their net income for tax purposes.

ITA: 56(1)(b) Support, 60(b) Support

On the other hand, child support payments have no impact on the tax of either the payer or recipient of the child support. The recipient of child support has no inclusion, while the payer has no deduction, which is also a mirror image. The following discussion is applicable to both the receipts and payments.

Important Cases Related to Support Payments

In the case of *Thibaudeau v. The Queen*, the Federal Court of Appeal ruled that a separated custodial parent did not have to include child support payments as part of her income. However, the Court did not rule on the deductibility of the husband's payments in this case. The Court's decision was based on a finding of instances of discrimination against separated custodial parents in the Act. As an example of such discrimination, the court indicated that a non-separated custodial parent is not required to include support payments from a spouse in income. (Of course, the payer spouse does not get a deduction in that case.) If this situation had been allowed to stand, such support payments, deductible to the payer but not includable by the recipient, would escape tax altogether.

Cases: *Suzanne Thibaudeau v. Her Majesty the Queen*, 94 DTC 6230 (FCA)

In the decision of the Supreme Court of Canada on the appeal of the case of *The Queen v. Thibaudeau*, the Court ruled that the custodial parent was required to include the child support payments in her income. The majority opinion concluded that the fact that the tax saving resulting from the inclusion/ deduction system does not benefit both parents equally does not infringe the equality rights protected by the *Canadian Charter of Rights and Freedoms*.

Cases: *The Queen v. Thibaudeau*, 95 DTC 5273 (SCC)

As a result of the *Thibaudeau* case, the inclusion – deduction system related to child support only was changed, as discussed below.

¶9,040.10 Spousal Support

The CRA is very strict on its interpretation of support receipts and deductions. All aspects of these rules must be adhered to. Support amounts, excluding child support, are deductible if the following five tests are met:

ITA: 56(1)(b) Support, 56.1(4) Definitions, 60(b) Support

- the payments are made as allowances on a periodic basis, as discussed below;
- the payments are made for the maintenance of the recipient;
- the recipient has discretionary use of the amounts;
- the payments are made to a spouse or common-law partner or former spouse or common-law partner who is living apart from the payer because of the breakdown of their marriage or common-law partnership, or paid by a natural parent of a child of the recipient; and
- the payments are made pursuant to an order of a competent tribunal or a written agreement.

Definitions

A spouse or common-law partner is described as an individual of either sex who cohabited with the recipient in a conjugal relationship or is the parent of the child of the recipient.

ITA: 248(1) common-law partner

The definition of an allowance for purposes of the above paragraphs is embodied in the definition of the term "support amount". The provision does not completely define an allowance, but does limit an allowance to an amount over which the recipient has discretion as to how the funds will be spent.

ITA: 56.1(4) support amount

In the case of *Gagnon v. The Queen*, the Supreme Court of Canada considered the meaning of allowance. Three conditions must be met for an amount to be regarded as an allowance in the Court's view:

Cases: *Jean-Paul Gagnon v. Her Majesty The Queen*, 86 DTC 6179 (SCC)

- the amount must be limited and predetermined;
- the amount must be paid to enable the recipient to pay a certain type of expense; and
- the recipient must be able to spend the payment in any way he or she wants.

The Court elaborated on the last condition. As long as the recipient benefits from the amount, it is not relevant that he or she has to account for it or that he or she cannot apply it to certain types of expense at his or her complete discretion.

As noted previously, all of these provisions require that the payments be made on a periodic basis. This concept is frequently litigated. The Federal Court of Appeal decision in *The Queen v. McKimmon* listed some of the criteria which should be used in determining whether a payment is made on a periodic basis and whether in fact the payment is a deductible allowance or an instalment of a lump or capital sum which is not deductible. The Court outlined the following list of factors to consider:

Cases: *Her Majesty the Queen v. Stanley John McKimmon*, 90 DTC 6088 (FCA)

> 1. The length of the periods at which the payments are made. Amounts which are paid weekly or monthly are fairly easily characterized as allowances for maintenance. Where the payments are at longer intervals, the matter becomes less clear. While it is not impossible, it would appear to me to be difficult to envisage payments made at intervals of greater than one year as being allowances for maintenance.
>
> 2. The amount of the payments in relation to the income and living standards of both payer and recipient. Where a payment represents a very substantial portion of a taxpayer's income or even exceeds it, it is difficult to view it as being an allowance for maintenance. On the other hand, where the payment is no greater than might be expected to be required to maintain the recipient's standard of living, it is more likely to qualify as such an allowance.
>
> 3. Whether the payments are to bear interest prior to their due date. It is more common to associate an obligation to pay interest with a lump sum payable by instalments than it is with a true allowance for maintenance.
>
> 4. Whether the amounts envisaged can be paid by anticipation at the option of the payer or can be accelerated as a penalty at the option of the recipient in the event of default. Prepayment and acceleration provisions are commonly associated with obligations to pay capital sums and would not normally be associated with an allowance for maintenance.
>
> 5. Whether the payments allow a significant degree of capital accumulation by the recip-ient. Clearly not every capital payment is excluded from an allowance for maintenance: common experience indicates that such things as life insurance premiums and blended monthly mortgage payments, while they allow an accumulation of capital over time, are a normal expense of living which are paid

from income and can properly form part of an allowance for maintenance. On the other hand, an allowance for maintenance should not allow the accumulation, over a short period, of a significant pool of capital.

6. Whether the payments are stipulated to continue for an indefinite period or whether they are for a fixed term. An allowance for maintenance will more commonly provide for its continuance either for an indefinite period or to some event (such as the coming of age of a child) which will cause a material change in the needs of the recipient. Sums payable over a fixed term, on the other hand, may be more readily seen as being of a capital nature.
7. Whether the agreed payments can be assigned and whether the obligation to pay survives the lifetime of either the payer or the recipient. An allowance for maintenance is normally personal to the recipient and is therefore unassignable and terminates at death. A lump or capital sum, on the other hand, will normally form part of the estate of the recipient, is assignable and will survive him.
8. Whether the payments purport to release the payer from any future obligations to pay maintenance. Where there is such a release, it is easier to view the payments as being the commutation or purchase of the capital price of an allowance for maintenance.

Payments to Third Parties

Certain payments to third parties made under an order or agreement are deductible as spousal support payments by the payer and included in the income of the person who benefits from the payment. Payments envisaged include medical bills, mortgage payments, or tuition fees.

ITA: 56.1 Support, 60.1 Support

Third-party payments, whether or not they are made on a periodic basis, will be deemed to be an allowance for the discretionary use of the recipient and, hence, deducted by the payer and included by the person who benefits, if they meet the following criteria:

ITA: 56.1(2) Agreement, 60.1(2) Agreement

- the payments are made in the year or preceding year under an order of a competent tribunal or written agreement;
- the expense was incurred for the maintenance of a spouse or common-law partner or former spouse or common-law partner; and
- the court order or written agreement alludes specifically to subsections 56.1(2) and 60.1(2).

Note that the use of this provision requires the agreement of both parties. If they do not agree to include the effects of these provisions in their documentation, the third-party amounts will not be deemed to be an allowance. These payments exclude the acquisition of tangible property, unless it involves an expenditure on medical expenses or educational expenses. The acquisition, improvement, or maintenance of a self-contained domestic establishment, as defined, also qualifies as payments that are deemed to be an allowance. Note that interest and principal payments are limited to 20% of the original principal amount of the debt.

ITA: 248(1) self-contained domestic establishment

Amounts that are received/paid in respect of support before a court order or written agreement is made are considered to have been received/paid under the order or agreement. However, the subsequent order or agreement must be made before the end of the year following the receipt/payment. In addition, the subsequent order or agreement must provide for the prior support to be deemed to have been received/paid under the order or agreement.

ITA: 56.1(3) Prior payments

¶9,040.20 Child Support

Amounts paid in respect of support or maintenance of a child are not deductible by the payer and are not included in the income of the recipient. Any amount not identified in the agreement or order as being solely for the support of the recipient spouse or former spouse will be considered to be an amount payable for child support.

For this purpose, the term "child support amount" is defined. These rules apply to new written agreements or court orders made or to existing written agreements or court orders changed.

ITA: 56.1(4) child support amount

¶9,040.30 Legal Fees in Connection With Support Payments

Under current common law, legal fees incurred to enforce pre-existing rights to support payments are deductible,[3] according to the CRA.[4] Subsequently, the CRA announced[5] that legal costs incurred to obtain spousal support under the Divorce Act, or under the applicable provincial legislation, in a separation agreement are considered to have been incurred to enforce a pre-existing right to support. This position is based on the case of *Gallien v. The Queen*. The CRA further indicated that it now accepts that legal costs of seeking to obtain an increase in support or to make child support non-taxable are also deductible.

Interpretation Bulletins: IT-99R5 Legal and Accounting Fees; Cases: *Gallien v. The Queen*, 2000 DTC 2514 (TCC)

¶9,045 Indirect Payments

Overview

These anti-avoidance provisions are put in place to discourage a taxpayer from attempting to avoid the inclusion of amounts in income by diverting income receipts through a third party so that the income is received indirectly. The rules invoke the principle of constructive or effective receipt and cause the taxpayer to impute the following amounts (impute refers to the inclusion in income of amounts that may not have been received, actually, by the taxpayer):

ITA: 56(1)(u) Social assistance payments, 56(1)(v) Workers' compensation

- income diverted at his or her direction to someone else either for the taxpayer's benefit or to satisfy the desire of the taxpayer to benefit the other person;
- any rights to income transferred by the taxpayer, while resident in Canada, to someone with whom he or she was not dealing at arm's length; and
- income earned on non-arm's length loans which do not yield a commercial rate of interest (see Chapter 6).

ITA: 56(2) Indirect payments

ITA: 56(4) Transfer of rights to income

ITA: 56(4.1) Interest free or low interest loans, 56(4.2) Exception, 56(4.3) Repayment of existing indebtedness

---

[3] See the *McColl* case, (T.C.C.) 2000 DTC 2148.

[4] Paragraph 18 of IT-99R5 also refers to the *Sembinelli* case (F.C.A.), 94 DTC 6636.

[5] Income Tax Technical News, No 24, October 10, 2002.

¶9,045.10 Conditions

The provision pertaining to indirect payments specifies the following four conditions:

ITA: 56(2) Indirect payments

- there must be a payment or transfer of property to a person other than the taxpayer;
- the payment or transfer must be made pursuant to the direction or with the concurrence of the taxpayer;
- the payment or transfer must be for the benefit of the taxpayer, or a benefit that the taxpayer desired to confer on the other person; and
- the payment or transfer would have been included in the taxpayer's income if it had been made to the taxpayer.

If all of these conditions are met, the payment or transfer is included in the taxpayer's income to the extent that it would be if the payment or transfer had been made directly to the taxpayer.[6]

The CRA has attacked certain family income splitting schemes by applying these indirect payments provisions. In the case of *Champ v. The Queen*, part of the dividends payable on shares owned by the taxpayer's wife was included in the taxpayer's income. It was found that the taxpayer had directed the payment of dividends on his wife's shares without the payment of dividends on his shares which were essentially the same. On the other hand, in the case of *The Queen v. McClurg*, subsection 56(2) was held not to be applicable in facts very similar to Champ but where there were contractual restrictions upon the payment of dividends. The case of *The Queen v. Neuman*, involved facts that were slightly different from those in the McClurg case. The decision to apply subsection 56(2) in the Neuman case was based on the power of the taxpayer to ratify the dividends paid to his wife and the distinction with the McClurg case on the wife's lack of contribution to the corporation

Cases: *Warren Champ v. Her Majesty The Queen*, 83 DTC 5029 (FCTD); *Her Majesty the Queen v. Jim A. McClurg*, 91 DTC 5001 (SCC); *Her Majesty the Queen v. Melville Neuman*, 96 DTC 6464 (FCA)

In its decision on the case of *Neuman v. The Queen*, the Supreme Court of Canada held that subsection 56(2) did not apply to the dividend income received by Neuman's wife. This decision established that there is no requirement for the shareholder to make a business contribution to the corporation in order to earn the dividend. Dividends are paid to shareholders simply as a return on their investment in the corporation, not as compensation for work done for the corporation. This conclusion clarifies the uncertainty left by the McClurg case on the issue.

Cases: *Melville Neuman v. Her Majesty the Queen*, 98 DTC 6297 (SCC)

¶9,055 Restrictive Covenants

Overview

The provisions on restrictive covenants set out rules with respect to amounts that are received or receivable in respect of a restrictive covenant.

ITA: 56.4 Restrictive Covenants

The term "restrictive covenant" is defined to mean an arrangement, an undertaking, or a waiver of a right or advantage that affects, in any way, the acquisition or provision of property or services by the taxpayer or someone not dealing at arm's length with the taxpayer. An example of a restrictive covenant is a payment as part of an agreement to limit services of a business to a certain geographical area.

ITA: 56.4(1) restrictive covenant

[6] For a more detailed analysis of this provision, see Robert E. Beam and Stanley N. Laiken, "Recent Developments on Subsection 56(2): Indirect Payments", Personal Tax Planning Feature (1995), vol. 43, no. 2, *Canadian Tax Journal*, pp. 447–469.

The starting point is to include in income the total of all amounts received or receivable by the taxpayer, or non-arm's length person, in respect of a restrictive covenant.

ITA: 56.4(2) Income — restrictive covenants

A deduction is provided for a bad debt if the amount was previously included in income as a payment for a restrictive covenant. Section 68 addresses the allocation of amounts between restrictive covenants and the other property being disposed of.

ITA: 56.4 Restrictive Covenants, 60(f) Restrictive covenant — bad debt

Generally, amounts received for restrictive covenants are included in income. The exceptions are for those amounts that are included in income somewhere else. The following are the three items that are not taxed as restrictive covenants because they are taxed elsewhere.

ITA: 56.4(2) Income — restrictive covenants, 56.4(3) Non-application of subsection (2)

¶9,055.10 Employment Income

The restrictive covenant inclusion rule will not apply if the amount is included in employment income or will be included when received. This might be the case where an employee leaves and is paid an amount not to work for a competitor. In this case there may not be any shares or assets sold that might cause part of the payments to be allocated in a different way. While employment income is normally taxed on the received basis, if the employee agreed to the covenant more than 36 months before the end of the taxation year, then the payments for the restrictive covenant may be included in employment income even though it is not actually received.

ITA: 56.4(3)(a); 6(3.1) Amount receivable for covenant

¶9,055.30 Proceeds of Disposition

The restrictive covenant inclusion rule will not apply to the extent that the amount is added to the proceeds of disposition of an "eligible interest". An "eligible interest" is capital property that is a partnership interest or a share of a corporation where the partnership or the corporation is carrying on a business. This might occur where the share or the partnership interest is disposed of and the shareholder or partner enters into a restrictive covenant. For this to be the case, the following conditions must be met:

ITA: 56.4(3)(c)

- the amount must directly relate to the taxpayer's disposition of an "eligible interest";

ITA: 56.4(1) eligible interest

- the disposition of the "eligible interest" must be to the purchaser of the restrictive covenant;
- the amount received or receivable must be consideration for an undertaking not to compete with the purchaser;
- the amount cannot exceed the amount determined by a formula;
- the amount is included in the proceeds of disposition of the "eligible interest"; and
- the taxpayer and the purchaser of the restrictive covenant have elected to apply this exception.

¶9,055.40 Schematic of the System for Restrictive Covenants

Figure 9-1 illustrates how section 56.4 fits into the taxation of restrictive covenant

Figure 9-1
Restrictive Covenants

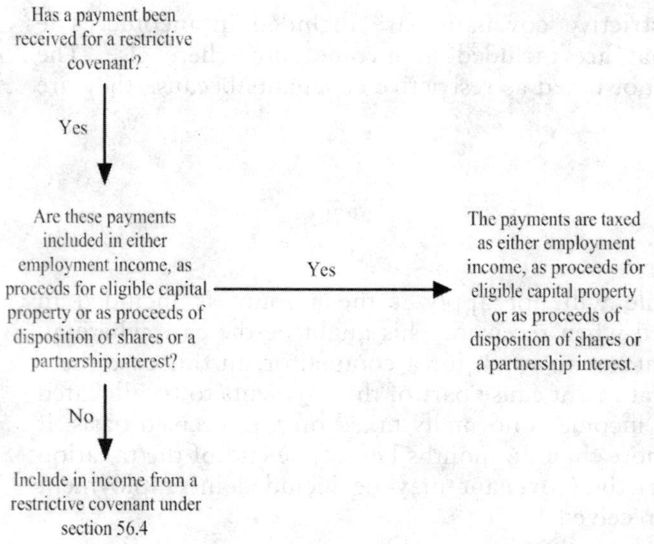
Has a payment been received for a restrictive covenant?
Yes
Are these payments included in either employment income, as proceeds for eligible capital property or as proceeds of disposition of shares or a partnership interest?
Yes
The payments are taxed as either employment income, as proceeds for eligible capital property or as proceeds of disposition of shares or a partnership interest.
No
Include in income from a restrictive covenant under section 56.4

¶9,060 Other Inclusions

In addition to those discussed in detail above, the Act requires the following amounts to be included in income:

ITA: 56(1)(l) Legal expenses

- Amounts received as legal costs awarded by a court on an appeal from an assessment of any tax, interest or penalties, as well as any reimbursement of costs received as a result of decisions under the *Employment Insurance Act* or *Canada Pension Plan*. These receipts are included if the expenses incurred are deducted or deductible. (See ¶9,220.)

ITA: 60(o) Legal expenses

- Amounts received as an award or reimbursement of legal expenses paid to collect or establish a right to a retiring allowance or benefits under a pension plan. The legal fees paid are deductible. (See ¶9,225.) A similar system is in place with respect to legal fees paid to collect or establish a right to salary or wages and other amounts that would be included in employment income. Reimbursements and awards of such costs are included in employment income and expenses are deductible from employment income. Excluded are legal expenses relating to a division or settlement of property arising from a marriage or other conjugal relationship. These legal fees are generally not deductible.

ITA: 56(1)(l.1) Idem; 60(0.1); 6(1)(j) Reimbursements and awards, 8(1)(b) Legal expenses of employee

- Amounts received as social assistance payments are included in income and, if the recipient is married, the amount received must be included by the spouse with the higher income.

ITA: 56(1)(u) Social assistance payments, 56(1)(v) Workers' compensation

- Amounts received as Workers' Compensation.

¶9,090 Pause and Reflect — Summary of Learning Goals

After working through this section, ¶9,000, you should be able to:

- Understand how pension income is taxed.
- Understand the pension splitting rules for pension and CPP income to minimize tax payable.
- Calculate the taxable portion of an annuity.
- Know how contributions and withdrawals from RESP and RDSP programs affect the calculation of net income for tax purposes.
- Explain the benefits of contributing to an RESP or RDSP.
- Understand the difference in tax treatment for spousal support and child support.

¶9,090.99 Practise What You've Learned

Refer to the following sections of the Study Guide to practise what you've learned:

¶9,800 — Review Questions

- Question 1 Termination of Employment
- Question 2 Termination of Employment
- Question 3 Support Receipts and Employments
- Question 4 Support Receipts and Employments

¶9,825 — Multiple Choice Questions

- Question 1 Termination of Employment

¶9,850 — Exercises

- Exercise 5 Termination of Employment

¶9,100 Amounts Not Included in Computing Income and Exempt Entities

Overview

The Act lists a number of specific types of income that would ordinarily have to be included in income subject to tax, but are excluded from the computation of income. Note the very limited scope of these exclusions each of which meets a specific problem area. ITA: 81 Amounts not included in income

¶9,110 Specific Examples

The more common components of this section are summarized below:

- amounts exempted by other federal statutes or foreign tax agreements;
- certain pension or other payments related to war services;
- war service pensions of a country which has reciprocal arrangements with Canada;
- compensation by the Federal Republic of Germany, for war victims;
- income and capital gains from personal injury award property for individuals under 21 years of age;
- social assistance payments based on a needs test;
- payments out of a profit sharing plan;
- expense allowances of elected municipal officers and members of provincial legislature;
- allowance for or reimbursement of part-time employment travel expenses (see Chapter 3 for a detailed discussion of this provision); and
- the first $1,000 of amounts received by an individual for work as a volunteer as an ambulance technician, a firefighter, or a search and rescue assistant, except in the case where a claim is made for the Volunteer Firefighter Tax Credit or the Search and Rescue Volunteer Tax Credit.

ITA: 81(1)(a) Statutory exemptions

ITA: 81(1)(d) Service pension, allowance or compensation

ITA: 81(1)(e) War pensions

ITA: 81(1)(g) Compensation by Federal Republic of Germany

ITA: 81(1)(g.1) Income from personal injury award property, 81(1)(g.2) Income from income exempt under para. (g .1)

ITA: 81(1)(h) Social assistance

ITA: 81(1)(k) Employees profit sharing plan

ITA: 81(2) M.L.A.'s expense allowance, 81(3) Municipal officers' expense allowance

ITA: 81(3.1) Travel expenses

ITA: 81(4) Payments for volunteer services; 118.06 [Volunteer firefighter tax credit], 118.07 [Search and rescue volunteers tax credit]

¶9,120 Tax-Free Savings Account (TFSA)

The tax-free savings account (TFSA) allows Canadian resident individuals who are 18 years of age and older to earn investment income, including interest, dividends, and capital gains, on a tax-free basis. Contributions to the TFSA are not deductible, but the income in the account is not taxed while in the account or upon withdrawal.

ITA: 146.2 [Tax-free savings accounts]

The following are the contribution limits for a TFSA:

ITA: 207.01 [Interpretation]

	Annual	Cumulative
2009–2012	$5,000	$20,000
2013–2014	5,500	31,000
2015	10,000	41,000
2016–2018	5,500	57,500

(indexed to inflation and rounded to the nearest $500)

Unused contribution room can be carried forward indefinitely. Withdrawals from the account add to the contribution room to allow individuals who access their TFSA savings the ability to recontribute an equivalent amount in the future. However, a recontribution made earlier than January 1st of the year following the year of withdrawal may give rise to an excess contribution. For example, assume Javid had no contribution room from previous years and that he made his $5,500 contribution for 2018 in January. If he withdrew his contribution in July and then recontributed it in October, he would have made an $11,000 contribution in 2018 when he is only allowed $5,500, thus, giving rise to an overcontribution of $5,500. Excess contributions are subject to a tax of 1% per month.

ITA: 207.02 Tax payable on excess TFSA amount

A TFSA is generally permitted to hold the same investments as an RRSP. However, it is not able to hold investments in any entities with which the holder does not deal at arm's length.

Interest on money borrowed to invest in a TFSA is not deductible since the income is not taxable.

ITA: 18(11) Limitation

The attribution rules do not apply to income earned in a TFSA which allows individuals to take advantage of contributions from their spouse or common-law partner.

ITA: 74.5(12) Where ss. 74.1 to 74.3 do not apply

Upon the death of the taxpayer, the TFSA generally loses its tax-exempt status. However, if the beneficiary is a surviving spouse, then the TFSA can be transferred to the surviving spouse and retain its tax-free status. Special rules also deal with marital breakdowns.

ITA: 207.01(2) Exempt contribution to survivor TFSA

¶9,130 Exempt Entities

The following are some of the entities that are not taxable under Part I of the Act:

- municipal authorities;
- Crown corporations, commissions, or associations;
- an agricultural organization, board of trade, or chamber of commerce;
- registered charities;
- non-profit corporations for scientific research and experimental development;
- labour organizations;
- non-profit clubs, societies, or associations that are not charities but are organized and operated for purposes such as social welfare, civic improvement, or recreation;
- pension trusts and corporations;
- trusts under a registered retirement savings plan or a deferred profit sharing plan;
- registered education savings plans; and
- registered retirement income funds.

Note that these entities involve government and not-for-profit organizations, which should not have income to be taxed, and retirement savings plans (and similar plans), which are designed to shelter income from tax.

¶9,140 Canada Child Benefit

The Canada Child Benefit (CCB) provides a non-taxable monthly payment to eligible families. The purpose of the benefit is to provide financial support for low and middle income families with children. The benefit began in July 2016 and replaced the Canada Child Tax Benefit and the Universal Child Care Benefit and coincided with the removal of the child fitness and arts credits.

The CRA provides a very helpful tool for calculating the Canada child benefit that can be found at: http://www.cra-arc.gc.ca/bnfts/clcltr/cfbc-eng.html.

¶9,190 Pause and Reflect — Summary of Learning Goals

After working through this section, ¶9,100, you should be able to:

- Understand the tax implications of contributing to, saving through, and removing funds from a Tax Free Savings Account;
- Understand the tax implications of the Canada Child Benefit; and
- Calculate the Canada Child Benefit Received.

¶9,200 Deductions in Computing Income

Overview

Subdivision (e) deals with deductions which are permitted but which are not attributed to a particular source of income like employment, business, property, or capital gains. This concept of a source is important because most deductions under Division B must be for expenditures incurred in order to earn specific types of income. However, this set of deductions applies to items which do not necessarily earn income themselves, such as tuition fees, alimony, etc.

ITA: 4(2) Idem

These deductions include:

- the capital element of annuity payments (discussed in ¶9,015);
- overpayments included in income;
- fees related to objections and appeals;
- legal fees to establish a right;
- OAS clawbacks;
- moving expenses;
- child care expenses;
- disability support deductions; and
- registered retirement savings plan (RRSP) contributions (discussed in ¶9,350).

¶9,210 Overpayments Included in Income

The Act permits the deduction of certain overpayments of receipts which have already been included in income, but to which the taxpayer was not entitled, and, hence, must repay (e.g., pension benefits, unemployment insurance, and education assistance payments).

ITA: 60(n) Repayment of pension or benefits, 60(q) Refund of income payments, 60(v.1) UI and EI benefit repayment

¶9,220 Objections and Appeals

Also, deductible are amounts paid in the year in respect of fees or expenses incurred in an objection or appeal under the Act and other specified legislation. The expenditures that are deductible could include accounting fees incurred in the preparation of an objection or appeal as well as legal costs.

ITA: 60(o) Legal expenses

¶9,225 Legal Fees To Establish a Right

Legal expenses paid by the taxpayer to collect or establish a right to a retiring allowance or pension benefits are deductible. The deduction of legal expenses is limited to the amount of retiring allowance or pension benefits at issue, net of any transfers of a retiring allowance to an RRSP or RPP. Excess legal expenses can be carried forward seven years to be deducted against related retiring allowance or pension benefits in those years.

ITA: 60(o.1) Idem, 60(j.1) Transfer of retiring allowances

¶9,230 OAS Clawback

A deduction is permitted for the amount of Old Age Security (OAS) benefits that a taxpayer must repay under the clawback provision of the Act. Where an individual's income under Division B, before deducting the clawback, exceeds $75,910 in 2018, all or some part of the Old Age Security benefits are taxed back. The amount of repayment is computed as:

ITA: 60(w) Tax under Part I.2, 180.2 Tax on Old Age Security Benefits

The lesser of:

(a)	OAS benefits		$xxx
(b)	income under Division B without par. 60(w) deduction	$ xxx	
	Less:	75,910	
	Excess, if any	$ xxx	
	15% of excess, if any		$xxx

Maximum OAS benefits are currently about $7,040 per year. Therefore, a Division B income of $80,000 (before the clawback deduction) would result in a clawback of $614 (i.e., 15% of ($80,000 - $75,910)). Since $614 of the benefits must be repaid as a special tax, the clawback is allowed as a deduction. In essence, the deduction equates net income effects with cash effects as follows:

ITA: 60(w) Tax under Part I.2; Part I.2 Tax on Old Age Security Benefits, 180.2 Tax on Old Age Security Benefits

	Income effect	Cash effect
Receipt	$7,040	$7,040
Clawback (Part I.2 tax)	(614)	(614)
Net effect	$6,426	$6,426

ITA: 146.01 [Home buyers' plan]

ITA: 60(w) Tax under Part I.2

¶9,240 Moving Expenses

Overview

The Act allows for deduction of certain expenses related to moving if the purpose of the move was related to work or to attend university, college or other post-secondary educational institution. The detailed rules are discussed below.

¶9,240.10 Deductible Expenditures

Taxpayers are permitted to deduct the moving expenses in respect of an eligible relocation under certain prescribed limitations imposed by the Act.

These deductible expenses include:

(a) reasonable travelling costs in moving the family members to the new residence;

(b) transporting or storing household effects;

(c) the cost of meals and accommodation near the old residence or an acquired new residence for a period not exceeding 15 days;

(d) lease cancellation costs in respect of the old residence;

(e) selling costs of the old residence;

(f) the cost of legal services, transfer taxes, or registration taxes, but not goods and services tax, in respect of the new residence but only where the old residence is being sold;

(g) mortgage interest, property taxes, insurance premiums, and costs associated with maintaining heat and power, to a maximum of $5,000, payable in respect of a vacant "old residence" for a period during which reasonable efforts are being made to sell the "old residence"; and

(h) the cost of revising legal documents to reflect the taxpayer's new address, replacing driving licenses and automobile permits and obtaining utility connections and disconnections.

Note that selling costs of the old residence may be deducted as moving costs or as selling cost of capital gains purpose.

ITA: 62(3) Definition of "moving expenses", 248(1) moving expenses

¶9,240.20 Flat-Rate Deductions by Administrative Practice

By administrative CRA practice, taxpayers may choose a simplified method to calculate certain travel expenses for moving. Instead of substantiating actual expenses by receipts, the taxpayer may use various pre-established flat rates. Individuals may claim a flat rate of $17 a meal, to a maximum of $51 per day, per person, without receipts. An individual may determine the deduction for vehicle expenses by multiplying the number of kilometres driven by the flat rate in the following list for the province or territory from which travel begins:

Province or Territory	2017 Cents/km[1]
Alberta	45.0
British Columbia	50.0
Manitoba	47.0
New Brunswick	50.5
Newfoundland and Labrador	54.0
Northwest Territories	59.5

Province or Territory	2017 Cents/km[1]
Nova Scotia	50.0
Nunavut	58.5
Ontario	55.5
Prince Edward Island	49.0
Quebec	50.5
Saskatchewan	46.0
Yukon	60.5

[1] www.cra.gc.ca/travelcosts — 2018 rates will be available on the CRA website in 2019.

Vehicle expenses covered by the flat rate include operating and ownership expenses as follows:

- operating expenses: fuel, oil, tires, licence fees, insurance, maintenance, and repairs; and
- ownership expenses: depreciation, provincial tax and finance charges.

¶9,240.30 Eligible Relocation

There are two distinct categories of taxpayers contained in the definition of "eligible relocation": ITA: 248(1) eligible relocation

(1) taxpayers who move within Canada, normally, to carry on business or be employed in Canada may deduct their moving expenses from that business or employment income; or

(2) students who move to attend a post-secondary institution on a full-time basis either in or out of Canada may deduct their moving expenses from student income. ITA: 62(2) Moving expenses of students

There are a number of specific limitations imposed upon the above two groups of taxpayers. The following are the most important:

(1) the taxpayer must move 40 kilometres (measured by the shortest normal route available to the travelling public)[7] closer (as discussed in Chapter 3, under the heading "Housing Loss and Housing Cost Benefits") to his or her work location or post-secondary institution;

(2) moving expenses, which exceed the income from the work location in the year of move, can be deducted, in any following year, against income from that new work location; and ITA: 248(28) Limitation respecting inclusions, deductions and tax credits

[7] The case of *Giannakopoulos v. The Queen*, 95 DTC 5477 (F.C.A.), appears to have established this method of measurement of the 40 kilometres.

(3) the taxpayer cannot be reimbursed by or be in receipt of an allowance from his or her employer for the moving expenses he or she is claiming, unless the reimbursement or allowance is included in income.

There has been some debate about how soon a move needs to take place after the change in employment location. Court cases have determined that there is no requirement that the work location be a new one at the time of the move and that there is no time period by which the taxpayer must move after a change in his or her work location.

Cases: *Beaudoin v. The Queen*, 2005 DTC 282 (TCC) *Wunderlich v. The Queen*, 2012 DTC 1040 (TCC) *Dierckens v. The Queen*, 2011 DTC 1136 (TCC)

The income limitation on moving expenses may not be clear in its application to the situation of an individual who fits both categories of taxpayer recognized in paragraph (*a*) of the definition of "eligible relocation". For example, a full-time student who moves to a university over 40 kilometres away may have both income from a research grant and part-time employment income from outside of the educational institution in the new location. The provision limits the *aggregate* of moving expenses,

ITA: 62(1)(c), 248(1) eligible relocation

(1) in the case of an employee or self-employed individual, to income from employment or business in the new location, *and*

(2) in the case of a full-time student, to income from a research grant.

The use of the word "and" between cases (1) and (2), above, may allow a deduction of moving expenses from the sum of both categories of income in the case of the student, as presented. The relevant Income Tax Folio (S1-F3-C4, par. 14.10) provides clarification that students that carry out an eligible relocation to be a full-time student and be employed may deduct moving expenses up to their income for the year from both educational and employment sources at the new location.

Income Tax Folio: S1-F3-C4 Moving Expenses

Also, it appears under common law that the actual move does not have to be accomplished in the same year as the change in the work location.

Example Problem 9-1

In October of last year, Kenzo moved from his rented Vancouver townhouse to his new home in Halifax to commence a sales position with a life insurance company. After training and client development time, his earnings from this new position were $3,000 for the year, but they were expected to increase as he developed his client base. As a result of his move, Kenzo incurred the following expenses:

Lease cancellation payments on his Vancouver townhouse	$1,000
Commissions and legal fees to acquire a new home	6,000
Moving van	3,800
Flight and five days' accommodation in Halifax	2,400
Shipping his car.	850

REQUIRED

What are the income tax consequences of the move for Kenzo?

SOLUTION

- Subject to the new work location income test, Kenzo can claim all of the moving costs, except for the $6,000 pertaining to the acquisition of his Halifax home. Those costs do not qualify, since he did not own (and, hence, sell) his Vancouver townhouse.
- While Kenzo can only claim $3,000 in moving expenses for last year, the excess can be carried forward to the next year.

¶9,240.90 Pause and Reflect — Summary of Learning Goals

After working through this section, ¶9,240, you should be able to:

- Identify moving expenses eligible to be deducted from net income for tax purposes.
- Apply your knowledge of the tax rules for moving expenses to calculate the appropriate tax deduction.

¶9,250 Child Care Expenses

Overview

The Act allows for the deduction of certain expenses related to child care if the purpose of the child care was to allow the parent to earn income and in some circumstances to attend school. The expenses are capped by a statutory limit. The details of the deduction are discussed below.

Income Tax Folio: S1-F3-C1 Child Care Expense Deduction

¶9,250.10 Eligibility

Child care expenses are permitted to be deducted in the same year that the taxpayer incurs these expenses in the process of earning income. Note that these provisions restrict the deduction to the parent or supporting individual with the lower income, except during a period where that individual is:

- a student in full-time or part-time attendance at a designated educational institution or a secondary school in Canada; ITA: 63(2)(b)(i)(A)
- infirm and incapable of caring for children for at least two weeks; ITA: 63(2)(b)(i)(B)
- confined to prison for at least two weeks; or ITA: 63(2)(b)(i)(C)
- living apart from the higher-income taxpayer throughout a period of at least 90 days commencing in the year due to a marital or common-law relationship breakdown. ITA: 63(2)(b)(i)(D)

Income for this purpose is determined to be the income before the child care expense deduction and the deduction for the clawback of certain social assistance payments like OAS. Where the incomes of two taxpayers are equal, the individuals must agree to treat the income of one of them as higher.

ITA: 63(2) Income exceeding income of supporting person, 63(2.1) Taxpayer and supporting person with equal incomes; 60(w) Tax under Part I.2

Important Child Care Cases

The case of *Fiset v. M.N.R.*, successfully challenged the above interpretation. In this particular situation, the Tax Court of Canada determined that since one spouse had no income and since nil is not an amount (of income), the provision could not be applied. However, section 3 was amended subsequently so that no income is zero amount, not nil. Therefore, a taxpayer with no income will have a zero "amount".

Cases: *Normand Fiset v. The Minister of National Revenue*, 88 DTC 1226 (TCC)

Another interesting judicial development involving child care expenses is the case of

Symes v. The Queen et al. In this case, the self-employed taxpayer claimed the expenses as a business expense rather than a child care expense. The CRA had denied the expenses as personal living expenses. The taxpayer also argued that there was a violation of rights under subsection 15(1) of the Canadian *Charter of Rights and Freedoms*. The Supreme Court of Canada held that the language of the child care expense deduction provision specifically encompasses the purpose for which the taxpayer had incurred her nanny expenses. As a result, the business expense deduction provisions could not be interpreted to permit her a child care business expense deduction. Furthermore, the taxpayer failed to show that women disproportionately pay child care expenses, to prove that the child care expense deduction provision violates subsection 15(1) of the Charter. The taxpayer's evidence showed only that women disproportionately bear the responsibility for caring for children in society.

ITA: 62 Moving expenses; 9 Income, 18(1)(a) General limitation, 18(1)(h) Personal and living expenses

¶9,250.20 Limitations

There are several additional restrictions which should be noted:

- an eligible child includes a child who turned 16 years of age during the year, since he or she was "during the year" under 16 years of age;

ITA: 63(3) eligible child

- the payments cannot be made to certain individuals listed under paragraph (*b*) of the definition of "child care expense", including persons under 18 years of age who are related to the taxpayer by blood, marriage or adoption and a person claimed as a dependant;

ITA: 63(3) child care expense, 251(6) Blood relationship, etc, 118 Personal credits

- the maximum amounts in 2018 are:

ITA: 63(3) annual child care expense amount

  - for each child who has a severe and prolonged mental or physical impairment — $275 (i.e., 1/40 of $11,000) per week,
  - for each child who is under the age of seven at the end of the year — $200 (i.e., 1/20 of $8,000) per week,
  - for any other eligible child — $125 (i.e., 1/40 of $5,000) per week;

ITA: 63(2.3) Amount deductible, 63(3) annual child care expense amount

- earned income, which is one of the limiting factors in determining the child care deduction, is defined very specifically (***note the difference between this definition*** *and the "earned income" definition for a registered retirement savings plan*). This definition of earned income reflects the original purpose of the child care expense deduction provision which was to encourage individuals who had to care for young children to enter the workforce as employees, to carry on a business, to carry on research under a grant, or attend an educational institution to upgrade work skills and knowledge; and

ITA: 63(3) earned income, 248(1) salary or wages; 146(1) earned income

- expenses must be substantiated by receipts bearing the social insurance number of the person performing the service.

ITA: 63(1) Child care expenses

¶9,250.30 Deduction Calculation

The following formulae reflect the maximum child care deduction.

The Lower-Income Spouse

ITA: 63(1) Child care expenses

The deduction is restricted to the least of:

(1) generally, an amount paid in the year by the taxpayer or supporting person;[8]

ITA: 63(1)(a)

(2) $5,000 for each eligible child seven years of age or older, $8,000 for each eligible child under age seven at the end of the year and $11,000 for each child who has a severe and prolonged mental or physical impairment; and

ITA: 63(3) annual child care expense amount

(3) ⅔ of the earned income of the taxpayer as defined

ITA: 63(2.3)(e), 63(3) Definitions

minus the amount deducted by the higher-income spouse below.

ITA: 63(2.3)(e), 63(3) Definitions

The Higher-Income Spouse

ITA: 63(2)(b)

The higher-income spouse is restricted to a deduction of the lesser of:

(1) the least of (1),[9] (2) and (3) described above and computed using the earned income of the higher-income supporting person; and

(2) the sum of:

(a) $275 (i.e., 1/40 of $11,000) times the number of children who have a severe and prolonged mental or physical impairment,

(b) $200 (i.e., 1/40 of $8,000) times the number of children under seven years of age at the end of the year, and

(c) $125 (i.e, 1/40 of $5,000) times the number of the other eligible children

times the number of weeks the lower-income spouse was a student, was incapable of caring for the children because of mental or physical infirmity, was in prison, or was living separate because of a breakdown of the marriage or common-law partnership.

ITA: 63(2)(b)

For the lower-income spouse to be considered a student, he or she must be a full-time student; that is, one who is enrolled in a program of not less than three consecutive weeks duration that requires not less than 10 hours per week on courses or work. The dollar limit on the deduction that may be claimed by the working spouse when the other spouse

---

[8] A "supporting person" is defined in subsection 63(3). However, where the taxpayer is the higher-income spouse, the payments made by a supporting person and deductible by the taxpayer are restricted by, and do not include, those payments made by a person living separate and apart from the taxpayer for a period of at least 90 days due to marital or common-law relationship breakdown.

[9] Paragraph 63(1)(*c*) excludes, from the deductible amount paid, amounts used in computing a child care deduction of another individual.

is a part-time student, described in subparagraph (ii) of the definition of factor C, is, also, $200 (i.e., 1/40 of $8,000) per child under age 7 and $125 (i.e., 1/40 of $5,000) per child age 7 to 16. However in the case of a part-time student, the limit is computed for each month or part-month of studies during which child care expenses are incurred. Months are counted where the part-time student is enrolled at an educational institution in Canada in an eligible program lasting at least three consecutive weeks and involving a minimum of 12 hours spent on courses each month.

ITA: 63(2)(b)

Ⓐ ¶9,250.40 Encouragement for Parent To Attend School

The legislation provides a child care expense deduction to single parents in full-time or part-time attendance at either a designated educational institution or a secondary school in Canada and to two-parent families when both parents are in full-time attendance in school at the same time. Full-time attendance is defined, for that purpose, as enrolment in a program of at least three consecutive weeks duration that requires the individual to spend at least 10 hours per week on courses or work in the program. Part-time attendance is defined as enrolment in a program of at least three consecutive weeks duration that requires the individual to spend not less than 12 hours per month on courses in the program. The limits of the deduction are the amounts paid in respect of child care to a maximum of $275 (i.e., 1/40 × $11,000) per week of attendance per child who has a severe and prolonged mental or physical infirmity, $200 (i.e., 1/40 of $8,000) per week of attendance per child under 7 at the end of the year and $125 (i.e., 1/40 of $5,000) per week of attendance per child over age 6 and under age 16 at any time during the year. The income limit for this deduction is based on all amounts included in computing the individual's Division B income for the year, not just earned income.

ITA: 63(2.2) Expenses while at school, 63(2.3) Amount deductible; 63(2.2)(a)(i); 63(2.2)(a)(ii); 63(2.3)(b)

¶9,250.50 Application

Example Problem 9-2

Evan and Mary are married. The cost of child care expenses for three eligible children (ages 4, 5, and 9) was $225 per week for 52 weeks.

Evan's earned income	$45,000
Mary's earned income	12,000

Mary was determined to be physically infirm by a qualified medical practitioner and she was confined to bed for a period of 10 weeks.

REQUIRED

Compute the child care expense deduction under section 63 for 2018.

SOLUTION

Since the lower-income spouse (Mary) is infirm and incapable of caring for children for at least two weeks in the year, it is possible for the higher-income spouse (Evan) to claim a deduction for part of the child care expenses as demonstrated below.

Evan's child care deduction is the lesser of:

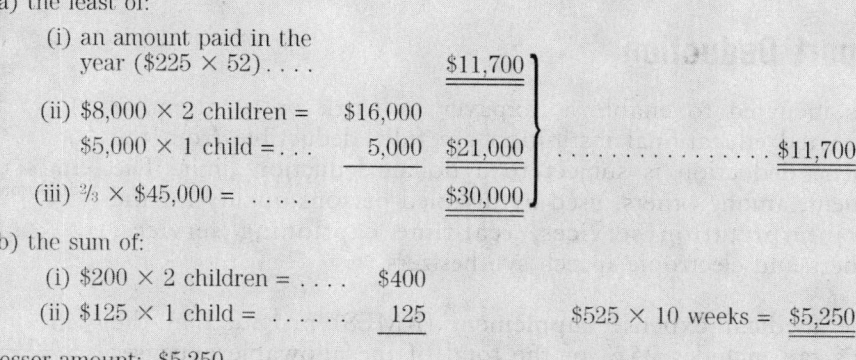

(a) the least of:			
(i) an amount paid in the year ($225 × 52)		$11,700	
(ii) $8,000 × 2 children =	$16,000		
$5,000 × 1 child = . . .	5,000	$21,000	. . . . $11,700
(iii) ⅔ × $45,000 = ...		$30,000	
(b) the sum of:			
(i) $200 × 2 children = ...	$400		
(ii) $125 × 1 child = ...	125	$525 × 10 weeks =	$5,250
Lesser amount: $5,250			

Mary's child care deduction is the least of:

(i) ($225 × 52 weeks) = ...	$11,700	
(ii) ($8,000 × 2 children) + ($5,000 × 1 child) = ...	$21,000	$8,000
(iii) (⅔ × $12,000) = ...	$ 8,000	
minus the amount deducted by Spouse A		5,250
		$2,750

Therefore, the sum of both spouses' claim ($5,250 + $2,750) is limited, in this case, to the $8,000 amount which is ⅔ of the lower-income spouse's earned income. The computational format used above is similar to that found in form T778. The format simplifies the effect on the calculation, which might otherwise require that the amount used in part (a)(i) of Evan's deduction calculation be determined as the minimum amount after all other parts of the calculation, so that only the $5,250 amount actually deductible by Evan is shown in part (a)(i). This follows from a possible strict interpretation of the rule, which would not permit Mary to deduct an amount that is "included in computing the amount deductible" by Evan, in this case. Technically, the full $11,700 used in part (a)(i) of Evan's calculation was included in computing the amount deductible by Mary. The simplified calculation used in the example problem, above, arrives at the correct distribution between Evan and Mary and is apparently acceptable evidenced by the computational format used in the authorized form, T778.

ITA: 63(1)(c)

¶9,250.90 Pause and Reflect — Summary of Learning Goals

After working through this section, ¶9,250, you should be able to:

- Identify child care expenses eligible to be deducted from net income for tax purposes.
- Apply your knowledge of the tax rules for child care expenses to calculate the appropriate tax deduction.

¶9,260 Disability Support Deduction

Disability support expenses incurred to enable a taxpayer to work or to attend a secondary school or a designated educational institution are fully deductible from the disabled person's income. The deduction is subject to a dollar deduction limit. The following services or equipment, among others, used by disabled persons qualify for the deduction: sign-language interpretation services, real-time captioning services, teletypewriters, optical scanners and electronic speech synthesizers.

ITA: 64 Disability supports deduction

In addition, the refundable medical expense supplement (RMES) provided in the calculation of an individual's tax includes 25% of the total of the allowable expenses claimed under the non-refundable medical expense tax credit and the new disability supports deduction. For details on this supplement, please refer to Chapter 10.

ITA: 122.51 [Refundable medical expense supplement]

An individual, who has a specified impairment in physical or mental function, such as speech, hearing, eyesight or learning or who has a severe and prolonged mental or physical impairment and who qualifies for the impairment credit, may deduct expenses paid to an unrelated attendant, who is at least 18 years of age, to enable the individual to work as an employee, carry on a business, carry on research, or attend a designated educational institution or a secondary school at which the individual is enrolled in an educational program. The deduction for disability support is limited to the lesser of:

ITA: 118.3 Credit for mental or physical impairment; 64 Disability supports deduction

(a) the amount paid in the year to the attendant, net of any reimbursement; and

(b) the sum of:

(i) the total of:

(A) employment income inclusions or the taxable portion, if any, of scholarships and bursaries or net research grants, or

(B) income from business, and

(ii) where the taxpayer is a student, the least of:

(A) $15,000,

(B) $375 times the number of weeks in the year during which the individual attends the institution or school, and

(C) the amount by which the individual's total income exceeds the individual's income, that is income aggregated in (b)(i), above.

Example Problem 9-3

Donalda was employed in the year for six months and attended school the other six months (i.e., 26 weeks). She requires the full-time care of an attendant. Her income for the year consisted of employment income inclusions of $12,000 and interest income of $2,000.

REQUIRED

What is the maximum that Donalda can claim for the attendant care deduction?

SOLUTION

To obtain the maximum deduction, the amount paid to the attendant cannot exceed:

The sum of:

(a) The total of:			
Employment income inclusions		$ 12,000	
Income from business		Nil	$ 12,000
(b) The least of:			
Dollar amount			$ 15,000
$375 × weeks of school attendance ($375 × 26)		$ 9,750	
Total income	$ 14,000		
Less: income in (a), above	12,000	$ 2,000	2,000
Total deduction			$ 14,000

¶9,270 Expenses of Residents Absent From Canada

The Act extends the deductibility of child care expenses and disability support expenses to an individual who is absent from, but still resident in, Canada. Such an individual, who is physically absent from Canada throughout all or some part of a taxation year, would otherwise be precluded from these deductions for expenditures made outside of Canada by the wording contained in the child care and disability support deduction provisions. This additional provision to extend deductibility is an apparent reaction to the strict interpretation of the child care expense and disability support deduction provisions taken by the courts in cases involving members of the Canadian Armed Forces. The provision appears to be directed to individuals who are physically absent from Canada for most of a year, but are deemed to be resident. However, the wording of the provision would also

ITA: 63 Child care expenses, 64 Disability supports deduction, 64.1 Individuals absent from Canada, 250(1) Person deemed resident; 64.1 Individuals absent from Canada

appear to apply to individuals who are considered to be resident by the common law principle of continuing ties to Canada.

¶9,290 Pause and Reflect — Summary of Learning Goals

After working through this section, ¶9,200, you should be able to:

- Explain when moving expenses are deductible and when they are not.
- Apply your knowledge to the calculation of deductible moving expenses.
- Apply your knowledge to the calculation of deductible child care expenses.
- Apply your knowledge to the calculation of disability support deductions.

¶9,290.99 Practise What You've Learned

Refer to the following sections of the Study Guide to practise what you've learned:

¶9,800 — Review Questions

- Question 6 OAS Clawback

¶9,825 — Multiple Choice Questions

- Question 3 Child Care Expenses
- Question 4 Moving Expenses
- Question 6 Moving Expenses

¶9,850 — Exercises

- Exercise 6 Moving Expenses
- Exercise 8 Childcare Expenses

¶9,300 Registered Savings Plans

Overview

There are several basic types of pension plans, and the pension legislation attempts to equalize the tax assistance provided to an individual whether he or she earns retirement income through a defined benefit registered pension plan (DBP), a money purchase registered pension plan (MPP), a deferred profit sharing plan (DPSP), or a registered retirement savings plan (RRSP). Generally, the Act allows for a deduction/exclusion for amounts contributed to a registered savings plan, investment income earned on contributions is tax-free while in the plan, and all amounts are taxed when they are subsequently withdrawn from the plan. The specific details of each type of plan are discussed below.

¶9,310 Harmonization Across Registered Plans

Although the Act, allows for a number of different registered savings plans with the objective of assisting taxpayers with saving for retirement, the Act has several provisions which harmonize policies across these distinct plans in a cohesive system. Specifically the Act attempts:

- to provide equal access to tax assistance regardless of the type of plan with which an individual funds his or her retirement; and
- to provide flexibility in the pension system.

These objectives have been accomplished through the integration of limits for various types of pension plans with the limits for RRSPs.

In order to provide the same amount of tax assistance to an individual for retirement savings, regardless of whether the retirement is funded through a registered pension plan (RPP), a deferred profit sharing plan (DPSP) or an RRSP, under pension reform a comprehensive annual limit for tax-assisted retirement savings is provided — 18% of earned income up to a maximum phased-in dollar limit. The fairly generous contribution limits give individuals an incentive to provide for their retirement years.

¶9,320 Defined Benefit Registered Pension Plans

Under a DBP, *the benefit that is to be paid* to each employee *is defined* usually in regard to a certain percentage of an employee's earnings in the last few years of employment, regardless of the cost to the employer or the earnings experience of the plan. The benefit that is tax-assisted is limited to a maximum. The employer contributions are deductible, provided that they are certified by an actuary to be necessary to fund the accruing benefits of the plan as registered with the CRA. The employee contributions are deductible, subject to a maximum.

The maximum tax-assisted benefit that may be provided to an individual under a defined benefit registered pension plan is 2% per year of the individual's average best three years of remuneration times the number of years of pensionable service, with a phased-in dollar limit. For example, if an individual has pre-retirement earnings of $147,222 in 2018, it would provide for a maximum tax-assisted pension of $103,055 or 70% of the individual's pre-retirement earnings. Assuming that the individual has 35 years of pensionable service, $147,222 × 2% = $2,944 per year, which buys a pension of $103,055, if expended annually over an effective period of 35 years.

The following table summarizes the scheduled increases.

Year	Money Purchase Limit	Maximum Pension Per year of Service	Maximum Pension (35 yrs)	Employment Income Needed
2017	$26,230	$2,914	$102,005	$145,722
2018	$26,500	$2,944*	$103,055	$147,222
2019	indexed	indexed	indexed	indexed

*Rounded to the nearest dollar, unrounded amount was $2,944.44, hence 35 × $2,944.44 = $103,055.40.

¶9,330 Money Purchase Registered Pension Plans

Under an MPP, which is sometimes called a defined contribution plan, *the contribution* that is required by the employer and the employee *is defined* rather than the benefit. The retirement benefit for the individual is acquired through the purchase of an annuity on the open market with the contributions made to the plan plus the earnings generated from those contributions while they are held in the plan. The tax-assisted contributions of both employees and employers are limited to a maximum each year as indicated in the above table in ¶9,330.10.

¶9,340 Deferred Profit Sharing Plans

Under this type of arrangement, only an employer may contribute a limited amount to a plan for the employee, which is based on the performance or the profits of the business. The funds must vest irrevocably in the employee after two years of employment, and the plan may invest in equity shares of the employer if they qualify.

¶9,350 Registered Retirement Savings Plans

Overview

Basically, an RRSP is a tax shelter provided under the Act to give an individual an incentive to save money for his or her retirement years. Within certain limits, the individual can claim tax deductions for contributions to his or her own RRSP, or a spousal RRSP., Income earned on contributions is tax free while in the plan and amounts are taxed when they are subsequently withdrawn from the plan. Certain exceptions exist for the taxation of withdrawals for situations where the amount removed is used for the purchase of a home through a home buyers plan or for educational costs through a lifelong learning plan. Since income can accumulate in the plan on a pre-tax basis, RRSPs can play an important part in an individual's overall retirement and tax planning.

If funds are withdrawn from an RRSP prior to maturity, the proceeds are subject to tax when received, as shown in Figure 9-2. If an RRSP is held until maturity, the accumulated RRSP funds may be received as a lump sum, in which case the funds are included in the individual's income and taxed at his or her marginal rate in the year received. Alternatively, the funds may be used to purchase a retirement annuity or may be transferred to a registered retirement income fund (RRIF). Both of these options would defer the receipt of the funds and, consequently, would defer tax on these funds until received in the form of retirement income. Tax savings will be realized if the funds are received and taxed in years when the individual's marginal tax rate is lower than in his or her pre-retirement years. The effect of the deferral of tax on income accumulating within the shelter can even offset the effect of a higher marginal tax rate on retirement income, making the RRSP shelter very attractive to most investors.

Figure 9-2
Taxation of RRSP Withdrawals

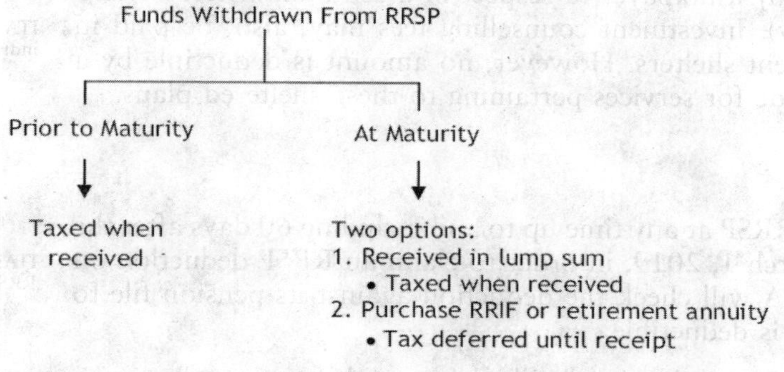

Technically, an RRSP is a contract, accepted for registration by the Minister of National Revenue, between an individual (the annuitant) and an entity that is authorized to carry on the business of selling such contracts (the carrier). RRSPs are available from banks, trust companies, life insurance companies, credit unions, caisses populaires, mutual funds and stockbrokerage firms.

¶9,350.10 Types of RRSPs

In general, the RRSPs available may be categorized into two types, both of which are of a money purchase nature:

- financial institution plans; and
- self-administered plans.

¶9,350.15 Financial Institution Plans

Financial institutions, such as insurance companies, banks, trust companies or credit unions, sponsor plans which are invested in savings deposits, term deposits and guaranteed investment certificates (GICs). They also offer plans which are invested in mutual funds or pooled fund trusts. These funds may be invested in mortgages, bonds, equities, money market instruments or a combination thereof. Some specialized funds are invested in high-risk investments providing venture capital. Others are invested in specific segments of the economy. Although one can select the type of fund for one's RRSP, the underlying investments are selected by the fund manager. Typically, investment management charges are levied against the underlying investment funds rather than the RRSP. However, sales or redemption charges may be applied against the RRSP on purchases or sales of units in the fund.

¶9,350.20 Self-Administered Plans

A self-administered RRSP can be set up with most financial institutions or a stock broker. A trustee will hold and administer the RRSP investments, but the individual can select investments or, if desired, an investment adviser can do it.

A self-administered RRSP can be invested in a wide variety of qualified investments, including publicly traded debt and equity securities, as well as publicly traded warrants or rights to acquire qualified investments. It can also be invested in certain mutual funds, mortgages, Canada Savings Bonds, treasury bills, and strip coupon bonds and certificates.

Often, administration fees are paid by a taxpayer in respect of a self-administered RRSP (or RRIF, as discussed subsequently). Investment counselling fees may, also, be paid in respect of property in these retirement shelters. However, no amount is deductible by a taxpayer in respect of payments made for services pertaining to these sheltered plans.

ITA: 18(1)(u) Fees — individual saving plans

¶9,350.25 Contributions

An individual may contribute to an RRSP at any time up to and including 60 days after the year end, or, for example, until March 1, 2019, in order to claim an RRSP deduction on his or her 2018 tax return. The CRA will check the deduction against its pension file to determine if the RRSP contribution is deductible.

ITA: 146(5) Amount of RRSP premiums deductible

An added advantage of the system is that if an individual is not able to contribute the maximum amount to an RRSP, he or she is allowed to "carry forward" any unused deduction limit. There is no time restriction on the carryforward of an individual's unused RRSP deduction room. This feature is discussed in more detail subsequently.

If funds are borrowed to make contributions to an RRSP (or an RPP or DPSP), interest on the borrowed funds is not deductible. The reason for this denial of an interest deduction is probably that the income from the investments in the sheltered retirement plans is not taxed as long as it remains in the plan.

ITA: 18(11) Limitation

¶9,350.30 Contribution Limits for RRSPs

Using these assumptions, a system has been put in place to determine an individual's RRSP deduction limit and RRSP dollar limit. These annual deduction limits and earned income requirements are defined in subsection 146(1) and are described for 2017 to 2020 in Exhibit 9-1.

Exhibit 9-1 2017 — 2020 Annual RRSP Deduction and Dollar Limits [ssec. 146(1)]

If the individual is:	The annual contribution limit for 2017–2020 is:
• a member of an RPP or a DPSP,	(A) the individual's unused RRSP deduction room carried forward from the previous year
	plus
	(B) the lesser of:
	(i) the RRSP dollar limit (below)
	and
	(ii) 18% of earned income for the prior year

If the individual is:	The annual contribution limit for 2017–2020 is:
	minus
	(C) the pension adjustment for the prior year reported to the CRA by the individual's employer and any past service pension adjustment reported by his or her employer during that particular year.
• a self-employed individual or an individual not described above,	(A) the individual's unused RRSP deduction room carried forward from the previous year
	plus
	(B) the lesser of:
	(i) the RRSP dollar limit (below)
	and
	(ii) 18% of earned income for the prior year.

RRSP Dollar Limits

	2017	2018	2019	2020
RRSP				
RRSP Dollar Limit	$26,010	$26,230	$26,500	indexed
Earned income needed @ 18%	$144,500	$145,722	$147,222	indexed

Employers are to report the pension adjustment (PA) (a measure of the pension benefits an employee is entitled to under an RPP and/or a DPSP) on an employee's T4 slip on or before February 28 of the year following the year in which the benefits accrued. From February to August of that year, the CRA will use the PA reported by the employer plus the prior year's earned income as calculated from the individual's personal tax return to create a pension account for each individual. The CRA will then provide an RRSP contribution limit statement with the taxpayer's Notice of Assessment for the tax return filed. For example, the Notice of Assessment for a taxpayer's 2017 tax return filed by April 30, 2018 will contain a calculation of the RRSP contribution limit for 2018.

The calculation of a taxpayer's RRSP limit requires three important inputs: the RRSP Dollar Limit described above and earned income and pension adjustment described in detail below.

Definition of Earned Income for RRSPs

If an individual was a resident of Canada throughout the year, earned income, as defined, will include the individual's income (for a period in the year throughout which the individual was a resident in Canada) from: ITA: 146(1) earned income

- an office or employment, generally including all taxable benefits, less all employment-related deductions, but not including any deduction for RPP contributions, employee contributions to a retirement compensation arrangement (RCA) or a clergyman's residence;
- a business carried on by the individual either alone, or as a partner actively engaged in the business;
- property, when derived from the rental of real property or from royalties in respect of a work or invention of which the individual was the author or inventor;
- support payments included in computing the individual's income;
- an amount included in income from supplementary unemployment benefit plans, net research grants, and support receipts in computing the individual's income; and
- the amount of disability pension received after 1990 by an individual under the Canada or Quebec Pension Plan;

less the total of the individual's loss or deduction (for a period in the year throughout which the individual was a resident in Canada) from:

- a business carried on by the individual either alone, or as a partner actively engaged in the business;
- property, where the loss is sustained from the rental of real property; and
- support payments deductible in computing the individual's income.

For the purposes of determining the earned income of such an individual, the income or loss of the individual for any period in a taxation year is the individual's income or loss computed as though that period were the whole taxation year.

Note that earned income does not include superannuation or pension benefits (including CPP/QPP and OAS benefits), retiring allowances, Employment Insurance benefits, death benefits, amounts received from an RRSP or taxable benefits from a DPSP or a revoked plan. It also does not include investment income, taxable capital gains, or scholarships and bursaries.

Also note that it is the earned income of the preceding year which is relevant for purposes of calculating the maximum deductible RRSP contribution.

The following chart provides a comparison of what is included in "earned income" for purposes of the RRSP deduction and child care expenses.

	RRSP	Child Care Expenses
Earned income definition	Individual's income from:	Individual's income from:
	• an office or employment, generally including all taxable benefits, less all employment-related deductions, but not including any deduction for RPP contributions, employee contributions to RCA or a clergyman's residence;	• all salaries, wages, and other remuneration and taxable benefits received from office or employment;
	• a business carried on by individual either alone, or as a partner actively engaged in the business;	• a business carried on by individual either alone, or as partner actively engaged in business;
	• property, when derived from rental of real property or from royalties in respect of a work or invention of which the individual was the author or inventor;	
	• support payments included in individual's income;	
	• an amount included in income from supplementary unemployment benefit plans, net research grants, and support receipts; and	• an amount included in income from supplementary unemployment benefit plans and net research grants; and
	• disability pension under CPP or QPP.	• disability pension received under CPP or QPP.

❹ Calculation of the Pension Adjustment (PA)

Since a pension adjustment is reported to the individual by his or her employer on a T4 slip, in most cases it will not be necessary for the individual to calculate his or her PA. To do some advance tax planning for an individual, it may be necessary to get a rough idea of what the individual's PA will be for future years. Conceptually, the PA represents the value of tax-assisted or sheltered benefits accruing to the taxpayer in a year. Hence, it reflects the amount of the dollar limit that has been used by employer and employee contributions to an RPP and/or DPSP, leaving the balance of the dollar limit available for a deductible RRSP contribution.

For example, if an individual's earned income is $72,000 and PA is $11,960, that individual's RRSP contribution would be limited to:

18% of earned income (18% of $72,000)	$12,960
Less: PA	11,960
Net limit for RRSP	$ 1,000

The following provides a non-technical indication of how the PA is determined.

(1) *PA for DBP*: The PA for a DBP is based on a formula which reflects the actuarial assumptions made about contributions providing pension income. The objective of the formula is to quantify the contribution room used by contributions to an RPP. The formula is beyond the scope of this text.

(2) *PA for MPP*: The PA for an MPP is equal to the total of the employer's and the employee's contributions in the year.

(3) *PA for DPSP*: The PA for a DPSP is equal to the employer's contributions in the year.

¶9,350.35 RRSP Contribution Room Carried Forward

An advantage of the system is that if an individual is not able to contribute the maximum amount, he or she is allowed to "carry forward" the unused deduction limit. There is no time restriction on this carryforward. The "unused RRSP deduction room" is a defined term. For example, if an individual's maximum annual RRSP contribution limit in 2013 is $10,000, but he or she made a contribution of only $7,000, he or she will be permitted to make an additional deductible RRSP contribution of $3,000 at any time in the future. However, even if he or she makes up the contribution in, for example, 2018, remember that he or she will lose the tax sheltering on the income that would have been earned on the $3,000 from 2013 until 2018, and on any future income earned on this amount for the balance of his or her career. Therefore, it is important to contribute the maximum to an RRSP as soon as possible.

ITA: 146(1) unused RRSP deduction room

¶9,350.40 Excess Contribution

The penalty provisions for RRSP overcontributions are fairly severe. There is a 1% per month penalty until the "excess" for the year is removed from the plan.

ITA: 204.1(2.1) Tax payable by individuals — contributions after 1990

In determining whether there is an excess, the individual includes all amounts contributed by the individual to the plan (other than specified transfers) and all gifts made to the plan, other than gifts made by the individual's spouse. Overcontributions of premiums in the 60-day grace period after the end of the year usually are not considered to be part of the "excess", since the individual can claim them in the year or in the following year.

In order to avoid the 1% per month penalty, the excess amount may be withdrawn from the plan, but it will be included in the individual's income in the year of receipt. This income can be reduced by an offsetting deduction if it is withdrawn in the year in which the excess was contributed or in the following year. The withdrawal of contributions on a tax-free basis is allowed only where the taxpayer is not deliberately making excess contributions.

ITA: 146(8) Benefits taxable; 146(8.2) Amount deductible

If the excess is not withdrawn in those particular years, but is instead left in the plan, then the individual will include in income this excess contribution when it is eventually withdrawn and yet there will have been no offsetting deduction in any year, resulting in double taxation. It is, therefore, not advisable to leave an excess contribution in an RRSP, as benefits of tax-free compounding in the plan are unlikely to offset the combination of the 1% per month penalty and the double taxation on withdrawal.

¶9,350.45 Additional Contribution

There is a threshold amount for an excess contribution, which has been set at a cumulative amount of $2,000. This means that at any point in time an individual may contribute up to $2,000 in excess of his or her deductible contribution limit without incurring a penalty. The purpose of this excess allowance is to provide a margin of error for inadvertent excess contributions and for the operation of group RRSP arrangements. In a family context, both spouses and common-law partners may contribute an additional $2,000, so that in total $4,000 may be sheltered without penalty. Children who did not attain the age of 18 in the previous year may not make this additional contribution. Individuals who contribute to both their own RRSP and a spousal RRSP may not make an additional contribution of more than $2,000 in total.

ITA: 204.2(1.1) Cumulative excess amount in respect of RRSPs

Even though the individual will not be able to deduct the excess $2,000 contribution for tax purposes as would be the case if it was a regular RRSP contribution, a sum of money could be accumulated using the benefits of tax-free compounding. If, however, the individual makes a maximum deductible contribution every year, when the excess is eventually withdrawn the individual may be subject to double tax, as the funds were not deductible when the contribution was made, but they are taxable when the individual withdraws them. This double tax may be avoided, since the rules provide for an indefinite carry forward of undeducted contributions. If the individual simply reduces the contribution that he or she would otherwise make in a later year (prior to the withdrawal) and claims the additional $2,000 contribution as a deduction under the carry forward provisions, no double tax will result, because all contributions will have been fully deducted.

Even if the individual was not certain that he or she would use the carry forward rules to eliminate double taxation, it may still be advantageous to make additional contribution. Assuming a 10% rate of return and a 50% personal tax rate, if the individual leaves the $2,000 in the RRSP for 15 years or longer, the benefits of tax-free compounding will outweigh the cost of the taxes that must be paid when the funds are withdrawn.

All or part of an individual's additional $2,000 contribution can be made by the individual to a spousal RRSP, but care must be taken so that the spousal attribution rules (see below) and the regular attribution rules do not apply.

ITA: 74.5(12) Where ss. 74.1 to 74.3 do not apply

Ⓐ ¶9,350.50 Contributions of Property

In addition to cash contributions, an individual may be able to contribute certain types of property, such as shares, units of a mutual fund, or Canada Savings Bonds, to an RRSP. The individual will generally need to have a self-administered RRSP if he or she wishes to make a non-cash contribution. If an individual contributes property, he or she is entitled to a deduction equal to the fair market value of the property at the time of the contribution, but keep in mind that the individual is still subject to the normal contribution limits and that the Act restricts the type of property that may be held in an RRSP.

The individual will be considered to have sold the property at its fair market value at the date of contribution. Although any resulting capital gain is subject to tax in the individual's hands, the individual cannot claim any capital loss that arises from a disposition to an plan under which the individual is a beneficiary or from a disposition to a spousal RRSP. (See ¶9,350.60.)

ITA: 40(2)(g)(iv)(A), 40(2)(g)(iv)(B)

¶9,350.55 Application

Example Problem 9-4

Mr. Clark reported the following income for tax purposes in 2017:

Employment income — Subdivision a.	$81,000
Dividend received from taxable Canadian corporation (grossed up).	1,200
Rental loss.	(2,500)
Total.	$79,700

Included in the employment income computation was a deduction for a current contribution to a registered pension plan of $3,200. His employer reported a PA on his T4 for 2017 of $10,000. Mr. Clark made $5,000 of tax-deductible support payments to his former spouse in 2017.

REQUIRED

Calculate the maximum RRSP contribution that Mr. Clark can deduct as an annual contribution in 2018, as determined under the definition of "RRSP deduction limit", and advise Mr. Clark as to when he can make his contribution. Is there any other advice that you might want to give Mr. Clark in 2018 regarding his contributions?

SOLUTION

ITA: 146(1) earned income

Mr. Clark's earned income for 2018 is calculated as follows:

Employment income — Subdivision a.	$81,000
Add back RPP contribution	3,200
Deduct: Support payment made.	(5,000)
Rental loss	(2,500)
Total earned income for 2017.	$76,700

In respect of 2018, Mr. Clark is able to deduct the following:

Lesser of:

(1) 18% of 2017 earned income of $76,700 = $13,806, and

(2) the dollar limit for 2018 of $26,230

less the PA for 2017 of $10,000 reported by his employer in respect of the year.

Mr. Clark is able to contribute $3,806 (i.e., $13,806 – $10,000) to his RRSP in respect of 2018. The contribution may be made at any time in 2018 and within the first 60 days of 2019, which is by March 1, 2019. However, Mr. Clark will probably have to wait until the end of February 2018 to make an early 2018 contribution, since he will not know his PA for 2017 until he receives his T4. If Mr. Clark was really cautious, he might want to wait until he receives his Notice of Assessment for his 2017 tax return in which the CRA will issue him a 2018 RRSP contribution limit statement. However, he will have lost the benefit of tax-free compounding on his contribution from March until he receives his Notice of Assessment and makes his contribution. You should inform him that if he has the information at hand respecting the pension benefits that he accrued in the year, you could assist him by calculating his PA and he could make his contribution on the first day of January 2018.

You should also advise Mr. Clark that because of the way the penalties for an overcontribution work, he may make a one-time additional contribution of up to $2,000 in 2018 and the funds may be left to accumulate tax-free in his RRSP. Although this contribution is not tax-deductible, a sum of money can be built up over the life of his RRSP. This will be preferable to Mr. Clark investing in debt instruments or stocks outside of his RRSP, since the income will not be taxed. In order to avoid tax when Mr. Clark withdraws the $2,000 from his plan, he may be able to use the carry forward rules to his advantage by making a contribution that is $2,000 less than his allowable contribution in a year just prior to the withdrawal of the $2,000 from the plan. Then, he will have room to deduct the $2,000. Even if Mr. Clark is not able to use the carryforward rules to eliminate the tax when he withdraws the funds from the plan, if Mr. Clark is able to leave the additional $2,000 in the plan for a period of about 15 years, assuming that his rate of return on the funds was 10%, he would still be better off making the additional contribution.

¶9,350.60 Contributions to Spousal (or Common-Law Partner) RRSP

A "spousal (or common-law partner) plan", which is a defined term, is a plan under which an individual makes contributions to an RRSP but his or her spouse (or common-law partner) is the annuitant. *An individual's contributions to both his or her plan and a spousal (or common-law partner) RRSP are restricted in total to the individual's own contribution limit.* Therefore, a contribution made by an individual to a spousal (or common-law partner) RRSP does not allow an individual any additional deduction or contribution room beyond his or her personal limit. At the time of contribution, a spousal (or common-law partner) plan contribution, therefore, has no different tax effect than a regular RRSP contribution. The benefit of such a contribution is instead at the time of withdrawal as the future withdrawal of the contribution and any related income generated within the plan will be included in the spouse or common law partners' return. Thus, it is an income splitting opportunity. Note as such, the contribution does not affect the spouse's or common-law partner's personal RRSP contribution limit for the year.

ITA: 146(1) spousal or common-law partner plan, 146(5.1) Amount of spousal RRSP premiums deductible

A spousal RRSP could be set up for a common-law partner. Two individuals of either sex are considered to be common-law partners of each other when they are cohabiting in a conjugal relationship and either (a) they have so cohabited throughout the preceding 12 months, or (b) they are parents of the same child. ITA: 248(1) common-law partner

A spousal (or common-law partner) RRSP can be used to achieve income splitting on retirement. Tax savings will be realized if the retirement income from the RRSP will be taxed at lower marginal tax rates in the spouse's or partner's hands. For example, assuming an individual intends to retire in 20 years and his or her RRSP earns a 10% annual rate of return, the individual could contribute $5,000 to a spousal (or common-law partner) RRSP for the next three years. At retirement, this would give the individual's spouse or partner a 15-year annuity of about $12,000 per year. If the spouse or partner will pay tax on this income at a marginal tax rate of about 26%, compared to about 46% in the individual's hands, the individual will realize annual tax savings of about $2,400 on this retirement income. To the extent that the contributions to a spousal (or common-law partner) RRSP exceed the individual's deductible limit, the income on withdrawal will be attributed back to the individual and will be subject to tax in his or her hands, because the non-deductible contribution would not meet the exception to the attribution rules. ITA: 74.5(12)(a)

Note that although the Act's allowance of income splitting for certain pension amounts may reduce the need for a spousal RRSP contribution in certain circumstances, it still provides a useful tax planning tool in a number of cases. Specifically, it would be beneficial in situations where a couple's retirement income will not be derived primarily from pension income which is often the case for individuals who are self-employed.

Provided an individual has earned income, contributions can be made to a spousal (or common-law partner) RRSP until the end of the year in which the spouse attains 71 years of age. These deductible contributions can be made even if the contributor is over 71.

There are other factors that an individual should consider when deciding whether to contribute to a spousal (or common-law partner) RRSP. The individual should be aware that amounts contributed to a spousal plan become the property of his or her spouse. This should be considered in view of any provincial laws governing the division of assets in the event of a marital breakdown.

¶9,350.65 Attribution on Spousal (or Common-Law Partner) RRSPs

An individual may contribute to a spousal (or common-law partner) RRSP to gain some benefit from income splitting. However, special rules apply to curtail such income splitting if the RRSP is used for short-term income splitting.

Attribution applies to include in the contributing individual's income all premiums paid to any spousal (or common-law partner) RRSP in a three-year period, even if the premiums are not deducted or deductible in the three years. As a consequence, attribution will apply on withdrawal of the funds by the spouse if: ITA: 146(8.3) Spousal or common-law partner payments

(1) the individual paid a premium to *any* spousal (or common-law partner) plan in the current year or the preceding two years; and ITA: 146.3(5.1) Amount included in income

(2) the premium is required to be included in computing the income of the individual's spouse or common-law partner. ITA: 146(8) Benefits taxable

If such withdrawals are included in the spouse's or partner's income, the amount withdrawn, up to the amount of the premiums paid by the individual in the three-year period, will also be included in the individual's income. In order to eliminate double counting, if the income is attributed to the individual who made the contribution, an offsetting deduction is allowed to the spouse or common-law partner.

ITA: 146(8.6) Spouse's [or common-law partner's] income

Similar rules apply where the individual's spouse or common-law partner receives an amount in excess of the minimum amount from a RRIF and the RRIF received property from an RRSP to which the individual paid a premium in the three-year period. The amount received by the individual's spouse or common-law partner in excess of the minimum amount will be included in the individual's income rather than the spouse's or partner's.

Example Problem 9-5

Christine and her spouse, Eric, have been setting money aside each year for retirement. A number of years ago, they decided that once they had children Christine would continue to work and Eric would stay home with the children. As a result, for the past five years Christine has been contributing $5,000 per year to a spousal RRSP owned by Eric. Early in 2018, Christine made her annual $5,000 contribution for 2018. However, in September Christine and Eric found they had a significant need for cash, so they withdrew $20,000 from the spousal RRSP set up for Eric.

REQUIRED

How much of the $20,000 withdrawal should be reported by Eric and how much by Christine?

SOLUTION

Christine must report the amount she contributed in the year and the preceding two years, i.e., $15,000.

Eric must report the remainder — $5,000.

Ⓐ ¶9,350.70 Integration of Limits

In order to provide the same amount of tax assistance to an individual for retirement savings, regardless of whether it is funded through an RPP, a DPSP, an RRSP or a combination thereof, a comprehensive annual limit for tax-assisted retirement savings is being phased in.

This comprehensive annual limit is determined using certain key assumptions with respect to retirement savings.

First, the maximum amount of tax-assisted retirement savings that the government is willing to fund through tax assistance for each individual is $103,055 in 2018. That amount was derived as a multiple of the average wage. Second, it is assumed actuarially that $9 of contributions buys $1 of annual pension income.

Under a DBP, an individual generally must have a combined pension contribution of $2,944.44 per year over the equivalent of 35 years to pay out the 2018 maximum pension of $103,055, and so at the maximum it will be possible to make combined employer/employee contributions equal to the lesser of 18% of the individual's compensation from the employer for the year, or $26,500 (= $2,944.44 × 9) per year.

Under an MPP, tax-assisted contributions at the maximum may equal the lesser of 18% (9 × 2%) of earnings or $26,500 per year (total contributions made by the employer and employee) and should result in an accumulation of funds in the plan of up to $103,055 of 2018 pension income, generally, after the equivalent of 35 years. The cap of $26,500 for 2018 limits the amount of pensionable earnings that may receive tax assistance to $147,222 (18% of $147,222 is $26,500).

Under a DPSP, the maximum contribution limit is the lesser of 18% of earnings and 50% of $26,500 for 2018, since only the employer may make contributions. This lower limit will leave more contribution room for the individual to make a deductible RRSP contribution.

To integrate the tax assistance provided to individuals who fund their retirement savings with a combination of RRSPs, pension plans, and deferred profit sharing plans, the RRSP contribution limit is 18% of earned income for the prior year to a 2018 maximum of $26,230, plus or minus any adjustments for benefits provided to the individual under an RPP or a DPSP in the prior year.

¶9,350.90 Pause and Reflect — Summary of Learning Goals

After working through this section, ¶9,350, you should be able to:

- Apply your knowledge to calculate the RRSP contribution limit for a taxpayer.
- Understand the difference between a RRSP contribution and a contribution to spousal RRSP and when it may benefit a taxpayer.

¶9,355 Withdrawals Before Retirement

Overview

An RRSP may generally be terminated at any time prior to maturity (generally retirement) and the proceeds distributed to the individual. However, the gross amount received must be included in his or her income. Of course, the benefit of a tax-free accumulation of funds will be lost. An individual may make partial withdrawals from an RRSP without terminating the plan.

The trustee of the RRSP must withhold tax from the amount withdrawn by the individual. The tax withheld may be claimed as a credit on the individual's income tax return as income taxes paid in the year. The withholding tax rate is based on the amount withdrawn — 10% of the amount if it is $5,000 or less; 20% of the amount if it is between $5,000 and $15,000; and 30% of the amount if it exceeds $15,000, except in Quebec. ITR: 103(4), 103(6)

Tax withheld at source from RRSP withdrawals may be minimized by making sure that each withdrawal is for $5,000 or less. Any tax liability related to the withdrawal in excess of the amount withheld must be paid when the individual files his or her tax return for the year.

¶9,355.10 Home Buyers' Plan (HBP)

Under the HBP, individuals may withdraw up to a total of $25,000 from any of their RRSPs to buy an owner-occupied home without having to pay tax on the withdrawal. Form T1036 must be used to report the withdrawal and to get the exclusion from income. These withdrawals must be repaid in annual instalments over a maximum period of 15 years. The repayment period begins in the second calendar year following the calendar year in which the withdrawal is made. However, the individual may elect to have a repayment made in the first 60 days of a year treated as having been made in the preceding year. Hence, if $25,000 is withdrawn in 2017, the minimum annual repayment of $1,667 (i.e., $25,000/15) must be made on or before March 1, 2020, being 60 days after 2019 which is the second calendar year after the 2017 year of withdrawal.

ITA: 146.01 [Home buyers' plan]

Figure 9-3 illustrates the timing.

Figure 9-3
HBP Payment Timing

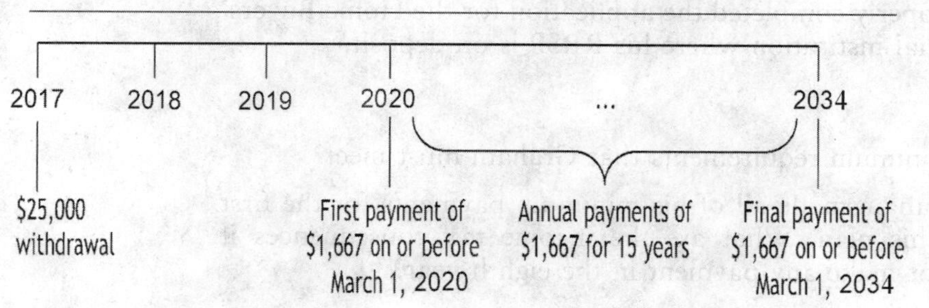

A qualifying home must generally be acquired before October 1 of the calendar year following the year of the withdrawal. Under specified conditions, this acquisition deadline can be extended. Only a first-time home buyer may make use of this plan. An individual will be considered to be a first-time home buyer, if neither the individual nor the individual's spouse or common-law partner owned a home and lived in it as the "principal place of residence" in any of the five calendar years beginning before the time of withdrawal. An individual is excepted from this five-year requirement on the termination of the marriage or common-law relationship.

An individual is allowed to participate in an HBP more than once in his or her lifetime. However, the individual must have repaid all amounts previously withdrawn under the HBP before the beginning of the year in which he or she participates in a new HBP.

The first-time home buyer condition need not be met under specific circumstances.

The conditions are that:

ITA: 118.3(1) Credit for mental or physical impairment

(1) the individual is entitled to claim the disability tax credit; and

(2) the HBP withdrawal by the disabled individual or a related individual is used to enable the disabled individual to acquire and live in a dwelling that is more accessible by the individual or that is better suited for the personal needs and care of the individual.

Ordinary contributions made to an RRSP within 90 days before a withdrawal will not be allowed as a deduction, except to the extent that the RRSP balance after the withdrawal is more than the amount of the contribution. Hence, an amount that is both contributed and withdrawn within the 90-day period will not be deductible as an RRSP contribution.

Any amount scheduled for repayment, but not repaid in the appropriate year will be included in the individual's income for the year. For example, if the minimum annual repayment is $1,667 and the individual only repays $1,000, the $667 will be included in income and subjected to tax. On the other hand, an individual may repay more than the minimum scheduled repayment for a year. In this case, there will be less to repay over the remainder of the 15-year period and the minimum annual repayments can, but need not, be reduced for subsequent years.

Example Problem 9-6

Graham plans to purchase his first home and withdraw $18,000 from his RRSP this year (Year 1). He properly completed the application for the Home Buyers' Plan (HBP) at the financial institution where his RRSP is on deposit.

REQUIRED

(1) What are the minimum requirements that Graham must meet?

(2) Assume that Graham made all of his minimum payments for the first seven years of his plan. What are the income tax consequences if Graham does not make any payment in the eighth year?

SOLUTION

(1) The following requirements must be met:

- The home must be purchased by October 1 of Year 2;
- The minimum annual repayment is $1,200 ($18,000/15);
- The first payment is due in Year 3 or in the first 60 days of Year 4.

(2) Since Graham did not make the Year 8 repayment, he must include $1,200 (i.e., the amount of the required payment) in his income in that year. The HBP remains in place and Graham must continue to make the minimum payments in subsequent years or be subject to the income inclusion of an amount that is not repaid.

¶9,355.20 Tax-Free RRSP Withdrawals for Lifelong Learning Plan (LLP)

Individuals are allowed to make tax-free withdrawals from their RRSPs for lifelong learning. The objective is to give taxpayers greater access to funds for retraining. Similar to the HBP, individuals must repay the amount they withdraw over a fixed period of time.

ITA: 146.02 [Lifelong learning plan]

A maximum of $10,000 per year can be withdrawn from an RRSP by an individual who is enrolled at a designated educational institution in full-time training or higher education requiring not less than 10 hours per week on courses or work in the program for at least three consecutive months during the year. Students with disabilities qualify if engaged in part-time studies. Further withdrawals can be made for a period of up to four years, but total withdrawals cannot exceed $20,000. Also, contributions made within 90 days of a withdrawal are not eligible for tax-free withdrawal. ITA: 118.6(1) designated educational institution

Amounts withdrawn are repayable in 10 equal annual instalments. The first repayment must be made at the earlier of:

(1) the year following the last year that the student was enrolled on a full-time basis, that is, where the student is not entitled to annual full-time education tax credits for at least three months in two consecutive years; or

(2) 60 days following the fifth year after the first withdrawal.

Repayments simply replenish, without interest, amounts withdrawn from the RRSP. Hence, these repayments are not deductible. If an amount is not repaid on time, it is included in the individual's income in that year.

Individuals may participate in this withdrawal program any number of times during their lifetime. However, no new withdrawals are permitted until all repayments from a previously started program have been made. Of course, while the funds are not in the RRSP, they are not earning sheltered income and there is no opportunity to replenish that income.

¶9,355.90 Pause and Reflect — Summary of Learning Goals

After working through this section, ¶9,355, you should be able to:

- Understand the tax implications of using the Home Buyer's Plan.
- Understand the tax implications of using the Lifelong Learning Plan.

¶9,360 Retirement Options

Overview

Although an RRSP must mature by the end of the year in which the individual reaches the age of 71, the individual does not have to wait until then to obtain retirement income from the RRSP. An RRSP can be matured at any time before the end of the year in which an individual reaches the age of 71. As an alternative, the individual can make withdrawals from the plan. This allows an individual the flexibility to take an early retirement should he or she so desire.

At maturity, the accumulated funds may be withdrawn from an RRSP. Tax must be paid at the individual's marginal tax rate on these funds. As an alternative, he or she may purchase one or a combination of available maturity options. These options provide an individual with retirement income in varying amounts over different periods of time. Tax is deferred until he or she actually receives retirement income.

Retirement options which are currently available are:

Fixed-term annuities	• provide benefits up to age 90, or if the spouse or common-law spouse is younger than the individual, and he or she so elects, until the spouse or common-law partner reaches age 90 • may provide fixed or fluctuating income
Life annuities	• provide benefits during the individual's life, or during the lives of the individual and his or her spouse or com-mon-law partner • may have a guaranteed pay-out option • may provide fixed or fluctuating income
Registered retirement income funds.	• are essentially a continuation of an RRSP • provide the individual with retirement income from the investment of the funds accumulated in a matured RRSP for the individual's life

Under federal and provincial pension legislation, the proceeds of locked-in RRSPs that arise on the transfer of a lump-sum payment of vested benefits from an RPP must be used to purchase a life annuity or RRIF at retirement.

¶9,360.10 Considerations When Choosing an Option

A number of factors should be considered when deciding which option or combination of options to choose upon maturity of an RRSP:

- the rate of return;
- current and future income needs;
- the tax that would be payable currently if an annuity or RRIF were not purchased to defer tax;
- the income stream that would result from a particular annuity or RRIF;
- the present age of the individual and that of his or her spouse or common-law partner;
- the extent to which the individual wants to personally manage his or her retirement income; and
- the size of the estate the individual wishes to leave to his or her beneficiaries.

¶9,360.20 Fixed-Term and Life Annuities

With a fixed-term annuity, all of the funds accumulated in an RRSP will be paid out over the term of the annuity. The monthly retirement income the individual receives will vary, depending on the interest rate the issuer anticipates earning on the funds. However, with a life annuity, the retirement income will also depend on the sex and age of the individual and the options he or she chooses to attach to the annuity. Retirement income is highest for a straight life annuity (i.e., payments cease upon death, even if this occurs shortly after purchasing the annuity). Retirement income is lower if a guaranteed pay-out or guaranteed term option is added. These options guarantee that a certain amount of funds will be paid out, or that funds will be paid for a specified number of years, regardless of when the individual dies.

When an annuity is purchased, the retirement income will be determined for the term of the annuity. Once the annuity is in place, no further involvement with regard to investment decisions is required on the individual's part. In addition, no adjustments in income occur if interest rates subsequently rise or fall.

¶9,360.30 Registered Retirement Income Fund (RRIF)

Generally, the following rules apply.

ITA: 146.3 Registered retirement income funds

- A RRIF may be established at any time before the end of the year in which the individual reaches the age of 71. Early retirement can therefore be accommodated by a RRIF.
- It is possible to have more than one RRIF at a time. As a result, several different RRIFs can be set up in order to diversify a RRIF portfolio.
- Although a minimum amount must be withdrawn each year, an individual may withdraw any amount in excess of this minimum.

The fact that an individual is able to withdraw any amount in excess of the minimum allows him or her to match cash needs in any given year. The minimum rate of withdrawal from an RRIF is based on a complicated formula. The Regulations provide a table of increasing factors that would be applied to the principal remaining to determine an estimate of the withdrawal for a particular year, starting at age 71. If a taxpayer were to establish an RRIF prior to reaching the age of 71, the minimum withdrawal factor is determined by the formula 1/(90 - age). Once the individual reaches age 94, the factor remains at 20% until all the money is withdrawn or the individual dies.

ITR: 7308(3); Information Circulars: IC 78-18R6 Registered Retirement Income Funds

Amounts withdrawn from a RRIF in excess of the minimum amount, however, will be subject to withholding tax at the same rates that are applicable to RRSP lump-sum withdrawals.

If an individual so elects at the commencement of the RRIF and his or her spouse or common-law partner is younger, the individual may have the minimum payment out of the RRIF based on the age of the spouse or common-law partner. This election does not automatically make the spouse or common-law partner the annuitant under the RRIF after the individual's death.

Generally, RRIF funds may be invested in the same types of investments as RRSPs. The RRIF may be self-administered. That is, an individual may personally determine, along with the trustees of the RRIF, what investments are made by it. As with an RRSP, a RRIF is not taxed on its earnings. Thus, income accumulates on a tax-free basis in the RRIF.

When choosing which investments to hold in a RRIF, an individual should consider the same factors that he or she would have considered in choosing investments for an RRSP. Liquidity is a particularly important factor when choosing investments to be held in a RRIF, since a portion of the funds must be withdrawn each year to provide retirement income.

Ⓐ ¶9,370 Treatment of RRSPs and RRIFs on Death

Overview

The tax treatment of RRSP's and RRIFs upon the death of the taxpayer is dependent on a number of factors, most importantly the ultimate beneficiary of the registered plan. The taxation of RRSPs and RRIFS upon the death of the taxpayer are discussed below across different beneficiary scenarios.

Ⓐ ¶9,370.10 Spouse or Common-Law Partner as Beneficiary

If the individual has a RRIF at the time of death, his or her spouse or common-law partner may continue to receive the income from the RRIF (become the annuitant under the RRIF) or receive a lump sum under the RRIF (become the beneficiary under the RRIF), provided that the individual specified that this was his or her intention, either in the RRIF contract or under the terms of his or her will.

If the spouse or common-law partner becomes the annuitant under the RRIF, payments may continue to be made to the spouse or partner, or to the estate for the benefit of the spouse or partner. If the spouse or partner becomes the beneficiary under the RRIF, the lump sum may be paid directly to him or her, or to an estate for the benefit of the spouse or partner. In the situation where the spouse or partner does not become the annuitant or the beneficiary under the RRIF, the RRIF must be collapsed and the value of the RRIF must be paid to any other named beneficiary or the individual's estate.

Amounts paid to a spouse or common-law partner as a named beneficiary from an RRSP (whether lump-sum or otherwise), or as an annuitant or beneficiary under a RRIF, will be taxable to the spouse or partner when received. Amounts paid from an RRSP to the individual's estate for the benefit of his or her spouse or partner will also be taxable to that spouse or partner, provided that the spouse or partner and the legal representatives of the estate file a joint tax election to this effect. If this election is not filed, the fair market value of all of the property of the RRSP fund at the time of his or her death will be included in the deceased's income for the year of death. If the individual intends to have his or her spouse or partner as beneficiary, it will generally be preferable for the individual to name the spouse or partner as beneficiary under the RRSP, rather than to file the election after death, in order to minimize probate fees. The election is made by filing T2019 (RRSP refunds of premiums designation — Spouse).

In the CRA's view, a similar election may not be available where an amount out of a RRIF is paid to an individual's estate for the benefit of his or her spouse or common-law partner. If the individual intends to have his or her spouse or partner as an annuitant or a beneficiary under the RRIF, the individual should name the spouse or partner as an annuitant or as a beneficiary under the contract or under the terms of the will, so that the RRIF amounts will not be included in the individual's income for the year of death.

Where amounts received out of an unmatured RRSP are taxed in the spouse's or partner's hands, he or she may defer tax on all or any portion of the amount by making either a direct or indirect transfer of the funds to an RRSP (if the spouse or partner is under the age of 71, a RRIF, or by purchasing a fixed-term or life annuity within 60 days after the taxation year of receipt.

ITA: 60(l) Transfer of refund of premiums under RRSP

If the value of an individual's RRSP or RRIF is taken into income at death and that value declines prior to the distribution from the plan, then the "loss" can be deducted on the individual's final return to offset the income that was originally reported.

ITA: 146.3(6.3) Deduction for post-death reduction in value

Ⓐ ¶9,370.20 Financially Dependent Child or Grandchild as Beneficiary

Where the spouse or common-law partner is not the beneficiary, or the beneficiary or annuitant in the case of a RRIF, the proceeds from a RRIF, an unmatured RRSP or the commuted value of an RRSP annuity must be included in the individual's income for the year of death. An exception occurs in certain circumstances where the beneficiary is a financially dependent child or grandchild even if the deceased individual had a surviving spouse or partner when he or she died, if the proceeds are considered to be a "refund of premiums" as defined.

ITA: 146(1) refund of premiums

A child or grandchild is not considered financially dependent if his or her income for the year preceding the year in which the annuitant died, for example 2019, exceeded the basic personal credit amount ($11,809 in 2018) for that preceding year. This amount is increased by $8,235 to $20,044 if that child or grandchild is infirm.

ITA: 146(1.1) Restriction — financially dependent

In these circumstances, it is possible to have, or to elect to have, such proceeds taxed in the hands of the child or grandchild. In the case where a dependent child or grandchild is mentally or physically infirm, tax may be deferred on such proceeds if either a direct or indirect transfer is made by the child or grandchild, or his or her representative, to an RRSP (if under the age of 71), a RRIF, or an annuity within 60 days after the taxation year of receipt.

ITA: 146(8.1) Deemed receipt of refund of premiums, 146.3(6.1) Designated benefit deemed received; 60(l) Transfer of refund of premiums under RRSP, 60.011 [Qualifying trust annuity]

In the case where the child or grandchild is not physically or mentally infirm, tax may be deferred on such proceeds if they are used to acquire an annuity with a term not exceeding 18 minus the age of the child or grandchild at the time the annuity is acquired. The annuity must be acquired in the year the proceeds are included in the child or grandchild's income. In these cases, it will generally be preferable for the individual to name the child or grandchild as the beneficiary under the terms of the will.

Ⓐ ¶9,370.30 Other Beneficiaries

If the individual names a person other than his or her spouse or common-law partner (or, in limited circumstances, a child or grandchild) as a beneficiary under the RRSP or as beneficiary or annuitant under the RRIF, the estate will be faced with paying any tax liability resulting from the individual's death, even though it may not have sufficient funds to do so because the proceeds have been paid to the named beneficiary.

Ⓐ ¶9,370.40 Transfer to an RDSP

The RRSP rollover rules allow a rollover of a deceased individual's RRSP proceeds to the RDSP of a financially dependent infirm child or grandchild. The amount of RRSP proceeds rolled over into an RDSP will not be permitted to exceed the beneficiary's available RDSP contribution room and will reduce the beneficiary's RDSP contribution room and will not attract Canada Disability Savings Grants. The lifetime contribution limit for RDSPs is $200,000.

ITA: 60.011 [Qualifying trust annuity]

Ⓐ ¶9,370.50 Contributions for Year of Death

If, at the time of death, the individual has not made an RRSP contribution for the year of death, his or her legal representative may make a spousal or common-law partner RRSP contribution under the normal rules. Such a contribution will be deductible in the year of death, provided the contribution is made within 60 days of the end of the year of death.

ITA: 146(5.1) Amount of spousal RRSP premiums deductible

¶9,380 Transfers of Retirement Income and Sheltered Amounts

Overview

In general, lump-sum amounts of retirement income can be transferred on a tax-free basis, but only where the amounts are transferred directly from one plan to another. When amounts are transferred directly, they generally are not included in income and consequently it is not necessary to claim an offsetting deduction.

ITA: 147.3 Transfer — money purchase to money purchase, RRSP or RRIF

The rollover of periodic pension income out of an RPP, DPSP, Old Age Security (OAS), and Canada Pension/Quebec Pension Plan (CPP/QPP) is generally prohibited. Restrictions are also placed on the amounts that may be transferred from defined benefit RPPs to money purchase RPPs and RRSPs. The result is to restrict the opportunity for individuals to obtain further tax deferral on receipts of periodic pension income.

¶9,380.10 Direct Transfer

Lump-sum RPP and DPSP amounts are transferable on a tax-free basis, but *only through a direct transfer* for:

- lump-sum amounts out of RPPs (other than lump-sum amounts that relate to an actuarial surplus) to another RPP or to an RRSP under which the individual is an annuitant;
- lump-sum amounts of DPSPs to an RPP, an RRSP or to certain DPSPs; and
- property from an unmatured RRSP to an RPP, to another RRSP or to a RRIF.

ITA: 147.3 Transfer — money purchase to money purchase, RRSP or RRIF

ITA: 147(19) Transfer to RPP, RRSP or DPSP, 147(20) Taxation of amount transferred

ITA: 146(16) Transfer of funds

When such direct transfers are made, the amount transferred is not included in income, and does not give rise to a deduction. If, however, the individual receives the funds personally, the amount will be included in his or her income for tax purposes in the year it is received and the individual will not be able to contribute the funds (i.e., transfer them indirectly) to his or her RRSP to avoid the income inclusion.

Unlimited lump-sum transfers may be made directly from one MPP to another, from an MPP to a DBP, from a DBP to another DBP, but transfers from a DBP to an MPP or RRSP are limited to prescribed amounts.

¶9,380.20 Retiring Allowances

A retiring allowance is defined to be an amount received (other than a superannuation or pension benefit, an amount received as a consequence of the death of an employee or employment benefits derived from certain specified counselling services):

ITA: 6(1)(a)(iv), 248(1) retiring allowance

(a) upon or after retirement of an individual from an office or employment in recognition of his or her long service, or

(b) in respect of a loss of an office or employment of an individual, whether or not received as, on account or in lieu of payment of damages or pursuant to an order or judgment of a competent tribunal

by the individual or, after his or her death, by a dependant or relation of the individual or by the legal representative of the individual.

A retiring allowance is generally included in income in the year it is received. It includes payments received on retirement; it also includes payments received on loss of employment. So a payment that arose as a result of a lawsuit filed by a terminated employee will also be included in income as a retiring allowance.

Ⓐ ¶9,380.30 Rollover

A retiring allowance may be transferred tax-free to an RRSP or RPP within the following limits:

ITA: 60(j.1) Transfer of retiring allowances

- $2,000 for each year or part thereof during which the individual was employed by the employer or related employer with respect to service before 1996;

  plus

- $1,500 for each year or part year of service counted for the $2,000 limit prior to 1989 for which the employer RPP and DPSP contribution did not vest at the time of retirement.

It should be noted that, as time goes by, there are fewer and fewer people who can take advantage of this rollover, since, to benefit from the rollover of a retiring allowance, you would need to have worked for your current employer at least since 1996, if not since before 1989.

The $1,500 limit is technically computed as the number of pre-1989 years or part years of employment in excess of the equivalent number of pre-1989 years in respect of which employer contributions had vested. The use of the term "equivalent number of years" allows for a fractional number of years to be used, when, to use the example presented in explanatory notes, an employee has worked seven pre-1989 years and 60% of the employer's contributions have vested. In that case, the non-vested years would be counted as 2.8 years (i.e., 7 years – 60% of 7 years) and, hence, at $1,500 per non-vested years, $4,200 (i.e., 2.8 × $1,500) could be deducted on a transfer of a retiring allowance.

The amount that may be deducted may not exceed the total of the amounts paid by the individual in the year or in the 60 days after the end of the year as a contribution to an RPP. Excluded from that limit are amounts deductible: (1) for employee contributions to an RPP, and (2) as a premium to an RRSP under which he or she is the annuitant, other than the portion that has been designated as a transfer of a refund of premiums to a spouse or child as a consequence of death or for certain direct transfers of amounts out of a RRIF or an RRSP.

ITA: 8(1)(m) Employee's registered pension plan contributions; 60(l) Transfer of refund of premiums under RRSP

The following is a *simplified* formula for the deductible amount of a retiring allowance transferred to an RRSP. The deductible transfer cannot exceed the least of:

(a)	the sum of:	
	(i) $2,000 × the number of pre-1996 years during which the individual was employed (as described above)	xxx
	(ii) $1,500 × the equivalent number of non-vested pre-1989 years (as described above)	xxx
		xxx
(b)[1]	total RRSP premium contributions	xxx
(c)	the amount of the retiring allowance	xxx

[1] Item (b) in the actual legislation consists of total RRSP contributions and non-deductible RPP contributions made by the employee. However, it would be unusual for an employee to have made a non-deductible RPP contribution under the current legislation (unless past service contributions were made) and, as a result, that part of the rule has been omitted for simplicity.

The limit in part (b), above, reflects the fact that an individual cannot deduct more than the amount actually transferred or contributed into a sheltered plan.

Example Problem 9-7

Consider the following facts:

Retiring allowance received by Lee Zhang in 2018.	$30,000
Earned income in 2017.	66,000
PA reported by employer in 2016	10,880
Number of pre-1996 years during which he was employed since November of 1984	12
Percentage of vesting for pre-1989 years of service.	60%

REQUIRED

Determine the amount that Lee is able to deduct if he transfers the maximum he can to his RRSP.

SOLUTION

Lee is only able to contribute $27,000 to his RRSP without overcontributing to the plan, determined as:

Sum of $2,000 × 12[(1)] =	$24,000
$1,500 × 2[(2)] =	3,000
Total	$27,000

Lee may deduct a $27,000 transfer in respect of his $30,000 retiring allowance to an RRSP, plus his annual contribution for 2018.

NOTES TO SOLUTION

[(1)] Since the legislation only refers to years, not full years, it is reasonable to assume part years would qualify.

[(2)] In the five pre-1989 years (i.e., 1984 to 1988, inclusive) during which the taxpayer was employed, 60% of the employer's contributions vested. Therefore, the equivalent non-vested years would be counted as two years (i.e., five years – 60% of five years) and, hence, an additional $1,500 may be deducted in respect of each of those two equivalent non-vested years.

¶9,380.90 Pause and Reflect — Summary of Learning Goals

After working through this section, ¶9,380, you should be able to:

- Understand the implications of transfer lump sums from different sources into a Registered Retirement Savings Plan.

¶9,385 Summary of Tax-Assisted Plans

The essential features of tax-assisted plans are summarized in Exhibit 9-2.

Exhibit 9-2 Summary of Registered Savings Plans

Plan	Purpose	Contributions Deductible	Contribution Limit	Taxation of Withdrawal
RRSP	Tax shelter to encourage individuals to save for retirement	Yes	Annually, lessor of: (i) RRSP dollar limit of $26,230 for 2018 (ii) 18% of earned income for prior year Less: Pension adjustment Plus: unused contribution room for prior years	Prior to maturity: 1. Taxed as received 2. Home Buyer's Plan (HBP)-up to $25,000 withdrawn tax-free if repaid in annual instalments over 15 years 3. Life long learning plan (LLP) up to $10,000 per year withdrawn tax-free for higher education if repaid in annual instalments over 10 years At maturity:

Plan	Purpose	Contributions Deductible	Contribution Limit	Taxation of Withdrawal
				1. Taxed as received 2. Purchase RRIF or retirement annuity so taxed deferred until receipt
RPP:				
DBP	Benefit to each employee is defined	Yes	$26,500 for 2018	Taxed as received
MPP	Contribution required by employer and employee is defined	Yes	$26,500 for 2018	Taxed as received
DPSP	Employer contributes to plan for employee based on performance of company	Yes — to employer	Annually lessor of (i) 18% of earnings (ii) 50% of $26,500 for 2018	Taxed as received
TFSA	Earn investment income on a tax-free basis	No	$5,500 annually	Not taxable
RESP	Fund post-secondary education for qualified beneficiary	No	$50,000 lifetime	Accumulated investment income taxable to beneficiary as funds received.
RDSP	Save for the long-term financial security of a child with a severe disability	No	$200,000 lifetime	Accumulated investment income taxable to beneficiary as funds received.

¶9,390 Pause and Reflect — Summary of Learning Goals

After working through this section, ¶9,300, you should be able to:

- Understand the taxation of contributions and withdrawals into registered savings plans.
- Explain the different tax treatments for contributions and withdrawals for TFSAs, RRSPs and RESPs.
- Know the tax impacts of transitioning RSPs into retirement income. Calculate a taxpayer's RRSP contribution limit.
- Calculate a taxpayer's RRSP contribution limit.

¶9,390.99 Practise What You've Learned

Refer to the following sections of the Study Guide to practise what you've learned:

¶9,800 — Review Questions

- Question 8 Defined Benefit Registered Plan
- Question 9 Money Purchase Registered Plan
- Question 10 RRSP Withdrawal Before Retirement
- Question 11 Treatment of RRSP at Death

¶9,825 — Multiple Choice Questions

- Question 2 RRSP Contribution

¶9,850 — Exercises

- Exercise 1 RRSP Contribution
- Exercise 2 RRSP Contribution
- Exercise 4 RRSP Withdrawal Before Retirement
- Exercise 7 RRSP Contribution

¶9,900 Pause and Reflect — Summary of Learning Goals for This Chapter

After working through all the sections of the chapter, you should know, understand, and be able to explain:

- The basic provisions of the *Income Tax Act* that relate to other income and other deductions.
- How pension income is taxed.
- How to calculate the taxable portion of an annuity.

- How contributions and withdrawals from RESP and RDSP programs affect the calculation of net income for tax purposes.
- The benefits of contributing to an RESP or RDSP.
- The difference in tax treatment for spousal support and child support.
- The difference between an RRSP contribution and a contribution to spousal RRSP and when it may benefit a taxpayer.
- The taxation of contributions and withdrawals into Registered Savings Plans.
- The different tax treatments for contributions and withdrawals for TFSAs, RRSPs and RESPs.
- The tax impacts of transitioning RSPs into retirement income.
- When moving expenses are deductible and when they are not.

You should be able to apply your knowledge and understanding to:

- Calculate deductible moving expenses.
- Calculate deductible child care expenses.
- Calculate disability support deductions.
- Calculate a taxpayer's RRSP contribution limit.
- Split pension and CPP income to minimize tax payable.

CHAPTER 10

Computation of Taxable Income and Taxes Payable for Individuals

ADVANCED CONTENT IN THIS CHAPTER

Learning Goals

Know, Understand and Explain

By the end of this chapter you will know, understand and be able to explain:

- The difference between net income for tax purposes and taxable income.
- Which deductions are used in the computation of net income for tax purposes and which deductions are used in the computation of taxable income.
- The difference between a tax credit and a tax deduction.
- The difference between a refundable and non-refundable tax credit.
- Non-refundable tax credits available to a taxpayer.
- Refundable tax credits available to a taxpayer.
- How computations of net income for tax purposes impact the calculation of refundable tax credits.
- The purpose of the minimum tax.
- Situations when minimum tax may apply.

Apply

By the end of this chapter you will be able to apply your knowledge and understanding to:

- Calculate the taxable income for an individual taxpayer.
- Calculate the tax owing for an individual taxpayer.
- Calculate tax credits for an individual taxpayer.

Review Questions

¶10,800 in the Study Guide

Multiple Choice Questions

¶10,825 in the Study Guide

Exercises

¶10,850 in the Study Guide

Assignment Problems

¶10,875 in the Study Guide

Overview

Chapter 10 completes the discussion of the subjects required to calculate the tax liability for individuals. It is important at this point to consider how the issues discussed previously and those discussed in this chapter fit into the overall calculation of an individual's tax liability.

The following illustrates the three distinct steps in computing the income tax liability for both corporations and individuals.

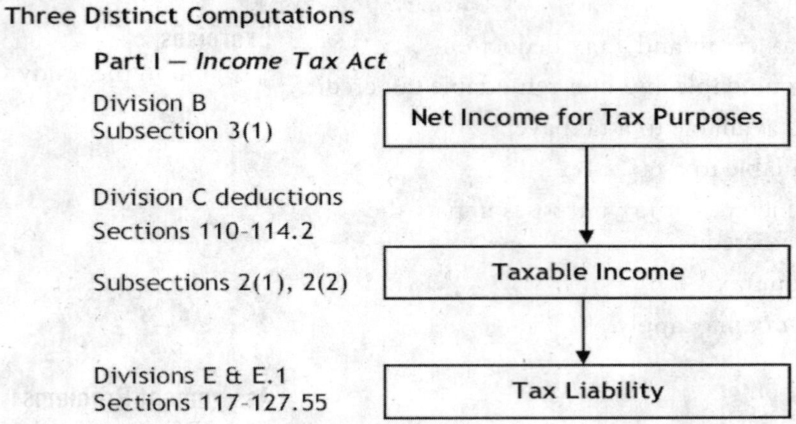

The content of Chapters 3 to 9 focused primarily on the computation of the first major computation "Net Income for Tax Purposes". Note that income and deductions discussed in those chapters generally are inputs to that distinct computation. Chapter 10 describes in detail the calculation of the remaining two computations: "Taxable income" and "Tax liability" for an individual. Note that the topics of "Taxable Income" and "Tax Liability" for a corporation will be discussed in Chapters 11 and 12.

The first major segment in Chapter 10 deals with a discussion of the provisions used to compute *taxable income*. The Act simply defines taxable income as income plus or minus amounts permitted under Division C. This chapter will cover a list of miscellaneous "amounts permitted" under Division C which specifically pertain to individuals. These items include the capital gains deduction which will be introduced briefly in this chapter and discussed more fully in Chapter 13 and the carryover of losses incurred in another year.

ITA: 2(2) Taxable income, 110.6 [Capital gains exemption]

The second major segment of this chapter discusses the computation of tax liability for individuals, including coverage of tax rates, tax credits, and minimum tax. This discussion follows a long list of tax credits for such things as marital status, dependants, age, pension income, charitable donations, medical expenses and disability, among others, and for transfers of certain of these credits to another taxpayer.

The following chart will help locate the major provisions of the Act considered in this chapter.

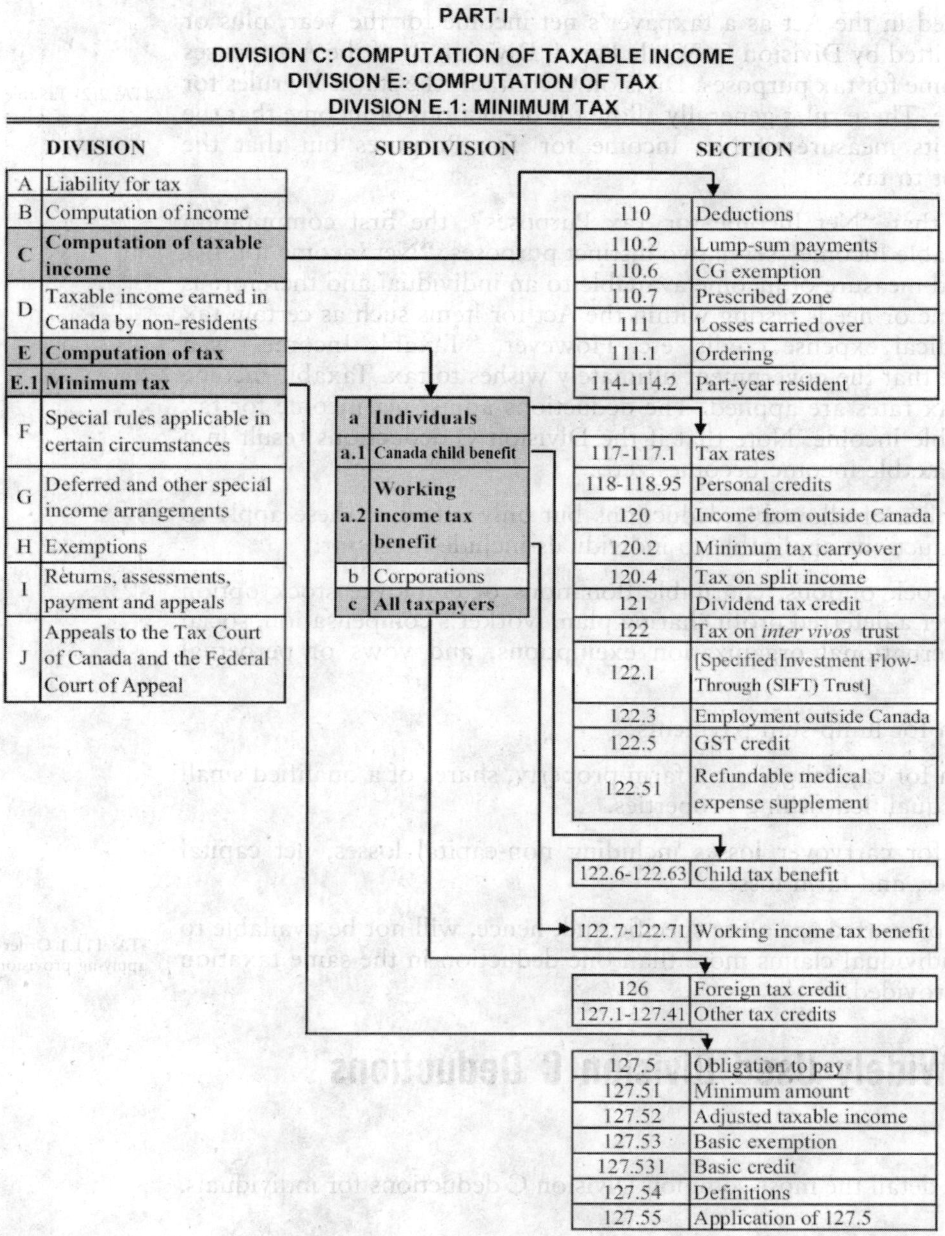
PART I
DIVISION C: COMPUTATION OF TAXABLE INCOME
DIVISION E: COMPUTATION OF TAX
DIVISION E.1: MINIMUM TAX
DIVISION
SUBDIVISION
SECTION
A Liability for tax
B Computation of income
C Computation of taxable income
D Taxable income earned in Canada by non-residents
E Computation of tax
E.1 Minimum tax
F Special rules applicable in certain circumstances
G Deferred and other special income arrangements
H Exemptions
I Returns, assessments, payment and appeals
J Appeals to the Tax Court of Canada and the Federal Court of Appeal
a Individuals
a.1 Canada child benefit
a.2 Working income tax benefit
b Corporations
c All taxpayers
110 Deductions
110.2 Lump-sum payments
110.6 CG exemption
110.7 Prescribed zone
111 Losses carried over
111.1 Ordering
114-114.2 Part-year resident
117-117.1 Tax rates
118-118.95 Personal credits
120 Income from outside Canada
120.2 Minimum tax carryover
120.4 Tax on split income
121 Dividend tax credit
122 Tax on inter vivos trust
122.1 [Specified Investment Flow-Through (SIFT) Trust]
122.3 Employment outside Canada
122.5 GST credit
122.51 Refundable medical expense supplement
122.6-122.63 Child tax benefit
122.7-122.71 Working income tax benefit
126 Foreign tax credit
127.1-127.41 Other tax credits
127.5 Obligation to pay
127.51 Minimum amount
127.52 Adjusted taxable income
127.53 Basic exemption
127.531 Basic credit
127.54 Definitions
127.55 Application of 127.5

¶10,000 Computation of Taxable Income for an Individual

Overview

"Taxable income" is defined in the Act as a taxpayer's net income for the year, plus or minus the deductions permitted by Division C. While Part I, Division B, of the Act focuses on the computation of income for tax purposes, Division C contains the statutory rules for determining taxable income. These rules generally allow for deductions of income that the Act wants to include in its measure of Net Income for Tax Purposes but that the government has chosen not to tax. ITA: 2(2) Taxable income

It is important to realize that "Net Income for Tax Purposes", the first computation described above, and "Taxable Income" serve two distinct purposes. "Net Income for Tax Purposes" provides a broad measure of income available to an individual and therefore is used as a measure of income or needs testing within the Act for items such as certain tax credits including the medical expense credit, etc. However, "Taxable Income" is a computation of the income that the government ultimately wishes to tax. Taxable income is the base to which the tax rates are applied. The deductions adjust net income for tax purposes to arrive at taxable income. Note that if the Division C deductions result in a negative taxable income, taxable income becomes zero.

Division C includes a number of allowable deductions but only a few of these apply to individuals. Division C deductions applicable to individuals include those for:

Section 110 — employee stock options, charitable donations of employee stock option shares, shares received under a deferred profit sharing plan, worker's compensation, social assistance, treaty and international organization exemptions, and vows of perpetual poverty.

Section 110.2 — deduction for lump-sum payments.

Section 110.6 — deduction for capital gains on farm property, shares of a qualified small business corporation, and qualified fishing properties.

Section 111 — deduction for carryover losses including non-capital losses, net capital losses, restricted farm losses, and farm losses.

As shown, the deductions permitted are quite specific and, hence, will not be available to all taxpayers. Where an individual claims more than one deduction in the same taxation year, an ordering rule is provided. ITA: 111.1 Order of applying provisions

¶10,100 Widely Used Division C Deductions

Overview

This section will discuss in detail the most common Division C deductions for individuals.

¶10,110 Stock Option Deduction

Overview

Employee stock options were discussed in detail in Chapter 3. Recall that one of the features that made employee stock options unique from regular payments of employment income such as salary was the opportunity to use the "stock option deduction", equal to half the employment income generated by the stock option. This deduction is a Division C deduction and is included in the computation of Taxable Income. Combined, the full amount of the employment income generated by the stock option and the stock option deduction in Division C to compute Taxable Income result in the stock option having an inclusion rate of 50%, equivalent to the inclusion rate for a capital gain. In summary, this outcome is accomplished by including the full employment income in the computation of net income for tax purposes and subsequently subtracting the "stock option deduction" (half the employment amount) as a Division C deduction during the computation of Taxable Income.

¶10,110.10 Granted by Corporations Other Than Canadian-Controlled Private Corporations

Employees who acquire shares from a corporation other than a Canadian controlled private corporation ("CCPC") under a stock option agreement are required to include a benefit in their employment income. The benefit is computed as the amount by which the fair market value of the shares at the time the shares were acquired exceeds the price actually paid (i.e., the exercise price). The employment benefit is then added to the adjusted cost base of the shares, so that any resultant capital gain reflects the increase in value since the acquisition date. Also, the adjusted cost base reflects the sum of amounts that have been previously taxed (that is, amounts that have been tax-paid).

ITA: 7(1) Agreement to issue securities to employees; 53(1)(j) [Adjustments to cost base — Share or fund unit taxed as stock option benefit]

There is a deduction of ½ of the employment benefit referred to as a "stock option deduction" available in the computation of taxable income. The stock option deduction can be claimed if the exercise price was not less than the value of the share at the time the option was granted. In addition, there are certain limitations on the type of shares issued (i.e., prescribed shares which are described as, in essence, common shares). Also, an arm's length relationship of the parties must exist before and after the exercising of the option. Note there are no tax consequences upon the granting of an option. This deduction is available for stock options that meet the conditions, from both non-CCPCs, like a public corporation, and CCPCs.

ITA: 110(1)(d) Employee options; ITR: 6204 Prescribed Shares

Ⓐ ¶10,110.20 Decline in Value of Shares

In some instances where employees have been granted stock options the value of the shares has subsequently declined to the point where the fair market value is less than the exercise price. As a result of this decline, employers may want to reduce the exercise price to the current fair market value. This, however, will disqualify the option for the Division C deduction, since the exercise price may be less than the fair market value at the time the option was granted. In recognition of this situation, employers are allowed to reduce the exercise price without jeopardizing the employee's Division C deduction, as long as the following conditions are met:

ITA: 110(1)(d) Employee options, 110(1.7) Reduction in exercise price, 110(1.8) Conditions for subsection (1.7) to apply

- the exercise price is reduced at a time when the fair market value of the securities is less than the old exercise price,
- the old exercise price was not less than the fair market value of the securities when the option was granted, and
- the new exercise price was not less than the fair market value of the securities at the time of the price reduction.

For example, assume that the original option was granted when the fair market value of the shares was $20 and the option had an exercise price of $22. This option would have qualified for the Division C deduction. If the share value drops to $10 and the company reduces the option price to $12 then this security will continue to qualify for the deduction.

ITA: 110(1)(d) Employee options

¶10,110.40 Granted by a Canadian-Controlled Private Corporation

An exception to the requirement to include the benefit in the year of exercise of the option is provided for stock options granted by a CCPC. There is an employment inclusion of the same amount, but the income is deferred until the year the shares are disposed of. Furthermore, the stock option deduction can only be claimed if the shares have not been sold or exchanged before the second anniversary date of the day of acquisition.

ITA: 7(1.1) Employee stock options, 110(1)(d.1) Idem

Note that for stock options granted by a CCPC, there are two possibilities for a stock option deduction.

(1) The shares acquired under the option are held for the two-year period and, thus, qualify for the CCPC deduction, or

ITA: 110(1)(d.1) Idem

(2) The exercise price is not less than the value of the shares at the date the option was granted and, thus, qualify for the general deduction.

ITA: 110(1)(d) Employee options

Only one of the two possibilities need apply.

¶10,110.50 Summary of Stock Option Rules

Where the stock option deduction is claimed in the computation of Taxable Income, only ½ of the employment benefit generated by the stock option (the difference between the exercise price and the value at the date of exercise) is taxable, equivalent to the inclusion rate of 50% for a capital gain. While the net numerical result is a ½ inclusion, the net amount is not a taxable capital gain and, therefore, not eligible for the capital gains deduction on qualified small business corporation shares ("QSBCS").

The schematic diagram on stock options introduced in Chapter 3 can be expanded now to include the effects of the stock option deduction.

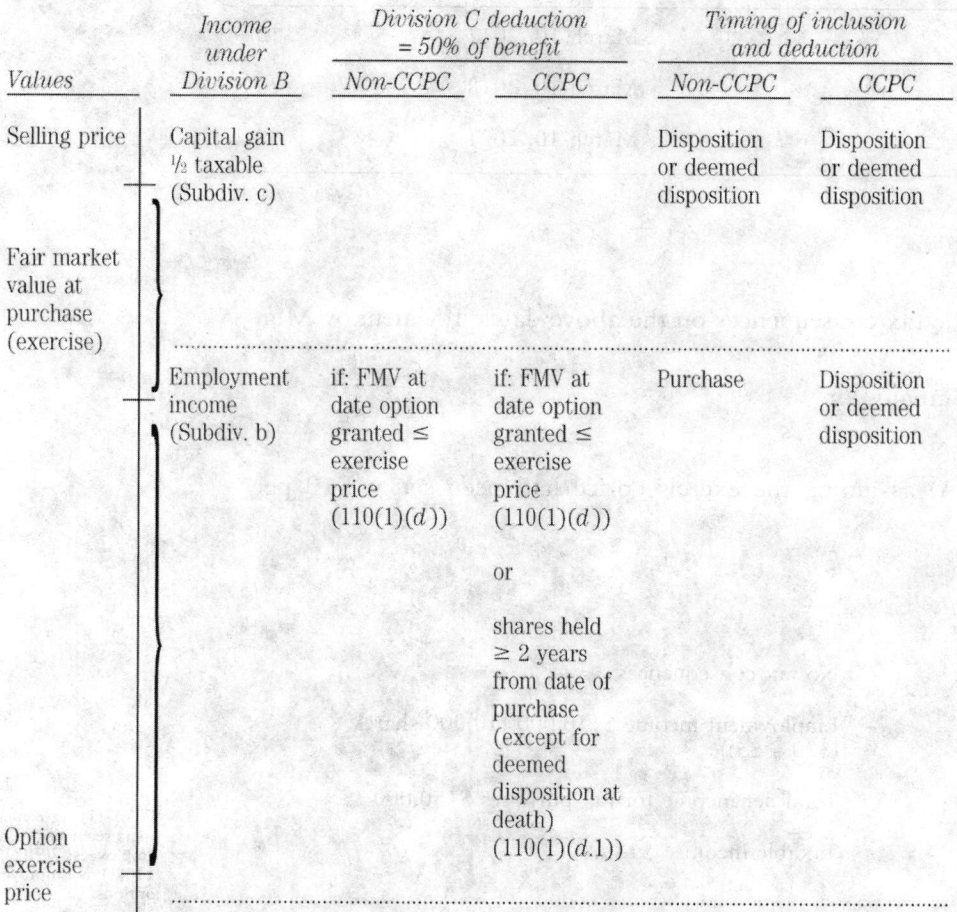

Values	*Income under Division B*	*Division C deduction = 50% of benefit*		*Timing of inclusion and deduction*	
		Non-CCPC	*CCPC*	*Non-CCPC*	*CCPC*
Selling price	Capital gain ½ taxable (Subdiv. c)			Disposition or deemed disposition	Disposition or deemed disposition
Fair market value at purchase (exercise)	Employment income (Subdiv. b)	if: FMV at date option granted ≤ exercise price (110(1)(*d*))	if: FMV at date option granted ≤ exercise price (110(1)(*d*)) or shares held ≥ 2 years from date of purchase (except for deemed disposition at death) (110(1)(*d*.1))	Purchase	Disposition or deemed disposition
Option exercise price					

Note that the fair market value of the shares at the date that the option is granted is relevant only for the condition that allows the ½ stock option deduction.

Example Problem 10-1

Malenkov Mfg. Ltd. granted Ms. Yampolsky, its vice-president, an option to purchase 10,000 shares for $5 per share. On March 10, 2018, she acquired the 10,000 shares under the option. The following pertains to the shares:

	Date	FMV
Option granted	March 10, 2012	$10
Option exercised	March 10, 2018	20
Shares to be sold	March 10, 2021	30

REQUIRED

(A) Determine the tax consequences on the above dates if Malenkov Mfg. Ltd. was:

(i) a public company, or

(ii) a CCPC.

(B) Redo Part (A) assuming the exercise price had been set at $10 per share.

SOLUTION

(A)(i)	March 10, 2012	—	No tax consequences
	March 10, 2018	—	Employment income $150,000 (10,000 shares × ($20 – $5))
			Total net income for tax purposes $150,000
			Taxable income[1] $150,000
		—	Adjusted cost base of each share increased by $15 per share to $20, so that the $15 per share benefit is not taxed again on disposition
	March 10, 2021	—	Taxable capital gain of $50,000 (½ ($30 – $20) × 10,000 shares)
			Total net income for tax purposes $50,000
			Taxable income $50,000
(ii)	March 10, 2012	—	No tax consequences
	March 10, 2018	—	No tax consequences
	March 10, 2021	—	Employment inclusion of $150,000 (10,000 shares × ($20 – $5))
			Taxable capital gain of $50,000 (½ ($30 – $20) × 10,000 shares)[2]

ITA: 7(1) Agreement to issue securities to employees; 7(9)(b), 110(1)(d) Employee options

ITA: 53(1)(j) [Adjustments to cost base — Share or fund unit taxed as stock option benefit]

ITA: 7(1.1) Employee stock options

Total net income for tax purposes $200,000

Stock option deduction of $75,000 (½ × $150,000)[3]   ITA: 110(1)(d.1) Idem

Taxable Income $75,000

— Adjusted cost base of each share increased by $15 per share to $20   ITA: 53(1)(j) [Adjustments to cost base — Share or fund unit taxed as stock option benefit]

[1] No stock option deduction, since the exercise price ($5) was less than the value on the grant date ($10)

[2] May qualify for the qualified small business corporation share capital gains deduction

[3] Since the shares were held over two years

(B) If the exercise price had been $10, equal to the fair market value of the shares at the date of grant, the two results would have been as follows:

	(B)(i)	(B)(ii)
Employment income (10,000 shares × ($20 – $10)).	$100,000	$100,000
Taxable capital gain	50,000	50,000
Net income for tax purposes	$ 150,000	$ 150,000
Division C deduction (½ × $100,000).	(50,000)	(50,000)
	$100,000	$100,000

ITA: 110(1)(d) Employee options, 110(1)(d.1) Idem

The primary difference between (A) and (B) is that the stock option deduction is available to the non-CCPC, since the exercise price is not less than the fair market value at the time the option was granted. Also, for the CCPC option, the benefit does not have to be reported until the year of disposal.   ITA: 110(1)(d) Employee options

The effect of these provisions is to give a treatment equivalent to capital gains for stock option benefits accruing up to the date of acquisition and included in employment income, without providing eligibility for the QSBC share capital gains deduction where applicable.

¶10,120 Deduction for Certain Receipts

A number of refundable and non-refundable tax credits provided to an individual taxpayer are designed to be based on a taxpayer's income level and are therefore reduced based on the individual's net income for tax purposes (also known as Division B income). The computation of net income for tax purposes is designed to be a broad measure to consider a wide range of income that a taxpayer may have earned and had available to them in the year. Certain social assistance payments received by individuals are included in their net income for tax purposes (Division B income) and may affect these tax credits. However, there is no intention to tax these payments in the hands of the recipient. To insure they are not included in taxable income, a deduction is provided in Division C, in the computation of taxable income, to remove these amounts that have previously been

ITA: 110(1)(f) Deductions for payments

included in the computation of net income for tax purposes. The sources of income which qualify for this treatment are:

- the Guaranteed Income Supplement,
- social assistance payments,
- workers' compensation, and
- amounts that are exempt income by virtue of a tax treaty.

¶10,140 Loss Carryovers

Overview

Income and losses are computed for a taxation year, which is a somewhat arbitrary period. Over a longer period, losses might be expected to offset income, with only the net income being taxable in that longer period. The availability of a carryover period for losses is intended to broaden the period within which losses can offset income. The statute provides for losses to be carried back against prior years' income or forward against future years' income. Taxpayers are provided some relief from the economic risk of an activity and are provided with encouragement to persevere. The necessity for limitations is crucial. Limitations, together with the broad general rules that apply to the utilization or restriction of various types of losses, will be discussed in this chapter.

Any losses which cannot be applied in the year in which they may be deducted in Division C by carrying the losses back three years through amended returns and/or applying the balance of the losses to future years, subject to any further restrictions as indicated below.

¶10,140.10 Non-Capital Loss Carryovers

A "non-capital loss" (non-CL) available for carryover is a defined term. For individuals, the definition can be summarized in computational form as follows: ITA: 111(1)(a) Non-capital losses, 111(8) Definitions

Aggregate of:			
Amounts computed as losses from non-capital sources:			ITA: 3(d)
Loss from an office or employment		$xxx	
Loss from business		xxx	
Loss from property		xxx	
Allowable business investment loss		xxx	
Amount deducted as capital gains deduction		xxx	ITA: 110.6 [Capital gains exemption]
Amount deducted as net capital losses		xxx	ITA: 111(1)(b) Net capital losses
Amount deductible as:			ITA: 110(1)(d) Employee options, 110(1)(d.1) Idem, 110(1)(d.2) Prospector's and grubstaker's shares, 110(1)(d.3) Employer's shares
Stock options	$xxx		
Social assistance and other payments	xxx	xxx	ITA: 110(1)(f) Deductions for payments
		$xxx	

ITA: 3(c)

ITA: 56 Amounts to be included in income for year, 59 Consideration for foreign resource property

ITA: 60 Other deductions, 66 [Exploration and development expenses]

Less: aggregate of net incomes:			
Income from office or employment		$xxx	
Income from business		xxx	
Income from property		xxx	
Income from other sources		xxx	
Taxable capital gains (other than from listed personal property)	$xxx		
Taxable net capital gain from listed personal property	xxx		
	$xxx		
Less: allowable capital losses (other than from listed personal property and allowable business investment losses)	xxx	xxx[1]	
		$xxx	
Less: other deductions		xxx	xxx[1]
			$xxx[1]
Less: farm loss (included in loss from business above)			xxx
Non-capital loss carryover			$xxx[1]

[1] Cannot be negative [sec. 257].

Note that in order to become a carryover non-capital loss, a current year's loss from non-capital sources must, in essence, exceed income from all other sources in the current year. Non-capital losses may be carried over by applying the earliest losses first. A non-capital loss incurred in the current year may be carried back three taxation years and carried forward 20 taxation years.

Allowable business investment losses are discussed in detail in Chapters 7 and 13. Note that the portion of an allowable business investment loss not used in the year the loss is incurred becomes a non-capital loss and is available for carryover equivalent to a non-capital loss described above. However, if the ABIL is not used up within a 10-year carryforward, then it reverts to its original nature and becomes a net capital loss available for indefinite carry forward, but only for deduction from net taxable capital gains.

¶10,140.20 Net Capital Loss Carryovers

ITA: 111(1)(b) Net capital losses; 111(8) net capital loss

Allowable capital losses that cannot be used in the current year (i.e., the excess allowable capital losses for the year after subtracting taxable capital gains for the year) generate a "net capital loss" ("net CL"). Net capital losses may be carried back three years and forward indefinitely. Note that the net CL also includes allowable business investment losses not absorbed in the 10-year carryforward period as a non-capital loss, as discussed above. It is important to note that net capital losses for a particular year are calculated using the inclusion rate of that year. This means that any net capital loss carryover balances will already have had the inclusion rate applied to it.

The following are the historical inclusion rates.

Capital Gains Inclusion Rate:

Years	Inclusion Rate
1990–February 27, 2000	3/4
February 28, 2000–October 17, 2000	2/3
After October 17, 2000	1/2

¶10,140.30 Carryovers From Periods With Different Inclusion Rates

Since net capital losses may arise in years with different capital gains inclusion rates to be deducted against other net taxable capital gains computed by other inclusion rates, it might be necessary to convert net capital losses to the capital gains inclusion rate appropriate to the carryover year in which the net capital loss is deducted. Conceptually, a capital loss from one period should offset an equivalent dollar value of capital gain from any other period.

Example

For example, a $10,000 capital loss from 1999 should completely offset a $10,000 capital gain in 2018. However, a $10,000 capital loss in 1999 would create a $7,500 net capital loss carryforward (75% inclusion rate × $10,000 capital loss) and the capital gain in 2018 would generate a $5,000 taxable gain ($10,000 capital gain × 50% inclusion rate). These two amounts cannot simply be netted as that would result in $2,500 of net capital loss still available to carryforward ($5,000 – 7,500) and conceptually they should net to nil. This situation calls for the net capital loss carryforward of $7,500 to be converted back into a full capital loss by reversing the inclusion rate of 75% when the loss was incurred in 1999. This is accomplished by dividing the net capital loss carryforward of $7,500 by 75% (the inclusion rate at the time the original loss was incurred) which results in a full loss of $10,000. The conversion is then completed by applying the current inclusion rate of 50% to the above full loss of $10,000 resulting in a converted net capital loss carryforward of $5,000 ($10,000 × 50%). This converted net capital loss carryforward of $5,000 perfectly offsets the taxable capital gain of $5,000 calculated above.

In summary, this conversion is completed by:

(1) Dividing the net capital loss carryforward by the inclusion rate at the time the loss was incurred to convert the fractional amount for that year to the full loss amount, and

(2) Multiplying the full loss calculated by step 1) by the current capital gains inclusion rate.

Example Problem 10-2

Larry Laplante had net capital losses of $15,000 in the taxation year ending December 31, 1999. He had capital gains of $7,000 in 2018. He has had no other capital gains or losses.

REQUIRED

Determine the maximum amount to be deducted in the 2018 taxation year.

ITA: 111(1)(b) Net capital losses, 111(1.1) Net capital losses

SOLUTION

		2018	
Net taxable capital gain:			ITA: 3(b)
Capital gains realized	$ 7,000		
Taxable capital gain	$ 3,500		
Adjusted deduction —			
Lesser of:			ITA: 111(1.1)(a)
(i) TCG above	$ 3,500		ITA: 3(b)
(ii) total of adjusted net capital losses of loss years (see carryover below)	$10,000**		
Lesser amount		$ 3,500	

**Net capital loss carryovers:

Year loss incurred	**1999**
Unadjusted net CL available in 2018	$15,000
Adjusted to 2018 inclusion rate	$10,000[1]

Year loss incurred	1999
Utilized in 2018	(3,500)
Available in 2019	$ 6,500

NOTE TO SOLUTION

(1) The losses are adjusted from the ¾ inclusion rate to the ½ inclusion rate as follows:

$$1999: (\$15,000 / 3/4) \times 1/2 = \$10,000$$

This adjustment factor does nothing more than convert the fractional loss of a particular year back into a full loss. The net capital loss is then calculated at the inclusion rate for the year of the deduction by multiplying the full loss by ½ . . . Hence, $15,000 divided by ¾ is $20,000 which was the full capital loss in 1999 before the ¾ inclusion rate was applied. Then $20,000 multiplied by ½ produces $10,000 which is the net capital loss stated in terms of a ½ inclusion rate used in 2018.

Note that the losses carried forward from the "loss year" are those from the earliest loss year. Note, also, how net capital losses deducted in a particular year, as modified by the adjustments for different inclusion rates, are limited to net taxable capital gains of that year. ITA: 111(3) Limitation on deductibility; 111(1)(b) Net capital losses, 111(1.1)(a)

¶10,150 Capital Gains Exemption/Capital Gains Deduction

The Capital Gains Exemption is an important tax break in the Canadian tax system as it has the potential to provide an individual with a large tax savings on the sale of certain property. It is available only to individuals (not corporations or trusts) and can allow individuals to shelter (i.e., not pay tax) on up to $848,252 of capital gains from the sale of qualifying properties over an individual's lifetime. Those qualifying properties include:

- Qualified small business corporation shares,
- Qualified farm property, or
- Qualified fishing property.

The capital gains exemption for 2018 is $848,252 (indexed) which generates up to a $424,126 capital gains deduction ($848,252 × 50% inclusion rate) that can be deducted as a Division C deduction. Note that the "capital gains exemption" refers to the amount without regard to the inclusion rate while the "capital gains deduction" has had the inclusion rate applied.

The entire taxable capital gain (capital gain × inclusion rate) on the sale of the qualifying property is included in the computation of net income for tax purposes. The capital gains deduction is then deducted during the computation of taxable income as a Division C deduction. The capital gains deduction available on qualified small business corporation shares will be discussed in detail in Chapter 13.

ITA: 110.6(2.1) Capital gains deduction — qualified small business corporation shares

¶10,160 Ordering of Division C Deductions

The act provides an order for deducting amounts under Division C. The act generally allows deductions that cannot be carried forward to be used first followed by deductions that allow for some carryforward to follow.

¶10,160.10 General Ordering Rules for Division C

Section 111.1 provides the following order of relevant deductions under Division C:

Sec. 110	Other deductions, such as employee stock options
Sec. 110.2	Lump-sum payments
Sec. 111	Loss carryovers, such as non- and net capital losses Sec. 110.6 Capital gains deduction
Sec. 110.7	Residing in prescribed zone.

¶10,160.20 Ordering of Section 111 Loss Carryovers

Loss carryovers can be applied in any order within section 111, subject to the general ordering rules for Division C, except that the oldest losses are always applied first. Therefore, careful consideration should be given as to which type of losses are used first. Generally speaking, the most restricted types of loss carryovers should be applied first. For example, since net capital losses can only be applied against net taxable capital gains, then net capital losses should be applied in years in which net taxable capital gains arise, unless it is expected that these gains will arise regularly in the future. Losses which have a carryback provision should be used immediately, if possible, so that taxes are refunded as soon as possible.

ITA: 111.1 Order of applying provisions, 111(3)(b)

Example Problem 10-3

The following information has been provided by your client, Karl Kraft:

	2016	2017	2018
Capital gains (CG)	—	$84,000	$44,000
Capital losses (CL) (excluding BIL)	$6,000	—	—
Business investment loss (BIL) before adjustment.	18,000	—	30,000

ITA: 39(9) Deduction from business investment loss

Additional Information

(1) Karl had a $10,000 net capital loss which arose in 1999, and has not been deducted previously.

(2) Karl had no capital gains prior to 2016 and he did not claim any net capital losses in any preceding years.

(3) In 2017, Karl had a rental property loss of $1,000 and had no property income in 2016 or 2017.

REQUIRED

(1) Determine Karl's income from the sources indicated for 2016 to 2018 according to the ordering rules in section 3.

(2) Determine Karl's taxable income from the sources indicated for 2016 to 2018 according to the ordering rules in Division C after amending the returns.

SOLUTION

	2016	2017	2018	
(1)				
Income from non-capital sources (≥ 0)	Nil	Nil	Nil	ITA: 3(a)
Net taxable capital gains (≥ 0):				ITA: 3(b)
taxable capital gains	Nil	$ 42,000	$ 22,000	
allowable capital losses	$ (3,000)	—	—	
	Nil	$ 42,000	$ 22,000	

	2016	2017	2018
Sum of non-capital and capital sources	Nil	$ 42,000	$ 22,000
Losses from non-capital sources and ABILs:			
rental property loss	—	—	(1,000)
ABIL	$ (9,000)	—	(15,000)
Division B income	0	$ 42,000	$ 6,000
(2)			
Division B income from (A)	0	$ 42,000	$ 6,000
Less: net capital losses	Nil	(9,667)[1]	Nil
non-capital losses (2016 ABIL carried forward to 2017)	Nil	(9,000)	Nil
Taxable income (Division C)	Nil	$ 23,333	$ 6,000

ITA: 3(d)

ITA: 3(e)

ITA: 111(1)(b) Net capital losses

The foregoing solution illustrates how the various components fit into the full calculation of Division B income and taxable income.

NOTE TO SOLUTION

[1]**Loss continuity schedule**	1999	2015	Total
Unadjusted net CL	$ 10,000	$ 3,000	
Adjusted to 2017 inclusion rate ($10,000 × 1/2 / 3/4)	$ 6,667	$ 3,000	$ 9,667
Utilized in 2017	(6,667)	(3,000)	(9,667)
Available in 2018	Nil	Nil	Nil

Example Problem 10-4

Larry Hewitt provides you with the following income (losses) for tax purposes for the years 2016 to 2018:

	2016	2017	2018
Employment income	$25,000	$ 32,000	$40,000
Business income:	20,000	(36,000)	40,000
Property income from Canadian interest.	3,000	4,000	5,000
Capital gains (capital losses):			
Listed personal property	6,000	(10,000)	12,000
Other	15,000	(14,000)	2,250

Larry also provides the following additional information:

(1) Loss carryovers:

Listed personal property loss arising in 2013	$ 2,000
Non-capital loss arising in 2014 from a business	35,000
Net capital loss arising in 2013	12,000

(2) Larry did not claim a capital gains deduction or net capital losses in the years prior to 2016.

REQUIRED

Dealing with each item line-by-line across the years, rather than one year at a time;

(1) determine Larry's income for 2016 to 2018 according to the ordering rules in section 3, and

(2) determine Larry's taxable income for 2016 to 2018 according to the ordering rule in Division C after amending the returns.

SOLUTION

	2016	2017	2018	
(1)				
Income from non-capital sources (≥0):				ITA: 3(a)
Employment	$25,000	$ 32,000	$ 40,000	
Business income	20,000	Nil	40,000	
Property from Canadian interest	3,000	4,000	5,000	
	$48,000	$ 36,000	$ 85,000	
Net taxable capital gains (≥0):				ITA: 3(b)
Listed personal property[1]	Nil	Nil	$ 3,000	
Other	$ 7,500	(7,000)	1,125	
	$ 7,500	Nil	$ 4,125	
Sum of non-capital and capital sources	$55,500	$ 36,000	$ 89,125	ITA: 3(c)
Losses from non-capital sources		(36,000)		ITA: 3(d)
Income — Division B	$55,500	Nil	$ 89,125	ITA: 3(e)
(2)				
Income — Division B	$55,500		$ 89,125	
Net capital loss[2]	(7,500)		(4,125)	ITA: 111(1)(b) Net capital losses
Non-capital loss[3]	(35,000)		Nil	ITA: 111(1)(a) Non-capital losses
Taxable income (Division C)	$13,000	Nil	$ 85,000	

NOTES TO SOLUTION

(1) The listed personal property loss from 2013 is applied against the 2016 listed personal property gain of $6,000 leaving $4,000, which will be offset by the listed personal property capital loss of 2017 carried back. The remaining 2017 listed personal property capital loss of $6,000 will be carried forward and applied against the 2018 listed personal property capital gain of $12,000 leaving a net capital gain of $6,000 of which ½ will be taken into income. Note that listed personal property losses are carried over in their full capital loss amounts.

ITA: 111(1)(b) Net capital losses, 111(1.1)(a), 111(8) Definitions

(2) (A) Net capital losses

	2016		2017	2018	
Lesser of:					
(i) net TCGs for the year	$ 7,500		N/A	$ 4,125	
(ii) total of net capital losses of prior loss years	$12,000		N/A	$11,500	
Lesser amount		$ 7,500			$ 4,125

(B) Net capital loss continuity schedule

	2013	2017	Total
Net CL	$12,000	N/A	$12,000
Utilized in 2016	(7,500)	N/A	(7,500)
Available in 2017	$ 4,500	—	$ 4,500
Realized in 2017	—	$7,000	7,000
Utilized in 2017	Nil	Nil	Nil
Available in 2018	$ 4,500	$7,000	$11,500
Utilized in 2018	(4,125)	Nil	(4,125)
Available in 2019	$ 375	$7,000	$ 7,375

[(3)] Non-capital loss continuity schedule

Non-capital loss — 2014		$35,000
2016 application		(35,000)
Balance of 2014 non-capital loss		Nil
Non-capital loss — 2017		
Business loss	$36,000	
less: sum of income sources for the year	(36,000)	Nil
Balance		Nil

ITA: 3(c)

Since individuals are eligible for non-refundable tax credits, it is advantageous to have at least $11,327 of taxable income in 2016. This amount increases to $11,474 in 2017 and $11,809 in 2018.

¶10,170 Taxable Income of Non-Residents

In the discussion of residence in Chapter 2, it was established that a part-year resident of Canada is taxed on worldwide income for the part of the year that the individual is resident in Canada. The taxable income for the period of part-year residence of an individual is calculated under Division D. A non-resident individual is subject to Part I tax on income from employment in Canada, from carrying on business in Canada and from the disposition of taxable Canadian property. In addition, a non-resident is subject to Canadian withholding tax on Canadian-source income such as interest, dividends, alimony, and pension receipts.

ITA: 114 Individual resident in Canada for only part of year; 115 Non-resident's taxable income in Canada; 212 Tax

Consider the case of an individual who is an international business consultant who decided to move the base of operations of the business to another country and to continue to provide service to Canadian clients from that base. Assume the individual ceases to be a resident on May 15 of the year, but continues to carry on the unincorporated business of providing consulting services in Canada periodically after that date. This individual would be taxed in that year.

ITA: 114(a), 114(b)

Income for the period of part-year residence is computed in the normal manner, including the deduction of most amounts allowed in Division B. The Division C deductions reasonably applicable to the period of part-year residence are also deductible. The taxable income of a non-resident with Canadian-source income is computed under Division D. Certain Division C deductions may be claimed in respect of that income earned in Canada.

Non-residents are required to pay tax on their "taxable income earned in Canada" for the year. "Taxable income earned in Canada" is the income that would be determined under section 3 with some adjustments to confine the calculation to Canadian-sources of the non-resident. In particular, the term "taxable Canadian property" necessary for the determination of income from its disposition is defined. Then, Division C deductions as

ITA: 2(3) Tax payable by non-resident persons, 2(3)(c), 110(1)(d) Employee options, 110(1)(d.1) Idem, 110.1(1) Deduction for gifts, 111

appropriate to the Canadian-source income may be claimed. These deductions include those in respect of stock options exercised, charitable donations, and loss carryovers reasonably applicable to Canadian-source income. The CRA's interpretation of these provisions is contained in their Interpretation Bulletin entitled "Non-residents — Income earned in Canada". See Chapter 19 for more information.

Losses deductible, 115(1)(b), 115(1)(f); Interpretation Bulletins: IT-420R3 Non-residents — Income earned in Canada

¶10,190 Pause and Reflect — Summary of Learning Goals

After working through this section, ¶10,100, you should be able to:

- Explain the different purposes for computing net income for tax purposes and taxable income.
- Identify which deductions are used in the computation of net income for tax purposes and which deductions are used in the computation of taxable income.
- Calculate taxable income starting from net income for tax purposes.

¶10,190.99 Practise What You've Learned

Refer to the following sections of the Study Guide to practise what you've learned:

¶10,800 — Review Questions

- Question 1 — Deduction of loss carryovers

¶10,825 — Multiple Choice Questions

- Question 1 — Employee stock options

¶10,850 — Exercises

- Exercise 2 — Loss carryovers
- Exercise 3 — Calculate income for tax purposes
- Exercise 15 — Taxable income for an individual

¶10,200 Computation of Tax for Individuals — General Rules

Overview

After taxable income is computed, the third computation, "tax liability", is calculated by applying the tax rates to the tax base of taxable income to arrive at total tax owing before credits. The taxpayer is then allowed to deduct credits for which they are eligible from that amount owing, as well as any tax payments already made via deduction from their employment income or instalments. The net result is the balance of tax owing or refundable. The following section discusses tax rates for individuals required to calculate the total tax owing followed by a discussion of the tax credits that may be available to the individual taxpayer.

¶10,210 Basic Computation of Tax

Our federal tax system has progressive tax rates for individuals. This means that as a person's taxable income increases from one income bracket to another (refer to the brackets below), the rate of tax on the next dollar earned also increases. This follows the tax policy argument that those who can afford to should pay a higher proportion of their income in tax. In a flat rate system, everyone would pay the same rate of tax regardless of their income.

¶10,220 Tax Rates

The Act sets out the rates of tax applicable to individuals. These amounts, which have been indexed for 2018, are presented in Exhibit 10-1.

ITA: 117(2) Rates for taxation years after 2015

Exhibit 10-1 2018 Federal Income Tax Brackets

Taxable income		Tax
$46,605 or less		15%
In excess of $46,605	$6,991[1]	+ 20.5% on next $46,603
In excess of $93,208	$16,544[2]	+ 26% on next $51,281
In excess of $144,489	$29,877[3]	+ 29% on next $61,353
In excess of $205,842	$47,669[4]	+ 33% on remainder

[1] Computed as 15% of $46,605 = $6,991 (rounded)
[2] Computed as $6,991 + 20.5% of $46,603 = $16,544 (rounded)
[3] Computed as $16,544 + 26% of $51,281 = $29,877 (rounded)
[4] Computed as $29,877 + 29% of $61,353 = $47,669 (rounded)

¶10,230 Annual Indexing Adjustment

The Act provides for the annual indexing of certain dollar amounts used in the calculation of tax or tax credits.

ITA: 117.1 Annual adjustment

The indexing formula is based on the annual increase in the Consumer Price Index for the 12-month period ending September 30 of the year before the year in which the indexing is to apply.

¶10,240 Overview of Tax Credit and Tax Calculation System

Exhibit 10-2 summarizes the key items in the calculation of tax credits and income tax payable. The first line in Exhibit 10-2 results from applying the tax table in Exhibit 10-1 to the taxpayer's taxable income for the year. Total federal income tax is reduced by two basic types of credits, non-refundable and refundable, which are deducted at one of three different stages of the calculation highlighted in italics below.

Exhibit 10-2 Summary of Income Tax Calculation

Total federal income tax on taxable income			$xxx	ITA: 117(2) Rates for taxation years after 2015, 117.1 Annual adjustment
Subtract:	Total non-refundable tax credits (see Exhibit 10-3)	$xxx		
	Federal dividend tax credit	xxx	xxx	ITA: 121 Deduction for taxable dividends
Basic federal tax			$xxx	
Subtract:	Federal foreign tax credits		xxx	ITA: 126 Foreign tax deduction
Federal tax			$xxx	
Subtract:	Federal political contributions tax credit	$xxx		ITA: 127(3) Contributions to registered parties and candidates
	Other federal tax credits	xxx	xxx	
Net federal tax			$xxx	
Add: Tax on Old Age Security benefits			xxx	ITA: 180.2 Tax on Old Age Security Benefits
Total federal tax			$xxx	
Add:	Provincial tax	$xxx		
	Provincial surtax	xxx	xxx	
Total payable			$xxx	
Subtract:	Total income tax deducted at source	$xxx		
	Federal refundable tax credits (e.g., employee and partner GST/HST rebate)	xxx		
	Tax paid by instalments	xxx		
	Provincial refundable tax credits	xxx	xxx	
Balance payable or refundable			$xxx	

¶10,240.10 Non-Refundable Versus Refundable Tax Credits

When an amount of federal tax owing is calculated, the taxpayer can pay by cash or by tax credits. This is similar in nature to paying a bill at a store where the consumer has both cash and some store credit, perhaps, from previously returned merchandise or reward points. The consumer can deduct the amount of the store credit from the bill and pay the remainder in cash. Similarly, the amount of tax credits is generally deducted from the tax owing.

Tax credits come in two general forms: refundable and non-refundable. With a non-refundable credit, if the amount of the credit exceeds the amount of tax owing, the excess credit is *not* refunded to the taxpayer and in the majority of cases will expire. Therefore if a taxpayer owes no tax, non-refundable credits provide no benefit to the taxpayer. This is the equivalent of having a store credit at a store you would never shop at.

Alternatively, when a tax credit is refundable, the excess portion is paid back to the taxpayer. It is the equivalent of receiving a store credit where any unused amount will result in cash back. Therefore, if a taxpayer has no amount of tax owing, a refundable credit will still benefit a taxpayer. This is why many credits aimed at taxpayers with low or potentially no income are refundable.

¶10,240.20 Non-Refundable Tax Credits

Non-refundable tax credits like the marital status tax credit or the dividend tax credit are subtracted from federal tax. To the extent that these credits exceed federal tax, the excess is not refundable and, therefore, is of no value to the taxpayer. Some non-refundable tax credits are referred to as "above-the-line tax credits", because they are subtracted from federal tax to arrive at basic federal tax. Alternatively, other non-refundable tax credits like federal foreign tax credits and federal political contributions tax credits can be termed "below-the-line tax credits", because they are subtracted after the calculation of basic federal tax. The important difference between the two is that "below-the-line tax credits" are not magnified by the territorial or non-resident tax effects, discussed below. Exhibit 10-3 lists many common non-refundable tax credits.

Exhibit 10-3 Types of Non-Refundable Tax Credits

- Basic personal amount
- Spousal amount
- Equivalent-to-spouse amount
- Canada caregiver credit
- Age amount
- Canada employment amount
- Adoption expense amount
- Home renovation tax credit

- Home accessibility tax credit
- First-time home buyers' tax credit
- Volunteer firefighters tax credit
- Search and rescue volunteers tax credit
- Canada or Quebec Pension Plan contributions
- Employment Insurance premiums
- Pension income amount
- Mental or physical impairment amount (disability)
- Disability amount transferred from a dependant other than spouse
- Tuition amount
- Tuition amount transferred from a child
- Amounts transferred from spouse
- Medical expenses
- Charitable gifts (donations)
- Interest paid on student loans
- Dividend tax credit

¶10,240.30 Refundable Tax Credits

Some tax credits are refundable and, hence, are subtracted last. To the extent that these tax credits, such as the federal credit for employment outside Canada or certain provincial tax credits, exceed total tax payable, the excess is refunded, along with excess tax withholdings from payroll or excess tax instalments on income not subject to withholdings. Other tax credits like the GST/HST credit and the child tax benefit involve a calculation of an amount that is deemed to be tax-paid and, hence, result in a "refund" of the deemed tax.

¶10,240.40 Tax Credit Versus Tax Deduction

It is important to understand the difference between a tax credit and a tax deduction. A tax deduction is really a misnomer since an expenditure, such as an RRSP contribution, reduces a taxpayer's income subject to tax at a particular marginal tax rate and does not reduce tax payable directly. Therefore, a deduction from income or taxable income saves the taxpayer an amount that increases with the taxpayer's level of income and, hence, tax rate. For some taxpayers, it may take $4 of deduction to save $1 in tax (i.e., at a 25% tax rate), while for other taxpayers only $2 of deduction will save the $1 in tax (i.e., at a 50% tax rate). A tax credit is a direct reduction of the taxpayer's tax bill at a specified rate. In general, a tax credit of $1 results in a tax reduction of $1. The objective of the tax credit system is to provide all taxpayers with the same level of tax reduction regardless of their marginal tax rate.

¶10,250 Provincial and Territorial Tax

All of the provinces and territories use a "tax on income" ("TONI") structure for computing provincial tax. In such a structure, provinces may adopt the federal calculation of taxable income or make adjustments to it. Provinces may use the federal brackets or change them. Provincial rates are specified for income in these brackets. Provinces specify their own non-refundable credit amounts. For provincial tax rates, tax brackets, and tax credit amounts, see the preface material in a current edition of the Wolters Kluwer Canada Limited *Canadian Income Tax Act with Regulations, Annotated*.

For the purposes of this book including problems in the Study Guide, where provincial tax is calculated for individuals, the following table, using the federal brackets, will be used. In addition, the provincial rate for the non-refundable credits will be assumed to be 10% of the federal base. For example, the provincial basic personal amount will be 10% of $11,809 or $1,181.

Taxable income	Tax
$46,605 or less	10%
In excess of $46,605	$4,661[1] + 12% on next $46,603
In excess of $93,208	$10,253[2] + 15% on next $51,281
In excess of $144,489	$17,945[3] + 17% on next $61,353
In excess of $205,842	$28,375[4] + 17% on remainder

[1] Computed as 10% of $46,605 = $4,661 (rounded)
[2] Computed as $4,661 + 12% of $46,603 = $10,253 (rounded)
[3] Computed as $10,253 + 15% of $51,281 = $17,945 (rounded)
[4] Computed as $17,945 + 17% of $61,353 = $28,375 (rounded)

¶10,260 Marginal Tax Rates

Marginal tax rates represent the amount of tax payable on the next dollar of income earned. This is the rate which is most pertinent to taxpayer and manager planning decisions that affect additional income or deductions. This is not to be confused with the average tax rate (calculated as federal tax/taxable income) which provides more of a historic perspective and may be useful for stakeholders in assessing a manager or firm's performance in a business or investment setting.

Since not all income is taxed in the same way, a calculation of the marginal tax will depend on the type of income being earned and the amount of income already earned. For example, assume that someone already earns $150,000 and wants to know what the federal and provincial marginal tax rate would be on an additional $1,000 of interest, dividends, and capital gains. Since this person is already in the federal bracket with income over $144,489, his or her marginal tax rate will be a 29% federal rate and a 17% provincial (notional) rate for a combined rate of 46%. However, the manner in which the types of income is taxed may result in a lower effective marginal tax rate, as follows:

		Interest	Eligible Dividends (38% Gross-Up)	Other Canadian Dividends (16% Gross-Up)	Capital Gains
Income	A	$1,000	$1,000	$1,000	$1,000
Gross-up			380	160	
Untaxed portion					(500)
Taxable		$1,000	$1,380	$1,160	$ 500
Federal @ 29%.		$ 290	$ 400	$ 336	$ 145
Federal DTC ($^8/_{11}$ gross-up)			(207)	(116)	
		290	193	220	145
Provincial @ 17%		170	235	197	85
Provincial DTC ($^3/_{11}$ × gross-up)			(173)	(44)	
	B	$ 460	$ 255	$ 373	$ 230
Effective marginal tax rate	B/A	46%	26%	37%	23%

Interest income does not receive any special tax treatment, so it is fully taxed at the marginal rate of 46%. Only 50% of capital gains are taxed, so the effective marginal tax rate on this type of income is 23%. Dividends receive special tax treatment to reflect the under- lying tax paid at the corporate level so, generally speaking, dividends from public companies have an effective marginal tax rate of 26% in this second-highest bracket and dividends from active business income and investment income of a CCPC taxed at the low corporate rate have a marginal rate of 37% in 2018 and later years.

¶10,290 Pause and Reflect — Summary of Learning Goals

After working through this section, ¶10,200, you should be able to:

- Explain the difference between a refundable and non-refundable tax credit
- Apply the tax rates to an amount of taxable income to calculate the amount of gross tax owing
- Understand the difference between a tax credit and a tax deduction
- Analyze the tax impact and give advice to a taxpayer situation to decide between activities generating a tax credit or tax deduction

¶10,290.99 Practise What You've Learned

Refer to the following sections of the Study Guide to practise what you've learned:

¶10,800 — Review Questions

- Question 3 — Calculate marginal tax rate
- Question 4 — Calculate marginal tax rate

¶10,825 — Multiple Choice Questions

- Question 4 — Calculate tax payable

¶10,850 — Exercises

- Exercise 4 — Calculate tax payable

¶10,300 Computation of Tax for Individuals — Personal Tax Credits

Overview

There is a collection of credits discussed in s. 118(1) that are collectively calculated at the lowest marginal tax rate of 15%. The amounts of the credits applicable to the individual taxpayer are aggregated and then multiplied by 15% to arrive at the amount of the tax credit from these sources. This group of tax credits is referred to as the "personal tax credits".

¶10,305 Calculation of Non-Refundable Personal Tax Credits

The provision for personal tax credits begins by presenting the following general formula:

ITA: 118(1) Personal credits

$$A \times B$$

where

A is the appropriate percentage for the year, defined to mean the lowest percentage rate of individual tax (i.e., 15%)

ITA: 117(2) Rates for taxation years after 2015, 248(1) Definitions

B is the aggregate of the following tax credit bases:

(a) married or common-law partnership status,

(b) wholly dependent person (i.e., equivalent-to-married status),

(c) single status, and

(d) Canada caregiver.

Therefore, the personal tax credits are computed as 15% of a dollar amount indexed for 2018.

Discussed in detail below, there are situations where the taxpayer may claim personal tax credits for another individual. The personal tax credits for individuals, other than the taxpayer, are limited by the net income for tax purposes (Division B income) of the dependant. However, dependants are allowed to earn a certain amount of net income for tax purposes before the tax credits are reduced.

For the purposes of this chapter, the amount of net income for tax purposes of a dependant before the tax credit is reduced will be called the "threshold income".

¶10,310 Basic Personal Tax Credit

Calculation of the personal tax credits begins with the basic personal tax credit available to all individuals. The base of the basic personal tax credit is set at $11,809 in 2018 and, when multiplied by 15%, provides a tax credit of $1,771 (rounded) for 2018. This essentially results in allowing every individual taxpayer to earn their first $11,809 of income without generating amount of tax owing.

ITA: 118(1)(c) Single status

¶10,315 Married or Common-Law Partnership Credit

Although individuals who are single calculate the basic personal tax credit above, individuals who are married or have a common-law partner instead calculate the married or common-law partner credit. This credit combines the taxpayer's basic personal amount with any unused portion of their spouse's or common law partner's basic personal credit for 2018:

ITA: 118(1)(a) Married or common-law partnership status

Basic personal tax credit base		$11,809
Spouse's tax credit base	$11,809[1]	
Less: spouse's Division B income	xxx	
Net amount (non-negative)		xxx
		$ xxx
Tax credit (15% of total)		$ xxx

ITA: 257 Negative amounts

[1] $13,991, if eligible for the Canada caregiver amount of $2,182, for a spouse or common-law partner who is dependent by reason of mental or physical infirmity.

The total tax credit is a maximum of $3,542 (i.e., 15% of $11,809 + 15% of $11,809), or $3,869 if eligible for the Canada caregiver amount of $2,182). This tax credit is available if an individual supports his or her spouse. Note, however, that the spouse's tax credit base is reduced by the Division B income of the dependent spouse for the whole year, even if the marriage occurred in the year.

On the other hand, if the individual was living apart from his or her spouse at the end of the year because of a marriage breakdown, only the spouse's income for the year, while married and not separated, is considered.

A common-law partner is treated like a spouse. The term "common-law partner" is defined as a person, regardless of sex, who cohabits with the taxpayer in a conjugal relationship and (a) has done so for a continuous period of at least one year, or (b) who is the parent of a child of whom the taxpayer is also a parent.

ITA: 248(1) common-law partner

Hence, the married status tax credit is allowed in a common-law relationship if the conditions in the extended meaning are met and the conditions in paragraph 118(1)(*a*) are met.

¶10,320 Equivalent-to-Married Status for Wholly Dependent Person Credit

A tax credit base equal to the tax credit base for married status is provided in respect of a wholly dependent person where the taxpayer is not entitled to a married credit (i.e., an individual who is not married or living in a common-law relationship). This provision might apply to an individual who, at any time in the year, was single, divorced, separated, or widowed and who supported a relative as, for example, a single parent. The calculation of the credit is the same as that shown for the married credit, with the Division B income of the wholly dependent person reducing the credit.

ITA: 118(1)(a) Married or common-law partnership status, 118(1)(b) Wholly dependent person

A number of additional conditions must apply for the tax credit to be available.

- The dependent person must live, at some time in the year, in the same self-contained domestic establishment as the taxpayer claiming the tax credit. The dependant must be wholly dependent for support on that taxpayer and/or other persons. The taxpayer need not own the residence. A rental unit qualifies.

ITA: 248(1) self-contained domestic establishment; Interpretation Bulletins: IT-513R Personal Tax Credits

- The dependant must be related to the taxpayer by blood, marriage, or adoption. Nieces, nephews, aunts, uncles, and cousins do not qualify as a marital equivalent under this provision (unless they fit the definition of child which is very broad and should be examined).

ITA: 251(6) Blood relationship, etc, 252(1) Extended meaning of "child"

- Unless the dependant is a child of the taxpayer, the dependant must be resident in Canada.
- Unless the dependant is the parent or grandparent of the taxpayer, the dependant must be either under 18 years of age at any time in the year or dependent by reason of physical or mental infirmity.
- Only one equivalent-to-married tax credit is available to a taxpayer.

ITA: 118(1)(b) Wholly dependent person, 118(4)(a)

- The dependant cannot be claimed under this tax credit if the dependant has been claimed under the married status credit by another taxpayer.

ITA: 118(4)(a.1)

- Where two taxpayers are eligible for the equivalent-to-married tax credit in respect of the same person or the same domestic establishment, only one person is permitted the tax credit and only one equivalent-to-married tax credit can be claimed for a given domestic establishment. If the taxpayers cannot agree as to who should have the tax credit, then neither can have the tax credit. For example, Tom and Donna, who are both single, support their mother in the same domestic establishment. Either Tom or Donna can have the tax credit, but not both. If they cannot agree, then neither can have the tax credit.

ITA: 118(1)(b) Wholly dependent person, 118(4)(b)

- Where an individual is required under the terms of a written agreement or court order to make payments in the year in respect of the support of a child, the individual is not entitled to claim any personal tax credit in respect of the child.

ITA: 118(5) Support

The interpretation of the phrase "at any time in the year is an unmarried person" appears to have the effect of enabling a person who presently qualifies for an equivalent-to-married tax credit and marries during the year to still qualify for this tax credit in the year of marriage, but not subsequently. Of course, the person claiming a dependent would not be allowed a claim for marital status.

ITA: 118(1)(b) Wholly dependent person, 118(1)(b) Wholly dependent person, 118(1)(a) Married or common-law partnership status; Interpretation Bulletins: IT-513R Personal Tax Credits

¶10,325 Canada Caregiver Credit

ITA: 118(1)(c) to (e) Canada caregiver credit

Individuals are entitled to a credit of:

- Up to $1,047 (i.e., 15% of $6,986) in respect of expenses for the care of dependent relatives with infirmities. This includes parents, brothers, sisters, adult children, and other specified relatives.
- Up to $327 (i.e., 15% of $2,182) in respect of expenses for the care of a dependent spouse/common-law partner or minor child with an infirmity.

The base amount of the credit is reduced when the dependent's income exceeds $16,405. The credit is not available if the dependent's income exceeds $23,391.

¶10,345 Age Credit

The non-refundable age tax credit is computed on a base of $7,333 for 2018. Since the appropriate percentage for the year is 15%, the tax credit for 2018 is $1,100 (rounded). It is available to an individual who has attained the age of 65 years before the end of the year.

ITA: 118(2) Age credit

However, this age tax credit is reduced by 15% of the excess of the individual's Division B income over $36,976 and is, thus, completely eliminated when the net income exceeds $85,863.

For example, if an individual's Division B income is $85,863, the age tax credit would be computed as:

Age tax credit base				$7,333
Less:	base reduction of lesser of:			
	(a) Credit base		$7,333	
	(b) Division B income	$85,863		
	Less: threshold	36,976		
	Excess, if any	$48,887 × 0.15 =	$7,333	
	Lesser amount			7,333
Net base				Nil
Age tax credit: 15% of Nil.				Nil

¶10,350 Pension Income Amount

This non-refundable pension tax credit is determined as follows:

ITA: 118(3) Pension credit

Age 65 and Older

The pension credit is equal to 15% of the lesser of:

(1) $2,000, and

(2) the "pension income".

Pension income includes, but is not limited to: ITA: 118(7) Definitions

(1) a payment in respect of a life annuity arising from a superannuation pension fund or plan;

(2) an annuity payment under a registered retirement savings plan or a payment under a registered retirement income fund;

(3) an annuity payment under a deferred profit sharing plan; and

(4) the income portion of other annuity payments.

Under Age 65

The pension credit is equal to 15% of the lesser of:

(1) $2,000, and

(2) the "qualified pension income".

The only difference is to change the definition of pension income to qualified pension income. Qualified pension income includes: ITA: 118(7) Definitions

(1) a payment in respect of a life annuity arising from a superannuation pension fund or plan; or

(2) certain annuities or payments received by the individual as a consequence of the death of the individual's spouse.

Certain amounts are not included in pension income or qualified pension income. These excluded amounts are: ITA: 118(8) Interpretation

(1) the Old Age Pension or Supplement;

(2) the Canada Pension Plan (or provincial plan) pension;

(3) a death benefit; ITA: 248(1) death benefit

(4) the amount of any payment which is included in income and then deducted under another provision, such as lump-sum payments from withdrawing from a pension fund, an RRSP or a DPSP, retiring allowances, or pension benefits or DPSP benefits transferred into a spousal RRSP; and

(5) a payment out of or under a salary deferral arrangement, a retirement compensation arrangement, an employee benefit plan, an employee trust, or a prescribed provincial pension plan.

¶10,355 Canada Employment Credit

This non-refundable credit is computed as 15% times the lesser of:

ITA: 118(10) Canada Employment Credit

- The individual's employment income for the year, and
- $1,195.

¶10,360 Summary of Personal Tax Credits

Exhibit 10-4 provides a summary of the numerical components of the most common personal tax credits.

ITA: 118 Personal credits, 118.3 Credit for mental or physical impairment

Exhibit 10-4 Section 118 Tax Credits (rounded)

Par. 118(1)*(a), (b), or (b.1)*:	Maximum tax credit	Tax credit base	Division B income threshold
Basic personal	$1,771	$11,809	N/A
Spouse or equivalent	1,771	11,809	N/A
Par. 118(1)(*c*): Single person	1,771	11,809	N/A
Par. 118(1)(*d*): Canada Caregiver	1,048	6,986	16,405
Ssec. 118(2): Age	1,100	7,333	36,976
Ssec. 118(3): Pension	300	2,000	N/A
Ssec. 118(10): Canada Employment Credit	179	1,195	N/A
Sec. 118.3: Disability amount (see ¶10,445)	1,235	8,235	N/A

Exhibit 10-5 Credits Available To Be Claimed With Respect to Children of a Taxpayer

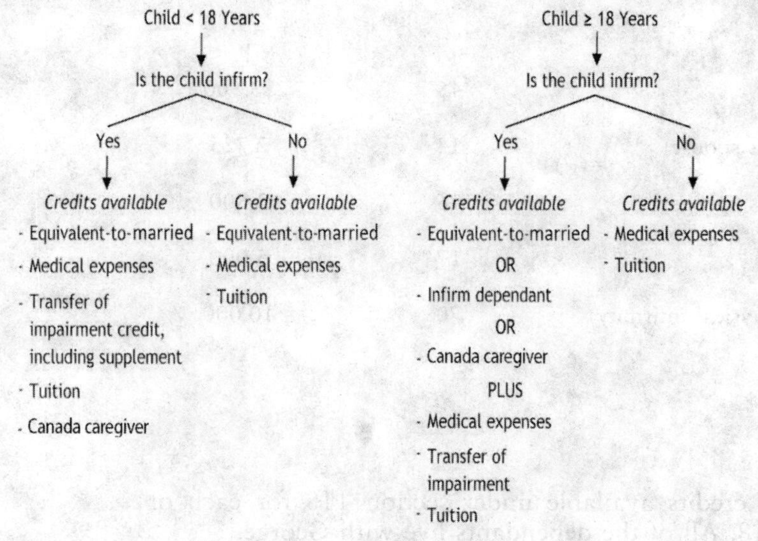

Notes:

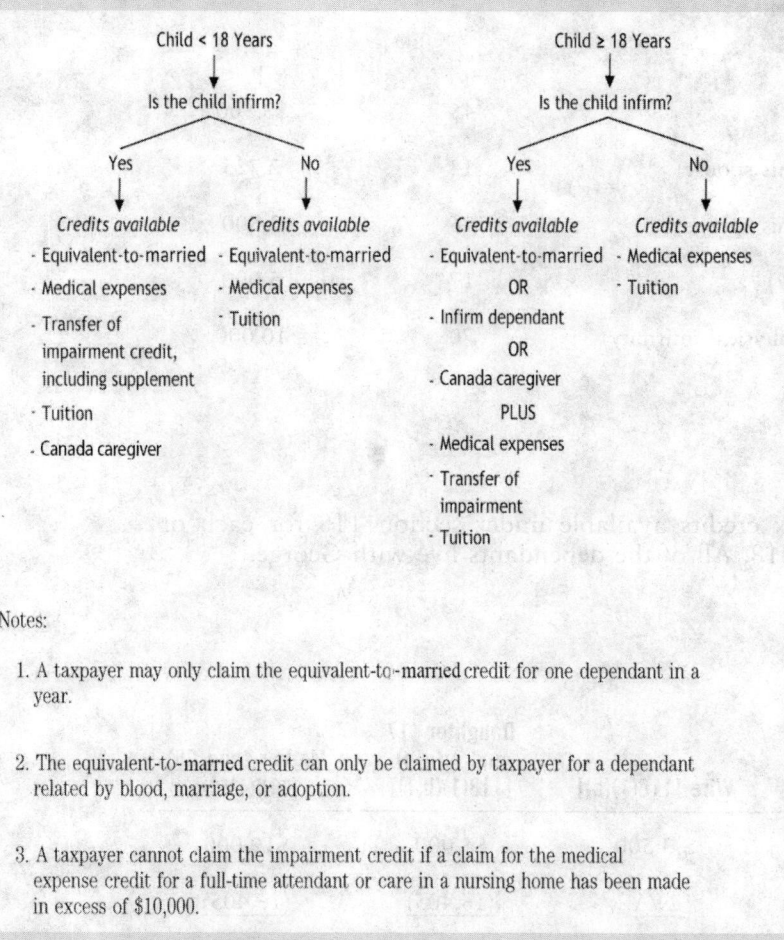

1. A taxpayer may only claim the equivalent-to-married credit for one dependant in a year.

2. The equivalent-to-married credit can only be claimed by taxpayer for a dependant related by blood, marriage, or adoption.

3. A taxpayer cannot claim the impairment credit if a claim for the medical expense credit for a full-time attendant or care in a nursing home has been made in excess of $10,000.

For the purposes of this book, where provincial tax credits are calculated for individuals, a rate of 10% (equal to the lowest provincial rate used in this book) will be applied to the above federal tax credit base, net of any applicable reduction for income in excess of the federal Division B income threshold.

Example Problem 10-5

George, age 50, has the following dependants, each of whom has Division B income as indicated for 2018:

Spouse	45	$3,500
Son (residing with George and his spouse)	14	2,725
Son (residing with George and his spouse)	16	2,800
Daughter (physically infirm)	17	5,000
Mother (dependent because of physical infirmity)	70	10,000

REQUIRED

Determine the personal tax credits available under section 118 for each of George's dependants for 2018. All of the dependants live with George.

SOLUTION

	Wife [118(1)(a)]	Daughter (17 and infirm) [118(1)(b.1)]	Mother (age 65) [118(1)(d)]
Division B income	$ 3,500	$5,000	$10,000
Threshold income	N/A	(16,405)	(16,405)
Excess income	$ 3,500	$ 0	$ 0
Tax credit base	$11,809	$2,182	$ 6,986
Excess income	(3,500)	0	0
Net tax credit base	$ 8,309	$2,182	$ 6,986
Tax credit @ 15% (rounded)	$ 1,246	$327	$ 1,048

Note that neither of the sons provides a dependant tax credit. They may be covered, depending on household income under the Canada Child Benefit.

¶10,390 Pause and Reflect — Summary of Learning Goals

After working through this section, ¶10,300, you should be able to:

- Identify personal tax credits available to a taxpayer
- Apply the rules to calculate the amount of personal tax credits for a taxpayer

¶10,390.99 Practise What You've Learned

Refer to the following sections of the Study Guide to practise what you've learned:

¶10,825 — Multiple Choice Questions

- Question 2 — Non-refundable credits

¶10,850 — Exercises

- Exercise 5 — Personal credits
- Exercise 14 — Calculate personal credit base amount

¶10,400 Computation of Tax for Individuals — Credits for Individuals Beyond the Personal Tax Credits

Overview

The personal tax credits discussed in section 118 are calculated together, use the lowest tax rate of 15% in the calculation across all credits, and are non-refundable with no options for carryforward. However, there are many other credits beyond the personal tax credits available to individuals that have unique features. For example, some allow carryforwards, use different rates for calculation, or are income tested. The following section discusses these tax credits.

¶10,405 Adoption Expense Tax Credit

The Act provides a non-refundable tax credit of up $2,351 (15% × $15,670) in the year in which an adoption is completed for eligible adoption expenses incurred during the adoption period.

ITA: 118.01 [Adoption expense tax credit]

Eligible adoption expenses include:

(1) fees paid to an adoption agency licensed by a provincial or territorial government,

(2) court costs, legal fees, and administrative expenses,

(3) reasonable travel and living expenses of the child and the adoptive parents,

(4) document translation fees,

(5) mandatory fees paid to a foreign institution, and

(6) any other reasonable expenses required by a provincial or territorial government or an adoption agency licensed by a provincial or territorial government.

The adoption period begins at the earlier of the time an application is made to register with a provincial ministry responsible for adoption or with a licensed adoption agency or the date an application is made to a Canadian court. The adoption period ends at the time of the adoption.

An eligible child is one who has not reached the age of 18 years at the time that the adoption is completed.

¶10,420 First-Time Home Buyers' Credit and Disability Home Purchase Credit

This is a non-refundable credit of $750 (i.e., 15% of $5,000) for the purchase of a qualifying home by a first-time home buyer. To be considered a first-time home buyer, neither the purchaser nor the purchaser's spouse or common-law partner can have lived or owned another home in the year of purchase, nor in any of the four preceding calendar years. The credit can be split between the spouses or common-law partners, but the total credit cannot exceed $750.

ITA: 118.05 [First-time home buyers' tax credit]

The credit may be claimed if a qualifying home is purchased for the benefit of an individual entitled to claim the disability credit to enable the disabled person to live a more accessible home or better suited home. In this case, the purchaser does not have to be a first- time home buyer.

A qualifying home can include a single-family house, a semi-detached house, a townhouse, a mobile home, and a condominium unit, among others. In addition, the following conditions must be met:

- The home is located in Canada.
- The home is registered in the name of the purchaser or the purchaser's common-law partner.
- The purchaser, the purchaser's common law partner, or a person eligible for the disability credit intends to inhabit the home as their principal residence within one year of the date of purchase.

¶10,425 Tax Credits for Firefighter and Search and Rescue Volunteers

Volunteering for search and rescue or firefighting can require significant amounts of time for training and potential expense for equipment. To recognize this contribution and its importance to communities within Canada, the Act provides a credit for volunteers in these areas. The details are described below.

¶10,425.10 Volunteer Firefighters Tax Credit

This credit enables eligible volunteer firefighters to claim a 15% non-refundable tax credit based on an amount of $3,000 for a credit of $450 (i.e., 15% of $3,000). However, individuals who claim this credit will not also be able to claim the exemption of up to $1,000 received for their volunteer firefighting activities.

ITA: 118.06(2) Volunteer firefighter tax credit; 81(4)(b)

To be eligible, the person must perform a minimum of 200 hours of volunteer firefighting services for one or more fire departments or eligible search and rescue volunteer services for an eligible search and rescue organization. They will be ineligible if they also provide firefighting services which are not voluntary to that fire department. Certification will be required from the fire department confirming the number of eligible volunteer firefighting hours.

ITA: 118.06(2) Volunteer firefighter tax credit; 118.06(3) Certificate

¶10,425.20 Search and Rescue Volunteer Tax Credit

Parallel to the Volunteer Firefighters Tax Credit, the Act provides for a Search and Rescue Volunteer Tax Credit also with a base of $3,000 for a credit of $450 (i.e., 15% of$3,000). The credit may be claimed by an individual who performs eligible search and rescue volunteer services in the year. The individual may not claim this credit and the Volunteer Firefighters Tax Credit in the same year. Again, the individual claiming this credit will not be eligible for the exemption.

ITA: 118.07(2) Search and rescue volunteer tax credit

ITA: 118.07(2) Search and rescue volunteer tax credit, 81(4) Payments for volunteer services

The individual must perform, in the year, not less than 200 hours of services in:

ITA: 118.07(1) Definitions

- eligible search and rescue volunteer service for an eligible search and rescue organization, as defined, or
- eligible volunteer firefighting services for a fire department, as defined.

ITA: 118.06(1) Definition of "eligible volunteer firefighting services"

Appropriate certification of the volunteer services and the hours may be required.

¶10,430 Home Accessibility Tax Credit

A non-refundable home accessibility tax credit for seniors and persons with disabilities is provided. This 15% credit applies on up to $10,000 of eligible home renovation expenditures per qualifying individual per eligible dwelling made in a calendar year. Eligible expenditures must allow the qualifying individual to gain access to, or to be more mobile or functional within, the dwelling, or reduce the risk of harm to the qualifying individual within the building or in gaining access to the building. The provision envisages such expenditures as wheel-chair ramps, walk-in tubs, wheel-in showers, and grab bars, all of an enduring nature.

ITA: 118.041 [Home Accessibility Tax Credit]

¶10,435 Charitable Gifts Credit

Overview

A tax credit is provided for charitable donations made by individuals. Unlike non-refundable credits discussed above, the charitable gifts credit provides a credit at a rate equivalent to the lowest tax bracket (15%) for the first $200 of donation, at a rate equivalent to the highest tax rate (33%) to the extent of income in excess of $205,842 at a rate equivalent to 29% on other donations, as computed by the formula below. The higher credit rates are provided as incentives to individuals in the higher tax bracket to make charitable donations beyond the first $200, to generate the same tax savings as other expenditures (such as an RRSP contribution) that would generate a tax deduction with the same value for the higher income taxpayer. Of course, those who make charitable donations in the lower brackets will also benefit from the higher credit rate.

ITA: 118.1 [Charitable and other gifts]; 118.1(3) Deduction by individuals for gifts

¶10,435.10 Basic Rules

The non-refundable charitable donation tax credit is calculated by the following formula:

$$(A \times B) + (C \times D) + (E \times F)$$

where

A is 15% (i.e., the appropriate percentage for the year);

B is the first $200 of total gifts; ITA: 118.1(1) total gifts

C is 33% (i.e., the highest federal marginal tax rate for the year);

D is the lesser of

(a) the individual's total gifts (if over $200) for the year, and

(b) the amount by which the individual's taxable income exceeds $205,842;

E is 29%; and

F is the amount by which the individual's total gifts for the year exceeds the total of $200 and the amount determined for D (i.e., the amount of the donation that is not eligible for the 33% rate).

Example

Scenario 1

An individual's taxable income is $210,000 and the individual made charitable donations of $5,000.

Tax Credit	
15% × $200 =	$ 30
33% × $4,800 =	1,584
Total Credit	$1,614

Scenario 2

An individual's taxable income is $210,000 and the individual made charitable donations of $15,000.

Tax Credit	
15% × $200 =	$ 30
33% × $4,158 =	1,372
29% × $10,642 =	3,086
Total Credit	$4,488

In essence, the tax credit amounts to

(1) 15% of total gifts up to $200

(2) 33% on total gifts to the extent of taxable income above $205,842

(3) 29% for total gifts in excess of 1) and 2)

For the purposes of this book, where provincial tax credits are calculated for individuals, a rate of 10% will be applied to total gifts up to $200 and 17% (equal to the highest provincial tax rate used in this book) for total gifts in excess of $200, whether providing a federal credit at the 29% or 33% rates.

The definition of total gifts indicates the following components:

(1) total charitable gifts, including gifts to:

- Canadian registered charities (including Canadian universities),
- registered Canadian amateur athletic associations,
- prescribed universities outside Canada,
- certain tax-free housing organizations in Canada,
- Canadian municipalities,
- the United Nations or its agencies,
- charities outside Canada to which the Government of Canada has made a donation in the year or the preceding year;
- municipal and public bodies performing a function of government in Canada,
- housing corporations in Canada constituted exclusively to provide low-cost housing for the aged,
- universities outside Canada, the student body of which ordinarily includes students from Canada, and
- certain other charitable organizations outside Canada that have received a gift from Her Majesty in right of Canada;

(2) total cultural gifts; and

(3) total ecological gifts.

By administrative practice, donations made by either spouse or common-law partner can be combined in one claim. This maximizes the tax savings as only one $200 threshold for the low credit rate need be applied.

¶10,435.20 Income Limit and Carryforward

If the eligible donations in a year exceed the maximum of 75% of Division B income, the excess amount should be carried forward and claimed first, before the current year gifts, in the next five years. Donations may only be carried forward five years subject to the 75% limitation in that year. The income limitation is found in the definition of "total gifts". This carryforward is permitted to the extent that the donations are not claimed in the current year, even though they may not exceed 75% of Division B income in the current year. The annual Division B income limitation of 75% of the donor's net income for the year is increased by 25% of:

ITA: 118.1(1) Definitions; 118.1(2.1) Ordering of gifts; 118(1) total gifts

- recapture of CCA arising on a gift of depreciable capital property; and
- taxable capital gains arising on the donation of a capital property.

A limit of 100% of Division B net income applies for gifts:

- made in the year of death; or

ITA: 118.1(4) Gifts — deaths before 2016

- of ecologically sensitive land.

ITA: 118.1(1) Definitions

The 75% of Division B income limit should not be expected to apply in most cases. However, the limit would become an effective limit, if gifts are made in an unusual year of relatively low income or a loss year.

¶10,435.30 Total Charitable Gifts

Gifts made to certain types of organizations listed under the definition of "total charitable gifts" may be eligible for the tax credit to a maximum tax credit base of 75% of Division B income. Only the gifts to these specified organizations are eligible and they must be supported by proper receipts.

ITA: 118.1(1) Definitions; 118.1(2) Proof of gift

Where gifts of capital property and works of art, which are inventory to the donor, have a fair market value greater than adjusted cost base or cost amount, and the gift is not cultural property, the taxpayer may make a designation of a transfer price. The taxpayer can designate a transfer price between fair market value and adjusted cost base or cost amount as proceeds of disposition and the value of the gift. Capital gains or income could, thus, be avoided by selecting the adjusted cost base or cost amount, but the value of the gift and the resultant tax credit under these paragraphs would be lower.

ITA: 118.1(1) Definitions; 118.1(6) Gifts of capital property; 118.1(7) Gift of art

If personal-use property is acquired as part of an arrangement under which the property is gifted to a charity, then the $1,000 rule will not apply. This rule is designed to prevent abuses connected with the donation of art and other personal-use property.

ITA: 46 Personal-use property

Ⓐ ¶10,435.40 Gifts of Publicly Traded Securities

The income inclusion rate for capital gains from gifts of publicly traded securities is reduced to zero for this purpose instead of the usual 50%. Securities eligible for this treatment include shares listed on a designated stock exchange. ITA: 38(a.1); ITR: 3200, 3201

Legislation eliminates tax on capital gains realized on the exchange of unlisted shares and partnership interests for publicly traded securities, if the publicly traded securities are then donated to a qualified donee within 30 days of the exchange (in which case, any further capital gain on the donation would also be nil). The unlisted securities must include, at the time they are issued, a condition allowing the holder to exchange them for publicly traded securities, and the publicly traded securities must be the only consideration received on the exchange. Special rules apply where the exchanged securities are partnership interests. ITA: 38(a.1), 38(a.2)

¶10,435.50 Total Cultural Gifts

Where an artist makes a cultural gift that is a work of art created by the individual and that is property in the artist's inventory, the artist is deemed to have received proceeds of disposition equal to the cost to the artist of the work of art. A cultural gift is included in the definition of "total cultural gifts" and means objects that the Cultural Property Export Review Board has determined meets certain conditions. The result of this provision is that the artist is entitled to a credit based on the full fair market value of the art donated, but has no income to report as a result of the donation and its consequent disposition of the art from inventory. There is no net income limitation and there is a five-year carryforward. ITA: 118.1(7.1) Gift of art; 118.1(1) Definitions

¶10,435.60 Tickets to Events

Where a charitable organization issues receipts for the price of tickets to fund-raising events involving an element of entertainment or other benefit for the donor, only the excess of the amount paid over the fair market value of the benefit received is allowed to be considered part of the charitable gift.

¶10,435.70 Total Ecological Gifts

A net income limitation of 100% applies to donations of certain ecologically sensitive land. An extended 10-year carry-forward period (rather than the usual five-year carry-forward period) is provided. This provision is meant to encourage the conservation and protection of Canada's environmental heritage and applies to qualified donations of land including qualified donations of covenants, servitudes, and easements. As a further incentive, for ecological gifts any capital gain realized on the donation (other than gifts to a private foundation) are subject to a zero capital gains inclusion rate. ITA: 38(a.2)

¶10,435.90 Pause and Reflect — Summary of Learning Goals

After working through this section, ¶10,435, you should be able to:

- Apply your knowledge to calculate the amount of charitable donation credit available to a taxpayer

¶10,440 Medical Expense Credit

Overview

A tax credit is provided for excess medical expenses beyond 3% of a taxpayer's net income for tax purposes (up to a statutory maximum threshold of $2,302). The credit has many features that make it unique from credits discussed previously in the chapter. One of the unique aspects of the medical expense credit is that the credit is income tested. This means that for the same amount of medical expenses, the credit generated may vary based on the taxpayer's net income for tax purposes. Another unique aspect of the credit is that it allows a taxpayer to include expenses for themselves, their spouse or common-law partner, dependants under 18 years of age and in certain circumstances dependants over 18 years of age. A third unique feature of this credit is that it allows the individual an opportunity to tax-plan to maximize the tax savings through the choice of the 12 month period for which the expenses are being aggregated. The Act allows the medical expenses for any 12 month period that ended during the tax year to be used for the calculation of the credit, subject to some limitations. The details of all of these unique features are discussed below.

¶10,440.10 Calculation of the Credit

Not all medical and health care costs are fully covered by a provincial health insurance plan or by a private health services plan. Expenses that must be borne by the taxpayer may qualify for the non-refundable medical expense credit. For example, certain cosmetic or elective procedures and a fraction of dental services may not be covered.

ITA: 118.2(1) Medical expense credit

The medical expense tax credit is calculated as:

$$A\,[(B - C) + D]$$

where

A is 15% (i.e., the appropriate percentage for the year)

B is medical expenses listed in the legislation for the individual, spouse or common law partner and children not reaching 18 before the end of the year

C is the lesser of:

- $2,302 (indexed for 2018), and
- 3% of the individual's net income

D applies only to dependants who are 18 and over and is calculated as

$$E - F$$

where

ITA: 118.2(2) Medical expenses, 118.2(3) Deemed medical expense

E is the total of all medical expenses incurred by the taxpayer on behalf of any other dependant, and

ITA: 118(6) Definition of "dependant"

F is the lesser of:

- $2,302 (indexed for 2018), and
- 3% of the other dependant's net income

The C and F calculations in the formula show that a certain level of medical expenses must be paid by the individual before a credit can be earned. This level of expense that is borne by the individual increases with net income until, at $76,733 ($2,302/0.03) of income or above, it remains the same.

In essence, the federal tax credit is 15% (10% used for provincial tax credit) of medical expenses in excess of the $2,302 for 2018 or 3% of the Division B income threshold. The medical expenses must be proven by filing receipts and must be paid within any 12-month period ending in the year unless the individual dies in the year. Where the individual dies in the year, the medical expenses must be paid by the claimant for the deceased person within any period of 24 months that includes the date of death.

¶10,440.20 Medical Expenses

The legislation includes about 40 detailed paragraphs outlining the very technical rules and conditions defining medical expenses. Medical expenses incurred in respect of the individual taxpayer, the individual's spouse or common-law partner, child who has not attained the age of 18 in the year, or other dependants may be claimed by the individual taxpayer. A brief description of these paragraphs is provided in Exhibit 10-6, below; however, a careful examination of these provisions and an Income Tax Folio must be made in order to determine the eligibility of each item. Reference to the Income Tax Folio entitled "Medical Expense Tax Credit" can be very helpful in this area.

ITA: 118.2(2) Medical expenses; ITR: 5700 [Prescribed devices and equipment], 5701 [Prescribed drugs and medicaments]; Income Tax Folio: S1-F1-C1 Medical Expense Tax Credit, S1-F1-C2 Disability Tax Credit, S1-F1-C3 Disability Supports Deduction

Exhibit 10-6 Summary List of Eligible Medical Expenses Discussed in Income Tax Folio S1-F1-C1

- Fees paid to medical professionals (including those licensed to provide a wide range of health care services)
- Cost of attendant care and care in certain types of facilities
- Transportation and travel expenses
- Artificial limbs, aids and other devices and equipment
- Products required because of incontinence
- Vision care
- Oxygen, insulin and injections for pernicious anaemia
- Guide and hearing ear dogs and other animals
- Bone marrow or organ transplants
- Alterations to an existing dwelling or construction of a new dwelling
- Rehabilitative therapy
- Sign language services
- Note-taking services
- Voice recognition software
- Reading services

- Deaf-blind intervening services
- Moving expenses
- Driveway alterations
- Van for wheelchair
- Caretaker training
- Therapy for eligible person with a disability
- Tutoring services
- Individualized therapy plan
- Devices and equipment prescribed by regulation
- Drugs, medicaments and other preparations or substances
- Preventive, diagnostic and other treatments
- Dentures
- Premiums paid to a private health services plan (PHSP)
- Gluten-free food
- Drugs not yet approved for sale
- Medical devices not yet approved for sale
- Medical marijuana
- Cosmetic procedures
- Reproductive technologies (e.g., in-vitro fertilization procedures)

Example Problem 10-6

Mr. Moyer has income under Division B of $25,000 and $30,000 for 2017 and 2018, respectively. His wife and children have no income in these years. He incurs the following receipted medical expenses on behalf of himself, his wife, and three dependent children.

2017 —	None prior to August			
	August	Dental bills for children	$ 325	
	September	Hospital bill and drugs	200[1]	
	November	Prescription drugs	65	
	December	Prescription drugs	125	
	Total medical expenses		$ 715	(B)

	Less the lesser of:			
	(a) $2,302			
	(b) 3% of Division B income (3% of $25,000)		750	(C)
	Net base for tax credit (B – C)		Nil	
2018 —	January	Eyeglasses for himself and wife	$ 225	
	February	Eyeglasses for three children	340	
	March	Orthodontic work for children	1,500	
	July	Chiropractor for Mr. Moyer	400[1]	
	Total medical expenses		$2,465	

[1] Excess over amount paid by a provincial medicare program.

REQUIRED

Determine the maximum amount Mr. Moyer can claim as a medical expense tax credit in 2018.

SOLUTION

Since the only restriction on the 12-month period is that it must end in the particular taxation year, Mr. Moyer should choose the 12 months ending in July 2018.

The medical expense tax credit is computed by the following formula:

$$A\ ((B - C) + D)$$

where

A = 0.15

B = total medical expenses (as computed below)

C = lesser of:

(a) $2,302

(b) 3% of Division B income (as computed below)

D = nil in this case

2017	— August to December: total medical expenses	$ 715	
2018	— January to July: total medical expenses	2,465	
	Total	$3,180	(B)

Less the lesser of:		
(a) \$2,302		
(b) 3% of Division B income (3% of \$30,000)	900	(C)
Net base for medical expense tax credit (B – C)	\$2,280	
Medical expense tax credit: A (B – C) = 0.15 × \$2,280 =	\$342	

Note that had Mr. Moyer's wife had some income that would attract tax in excess of her other tax credits, but less than her husband's, there may be a greater benefit to the family if she claimed the medical expense tax credit because the 3% threshold would be lower.

Note, also, that the CRA has indicated that prepaid medical expenses only qualify as valid medical expenses when they are made in the same 12-month period during which the medical services are rendered.[1]

¶10,440.30 Notch Provision for Dependants

As indicated above, a taxpayer may claim a medical expense tax credit for the medical expenses of the taxpayer, the taxpayer's spouse or a dependent individual. Where a person, other than the taxpayer's spouse, qualifies as a dependant (including a child who has reached the age of 18, grandchild or parent, grandparent, brother, sister, uncle, aunt, niece, or nephew, if resident in Canada), the taxpayer may include the medical expenses of that person when computing the medical expense tax credit.

Specifically, medical expense claims made on behalf of minor children are pooled in item B of the medical expense tax credit formula with those of the taxpayer and his or her spouse or common-law partner, subject to the taxpayer's minimum expense threshold (the lesser of 3% of net income and \$2,302) without regard to the income of the minor child.

For medical expenses paid on behalf of other dependent relatives (e.g., child who has reached the age of 18, parent, grandparent, niece, nephew, etc.) taxpayers can claim qualifying medical expenses paid on behalf of such a dependant that exceed the lesser of 3% of the dependant's net income and \$2,302. This reduction is embedded in item D of the medical expense tax credit formula.

[1] See Tax Window Files, Document No. 2005-0133261I7.

Example Problem 10-7

Mr. Jones' father is a dependant. His father's Division B income is only $8,500 for 2018. During the year, Mr. Jones paid medical expenses of $1,000 on behalf of his father and $2,500 for himself. Mr. Jones' Division B income is $100,000 for 2018.

REQUIRED

Determine the maximum amount that Mr. Jones can claim as a medical expense tax credit in 2018.

SOLUTION

The medical expense tax credit is computed by the following formula

$$A\,[(B - C) + D]$$

If Mr. Jones claims his father's medical expenses:

A = 0.15

B = total medical expenses (i.e., $2,500 for taxpayer)

C = lesser of $2,302 and 3% of $100,000 (i.e., taxpayer's Division B income)

D for the dependent father is

$$E - F$$

where

E = the total of all medical expenses incurred by the taxpayer on behalf of the father (i.e., $1,000), and

F = lesser of:

- $2,302, and
- 3% of the father's net income (i.e., 3% of $8,500 = $255)

15% × [($2,500 – $2,302) + ($1,000 – $255)] = $141

¶10,440.90 Pause and Reflect — Summary of Learning Goals

After working through this section, ¶10,440, you should be able to:

- Identify medical expenses that qualify for the medical expense credit
- Apply your knowledge to identify the twelve-month period that maximizes the medical expense credit for the taxpayer
- Apply your knowledge to calculate the maximum medical tax credit for a taxpayer

¶10,445 Credit for Mental or Physical Impairment (Disability Tax Credit)

Overview

The Act provides the formula for calculating the non-refundable tax credit for an individual with a mental or physical impairment and the conditions for entitlement to the credit.

ITA: 118.3(1) Credit for mental or physical impairment

¶10,445.10 Calculation of the Credit

The tax credit for 2018 is $1,235 (i.e., 15% of $8,235). This tax credit is available to taxpayers who have "one or more severe and prolonged impairments in physical or mental functions" that has been certified by a medical doctor. A health professional, other than a medical doctor, may be eligible to certify the impairment. Nurse practitioners are eligible to certify the impairment. An optometrist may certify the existence of an impairment of sight. An audiologist may certify an impairment of hearing. An occupational therapist may certify the existence of an impairment with respect to an individual's ability to walk or to feed or to dress himself or herself. A psychologist may certify to the existence of an impairment with respect to an individual's ability to perceive, think, and remember. A speech- language pathologist may certify a severe and prolonged speech impairment. A physical therapist may certify a marked restriction in walking. Cumulative effects of multiple restrictions must usually be certified by a medical doctor.

The impairment, or the cumulative effect of multiple restrictions, must have caused the individual to be markedly restricted all or almost all of the time in his or her basic activities of daily living. The impairment must have lasted or be expected to last for a continuous period of at least 12 months. Such impairment would include blindness, deafness, and other listed impairments. It would also occur where, even with the use of appropriate devices, medication or therapy, the individual is generally unable (or requires an inordinate amount of time) to feed or to dress himself or herself or perform specified fundamental functions.

ITA: 118.4(1) Nature of impairment

No claim can be made under this subsection if a claim has been made for a medical tax credit for a full-time attendant or care in a nursing home. However, a claim for expenses of an attendant costing up to $10,000 in computing the medical expense tax credit will not deny this impairment tax credit.

ITA: 118.2(1) Medical expense credit; 118.2(2)(b.1)

A supplement amount of $4,804 for 2018 is available for each disabled child under the age of 18 years at the end of the year. The supplement amount is reduced by the excess of the total of child care and attendant care expenses, paid in the year and deducted in respect of the child, over $2,814 (for 2018).

¶10,445.20 Transfer of Impairment Credit

A transfer of this credit is available to a taxpayer if the dependants themselves cannot use all or some part of this credit. The impaired dependant must use as much of the credit as necessary to reduce his or her federal income tax to zero before the remainder can be transferred. The transfer of the unused part of the impairment credit is available to a taxpayer if:

ITA: 118(1)(c.1) In-home care of relative, 118.3(2) Dependant having impairment

- the taxpayer claimed an equivalent-to-married credit for the dependant;

ITA: 118(1)(b) Wholly dependent person

- the dependant was the taxpayer's child, grandchild, parent, grandparent (including in-laws), brother, sister, aunt, uncle, nephew, or niece, and the taxpayer could have claimed an equivalent-to-married credit for that dependant if the taxpayer did not have a spouse or common-law partner and if the dependant did not have any income;

ITA: 118(1)(d) Canada caregiver credit

- the dependant was the taxpayer's child or grandchild and the taxpayer claimed them as a dependant or for the Canada caregiver credit;

ITA: 118(1)(d) Canada caregiver credit, 118(1)(c.1) In-home care of relative

- the dependant was the taxpayer's child or grandchild and the taxpayer could have claimed them as a dependant or for the Canada caregiver credit if they had no income; or

ITA: 118(1)(c.1) In-home care of relative, 118(1)(d) Canada caregiver credit

- the dependant was the taxpayer's parent or grandparent (including in-laws) and the taxpayer could have claimed them as a dependant or for the Canada caregiver credit if they had no income.

The net result of these rules is that if a parent supports two or more disabled children, the parent is entitled to the transfer of the unused portion of the impairment tax credit of those children, even though only one child may be claimed as an equivalent-to-married tax credit. The spousal transfer of this credit is discussed later.

ITA: 118.8 Transfer of unused credits to spouse or common-law partner

The legislation deals with the allocation of the impairment tax credit where more than one individual is entitled to the credit for the same dependant. A definition of impairment is contained in the provision and applies not only to the disability credit, but also to the medical expenses credit. A definition of the term used to describe a medical practitioner is also contained in the provision and appears to codify the description in an Interpretation Bulletin.

ITA: 118.2 Medical expense credit, 118.3 Credit for mental or physical impairment, 118.3(3) Partial dependency, 118.4 Nature of impairment, 118.4(2) Reference to medical practitioners, etc; Income Tax Folio: S1-F1-C1 Medical Expense Tax Credit, S1-F1-C2 Disability Tax Credit, S1-F1-C3 Disability Supports Deduction

¶10,450 Post-Secondary Education Tuition Credit and Student Loan Interest

Overview

The Act provides a series of credits as an incentive and support for individuals taking post-secondary education. These include credits for tuition and student loan interest.

¶10,450.10 Tuition Tax Credit

The federal tuition fee tax credit is equal to 15% (10% used for provincial tax credit) of eligible tuition fees paid in respect of that year. The Act provides for a tax credit in respect of tuition fees paid to an educational institution in Canada. The fees must be paid to a university, college, or other educational institution in respect of courses at a post-secondary school level, or an institution certified by the Minister of Human Resources Development providing courses that furnish a person, who is at least 16 years of age at the end of the year, with skills for an occupation. The total of fees paid to a qualified institution in a year must exceed $100.

ITA: 118.5 Tuition credit, 118.5(1)(a)

Tuition fees for full-time and part-time students include items such as library and laboratory charges. Also, eligible for the credit are mandatory ancillary fees, other than student association fees, required to be paid by all full-time and part-time students for courses at the post-secondary school level. Eligible fees include those charged for health services and athletics. In addition to student association fees, the following are excluded: charges for property to be acquired by students, services not ordinarily provided at post-secondary educational institutions in Canada, and tax exempt financial assistance to students. Also, mandatory charges paid for the construction, renovation, or maintenance of a building or facility, generally, do not qualify for the credit. A fee that would be eligible, but for the fact that it is not required from all students, may be claimed to a limit of $250.

The tax credit for tuition paid in the year to a university outside Canada is more restricted. The student must be in full-time attendance at a university in a course leading to a degree. The course must be of at least three consecutive weeks' duration. A tax credit for fees paid by a Canadian resident who commuted to an educational institution providing courses at the post-secondary level in the United States is allowed. Again, the amount of the fees paid in the year to a particular institution must exceed $100. ITA: 118.5(1)(b), 118.5(1)(c)

Examination fees paid to an educational institution, professional association, provincial ministry, or other institution for an examination required to obtain a professional status recognized by federal or provincial statute, or to be licensed or certified to practise a trade or profession in Canada, will be eligible for the tuition tax credit. ITA: 118.5(1)(d)

Fees for an individual's tuition for occupational skills courses that are not at the post-secondary level but are paid to a university, college, or other post-secondary institution in Canada may also be eligible for the credit. To qualify, the course must provide new skills or improve the individual's skills in an occupation. For these fees to qualify, the individual must have attained the age of 16 before the end of the year.

¶10,450.40 Carryforward

The unused portion of a student's tuition fee credit can be claimed by the student in a subsequent taxation year. This allows an indefinite carryforward of these credits by the student to the extent that they are not transferred in the year earned to a spouse or supporting individual. Students are permitted to transfer part of the unused credits and carry forward the remainder. ITA: 118.61 Unused tuition, textbook and education tax credits

¶10,450.50 Transfer of Tuition Credit to Spouse, Parent, or Grandparent

The tuition fee credit may be transferred to a spouse or to a parent or grandparent of the student. To qualify, the student must designate, in writing, an amount transferred to a spouse or to a parent or grandparent. The formula for calculating the amount that may be claimed as a tax credit by the spouse or by the parent or grandparent is the lesser of: ITA: 118.8 Transfer of unused credits to spouse or common-law partner, 118.81 Tuition tax credit transferred, 118.9 Transfer to parent or grandparent

(1) the amount determined by the formula A – B

where A is the lesser of: ITA: 118.01 [Adoption expense tax credit], 118.02 [Transit pass tax credit], 118.03

(a) $750 (i.e., 15% of $5,000), and

(b) the student's tuition credit (excluding unused amounts carried forward).

B is the amount of the student's Part I tax payable after deducting credits for personal, age, pension, and employment, public transit passes, mental or physical impairment, EI and CPP, and unused tuition, and ITA: 118 Personal credits, 118.3 Credit for mental or physical impairment, 118.7 Credit for EI and QPIP premiums and CPP contributions

(2) the amount designated by the student in writing for the transfer to a spouse or to a parent or grandparent.

In effect, this formula allows the transfer of the excess of up to $750 of a student's tuition credit over those credits required by the student to reduce federal tax to nil.

Example Problem 10-8

Debbie, who is not dependent upon any person, was enrolled as a full-time student at the University of Toronto for eight months during 2018. Debbie provides you with the following information for 2018:

Scholarship income	$12,000
Summer employment	15,000
Interest income — Canadian	1,000
Qualified tuition fees paid in 2018 (8 months)	9,000

REQUIRED

(1) Determine the amount of Debbie's federal tuition credit which can be transferred to her parent.

(2) Determine the amount of Debbie's unused federal tuition tax credit at the end of 2018, assuming she transfers the maximum amount.

SOLUTION

(1)

Scholarship income [not taxable]	$ Nil
Employment income	15,000
Interest	1,000
Division B and taxable income	$16,000
Federal tax @ 15%	$ 2,400
Basic personal tax credit ($11,809 × 15%)	(1,771)
Canada employment credit ($1,195 × 15%)	(179)
Federal tax payable	$450
Tuition fee tax credit:	
Tuition fee tax credit (15% of $9,000)	$ 1,350

Tuition fee tax credit transfer to parent:

Lesser of:		
(a) $750		
(b) Student's tuition fee credit ($1,350)		$ 750
Less: amount of student's Part I tax net of secs. 118 to 118.07, 118.3, 118.61, and 118.7 credits		450
Net amount available for transfer		$ 300

(2)

Unused tuition credit at December 31, 2017		Nil
Plus: 2017 tuition	$1,350	
Less: Debbie's tax payable before deducting the current year's tuition, education, and textbook credits	(450)	$900
Minus: Unused tuition credit deducted in 2018		(Nil)
Tuition credit transferred		(300)
Unused tuition tax credit at December 31, 2018		$ 600

¶10,450.60 Credit for Interest on Student Loans

A student may deduct a federal tax credit of 15% (10% used for provincial tax credit) of interest on a federal or provincial student loan payable in respect of the year or in any of the five preceding taxation years. Qualifying loans are those made under the *Canada Student Loans Act*, the *Canada Student Financial Assistance Act*, the *Apprentice Loan Act*, or a similar provincial statute.

ITA: 118.62 Credit for interest on student loan

¶10,455 Credit for Employment Insurance Premiums and CPP Contributions

The federal tax credit is equal to 15% (10% used for provincial tax credit) of:

ITA: 118.7 Credit for EI and QPIP premiums and CPP contributions

(1) all amounts payable by the individual in respect of an employee's premiums for Employment Insurance;

(2) all amounts payable by the individual as an employee's contributions under the Canada (or Quebec) Pension Plan; and

(3) all amounts payable by the individual as a contribution for self-employed earnings under the Canada (or Quebec) Pension Plan.

For 2018, the Employment Insurance premium rate for the employee is 1.66% of earnings to a maximum annual earnings amount of $51,700. At this level of earnings the maximum level of premium of $858 is reached. (Employers must pay a premium of 2.32% (i.e., 1.4 times the employee payment), for a total maximum of $1,202.)

The rate of contribution to the Canada Pension Plan for 2018 is 4.95% of pensionable earnings. The maximum pensionable earnings are $55,900 with a basic exemption of $3,500. Thus, the maximum contribution is calculated as follows:

4.95% of ($55,900 – $3,500) = $2,594

For a self-employed individual, the maximum is twice the above amount or $5,188. Half of this amount provides a deduction in Subdivision e. This is the equivalent of the treatment of the amount paid by an employer.

ITA: 60(e) CPP/QPP contributions on self-employed earnings

¶10,460 Dividend Tax Credit

Overview

The federal dividend tax credit available to an individual is a non-refundable tax credit. As dividends are generated by the earnings of a corporation that have already been taxed, the dividend tax credit attempts to give the individual credit for the corporate tax already paid on those earnings. Together with the dividend gross-up included in the computation of net income for tax purposes (discussed in detail in chapter 6), the dividend tax credit's purpose is to eliminate or reduce double taxation on income earned and taxed at the corporation and then taxed again in the hands of the individual as a dividend.

ITA: 121 Deduction for taxable dividends

¶10,460.10 Calculation of the Dividend Tax Credit

There are two rates of dividend tax credit. Classification is meant to approximate the corporate tax rate applied to the earnings when they were generated in the corporation. This is accomplished by classifying the dividends as:

- "Eligible" for the larger tax credit because the earnings faced a higher corporate tax rate when they were earned in the corporation (i.e., corporate income that was not subject to the reduced small business tax rate). The rate of 20.7% of the dividend paid applies to dividends paid by

  ITA: 82(1)(b)(ii)

  (1) a public corporation resident in Canada (and any other non-CCPC resident in Canada) from income subject to tax at the general corporate tax rate, and

  (2) a CCPC resident in Canada to the extent that its income (other than investment income) is taxed at the general corporate rate.

- "Non-Eligible" for the larger tax credit because the earnings faced a lower corporate tax rate when they were earned in the corporation (i.e., corporate income that was taxed at the reduced small business tax rate) and therefore receiving a reduced credit. A rate of 11.63% of the dividend paid applies to dividends paid by a CCPC from income subject to tax at the low rate applicable to active business income and aggregate investment income.

The dividend tax credit can be calculated in three different ways depending on the information available:

Source of dividend	CCPC, on income taxed at the low rate on ABI and AII	Canadian-resident public corporation or other corporations on income taxed at the general rate
Dividend paid	100%	100%
Gross-up	16%	38%
Dividend tax credit		
Fraction of gross-up	8/11	6/11
Percentage of dividend paid	11.6%	20.7%
Percentage of grossed up dividend	10% (rounded)	15% (rounded)

For the purposes of this book, unless otherwise stated, where provincial tax credits are calculated for individuals, a theoretical dividend tax credit rate will be applied to the dividend gross-up as follows:

- a provincial rate of 3/11 where the 16% gross-up applies; and
- a provincial rate of 5/11 where the 38% gross-up applies.

Theoretically, the combined federal and provincial dividend tax credit should equal the gross-up of 16% or 38% of the dividend. This will be explored in Chapter 12. This would imply a provincial dividend tax credit rate applied to the grossed-up dividend of:

Low-rate income

- 8/11 federal + 3/11 provincial, for a total of 100% of the gross-up.

High-rate income

- 6/11 federal + 5/11 provincial, for a total of 100% of the gross-up.

However, provinces, in their use of the tax-on-income ("TONI") structure, may specify their own rate of dividend tax credit.

Ⓐ ¶10,460.20 Election to Transfer Dividends to Spouse

An election is available to deem taxable dividends from taxable Canadian corporations received by one spouse or common-law partner, who cannot use the dividend tax credit because of low income, to be received by the other spouse or common-law partner. However, this election can only be used if the married personal tax credit claimed by the higher income spouse for the dependent spouse or common-law partner is increased or created by transfer ring the dividend income in this way. If the election can be made, the taxpayer must include the grossed up dividends transferred from the spouse or common-law partner, but may deduct the dividend tax credit available on the dividends.

ITA: 82(3) Dividends received by spouse or common-law partner

Consider the following situations where the low-income spouse has $300 of grossed up dividends from Canadian-resident public corporations plus some other source of income.

Calculation of taxpayer's married tax credit	Case 1	Case 2	Case 3
Spouse's Division B income before election	$11,400	$ 8,000	$12,000
Married credit:			
Spouse base	$11,809	$11,809	$11,809
Spouse's Division B income	(11,400)	(8,000)	(12,000)
Net credit base	$ 409	$ 3,809	Nil
Credit @ 15% of net credit base	$ 61	$ 571	Nil
Spouse's Division B income after election	$11,100	$ 7,700	$11,700
Married credit:			
Spouse tax credit base	$11,809	$11,809	$11,809
Spouse's Division B income	(11,100)	(7,700)	(11,700)
Net credit base	$ 709	$ 4,109	Nil
Credit @ 15% of net credit base (rounded)	$ 106	$ 616	Nil

In Case 1, an election is available, since after the election, the spousal credit has increased from $61 to $106. In Case 2, the spousal credit has increased from $571 to $616 by the transfer of the dividends and, hence, the election is available. In Case 3, the election is not available, since the spousal credit is not available either before or after the transfer.

¶10,470 School Supplies Tax Credit

An "eligible educator" may claim a refundable school supplies tax credit at 15% on up to $1,000 of "eligible supplies expense".

An "eligible educator" is defined as an individual, who at any time during the year:

(a) is employed in Canada as a teacher or early childhood educator at:

(i) an elementary or secondary school, or

(ii) a regulated child care facility, and

(b) holds a valid and recognized (by a province or territory of Canada)

(i) teaching certificate, licence, permit, or diploma, or

(ii) certificate or diploma in early childhood education.

"Eligible supplies expense" is a defined term. It covers expenditures for teaching supplies that were purchased by the educator for teaching or facilitating student learning and directly consumed or used in the educator's employment. The CRA may demand written certification of these expenditures from the educator's employer. Also, the educator may not be entitled to receive any non-taxable reimbursement, allowance, or other form of assistance for these expenditures.

"Teaching supplies" is defined to mean consumable supplies such as construction paper, items for science experiments, art supplies, and stationery. The definition also includes "prescribed durable goods" which are listed in a Regulation as books, games and puzzles, containers for storage, and educational support software.

¶10,475 Foreign Tax Credits

Since a resident of Canada is subject to tax on worldwide income, any income earned from a foreign source must be included in total income being taxed in Canada. However, the foreign income may also have been taxed in the country in which it was earned. In the absence of a tax treaty which removes the income from the tax base of either Canada or the other country, the income would be taxed twice. The Act provides tax credits deductible from tax payable in Canada for income tax paid in another country. Residents of Canada may claim a tax credit for non-business income tax paid (such as tax on investment income) in another country and a tax credit for business income tax paid in another country. Both credits are limited to a proportion of tax payable in Canada that can be considered to be attributed to the income from the foreign source. This limit is computed by formula.

ITA: 126 Foreign tax deduction, 126(1) Foreign tax deduction, 126(2) Idem; Income Tax Folio: S5-F2-C1 Foreign Tax Credit

For individuals, the foreign non-business tax credit is computed as the lesser of:

ITA: 126(1) Foreign tax deduction

(a) non-business income tax paid to a foreign country, and

(b) $\dfrac{\text{net non-business foreign income}}{\text{total income included under Division B net of certain adjustments}} \times$ tax for the year otherwise payable under Part I

Note that part (b) attempts to estimate the Canadian tax paid on the foreign income. As a result, the credit against Canadian tax cannot exceed the estimated Canadian tax paid on the foreign income.

The definition of "non-business income tax" excludes an amount that was deductible from property income in respect of foreign taxes in excess of 15% on income from property and an amount that was deducted in respect of foreign non-business income tax paid.

ITA: 20(11) Foreign taxes on income from property exceeding 15%, 20(12) Foreign non-business income tax, 126(7) Definitions

The denominator of the fraction, which uses total income under Division B as the base, is reduced by amounts that are attributable to specific types of income which are offset by Division C deductions and, hence, do not generate tax. These amounts include:

(1) amounts deducted as net capital losses; or

ITA: 111(1)(b) Net capital losses

(2) amounts deductible in respect of:

ITA: 110(1)(d) Employee options, 110(1)(d.1) Idem, 110(1)(d.2) Prospector's and grubstaker's shares, 110(1)(d.3) Employer's shares

(a) shares, or

(b) a deduction for workers' compensation or social assistance.

ITA: 110(1)(f) Deductions for payments

The term "tax for the year otherwise payable under this Part" is defined for the purposes of the foreign non-business income tax credit. As it applies generally to individuals, it is the tax payable under Part I of the Act before specified deductions from tax, including the deduction of the dividend tax credit and the credit for employment outside Canada.

ITA: 126(7) tax for the ear otherwise payable under this Part (a)

The foreign business income tax credit, also, applies to individual taxpayers and is similar in its calculation. The major difference is that any business income tax paid but not deducted is available as an "unused foreign tax credit" to be carried back three years and forward 10 years. This foreign tax credit will be dealt with in more detail, as it applies to corporations, in the next chapter.

ITA: 126(7) Definitions

¶10,480 Federal Political Contribution Tax Credit

A tax credit is available for contributions to a registered federal political party, a registered association, or a candidate for election to the House of Commons. Receipts signed by the registered agent of the party or the official agent of the candidate are required to substantiate the credit claimed. The maximum credit is $650 which is reached with a contribution of $1,275 or more on the following sliding scale:

ITA: 127(3) Contributions to registered parties and candidates

Contribution	Credit
$400 or less	75% of the contribution
More than $400, but not more than $750	$300 + 50% of the contribution over $400
More than $750, but not more than $1,275	$475 + 33⅓% of the contribution over $750
More than $1,275	$650

¶10,485 Tax on Old Age Security Benefits

The Part I.2 tax results in the repayment of federal Old Age Security benefits included in computing the taxpayer's income, to the extent that the taxpayer's income is in excess of an indexed threshold ($75,910 for 2018). The repayment is computed as:

ITA: 60(w) Tax under Part I.2, 180.2 Tax on Old Age Security Benefits

the lesser of:

(a)	Old Age Security benefits		$xxx
(b)	income under Division B without par. 60(*w*) deduction	$ xxx	
	less	75,910	
	excess, if any	$ xxx	
	15% of excess, if any		$ xxx

Note that the amount of this tax is deductible from income; however, offsetting the Part I.2 tax in part (b), above, through the deduction removes the potential double tax on this amount, as discussed in Chapter 9 at ¶9,230.

ITA: 60(w) Tax under Part I.2

Example Problem 10-9

Joanne, a widow, received the Old Age Security benefit of $7,040 in 2018. Her Division B income, excluding the deduction for the Part I.2 tax, is $77,000.[1]

ITA: 60(w) Tax under Part I.2

REQUIRED

Outline all of the tax implications of receiving the Old Age Security benefit in this case.

SOLUTION

(1) The amount of the Old Age Security benefit received must be included in Joanne's income

ITA: 56(1)(a) Pension benefits, unemployment insurance benefits, etc.

(2) The following repayment of the Old Age Security payment is required:

ITA: 180.2 Tax on Old Age Security Benefits

the lesser of:		
(i) Old Age Security benefit		$ 7,040
(ii) Division B income (excluding clawback deduction)	$77,000	
less	75,910	
excess, if any	1,090	
15% of excess		$ 164

ITA: 60(w) Tax under Part I.2

(3) The $164 repayment is deductible.

ITA: 60(w) Tax under Part I.2

(4) The net effect is as follows:

(i) inclusion of Old Age Security benefit	$ 7,040	
(ii) deduction of repayment	(164)	$ 6,876
(iii) cash received	$ 7,040	
(iv) repayment of Old Age Security benefit (paid special Part I.2 tax)	(164)	$ 6,876

NOTES

[1] This is the amount for the first quarter 2018 ($7,040), annualized maximum amount.

Ⓐ ¶10,490 Tax Reduction on Retroactive Lump-Sum Payments

When an individual receives a lump-sum payment in a year that relates to prior years, the graduated tax rate schedule, when applied to the lump sum, may result in more income tax payable in the year of receipt than in the prior years had the lump sum been spread over those previous years. The legislation provides for a reduction of tax on the following lump sums:

ITA: 120.31 Lump-sum Payments, 110.2 Lump-sum payments

- income from an office or employment or income received because of the termination of an office or employment, received under the terms of a court judgment, arbitration award, or in settlement of a lawsuit;
- superannuation or pension benefits, other than non-periodic benefits;
- spouse or child support payments; and
- employment insurance and other benefits that may be prescribed by regulations.

The right to receive the lump sum must have existed in a prior year. For the tax reduction to apply, the lump sum received in the year must be at least $3,000.

The amount of income that is eligible for this special treatment is deducted in arriving at taxable income and then subject to notional tax. The notional tax is calculated as if the lump- sum payment had actually been received in the year to which it related. Interest, calculated at a prescribed rate, is added to the tax to reflect the fact that the notional tax was not actually paid in a previous year.

ITA: 120.31 Lump-sum Payments, 110.2 Lump-sum payments

This calculation will not affect any income-based benefits or deductions in those prior years.

¶10,495 Additional Features and Rules Applicable to Tax Credits

¶10,495.10 Transfer of Unused Credits to Spouse or Common-Law Partner

Certain unused tax credits may be transferred to a spouse or common-law partner. These tax credits are:

ITA: 118.8 Transfer of unused credits to spouse or common-law partner

(1) the tuition credit (to a maximum of $750);

ITA: 118.5 Tuition credit, 118.6 [Education and textbook tax credits]

(2) the age amount;

ITA: 118(2) Age credit

(3) the pension income amount; and

ITA: 118(3) Pension credit

(4) the mental or physical impairment credit.

ITA: 118.3(1) Credit for mental or physical impairment

The amount that may be transferred is calculated by the following formula:

$$A + B - C$$

where

A is the lesser of:

- $750, and
- the spouse's tuition fee credit;

B is the sum of the following tax credits available to the spouse:

- the age amount,
- the pension income amount, and
- the mental or physical impairment credit; and

C is the amount, if any, by which

ITA: 118(1)(c) Single status

(a) the spouse's Part I tax payable after deducting:

- the basic single personal credit,
- unused tuition credit, and
- the EI and CPP credits

ITA: 118.61 Unused tuition, textbook and education tax credits

ITA: 118.7 Credit for EI and QPIP premiums and CPP contributions

exceeds

(b) the lesser of:

(i) the tuition credit deductible by the spouse; and

(ii) the spouse's Part I tax payable after deducting:

- the basic personal credits for married status, equivalent-to-married status, single, dependants, and Canada caregiver,
- the adoption expense credit,
- the Canada employment credit,
- the home accessibility tax credit,
- the first-time home buyers' tax credit,
- the volunteer firefighters tax credit,
- the search and rescue volunteer tax credit,
- the impairment (disability) credit,
- the unused tuition credit, and
- the EI and CPP credits.

ITA: 118(1) Personal credits

ITA: 118.01 [Adoption expense tax credit]

ITA: 118(10) Canada Employment Credit

ITA: 118.041 [Home Accessibility Tax Credit]

ITA: 118.05 [First-time home buyers' tax credit]

ITA: 118.06 [Volunteer firefighter tax credit]

ITA: 118.07 [Search and rescue volunteers tax credit]

ITA: 118.3 Credit for mental or physical impairment

ITA: 118.61 Unused tuition, textbook and education tax credits

ITA: 118.7 Credit for EI and QPIP premiums and CPP contributions

Example Problem 10-10

Mrs. Ahmed, age 75, received the following income in 2018:

Registered pension plan payments	$ 700
Old Age Security pension	7,040
Canada Pension Plan payments	600
Interest from Canadian corporations	400
Division B income	$8,740

Mrs. Ahmed has been confined to a wheelchair for several years but is quite active and is registered as a full-time student at a post-secondary institution for eight months, paying tuition of $2,000 at the senior citizen's rate.

REQUIRED

Calculate the amount of federal tax credit transfer available to her husband for 2018.

SOLUTION

Transfer of credits to Mr. Ahmed in accordance with the formula:

A + B − C

(A)	Tuition credit transferred			
	Lesser of:	(a) dollar limit	$ 750	
		(b) tuition credit (15% × $2,000)	$ 300	
		lesser amount		$ 300
(B)	Age credit		$1,100	
	Pension credit[(1)]		105	
	Disability credit		1,235	2,440
				$2,740

(C)	Mrs. Ahmed's Part I tax ($1,311 = 15% of $8,642) net of the basic personal tax credit ($1,771), unused tuition credits (nil), and CPP and EI credits (nil)		Nil	
	Minus lesser of:			
	(i) tuition credit deductible by Mrs. Ahmed	Nil		
	(ii) Mrs. Ahmed's Part I tax ($1,296) net of the basic personal tax credit ($1,771), the disability credit ($1,235), Canada employment (nil), adoption (nil), public transit passes (nil), the unused tuition, education, and textbook credits (nil), and CPP and EI credits (nil)	Nil		
	Lesser amount		Nil	(Nil)
				$2,740

NOTE TO SOLUTION

(1) The Old Age Security pension and CPP payments do not qualify for the pension tax credit. The pension credit is calculated as 15% of the lesser of:

ITA: 118(8) Interpretation

(1) $2,000; and

(2) pension income of $700.

¶10,495.20 Credits for Part-Year and Non-Residents

Generally, for the period of residence in Canada of a part-year resident, the individual can deduct specified tax credits prorated by the number of days that the individual is resident in the year divided by the number of days in the calendar year:

ITA: 118.91 Part-year residents

- basic personal amount, married amount, equivalent-to-married amount, dependant amount, and Canada caregiver amount;

ITA: 118(1) Personal credits

- age amount;

ITA: 118(2) Age credit

- disability amount either for the taxpayer or transferred from a dependant;

ITA: 118.3 Credit for mental or physical impairment

- unused credits transferred from a spouse; and

ITA: 118.8 Transfer of unused credits to spouse or common-law partner

- unused tuition and education amounts transferred from a child or grandchild

ITA: 118.9 Transfer to parent or grandparent

All other personal amounts may fully be claimed if they relate to the period of residence. These include:

- the pension credit; — ITA: 118(3) Pension credit
- Canada employment credit; — ITA: 118(10) Canada Employment Credit
- the adoption expense credit; — ITA: 118.01 [Adoption expense tax credit]
- first-time home buyers' credit and disability purchase credit; — ITA: 118.05 [First-time home buyers' tax credit]
- volunteer fire-fighter tax credit; — ITA: 118.06 [Volunteer firefighter tax credit]
- volunteer search and rescue volunteer tax credit; — ITA: 118.061
- charitable gifts; — ITA: 118.1 [Charitable and other gifts]
- medical expenses; — ITA: 118.2 Medical expense credit
- tuition credit; — ITA: 118.5 Tuition credit
- credit for interest on student loan; and — ITA: 118.6 [Education and textbook tax credits], 118.62 Credit for interest on student loan
- EI and CPP credits. — ITA: 118.7 Credit for EI and QPIP premiums and CPP contributions

A non-resident individual (i.e., an individual who at no time in the year is resident in Canada) may deduct tax credits for the following amounts:

ITA: 118.94 Tax payable by non-residents (credits restricted)

- charitable donations, including Crown gifts and cultural gifts; — ITA: 118.1 [Charitable and other gifts]
- impairment amount for the taxpayer, but not for a dependant; — ITA: 118.3(1) Credit for mental or physical impairment
- tuition credit; and — ITA: 118.5 Tuition credit
- EI and CPP (or QPP) credits. — ITA: 118.7 Credit for EI and QPIP premiums and CPP contributions

Credits for all other personal amounts may be deducted if all or substantially all of the individual's worldwide income for the calendar year is included on the return.

¶10,495.30 Ordering of Credits

The Act provides an ordering rule for computing basic federal tax payable by an individual under Part I of the Act. The tax credits discussed, all of which are above-the-line non- refundable tax credits, must be applied in the following order:

ITA: 118.92 Ordering of credits

Ssec. 118(1)	— married, equivalent-to-married, single, dependant, and Canada caregiver tax credits;
Ssec. 118(2)	— age credit;
Sec. 118.7	— Employment Insurance and Canada (or Quebec) Pension Plan credits;
Ssec. 118(3)	— pension credit;
Ssec. 118(10)	— Canada employment credit;
Sec. 118.01	— adoption expense credit;
Sec. 118.041	— home accessibility tax credit;

Sec. 118.05	— first-time home buyers' credit and disability home purchase credit;
Sec. 118.06	— volunteer firefighters tax credit;
Sec. 118.07	— search and rescue volunteer tax credit;
Sec. 118.3	— mental or physical impairment credit (including dependant's unused credit);
Sec. 118.61	— unused tuition credit carryforward;
Sec. 118.5	— tuition fee credit;
Sec. 118.9	— transfer of tuition credit;
Sec. 118.8	— transfer of unused spouse's credits;
Sec. 118.2	— medical expense credit;
Sec. 118.1	— charitable gifts credit;
Sec. 118.62	— credit for interest on student loan;
Sec. 119.1	— family tax cut credit; and
Sec. 121	— dividend tax credit.

Example Problem 10-11

The following list of income inclusions, deductions, losses, and tax credits has been determined correctly by a junior staff accountant prior to the preparation of the tax return for Ms. Samara Lowen.

Inclusions	
Salary	$60,000
Canadian bank interest	1,200
Taxable capital gains	7,500
Taxable benefits from employment	1,780
Pension income	5,000
Taxable amount of dividends from taxable Canadian corporations	750

Deductions, Losses, and Tax Credits	
Non-capital losses claimed	$2,000
Net capital losses carried forward	6,000
Basic personal and spousal tax credits	3,542
Registered pension plan contributions	1,000
Medical expenses tax credit	80
Interest expense to acquire Canadian shares	300
Moving expenses	600
Charitable donations tax credit	202
Pension tax credit	300
Canada Pension Plan contributions tax credit	389
Employment Insurance premiums tax credit	129
Dividend tax credit	100
Allowable capital losses	650
Business loss	3,080
Canada employment credit	179

REQUIRED

(1) From the structural outlines and exhibits on the preceding pages, determine the income, taxable income, and basic federal tax net of non-refundable tax credits based upon the above correct information using the ordering rules in sections 3, 111.1, and 118.92.

(2) Cross-reference each amount to the appropriate section of the Act. (Refer to Sectional List of the Act.)

SOLUTION

Division B — Section 3

Par. 3(*a*)	*Subdivision a*			
	Sec. 5	Salary	$ 60,000	
	Par. 6(1)(*a*)	Taxable benefits	1,780	$ 61,780
	Less			
	Par. 8(1)(*m*)	Registered pension plan contributions		(1,000)
				$60,780
	Subdivision b			
	Business		Nil	
	Property			
	Par. 12(1)(*c*)	Canadian bank interest	$ 1,200	
	Par. 12(1)(*j*)	Dividends (taxable amount)	750	
			$ 1,950	
	Par. 20(1)(*c*)	Interest expense	(300)	$ 1,650
	Subdivision d			
	Ssec. 56(1)	Pension income		5,000
				$ 67,430
Par. 3(*b*)	*Subdivision c*			
	Sec. 38	Taxable capital gains	$ 7,500	
	Sec. 38	Allowable capital losses	(650)	6,850
				$ 74,280
Par. 3(*c*)	*Subdivision e*			
	Sec. 62	Moving expenses		(600)
				$ 73,680
Par. 3(*d*)	Sec. 9	Business loss		(3,080)
		Division B income		$ 70,600

Division C — Section 111.1

Par. 111(1)(*a*)	Non-capital losses	$ (2,000)	
Par. 111(1)(*b*)	Net capital losses	(6,000)	(8,000)
Taxable income			$ 62,600

Division E — Section 118.92

Sec. 117	Federal tax on first	$ 46,605	$ 6,991
	Tax on balance	15,995 @ 20.5%	3,279
Federal tax before credits			$ 10,270
Less tax credits:			
Sec. 118	Personal tax credits	$ 3,542	
Sec. 118.7	CPP tax credit	389	
Sec. 118.7	EI premium tax credit	129	
Ssec. 118(3)	Pension tax credit	300	
Ssec. 118(10)	Canada employment credit	179	
Sec. 118.2	Medical expense credit	80	
Sec. 118.1	Donation tax credit	202	
Sec. 121	Dividend tax credit	100	(4,921)
Basic federal tax			$ 5,349

¶10,495.40 Income Not Earned in a Province

This provision imposes a surtax of 48% on federal tax of an individual applicable proportionally to income for the year not earned in a province. A definition of the term "income earned in the year in a province" is provided.

ITA: 120(1) Income not earned in a province, 120(4) Definitions; ITR: 2600 Interpretation

The purpose of this provision is to achieve a tax rate on income earned outside of Canada and taxable in Canada which approximates the total federal and provincial income tax on income earned in Canada.

¶10,495.50 Application of Rules for Computation of Tax and Credits

Example Problem 10-12

The following 2018 correct computation of taxable income for John Q. Citizen has been prepared for your analysis:

Income — Division B			
Employment income for tax purposes			$52,000
Business and property income, composed of:			
	Dividends from Canadian-resident public corporations	$ 3,000	
	Gross-up 38%	1,140	
	Dividends — Foreign ($150 of tax withheld)	1,000	5,140
Pension income (including OAS benefit of $7,040)			16,219
Taxable capital gain			2,500
			$75,859
Less: Subdivision e deductions:			
RRSP contributions		$ 1,000	
Old Age Security benefit clawback		Nil	
Moving expenses		1,050	(2,050)
Division B income			$73,809

Less: net capital losses	(1,000)
Taxable income	$72,809

Additional Information

(1) John, age 67, and his wife Jill, age 64, are both resident in your province. Jill has no income and is blind.

(2) John has made the following selected payments in 2018:

Donations:	
Federal political party (registered)	$ 500
Provincial political party (registered)	400
United Appeal (registered) (made annually)	500

(3) John's employer correctly withheld the following amounts:

Employment Insurance	$ 858
Canada Pension Plan	2,594

(4) John filed his return on April 30, 2018.

REQUIRED

Compute the total amount of federal taxes payable for the year.

SOLUTION

Sec. 117	Federal tax on first	$46,605		$ 6,991
	Tax on balance	26,204	@ 20.5%	5,372
		$72,809		
	Total			$12,363
	Less: federal non-refundable tax credits:			
Ssec. 118(1)	Basic personal credit base		$11,809	
	Married credit base (with family caregiver credit)		11,809	

	Canada caregiver credit		2,182	
Ssec. 118(10)	Canada employment credit base		1,195	
Ssec. 118(2)	Age credit base[(1)]		1,808	
Sec. 118.7	Employment Insurance credit base		858	
	Canada Pension Plan credit base		2,594	
Ssec. 118(3)	Pension credit base		2,000	
Sec. 118.8	Transfer of spouse's impairment credit base		8,235	
				$42,490
	15% thereof			(6,374)
				$ 5,989
Sec. 118.1	Charitable donations tax credit			
	First	$200 @ 15%	$ 30	
	Excess	$300 @ 29%	87	(117)
		$500		
Sec. 121	Federal dividend tax credit ($^6/_{11}$ × $1,140)			(622)
	Basic federal tax			$ 5,250
	Less: other federal tax credits:			
Sec. 126	Federal foreign tax credit[(2)]			
	Lesser of:			
	(a) $150			
	(b) $1,000/($73,809 – $1,000) × ($5,250 + $622) = $81			(81)
	Federal tax			$ 5,169
Ssec. 127(3)	Federal political donations[(3)]			(350)
	Net federal Part I tax payable			$ 4,819
Sec. 180.2	Old Age Security benefit clawback[(4)]			0
	Net federal tax payable			$ 4,819

NOTES TO SOLUTION

(1) Age tax credit base

Age tax credit base			$7,333
Less: base reduction of lesser of:			
(a) Amount of credit base		$7,333	
(b) Division B income	$73,809		
Less: threshold	36,976		
	$36,833 × 0.15 =	$5,525	
Lesser amount			5,525
Net base			$1,808

(2) In this case, the foreign non-business tax credit is computed as the lesser of:

(a) the foreign non-business tax paid, and

(b) $$\frac{\text{foreign non-business income included under Division B}}{\text{Division B income less net capital losses claimed}} \times \text{basic federal tax plus dividend tax credit}$$

(3) The Act permits the deduction of a contribution to a federal registered party or person nominated as a candidate to serve in the House of Commons. The formula is:

ITA: 127(3) Contributions to registered parties and candidates

75% of first $400	$300
50% of next $350 ($500 – $400 in this situation)	50
33⅓% on next $525 (none in this situation)	Nil
	$350

(4) Lesser of:

(a)	Old Age Security benefit		$7,040
(b)	income under Division B (excluding clawback deduction)	$73,809	
	less	75,910	
	excess, if any	Nil	
	15% of excess		Nil

ITA: 60(w) Tax under Part I.2

Example Problem 10-13

Joshua's computation of taxable income for 2018 is as follows:

Income from employment	$57,500
Net income from rental properties	1,230
Public company dividend income	2,000
Gross-up 38%	760
Taxable capital gain	1,200
RRSP contribution	(4,000)
Child care expenses	(2,500)
Net income for tax purposes	56,190
Less: Net capital loss carryforward	(1,200)
Taxable income	$54,990

NOTES:

(a) Assume Joshua was resident in Canada on December 31, 2018.

(b) Assume that Joshua's taxable income was prepared correctly.

(c) Joshua is divorced and lives with his 7-year-old son, Jamie.

(d) During the year Joshua incurred the following expenses:

United Way donation (made annually)	$50
Cancer Society donation	20
Registered political party contribution	100
Transit passes (purchased monthly)	1,140
Tuition (part-time university course — 3 months)	175
Medical expenses for Jamie (dental and ophthalmic)	1,755

(e)	T4 information:	
	Employment insurance	858
	Canada Pension Plan	2,594
	Tax withheld by employer	9,800

REQUIRED

Compute Joshua's federal and provincial taxes payable. Assume the provincial tax rates are as set out in ¶10,250. Also assume that the provincial tax credit base amounts are the same as the federal amounts; there are no over/under payments of EI and CPP.

SOLUTION

Federal tax on the first	$46,605		$ 6,991
Excess	$8,385	× 20.5%	1,719
Federal tax on taxable income	$54,990		$ 8,710
Less:			
Non-refundable tax credits (Sch. 1)			($4,287)
Dividend tax (6/11 × $760)			(415)
Basic federal tax			$ 4,008
Less: federal political tax credit			(75)
Net Federal Tax			$ 3,933
Provincial Tax (Sch. 2)			2,464
Total Tax Payable			$ 6,397
Less: tax deducted			(9,800)
Total tax refund			$ 3,403

Schedule 1: Federal non-refundable tax credits		Tax Base	Federal Credit (15%)
Basic personal credit		$11,809	$1,771
Equivalent-to-spouse credit		11,809	1,771
Canada Pension Plan credit		2,594	389
Employment Insurance credit		858	129
Canada Employment credit		1,195	179
Tuition fees		175	26
Medical expense credit			
Total medical expenses	$ 1,755		
3% × $56,190 (net income)	1,686		
Excess		69	10
Charitable donations credit		70	11
Non-refundable credits		$28,579	$4,287
Federal political tax credit		$ 100	$ 75

Schedule 2: Provincial tax calculation			
Provincial tax on the first	$46,605		$4,661
Excess	8,385	× 12%	1,006
Provincial tax on taxable income	$54,990		$5,667
Less:			
Provincial non-refundable credits	28,579	× 10%	(2,858)
Provincial dividend tax credit		($760 × 5/11)	(345)
Provincial tax			$2,464

¶10,499 Pause and Reflect — Summary of Learning Goals

After working through this section, ¶10,400, you should be able to:

- Identify all tax credits available to a taxpayer.
- Apply the rules to calculate the amount of all tax credits for a taxpayer.
- Apply the rules to calculate amount of tax owing or refund available to a taxpayer.

¶10,499.99 Practise What You've Learned

Refer to the following sections of the Study Guide to practise what you've learned:

¶10,800 — Review Questions

- Question 2 — Taxation of dividends
- Question 5 — Charitable donation tax credits
- Question 6 — Tax credits

¶10,825 — Multiple Choice Questions

- Question 3 — Transfer of education credits

¶10,850 — Exercises

- Exercise 7 — Transfer of credits to spouse
- Exercise 8 — Transfer of dividends
- Exercise 9 — Foreign and dividend tax credits

¶10,500 Refundable Amounts

Overview

As discussed previously, the Act provides both non-refundable and refundable tax credits. The non-refundable credits discussed above factor into the calculation of the balance of tax owing. However, the refundable credits generally do not impact the calculation of tax owing but instead generate a refund in the form of a cash payment to the individual taxpayer. The following section discusses the calculations of and rules applicable to these payments.

¶10,520 Refundable Medical Expense Supplement

A refundable medical expense supplement ("RMES") is provided for eligible individuals. An eligible individual is an individual who is resident in Canada throughout the year and 18 years of age or older at the end of the year. The individual's adjusted income for a taxation year is defined as being the total of the income of the individual and of the individual's cohabiting spouse.

ITA: 122.51 [Refundable medical expense supplement], 122.51(1) Definitions

The supplement is calculated as follows:

lesser of:

(1) $1,222, and

(2) the total of

(a) $^{25}/_{15}$ of the medical expense tax credit claimed by the eligible individual for the year, and

(b) 25% of the amount deductible for disability support

less: 5% of the amount, if any, by which

(1) the individual's adjusted income

exceeds

(2) $27,044 for 2018.

ITA: 118.2 Medical expense credit

ITA: 64 Disability supports deduction

Since this is a refundable federal tax credit, it does not affect provincial tax. However, an adjustment for the effect of provincial tax is contained in the $^{25}/_{15}$ fraction used in the above calculation.

This supplement is completely eroded by the 5% reduction, when adjusted income is $51,484 (i.e., ($1,222/0.05) + $27,044).

The supplement is deemed to be tax paid as part of the individual's tax liability for the year, like income tax withheld. Thus, it is available for refund if total tax paid or deemed paid exceeds tax payable for the year.

ITA: 122.51(1) Definitions

The addition of 25% of the disability support deduction to the RMES ensures that disabled persons do not see their refundable medical expense credit reduced if they claim their cost of disability support as a deduction instead of a credit. The purpose of the RMES is to provide an incentive for Canadians with disabilities to work. The RMES is intended to offset the loss of coverage for medical and disability-related expenses when individuals move from social assistance to work.

¶10,550 Working Income Tax Benefit ("WITB")

Overview

For many low-income Canadians, taking a job can mean being financially worse off. To improve their incentives and lower their barriers to employment the WITB was introduced.

ITA: 122.7 [Working Income Tax Benefit]

The WITB provides a refundable tax credit equal to 25% of each dollar of earned income in excess of $3,000 to a maximum credit of $1,059 for single individuals without dependants (single individuals) and $1,922 for families (couples and single parents).[3] Earned income for purposes of the WITB means the total amount of an individual's or family's income for the year from employment and business and is determined without reference to any losses arising or claimed in that year.

To target assistance to those with low income, the credit is reduced by 15% of net family income in excess of $12,016 for single individuals and $16,593 for families in 2017.

[3] Note the numbers in this section are for the 2017 tax year as the 2018 numbers were not released by the CRA at the time of writing.

Hence, no WITB is available when a single individual's earned income reaches $19,076 (i.e., $1,059/0.15 + $12,016) or a family's earned income reaches $29,406 (i.e., $1,922/0.15 + $16,593) in 2016. Net income is calculated on the same basis as is currently used for the GST/HST credit.

An individual is eligible for the WITB if resident in Canada throughout the year and 19 years of age at the end of the year. In addition, a single parent must be the primary caregiver to the dependent child in Canada.

Students, as defined for the education tax credit, with no dependent children, who are enrolled as full-time students for more than three months in the year are not eligible for the WITB.

Example Problem 10-14

Bill is single and working as a mechanic in a bicycle shop earning $15,000 per year. His sister, Mary, is married and she and her husband make $22,000 per year.

REQUIRED

Will they qualify for the working income tax benefit?

SOLUTION

	Bill	Mary
Income	$15,000	$22,000
Base amount	(3,000)	(3,000)
Net working income over base	$12,000	$19,000
Lesser of $1,059/$1,922 and 25% of above amount	$1,059	$ 1,922
Reduction (below)	(448)	(811)
WITB	$ 611	$ 1,111
Income	$15,000	$22,000
Threshold	(12,016)	(16,593)
Base of reduction	$ 2,984	$ 5,407
Reduction: 15% of base	(448)	(811)

Both Bill and Mary will qualify for the working income tax benefit.

¶10,550.10 WITB Supplement for Persons With Disabilities

Persons with disabilities face significant barriers to their participation in the labour force. The WITB provides an additional supplement for each individual, other than a dependant, who is eligible for the disability tax credit and who has at least $1,150 of earned income and who meets the other eligibility requirements for the WITB. For each dollar in excess of $1,150, the individual is supplemented at a rate of 25% up to a maximum credit of $529. This supplement is reduced by 15% of net family income in excess of $19,073 for single individuals and $29,410 for families in 2017.

¶10,550.20 WITB Prepayment

To maximize the effectiveness of the WITB, a prepayment mechanism was put in place. Individuals and families who are eligible for the GST/HST credit, and who are eligible for the WITB, are eligible to apply to the CRA for a prepayment of one-half of their estimated WITB.

¶10,590 Pause and Reflect — Summary of Learning Goals

After working through this section, ¶10,500, you should be able to:

- Identify refundable tax credits available to a taxpayer
- Apply the calculation of the working income tax benefit
- Understand how computations of net income for tax purposes impact the calculation of refundable tax credits
- Understand how refundable tax credits are calculated outside of the calculation of net tax owing

¶10,590.99 Practise What You've Learned

Refer to the following sections of the Study Guide to practise what you've learned:

¶10,800 — Review Questions

- Question 16 — Working income tax benefit

¶10,600 Minimum Tax

Overview

The minimum tax addresses a government concern about the ability of individuals to have a tax year where the individual has significant income yet owe little income tax payable. An example of this is when individuals use their lifetime capital gains exemption or have a significant amount of their income comprised of eligible dividends. To address this situation, a minimum tax is calculated using a different tax base than taxable income and

ITA: 120.2 Minimum tax carry-over, 127.5 Obligation to pay minimum tax

the taxpayers may be required to pay minimum tax to the extent that their income tax payable is less than the minimum tax payable.

¶10,610 Minimum Amount

An individual's minimum tax is calculated by the following formula:

ITA: 127.51 Minimum amount determined

$$A\,(B - C) - D$$

where

A is 15% (i.e., the appropriate percentage for the year),

B is adjusted taxable income,

ITA: 127.52 Adjusted taxable income determined

C is the basic exemption ($40,000), and

ITA: 127.53 Basic exemption

D is the basic minimum tax credit.

ITA: 127.531 Basic minimum tax credit determined

This "minimum amount" minus a special foreign tax credit is then compared to regular Part I tax, net of all non-refundable tax credits (generally, before adding the 48% surtax for income not earned in a province). The greater amount becomes the basis of federal Part I tax for the year. The special foreign tax credit is basically equal to the greater of the foreign tax credit determined under normal rules or 15% of foreign income.

ITA: 127.54(2) Foreign tax credit

Other tax credits, such as dividend tax credits and political donation credits, will not be deductible from the minimum amount. In addition, even where the minimum amount is less than Part I tax, the restricted tax credits will be available only to the extent that Part I tax payable for the year does not go below the minimum amount.

¶10,620 Adjusted Taxable Income

This provision of the Act sets out the rules for computing adjusted taxable income, being a recalculation of taxable income using certain assumptions set out in the section. The CRA's form T691, for simplicity, starts with regular taxable income and adds back or subtracts amounts to arrive at adjusted taxable income. The amounts added back include:

ITA: 127.52 Adjusted taxable income determined

- the portion of the loss (including a share of a partnership loss) from certified film or videotape properties that relates to CCA or carrying charges such as interest and financing charges;
- losses on resource properties as a result of certain incentive deductions such as Canadian exploration expense, Canadian development expense, depletion allowance, or Canadian oil and gas property expense;
- 30% of the excess of capital gains over capital losses for the year;
- 3/5 of the employee stock option deductions and the other share deductions; and
- losses on investments required to be identified under the tax shelter identification rules.

ITA: 110(1)(d) Employee options, 110(1)(d.1) Idem, 110(1)(d.2) Prospector's and grubstaker's shares, 110(1)(d.3) Employer's shares

Deducted in computing adjusted taxable income are:

- the gross-up of Canadian dividends; and

- the non-deductible fraction of allowable business investment losses claimed in the year.

¶10,630 Basic Minimum Tax Credit

An individual's basic minimum tax credit is the sum of the tax credits that may be deducted in computing tax payable under Part I of the Act:

Ssec. 118(1)	–Personal credits for married status, equivalent-to-married status, single, dependants, and Canada caregiver;
Ssec. 118(2)	–Age credit;
Ssec. 118(10)	–Canada employment credit;
Ssec. 118.01	–Adoption expense credit;
Sec. 118.041	–Home accessibility tax credit;
Sec. 118.05	–First-time home buyers' tax credit;
Sec. 118.06	–Volunteer firefighter tax credit;
Sec. 118.07	–Search and rescue volunteer tax credit;
Sec. 118.1	–Charitable gifts credit;
Sec. 118.2	–Medical expense credit;
Ssc. 118.3(1)	–Mental or physical impairment credit;
Sec. 118.5	–Tuition credit;
Sec. 118.61	–Unused tuition credit;
Sec. 118.62	–Credit for interest on student loan;
Sec. 118.7	–Credit for Employment Insurance premium and CPP contribution:
Sec. 119	–Former resident-credit for tax paid; and
Sec. 127(1)	–Investment tax credit

¶10,640 Minimum Tax Carryforward

To recognize that a taxpayer who is not normally subject to minimum tax may, through unusual circumstances, be subject to minimum tax in a given year, the Act contains a carryforward provision. A taxpayer may carry forward for seven years the excess of the minimum tax over regular Part I tax for a particular year. The amount of the carryforward deductible in a subsequent year is restricted to the excess of regular Part I tax over the minimum tax in that subsequent year. As a result, in a carryforward year in which Part I tax exceeds the minimum tax, all or some part of the minimum tax paid in the previous year is recoverable as, in essence, a tax credit against Part I tax payable.

ITA: 120.2 Minimum tax carry-over

¶10,650 Impact of the Minimum Tax

The minimum tax directly affects only a small minority of Canadian taxpayers. Most top bracket taxpayers who do not invest in tax shelters are also unlikely to be affected by the minimum tax. However, it is necessary for taxpayers who could potentially be affected to do minimum tax calculations as a part of their tax planning each year. Thus, the tax adds a significant additional degree of complexity to the tax system.

Example Problem 10-15

Determine the federal tax payable in 2018 by Scoop, an unmarried taxpayer, with the following sources of income and deductions and a $400 federal political donation tax credit.

Employment income for tax purposes	$ 90,000
Interest income	15,512
Cash dividend from Canadian-resident public corporation	12,800
Gross-up on dividend @ 38%	4,864
Taxable capital gain (½ × $112,500)	56,250
RRSP contribution	(7,500)
Support of former spouse	(20,000)
Tax shelter loss due to film CCA	(25,000)
Net income for tax purposes	$126,926
QSBC share capital gains deduction	(50,000)
Taxable income.	$ 76,926

Maximum Employment Insurance of $858 and CPP of $2,594 were withheld from salary.

SOLUTION

Regular Part I tax			
on first	$46,605		$ 6,991
on balance of	30,321	@ 20.5%	6,216
	$76,926		$ 13,207

Less tax credits:			
Basic personal (15% of $11,809)		$1,771	
Employment Insurance (15% of $858)		129	
CPP (15% of $2,594)		389	
Employment (15% of $1,195)		179	
Dividend tax credit (6/11 of $4,864)		2,653	$ (5,121)
Basic federal tax under regular rules			$ 8,086(A)
Less: political donation tax credit (75% of $400).			(300)
Federal tax under regular rules			$ 7,786(B)
Adjusted taxable income:			
Taxable income			$ 76,926
Add back:	30% of capital gain.		33,750
	CCA loss		25,000
Less: dividend gross-up			(4,864)
Adjusted taxable income			$130,812
Less: basic exemption			(40,000)
Net			$90,812
Minimum tax before minimum tax credit (15% of 90,812)			$ 13,622
Less basic minimum tax credit:			
	Basic personal	$1,771	
	Employment Insurance premium	129	
	CPP	389	
	Employment	179	(2,368)
Minimum amount $			11,254(C)
Federal tax — greater of (B) and (C).			$ 11,254

Therefore, minimum tax is incurred in this situation.

¶10,690 Pause and Reflect — Summary of Learning Goals

After working through this section, ¶10,600, you should be able to:

- Understand the purpose of the minimum tax
- Identify situations when minimum tax may apply
- Understand the differences between the calculation of minimum tax and income tax
- Apply the rules to calculate minimum tax

¶10,690.99 Practise What You've Learned

Refer to the following sections of the Study Guide to practise what you've learned:

¶10,800 — Review Questions

- Question 17 — Minimum tax

¶10,825 — Multiple Choice Questions

- Question 5 — Minimum tax

¶10,850 — Exercises

- Exercise 10 — Minimum tax
- Exercise 12 — Minimum tax

CHAPTER 11

Computation of Taxable Income and Tax After General Reductions for Corporations

ADVANCED CONTENT IN THIS CHAPTER

Learning Goals

Know

By the end of this chapter you will know:

- The key components in the calculation of taxable income and tax payable for a corporation.

Understand and Explain

By the end of this chapter you will understand and be able to explain:

- Why the various items in Division C are deductible.
- How loss carryovers are restricted.
- How an acquisition of control impacts a corporation.
- Why the various taxes and tax reductions are part of the tax system.

Apply

By the end of this chapter you will be able to apply your knowledge and understanding to:

- Calculate taxable income including the carryover of losses.
- Calculate basic tax payable for a corporation.
- Calculate the tax consequences of an acquisition of control.

Review Questions
¶11,800 in the Study Guide

Multiple Choice Questions
¶11,825 in the Study Guide

Exercises
¶11,850 in the Study Guide

Assignment Problems
¶11,875 in the Study Guide

Overview

This chapter addresses two key elements in the taxation of corporations:

(1) Deductions from income in arriving at taxable income, such as charitable donations, loss carryovers and intercompany dividends, and

(2) The computation of tax payable.

The following chart will help to position in the Act some of the major provisions dealt with in this Chapter.

DIVISION C: COMPUTATION OF TAXABLE INCOME
DIVISION E: COMPUTATION OF TAX

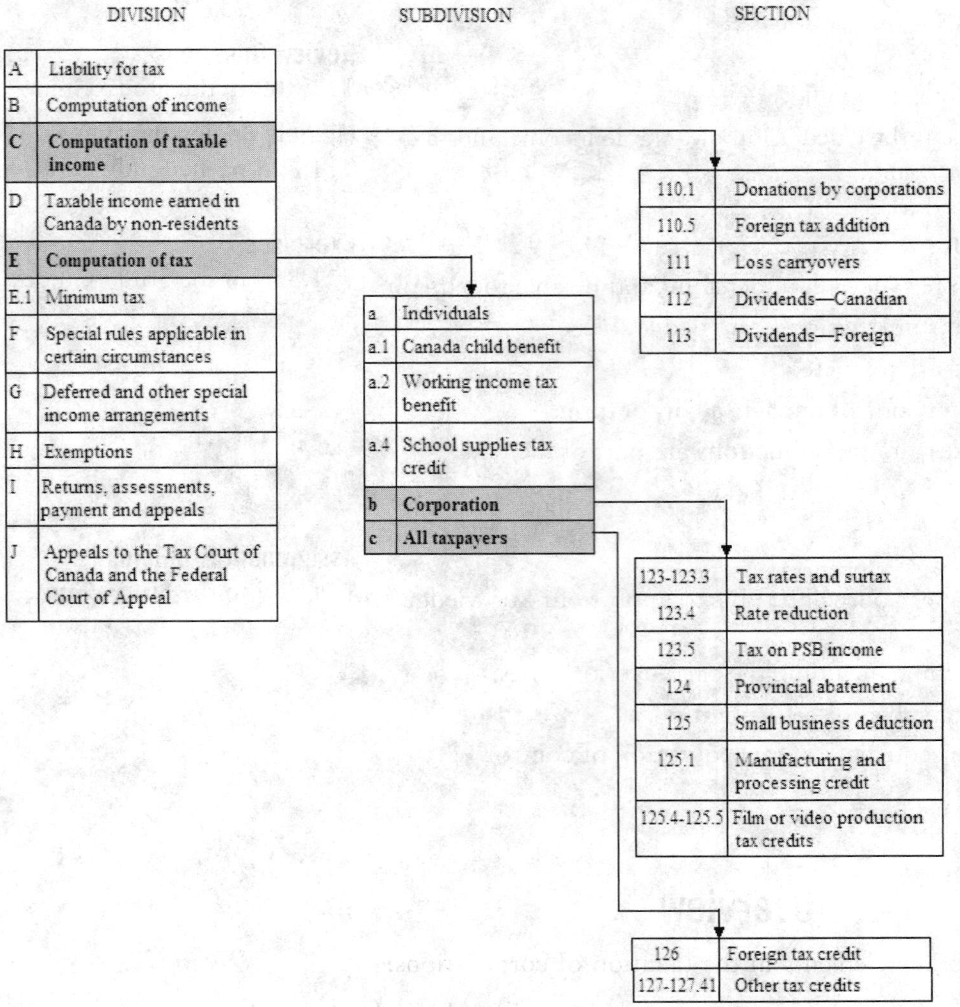
DIVISION
SUBDIVISION
SECTION
A Liability for tax
B Computation of income
C Computation of taxable income
D Taxable income earned in Canada by non-residents
E Computation of tax
E.1 Minimum tax
F Special rules applicable in certain circumstances
G Deferred and other special income arrangements
H Exemptions
I Returns, assessments, payment and appeals
J Appeals to the Tax Court of Canada and the Federal Court of Appeal
a Individuals
a.1 Canada child benefit
a.2 Working income tax benefit
a.4 School supplies tax credit
b Corporation
c All taxpayers
110.1 Donations by corporations
110.5 Foreign tax addition
111 Loss carryovers
112 Dividends—Canadian
113 Dividends—Foreign
123-123.3 Tax rates and surtax
123.4 Rate reduction
123.5 Tax on PSB income
124 Provincial abatement
125 Small business deduction
125.1 Manufacturing and processing credit
125.4-125.5 Film or video production tax credits
126 Foreign tax credit
127-127.41 Other tax credits

¶11,000 Computation of Taxable Income for a Corporation

¶11,010 Overview

The formula to calculate income for tax purposes included in section 3 of the Act applies to corporations as well as individuals. Generally, financial statements are prepared in accordance with GAAP. Canada has required the adoption of International Financial Reporting Standards (IFRS) by public enterprises since 2011. As a result, the term "generally accepted accounting principles" (GAAP) for public enterprises will refer to IFRS. A private corporation may choose to use IFRS, but it is not required to do so. The alternative for a private corporation is to use Accounting Standards for Private Enterprise (ASPE).

From those financial statements, adjustments are required to reconcile accounting income to income for tax purposes. There can be many or few additions and deductions to determine the income for tax purposes. For example, accounting amortization is not allowed as a deduction for tax purposes so it is added back to accounting income and then the allowable CCA is deducted to compute income for tax purposes. In order to correctly calculate net income for tax purposes, we must understand how an item was recorded for accounting purposes. For example, a warranty provision is deductible for accounting purposes, but for tax purposes, it is not an allowed deduction. Given that we start with accounting income to calculate the net income for tax purposes, we know that we have a deduction for warranty expense in the accounting net income. We know that if it was expensed for accounting, we would need to add it back (to remove the expense) for tax purposes.

Computing income for tax purposes for an incorporated business follows the same rules as computing income for a proprietorship business. Incorporating a business does not mean that more expenses may be deducted. Sections 9 to 20 of Subdivision b apply to income or loss from a business or property whether incorporated or not. The taxpayer who earns the income is irrelevant. A corporation, a trust, and an individual are all subject to the same basic rules. Chapter 4 discusses the calculation of business income in detail. Chapter 5 discusses the rules for deducting capital cost allowance.

The rules for computing taxable capital gains and allowable capital losses also apply to corporations. The only difference in the taxation of capital gains is that the capital gains deduction (section 110.6) applies to individuals only.

Taxable income results from the deduction from income for tax purposes of certain amounts listed in Division C of Part I. The following is the calculation of taxable income showing the different components of income for tax purposes and the deduction of Division C deductions.

ITA: 110.1 Deduction for gifts, 111 Losses deductible, 112 Deduction of taxable dividends received by corporation resident in Canada

Sources of Income:	**Individuals**	**Corporations**
Employment	$xxx	$ — [1]
Business & property	xxx	xxx
Capital gains & losses	xxx	xxx
Other income	xxx	— [1]
Other deductions	(xxx)	— [1]
Division B Income — income for tax purposes	$xxx	$xxx
Division C Deductions	(xxx)	(xxx)
Taxable Income	$xxx	$xxx

[1] Employment income earned by a corporation would be classified as "personal services business" income (¶12,155). Very few items of "other income" or "other deductions" pertain to most corporations.

Exhibit 11-1 lists the common Division C deductions and indicates which of these are available to corporations.

Exhibit 11-1 Selected Division C Deductions

Provisions	Deduction	Individuals	Corporations
Par. 110(1)(*d*), (*d*.1)	Employee stock options	X	
Par. 110.1(1)	Charitable gifts[1]		X
Sec. 110.6	Capital gains deduction	X	
Par. 111(1)(*a*)	Carryover of non-capital losses	X	X
Par. 111(1)(*b*)	Carryover of net capital losses	X	X
Par. 111(1)(*c*)	Carryover of restricted farm losses	X	X
Par. 111(1)(*d*)	Carryover of farm losses	X	X
Par. 111(1)(*e*)	Carryover of limited partnership losses	X	X
Sec. 112	Dividends from Canadian corporations		X
Sec. 113	Dividends from foreign affiliates.		X

[1] Non-refundable tax credits available in subsection 118.1(3) for an individual.

¶11,020 Deduction of Taxable Dividends

Certain dividends received by a corporation are deductible in the calculation of its taxable income. This deduction offsets the inclusion of the dividend in income so that qualifying dividends have no effect on the taxable income of the corporation and no effect on Part I tax. The dividends that qualify for the deduction are from:

ITA: 112(1) Deduction of taxable dividends received by corporation resident in Canada

(1) taxable Canadian corporations; ITA: 112(1)(a)

(2) taxable subsidiary corporations resident in Canada; and ITA: 112(1)(b)

(3) foreign affiliates which have been appropriately taxed in a foreign jurisdiction which has a treaty with Canada (refer to Chapter 19). ITA: 113 Deduction in respect of dividend received from foreign affiliate

¶11,025 Purpose

The purpose of the deduction is to prevent the double taxation of corporate income. When dividends are paid, the source of the dividends is usually after-tax retained earnings of the payer corporation. If a recipient corporation were to pay tax on the dividends it receives, the income that gave rise to the dividends would effectively be taxed twice. This provision prevents that second imposition of tax at the level of the recipient corporation. In fact,

ITA: 112(1) Deduction of taxable dividends received

by corporation resident in Canada

retained earnings can, in many cases, be flowed through any number of shareholder corporations in the form of taxable dividends without attracting tax under Part I. When the retained earnings are ultimately paid as dividends to an individual shareholder, the dividend gross-up and tax-credit mechanism will operate to reduce, at the individual taxpayer level, the potential double taxation of income generated by a corporation.

¶11,025.10 Concept of Integration of Individual and Corporate Tax on Income

The dividend deduction for corporate shareholders is the second building block of the theory of integration. The first building block, the dividend gross-up and tax credit for individual shareholders, was previously discussed in Chapters 6 and 10. The function of the dividend deduction for a corporation is to remove some of the potential multiple taxation of dividend income as the income moves through a series or chain of corporations.

Simply stated, the integration concept, discussed in more detail in Chapter 12, requires that a tax system should be designed so that a taxpayer is indifferent (i.e., pays the same amount of tax), no matter what type of entity or person earns the income. In the context of corporations and their shareholders under a perfectly integrated tax system, the total tax burden should be identical whether the individual receives the income directly or indirectly, as a shareholder, from dividends through the corporate structure.

The Canadian income tax system is not perfectly integrated. As shown in Exhibit 12-1 near perfect integration occurs numerically where the combined corporate rate of tax (federal and provincial) is equal to:

- about 13.8% for dividends paid by Canadian-controlled private corporations on their business and investment income eligible for a low rate of tax, and
- about 27.5% for Canadian-resident corporations on their income subject to the higher general rate of tax.

However, even at these rates there are flaws in the system. For example, the dividend tax credit should represent the underlying tax paid by the corporation. However, under our present income tax system, even when the corporation has not paid any tax due to losses, for example, shareholders still receive a dividend tax credit.

¶11,025.20 Application of the Concept of Integration

To illustrate the corporate dividend deduction aspect of integration, assume that there is a chain of three taxable Canadian corporations:

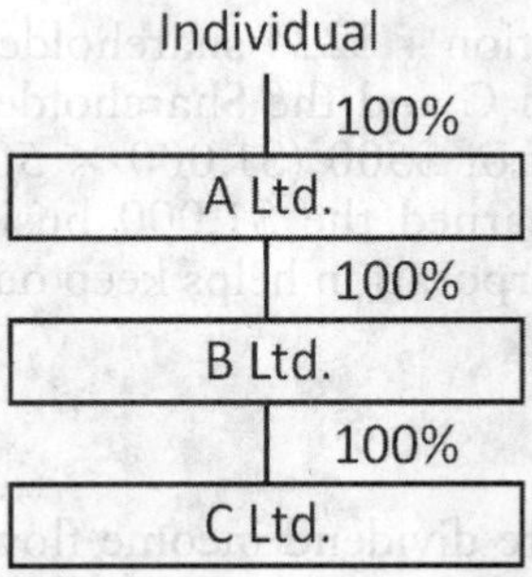

A Ltd., a Canadian-resident public corporation, owns 100% of B Ltd., which in turn owns 100% of C Ltd. Also, assume that each of the corporations is taxed at a combined rate of 27.5%, and the individual shareholders of A Ltd. are all taxed at a combined federal and provincial rate of 50%; all of the after-tax income is passed up to the next level in the form of eligible dividends, i.e., eligible for the 38% gross-up and tax credit in the hands of an individual shareholder. In the absence of a corporate deduction for dividends received from another corporation the following would result:

Person	Income	Tax	Dividend
C Ltd	$1,000	$275	$725
B Ltd	725	199	526
A Ltd	526	145	381
Shareholders of A Ltd.	526[1]	118[2]	284[3]
		$737	

[1] $381 × 1.38 (i.e., the grossed-up dividend)

[2] ($526 × 0.50) – ($526 – $381) = $118 where $526 – $381 reflects the combined federal and provincial dividend tax credit being equal to the gross-up.

[3] Cash received (i.e., $381 – $118).

The result of this example is that on the $1,000 of income initially earned by C Ltd., the ultimate tax burden is $737. The dividend deduction, as discussed above, eliminates the corporate tax in both B Ltd. and C Ltd. The tax burden remaining would be composed of the $275 on the income earned initially by C Ltd. and the tax of $224 on the $1,001 grossed-up dividend received by the individual shareholders calculated as follows:

Dividend received by shareholders of A Ltd	$ 725
Gross-up (0.38 × $725)	276
Grossed-up dividend	$ 1,001
Tax @ 50%	$ 500
Dividend tax credit (6/11 federal + 5/11 provincial) of $276	(276)
Net tax on shareholders of A Ltd	$ 224

The total income tax is now $499 (i.e., $275 corporation + $224 shareholder) compared to $737. Note that the total tax paid by Corporation C and the Shareholders of A Ltd. corporation is $499. This is the equivalent of the tax of $500 ($1,000 × 50%) that the shareholders of A Ltd. would have paid had they earned the $1,000 business income directly. The deduction of dividends received by the corporation helps keep our tax system integrated.

¶11,025.30 Conclusion

From the above example, one can conclude that where dividend income flows through a series of corporations there will be only two incidents of income tax. Initially, the corporation that earns the business or property income will pay income tax and eventually the individual shareholder or trust who receives the income in the form of a dividend will also pay some income tax. In the next chapter, the topic of integration will be expanded on with different corporate rates and other factors.

¶11,050 Charitable Donations

While individuals are provided with a non-refundable tax credit for various donations, as discussed in Chapter 10, corporations are permitted a deduction in Division C. The types of donation that provide a corporation with this deduction are the same as the types of donation that provide an individual with a tax credit. Also, a corporation's deduction for gifts is, generally, limited to 75% of the corporation's income for tax purposes under Division B.

ITA: 110.1(1) Deduction for gifts

Any unused donations for a given year can be carried forward five years to be deducted in a future year. The total claim for donations carried forward to a year and current donations made in that year cannot exceed the 75% of Division B income limit. The maximum donation need not be deducted in a given year, such that undeducted amounts are available within the carryforward period. To be deducted, a donation must be proven, if necessary, by a receipt that contains prescribed information.

ITA: 110.1(2) Proof of gift

¶11,060 Loss Carryovers

The rules governing the deductibility of net capital losses and non-capital losses are the same for corporations and individuals. A net capital loss carryover from the current year may be carried back three years and forward indefinitely and deducted against net taxable capital gains in those years. The carryforward of non-capital losses, restricted farm losses, and farm losses is back three years and forward 20 years.

ITA: 111 Losses deductible

The following table shows the carryover period for net and non-capital losses.

	Back	Forward
Net capital loss	3	Indefinitely
Non-capital loss	3	20

¶11,065 Non-Capital Loss

A non-capital loss for a particular year, as it affects a corporation (for the purposes of this text), is generally defined to include:

ITA: 12(1)(j) Dividends from resident corporations

Total losses:

losses from business	$ XXX
losses from property	XXX
allowable business investment losses	XXX
net capital losses deducted in the year (Division C)	XXX

dividends deducted (Division C)			XXX	
			$ XXX	(E)
Less total income:				
income from business		$ XXX		
income from property (including dividends deductible (Division C)		XXX		
taxable capital gains	$ XXX			
less: allowable capital losses	(XXX)[1]	XXX[1]		
			$(XXX)[1]	(F)
Non-capital loss			$ XXX[1]	

[1] Cannot be negative.

This definition is designed to offset the current year's losses from various sources (item (E)) against the current year's income from other sources (item (F)). Then the balance or the unabsorbed excess loss can be carried over and deducted in another year. Non-capital losses and farming and fishing losses may be carried back three taxation years and forward 20 taxation years. To carry losses back to a taxation year for which a return has been filed, the corporation need only file one form (Schedule 4) and not a full, amended tax return.

ITA: 111(1)(d) Farm losses, 111(8) Definitions, 111(1)(a) Non-capital losses, 112 Deduction of taxable dividends received by corporation resident in Canada

Although a 20-year carryforward period is quite long, it is possible for carried-over losses to expire. Recognize that 20 years is a very long time for a business to sustain losses with no income earned to offset those losses. Most businesses would not last that long with those losses. However, planning should be undertaken to ensure that the losses are utilized within the carryover period. Income can be increased to absorb non-capital losses by omitting optional or permissive deductions such as capital cost allowances, scientific research and experimental development expenditures or reserves. The deduction of these amounts can be deferred to future years when there is offsetting income.

Information Circulars: IC 84-1 Revision of capital cost allowance claims and other permissive deductions

The Canada Revenue Agency (CRA) usually permits the revision of a permissive deduction for a prior year. An Information Circular indicates that a letter to the director of the taxpayer's district taxation office that outlines the requested revisions will be sufficient if specified conditions are met. In addition, the corporation should consider the sale of unnecessary or redundant assets to generate income which could be used to absorb losses. The CRA may also allow the substitution of one type of loss for another, as long as the year in which the substitution is made is still open to assessment (as discussed in Chapter 14). For example, a non-capital loss may have been carried back to a year in which there was a net taxable capital gain. Subsequently, an allowable capital loss may arise. The resultant net capital loss may be carried back and substituted for the non-capital loss, leaving the freed non-capital loss available for carryforward.

Information Circulars: IC 84-1 Revision of capital cost allowance claims and other permissive deductions

Example Problem 11-1

The operations of Balloons Ltd. generated the following data for its current December 31 taxation year:

Business losses	$(60,000)
Dividends received and deducted (Division C)	10,000
Bond interest	5,000
Allowable business investment loss	(3,000)
Taxable capital gains	15,000
Allowable capital losses	(7,000)
	$(40,000)

In the prior taxation year (last year), its first profitable year in several, Balloons Ltd. had taxable income of $40,000.

REQUIRED

Compute the non-capital loss for Balloons Ltd. in the current year and determine the amount of that loss that can be carried back to the prior year.

SOLUTION

Before calculating the non-capital loss for the current year, a review of the construction of section 3 income would be useful in understanding the basic concept. The following calculation reorganizes the above information using the ordering and application rules in section 3.

Par. 3(*a*)	Income — business		Nil	
	— property:	dividends	$10,000	
		interest	5,000	$15,000
Par. 3(*b*)	Net taxable capital gains:			
		Taxable capital gains	$15,000	
		Allowable capital losses	(7,000)	8,000
Par. 3(*c*)	(No Subdivision e deductions taken).			$23,000
Par. 3(*d*)	Business loss		$60,000	
	Allowable business investment loss		3,000	(63,000)
Net income from Division B				Nil

Calculation of Non-capital Loss:

Losses arising in the current year

Business loss			$ 60,000
Allowable business investment loss			3,000
Dividends			10,000
			$ 73,000
Less: Par. 3(*c*) income (as shown above):			
Income from property			
Bond interest	$ 5,000		
Dividends (see commentary below)	10,000	$15,000	
Net taxable capital gains			
Taxable capital gains.	$15,000		
Allowable capital loss	(7,000)	8,000	(23,000)
Non-capital loss for the current year			$ 50,000

ITA: 112(1)(j), 112 Deduction of taxable dividends received by corporation resident in Canada

ITA: 3(b)

Carryback of non-capital loss to the prior year:

Lesser of:

(a) Non-capital loss (as calculated above)	$ 50,000
(b) Taxable income for the prior year	$ 40,000

Thus, $40,000 of the current year non-capital loss could be carried back to the prior year leaving $10,000 to carry forward for 20 years.

Dividend income deductible in the calculation of a corporation's taxable income (i.e., $10,000), when added to the business loss and the allowable business investment loss, has the effect of offsetting the dividend income included in the paragraph 3(*c*) income under paragraph 3(*a*). As a result, this dividend income has no effect on the amount of losses available for carryover. As previously discussed, dividends are deductible to offset the dividend income inclusion and, therefore, have no effect on the taxable income of a corporation. Therefore, a similar adjustment is necessary to the non-capital loss calculation to remove the effect of the inclusion of these dividends in property income, as shown above.

ITA: 3(a)

¶11,070 Treatment of Allowable Business Investment Loss

A "business investment loss" is a capital loss that arises from the disposition of shares or debt of a "small business corporation". The concept of a small business corporation (SBC) is discussed in some detail in Chapter 13 (¶13,345). A business investment loss (BIL) must arise from either an arm's length disposition of the shares and/or debt, establishing a debt to be bad, or a bankruptcy action.

ITA: 50(1) Debts established to be bad debts and shares of bankrupt corporation, 39(1)(c), 248(1) small business corporation

An "allowable business investment loss" (ABIL) is defined as ½ of a business investment loss. Unlike an allowable capital loss, an allowable business investment loss may, in the year in which it is realized, be deducted against any source of income. Hence, the deductibility of an allowable business investment loss is less restricted than an allowable capital loss.

ITA: 3(d), 38(c)

To the extent that it cannot be absorbed against these other sources of income in the year in which it is incurred, it becomes part of the aggregate of non-capital losses to be carried over in the manner discussed above. However, if the ABIL cannot be deducted as a non-capital loss in the 3-year carryback period or within a 10-year carryforward period, then it can be added to net capital losses which can be carried forward indefinitely as discussed next. See Figure 7-2 in ¶7,510.50 for a flow-chart summary of these rules.

Example Problem 11-2

The operations of Blyth Limited generated the following data for the year ended December 31 in the current year:

Business investment loss on sale of shares	$116,000
Capital gains	4,000
Other capital losses	10,000
Other Division B income	30,000

REQUIRED

Compute the taxable income of the corporation for the current year and indicate the loss carryovers available for other years.

SOLUTION

Par. 3(*a*)	Other Division B income		$30,000
Par. 3(*b*)	Taxable capital gains (½ × $4,000)	$ 2,000	
	Allowable capital losses (½ × $10,000)	(5,000)	Nil
Par. 3(*c*)	Income		$30,000

Par. 3(*d*)	Allowable business investment loss deductible (max: ½ × $116,000 = $58,000)	(30,000)
	Income and taxable income	Nil
	Net capital loss available for carryover	$ 3,000[1]
	Non-capital loss available for carryover	$28,000[2]

[1] (½ × $10,000 capital loss incurred in the year) *less* ($2,000 claimed in the year as an allowable capital loss) = $3,000.

[2] (½ × $116,000 business investment loss incurred in the year) *less* ($30,000 claimed in the year as an ABIL) = $28,000. Available to carryforward 10 years as a non-capital loss.

¶11,075 Net Capital Losses

¶11,075.10 Definition

For corporations, a "net capital loss" (net CL) is, essentially, the excess of allowable capital losses, excluding losses on listed personal property and allowable business investment losses, over taxable capital gains, including taxable net gains from listed personal property. ITA: 111(8) Definitions

This is given by the following computational format:

Allowable capital losses excluding allowable business investment losses	(A)	$XXX
Less: taxable capital gains	(B)	(XXX)
	(A – B)	$XXX
Add: allowable business investment loss unutilized in the tenth year of its carryforward as a non-capital loss (see comment in previous section)		XXX
Net capital loss		$XXX

Remember, the term net capital loss captures the excess of allowable capital losses over taxable capital gains. Therefore, the term net capital loss is always at 50%.

¶11,075.20 Adjustment for Years With Different Inclusion Rates

Net capital losses can be carried back three taxation years and forward indefinitely. However, they can only be deducted to the extent of the excess, if any, of taxable capital gains over allowable capital losses in the carryover years. Rules which determine the amount that a person may deduct in respect of net capital losses are the result of the differing inclusion rates for capital gains and capital losses discussed in Chapter 10. ITA: 111(1.1) Net capital losses

The historical inclusion rates are as follows:

1990 to February 27, 2000	3/4
February 28 to October 17, 2000	2/3
After October 17, 2000	1/2

The purpose of the rules is to ensure that the amount of net capital losses, carried forward or carried back from a taxation year with a particular inclusion rate, is converted to the inclusion rate of the taxation year in which the net capital losses are deducted.

¶11,080 Restrictions and Ordering of Deductions

A taxpayer can choose how much, if any, of its previously unclaimed carried-over losses to deduct in a particular year and in which order to deduct such losses and other Division C deductions. However, the taxpayer must deduct a loss of a particular type (that is, non-capital loss, net capital loss, restricted farm loss or farm loss) in the chronological order in which the loss was incurred. Logic would suggest that those deductions in Division C, which are more restricted in their deductibility, be claimed as soon as possible and before those deductions which are less restricted.

ITA: 111(3) Limitation on deductibility

There are two basic types of restriction on losses available for carryover.

(1) The first is a restriction on the type of income against which the loss carryover can be deducted.

(2) The other is a restriction on the number of years a loss can be carried over.

For example, a net capital loss can only be applied against net taxable capital gains, but is unrestricted as to carryforward time. A non-capital loss can be applied against any source of income, but is time-restricted. Between net capital losses and non-capital losses, the decision depends on whether taxable capital gains are anticipated in future years. If there are current taxable capital gains and an examination of the corporation's balance sheet indicates no accrued or prospective capital gains, then net capital losses should probably be deducted before non-capital losses.

Exhibit 11-2 Summary for Carryover Rules for Division C Deductions

		Carryover	
Type of deduction	**Type of income applied against**	**Back**	**Forward**
Dividends	Any type	Note [(1)]	Note [(1)]
Donations	Any type	0	5

		Carryover	
Type of deduction	Type of income applied against	Back	Forward
Net capital losses	Net taxable capital gains	3	Indefinitely
Non-capital losses	Any type	3	20

(1) No carryover rule applies specifically to dividends, but they have an impact on the non-capital loss carryover balance.

Consider:

(1) Type of income the deduction can be applied against.

(2) Number of years available in the carryover period.

(3) The likelihood that the type of income needed will arise in the carry-over period.

Generally apply most restrictive first.

¶11,085 Choice To Deduct Net Capital Losses To Preserve Non-Capital Losses

Taxpayers, at their option, can deduct net capital losses under Division C to preserve non-capital losses. The purpose of this choice is to correct a long-standing anomaly in the legislation which inadvertently penalized taxpayers in certain specific situations, as shown in the example below. Whether a taxpayer decides to utilize this option depends upon whether the corporation is expected to generate, in the near future, adequate business income or taxable capital gains. ITA: 111(8) Definitions

The non-capital loss can be increased by the amount of any net capital loss actually deducted under Division C for that year. The only restriction on the deduction of a net capital loss is that there is a net taxable capital gain in the year that is at least equal to the net capital loss being deducted. For example, assume that a corporation (or an individual) has a business loss of $100,000, a net taxable capital gain of $40,000 and a net capital loss of $60,000 carry forward. The tax consequences are as follows:

Par. 3(*a*): Income from business	Nil
Par. 3(*b*): Net taxable capital gain	$ 40,000
Par. 3(*c*):	$ 40,000
Par. 3(*d*): Business loss	(100,000)
Par. 3(*f*): Division B income	Nil

If the definition of non-capital loss did not contain the addition for net capital losses deducted under Division C, a corporation could deduct $40,000 of the net capital loss of $60,000 (equal to the net taxable capital gain) but would not do so because such a deduction would have no impact upon the taxable income which would still be zero. In addition, if the $40,000 was deducted, the taxpayer would no longer have a potential use of the $40,000 net capital loss in the future when the taxpayer is in a taxable position.

ITA: 3(b), 111(8) Definitions

The non-capital loss without the addition would be:

Par. 3(*d*): Business loss	$ 100,000
Par. 3(*c*): — see above calculation	(40,000)
Non-capital loss	$ 60,000

The result is that the net taxable capital gain has been used to offset the business loss resulting in a lower non-capital loss (i.e., $60,000 versus $100,000). The taxpayer may or may not be happy with this result depending upon the taxpayer's expected future income sources. Since net capital losses can only be applied to net taxable capital gains (i.e., $40,000) a potential net capital loss deduction has been blocked by the current business loss of $100,000.

The addition of deducted net capital losses to the non-capital loss balance provides a positive tax consequence to claiming a net capital loss deduction, even though the deduction has no impact upon the taxable income as shown below.

Division B income — see previous sec. 3 computation	Nil
Division C — net capital loss deduction limited to par. 3(*b*) amount	$(40,000)
Taxable income	Nil

ITA: 111(1)(b) Net capital losses

However, as a result of the deduction of net capital losses, the non-capital loss is increased by a net capital loss deducted:

Par. 3(*d*): Business loss	$100,000
Add: Net capital loss deducted in the year	40,000
	$140,000
Less: Par. 3(*c*) balance — see above	40,000
	$100,000

The result is that $40,000 of the net capital loss carryover has been deducted under Division C to offset the $40,000 of net taxable capital gain under paragraph 3(*b*). This preserves the full $100,000 of business loss to be carried over as a non-capital loss, which can be deducted from any source of income in a carryover year.

Example Problem 11-3

The following data summarize the operations of Parliamentary Fertilizers Limited, a Canadian-controlled private corporation, for the years 2015 to 2018 ended December 31.

	2015	2016	2017	2018
Income (loss): fertilizer business	$ 62,500	$(187,500)	$75,000	$100,000
Dividend income — taxable Cdn. corporation	37,500	62,500	12,500	—
Capital gains (losses)	25,000	(50,000)	7,500	12,000
Charitable donations made	(18,750)	(10,000)	(12,500)	(6,000)
Income (loss): other business	7,500	(20,000)	2,500	5,000
Income (loss) per financial accounting statements	$113,750	$(205,000)	$85,000	$111,000

The corporation has a net capital loss balance of $12,500 which arose in 2010.

REQUIRED

Calculate the taxable income of the company for each of the years indicated, on the assumption that future other business income and taxable capital gains are uncertain, and tabulate the losses available for carryover at the end of 2018. (For the purposes of this type of problem, dealing with each item, line by line, across the years, will help keep track of carryovers more easily than dealing with income one year at a time.)

SOLUTION

		2015	2016	2017	2018
Par. 3(*a*)	Income from business				
	— fertilizer	$ 62,500	—[(1)]	$75,000	$100,000
	— other	7,500	—[(1)]	2,500	5,000

		2015	2016	2017	2018
	Income from property	37,500	$ 62,500	12,500	—
		$107,500	$ 62,500	$90,000	$105,000
Par. 3(*b*)	Taxable capital gain	12,500	—	3,750	6,000
	Allowable capital loss	—	— [(2)]	—	—
Par. 3(*c*)	Total	$120,000	$ 62,500	$93,750	$111,000
Par. 3(*d*)	Loss from business				
	— fertilizer	—	(187,500)[(3)]	—	—
	— other	—	(20,000)	—	—
	Income for the year[(4)]	$120,000	Nil[(3)]	$93,750	$111,000
Sec. 112	Dividends from taxable Canadian corporations	(37,500)[(5)]	— [(6)]	(12,500)[(5)]	—
		$ 82,500	Nil	$81,250	$111,000
Sec. 110.1	Donations made				
	— carryover	—	—	(10,000)	—
	— current	(18,750)	—	(12,500)[(7)]	(6,000)
		$ 63,750	Nil	$58,750	$105,000
Par. 111(1)(*b*)	Net capital losses	(12,500)	—	(3,750)[(8)]	(6,000)[(8)]
		$ 51,250	Nil	$55,000	$ 99,000
Par. 111(1)(*a*)	Non-capital losses	(51,250)[(9)]	—	(55,000)[(9)]	(99,000)[(9)]
	Taxable income	Nil	Nil	Nil	Nil

NOTES TO SOLUTION

(1) Items aggregated from the various non-capital sources under paragraph 3(*a*) cannot be negative. Losses from these sources are deducted under paragraph 3(*d*).

(2) Allowable capital losses are only deductible to the extent of taxable capital gains under paragraph 3(*b*). The remainder is available for carryover to another year.

(3) Losses from the various non-capital sources and from allowable business investment losses are only deductible under paragraph 3(*d*). However, the net income amounts after the deductions in paragraph 3(*d*) cannot be negative. Note that the excess of the deductions in paragraph 3(*d*) over the aggregate income in paragraph 3(*c*) is only one component of the addition to the non-capital loss carryover balance computed below.

(4) Income for the year cannot be negative. There is no statutory order in which Division C deductions must be taken. However, the time and source restrictions of loss carryovers, as previously discussed, should be taken into account. Dividends from taxable Canadian corporations are the only Division C deduction for corporations that do not have a carryover clause. There is no need for a carryover provision for these dividends, because the amount deductible is added to the non-capital loss carryover pool. As a result, this addition to the pool offsets the inclusion of the dividend in the non-capital loss definition, leaving more non-capital loss from other sources, like business, to be carried over. In essence, this makes the priority for the deduction of these dividends in Division C the same as non-capital losses. Nevertheless, in this book, these dividends will generally be deducted first, following general practice.

(5) Dividends from taxable Canadian corporations are deducted first, following general practice for Division C, although an equal amount of non-capital losses carried over could be deducted with the same effect on both taxable income and the non-capital loss pool carried over. As long as the dividends are deductible in Division C, they are added to the non-capital loss pool. They need not be actually deducted in the same way that net capital losses must actually be deducted to be added to the non-capital loss pool.

(6) A deduction in the computation of taxable income should not be taken if it reduces the balance to a negative number, since normally negative taxable income has no meaning. The one exception to this rule is in respect of net capital losses which can be added to the non-capital loss balance if they are actually deducted in a particular year. The only limit on the deduction of net capital losses carried over is the amount of net taxable capital gains included under paragraph 3(*b*) for the year.

(7) The deduction of charitable donations is limited to 75% of Division B income for the year. Donations not deducted in the year they are made, can be carried forward to the next five taxation years. However, the Division B income limitation applies to the sum of donations carried forward and current donations. Since the unused donations of a particular taxation year have a time

restriction of 5 years, it would be advisable to claim them prior to claiming current year donations.

(8) Deductions for net capital loss carryovers are restricted to the extent of the net taxable capital gains included in paragraph 3(*b*) for the carryover year.

Net capital loss for 2016 (½ × $50,000)	$25,000
Loss deductible to the extent of net capital gains under par. 3(*b*):	
2017 — limited to TCG	(3,750)
	$21,250
2018 — limited to TCG	(6,000)
Remaining carryforward	$15,250

(9) "Non-capital loss" is computed for carryforward in: ITA: 111(8) Definitions

	2015	2016	2017	2018
Sum of:				
(a) loss from business or property	Nil	$207,500	Nil	Nil
(b) ABIL	Nil	Nil	Nil	Nil
(c) dividends deductible under sec. 112	$ 37,500	62,500	$ 12,500	Nil
(d) net capital loss deducted	12,500	Nil	3,750	$ 6,000
	$ 50,000	$270,000	$ 16,250	$ 6,000
Less:				
(e) par. 3(*c*) total	(120,000)	(62,500)	(93,750)	(111,000)
Non-capital loss for the year	Nil	$207,500	Nil	Nil
Non-capital loss carryforward balance:				
Non-capital loss carryforward to the year	Nil	Nil	$156,250	$101,250
Added in the year	Nil	$207,500	Nil	Nil

	2015	2016	2017	2018
Applied	Nil	(51,250)[1]	(55,000)	(99,000)
Non-capital loss carryforward balance	Nil	$156,250	$101,250	$ 2,250

[1] Carried back to 2015.

¶11,085.99 Practise What You've Learned

Refer to the following sections of the Study Guide to practise what you've learned:

¶11,800 — Review Questions

- Question 1 — Donations
- Question 2 — Non-capital losses

¶11,825 — Multiple Choice Questions

- Question 5 — Calculate taxable income

¶11,850 — Exercises

- Exercise 1 — Calculate taxable income
- Exercise 2 — Maximizing charitable donations
- Exercise 3 — Calculate non-capital losses
- Exercise 4 — Calculate net capital losses
- Exercise 5 — Calculate net and non-capital losses
- Exercise 6 — Calculate taxable income

¶11,090 Acquisition of Control of a Corporation and Its Effect on Losses

¶11,095 Conceptual Overview

Corporations are often unable to generate appropriate or sufficient income to utilize losses and, hence, are unable to recover taxes previously paid or reduce taxes payable. Consequently, such loss corporations become attractive targets for acquisition by profitable corporations which, through a variety of strategies, could shelter their income from tax by utilizing the losses of the acquired corporation. Because such strategies ultimately result in reduced tax revenues, the government, understandably, does not view such transactions with favour. As a result, over the years the government has introduced increasingly restrictive legislation to curb such transactions which are sometimes referred to as "tax-loss trading".

Two of the more common loss utilization strategies are outlined as follows:

(1) After control of the loss corporation is acquired, the operations of the income-earning acquirer corporation and the loss corporation are restructured so that income is generated in the latter corporation. For example, the assets of a profitable business or division in the income-generating corporation are transferred to the loss corporation. Usually the transfer will be accomplished by means of a tax-free rollover by moving profit-generating assets to the loss corporation (discussed in Chapter 16). The income that is so generated is used to absorb the losses of the loss corporation.

ITA: 85(1) Transfer of property to corporation by shareholders

(2) The second strategy involves implementing intercompany transactions which produce expense deductions to the income-generating corporation while generating income for the loss corporation. Interest on loans, rental contracts, management contracts, and commission contracts are examples of such intercompany transactions.

When legal control of the corporation is acquired a corporation's ability to carry forward or carry back non-capital losses is severely restricted. In addition, net capital losses, losses from property and allowable business investment losses (ABILs) that are unutilized at the time of the acquisition of control may not be carried forward — they simply expire.

ITA: 111(4) Loss restriction event — capital losses, 111(5) Loss restriction event — non-capital losses and farm losses, 111(5.1) Loss restriction event — UCC computation, 111(5.2) Loss restriction event — CEC computation, 111(5.3) Loss restriction event — doubtful debts and bad debts

The loss utilization restrictions become operative when control of a corporation is acquired by another person or another group of persons. The acquisition of control is considered to occur when control over the voting rights (i.e., *de jure* or legal control that exists where more than 50% of the votes necessary to elect the Board of Directors is held) of the corporation is acquired by a person or group of persons. While it is clear that control refers to voting control, some uncertainty exists as to how the CRA will interpret the phrase "group of persons" for the purposes of these rules. The CRA has indicated that it will look for evidence of a group's intention to "act in concert" to control a corporation.

Interpretation Bulletins: IT-302R3 Losses of a Corporation — The Effect that Acquisitions of Control, Amalgamations, and Windings-Up Have on their Deductibility — After January 15, 1987

The current legislative restrictions which are aimed at curtailing the utilization of tax losses, are based on certain transactions and events which are deemed to occur when there has been an acquisition of control. These transactions and events, as well as other rules that comprise the restrictions, are discussed below. The government policy in implementing these restrictions appears to be to restrict the tax-shielding benefits of losses where control over the losses passes to controlling shareholders who did not bear the risks that generated the losses.

The following are the steps we will follow as we analyze an acquisition of control (refer to Exhibit 11-3 for more details):

(1) Establish a deemed year end on the day before.

(2) Determine any accrued losses and unrealized gains.

(3) Determine the tax position of the company with the automatic realization of the accrued losses.

(4) Consider election to create income.

(5) Recalculate Division B and taxable incomes after the election.

(6) Recalculate cost base of properties.

(7) Determine whether the business losses can be used after the acquisition of control.

(8) Determine the steps needed to use up the business losses that survived.

¶11,100 Deemed Year End

The corporation is deemed to have a taxation year end immediately before the time of the acquisition of control of the corporation (referred to hereinafter as the "deemed taxation year end").

ITA: 249(4) Loss restriction event — year end

The result is that various adjustments that are normally made at a year end, are required to be made before the acquisition of control. For example, the requirement that inventory be valued at the lower of cost or market at a taxation year end will cause any accrued losses in inventory to be realized. This adjustment will increase the corporation's pre-acquisition non-capital losses or farm losses. As will be explained later, such pre-acquisition losses are available for carryforward, but only after certain restrictive conditions are satisfied. The advent of the deemed year end causes other adjustments (discussed below) to increase the corporation's pre-acquisition of control non-capital losses.

ITA: 10 Valuation of inventory; ITR: 1801 Valuation

As a result of the deemed year end, the corporation is required to satisfy the normal compliance requirements of filing tax returns, reviewing unpaid amounts, determining the status of charitable donations and loss carryovers and their carryforward period, etc.

ITA: 78(1) Unpaid amounts, 78(4) Unpaid remuneration and other amounts, 13(4) Exchanges of property, 44(1) Exchanges of property

Unless the deemed year end coincides with the corporation's normal year end, the corporation may have two taxation years lasting less than 24 months in total. To illustrate this, assume that a corporation whose normal taxation year end is December 31, experiences an acquisition of control on April 1, 2018. The corporation will have a deemed year end of March 31, 2018. If the corporation chooses to return to its original taxation year end of December 31, the corporation will have two taxation years ending in the 12-month period ending December 31, 2018. The first taxation year will be three months long, the second nine months long. If the corporation chose a date for its subsequent taxation years to be, say, March 31, as permitted, it would then have two taxation years lasting a total of only 15 months — namely, the deemed taxation year ending on March 31, 2018 will be three months long and the taxation year ending March 31, 2019 will be 12 months long. The foregoing example can be illustrated with the following diagram:

ITA: 249(4) Loss restriction event — year end, 249(4)(d)

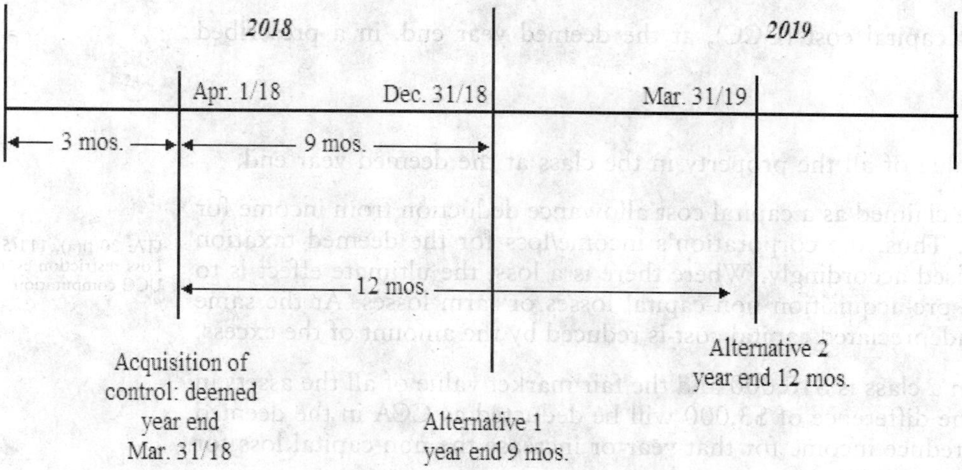

The result is that the normal 276-month (3 years back plus 20 years forward) carryover period for non-capital losses is reduced. This, in itself, represents a constraint in that the corporation has a shorter period over which to generate income to utilize the losses. A short taxation year will also cause any capital cost allowance or small business deduction (discussed in Chapter 12) to be proportionately reduced.

¶11,105 Accrued or Unrealized Losses on Inventory

A taxpayer is required to value its inventory at the end of each taxation year. The Act requires that each item of inventory be valued at the lower of cost and market (LCM), while the Regulations permit valuation at the fair market value of the entire inventory. Either way, the result is that any accrued or unrealized inventory losses are realized in the deemed taxation year, thus, decreasing the taxpayer's income or increasing its non-capital losses in the pre-acquisition period.

ITA: 10(1) Valuation of inventory; ITR: 1801 Valuation

¶11,110 Accrued or Unrealized Losses on Accounts Receivable

The restrictions and their consequences that apply to accrued inventory losses are paralleled in the provisions that relate to accrued losses on accounts receivable. The largest amount that a corporation could deduct as a reserve for doubtful accounts for each separate trade receivable, must be claimed as an actual bad debt in the deemed taxation year. That is, where there has been an acquisition of control, the normal method of computing a reserve by aging the accounts and applying a fixed percentage to each age category is not permitted. Instead, each debt must be considered individually as to its collectibility and, if collection is doubtful, the debt must be written off as a bad debt. The amount deducted is deemed to be a separate debt and any amount or amounts subsequently received in respect of the separate debt must be included in income.

ITA: 20(1)(l) Doubtful or impaired debts, 20(1)(p) Bad debts, 111(5.3) Loss restriction event — doubtful debts and bad debts, 12(l)(i); Interpretation Bulletins: IT-442R Bad Debts and Reserves for Doubtful Debts

As is the case with accrued inventory losses, accrued losses on accounts receivable become part of time-limited non-capital or farm losses, which are deductible only if certain restrictive conditions are satisfied.

¶11,115 Accrued or Unrealized Losses on Depreciable Property

Accrued or unrealized losses on depreciable property are measured as the amount by which:

(1) the undepreciated capital cost (UCC), at the deemed year end, in a prescribed class

exceeds:

(2) the fair market value of all the property in the class at the deemed year end.

The excess is deemed to be claimed as a capital cost allowance deduction from income for the deemed taxation year. Thus, the corporation's income/loss for the deemed taxation year is increased or decreased accordingly. Where there is a loss, the ultimate effect is to increase the corporation's pre-acquisition non-capital losses or farm losses. At the same time, the balance of the undepreciated capital cost is reduced by the amount of the excess.

ITA: 20(l)(a), 111(5.1) Loss restriction event — UCC computation

For example, if the UCC in a class is $10,000 and the fair market value of all the assets in the class is $7,000, then the difference of $3,000 will be deducted as CCA in the deemed year end. This will either reduce income for that year or increase the non-capital loss for the year.

If the asset is used in an active business, then this deduction reduces business income but if the asset is used to earn property income then this deduction reduces property income.

The restrictive aspects of the rule are, therefore, as follows:

- first, an accrued loss (i.e., unclaimed capital cost allowance) that would otherwise not be subject to any time limitation, as far as its deductibility is concerned, becomes part of a time-limited non-capital loss or farm loss;
- second, the corporation commences the first post-acquisition of control taxation year with a reduced undepreciated capital cost balance in the particular class.

¶11,125 Accrued or Unrealized Losses on Non-Depreciable Capital Property

Accrued or unrealized capital losses on non-depreciable capital property are deemed to have been realized at the deemed taxation year end. The accrued capital losses are measured as the excess of:

ITA: 111(4)(c), 111(4)(d)

(1) the adjusted cost base (ACB)

over

(2) the fair market value,

at the deemed year end, of each non-depreciable capital property (e.g., marketable securities, land used in the business) of the corporation. These rules result in the following:

(1) the capital losses that are so triggered, offset any capital gains produced in the deemed taxation year or increase any existing net capital losses of the corporation;

(2) the adjusted cost base of each affected capital property is reduced by the amount of the applicable excess.

Therefore, any deemed realized allowable capital losses that cannot be utilized against taxable capital gains realized in the deemed taxation year become part of the corporation's net capital losses immediately before the acquisition of control. If nothing further is done, these allowable capital losses, now embedded in the net capital loss balance, will expire.

However, there are two possible remedies to this situation:

(1) First, the net capital losses can be deducted in arriving at taxable income for the deemed taxation year to the extent of net taxable capital gains in that year. As previously discussed, these deducted net capital losses will increase the non-capital loss balance. However, a further set of restrictions (discussed later in the chapter) is imposed on the utilization of non-capital losses on an acquisition of control.

(2) The second alternative is to create elective taxable capital gains to offset the deemed allowable capital losses as described in the next section.

¶11,130 Elective Capital Gains and Recapture

¶11,130.10 Election Range

A corporation is permitted to elect to have a deemed disposition for any depreciable or non-depreciable capital property on which capital gains or recapture have accrued. The objective of the elective provision is to permit the corporation to trigger capital gains or recapture, which is income from business, to reduce the amount of net capital losses or non-capital losses that would otherwise expire on account of the acquisition of control. ITA: 111(4)(e)

Upon making the election, the corporation must also choose (i.e., designate) an amount to represent the deemed proceeds of disposition. The designated amount or deemed proceeds must be equal to the lesser of:

(1) the fair market value of the property; and

(2) the greater of:

(a) the adjusted cost base of the property, and

(b) an amount designated (or chosen) by the corporation.

The effect of the above rule is that the corporation can choose proceeds of disposition (amount designated) at any point between fair market value and the adjusted cost base of the particular capital property.

This rule also prevents the designated amount from being greater than the fair market value of the property. In addition, the designated amount (proceeds of disposition) cannot be less than the adjusted cost base (capital cost in respect of depreciable property).

Note that the election is not available where an accrued terminal loss exists since that loss is deemed to be realized automatically. However, the above formula does allow a corporation to elect proceeds of disposition which would trigger recapture on depreciable property. ITA: 111(5.1) Loss restriction event — UCC computation

¶11,130.20 Election Strategy

In determining the partial amount which should be designated where there are losses about to expire, the following formula should be used to trigger a taxable capital gain. This taxable capital gain should be sufficient to offset expiring losses. The elected proceeds will be: ITA: 111(4)(e)

the sum of:

(1) 2 (based on a 50% inclusion rate) times the sum of:

(a) any allowable capital loss arising in the deemed taxation year about to expire,

(b) the net capital losses about to expire, and

(c) the sum of the property losses and ABILs about to expire; and

(2) the adjusted cost bases of the properties chosen to be elected upon.

The taxable capital gain, using the above deemed proceeds of disposition, should result in the utilization of all of the losses about to expire upon the acquisition of control.

This procedure of creating only enough taxable capital gains to offset the property losses and capital losses about to expire also optimizes the step-up in the cost base of an asset elected upon as discussed below. In addition, this minimum elected amount preserves the business losses which can be utilized after the acquisition of control.

In summary, the deemed proceeds on the asset(s) chosen to be elected upon can be determined as follows:

Deemed proceeds of disposition = 2 × ((a) + (b) + (c)) (as described above) + the ACB(s) of properties chosen to be elected upon

¶11,130.30 Consequences of the Election

The properties and amounts elected upon must be designated in the corporation's tax return for the deemed taxation year. While a corporation will focus mainly on the capital gain implications of an election, an election made in respect of a depreciable property may, also, give rise to recaptured capital cost allowance which may affect the non-capital losses of the corporation. Consequently, both the capital gain and recaptured capital cost allowance implications must be carefully considered when an election is contemplated. ITA: 111(4)(e)

The rules also provide for a deemed reacquisition of the depreciable or non-depreciable capital properties that are elected upon. A non-depreciable property is deemed to be reacquired at a cost equal to the amount of the deemed proceeds of disposition. For the purpose of computing future capital gains or losses, a depreciable property is deemed to be reacquired at a cost equal to the amount of the deemed proceeds of disposition. On the other hand, for the purpose of determining future capital cost allowance and recapture amounts, a depreciable property is deemed to be reacquired at a cost equal to the amount that is the capital cost plus the realized taxable capital gain (i.e., ½ of the capital gain elected). Thus, the increase in the base for capital cost allowance is limited to the amount of the gain that has been included in income, i.e., the taxable capital gain plus recapture. ITA: 111(4)(e), 13(7)(f)

Where the deemed proceeds give rise to recapture, but no capital gain is triggered at the same time, the capital cost is deemed to be that amount immediately before the disposition (original capital cost). Capital cost allowance is deemed to have been taken equal to the excess of the original capital cost over the deemed proceeds calculated according to the formula described above. The result of this provision is to retain the original capital cost for purposes of future recapture calculations and to prevent double counting of the recapture recognized on the exercise of the election. ITA: 111(4)(e)(iii), 111(4)(e)(iv)

Example

Mentors Inc. has just been acquired. It has $10,000 of property losses that will expire as a result of the acquisition of control. The only asset involved is a depreciable one that has a capital cost of $70,000, an undepreciated capital cost of $35,000 and fair market value of $60,000.

Obviously, there is no accrued capital gain on the depreciable asset. In fact, there has been a decline in value. Capital losses are denied on depreciable assets, because a decline in value is handled through the CCA system. There is, however, potential recapture to a current maximum amount of $25,000 (i.e., $35,000 – $60,000), depending upon the designated amount or proceeds of disposition. Therefore, Mentors Inc. may attempt to designate, in this fact situation, an amount of $45,000 as the proceeds of disposition so that a desired $10,000 of recapture will be triggered. ITA: 39(1)(b)(i)

In this case, however, the elected amount or deemed proceeds must be equal to the lesser of:

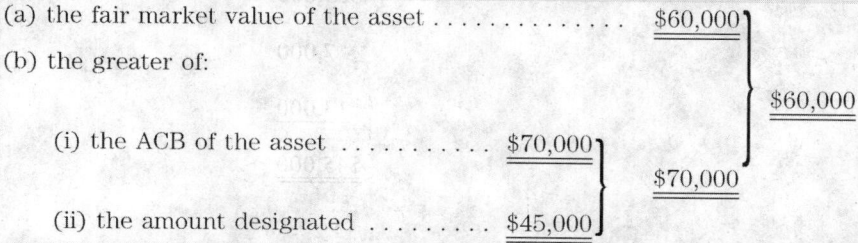

(a) the fair market value of the asset		$60,000	
(b) the greater of:			$60,000
(i) the ACB of the asset	$70,000		
		$70,000	
(ii) the amount designated	$45,000		

As a result of the formula, the full $25,000 of recapture must be included in income, calculated as:

UCC		$35,000
Less: the lower of:		
(a) capital cost	$70,000	
(b) proceeds	60,000	60,000
Recapture		$25,000

Therefore, in some cases, it may not be worthwhile to elect, because all of the unrealized recapture will be triggered.

From the perspective of the Mentors Inc., the capital cost is deemed to be the original capital cost of the acquired corporation, i.e., $70,000. In addition, Mentors Inc. is deemed to have taken capital cost allowance equal to the difference between the capital cost of $70,000 and the proceeds of $60,000. The effect of these two deeming provisions is to make Mentors Inc. assume responsibility for the remaining potential recapture of $10,000. The undepreciated capital cost, on which future capital cost allowance may be computed, is now set at $60,000.

¶11,135 Allowable Business Investment Losses and Losses From Property

As a general rule, non-capital losses include allowable business investment losses (ABILs) and losses from property. However, when there has been an acquisition of control of a corporation, the rules restrict the carryover of non-capital losses to those losses which can reasonably be attributed to the carrying on of a business. As a result, unutilized allowable business investment losses and losses from property expire after the deemed taxation year and must be removed from the non-capital loss balance. Even ABILs and property losses created in years prior to the acquisition of control are removed from the non-capital loss balance.

ITA: 111(4)(e); 111(5) Loss restriction event — non-capital losses and farm losses

For example, consider the case where a non-capital loss is made up of the following types of losses:

Business loss	$25,000
Property loss	7,000
ABIL	13,000
Total non-capital loss	$45,000

In this situation the property loss and the ABIL will expire and the business loss of $25,000 will be the only loss to survive after the deemed year end.

¶11,140 Unused Charitable Contributions

A corporation's unused charitable contributions cease to be deductible after the deemed year end resulting from an acquisition of control. Furthermore, the deduction of a gift of property made after an acquisition of control is denied if the property was owned at the time of the acquisition of control and it was expected that a gift of the property would be made after the acquisition of control. The purpose of these provisions is to discourage charitable deduction trading transactions.

ITA: 110.1(1.2) Where control acquired

¶11,145 Deductibility of Non-Capital Losses After an Acquisition of Control

¶11,145.10 Requirement That the Loss Business Be Carried on With a Reasonable Expectation of Profit

Non-capital losses and farm losses carried forward to taxation years beyond the deemed taxation year are deductible only if the following conditions are satisfied:

ITA: 111(5)(a)(i)

(1) the business that generated the losses must be carried on throughout the year in which the corporation seeks to make a deduction for non-capital losses; and

ITA: 111(1)(a) Non-capital losses, 111(1)(d) Farm losses

(2) the particular business must be carried on for profit or with a reasonable expectation of profit.

An important feature of this rule is that the legislation identifies the non-capital losses with a particular business. Note that the word "business" is not synonymous with the word "corporation"; that is, a corporation can carry on more than one business.

With regard to the condition (ii), above, there are no guidelines in the Act dealing with the "expectation of profit" test in this context. Accordingly, there is some uncertainty as to how the CRA will apply this test. One court case on the issue is *Garage Montplaisir Ltée v. M.N.R.*, where the Court discovered that the acquisition of the loss corporation was for the purpose of eliminating a competitor, not for the purpose of earning income from the loss business. On appeal to the Federal Court–Trial Division, it was found that there was no evidence that the taxpayer had continued to carry on any significant part of the loss business "for profit or with a reasonable expectation of profit". The latter decision was affirmed by the Federal Court of Appeal. It would be advisable to develop a turnaround plan for the loss business to help establish a "reasonable expectation of profit". The checklist in Exhibit 4-3 can be consulted in the development of that plan.

Cases: *Garage Montplaisir Ltée v. The Minister of National Revenue*, 92 DTC 2317 (TCC)*Garage Montplaisir Ltée v. Her Majesty the Queen*, 96 DTC 6557 (FCTD)*Garage Montplaisir Inc. v. Her Majesty the Queen*, 2001 DTC 5366 (FCA)

¶11,145.20 Requirement That Non-Capital Losses Must Be Applied Only Against Income From the Same or Similar Products or Services

The principle of identifying non-capital losses and farm losses with a particular business is only the first step in determining the deductibility of these losses. As a second step in the determination, non-capital losses that are carried forward beyond the deemed taxation year are deductible only against income generated by the particular business and by any other business substantially all of whose income is derived from the sale, leasing, rental or development of similar properties or the rendering of similar services.

ITA: 111(5)(a)(ii); Interpretation Bulletins: IT-302R3, par. 13

This other business is often referred to, generally, as a "similar" business, but the wording of the Act may be more restrictive in specifying "similar properties" or "similar services". The CRA's opinion of the meaning of the word "similar" in this context is interpreted as "of the same general nature or character". The determination is highly fact-dependent.

Interpretation Bulletins: IT-302R3, par. 14, IT-206R, par. 5

Note that, in addition to the more obvious horizontally integrated business, a vertically integrated business is also considered a similar business. It is not clear whether products or services from various stages of a vertically integrated business are considered to be similar for the purposes of this provision. The case of *Manac Inc. Corp. v. The Queen* presents facts to address this issue. Although the decision in this case was based on the "substantially all" condition in the provision, the court made the following comments on the vertical integration and the "similar properties" issue: "we do not see how property which loses its identity when incorporated into an end product can be described as property similar to the end product".[2]

Cases: *Manac Inc. Corp. v. The Queen*, 98 DTC 6605 (FCA)

In any case, only income from a business can be offset by losses that are carried over. The wording of the Act, therefore, precludes income from property, for example, from being offset by these carryover losses.

The principle of matching the losses of a particular business against income from that business or the income of similar products and services is sometimes referred to as "streaming". Because the stream of income against which the losses can be applied is limited, there is an increased possibility that losses will not be deductible in the appropriate carryover period. Hence, the principle of streaming is inherently restrictive as far as the utilization of losses is concerned.

[2] For a more liberal interpretation of a different set of facts, consider the case of *Crystal Beach Park Limited v. The Queen*, 2006 DTC 2845 (T.C.C.), in which the corporation redeveloped an amusement park property into a marina and condominium development, and utilized the park losses to offset profits from the redeveloped property. The Court concluded, at 2854, that "the business ... was the exploitation of a recreational site".

¶11,150 Loss Carryback Rules

The preceding commentary focuses on the carryforward of non-capital losses. In general, the restrictions that were described above apply with equal effect in situations where post-acquisition of control losses are carried back to a taxation year preceding the acquisition of control. Again, only income from a business can be offset by these carryover non-capital losses. ITA: 111(5)(b)

¶11,155 Summary and Application

The effects of the restrictive legislation on loss utilization, following an acquisition of control, may be summarized as follows:

(1) net capital losses, allowable business investment losses, property losses and unused charitable contributions expire and are not carried forward beyond the deemed taxation year;

(2) accrued losses of various kinds are deemed to be realized and, thus, increase the amount of non-capital losses of a corporation; as non-capital losses, they are subject to time restrictions as to their deductibility; and

(3) the principle of streaming, which matches losses from a particular business against income from the particular business and a similar business, increases the likelihood that non-capital losses will not be deductible within their carryforward periods.

Example Problem 11-4

Wonder Inc.'s tax return for its year ended December 31, 2017, showed the following balances in its loss accounts:

Type of Loss	Balance	Year Incurred
Net capital loss	$ 8,000	2014
Non-capital loss	$10,000	2015

During the period January to December 2018, Wonder Inc. earned business income of $1,000 per month, computed in accordance with the *Income Tax Act*. On April 1, 2018, an unrelated person acquired 51% of the voting shares of Wonder Inc.

REQUIRED

Discuss the tax implications of the above information.

SOLUTION

Legal control (greater than 50% of the voting shares) of Wonder Inc. has been acquired by an unrelated person. This has the following tax implications for Wonder Inc.: ITA: 256(7)(a)

(1) The taxation year of Wonder Inc. is deemed to have ended on March 31, 2018, being immediately before the acquisition of control. ITA: 249(4)(a)

(2) A new taxation year is deemed to begin April 1, 2018. ITA: 249(4)(b)

(3) Wonder Inc. can choose any date up to 53 weeks in the future as its new taxation year end. ITA: 249(4)(d)

(4) The net capital loss expires on March 31, 2018, and can never be deducted by Wonder Inc. after that date. ITA: 111(4)(a)

(5) The non-capital loss, to the extent that it is a loss from carrying on business (not a loss from a property source), can be deducted in future taxation years, provided the following tests are met:

(a) the business in which the loss was incurred is carried on at a profit or with a reasonable expectation of profit throughout the taxation year the loss is claimed, and ITA: 111(5)(a)(i)

(b) the non-capital loss is deducted against income from the business that generated the non-capital loss and/or income from a business selling similar products or providing similar services. ITA: 111(5)(a)(ii)

Thus, Wonder Inc. will claim $3,000 of its non-capital loss to offset its taxable income (i.e., three months × $1,000) for the three-month deemed taxation year ended March 31, 2018. As to whether the remaining $7,000 will ever be deducted depends on point (5), above.

The net capital loss cannot be deducted in the deemed year ended March 31, 2018, as there are no capital gains to deduct it against. Since it expires on March 31, 2018, it will never be used.

Example Problem 11-5

On May 1, 2018, an unrelated person acquired 60% of the voting shares of Novell Inc. The values of the assets owned by Novell Inc. at May 1, 2018, were as follows:

Assets	Cost	UCC	FMV
Inventory	$10,000	N/A	$ 8,000
Accounts receivable	20,000	N/A	15,000

Assets	Cost	UCC	FMV
Equipment	30,000	$28,000	12,000
Marketable securities	40,000	N/A	10,000
Goodwill	50,000	36,000	30,000

In determining the value of the receivables, the collectability of each debt was considered individually.

REQUIRED

Which of the accrued (unrealized) losses in the above assets must be recognized by Novell Inc. in determining its income for tax purposes for the deemed year ended April 30, 2018?

SOLUTION

The accrued loss in the inventory must be recognized. Inventory is valued at the lower of cost or market	$ 2,000	ITA: 10(1) Valuation of inventory; ITR: 1801 Valuation
The largest amount that Novell Inc. could deduct as a reserve for doubtful accounts for each trade receivable, must be claimed as a bad debt	5,000	ITA: 20(1)(l) Doubtful or impaired debts, 20(1)(p) Bad debts, 111(5.3) Loss restriction event — doubtful debts and bad debts
The UCC of the equipment is reduced to $12,000. The reduction is deducted as CCA in the deemed year end.	16,000	ITA: 111(5.1) Loss restriction event — UCC computation
The ACB of the marketable securities is reduced to $10,000. The reduction is deemed to be a capital loss in the deemed year end. The allowable capital loss is $30,000 × ½ = $15,000 and is deductible only to the extent there are taxable capital gains in the deemed year ended April 30, 2018, or in any of the three preceding years. No such gains are evident in this case.		ITA: 111(4)(c), 111(4)(d)
The UCC for the goodwill (Class 14.1) is reduced to $30,000, being equal to FMV. The reduction is deducted as CCA in the deemed year end.	6,000	
Total reduction to the business income of Novell Inc. for its deemed year ended April 30, 2018.	$29,000	

Example Problem 11-6

Universal Ltd.'s tax return for its year ended December 31, 2017, showed the following balances in its loss accounts:

Type of Loss	Balance	Year Incurred
Net capital loss	$ 8,000	2007
Non-capital loss	$10,000	2014

On June 1, 2018, an unrelated person acquired 75% of the voting shares of Universal Ltd. The accountant has calculated the business loss for the deemed year ended May 31, 2018, to be $25,000, including the accrued losses required to be recognized on the acquisition of control. The capital assets owned by Universal Ltd. at June 1, 2018, had the following values:

Capital Assets	Cost	UCC/CEC	FMV
Land	$ 40,000	N/A	$ 70,000
Building	60,000	$45,000	90,000
	$100,000		$160,000

The accountant is projecting income of $100,000 for Universal Ltd. over the next 12 months. The projected income is from the business that incurred the losses.

REQUIRED

Universal Ltd. is considering making an election. Recommend the asset(s) that should be designated and the amount(s) which should be designated in the election. ITA: 111(4)(e)

SOLUTION

Universal Ltd. should elect to recognize a taxable capital gain of $8,000 in order to utilize the $8,000 adjusted net capital loss expiring May 31, 2018. The election should be made on the land and not on the building as recapture would be incurred on the building. Such recapture would reduce the current (deemed) year's business loss and, thus, would be disadvantageous, because there would be $15,000 (i.e., $60,000 – $45,000 = $15,000 recapture) less in non-capital losses to carry forward to the next 20 years.

To trigger a $8,000 taxable capital gain on the land, proceeds of $56,000 should be designated. (Current ACB of the land ($40,000) + desired taxable capital gain grossed up to the full capital gain ($8,000 × 2) = $56,000). The resulting income under section 3 and taxable income for the year would be calculated as follows:

par. 3(*a*) income from business, property		$ Nil
par. 3(*b*) taxable capital gains ($56,000 – $40,000) × ½	$ 8,000	
allowable capital loss	0	8,000
par. 3(*c*)		$ 8,000
par. 3(*d*) loss from business	$(25,000)	
loss from property	0	(25,000)
Division B net income (technically cannot be negative)		$(17,000)
Division C deductions:		
Net capital losses (only restricted by par. 3(*b*) amount)		(8,000)
Non-capital losses		0
Non-capital loss for the deemed year ended May 31, 2018		$(25,000)

Universal has non-capital losses of $10,000 + $25,000 = $35,000 at May 31, 2018. This amount can be used to offset the prospective $100,000 of income from the business that generated the loss, if at least $35,000 of the income is actually earned. This is the same with or without the election. The advantage of the election is that the ACB of the land is bumped up to $56,000. The higher ACB of the land will reduce a future capital gain on a disposition. ITA: 111(4)(e)

Once an acquisition of control is recognized, the steps outlined in Exhibit 11-3 can be taken. An acquisition of control should be recognized, in its basic form, when shares of a corporation (or its parent corporation) are acquired by a third party that obtains control of the target corporation. While the rules apply even when a target corporation has no realized or unrealized losses at the time of the acquisition of control, the rules are designed to restrict the utilization of realized or unrealized losses where a purchaser acquires control of a loss company. The rationale is that the purchaser will not have taken the risks that generated the losses, particularly those that expire, and should not gain the benefit of the tax shields from those losses against the purchaser's income.

Exhibit 11-3 Acquisition of Control (AOC)

Steps to Take

(1) **Establish a deemed year end on the day before the AOC**

(2) **Determine any accrued losses and unrealized gains**

- Realize "accrued" losses automatically
  - Terminal losses
  - Inventory losses
  - Allowance for doubtful accounts
  - Capital losses
- Identify "accrued" gains for purposes of an election
  - Recapture
  - Capital gains

(3) **Determine the tax position of the company with the automatic realization of the accrued losses**

- Calculate non-capital and net capital losses carried forward from previous years
- Calculate Division B income, using the ordering rules of section 3, and losses from non-capital sources and allowable capital losses for the deemed year
- Identify expiring property losses, ABILs, and capital losses in the carryforward balances and in the deemed year
- Determine whether any losses that will survive the acquisition of control restrictions are likely to be utilized in their remaining carryover period

(4) **Consider election to create income**

- Offset losses that will expire at the deemed year end, or
- Offset losses that may expire after the deemed year end
  - Due to carryforward period running out
  - Due to restrictions on use of carryforwards
- Avoid electing recapture that offsets losses that will survive the acquisition of control restrictions

(5) **Recalculate Division B and taxable income after the election**

- Apply loss carryovers
- Determine which losses expire
  - Net capital losses

- Non-capital losses
  - Property losses
  - ABILs
- Recalculate non-capital losses by year

(6) **Recalculate cost base of properties**

- For purposes of
  - Capital gains
  - Recapture

(7) **Determine whether**

- The loss business is being carried on with a reasonable expectation of profit, and
- The company is carrying on the same business or selling the same or similar products or services in order to see whether the losses being carried over can be applied against future income

(8) **Determine the steps needed to use up the non-capital loss carryovers with loss utilization planning tools**

- Create a source of intercompany income in the loss company
- Transfer of income-producing assets
- Amalgamation
- Winding-up

¶11,155.99 Practise What You've Learned

Refer to the following sections of the Study Guide to practise what you've learned:

¶11,800 — Review Questions

- Question 3 — Acquisition of control
- Question 4 — Restrictions on acquisition of control
- Question 5 — Restrictions on acquisition of control

¶11,825 — Multiple Choice Questions

- Question 1 — Acquisition of control — year end
- Question 2 — Acquisition of control — loss recognition
- Question 3 — Acquisition of control — deemed CCA

- Question 4 — Acquisition of control

¶11,850 — Exercises

- Exercise 8 — Acquisition of control
- Exercise 12 — Acquisition of control

¶11,160 Taxable Income of a Corporation in General

Recall that the starting point for the calculation of a corporation's taxable income is its net income for tax purpose computed under Division B. Where financial statements have been prepared using generally accepted accounting principles, it may be necessary to adjust income for financial accounting purposes to income for tax purposes as determined by Division B. This usually involves a reconciliation process, introduced in Chapter 4. Generally, expenditures deducted for financial accounting purposes but not deductible for tax purposes, must be added to financial accounting income, and expenditures not deducted for financial accounting purposes but deductible for tax purposes may be deducted in the reconciliation. To perform this reconciliation in the preparation of a corporate tax return, Schedule 1 is completed.

ITA: 110 Deductions permitted, 111 Losses deductible, 112 Deduction of taxable dividends received by corporation resident in Canada

Example Problem 11-7

The following information has been taken from the financial records of the FT Limited:

	2017	2018
Net income (loss) for financial accounting	$(53,000)	$126,000
Provision for income taxes	–	113,000
Financial accounting expenses include:		
– Charitable donations	15,000	15,000
– Depreciation	105,000	105,000
– Bond discount amortization	5,000	5,000
Financial accounting income included:		
– Dividends from taxable Canadian corporations	23,000	23,000

	2017	2018
– Dividends from foreign corporations (not foreign affiliates and net of 15% withholding tax)	15,300	15,300
– Capital gains	–	–

In 2017, capital cost allowance of $10,278 had been taken on a brick building purchased in 2014 (Class 1 (separate): 6%) leaving an undepreciated capital cost balance of $246,667 on January 1, 2018, the beginning of the 2018 taxation year. In addition, $44,800 in capital cost allowance had been taken on equipment leaving an undepreciated capital cost balance of $179,200 on January 1, 2018. In 2018 no additions or disposals were made to these classes of assets.

The corporation had non-capital losses of $18,000 available for carryover until 2031 and a 2012 net capital loss of $5,000 available for carryover.

REQUIRED

Calculate the taxable income of the corporation for the years indicated.

SOLUTION

	2017		2018	
Net income (loss) per financial statements		$(53,000)		$126,000
Add items not deductible for tax purposes:				
Provision for income taxes[(1)]		—	$113,000	
Withholding tax on foreign dividends[(2)]	$ 2,700		2,700	
Charitable donations[(3)]	15,000		15,000	
Depreciation	105,000		105,000	
Amortized bond discount[(4)]	5,000	127,700	5,000	240,700
Deduct items tax deductible:				
Capital cost allowances[(5)]		(55,078)		(50,640)
Income for tax purposes		$ 19,622		$316,060

	2017		2018	
Deductions in computation of taxable income:				
Inter-company dividends	$ 23,000		$ 23,000	
Charitable donations				
— carried over	—		15,000[6]	
— current	Nil[6]		15,000[6]	
Non-capital loss carryover[7]	—		18,000	
Net capital loss carryover[8]	—	(23,000)	—	(71,000)
Taxable income		Nil		$245,060

ITA: 112 Deduction of taxable dividends received by corporation resident in Canada

ITA: 110.1(1)(a) Charitable gifts

ITA: 111(1)(a) Non-capital losses

ITA: 111(1)(b) Net capital losses

NOTES TO SOLUTION

(1) Income tax is not an expenditure made to produce income. It is an appropriation of profits after they have been earned.

(2) This is not an expenditure made to produce income for tax purposes, but an appropriation of profits after they have been earned. However, a foreign tax credit may be available in the computation of tax.

(3) Donations, normally, are not deductible in the computation of income, but are deductible in the computation of taxable income of a corporation.

ITA: 18(1)(f) Payments on discounted bonds, 20(1)(f) Discount on certain obligations

(4) Bond discount amortizations are prohibited, but payments reflecting bond discounts are deductible at the earlier of redemption or maturity.

(5) Capital cost allowances for 2018 were computed as follows:

	Building Class 1: 6%	Equipment Class 8: 20%
2018: UCC, January 1, 2018	$246,667	$179,200
CCA for 2018 (total expense: $50,640)	(14,800)	(35,840)
2019: UCC, January 1, 2019	$231,867	$143,360

(6) The amount of charitable donations that may be deducted in a year is limited to 75% of income as computed in Division B of Part I. However, charitable donations not deducted in the current year can be carried forward five years.

ITA: 110.1(1)(a) Charitable gifts

[7] Non-capital losses would not be deducted in 2017, because after the dividends have been deducted, there is no income against which to absorb them in that year. Non-capital losses increase by $3,378 to $21,378.

[8] Net capital loss carryovers cannot be deducted in 2017 and 2018 because there were no taxable capital gains against which to absorb them in these years. However, if there are net taxable capital gains available under paragraph 3(*b*) in the future or in the three years before 2017 (to the extent the taxable capital gains have not been offset by allowable capital losses), there is a potential increase in the non-capital losses at the taxpayer's discretion. The decision to utilize this option will depend upon which source of income will be generated first, business income or net taxable capital gains.

¶11,200 Basic Computation of Tax for All Corporations

¶11,210 Objectives of Provisions Affecting Taxation of Corporations

Although a corporation is regarded as a separate entity, in an economic sense the separation of a corporation and its shareholders may be artificial. However, the flexibility provided by corporations, often involving tax planning, has resulted in considerable complexity of the legislation pertaining to the taxation of corporations. This legislation appears to have two main objectives.

The first objective is the alleviation of the multiple taxation of corporate income by taxing income at the level of the corporation and, then, at the level of the shareholder on dividends received from after-tax corporate earnings. The Act attempts to integrate these two taxes primarily by way of the dividend gross-up and tax credit mechanism. If the system of integration were perfect, it would completely eliminate the double taxation of corporate income, as previously discussed at the beginning of this chapter and demonstrated in Chapter 12. The Canadian system of integration is not perfect in this sense, but it does remove much of the effect of double taxation on investment income and some types of business income. The examination of this aspect will be continued in detail in the next chapter.

The second objective of these provisions is to provide tax incentives to certain types of corporations. The small business deduction, which will be discussed in the next chapter, is probably the most important of these. The small business deduction will be shown to substantially reduce tax for a Canadian-controlled private corporation. The manufacturing and processing profits deduction will be alluded to. Investment tax credits, including the credit for scientific research expenditures, will be discussed.

ITA: 55(2) Deemed proceeds or gain, 110.6 [Capital gains exemption], 245 [General anti-avoidance rule], 246 Benefit conferred on a person

¶11,212 Types of Corporations

The Canadian corporate tax system draws a distinction among types of corporations. For the purpose of this text, we need to consider three types:

- a private corporation;
- a Canadian-controlled private corporation; and

- a public corporation.

Certain tax preferences, such as the small business deduction, or tax accounts, such as the capital dividend account, apply to only certain types of corporations. Hence, the need to distinguish the types of corporations is important.

¶11,213 Private Corporation

The Act defines a "private corporation" as one that is resident in Canada and not controlled by one or more public corporations (or a prescribed federal Crown corporation). A private corporation has certain tax preferences or considerations, as discussed in Chapter 12, such as a capital dividend account and a refundable dividend tax on hand account. ITA: 89(1) Definitions

Some types of private corporations enjoy the most favourable tax rates. Some tax credits are also more favourable for private corporations than for public corporations, such as the investment tax credit on scientific research and experimental development expenditures.

¶11,214 Canadian-Controlled Private Corporation (CCPC)

A "CCPC" is defined as a private corporation that is a Canadian corporation that is not controlled, directly or indirectly, in any manner whatever, by one or more non-residents, by one or more public corporations, or by a combination of the two. Also, no class of its shares are listed on a designated stock exchange. Notice that the definition is negative. That is, there is no requirement that it be Canadian-controlled, it just cannot be controlled by non-residents or public corporations. Consequently, a Canadian private corporation that is controlled 50% by Canadian residents and 50% by non-residents is a CCPC. ITA: 125(7) Definitions

One of the principal tax advantages of a CCPC is the small business deduction. From an individual's perspective, capital gains deduction eligibility requires the corporation having CCPC status.

¶11,215 Public Corporations

Public corporations are those resident in Canada and which have a class of shares listed on a "designated stock exchange" in Canada, as designated by the Minister of Finance. Public corporations do not enjoy any of the tax preferences available to private corporations. The tax system has become almost fully integrated at the public corporation level, as a result of the higher gross-up and the tax credit for eligible dividends. Canadian corporations that are controlled by public corporation are treated the same as public corporations for Canadian tax purposes and do not have the tax preferences available to a private corporation. ITA: 89(1) Definitions, 248(1) Definitions, 262 Authority to designate stock exchange

¶11,216 Diagrammatic Summary of Types of Corporations

Figure 11-1 shows the three basic types of corporations.

Figure 11-1 Types of Corporations

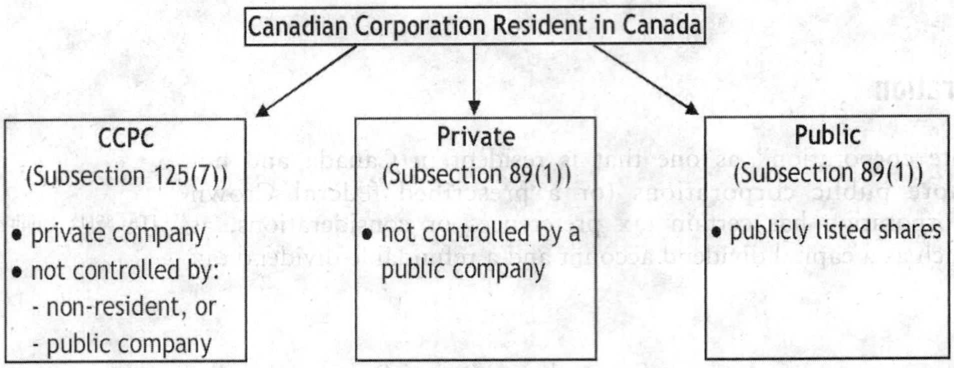

¶11,220 General Rates for Corporations

¶11,225 Overview of Rates and Credits

ITA: 123 Rate for corporations, 124 Deduction from corporation tax, 125 Small business deduction, 126 Foreign tax deduction, 127 [Investment tax credit, etc.]

The general federal rate of tax to be paid on the taxable income of all corporations under Part I of the Act is 38%. However, the basic federal rate of 38% is subject to modification, depending on the type of corporation. The Act provides for the following adjustments to the tax rate:

- 10% abatement from federal tax payable, in recognition of provincial income taxes;
- 18% small business deduction;
- 13% general rate reduction on certain business income;
- 13% manufacturing and processing profits deduction for certain corporations;
- foreign tax credits; and
- other tax credits including political contribution tax credit and the investment tax credit.

¶11,235 Effect of Provincial Corporate Tax Rates

In addition to the federal taxes imposed, each province levies an additional income tax on a corporation's taxable income. Furthermore, the taxable income calculation may vary from province to province because of provincial taxing statutes. The provincial rate varies from province to province, but on the whole lies between 0.0% and 16%.

¶11,240 Effect of Corporation Type

As mentioned previously, the type and status of the corporation has a bearing on how its income is taxed. There are three major classifications of corporations to be concerned with. These are described in ¶11,212 to ¶11,216.

As a result of the combined federal and provincial rate and several of the modifications to that rate, the rates of tax applicable to business income earned by Canadian corporations will vary from a low of about 11% to a high of about 31%, depending on the classification of the corporation and the type of income earned.

¶11,245 General Rate Reduction

The Act provides a corporation with a deduction from tax, computed by multiplying the corporation's "general rate reduction percentage" by its "full-rate taxable income". The "general rate reduction percentage" is 13%. The full-rate taxable income of a corporation, generally, is a corporation's taxable income that has not benefited from special rate reductions, such as the manufacturing and processing profits deduction (alluded to later in this chapter) and the small business deduction (discussed in Chapter 12), among others. The amount of the rate reduction is dependent on the nature of the corporation.

ITA: 123.4(2) General deduction from tax, 123.4(1) Definitions

The general rate reduction is 13% of the following:

Taxable income

Less:

- The amount of income eligible for the small business deduction
- The amount of income eligible for the M&P profits deduction
- The amount of income from a personal services business
- Aggregate investment income

The following shows the net federal corporate tax rate on general business income:

Basic	38%
Abatement	(10)
General rate reduction	(13)
	15%

¶11,250 Abatement From Federal Tax for Income Earned in a Province

¶11,255 Purpose of the Provision

A federal abatement of 10% of a corporation's taxable income earned in Canada is deducted from income tax otherwise calculated. This abatement is based on taxable income earned in a Canadian province or territory; that is, the reduction allows for the imposition of such a provincial tax. All of the provinces and the territories impose an income tax on corporations at general rates, which vary.

ITA: 124(1) Deduction from corporation tax

Exhibit 11-4 shows a hypothetical calculation, applicable to most corporations, of effective total tax on taxable income eligible for the abatement. Note that the provincial tax is calculated separately on a tax base that may or may not equal taxable income under the federal Act depending on the particular province levying the tax. For illustrative purposes only, Exhibit 11-4 *assumes* that the tax base for income earned in a hypothetical province is equal to taxable income for federal corporate income tax. The exhibit also assumes that the provincial corporate rate of tax is 13% of the taxable income earned in that province.

Exhibit 11-4 Hypothetical Tax Rates Applicable to Taxable Income Eligible for Abatement

Basic federal tax rate	38%
Federal abatement for provincial tax (i.e., General Rate Reduction)	(10)
Net federal tax	28%
Federal tax reduction (i.e., General Rate Reduction)	(13)
Net federal tax	15%
Provincial tax (assumed)	13
Effective total tax	28%

ITA: 123(1) Rate for corporations

ITA: 124(1) Deduction from corporation tax

¶11,260 Applicable Income Tax Regulations

Part IV of the Regulations provides the prescribed method to determine the taxable income earned in a province by a corporation. The term "taxable income earned in the year in a province" by a corporation is defined as being the aggregate of the taxable incomes of the corporation earned in the year in each of the provinces. The Regulations also set out the method of calculating the taxable income earned in a particular province during the year. The taxable income earned in a particular province is that taxable income which is attributable to a *permanent establishment* that the corporation has in the province. If a company has no permanent establishment in a province, it will not have earned any taxable income in that province for the purposes of the abatement. The formula for determining the attributable amount is discussed in great detail in ¶11,270 below.

ITR: 400(1), 402 General Rules

The term "permanent establishment" is defined as a fixed place of business of the corporation, including an office, a branch, a mine or oil well, a farm, a timber land, a factory, a workshop or a warehouse. Where the corporation does not have a fixed place of business, its permanent establishment is the principal place in which the corporation's business is carried out. A corporation is deemed to have a permanent establishment in a place, if the corporation carries on business through an employee or agent, established in a particular place:

ITR: 400(2), 400(2)(b)

(1) who has general authority to contract for his or her employer or principal; or

(2) who has a stock of merchandise owned by his or her employer or principal from which he or she regularly fills orders which he or she receives.

However, the fact that a corporation has business dealings through a commission agent, broker or other independent agent, or maintains an office solely for the purchase of merchandise, does not of itself mean that the corporation has a permanent establishment. The use of substantial machinery or equipment in a particular place at any time in a taxation year constitutes a permanent establishment in that place as does the ownership of land in a province by a corporation that, otherwise, has a permanent establishment in Canada. The CRA indicates that the application of the criteria for a permanent establishment set out in the Regulations will often involve questions of fact that must be answered by the circumstances of each case.

ITR: 400(2), 400(2)(d), 400(2)(e), 400(2)(f); Interpretation Bulletins: IT-177R2

¶11,265 Cases on the Meaning of Permanent Establishment

The case of *M.N.R. v. Panther Oil and Grease Manufacturing Co. of Canada Ltd.* presents a specific fact situation. Here the taxpayer had a factory in Ontario, but maintained a sizable sales force throughout Canada under the direction of district sales managers. These sales managers were under the direction of division managers, one of whom lived in Quebec. He had an office, not listed as the company's, in his home. The division and district managers kept a small quantity of the company's goods on hand for small orders when quick delivery was requested. However, most orders were filled from Ontario.

ITR: 400(2); Cases: *Minister of National Revenue v. Panther Oil & Grease Manufacturing Co. of Canada Ltd*, 61 DTC 1222 (EC)

It was held that the extensive sales organization in Quebec, itself, constituted a branch in that province and district managers constituted "agencies" of the company. It was also found that the stock of merchandise from which small orders were filled qualified as a permanent establishment.

In the case of *Enterprise Foundry (N.B.) Ltd. v. M.N.R.*, the appellant was incorporated in New Brunswick, but all of its sales were made to customers in Quebec. About 40% of its orders were filled from a stock of merchandise maintained in a public warehouse in Montreal. The taxpayer's key employee had the authority to deliver goods from the stock of merchandise and also had general authority to contract for his employer. It was held that there was a permanent establishment in Quebec.

ITR: 400(2)(b); Cases: *Enterprise Foundry (N.B.) Limited v. Minister of National Revenue*, 64 DTC 660 (TAB)

¶11,270 Taxable Income Earned in a Province or Territory

Once it is determined that a corporation has a permanent establishment in a province or territory, a portion of the company's taxable income is attributed to that jurisdiction. To determine the attribution, a formula must be used. The formula is based on the proportion of gross revenues earned through a permanent establishment in a province or territory and the proportion of salaries and wages expense paid through the same permanent establishment in that jurisdiction, relative to total gross revenues and salaries and wages expense, respectively, of the corporation. The total taxable income allocated to all provinces and territories provides the basis for the 10% abatement. The allocations to individual jurisdictions, other than Alberta and Quebec, provide the basis for provincial or territorial corporate income tax. Refer to Example Problem 11-8 to see how this calculation works.

ITR: 402 General Rules

A taxpayer must first determine the gross revenue for the year which is reasonably attributable to each permanent establishment. Rules are provided for determining the permanent establishment to which gross revenue is attributable where merchandise is shipped by a corporation to its customers outside of Canada.

ITR: 402(3)(a), 402(4)

Where the gross revenue reasonably attributable to a permanent establishment in a province has been determined, this amount will be divided by the corporation's total gross revenue for the year. Certain types of investment income including interest on securities, dividends and rentals or royalties from properties not used in the main business of the corporation are excluded from gross revenue. ITR: 401 Computation of Taxable Income, 402(5)

It will also be necessary to determine the aggregate of the salaries and wages paid in the year by the corporation to employees of a permanent establishment in each particular jurisdiction. This will then be divided by the aggregate of all salaries and wages paid in the year by the corporation. To determine the percentage of taxable income to allocate to each province, we take the average of the two percentages determined by the gross revenues and aggregate salaries. ITR: 401 Computation of Taxable Income, 402(3)(b)

Example Problem 11-8

Barry and the Wild Bunch Limited, with its head office in Ottawa, Ontario and other permanent establishments in the provinces of New Brunswick and Quebec, and in the United States, has taxable income of $325,000.

Assume that the corporation's gross revenue and salaries and wages are attributable to its permanent establishments as follows: ITR: 402 General Rules

	Gross revenue	Salaries and wages
Ontario	$ 780,000	$ 130,000
New Brunswick	2,340,000	520,000
Quebec	2,600,000	585,000
United States	390,000	65,000
Total	$6,110,000	$1,300,000
Dividends not attributable	130,000	—
	$6,240,000	$1,300,000

ITR: 402(5)

REQUIRED

Compute the amount of the company's taxable income attributable to each province and determine the amount of the company's abatement. ITA: 124(1) Deduction from corporation tax

SOLUTION

The proportion of taxable income attributable to each province would be computed as follows: ITR: 402 General Rules

	Gross revenue		Salaries and wages		
	Amount	%	Amount	%	Average %
Ontario	$ 780,000	12.8%	$ 130,000	10.0%	½ (12.8% + 10.0%) = 11.4%
New Brunswick	2,340,000	38.3	520,000	40.0	½ (38.3% + 40.0%) = 39.2%
Quebec	2,600,000	42.6	585,000	45.0	½ (42.6% + 45.0%) = 43.8%
Subtotal	$5,720,000	93.7%	$1,235,000	95.0%	½ (93.7% + 95.0%) = 94.4%
U.S	390,000	6.3	65,000	5.0	
Total	$6,110,000	100.0%	$1,300,000	100.0%	

Allocation of taxable income to each province:

Ontario	11.4% of $325,000 =	$ 37,050
New Brunswick	39.2% of $325,000 =	127,400
Quebec	43.8% of $325,000 =	142,350
Total taxable income earned in a province or territory		$306,800

Note that the remaining $18,200 (i.e., $325,000 – $306,800) of taxable income earned in the U.S. does not have the 10% abatement applied, since it is not earned in a province or territory of Canada.

The amount deductible from the corporation tax otherwise payable would be computed as follows:

ITA: 124(1) Deduction from corporation tax

10% of $306,800	$30,680

¶11,300 Tax Deductions/Credits

The Act provides for the following deductions/credits, applicable to all corporations:

- Manufacturing and Processing (M&P) Profits Deduction
- Foreign Tax Credit (FTC)
- Investment Tax Credit (ITC)

Ⓐ ¶11,310 Manufacturing and Processing Profits Deduction

Both the M&P Profits Deduction and the General Rate Reduction are a 13% rate reduction. Either will result in the same net federal tax of 15% shown in Exhibit 11-4. The only difference in rates results from a lower provincial rate where a province provides for an M&P deduction.

ITA: 125.1 Manufacturing and processing profits deductions; Income Tax Folio: S4-F15-C1 Manufacturing and Processing

Apparently, the main reason for the continued existence of the M&P profits deduction legislation in the federal Act is to accommodate provinces that offer an M&P profits deduction from provincial tax based on the federal calculation of M&P profits. The technical details of the federal M&P legislation are beyond the scope of this book.

¶11,320 Foreign Tax Credit

¶11,325 Purpose and Approach

Residents of Canada, including corporations, are taxable on their world income even though part of this income may have been subject to tax in a foreign country. Foreign tax credits are designed to mitigate the effects on a Canadian individual or corporate taxpayer of double taxation on income arising from a source outside Canada. Relief is granted by means of a credit, from the Canadian tax otherwise payable, of all or part of the foreign tax paid.

ITA: 126 Foreign tax deduction; Income Tax Folio: S5-F2-C1 Foreign Tax Credit

The theory underlying this arrangement for a tax credit is that the country where the income is earned has the first right to tax the income. If the country of the taxpayer's residence levies a higher rate of tax on the income, the taxpayer will pay tax at the higher rate, but part of that tax is paid to the country where the income was earned while the remainder will be paid to the country of the taxpayer's residence.

Since the foreign tax credit is meant to reduce Canadian tax on foreign income that has been taxed elsewhere, there is no foreign tax credit available on foreign income that is not taxed in Canada. If a source of income is exempt from tax in Canada, there is no Canadian tax to reduce with a foreign tax credit.

ITA: 113 Deduction in respect of dividend received from foreign affiliate, 112 Deduction of taxable dividends received by corporation resident in Canada, 126(1)(a), 95(1) Definitions for this subdivision

For example, certain dividends received by corporations resident in Canada from corporations, such as foreign subsidiaries, resident in another country are not taxable in Canada. Such dividends are, effectively, not taxable in Canada because, although they are included in Division B income, they are deductible in the calculation of taxable income in Division C. This provision is similar to the provision which provides a deduction for dividends received from taxable Canadian corporations. These dividends, from foreign affiliates, that are deductible in Division C are not eligible for the foreign tax credit, since any tax "that may reasonably be regarded as having been paid by the taxpayer in respect of income from a share of the capital stock of a foreign affiliate of the taxpayer" is excluded from foreign tax which is eligible for the credit. A foreign affiliate is defined, basically, as a corporation in which the taxpayer has at least 10% equity ownership.

On the other hand, types of foreign income that are included in Canadian income and, hence, are eligible for a foreign tax credit include: income from an unincorporated foreign branch, dividend income that is not eligible for deduction in the calculation of taxable income, e.g., or dividend income from a corporation which is not a foreign affiliate.

ITA: 113 Deduction in respect of dividend received from foreign affiliate

This text will focus on "non-business-income tax" and "business-income tax". Where the taxpayer is eligible for a foreign tax credit for "non-business-income tax" or on "business-income tax" paid to more than one foreign country, the taxpayer is required to compute separate deductions for each country. It should be emphasized that with few exceptions, the same rules apply to both individuals and corporations. However, the following discussion will focus on the foreign tax credit rules as they apply to corporations.

ITA: 126(1) Foreign tax deduction, 126(2) Idem, 126(6) Rules of construction

¶11,330 Non-Business Income Tax Deduction

¶11,330.10 Calculation

Where a taxpayer has non-business income (e.g., interest income) from another country and has paid foreign income or profits taxes to the government of that country or to the government of a state, province or other political subdivision of that country, the taxpayer may take a deduction from Canadian tax equal to the lesser of:

ITA: 126(1) Foreign tax deduction, 126(7) Definitions

(1) the foreign non-business-income tax paid in respect of that foreign income; and

(2) $\dfrac{\text{foreign non-business income (Div. B)}}{\text{Income (Div. B) for the year (from all sources) plus or minus certain amounts}} \times \text{tax otherwise payable [sec. 126(7)]}$

Note that part (2) attempts to estimate the Canadian tax paid on the foreign income. As a result, the credit against Canadian tax cannot exceed the estimated Canadian tax paid on the foreign income.

The amounts to be subtracted from the Division B income of a corporation in the denominator of the fraction are:

(1) the claims for net capital losses deducted in the year because they directly offset taxable capital gains, with the result that they are not taxed; and

ITA: 111(1)(b) Net capital losses

(2) the amount of taxable dividends received and deductible and the amount of dividends received from a foreign affiliate and deductible, because they are not taxed under Part I.

ITA: 112 Deduction of taxable dividends received by corporation resident in Canada, 113 Deduction in respect of dividend received from foreign affiliate

¶11,330.20 Definition of "Tax Otherwise Payable" for the Non-Business Foreign Tax Credit

The term "tax otherwise payable" is defined in the Act under the heading "tax for the year otherwise payable under this Part". For purposes of the foreign non-business income tax credit, "tax otherwise payable" is defined for corporations as federal taxes less:

ITA: 126(7) Definitions

(1) 10% abatement

(2) general tax reduction (other than CCPC)

ITA: 123.4 Corporation tax reductions, 124 Deduction from corporation tax, 125 Small business deduction, 125.1 Manufacturing and processing profits

Note that the "tax otherwise payable" is determined before deducting the small business deduction, the manufacturing and processing profits deduction and the foreign tax credit.

deductions, 126 Foreign tax deduction

ITA: 127 [Investment tax credit, etc.], 127.2 Share-purchase tax credit, 127.3 Scientific research and experimental development tax credit, 127.4 [Labour-sponsored funds tax credit]

The net result is to determine the Canadian tax that would apply to the foreign non-business income. That amount would be net of the abatement and the general rate reduction for a corporation, other than a Canadian-controlled private corporation.

There is no carry over of unused non-business foreign tax credits.

¶11,330.30 Interpretation of Terms

ITA: 126(1) Foreign tax deduction, 127(7) Investment tax credit of certain trusts

The following should be noted about the term "non-business income tax paid" as it applies to a corporation:

(1) the foreign tax must be paid, not merely payable and the conversion of the foreign tax into its Canadian-dollar equivalent must be made at the rate of exchange prevailing at the time payment is made;

(2) the foreign tax must generally be in the nature of an income or profits tax;

(3) the term includes such income tax paid to the government of another country or to the government of a state, province or other political subdivision of that country;

(4) the term excludes "business income tax" paid in the other country; and

(5) foreign non-business income tax deducted as an expense in Division B must be excluded. Unlike a foreign "business" income credit, described below, an unused foreign non-business income credit cannot be carried forward. Therefore, consideration should be given to using the deduction from income for these amounts. Since a deduction from tax (i.e., a tax credit) is preferable to a deduction from income, eligibility for a foreign tax credit should be determined first, with any unused balance of foreign taxes paid being taken as a deduction. This may result in a circular calculation because of the credit's dependence on net income after the deduction. An algebraic approach may be necessary to solve this problem.

ITA: 20(12) Foreign non-business income tax

¶11,335 Business Income Tax Deduction

In the case of a corporation resident in Canada, it would be considered to carry on business in a foreign country if the corporation had an *unincorporated* branch in that foreign country. If the Canadian resident corporation established a subsidiary in the foreign country, the business income of the subsidiary would be taxed by the foreign country as a separate entity and no business foreign tax credit would be available to the parent. Where the corporation operates in foreign countries through unincorporated branches, a business foreign tax credit will arise.

Unused business foreign tax credits can be carried back and applied in any of the previous three years or carried forward and applied in any of the next ten years.

¶11,335.10 Calculation

The credit, as it applies to a corporation, is computed as the least of: ITA: 126(2) Idem

(1) the total of the "business-income tax paid" for the year in respect of all businesses carried on through an unincorporated branch by the taxpayer in a particular country, plus any "unused foreign tax credit" from other years in respect of the same country as the taxpayer may wish to claim;

(2) $$\frac{\text{foreign business income}}{\text{income (Div. B) for the year (from all sources) plus or minus certain amounts}^{1}} \times \text{tax otherwise payable before abatement minus general tax reduction}$$

ITA: 126(7) business-income tax paid

(3) the tax otherwise payable before abatement minus general rate reduction less any non-business income tax deduction under subsection 126(1).

¶11,335.20 Definition of "Tax Otherwise Payable" for the Business Foreign Tax Credit

For the foreign business income tax credit, the "tax otherwise payable" is defined as the federal tax before any deduction for the federal tax abatement minus the general tax reduction. Note that, if foreign business income were a Canadian resident corporation's only source of income, none of its taxable income would likely be considered to be earned in a province and the corporation would receive no tax abatement. Therefore, the Canadian tax otherwise payable on that income, conceptually, would be before the 10% abatement. However, the foreign business income of a non-CCPC (see Chapter 12) would be eligible for the general tax reduction.

ITA: 126(7) Definitions, 124 Deduction from corporation tax, 125 Small business deduction, 126 Foreign tax deduction, 127 [Investment tax credit, etc.]

The "tax otherwise payable", in this case, for part (2) and part (3) of the calculation, above, is the same amount.

ITA: 127(7) Investment tax credit of certain trusts

Example Problem 11-9

You have audited the books of International Money Limited, a public corporation, and have determined that the income for tax purposes of $472,000 for the year ended December 31, 2018, has been calculated correctly. The following additional data are available:

Interest received from:

an Australian company (net of $3,000 tax withheld)	$17,000

[1] The amounts to be added to and subtracted from Division B income are the same as those that were identified for the non-business income tax deduction.

a British company (net of $1,500 tax withheld)	8,500
Business income (net of $9,800 tax paid) earned from an unincorporated branch in Turkey	18,200
Donations	20,000
Dividend received from a taxable Canadian corporation	52,000
Taxable income earned in a province (computed by Reg.)	375,000

REQUIRED

Compute the maximum foreign tax credit available to the corporation for 2018.

SOLUTION

(1) Calculation of taxable income:

Income for tax purposes		$472,000
Less: donations	$20,000	
dividends	52,000	72,000
Taxable income		$400,000

ITA: 110(1)(a) Charitable gifts

ITA: 112 Deduction of taxable dividends received by corporation resident in Canada

(2) Calculation of tax otherwise payable:

ITA: 126(1) Foreign tax deduction

(i) For foreign non-business income tax credit:

Tax otherwise payable (38% of $400,000)	(A)	$152,000
Less: 10% of $375,000		37,500
Net		$114,500
Tax rate reduction @ 13% of $400,000		(52,000)
Tax otherwise payable	(B)	$ 62,500

(ii) For foreign business income tax credit:[(1)]

Tax otherwise payable, per (A), above	$152,000

Less: tax rate reduction		(52,000)
Tax otherwise payable	(C)	$100,000

(3) Calculation of foreign tax credit:[2]

(i) Foreign non-business income:

Interest from the Australian company

lesser of:

(I) tax paid $3,000

(II) $\frac{\text{income from Australia}}{\text{income less dividends}}$ × tax otherwise payable (B)

$= \frac{\$20,000}{\$472,000 - \$52,000} \times \$62,500$ $2,976 → $2,976

Interest from British company

lesser of:

(I) tax paid $1,500

(II) $\frac{\text{income from Britain}}{\text{income less dividends}}$ × tax otherwise payable (B)

$= \frac{\$10,000}{\$472,000 - \$52,000} \times \$62,500$ $1,488 → $1,488

(ii) Foreign business income:

least of:

(I) tax paid $9,800

(II) $\frac{\text{income from Turkey}}{\text{income less dividends}}$ × tax otherwise payable (C)

= $28,000 / ($472,000 – $52,000)	× $100,000	$6,667	→	$6,667
(III) tax otherwise payable (C) less non-business income tax deduction ($100,000 – ($2,976 + 1,488))		$95,536		

(4) Total foreign tax credit:

ITA: 126(2) Idem

Foreign non-business income		
U.S. source	$2,976	
British source	1,488	$ 4,464
Foreign business income		6,667
Total credit		$11,131

NOTES TO SOLUTION

(1) If the Canadian income tax effects on foreign investment income could be isolated, as in the case where the corporation's only source of income was foreign non-business income (other than from real property), such as interest income, it would be considered to be earned in the province of which the taxpayer is a resident and, therefore, would be eligible for the federal tax abatement. As a result, it is the tax otherwise payable (B) after the abatement on which the non-business income tax deduction is based. On the other hand, foreign business income is assumed to be earned in a permanent establishment in the foreign country and, therefore, is not eligible for the federal tax abatement. Thus, the tax otherwise payable (C) before the abatement is the relevant base for the business income tax credit.

(2) Note how these credits against Canadian tax do not exceed foreign tax paid on the foreign income. These reductions of Canadian tax are also restricted to the estimated amount of Canadian tax paid on the foreign income.

¶11,340 Investment Tax Credits

¶11,345 Overview

¶11,345.10 Purpose

The investment tax credit (ITC) was introduced as an incentive to stimulate new investment in Canada in certain specific business sectors and regional locations. Certain credits apply regionally only to the Gaspé and the Atlantic provinces for certain specific capital expenditures. Three credits apply to all of Canada:

- scientific research and experimental development (SR&ED) expenditures,
- apprenticeship job creation tax credit, and
- child care spaces tax credit.

Conceptually, the available investment tax credit is simply calculated by applying a "specified percentage" or other limit for one of the categories described above to the capital cost of the asset acquired or the expenditure incurred. The actual amount of the ITC claimed by the taxpayer is deducted in the following taxation year from the capital cost of the asset acquired or the SR&ED pool. In addition, there is a carryover mechanism for available investment tax credits not claimed in a particular year.

The purpose of this section is to introduce, conceptually, the ramifications of this important tax credit and to provide some simple examples of its application.

¶11,345.20 Computation of Investment Tax Credit

One provision defines the basis for the computation of the available investment tax credit. It sets out the category of the asset or expenditure that is eligible for a credit, the "specified percentage" or the expenditure limit applicable to that category and the carryover rules.

ITA: 127(9) Idem

The cost of the capital asset to which the "specified percentage" is applied must be reduced by all government assistance (e.g., grants, subsidies, loans, etc.) and non-arm's length third-party assistance including certain specified contract payments for goods and services.

ITA: 127(11.6) Non-arm's length costs, 127(11.7) Definitions, 127(11.8) Interpretation for non-arm's length costs, 127(16) Non-arm's length parties, 127(17) Assessment, 127(18) Reduction of qualified expenditures, 127(19) Reduction of qualified expenditures, 127(20) Agreement to allocate, 127(21) Failure to allocate

The amount of the *available* investment tax credit which can be applied in a year is limited only by the Part I tax remaining after the deduction of any of the other corporate tax credits. Those available ITCs that are not applied in the year of acquisition or expenditure can be carried back three taxation years and forward 20 taxation years. Because of the generous carryforward time-frame, it is reasonable that ITCs should be deducted last.

Exhibit 11-5 lists the investment tax credit rates which apply to the most common types of properties and expenditures, incurred by taxpayers other than Canadian-controlled private corporations (which are discussed in Chapter 12), which give rise to such credits. The specified percentages listed in the Exhibit vary, depending on the geographic location and nature of the property or expenditure.

All of the terms describing property will be discussed in more detail following the Exhibit.

Exhibit 11-5 General Rates of Investment Tax Credits (Other Than CCPCs)[1] [ssec. 127(9)]

	Atlantic provinces and Gaspé	Balance of Canada
Qualified property	10%	0%
Qualified SR&ED[2]	15	15
Apprenticeship expenditure[3]	10	10
Child care spaces[4]	25	25

[1] Rates applicable to Canadian-controlled private corporations are discussed in Chapter 12.

[2] SR&ED refers to scientific research and experimental development as discussed in Chapter 4.

[3] Limited to $2,000 per eligible apprentice.

[4] Limited to $10,000 per eligible space.

Ⓐ ¶11,355 Qualified Scientific Research Expenditure

According to the CPA Knowledge Supplement, the topic of scientific research and experimental development credits is generally viewed as an advanced topic to be covered in detail in the *elective* stage. Therefore, our advanced symbol (Ⓐ) in this section identifies material within this subject that is more complex and non-routine in nature.

¶11,355.05 Scientific Research and Experimental Development Expenses

Overview of Expense Deduction

Expenses incurred by a business for the purpose of scientific research and experimental development (SR&ED) receive special treatment within the Act as they may not only generate a deductible expense that can be deducted in the year of the taxpayer's choosing but also a tax credit from the same expenditure. The specific details of scientific research and experimental development expenditures is discussed in this section.

Meaning of Scientific Research and Experimental Development

"Scientific research and experimental development" (SR&ED) is defined to mean the "systematic investigation or search carried out in a field of science or technology by means of experiment or analysis ...", including basic research, applied research, and experimental development. ITA: 248(1) Definitions

Activities which result in deductible expenditures in support of the three types of research include engineering or design, operations research, mathematical analysis or computer programming, data collection, testing, and psychological research.

However, activities which do not result in a deductible expenditure include market research or sales promotion, quality control or routine testing, social sciences or humanities research, natural resource exploration, commercial development of material, products or processes, and style changes or routine data collection. The CRA has issued an Information Circular and an Interpretation Bulletin that offer some guidelines in the area.

Interpretation Bulletins: IT-151R5 Scientific Research and Experimental Development Expenditures

The term "scientific research and experimental development" recognizes that the bulk of industrial scientific research is concentrated on the experimental development of new products or processes rather than pure or applied research. The inclusion of the words "experimental development" confirms that research does not include projects involving only routine engineering or routine development.

General Deduction of Expenditures

Generally, research and development expenditures of a current (i.e., non-capital) nature made in a year are fully deductible. However, any allowable expenditures that are not deducted in a year are placed in a pool and may be deducted in any future year in which the taxpayer carries on business in Canada.

This "pool" is made up of current SR&ED expenditures, less any investment tax credit (ITC) deducted from tax that is related to these expenditures. Each year, the company can determine how much, if any, of this pool is deducted from income for tax purposes. This is especially useful for companies that have heavy research expenditures and little income, since it allows them to defer the expense into a future period when there is income to deduct it against.

ITA: 37(1) Scientific research and experimental development

Certain scientific research and experimental development expenditures made in the year can be deducted from income of a business carried on in Canada. The following is a list of expenditures of a current (i.e., non-capital) nature that are deductible:

ITA: 37(1)(a)

(1) expenditures on scientific research and experimental development related to the business and directly undertaken by or on behalf of the taxpayer;

(2) expenditures to an approved association that undertakes scientific research and experimental development related to the class of business of the taxpayer;

(3) expenditures to an approved university, college, research institute or other similar institution to be used for scientific research and experimental development related to the class of business of the taxpayer;

(4) expenditures for scientific research and experimental development in Canada to non-profit corporations resident in Canada; or

(5) expenditures to a corporation resident in Canada for scientific research and experimental development in Canada related to the business of the taxpayer.

To qualify as SR&ED, expenditures must be related to a business carried on by the person making the expenditure. As indicated, SR&ED expenditures are added to a pool of such costs. They are eligible for a 100% deduction in the year incurred or may be carried forward indefinitely.

ITA: 37(1)(a), 37(1)(b)

As a further incentive to invest in SR&ED activity, the Act provides for an investment tax credit (ITC, discussed in Chapter 12) that is a direct reduction of the taxpayer's tax liability. The investment tax credit is calculated as a specified percentage of the SR&ED expenditures made. Since an investment tax credit in respect of SR&ED lowers the cost of the research and development activity, the amount of the investment tax credit reduces the amount of the pool available for deduction in the year following the year of the investment tax credit claim. If there is no balance in the pool in that year, because all amounts were previously deducted and no new expenditures were made in the current year, then the investment tax credit is included in income. The investment tax credit reduction of the balance in the pool reduces the future deduction and has the same effect as the income inclusion. The effect of this adjustment for the investment tax credit is to permit a deduction of the net cost of the expenditure after the partial recovery of cost through the investment tax credit. This effect can be illustrated with the following two options:

ITA: 12(1)(v) Research and development deductions, 37(1)(e), 127(9) Idem

	Fully deducted	Pooled
Expenditure in year 1	$1,000	$1,000
Deducted in year 1	(1,000)	Nil
Available for future deduction	Nil	$1,000
ITC @ 15% of $1,000 claimed in year 1:		
Income inclusion in year 2	$150	
Reduction of pool in year 2		(150)
Available for future deduction		$850
Net deduction:		
Deduction in year 1 net of inclusion in year 2 (i.e., net deduction over 2 years)	$850	
Available for future deduction		$850
Net cost:		
Initial expenditure	$1,000	$1,000
ITC claimed in year 1	(150)	(150)
Tax saving at, say 20%:		
year 1 — $1,000 × 0.20	(200)	
later years — $1,000 × 0.20		(200)
Tax cost: year 2 ($350 × 0.20)	70	70
Net cost	$720	$720

Only certain expenditures of a current (i.e., non-capital) nature made for scientific research and experimental development carried on outside Canada may be deducted and only in the year that they are incurred. They are not pooled.

ITR: 2900(3) [Expenditures directly attributable to premises, facilities and equipment]

Current expenditures that are "directly attributable" to scientific research also qualify. This allows for the prorating of the direct costs of personnel who, while not solely involved with research, do directly perform scientific research part of the time, support scientific research personnel or directly supervise researchers.

Election Method to Determine Deduction

An election is available as an alternative method for determining which expenditures incurred in Canada will qualify as SR&ED, to be included in the pool. This alternative method, which must be elected in prescribed form each year, is generally simpler for the taxpayer. If the election is used, the Act specifically lists three types of expenditures that will be considered to be for SR&ED carried on in Canada and, therefore, will be included in the taxpayer's SR&ED pool under subsection 37(1).

This elective method for determining SR&ED expenditures does not account for general overhead expenditures, even if they are directly attributable to the prosecution or the provision of premises for the prosecution of SR&ED in Canada. Such overhead expenditures are treated, under the elective method, as ordinary expenses which are, generally, deductible in the year incurred or eligible for capital cost allowance. However, general overhead expenses are recognized in the method of calculating the investment tax credit discussed in Chapter 12.

¶11,355.10 Overview of the SR&ED Investment Tax Credit

Scientific research and experimental development expenditures are very generously treated by Canadian tax legislation. Not only is there a potential 100% write-off of qualifying expenditures, but there is also a 15% investment tax credit available. In addition, many of the provincial governments provide additional incentives for SR&ED expenditures. In the next chapter it will be shown that certain qualifying Canadian-controlled private corporations benefit from an even greater "specified percentage" and a potential refund for unclaimed ITCs.

ITA: 37 Scientific research and experimental development

¶11,355.20 Qualified SR&ED Expenditure

"Qualified expenditure" is defined to include scientific research and experimental development expenditures on new property and described in the Act as current expenditures. Capital expenditures are not included.

ITA: 127(9) Idem, 37(1)(a), 37(8)(d); ITR: 2902 Prescribed Expenditures, 2903 Special-Purpose Buildings

¶11,355.30 Application

In the taxation year following the year in which an ITC deduction is made, the amount of the ITC claimed is deducted from the pool of unclaimed SR&ED expenditures. Remember that current expenditures that are eligible SR&ED expenditures are either written off, i.e., deducted, in the year of the expenditure or placed in a pool of unclaimed expenditures.

ITA: 12(1)(t) Investment tax credit

Example Problem 11-10

In 2017, Developit Limited incurred $100,000 of qualified scientific research and experimental development expenditures eligible for the 15% investment tax credit. The corporation's federal income tax rate after the abatement and the general rate reduction is 15%. Its taxable income before the deduction of the SR&ED expenditures under section 37 is $150,000.

The corporation is not eligible for any other tax credits and paid no tax in the preceding three years.

REQUIRED

(1) What is the maximum investment tax credit available?

(2) Compute the net federal Part I tax payable after the investment tax credit.

(3) What is the amount, if any, of the investment tax credit carryover?

(4) Compute the corporation's deduction or income included in the following year if no further SR&ED expenditures are made.

SOLUTION

(A) The maximum investment tax credit is: 15% of $100,000 = $15,000

(B)	Taxable income before sec. 37 deduction.	$150,000
	Sec. 37 deduction	(100,000)
	Taxable income	$ 50,000
	Net tax @ 15%	$ 7,500
	Investment tax credit (maximum)	(7,500)
	Net federal tax payable under Part I	Nil

(C) The remaining investment tax credit of $7,500 (i.e., $15,000 – $7,500) may be carried back three years and forward 20 years. In this particular case, the corporation paid no tax in the preceding three years, so it must carry the balance of ITC forward.

(D)	Sec. 37 SR&ED expenditures in 2018	$100,000
	Sec. 37 SR&ED deduction in 2018	(100,000)
	Balance in the pool at the beginning of 2019	Nil
	Income in 2019 based on ITC claimed in 2018	7,500
	Income effect in 2019	$ 7,500

ITA: 12(1)(t) Investment tax credit

When the remaining ITC of $7,500 is claimed in a carryforward year, the amount claimed must be brought into income, as recapture, in the year following the year of claim.

Had there been a balance of the $100,000 that was not deducted under section 37, the balance would form a pool of SR&ED expenditures that could be deducted in a future year. Where a balance in the SR&ED pool exists, the amount claimed as ITC in a year is deducted from the balance in the SR&ED pool in the following year.

The following diagram shows the process of handling the SR&ED expenditures and ITC in this example problem.

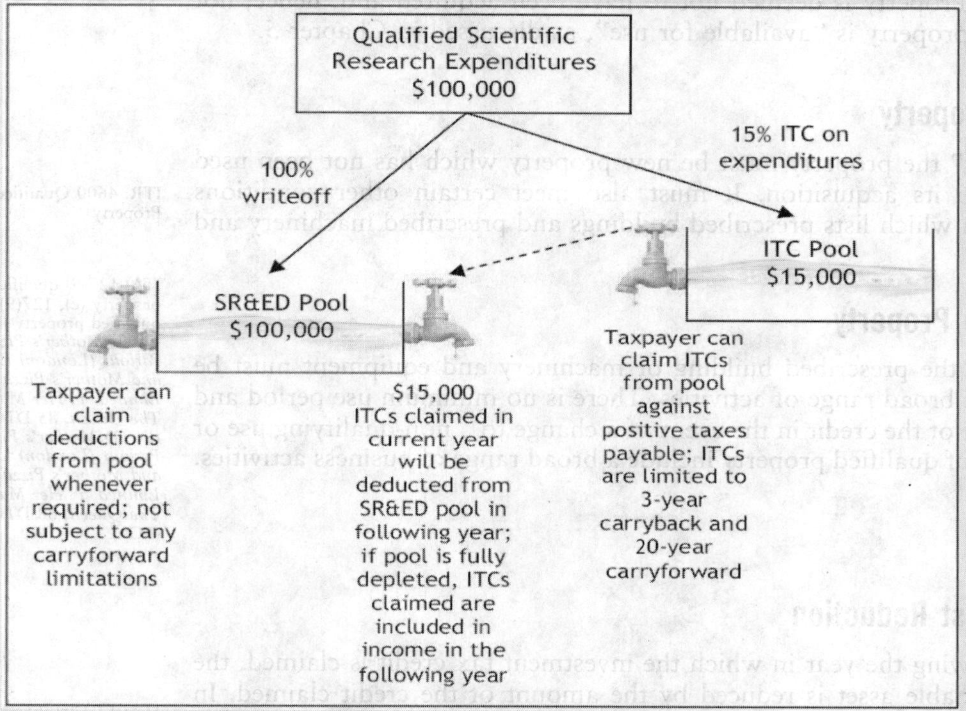

¶11,355.40 Prescribed Proxy Amount

Where business overhead expenses can be allocated to scientific research and experimental development costs, such overhead expenses will be included in the base on which the 15% investment tax credit for SR&ED expenditures is calculated. In a situation where a business is unable to allocate overhead expenses to SR&ED, the investment tax credit base would be relatively lower, resulting in a lower investment tax credit. As an alternative to allocating overhead expenses, for the purposes of computing the investment tax credit, use of a prescribed proxy amount (PPA) is permitted. The PPA is computed by a formula, provided in the Regulations, which is based on salaries paid to employees directly engaged in SR&ED in Canada. Use of the PPA method to account for overhead expenses in the calculation of the SR&ED investment tax credit must be elected annually. A more elaborate discussion of the PPA method and an example in which the calculation is demonstrated is presented in Chapter 12, where the application of the SR&ED investment tax credit to Canadian-controlled private corporations is discussed. However, it should be recognized that the PPA election is available to all taxpayers eligible for a SR&ED investment tax credit.

¶11,360 Qualified Property

¶11,360.10 Time of Acquisition

"Qualified property" is property that is a prescribed building, grain elevator or machinery and equipment. Generally, a taxpayer is considered to have acquired depreciable property when title passes or when the taxpayer obtains all the incidents of title including possession, use and risk. Property is deemed not to have been acquired and, hence, not eligible for ITC until the property is "available for use", as discussed in Chapter 5.

ITA: 127(9) Idem, 127(11.2) Time of acquisition; ITR: 4600 Qualified Property

¶11,360.20 Type of Property

To be "qualified property" the property must be new property which has not been used for any purpose prior to its acquisition. It must also meet certain other conditions prescribed by a regulation which lists prescribed buildings and prescribed machinery and equipment.

ITR: 4600 Qualified Property

¶11,360.30 Use of the Property

To qualify for the credit, the prescribed building or machinery and equipment must be used primarily in one of a broad range of activities. There is no minimum use period and no provision for recapture of the credit in the event of a change to a non-qualifying use or the sale of the asset. Uses of qualified property include a broad range of business activities.

ITA: 127(9) qualified property (c), 127(9) qualified property (d); Cases: *Mother's Pizza Parlour (London) Limited and Mother's Pizza Parlour Limited v. Her Majesty The Queen*, 85 DTC 5271 (FCTD)*Mother's Pizza Parlour (London) Limited and Mother's Pizza Parlour Limited v. Her Majesty The Queen*, 88 DTC 6397 (FCA)

¶11,360.40 Capital Cost Reduction

In the taxation year following the year in which the investment tax credit is claimed, the capital cost of the depreciable asset is reduced by the amount of the credit claimed. In situations where the asset no longer exists (i.e., the property has been disposed of), there would be an income inclusion as a substitute for the capital cost reduction of the capital asset.

ITA: 12(1)(t) Investment tax credit, 13(7.1)(e)

Example Problem 11-11

In 2018, Investit Limited has acquired $100,000 of Class 8 (20%) assets eligible as "qualified property" for the 10% investment tax credit in the Gaspé area. The corporation's federal income tax rate after the abatement and the general rate reduction is 15%. Its taxable income before capital cost allowance on the eligible property is $30,000.

The corporation is not eligible for any other tax credits and paid no tax in the preceding three years.

REQUIRED

(1) What is the maximum investment tax credit available?

(2) Compute the net federal Part I tax payable after the investment tax credit.

(3) What is the amount of the investment tax credit available for carry-over?

(4) Compute the UCC balance in Class 8 at the end of the following year, assuming the new assets are the only assets in the class.

SOLUTION

(A)	The maximum investment tax credit available will be $10,000 (i.e., 10% of $100,000)	
(B)	Taxable income before capital cost allowance on qualified property	$30,000
	Less: capital cost allowance on qualified property: ½ × 20% of $100,000	(10,000)
	Taxable income	$20,000
	Net federal tax @ 15%	$ 3,000
	Less: investment tax credit	(3,000)
	Net federal tax payable under Part I	Nil
(C)	The remaining investment tax credit of $7,000 (i.e., $10,000 – $3,000) may be carried back three and forward 20 years	
(D)	UCC in Class 8 before CCA in first year	$100,000
	Less: CCA claimed in first year	(10,000)
	UCC at beginning of second year	$ 90,000
	Less: ITC claimed in first year	(3,000)
	UCC before CCA in second year	$ 87,000
	Less: CCA claimed in second year @ 20%	(17,400)
	UCC balance after CCA	$ 69,600

Note that any investment tax credit for depreciable property carried over to another year and used to reduce tax in that year will reduce the undepreciated capital cost balance in the year following the year of use or the year following the purchase, whichever is later. This will occur until the remaining investment tax credit is fully utilized or expires. The undepreciated capital cost balance will not be reduced by expired investment tax credits. Under certain conditions, it may be worthwhile to deduct no capital cost allowance in order to be able to claim more investment tax credit that would otherwise expire. However, the facts of each case must be analyzed carefully.

¶11,360.99 Practise What You've Learned

Refer to the following sections of the Study Guide to practise what you've learned:

¶11,800 — Review Questions

- Question 6 — Objective of tax provisions
- Question 7 — Permanent establishments
- Question 8 — Foreign tax credit
- Question 9 — Non-business foreign tax credit
- Question 10 — Foreign tax credit

¶11,825 — Multiple Choice Questions

- Question 6 — Calculate federal tax payable

¶11,850 — Exercises

- Exercise 9 — Business foreign tax credit
- Exercise 10 — Calculate Part I tax — various sources of income
- Exercise 11 — Investment tax credit
- Exercise 13 — Federal abatement & permanent establishment

CHAPTER 12

Integration for Business and Investment Income of the Private Corporation

ADVANCED CONTENT IN THIS CHAPTER

Learning Goals

Know

By the end of this chapter you will know:

- How the tax system works to integrate the tax on individual shareholders with the tax on private corporations for business and investment income.

Understand and Explain

By the end of this chapter you will understand and be able to explain:

- How the small business deduction helps to achieve the integration of business income.
- The rules for associated corporations.
- The investment tax credit for scientific research and experimental development.
- How investment income is taxed in a private corporation.

Apply

By the end of this chapter you will be able to apply your knowledge and understanding to:

- Determine if corporations are associated.
- Compute the small business deduction.
- Calculate the investment tax credit.
- Compute tax payable and refundable tax on investment income in a private corporation.
- Assess whether various types of income should be incorporated.

Review Questions

¶12,800 in the Study Guide

Multiple Choice Questions

¶12,825 in the Study Guide

Exercises

¶12,850 in the Study Guide

Assignment Problems

¶12,875 in the Study Guide

Overview

This chapter deals with the provisions of the Act which attempt to integrate the taxation of private corporations with the taxation of the shareholders of those corporations. Following an introduction to the concept of integration, this chapter will consider both the integration of business income and investment income. While the word "integration" is not used in the Act, a series of provisions attempts to implement a system of integration which is designed to achieve certain objectives.

One of the most important reductions of tax available to corporations is the small business deduction which applies to Canadian-controlled private corporations as defined in the Act. This chapter will discuss the rules for computing the small business deduction. It will also deal with the rules for computing the additional investment tax credit where a corporation is eligible for the small business deduction. Then the chapter considers the integration of investment income, including the refundable tax system. This chapter

ITA: 125(7) Definitions

presents the remaining rules that must be followed to make a complete calculation of the tax payable by a corporation.

The following chart will help to position in the Act some of the major provisions dealt with in this chapter.

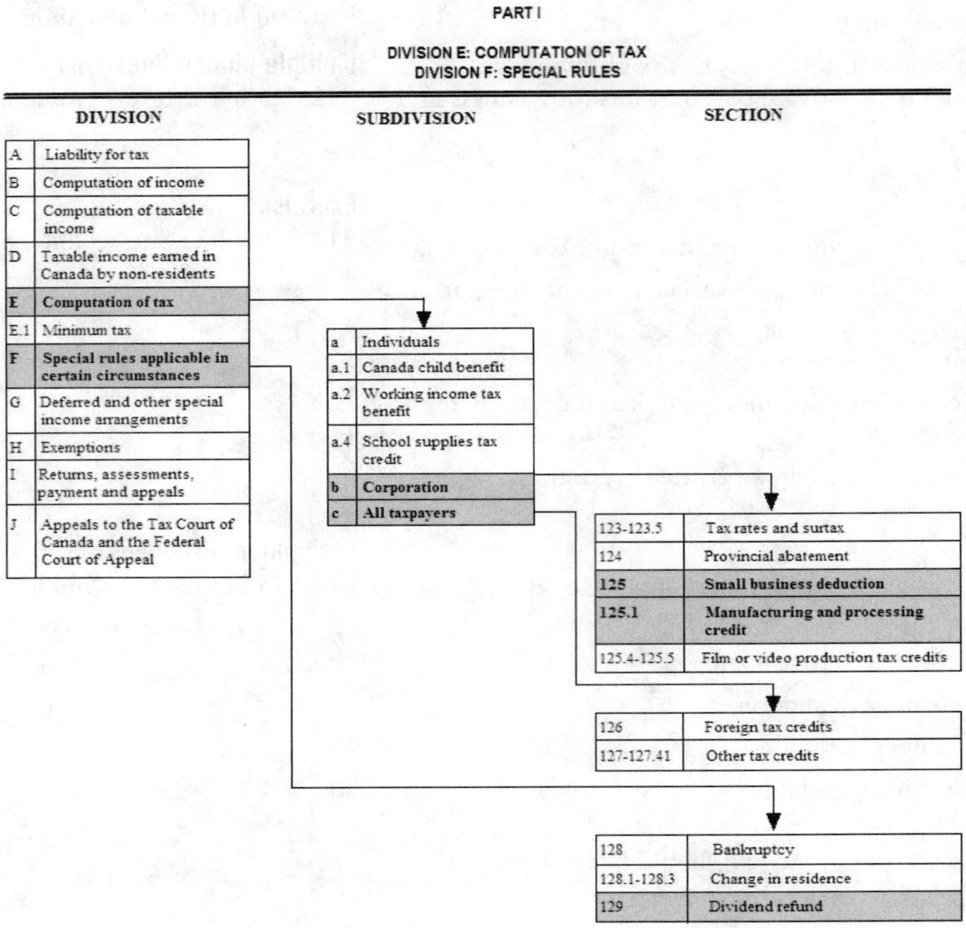
PART I
DIVISION E: COMPUTATION OF TAX
DIVISION F: SPECIAL RULES
DIVISION
SUBDIVISION
SECTION
A Liability for tax
B Computation of income
C Computation of taxable income
D Taxable income earned in Canada by non-residents
E Computation of tax
E.1 Minimum tax
F Special rules applicable in certain circumstances
G Deferred and other special income arrangements
H Exemptions
I Returns, assessments, payment and appeals
J Appeals to the Tax Court of Canada and the Federal Court of Appeal
a Individuals
a.1 Canada child benefit
a.2 Working income tax benefit
a.4 School supplies tax credit
b Corporation
c All taxpayers
123-123.5 Tax rates and surtax
124 Provincial abatement
125 Small business deduction
125.1 Manufacturing and processing credit
125.4-125.5 Film or video production tax credits
126 Foreign tax credits
127-127.41 Other tax credits
128 Bankruptcy
128.1-128.3 Change in residence
129 Dividend refund

¶12,000 The Concept of Integration

¶12,005 Changes to Integration

In December 2015 when the government introduced its 4 percentage point increase in the top personal marginal tax rate it also introduced a number of changes to the corporate tax rates for Canadian private corporations in order to preserve integration. The concept of integration will be discussed in detail in this chapter.

In addition, previously announced changes to the small business deduction and the dividend gross-up and tax credit for non-eligible dividends came into effect in 2016 and remained unchanged in 2017. For 2018, the small business deduction is 18%, while the dividend gross-up and tax credit federally for non-eligible dividends has changed to 16% and 8/11 respectively. The provincial dividend tax credit will vary from province to province.

The following are the changes to the tax rates that apply starting in 2016.

		Starting in	
	Pre 2016	2016/2017	2018
	%	%	%
Private Corporations			
Additional refundable tax	6.67	10.67	10.67
Part IV tax	33.33	38.33	38.33
Refundable Part I tax	26.67	30.67	30.67
Dividend refund rate	33.33	38.33	38.33
Canadian-Controlled Private Corporations			
Small business deduction rate	17	17.5	18
Non-Eligible Dividends			
Gross-up	18	17	16
Dividend tax credit			
Federal	13/18	21/29	8/11
Provincial (assumed)	5/18	8/29	3/11

The dividend gross up and dividend tax credit on eligible dividends are not impacted.

¶12,010 Issues Addressed by Integration

From a legal perspective, a corporation is an entity separate from its shareholders. In economics, however, there is no more separation between a corporation and its shareholders than between a proprietorship and its proprietor, a partnership and its partners or an investment portfolio and its owner.

As a taxpayer, a corporation is a person which is taxed separately from the natural persons (individuals) who are its shareholders. Hence, this could give rise to double taxation, with the same income being taxed, first, at the corporate level and then, again, at the individual shareholder level. Conceptually, a corporation should really be treated as a non-taxable conduit through which income flows to the individual shareholders, in the same way that a proprietorship business or a partnership business is a conduit through which income flows to the individual proprietor or partners. However, as subsequent comments in this chapter will illustrate, if only individuals and not corporations are subject to tax, problems of an economic or political nature may arise.

¶12,020 Objectives of Integration

Ideally, integration should cause the total tax paid by a corporation and its shareholders to be equal to the total tax paid by an individual who carries on the same economic activity directly and not through the corporation. By integrating the corporate and personal tax systems, the double taxation of corporate income can be avoided. This would make the tax system neutral with respect to the form of organization, used to carry on an economic activity, because there would be no tax advantage or disadvantage to one form of organization over another. Integration would also make the system equitable by ensuring that the tax imposed on income passed through a corporation to an individual is equal in amount to the tax that is imposed on the same amount and type of income earned directly by an individual. Stated differently, the total tax levied on the corporation and the individual in the former situation should be equal in amount to the tax imposed on the individual in the latter situation.

Perfect integration depends on the existence of two assumptions in the tax system. First, where the corporation itself pays tax, the shareholder should include in income and pay taxes on the full pre-tax income earned by the corporation and then receive a full credit for all of the income tax paid by the corporation. To the extent that the shareholder's tax on this income is less than the corporation's tax paid on behalf of the shareholder, the shareholder should get a refund of the difference. This approximates the approach that is taken for employment income. Salaries or wages are subject to withholding, but the employee gets full credit for all taxes withheld. If taxes withheld exceed taxes payable for the year, a refund is due.

The second assumption is that all after-tax income of the corporation should be either paid out as dividends in the year earned or taxed at the shareholder level in that year to avoid the indefinite deferral of tax. This potential deferral would occur if corporate tax rates were lower than individual tax rates. This assumption equates the position of the shareholder with the position of the proprietor, partner or owner of investments who must pay tax on income from his or her economic activity whether or not it is distributed. It is important to understand that the payment of the dividend to the shareholder may be delayed indefinitely providing the shareholder does not have a need for the after-tax cash in the corporation. Chapter 13 discusses different methods for an owner-manager to withdraw funds from the corporation and the tax implications of each method.

¶12,030 The Major Tool for Integration in the *Income Tax Act*

¶12,035 The Concept of Integration

The mainstay of the integration system as it applies to individual shareholders of all taxable Canadian corporations is the gross-up and tax credit procedure which is illustrated in Exhibit 12-1. The gross-up is intended to add to the dividend received by the individual shareholder an amount equal to the total income tax (including provincial tax) paid by the corporation on the income that gave rise to the dividend. Thus, the grossed-up dividend is intended to represent the corporation's pre-tax income. The shareholder will pay tax on the grossed-up dividend at his or her personal rate. The combined federal and provincial tax credit is intended to give the shareholder credit for the total tax paid by the corporation on the shareholder's behalf. This procedure is intended to equalize the tax paid on the income that is flowed through the corporation to its shareholders, with the tax paid on the same income that is earned directly. The potential double taxation of corporate income is thereby avoided.

Exhibit 12-1 Theoretical Taxation of Dividends to Individuals That Demonstrates Perfect Integration

Facts: An individual can earn $1,000 of active business income either personally or in a corporation. The personal tax rate is 50% and the corporate tax rate is either 13.8% or 27.5%.

Calculate

(1) A = the personal after-tax cash available, if the income is earned by an individual

		Personal
Combined federal and provincial tax rate		50%
Active business income		$1,000
Personal tax		$500
After-tax cash — personal	**A**	$ 500

(2) B = the corporate after-tax cash available for payment of a dividend, if the income is earned in a corporation owned by the individual

Corporate tax rate	**13.8%**	**27.5%** [1]
Corporate income	$1,000	$1,000
Corporate tax, including provincial tax (theoretical rate, i.e., 13.8% and 27.5%)	138	275
After-tax income available for distribution as a dividend	$ 862	$ 725

[1] Possible imperfections in corporate tax rate, given a fixed gross-up and a theoretical total dividend tax credit of 38%.

(3) C = the personal after-tax cash available, if the corporation distributed its after-tax income as a dividend to the individual as the shareholder

Corporate tax rate	**13.8%**	**27.5%** [1]
Individual Shareholder		
Dividend	$ 862	$ 725
Gross-up (theoretically equal to corporate tax or 16% and 38% of the dividend)	138	275
Taxable income (theoretically equal to pre-tax corporate income)	$1,000	$1,000

Combined personal tax at 50% — federal and provincial	$ 500	$ 500
Less: Combined dividend tax credit	138	275
Combined personal tax paid on the dividend. **B**	$ 362	$ 225
After-tax cash available to the individual shareholder from the dividend **C**	$ 500	$ 500

To determine savings or cost, compare A to C

A = the personal after-tax cash available, if the income is earned personally, to

C = the corporate after-tax cash available, if the income earned in a corporation and, then, the after-tax corporate retained earnings are distributed as a dividend to the individual as a shareholder

If A = C, integration is perfect and there is no tax savings or cost of incorporation.

If C > A, then there is a tax savings from flowing the income through a corporation.

If C < A, then there is a tax cost from flowing the income through a corporation.

To determine deferral or prepayment, look at B

B = the personal tax paid on the dividend received from the corporation. This amount is deferred until the dividend is actually paid.

Another way to look at perfect integration is to examine tax rates paid by the individual and the corporation. If the income is earned directly by the individual, he or she will be taxed at the assumed marginal tax rate of 50%. Under perfect integration, the corporation and shareholder will pay 50% in total, if the income is earned through a corporation. Thus, theoretically, under perfect integration, the potential deferral of shareholder tax is simply the difference between the corporate and individual rate as shown below:

Individual tax rate	50%	50%
Corporate tax rate	13.8%	27.5%
Shareholder net tax rate (potential deferral)	36.2%	22.5%

¶12,040 Dividends From GRIP and LRIP

General Rate Income Pool (GRIP)

The general rate income pool represents income taxed at the high corporate rate. It is assumed that all income earned by public corporations is part of this pool. Canadian-controlled private corporations are generally assumed to earn low-rate income so they only need to specifically keep track of any GRIP they earn. GRIP would include active business income on which the corporation did not get the small business deduction and eligible dividends received from the GRIP of other corporations.

ITA: 89(1) Definitions; 82(1) Taxable dividends received

Dividends paid from GRIP are "eligible dividends" subject to the 38% gross-up and dividend tax credit for individual recipients.

Simplified GRIP Formula for CCPCs

GRIP balance at the end of the previous year

+ After-tax taxable income excluding both income eligible for the small business deduction and aggregate investment income

+ Eligible (high-rate) Canadian dividends received

- Eligible dividends paid

The after-tax taxable income mentioned above is calculated as follows:

72% × (taxable income – small business deduction × 100/17 – lesser of aggregate investment income and taxable income)

Canadian-controlled private corporations can choose to designate that a dividend is paid out of either the GRIP or LRIP.

ITA: 89(14) Dividend designation

Low Rate Income Pool (LRIP)

The low rate income pool represents income taxed at the low corporate rate in Canadian-controlled private corporations. This income includes income eligible for the small business deduction, aggregate investment income eligible for refundable Part I tax and dividends received from the LRIP of other corporations.

ITA: 89(1) Definitions

Canadian public corporations are assumed to earn high-rate income so they only need to specifically keep track of any LRIP they earn.

Dividends paid from LRIP are non-eligible dividends subject to the 16% gross-up and dividend tax credit for individual recipients.

ITA: 82(1) Taxable dividends received

Simplified LRIP Formula for Canadian Public Corporations

LRIP balance at the end of the previous year

+ After-tax taxable income eligible for the small business deduction (normally this will be nil unless a CCPC became a public corporation)

+ Non-eligible (low-rate) Canadian dividends received

– Non-eligible dividends paid

However, public corporations need to pay dividends out of their LRIP balance before they can designate a dividend as an eligible (high-rate) dividend. If not, they will be subject to Part III.1 tax. Since it is rare for a public corporation to have a LRIP balance we will not discuss Part III.1 tax further.

¶12,040.10 Dividends From Low-Rate Business Income and Investment Income Earned by a Canadian-Controlled Private Corporation

Integration works for this type of income where the corporate tax rate is 13.8%. As shown in the 13.8% column of Exhibit 12-1, $1,000 of corporate income attracts tax of $138. The resulting $862 is paid as a dividend to an individual who then grosses this up by 16%, or $138, resulting in taxable income of $1,000, which is equal to the pre-tax corporate income. The individual then pays personal tax on the dividend at, for example, 50%, or $500, and receives a dividend tax credit equal to the underlying corporate tax of $138. The end result is that the corporation and individual together pay the same amount of tax ($500) as if the individual earned the income directly. This is an example of perfect integration.

¶12,040.20 Eligible Dividends From General-Rate Business Income

A different gross-up and tax credit for "eligible dividends" paid out of the general rate income pool (GRIP) applies. The 27.5% column of Exhibit 12-1, assumes an underlying corporate tax rate of 27.5%. Then, the gross-up is 38% to return the personal income to the pre-tax corporate level. Again, the dividend tax credit is equal to the underlying corporate tax and gross-up to result in the shareholder being indifferent between earning the $1,000 personally or through a corporation. The end result is that the corporation and individual together pay the same amount of tax ($500) as if the individual earned the income directly. Again, this is an example of perfect integration.

"Eligible dividends" are, generally, dividends paid by: ITA: 89(1) Definitions

(1) public corporations resident in Canada and subject to the general corporate tax rate, and

(2) CCPCs resident in Canada to the extent that their business income, but not investment income, is subject to tax at the general corporate tax rate; that is, business income on which the corporation does not get the small business deduction. For a CCPC this is added to its "general rate income pool" (GRIP). For example, if a CCPC has Canadian active business income of $600,000 then conceptually it will have $100,000 (less tax) in GRIP since the first $500,000 will receive the benefits of the small business deduction and the remaining $100,000 will be taxed at the general corporate tax rate. ITA: 89(1) Definitions

Under perfect integration, the corporate tax is like a withholding tax on the shareholder's income which the corporation earns on behalf of the shareholder. In a sense, it is similar to the withholding of tax on the salary or wages of an employee. Thus, the corporate tax prevents the tax on income earned by a corporation from being deferred until a dividend is paid and is then taxed in the hands of the shareholder. When the shareholder receives a dividend, the full pre-tax income earned by the corporation is reported by the shareholder, through the gross-up mechanism, just as an employee reports gross salary or wages. Then, tax is computed at the shareholder's personal rate. In the same way that taxes withheld from salary or wages are used to reduce the employee's final tax payable, so the dividend tax credit (representing the tax paid by the corporation) reduces the shareholder's tax payable on the dividend income.

¶12,045 Basis for the Calculation of the Dividend Tax Credit

A major assumption in Exhibit 12-1 is that the dividend tax credit for individuals is equal to the underlying corporate tax and the gross-up. Using the facts in Exhibit 12-1, this can be illustrated as follows:

ITA: 121 Deduction for taxable dividends

Total corporate tax rate	**13.8%**	**27.5%**
Dividend	**Non-eligible**	**Eligible**
Calculation based on gross-up (per ss. 82(1))		
Dividend gross-up from Exhibit 12-1	$ 138	$ 275
Federal dividend tax credit		
$^{8}/_{11}$ of the gross-up	$ 100	
$^{6}/_{11}$ of the gross-up		$ 150
Provincial dividend tax credit (theoretical)		
$^{3}/_{11}$ of the gross-up	38	
$^{5}/_{11}$ of the gross-up		125
	$ 138	$ 275

The federal dividend tax credit provides for the credit to be equal to $^{8}/_{11}$ of the gross-up on taxable dividends, other than eligible dividends, from a corporation resident in Canada, and $^{6}/_{11}$ of the gross-up on eligible dividends received.

ITA: 82(1)(b), 121 Deduction for taxable dividends

Dividends subject to the 16% gross-up are:

- dividends from the active business income of CCPCs that is eligible for the small business deduction
- dividends from the investment income of CCPCs

Dividends subject to the 38% gross-up are:

- dividends from the active business income of CCPCs that is **not** eligible for the small business deduction
- dividends from Canadian public companies, and other corporations that are not CCPCs, that are resident in Canada and subject to the general corporate income tax rate

Where the combined federal and provincial corporate rate of tax is anything other than 13.8% or 27.5%, the system of integration breaks down. The imperfections in the integration system will be considered in more detail in this chapter. The chapter will also consider some tools of integration that help to bring the corporate rate of tax close to the perfect 13.8% on the first $500,000 of active business income and on all of the investment income earned by a Canadian-controlled private corporation.

¶12,060 Taxation of Income in a CCPC — An Overview

Exhibit 12-2 Types and Tax Rates for CCPC Income

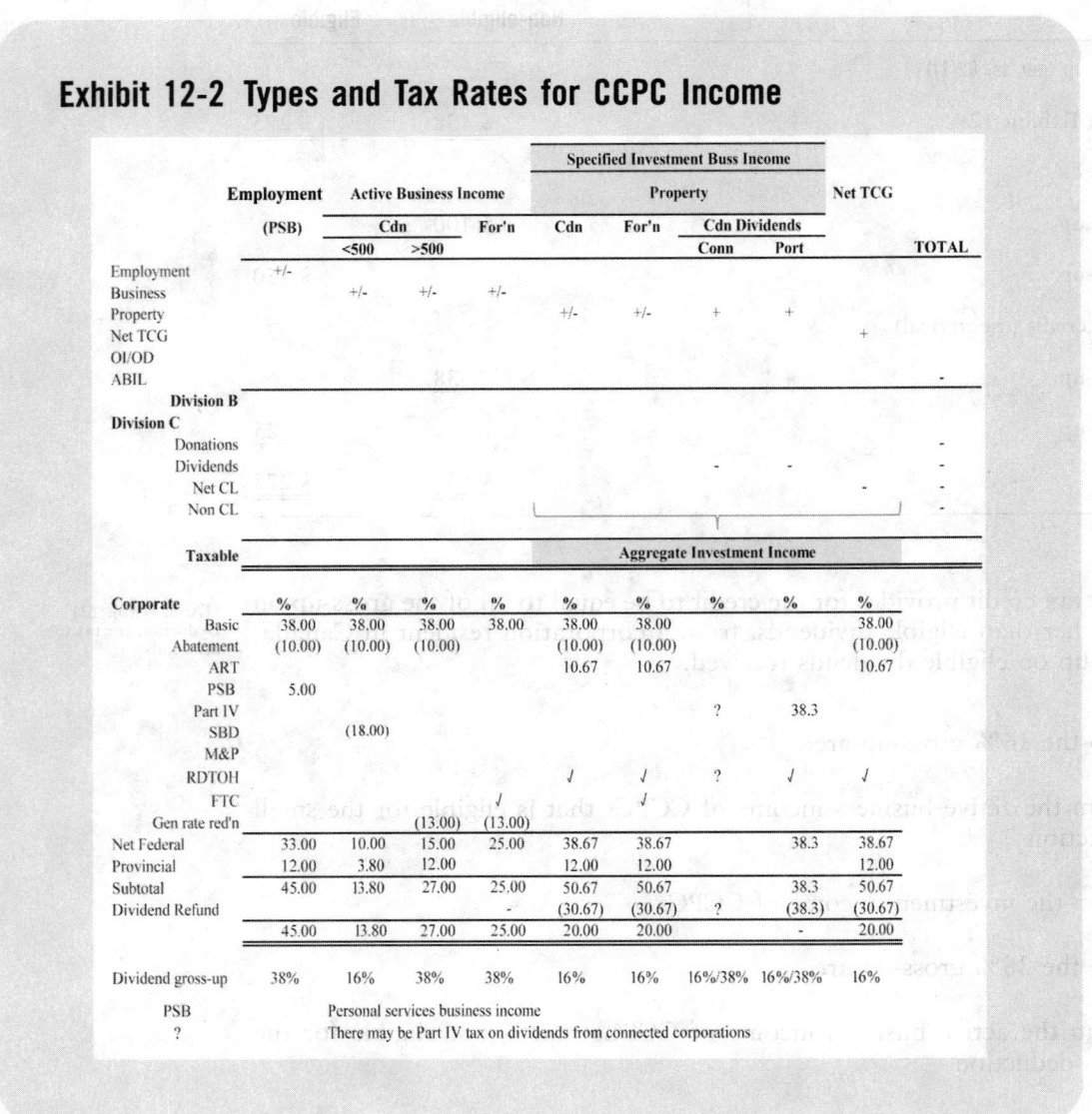

	Employment	Active Business Income			Specified Investment Buss Income — Property				Net TCG	
	(PSB)	Cdn		For'n	Cdn	For'n	Cdn Dividends			
		<500	>500				Conn	Port		TOTAL
Employment	+/-									
Business		+/-	+/-	+/-						
Property					+/-	+/-	+	+		
Net TCG									+	
OI/OD										
ABIL										-
Division B										
Division C										
Donations										-
Dividends							-	-		-
Net CL									-	-
Non CL										-
Taxable					Aggregate Investment Income					
Corporate	%	%	%	%	%	%	%	%	%	
Basic	38.00	38.00	38.00	38.00	38.00	38.00			38.00	
Abatement	(10.00)	(10.00)	(10.00)		(10.00)	(10.00)			(10.00)	
ART					10.67	10.67			10.67	
PSB	5.00									
Part IV							?	38.3		
SBD		(18.00)								
M&P										
RDTOH					√	√	?	√	√	
FTC				√		√				
Gen rate red'n			(13.00)	(13.00)						
Net Federal	33.00	10.00	15.00	25.00	38.67	38.67		38.3	38.67	
Provincial	12.00	3.80	12.00		12.00	12.00			12.00	
Subtotal	45.00	13.80	27.00	25.00	50.67	50.67		38.3	50.67	
Dividend Refund				-	(30.67)	(30.67)	?	(38.3)	(30.67)	
	45.00	13.80	27.00	25.00	20.00	20.00		-	20.00	
Dividend gross-up	38%	16%	38%	38%	16%	16%	16%/38%	16%/38%	16%	

PSB Personal services business income

? There may be Part IV tax on dividends from connected corporations

The above table identifies the various types of income that can be earned by a CCPC along with the tax treatment of each type and the dividend gross-up that applies to dividends paid out of these types of income.

For example, Canadian active business income eligible for the small business deduction has an effective federal tax rate of 10%. With an additional 3.8% of provincial tax the combined tax rate is 13.8%. Since this is low-rate income any dividend paid out of this type of income will be a non-eligible dividend with an 16% gross-up.

Contrasting this is active business income over $500,000 which does not receive the small business deduction but does receive the general rate reduction giving it a combined federal and provincial tax rate of 27.5%. Dividends paid out of this type of income come out of the general rate income pool (GRIP) and are eligible dividends with a gross-up of 38%.

Investment income will be discussed in detail later in this chapter.

¶12,100 Income From an Active Business of a CCPC

¶12,110 Introduction to the Small Business Deduction

The small business deduction represents a credit against the tax otherwise payable on income "from an active business carried on in Canada" and is designed only for small "Canadian-controlled private corporations" in order to assist them to retain capital to expand their businesses. Note, however, that the corporation does not have to be "small" in order to qualify for the credit.

Exhibit 12-3 illustrates the tax rates on the following types of income:

(1) Personal services business income (PSB)

(2) Canadian active business income eligible for the small business deduction

(3) Canadian active business income not eligible for the small business deduction

(4) Foreign active business income

Exhibit 12-3 Taxation of Income in a CCPC

	Employment (PSB)	Active Business Income Cdn <500	Active Business Income Cdn >500	Active Business Income For'n
Employment	+/-			
Business		+/-	+/-	+/-
Property				
Net TCG				
OI/OD				
ABIL				
Division B				
Division C				
Donations				
Dividends				
Net CL				
Non CL				
Taxable				
Corporate	**%**	**%**	**%**	**%**
Basic	38.00	38.00	38.00	38.00
Abatement	(10.00)	(10.00)	(10.00)	
ART				
PSB	5.00			
Part IV				
SBD		18.00		
M&P				
RDTOH				
FTC				✓
Gen rate red'n			(13.00)	(13.00)
Net Federal	33.00	10.00	15.00	25.00
Provincial	12.00	3.80	12.00	-
Subtotal	45.00	13.80	27.00	25.00
Dividend Refund				
	45.00	13.80	27.00	25.00
Dividend gross-up	38%	16%	38%	38%

PSB Personal services business income

Note that the effective total tax rate is the same as the 13.8% total corporate tax rate that results in perfect integration. Many provinces have a lower rate than the 3.8% used in the exhibit, making the effective total tax even lower. The significance of a total corporate rate under 13.8% will be discussed later in this chapter.

The hypothetical provincial tax rate of 3.8% used in Exhibits 12-2 and 12-3, above, reflects an average provincial equivalent of the federal small business deduction. Remember that in Chapter 11, Exhibit 11-4 used an assumed provincial rate of 13% because most provincial basic tax rates lie between 10% and 16%. Most provinces also give an equivalent small business tax credit, resulting in an effective provincial rate ranging from 0% to 8% on the first $500,000 of active business income.

The prime qualification that a corporation must meet to get the benefit of the small business deduction is that it be, throughout the taxation year, a "Canadian-controlled private corporation" (CCPC). A CCPC is "Canadian controlled" if it is not controlled by a non-resident. And, it is a private corporation if it is not controlled by a public corporation or its shares are not listed on a designated Canadian or foreign stock exchange.

ITA: 89(1) Definitions, 125(7) Definitions; Interpretation Bulletins: IT-458R2 Canadian-Controlled Private Corporation

¶12,120 Mechanics of Calculation of Small Business Deduction

¶12,125 The Basic Limits

¶12,125.10 Eligibility

A Canadian-controlled private corporation calculates its tax liability by first applying the standard corporate rate to its total taxable income. After this basic tax amount is determined, the corporation makes various deductions (e.g., M&P profits deduction, investment tax credit, etc.) to determine the final taxes payable. One such deduction is the small business deduction.

A corporation must be a Canadian-controlled private corporation *throughout* the year to qualify for the small business deduction which is a deduction from the tax otherwise payable. For such a corporation, the deduction is calculated by the following formula:

ITA: 125(1) Small business deduction

¶12,125.20 The Formula

Small business deduction = 18% of the least of:

ITA: 125(1) Small business deduction, 125(1.1) Small business deduction rate

(1) net Canadian active business income (i.e., income minus losses);

(2) taxable income fully taxed in Canada achieved by removing from the total taxable income, foreign-source income estimated as the sum of:

(a) foreign-source investment income, estimated as $^{100}/_{28}$ times the foreign tax credit on foreign non-business income, determined without reference to the additional refundable tax on investment income,

ITA: 126(1) Foreign tax deduction

(b) foreign-source business income, estimated as the relevant factor (i.e., 4)[1] times the foreign tax credit on foreign business income, and

ITA: 126(2) Idem, 248(1) definition of relevant factor

(c) taxable income exempt from Part I tax by reason of an enactment of Parliament; and

(3) the business limit, i.e., $500,000 *less* any portion allocated to associated corporations (to be discussed later in this chapter).

ITA: 125(2) Business limit, 125(3) Associated corporations

¶12,125.30 Interpretation of the Formula

Items (b)(i) and (ii) ensure that foreign income not taxed in Canada, because of a foreign tax credit, is removed from taxable income. This is necessary since Canada should not allow the small business deduction on income on which the corporation does not pay tax as a result of a foreign tax credit.

[1] The definition of "relevant factor" in subsection 248(1) provides a formula that results in a factor of 4 (i.e., 1/(.38 –.13). The .13 in the formula represents the general rate reduction.

Conceptually, the adjustment in item (b)(i), above, removes from taxable income an estimate of foreign investment income by multiplying by 100/28 the tax credit which is assumed to be 28% of the foreign investment income. The 28% rate is based on an assumed corporate rate of 38% reduced by the 10% federal abatement for income earned in a province or territory. Investment income is subject to that abatement, because it is thought to be earned in a province or territory where the corporation is established, as explained in the previous chapter in the discussion of the foreign tax credit calculation.

Conceptually, the adjustment in item (b)(ii), above, removes from taxable income an estimate of foreign business income by multiplying by 4 the tax credit which is assumed to be 25% of the foreign business income. The 25% rate is intended to approximate corporate income tax rates on this type of income, i.e., 38% – 13%.

Similarly, item (b)(iii) removes from the base for the small business deduction an amount that is not subject to tax. This removal follows from the concept that an amount that is not taxed in Canada should not be in the base for a tax credit which reduces taxes payable in Canada.

¶12,130 Elimination of Small Business Deduction for Large CCPCs

Large Canadian-controlled private corporations are not fully eligible for the small business deduction. The amount of the small business deduction is phased out or "clawed back" with a formula based on the amount of taxable capital employed in Canada for the preceding taxation year. The phase-out range is taxable capital employed in Canada between $10 and $15 million. The business limit of $500,000 for purposes of the small business deduction is reduced by $1 for every $10 (i.e., ($15,000,000 – $10,000,000) ÷ $500,000) of taxable capital employed in Canada in excess of $10 million.

ITA: 125(5.1) Business limit reduction

The above limitation also applies to a group of associated corporations. Therefore, the associated corporations' total taxable capital employed in Canada in excess of $10 million serves as the basis for the corporate group's business limit reduction.

"Taxable capital employed in Canada" is a term that is defined in the Act. The calculation of this amount is beyond the scope of this book, but in general terms it represents the capital of the corporation invested in its business. The basic calculation is the total of the share capital and borrowings of the corporation less amounts it has invested in shares or debt of other corporations.

ITA: 181.2 Taxable capital employed in Canada

As shown in the following example problem, an easy, but less technical way to obtain the statutory result is to multiply the business limit allocated to the corporation by the fraction where the numerator is the excess of taxable capital over $10 million and the denominator is $5 million, which is the range of taxable capital over which the clawback occurs.

Example Problem 12-1

Lennox Inc., a Canadian-controlled private corporation, has a fiscal year end of December 31. Little-Big Inc. is not associated with any other corporation and all of its income is earned in Canada. The following selected tax information has been provided for 2018:

Active business income	$ 350,000
Taxable income	500,000
Taxable capital employed in Canada in 2017	13,000,000

REQUIRED

Determine Little-Big Inc.'s small business deduction for the 2018 taxation year.

SOLUTION

Business limit:

Before reduction	$ 500,000
Reduction:	
$500,000 × ($13,000,000 – $10,000,000) / $5,000,000	
= $500,000 × $3,000,000 / 5,000,000	(300,000)
Business limit	$ 200,000

Small business deduction for 2018:

18% of least of:

(a) active business income	$350,000	
(b) taxable income	$500,000	
(c) business limit	$200,000	
Least amount		$ 200,000
18% of $200,000		$ 36,000

¶12,135 Elimination of the Small Business Deduction for CCPCs with Significant Income from Passive Investments

Effective for taxation years beginning after 2018, the February 27, 2018 Budget proposes to reduce the small business deduction limit for CCPCs (and their associated corporations) that have significant passive income. For CCPCs with passive investment income in excess of $50,000, the small business deduction will be reduced by $5 for every $1 of investment income over $50,000. Specifically, the small business deduction (SBD) limit will be reduced on a straight-line basis for CCPCs (with associated companies) having between $50,000 and $150,000 in investment income, and completely eliminated if passive investment income is greater than $150,000 (for the associated group).

For example, assume John is the sole shareholder of ACB Corporation, which earned active business income (ABI) of $500,000, along with $120,000 in passive investment income. ACB corporation pays tax at the following tax rates: ABI below the SBD limit is 13.8%, ABI above the SBD limit is 27%, and aggregate investment income is 50.67% (assuming a provincial rate of 12%). Under the old rules the ABC would pay $129,804[2] in tax. The ABI for the corporation is below the small business deduction limit and therefore will be subject to the lower income tax rates. Under the new rules, the small business deduction will be eroded which means a portion of the ABI earned by ABC corporation will be subject to the higher tax rate of 27%. The SBD would be reduced by $350,000.[3] Under the new proposed rules ABC corporation will pay tax equal to $176,004.[4] The proposed rules penalize the corporation for excess passive investment income.

Since all associated corporations must be considered in determining the SBD, excess passive investment income in a holding corporation would affect the SBD for an active corporation.

¶12,135.10 Business Limit Reduction

For taxation years beginning after 2018, the reduction of the corporation's business limit will be equal to the greater of:

(a) the reduction based on taxable capital, and

(b) the reduction based on aggregate investment income.

¶12,140 Definition of "Active Business"

¶12,145 The "Default" Definition

The definition of the term "active business" reads as follows: ITA: 125(7) Definitions

> "active business carried on by a corporation" means any business carried on by the corporation other than a specified investment business or a personal services business and includes an adventure or concern in the nature of trade.[5]

[2] [($500,000 × 13.8%) + (120,000 × 50.67%)].

[3] [(120,000 − 50,000) × $5].

[4] [($150,000 × 13.8%) + (350,000 × 27%) + (120,000 × 50.67%)].

[5] Note that this definition is used only for the purpose of section 125. A definition of "active business" can be found in subsection 248(1) which is to be used whenever the term is used elsewhere in the Act. The phrase, "an adventure or concern in the nature of trade", is not included in the definition of "active business" in subsection 248(1). However, the phrase is part of the definition of "business" in subsection 248(1).

Note how this definition is a "default" definition, since the income must be determined not to be from a specified investment business or a personal services business.

¶12,150 Specified Investment Business

As noted in the definition of active business income, all income from carrying on a business is considered to be active *other than* for a specified investment business or a personal services business. Consequently, income earned by a specified investment business (SIB) does not qualify for the small business deduction. The purpose of introducing the small business deduction (SBD) was to establish a special low rate of tax applicable to the income of a CCPC from an "active business carried on in Canada". The concept of specified investment business was introduced as the mechanism by which property income is excluded from enjoying the benefits of the small business deduction. This provision ensures that no incentive is provided for individuals who might incorporate in order to obtain lower tax rates by having income from property earned by a private corporation.

ITA: 125(7) Definitions

A "specified investment business" (SIB), which is excluded from that definition of "active business", is defined to mean:

ITA: 125(7) Definitions

- a business (other than the business of a credit union or of leasing property other than real property),
- the principal purpose of which is to derive income from property (including interest, dividends, rents, and royalties),
- *unless* the corporation employs in the business throughout the year *more than* five full-time employees.

In the decision of *489599 B.C. Ltd. v. The Queen*, the Tax Court of Canada, based on strong reasoning, concluded that five full-time and two part-time employees met the condition requiring more than five full-time employees. This conclusion was not appealed by the Crown. The CRA has announced that it will follow the decision in *489599 B.C. Ltd.*

Cases: *489599 B.C. Ltd. v. The Queen*, 2008 DTC 4107 (TCC)

In paragraph (*b*) of the definition "specified investment business", the Act goes on to allow an exception where a corporation would have employed more than five full-time employees but does not because another corporation associated with it provides the services that would otherwise have been performed by its own employees.

A specified investment business is restricted to a business which generates property income, including dividends, interest, rent (leasing), and royalties. Note that by virtue of the exception contained in the brackets in the definition, the business of leasing movable property (i.e., not real property) is an active business. The taxation of investment income, including income from a specified investment business, will be discussed later in the chapter.

Example Problem 12-2

Ava Ltd. owns an apartment building in downtown St. John's. The only employees of Ava are the two shareholders. Ava earns income from rents and has some interest income.

REQUIRED

(1) Is Ava a specified investment business?

(2) Would it matter if all the apartments were on leases and not month-to-month tenancies?

(3) What if Ava had seven full-time employees?

SOLUTION

(1) Yes, as Ava earns its income in the form of rents and does not have more than five full-time employees.

(2) No, that makes no difference, as the leasing income is from leasing real property.

(3) In that case, Ava would be eligible for the small business deduction. Whether the interest income would qualify for the SBD depends on whether the interest is from a "permanent" investment (no SBD) or is ancillary income (SBD applies). See ¶12,160 for a discussion of this concept.

¶12,155 Personal Services Business

A personal services business (PSB) is the second type of business income specified as ineligible for the small business deduction. A "personal services business" can be thought of as an incorporated employee. In such a situation, income from the personal services business does not qualify as ABI. In addition, deductions are limited (discussed below). A company that would otherwise constitute a PSB is exempt if it has more than five full-time employees or when the service is provided to, and the income is received from, an associated corporation.

ITA: 125(7) Definitions, 18(1)(p) Limitation re personal services business expenses

A "personal services business" (PSB) is also excluded from the definition of the term "active business". A "personal services business" is defined to mean:

ITA: 125(7) Definitions

- a business of providing services where
  - (*a*) an individual who performs services on behalf of the corporation ("incorporated employee"), or
  - (*b*) any person related to the incorporated employee

  is a specified shareholder defined to mean, in part, an owner, directly or indirectly, of 10% or more of the shares of the corporation;

ITA: 248(1) specified shareholder

- the incorporated employee would reasonably be regarded as an officer or employee of the entity to which services are provided;

- *unless*

  (*c*) the corporation employs throughout the year more than five full-time employees, or

  (*d*) services are provided to an associated corporation (to be discussed subsequently).

To determine whether "the incorporated employee would reasonably be regarded as an officer or employee of the entity to which services are provided", it may be necessary to perform an employee versus self-employed analysis, as presented in Chapter 3. The package of common law tests should be applied to the facts pertaining to the relationship between the incorporated employee and the entity to which services are provided. This was done in the case of *Criterion Capital Corporation v. The Queen.* Criterion was held not to be carrying on a PSB and, hence, was eligible for the small business deduction, in part, on the application of the "control" and "ownership of tools" tests.

Cases: *Criterion Capital Corporation v. Her Majesty the Queen*, 2001 DTC 921 (TCC)

Classification as a PSB is not advantageous. The category exists to discourage individuals (who would otherwise be employees of the entity to which services are provided) from incorporating, in an attempt to gain the tax advantage of the small business deduction with its low corporate rate. The only deductions allowed to a PSB are:

ITA: 18(1)(p) Limitation re personal services business expenses

- salary/wages paid to the incorporated employee;
- cost of benefits/allowances paid to the incorporated employee;
- amounts that would have been deductible under section 8 by the employee; and
- legal expenses to collect amounts owing for services.

As shown in Exhibit 12-3, PSB income is taxed at a very high rate. A corporation carrying on such a personal services business is not eligible for a small business deduction or the general rate reduction in respect of its PSB income. In fact, an additional tax of 5% is levied on income from a PSB. As indicated in Chapter 11, the credit for employment outside Canada is not available to a corporation carrying on a PSB.

ITA: 18(1)(p) Limitation re personal services business expenses, 123.4(1) Definitions

¶12,160 Income Incidental to an Active Business

"Income of the corporation for the year from an active business" includes any income for the year from an "active business", including any income for the year pertaining to or incident to that business; income from a property held for investment in Canada is specifically excluded.

ITA: 125(7) Definitions

Ancillary income incidental to the carrying on of an active business will, therefore, be considered as income from an active business in addition to income directly from an active business. Examples of such ancillary income include interest from short-term investment of surplus cash, recaptured capital cost allowance on assets used in the active business, interest on accounts receivable and bad debt recoveries, among others. An Interpretation Bulletin indicates the CRA's interpretation of the concept of ancillary income.

Interpretation Bulletins: IT-73R6 The Small Business Deduction

It is important to note that a corporation may have income from more than one source. Therefore, it is necessary to analyze the corporate income (Division B) and break it down into its components.

Ⓐ ¶12,161 Specified Corporate Income & Specified Partnership Income

Prior to the discussion of associated corporations in ¶12,170, it is important to understand the implication of specified corporate or partnership income. Where a CCPC is providing services or property to a private corporation or a partnership, that income may be excluded from the ABI eligible for the small business deduction (SBD). This requirement is designed to discourage the multiplication of the $500,000 business limit from one source of income.

The 2016 Federal Budget introduced the concept of specified corporate income (SCI), that may limit the corporation's ability to use the SBD. These new rules are complex and very broad. The rules outline that income from active business earned by a CCPC to be ineligible for the SBD if the following conditions are met:

- The corporation (Corp 1) provides a service or property to a private corporation (Corp 2), and all or substantially all of its corporation's income (Corp 1) is **not** from property or services to an arm's length person or partnership.
- The corporation, or one of its shareholders, or a person who does not deal at arm's length with the corporation (or one of its shareholders) holds an interest (directly or indirectly) in the private corporation (Corp 2).

If the income meets the two criteria, this income would not be eligible for the small business deduction under these SCI rules. Note that the first criteria includes the term "all or substantially all", which the CRA's administrative policy treats as meaning 90% or more. This indicates that where a corporation provides services or property, 90% or more of which is to an arm's length source, the SCI rules would not apply to limit the SBD.

Example — SCI and Spousal Corporations

Mr. A owns 100% of the shares of ABC Corporation (ABC), which carries on active business income by providing architectural services. Mrs. A (Mr. A's wife) owns 100% of XYZ Corporation (XYZ), which only earns management fees from ABC corporation.

Prior to the introduction of specified corporate income (SCI), the management fees earned by XYZ corporation would be eligible for the small business deduction. ABC and XYZ would be related but since they are not associated, they would not have to share the small business deduction.

ABC and XYZ are not dealing at arm's length because they are related. Under the new rules, the management fees would be considered to be specific corporate income to XYZ and would not be eligible for the SBD. The new rules apply because XYZ is a private corporation, and the shareholders of ABC (Mr. A) do not deal at arm's length with XYZ.

Example — SCI and Multiple Holding Corporations

Consider the following corporate setup:

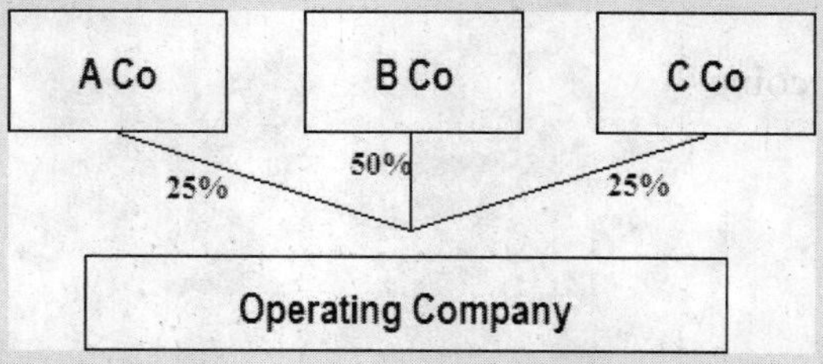

A Co, B Co and C Co are not related as they are controlled by individuals who are not related. Operating company pays management fees to each of the shareholder corporations.

Prior to the introduction of the specified corporate income (SCI) rules, the management fees paid to A Co, B Co and C Co would be eligible for the small business deduction (SBD). Each of the three shareholder corporations would have their own SBD as they are not associated.

Under the new SCI rules, the management fees earned by the three corporate shareholders (A Co, B Co and C Co) would not be eligible for the SBD unless the corporations (A Co, B Co and C Co) earn 90% or more of its income for the year from arm's length parties (i.e., less than 10% of its income if from the operating company) or the Operating company allocates some of its SBD.

¶12,161.99 Practise What You've Learned

Refer to the following sections of the Study Guide to practise what you've learned:

¶12,800 — Review Questions

- Question 1 — Integration

- Question 2 — Ideal integration
- Question 3 — Dividend gross-up and integration
- Question 4 — Purpose of small business deduction
- Question 12 — Purpose of the dividend gross-up
- Question 13 — Dividend tax credit
- Question 14 — Integration

¶12,825 — Multiple Choice Questions

- Question 1 — Small business deduction
- Question 2 — Identify type of income

¶12,850 — Exercises

- Exercise 1 — Identify types of income
- Exercise 9 — Type of income

¶12,170 Associated Companies

¶12,175 Overview

When two or more Canadian-controlled private corporations are associated for tax purposes, the business limit of $500,000, or the reduced amount, must be allocated annually, in any manner, among the associated companies for the purpose of determining the small business deduction in each company. A number of other provisions of the Act, also, rely on the concept of association. These include the definitions of the terms "specified investment business" and "personal services business" which were introduced previously in this chapter. The concept of association is, also, used to determine certain limits and rates for the investment tax credit, as discussed later in this chapter.

ITA: 125(3) Associated corporations, 127(10.1) Additions to investment tax credit, 127.1 Refundable investment tax credit, 125(7) Definitions, 125(10.1); Interpretation Bulletins: IT-73R6 The Small Business Deduction

The deeming rule, which will be discussed subsequently in this chapter, pertaining to certain intercorporate payments, depends on association between corporations.

ITA: 129(6) Investment income from associated corporation deemed to be active business income

¶12,180 Related Persons

The term "associated corporations" may depend on the definition of "related persons". Related persons include relationships between individuals, between individuals and corporations and between corporations.

ITA: 251 Arm's length, 256 Associated corporations

¶12,180.10 Related Individuals

The key to the definition of relationships is found in relationships between individuals who are connected by blood relationship, marriage or adoption. Exhibit 12-4 (which was introduced in Chapter 6 as Exhibit 6-2) attempts to diagram these relationships (i.e., individuals who are related to a taxpayer (i.e., "you")) schematically. On the horizontal axis, do not attempt to relate individuals at the extreme outer limits (i.e., the second bullet) to each other. They are related to "you".

Exhibit 12-4 Schematic Diagram of Related Individuals

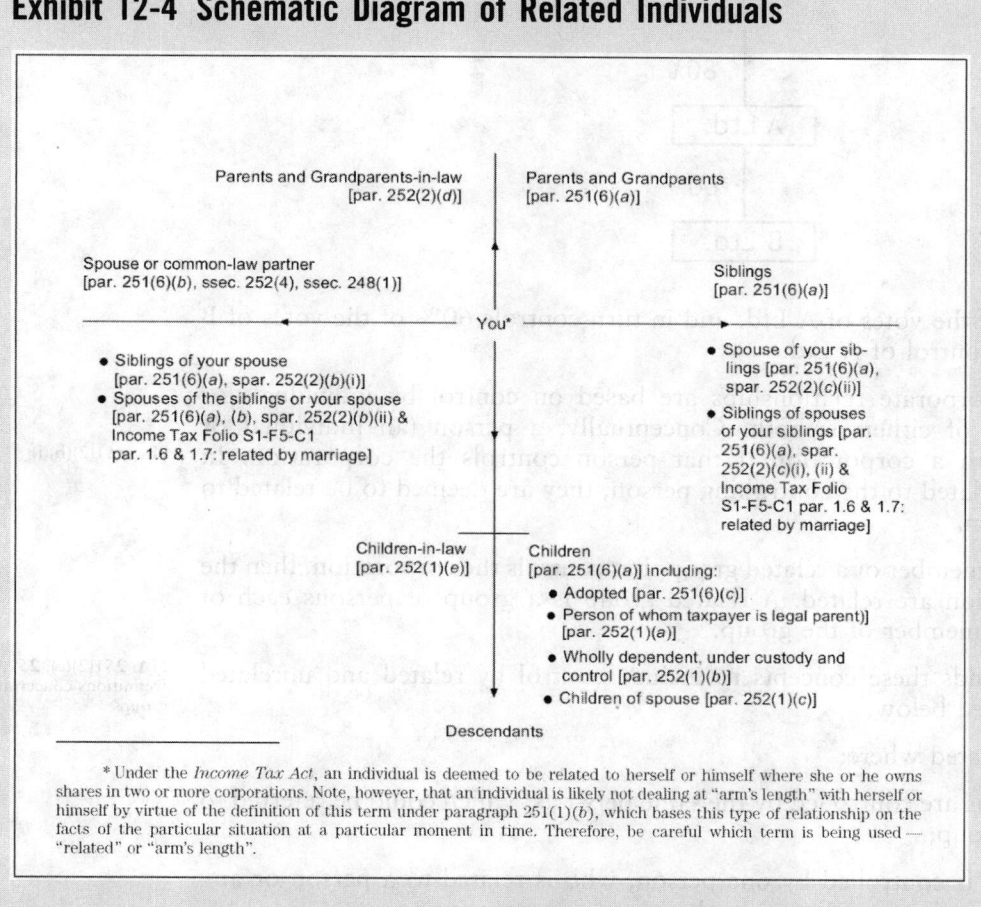

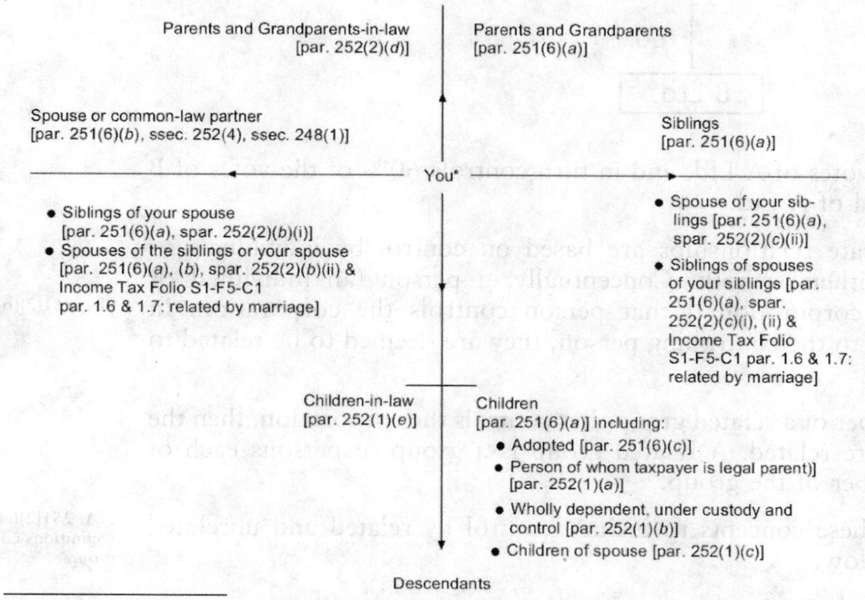

* Under the *Income Tax Act*, an individual is deemed to be related to herself or himself where she or he owns shares in two or more corporations. Note, however, that an individual is likely not dealing at "arm's length" with herself or himself by virtue of the definition of this term under paragraph 251(1)(*b*), which bases this type of relationship on the facts of the particular situation at a particular moment in time. Therefore, be careful which term is being used — "related" or "arm's length".

ITA: 251(5)(c), 256(1.5) Person related to himself, herself or itself; 248(1) common-law partner

Certain individuals who would normally be regarded as related to other individuals are not considered to be related for tax purposes. These individuals, who do not appear in Exhibit 12-4, include: aunts, uncles, nieces, nephews and cousins.

Note that where the word "spouse" is used, the provision extends to a "common-law partner". This term is defined as two persons, regardless of sex, who cohabit in a conjugal relationship and have done so for a continuous period of at least 12 months.

¶12,180.20 Relationships Involving Corporations

Corporations can be related to individuals and other corporations. The key to understanding corporate relationships is the concept of control. In this context, control refers to legal (*de jure*) control which is generally understood to mean the right of control that rests in the ownership of such number of shares of the corporation as to give a majority of the voting power in the corporation. Control can either be direct or indirect. The latter, for example, could be accomplished through an intermediary corporation.

An example of indirect control would be where A, an individual, owns 80% of the voting shares of A Ltd. which in turn owns 60% of the voting shares of B Ltd.

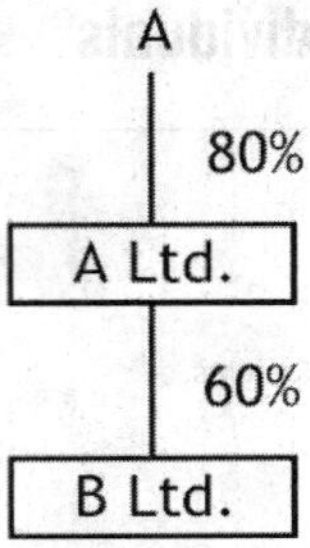

A has more than 50% of the votes of A Ltd. and in turn controls 60% of the votes of B Ltd. through his or her control of A Ltd.

The rules that govern corporate relationships are based on control by individuals or corporations, or groups of either or both. Conceptually, a person (an individual or corporation) is related to a corporation if that person controls the corporation. In addition, if a person is related to the controlling person, they are deemed to be related to the controlled corporation. ITA: 251(2)(b)(i)

Similarly, if a person is a member of a related group that controls the corporation, then the person and the corporation are related. A related group is a group of persons each of whom is related to each member of the group.

A relationship rule expands these concepts to include control by related and unrelated groups, and is summarized below. ITA: 251(2)(c), 251(4) Definitions concerning groups

Two corporations are related where:

(1) both corporations are controlled by the same person(s) which could be referred to as a common group;

(2) one corporation is controlled by one person, who is related to a person or any member of a related group that controls the other corporation;

(3) one corporation is controlled by one person or a related group and that person or one member of the related group is related to each member of an unrelated group which controls the other corporation; and

(4) two corporations are controlled by unrelated groups and at least one member of one of the groups is related to each member of the other group.

Example Problem 12-3

Consider the following two groups, each of which controls a corporation with a 50/50 ownership of the shares:

Group One Ltd. — Mom and Dad

Group Two Ltd. — Child of Mom and Dad and Mom's brother

REQUIRED

Determine whether Group One Ltd. and Group Two Ltd. are related.

SOLUTION

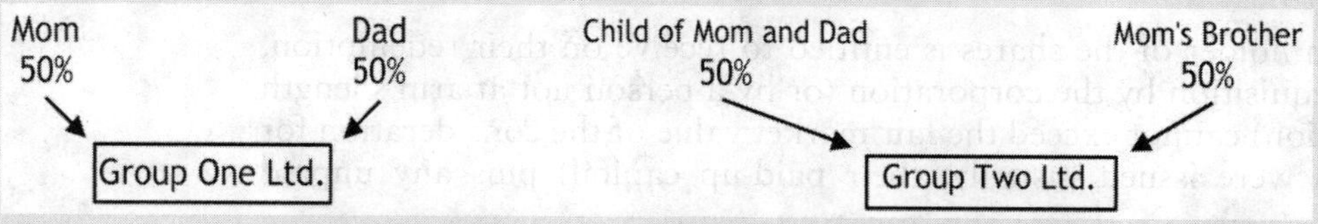

Group Two Ltd. is controlled by an unrelated group since it is composed of an uncle and a niece/nephew. Group One Ltd. is controlled by a related group, because Mom and Dad are related through marriage. In this situation, each member of the related group that controls Group One Ltd. is related to each member of the unrelated group that controls Group Two Ltd.

Therefore, the corporations are related.

ITA: 251(2)(c)(v)

¶12,185 Basic Association Rules

Conceptually, two companies are associated for tax purposes, when one company controls the other, or both companies are controlled by the same person or group of persons. However, the definition of associated corporations goes on to list other conditions for association. Therefore, the definition must be consulted to properly evaluate a particular set of facts. The first two general rules each require that only one straightforward condition be met in order to apply.

ITA: 256 Associated corporations, 256(1)(a), 256(1)(b)

The last three general rules each contain three conditions, all joined by the word "and", which means that all three conditions must be satisfied for the rule to apply.

ITA: 256(1)(c), 256(1)(d), 256(1)(e)

¶12,185.10 Paragraph 256(1)(c)

The three conditions that must be met for this rule to apply are:

(1) each of the corporations must be controlled, directly or indirectly in any manner whatever, by a person (which includes an individual or another corporation) (hereinafter referred to as the "control test");

(2) the person who controls one of the corporations must be related to the person who controls the other corporation (hereinafter referred to as the "related test"); and

(3) either of the two related persons owns not less than 25% of the issued shares of any class, other than a specified class (as defined below), of the capital stock of each corporation (hereinafter referred to as the "cross-ownership test").

Shares of a "specified class" are excluded from the cross-ownership conditions. The term "specified class" is defined to mean a class of shares where:

ITA: 256(1.1) Definition of "specified class"

(1) the shares are neither convertible nor exchangeable;

(2) the shares are non-voting;

(3) dividends payable on the shares are fixed in amount or rate;

(4) the annual rate of dividend on the shares, expressed as a percentage of the fair market value of the consideration for which the shares were issued, does not exceed the prescribed rate of interest at the time the shares were issued; and

(5) the amount that a holder of the shares is entitled to receive on their redemption, cancellation or acquisition by the corporation (or by a person not at arm's length with the corporation) cannot exceed the fair market value of the consideration for which the shares were issued (usually, their paid-up capital) plus any unpaid dividends.

The exclusion of a specified class of shares as it relates to the 25% cross-ownership test allow a person to invest funds in a corporation controlled by a related person without subjecting his or her own corporation to the consequences of association.

Example Problem 12-4

Dad and Son (age 25) both own 100% of the common shares of their respective corporations: Dadco Ltd. and Sonco Ltd. Dad owns 100% of the preferred shares of Sonco Ltd. The preferred shares are voting, bear a dividend rate of 8%, and are redeemable at $100,000. At the time the preferred shares were issued, the prescribed rate was 10% and the fair market value was $100,000.

REQUIRED

Determine whether Dadco Ltd. and Sonco Ltd. are associated under subsection 256(1). Substantiate your conclusions by reference to the related provisions of the Act and the conditions contained therein.

SOLUTION

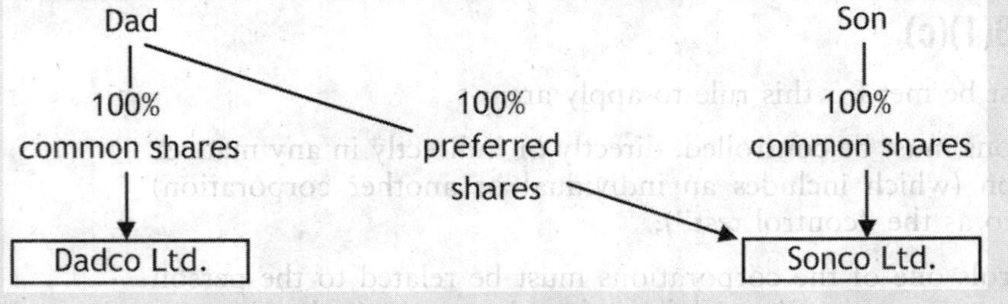

Dadco Ltd. and Sonco Ltd. are associated because: ITA: 256(1)(c)

(1) the corporations are controlled directly by either Dad or Son;

(2) Dad and Son are related by blood (i.e., parent–child); ITA: 251(1)(a), 251(6) Blood relationship, etc.

(3) one of the related persons (Dad) owns not less than 25% of issued shares of any class of both corporations, other than specified shares

(i.e., 100% of the common shares of Dadco Ltd. and 100% of the preferred shares of Sonco Ltd.); and

(4) the preferred and common shares are not specified shares since both classes have voting rights. ITA: 256(1.1) Definition of "specified class"

¶12,185.20 Paragraph 256(1)(d)

Whereas the preceding rule applies to two corporations each controlled by a single person, this rule applies to a situation in which one corporation is controlled by a single person and the other corporation is controlled by a group of persons. The three conditions (involving a control test, a related test and a cross-ownership test) that must be met are:

(1) one of the corporations must be controlled, directly or indirectly in any manner whatever, by one person (control test);

(2) that person must be related to each member of a group of persons (not necessarily a related group) that controls the other corporation (related test); and

(3) that person must own not less than 25% of the issued shares of any class, other than specified shares, of the capital stock of the other corporation (cross-ownership test).

Example Problem 12-5

Mom owns 100% of the common shares of Momco Ltd. Her adult daughters, No. 1 and No. 2, each own 35% of the common shares of Sibco Ltd. Mom owns the remaining 30% of the outstanding common shares of Sibco Ltd.

REQUIRED

Determine whether Momco Ltd. and Sibco Ltd. are associated. Substantiate your conclusions by reference to the related provisions of the Act and the conditions contained therein.

SOLUTION

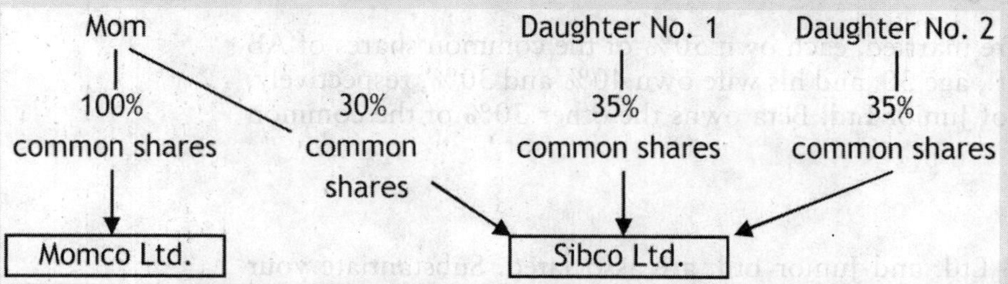

Momco Ltd. and Sibco Ltd. are associated because: ITA: 256(1)(d)

(1) one person (Mom) controls one corporation (Momco Ltd.);

(2) that person (Mom) is related to each person (daughters No. 1 and No. 2) in the group that controls the other corporation (Sibco Ltd.) because of the parent–child relationship. Note that the condition would also be met if the controlling group was either Mom and Daughter No. 1 or Mom and Daughter No. 2, since Mom is deemed to be related to herself as a shareholder of both corporations; ITA: 251(1)(a), 251(5)(c), 251(6)(a)

(3) that person (Mom) owns not less than 25% of non-specified shares in the other corporation (30% of the common shares of Sibco Ltd.); and

(4) the common shares of Sibco Ltd. are not specified shares since these shares have voting rights and no restriction on the amount of dividends.

¶12,185.30 Paragraph 256(1)(e)

Finally, this rule applies to two group-controlled corporations if the following three conditions (involving a control test, a related test and a cross-ownership test) are met:

(1) each of the corporations must be controlled, directly or indirectly in any manner whatever, by a related group, i.e., a group in which each member of the control group is related to each other member of that control group (control test);

(2) each member of one of the related groups must be related to all of the members of the other related group (related test); and

(3) one or more members of both related groups must own, either alone or together, not less than 25% of the issued shares of any class, other than a specified class, of shares of the capital stock of the other corporation (cross-ownership test).

Example Problem 12-6

Alpha and Beta, who are married, each own 50% of the common shares of AB Ltd. Their son, Alpha Jr., age 30, and his wife own 40% and 30%, respectively, of the common shares of Junior Ltd. Beta owns the other 30% of the common shares of Junior Ltd.

REQUIRED

Determine whether AB Ltd. and Junior Ltd. are associated. Substantiate your conclusions by the related provisions of the Act and the conditions contained therein.

SOLUTION

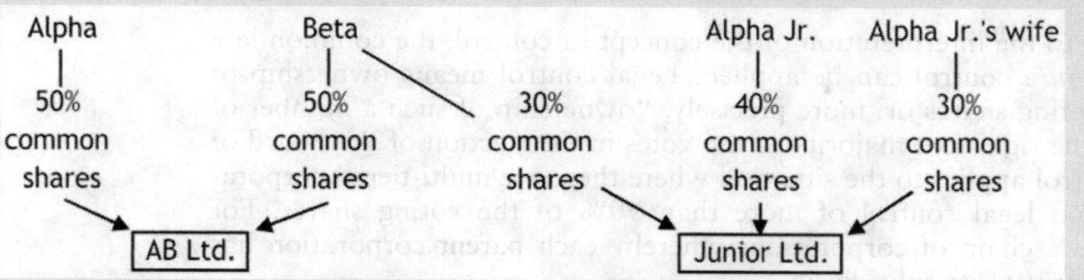

AB Ltd. and Junior Ltd. are associated because: ITA: 256(1)(e)

(1) each corporation (AB Ltd. and Junior Ltd.) is controlled by a related group:

- AB Ltd. is controlled by Alpha (50%) and Beta (50%) who are related by marriage; ITA: 251(1)(a), 251(6)(b)
- Junior Ltd. is controlled by any of: ITA: 251(1)(a), 251(6)(b)

  (a) Alpha Jr. (40%) and his wife (30%) who are related by marriage, ITA: 251(1)(a), 251(6)(a)

  (b) Beta (30%) and Alpha Jr. (40%) who are related by blood, ITA: 252(1)(e)

  (c) Beta (30%) and Alpha Jr.'s wife (30%) who are related through the extended definition of child, ITA: 251(5)(c)

  (d) Alpha Jr. (40%), Alpha Jr.'s wife (30%) and Beta (30%), all of whom are related;

(2) each member of one related group (Alpha and Beta) is related to all members of the other related group. Note that in cases (ii), (iii), and (iv), above, Beta is related to herself as a shareholder of both corporations;

(3) one (or more) member of *both* related groups (Beta) must own not less than 25% (Beta owns 30% in Junior Ltd.) of the issued shares of any class other than specified shares of the other corporation; and

(4) common shares are not specified shares. ITA: 256(1.1) Definition of "specified class"

The following is a list of the key words used in each of the paragraphs of subsection 256(1).

Par. (*a*)	controlled
Par. (*b*)	controlled, person, group of persons
Par. (*c*)	controlled, person, related, owned not less than 25%, specified class
Par. (*d*)	controlled, person, group of persons, related, owned not less than 25%, specified class
Par. (*e*)	controlled, related group, owned not less than 25%, specified class

¶12,190 Concept of Control

¶12,190.10 Legal Control

As a first approximation to the interpretation of the concept of control, the common law definition of legal or *de jure* control can be applied. Legal control means ownership of more than 50% of the voting shares or, more precisely, "ownership of such a number of shares as carries with it the right to a majority of the votes in the election of the Board of Directors".[6] Indirect control applies to the situation where there are multi-tiered corporations but is still based on legal control of more than 50% of the voting shares. For example, assume there is a chain of corporations whereby each parent corporation has 60% of all the voting shares of its subsidiary:

A Ltd. —60%→ B Ltd. —60%→ C Ltd. —60%→ D Ltd.

In each situation, the parent corporation controls its subsidiary. A Ltd. directly controls B Ltd. and indirectly controls C Ltd. and D Ltd. B Ltd. directly controls C Ltd. and indirectly controls D Ltd. Note that control is not multiplicative. Since A Ltd. controls B Ltd., A Ltd. can cause B Ltd. to vote all of B Ltd.'s shares in C Ltd. according to A Ltd.'s wishes. Therefore, A Ltd. controls, indirectly, C Ltd. Furthermore, the Interpretation Bulletin should be consulted for the CRA's view of these rules.

Interpretation Bulletins: IT-64R4 Corporations: Association and Control

¶12,190.20 Factual Control

A broadening of the concept of legal control may occur in fact situations to which the concept of "control in fact" applies. Using factual control to determine association further restricts the multiplication of the small business deduction by extending the circumstances under which corporations are considered to be associated. As indicated, the concept of control has been interpreted to mean legal or *de jure* control that vests in the ownership of more than 50% of the voting shares, as set out in the *Buckerfield's* case.[7] The expression "controlled, directly or indirectly in any manner whatever" when used throughout the Act, extends the concept of control to *de facto* control which might exist by virtue of a person having any direct or indirect influence.

ITA: 256(5.1) Control in fact

The Federal Court of Appeal has stated "that in order for there to be a finding of *de facto* control, a person or group of persons must have the clear right and ability to effect a significant change in the board of directors or the powers of the board of directors or to influence in a very direct way the shareholders who would otherwise have the ability to elect the board of directors." Subsequent cases have affirmed this test of *de facto* control and have clarified that this test has no basis in the concept of effective control that derives from operating or managerial control. The FCA did suggest that, in determining whether *de facto* control exists, it is necessary to examine external agreements; shareholder resolutions and whether any party can change the board of directors or whether any shareholders' agreement gives any party the ability to influence the composition of the board of directors.

Cases: *Silicon Graphics Limited v. The Queen*, 2002 DTC 7112, pars. 66 and 67*McGillivray Restaurant Ltd. v. The Queen*, 2016 DTC 5048 (FCA)

Perhaps, as a reaction to this line of cases restricting the application of the concept of factual control, the 2017 Federal Budget added a subsection that would require the consideration of all of the relevant factors in the circumstances, as outlined in the common law. Furthermore, the factors need not include "whether the taxpayer has a legally

ITA: 256(5.11) Factual control — interpretation

[6] Stated in the case of *Buckerfield's Limited et al. v M.N.R.*, (Ex. Ct.) 64 DTC 5301.

[7] See also the case of *The Queen v. Imperial General Properties*, 85 DTC 5500 (S.C.C.).

enforceable right or ability to effect a change to the board of directors or its powers, or to exercise influence over the shareholder or shareholders who have that right and ability."

¶12,195 Extended Meaning of Control

The concept of control is further broadened by another provision. In determining whether a corporation was controlled by a group of persons, a group means any two or more persons each of whom owned shares of the same corporation. A corporation can be considered to be controlled at the same time by several persons or groups of persons. This concept is shown in the preceding example problem dealing with paragraph 256(1)(*e*). Note how four different groups control Junior Ltd.

ITA: 256(1.2)(a), 256(1.2)(b)

A person or group of persons will be deemed to control a corporation when the person or group owns:

ITA: 256(1.2)(c)

(1) shares representing more than 50% of the fair market value of all issued and outstanding shares of the corporation, or

(2) common shares representing more than 50% of the fair market value of all issued and outstanding common shares of the corporation.

Note how this rule ignores the voting rights of the shares and looks at the underlying value of the shares in question. For example, assume that a corporation is capitalized with $1,000,000 of non-voting retractable shares owned by Individual A and $1,000 of common shares owned by Individual B. Both A and B control the corporation — Individual B through his or her voting rights and Individual A through the preferred shares which represent more than 50% of the total fair market value of the share capital of $1,001,000.

Since the value of a share can be affected by voting rights and certain other special features, these features are to be disregarded for the purposes of determining the fair market value of a share in this context. Likewise, "term preferred shares" and shares included in a "specified class" should be disregarded for purposes of making the fair market valuation.

ITA: 256(1.2)(g), 248(1) Definitions, 256(1.1) Definition of "specified class", 256(1.2) Control, etc, 256(1.6) Exception

¶12,200 Ownership of Shares

¶12,200.10 Look-Through Rules

The association rules use both of the words "controlled" and "owned". As previously demonstrated, indirect control of a corporation can flow through a chain of corporations through *de jure* control. However, the courts have held that ownership, including indirect ownership, cannot be traced through a chain of corporations. Therefore, provisions were enacted to provide a series of indirect ownership rules which are referred to as the "look-through" rules. These rules apply where shares of a corporation are held by another corporation, a partnership or a trust. A shareholder of a corporation, a member of a partnership or a beneficiary of a trust that holds shares in a corporation would be deemed to own a number of the shares of the corporation as is proportionate to his or her economic interest in the corporation, partnership or trust that actually owns the shares.

ITA: 256(1.2)(d), 256(1.2)(e), 256(1.2)(f)

¶12,200.20 Example of Control and Ownership Through a Corporation

Consider the facts in the following diagram:

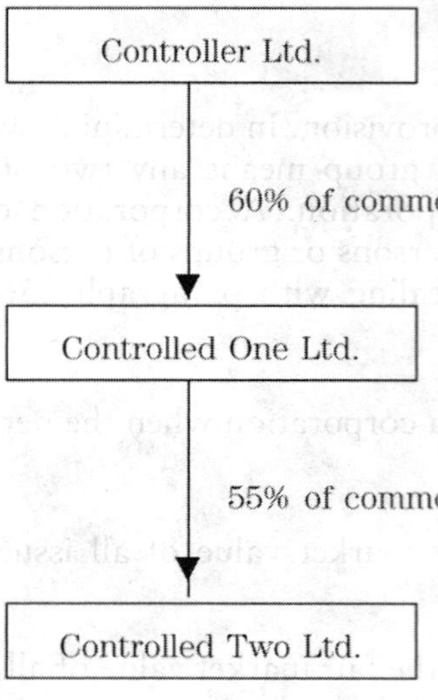

With its 60% ownership of the common shares of Controlled One Ltd., Controller Ltd. controls Controlled One Ltd. Since Controller Ltd. controls Controlled One Ltd., it can cause Controlled One Ltd. to vote the latter's 55% controlling interest in Controlled Two Ltd. in the interest of Controller Ltd. Therefore, Controller Ltd. controls Controlled Two Ltd. through Controlled One Ltd. Controller Ltd. does not own any shares directly in Controlled Two Ltd. through its ownership of shares in Controlled One Ltd. However, paragraph 256(1.2)(*d*) deems Controller Ltd. to *own* 33% (i.e., 60% of 55%) of Controlled Two Ltd.

¶12,200.30 Shares Owned by a Minor

Another such rule deems that shares of a corporation owned by a minor child are owned by each parent of the child. Even if the shares are deemed to be owned by the minor child by another provision of section 256, the shares will be deemed to be owned by each parent. However, an exception is provided if it may reasonably be considered that the child manages the business and affairs of the corporation and does so without a significant degree of influence by the parent. This exception is intended to accommodate young entrepreneurs.

ITA: 256(1.3) Parent deemed to own shares

¶12,200.40 Two Other Deeming Rules

One of these rules pertains to rights to acquire shares (e.g., options) or rights to cause a corporation to redeem shares of other shareholders. The holder of such rights is deemed to be in the same position as if the rights were exercised. The other rule deems a person to be related to himself or herself in his or her capacity as shareholder of two or more corporations.

ITA: 256(1.4) Options and rights

¶12,205 Association With Third Corporation

Where two corporations, that would not otherwise be associated, are both associated with a third corporation, the two corporations are normally deemed to be associated with each other. However, relief from this deeming rule is available, for the purposes of the small business deduction only, if the third corporation is not a Canadian-controlled private corporation or if the third corporation elects this deeming rule to apply. The business limit of the third corporation is deemed to be nil. Since the two deemed non-associated corporations are still each separately associated with the third corporation, for the purposes of computing the business limit of each of the two non-associated corporations, the taxable capital of the third corporation must be included. For this election to apply, the two corporations associated through a third corporation cannot be associated by any other rule. Note that the election is an annual one. The result of the election is that the business limit of the third corporation is deemed to be nil.

ITA: 256(2) Corporations associated through a third corporation, 125 Small business deduction

Example Problem 12-7

H and W, a married couple, have incorporated their separate businesses, H Ltd. and W Ltd., both of which are CCPCs. In order to avoid duplication of administrative costs, H and W incorporated a management corporation, M Ltd., to provide support services for H Ltd. and W Ltd. H and W each own 50% of the common shares of M Ltd.

REQUIRED

Determine whether H Ltd., W Ltd. and M Ltd. are associated.

SOLUTION

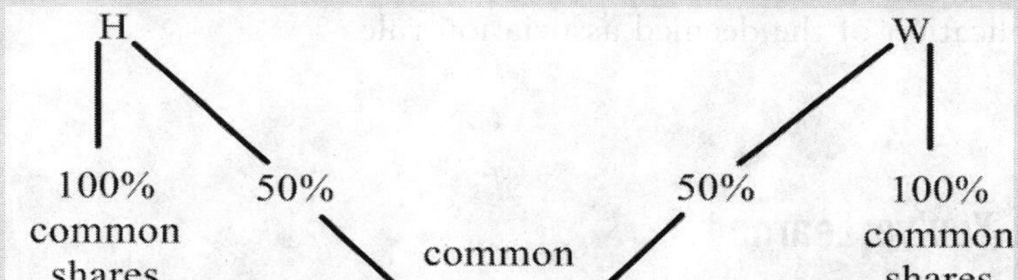

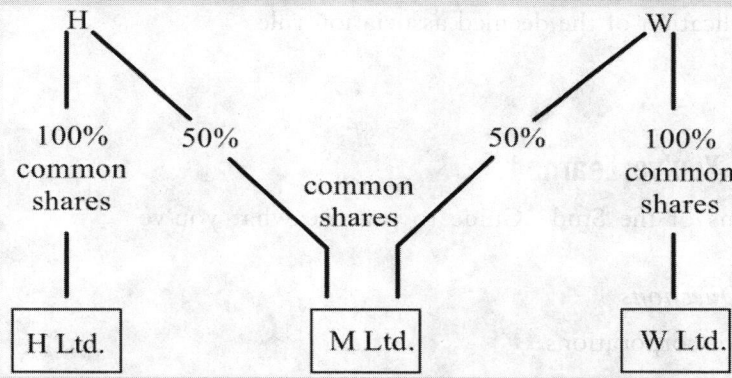

H Ltd., W Ltd. and M Ltd. are all associated with each other.

H Ltd. and M Ltd. are associated:

ITA: 256(1)(d)

- H controls (100% of common shares) H Ltd.;
- H and W control M Ltd. (50% of common shares each);
- H is related to:

  (1) W through marriage; and

  (2) H through the deemed related rule for a shareholder; and

ITA: 252(1)(a), 252(6)(b)

ITA: 256(1.5) Person related to himself, herself or itself

- H owns not less than 25% of non-specified shares of the other corporation (100% of H Ltd. and 50% of M Ltd.).

W Ltd. and M Ltd. are associated also, using the same logic. ITA: 256(1)(d)

Therefore, H Ltd. and W Ltd. are associated through a common third corporation, M Ltd. Note that without M Ltd., H Ltd. and W Ltd. would not be associated.

ITA: 256(2) Corporations associated through a third corporation

However, if M Ltd. elects, in prescribed form and on a year-by-year basis, then H Ltd. and W Ltd. are deemed not to be associated for that particular year for purposes of the small business deduction. The business limit of M Ltd. is deemed to be nil for the taxation year, so that M Ltd. cannot, itself, benefit from the small business deduction. However, the taxable capital of M Ltd. must be included in the total taxable capital for each of H Ltd. and W Ltd., in the calculation of the business limit of the latter two. No election is needed if M Ltd. is not a Canadian-controlled private corporation.

¶12,210 Deemed Association

Where one of the main reasons for the separate existence of two corporations that are otherwise not associated is tax considerations, the two corporations may be deemed to be associated. The provision also contains a reasonableness test. If the taxpayer can show a valid, non-tax reason for the separate existence of a corporation, the presence of a tax reason should not result in the application of the deemed association rule.

ITA: 256(2.1) Anti-avoidance

¶12,210.99 Practise What You've Learned

Refer to the following sections of the Study Guide to practise what you've learned:

¶12,825 — Multiple Choice Questions

- Question 5 — Associated corporations
- Question 6 — Associated corporations

¶12,850 — Exercises

- Exercise 2 — Arm's length
- Exercise 3 — Associated corporations
- Exercise 4 — Sharing small business deduction
- Exercise 5 — Associated corporations
- Exercise 12 — Association
- Exercise 13 — Association

- Exercise 15 — Association

Ⓐ ¶12,220 Corporate Partnerships

The associated corporation rules were designed to prevent the splitting of a business into numerous corporations each of which could qualify for the maximum small business deduction. To prevent the splitting of a business into numerous multiple non-associated corporations operating as partners and each qualifying for the maximum small business deduction, further rules were designed to require that the maximum annual small business deduction limit of $500,000 be shared by corporate partners or groups of corporate partners. These rules are necessary because partnerships are not taxed as separate entities as will be discussed in Chapter 18.

ITA: 125(5.1) Business limit reduction

In addition, an anti-avoidance rule is provided where one of the reasons for CCPC providing services or property to a partnership or another corporation is to avoid the application of the restriction on the business limit. In that case, no amount of the income for that source is included in active business income eligible for the small business deduction.

ITA: 125(9) Anti-avoidance

Ⓐ ¶12,230 Manufacturing and Processing Profits and the Small Business Deduction

In the previous chapter, the manufacturing and processing profits deduction was alluded to without reference to the effect of the small business deduction on the manufacturing and processing profits deduction. Essentially, there is no manufacturing and processing profits deduction on that portion of Canadian manufacturing and processing profits eligible for the small business deduction. The amount of manufacturing and processing profits deduction for a CCPC is derived conceptually as the excess of manufacturing and processing profits over the amount of income eligible for the small business deduction. Hence, income eligible for the small business deduction will not be eligible for the M&P profits deduction as well.

ITA: 125.1(1) Manufacturing and processing profits deductions; Income Tax Folio: S4-F15-C1 Manufacturing and Processing

Since the M&P profits are also eligible for the general rate reduction (GRR), and the two rates are the same at 13%, we will ignore the M&P profits deduction in this text; the GRR is much easier to calculate and results in the same reduction in tax. Also, if income is eligible for the small business deduction, it is not also eligible for either the M&P profits deduction or the GRR.

Example Problem 12-8

During its first taxation year (of 365 days) which ended December 31, 2018, Logic Ltd., a Canadian-controlled private corporation, reported the following incomes:

Manufacturing and processing profits	$ 80,000
Total active business income earned in Canada (including M&P)	110,000
Taxable income	75,000
Division B income	110,000
Taxable dividends paid in the year	40,000

The corporation carries on business in Canada and is not associated with any other Canadian-controlled private corporation.

REQUIRED

Compute the tax payable for 2018 by the corporation under Part I of the Act, assuming a 4% provincial rate of tax.

SOLUTION

Taxable income		$ 75,000
Basic federal tax (38% of $75,000)		$ 28,500
Federal abatement (10% of $75,000)		(7,500)
Small business deduction:		
18% of least of:		
(a) Income from active business carried on in Canada	$110,000	
(b) Taxable income	$75,000	
(c) Business limit	$500,000	
18% of $75,000		(13,500)
Manufacturing and processing profits deduction (all of this income is eligible for the small business deduction)		Nil
General rate reduction (all of this income is eligible for the small business deduction)		Nil
Federal Part I tax payable		$ 7,500
Provincial tax @ 4% of $75,000		3,000
Total tax payable		$ 10,500

¶12,235 The General Rate Reduction Revisited

The 13% general rate reduction was introduced in Chapter 11. The objective of this provision is to reduce corporate business income taxed at the full corporate tax rate. Where the corporation is a Canadian-controlled private corporation, some of its income, like income eligible for the small business deduction and aggregate investment income (to be discussed later in this chapter) are not taxed at full corporate rates and, hence, are not eligible for the general rate reduction. Personal services business income is not eligible for the general rate reduction to discourage the formation of a corporation to undertake such a business for tax purposes. As a result, it must be removed from taxable income and that is done by the following calculation:

ITA: 123.4 Corporation tax reductions

Taxable income

Less:

- income from a personal services business
- the amount of income eligible for the small business deduction
- aggregate investment income

The net is the base for the 13% general rate reduction for a CCPC. That base is the business income of the corporation that is taxed at the full corporate rate. Refer to Exhibit 12-2 to see how this applies.

Ⓐ ¶12,240 Investment Tax Credit Revisited

According to the CPA Knowledge Supplement, the topic of scientific research and experimental development credits is generally viewed as an advanced topic to be covered in detail in the *elective* stage. Therefore, our advanced symbol (Ⓐ) in this section identifies material within this subject that is more complex and non-routine in nature.

¶12,245 Overview

The investment tax credit (ITC), as described in Chapter 11, is also available for Canadian-controlled private corporations. Refer to the diagram at the end of Example Problem 11-13 for a conceptual overview of the process of dealing with the deduction of the expenditures and the ITC. However, additional incentives are provided for CCPCs. These incentives are obtained by adhering to a strict set of limitations many of which are similar to the restrictions for the small business deduction. This section will describe the advantages and limitations imposed by the legislation.

¶12,250 The ITC Rate for CCPCs

¶12,250.10 Basic Rates

Investment tax credits are presently restricted to qualifying scientific research and experimental development (SR&ED) expenditures for all jurisdictions within Canada. [The one very limited exception is the credit for qualifying property expenditures for the Atlantic provinces and the Gaspé at a rate of 10% as described in Chapter 11.] The basic SR&ED rate is 15% for all taxpayers including individuals, trusts and corporations. This basic ITC rate of 15% has no dollar limit, except that all of the qualifying expenditures must meet the rules set out in section 37, as described in Chapter 11.

ITA: 127(9) Idem

¶12,250.20 Additional Rate of ITC for SR&ED Expenditures

An additional ITC incentive of 20% is provided where the taxpayer is a CCPC throughout the taxation year in which the expenditure is made. This additional rate results in a combined tax credit rate of 35%. However, the 20% additional credit bears additional restrictions as described below.

ITA: 127(10.1) Additions to investment tax credit

The additional 20% credit is restricted in total to $3 million of qualifying expenditures, referred to as the SR&ED expenditure limit, but only where the preceding year's taxable income of the corporation and all associated corporations does not exceed the $500,000 small business deduction limit for the year. Where the preceding year's taxable income of the corporation and all associated corporations exceeds $500,000, the SR&ED expenditure limit of $3 million is reduced by $10 for every dollar of excess. Once the corporate group's taxable income reaches $800,000, the SR&ED expenditure limit is reduced to zero. The actual calculation of the expenditure limit in the provision is, generally, $8 million minus 10 times the greater of $500,000 and the taxable income of the associated group for the immediately preceding taxation year.

ITA: 127(10.2) Expenditure limit determined

The $3 million expenditure limit is further reduced if the taxable capital of the corporation and any associated corporations exceeds $10 million. The expenditure limit is reduced by $3 for every $40 in taxable capital in excess of $10 million. At $50 million of taxable capital, the expenditure limit is nil.

¶12,255 Refundable Investment Tax Credit

Since many small Canadian businesses may not be in a position to pay taxes because of a weak profit position or losses incurred, the investment tax credit is not a strong incentive to invest. Therefore, cash refunds are available to certain taxpayers, in respect of available investment tax credits which cannot be used to offset taxes payable in a particular year. The extent to which a refund is available is a function of the status of the taxpayer, the nature of the expenditure that gave rise to the credit and when the expenditure was made. Investment tax credits that are available for deduction in a taxation year and which cannot be offset against taxes payable or converted into a cash refund, are available for carryover back three taxation years and forward 20 taxation years. However, any ITC that is deducted or refunded in the year must be included in income for the following year in respect of current SR&ED expenditures or deducted from the capital cost of qualifying depreciable capital property acquisitions.

ITA: 12(1)(t) Investment tax credit, 13(7.1) Deemed capital cost of certain property, 12(1)(r) Inventory adjustment

The refundable investment tax credit rates available to a qualifying CCPC, i.e., a CCPC or an associated group with total taxable income of less than the $500,000 small business deduction limit, are:

(1) 100% cash refund of the available 35% ITC based on qualifying SR&ED current expenditures not in excess of the expenditure limit for the year; and

(2) 40% cash refund of the available 15% ITC on qualifying SR&ED current expenditures in excess of the expenditure limit.

Note that the available ITC refers to the ITC as determined by the rules described in the previous section of this chapter.

Example Problem 12-9

Small Limited, a CCPC with a December 31 year end, spent $4 million in current qualifying SR&ED expenditures in 2018. Small Limited is not associated with any other corporation and may be eligible for an ITC of 35%. Its taxable capital for the preceding year was $9 million.

REQUIRED

Determine the amount of ITCs and refundable ITCs for 2018 on the assumption that its taxable income for the preceding year was:

(1) $500,000,

(2) $600,000, and

(3) $800,000.

SOLUTION

Taxable income of preceding year (2017)	Expenditure limit	Refundable ITC	Non-refundable ITC
(a) $500,000	$3,000,000	$1,110,000[(1)]	$ 90,000[(2)]
(b) $600,000	2,000,000[(3)]	Nil[(4)]	1,000,000[(6)]
(c) $800,000	Nil[(6)]	Nil[(7)]	600,000[(8)]

NOTES TO SOLUTION

(1) (35% × $3,000,000 × 100%) + (15% × $1,000,000 × 40%)

(2) 15% × $1,000,000 × 60%

(3) $8,000,000 – ($600,000 × $10)

(4) Refundable ITC is nil because taxable income in the prior year was in excess of the small business deduction limit.

(5) $2,000,000 × 35% + $2,000,000 × 15%

(6) $8,000,000 – ($800,000 × $10)

(7) Refundable ITC is nil because taxable income in the prior year was in excess of the small business deduction limit.

(8) $4,000,000 × 15%

¶12,260 Prescribed Proxy Amount

As indicated in Chapter 11, an elective alternative for the treatment of SR&ED overhead expenditures eligible for the investment tax credit was introduced to reduce the amount of record-keeping required. Under this annual election, referred to as a prescribed proxy amount (PPA), a prescribed amount rather than the actual overhead expenditure is eligible for ITC. Under the PPA election, the actual overhead expenditures are deductible from business income as ordinary expenditures rather than as SR&ED expenditures, which are credited to the SR&ED expenditure pool and written off as required. For a more detailed explanation of the treatment of SR&ED expenditures, see Chapter 11. The major difference in the write-off treatment of the two methods is the 20-year limited period of carryforward for ordinary business expenses, as compared to the indefinite carryover for the SR&ED expenditure pool.

ITA: 37 Scientific research and experimental development

The PPA is only used in respect of the determination of ITCs related to SR&ED expenditures, not the deduction of overhead expenditures. The statutory reference to a PPA is found in the definition of the ITC base, a qualified expenditure. The PPA itself is defined in and computed by the Regulations.

ITA: 127(9) Idem; ITR: 2900(4) [Calculation of prescribed proxy amount], 2900(5) [All or substantially all salaries or wages]

The PPA is basically a substitute for an item-by-item accounting for and allocating of overhead expenditures *directly* attributable to SR&ED in Canada. The PPA (i.e., the amount eligible for the ITC) is 55% of the salary base which is the portion of the salaries of employees directly engaged in SR&ED in Canada. The "portion", referred to above, is determined on a reasonable time allocation basis for each employee engaged in SR&ED, including direct technical management activities. For employees who spend all or substantially all (i.e., 90%) of their time on qualifying SR&ED activities, the whole amount of their salaries is included in the salary base.

ITR: 2900(4) [Calculation of prescribed proxy amount]

A modification to this rule relates to "specified employees". A specified employee is one who is a specified shareholder of the corporate employer or who does not deal at arm's length with the employer-entity. A specified shareholder is defined as a person who owns, together with the shares of related persons, 10% or more of any class of shares of the corporation. The salary base for specified employees is limited to the lesser of three-quarters of their full salary and 2.5 times the year's maximum pensionable earnings for CPP purposes (i.e., 2.5 × $55,900 = $139,750 for 2018).

ITA: 248(1) specified employees, 248(1) specified shareholder; ITR: 2900(7) [Restrictions for specified employees]

Where a PPA election is used, eligible expenditures for SR&ED and the related ITC are restricted to the following non-overhead expenditures:

ITA: 37 Scientific research and experimental development

(1) wages and benefits of employees *directly* engaged in SR&ED activities;

(2) leasing expenses of equipment, other than general-purpose office equipment or furniture, used *all or substantially all* in SR&ED activities;

(3) qualifying third-party payments for subcontracted SR&ED activities; and

(4) costs of materials used directly in SR&ED activities.

A restriction prevents the PPA from being greater than the total amount, with some adjustments, that would otherwise be deductible as business expenses.

ITR: 2900(6) [Maximum prescribed proxy amount]

As a consequence of this election, the definition of a qualified expenditure includes PPAs. Therefore, ITCs in respect of a PPA are treated in the same manner as all ITCs in respect of SR&ED and reduce the SR&ED expenditure pool. ITCs in respect of PPAs are also eligible for refundable investment tax credit treatment as previously discussed.

Example Problem 12-10

Mr. A owns all the common shares of ABC Limited, a Canadian-controlled private corporation. ABC Limited incurred certain costs in the development of a new process that qualifies for SR&ED expenditures treatment.

Direct material	$250,000
Direct labour	200,000
Indirect costs — overhead	150,000

Of the indirect costs, Mr. A believes that approximately 20% is applicable to the development of the new process, but the corporation's accounting system is not sophisticated enough to identify the direct overhead costs.

Included in the direct labour costs is a salary of $50,000 paid to Mr. A's daughter, a professional engineer who spent 90% of her time on SR&ED activities.

ABC Limited has not had any SR&ED expenditures in the past and had taxable income for the preceding year of $135,000. Taxable capital in the preceding taxation year was $800,000. ABC Limited is not associated with any other corporation. The corporation does not anticipate that it will have any taxable income for this taxation year.

REQUIRED

Describe the tax treatment of the direct and indirect development costs of the current process on the assumption that the new process meets the current requirements as SR&ED expenditures.

SOLUTION

All of the direct material and direct labour costs, for a total of $450,000, are deductible as current SR&ED expenditures since they are directly attributable to the development of the new process. Any amount of these expenses that are not deductible this year will qualify for the SR&ED expenditure pool and can be deducted in any future year. Any ITC deducted from taxes payable or refunded in this year or in future years is deducted from the expenditure pool.

ITA: 37 Scientific research and experimental development

In addition, all of the direct material and direct labour costs qualify for an ITC of 35% since ABC Limited's taxable income in the preceding year was under the small business deduction limit (i.e., $500,000) and the total of these direct costs was less than the expenditure limit of $3 million. Also, taxable capital was less than $10 million. The ITC would be $157,500, i.e., 35% of $450,000.

Since the indirect material and labour costs cannot be traced directly to the development of the new process, they are not deductible under section 37 but are expensed in the normal manner under section 9. An ITC can also be claimed on the indirect material and labour costs of $150,000 by electing the proxy amount method for the current taxation year. The amount of the ITC is calculated below:

Direct labour costs		$200,000
Less: Daughter's salary (a specified employee)		50,000
		$150,000
Plus: Eligible portion of the daughter's salary — Lesser(1) of:		
(a) 75% of $50,000	= $ 37,500	
(b) 2.5 × $55,900(2)	= $139,750	$ 37,500
		$187,500
Amount eligible for the proxy amount 55% of $187,500)		$103,125
ITC 35% thereof		$ 36,094

Note that these labour costs are used as the basis of the proxy amount for overhead. The deduction of labour expenses and other overhead expenses as business expenses is not affected by this proxy amount calculation.

Mr. A's daughter is considered to be a specified shareholder since she is *deemed* to own all of her father's shares and, therefore, owns not less than 10% of the issued shares (i.e., 100% in this situation).

ITA: 248(1) specified shareholder (a)

Since ABC Limited does not expect to have any taxable income this year it can apply for a 100% cash refund of the total ITCs of $193,594 ($157,500 + $36,094). Alternatively, ABC Limited can apply these ITCs against taxes payable in the three preceding years or against future taxes in the next 20 years.

In the following taxation year, ABC Limited will have to include in income the amount of the ITC deducted or refunded of $193,594.

ITA: 12(1)(t) Investment tax credit

NOTES TO SOLUTION

(1) Limited by Regulation for a specified employee, but cannot exceed the portion of actual salary allocated to SR&ED (i.e., 90% of $50,000 or $45,000, in this case).

ITR: 2900(7) [Restrictions for specified employees]

(2) The year's maximum pensionable earnings for CPP purposes (i.e., $55,900 for 2018).

¶12,270 Incorporated Business Income and Integration

¶12,275 Corporate Tax Rate Incentives To Incorporate in General

Now that the complete system for the taxation of business income has been presented, an analysis can be done to determine whether there is a tax advantage to incorporating business income. The answer to the question is affected largely by the combined federal and provincial corporate tax rate applicable to the business income. Generally, business income not eligible for the small business deduction at the corporate level will attract higher tax costs when earned through a corporation than when earned directly by an individual even with the 38% gross-up and tax credit when the provincial tax rate exceeds

12.5%. Exhibit 12-5 illustrates this point using a provincial tax rate of 13% instead of the 12.5% rate that results in perfect integration.

Exhibit 12-5 Tax Impact of Incorporating Active Business Income Not Eligible for the Small Business Deduction

Facts: An individual earns $1,000 of active business income and is deciding whether to incorporate.

The company is not able to claim the small business deduction and has a combined federal and provincial tax rate of 28% including a provincial rate of 13%.

The individual pays tax at a combined federal and provincial rate of 50%.

The dividend gross-up will be 38% and the dividend tax credit will be 6/11 federally and 5/11 provincially.

Calculate

(1) A = the personal after-tax cash available, if the amount and type of income is earned by an individual

		Personal
Combined federal and provincial tax rate		50%
Active business income		$1,000
Personal tax		$ 500
After-tax cash — personal	A	$ 500

(2) B = the corporate after-tax cash available for payment of a dividend, if the amount and type of income is earned in a corporation owned by the individual

		Corporate
Active business income		$1,000
Corporate tax @ 28% (38% – 10% – 13% + 13%)		280
After-tax income available for distribution as a dividend	B	$ 720

(3) C = the personal after-tax cash available, if the corporation distributed its after-tax income as a dividend to the individual as the shareholder

		Personal
		50%
Dividend paid — from Calculation 2		$ 720
Gross-up @ 38%		274
Taxable dividend		$ 994
Combined federal and provincial tax		$ 497
Combined dividend tax credit (($^6/_{11}$ + $^5/_{11}$) × gross-up)		(274)
Personal tax paid on the dividend		$ 223
After-tax cash — Personal	C	$ 497

Determine tax savings or cost

To determine if a tax savings or a tax cost will result from incorporation, perform the following analysis:

		Personal
Combined federal and provincial tax rate		50%
Tax savings (if C > A)	C – A	$ —
Tax cost (if A > C)	A – C	$ 3

(1) Compare

A = the personal after-tax cash available, if the income is earned personally, to

C = the corporate after-tax cash available, if the income earned in a corporation and, then, the after-tax corporate retained earnings are distributed as a dividend to the individual as a shareholder

(2) Determine the tax savings from incorporation — (if C > A)

(C – A) = the amount of tax savings that will be realized if C is greater than A

Since the total corporate tax on the income and personal tax paid on the dividend when flowed through the corporation is greater than the personal tax on the original income there is not a tax savings.

(3) Determine the tax cost from incorporation — (if A > C)

(A – C) = the amount of tax cost that will be incurred if A is greater than C

Since the total corporate tax on the income and personal tax paid on the dividend when flowed through the corporation is greater than the personal tax on the original income, there is a tax cost to incorporating of $3 at the 50% tax rate.

Determine tax deferral or prepayment

A tax deferral is realized by having the income earned and taxed in the corporation and then not paying a dividend but leaving the money in the company. This deferral possibility exists when the personal taxes which must be paid immediately on directly earned business income exceed the corporate taxes on the same business income.

To determine the amount of the tax deferral or prepayment, perform the following analysis:

		Personal
Combined federal and provincial tax rate		50%
Deferral (if B is greater than A)	B – A	$220
Prepayment (if A is greater than B)	A – B	$ —

(1) Compare

A = the personal after-tax cash available, if the income is earned personally, to

B = the corporate after-tax cash available, if the income is earned and retained by the corporation by not distributing the income immediately as a dividend

(2) Determine the tax deferral from incorporation — (if B > A)

(B – A) = the amount of tax deferred that will be realized if B is greater than A

(3) Determine the tax prepayment from incorporation — (if A > B)

(A – B) = the amount of tax prepayment that will be realized if A is greater than B

Alternative View on the Calculation of the Deferral

The above calculation of deferral revolves around the decision of whether to incorporate. For this decision, the calculation above is appropriate.

However, once you have incorporated you are no longer faced with that decision. Instead, your decision is whether to pay out a dividend or leave the cash in the corporation.

At the 50% personal tax rate, $223 of personal tax on the dividend can be deferred by leaving the money in the corporation to be paid out at a later date.

On active business income eligible for the small business deduction, a small tax saving results from the incorporation of such income compared to receiving it directly if the total corporate tax rate is lower than the theoretical 13.8% where integration is perfect, using the 16% gross-up and tax credit on low-rate business income. There is, however, the possibility of deferring tax on dividends ultimately distributed to the shareholders by delaying that distribution. Exhibit 12-6 illustrates these effects. Remember that, although most provincial corporate rates lie between 10% and 16%, the equivalent of the federal small business deduction is also given by most provinces to give an approximate effective rate of 3.8%.

Exhibit 12-6 Tax Impact of Incorporating Active Business Income Eligible for the Small Business Deduction

Facts:

An individual earns $1,000 of active business income and is deciding whether to incorporate.

The company is able to claim the small business deduction on this income and has a combined federal and provincial corporate tax rate of 13.8% including a provincial rate of 3.8%.

The individual pays tax a combined federal and provincial rate of 50%.

The dividend gross-up is 16% and the dividend tax credit is 8/11 federally and 3/11 provincially of the gross-up.

Calculate

(1) A = the personal after-tax cash available, if the amount and type of income is earned by an individual

		Personal
Combined federal and provincial tax rate		50%
Active business income		$1,000
Personal tax		$ 500
After-tax cash — personal	A	$ 500

(2) B = the corporate after-tax cash available for payment of a dividend earned in a corporation owned by the individual

		Corporate
Active business income		$1,000
Corporate tax @ 13.8% (38% – 10% – 18% + 3.8%)		138
After-tax income available for distribution as a dividend	**B**	$ 862

(3) C = the personal after-tax cash available, if the corporation distributed its after-tax income as a dividend to the individual as the shareholder

		Personal
		50%
Dividend paid — from Calculation 2		$ 862
Gross-up @ 16%		138
Taxable dividend		$1,000
Combined federal and provincial tax		$ 500
Combined dividend tax credit (($^{8}/_{11}$ + $^{3}/_{11}$) × gross-up)		138
Personal tax paid on the dividend		$ 362
After-tax cash — Personal ($862 - $362)	**C**	$ 500

Determine tax savings or cost

To determine if a tax savings or a tax cost will result from incorporation, perform the following analysis:

		Personal
Combined federal and provincial tax rate		**50%**
Tax savings (if C > A)	**C – A**	$ —
Tax cost (if A > C)	**A – C**	$ —

(1) Compare

A = the personal after-tax cash available, if the income is earned personally, to

C = the corporate after-tax cash available, if the income earned in a corporation and, then, the after-tax corporate retained earnings are distributed as a dividend to the individual as a shareholder

(2) Determine the tax savings from incorporation — (if C > A)

(C – A) = the amount of tax savings that will be realized if C is greater than A

Since the total corporate and personal tax paid is the same when flowed through the corporation than if the income is earned personally, there is no tax savings.

(3) Determine the tax cost from incorporation — (if A > C)

(A – C) = the amount of tax cost that will be incurred if A is greater than C

Since the total corporate and personal tax paid is less when flowed through the corporation, there is not a tax cost to incorporating.

Determine tax deferral or prepayment

A tax deferral is realized by having the income earned and taxed in the corporation and then not paying a dividend but leaving the money in the company. This deferral possibility exists when the personal taxes, which must be paid immediately on directly earned business income, exceed the corporate taxes on the same business income.

To determine the amount of the tax deferral or prepayment, perform the following analysis:

		Personal
Combined federal and provincial tax rate		50%
Deferral (if B > A)	B – A	$362
Prepayment (if A > B)	A – B	$ —

(1) Compare

A = the personal after-tax cash available, if the income is earned personally, to

B = the corporate after-tax cash available, if the income is earned and retained by the corporation by not distributing the income immediately as a dividend

(2) Determine the tax deferral from incorporation — (if B > A)

(B – A) = the amount of tax deferred that will be realized if B is greater than A. In this case, the deferral is $362.

(3) Determine the tax prepayment from incorporation — (if A > B)

(A – B) = the amount of tax prepayment that will be realized if A is greater than B

Alternative view on the calculation of the deferral

The above calculation of deferral revolves around the decision of whether to incorporate. For this decision, the calculation above is appropriate.

However, once you have incorporated you are no longer faced with that decision. Instead, your decision is whether to pay out a dividend or leave the cash in the corporation. Then, the amount of the deferral is calculated by determining the amount of personal tax on the dividend that will be paid at some future date.

At the 50% personal tax rate, $362 of personal tax on the dividend can be deferred by leaving the money in the corporation.

It will take a provincial rate of tax below 3.8% (13.8% – (38% – 10% – 18%)) to provide tax savings from the incorporation of income eligible for the small business deduction. For all higher corporate provincial income tax rates, the total corporate tax rate will be above the 13.8% rate necessary for perfect integration of the tax on low-rate income and, as a result, there will be a tax cost to incorporation.

¶12,285 Summary of Advantages and Disadvantages of Incorporating Active Business Income

From the foregoing analysis, it should be possible to draw some conclusions of both a tax and non-tax nature regarding the incorporation of business operations.

¶12,285.10 Advantages of Incorporation

The advantages of incorporation appear to include the following:

- limited liability, although it should be recognized that to the extent creditors of an incorporated business demand personal guarantees from shareholders, limited liability is negated;
- tax savings if the combined corporate tax rate is under 13.8%;
- a tax savings will result from a provincial corporate tax rate of less than 3.8%;
- tax deferral at higher personal income levels on business income not eligible for the small business deduction and at all personal income levels on business income eligible for the small business deduction;
- income splitting potential in carefully planned and very restrictive situations (as discussed previously with respect to the attribution rules and tax on split income) with family members as employees or shareholders. Chapter 13 provides further discussion on the Tax on Split Income (TOSI);

- estate planning advantages on the transfer of future growth in the corporation's shares to children, subject to restrictions on the new TOSI rules (as discussed in a subsequent chapter);
- availability of registered pension plans, including defined benefit plans, to the owner as an employee of a corporation is not possible in the unincorporated form;
- separation of business and personal activities;
- stabilization of income of the individual through salary payments or greater flexibility in the timing of the receipt of income subject to personal tax;
- continuity of the separate legal entity;
- deferral of accrued capital gains on transfer of shares to a spouse (as discussed in a subsequent chapter);
- potentially easier access to financing;
- availability of the capital gains exemption for qualified small business corporation shares or business investment loss treatment for securities of a small business corporation; and
- availability of the deferral of capital gains on the sale of eligible small business corporation shares, if replacement shares are acquired. ITA: 44.1(1) Definitions

¶12,285.20 Disadvantages of Incorporation

The disadvantages of incorporating business operations appear to include:

- a tax cost if the combined corporate tax rate is over 13.8% for income eligible for the small business deduction and 27.5% for other business income;
- a prepayment of tax at lower levels of personal income on business income not eligible for the small business deduction;
- the additional legal and accounting costs of maintaining a corporation;
- a loss of the availability of business and capital losses to offset personal income. While this disadvantage may be offset, to some extent, by the availability of allowable business investment loss treatment for shares of a small business corporation, the loss is only one-half deductible and it is deductible only on sale of the shares or bankruptcy of the corporation; and
- administrative costs such as maintaining corporate records, dividend resolutions and T5 reporting.

Often the tax saving, if any, or deferral will, in many cases, outweigh the disadvantages of incorporating such income. This is particularly so where business income eligible for the small business deduction is earned through a corporation.

¶12,285.99 Practise What You've Learned

Refer to the following sections of the Study Guide to practise what you've learned:

¶12,800 — Review Questions

- Question 6 — Small business deduction
- Question 7 — Advantages of incorporation
- Question 8 — Disadvantages of incorporation
- Question 9 — Small business deduction vs. general rate reduction

¶12,825 — Multiple Choice Questions

- Question 3 — General rate reduction

¶12,850 — Exercises

- Exercise 6 — Calculate Part I tax

¶12,300 Income From Investments of a CCPC

¶12,310 Overview of Integration for Income From Investments of a CCPC

¶12,315 Purpose

¶12,315.10 Investment Income

(i) The theory

The tax system provides special rules for private corporations which are meant to eliminate some of the tax biases between income earned by an individual and income earned by a corporation. One bias arises from the potential double taxation of investment income. For the moment, think of investment income as property income (i.e., interest, rents, etc., but not dividends). Later on, a more precise definition will be given. Without special rules, investment income would be taxed once in the corporation and again at the shareholder level when dividends are paid. To eliminate this bias, the concept of a refundable tax was developed, whereby a portion of the initial corporate tax on such income is refunded when dividends are paid. The corporate tax on investment income would have to be reduced to an approximate rate of tax of 13.8%. The 16% gross-up and dividend tax credit then would allow the shareholder credit for that 13.8% tax paid by the company and complete integration of corporate and personal taxes would be achieved. Thus, a Canadian who transfers his or her investments to a private corporation and flows the income through the corporation, would, theoretically, retain the same amount of after-tax investment income as he or she would if the investments were held personally and had received the income from the investments directly.

When investment income is flowed through a corporation, an indefinite deferral of tax is possible if the initial corporate tax rate is relatively low and if the investment income is left in the corporation and not distributed by way of dividends to the shareholders. In contrast, an individual Canadian who holds his or her investments personally, is required to pay tax on the income as it is received or accrued. The tax system attempts to eliminate this bias by ensuring that investment income earned in a corporation is taxed initially at a high corporate rate. Then the corporate tax is partially refunded when the investment income is distributed, by way of taxable dividends, to the corporation's shareholders who then pay tax on the income at their personal rate. The system removes the ability to defer the tax on investment income earned in the corporation. As mentioned earlier in the chapter, significant investment income in a corporation will affect the corporation's ability to access the lower tax rate on the first $500,000 in active business income.

The system of integration was intended to bring the effective corporate rate of tax on investment income down to 13.8%. This rate is the same rate that was intended to apply on up to $500,000 of active business income. As mentioned previously, at a corporate rate of 13.8% the objective of theoretically perfect integration is achieved. However, the specific rules applied to each type of income attempt to achieve the objective in opposite ways. On the one hand, the rules applied to active business income provide for a low initial rate of corporate tax, after the small business deduction, to allow for greater retention of income for reinvestment in the business. On the other hand, the rules applied to investment income provide for a high initial rate of corporate tax to prevent the use of a corporation as a means of deferring tax on investment income. When retained earnings are distributed as dividends, the dividend refund was intended to bring the total effective corporate tax rate on that investment income down to 13.8%.

The provisions which increase the dividend gross-up and tax credit on eligible dividends do not apply to investment income earned in a Canadian-controlled private corporation. As a result, for dividends from investment income, the gross-up is 16% and the federal dividend tax credit is $^{8}/_{11}$ of the gross-up.

(ii) The reality: Imperfection

Close to perfect integration of active business income up to the $500,000 limit at a corporate rate of about 13.8% is, generally, achieved with a combined federal and provincial small business deduction. However, perfect integration of investment income is, generally, not achieved. Imperfections result from refundable tax rates and provincial corporate rates that are either too high or too low.

Exhibit 12-7 shows the effective tax rate on aggregate investment income, including the additional refundable tax (ART) of $10^{2}/_{3}$%. The ART is necessary to discourage the use of a corporation to defer tax on investment income. The ART results in the total initial tax at the corporate level being higher than the top personal rate of tax in most provinces.

Two terms used in this Exhibit are Specified Investment Business (SIB) Income and Aggregate Investment Income (AII). SIB is defined in ¶12,150 and AII is defined in ¶12,315.

Exhibit 12-7 Taxation of Income in a CCPC

	Specified Investment Buss Income			
	Property			Net TCG
	Cdn	Cdn Dividends		
		Conn	Port	
Employment				
Business				
Property	+/-	+	+	
Net TCG				+
OI/OD				
ABIL				
Division B				
Division C				
Donations				
Dividends		-	-	
Net CL				-
Non CL				
Taxable	**Aggregate Investment Income**			
Corporate	%	%	%	%
Basic	38.00			38.00
Abatement	(10.00)			(10.00)
ART	10.67			10.67
Part IV		?	38.3	
SBD				
M&P				
RDTOH	√	?	√	√
FTC				
Gen rate red'n				
Net Federal	38.67		38.3	38.67
Provincial	12.00			12.00
Subtotal	50.67		38.3	50.67
Dividend Refund	(30.67)	?	(38.3)	(30.67)
	20.00		-	20.00
Dividend gross-up	16%	16%/38%	16%/38%	16%

Exhibit 12-8 shows a calculation of effective total tax applicable to taxable investment income of a Canadian-controlled private corporation eligible for a refund on the payment of dividends, referred to as a dividend refund, using a hypothetical provincial rate of 12% and including the $10\frac{2}{3}$% additional refundable tax on investment income.

Exhibit 12-8 Comparison of Tax Rates Applicable to Investment Income Eligible for a Dividend Refund and on the First $500,000 Active Business Income of a Canadian-Controlled Private Corporation

	Investment income[1]	Active business income[2]
Federal tax rate	38.00%	38.00%
Abatement for provincial tax	(10.00)	(10.00)
Net federal tax	28.00%	28.00%
Additional refundable tax on investment income	10.67	Nil
Small business deduction	—	(18%)
Refund on payment of dividends from investment income	(30.67)	—
Net federal tax after dividend refund	8.00%	10.00%
Provincial tax (theoretical)	12.00[3]	3.80[4]
Effective total tax	20.00%	13.80%

ITA: 123(1)(a)

ITA: 124(1) Deduction from corporation tax

ITA: 129(1) Dividend refund to private corporation

[1] Investment income includes all types of property income except dividends from taxable Canadian corporations.

[2] This column of the table reflects the tax on the first $500,000 of active business income. Over $500,000, there is no small business deduction, but there is a 13% general rate reduction; therefore, the effective tax rate would be 28%, assuming a full hypothetical provincial tax rate of 12%.

[3] A provincial corporate tax rate of 5.8% on investment income would result in an effective total tax of 13.8%, which would allow for perfect integration. However, provincial tax rates average around 12%.

[4] Several provinces also give a small business deduction on the first $500,000 of active business income. In this example, a net 3.8% provincial rate after a provincial small business deduction was assumed.

Exhibit 12-8 clearly demonstrates that effective tax rates for investment income are above the 13.8% rate at which integration is perfect with the applicable 16% gross-up for dividends paid. Active business income, at or below $500,000, is taxed at a corporate rate that results in close to perfect integration. However, for a CCPC with active business income over $500,000 or investment income, there is a significant difference in the effective tax rates on these two types of income (i.e., 27.5% for business income versus 21% for investment income). This difference may encourage some taxpayers to attempt to recharacterize some of their active business income (over $500,000) as investment income so as to attract the investment income net rate (20%) which has no cap (like the $500,000 business limit). Remember, however, that one important downside of investment income is that the initial corporate tax rate before the dividend refund is at the high 50⅔% (i.e., 28% + 10⅔% + 12%) rate (i.e., no general rate reduction), including a 10⅔% additional refundable tax, and that dividends must be paid in order to trigger the refund of Part I tax of 30⅔%. While the corporate rate after the refund is low at 20% (i.e., 50⅔% – 30⅔%), the shareholders receive a dividend which is taxable to complete the integration process.

Remember too that the higher 38% dividend gross-up and tax credit apply to business income taxed at the high rate. On high-rate income the theoretical rate for integration is 27.5%. As a result, the discrepancy is not as great, and the incentive to recharacterize high-rate business income as investment income is greatly reduced.

¶12,315.20 Portfolio Dividends

Another bias arises because intercorporate dividends are deductible in order to arrive at taxable income and, therefore, not subject to tax under Part I of the Act. By placing dividend-yielding investments in a corporation, an individual, particularly one in a high tax bracket, could defer tax on dividend income indefinitely. A 38⅓ Part IV refundable tax that certain corporations pay on such dividends is intended to eliminate this bias.

ITA: 186 Tax on assessable dividends

If it were not for the Part IV tax on what are referred to as "portfolio dividends", it would be extremely attractive for an individual to make portfolio investments in dividend-producing shares through an investment holding corporation. No tax would be paid under Part I on the dividends received by the holding corporation. By contrast, an individual who owned the portfolio investments directly, would pay tax under Part I at his or her personal rate on any dividends received. Thus, the Part IV tax of 38⅓% levied on the recipient corporation is an initial tax roughly equivalent to the tax that would be paid by the individual in the top federal tax bracket receiving a dividend from a taxable Canadian corporation. The Part IV tax is fully refundable when the recipient corporation itself pays a taxable dividend to its shareholders. Thus, after the refund, the corporation is effectively not taxed on the dividend that it received from another corporation and passed on to its shareholders. This preserves the integration system by preventing double taxation of the income that gave rise to the original dividend from the originating corporation to the holding corporation.

¶12,320 Conceptual Illustration of Integration

Exhibit 12-9 illustrates conceptually how investment income, such as interest income, capital gains and portfolio dividends are integrated through a private corporation that qualifies for refundable tax treatment. Recall that one of the objectives of the integration system is to ensure that income from investments, which flows through a qualifying private corporation to its shareholders, bears the same total tax burden (at the combined corporate and individual level) that would be borne on that income if it were earned directly by an individual. For simplicity of illustration, and to demonstrate total integration, the combined federal and provincial corporate tax is assumed to be 40% plus the additional refundable tax of 10⅔% and the dividend tax credit, including the provincial tax effect, is assumed to be equal to the 16% gross-up, except for portfolio dividends from Canadian-resident public corporations eligible for the 38% gross-up. Remember that CCPCs that receive "eligible dividends" can flow those dividends out to the shareholders as dividends eligible for the 38% gross-up. The combined federal and provincial tax rates for individuals is assumed to be 50% for this illustration, although *any individual's combined federal and provincial marginal tax rate* could have been used to show perfect integration. Under these assumptions, this objective of integration is met perfectly.

Exhibit 12-9 Conceptual Illustration of Integration (or Tax Impact of Incorporating Investment Income)

Facts: An individual earns $1,000 of each of interest income, capital gains, and portfolio dividends and is deciding whether or not to incorporate.

	Investment Income	Dividends
Corporate tax		
Part I combined federal (28%) & provincial (12%)	40%	
Additional refundable tax	10⅔%	
Part IV tax rate		38⅓%
Dividend refund	30⅔%	38⅓%

	Investment Income	Flow through of low-rate dividends	Flow through of eligible dividends
Dividend gross-up	16%	16%	38%
Dividend tax credit — federal (fraction of gross-up)	8/11	8/11	6/11
Dividend tax credit — provincial (fraction of gross-up)	3/11	3/11	5/11

The individual will pay tax at a combined federal and provincial rate of 50%.

Calculate

(1) A = the personal after-tax cash available, if the amount and type of income is earned by an individual

	Personal				
		Capital Gain		Dividend	
	Interest	50% Taxable	50% Non-taxable	16% Gross-up	38% Gross-up
Income	$1,000	$1,000	$1,000	$1,000	$1,000
Gross-up				160	380
Taxable income	$1,000	$1,000	$1,000	$1,160	$1,380
Tax @ 50%	$ 500	$ 500		$ 580	$ 690
Dividend tax credit				160	380
Total personal tax	$ 500	$ 500		$ 420	$ 310
After-tax cash — personal **A**	$ 500	$ 500	$1,000	$ 580	$ 690

The non-taxable portion of the capital gain can be distributed by the corporation as a capital dividend and received tax-free by the shareholder (discussed in a subsequent chapter).

(2) B = the corporate tax that would be paid, if the amount and type of income is earned in a corporation owned by the individual

	Corporate				
		Capital Gain		Portfolio Dividends	
	Interest	50% Taxable	50% Non-taxable	16% Gross-up	38% Gross-up
Income	$1,000	$1,000	$1,000	$1,000	$1,000
Division C deduction				$1,000	$1,000
Taxable income	$1,000	$1,000	$1,000	$ —	$ —
Part I Tax @ 40%	$ 400	$ 400			
Part IV Tax @ 38⅓%				$ 383	$ 383
Additional refundable tax @ 10⅔% of $1,000	107	107			
Total tax — initially before refund	507	507		383	383

Corporate

		Capital Gain		Portfolio Dividends	
	Interest	50% Taxable	50% Non-taxable	16% Gross-up	38% Gross-up
Corporate after-tax cash available before dividend refund **B**	$ 493	$ 493		$ 617	$ 617
Dividend refund @ 30⅔%	307	307			
Dividend refund @ 38⅓%				383	383
Net corporate tax	$ 200	$ 200		$ 0	$ 0
Cash available for dividends	$ 800	$ 800		$1,000	$1,000

(3) C = the personal after-tax cash available, if the corporation distributed its after-tax income as a dividend to the individual as the shareholder

Personal

		Capital Gain		Portfolio Dividends	
	Interest	Taxable	Non-taxable	16% Gross-up	38% Gross-up
Dividend paid — from Calculation 2	$ 800	$ 800	$1,000	$1,000	$1,000
Gross-up @ 16%/38%	128	128		160	380
Taxable income	$ 928	$ 928	$1,000	$1,160	$1,380
Combined federal and provincial personal tax @ 50%	$ 464	$ 464		$ 580	$ 635
Dividend tax credit	(128)	(128)		(160)	(380)
Net personal tax	$ 336	$ 336		$ 420	$ 255
After-tax cash — personal **C**	$ 464	$ 464	$1,000	$ 580	$ 745

Notice that the dividend gross-up does not bring taxable income back up to $1,000 for interest and taxable capital gains. This imperfection will cause the tax cost shown in the next step.

Determine tax savings or cost

To determine if a tax savings or a tax cost will result from incorporation, perform the following analysis:

		Personal				
			Capital Gain		Portfolio Dividends	
		Interest	50% Taxable	50% Non-taxable	16% Gross-up	38% Gross-up
Tax savings (if C > A)	**C – A**					
Tax cost (if A > C)	**A – C**	$ 36	$ 36			

(1) Compare

A = the personal after-tax cash available, if the income is earned personally, to

C = the corporate after-tax cash available, if the income earned in a corporation and, then, the after-tax corporate retained earnings are distributed as a dividend to the individual as a shareholder

(2) Determine the tax savings from incorporation — (if C > A)

(C – A) = the amount of tax savings that will be realized if C is greater than A

Interest and Taxable Capital Gains

Since the total corporate and personal tax paid is more when flowed through the corporation than if the income is earned personally, there is not a tax savings.

Portfolio Dividends

Since the total corporate and personal tax paid when flowed through the corporation is equal to the personal tax paid if the income is earned personally, there is not a tax savings.

(3) Determine the tax cost from incorporation — (if A > C)

(A – C) = the amount of tax cost that will be incurred if A is greater than C

Interest and Taxable Capital Gains

Since the total corporate and personal tax paid is more when flowed through the corporation than if the income is earned personally, there is a tax cost of $36.

Portfolio Dividends

Since the total corporate and personal tax paid when flowed through the corporation is equal to the personal tax paid if the income is earned personally, there is not a tax cost.

Determine tax deferral or prepayment

A tax deferral is realized by having the income earned and taxed in the corporation and then not paying a dividend but leaving the money in the company. This deferral possibility exists when the personal taxes which must be paid immediately on directly earned investment income exceed the corporate taxes on the same investment income. A prepayment results in the opposite scenario where the corporate tax exceeds the personal tax.

To determine the amount of the tax deferral or prepayment, perform the following analysis:

			Personal			
			Capital Gain		Portfolio Dividends	
		Interest	50% Taxable	50% Non-taxable	16% Gross-up	38% Gross-up
Deferral (if B > A)	B – A				$37	
Prepayment (if A > B)	A – B	$7	$7			$73

(1) Compare

A = the personal after-tax cash available, if the income is earned personally, to

B = the corporate after-tax cash available, if the income is earned and retained by the corporation by not distributing the income immediately as a dividend

(2) Determine the tax deferral from incorporation — (if B > A)

(B – A) = the amount of tax deferred that will be realized if B is greater than A. In this case there is a deferral for non-eligible portfolio dividends (16% gross-up).

(3) Determine the tax prepayment from incorporation — (if A > B)

(A – B) = the amount of tax prepayment that will be realized if A is greater than B. In this case there is a prepayment of tax for interest, taxable capital gains and eligible portfolio dividends (38% gross-up).

Alternative view on the calculation of the deferral

The above calculation of deferral revolves around the decision of whether to incorporate. For this decision, the calculation above is appropriate.

However, once you have incorporated you are no longer faced with that decision. Instead, your decision is whether to pay out a dividend or leave the cash in the corporation. In this case the deferral is measured by the personal tax the individual would pay on the dividend being deferred.

¶12,330 Special Refundable Taxes in Respect of Income From Investments of a CCPC

¶12,335 Aggregate Investment Income

Aggregate investment income is broadly defined to include income from property, plus net taxable capital gains, less certain adjustments. Property income, for the purposes of this definition, includes net income from all property, other than (a) exempt income, and (b) dividends which are deductible in computing taxable income. The meaning of the term "income from property" is amplified by the definition "income" or "loss" which includes income from a specified investment business *carried on in Canada*, but excludes income from the following sources: ITA: 129(4) Definitions

(1) from any property that is incident to or pertains to an active business carried on by a corporation, or

(2) from any property used or held primarily for the purpose of earning income from an active business carried on by the corporation.

Net losses from property are deducted from the foregoing amounts of property income.

Foreign investment income is calculated as aggregate investment income from foreign sources. Hence, aggregate investment income includes that income from both Canadian and foreign sources. ITA: 129(4) Definitions

As part of the system of integration, one-half of the capital gains and capital losses that is not included in income, is included in the corporation's capital dividend account (discussed in a subsequent chapter). The Act permits the corporation to pay a dividend out of the capital dividend account. The capital dividend is received free of tax by the shareholder. This completes the full integration of capital gains through a private corporation or Canadian-controlled private corporation and, with respect to the tax-free portion of the capital gains, places the shareholder in the same position as if he or she received the gain directly. ITA: 89(1) Definitions, 83(2) Capital dividend

¶12,340 Additional Refundable Tax (ART)

¶12,340.10 Basic Rules

For Canadian-controlled private corporations, a refundable tax is imposed on "aggregate investment income". This tax can be summarized as follows: ITA: 123.3 Refundable tax on CCPC's investment income

$10\frac{2}{3}\% \times$ the lesser of:

(1) aggregate investment income, and ITA: 129(4) Definitions

(2) taxable income minus the amount on which the small business deduction is based.

Aggregate investment income (AII) can be summarized as follows: ITA: 129(4) Definitions

- Net taxable capital gains for the year,
- Less: net capital losses deducted under Division C,
- Plus: income from property (Canadian and foreign),[8]
- Less: dividends deducted under Division C,
- Less: losses from property (Canadian and foreign).

¶12,345 "Refundable Dividend Tax on Hand" (RDTOH)

Beginning with taxation years after 2018, the February 27, 2018 Federal Budget proposed two measures to limit the tax advantages that a Canadian-controlled private corporation (CCPC) can obtain: (1) the limitation of the small business deduction for CCPCs with a significant level of passive income, discussed earlier in the chapter, and (2) the introduction of a second refundable dividend tax on hand (RDTOH). The introduction of the second RDTOH account will limit the CCPC's ability to access the refundable taxes on investment income. This section will first discuss the concept of the RDTOH to enable the reader to understand the concept and then will discuss the new proposed rules that will limit the CCPCs use of the RDTOH account.

¶12,345.10 The Concept

"Refundable dividend tax on hand" (RDTOH) may be viewed as an account which accumulates all of the tax paid by a private company on its portfolio dividend income (i.e., Part IV tax at 38.33%) and a portion of the Part I tax paid by a Canadian-controlled private corporation on other investment income. The principal components of the account are as follows:

- the refundable portion of Part I tax (including the ART) that is paid on investment income; ITA: 129(3)(a)
- the amount of Part IV tax that is paid on taxable dividends (the Part IV tax is discussed in more detail below); and ITA: 129(3)(b), 186 Tax on assessable dividends
- the RDTOH balance at the end of the previous year, less "dividend refunds" (explained below) of the previous year that arise when the corporation pays taxable dividends. ITA: 129(3)(c), 129(3)(d)

The February 27, 2018 Budget did not change the components of the RDTOH account but did outline special rules related to Part IV tax paid on eligible dividends received. The taxes that are accumulated in the RDTOH account are refundable to the company at the rate of $38.33 of refund for every $100 of taxable dividends paid. These refunds are commonly referred to as "dividend refunds", which reduce the balance in the RDTOH account. ITA: 129(1)(a)(i), 129(3)(d)

[8] Includes interest, royalties, rents, and dividends.

The following diagram illustrates these rules conceptually:

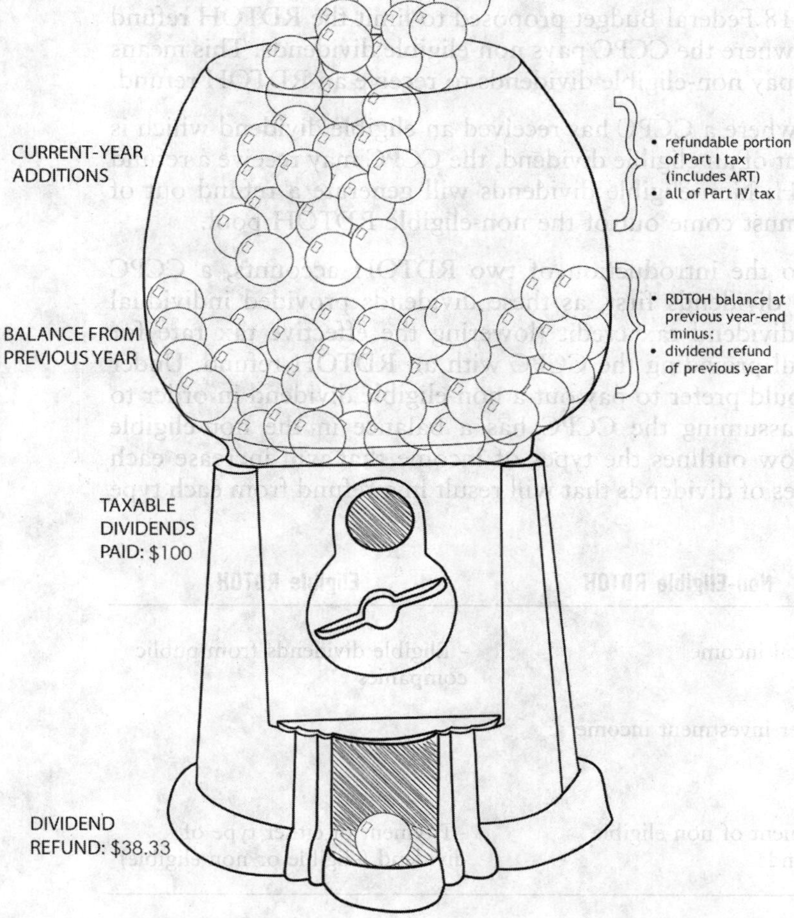

¶12,345.20 Interpretation of the Law

RDTOH is illustrated, in part, in Exhibit 12-10. The basic purpose of the calculation is to aggregate the two types of refundable taxes (i.e., refundable portion of Part I tax for investment income (shown in the Exhibit) and Part IV tax), net of the amount of refundable taxes actually received. The current rules related to refundable dividend tax on hand tracks all the additional tax in one RDTOH account.

ITA: 129(3) Definition of "refundable dividend tax on hand"

¶12,345.30 Proposed RDTOH for taxation years beginning after 2018

For taxation years beginning after 2018, the February 27, 2018 Budget proposed the introduction of two RDTOH accounts for CCPCs: eligible RDTOH and non-eligible RDTOH. The eligible RDTOH pool will track Part IV refundable taxes paid on eligible dividends received by the CCPC (generally dividends received from public companies). The non-eligible RDTOH will track the additional Part I and Part IV tax paid on all other investment income.

The purpose of the two RDTOH pools is to restrict the CCPC's ability to get a refund from the RDTOH account on the payment of eligible dividends. As discussed earlier in this chapter, along with other previous chapters, eligible dividends allow an individual to access an enhanced dividend tax credit, thus lowering the tax implications for an individual taxpayer. The February 27, 2018 Federal Budget proposed to limit the RDTOH refund a CCPC will receive to situations where the CCPC pays non-eligible dividends. This means that CCPCs will be motivated to pay non-eligible dividends to receive an RDTOH refund.

The one exception to this rule is where a CCPC has received an eligible dividend which is subject to Part IV tax. On payment of an eligible dividend, the CCPC may receive a refund of balance in the eligible RDTOH. Non-eligible dividends will generate a refund out of either pool, but the refund first must come out of the non-eligible RDTOH pool.

Under the current rules, prior to the introduction of two RDTOH accounts, a CCPC would generally pay out eligible dividends first, as these dividends provided individual shareholders with an enhanced dividend tax credit (lowering the effective tax rate for individual shareholders) while still providing the CCPC with an RDTOH refund. Under the proposed rules, the CCPC would prefer to pay out a non-eligible dividend in order to maximize the RDTOH refund (assuming the CCPC has a balance in the non-eligible RDTOH account). The table below outlines the types of income that will increase each type of RDTOH pool and the types of dividends that will result in a refund from each type of pool.

	Non-Eligible RDTOH	**Eligible RDTOH**
Additions to the pool	- Rental income	- Eligible dividends from public companies
	- Other investment income	
Decreases to the pool	- Payment of non-eligible dividends	- Payment of either type of dividend (eligible or non-eligible)

Exhibit 12-10 Refundable Portion of Part I Tax [par. 129(3)(a)]

The amount added to non-eligible RDTOH in a taxation year in respect of Part I tax is the total of:

(1) where the corporation was a CCPC throughout the year, the least of:

(a) 30⅔% × aggregate investment income

less the net of: non-business foreign tax credit minus: 8%[1] × foreign investment income

[1] The notional federal tax rate for non-business income is 38.67% (i.e., approximately 38% – 10% + 10.67% = 38.67%). 8% is the notional 38.67% rate less 30⅔%.

(b) $30\frac{2}{3}\%$ × (taxable income less the total of:

- the amount eligible for the small business deduction
- $\frac{100}{38.67}$[2] × non-business foreign tax credit
- 4 (i.e., the "relevant factor")[3] × business foreign tax credit

(c) Part I tax

The refundable portion of the Part I tax is designed to produce a refundable tax equal to $30\frac{2}{3}\%$ of investment income (excluding most dividends). The provisions establish aggregate investment income, net of expenses, from which net capital losses deducted in the year and losses for the year from property sources are subtracted. The justification for deducting the net capital losses is that since investment income is computed at the net income level, it is possible that taxable capital gains included in income could be offset by net capital losses which are deducted at the taxable income level after the computation of income for tax purposes. Since no Part I tax would be payable on such taxable capital gains, no refund of unpaid tax should apply to such gains. Hence, net capital losses claimed are deducted from aggregate investment income eligible for refundable treatment.

ITA: 129(4) Definitions, 111(1)(b) Net capital losses

The calculations ensure that no refundable tax is calculated on foreign investment income which gives rise to a foreign tax credit in the year. Such foreign income will, therefore, not result in a refund of Canadian taxes that have not been paid as a result of the foreign tax credit.

The adjustments to taxable income are made to restrict the amount of the refund where other items (i.e., the small business deduction and foreign-source income) have reduced the taxable income below the investment income subject to tax.

Finally, the refundable portion of Part I tax is limited by the amount of tax payable under Part I, because there should not be a potential refund of a portion of Part I tax that has not been paid. Such non-payment of Part I tax may be due to the carryover of losses, deductions such as the small business deduction and the M&P profit deduction, or credits such as foreign tax credits, investment tax credits and political donations credits.

Ⓐ ¶12,350 "Deeming Rules"

What are known in practice as "deeming rules" are provided as an anti-avoidance provision that converts what would be property income (e.g., rent and interest) into active business income. However, this deeming provision only applies in situations where the income was derived from an associated corporation that had deducted the same amount in determining its active business income.

ITA: 129(6) Investment income from associated corporation deemed to be active business income

[2] Based on a 38.67% rate as above.

[3] 4 = 1/(0.3867 − 0.13), as found in the definition of "relevant factor" in subsection 248(1) and as discussed in ¶12,125.20.

Were it not for these deeming rules, it would be possible for a corporation that was approaching the $500,000 business limit for its small business deduction, for example, to transfer certain of its assets to an associated corporation which would rent the assets back to the original corporation. The rental expense incurred by the original corporation would be deductible, thereby reducing its active business income and preventing income in excess of $500,000 from being taxed at full corporate rates. The rental income to the associated corporation would be considered income from property or income from a specified investment business and would, therefore, be eligible for refundable treatment. However, as a result of the deeming rules, the amounts received are deemed to be active business income of the recipient.

As a result, the combined active business income of the original corporation and of the associated corporation, which receives the rent deemed to be active business income is the same as it would have been if the new corporation had not been set up; that is, the fact that the two corporations must share the $500,000 business limit has no effect on the total active business income of the group. Thus, any active business income in excess of $500,000 within the associated group will be taxed at full corporate rates as it would have been without the associated corporation. These deeming rules are summarized in Exhibit 12-11.

Exhibit 12-11 "Deeming Rules" [ssec. 129(6)]

Conditions	(1) Amount that would be income of the recipient corporation from property.
	(2) Amount deductible in computing income from an active business of an *associated* payer corporation.
Effect	(1) Amount not included in income from property.
	(2) Amount deemed to be income of the recipient from an active business [spar. 129(6)(*b*)(i)].
Application of small business deduction	Eligible for the small business deduction to the extent that the associated group of corporations has not exceeded the $500,000 business limit [ssec. 125(1)].

Special rules apply where companies are deemed not to be associated because both companies are associated with a third company as discussed in ¶12,205 above. Where the third company is not a CCPC or has a business limit that is deemed to be Nil because of any election, the eligibility of the recharacterized income for the small business deduction is impacted. In such case, amounts paid from the third corporation to one of the other corporations that would be deemed to be active business income under subsection 129(6) would not be eligible for the small business deduction by the corporation receiving the payment. This restriction on eligibility for the small business deduction was added to prevent planning that involved transferring income from a non-CCPC or other company that was not eligible for the small business deduction to a corporation that could use the small business income against such income.

ITA: 256(2)(a), 256(2)(b)

¶12,355 Part IV Tax on Portfolio and Other Dividends

Normally, when a private corporation (or a "subject corporation", which is discussed below) receives a taxable dividend from another Canadian company (or an exempt dividend from a foreign affiliate), the dividend is deductible, in Division C, in computing taxable income. This indicates that dividends between corporations would be tax free. However, a 38⅓% tax may be required to be paid on some of these dividends. A calculation of the Part IV tax is made in the T2 corporate tax return to meet the filing requirements for this tax. Late-filed payments of this tax are subject to interest at the prescribed rate. This special Part IV tax is fully refundable to the corporation when the dividend income is passed on to its shareholders as previously discussed.

ITA: 186(1)(a), 187(1) Information return, 187(2) Interest, 129(1)(b), 125(1)(a)(i)(C)

Part IV tax is fully refundable tax, i.e., temporary tax of 38⅓% levied on "assessable dividends" received by a "private corporation" or a "subject corporation" with an exception for dividends received from "connected corporations". Terms are discussed below. The objective of this tax is to discourage the use of a corporation to hold dividend-paying shares to defer tax to be paid by an individual shareholder on those dividends.

For taxation years beginning after 2018, the February 27, 2018 Federal Budget separates the refundable portion of Part IV tax. Part IV tax paid on eligible dividends will now be tracked in the eligible refundable dividend tax on hand (RDTOH) while all other Part IV tax will be tracked in the non-eligible RDTOH.

¶12,355.10 Assessable Dividends

Dividends subject to the 38⅓% Part IV tax have often been referred to as "portfolio dividends" even though the Act does not use this term. The term "assessable dividend" is defined to include dividends that are deductible under Division C.

ITA: 186(3) Definitions

¶12,355.20 Private Corporation

A private corporation is a corporation that is resident in Canada and that is neither a public corporation nor controlled by a public corporation.

¶12,355.40 Connected Corporation

ITA: 186(4) Corporations connected with particular corporation

A corporation is connected with another corporation where:

(1) the corporation is controlled by the other corporation (where control represents ownership of more than 50% of the voting shares by any combination of the other corporation and persons with whom it does not deal at arm's length); or

(2) the corporation's shares are held by the other corporation and these shares represent more than 10% of the voting shares and more than 10% of the fair market value of all the issued shares in the corporation.

ITA: 186(2) When corporation controlled

The definition of control is expanded for the purposes of the concept of connected corporation. The provision requires that in determining "control", shares owned by non-arm's length persons must be included in that determination. For example, this provision allows avoidance of the Part IV tax where the share ownership is split in lots of 10% among family members.

This concept of a "connected corporation" is illustrated in Exhibit 12-12.

Exhibit 12-12 Concept of Connected Corporations

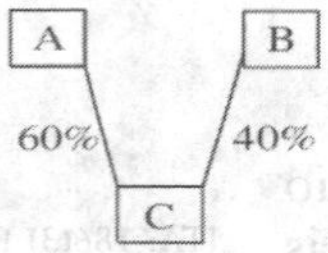

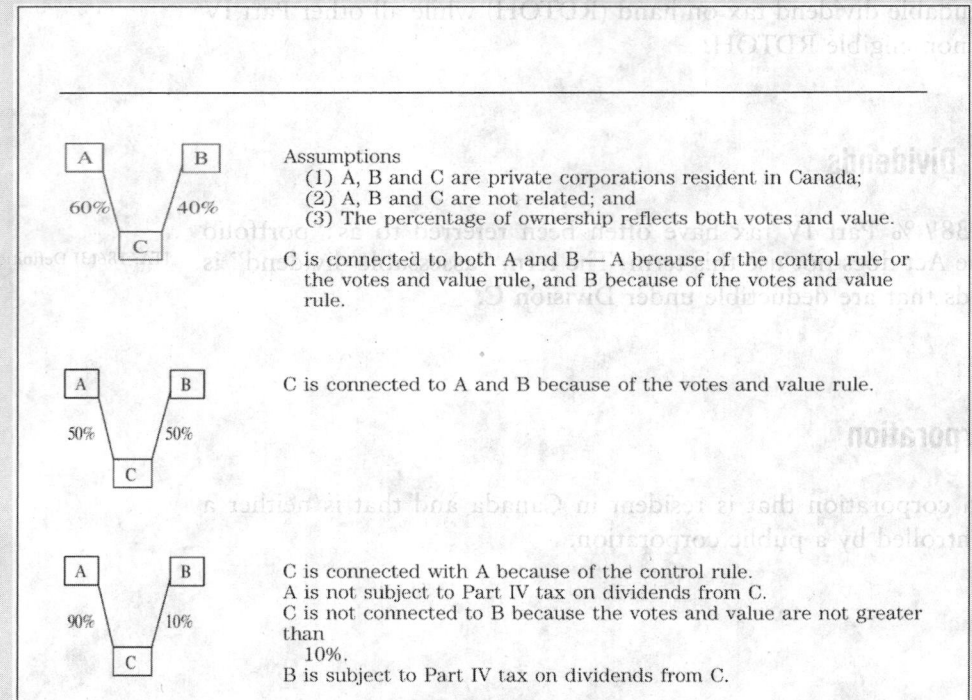

Assumptions
(1) A, B and C are private corporations resident in Canada;
(2) A, B and C are not related; and
(3) The percentage of ownership reflects both votes and value.

C is connected to both A and B — A because of the control rule or the votes and value rule, and B because of the votes and value rule.

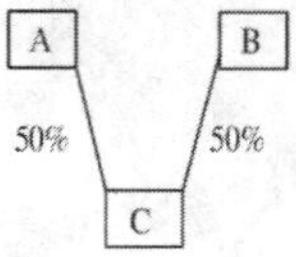

C is connected to A and B because of the votes and value rule.

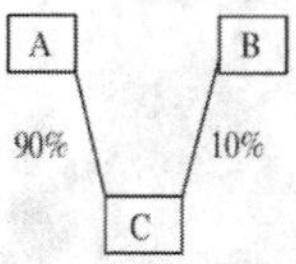

C is connected with A because of the control rule.
A is not subject to Part IV tax on dividends from C.
C is not connected to B because the votes and value are not greater than 10%.
B is subject to Part IV tax on dividends from C.

Note that the "connected" concept flows from C to A and B. Therefore, C may be connected to A and B, but A and B are not connected to C.

Example Problem 12-11

Mr. and Ms. Cheng hold common shares in two private corporations resident in Canada, as shown in the chart below. These corporations in turn hold common shares in another private corporation, Opco Ltd. The balance of the common shares are held by unrelated individuals. Assume that the share-ownership percentage also reflects their underlying value.

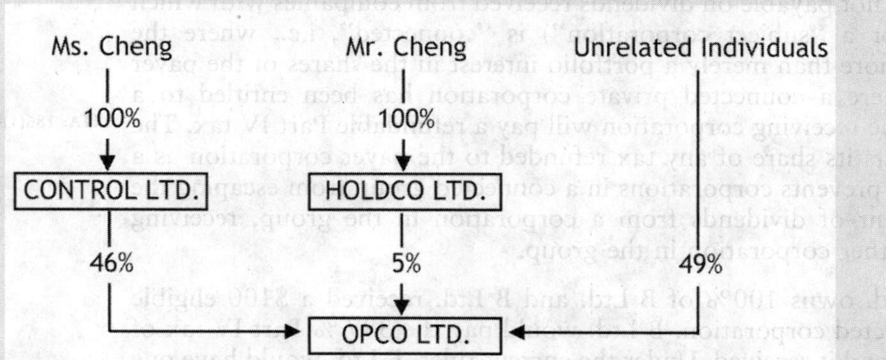

REQUIRED

Determine whether Opco Ltd. is connected to Holdco Ltd. and Control Ltd.

SOLUTION

Opco Ltd. is not connected to Holdco Ltd. through the votes and value rule since Holdco Ltd. holds less than 10% of the common shares (i.e., 5%). However, Opco Ltd. is connected to Holdco Ltd. by virtue of the control rule as modified by the extended meaning of control. This latter provision extends the meaning of control by including shares belonging to non-arm's length persons, including other corporations and persons who do not deal at arm's length with the other corporations. In this situation, Control Ltd. and Holdco Ltd. are not dealing at arm's length since both corporations are related because Mr. and Ms. Cheng are related through marriage. Therefore, for purposes of determining control, Holdco Ltd. is deemed to own the shares held by Control Ltd. (i.e., 46%) plus the shares owned directly (i.e., 5%) giving Holdco Ltd. effective voting control of Opco Ltd.

ITA: 186(4) Corporations connected with particular corporation, 186(4)(a), 186(2) When corporation controlled, 251(2)(a), 251(2)(b), 251(2)(c)(ii)

Opco Ltd. is connected to Control Ltd. through both the votes and value rule and the extended meaning of control rule as described above.

ITA: 186(4)(a), 186(4)(b), 186(2) When corporation controlled

¶12,360 Dividend Refund

The private corporation will obtain a dividend refund each year equal to the lesser of

ITA: 129(1)(a)

(1) 38.33% of all taxable dividends paid in the year, and

(2) the corporation's RDTOH at the end of the year.

A dividend refund is only available to a private corporation if it has that status at the time that it pays the taxable dividend. Thus, where plans exist for control of a private corporation to be acquired by a public corporation, consideration should be given to paying taxable dividends to shareholders prior to the time when control changes in order to maximize the dividend refund to the corporation.

¶12,365 Dividend Refund in Connected Payer Corporation

The Part IV tax is generally not payable on dividends received from companies with which the private corporation (or a "subject corporation") is "connected", i.e., where the recipient corporation has more than merely a portfolio interest in the shares of the payer corporation. However, where a connected private corporation has been entitled to a refund of tax in the year, the receiving corporation will pay a refundable Part IV tax. The amount of the tax represents its share of any tax refunded to the payer corporation as a result of the dividend. This prevents corporations in a connected group from escaping the Part IV tax by the payment of dividends from a corporation in the group, receiving portfolio dividends, to another corporation in the group. ITA: 186(1)(b)

For example, assume A Ltd. owns 100% of B Ltd. and B Ltd. received a $100 eligible dividend from a non-connected corporation. B Ltd. would pay the 38⅓% Part IV tax of $38.33 on the eligible dividend it received. Under the current rules, B Ltd. would have one RDTOH account to track the additional Part I and Part IV tax. If B Ltd. then paid A Ltd. an eligible dividend of $100, B Ltd. would receive its dividend refund of $38.33. The $100 dividend would not be a portfolio dividend to A Ltd. because A Ltd. controls B Ltd. and, therefore, is "connected" (as discussed above) with B Ltd. If it were not for this anti-avoidance rule, A Ltd. would thus not be taxable on the dividend from B Ltd. This would defeat the purpose of the Part IV tax which is to avoid indefinite deferrals of tax on dividends of this nature. Thus, the anti-avoidance rule prevents such an escape from the Part IV tax by taxing A Ltd. under Part IV on the $38.33 dividend refund received by B Ltd. on the payment of the $100 dividend. Had A Ltd. owned only 51% of B Ltd., A Ltd. would have paid the Part IV tax only on its share of the dividend refund to B Ltd., i.e., on 51% of $38.33 for a tax of $19.55. Thus, A Ltd. pays Part IV tax on its proportionate share of the B Ltd. dividend refund triggered by the dividend paid by B Ltd. ITA: 186(1)(b)

Beginning with taxation years after 2018, the February 27, 2018 Budget will separate the additional Part IV tax paid on eligible dividends from all other additional Part I and Part IV tax. In the example above, the Part IV tax paid by A Ltd. would increase A Ltd.'s eligible RDTOH account.

Ⓐ ¶12,375 Application of Non-Capital Losses

The recipient private corporation may *choose* to reduce the amount subject to the Part IV tax by applying otherwise available non-capital losses of the year or of a carryover year. These losses *cannot* be deducted subsequently from other income under Division C. Either the non-capital losses can be deducted, in effect, from dividend income subject to Part IV tax or they can be deducted in the calculation of taxable income subject to Part I tax. The same non-capital losses *cannot* be deducted under both provisions. It is, therefore, usually preferable to use the losses against income taxed at normal corporate rates, under Part I if that is possible, since the tax savings are usually greater and the Part IV tax otherwise payable is potentially refundable to the corporation. ITA: 186(1)(c), 186(1)(d)

¶12,380 Actual Application of the Scheme

The following two examples demonstrate the interaction of Part I tax and the refundable taxes. These examples follow the current rules relating to the RDTOH account and do not reflect the proposed rules outlined in the February 27, 2018 Federal Budget. The first example problem deals with Canadian investment income and active business income. The second example adds the element of portfolio dividends subject to Part IV tax and then demonstrates the interaction of the two refundable taxes on RDTOH and the dividend refund.

Example Problem 12-12

Murphy Corporation Limited, a Canadian-controlled private corporation with a December 31, 2018 year end, has made the following calculation of its taxable income.

Canadian investment income	$1,000
Canadian active business income	1,000
	$2,000
Donations	500
Taxable income	$1,500

REQUIRED

Compute the refundable portion of the corporation's Part I tax for 2018. Assume a 13% provincial tax rate.

SOLUTION

Part I tax on taxable income:

Tax @ 38% on $1,500		$ 570
Deduct: Federal tax abatement (10% of $1,500)		150
Net amount		$ 420
Add: Additional refundable tax ($10\frac{2}{3}$ × $500[(1)])		53
Deduct:		
Small business deduction (18% of $1,000)	180	
General rate reduction[(2)]	Nil	180
Total federal tax under Part I		$ 293

Provincial tax @ 13% of $1,500		195
Total tax		$ 488

Refundable portion of Part I tax:

Least of:

(a) $30\frac{2}{3}$ × aggregate investment income (AII) ($30\frac{2}{3}$% × $1,000)		$307
(b) Taxable income	$ 1500	
Less: Amount eligible for the SBD	(1,000)	
	$30\frac{2}{3}$% × $ 500 =	$153
(c) Part I tax		$293
Least amount		$153

NOTES TO SOLUTION

(1) $10\frac{2}{3}$% lesser of:

Aggregate investment income (AII)	$1,000
Taxable income (TI) – income eligible for SBD ($1,500 – $1,000)	$ 500

Note that the Division C deduction for the donations effectively reduced the aggregate investment income first, thereby, leaving the active business income for the small business deduction.

(2) There is no tax reduction in this case since all active business income is eligible for the small business deduction and any other income of this CCPC is aggregate investment income.

Example Problem 12-13

VTL Limited is a Canadian-controlled private corporation with its first fiscal year ended December 31, 2018. The following data resulted in the indicated computation of taxable income and Part I tax payable:

Taxable dividends paid during the year		$ 30,000
Active business income (assume equal to income eligible for the small business deduction)		$148,560
Investment income:		
Taxable capital gains less allowable capital losses	$ 3,000	
Net income from property:		
Canadian-source rental income	4,500	
Total investment income		7,500
Dividends (eligible for deduction under sec. 112 from non-connected Canadian-resident public corporations)		13,000
Total net income		$169,060
Deduct: dividends		13,000
net capital losses		700
Taxable income		$155,360
Part I tax on taxable income:		
Tax @ 38% on $155,360		$ 59,037
Deduct: Federal tax abatement (10% of $155,360)		15,536
Net amount		$ 43,501
Add: Additional refundable tax (10⅔% × $6,800[1])		725
		$ 44,226
Deduct:		
Small business deduction (18% of $148,560)	26,741	
Tax reduction[2]	Nil	26,741
Total federal tax under Part I		$ 17,485
Provincial tax (assumed) @ 13% of $155,360		20,197
Total tax		$ 37,682

ITA: 112 Deduction of taxable dividends received by corporation resident in Canada

[1] 10⅔% × lesser of:

(1) All ($3,000 + $4,500 – $700) = $6,800

(2) TI – SBD amount ($155,360 – $148,560) = $$6,800

[2] There is no tax reduction in this case, since all active business income is eligible for the small business deduction and any other income of this CCPC is aggregate investment income.

REQUIRED

Compute the refundable dividend tax on hand at the end of the 2018 taxation year and the dividend refund for the 2018 taxation year.

SOLUTION

Part IV tax on taxable dividends received:		
Taxable dividends subject to Part IV tax		$13,000
Part IV tax payable: 38⅓% of $13,000		$ 4,983[(1)]
Refundable dividend tax on hand:		
Refundable portion of Part I tax:		
Least of:		
(a) 30⅔% × aggregate investment income (AII) (30⅔% × $6,800)		$ 2,085
(b) Taxable income	$ 155,360	
Less: Amount eligible for SBD	(148,560)	
4 × business FTC	—	
30⅔% ×	$ 6,800 =	$ 2,085
(c) Part I tax		$18,228
Refundable portion of Part I tax		$ 2,085
Part IV tax payable		4,983
Refundable dividend tax on hand		$ 7,068
Dividend refund:		
Lesser of:		
(a) Taxable dividends paid: $30,000 × 38.33%	$11,500	
(b) Refundable dividend tax on hand at year end	$ 7,068	
Dividend refund: lesser of (a) and (b)		$ 7,068
Summary of taxes payable:		
Part I tax (including assumed provincial tax)		$37,682

Part IV tax	4,983
	$42,665
Less: dividend refund	7,068
Net taxes payable	$35,597

NOTE TO SOLUTION

(1) Had any of the dividends deductible under section 112 been received from a connected corporation, such dividends would not have been subject to the Part IV tax, unless those dividends gave rise to a dividend refund to the connected corporation.

¶12,390 Summary of Advantages and Disadvantages of Incorporating Investment Income Eligible for Refundable Tax

¶12,390.10 Advantages

The advantages of incorporating investment income eligible for refundable tax would appear to include the following:

- a tax deferral from incorporation if the shareholder's combined personal marginal tax rate is greater than the combined corporate rate before the dividend refund;
- a tax savings occurs when the personal tax on the investment income is greater than the personal and corporate tax on the same income earned in a corporation with the after-tax income paid out to the individual as a dividend and taxed personally;
- greater flexibility in the timing of the receipt of income subject to personal tax;
- estate planning advantages on the transfer of property and the transfer of future growth to children (as discussed in a subsequent chapter);
- possible family income splitting in carefully planned and very restrictive situations (to be discussed subsequently with respect to the corporate attribution and TOSI rules) through family members as shareholders and, perhaps, employees; and
- possible avoidance of foreign estate taxes by placing foreign property in a Canadian corporation.

¶12,390.20 Disadvantages

On the other hand the disadvantages of incorporating investment income would appear to include the following:

- a tax prepayment (as opposed to a deferral) from incorporation occurs if the shareholder's combined marginal tax rate is less than the combined corporate rate before the dividend refund;

- a tax cost occurs when the personal tax on the investment income is less than the personal and corporate tax on the same income earned in a corporation with the after-tax income paid out to the individual as a dividend and taxed personally;
- an additional cost of maintaining a corporation in the form of administrative, accounting and legal costs; and
- a loss of the availability to the individual of investment and capital losses.

Given the likely prepayment of tax and tax cost resulting from the incorporation of investment income, these disadvantages may outweigh the advantages. However, the beneficial effects of estate planning and income splitting must be analyzed.

¶12,400 Imperfections and Policy Choices in the Integration System for Income of a CCPC

As discussed and illustrated, perfect integration results where corporate income, taxed at the corporate level and then at the individual shareholder level on dividends attracts the same total tax as the same income in the hands of an individual. Given the gross-up and dividend tax credit system, the major tool of integration, specified by the Act, perfect integration arises from:

(1) a combined federal and provincial corporate tax rate of:

(a) 27.5% on business income producing dividends eligible for the 38% gross-up (i.e., eligible dividends), or

(b) 13.8% on business income that has benefited from the small business deduction and investment income that has benefited from the refundable tax system eligible for the 16% gross-up; and

(2) a combined federal and provincial dividend tax credit equal to the gross-up.

¶12,405 Imperfections

¶12,405.10 The High Corporate Rate on Business Income

Imperfections from the combined federal and provincial corporate tax rate not being the perfect 27.5% or 13.8% result because of variations in the provincial corporate rates of tax. For a combined federal and provincial corporate rate of tax of 27.5% to exist, the provincial component of that corporate tax rate must be 12.5% (i.e., 38% – 10% – 13% + 12.5% = 27.5%). In fact, provincial corporate rates on this type of income range from 10% to 16%. Where the combined corporate rate is less than 27.5%, due to a provincial rate of less than 12.5%, a tax savings imperfection will result from incorporation, relative to earning the income in an unincorporated form, like a proprietorship or a partnership. On the other hand, where the combined corporate rate is greater than 27.5%, due to a provincial rate of greater than 12.5%, a tax cost imperfection will result from incorporation relative to an individual earning the same income directly in an unincorporated form.

¶12,405.20 The Low Corporate Rate on Business Income

At the low combined federal and provincial corporate rate of 13.8%, the provincial component of the tax rate has to be 3.8% (i.e., 38% – 10% – 18% + 3.8% = 13.8%) on income eligible for the small business deduction. In fact, provincial rates of tax on income eligible for the small business deduction range from 0 to 8%. Where the provincial corporate rates are lower than the perfect rate of 3.8%, a tax savings results, and where the provincial corporate rates are higher, a tax cost results from incorporation.

¶12,405.30 The Low Corporate Rate on Investment Income

On investment income eligible for refundable tax, the provincial corporate rate of tax has to be 5.8% (i.e., 38% – 10% + 10.67% – 30.67% + 5.8% = 13.8%). The actual provincial rates on this type of income range from 10% to 16%. Where the provincial corporate rates are lower than the perfect rate of 5.8%, a tax savings results, and where the provincial corporate rates are higher, a tax cost results from incorporation.

¶12,405.40 The Part IV Tax on Dividend Income

On dividend income subject to Part IV tax, there is no provincial tax and the Part IV tax is fully refundable when this income is paid out as a dividend to the shareholders. There is no tax savings or cost on this type of income earned through a corporation.

¶12,405.50 The Dividend Tax Credit

Perfect integration requires a dividend tax credit that is equal to the gross-up. The federal component of the dividend tax credit for dividends subject to the 38% gross-up is 6/11 of the gross-up. That means that the provincial component of the dividend tax credit has to be equal to 5/11 of the gross-up. If the provincial tax credit rate is less than 5/11 of the gross-up, then the total dividend tax credit will be less than the gross-up and there will be a tax cost to distributing after-tax corporate income as dividends with the result that there would be a tax advantage to paying salary. Of course, if the provincial dividend tax credit is higher than 5/11 of the gross-up, then there will be a tax advantage to paying dividends.

The federal component of the dividend tax credit for dividends subject to the 16% dividend tax credit is 8/11 of the gross-up. To be perfect, the provincial component has to be 3/11 of the 16% gross-up. A provincial tax credit rate of less than the perfect 3/11 of the gross-up results in a tax cost to paying a dividend relative to paying a salary or bonus, whereas a provincial tax credit rate of more than 3/11 of the gross-up results in a tax savings from paying dividends rather than a salary or bonus.

¶12,410 A Deferral of Tax as a Government Policy Choice

A corporation can be used to defer tax on income earned by a corporation compared to the same income earned directly by an individual, if the combined federal and provincial corporate tax rate is less than the combined federal and provincial personal tax rate on that income. In this case of a lower corporate tax rate compared with the personal tax rate, the deferral that results is a deferral of tax on the dividend paid out of after-tax corporate income to an individual shareholder, until the time that the dividend is paid.

The availability of this deferral is not an imperfection in the system, but a government policy choice for corporate tax rates. The government may wish to maintain lower corporate tax rates on, say, business income, for international competition purposes. One way of achieving this is to introduce a general rate reduction on that income. The government may wish to provide more internally generated funds for reinvestment in the corporate business to allow that business to grow. One way of achieving this is to provide a small business deduction. Of course, the lower the corporate rate, the more deferral is possible, if the income is retained in the corporation and not paid out as dividends to attract tax in the hands of the individual shareholder.

If the government's objective was to eliminate a tax deferral altogether, it could implement a system of taxing all corporate income at the same tax rate as an individual would pay on the same income, whether it is distributed as a dividend or not. That is the way income from an unincorporated entity, like a proprietorship or a partnership is taxed. In the unincorporated form, income is taxed in the hands of the owners, whether or not they withdraw it. In this system, there would be no deferral, but the benefits of a lower corporate tax rate would not be available.

The opposite of a deferral effect is a prepayment of tax through an initial corporate rate that is higher than personal tax rates. This occurs by design for investment income, because there is no economic advantage to the government from encouraging the formation of corporations to generate investment income, compared to generating business income. Therefore, the system applicable to investment income of a CCPC has been designed to tax the corporation, initially, at a corporate rate that is, generally, higher than the top personal tax rate. This has necessitated the additional refundable tax and, of course, no eligibility for the general rate reduction. That results in a combined initial federal and provincial corporate tax rate of 50⅔% (i.e., 38% – 10% + 10⅔% + 12%), using a hypothetical provincial corporate rate of 12%. At this total corporate rate, there is virtually no deferral advantage from incorporating a source of investment income. Further, at that high corporate rate, there is a considerable tax cost to incorporating that type of income which is only eligible for the 16% gross-up and tax credit. That is why the system allows for a refund of some of the corporate tax at the high rate to bring the corporate rate, after the dividend refund, closer to the corporate rate necessary for perfect integration where the tax cost is substantially reduced. The corporation receives the dividend refund when it pays a taxable dividend, so there is no deferral possibility at that time. In fact, at the time that the corporation receives the refund to lower its effective tax rate, the individual pays the tax on the dividend.

¶12,500 Comprehensive Summary of Types of Corporate Income and Federal Corporate Income Tax Rates

Exhibit 12-13 presents a comprehensive summary of types of corporate income that can be earned by a Canadian corporation and the marginal income tax rates applicable to each type of income.

Exhibit 12-13 Summary of CCPC Income Types and Applicable Tax Rates

	Employment	Active Business Income			Specified Investment Buss Income — Property				Net TCG	
	(PSB)	Cdn		For'n	Cdn	For'n	Cdn Dividends			
		<500	>500				Conn	Port		TOTAL
Employment	+/-									
Business		+/-	+/-	+/-						
Property					+/-	+/-	+	+		
Net TCG									+	
OI/OD										
ABIL										
Division B										
Division C										
Donations										-
Dividends							-	-		-
Net CL									-	-
Non CL										-
Taxable					Aggregate Investment Income					
Corporate	%	%	%	%	%	%	%	%	%	
Basic	38.00	38.00	38.00	38.00	38.00	38.00			38.00	
Abatement	(10.00)	(10.00)	(10.00)		(10.00)	(10.00)			(10.00)	
ART					10.67	10.67			10.67	
PSB	5.00									
Part IV							?	38.3		
SBD		(18.00)								
M&P										
RDTOH					√	√	?	√	√	
FTC				√		√				
Gen rate red'n			(13.00)	(13.00)						
Net Federal	33.00	10.00	15.00	25.00	38.67	38.67		38.3	38.67	
Provincial	12.00	3.80	12.00	-	12.00	12.00			12.00	
Subtotal	45.00	13.80	27.00	25.00	50.67	50.67		38.3	50.67	
Dividend Refund					(30.67)	(30.67)	?	(38.3)	(30.67)	
	45.00	13.80	27.00	25.00	20.00	20.00		-	20.00	
Dividend gross-up	38%	16%	38%	16%	16%	16%	16%/38%	16%/38%	16%	

PSB — Personal services business income

? — There may be Part IV tax on dividends from connected corporations

Corporate marginal income tax rates are summarized in the above table. In the calculation of income tax for a corporation, these marginal rates are not applied to the various sources of income separately. However, these marginal rates may be helpful in planning analyses. The table also indicates the opportunity to save and to defer tax at the corporate rates shown.

Example Problem 12-14

James Fish Distributors Inc. (JFDI) is a Canadian-controlled private corporation located in Burnaby, British Columbia. The company's income for tax purposes for its December 31, 2018 taxation year end was calculated correctly as follows:

Distributing income	$ 210,000
Wholesaling income	195,000
Maintenance service contract loss	(65,000)
Patent income[1]	45,000
Rental income[2]	35,000
Taxable capital gains net of losses[3]	55,000
Recapture of CCA[3]	15,000
Interest income on outstanding account receivable on wholesaling income	10,000
Interest income from loan to wholly owned subsidiary[4]	20,000
Interest income from a sinking fund trust for replacement of a building	50,000
Dividends from CCPCs (non-connected)	12,500
Dividends from the wholly owned subsidiary which received a $1,500 dividend refund as a result of paying this dividend	17,500
Profit on sale of excess land[5]	90,000
Net income for tax purposes — Division B	$ 690,000

[1] The patent income has been determined to be property income.

[2] The rental income was derived from leasing the entire space on a 5-year lease in an unused warehouse in a small town in the northern part of the province.

[3] The net taxable capital gain and the recapture concerned the disposition of certain specialized maintenance service equipment.

[4] The funds were used to buy equipment for its active business.

[5] The land had been held for approximately 5 years. It was purchased with the intent of realizing a profit on sale.

Additional Information:

(1) JFDI made the following selected payments during the year:

Charitable donations	22,500

Dividends paid in 2018	37,500

(2) The balances in the tax accounts on January 1, 2018 were:

Charitable donation carryforward	$ 2,500
Non-capital losses	42,500
Net capital losses (arising in 2012)	9,000
RDTOH balance	Nil

(3) Taxable income earned in British Columbia, which is the only Canadian jurisdiction in which JFDI operates. Assume a provincial tax rate of 10%.

(4) The full business limit is allocated to JFDI.

REQUIRED

(1) Calculate the federal tax and provincial tax at an assumed net rate of 10% on federal taxable income payable by the company for 2018.

(2) Compute the refundable dividend tax on hand balance as at December 31, 2018, and compute the dividend refund for 2018.

SOLUTION

Analysis of Division B Income

	ABI			Investment		Dividend		
Source	**Cdn.**	**For'n.**	**PSB**	**Cdn.**	**For'n.**	**Conn.**	**Port.**	**Total**
Distributing	$210,000							$210,000
Wholesaling	195,000							195,000
Maintenance service	(65,000)							(65,000)
Patent				$ 45,000				45,000
Rental				35,000				35,000
Net taxable capital gains				55,000				55,000
Recapture	15,000							15,000

	ABI			Investment		Dividend		
Source	Cdn.	For'n.	PSB	Cdn.	For'n.	Conn.	Port.	Total
Interest — A/R	10,000							10,000
loan	20,000(1)							20,000
sinking fund				50,000				50,000
Dividend						$17,500	$12,500	30,000
Profit	90,000							90,000
Division B income	$475,000		Nil	$185,000		$17,500	$12,500	$690,000

(A) *Tax Payable*

Division B income		$ 690,000
Division C deductions:		
Charitable donations ($22,500 + $2,500) — max. 75% of $690,000	$25,000	
Dividends from taxable Canadian corporations ($17,500 + $12,500)	30,000	
Non-capital losses	42,500	
Net capital losses	9,000	(106,500)
Taxable income		$ 583,500
Federal tax @38% of $583,500		$ 221,730
Deduct: Federal abatement (10% of $583,500)		58,350
Net amount		$ 163,380
Add: Additional refundable tax (Schedule 1)		11,573
		$ 174,953
Deduct:		
Small business deduction (Schedule 4)	85,500	
General rate reduction (Schedule 5)	Nil	
		(85,500)

Part I tax payable		$ 89,453
Provincial tax @ 10% of $583,500		58,350
Part IV tax payable (($38\frac{1}{3}\%$ of $12,500) + $1,500)		6,292
Total tax		154,095
Less: dividend refund		(14,375)
Net tax		$ 139,720
Schedule 1: Additional refundable tax		
$10\frac{2}{3}\%$ of lesser of:		
(a) AII ($185,000 + $17,500 + $12,500 – $9,000 – $30,000)		$ 176,000
(b) Taxable income – SBD amount[2] ($583,500 – $475,000)		$ 108,500
$10\frac{2}{3}$ of $108,500 = $11,573		
Schedule 2: Small business deduction		
18% of least of:		
(a) Active business income (Canadian-source)		$475,000
(b) Taxable income		$583,500
(c) Business limit		$500,000
18% of $475,000 = $85,500		
Schedule 3: General rate reductions		
Taxable income		$583,500
Less: income eligible for the small business deduction	$475,000	
AII	176,000	(651,000)
Net		Nil
13% of Nil		Nil

(B) *Refundable Portion of Part I Tax*

Least of:

(a) $30\frac{2}{3}\%$ of AII ($30\frac{2}{3}\%$ of $176,000)		$ 53,973
(b) Taxable income	$583,500	

Less: Amount eligible for SBD	475,000	
30⅔% of	$108,500	$ 33,273
(c) Part I tax		$ 89,453
Least amount = $33,273		
RDTOH		
Balance, January 1, 2018		Nil
Add: Refundable portion of Part I tax		$ 33,273
Part IV tax		6,292
Balance, December 31, 2018		$ 39,565

Dividend refund

Lesser of:

(a) Taxable dividends paid × 38⅓% ($37,500 × 38.33%)	$ 14,375
(b) RDTOH balance, December 31, 2018	$ 39,565
Lesser amount = $14,375	

NOTES TO SOLUTION

ITA: 129(6) Investment income from associated corporation deemed to be active business income

(1) The interest on the loan to the subsidiary is deemed to be active business income. JFDI and the subsidiary are associated. The interest is ordinarily income from property, but is deducted from the ABI of the associated payer.

(2) Initially, the SBD amount is assumed to be $475,000, since Canadian-source ABI is $475,000 and taxable income is $583,500. This assumption, which is verified later in Schedule 4, allows for a calculation of ART.

¶12,500.99 Practise What You've Learned

Refer to the following sections of the Study Guide to practise what you've learned:

¶12,800 — Review Questions

- Question 10 — Part IV tax

- Question 11 — Five tools to integrate investment income in a corporation
- Question 15 — Investment income in a corporation

¶12,825 — Multiple Choice Questions

- Question 4 — Part IV tax

¶12,850 — Exercises

- Exercise 7 — Calculate Part I tax, RDTOH, dividend refund
- Exercise 8 — Type of income, Part IV tax
- Exercise 11 — Interest income from a US subsidiary
- Exercise 14 — Discussion of corporate tax & rates on various types of income earned by a CCPC
- Exercise 16 — Intercompany payments
- Exercise 17 — Part IV tax; Dividend refund
- Exercise 18 — Intercompany payments

CHAPTER 13

Shareholder-Manager Remuneration and Tax Planning for the Owner-Manager

ADVANCED CONTENT IN THIS CHAPTER

Learning Goals

Know

By the end of this chapter you will know:

- The common elements of compensation for a corporation's shareholder-manager.
- The basic elements of the capital gains exemption.
- The issues related to the general anti-avoidance rule.

Understand and Explain

By the end of this chapter you will understand and be able to explain:

- The issues related to the choice of different types of compensation for a shareholder-manager.
- The benefits of the capital gains exemption.
- The rewards and risks of income splitting using a corporation.
- Why the general anti-avoidance rule is designed the way it is.

Apply

By the end of this chapter you will be able to apply your knowledge and understanding to:

- Choose the compensation plan for a shareholder-manager.
- Determine whether the capital gains exemption applies.
- Calculate the capital gains exemption.
- Calculate the benefits and penalties from income splitting using a corporation.

Review Questions

¶13,800 in the Study Guide

Multiple Choice Questions

¶13,825 in the Study Guide

Exercises

¶13,850 in the Study Guide

Assignment Problems

¶13,875 in the Study Guide

OVERVIEW

The previous chapter demonstrated that the integration system, when applied to business income earned by a corporation, can result in tax savings in certain cases where the combined federal and provincial rate of tax on corporations is less than the 13.8% or the 27.5% rate on which the gross-up and tax credit rates are based. Further tax savings and flexibility through the use of a corporation for business income are possible, if proper planning is undertaken. This chapter discusses planning considerations by beginning with the planning of employment remuneration for the shareholder-manager. It then examines the question of whether to pay salaries and similar income or to pay dividends. While much of the discussion is set out in terms pertaining to an individual owner of a business, the principles can be applied, with appropriate modification, to a group of owners controlling the business. Some other planning aspects of using corporations pertaining to holding companies, the qualified small business corporation share (QSBCS) capital gains exemption and attribution are discussed next. The final section of the chapter discuss the

ITA: 74.4 [Transfers and loans to corporations], 110.6 [Capital gains exemption], 245 [General anti-avoidance rule]

general anti-avoidance rule (GAAR) of the *Income Tax Act*, which may limit more aggressive planning and, hence, must be considered.

For the purposes of computing the total income tax of an individual, the following table will be used in this chapter. Provincial rates of tax used in the table are hypothetical. Actual provincial rates vary. In addition, provincial tax brackets may vary, due to the use of a provincial Consumer Price Index and the impact of provincial surtaxes. Provinces may also establish a different number of tax brackets.

Combined Federal and Hypothetical Provincial Tax Rates

Taxable Income		Federal		Provincial		Total	
		Tax on lower limit	Tax rate on excess	Tax on lower limit	Tax rate on excess	Tax on lower limit	Tax rate on excess
—	$ 46,605	—	15.0%	—	10%	—	25.0%
$ 46,606	93,208	$ 6,991	20.5%	$ 4,661	12%	$11,652	32.5%
93,209	144,489	16,545	26.0%	10,253	15%	26,798	41.0%
144,490	205,842	29,878	29.0%	17,945	17%	47,823	46.0%
205,843		47,670	33.0%	28,375	17%	76,045	50.0%

¶13,000 Employment Remuneration

¶13,050 Salaries, Bonuses, and Other Payments to the Shareholder-Manager

¶13,060 Salaries and Bonuses

In order to be deductible by the corporation, salaries and bonuses paid, must be reasonable in the circumstances. There are no concrete guidelines as to what is meant by the word "reasonable". Where the employee is at arm's length with the corporation, generally any salary and/or bonus would qualify as "reasonable". However, this is not the case in the situation of a controlling shareholder-manager. In such a case, the value of his or her services may be assessed. The Canada Revenue Agency (CRA) could look at what executives in other corporations are being paid. The gross revenue and profitability of the corporation are probably the major factors to consider when justifying a large salary or bonus to a key person.[1]

ITA: 67 General limitation re expenses

[1] For a case on the issue of the reasonableness of bonuses, see *La Compagnie Idéal Body Inc. v. The Queen*, 89 DTC 5450 (F.C.T.D.). See also "Shareholder/Manager Remuneration" in *Income Tax Technical News* No. 22, Canada Customs and Revenue Agency, January 11, 2002.

On the other hand, there may be no incentive for the CRA to challenge the amount of salary paid to a controlling shareholder-manager. While the salary may be deductible to the corporation, it is included in the income of the recipient shareholder-manager. At high salary levels, the tax on the income in the hands of the shareholder-manager will generally be higher than the tax saving from the deduction of salary by the corporation.

In the case of *Totem Disposal Co. Ltd. v. M.N.R.*, the Tax Review Board held that the company's policy of limiting its net income to below the small business deduction limit by the accrual of management salary was for the purpose of tax reduction and not for the purpose of gaining or producing income. Therefore, the accrued salary expense was not allowed. This decision would not necessarily preclude the actual payment, as opposed to accrual, of a reasonable salary or bonus to achieve the same objective. In contrast to the *Totem Disposal* case, the Tax Court of Canada, in rejecting the argument that accruals were not made to produce income, set out the following criteria[2] for deductibility:

Cases: *Totem Disposal Co. Ltd. v. M.N.R.*, 81 DTC 493 (TRB)

- reasonableness of the bonus in relation to profit and services rendered;
- payment for real and identifiable service;
- some justification for expecting a bonus over regular salary (e.g., a company policy);
- reasonableness of the time between determining profit and establishing the bonus; and
- a legal obligation to pay the accrued bonus.

Where a director's resolution authorizing payment of management bonuses contained uncertainties regarding the actual payment, the Tax Court of Canada, in *Samuel F. Investments Limited v. M.N.R.*, held that the liability was contingent in nature and, therefore, not deductible.

Cases: *Samuel F. Investments Limited v. The Minister of National Revenue*, 88 DTC 1106 (TCC)

The CRA's position on the issue of reasonableness of salaries or bonuses is that the reasonableness of salaries or bonuses paid to employee-shareholders is to be determined based on the facts of the case. However, they will generally not challenge the reasonableness of salaries or bonuses to shareholder-managers if profits are usually distributed by way of bonuses to the shareholder-managers or the company has a policy of paying bonuses to compensate them for their special knowledge or skills.[3]

¶13,065 Accrued Bonuses and Other Amounts

¶13,065.10 Unpaid Remuneration

Where an amount in respect of employee remuneration (including salaries, wages, pension benefits, and retiring allowances) is unpaid 180 days after the end of the employer's fiscal period, the amount is deductible only in the employer's fiscal period in which the amount is actually paid. (By administrative practice, the CRA allows payment on the 180th day, despite the clarity of the legislation on this point.) Thus, the accrual method is denied to the employer on amounts unpaid after the 179-day period. Note that a shareholder-manager has far greater flexibility when the corporation's fiscal year ends during the last 179 days of the calendar year. Since a bonus can be paid at any time during the following 179 days from the year end of the accrual, income can be triggered in the current calendar year by a payment to the owner-manager. Alternatively, income can be

ITA: 78(4) Unpaid remuneration and other amounts; Interpretation Bulletins: IT-109R2 Unpaid Amounts

[2] These criteria were quoted in the case of *Earlscourt Sheet Metal Mechanical Limited v. M.N.R.*, 88 DTC 1029 (T.C.C.).

[3] Question 42 of the "CRA Round Table" in the *1981 Conference Report* of the Canadian Tax Foundation.

deferred to the following year by an accrual in the fiscal period and a payment in the following year, if this is more beneficial.

Example

JP Inc. has a fiscal year end of August 31, 2017. For its current year end, JP Inc. declared a bonus of $50,000 to its manager, Jeff Scope, who is also the sole shareholder. The bonus will be paid on January 31, 2018.

JP Inc. has paid the bonus within 179 days of its fiscal year end. It can deduct the bonus in the year ending August 31, 2017. Jeff is receiving payment for the bonus on January 31, 2018. As an employee, Jeff would include this bonus on a cash basis and would therefore include the bonus in his 2018 tax return.

Of course, the benefit from deferring the payment of the bonus to the employee is reduced considerably by the requirement by the employer to withhold tax at the time of paying the bonus. With a fiscal year end in the first half of the calendar year, the accrued bonus must be paid in the same calendar year, as it is accrued, thereby reducing the deferral flexibility.

¶13,065.20 Non-Arm's Length Accruals Other Than Remuneration

Where an amount, other than remuneration, is deductible by a taxpayer, like a corporation, and owed to a non-arm's length person, like a majority shareholder, another limited accrual rule applies to the unpaid amount.

ITA: 78(1) Unpaid amounts, 78(1)(a), 78(1)(b), 80(1) Definitions

Consider a situation where *property* owned by a majority shareholder personally is transferred to a corporation in return for certain income payments, such as, a royalty payment. The royalties can be accrued by the corporation as an expense in one year and paid up to two years after the taxation year of the corporation in which the amount was accrued. This gives the company an immediate expense deduction, but the shareholder, if using the cash basis, has no income until the amount is paid. However, if the amount is not paid prior to the end of the second taxation year after the year in which it is expensed, the amount must be added back to the income of the corporation in the third taxation year of the corporation following the year of accrual. The ultimate payment of the amount by the corporation to the shareholder will result in double taxation as it will be included in the shareholder's income at that time and the corporation would not get a deduction.

If instead the shareholder forgives the debt owing by the corporation, there will not be any income to report by the shareholder. On the forgiveness of a debt of this nature, normally the forgiven amount would be included in income. However, if section 78 applies, the amount payable is considered "an excluded obligation" and the debt forgiveness rules will not apply.

Instead of forgiving the balance owing to avoid double taxation, the corporation and the shareholder-manager may file an agreement on or before the date on which the corporation must file its tax return for the third taxation year following the year of accrual. This agreement will deem the amount to have been paid by the corporation and received by the shareholder-manager on the first day of the third taxation year following the year of accrual. The shareholder-manager must report the amount as income. In addition, the amount deducted is deemed to have been lent back to the corporation by the shareholder-manager. The ultimate payment of the balance owing by the corporation will have no tax consequences as a result.

¶13,065.30 Example of Non-Arm's Length Accrual Effects

Assume a corporation's year end is December 31. Royalties accrued on December 31, 2016 must be paid by December 31, 2018 or added back to the corporation's income for the year ended December 31, 2019 unless an agreement is filed on or before June 30, 2020. In that case, the royalties are deemed to have been received by the non-arm's length shareholder-manager and loaned back to the corporation on January 1, 2019. The effect of the agreement is to put the shareholder in the same position as he or she would have been had the royalties actually been paid, meaning the shareholder would have to include the royalty payment in their taxable income. When the corporation ultimately repays the loan resulting from the unpaid royalties, there are no further tax consequences because the royalties were already taxed on their deemed receipt under the agreement. ITA: 78(1)(b)

The agreement can be filed late, that is, after the filing deadline. However, if the agreement is filed late, 25% of the unpaid amount is added back in the third year to the corporation's income. This will not affect the treatment of the full unpaid amount. Thus, in the above example, 25% of the unpaid amount would be added back to the corporation's income in the 2019 taxation year, but under the agreement the entire amount of unpaid royalties would be deemed to have been paid by the corporation and received by the shareholder-manager and to have been loaned back on January 1, 2019. When the corporation ultimately pays back the loan, there will be no further tax consequences. The corporation will have deducted the entire amount of royalties in its 2016 taxation year, but will have added back 25% in its 2019 taxation year. Thus, the 25% amount will, in effect, not have been deducted, thereby creating a penalty for a late-filed agreement. ITA: 78(3) Late filing, 78(1)(a)

The foregoing non-arm's length accrual rules and their effects, which apply if the accrual is not actually paid within two years, can be diagrammed as follows, assuming a $10,000 royalty accrual:

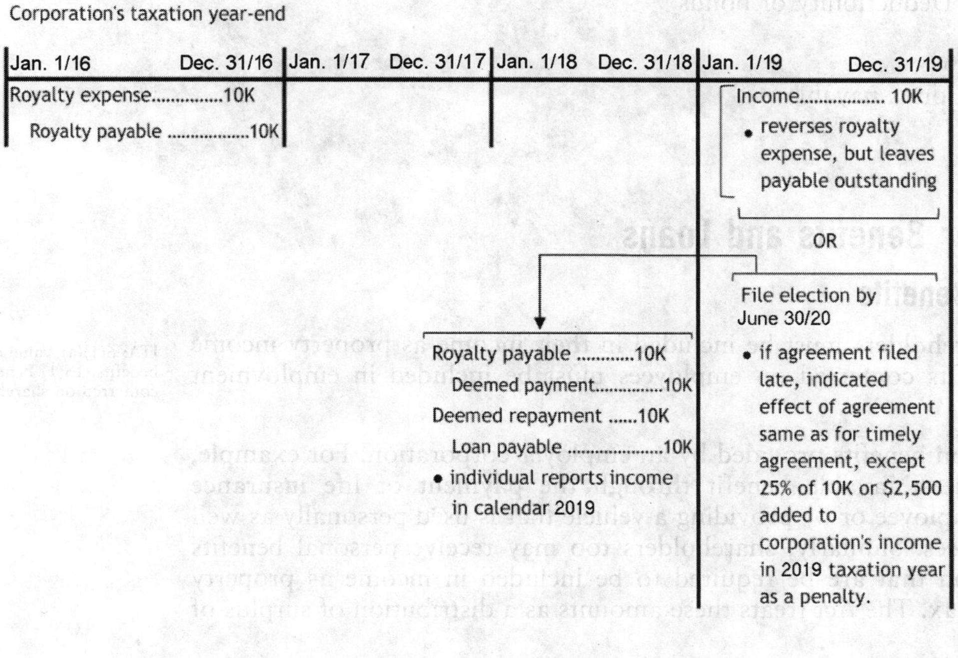

¶13,065.40 Genuine, Not Contingent Liability

There are other potential problems with the accrual of amounts. In order to be deductible in the year accrued, there must be a legal obligation to pay the amount. If the legal obligation is not established, then a deduction would be allowed only in the year of payment and not in the year of accrual. Thus, the liability should be established by recording the amount in the minutes of the directors' meeting prior to the year end and by attempting to establish, in the case of a bonus, some formula for computing the bonus representing objective standards. The payment should not be made contingent on some event which might take place after the year end. Having established a real liability in this manner, if the amount is not paid on time and if the election is not filed, the shareholder may decide to forgive the amount so that the corporation need not pay it and avoid the double taxation previously mentioned.

An Interpretation Bulletin suggests that if an unpaid amount does not constitute a genuine liability, no deduction will be allowed. The Interpretation Bulletin states that "for genuine liability to exist, there must be an enforceable claim by the creditor with a reasonable expectation that the debt will in fact be paid by the debtor." ITA: 15(e), 18(1)(e) Reserves, etc; Interpretation Bulletins: IT-109R2 Unpaid Amounts

¶13,065.99 Practise What You've Learned

Refer to the following sections of the Study Guide to practise what you've learned:

¶13,800 — Review Questions

- Question 3 — Bonus payments
- Question 4 — Bonus accruals

¶13,825 — Multiple Choice Questions

- Question 3 — Deductibility of bonus

¶13,850 — Exercises

- Exercise 1 — Bonus payable

¶13,070 Shareholder Benefits and Loans

¶13,075 Shareholder Benefits

Benefits conferred on shareholders must be included in their income as property income just as employment benefits conferred on employees must be included in employment income. ITA: 6(1)(a) Value of benefits, 15(1) Benefit conferred on shareholder

Employees may be taxed on benefits provided by an employer corporation. For example, an employer may provide a taxable benefit through the payment of life insurance premiums on behalf an employee or by providing a vehicle that is used personally as well as for employment purposes. Similarly, shareholders too may receive personal benefits conferred by a corporation that are be required to be included in income as property income and be subject to tax. The Act treats these amounts as a distribution of surplus of the corporation and thus requires an amount to be included in property income. However, the amount is not deemed to be a dividend and, therefore, is not eligible for the dividend tax credit. In addition, these amounts are not deductible by the corporation; they are treated the same as dividends at the corporate level.

The provisions are designed to prevent the distribution of part of the accumulated surplus of a corporation (other than by way of taxable dividends) to shareholders while the corporation is a going concern. There are exceptions to the broad application of these rules for particular situations that are dealt with elsewhere in the Act, notably in the provision dealing with the taxation of dividends and options.

For example, this provision was applied in the case of *No. 403 v. M.N.R.*, in which a controlling shareholder purchased a house from his company at $38,000 when it had been purchased a year earlier by the company for $45,000. The $7,000 benefit to the shareholder was included in his income from property. The corporation was considered to have received proceeds equal to the fair market value of the house at the time of the sale to the shareholder and include the income or taxable capital gain in Division B income.

ITA: 69(4) Shareholder appropriations; Cases: *Income Tax Appeal Board*, 57 DTC 120 (T.A.B.)

Where a loan to a shareholder is forgiven by a corporation, that is, the shareholder is not required to repay all or some part of the principal amount of the loan, a rule provides that the amount of the principal forgiven must be included in the shareholder's income.

ITA: 15(1) Benefit conferred on shareholder, 15(1.2) Forgiveness of shareholder debt

Many of the related subsections in section 15, applicable to shareholders, provide a treatment similar to section 6, applicable to employees, as shown in Exhibit 13-1.

Exhibit 13-1 Selected Shareholder and Employee Benefits

	Shareholder subsection 15(1) and	**Employee paragraph 6(1)(*a*) *and/or***
Automobile	Subsection 15(5)[1]	Paragraphs 6(1)(*e*), (*k*) and subsection 6(2)
Interest on loans	Subsections 15(9) and 80.4(2)	Subsections 6(9) and 80.4(1)
Forgiveness of loans	Subsection 15(1.2)	Subsection 6(15)

[1] Refers to subparagraph 6(1)(*e*)(i) and subsections 6(1.1) and (2).

The question often arises, when dealing with a shareholder-manager, as to which provision is applicable — section 6 dealing with employees or section 15 dealing with shareholders. The capacity (often referred to by the Latin word *qua*) in which the person is operating and which, in turn, depends upon the specifics of the particular relationship, will determine which provision will apply. A good rule of thumb is that a person operates in his or her capacity as shareholder (that is, *qua* shareholder) if he or she receives a benefit which he or she would not have received if he or she was an ordinary employee.[4]

[4] For a more detailed discussion of this topic see Robert E. Beam and Stanley N. Laiken, "The "Capacity" Issue in Corporate Transactions with Shareholders", Personal Tax Planning Feature (1992), Vol. 40, No. 2, *Canadian Tax Journal*, pp. 412–439.

The word "benefit" is another of those key words that is undefined and yet sprinkled liberally throughout the Act. The standard test to determine whether a benefit has been conferred on a shareholder is the "*bona fide* transaction" test as set out in *M.N.R. v. Pillsbury Holdings Ltd.* The court made the distinction between a *bona fide* transaction and transactions that are devices and arrangements for conferring benefits or advantages on a shareholder. A *bona fide* transaction might occur where a shareholder deals with the corporation in the same manner or capacity as a customer (i.e., *qua* customer) or as a supplier (i.e., *qua* supplier). Further comments on the concept of a benefit are made in ¶3,105 of Chapter 3.

Cases: *M.N.R. v. Pillsbury Holdings Limited*, 64 DTC 5184 (Ex. Crt.)

Once it has been established that a benefit has been conferred, then the next step is to determine its value, if any. In *Youngman v. The Queen*, the Federal Court of Appeal determined that the value of a benefit of a house provided to its shareholders was not based on the equivalent rental fair market value, but instead was based on the value of the house itself.

Cases: *Lloyd Youngman v. Her Majesty the Queen*, 90 DTC 6322 (FCA)

Example Problem 13-1

Smart Manufacturing Ltd. built a 21-room house for its principal shareholder-officer on a country property owned by him. The company expensed the costs as promotion expenses on the basis that he would use the property to entertain distributors of the company's products to ensure continuing outlets for the company's products.

REQUIRED

Consider the tax consequences to the individual and the company in this case.

SOLUTION

The value of the house plus the HST, if any, on that value must be included in the income of the shareholder since it represents a benefit conferred on the shareholder. Since the company does not own the property on which the house was built and it has expensed the cost on its books, it appears clear that the shareholder has received a taxable benefit.

ITA: 15(1) Benefit conferred on shareholder

The company would ordinarily be allowed to deduct an expenditure made or incurred to produce income. In this case, the house would be a capital asset subject to the capital cost allowance system to the extent that some part of the house was used for business purposes. However, if the house is considered to be a lodge, in any way, the Act would prohibit the corporation from deducting any expense or outlay considered for the use or maintenance of that property.

ITA: 18(1)(l)(i)

Example Problem 13-2

Mr. Edwards owns all of the outstanding shares of Edwards Inc., a large property management company, which manages over 20 large apartment buildings. One spring Mr. Edwards had the repair crew spend five days at his cottage making extensive repairs to the building. The value of these repairs was $8,500 (including HST). Because of his busy schedule, Mr. Edwards apparently forgot to tell his controller to send him a bill for the work done.

REQUIRED

If the CRA were to discover this transaction during their audit, how would they reassess?

SOLUTION

The CRA would begin by assessing Mr. Edwards a shareholder benefit in the amount of $8,500, since funds of the corporation were directed to the benefit of a shareholder. This amount would be treated as income from property in the calendar year that the repairs were made.

ITA: 15(1) Benefit conferred on shareholder

The company, Edwards Inc., would probably also be reassessed to deny the deduction for the cost to the company of the repairs on the basis that the expenses were not incurred to earn income since no billing was ever sent, or on the basis that the expense was a personal or living expense.

ITA: 18(1)(a) General limitation, 18(1)(b) Capital outlay or loss, 18(1)(h) Personal and living expenses

As a result, there is double taxation. Mr. Edwards includes an amount in income for which the company does not receive a deduction.

¶13,080 Shareholder Loans or Indebtedness

¶13,080.10 Principal

Normally, when funds are borrowed, the principal amount of the debt, that is, the amount borrowed, is not considered to be income and the amount of the debt repaid is not deductible. Incurring and repaying the debt is a capital transaction. However, in the case of a shareholder, particularly a significant shareholder who can influence the decisions of the corporation, it would be easy to escape tax on the distribution of corporate surplus by removing surplus as a shareholder loan. A shareholder could borrow funds from the corporation, instead of receiving taxable salary, interest or dividends from the corporation, and never repay these funds. The shareholder loan provisions require the loan to be subject to tax as property income unless specific exceptions are met.

ITA: 15(2) Shareholder debt, 15(2.2) When s. 15(2) not to apply — non-resident persons

Income Inclusion

Loans and other forms of indebtedness to non-corporate shareholders or to persons not at arm's length with the shareholder are required to be included in income of the borrower for the year in which the loan was made. In the case of *The Queen v. Silden*, the Federal Court of Appeal confirmed that subsection 15(2) must be applied where a loan is made to a shareholder. The capacity in which the individual receives the loan, i.e., as a shareholder or as an employee, is not relevant to the application of that rule, but may be relevant for certain specific exceptions. Related persons, discussed in a previous chapter, do not deal with each other at arm's length.

ITA: 15(2.1) Meaning of connected, 251 Arm's length, 252 Extended meaning of "child"; Cases: *The Queen v. Jan Silden*, 93 DTC 5362 (FCA)

A loan received by a corporate shareholder is not taxable under the shareholder loan provisions just as distributions of surplus to a corporation as a dividend would not be taxable under Part 1 because of the Division C deduction for dividends.

¶13,080.20 Exceptions

Loans Arising in the Ordinary Course of the Lender's Business

Debt that arises in the ordinary course of the lender's business is not subject to the shareholder loan inclusion rule, as long as *bona fide* arrangements are made at the time the loan is made for repayment within a reasonable time. For example, this exception protects a borrower who happens to be a minority shareholder of a bank from which he or she borrowed money.

Short-Term Loans

A loan or indebtedness that is repaid within one year of the end of the taxation year of the lender in which it was made or incurred is excluded if the repayment is not part of a series of loans and repayments. If a loan is outstanding beyond one year from the end of the tax year in which it is made, the loan must be included in the income of the shareholder for the year in which the loan was received.

ITA: 15(2) Shareholder debt, 15(2.4)(e), 15(2.6) When s. 15(2) not to apply — repayment within one year, 15(4.2); Interpretation Bulletins: IT-119R4 Debts of Shareholders and Certain Persons Connected with Shareholders

Where a shareholder loan is received by virtue of the individual's shareholdings, this is the only exception available to the income inclusion requirement. See below regarding the CRA's administrative position on when a loan is considered to have been received by virtue of employment.

Shareholder Loans Received By Virtue of Employment

Where a shareholder loan arises because of the employee's employment (often referred to, using the Latin, as in, *qua* employee) and not because of his or her shareholdings (*qua* shareholder) there are four additional potential exceptions to the shareholder loan inclusion rule.

ITA: 15(2.4)(e), 15(2.4)(f)

The principal amount can be excluded from a shareholder's income if they received:

ITA: 15(2.2) When s. 15(2) not to apply — non-resident persons, 15(2.3) When s. 15(2) not to apply — ordinary lending business

(1) a loan made by the corporation to a shareholder who is also an employee, but not a specified employee (defined, very generally, as an employee who, together with non-arm's length persons, owns at least 10% of the shares of any class of a corporation or who does not deal at arm's length with the corporation); or

ITA: 15(2.4) When s. 15(2) not to apply — certain employees, 248(1) specified employee

(2) a loan made by the corporation to a shareholder who is also an employee to assist him or her to acquire:

(a) a home for his or her own occupation (even if the loan is made to the employee's spouse), ITA: 15(2.4)(b)

(b) previously unissued, fully paid shares of the corporation purchased directly from the corporation, or ITA: 15(2.4)(c)

(c) a motor vehicle (as defined) to be used in the performance of his or her duties of employment. ITA: 15(2.4)(d), 248(1) Definitions

For the principal amount of the loan to be excluded, *bona fide* arrangements must be made at the time of the loan for repayment within a reasonable period of time. An Interpretation Bulletin suggests that normal commercial practice is used as the basis for *bona fide* arrangements. For example, a 25-year amortization period would be appropriate for a housing loan and the security of a mortgage on the property should be taken for large loans.

Thus, for the shareholder loan inclusion rule, the recipient of the loan must be a shareholder. To exclude the principal amount of the loan under all four of the exceptions, the recipient must also be an employee. An employee-capacity condition is imposed on these exceptions, which results in exclusion of the principal, if the other conditions are met. That is, the loan must be received by the employee in his or her capacity as an employee, in addition to meeting the other conditions, for the loan to be excluded.

Administratively, the CRA indicates that where other employees receive loans with the same terms and conditions as the shareholder loan, the loan is considered to be received by virtue of employment. However, when the terms and conditions are more favourable or where loans are available only to shareholders, the loan would be received by virtue of shareholdings and the exceptions would not be available.

Interpretation Bulletins: IT-119R4 Debts of Shareholders and Certain Persons Connected with Shareholders

¶13,080.30 Deduction of Repayment

Where an amount has been included in income for a preceding year, the taxpayer is permitted to deduct any repayment of the loan or indebtedness from his or her income in the year of repayment provided the repayment was not part of a series of loans and repayments. While the CRA states in an Interpretation Bulletin that whether a repayment is part of such a series is a question of fact, it also states that a shareholder's loan account with several loan and repayment transactions will give rise to a series unless there is clear evidence otherwise.

ITA: 15(2) Shareholder debt, 20(1)(j) Repayment of loan by shareholder; Interpretation Bulletins: IT-119R4 Debts of Shareholders and Certain Persons Connected with Shareholders

The CRA also states in the same Interpretation Bulletin that, notwithstanding that there is a series of loans and repayments, they will administratively allow a deduction for a decrease in the loan account, unless the decrease is temporary. A numerical example of the application of the CRA's policy on how the net decrease should be calculated is provided, based on a FIFO allocation of repayments of the loan balance. However, the calculation of both the inclusion in income and the deduction are based on administrative practice only. Since this is a particularly tricky area in practice, the Bulletin should be studied carefully.

ITA: 20(1)(j) Repayment of loan by shareholder; Interpretation Bulletins: IT-119R4 Debts of Shareholders and Certain Persons Connected with Shareholders

The CRA's practice is to consider that dividends, salaries or bonuses paid or credited to the shareholder loan account (i.e., amounts owing to the shareholder by the corporation) to repay the balance at the end of the previous year are not part of a "series of loans or other transactions and repayments" for purposes of these two provisions. *Income Tax Technical News*, No. 3, dated January 30, 1995 and the Interpretation Bulletin, indicate that the Agency has based its position on two Tax Court of Canada cases.[5]

Interpretation Bulletins: IT-119R4 Debts of Shareholders and Certain Persons Connected with Shareholders

[5] *Joel Attis v. M.N.R.*, 92 DTC 1128, and *Uphill Holdings Ltd. et al. v. M.N.R.*, 93 DTC 148.

It is necessary to properly document loans. Not all charges to a shareholder loan account are necessarily *bona fide* loans. Some charges might be construed as salary, dividends or an appropriation.

ITA: 20(1)(c)(vi), 80.4 Loans; Income Tax Folio: S3-F6-C1 Interest Deductibility

Example Problem 13-3

Sally owns all the outstanding shares of Sally Inc. On July 15, 2017, Sally Inc. loans Bob, Sally's brother, $10,000 to buy a sailboat. Sally Inc. has a December 31 year end. On January 1, 2019, the loan is still outstanding.

REQUIRED

What are the income tax consequences to Bob?

SOLUTION

In this case, Bob received a loan from Sally Inc. and Bob is connected to his sister Sally, the shareholder, because they are related. Since the loan was not repaid before January 1, 2019, Bob will have to take the principal amount of the loan, $10,000, into income in the year the loan was received which was 2017. The following timeline of the facts and consequences may be helpful.

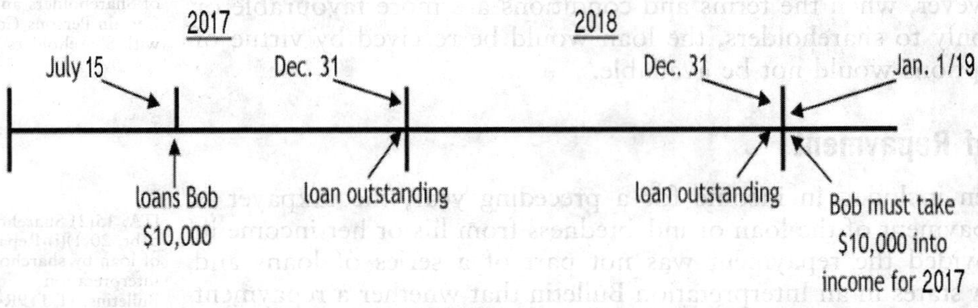

Example Problem 13-4

Ms. Alpha owns 100% of the shares of Xenon Ltd., which carries on a retailing business and has a December 31 year end. At the beginning of January 2018, Xenon Ltd. loaned Ms. Alpha $200,000 for personal purposes that would not result in an exclusion of the principal amount of the loan, by virtue of subsection 15(2.4). Under the terms of the loan, the principal was to be repaid in five equal annual instalments, commencing December 31, 2018.

REQUIRED

If repayments are made on schedule, how much of the principal amount of the loan must be included in Ms. Alpha's income for 2018?

SOLUTION

This particular fact situation does not seem to have been resolved in case law or in published commentary by practitioners or the CRA. The CRA's Interpretation Bulletin IT-119R4 does not address this fact pattern. The following discusses some possible interpretations.

ITA: 15(2) Shareholder debt, 15(2.6) When s. 15(2) not to apply — repayment within one year, 20(1)(j) Repayment of loan by shareholder; Interpretation Bulletins: IT-119R4 Debts of Shareholders and Certain Persons Connected with Shareholders

One interpretation that is not supported in common law but reflects administrative practice has been offered by the CRA.[6] Using this approach would include in 2018 income the $120,000 (i.e., $200,000 - ($40,000 + $40,000)) that is outstanding after the one-year repayment period. This interpretation would allow any repayments within that period to be excluded from the taxpayer's income in the year that the loan is received. Repayments of the loan made after December 31, 2019 would be deducted in the year in which they were made. While the CRA did not offer support in the law for its administrative position, it may be possible to interpret subsection 15(2.6) with an emphasis on the word "indebtedness". A part of a loan might be considered to be an indebtedness, which if repaid within the one-year period, as specified, could be excluded from income.

Another perspective on the provisions in question is based on a conservative interpretation. The basic rule on the inclusion of shareholder debt requires that the "*amount* of the loan" be included in income in the year that the loan is received. Focusing on the use of the word "loan", this inclusion rule "does not apply to *a loan* . . . repaid within one year after the end of the taxation year of the lender . . . in which *the loan* was made". The use of the words "a loan" and "the loan" might be interpreted to mean that the exclusion of the loan from income will only arise if the full amount of the loan is repaid within the one-year period.

ITA: 15(2) Shareholder debt, 15(2.6) When s. 15(2) not to apply — repayment within one year

This interpretation might be supported by the use of slightly different wording in the provision that allows for a deduction of "*such part* of any loan . . . repaid by the taxpayer in the year . . . as was included in computing the taxpayer's income for a preceding taxation year". The use of the words "such part" in the deduction provision but not in the exclusion provision might suggest that the exclusion only applies in the case of a repayment of the full amount of the loan within the one-year period because the "such part" wording could have been used in the exclusion provision but was not.

ITA: 20(1)(j) Repayment of loan by shareholder

This conservative interpretation would result in the inclusion of the full $200,000 amount of the loan in this case since it was not fully repaid within the one-year period. Then, repayments of the loan could be deducted as those repayments were made. The problem with this interpretation is that the

[6] Corporate Finance Section, Income Tax Rulings directorate, Legislative Policy and Regulatory branch, Document No. 2012-044252, August 12, 2012.

repayment made on December 31, 2018, at the end of the year in which the loan was made, may not be deductible. That $40,000 would not have been made in respect of a loan included "in income for a preceding taxation year". This does not seem to fit the inclusion/deduction scheme that the Act contemplates in these provisions. If this interpretation were to prevail, then planning would suggest that repayment conditions for the loan be established so that the first repayment is made on January 1, 2019, rather than on December 31, 2018, in this type of loan situation.

As an intermediate position, it may be possible to consider the amount of the loan in 2018 to be $160,000, that is, net of the repayment made in 2018. Then, any subsequent repayment would be deducted in the year that it is made.

While the fact situation presented is realistic, there is no definitive answer to the question that can be found in common law or published administrative practice at this time. Since the apparent CRA administrative practice is favourable and can possibly be supported, in this case, it should be used with caution, because it is not necessarily supported in law.

¶13,080.40 Imputed Interest Benefit

Where the principal amount of the loan is not included in income because it meets one of the exceptions discussed above, a provision dealing with imputed interest on loans may apply. The Act requires any person who received a loan or otherwise incurred a debt by virtue of: ITA: 80.4 Loans

- an individual's employment or intended employment (as discussed in Chapter 3),
- shareholdings in a corporation, or
- a shareholding of a person who does not deal at arm's length with a shareholder,

to include in his or her income an amount in respect of interest on low-interest or interest-free loans. The *qua* or capacity issue is relevant for purposes of the imputed interest benefit rules. It is always a question of fact whether a person will receive a benefit under this section by virtue of his or her employment or by virtue of his or her shareholdings. ITA: 6(9) Amount in respect of interest on employee debt, 15(9) Deemed benefit to shareholder by corporation

An interest benefit is imputed by one rule as a consequence of a previous, a current or an intended office or employment. Another rule imputes an interest benefit by virtue of the taxpayer's shareholdings in the lending corporation or a related corporation. A taxpayer may fall into either category, depending on the facts under which the loan was granted. Therefore, a decision will have to be made as to the source of this benefit based on the facts of the situation. ITA: 80.4(1) Loans, 80.4(2) Idem

By virtue of employment

An interest benefit is imputed to a person who receives a loan by virtue of employment rather than as a consequence of shareholdings. The individual must include in income the amount by which interest on the loan computed at the prescribed rate tied to the treasury ITA: 80.4(4) Interest on loans for home purchase, bill rate exceeds the interest actually paid in the year or within 30 days after the end of the taxation year on such a loan. Special rules apply to compute the interest benefit for a "home purchase loan". 80.4(7)(a), 248(1) Definitions

If the loan is a "home purchase loan", the definition of which is applicable only to loans by virtue of employment, the imputed interest benefit is calculated for each quarter[7] as the lesser of:

(1) the prescribed rate in effect at the time the loan was received; and

(2) the prescribed rate (changed on a quarterly basis) in effect during that quarter.

However, a new loan will be deemed to have been received every five years on longer-term home purchase loans. This deemed disposition will have the effect of changing the rate of imputed interest at least every five years. Finally, the interest benefit is the amount of imputed interest in excess of the interest actually paid in the year or within 30 days after the end of the taxation year on the loan. ITA: 80.4(6) Deemed new home purchase loans

By virtue of shareholdings

An interest benefit is imputed to a person who receives a loan by virtue of shareholdings rather than as a consequence of employment. The recipient of the loan may include a shareholder or a person not at arm's length with a shareholder of a corporation who receives a loan from, or incurs a debt to, the corporation or a related corporation. Since the special provisions for a home purchase loan refer only to a loan received by virtue of an office or employment, these provisions cannot apply where the loan is received by virtue of shareholdings. In this case, the individual must include in income the amount by which interest on the loan computed at the prescribed rate tied to the treasury bill rate exceeds the interest actually paid in the year or within 30 days after the end of the taxation year on such a loan. ITA: 80.4(2) Idem, 80.4(4) Interest on loans for home purchase; ITR: 4300(7)

Two additional exceptions to the application of the imputed interest rules are provided. First, a benefit will not arise where the rate of interest payable is equal to or greater than the rate of interest that would have been agreed upon in an arm's length transaction at the time the obligation was incurred. Second, where the principal amount of the loan has already been included in the income of a person, the loan is exempt from imputed interest, whether the loan is received by virtue of employment or shareholdings. ITA: 80.4(3) Where ss. (1) and (2) do not apply, 80.4(3)(a), 80.4(3)(b)

Receiving a loan by virtue of shareholding is more likely to result in the loan principal being included in income. Only short-term loans repaid within one year of the end of the tax year are exempted from the income inclusion. Where the individual does repay the loan within the time period required to avoid including the principal in income, then there will be a deemed interest benefit by virtue of shareholdings included in income for the period the loan is outstanding. One key takeaway is that a loan taken by virtue of shareholdings will never have both an income inclusion and an interest benefit.

The Act deems the interest benefit to be interest paid or payable in the year pursuant to a legal obligation for purposes of interest deduction provisions, as long as the conditions of the interest deduction provisions are met. Thus, an offsetting deduction may be available for interest deemed to have been paid, depending on the use of the borrowed funds. For

[7] The quarter-by-quarter method is used by the CRA for the "lesser of" calculation and may result in a slightly smaller income inclusion than the traditional annual calculation.

instance, if a loan received by virtue of employment by a shareholder is used to acquire previously unissued shares of a corporation and *bona fide* repayment terms were in place at the time the loan was made, the shareholder will not be required to include the loan in income in the year of receipt. Instead, there will be an imputed interest benefit for the period the loan is outstanding that must be included in the shareholder's employment income. The interest benefit will be deemed to have been paid and will be deductible in computing property income of the shareholder. The deduction is allowed because the loaned funds were invested for the purpose of earning property income in the form of dividends on the shares acquired.

ITA: 80.5 Deemed interest, 8(1)(j) Motor vehicle and aircraft costs, 20(1)(c) Interest

Deductibility of Interest on Funds Borrowed to Make a Shareholder Loan

If the corporation borrows money to make a loan to a shareholder and incurs interest charges, it should in turn charge interest to the shareholder or some of the interest it pays may be disallowed as not for the purpose of earning income. This applies even if the loan falls under the exception rules discussed above. An Income Tax Folio comments on the deductibility of interest on borrowed money used to make interest-free loans to employees and shareholders. However, the CRA makes the statement that "interest on money borrowed to make interest-free loans to individuals in their capacity as shareholders would not generally qualify."

Income Tax Folio: S3-F6-C1 Interest Deductibility

¶13,080.50 Application of Shareholder Loan Rules

Exhibit 13-2 provides a flow chart of the shareholder loan rules in sections 15 and 80.4 and the consequences of their application.

Exhibit 13-2 Shareholder Loans, Section 15 and Section 80.4

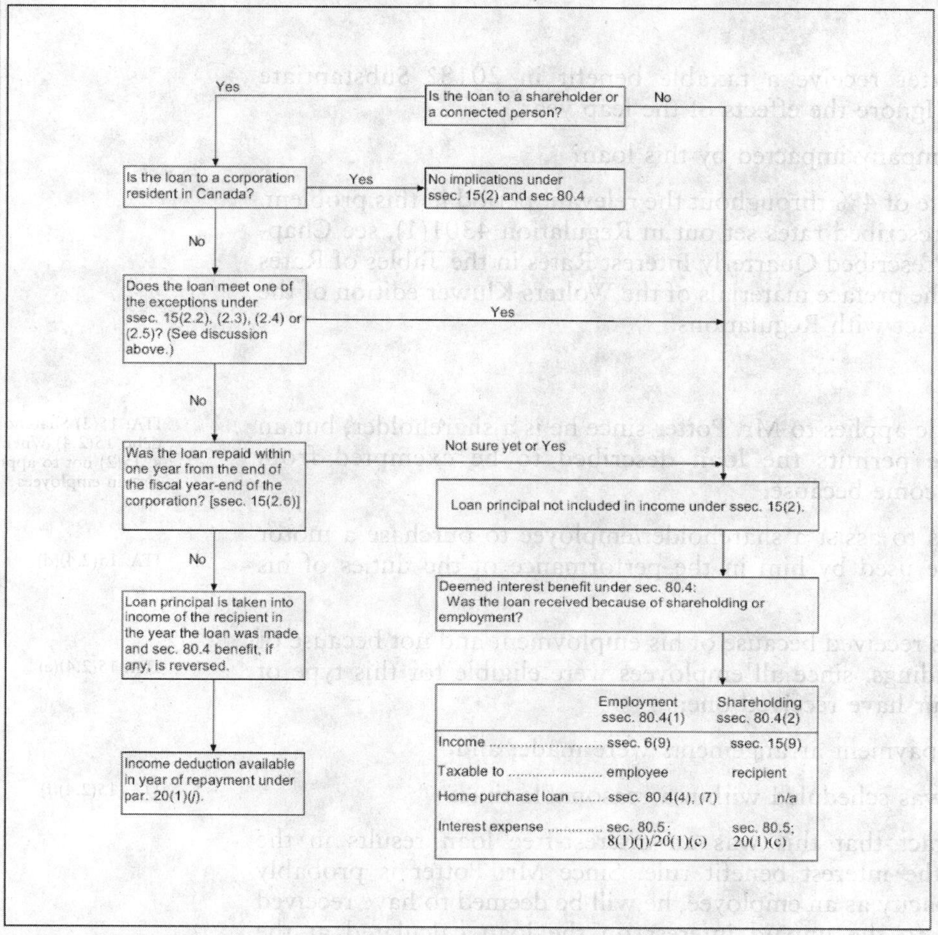

Example Problem 13-5

Mr. Potter owns all the outstanding shares of Run for Your Life Limited, a health and fitness club. He is the company president. On July 1, 2018 the company made a loan to Mr. Potter of $19,500 which he used to acquire an automobile at fair market value. All of the other six employees of the corporation are eligible to receive this type of loan on the same terms and four have, in fact, taken advantage of the opportunity. He requires the automobile to carry out his business duties for the company. (He drives behind members of the club in case of an emergency while they are jogging.) The loan is repayable in two equal annual instalments starting July 2019 without interest.

REQUIRED

(1) Does Mr. Potter receive a taxable benefit in 2018? Substantiate your answer. (Ignore the effects of the leap year.)

(2) How is the company impacted by this loan?

Assume a prescribed rate of 4% throughout the relevant period in this problem. For a table of actual prescribed rates set out in Regulation 4301(1), see Chapter 14, or the table of Prescribed Quarterly Interest Rates in the Tables of Rates and Credits section in the preface materials of the Wolters Kluwer edition of the Canadian Income Tax Act with Regulations.

SOLUTION

(1) The general rule applies to Mr. Potter since he is a shareholder, but an exception rule permits the loan described to be exempted from inclusion in income because: ITA: 15(2) Shareholder debt, 15(2.4) When s. 15(2) not to apply — certain employees

(a) the loan was to assist a shareholder/employee to purchase a motor vehicle to be used by him in the performance of the duties of his office; ITA: 15(2.4)(d)

(b) the loan was received because of his employment and not because of his shareholdings, since all employees were eligible for this type of loan and four have received one; ITA: 15(2.4)(e)

(c) *bona fide* repayment arrangements were made; and

(d) repayment was scheduled within a reasonable time. ITA: 15(2.4)(f)

However, the fact that this was an interest-free loan results in the application of the interest benefit rule. Since Mr. Potter is probably acting in his capacity as an employee, he will be deemed to have received a benefit equal to the unpaid interest on the loan calculated at the prescribed rate in effect during the period in the year that the loan was outstanding. The prescribed rate, for this purpose, is given as 4% for all relevant quarters. Therefore, the amount of the benefit would be calculated as follows: ITA: 80.4(1) Loans

4% of $19,500 × 92/365	=	$ 196.60
4% of 19,500 × 92/365	=	196.60
		$ 393.20

The $393.20 will be considered interest paid on a car loan for purposes of determining Mr. Potter's deduction of interest paid from employment income. This will allow him to deduct the business-use portion of the interest deemed to have been paid within the limits for the deduction of interest.

ITA: 80.5 Deemed interest, 8(1)(j) Motor vehicle and aircraft costs, 67.2 Interest on money borrowed for passenger vehicle

(2) From the company's position, a loan is a capital transaction and does not impact corporate taxable income unless interest is charged. There is no need to charge interest on a *bona fide* loan and no interest will be imputed to the corporation in a fair market value transaction.

Income Tax Folio: S3-F6-C1 Interest Deductibility

If the company borrowed the funds which it loaned to Mr. Potter, it would be able to deduct the interest it paid provided it was part of reasonable total remuneration to Mr. Potter as an employee.

The company would be required to report the interest benefit to Mr. Potter on his T4 slip.

¶13,080.99 Practise What You've Learned

Refer to the following sections of the Study Guide to practise what you've learned:

¶13,800 — Review Questions

- Question 5 — Shareholder loan
- Question 6 — Shareholder loan

¶13,825 — Multiple Choice Questions

- Question 1 — Shareholder loan — home
- Question 2 — Shareholder loans

¶13,850 — Exercises

- Exercise 2 — Shareholder loan
- Exercise 3 — Shareholder loan — series of transactions
- Exercise 4 — Shareholder loan — car
- Exercise 5 — Shareholder loan — car
- Exercise 13 — Shareholder loans
- Exercise 15 — Shareholder loan & unpaid amounts

¶13,090 Other Planning Considerations for Shareholder-Manager Remuneration

¶13,095 Income Splitting Through Salary Payments

It is possible to pay a spouse or other family members a tax-deductible salary. Of course, the salary must be reasonable in the circumstances and based on the value of the actual services performed for the business, as discussed previously. Such payments will split the income of a business so that it is subject to tax at lower personal tax rates. The trade-off for this benefit is the possible loss of a marital status tax credit for the spouse.

Unlike the case of remunerating a controlling shareholder-manager with salary, there may be an incentive for the CRA to challenge, on the basis of reasonableness, the deduction of the amount of salary paid to relatives, because they may be in a lower tax bracket than the corporation after the payment of salary. The case of *Gabco Limited v. M.N.R.* presents an interesting situation of this nature. Late in 1962, Jules, the president of a construction company, hired Robert, his brother aged 19, with the intention of making him the number two man. Robert immediately became an energetic and innovative driving force in the company and, according to his brother Jules, gave better service than anyone in the company, including the superintendent who was Robert's immediate superior. The company deducted the following sums from its income as expenses for Robert's remuneration: $20,371 for three months in 1962 consisting of $851 in salary and $19,520 in bonus and $35,673 in 1963 consisting of $5,280 in salary and $30,393 in bonus. These bonuses were paid in accordance with the company's practice of paying its permanent employees mainly by way of a yearly bonus proportionate to each employee's shareholdings which were based on service.

ITA: 67 General limitation re expenses; Cases: *Gabco Limited v. Minister of National Revenue*, 68 DTC 5210 (EC)

The CRA took the position that only $1,800 in 1962 and $7,200 in 1963 was a reasonable deduction for remuneration in the circumstances. This position was based on Robert's youth, his record of academic failures and the fact that his earnings for the three months in 1962 were greater than the superintendent's salary for that year. An expert appearing for the company testified that Robert was, in fact, the number two man in the company and that, as such, he would normally receive 70% of the most senior man's salary. Jules' salary was $48,000 in 1962 and $57,000 in 1963.

The company's position was upheld on the basis that Robert's remuneration was reasonable in the circumstances. The question to be answered was: would a reasonable business person have paid the remuneration in the circumstances? It was found that the bonus arrangement was a legitimate way of remunerating the company employees. Having regard to Robert's contemplated status in the company, which was subsequently fulfilled, and to the legitimate consideration of future benefits to be derived from his employment, the court found that his remuneration for the three-month period in 1962 was not unreasonable but in proportion to the value of his services to the company. The court also found, on the basis of the evidence that 70% of the most senior person's salary was a normal salary for his second in command, that Robert's remuneration for 1963 was reasonable.

¶13,100 Employment Benefits

¶13,100.10 Contributions to RPP

The remuneration package for a shareholder-manager may include a number of employment benefits such as private health insurance and group sickness or accident insurance, among others. It might include retirement benefits from an employer's contribution to a registered pension plan. Since only employees are eligible, the owner of an unincorporated business, who is not considered to be an employee, cannot participate in such a pension plan. However, a personal contribution to a registered retirement savings plan could still be made. There are criteria which must be met by a registered pension plan for a shareholder-manager.

¶13,100.20 Payment of Premiums For Life and/or Disability Insurance

Sometimes the life and disability insurance coverage provided in the group insurance package is not adequate to meet the needs of the shareholder-manager. If the company were to pay for additional life insurance premiums on an individual policy owned by the shareholder-manager (in his or her capacity as a shareholder), then the full premium would be a shareholder benefit. Similarly, if the company were to pay the premiums on a disability insurance policy owned by the shareholder-manager, and if the benefit was received in his or her capacity as shareholder, then the full amount of the premium would be a shareholder benefit.

ITA: 15(1) Benefit conferred on shareholder

¶13,100.30 Retiring Allowance

A retiring allowance could also be paid by the company which would receive a tax deduction. The tax on that income could be deferred by the shareholder-manager by rolling the allowance into a registered retirement savings plan or a registered pension plan. Note, however, that the Act will restrict the amount that can be rolled in this manner. A limit, for years of service prior to 1989, of $3,500 will apply for each year that the taxpayer was not a member of a registered pension plan, or was a member of a plan whose benefits for those years did not vest, and $2,000 for each year that the taxpayer was a member of such a plan whose benefits did vest. For years of service after 1988 and before 1996, there is a single limit of $2,000 for each year of service. Therefore, no amount in respect of years of service after 1995 can be rolled into an RRSP.

ITA: 60(j.1) Transfer of retiring allowances

¶13,100.40 Company Car

Finally, a company car can be provided as an employment benefit. Exhibit 13-3 presents an example which shows the possible advantage of the company providing a car subject to the standby charge in comparison with the individual providing himself or herself with the same car. The decision in this comparison will depend on the specific facts of each case. However, the calculation at the bottom of Exhibit 13-3 would suggest a benefit to a company car when the actual cost of the personal use of the company car exceeds the amount of the benefit that must be added to the shareholder-manager's employment income for the particular car in question. It should be noted that if the car is used primarily for personal purposes as a perquisite, there may be a reduction in the standby charge, but the decision in this case will not change. Note that the example neutralizes the company's position by assuming that lease costs and operating costs would be added to the salary of the shareholder-manager where he or she assumed these expenses. Exhibit 13-3 is a relatively simple example. The analysis can be much more complex (e.g., luxury cars with a cost or lease payments over $30,000 or $800, respectively).

Exhibit 13-3 Company Car as an Employment Benefit

Assumptions:

Annual car lease cost (added to salary if leased by shareholder-manager), including HST (13%)	$ 6,000
Annual operating costs of car (added to salary if leased by shareholder-manager), including HST (13%)	$ 2,880
Shareholder-manager has taxable income before car benefit of:	
if car leased by company	$154,000
if car leased personally ($154,000 + $6,000 + $2,880)	$162,880
Employment use of car (4,800/24,000 km)	20%

Company Leases Car		*Shareholder-Manager Leases Car Personally*	
Benefit from use of car:		Incremental taxable income	$ 8,880
— value of operating costs of personal use [par. 6(1)(*k*)] (25¢ × 19,200 km)	4,800	Less: deduction for employment use of car (20% of ($2,880 + $6,000))	(1,776)
			$ 7,104
— standby charge* [par. 6(1)(*e*)] (⅔ × $6,000)	4,000	HST rebate (13/113 × $1,776) . . .	$ 204
	$ 8,800	Tax @ 50% on income	$ 3,552
Tax @ 50%	$ 4,400	Tax @ 50% on HST rebate	$ 102
		Net tax ($3,552 − $204 + $102) . . .	$ 3,450

Difference: $950

Conclusion: If considering only net cash in shareholder-manager's hands he or she would choose to lease the car personally.

Reason:

Cost of personal use of car ($8,880 −$1,776) + HST rebate included in the year of receipt ($204)	$7,308
Less: benefit added to income under ssec. 6(1) ($4,800 + $4,000)	8,800
Net income difference	$1,492
Tax on net saving @ 50%	$ 746
HST rebate received	204
Total cash difference	$ 950

Note that present value considerations on the rebate which is received and taxed in the following year have been ignored, although the tax on the rebate inclusion is considered by the inclusion of the rebate in income. Also, ignored is the effect of the input tax credit (ITC) received by the corporation if it incurs the annual lease and operating costs. If the corporation pays additional salary equal to its net costs for these items after ITC and, hence, if the shareholder-manager must pay the HST from other sources, it can be shown that the shareholder-manager's after-tax retention is reduced by the after-tax equivalent of the HST costs.

* Since business travel does not comprise the primary (usually more than 50%) purpose of the distance travelled, the reduction factor in subsection 6(2) does not apply (i.e., A/B = 1 in the formula). Lease costs in this calculation include HST @ 13%.

Considerations in Choosing Elements of Shareholder-Manager Remuneration

Cash Needs

The optimum compensation paid to a shareholder-manager is a complex matter. Considerations include:

- Cash needs of the shareholder-manager
- Cash needs of the business
- Tax rate of the corporation
- Personal tax rate of the shareholder-manager
- Personal preferences of the shareholder-manager on such issues as making RRSP contributions and contributing to the Canada Pension Plan

The decision is not necessarily simple and the answer is different from one client to the next as their circumstances and preferences vary.

Individual's Tax Bracket

Important to the remuneration decision are all the sources of income that the shareholder-manager may have. If he or she is already in a high tax bracket, it might be wise to freeze salaries and bonuses to take advantage of a tax deferral on the income left in the corporation, even though the ultimate total tax may be higher. The time value of money may make the saving now greater than the added cost at some time in the future.

For example, consider the case of a corporation taxable at a net 15% rate, including provincial tax on its active business income eligible for the small business deduction and at a net 28% rate on its business income not eligible for the small business deduction. This corporation faces the choice of whether to pay a bonus of $1,000 now or a dividend of $1,000 at some time in the future. Exhibit 13-4 shows the comparative calculation that might be made assuming that the individual tax rate (federal plus provincial) is approximately 50%. The "dividend later" column is broken down into two options. Column A shows the results if the dividend gross-up and tax credit is 16% on non-eligible dividends from the low rate income pool (LRIP). Column B assumes that active business income not eligible for the small business deduction would qualify for the enhanced gross-up and credit of 38% on eligible dividends from the general rate income pool (GRIP).

Exhibit 13-4 Comparison of $1,000 Paid as a Bonus Now or as a Dividend in the Future

	Bonus now		Non-eligible LRIP A		Eligible GRIP B
Corporation					
Corporate income	$1,000		$ 1,000		$1,000
Bonus	1,000		—		—
Corporate taxable income	Nil		$ 1,000		$1,000
Corporate tax @ 15%/28% (rounded)	—		(150)		(280)
Funds available for dividend	Nil		$ 850		$ 720
Shareholder					
Income	$1,000		$ 850		$ 720
Dividend gross-up 16%/38%	—		136		274
Taxable income	$1,000		$ 986		$ 994
Combined federal and provincial tax @ 50% (rounded)	$ 500		$ 493		$ 497
Dividend tax credit @ 16%/38% of actual dividend (combined federal and provincial effect)	—		(136)		(274)
Net tax	$ 500		$ 357		$ 223
Cash available	$ 500		$ 493		$ 497
Tax deferral (personal tax on dividend)		$357		$223	
Tax savings (cost) ($500 − ($150 + $357)) and ($500 − ($280 + $223))		$ (7)		$ (3)	

Where the gross-up is 16% for non-eligible dividends out of the LRIP, there is a tax deferral benefit of $357 (i.e., the personal tax on the dividend) to be gained through retaining the funds in the corporation. When the dividend is paid, personal tax of only $357 must be paid on the dividend. Thus, the tax on the dividend, at $357, is the tax deferred until the dividend is paid. Overall there is a tax cost of $7 incurred when the dividend is paid in the future. The PV of this tax cost depending on when the dividend is paid in the future will be offset by the benefit gained through the reinvestment of the $357 of deferred tax in the corporation. Column B (GRIP) in Exhibit 13-4 shows the effect of the 38% gross-up on eligible dividends, i.e., dividends paid from active business income not eligible for the small business deduction. In this case, the tax deferral benefit of $223 is lower than in Column A (LRIP) since the corporate tax rate is higher and the gross-up/credit system is different. Again, the tax on the dividend of $223 is deferred until the dividend is paid. Overall there is a tax cost of $3 incurred when the dividend is paid in the future. Again, this cost will be offset by the benefit gained through the reinvestment of the $223 of deferred tax in the corporation.

Tax Deferral Benefit To Retaining Funds in the Corporation

As shown in the previous chapter and above, the availability of the small business deduction maximizes the tax deferral benefit to retaining funds in a corporation for income below the business limit of $500,000 with very little tax cost when dividends are paid in the future depending on the provincial tax rate. Thus, a remuneration policy might be designed to maintain corporate income below the business limit of $500,000 maximizes the tax deferral benefit. However, Canadian business income that is taxed at full corporate rates is also usually almost perfectly integrated with the higher gross-up and tax credit. The tax deferral benefit to retaining funds in a corporation is lower for income not eligible for the small business deduction but still significant and there is very little tax cost when dividends are paid in the future depending on the provincial tax rate. With the 38% gross-up and tax credit, there may be some tax cost if combined federal and provincial corporate tax rates exceed 27.5%. If the deferral advantage cannot be achieved, because corporate earnings are to be distributed immediately, to meet owner-manager needs, the payment of salary or bonuses down to the $500,000 small business deduction limit may be slightly better than the payment of dividends where the corporate tax rate exceeds 27.5%. A remuneration policy must recognize that added salary or bonuses to maintain business income at under $500,000 will likely be taxed at a high personal rate of a shareholder-manager and may have adverse tax consequences not considered in the above breakeven analysis.

Payroll Costs and Administration

Salary may increase a payroll tax such as the health levy used in several provinces to finance health care. Further, the corporation must incur the cost of remitting the employer portion of Canada Pension Plan and possibly Employment Insurance contributions. The employee portion of CPP, EI and the income tax withholdings must be remitted to CRA.

Cumulative Net Investment Loss (CNIL) Account

The payment of interest or dividends is favoured, if it is desirable to reduce the cumulative net investment loss (CNIL) account, as will be discussed later in this chapter, to preserve access to the QSBCS capital gains deduction. Note that interest paid on shareholder debt has the same effect as salary in reducing corporate income to the business limit of $500,000. However, interest income reduces the cumulative net investment loss and salary does not. Interest on shareholder debt may be subject to TOSI under the draft legislative proposals released December 13, 2017 on split income. This will be of little consequence if the shareholder is already in the highest tax bracket.

Cash Needs in the Corporation

Another consideration would include the company's need for funds to be used in the business. As shown in Exhibit 13-4, the tax savings/cost is nominal and the tax deferral is significant so leaving the cash in the corporation is a viable option.

Use of Personal Tax Credits

It is generally desirable to ensure that various basic deductions and personal tax credits available to employees and individuals, in general, are fully utilized by the payment of salaries and bonuses or other similar amounts of employment income. These basic deductions and credits would include items listed in section 8 of the Act (Chapter 3) and Division C and personal tax credits listed in Division E (Chapter 10).

¶13,200 Salary Versus Dividends

¶13,210 The Basic Trade-Off

On the one hand, salaries which are deductible by the corporation are subjected to personal tax. On the other hand, dividends which are not deductible by the corporation must be generated from income that is subjected to corporate tax; in turn, such dividends are subjected to personal tax which is reduced by the dividend tax credit.

Exhibit 12-1 demonstrated that integration of personal and corporate income tax works perfectly if the combined corporate tax rate is 13.8% where the proposed 16% gross-up applies and about 27.5% where the 38% gross-up applies. Since the federal tax rate on income eligible for the small business deduction is 10%, a provincial corporate tax rate of 3.8% (13.8% – 10%) on this type of income would provide perfect integration. If the provincial tax rate is less than 3.8%, then there is a tax saving advantage from incorporating income eligible for the small business deduction and receiving dividends, since the dividend tax credit claimed on the personal tax return will be greater than the underlying corporate tax. If the provincial corporate tax rate is higher than 3.8%, then there will be a tax cost disadvantage from incorporating this type of income, since the dividend tax credit will be less than the underlying corporate tax. In this case, salary, and not dividends, will generally be preferred. Since the federal tax rate on business income subject to the higher corporate tax rate is 15%, the breakeven provincial corporate tax rate on that income must be 12.5% (27.5% – 15%).

Further, salaries can reduce income to maintain corporate income at or below the $500,000 business limit for the small business deduction, whereas dividends will not. On the other hand, dividends reduce the cumulative net investment loss balance, to help preserve access to the capital gains deduction and may generate a dividend refund out of the company's RDTOH, but salaries do not. Maintaining active business income below the $500,000 business limit may not be very important where business income in excess of that limit is taxed at a combined federal and provincial rate close to 27.5% at which that income is perfectly integrated. Then, the need for salary or bonus for other tax purposes becomes more important than maintaining income below the business limit.

¶13,220 Distribution Out of Income Taxed at Small Business Rate

Exhibit 13-5 shows the small tax saving resulting from the payment of a dividend rather than salary from income eligible for the small business deduction in a province with a 3% corporate tax rate. Generally, dividends from the active business income of a CCPC taxed at the low rate are preferred to salary at all personal rates when total corporate rates are less than 13.8%. This is because the dividend tax credit is larger than the tax paid by the corporation, resulting in what is known as "over integration" which produces a small tax savings from the use of a corporation. Corporate rates will be less than 13.8% where a corporation is eligible for the federal small business deduction and where the provincial corporate tax rate is 3.8% or less.

When corporate tax rates total 13.8% or more on income eligible for the small business deduction, salaries alone will result in the lowest tax cost.

Exhibit 13-5 Eligible for Small Business Deduction

		Individual	
		Combined federal and provincial tax bracket	
		25% (up to $45,605)	50% (over $205,842)
Tax on $1,000 of salary	(A)	$ 250	$500
Tax on $1,000 corporate income distributed as a dividend after corporate tax:			
Corporate tax @ 13% (i.e., 38% - 10% - 18% + 3.0% (assumed prov.))		$ 130	$130
Combined federal and provincial personal tax[1] on remainder distributed as a dividend (tax on $1,000 - $130 = $870 dividend)		$113	$365
	(B)	$ 243	$495
Tax saving on dividend alternative (A) - (B)		$7	$5
Tax deferred while funds left in corporation (personal tax on dividend)		$113	$365

[1] Includes the effect of the combined federal and provincial rates on the grossed-up dividend and dividend tax credit — e.g., at the lower personal rate: 0.13 [25% × (1.16 × $870) - (0.16 × $870)] and at the higher personal rate: 0.42 [50% × (1.16 × $870) - (0.16 × $870)].

However, there is a range which will vary annually with indexing within which a combination of salaries and dividends will provide the lowest tax cost. Below the lower limit of the range, which is approximately equal to the level of the individual's total personal credit base (i.e., the level of income at which tax is offset by personal tax credits), salaries alone result in the lowest tax cost because they are deductible by the corporation and in the hands of the individual are offset by personal credits and, therefore, not taxable. For example, a salary of $11,809 (for 2018) will be fully deductible by the corporation, and the individual can offset his or her taxes payable using just the basic personal amount. Above the upper limit of the range, dividends alone result in the lowest tax cost at a combined rate of less than 13.8%. The latter case is demonstrated in Exhibit 13-7 using a $120,000 level of pre-tax corporate income. In that case, the payment of the salary is not fully integrated. The salary is deductible by the corporation at a relatively low tax rate, assumed to be 13%, and taxable to the individual at a relatively high rate. On the other hand, the dividend benefits from "over-integration" because the total corporate rate of tax is less than 13.8%.

Exhibit 13-6 Salary Versus Dividends

A. Data

Company earns $120,000 of active business income eligible for small business deduction. Shareholder has no other income and has federal personal tax credits of $2,100 and provincial personal tax credits of $1,400 that are allowable for both regular Part I tax and minimum tax.

B. Comparison

	Salary	Dividend
Pre-tax corporate income	$120,000	$120,000
Salary	(120,000)	—
Taxable income of corporation	—	$120,000
Combined federal and provincial corporate tax @ 13% (i.e., 38% - 10% - 18% + 3%)	—	(15,600)
Available for payment of dividend	—	$104,400
Combined federal and provincial personal tax on salary or dividend (using graduated rates)	$34,282[1]	$18,031[2]
Add: corporate tax	—	15,600
Total tax paid	$34,282	$33,631
Difference (tax saved from dividends)	$651	

[1] Federal Tax [16,545+.26(120,000-93,209) - 2,100] + Provincial Tax [10,253+.15(120,000-93,209) -1,400] = 34,282

[2] Federal Tax [16,545+.26(104,400+16,704-93,209)-2,100 – 8/11(16,704)] + Provincial Tax [14,437+.15(104,400+16,704-93,209)-2,100-3/11(16,704)] = 18,031

Note that in this situation federal minimum tax would not apply to the dividend, as shown by the following calculation of federal tax:

Greater of:

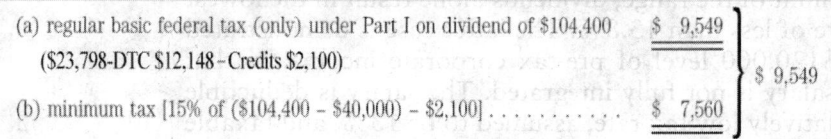

(a) regular basic federal tax (only) under Part I on dividend of $104,400 ($23,798-DTC $12,148 – Credits $2,100)	$ 9,549	$ 9,549
(b) minimum tax [15% of ($104,400 – $40,000) – $2,100]	$ 7,560	

A salary and dividend combination can provide a better result where not all of the dividend tax credit can be used against the shareholder's tax liability. Examples 13-5 and 13-6 illustrate an optimal salary/dividend mix in such circumstance.

Example Problem 13-6

Ethan Corporation Limited, a Canadian-controlled private corporation carrying on business in a province with a 3% corporate tax rate on its income (i.e., a total corporate tax rate of 13%), has earned $36,000 in its taxation year ended December 31 before a salary has been paid to the shareholder-manager. The shareholder-manager has federal personal tax credits of $2,500 and provincial personal tax credits of $1,600 and no income from other sources.

REQUIRED

(1) If the full $36,000 is to be distributed either by way of salary or dividends, which should be chosen? Use the 16% gross-up for dividends paid.

(2) Is there a combination of salary and dividends that is better?

SOLUTION

		Part A		Part B
		Salary	Dividend	Combination
Corporation:				
Income before salary	(I)	$36,000	$36,000	$36,000
Salary		(36,000)	—	(6,960)
Taxable income		Nil	$36,000	$29,040
Corporate tax @ 13% (i.e., 38% - 10% - 18% + 3%)	(II)	Nil	(4,680)	(3,775)
Available for dividend		Nil	$31,320	$25,265
Shareholder:				
Income from salary and/or dividend[1]		$36,000	$31,320	$32,225
Gross-up @ 16%		—	5,011	4,042
Taxable income		$36,000	$36,331	$36,267
Federal tax (15%)		$ 5,400	$ 5,450	$ 5,440
Personal tax credits		(2,500)	(2,500)	(2,500)

		Part A		Part B
		Salary	Dividend	Combination
Dividend tax credit @ 8/11 of gross-up		—	(3,645)	(2,940)
Basic federal tax[2]		$ 2,900	Nil	Nil
Provincial tax (10%)		3,600	3,633	3,601
Provincial personal tax credits		(1,600)	(1,600)	(1,600)
Provincial dividend tax credit @ 3/11 of gross-up		Nil	(1,367)	(1,102)
Total tax[2]	(III)	$ 4,900	$ 666	$ 924
Cash retained (I - (II + III))		$31,100	$30,654	$31,301

[1] A dividend of these amounts would not be affected by the minimum tax.

[2] Cannot be negative.

Note that the mix of salary and dividend in Part B is better, as measured by after-tax cash, than the all-salary alternative by $201 (i.e., $31,301 - $31,100). The salary/dividend mix chosen in Part B is determined as the amount that will result in the full use of the personal and dividend tax credits against federal tax. This combination results in more after-tax cash than the dividend option in Part A because of the full utilization of the credits. This combination also takes advantage of the tax savings available through paying dividends when the corporate tax rate is below 13.8% and is more tax effective than the salary option in Part A.

However, there are other factors to consider when making the salary/dividend decision, such as:

- Canada Pension Plan and Employment Insurance premiums on salary income
- The ability to make RRSP contributions, which requires salary income
- The need for personal earned income (salary) to claim child care expenses
- No withholding tax on dividends, but instalments may be required

Example Problem 13-7

Bryan Hill owns all of the issued shares of Hill & Associates Inc., a consulting firm he started five years ago. Bryan's only source of income is from the corporation and he has federal personal, non-refundable tax credits of $2,500 and provincial tax credits of $1,700. The corporation has a tax rate of 14% on its income eligible for the small business deduction.

REQUIRED

Determine the best combination of salary and/or dividend that Bryan should take in order to minimize the total corporate and personal tax for the year, assuming that the corporation earned net income of $100,000 before owner compensation and income tax. Bryan needs a pre-tax amount of $36,000 in cash to meet his personal expenses. Use the 16% gross-up.

SOLUTION

		Salary	Dividend	Combination[1]
Corporation				
Income before salary	(I)	$100,000	$100,000	$100,000
Salary		(36,000)	—	(4,600)
Taxable income		$ 64,000	$100,000	$ 95,400
Corporate tax @ 14% (i.e., 38% - 10% - 18% + 4%)	(II)	(8,960)	(14,000)	(13,356)
Available for dividend		$ 55,040	$ 86,000	$ 82,044
Paid as dividend		—	(36,000)	(31,400)
Retained by corporation		$ 55,040	$ 50,000	$ 50,644
Shareholder				
Income from salary		$ 36,000	—	$ 4,600
Income from dividend		—	$ 36,000	31,400
Gross-up @ 16%		—	5,760	5,024
Taxable income		$ 36,000	$ 41,760	$ 41,024
Federal tax		$ 5,400	$ 6,264	$ 6,154
Personal tax credits		(2,500)	(2,500)	(2,500)
Dividend tax credit (8/11 gross-up)		—	(4,189)	(3,654)
Basic federal tax		$ 2,900	Nil	Nil

		Salary	Dividend	Combination[1]
Provincial tax		3,600	4,176	4,102
Provincial personal tax credits		(1,700)	(1,700)	(1,700)
Provincial dividend tax credit (3/11 of gross-up)		Nil	(1,571)	(1,370)
Total tax	(III)	$ 4,800	$ 905	$ 1,032
Net cash retained initially (I - (II + III))		$ 86,240	$ 85,095	$ 85,612
Ultimate tax on dividend[2]		(23,117)	(21,000)	(21,270)
Net retained ultimately after tax		$ 63,123	$ 64,095	$ 64,342

[1] Note that, when the remuneration is paid as a dividend, there is an excess of $425 in federal non-refundable dividend tax credit and personal tax credits that cannot be used to offset tax on other income. By increasing the salary to $4,600 this excess federal credit can be used resulting in a slightly lower tax.

[2] When the amount retained by the corporation is paid out as a dividend, it will attract personal tax at that time. The combined federal and provincial tax can be estimated at a top rate of 42% (i.e., (.50 × 1.16) - .16) of the cash dividend paid. If the shareholder is in a lower tax bracket at the time that the dividend is paid, the effective tax rate on the dividend will be lower. When this amount is deducted from the net cash retained initially, the ultimate net after-tax retention is computed. Of course, the tax on the dividend paid from corporate retention has not been reduced by the time value of money, which depends on when the dividend is ultimately paid.

The salary level of $4,600 determined in the combination option is the amount of salary needed to ensure full utilization of the personal and dividend tax credits against federal tax.

This situation shows that it would be marginally better to pay a combination of salary and dividends since it results in $247 (i.e., $64,342 – $64,095) of additional after-tax cash. The difference is small because we have almost perfect integration at a combined rate of 14%. The combination option is also better than the salary option in the current year because Bryan will have $3,768 more available after-tax for personal expenses. However, the trade-off is $4,396 less cash available for reinvestment in the corporation relative to the salary option in the current year.

¶13,230 Distributions Out of Income Not Eligible for the Small Business Deduction

To this point the analysis has focused on the question of salaries versus dividends as remuneration from income eligible for the small business deduction. Exhibit 13-8 presents the comparison for income *not* eligible for the small business deduction. At a corporate tax rate of 27.5% for income not eligible for the small business deduction there is perfect integration and the preference to pay out salary vs. dividends is negligible as there is no overall tax cost or savings to one option over the other. However, similar to dividends paid from income eligible for the small business deduction where income is taxed at the high corporate business income rate, the dividend alternative produces a tax deferral advantage for individuals in the higher tax brackets. An individual taxed at the highest corporate rate of 50% can retain the funds in the corporation to be taxed at a rate of 27.5%. Recognize that the amount of tax deferred can be reinvested in the corporation to, perhaps, make up any tax cost on the payment of the funds as a dividend in the future. The deferral advantage of dividends can be taken advantage of if there is no immediate need for the funds. In making this comparison, it is important to consider the amount of this deferral advantage and the length of time any tax cost can be deferred by delaying the payment of dividends.

Exhibit 13-8 uses the 38% dividend gross-up and related tax credit on dividends paid out of high tax rate active business income. In this case, we are assuming that the income under consideration is above the small business deduction business limit of $500,000. The tax rate used in the exhibit is a 28% combined corporate rate which is higher than the rate of 27.5%, which provides for perfect integration, i.e., no tax cost to paying corporate funds out as dividends in the future. At the 28% combined corporate rate, there is a small tax cost to paying dividends of $5 for dividends taxed at the lowest personal rate of 25% and a small tax cost of $3 for dividends taxed at the highest personal rate of 50%.

Under the 25% tax column, the personal tax on the dividend is actually negative. This is as a result of the fact that the dividend tax credit is greater than the tax on the gross-up and, therefore, available to offset tax on other income.

The result is that the tax cost on the dividend alternative is not significant, and offset by the tax deferral at the 50% personal tax rate that provides an advantage to leaving the money in the corporation and paying a dividend at a later date.

Exhibit 13-7 Canadian Business Income Not Eligible for Small Business Deduction

		Individual	
		Combined federal and provincial tax bracket	
		25% (up to $46,605)	50% (over $205,842)
Tax on $1,000 of salary	(A)	$ 250	$500
Tax on $1,000 corporate income distributed as a dividend after corporate tax:			
Corporate tax @ 28% (i.e., 38% - 10% - 13% + 13%)		$ 280	$280
Personal tax[1] on remainder distributed as a dividend (tax on $1,000 - $280 = $720)		(25)	223
	(B)	$ 255	$503
Tax cost on dividend alternative (B) - (A)		$ 5	$ 3
Tax deferral (prepayment) while funds left in corporation (personal tax on dividend)		$ (25)	$223

[1] Includes the effect of the combined federal and provincial rates on the grossed-up dividend and dividend tax credit — e.g., at the lower personal rate, -0.035 calculated as [[25% × (Dividend × 1.38)] - (0.38 × Dividend) = -0.035 × Dividend], and at the higher personal rate, 0.31 calculated as [[50% × (Dividend × 1.38)] - (0.38 × Dividend) = 0.31 × Dividend].

The following table summarizes the results of Exhibit 13-5 and Exhibit 13-7.

Cases: *Warren Champ v. The Queen*, 83 DTC 5029 (FCTD)

Summary of Tax Savings/Cost and Deferrals for $1,000 Paid as Salary or Dividend

	Individual	
	Combined federal and provincial tax bracket	
	25% (up to $46,605)	50% (over $205,842)
Income Eligible for Small Business Deduction [Exhibit 13-5]		
At a combined corporate tax rate of 13%		
Tax savings/(cost) on dividend alternative	$7	$5
Tax deferred while funds left in corporation	$113	$365
Canadian Business Income Not Eligible for Small Business Deduction [Exhibit 13-7]		
At a combined corporate tax rate of 28%		
Tax saving/(cost) on dividend alternative	$ (5)	$ (3)
Tax deferred/(prepayment) while funds left in corporation	$(25)	$223

¶13,240 Approximate Amounts of Taxable Dividends That Can Be Distributed Tax-Free

Exhibit 13-8 demonstrates that it is possible to distribute a considerable amount of dividends which will be received tax-free by the shareholder, if he or she has no other sources of income. This fact might be advantageous in family income splitting where various members of a family hold different classes of shares.

Cases: *Warren Champ v. Her Majesty The Queen*, 83 DTC 5029 (FCTD)

The case of *The Queen v. McClurg* supports the ability to pay dividends on separate classes of shares even where the shares are similar in nature (e.g., different classes of common shares). The case was resolved in favour of the taxpayer paying dividends to a spouse on a separate class of common shares because the Articles of Incorporation allowed the "sprinkling" of dividends among various classes of shares at the discretion of the directors. However, it must be remembered that in order for the company to pay the dividends indicated it must generate income which will be subjected to corporate taxes.

Cases: *Her Majesty the Queen v. Jim A. McClurg*, 91 DTC 5001 (SCC)

Draft legislative proposals released December 13, 2017 and discussed in ¶13,260 below greatly restrict the ability to split income in this manner with family members unless they are actively engaged in the business of the corporation, have made a contribution of property to, or assumed risks in respect of the business. Tax on split income (TOSI) will apply to such dividends unless the dividend meets the definition of an excluded amount. If the dividend is subject to TOSI, it will be taxed at the highest graduated tax rate, eliminating any benefit gained through income splitting.

Dividends distributed out of low-rate active business income (small business deduction) are subject to the 16% gross-up, while dividends distributed out of high-rate active business income are subject to the 38% gross-up. Exhibit 13-8 shows the possibility of receiving a significant dividend without any personal tax should the dividend be an excluded amount under the TOSI provisions of the Act.

Exhibit 13-8 Approximate Amounts of Taxable Dividends That Can Be Distributed Tax-Free

	Non-eligible LRIP 16% Gross-up	Eligible GRIP 38% Gross-up
Taxable dividend[1, 2]	$22,710	$76,014
Gross-up (16%/38%)	3,634	28,885
Taxable dividend	$26,344	$104,899
Federal and provincial tax	$ 6,586	$ 31,837
Less: assumed personal tax credits	(2,952)	(2,952)
dividend tax credit	(3,634)	(28,885)
Total tax[3]	$ —	$ —
Net cash retained	$22,710	$ 76,014

[1] Amounts will change with indexing of tax brackets. The increase in dividends will be approximately equal to the increase in the indexing factor for the year.

[2] None of these amounts will be affected by the minimum tax.

[3] In this exhibit, federal and provincial tax and credits were combined. In reality, the federal and provincial calculations are done separately. As a result, federal credits can exceed federal tax, but federal tax cannot be negative, since the tax credits are non-refundable. Therefore, the dividend would be calculated to arrive at a basic federal tax of nil. As a result, some provincial tax would be paid, but the provincial tax rate is lower than the federal tax rate.

¶13,250 Summary of the Salary Versus Dividends Issue

Once the decision to incorporate has been made, the key issue becomes how to compensate the owner-manager. Should the compensation be in the form of salary/bonus or in the form of dividends or a combination of both? Exhibit 13-9 outlines the steps that should be taken in the analysis of that decision.

Exhibit 13-9 Steps to Take in the Analysis of the Salary or Dividend Decision

Consider:

(1) The corporate tax that would be paid, based on the type of income that is earned in a corporation owned by the individual. Is the combined corporate rate above or below the rate of perfect integration?

(2) The personal tax that would be paid by the individual, if the corporation paid some or all of its after-tax income out as a dividend to the individual as the shareholder. Is there an overall personal/corporate tax cost or tax saving when dividends are paid from corporate income?

(3) The personal tax that would be paid by the individual if the corporation paid some or all of its after-tax income out as a salary/bonus to the individual as the employee. How much of a tax deferral can be gained through retaining and reinvesting funds in the corporation?

(4) If an all-dividend option will result in excess non-refundable federal tax credits, consider a combination of salary and dividends to eliminate the excess federal credits.

(5) Can dividends be paid out to low income shareholders and received tax free considering the impact of proposed legislation dealing with TOSI?

Determine tax savings or cost

Determine if a savings occurs from using one option compared to the other. A savings occurs when overall tax is reduced by choosing to take money out of the corporation through dividends.

(1) Compare

- The total of personal and corporate tax paid when the specified salary/bonus is paid to the individual to,
- The total of personal and corporate tax paid when the specified salary/bonus is left in the corporation to be taxed and the after-tax cash is paid as a dividend to the individual.

(2) A savings is realized by paying a dividend if the individual has more after-tax personal cash when the income is flowed through the corporation and paid as a dividend compared to paying a salary/bonus.

(3) A savings is realized by paying a salary/bonus if the opposite is true.

Determine tax deferral or prepayment

Determine if a deferral occurs from using one option compared to the other. A deferral occurs when after-tax money is left in the corporation and not paid out.

(1) Compare

- The total of personal tax paid when the specified salary/bonus is received by the individual to
- The corporate tax paid when the specified salary/bonus is left in the corporation to be taxed and not paid as a dividend to the individual.

(2) A "deferral" is realized if the tax on the salary/bonus is greater than the tax in the corporation.

(3) A "prepayment" is realized if the tax on the salary/bonus is less than the tax in the corporation.

The factors affecting a decision on whether to remunerate the shareholder-manager of a corporation by salary or by dividends include the following:

- the corporate tax rate, including both federal and provincial components, applicable to the type of income of the corporation;
- the personal tax rate, including both federal and provincial components with surtaxes, applicable to the shareholder as a result of income other than that from the corporation;
- the amount of the shareholder's personal tax credits and deductions; and
- the shareholder's participation in the Canada Pension Plan, registered pension plans and registered retirement savings plans, eligibility for child care deductions, which require income in the nature of salary rather than dividends. If no salary is paid, the owner-manager does not have income that will qualify him or her to make Canada Pension Plan or registered retirement savings plan contributions. Each of these provides for an initial tax benefit, the sheltering of income and the deferral of the ultimate payment of tax until the receipt of benefits.

The number of variables involved in a specific set of circumstances make it necessary to do a set of calculations similar to those presented in this chapter to determine the best mix of salaries and/or dividends in the particular case.

¶13,250.99 Practise What You've Learned

Refer to the following sections of the Study Guide to practise what you've learned:

¶13,800 — Review Questions

- Question 1 — Bonus payments
- Question 2 — Bonus payments
- Question 7 — Compensation decisions

- Question 8 — Non-eligible dividends

¶13,850 — Exercises

- Exercise 6 — Salary vs. dividend
- Exercise 7 — Salary vs. dividend
- Exercise 17 — Salary vs. Dividends

¶13,260 Tax on Split Income ("TOSI")

Tax on split income (TOSI) was added to the *Income Tax Act* in 2000 to eliminate income splitting opportunities with minor children. The tax applies to a specified individual who receives split income. In such a case, income tax computed at the top marginal rate is levied.

ITA: 120.4(2) Tax on split income

Prior to 2018, a specified individual included individuals under 18 years of age at the end of a calendar year. As a result, this tax has been commonly referred to as kiddie tax.

Prior to 2018, split income included:

- taxable dividends and shareholder benefits derived from a private corporation, received either directly or indirectly through a trust or partnership;
- income from a trust or partnership which derives income from the business of providing property or services to a business carried on by a relative of the minor or a corporation in which the relative is a specified shareholder; and
- taxable capital gains of a minor from a disposition of shares to a non-arm's length person if taxable dividends on such shares would have been subject to the tax on split income (added in 2011).

Where the split income consists of taxable capital gains in the above list, an amount equal to two times the taxable capital gain is deemed to be a non-eligible dividend and is subject to tax at the top marginal rate. Since capital gains are considered to accrue from reinvested retained earnings, it would otherwise be possible to avoid the tax on split income in a non-arm's length situation by retaining income and maximizing capital gains rather than paying income out as a dividend subject to TOSI.

ITA: 120.4(4) Taxable capital gain, 120.4(5) Taxable capital gain of trust

The income-splitting tax is not applicable to:

ITA: 120.4(1) Definitions

- minors with parents who are not resident in Canada;
- income from property and taxable capital gains from the disposition of property inherited by a minor from a parent; and
- income from property and taxable capital gains from the disposition of property inherited by a minor from anyone else if, during the year in which the minor receives the income, the minor is:
  - in full-time attendance at a post-secondary educational institution, or
  - eligible for the disability tax credit.

Income subject to TOSI is deductible from the Part I income of the specified individual, so that it is not taxed twice. Also, the only tax credits permitted in computing TOSI are the dividend tax credit and the foreign tax credit.

ITA: 56(5) Exception for split income

To the extent that income is subject to TOSI, that same income is not subject to the regular attribution rules. In addition, if taxable dividends are subject to TOSI, then they may reduce the deemed interest penalty calculated for corporate attribution purposes discussed below at ¶13,390.

ITA: 74.4(2)(g)

If a parent was active in the business from which the income subject to the income-splitting tax was derived, then the parent is jointly liable for the income-splitting tax payable by a minor.

Note that under the above TOSI rules, prior to 2018 it was possible to split dividends of private corporations with non-minor children and other adult family members to minimize and in some cases completely eliminate tax. As noted in paragraph ¶13,240 above, an owner-manager could arrange for dividends to be paid on separate classes of shares held by low-income family members allowing for significantly lower rates of tax and in some cases no tax whatsoever. Exhibit 13-8 provides a calculation of the dividend that could be received tax-free by an individual without any other source of income. A non-eligible dividend of $22,710 and an eligible dividend of $76,014 can be received tax free by such an individual because the basic personal and dividend tax credits will offset the tax applicable. This ability to split income created a significant tax savings opportunity for owner-managers with low-income family members.

December 13, 2017 Draft Legislation — Applicable to 2018 and later years

Proposed amendments to the *Income Tax Act* released July 18, 2017 and a later revision to the amendments in draft legislation released December 13, 2017 drastically limits the ability to split income with low-income family members through an extension of the TOSI rules effective January 1, 2018.

Any individual receiving dividends on shares of a private corporation, income from a debt obligation owing from a private corporation or realizing a capital gain on private corporation shares now must consider whether TOSI will apply to levy tax at the highest marginal rate. The rules are no longer restricted to only minor children.

The definition of "split income" has been expanded and includes (but is not limited to) the following;

- taxable dividends and shareholder benefits derived from a private corporation, received either directly or indirectly through a trust or partnership;
- taxable capital gains of a minor from a disposition of shares to a non-arm's length person if taxable dividends on such shares would have been subject to the tax on split income;
- income derived from a "**related business**" in respect of the individual;
- an amount in respect of a debt obligation of a private corporation, partnership or trust; and
- a taxable capital gain or profit of the individual from the disposition of a share or debt obligation in a private corporation.

See the definition of "split income" for a full list of amounts included.

It should be noted that as long as the taxable capital gain on the disposition of shares of a private corporation is realized on a QSBC share as discussed in paragraph ¶13,340 below, TOSI will not apply. This heightens the importance of ensuring shares are QSBC shares prior to sale for an individual subject to tax at rates below the highest marginal rate on the taxable capital gain. Note that for minors, a taxable capital gain realized on the disposition of a share to a non-arm's length person remain to be treated as a non-eligible dividend as described under the pre-2018 rules above.

A "**related business**" includes a business carried on by a related person or a partnership, corporation or trust in which the related person is actively engaged on a regular basis in its activities or a business of a corporation of which a related person owns 10% of the value of the shares.

The exceptions available to exclude an amount from TOSI depend on the age category in which the taxpayer falls.

Taxpayers under the age of 18

Split income received by a taxpayer under the age of 18 is always subject to tax at the highest tax rate. As noted above, the only exceptions apply to income from property acquired by the minor child upon the death of a parent or, the death of any person while the individual was a full-time student or eligible for the disability credit.

Taxpayers aged 18 to 23 years of age

Split income received by a taxpayer who is age 18 to 23 is subject to tax at the highest tax rate unless the amount meets the definition of an "**excluded amount**".

Excluded Business Exception

Split income from an excluded business is an excluded amount and will not be subject to TOSI. If the individual is actively engaged on a regular, continuous and substantial basis in the business in the taxation year the split income is received, **or** in any five prior taxation years, the income is considered to have been received from an **excluded business**. The five taxation years do not need to be consecutive. Further, a person who works in the business at least twenty hours per week during the portion of the year in which the business operates is deemed to be actively engaged in the business.

Example 1

21-year-old child of the owner-manager works a minimum of 20 hours a week in the portion of the year in which business operates and receives a dividend that year. TOSI will not apply to the income.

Example 2

23-year-old child is attending university full time but in the past worked a minimum of 20 hours a week in the business for any of a total of five earlier years. TOSI will not apply to the income.

Note that it would be difficult for a child who is enrolled in a post-secondary educational program to meet this exception. Summer employment with the parent's business will not be sufficient for the individual to be considered to be actively engaged in the business and it is unlikely that they will have worked sufficiently in the business for a total of five earlier years.

Safe Harbour Capital Return Exception

Split income that represents a safe harbour capital return on property contributed to the related business is an **excluded amount** and is not subject to the high rate of tax. The safe harbour return is calculated using the highest prescribed rate in effect for a quarter in the year and is applied to the fair market value of the property contributed for the timeframe it is used in the business during the year. The fair market value of the property at the time of the contribution is used to calculate the return.

Example

23-year-old child invests $20,000 of his/her funds into a parent's corporation or borrows funds from a bank to invest in shares of the corporation. The funds are used to purchase equipment used in the business throughout the year. A safe harbour return of 1% (the highest prescribed rate for the year) would be allowed as a dividend during the year. As a result, a $200 dividend could be received in relation to the contribution and not be subject to TOSI.

Note that the income splitting possibilities available through this exception will be minimal because of the current low prescribed rate and the potentially unlikely ability of an individual in this age group to have sufficient resources to invest in the business.

Reasonable Return on Arm's Length Capital Exception

Split income that represents a **reasonable return** on contributions by the individual of **arm's length capital** is an **excluded amount** and is not subject to TOSI.

The determination of whether an amount is considered a reasonable return is a question of fact taking into consideration work performed, property contributed, risks assumed, amounts paid or payable in respect of the business, and other factors. The CRA has provided some guidance on how this exception will be applied and what will be considered to be a reasonable return.

Further, for an individual in this age group to meet this exception, the contribution to the corporation must meet the definition of "**arm's length capital**". Funds that are borrowed from any source or funds provided by a related person (unless on death) or related business do not qualify. This restricts the eligible contributions on which a reasonable return could be received to either inheritances or after-tax funds received from employment or from unrelated businesses.

Example 1

21-year-old child invests $30,000 of investment funds that were derived from prior years' dividends from the related corporation. The return on the funds would be subject to TOSI because it would not be a return on arm's length capital.

Example 2

21-year-old child invests $30,000 of investment funds that were derived from salaries earned from summer employment with unrelated employers.The return on the funds would not be subject to TOSI as long as a reasonable return is received on that contribution. It is a question of fact whether the CRA will consider a return to be reasonable.

The income splitting possibilities available through this exception will be limited as most individuals in this age group are unlikely to have arm's length capital available to invest in the related business.

Overall, the ability of an owner-manager to split dividend income of his private corporation with a child who is age 18 through to 23 is restricted to primarily children who have been actively involved in the business and can meet the **excluded business** exception.

Taxpayers aged 24 and older — Tax on Split Income

Income splitting opportunities are less restrictive once the individual receiving the income reaches the age of 24. The **excluded business** exception noted above can apply. Therefore, where the individual is actively engaged on a regular, continuous and substantial basis in the business, income splitting may be possible.

As well, the **reasonable return** exception can be relied on without the requirement that the individual's contribution meet the definition of "arm's length capital". Again, the determination of whether an individual has received a reasonable return is a question of fact and must be supportable based on work performed, property contributed, risks assumed, etc.

Excluded Share Exception

An individual who has reached the age of 24 can also avoid TOSI in relation to excluded shares. Income from or taxable capital gains from the disposition of **excluded shares** are **excluded amounts.**

Shares in professional corporations and shares of corporations that earn 90% or more of their income from services are not excluded shares. This restricts the ability of professionals and owner-managers with serviced-based businesses from splitting income with family members unless they are actively engaged in the business or have made a contribution to the business [i.e., the excluded business or reasonable return exceptions have been met].

For a corporation that is not a professional corporation or earns less than 90% of its income from services, the shares are excluded shares if the individual owns 10 percent of the votes and value of all of the shares of the capital stock of the corporation. As a result, it is possible for the owner-manager who owns and operates a corporation operating a retail (non-service) business to split income with any family member who owns at least 10% of the votes and value of the shares of the corporation.

It should be noted that shares of a corporation can only be considered to be "**excluded shares**" if all or substantially all (90%) of the income of the corporation was not derived from a related business in respect of the individual. This restricts income splitting opportunities with family members owning shares of holding companies or real estate holding companies where they are not actively engaged in the related business. If the holding company has 90% or more of its income for the relevant tax year derived from a related business, the shares held by family members would not meet the definition of an excluded share. The only exception allowing income splitting in such a case would be the excluded business exception.

Example 1

John and his wife, Jane, both 40 years of age, own 50% of the common shares of a corporation. John is actively engaged in the company's manufacturing business. John owns Class A common shares and Jane owns Class B common shares, and the shares were issued on incorporation for nominal amounts. Jane is not involved in the business. For 2018, the corporation declares a $20,000 dividend to Jane on her Class A common shares. TOSI will not apply to the dividend received by Jane. She would not meet the excluded business or reasonable return exception. However, Jane's shares would be excluded shares because she owns shares that provide 10% or more of the votes and 10% or more of the fair market value of all of the issued and outstanding shares of the capital stock of the corporation. Also, if either Jane or John disposed of the shares of the corporation, TOSI would not apply to the taxable capital gain as long as the shares were QSBC shares at the time of disposition.

Example 2

A medical practitioner, Jane, age 45, owns 100% of the shares of her professional corporation. Her spouse holds non-voting preferred shares of the corporation and is not involved in the practice. Dividends paid to Jane would be excluded amounts not subject to TOSI because of either of the excluded business or reasonable return exceptions. Her shares would not be excluded shares because the shares are of a professional corporation. Dividends paid to Jane's spouse would be subject to TOSI as none of the exceptions would be available. The spouse's shares would not be excluded shares because they are shares in a professional corporation.

Example 3

Jane also holds the real estate used in her professional corporation in a separate real estate holding company, Realco. The only income earned in Realco is rent from the real estate rental to the professional corporation. Jane and her spouse each own 50% of the common shares of Realco. Dividends paid to Jane on her common shares would be excluded amounts not subject to TOSI because of the excluded business exception. Dividends paid to Jane from Realco would be amounts derived indirectly from an excluded business of Jane. Dividends paid to Jane's spouse would be subject to TOSI as none of the exceptions would be available. The spouse's shares would not be excluded shares because 90% or more of the income in Realco is derived from a related business.

Overall, as long as a business is not a service-based business, or incorporated as a professional corporation, income splitting with family members who are either actively engaged in the business, have made contributions in terms of work, property or risk to the business or who own at least 10% of the votes of value of the corporation is still possible. Note that tax savings can be significant where such a family member is in a tax bracket that is lower than the owner-manager.

Taxpayers aged 65 and older — Tax on Split Income

Income splitting opportunities also exist once individuals are in their retirement years. Along with all of the exceptions applicable to taxpayers aged 24 and older, a deeming provision applies to deem amounts as excluded once the taxpayer's spouse is in his or her 65th year.

An amount of income or taxable capital gain is deemed to be an "**excluded amount**" if it would have been an excluded amount if instead received by the individual's spouse. The spouse must have reached the age of 64 before the year.

Example

Jane in Example 2 above is instead 67 years old, semi-retired and works part time providing medical services to patients through her professional corporation. A dividend is paid on the preferred shares of the corporation held by her 64-year-old spouse who does not actively work for the corporation. Dividends received by Jane on her common shares are excluded amounts because of the excluded business exception. The dividend received by Jane's spouse would not be subject to TOSI because Jane, who is 65 and older, is able to receive dividends from the corporation that are excluded amounts under the **excluded business** exception.

This deeming provision is designed to align the rules with pension income splitting legislation.

Summary

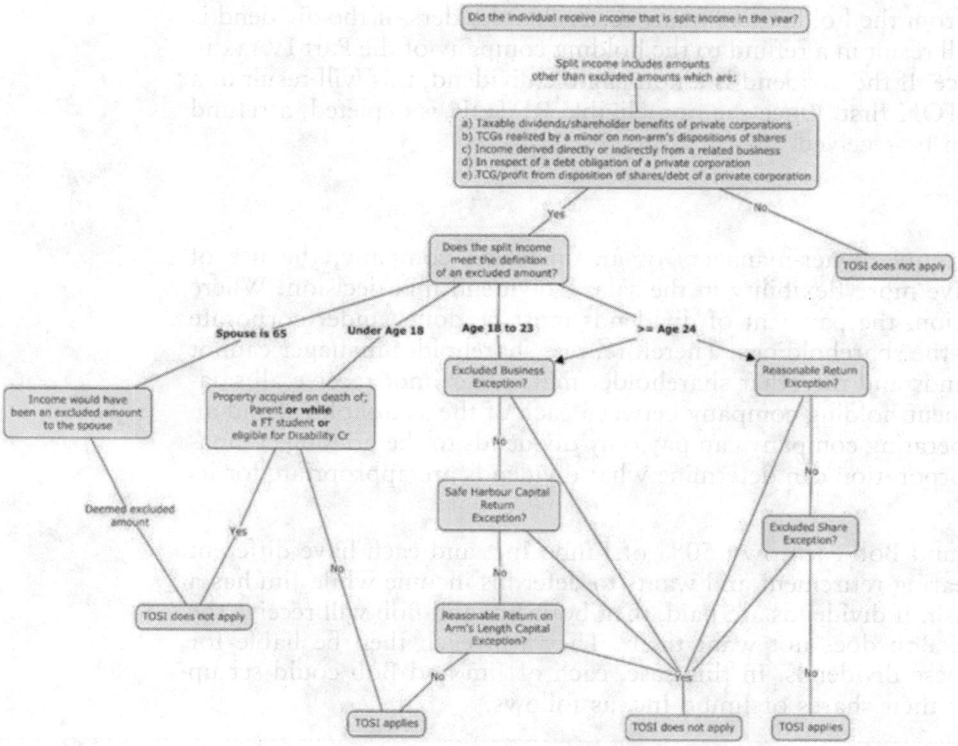

¶13,300 Other Planning Aspects of Using Corporations

¶13,310 Use of Holding Companies

¶13,315 An Extension of Integration

Inserting a holding company between a shareholder and another company requires an extension of the concept of integration, discussed in the previous chapter, to allow income ultimately to flow through the holding company to the shareholder to be taxed in his or her hands. To put this into effect, dividends must not be taxed at the corporate shareholder's level. This occurs under Part I since intercorporate dividends between Canadian companies are deductible under Division C leaving the taxable income of the recipient unaffected. However, there is the possibility of a tax under Part IV of the Act on such dividends received by a private corporation. This tax is refundable when the recipient corporation pays a taxable dividend to its shareholders such that the recipient corporation itself is not ultimately taxable on the dividends that pass through to the individual shareholder.

Note that the February 27, 2018 Federal Budget introduces both an eligible and non-eligible RDTOH account to capture Part IV tax paid on dividends. Part IV tax on eligible dividends, i.e., dividends on portfolio investments will be included in the eligible RDTOH balance. Part IV tax on dividends from connected corporations will be included in the RDTOH balance that matches the RDTOH account from which the payor corporation obtained its refund. Thus, when using a holding company, it will be necessary to consider which RDTOH balance any Part IV tax paid will be impacted when dividends are received.

When dividends are paid from the holding company to its shareholders, if the dividend is an eligible dividend this will result in a refund to the holding company of the Part IV tax in the eligible RDTOH balance. If the dividend is a non-eligible dividend, this will result in a refund of non-eligible RDTOH first. Once the non-eligible RDTOH is depleted, a refund of the eligible RDTOH can be received.

¶13,320 Compensation

Where there are two or more owner-managers of an operating company, the use of holding companies may give more flexibility in the salary–dividend mix decision. Where there is only one corporation, the payment of dividends must be done, under corporate law, *pro rata* according to the shareholdings. Therefore, one shareholder-manager cannot normally receive all dividends and the other shareholder-manager cannot receive all salary. By inserting a management-holding company between each of the shareholders and an operating company, the operating company can pay only dividends to the holding companies. Then each holding corporation can determine what dividends are appropriate for its shareholder(s).

For example, assume Jim and Bob each own 50% of Jimbo Inc. and each have different cash flow needs. Bob is nearing retirement and wants to defer his income while Jim has a young family and needs cash. If dividends are paid, then both Jim and Bob will receive the dividends *pro rata* even if Bob does not want them. They will each then be liable for personal income tax on these dividends. In this case, each of Jim and Bob could set up holding companies to own their shares of Jimbo Inc. as follows:

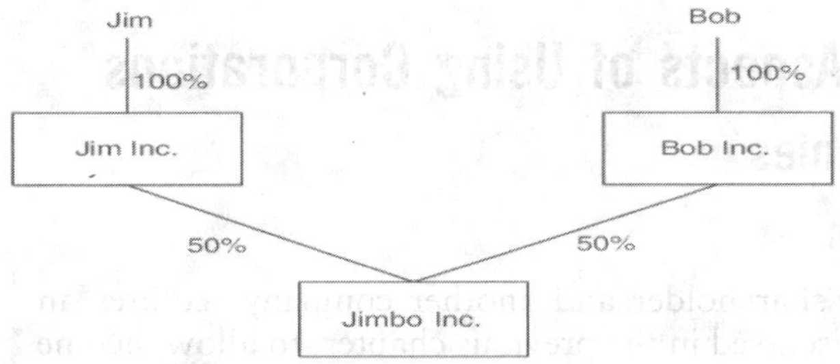

As dividends are paid from Jimbo Inc. they will be received by the holding companies without either Part I or Part IV tax as long as Jimbo Inc doesn't have a refundable dividend tax on hand balance. Bob can then defer his personal tax liability by leaving his dividends in Bob Inc. while Jim could take the cash he needs by paying a dividend to himself from Jim Inc.

As long as both Jim and Bob are actively engaged in the Jimbo Inc. business, the draft legislative proposals released December 31, 2017 and taking affect January 1, 2018 will not impose dividends paid by the respective holding companies to each of Jim and Bob to TOSI. See the discussion on TOSI in ¶13,260 above.

¶13,325 Deferral of Tax on Dividends

The use of a holding company may be advisable in the situation of a non-controlling shareholder-employee of an operating company that is paying out more taxable dividends than necessary for the shareholder-employee's immediate needs. In such a case, the shareholder could transfer his or her shares in the operating company to a holding company which he or she controls. If the holding company owned more than 10% of the total voting shares and more than 10% of the fair market value of all the issued shares in the operating company, the two corporations are connected. The dividends then could be received by the holding company without attracting the Part IV tax as long as the holding company and the operating company which had no investment income or portfolio dividends were connected.

A much smaller deferral of tax (if any) is possible on dividends from non-connected corporations on which Part IV tax is payable. The Part IV tax is levied at a 38⅓% rate. Therefore, there will only be a deferral benefit when the personal combined rate of federal and provincial tax plus surtaxes exceeds 38⅓%.

¶13,330 Implementing an Estate Freeze

Another reason for the use of a holding company to own shares of an operating company would be to effect a planning device known as an estate freeze. To give a very simple example, the owner of an operating company may wish to freeze or stop the growth in his or her interest in the operating company to avoid further capital gains on these shares which would ultimately be triggered at his or her death. The owner could arrange to transfer his or her common shares in the operating company to a holding company in which the common shares were owned by the next generation in the family, the children. The owner could take back in return, perhaps, preferred shares with voting rights in the holding company. These preferred shares would not grow in value, but could pay a sufficient dividend to meet his or her personal needs and would maintain control over the operating company through the voting privileges. Dividends paid on the common shares of the operating company would flow to the holding company free of Part IV tax as long as the operating company had no investment income or portfolio dividends to trigger a dividend refund while the two companies were connected. Estate planning will be discussed in greater detail in Chapter 17.

¶13,335 Lifetime Capital Gains Exemption

¶13,337 Overview

The lifetime capital gains exemption allows an individual to shelter from tax up of $848,252 (2018) of a capital gain on the disposition of shares of qualifying small business corporations (QSBC) and $1,000,000 on qualified farm and fishing property.

The current capital gains deduction applies to individuals (other than trusts) who are resident in Canada throughout the year. There is, however, a deeming provision which extends the definition of a resident, for purposes of this section only, to include individuals who were resident at any time in the year and who were resident in Canada throughout either the preceding or the following taxation year. This rule allows an individual who has either ended or commenced residence in Canada during a particular year to qualify for the deduction on a disposition.

The deduction applies to net taxable capital gains (the excess of taxable capital gains (TCGs) over allowable capital losses (ACLs)) on QSBC shares and qualified farm and fishing property. Also eligible for the deduction are capital gains reserves on dispositions of QSBC shares, farm and fishing property.

The maximum fractional capital gains deduction for qualified small business corporation shares is $424,126 (i.e., ½ × $848,252). Note that in this text the term "exemption" is used to refer to the full amount of a capital gain and the term "deduction" is used to refer to the fractional amount of the capital gain that gives rise to the actual deduction from taxable income of an individual.

¶13,340 Qualified Small Business Corporation (QSBC) Share

¶13,350 Basic QSBC Rules

There are three tests that must be met for shares to meet the definition of a QSBC share which will be referred to, respectively, as:

(1) the SBC Test,

(2) the Holding Period Test, and

(3) the Basic Asset Test (50% Test).

The term "qualified small business corporation share" of an individual is defined as follows: ITA: 110.6(1) Definitions, 110.6(14)(d)

The SBC Test

(*a*) a share of the capital stock of a corporation that is a small business corporation (SBC) at the time of disposition (i.e., the determination time) and is owned by the individual, by the individual's spouse or by a partnership related, as specifically defined for this purpose, to the individual;

The Holding Period Test

(*b*) the share was not owned by anyone, other than the individual or a person (including a personal trust) or partnership related to the individual throughout the 24-month period preceding the disposition (without exception to the 24-month period in the case of a deemed disposition caused by death);

The Basic Asset Test

(*c*) the share was, throughout that part of the 24-month period ending immediately before the disposition that the share was owned by the individual or a person or partnership related to the individual:

(i) a share of a corporation that was a Canadian-controlled private corporation, and

(ii) more than 50% of the fair market value of the corporation's assets were used principally in an active business carried on primarily in Canada by the corporation or a related corporation.

Exhibit 13-10 presents the foregoing tests in point form for ease of reference.

Exhibit 13-10 Qualified Small Business Corporation (QSBC) Share [ssec. 110.6(1)] Basic Tests

A Qualified Small Business Corporation Share is:

- at any time (i.e., determination time)
  - typically at time of disposition or deemed disposition;
- a share that meets the following tests:

  (1) SBC Test
  - an SBC at the determination time
  - owned by:
    - the individual

  (2) Holding Period Test
  - throughout the 24 months preceding the determination time
  - owned by no one other than
    - the individual, or
    - a person related to the individual;

  (3) Basic Asset Test (50% Test)
  - throughout that part of the 24 months preceding the determination time while owned by the individual or related party
    - share of a CCPC for which more than 50% of the fair market value of its assets were used principally in an active business carried on primarily in Canada by the corporation or by a related corporation.

Graphically, the timing factor in each of the three tests could be depicted as follows:

				Determination time
(a) SBC Test				I
(b) Holding Period Test	I←	24 months		→I
(c) Basic Asset Test	I←	24 months		→I

The SBC Test (see below) and the Basic Asset Test are calculated similarly, but the SBC Test is determined at a particular point in time, while the Basic Asset Test is determined over a period of 24 months.

¶13,353 Small Business Corporation (SBC)

The corporate entity referred to as a "small business corporation" (SBC) is widely used throughout the Act. For example, the term is used in connection with a business investment loss and an exemption from the effects of the corporate attribution rules.

ITA: 74.4 [Transfers and loans to corporations]

A small business corporation (SBC) is defined as a Canadian-controlled private corporation of which all or substantially all of the assets, on a fair market value basis, are used principally in an active business, carried on primarily in Canada by the corporation or a related corporation. The reference to a related corporation means that assets leased or loaned to a related corporation also qualify. The assets meeting the "all or substantially all" test may include shares or debt in an SBC that is a connected corporation.

ITA: 110.6(2.1) Capital gains deduction — qualified small business corporation shares, 110.6(4) Maximum capital gains deduction, 186(4) Corporations connected with particular corporation

The CRA's interpretation of the phrase "all or substantially all", as stated in about 10 different Interpretation Bulletins, is that it means at least 90%. However, in the case of Wood v. M.N.R., on another issue, but in respect of the phrase "all or substantially all", the Tax Court of Canada concluded that the CRA "might be hard pressed to refuse a claim where the percentage was 89%, maybe even 85% or 80% or lower". The court concluded that the "term "substantially all" does not lend itself to a simple mathematical formula" like at least 90%. The court preferred the meaning given by "small unrelated amounts" reducing the total to arrive at substantially all. The word "primarily", while not defined in the Act, is generally considered to mean more than 50%. Elsewhere, the CRA states that the word "principal" is not defined in the Act but it is considered that the words "chief" and "main" are synonymous to it. While a principal or main use may be less than 50% if the use is the most of many uses, the CRA has generally interpreted the word to mean more than 50%. Exhibit 13-11 presents the definition of a small business corporation in point form.

Interpretation Bulletins: IT-151R5 Scientific Research and Experimental Development Expenditures, IT-73R6 The Small Business Deduction; Cases: *Douglas Wood v. The Minister of National Revenue*, 87 DTC 312 (TCC)

Exhibit 13-11 Small Business Corporation (SBC) [ssec. 248(1)]

A Small Business Corporation is a corporation which was at any particular time:

- a Canadian-controlled private corporation, and
- all or substantially all (90% test) of the fair market value of assets (including unrecorded assets but excluding liabilities) were
  - (1) used principally in an active business carried on primarily (>50%) in Canada by
    - the particular corporation, or
    - a corporation related [sec. 251] to the particular corporation; or
  - (2) shares or debt
    - of a SBC that was connected [ssec. 186(4)] with the particular corporation; or
  - (3) a combination of (1) and (2).

Example Problem 13-8

Maya lives in Toronto and owns 100% of Maya's Ltd. The corporation was incorporated 10 years ago, in Ontario, to operate a retail clothing establishment in Toronto. The following is the recent balance sheet for the corporation.

Maya's Ltd.
BALANCE SHEET
as at December 31, 2018

Assets	
Current	
Cash	$ 2,500
Marketable securities	200,000
Accounts receivable (net of reserve)	95,000
Inventory	270,000
Prepaid expenses	2,000
Total (equal to fair market value)	$ 569,500
Fixed	
Land, at cost (FMV: $225,000)	150,000
Building, at net book value (FMV: $350,000)	160,000
Equipment, at net book value (FMV: $100,000)	120,500
	$1,000,000
Liabilities	
Current	
Accounts payable	$ 265,000
Income taxes payable	5,000
Due to shareholder	80,000
	$ 350,000
Mortgage payable	275,000
	$ 625,000

Shareholder's Equity	
Share capital	1,000
Retained earnings	374,000
	$1,000,000

The goodwill of the business has been valued at $250,000.

REQUIRED

Determine whether Maya's Ltd. is a small business corporation, assuming that the marketable securities were held:

(1) as a short-term investment of surplus cash at the low-point of the corporation's inventory cycle, and

(2) as a long-term investment to produce investment income.

SOLUTION

In this case the critical condition in the definition of a small business corporation is the 90% test. It must be determined whether all or substantially all of the fair market value of the assets, including unrecorded goodwill, was used principally in an active business carried on primarily in Canada by Maya's Ltd. Retailing is an active business and it is being carried on exclusively in Canada in this case.

(1) If the marketable securities are held for use in the business, as would be the case if they represented a short-term investment of cash surplus, pending the build-up of inventory, then it can be concluded that all of the fair market value of the assets is used principally in an active business carried on primarily in Canada. Therefore, the company meets the 90% test and is a small business corporation.

(2) If the marketable securities are not considered to be used in the active business of retailing, then their relative value must be determined as follows:

	Fair market value	%
Cash	$ 2,500	0.17
Marketable securities	200,000	13.38
Accounts receivable	95,000	6.36
Inventory	270,000	18.07
Prepaid expenses	2,000	0.13

	Fair market value	%
Land	225,000	15.06
Building	350,000	23.42
Equipment	100,000	6.69
Goodwill	250,000	16.72
Total	$1,494,500	100.00%

Since the marketable securities comprise more than 10% of the fair market value of the assets, the 90% test in the definition of a small business corporation is not met. (Note that the legislation does not quantify the term "all or substantially all". The courts may not interpret this term as meaning at least 90% as used administratively by the CRA.) Note that the definition of a small business corporation applies at a particular point in time. Therefore, if some of the marketable securities can be removed from the corporation: either sold with the proceeds used to pay off liabilities or invested in assets used in the active retailing business, the 90% test can be met after the removal or reinvestment. Thus, the corporation can be "purified" to meet the 90% test. It is not enough to convert the marketable securities into cash, if the cash is not used in an active business carried on by the corporation.

Example Problem 13-9

Reconsider the facts of the previous example problem. Assume that the problem raised by the marketable securities has been resolved by removing the marketable securities from the corporation. Also, assume that the relative proportion of assets held at December 31, 2018 has not changed in the last five years.

REQUIRED

Determine whether the shares are eligible for the capital gains exemption, assuming:

(1) the shares were acquired on incorporation 20 years ago, and

(2) the shares were acquired from the brother of Maya in blocks of 200 shares annually for the last five years.

SOLUTION

At the time of their disposition or deemed disposition, to qualify for the capital gains exemption, the shares must meet three tests. The difference between parts (A) and (B) of the Required will be seen in the application of the second test.

(1) SBC Test

The shares must be of an SBC at the time of the disposition or deemed disposition. In this case, steps have been taken to make the corporation an SBC, if it did not already qualify as such, as discussed in the previous example problem.

(2) Holding Period Test

Throughout the 24 months preceding the disposition, the shares cannot be owned by anyone other than Maya or a related party (i.e., Maya's brother).

(1) This test is met because the shares were held for the preceding two years by Maya.

(2) Where the shares have been acquired from the related individual (i.e., Maya's brother) even within the previous 24-month period, the test is still met. If the individual from whom the shares were acquired was not related, then the shares would have to be held by the present shareholder for the full 24 months. Since the holding period test is applied to each share, a series of dispositions can be staged as the shares meet the 24-month test on a first-in, first-out basis as permitted.

(3) Basic Asset Test (50% Test)

This test requires that throughout the 24 months preceding a disposition or deemed disposition, while the shares were held by a particular individual (i.e., Maya) or related party (i.e., Maya's brother), the shares were of a Canadian-controlled private corporation in which more than 50% of the fair market value of the assets were used principally in an active business carried on primarily in Canada by the corporation or by a related corporation. Since no other corporation is involved in this situation, the other parts of the test pertaining to a connected corporation do not apply. In this case, even with a 13.38% investment in marketable securities which may not be considered to have been used in the active business of the corporation, the 50% asset test is still met throughout the 24 months preceding a contemplated disposition or deemed disposition at this time, since the proportion of marketable securities has been stable throughout those 24 months. Remember that, even though the securities have been disposed of to meet the SBC test, they were still assets of the corporation during the 24 months preceding the disposition.

Ⓐ ¶13,355 Modification of the Basic Asset Test (Stacking Rule)

Even where there are a number of connected corporations, the basic rules as described above must be applied, including the 50% basic asset test in the definition paraphrased above. If the particular corporation to be sold (i.e., a parent corporation) can meet the 50% basic active business asset test with its own active business assets, its shares will meet the test and the modification can be ignored.

ITA: 110.6(1) qualified small business corporation share (c)(i)

Where the active business assets of the parent corporation are 50% or less, then the parent corporation may still qualify by including shares and indebtedness of corporations connected with it. The modification of the basic asset test must be considered. In such case, the basic asset test is modified to ensure that one of the two levels of corporations (i.e., parent or connected subsidiaries) meets an all or substantially all test (90%) while the other level of corporations meets a "primarily" test (50%) of the aggregate of active business assets and debts or shares of a connected CCPC.

ITA: 110.6(1) qualified small business corporation share (d)

Recall, from the discussion of the Part IV tax in Chapter 12, that a connected corporation is a defined term. A corporation is connected with another corporation where:

ITA: 186(4) Corporations connected with particular corporation

(*a*) the other corporation controls the corporation, or

(*b*) the other corporation holds more than 10% of the votes and fair market value in shares of the corporation.

If the parent meets the 90% test throughout the 24-month period before the disposition with a combination of its own active business assets and shares and debt of a connected corporation, the connected subsidiary need only meet the 50% test on its assets.

Alternatively, if the parent meets the 50% test but does not meet the 90% test throughout the 24-month period before the disposition when taking into account the shares and debt of a connected corporation, the connected subsidiary must meet the 90% test. The connected subsidiary must meet a 90% test for its shares/debt to be considered as assets of the parent company for meeting the 50% test. This modification of the 50% test is presented in Exhibit 13-12 in point form.

Another way of stating the conclusions on the application of these tests is as follows.

- Where more than 50% of the assets of a particular corporation are active business assets, the Basic Asset Test (50% Test) discussed in the previous segment is met and the type of assets held by connected corporations in the chain below the particular corporation is not relevant. The modified test need not apply.

- It is only when the 50% Asset Test is not met by the given corporation with its own active business assets that the Modified Asset Test must be used.

- Where the modification applies in a two-corporation chain, the given corporation and the other connected corporation below it in the chain must meet the 50% Asset Test with their own active business assets in combination with the shares and debt of connected corporations and one of the parent or the connected corporation must meet the 90% test.

Note that the modification must be met for the entire 24-month period prior to the sale of the shares. Further, the company may still require purification prior to the share sale to meet the SBC test.

Exhibit 13-12 Qualified Small Business Corporation (QSBC) Share [ssec. 110.6(1)] Modification of the Basic Asset Test (50% Test)

- Modification of the 50% Basic Asset Test where:
  - there is a corporation (subsidiary) connected [ssec. 186(4)] to a particular corporation (parent); the subsidiary must be connected, but not necessarily a SBC,
  - the particular corporation (parent) does not meet the 50% Test (on its own active business assets (i.e., excluding the shares and debt of a connected corporation)).
- Conclusion on modification of Asset Test:
  - throughout the 24 months ending at the determination time,
    - both the parent and the connected corporation must each meet the 50% Test with a combination of their own active business assets and shares and debt of a connected corporation;
    - one of either the parent or the connected corporation must meet the 90% Test with a combination of its own active business assets and shares and debt of a connected corporation.
- Therefore,
  - conceptually, the test is
    - 90/50 for parent/connected, or
    - 50/90 for parent/connected.

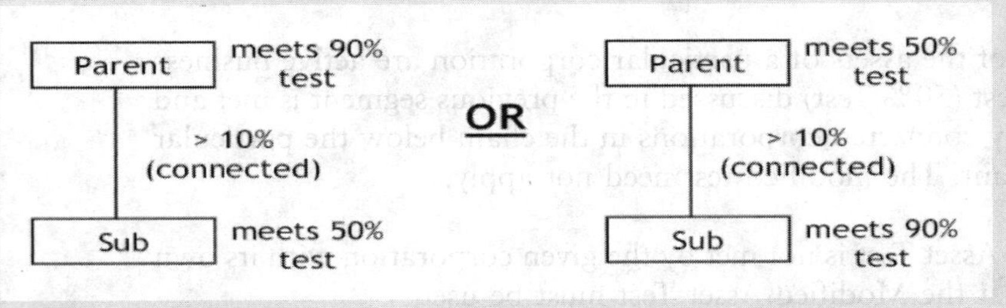

If a holding company owns more than one connected subsidiary corporation, then the modified asset test applies as follows.

(1) If the holding company meets the 90% test with a combination of its own active business assets and shares or debt of a connected corporation that meets the 50% test, the modified asset test is passed.

(2) If the holding company meets the 50% test with a combination of its own active business assets and shares or debt of a connected corporation that meets the 90% test, the modified asset test is passed.

Example Problem 13-10

Zeto, a resident of Canada, has owned 100% of the shares of Zeto's Manufacturing Limited (ZML), a Canadian-controlled private corporation, since its incorporation 20 years ago. The corporation carries on a manufacturing business in Canada. He is presently considering the sale of his shares. The fair market value of the assets of ZML is comprised as follows:

	FMV at present	%	FMV throughout past 24 months	%
Active business assets	$200,000	40	$160,000	40
Shares of 100%-owned subsidiary	250,000	50	120,000	30
Investments	50,000	10	120,000	30
	$500,000	100	$400,000	100

The subsidiary, Zeto Wholesale Ltd. (ZWL), was incorporated by ZML 15 years ago to carry on a wholesaling business in Canada. The fair market value of its assets consist of the following:

	FMV at present	%	FMV throughout past 24 months	%
Active business assets	$270,000	90	$157,500	90
Investments	30,000	10	17,500	10
	$300,000	100	$175,000	100

REQUIRED

Determine whether the shares of ZML are qualified small business corporation shares at the present time.

SOLUTION

For the shares of ZML to be qualified small business corporation shares, the following tests must be met:

(1) SBC Test

At the time of sale the shares of ZML must be of a small business corporation (SBC). An SBC is defined to be a Canadian-controlled private corporation (CCPC) which ZML is. In addition, all or substantially all (i.e., at least 90%) of the fair market value of the assets of ZML must be used, at the present time, principally in an active business carried on primarily in Canada by ZML or a related corporation or must be shares or debt of a connected SBC. This test is met by a combination of ZML's own active business assets presently comprising 40% and the shares of the wholly owned subsidiary (ZWL) presently comprising the other 50%. The subsidiary is connected with ZML because it is controlled by ZML and the subsidiary is an SBC because 90% of the present fair market value of its assets are active business assets at the time of the sale.

ITA: 248(1) Definitions, 186(2) When corporation controlled, 186(4) Corporations connected with particular corporation

(2) Holding Period Test

Throughout the 24 months preceding the present time, the shares cannot have been owned by anyone other than Zeto or a related party. This test is met because only Zeto owned the shares for the past 10 years.

(3) Basic Asset Test (50% Test)

Throughout the 24 months preceding the present time, the shares must be of a CCPC with more than 50% of the fair market value of its assets used principally in an active business carried on primarily in Canada. However, ZML does not meet the 50% Test based on its active business assets alone. Therefore, the Modified Asset Test must be applied.

(4) Modified Asset Test

This test requires, first, that both corporations, ZML and ZWL, must hold more than 50% of their assets in a combination of active business assets and shares or debt of a connected corporation throughout the 24 months preceding the present time. This condition is met by ZML with its 40% active business assets in combination with its 30% in shares of the subsidiary. The subsidiary meets the test with its 90% active business assets. Then, one of the corporations must meet the 90% test with a combination of its active business assets and shares or debt of a connected corporation throughout the preceding 24 months. This condition is met by the subsidiary with its active business assets.

Since all of the relevant tests have been met, the shares of ZML are qualified small business corporation shares.

¶13,370 Computation of the Capital Gains Deduction

The amount of the deduction is discretionary and is limited by cumulative taxable capital gains net of allowable capital losses, that is, net taxable capital gains exposed to tax over an individual's lifetime, to the extent of the maximum permissible deduction. The limit on the QSBC capital gains deduction in a particular year is set at the least of three amounts.

(1) Unused lifetime deduction — This restriction limits the deduction to \$424,126 (½ × \$848,252) *minus* all previously claimed capital gains deductions adjusted to the appropriate inclusion rate for the year in which the limit is being computed.

ITA: 110.6(2.1)(a)

The following table shows the factor to use to convert a capital gains deduction claimed in a prior year to the inclusion rate in use after October 17, 2000:

Year capital gain deduction claimed	Inclusion rate in that year	Factor to convert to post–Oct. 17, 2000 period
1990-Feb. 27, 2000	3/4	1/2 / 3/4 = 2/3
Feb. 28, 2000–Oct. 17, 2000	2/3	1/2 / 2/3 = 3/4
After Oct. 17, 2000	1/2	

(2) Annual gains limit — This amount is the lesser of the net taxable capital gains (net TCG) for the particular year and the amount of the net TCG that would be determined only taking into account dispositions of QSBC shares and qualified farm property, *minus* ITA: 3(b), 110.6(1) Definitions

(a) net capital losses of other years deducted in the current year, and

(b) the allowable business investment losses (ABILs) realized during the year whether or not they are claimed. ITA: 3(d)

(3) Cumulative gains limit — This amount aggregates, without an adjustment for changing inclusion rates, *all the components* of the "annual gains limit for all years" *minus* two additional amounts: ITA: 110.6(1) Definitions

(a) the capital gains deductions claimed in preceding years, without an adjustment for changing inclusion rates, and

(b) the cumulative net investment loss (CNIL) — a limitation which is defined below.

This description of the computation is relatively conceptual, rather than technical. However, it is complicated by the allowable business investment loss (ABIL) rules and the cumulative net investment loss (CNIL).

¶13,375 Allowable Business Investment Losses

As previously discussed in Chapter 7, allowable business investment losses are deductible from all sources of income. The definition of a business investment loss includes capital losses arising from the disposition of shares and debts of a small business corporation (SBC). Reference should be made to the material on allowable business investment losses in Chapter 7. In particular, Figure 7-2 should be reviewed for details on the treatment of a business investment loss. ITA: 3(d), 39(1)(c), 248(1) Definitions

❹ ¶13,380 Cumulative Net Investment Loss (CNIL)

As previously indicated, there is a further restriction to the "cumulative gains limit" which reduces the potential availability of the capital gains deduction. This reduction is basically the excess of property expenses over property income. The purpose of this restriction is to remove the perceived double benefit of capital gains offset by a capital gains deduction and non-capital sources of income offset by excess investment expenses at the same time.

The cumulative net investment loss (CNIL) is defined as the excess of investment expenses (a defined term) over investment income (another defined term) aggregated for all years after 1987. ITA: 110.6(1) Definitions

"Investment expense" which, generally, relates to expenses incurred to earn investment income includes the following:

(a) all property expenses, including interest (either actually incurred or deemed to have been paid by section 80.5) and carrying charges, deducted by the taxpayer in computing property income;

(b) certain specific expenses, including interest and carrying charges, deducted from the income of a partnership of which the taxpayer is a specified member (basically defined as a limited partner or a member who is not actively engaged in the business or a similar business on a regular, continuous, and substantial basis);

(c)

(i) losses incurred in the year from a partnership of which the taxpayer is a specified member, and

ITA: 111(1)(e) Limited partnership losses

(ii) limited partnership loss carryovers deducted in the year;

(d) losses from all property and, specifically, rental properties (i.e., business losses from rental properties) deducted by the taxpayer or a partnership of which he or she was an *ordinary* member; and

(e) net capital losses carried over and deducted against certain net taxable capital gains of the carryover year that were not eligible for the capital gains deduction.

"Investment income" includes the following:

ITA: 110.6(1) Definitions

(a) income from all property, including recaptured capital cost allowance that was considered to be income from property and not from a business;

(b) income from a partnership of which the taxpayer is a specified member;

(c) income (including recapture) from rental property of the taxpayer or partnership of which he or she was an ordinary member; and

(d) net taxable capital gains on certain property not eligible for the capital gains deduction.

ITA: 56(1)(d) Annuity payments, 60(a) Capital element of annuity payments

¶13,385 Other Related Provisions

At this stage, there are several other provisions related to the capital gains deduction worth noting:

- An individual must file a tax return if a taxable capital gain was realized or a disposition of capital property has occurred in the taxation year.

ITA: 150(1) Filing returns of income — general rule

- An individual who is resident in Canada for only part of a taxation year is deemed to be a resident throughout the entire year if he or she is resident in Canada throughout the immediately preceding or the following taxation year.

ITA: 110.6(5) Deemed resident in Canada

- A capital gains deduction in respect of a particular transaction is denied forever where the capital gain was not reported on a filed tax return or where the tax return is not filed within a one-year grace period and where the Minister can prove the taxpayer knowingly or under circumstances amounting to gross negligence did not report the gain.

ITA: 110.6(6) Failure to report capital gain

- A number of anti-avoidance provisions prevent abuses of the capital gains deduction.

ITA: 110.6(7) Deduction not permitted, 110.6(12) Trust deduction — death of spouse or common-law partner

- An individual may elect to use the capital gains deduction in respect of qualified small business corporation shares when the corporation becomes a public corporation because its shares are listed on a designated stock exchange in Canada.

ITA: 48.1 Gain when small business corporation becomes public

Example Problem 13-11

Lenny disposed of some shares of Underground Airways Limited, a QSBC, in January 2018 and realized a taxable capital gain of $305,000. In addition, he received $13,750 in interest and incurred a net rental loss of $2,500.

Also in 2018, Lenny realized a business investment loss (before any adjustment) of $50,000.

ITA: 39(9) Deduction from business investment loss

Prior to 2018, Lenny received cumulative interest income of $6,875 and grossed-up taxable dividends of $1,563. He also incurred a cumulative net rental loss of $12,500 and carrying charges of $12,188. In 2010, Lenny realized taxable capital gains of $15,000 on QSBC shares which he fully offset with the capital gains deduction. Lenny had no previous capital transactions.

REQUIRED

ITA: 110.6(2.1) Capital gains deduction — qualified small business corporation shares

Compute Lenny's capital gains deduction for 2018 supported by all the necessary calculations.

SOLUTION

(A) Unused lifetime deduction in 2018:		
Lifetime cumulative deduction limit		$424,126
Less: prior years' deductions:		
Capital gains deduction claimed in 2000		(15,000)
Unused lifetime capital gains deduction available for 2018		$409,126
(B) Annual gains limit for 2018:		
Net TCGs for 2018[1]		$290,000
Minus:		
Net CLs deducted in 2018	Nil	
ABILs realized in 2018[1]	$10,000	10,000
Annual gains limit for 2018		$280,000
(C) Cumulative gains limit for 2018:[2]		
Cumulative net TCGs ($15,000 + $290,000)		$305,000
Minus:		

Cumulative net capital losses deducted		Nil	
Cumulative ABILs realized		$10,000	
Cumulative CGs deductions		15,000	
Cumulative net investment loss:			
Investment expenses:			
Cumulative interest expenses and carrying charges	$12,188		
Cumulative net rental losses ($2,500 + $12,500)	15,000		
	$27,188		
Investment income:			
Cumulative investment income ($6,875 + $1,563 + $13,750)	(22,188)	$5,000	$30,000
Cumulative gains limit for 2018			$275,000
(D) Least of (A), (B), (C)			$275,000

NOTES TO SOLUTION

(1) Allowable business investment loss (ABIL):

ITA: 39(9) Deduction from business investment loss

BIL before reduction			$50,000
Disallowed portion — Lesser of:			
(a) BIL		$50,000	
(b) Adjustment factor × cumulative CG deductions of previous years (2 × $15,000)	$30,000		
Minus: Cumulative disallowed BIL of prior years	Nil	$30,000	
Lesser of (a) and (b)			(30,000)
BIL after adjustment			$20,000
ABIL (1/2 × $20,000)			$10,000
Allowable capital loss (ACL):			
Disallowed portion of BIL			$30,000

ACL (½ × $30,000)	$15,000
Net TCG for 2018:	
TCG	$305,000
Less: ACL	15,000
Net TCG	$290,000

(2) The components of the cumulative gains limit are not adjusted for inclusion rate changes over the period of accumulation.

¶13,390 Attribution Through a Corporation

Since the attribution rules for spouses and minors includes loans affecting such individuals, corporations have become the obvious vehicle to attempt income splitting among family members. Consider the situation where the low-income spouse incorporates a company using a nominal amount of his or her own funds. The high-income spouse then loans to the corporation a large amount of money through a non-interest bearing note. Income earned on these loans and subsequently paid out in the form of dividends is not caught by the attribution rules since these provisions deal with individuals and trusts only. Hence, the Act contains a series of rules to attribute back to the transferor income in the form of a deemed interest receipt on property transferred or loaned to a corporation.

ITA: 74.1(1) Transfers and loans to spouse or common-law partner, 74.1(2) Transfers and loans to minors, 74.4 [Transfers and loans to corporations]

These rules only apply during the period in which there were "designated persons" who benefit from the transfer or loan to a corporation and the corporation was not a small business corporation (SBC) as discussed above in relation to qualified small business corporation shares.

ITA: 74.5(5) Definition of "designated person", 251 Arm's length

A designated person is the transferor's spouse or a minor who is either not at arm's length with the transferor or who is a niece or nephew of that individual. The designated person must also be a specified shareholder defined, generally, as a person who owns at least 10% of the shares of any class of the corporation. Note that a small business corporation is one that, by definition, would generate mostly active business income which, if earned on a direct transfer or loan of funds, would not be subject to attribution. Also, note how designated persons are the same individuals to whom direct transfers or loans would be subject to income attribution. If the corporation, with designated persons as shareholders, ceased to be a small business corporation at some point during the year, the imputed interest benefit would be prorated for the part of the year that the corporation was not an SBC.

ITA: 248(1) specified shareholder

¶13,395 Imputed Interest

The corporate attribution rule applies where one of the main purposes of the transfer or loan may reasonably be considered to be to reduce the income of the transferor and to benefit a designated person. If this rule applies, the transferor is deemed to receive, as *interest*, the following amount:

ITA: 74.4(2) Transfers and loans to corporations

- interest imputed on the outstanding amount of the loan or transferred property at the basic prescribed rates in effect during the year, for the period when the corporation was not an SBC and designated persons were specified shareholders

ITA: 74.4(3) Outstanding amount; ITR: 4301(c)

less the sum of:

- interest received by the transferor in respect of the loan or transfer,
- all grossed-up taxable dividends received by the transferor on shares received as consideration for the loan or transfer of property, and
- taxable dividends that are received by the designated person and that can reasonably be considered to be part of the benefit sought to be conferred and are included in the designated person's "split income".

ITA: 120.4 Tax on split income [Kiddie tax]

The term "outstanding amount", which is the base for the deemed interest receipt, is defined to be the fair market value of property "transferred or loaned" to the corporation in excess of the fair market value of consideration *received* from the corporation in return. Consideration that reduces the outstanding amount would include, for example, cash. It does not include debt or shares of the corporation or rights to receive debt or shares of the corporation received as consideration for the transfer. Debt and shares received by the transferor are considered to be "excluded consideration" for determining the outstanding amount on which the deemed interest is calculated. While debt or shares received from the corporation do not reduce the outstanding amount, interest and the grossed-up amount of taxable dividends paid to the transferor on the debt or shares received reduce the deemed interest receipt to the transferor, as shown by the above computational formula.

ITA: 74.4(3) Outstanding amount, 74.4(1) Definitions

Note how the reduction of the deemed interest income is as a result of the payment by the corporation of actual income that would attract tax in the hands of the transferor or lender and, therefore, would reduce the benefits of income splitting. It should also be noted that the deemed interest income included in the individual's income is not allowed as a deduction to the corporation.

The "outstanding amount" is reduced by repayments of any debt consideration or on the redemption of share consideration received on the transfer.

Example Problem 13-12

Fresser and Klutz are spouses. Fresser owns and operates a construction company, Fresser Inc., which uses all of its assets (fair market value of $1.2 million) in its active business carried on in Calgary. Klutz received an inheritance of $100,000 which he invested in Fresser Inc. 4% non-voting preference shares on January 1, 2016. Fresser Inc. immediately used this cash to pay down a bank loan. On January 1, 2017, Fresser Inc. ceased operations and liquidated its assets leaving $200,000 of cash in the company until January 31, 2018, when the 4% preference shares were redeemed for $100,000. In each of 2016 and 2017, dividends of $4,000 were paid on the preference shares.

REQUIRED

Determine the amount attributed to Klutz over the three years, assuming that the prescribed interest rate is a constant 3% and that dividends were paid from the low-rate income pool.

SOLUTION

2016: The rule would not attribute any amount to Klutz since Fresser Inc. was a "small business corporation" throughout the taxation year of Klutz. Klutz's income would include only the $4,000 of dividends paid on the preference shares.

ITA: 74.4(2) Transfers and loans to corporations

2017: Fresser Inc. was not a small business corporation throughout 2017; therefore, the rule applies as follows:

ITA: 74.4(2) Transfers and loans to corporations

Interest imputed at 3% on the outstanding amount	
($100,000 × 3%)	$3,000
Less: 1.16 × dividends received ($4,000 × 1.16)	(4,640)
Interest received	Nil
Amount deemed to be received by Klutz as interest	Nil

Klutz will report the $4,000 of dividends ($4,640 grossed up) received from the company.

2018: Fresser Inc. was not a small business corporation during that portion of the year when the shares were outstanding; therefore, the rule applies as follows:

ITA: 74.4(2) Transfers and loans to corporations

Interest imputed at 3% on the outstanding amount	
($100,000 × 3% × 30/365)	$ 247
Less: 1.16 × of dividends received	Nil
Interest received	Nil
Amount deemed to be received by Klutz as interest	$ 247

Remember that there is a purpose test. It may be possible to argue that, since the purpose of the loan was to finance an active business, these attribution rules do not apply. On the other hand, it may be argued that since the money was used in the business for such a short period (13 months) that "one of the main purposes of the transfer" must have been to reduce the income of Klutz and benefit Fresser.

ITA: 74.4(2) Transfers and loans to corporations

¶13,395.99 Practise What You've Learned

Refer to the following sections of the Study Guide to practise what you've learned:

¶13,800 — Review Questions

- Question 9 — ABILs
- Question 10 — SBC status
- Question 11 — QSBC shares
- Question 12 — Corporate attribution

¶13,825 — Multiple Choice Questions

- Question 6 — Corporate attribution
- Question 7 — Small business corporation

¶13,850 — Exercises

- Exercise 8 — Small business corporation
- Exercise 9 — Capital gains deduction
- Exercise 10 — Corporate attribution
- Exercise 16 — Capital gains deduction, personal tax credits, donations — charitable & political
- Exercise 18 — QSBC shares
- Exercise 19 — QSBC shares

¶13,500 General Anti-Avoidance Rule Under the *Income Tax Act*

¶13,510 The Statutory Provision

¶13,515 Purpose

The technical notes released to explain this provision when it was first introduced made the following statement: ITA: 245 [General anti-avoidance rule]

> New section 245 of the Act is a general anti-avoidance rule which is intended to prevent abusive tax avoidance transactions or arrangements but at the same time is not intended to interfere with legitimate commercial and family transactions. Consequently, the new rule seeks to distinguish between legitimate tax planning and abusive tax avoidance and to establish a reasonable balance between the protection of the tax base and the need for certainty for taxpayers in planning their affairs.

The main statement of the general anti-avoidance rule (GAAR), or provision, in essence, provides that the tax benefit that results from an avoidance transaction is denied. In order to determine the amount of the tax benefit that is denied, the provision indicates that the tax consequences of the transaction to a person will be determined as is reasonable in the circumstances.

ITA: 245(2) General anti-avoidance provision

¶13,520 Defined Terms

The term "avoidance transaction" is defined as any transaction that by itself or as part of a series of transactions (i.e., a "step transaction") results in a tax benefit, unless the transaction can reasonably be considered to have a *bona fide* purpose other than obtaining the tax benefit. The technical notes indicate that "the vast majority of business, family or investment transactions will not be affected by proposed (as it was then) section 245 since they will have *bona fide* non-tax purposes". The notes go on to state that "a transaction will not be considered to be an avoidance transaction because, incidentally, it results in a tax benefit or because tax considerations were significant, but not the primary purpose for carrying out the transaction". On the other hand, the notes indicate that:

ITA: 245(3) Avoidance transaction

> Ordinarily, transitory arrangements would not be considered to have been carried out primarily for *bona fide* purposes other than the obtaining of a tax benefit. Such transitory arrangements might include an issue of shares that are immediately redeemed or the establishment of an entity, such as a corporation or a partnership, followed within a short period by its elimination.

The term "tax benefit" is defined to mean "a reduction, avoidance or deferral of tax or other amount payable under this Act or an increase in a refund of tax or other amount under this Act". According to the technical notes, "the references to "other amount payable under this Act" and "other amount under this Act" are intended to cover interest, penalties, the remittance of source deductions, and other amounts that do not constitute tax". The term "tax consequences" is, also, defined and is necessary, as indicated previously, to determine the amount of the benefit that will be denied. The actual determination of the tax consequences is provided by a rule which sets out some of the methods by which a benefit will be denied.

ITA: 245(1) Definitions, 245(5) Determination of tax consequences

¶13,525 Limitation

A limitation on the application of the GAAR is provided. In the overview commentary on the GAAR, the technical notes make the following statement:

ITA: 245(4) Application of subsection (2)

> Transactions that comply with the object and spirit of other provisions of the Act read as a whole will not be affected by the application of this general anti-avoidance rule. For example, a transaction that qualifies for a tax-free rollover under an explicit provision of the Act, and that is carried out in accordance not only with the letter of that provision but also with the spirit of the Act read as a whole, will not be subject to new section 245. However, where the transaction is part of a series of transactions designed to avoid tax and results in a misuse or abuse of the provision that allows a tax-free rollover, the rule may apply. If, for example, a taxpayer, for the purposes of converting an income gain on a sale of property into a capital gain, transfers the property, on a rollover basis to a shell corporation in exchange for shares in a situation where

new section 54.2 of the Act does not apply and subsequently sells the shares, the new section could be expected to apply.

The new rule applies as a provision of last resort after the application of the other provisions of the Act, including specific anti-avoidance measures.

¶13,530 Examples in the Technical Notes

The commentary in the technical notes states that "the application of new subsection 245 [*sic*] must be determined by reference to the facts in a particular case in the context of the scheme of the Act". The notes then provide the following three examples of planning that would not be affected by the GAAR.

ITA: 245(4) Application of subsection (2)

> . . . the attribution provisions of the Act set out detailed rules that seek to prevent a taxpayer from transferring property by way of a gift and thereby transferring income to a spouse or minor children. A review of the scheme of these provisions indicates that income splitting is only of concern in transfers of property involving spouses or children under 18 years of age. The attribution rules are not intended to apply to other transfers of property such as gifts to adult children. This can be discerned from a review of the scheme of the Act, its relevant provisions and permissible extrinsic aids. Thus, a straightforward gift from a parent to his adult child will not be within the scope of section 245 either because it is made primarily for non-tax purposes or because it may reasonably be regarded as not being an abuse of the provisions of the Act. If, however, the gift is made so that the adult child acquires an investment and, through a series of transactions, disposes of it and subsequently transfers the proceeds, including any income therefrom, to the parent, proposed section 245 should apply where the purpose of the transaction is the reduction, avoidance or deferral of tax. (Note that subsection 56(4.1) deals with this type of avoidance where a *loan* is made to a related person.)
>
> As another example, "estate freezing" transactions whereby a taxpayer transfers future growth in the value of assets to his children or grandchildren will not ordinarily be avoidance transactions to which the proposed rules would apply despite the fact that they may result in a deferral, avoidance or reduction of tax. Apart from the fact that many of these transactions may be considered to be primarily motivated by non-tax considerations, it would be reasonable to consider that such transactions do not ordinarily result in a misuse or abuse given the scheme of the Act and the recent enactment of subsection 74.4(4) of the Act to accommodate estate freezes. (See also IC 88-2, paragraph 10.)
>
> Another example involves the transfer of income or deductions within a related group of corporations. There are a number of provisions in the Act that limit the claim by a taxpayer of losses, deductions and credits incurred or earned by unrelated taxpayers, particularly corporations. The loss limitation rules contained in subsections 111(4) to (5.2) of the Act that apply on a change of control of a corporation represent an important example. These rules are generally restricted to the claiming of losses, deductions and other amounts by unrelated parties. There are explicit exceptions intended to apply with respect to transactions that would allow losses, deductions or credits earned by one corporation to be claimed by

related Canadian corporations. In fact, the scheme of the Act as a whole, and the expressed object and spirit of the corporate loss limitation rules, clearly permit such transactions between related corporations where these transactions are otherwise legally effective and comply with the letter and spirit of these exceptions. Therefore, even if these transactions may appear to be primarily tax-motivated, they ordinarily do not fall within the scope of section 245 since they usually do not result in a misuse or abuse. (See also IC 88-2, paragraph 8.)

¶13,535 Administration and Application

Finally, it should be noted that the Act provides rules that pertain to the administration of the legislation in the GAAR.

ITA: 245(6) Request for adjustments, 245(8) Duties of Minister

The CRA issued an Information Circular which is intended to provide guidance on the application of the GAAR. It contains over 20 fact situations which are interpreted by the CRA in the context of the application of the GAAR.

Information Circulars: IC 88-2

The GAAR applies, not only to a misuse or abuse of the provisions of the *Income Tax Act*, but also to the provisions of the *Income Tax Regulations*, the *Income Tax Application Rules*, or a tax treaty. The *Excise Tax Act* (ETA) contains a GAAR almost identical in nature to the provision in the *Income Tax Act*.

ETA: 274 Definitions; ITA: 245(1) Definitions

A paper,[8] which resulted from a panel discussion held at the 1989 Annual Conference of the Canadian Tax Foundation, presented a "GAAR Decision Tree" to outline the logic that can be used to determine whether the GAAR would apply. Exhibit 13-13 attempts to diagram the logic used.

[8] Robert D. Brown, Robert Couzin, Cy M. Fien, William R. Lawlor and William J. Strain, "GAAR and Tax Practice: More Questions than Answers", *1989 Conference Report: Report of the Proceedings of the Forty-First Tax Conference*, Canadian Tax Foundation, Toronto, 1989, pp. 11:3-4.

Exhibit 13-13 GAAR Application Logic

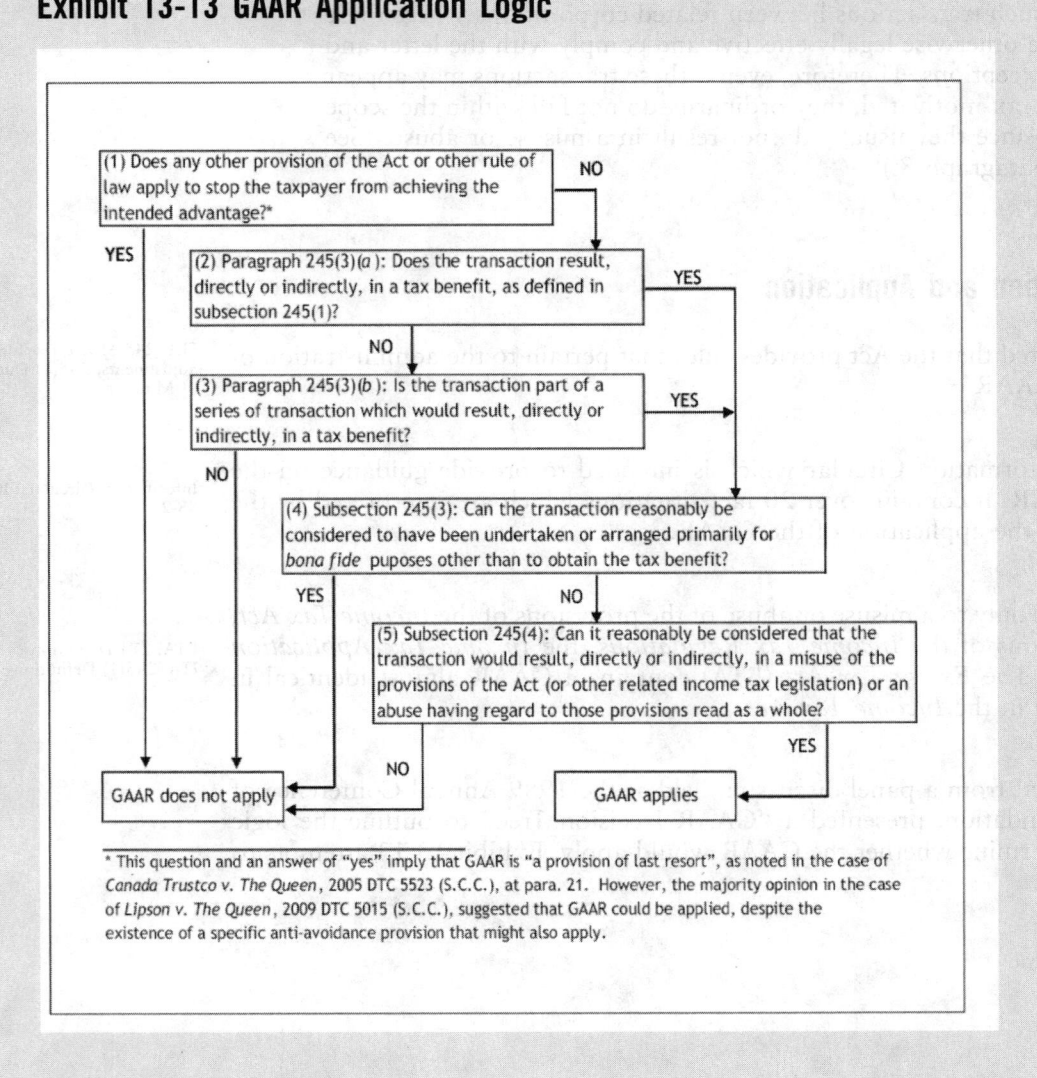

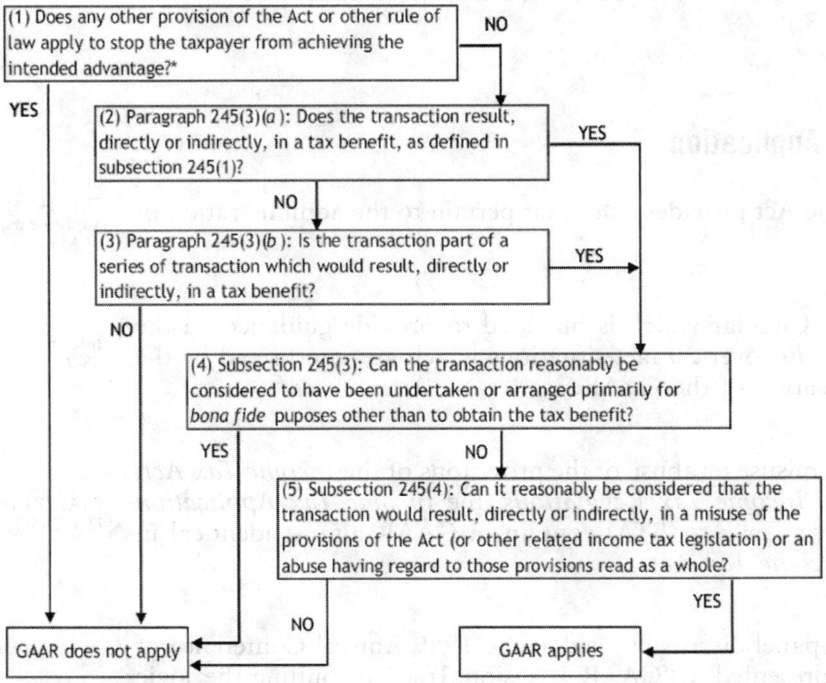

(1) Does any other provision of the Act or other rule of law apply to stop the taxpayer from achieving the intended advantage?*
NO
YES
(2) Paragraph 245(3)(*a*): Does the transaction result, directly or indirectly, in a tax benefit, as defined in subsection 245(1)?
YES
NO
(3) Paragraph 245(3)(*b*): Is the transaction part of a series of transaction which would result, directly or indirectly, in a tax benefit?
YES
NO
(4) Subsection 245(3): Can the transaction reasonably be considered to have been undertaken or arranged primarily for *bona fide* puposes other than to obtain the tax benefit?
YES
NO
(5) Subsection 245(4): Can it reasonably be considered that the transaction would result, directly or indirectly, in a misuse of the provisions of the Act (or other related income tax legislation) or an abuse having regard to those provisions read as a whole?
YES
NO
GAAR does not apply
GAAR applies

* This question and an answer of "yes" imply that GAAR is "a provision of last resort", as noted in the case of *Canada Trustco v. The Queen*, 2005 DTC 5523 (S.C.C.), at para. 21. However, the majority opinion in the case of *Lipson v. The Queen*, 2009 DTC 5015 (S.C.C.), suggested that GAAR could be applied, despite the existence of a specific anti-avoidance provision that might also apply.

¶13,540 Federal Court of Appeal — *OSFC Holdings Ltd.*

¶13,545 The Findings

The appeal by the taxpayer in *OSFC Holdings Ltd. v. The Queen* was the first decision of the Federal Court of Appeal on the GAAR.[9] After a thorough analysis of the GAAR, the court dismissed the taxpayer's appeal. It held that a series of transactions resulted in a tax benefit. The court upheld the finding of the Tax Court that the primary purpose of the transaction was to obtain a tax benefit. It also found that the transactions in question violated a clear and unambiguous general policy of the Act and, hence, concluded that the

Cases: *OSFC Holdings Ltd. v. Her Majesty the Queen*, 2001 DTC 5471 (FCA)

[9] An extensive commentary on this case by Thomas B. Akin appears in *Tax Topics*, Number 1546, Wolters Kluwer Limited, October 25, 2001, pp. 5-8.

avoidance transaction resulted in an abuse of the provisions of the Act read as a whole. In June 2002, the Supreme Court of Canada refused to grant OSFC Holdings Ltd. leave to appeal.

¶13,550 Application of OSFC Case Analytical Framework

The analytical framework used in the *OSFC* case was applied in the Crown's appeal in *The Queen v. Canadian Pacific Limited*. First, the court concluded that there was a tax benefit. The court, then, upheld the Tax Court finding that the primary purpose of the transaction in question was not to minimize tax. Although the latter finding was sufficient to dismiss the Crown's appeal, the court considered the argument that there had been an abuse of the provisions of the Act read as a whole on the basis that the transaction in question contravened a policy of the Act. This argument was rejected. The court concluded that the conditions for the GAAR did not apply to the facts of this case.[10]

Cases: *Her Majesty the Queen v. Canadian Pacific Limited*, 2002 DTC 6742 (FCA)

The three-step analytical framework developed by the Federal Court of Appeal in the *OSFC* case was applied in the case of *The Queen v. Imperial Oil Limited*. The following summary of the three steps is quoted from the *Imperial Oil* case, in the indicated paragraphs.

Cases: *The Queen v. Imperial Oil Limited*, 2004 DTC 6044 (FCA)

(1) First, a court must determine if there is a "tax benefit", as defined. If there is not, GAAR will not apply and the inquiry ends [par. 34].

ITA: 245(3) Avoidance transaction

(2) If there is a "tax benefit", a court must take the second step and determine whether there is an "avoidance transaction", as defined. If there is no "avoidance transaction", GAAR will not apply and, again, the inquiry ends [par. 34].

ITA: 245(3) Avoidance transaction

(3) If the transaction confers a "tax benefit" and constitutes an "avoidance transaction", a court must take the third step and determine whether the transaction is a "misuse" or an "abuse". This inquiry involves taking two smaller steps [par. 35].

ITA: 245(4) Application of subsection (2)

(a) First, a court must determine "if it may reasonably be considered that the transaction would not result directly or indirectly in a misuse"[11] of the provisions of the Act. To determine if there has been a misuse, a court must identify the object, or underlying policy or policies, of the relevant provision or provisions of the Act, and decide if the avoidance transaction is contrary to those objectives or policies. If it is, the transaction constitutes a misuse and GAAR applies [par. 36].

One must infer from the statutory language the policy, if any, on which the relevant provisions of the Act are unambiguously based. This exercise in statutory interpretation must be undertaken with the assistance of such extrinsic aids as: judicial statements, Hansard, ministerial or departmental statements, explanatory notes, bulletins, circulars, texts, periodicals and others [par. 49].

(b) However, if there is no misuse, the second smaller step must be taken. This requires a court to decide if the transaction is an abuse, having regard to the provisions of the Act, other than those dealing with GAAR, when read as a whole. The question is whether the transaction contravenes any policy or policies

[10] The Crown's appeals were also dismissed in the cases of *The Queen v. Produits Forestiers Donohue Inc.*, 2002 DTC 7512 (F.C.A.), and *The Queen v. Jabin Investments Ltd.*, 2003 DTC 5027 (F.C.A.). In both of these cases the OSFC framework was applied in the analysis of the applicability of the GAAR. In the latter case, the "clear and unambiguous" threshold for policy was clarified.

[11] In 2004, the wording of this part of the provision was changed to remove the word "not" and, in effect, to change the test to a positive test for the application of the GAAR.

> underlying the provisions of the Act as a whole. If it does, the transaction may constitute an abuse for the purpose of GAAR [par. 37].

ITA: 245(4) Application of subsection (2)

While the Act does not expressly provide that the policy must be "clear and unambiguous", this is implicit in the language of the GAAR, which permits the exemption for a tax avoidance scheme where "it may reasonably be considered that the transaction would not result directly or indirectly in a misuse of the provisions of this Act or an abuse having regard to the provisions of this Act . . . read as a whole [based on former wording of the provision]." [par. 39]

Thus, if the scheme may reasonably be considered not to result directly or indirectly in a misuse or an abuse, GAAR does not apply: in effect, the taxpayer is given the benefit of any doubt. Consequently, for GAAR to apply it must be clear that the provisions of the Act are being misused or the Act as a whole is being abused. It is not enough that a court might reasonably consider them to be misused or abused [par. 40].

¶13,560 Supreme Court of Canada — *Canada Trustco and Mathew et al.*

Cases: *Canada Trustco Mortgage Co. v. Canada*, 2005 DTC 5523 (SCC)*Mathew v. Canada (sub nom. Kaulius v. The Queen)*, 2005 DTC 5538 (SCC)

In 2005, the Supreme Court of Canada (S.C.C.) released two decisions on the GAAR, *Canada Trustco Mortgage Co.* and *Mathew et al.* (sub nom. *Kaulius*).

¶13,565 The Transactions

In the *Canada Trustco* case, the taxpayer had purchased trailers and then leased them back to the vendor. A major purpose for this transaction was to allow Canada Trustco to claim CCA on these trailers while the arrangements were structured so the taxpayer had little or no financial risk. While there are special rules in the Act to counter this type of transaction, trailers were exempt from them. The CRA reassessed under the GAAR to deny the CCA claimed. The Supreme Court of Canada decision held in favour of the taxpayer, dismissing the Crown's appeal.

Cases: *Canada Trustco Mortgage Co. v. Canada*, 2005 DTC 5523 (SCC)

In the *Mathew* case, Standard Trust, an insolvent trust company, transferred a loan portfolio, with accrued losses of $52 million, to a partnership that had arm's length partners. The losses were then realized and allocated to these arm's length partners. The CRA reassessed under the GAAR to deny the losses claimed. The Supreme Court of Canada held in favour of the Crown, dismissing the taxpayer's appeal.

Cases: *Mathew v. Canada (sub nom. Kaulius v. The Queen)*, 2005 DTC 5538 (SCC)

¶13,570 Application of GAAR and Interpretations

In both cases, the Court applied the three tests set out in *OSFC Holdings* with the following results.

Test 1: There was a tax benefit.

Test 2: There was an avoidance transaction.

Test 3: The issue before the Court was whether there was a misuse of the provisions of the Act or an abuse of those provisions read as a whole.

The Supreme Court stated, at paragraph 66 of the *Canada Trustco* case,

Cases: *Canada Trustco Mortgage Co. v. Canada*, 2005 DTC 5523 (SCC)

> [t]he approach to s. 245 of the *Income Tax Act* may be summarized as follows.

1. Three requirements must be established to permit application of the GAAR:

   (1) A tax benefit resulting from a transaction or part of a series of transactions (s. 245(1) and (2));

   (2) that the transaction is an avoidance transaction in the sense that it cannot be said to have been reasonably undertaken or arranged primarily for a *bona fide* purpose other than to obtain a tax benefit; and

   (3) that there was abusive tax avoidance in the sense that it cannot be reasonably concluded that a tax benefit would be consistent with the object, spirit or purpose of the provisions relied upon by the taxpayer.

2. The burden is on the taxpayer to refute (1) and (2), and on the Minister to establish (3).

3. If the existence of abusive tax avoidance is unclear, the benefit of the doubt goes to the taxpayer.

4. The courts proceed by conducting a unified textual [words used], contextual [context of provision] and purposive [purpose of analysis] analysis of the provisions giving rise to the tax benefit in order to determine why they were put in place and why the benefit was conferred. The goal is to arrive at a purposive interpretation that is harmonious with the provisions of the Act that confer the tax benefit, read in the context of the whole Act.

5. Whether the transactions were motivated by any economic, commercial, family or other non-tax purpose may form part of the factual context that the courts may consider in the analysis of abusive tax avoidance allegations under s. 245(4). However, any finding in this respect would form only one part of the underlying facts of a case, and would be insufficient by itself to establish abusive tax avoidance. The central issue is the proper interpretation of the relevant provisions in light of their context and purpose.

6. Abusive tax avoidance may be found where the relationships and transactions as expressed in the relevant documentation lack a proper basis relative to the object, spirit or purpose of the provisions that are purported to confer the tax benefit, or where they are wholly dissimilar to the relationships or transactions that are contemplated by the provisions.

The following are some of the other comments made in the *Canada Trustco* case that might shed some light on the third requirement for the application of the GAAR.

> [36] The third requirement for application of the GAAR is that the avoidance transaction giving rise to a tax benefit be abusive. The mere existence of an avoidance transaction is not enough to permit the GAAR to be applied. . . .
>
> [43] For these reasons we conclude, as did the Tax Court judge, that the determinations of "misuse" and "abuse" under s. 245(4) are not separate inquiries. Section 245(4) requires a single, unified approach to the textual,

contextual and purposive interpretation of the specific provisions of the *Income Tax Act* that are relied upon by the taxpayer in order to determine whether there was abusive tax avoidance.

. . .

[45] . . . An abuse may also result from an arrangement that circumvents the application of certain provisions, such as specific anti-avoidance rules, in a manner that frustrates or defeats the object, spirit or purpose of those provisions. By contrast, abuse is not established where it is reasonable to conclude that an avoidance transaction under s. 245(3) was within the object, spirit or purpose of the provisions that confer the tax benefit.

. . .

[52] In general, Parliament confers tax benefits under the *Income Tax Act* to promote purposes related to specific activities. For example, tax benefits associated with business losses, CCA and RRSPs, are conferred for reasons intrinsic to the activities involved. Unless the Minister can establish that the avoidance transaction frustrates or defeats the purpose for which the tax benefit was intended to be conferred, it is not abusive.

¶13,580 The Saga Continues — Decisions Since *Canada Trustco*

The following two cases have been decided by the Supreme Court since *Canada Trustco*.

¶13,585 *Earl Lipson* and *Jordan B. Lipson* (2006 DTC 2687 (T.C.C.)/2007 DTC 5172 (F.C.A.)/2009 DTC 5015 (S.C.C.))

This is a case about the conversion of interest expense from being non-deductible to being deductible. Earl and his wife, Jordanna, agreed to purchase a home for $750,000. A few months later, on closing, Jordanna borrowed $560,000 from the bank to buy shares of a family company from Earl. Earl agreed to repay the loan the next day. Jordanna and Earl then borrowed an additional $560,000 from the bank, secured by a mortgage on their new home, to pay off the original loan to buy the shares. By not electing under subsection 73(1) on the sale of shares from Earl to Jordanna, there was no gain on this transaction and the attribution rules would then cause any dividend income and interest expense to be reported in Earl's return. The judge concluded that there was a "tax benefit" and that it could not be said "to have been reasonably undertaken or arranged primarily for a *bona fide* purpose other than to obtain a tax benefit", as required by the Act.

Cases: *Lipson et al. v. The Queen*, 2006 DTC 2687 (TCC)

As a result, the third test of misuse or abuse was the determining factor. On this issue, at the Tax Court of Canada, the judge found, at paragraphs 31 and 32,

> This case is, in my view, an obvious example of abusive tax avoidance. Whatever commercial or other non-tax purpose, if any, is served by transferring Earl's shares to Jordanna, it is subservient to the objective of making the interest on the purchase of the house deductible by Earl.
>
> In this case I am not looking to any "overarching policy" that supersedes the specific provisions of the ITA. I am simply looking at the obvious purpose of the various provisions that are relied on and have concluded that those purposes have been subverted and those sections turned on their heads. I mentioned above that section 245 must itself be subjected to a

> textual, contextual and purposive analysis. If there ever was a case at which section 245 was aimed, it is this one.

The Federal Court of Appeal confirmed the decision of the Tax Court of Canada in the *Lipson* case. The Supreme Court of Canada also held that the GAAR applied. It was a majority decision of four judges with two dissenting opinions given by three judges. It was the use of the attribution rules and not the interest deductibility rules that resulted in the conclusion that the GAAR applied in this particular case.

Cases: *Lipson et al. v. The Queen*, 2007 DTC 5172 (FCA)*Lipson et al. v. The Queen*, 2009 DTC 5015 (SCC)

¶13,586 *Copthorne Holdings Ltd. v. The Queen*, 2012 DTC 5007 (S.C.C.)

In a unanimous decision by a full panel of nine judges, the Supreme Court of Canada applied the GAAR to a series of transactions involving a form of amalgamation that resulted in the preservation of paid-up capital (PUC) that was paid to a non-resident shareholder as a tax-free return of capital, thereby avoiding withholding tax on a dividend. An avoidance transaction was held by the Court to exist; it was further held that the transaction defeated the purpose of a provision of the Act and was, therefore, abusive.

In its decision, the Court addressed the three questions that it had set out in *Canada Trustco* to be decided in a GAAR analysis:

(1) Was there a tax benefit?

(2) Was the transaction giving rise to the tax benefit an avoidance transaction?

(3) Was the avoidance transaction giving rise to the tax benefit abusive?

In its analysis of the third question, the Court made the following comments of a general nature, at the indicated paragraphs:

> [65] The most difficult issue in this case is whether the avoidance transaction was an abuse or misuse of the Act. The terms abuse or misuse might be viewed as implying moral opprobrium regarding the actions of a taxpayer to minimize tax liability utilizing the provisions of the *Income Tax Act* in a creative way. That would be inappropriate. Taxpayers are entitled to select courses of action or enter into transactions that will minimize their tax liability (see *Duke of Westminster*).
>
> [66] The GAAR is a legal mechanism whereby Parliament has conferred on the court the unusual duty of going behind the words of the legislation to determine the object, spirit or purpose of the provision or provisions relied upon by the taxpayer. While the taxpayer's transactions will be in strict compliance with the text of the relevant provisions relied upon, they may not necessarily be in accord with their object, spirit or purpose. In such cases, the GAAR may be invoked by the Minister. The GAAR does create some uncertainty for taxpayers. Courts, however, must remember that s. 245 was enacted "as a provision of last resort" ([*Canada*] *Trustco*, at para. 21).
>
> [67] A court must be mindful that a decision supporting a GAAR assessment in a particular case may have implications for innumerable "everyday" transactions of taxpayers. A decision affecting PUC is a good example. There are undoubtedly hundreds, and perhaps thousands of share transactions each year in which the PUC of a certain class of shares may be a relevant consideration. Because of the potential to affect so many transactions, the court must approach a GAAR decision cautiously. It is neces-

sary to remember that "Parliament must . . . be taken to seek consistency, predictability and fairness in tax law" ([*Canada*] *Trustco*, at para. 42). As this Court stated in *Trustco*:

> Parliament intends taxpayers to take full advantage of the provisions of the *Income Tax Act* that confer tax benefits. Indeed, achieving the various policies that the *Income Tax Act* seeks to promote is dependent on taxpayers doing so. [para. 31]

[68] For this reason, "the GAAR can only be applied to deny a tax benefit when the abusive nature of the transaction is clear" ([*Canada*] *Trustco*, at para. 50). The court's role must therefore be to conduct an objective, thorough and step-by-step analysis and explain the reasons for its conclusion.

[69] In order to determine whether a transaction is an abuse or misuse of the Act, a court must first determine the "object, spirit or purpose of the provisions . . . that are relied on for the tax benefit, having regard to the scheme of the Act, the relevant provisions and permissible extrinsic aids" ([*Canada*] *Trustco*, at para. 55). The object, spirit or purpose of the provisions has been referred to as the "legislative rationale that underlies specific or interrelated provisions of the Act" (V. Krishna, *The Fundamentals of Income Tax Law* (2009), at p. 818).

[70] The object, spirit or purpose can be identified by applying the same interpretive approach employed by this Court in all questions of statutory interpretation — a "unified textual, contextual and purposive approach" ([*Canada*] *Trustco*, at para. 47; *Lipson v. Canada*, [2009 DTC 5015] 2009 SCC 1, [2009] 1 S.C.R. 3, at para. 26). While the approach is the same as in all statutory interpretation, the analysis seeks to determine a different aspect of the statute than in other cases. In a traditional statutory interpretation approach the court applies the textual, contextual and purposive analysis to determine what the words of the statute mean. In a GAAR analysis the textual, contextual and purposive analysis is employed to determine the object, spirit or purpose of a provision. Here the meaning of the words of the statute may be clear enough. The search is for the rationale that underlies the words that may not be captured by the bare meaning of the words themselves. However, determining the rationale of the relevant provisions of the Act should not be conflated with a value judgment of what is right or wrong nor with theories about what tax law ought to be or ought to do.

[71] Second, a court must consider whether the transaction falls within or frustrates the identified purpose ([*Canada*] *Trustco*, at para. 44). As earlier stated, while an avoidance transaction may operate alone to produce a tax benefit, it may also operate as part of a series of transactions that results in the tax benefit. While the focus must be on the transaction, where it is part of a series, it must be viewed in the context of the series to enable the court to determine whether abusive tax avoidance has occurred. In such a case, whether a transaction is abusive will only become apparent when it is considered in the context of the series of which it is a part and the overall result that is achieved (*Lipson*, at para. 34, *per* LeBel J.).

> [72] The analysis will then lead to a finding of abusive tax avoidance: (1) where the transaction achieves an outcome the statutory provision was intended to prevent; (2) where the transaction defeats the underlying rationale of the provision; or (3) where the transaction circumvents the provision in a manner that frustrates or defeats its object, spirit or purpose ([*Canada*] *Trustco*, at para. 45; *Lipson*, at para. 40). These considerations are not independent of one another and may overlap. At this stage, the Minister must clearly demonstrate that the transaction is an abuse of the Act, and the benefit of the doubt is given to the taxpayer.
>
> [73] When applying this test, there is no distinction between an "abuse" and a "misuse". Instead, there is a single unified approach ([*Canada*] *Trustco*, at para. 43 . . .

¶13,600 Requirement For Information Reporting of Tax Avoidance Transactions

Legislation implements a reporting regime requiring taxpayers to report aggressive tax avoidance transactions.

ITA: 237.3 [Reporting for tax avoidance transactions]

The objective of the reporting regime is to help the CRA to identify potentially abusive transactions and their participants. The determination of whether a transaction or series of transactions must be reported is based on the existence of specified "hallmarks" of aggressive tax planning. These hallmarks are thought to reflect certain situations that are present in tax avoidance transactions of interest. Identification of these transactions through the reporting requirements may lead to a challenge under other provisions such as the GAAR.

Under these proposals, a "reportable transaction" is defined as a transaction that is classified as an "avoidance transaction" under the GAAR or a transaction that is part of a series of transactions that includes an avoidance transaction if, at any time, two of the following three hallmarks come into existence in respect of the transaction or series:

ITA: 237.3(1) Definitions

(1) a promoter or tax adviser in respect of the transaction is entitled to fees that are to any extent

- based on the amount of the tax benefit from the transaction,
- contingent upon the obtaining of a tax benefit from the transaction, or
- attributable to the number of taxpayers who participate in the transaction or who have been provided access to advice given by the promoter or adviser regarding the tax consequences from the transaction;

(2) a promoter or tax adviser in respect of the transaction requires "confidential protection" with respect to the transaction. In this respect, a "confidential protection" is defined as any limitation on disclosure to any other person, including the CRA, that is placed by a promoter or tax adviser on the taxpayer, or on a person who entered into the transaction for the benefit of the taxpayer, in respect of the details or structure of the avoidance transaction that give rise to any tax benefit;

(3) the taxpayer or the person who entered into the transaction for the benefit of the taxpayer obtains "contractual protection" in respect of the transaction (otherwise than as a result of a fee described in the first hallmark).

A penalty for failure to report is imposed.

ITA: 237.3(8) Penalty

¶13,600.99 Practise What You've Learned

Refer to the following sections of the Study Guide to practise what you've learned:

¶13,825 — Multiple Choice Questions

- Question 4 — GAAR
- Question 5 — GAAR

¶13,850 — Exercises

- Exercise 11 — GAAR
- Exercise 12 — GAAR

CHAPTER 14

Rights and Obligations Under the *Income Tax Act*

ADVANCED CONTENT IN THIS CHAPTER

Learning Goals

Know

By the end of this chapter you will know:

- The basic rules related to tax compliance.
  - Filing deadlines
  - Payment deadlines
  - Instalment payments
  - Appeal deadlines
- The tax issues related to death of a taxpayer.

Understand and Explain

By the end of this chapter you will understand and be able to explain:

- The basic rules related to tax compliance.
- How a deceased taxpayer is taxed.

Apply

By the end of this chapter you will be able to apply your knowledge and understanding to:

- Calculate instalments payable.
- Calculate penalties.
- Calculate the taxable income and tax payable for a deceased taxpayer.

Review Questions

¶14,800 in the Study Guide

Multiple Choice Questions

¶14,825 in the Study Guide

Exercises

¶14,850 in the Study Guide

Assignment Problems

¶14,875 in the Study Guide

Overview

Canadian income tax is based on the self-assessment system. The obligation of calculating taxable income and taxes payable and of paying taxes owing is that of the taxpayer and not the CRA. The *Income Tax Act* (the Act) enumerates these obligations and also specifies the rights and powers of the CRA to enforce the system. Finally, taxpayers are given the right to appeal any actions taken by the CRA.

In the interest of efficiency and enforcement, the Act shifts some of the obligations from the taxpayer to other persons. These include employers and persons paying interest, dividends, and other payments to non-residents. The obligations of these persons to report payments and/or withhold tax and remit it to the CRA will also be discussed.

The following chart outlines the major provisions of Part I, Division I of the *Income Tax Act*, pertaining to returns, assessments, payments, and appeals discussed in this chapter.

PART I — DIVISION I

RETURNS, ASSESSMENTS, PAYMENT AND APPEALS

DIVISION — SUBDIVISION — SECTION

DIVISION	
A	Liability for tax
B	Computation of income
C	Computation of taxable income
D	Taxable income earned in Canada by non-residents
E	Computation of tax
E.1	Minimum tax
F	Special rules applicable in certain circumstances
G	Deferred and other special income arrangements
H	Exemptions
I	**Returns, assessments, payment and appeals**
J	Appeals to the Tax Court of Canada and the Federal Court of Appeal

SECTION	
150	Returns
150.1	Electronic filing
151	Estimate of tax
152	Assessment
153-160.4	Payment of tax
161	Interest
161.1-161.2	Offset of refund interest and arrears interest
161.3-161.4	Small amounts owing
162-163.1	Penalties
163.2	Misrepresentation of a tax matter by a third party (civil penalty)
164	Refunds
165	Objections to assessments
166-167	General
168	Revocation of registration of certain organizations and associations

¶14,000 Obligations of the Taxpayer Under the *Income Tax Act*

¶14,010 Returns, Penalties, and Criminal Offences

¶14,015 Returns

¶14,015.10 Filing Deadlines

The Act requires taxpayers to file returns in prescribed form and containing prescribed information, and specifies the date by which the returns must be filed as follows:

(1) Corporations — within six months after the end of the taxation year. ITA: 150(1)(a) Corporations

(2) Individuals — on or before April 30 of the next year, unless an individual or the individual's cohabiting spouse carried on a business in the year, in which case the filing deadline is June 15 of the following year. ITA: 150(1)(d) Individuals

(3) Deceased individuals — where an individual has died after October of a particular year and before the filing date for that year (April 30th or June 15th, as discussed above), the return for the particular year of the deceased must be filed by the legal representative by the later of:

(a) six months after the date of death, and

(b) the usual filing date (i.e., April 30th or June 15th) following the particular year. ITA: 150(1)(b) Deceased individuals

Where the death has occurred outside of these time limits, the normal filing dates as discussed in (b), above, apply.

The objective of these rules is to provide the legal representative of the deceased a minimum of six months after the date of death within which to file a return. These rules are discussed in more detail later in this chapter.

(4) Trusts or estates — within 90 days after the end of the taxation year. ITA: 150(1)(c) Trusts or estates

The following summarizes the filing deadlines:

Income tax return	Filing date	
Corporations	6 months	ITA: 150(1)(a) Corporations
Individuals	April 30 or June 15	ITA: 150(1)(d) Individuals
Deceased individuals	Later of 6 months after death and the normal due date	ITA: 150(1)(b) Deceased individuals
Trusts or estates	90 days	ITA: 150(1)(c) Trusts or estates

¶14,015.20 Requirements To File a Return

Note that corporations that are resident in Canada or carry on business in Canada must file for each taxation year, but individuals are only required to file if one of the following applies:

(1) a balance of tax is owing for the year; ITA: 150(1.1)(b)(i)

(2) a capital property has been disposed of in the year; ITA: 150(1.1)(b)(ii)

(3) a non-resident individual has a taxable capital gain (e.g., claimed a capital gains reserve in the previous year); ITA: 150(1.1)(b)(iii)

(4) the individual's Home Buyer Plan (HBP) balance or Lifelong Learning Plan (LLP) is a positive amount; or ITA: 146.01(1) Definitions, 146.02(1) Definitions, 150(1.1)(b)(iv)

(5) a return is demanded by the Minister. ITA: 150(2) Demands for returns

Of course, individuals entitled to a refund due to over-withholding or refundable tax credits should file in any case. Low-income taxpayers should file to receive income-based benefits such as the GST/HST credit, the Canada Child Benefit (CCB) and the Guaranteed Income Supplement (GIS). If they do not file a tax return, they are not eligible to receive these amounts.

The February 27, 2018 federal Budget proposes to impose an obligation for certain (express) trusts to file a tax return (T3) along with new reporting requirements of such a trust's trustees, beneficiaries, and settlors. Graduated rate estates and trusts that hold only cash, government debt, and listed securities of less than $50,000 throughout the year will be exempt from the additional reporting requirements.

¶14,015.30 Electronic and Other Filing Options

Individuals can file their personal returns electronically. The CRA encourages this by not mailing return forms to individual taxpayers who have used software to prepare their previous returns. The primary benefit of the electronic filing program for taxpayers is that processing of a tax refund can be much faster. The primary benefit to the CRA is the elimination of data inputting errors on their computer system.

ITA: 150.1 [Electronic filing]

Taxpayers who electronically file their tax return are not required to submit any receipts or other supporting documentation. The CRA, however, has the right to request supporting documentation.

Taxpayers are eligible to NETFILE their personal return if specified conditions are met.

While there are some exceptions, corporations that have annual gross revenues in excess of $1 million in a taxation year are required to file their income tax returns electronically. There are penalties for non-compliance.

ITA: 150.1(2.1) Mandatory filing of return by electronic transmission, 162(7.2) Failure to file in appropriate manner — return of income

¶14,018 Functional Currency Tax Reporting

Under specified conditions, Canadian-resident corporations are allowed to report their Canadian tax results in their elected functional currency, other than the Canadian dollar. An election into the foreign functional currency for tax reporting removes the need to convert financial results into Canadian dollars. This is a benefit to corporate taxpayers that maintain their books and records for financial reporting purposes in a foreign currency. In these cases, the taxpayers would otherwise have to translate their financial results to Canadian dollars only to compute their Canadian tax liabilities. Opting for functional currency tax reporting in Canada reduces the distortions that may arise under conditions of currency volatility when foreign currency results have to be translated into Canadian dollars. For the purposes of the functional currency election, a "qualifying currency" is limited to the currency of the United States, the European Monetary Union, the United Kingdom, Australia, and a currency prescribed by regulation.

ITA: 261 [Functional currency reporting]

¶14,020 Penalties

¶14,020.10 Failure To File Return

The Act provides penalties for failure to file a tax return as and when required. The penalty is 5% of the tax unpaid at the date on which the return was due to be filed. In addition, a further penalty of 1% of the unpaid tax is levied for each complete month that the return was late, for up to 12 months.

ITA: 150(1) Filing returns of income — general rule, 162(1)(a), 162(1)(b)

A higher penalty is imposed for a taxpayer who has already been assessed a penalty for failure to file a return in any of the three preceding years. This penalty equals 10% of unpaid tax plus 2% per month, for up to 20 months.

ITA: 162(2) Repeated failure to file

The February 27, 2018 federal Budget proposes to introduce new penalties for a failure to file a T3 return, including a new beneficial ownership reporting schedule. The penalty will be $25 per day with a minimum penalty of $100 and a maximum penalty of $2,500. An additional penalty of 5% of the maximum fair market value of property held by the trust with a minimum penalty of $2,500 will apply where failure to file the return was made knowingly, or due to gross negligence.

¶14,020.20 Failure To Report an Amount of Income

A penalty of the lesser of 10% of the income that a taxpayer has failed to report and 50% of the understated unpaid tax is imposed if there had been a previous failure to report in the preceding three years. The penalty only applies if the unreported income in the current and any of the three prior years was equal to or greater than $500. However, no penalty will apply where the more severe penalty for false statements or omission (below) has been applied or where the previous failure was more than three years ago.

ITA: 163(1) Repeated failure to report income, 163(1.1) Amount of penalty

¶14,020.30 False Statements or Omission

Where taxpayers knowingly or under circumstances amounting to gross negligence under-report income, the Act imposes a penalty equal to the greater of $100 and 50% of the difference in tax liability. This provision is invoked frequently in cases involving omission of income on returns. The term "gross negligence" has been interpreted to include errors which amount to little more than careless omissions, if the taxpayer knew or should have known that the amount was omitted. This provision would not be applied to amounts excluded because of an honest dispute as to their taxability.

ITA: 163(2) False statements or omissions

¶14,020.40 Interplay of Penalty Provisions

The interplay between the penalties for failure to report and for false statements or omission should be noted. On the first failure to report income, the first penalty would not apply, so the CRA could impose the penalty for false statements or omissions. On a repeated failure to report income within the three years specified, the CRA may have a choice between the failure to report penalty and the false statement or omission penalty.

ITA: 163(1) Repeated failure to report income, 163(2) False statements or omissions

¶14,020.50 Penalty for Late or Deficient Instalments

The Act imposes a penalty of 50% of the interest, charged on late or underpaid instalment payments, in excess of the greater of $1,000 or 25% of the interest calculated as if no instalments had been paid. This section applies if *any* instalment for the year is late or deficient, as discussed later in this chapter.

ITA: 161 [Interest], 163.1 Penalty for late or deficient instalments

¶14,020.55 Penalty for Failure To Provide Information on Form

The Act imposes a penalty of $100 for each failure to provide any information required on a prescribed form unless a reasonable effort was made to obtain the information in respect of another person.

ITA: 162(5) Failure to provide information on form

¶14,020.60 Civil Penalties for Misrepresentation of a Third Party

The Act imposes civil penalties for misrepresentations by third parties in respect of another person's tax matters. The penalty is directed to tax professionals, appraisers and valuators and promoters of tax shelters and other tax minimization schemes. Two penalties are imposed.

ITA: 163.2 [Misrepresentation of a tax matter by a third party]

The first penalty, referred to as the planner's penalty, is a penalty that is imposed when the third-party person is involved in the making of, or causes another person to make a statement that the person knows, or would reasonably be expected to know but for circumstances amounting to "culpable conduct" (as defined in the provision) is a false statement or omission that may be used by another person for tax purposes.

ITA: 163.2(2) Penalty for misrepresentations in tax planning arrangements, 163.2(1) Definitions

The penalty is one of two amounts. The first amount applies where a "false statement" (as defined in the provision) is made in the course of a "planning activity" or a "valuation activity" (as defined). The penalty is the greater of $1,000 and the total of the person's "gross entitlement" (as defined) in respect of the planning/valuation activity calculated at the time at which the notice of assessment of the penalty is sent to the person. The second amount is $1,000, which applies in the case of a false statement in a situation that falls outside of the definition of a "planning activity" or a "valuation activity" or, perhaps, in which there is no gross entitlement.

ITA: 163.2(3) Amount of penalty, 163.2(1) Definitions

The second penalty, referred to as the preparer's penalty, is a penalty imposed on a third-party person involved in the making of a false statement or omission statement to, or by or on behalf of, another person.

The statement must be established as one that the person knows, or would be reasonably expected to know but for circumstances amounting to "culpable conduct", is a false statement or omission that may be used for tax purposes by or on behalf of the other person. The penalty is the greater of two amounts. The minimum amount is $1,000. The maximum amount is, generally, 50% of the amount of tax sought to be avoided, or the amount of excess refund sought to be obtained, but the upper limit is $100,000 plus the fee charged by the preparer. Additional discussion and clarification of the CRA's position on third party civil penalties, with examples, is contained in an Information Circular.

ITA: 163.2(4) Penalty for participating in a misrepresentation, 163.2(5) Amount of penalty; Information Circulars: IC 01-1 Third-Party Civil Penalties

The following flow chart may be helpful in applying these civil penalties.

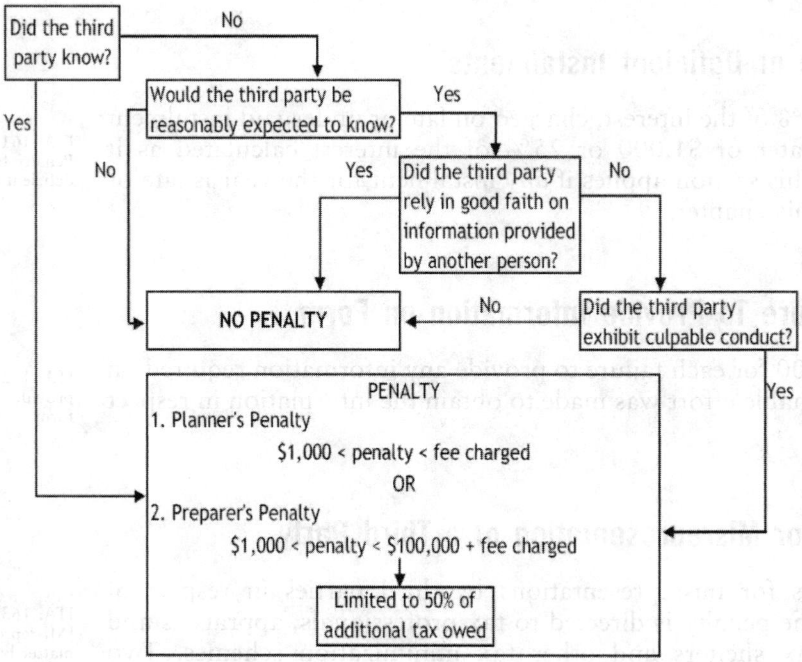

¶14,020.70 Summary of Penalties

The following table summarizes the above penalties.

Offence	Penalty	
Late-filed tax return	Balance of tax owing × 5% + 1% for each complete month late: Maximum = 17%	ITA: 162(1) Failure to file return of income
Late-filed tax return — repeat offender	Balance of tax owing × 10% + 2% for each complete month late: Maximum = 50%	ITA: 162(2) Repeated failure to file
Failure to report income — repeat offender	Lesser of income not reported × 10% and 50% of tax liability	ITA: 163(1) Repeated failure to report income, 163(1.1) Amount of penalty
False statement or omissions — knowingly or gross negligence	Minimum = $100 Maximum = increased tax liability × 50%	ITA: 163(2) False statements or omissions
Late or deficient instalments	[Interest charged — greater of (a) $1,000 and (b) 25% of interest that would have been charged if no instalments were made] × 50%	ITA: 163.1 Penalty for late or deficient instalments
Third party civil penalty Planner's penalty	Minimum = $1,000 Maximum = Fee charged for the planning	ITA: 163.2(2) Penalty for misrepresentations in tax planning arrangements, 163.2(3) Amount of penalty
Preparer's penalty	Minimum = $1,000 Maximum = $100,000 + Fee charged Limited to 50% × tax on unreported income	ITA: 163.2(4) Penalty for participating in a misrepresentation, 163.2(5) Amount of penalty
Failure to provide information	$100 per failure	ITA: 162(5) Failure to provide information on form

Example Problem 14-1

Mr. Shinh, the new controller of Secret Ltd., a CCPC, is in the process of preparing the company's current-year T2 return. He notices a section of the return asking for information about the percentage ownership of the top three shareholders of the company. Secret Ltd. is so secretive that even Mr. Shinh does not know exactly how many shares the president and vice-president own. He, therefore, sends the return to Mr. Clements, the president. Mr. Clements writes "None of your business" in that section of the return, signs it, and returns it to Mr. Shinh for filing.

Mr. Shinh, worried, calls you, Secret Ltd.'s tax adviser, and asks you to speak to Mr. Clements. Mr. Shinh says that all tax owing for the year has been paid and that the return will be filed on time.

REQUIRED

What would you tell Mr. Clements about the risks, if any, Secret Ltd. is running by not completing the section of the T2 return?

SOLUTION

Secret Ltd. is required to file a tax return containing prescribed information. Any information asked for on a form issued by the CRA is prescribed information, since such forms are prepared and released (in theory) by order of the Minister.

ITA: 150(1) Filing returns of income — general rule

The CRA could, therefore, take the position that Secret Ltd. failed to file a return "as required" and assess a penalty. No amount would be payable since the penalty for a first offence is 5% plus 1% per month of unpaid tax. However, should the CRA disagree with the company's calculation of tax payable, the penalty would be based on tax unpaid per the assessment or reassessment.

ITA: 162(1) Failure to file return of income

In any case, Secret Ltd. would likely be assessed the $100 minimum penalty for failing to provide complete information on a prescribed form.

ITA: 162(5) Failure to provide information on form

¶14,020.80 Voluntary Disclosures and CRA's Power To Waive or Cancel Interest and Penalties

The CRA has the legislative authority to waive or cancel penalties, if the taxpayer makes a voluntary disclosure. The CRA's voluntary disclosure program is outlined in an Information Circular. Where a taxpayer makes voluntary disclosures to correct inaccurate or incomplete information or to disclose previously unreported information, the taxpayer will have to pay taxes owing plus interest, but monetary penalties and prosecution may be waived.

ITA: 220(3.1) Waiver of penalty or interest; Information Circulars: IC 00-1R6 Voluntary Disclosures Program

In 2017, the CRA introduced a more restricted voluntary disclosure program through substantial revisions to the Information Circular. The new program provides for two tracks of income tax disclosures available to a taxpayer.

A disclosure made by a taxpayer under the General Program will provide for penalty and criminal prosecution relief and partial interest relief. Full interest will apply to tax owing for the prior three taxation years. For preceding years, partial relief of up to 50% of the normal interest charges on unpaid tax will be provided.

A disclosure must be made by a taxpayer under the Limited Program where there is an element of intentional conduct by the taxpayer or a closely related party. An example would include a Canadian resident taxpayer who has failed to disclose income on investments in an offshore account set up to hold undeclared business income. A disclosure by a taxpayer under the Limited Program will provide for relief from criminal prosecution and gross negligence penalties, but all other applicable penalties such as late filing penalties will stand. Further, no interest relief will be provided under the Limited Program. Corporations with gross revenue of more than $250 million in two of the past five years must make a voluntary disclosure under the Limited Program.

The estimated income tax owing must be paid with the voluntary disclosure application.

The Act also allows the CRA to cancel or waive interest and penalties in a number of other circumstances. Another Information Circular sets out three types of circumstances that would warrant a waiver.

ITA: 220(3.1) Waiver of penalty or interest; Information Circulars: IC 07-1 Taxpayer Relief Provisions

(1) Circumstances beyond the taxpayer's or employer's control such as natural disasters, postal strikes, serious illness or accident or serious emotional or mental distress.

(2) Actions of the Department such as processing delays, errors in CRA materials, errors in CRA advice, processing errors or CRA delays in providing information.

(3) To facilitate collection when there is an inability to pay or where a reasonable repayment arrangement is not possible due to the heavy interest charges.

¶14,025 Criminal Offences

In addition to the penalties described above, the Act prescribes a number of more serious penalties that can be imposed for a variety of offences.

ITA: 238 Offences and punishment; Information Circulars: IC 00-1R6 Voluntary Disclosures Program

A person is liable for a fine of $1,000 to $25,000 or both the fine and imprisonment for up to 12 months on summary conviction for failing to file a return as and when required. A person convicted under this section is not liable to pay a penalty under specified sections of the Act unless that penalty was assessed before he or she was charged under this section.

ITA: 238(3) Saving, 162 Failure to file return of income, 227 Withholding taxes

On summary conviction, there is a fine of between 50% and 200% of tax sought to be evaded or both the fine and imprisonment for up to two years for:

ITA: 239(1) Other offences and punishment

(1) making a false statement in a return;

(2) destroying books and records;

(3) falsifying books and records;

(4) wilfully attempting to evade compliance with the Act; and

(5) conspiring to commit any of the above four offences.

If the foregoing five offences are prosecuted by indictment at the election of the Attorney General of Canada, as indicated in the case of *The Queen v. Smythe*, a conviction can result in a fine of 100% to 200% of the tax sought to be evaded and imprisonment for up to five years. Again, a person convicted under this section is not liable for the penalty under specified sections of the Act for the same attempt to evade tax unless that penalty was assessed before charges were laid under this section.

ITA: 239(2) Prosecution on indictment, 239(3) Penalty on conviction; Cases: *The Queen v. Conn Stafford Smythe*, 70 DTC 6382 (Ont. Sup. Crt.)

¶14,025.99 Practise What You've Learned

Refer to the following sections of the Study Guide to practise what you've learned:

¶14,825 — Multiple Choice Questions

- Question 1 — Late-filing penalty

¶14,850 — Exercises

- Exercise 5 — Late-filing penalty
- Exercise 8 — Preparer penalties
- Exercise 15 — Penalties

¶14,030 Payments and Interest

The following is a summary of the payment deadlines.

ITA: 248(1) Definitions

Taxpayers	Balance-due day
Individuals	April 30
Corporations	2 months after year end
CCPC claiming Small Business Deduction with taxable income under the business limit in the previous year	3 months after year end
Trusts	Due date for trust return

¶14,035 Individuals

¶14,035.10 Instalment Threshold

Individuals whose primary sources of income are wages and salary generally do not have to pay instalments because their employers are remitting withholding tax on a monthly basis. However, not all of a taxpayer's income may be subject to withholding in a year. If the difference between the total tax liability (federal and provincial for all provinces, except Quebec) in the current year and one of the two preceding years exceeds the amount of tax withheld at source by the instalment threshold, then, quarterly instalments must be paid. That threshold is $3,000 ($1,800 if resident in Quebec). For example, if the total tax liability on income not subject to withholding (that is, net tax owing) for an individual living in a province other than Quebec is $2,900 in 2016, $3,100 in 2017, and $3,300 in 2018, then quarterly instalments must be paid in 2018. In this case, the net tax owing in 2018, the current year, and in 2017, one of the two preceding years, exceeds the $3,000 threshold.

ITA: 156(1) Other individuals, 156(2) Payment by mutual fund trusts, 156.1(1) Definitions

¶14,035.20 Instalment Amounts and Timetable

These instalments must be paid by the 15th day of each calendar quarter (i.e., the 15th day of March, June, September, and December), with the balance of tax due the following April 30. Each instalment is computed as the least of:

(1) one-quarter of the estimated tax payable for the current year;

(2) one-quarter of the instalment base (defined for this purpose in a regulation, in essence, as tax payable excluding the effect of certain tax credits) for the immediately preceding year; and

ITR: 5300 Individuals

(3) one-quarter of the instalment base for the second preceding year for the March and June instalments, and one-half of the instalment base for the preceding taxation year net of the March and June payments for the September and December instalments.

Individuals are informed by the CRA with respect to the exact amount of their instalment requirement under option (3) above. For example, in respect of 2018, the March and June instalments are based on one-quarter of the 2016 instalment base. The September and December instalments are equal to 50% of the excess of the individual's 2017 instalment base over 50% of the 2016 instalment base. Instalments can be based on the estimated liability for the year under option (1) above, but will be subject to interest on understated amounts where an estimate is too low, as discussed below.

¶14,035.30 Interest on Deficient or Late Instalments

The Act charges interest on deficient and late instalments from the day the instalment should have been made to the day the final payment of tax is due (e.g., April 30 for individuals). An instalment interest offset is available on prepaid or overpaid instalments. However, this credit offset can only be applied against instalment interest owing; it is not refundable and may not be applied against any other debts. Interest is calculated from the date the final payment is due until the amount is paid. Interest charges on deficient instalments can be avoided by computing instalments on a preceding year's instalment base as in options (2) or (3) outlined in ¶14,035.20, above, even if the current year's income is likely to be higher. Interest on deficient instalments may be cancelled if the interest does not exceed $25 for a taxation year.

ITA: 161(2) Interest on instalments, 161(2.2) Contra interest, 161(1) General, 161(4.01) Limitation — other individuals, 161.3 Interest and penalty amounts of $25 or less

The prescribed interest rate is set quarterly in relation to the average interest rate on 90-day treasury bills during the first month of the preceding quarter. Exhibit 14-1 lists the recent prescribed rates under Part XLIII of the Regulations.

Exhibit 14-1 Prescribed Interest Rates Under Part XLIII of Regulations

			CRA refunds[1]		
Year	**Quarter**	**Employee or shareholder loans**	**Non-corp.**	**Corp.**	**Unpaid tax and instalments**
2017	1	1	3	1	5
	2	1	3	1	5
	3	1	3	1	5
	4	1	3	1	5
2018	1	1	3	1	5
	2	2	4	2	6

[1] The interest rate paid by the CRA to corporations is the basic prescribed rate (i.e., without the additional 2%).

The lowest prescribed rate applies to imputed interest benefit calculations on employee or shareholder loans. The lowest rate also applies for the purpose of calculating interest on refunds owed by the CRA to a corporate taxpayer. The basic prescribed rate is increased by two percentage points for the purpose of calculating interest on refunds, owed by the CRA to a non-corporate taxpayer. The rate applicable to late and deficient instalments and tax payments is increased by four percentage points. Also, subject to the highest rate of interest are unpaid employee source deductions and other amounts withheld at source.

ITR: 4301 Prescribed Rate of Interest

Interest paid on unpaid tax and instalments, arrears interest, is not deductible for tax purposes. However, interest received must be included in income. Refund interest accruing over a period can offset any arrears interest that accrues over the same period, to which the refund interest relates. Hence, only the excess refund interest is taxed to the individual.

ITA: 18(1)(t) Payments under different acts, 161.1 [Interest offset and arrears]

As noted above, the rate of interest paid on refunds is calculated at the basic rate for corporations and with an additional two percentage points for taxpayers other than corporations (e.g., individuals or trusts). However, contra-interest, as an interest offset on overpayments of tax, contains the additional four percentage points indicated for deficient payments. For example, where an instalment payment is made early to create contra-interest to offset the interest on an earlier late instalment payment, the contra-interest is calculated at the 5% rate in computing the net interest liability to the taxpayer.

ITA: 161(2.2) Contra interest

Note that all interest is compounded daily, based on the quarterly prescribed rates.

ITA: 248(11) Compound interest

¶14,040 Corporations

¶14,040.10 Instalment Threshold and Interest Considerations

Corporations must make instalment payments of their tax with the number of instalments dependent on the type of the corporation. A private corporation is permitted to reduce its monthly instalments by 1/12 of the corporation's dividend refund on the payment of dividends for the year. A corporation is not required to make instalments if taxes payable for the current or preceding year do not exceed $3,000. Corporate instalments will only be considered to have been received on time if received by the due date, i.e., postmarks will not suffice.

ITA: 157(1) Payment by corporation, 157(3) Reduced instalments, 157(2.1) $3,000 threshold, 248(7) Receipt of things mailed

The offsetting of interest on corporate tax overpayments and underpayments is permitted. This is different from the contra interest mechanism previously discussed. The provision is aimed at situations most commonly encountered by corporations with complex tax matters, where multiple taxation years may be reassessed concurrently to reallocate income and expenses from one taxation year to another. The provision allows a corporation to avoid paying non-deductible arrears interest for a period for which refund interest is being calculated in the corporation's favour. A written application will be required for the interest offset mechanism to be implemented.

ITA: 161.1 [Interest offset and arrears], 161(2.2) Contra interest, 161.1(2) Concurrent refund interest and arrears interest

¶14,040.20 Quarterly Instalments For Eligible Canadian-Controlled Private Corporations (Small CCPCs)

Only an eligible CCPC may pay quarterly instalments, which are due on the last day of each quarter of the CCPC's taxation year. A CCPC will be considered to be an eligible CCPC if:

ITA: 157(1.1) Special case

(1) the corporation has, together with any associated corporation, in either the current or the previous taxation year:

   (a) taxable income not exceeding $500,000 (i.e., the small business deduction limit), and

   ITA: 157(1.2)(a), 157(1.3) Taxable income — small-CCPC

   (b) taxable capital employed in Canada for the taxation year not exceeding $10,000,000;

   ITA: 157(1.2)(b), 157(1.4) Taxable capital — small-CCPC

(2) a small business deduction was claimed in computing the corporation's income tax payable for either the current or the previous taxation year; and

ITA: 157(1.2)(c)

(3) the corporation has a "perfect compliance history", as outlined below, at the time that the quarterly instalment is due.

ITA: 157(1.2)(d)

A corporation will be considered to have a "perfect compliance history" at the time that a quarterly instalment is due if, throughout the 12-month period before that time, it has no compliance irregularities pertaining to remittance of tax and filing of returns under the *Income Tax Act* or the GST/HST portion of the *Excise Tax Act*.

ITA: 157(1.2)(d)

Eligible CCPCs will be permitted three options to determine the amount of their quarterly instalments, computed as follows:

ITA: 157(1.1)(a)

(1) four instalments equal to 1/4 of the estimated tax payable for the current taxation year;

ITA: 157(1.1)(a)(i)

(2) four instalments equal to 1/4 of the tax payable for the previous taxation year; or

ITA: 157(1.1)(a)(ii)

(3)

(a) a first instalment equal to 1/4 of the tax payable for the second preceding year, and ITA: 157(1.1)(a)(iii)

(b) three instalments equal to 1/3 of the amount by which the tax payable for the previous taxation year exceeds the first instalment paid for the current year.

This pattern of three options is similar to that for quarterly instalments paid by individuals, as outlined above, and for monthly instalments paid by corporations that are not eligible for quarterly instalments, to be discussed next.

Interest and penalty provisions that are applicable to other corporations are discussed in the following section.

Example Problem 14-2

Abigail Ltd. is a small CCPC eligible to make quarterly instalments of its corporate income taxes. The corporation has a December 31 year end. Ava, the owner-manager, has estimated that the corporation's tax liability for the 2018 taxation year will be $50,000. Your files indicate that the 2017 tax liability was assessed at $45,000 and the 2016 tax liability was assessed at $40,000.

REQUIRED

What are the options available to Abigail Ltd. to calculate quarterly income tax instalments?

SOLUTION

An eligible CCPC may pay its quarterly instalments on the last day of each quarter in its taxation year. In this case, with a December 31 year end, the instalments are due on March 31, June 30, September 30, and December 31. The three options are computed as follows: ITA: 157(1.1) Special case

(1)		1/4 × $50,000 (estimated tax liability for 2018)	$12,500
(2)		1/4 × $45,000 (actual tax liability for 2017)	$11,250
(3)	(a)	1/4 × $40,000 (actual tax liability for 2016), payable on March 31, 2018	$10,000
	(b)	1/3 × ($45,000 − $10,000), payable on June 30, September 30, and December 31, 2018	$11,667

¶14,040.30 Monthly Instalments for Other Corporations

Corporations that are not eligible small CCPCs must make monthly instalment payments of their tax at the end of each month. The corporation must compute the instalments on one, usually the least, of the following bases:

(1) $\frac{1}{12}$ of the estimated tax liability calculated at current rates on the estimated taxable income for the current year;

(2) $\frac{1}{12}$ of the instalment base (defined, in essence, as tax payable for the company) for the immediately preceding taxation year; or

(3) $\frac{1}{12}$ of the instalment based (defined as above) for the second preceding taxation year for the first two months, then for the next ten months $\frac{1}{10}$ of the quantity computed as the instalment base (defined as above) for the immediately preceding taxation year minus the amount paid in instalments for the first two months.

The basics of the calculation of monthly instalments, along with the liability of all corporations for interest and penalties, are illustrated by the following problem.

Example Problem 14-3

No Flab Enterprises Limited is an incorporated company involved in the sale of muscle building and physical fitness equipment. For the fiscal year ended March 31, 2016, the company generated taxes payable of $1.86 million. In fiscal 2017, taxes payable were $1.9 million.

Mr. Fiennes, president and controlling shareholder of the company, planned a reduced sales effort on his part for the fiscal year ended March 31, 2018. As a result, he estimated the company's taxes payable at $1.524 million for the year and paid 12 equal monthly instalments based on this amount. By March 2018, Mr. Fiennes had tabulated the profits and knew that the company's taxes payable would be $2.154 million.

Since Mr. Fiennes had reinvested all of the profits for fiscal 2018, he did not have the cash to pay the additional $630,000 in tax, so he paid nothing further. He filed the corporation's tax return on December 31, 2018, and, in order to avoid showing the further taxes payable, he did not report income for the corporation's 2018 fiscal year, thereby reducing taxes for the year by the $630,000. He reasoned that he would declare this income in the following year and pay the taxes on that income then.

Furthermore, instead of using the corporate tax return form readily available at his local District Tax Services Office, he filed his corporation's return on some accounting paper. As a result of filing in this way, however, his return did not contain all of the information required to be filed by the corporation.

In May 2019, the corporation's file was randomly selected for a full-scale audit during which discussions with Mr. Fiennes revealed the omitted taxable income. He argued with the tax auditor that the added taxable income resulted from his forgetting to record the sales of 123,000 units in September 2018. He was forcefully requested to pay the added tax by June 30, 2019 which he planned to do by that date. In addition to the added tax and interest, the tax auditor decided to assess the corporation for appropriate penalties, in this case, based on the evidence on hand. These were included in the notice of assessment requiring payment by June 30, 2019.

REQUIRED

(1) Set out the basis on which the interest that the corporation must pay on June 30, 2019 would be computed, assuming it was not eligible for the small business deduction.

ITA: 125 Small business deduction

(2) Indicate which penalties would be imposed.

SOLUTION

(1) Interest

ITA: 157(1) Payment by corporation

As indicated above, the corporation must compute the instalments on one, usually the least, of the following bases:

(A) 1/12 of the estimated tax liability calculated at current rates on the estimated taxable income for the current year (estimated to be $1.524 million in taxes payable for the year in this case);

(B) 1/12 of the instalment base (defined, in essence, as tax payable for this company) for the immediately preceding taxation year (amounting to $1.9 million for the year in this case); or

ITR: 5301 Corporations Under Part I of the Act

(C) 1/12 of the instalment base (defined as above) for the second preceding taxation year (amounting to $1.86 million for the year in this case) for the first two months, then for the next 10 months 1/10 of the quantity computed as the instalment base (defined as above) for the immediately preceding taxation year minus the amount paid in instalments for the first two months.

Whichever base is used for instalments, the difference between the estimate of the tax payable at the end of the fiscal period and the instalments paid must be paid two months after the end of the taxation year. Prudent financial management would suggest that a corporation use the base which allows it to pay the lowest amount in monthly instalments, while avoiding interest on a deficiency of instalments. In periods of rising income, this will generally be the third alternative.

The monthly instalments of corporate tax and other amounts payable by corporations will be deemed for the rules relating to interest and penalties to have been remitted only when received by the Receiver General or his or her representative, not on the date of mailing.

ITA: 248(7) Receipt of things mailed

Interest paid on a deficiency of instalments of a corporation is limited to interest on the difference between the amount of instalments actually paid and an amount based on the least of:

ITA: 161(4.1) Limitation — corporations, 157(1) Payment by corporation

(A) the tax payable for the year (in this case $2.154 million);

(B) the instalment base for the immediately preceding taxation year (in this case $1.9 million); and

(C) the instalment base for the second preceding taxation year (in this case $1.86 million) and the immediately preceding taxation year (in this case $1.9 million).

The deficiency of instalments in this case could be set out as follows (000s omitted from chart):

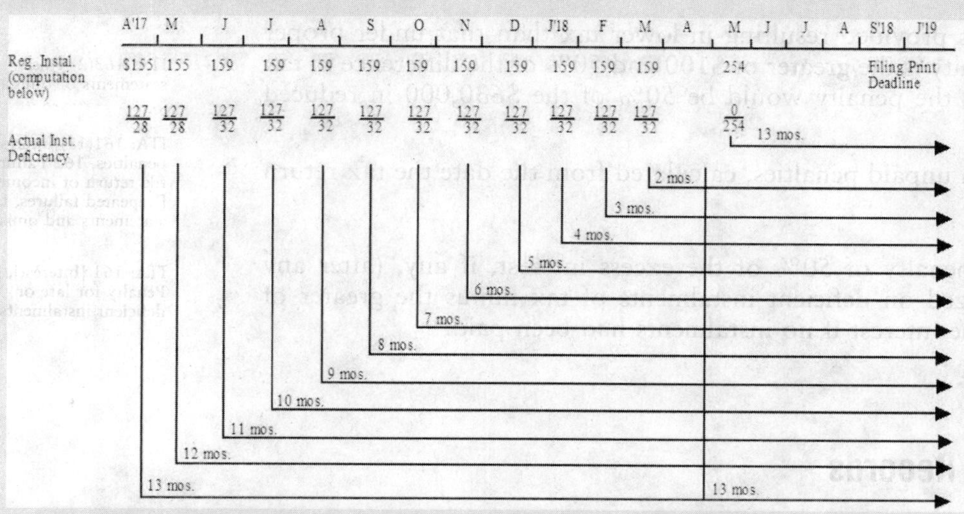

The required instalments are computed as follows:

(A) first two months: $\frac{1}{12}$ × $1,860,000 = $155,000

(B) next 10 months: $\frac{1}{10}$ × [$1,900,000 – (2 × 155,000)] = $159,000

(C) final instalment: $2,154,000 – [(10 × $159,000) + (2 × $155,000)] = $254,000

Interest is imposed at prescribed rates on underpaid instalments. This interest runs from the time when the instalment payment was due to either the date of payment or the date when the remainder of tax payable should be paid, whichever is earlier, and is compounded daily. Interest is imposed on the tax *and interest* owing on May 31, 2018 from the date the remainder of tax payable and interest payable is due until it is paid on June 30, 2019.

ITA: 161(2) Interest on instalments, 157(1)(b), 161(1) General; ITR: 4301 Prescribed Rate of Interest

(2) Penalties

A penalty is provided for failure to file the corporate tax return on September 30, 2018. The penalty is 5% of the tax unpaid at the date on which the return was due for filing. In this case, since the return was not filed on time in the prescribed form, the penalty would be 5% of the $630,000 in unpaid taxes or $31,500. In addition, the provision levies a further penalty of 1% of the unpaid tax per complete month that the return was past due for up to 12 months. In this case, the penalty would be 1% of the unpaid taxes of $630,000 for three months or $18,900.

ITA: 162(1)(a), 162(1)(b)

The Act imposes a penalty of $100 for failing to provide the required information on a prescribed form.

ITA: 162(5) Failure to provide information on form

The requirement for a corporation to file electronically applies to a corporation with gross revenue exceeding $1 million. The penalty for failing to file a return of income in the appropriate manner applies.

ITA: 150.1(2.1) Mandatory filing of return by electronic transmission, 162(7.2) Failure to file in appropriate manner — return of income

Where information is provided resulting in lower tax than that under proper information, the penalty is the greater of $100 and 50% of the difference in tax liability. In this case, the penalty would be 50% of the $630,000 in reduced taxes or $315,000.

ITA: 163(2) False statements or omissions

Interest is charged on unpaid penalties, calculated from the date the tax return was due.

ITA: 161(11) Interest on penalties, 162 Failure to file return of income, 163 [Repeated failures, false statements and omissions]

The Act imposes a penalty of 50% of the excess interest, if any, (after any interest offsets) charged on deficient instalments of tax minus the greater of $1,000 or 25% of the interest if no instalments had been paid.

ITA: 161 [Interest], 163.1 Penalty for late or deficient instalments

¶14,050 Books and Records

Taxpayers are required to keep adequate books and records. This requirement is for all persons carrying on a business and persons required to pay or collect taxes, among others. While the word "adequate" is not defined or illustrated, the records (including inventory documentation) must be sufficient to support a determination of income subject to tax or of amounts to be remitted. In an Information Circular, the CRA implies that basic transaction data, including invoices, receipts, contracts, bank statements and cancelled cheques, would be the minimum required. Electronic images of this data are acceptable as a method of keeping records.

ITA: 230 Records and books; Information Circulars: IC 78-10R5 Books and Records Retention/Destruction

All such books and records must be maintained at the taxpayer's place of business or residence in Canada until the taxpayer receives written permission to dispose of these materials. A set of rules prescribes a period for keeping certain records or books together with accounts and vouchers necessary to verify them and establishes a period of six years from the end of the last taxation year to which the records and books relate for all other cases not prescribed. Further subsections deal with a person who has not filed a return or a person who has a case under appeal, with a special request from the Minister and with permission to dispose of records and books before the expiration of the required period. If such materials are maintained in an electronically readable format to save space, guidelines for this procedure are set out in an Information Circular.

ITA: 230(4) Limitation period for keeping records, etc; ITR: 5800 [Required retention period]; Information Circulars: IC 78-10R5 Books and Records Retention/ Destruction

Failure to keep adequate books and records is a punishable (criminal) offence. Punishable offences were discussed earlier in this chapter at ¶14,025.

ITA: 238(1) Offences and punishment

¶14,050.99 Practise What You've Learned

Refer to the following sections of the Study Guide to practise what you've learned:

¶14,825 — Multiple Choice Questions

- Question 5 — Instalments — CCPC
- Question 6 — Instalments — Individual

¶14,850 — Exercises

- Exercise 3 — Instalments — Individual
- Exercise 4 — Instalments — CCPC
- Exercise 14 — Instalments — Corporation
- Exercise 16 — Filing due date; Balance due date; Instalments

¶14,100 Powers and Obligations of the CRA

While the Department of Finance formulates tax policy, the CRA controls, regulates, manages and supervises the income tax system. The duties of the Minister of National Revenue and the employees of his or her agency are set out in the Act. The Commissioner of the Canada Revenue Agency, the CRA's chief executive officer, is empowered to exercise all the powers and perform all of the duties of the Minister under the Act.

ITA: 220 Minister's Duty

¶14,110 Assessments and Reassessments

Having made a quick check of the return in the initial assessment process for verifying the basic information and calculations, the CRA can do a detailed review of the return, subject to the time restrictions, where applicable. The CRA may assess tax, interest, and penalties and, furthermore, it may reassess or make additional assessments in the following situations:

ITA: 152(4) Assessment and reassessment

(1) at any time, if the taxpayer or person filing the return has made any misrepresentation that is attributable to neglect, carelessness or wilful default or has committed any fraud in filing the return or in supplying any information under the Act;

(2) within the normal reassessment period, which is defined to be four years from the date of mailing a notice of assessment for all corporations, other than Canadian-controlled private corporations, and three years from the date of mailing of a notice of assessment for Canadian-controlled private corporations and all other taxpayers;

ITA: 152(3.1) Definition of "normal reassessment period"

(3) within three years of the expiration of the normal reassessment period, to allow for carrybacks to an earlier year. This allows the CRA to reassess, for example, for both a given year and any of the previous years to which, for instance, a loss or an investment tax credit may have been carried back;

ITA: 152(6) Reassessment where certain deductions claimed

(4) at any time, if the taxpayer has filed, within the normal assessment period, a waiver of the statutory assessment period. A waiver might be used where the taxpayer wishes to be able to re-open a return for a year in which there was a very complex problem that is expected to take longer than the normal assessment period to sort out. The ability to reassess is *limited* to the matter(s) specified in the waiver, and the waiver can be revoked upon six months' notice;

(5) within three years of the expiration of the normal reassessment period related to a transaction between a taxpayer and a non-arm's length non-resident person (e.g., transfer pricing adjustments). The February 27, 2018 federal Budget proposes to extend this period by three years to allow for adjustments to carrybacks to an earlier year (similar to (3) above).

The normal reassessment period can be summarized as follows.

Taxpayers	Normal reassessment period
Individuals	three years
Trusts	three years
CCPCs	three years
Corporations other than CCPCs	four years

The Act gives the Minister the discretion to reassess beyond "the normal reassessment period" where an application has been made by an individual or a graduated rate estate for a reduction of taxes, interest and penalties. Taxpayers might make such an application where they inadvertently forget to claim a deduction or tax credit. However, it should be remembered that the provision gives the Minister the discretion to either reject or accept the application. In addition, the Minister also has the discretion to waive any assessed interest and penalties. There is a 10-year limit on a reassessment and a waiver in these circumstances.

ITA: 152(4.2) Reassessment with taxpayer's consent, 220(3.1) Waiver of penalty or interest

The Minister is permitted to reassess beyond "the normal reassessment period" in situations where a reassessment within "the normal reassessment period" affects the tax liability for a year which is outside "the normal reassessment period". However, a reassessment of this type is permitted only to the extent that it relates to the change in a particular balance of a taxpayer for a particular year. For example, if the amount of a net capital loss is redetermined by a subsequent assessment within "the normal reassessment period" but impacts on the carryback or carryforward of taxation periods outside of "the normal reassessment period", then the Minister has the authority to reassess those statute-barred taxation years. Obviously, this provision can work either in favour of or to the disadvantage of the taxpayer.

ITA: 152(4.3) Consequential assessment, 152(4.4) Definition of "balance"

Where fraud or misrepresentation is alleged through the issue of a reassessment after the normal assessment period, the onus is on the CRA to prove it if the taxpayer appeals the assessment. However, having proved it, the onus shifts to the taxpayer to show that the assessment of tax resulting from the fraud or misrepresentation is incorrect. In tax matters, the taxpayer always has the burden of proving that an assessment is incorrect, since it is assumed that under our self-assessment system the taxpayer has all of the basic data under his or her own control.[1]

In the case of *M.N.R. v. Taylor*, it was established that the standard of proof need only be that of the "balance of probabilities" used in civil cases rather than the more rigorous standard of "beyond reasonable doubt" used in criminal proceedings.

Cases: *Minister of National Revenue v. Maurice Taylor*, 61 DTC 1139 (EC)

It should also be noted that misrepresentation has been interpreted to include "innocent" misrepresentation, that is, a false statement made in the honest belief that it is true, but under the current wording of the Act it may be more restricted in concept. Finally, it should be noted that where the Minister reassesses beyond the normal reassessment period, the reassessment may only be made in respect of an amount which the taxpayer failed to include in the situation under consideration either for fraud or misrepresentation or for the waiver of the normal reassessment period.

ITA: 152(4.01) Extended period assessment, 152(5) Limitation on assessments

Example Problem 14-4

Mr. Don Godfather filed a personal tax return on April 30, 2018 declaring income of $25,000 for the year ended December 31, 2017. As a result of an investigation, the CRA determined that, at December 31, 2016, Mr. Godfather had total assets estimated at $1,250,000 and total liabilities estimated at $900,000. At December 31, 2017, the taxpayer had total assets estimated at $1,400,000 and total liabilities estimated at $1,025,000. It was also determined by the CRA that a sum of $65,500 represented personal or living expenses of the taxpayer and it was further established that the taxpayer won $10,000 from playing poker with friends during the course of the year.

REQUIRED

(1) What legal right given by the Act does the CRA have to dispute Mr. Godfather's signed declaration of income?

(2) What will the CRA argue is the income of Mr. Godfather for 2017?

(3) What are the possible arguments available to him to substantiate a lower income figure?

SOLUTION

[*See Philippe Tremblay v. M.N.R.*, 54 DTC 132 (T.A.B.).]

(1) The Minister of National Revenue is not bound by a return of information supplied by or on behalf of a taxpayer, and may, notwithstanding such a return of information, assess the taxpayer. It is under this provision that the Minister of National Revenue, where he or she is dissatisfied with a return, makes what are known as arbitrary assessments, in which he or she assesses the income which he or she believes the taxpayer to have had.

ITA: 152(7) Assessment not dependent on return or information

[1] This onus of proof was affirmed in the case of *Violi v. M.N.R.*, 80 DTC 1191 (T.R.B.).

(2) The most common method used is the "net worth" method which involves ascertaining the taxpayer's net worth at the beginning and end of the period. The income for the period is arrived at by adding the increase in net worth to his estimated non-deductible expenditures and deducting non-taxable receipts such as gifts. In the problem at hand, the following estimate of income might be made:

(i) net worth ('16)	= assets ('16) – liabilities ('16)
	= $1,250,000 – $900,000
	= $350,000
(ii) net worth ('17)	= assets ('17) – liabilities ('17)
	= $1,400,000 – $1,025,000
	= $375,000
(iii) increase in net worth	= $375,000 – $350,000 = $25,000
(iv) income	= increase in net worth + personal or living expenses – windfalls
	= $25,000 + $65,500 – $10,000
	= $80,500

(3) The onus is on the taxpayer to show that this assessment is incorrect. The taxpayer might, therefore, argue using appropriate evidence that:

(a) net worth ('16) was actually higher than estimated because assets ('16) were higher or liabilities ('16) were lower;

(b) net worth ('17) was actually lower than estimated because assets ('17) were lower (e.g., they belonged to a spouse) or liabilities ('17) were higher;

(c) personal or living expenses were actually lower than estimated; or

(d) windfalls (e.g., inheritance, gambling winnings) were actually higher.

¶14,120 Refunds and Interest

The Act also requires the Minister to determine the amount of any refund owing to a taxpayer as a result of overpayment of tax. The Minister *may* pay the refund upon assessment but *must* pay it upon application in writing by the taxpayer within the normal reassessment period. However, the Minister is given the authority to make refunds of tax paid beyond "the normal reassessment period". There is a 10-year limit on such refunds. As a practical matter, refunds are generally made by direct deposit or

ITA: 152 Assessment, 164 Refunds, 164(1.5) Exception

cheque mailed out with notices of assessment. If the taxpayer has other tax liabilities, the Minister may apply the refund to that liability.

Interest, compounded daily at the prescribed rate shown in Exhibit 14-1, is paid in most cases on overpayments of tax from the latest of: ITA: 164(3) Interest on refunds and repayments

(1) the day the overpayment arose;

(2) for individuals, 30 days after the balance-due day for the year, which is April 30 of the following year;

(3) for corporations, 120 days after the end of the taxation year; and

(4) where the return was filed after the filing-due date, 30 days after the date the return was filed for individuals, and the day the return was filed for corporations.

Where a refund arose from a loss carryback or other provision that changed the tax payable in a previous year, no interest is payable for the period prior to the filing of the tax return for the subsequent year in which the loss was established. Similar rules are provided for other carryback provisions in the Act. The effect of the loss carryback is also ignored in computing interest charged on deficient instalments in that carryback year. ITA: 164(5) Effect of carryback of loss, etc., 164(5.1) Interest — disputed amounts, 161(7) Effect of carryback of loss, etc.

Note that any refund interest received is taxable as interest income in the year received.

¶14,120.99 Practise What You've Learned

Refer to the following sections of the Study Guide to practise what you've learned:

¶14,825 — Multiple Choice Questions

- Question 2 — Normal reassessment period — Corporation
- Question 6 — Notice of reassessment

¶14,850 — Exercises

- Exercise 2 — Windfalls
- Exercise 7 — Compare interest paid to and by CRA
- Exercise 11 — Interest on tax refunds

¶14,200 Rights of the Taxpayer

¶14,210 Objections and Appeals

A taxpayer may discover that the CRA disagrees with his or her calculation of tax payable either when a CRA auditor questions particular items (more usual for large corporations which routinely undergo an audit every few years) or when a notice of assessment or reassessment is received. If matters cannot be resolved favourably through informal negotiation, the next step is to file a notice of objection. All taxpayers, except individuals, must file a notice of objection within 90 days of the mailing of the notice of assessment. ITA: 165(1)(b)

The due date for the notice of objection for individuals and a graduated rate estate is the later of:

(1) one year after the filing-due date of the taxpayer for the year; and

(2) 90 days after the day of mailing of the notice of assessment.

The "filing-due date" is defined to be the day on or before which the taxpayer's return for the year is required to be filed as summarized in ¶14,015.10.

ITA: 248(1) filing-due date

Deadlines for the filing of a Notice of Objection are summarized as follows.

Taxpayers	Notice of objection due date
Individuals & a graduated rate estate	Later of: - Mailing date on the Notice + 90 days - Tax return filing-due date + 1 year
Other taxpayers	Mailing date on the Notice + 90 days

Even if the dispute appears headed for a favourable resolution, taxpayers often file a notice of objection as protection if the 90-day period is about to expire. Limits are placed upon the right to object to assessments and determinations in respect of court decisions and specified provisions.

ITA: 165(1.1) Limitation of right to object to assessments or determinations, 165(1.2) Limitation on objections

A notice of objection can be delivered or mailed to the Chief of Appeals in a Tax Services Office or Taxation Centre of the CRA. The objection may be submitted on Form T400A. The use of this form is not mandatory. The only requirement is that the notice must contain the facts and reasons for the appeal. Large corporations are required to provide extensive detail on the notice of objection and pay 50% of the tax amount assessed. The notice of objection is limited for individuals and trusts to assessments under Part I of the Act, individual surtax and tax on Old Age Security benefits.

ITA: 164(1.1) Repayment on objections and appeals, 165(1.11) Objections by large corporations, 165(2) Service, 165(2.1) Application

¶14,220 Amended Returns

The Act does not provide general procedures for filing an amended tax return, other than:

- situations relating to reassessments where options granted by a taxpayer are exercised in a subsequent year;

ITA: 49(4) Reassessment where option exercised in subsequent year

- a situation which requires the Minister to amend a return if a loss or tax credit is being carried back to that year; and

ITA: 152(6) Reassessment where certain deductions claimed

- situations relating to amendments made by a legal representative of a deceased taxpayer.

ITA: 164(6) Disposition by legal representative of deceased

With respect to the carryback of a loss, it should be noted that the Minister is only required to do so if the prescribed form (e.g., the T1A for individuals or T2A for corporations) or an amended return is filed by the date the tax return for the year the loss is incurred is required to be filed.

To amend other items, if the 90-day period for filing a Notice of Objection has not expired, the return may be amended by filing the Notice of Objection. Otherwise, the CRA's administrative policy is that a return may only be amended if the taxpayer makes a written request for a refund within three years of the end of the year in question and:

Information Circulars: IC 75-7R3 Reassessment of a return of income

(1) the CRA is satisfied that the previous assessment was wrong;

(2) the reassessment can be made within the normal reassessment period or the taxpayer has filed a waiver;

(3) the requested decrease in taxable income assessed is not based solely on a permissive deduction such as an increased claim for capital cost allowance where the taxpayer originally claimed less than the allowable amount; and

(4) application for a refund is not based solely on a successful appeal to the courts by another taxpayer.

Often, a previous assessment was not wrong but the taxpayer wishes to amend the discretionary deductions he or she claimed (or failed to claim) in a previous year. For example, a company in a loss position may choose not to claim capital cost allowance in the loss year because unclaimed capital cost allowance can be carried forward indefinitely whereas non-capital losses expire in twenty years. Two years later, the company may find itself profitable, and may wish to claim the capital cost allowance for the previous year to increase the loss carryforward.

The CRA allows such amendments to change discretionary deductions where the amendment would not alter taxes payable for that year. Where a loss is increased by claiming additional capital cost allowance, no increase in taxes payable could, of course, result.

Information Circulars: IC 84-1 Revision of capital cost allowance claims and other permissive deductions

¶14,220.99 Practise What You've Learned

Refer to the following sections of the Study Guide to practise what you've learned:

¶14,825 — Multiple Choice Questions

- Question 3 — Notice of objection — Individual

¶14,850 — Exercises

- Exercise 9 — Appeal procedure

¶14,300 Obligations of Payers and Other Persons

¶14,310 Employers

Every person paying salary, wages, or other remuneration or any of the other amounts listed in section 153 is required to withhold prescribed amounts from the payments and remit them to the Receiver General. Where the average monthly remittances, including CPP and EI premiums, in the second preceding calendar year are between $25,000 and $100,000, tax withheld from remuneration paid in the first 15 days of a month is due on

ITR: 108(1.1)

the 25th of that month, and from remuneration paid in the balance of the month on the 10th of the following month. Where the average monthly remittances in any particular month exceed $100,000, employers are required to remit up to four times a month.

A regulation relaxes these rules on an elective basis as follows:

(1) employers with average monthly remittances in the preceding calendar year of less than $25,000 are required to remit on the 15th of the month following payment; and ITR: 108(1)

(2) employers with average monthly remittances between $25,000 and $100,000 for the preceding calendar year (and over $100,000 in the second preceding year) are allowed to remit on the 25th and 10th days as described above. ITR: 108(1.11)

Small employers with average monthly withholding amounts of less than $3,000 for the second preceding calendar year and no compliance irregularities in the preceding 12 months are allowed to remit quarterly. Remittances for each quarter are due April 15, July 15, October 15, and the following January 15. ITR: 108(1.12)

The employee completes a TD1 form listing personal credits and certain other deductible amounts, and the withholding amount is based on gross salary less these amounts. The amounts of withholding on both periodic and lump-sum payments are prescribed. The employee can elect to increase the amount withheld if he or she so chooses. Lump-sum payments such as bonuses require tax withholdings (combined federal and provincial) of 10% for bonuses up to $5,000, 20% for bonuses above $5,000 up to $15,000, and 30% thereafter (for all provinces other than Quebec). ITA: 153(1.1) Undue hardship; ITR: 103(4), 100 Interpretation

In addition, the Act provides for a reduction in the amount withheld if the amount required to be withheld would cause "undue hardship". The CRA district offices will generally approve applications by employees for reduced withholding if a *pro forma* tax return indicates that a substantial refund will be forthcoming due to substantiated deductions such as RRSP contributions or support payments. ITR: 205 Date Returns to be Filed

The payer is also required to file information returns as prescribed. Employers, for example, must complete forms T4 Summary and T4 Supplementary by the last day in February, and send two copies of the T4 Supplementary to the employee.

Every person paying a fee, commission or other amount to a non-resident in respect of services rendered in Canada is required to withhold 15%. Non-residents exempt from paying Canadian tax by virtue of the Act or a tax treaty can apply for a waiver of this requirement. ITR: 105 Non-Residents

While paragraph 153(1)(*a*) requires an employer to withhold on payments of "salary, wages, or other remuneration", stock option benefits appear to escape this withholding requirement because the employer does not "pay" this form of remuneration. As a result, the provision in subsection 153(1.01) is required to consider a stock option benefit to have been remuneration paid as a bonus. This makes the stock option benefit subject to withholding. ITA: 153(1)(a), 153(1.01) Withholding — stock option benefits

Any person required to withhold by section 153 who fails to withhold tax is liable for a penalty of 10% of the tax that should have been withheld, together with interest. A second or further occurrence of failure to withhold under section 153 will result in a penalty of 20% of the tax that should have been withheld. Withholding taxes will only be considered to have been received on time if received by the due date (i.e., postmarks will not suffice). Any person who withheld tax but failed to remit it is required to pay, in addition to the ITA: 227(8) Penalty, 227(9) Penalty, 248(7) Receipt of things mailed;

tax withheld, a penalty of 10% of the amount that should have been remitted. Once again, the penalty doubles to 20% of the tax withheld for second-time offenders. If a taxpayer had tax withheld at source and the withholder did not remit the amount, the CRA cannot require the taxpayer to pay the amount. See, for example, *Lalonde v. M.N.R.*, in which the employee was paid in cash and the employer neither remitted the tax nor provided a T4 or other documentation that tax had been withheld. Cases: *Robert Lalonde v. M.N.R.*, 82 DTC 1772 (T.R.B.)

Example Problem 14-5

The *Toronto Gazette* employs a number of foreign correspondents who are often required to report from war zones. On September 30, 2018, "Ace" Johnson, a veteran reporter, is killed while reporting from Iraq. The *Gazette* decides to continue his monthly salary of $4,000 to his widow for the balance of 2018.

REQUIRED

What are the obligations of the *Gazette* in terms of withholding tax under the Act?

SOLUTION

The payer is required to withhold tax on a death benefit, which is defined as an amount received "upon or after the death of an employee in recognition of the employee's service". The amount of withholding for periodic payments of remuneration is prescribed. Remuneration is defined as including a death benefit. However, the definition of death benefit excludes the lesser of $10,000 or the amount received as the death benefit. Thus, withholding would only be required on the amount received in excess of $10,000 (i.e., $2,000 = ($4,000 × 3) – $10,000, in this case). ITR: 103(4)

¶14,320 Obligations of Other Payers, Trustees, etc.

¶14,322 Liability of Directors

Where a corporation has failed to: ITA: 227.1 Liability of directors for failure to deduct

- deduct or withhold certain amounts under the Act,
- remit such amounts, or
- pay certain amounts of tax for a taxation year,

the directors of the corporation at the time that the corporation was required to deduct, withhold, remit, or pay are jointly and severally liable together with the corporation to pay the amount and any interest or penalties relating to it. Note that the liability of the director does not include the corporation's ordinary liability for Part I tax. Joint and several liability means that each director is liable for the amount of the liability, although the liability can be shared among directors. This liability is limited to situations in which the corporation is being dissolved or the corporation has made an assignment in bankruptcy.

A director is not liable for a failure of the corporation, where the director exercised the degree of care, diligence, and skill to prevent the failure that a reasonably prudent person would have exercised in comparable circumstances. Any proceedings to recover an amount from a director must be commenced within two years after the director ceased to be a director.

¶14,324 Taxpayer's Legal Representative

Before making a distribution of a taxpayer's property, the taxpayer's representative, with possession or control of the property, must obtain a clearance certificate from the CRA. The certificate certifies that all amounts owed or expected to be owed by the taxpayer have been paid or secured in a manner acceptable to the CRA. If the taxpayer's legal representative fails to obtain a clearance certificate, the legal representative is personally liable for the payment of the amounts owed by the taxpayer to the extent of the value of the property distributed. For example, an executor who distributes property of an estate without obtaining a clearance certificate is personally liable for the deceased's unpaid taxes and interest. A trustee in bankruptcy is excluded from the application of this provision.

ITA: 159(2) Certificate before distribution, 159(3) Personal liability

¶14,325 Payments to Residents of Canada

The Act allows the Governor in Council to make any regulations requiring "any class of person to make information returns respecting any class of information required in connection with assessment under the Act". The provisions also require any such person to supply copies of the information to the person whose income is being reported. The Minister is allowed to demand a prescribed information return, and penalties for failure to make such returns are prescribed. In addition, the offences on which penalties are imposed apply to failure to make information returns, or giving false information on such returns.

ITA: 221(1)(d), 162(7) Failure to comply, 233 Information return, 238 Offences and punishment, 239 Other offences and punishment

Regulations prescribe which persons are required to make information returns, and other information such as filing dates. In addition to employers, these regulations affect payers of interest, dividends and royalties and persons making payments to non-residents. Other persons required to make information returns include trustees of RRSPs and other deferred income plans. Unless otherwise indicated, such returns are due the last day of February (e.g., the T5 Summary and Supplementary in respect of dividends and interest).

ITR: 200 Remuneration and Benefits

Promoters of tax shelters are required to file an information return in prescribed form containing information on the persons who acquired interests and the amount paid for each interest. There are also filing requirements for partnerships and securities dealers handling sales of shares, commodities, etc., with penalties for failure to file, as discussed earlier.

ITA: 237.1 [Tax shelters]; ITR: 229 Partnership Return, 230 Security Transactions

Ⓐ ¶14,330 Payments to Non-Residents

The Act specifies the payments on which tax must be withheld by Canadians remitting amounts to non-residents. The rate of withholding specified is 25%, but this is often reduced or eliminated by the applicable tax treaty. Such payers are also required to file information returns (e.g., NR4 Summary and Supplementary). Some forms of interest payments are subject to withholding tax. However, all arm's length payments of interest to non-residents are exempted from this withholding tax. Also exempted are interest payments to non-arm's length U.S. residents under the treaty between Canada and the United States.

ITA: 212 Tax, 212(1)(b) Interest; Information Circulars: IC 76-12R6 Applicable Rate of Part XIII Tax on Amounts Paid or Credited to Persons in Countries with which Canada has a Tax Convention

Non-residents receiving rent from real property in Canada or a timber royalty in Canada can elect to file a Canadian income tax return reporting the net rental or royalty income, rather than paying the flat withholding tax (under Part XIII) on the gross rents or royalties. There are no personal credits permitted on such returns, but the graduated tax rates do apply to individuals. A return must be filed within two years from the end of the year in which the rent or royalty was paid and is in addition to any other returns that may be required under Part I. While withholdings must still be made by the non-resident's agent on the gross rent or royalty, the election allows for a refund of excess Part XIII tax withheld, where Part I tax on the net rental or royalty income is lower.

ITA: 216 Alternatives re rents and timber royalties, 215(3) Idem

If, in addition to the general election, the non-resident files an election on form NR6 with the CRA, committing to file a Canadian return relating to the rents or royalties, an agent for the non-resident can withhold tax on the basis of net (instead of gross) income. However, the same withholding rate applies. In this case, the tax return must be filed within six months from the end of the year that the rents or royalties are paid.

ITA: 216 Alternatives re rents and timber royalties, 216(4) Optional method of payment

Failure to withhold, remit, or file information returns results in the same penalties imposed on persons making payments to residents in Canada.

¶14,335 Foreign Reporting Requirements

The Act imposes reporting requirements on Canadian corporations with respect to transactions with non-arm's length non-residents to be filed within six months from the end of the year.

ITA: 233.1 [Reporting for non-arm's length transactions with non-residents]

Canadian taxpayers and partnerships are required to report certain information relating to foreign investments.

The Act requires a person who transfers or loans property to certain foreign trusts to file information returns. Certain resident taxpayers and partnerships are required to file information returns relating to foreign property held, if the cost of such property exceeds $100,000. Resident taxpayers and partnerships are required to file information returns with respect to foreign affiliates Certain Canadian entities that own a beneficial interest in a non-resident trust and are not required to file an information return for transfers or loans to a foreign trust are required to file an information return in each year they receive a distribution from or become indebted to the trust.

ITA: 233.2 [Reporting for loans or transfers to non-resident trusts], 233.3 [Reporting for ownership of specified foreign property], 233.4 [Reporting in respect of foreign affiliates], 233.5 Due diligence exception

There are penalties for failure to file such returns and for providing false statements or omissions in these information returns.

ITA: 162(7) Failure to comply, 162(10.1) Additional penalty, 163 [Repeated failures, false statements and omissions]

Example Problem 14-6

Reconsider the previous example problem.

REQUIRED

If the death benefit had been paid to a resident of the U.K. instead of Canada, what would the withholding tax requirement have been?

SOLUTION

A 25% withholding tax is imposed on a death benefit as defined by the Act (i.e., the amount in excess of $10,000). The Canada–U.K. Tax Convention is silent on the issue of death benefits and, thus, the 25% rate would still apply. ITA: 212(1)(j) Benefits

¶14,335.99 Practise What You've Learned

Refer to the following sections of the Study Guide to practise what you've learned:

¶14,825 — Multiple Choice Questions

- Question 1 — Withholding tax requirements

¶14,850 — Exercises

- Exercise 10 — Rents earned by non-resident
- Exercise 17 — Taxation of non-resident; Filing due dates
- Exercise 18 — Taxation of non-resident; Filing due dates

¶14,340 Deceased Taxpayers

According to the CPA Knowledge Supplement, the topics of returns for deceased taxpayers is viewed as an advanced topic to be introduced in the core level and covered in detail in the *elective* stage. Therefore, our advanced symbol (Ⓐ) in this section identifies material within these subjects that is more complex and non-routine in nature.

A number of special rules apply to tax returns and payment of tax for deceased taxpayers. Note that rules governing the deemed disposition of the deceased's capital property are covered in Chapter 7, ¶7,300.

¶14,345 Tax Returns

There are two provisions which govern the filing of deceased taxpayers' tax returns. Where the individual has died after October of a year and on or before the usual filing due date for the year (i.e., April 30 or June 15 of the following year), the individual's legal representative has six months or until the day the return would otherwise have to be filed, whichever is later, to file the return. Where the taxpayer has died outside of this time period, the normal filing deadline of April 30 (or June 15 where the deceased individual or his or her spouse carried on business in the year) is imposed. The key to understanding how these two provisions interact is to identify the particular tax return year to which these rules apply.

ITA: 150(1)(b) Deceased individuals, 150(1)(d) Individuals

¶14,345.10 Prior Taxation Year

Where the taxpayer has died in the period from January 1 to the usual filing due date for the prior year, the legal representative of the taxpayer has six months after the date of death to file a tax return for the immediately preceding year and pay the balance of tax. For example, for a taxpayer who died on March 1, 2018 without filing his or her 2017 tax return, the return and balance would be due September 1, 2018.

ITA: 150(1)(b) Deceased individuals

¶14,345.20 Terminal Return

The legal representative of the taxpayer must also file a final or terminal return for the period in the year to the date of death (e.g., January 1 to March 1 in the above example). The deadline for the terminal return and the payment of any balance owing depends on the date of death. For those persons who have died between January 1 and October 31, the terminal return is due April 30 or June 15 of the following year. For those persons who have died between November 1 and December 15, the terminal return is due 6 months from the date of death, or in the case of an individual who carried on business in the year, June 15, and for deaths between December 16 and December 31, six months from the date of death. Therefore, in the example of a death on March 1, 2018, the terminal return for 2018 is due April 30 or June 15, 2019. No instalments are required in respect of a terminal return.

Amounts in respect of periodic payments, such as interest, rent, salary, etc., must be accrued on a daily basis to the date of death and reported on the terminal return.

ITA: 70(1) Death of a taxpayer

The full year's personal tax credits may be claimed, although the taxpayer was alive for only part of the year. The reserves that may be claimed on a terminal return are limited.

ITA: 72 Reserves, etc., for year of death

¶14,350 Rights or Things

The legal representative of the taxpayer is allowed to report the income from "rights or things" of the deceased on a separate tax return. The return is due on the date that is the later of one year after death and 90 days after assessment of any return for the year of death. This alternative return is generally advantageous, since personal tax credits equal to those claimed in the terminal return may be claimed on the rights or things return as well as on the terminal return, in addition to the benefit of lower marginal tax brackets on both returns.

ITA: 70(2) Amounts receivable, 118(1) Personal credits, 118(2) Age credit, 118.93 Credits in separate returns

Rights or things are amounts which are receivable at the date of death but have not been received, such as:

- matured, uncashed bond coupons;
- declared, unpaid dividends;
- declared, unpaid salary, commissions, and vacation pay if owed to the deceased on the date of death and if pertaining to pay periods *completed* before the date of death;

- lump-sum payments out of a pension plan; and
- partner's right to a share of income of a partnership to the date of death.

Alternatively, the legal representative can assign, under the directions of a will, the income from "rights or things" to a particular beneficiary or beneficiaries. However, the income must be distributed to the beneficiary prior to the expiry of the deadline for the rights or things election as described above. This alternative would be advantageous where the beneficiary would be taxed at a lower rate as compared to the rights or things election for a separate return of the deceased.

ITA: 70(2) Amounts receivable, 70(3) Rights or things transferred to beneficiaries

The CRA states that where there is genuine doubt about whether the income is a periodic payment or a right or thing, its treatment is generally resolved in favour of the taxpayer.

Interpretation Bulletins: IT-212R3 Income of Deceased Persons — Rights or Things

Rights or things do not include accrued periodic amounts taxable in the terminal return. With the provision of acceptable security, tax owing on a rights or things return may be paid in up to 10 annual instalments. Of course, interest will be charged until the balance owing is paid in full.

ITA: 70(1) Death of a taxpayer, 159(5) Election where certain provisions applicable, 70(2) Amounts receivable

¶14,355 Other Return

One other return may be used to report income of the deceased taxpayer.

Beneficiaries of a trust report their trust income based on the income earned by the trust in the trust year that ends in the taxation year of the beneficiary. Also, a testamentary trust that is a graduated rate estate can have a year end other than December 31 as long as the first year end chosen is not more than 12 months from the death of the individual who created the trust. As a result, an individual beneficiary of the trust who dies after the trust year end will have to report not only the income from the trust (12 months), but also any further income earned by the trust after the trust year end and before the date of death that is payable to the deceased individual. For example, assume that a graduated rate estate had a year end of March 31, 2018, and that the sole beneficiary died on July 31, 2018. On the final return, the deceased would report the 12 months of income from the trust year that ended March 31, plus the four months of income earned by the trust from March 31 to July 31. To alleviate this burden, the Act allows the representative of the deceased to file a separate return that includes the "stub period" income, being that income earned by the trust from March 31 to July 31.

ITA: 104(23) Deceased beneficiary of graduated rate estate, 104(23)(d)

In this case, personal tax credits equal to those claimed in the terminal return may be claimed in the separate return.

ITA: 118(1) Personal credits, 118(2) Age credit, 118.93 Credits in separate returns

This return is due on the date that is the later of six months after the date of death and April 30 or June 15 of the year following the year of death.

¶14,360 Personal Tax Credits

As previously noted, the personal tax credits can be claimed on all of the three tax returns. This includes the basic personal credit, the married or equivalent-to-married credit, the infirm dependant credit and the age credit. The marital status tax credit must be reduced by the income of the surviving spouse for the full year of death in excess of the threshold for that credit. For the remainder of the credits, the claim on the terminal return and the elective returns, combined, cannot exceed the credits that could have been claimed on the terminal return, if no elective returns were filed. Some credits can only be claimed on the return on which the related income is reported (e.g., pension credit, CPP and EI

ITA: 118(1) Personal credits, 118(2) Age credit, 118.93 Credits in separate returns, 118.8 Transfer of unused credits to spouse or common-law partner; Interpretation Bulletins: IT-513R Personal Tax Credits

credits). Note that the credit for the transfer of unused credits for a spouse can only be deducted in the terminal return according to CRA administrative practice.

¶14,365 Summary of Filing Deadlines

The following summarizes the returns and respective filing deadlines for deceased individuals:

Income Tax Return	Filing date
Prior taxation year	Later of six months after the date of death and April 30 or June 15 of the year following the year for which the return is being filed (i.e., the usual filing deadline for that year).
Terminal or final return	Later of six months after death and April 30 or June 15 of the year following the year of death (i.e., the usual filing deadline for the year of death).
Rights or things return	Later of one year after death and 90 days after assessment of any return for theyear of death.
Trust beneficiary's return	Later of six months after the date of death and April 30 or June 15 of the year following the year of death (i.e., the usual filing deadline for the year of death).

¶14,365.99 Practise What You've Learned

Refer to the following sections of the Study Guide to practise what you've learned:

¶14,825 — Multiple Choice Questions

- Question 4 — Final return due date

¶14,850 — Exercises

- Exercise 12 — Death of a taxpayer
- Exercise 13 — Death of a taxpayer
- Exercise 19 — Deceased taxpayer

CHAPTER 15

Corporate Distributions, Windings-Up, and Sales

ADVANCED CONTENT IN THIS CHAPTER

Ⓐ The Effect of Corporate Law ¶15,035

Ⓐ Deemed Dividends and Capital Gains on PUC Reductions ¶15,170

Learning Goals

Know

By the end of this chapter you will know:

- The basic provisions of corporate surplus and the implication of its distribution.

Understand and Explain

By the end of this chapter you will understand and be able to explain:

- The tax paid or tax-free components of corporate surplus.
- The process for analyzing the tax consequences of selling the assets or shares of a corporation.

Apply

By the end of this chapter you will be able to apply your knowledge and understanding to:

- Calculate the corporate surplus components and the tax consequences of its distribution.
- Calculate whether the shareholders should sell shares or assets of a corporation.

Review Questions
¶15,800 in the Study Guide

Multiple Choice Questions
¶15,825 in the Study Guide

Exercises
¶15,850 in the Study Guide

Assignment Problems
¶15,875 in the Study Guide

OVERVIEW

This chapter deals primarily with transactions between corporations and their shareholders involving the accumulated surplus of a corporation or the value of its shares. The discussion begins with distributions of corporate surplus. The chapter follows with a discussion of the winding-up of a corporation and the sale of a corporation in terms of assets or shares. This chapter will introduce only the general concepts and the basic calculations, rather than cover all aspects of the topics.

The following chart will help to locate the major provisions of the Act discussed in this chapter.

PART I — DIVISION B, SUBDIVISION h

CORPORATIONS RESIDENT IN CANADA AND THEIR SHAREHOLDERS

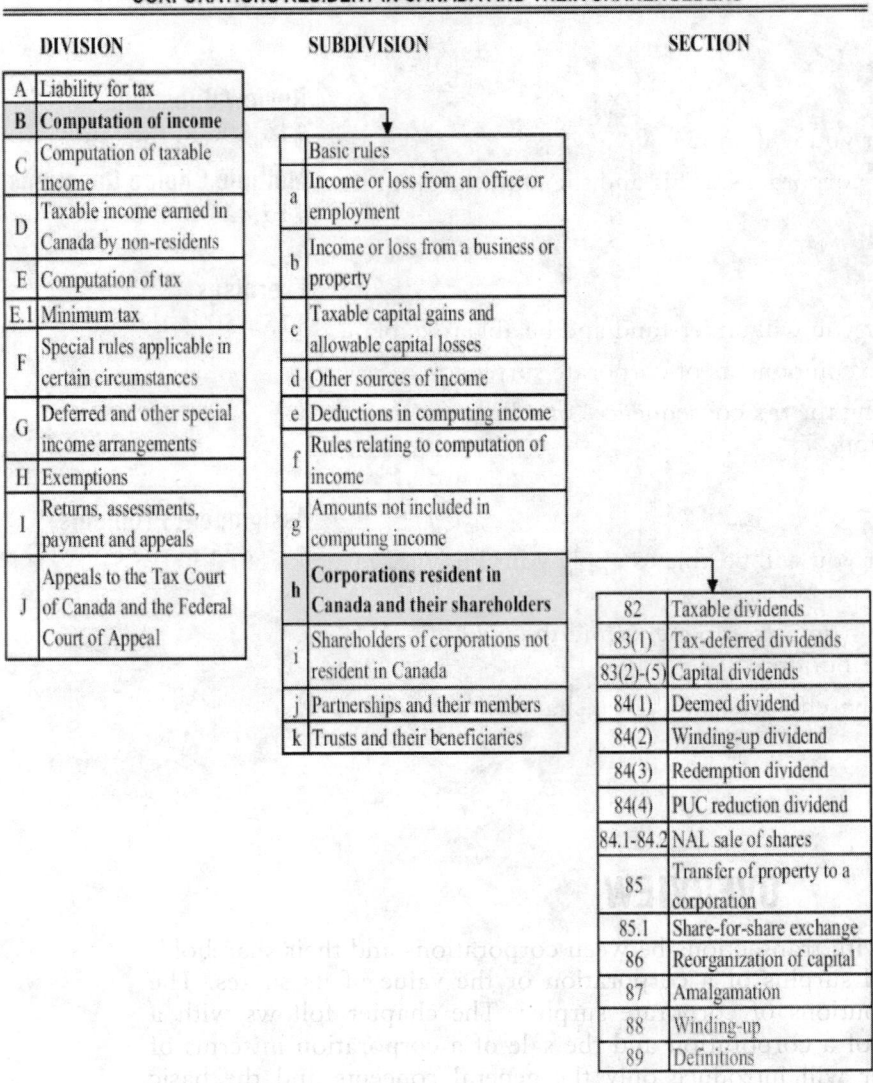

DIVISION

A	Liability for tax
B	**Computation of income**
C	Computation of taxable income
D	Taxable income earned in Canada by non-residents
E	Computation of tax
E.1	Minimum tax
F	Special rules applicable in certain circumstances
G	Deferred and other special income arrangements
H	Exemptions
I	Returns, assessments, payment and appeals
J	Appeals to the Tax Court of Canada and the Federal Court of Appeal

SUBDIVISION

	Basic rules
a	Income or loss from an office or employment
b	Income or loss from a business or property
c	Taxable capital gains and allowable capital losses
d	Other sources of income
e	Deductions in computing income
f	Rules relating to computation of income
g	Amounts not included in computing income
h	**Corporations resident in Canada and their shareholders**
i	Shareholders of corporations not resident in Canada
j	Partnerships and their members
k	Trusts and their beneficiaries

SECTION

82	Taxable dividends
83(1)	Tax-deferred dividends
83(2)-(5)	Capital dividends
84(1)	Deemed dividend
84(2)	Winding-up dividend
84(3)	Redemption dividend
84(4)	PUC reduction dividend
84.1-84.2	NAL sale of shares
85	Transfer of property to a corporation
85.1	Share-for-share exchange
86	Reorganization of capital
87	Amalgamation
88	Winding-up
89	Definitions

¶15,000 Corporate Surplus Balances

¶15,010 Overview

The shareholders' equity section of a balance sheet has to be analyzed to arrive at the balances in the tax surplus accounts. The basic components are share capital and equity. Exhibit 15-1 is a schematic representation of a tax-basis balance sheet.

Exhibit 15-1 Tax Basis Balance Sheet

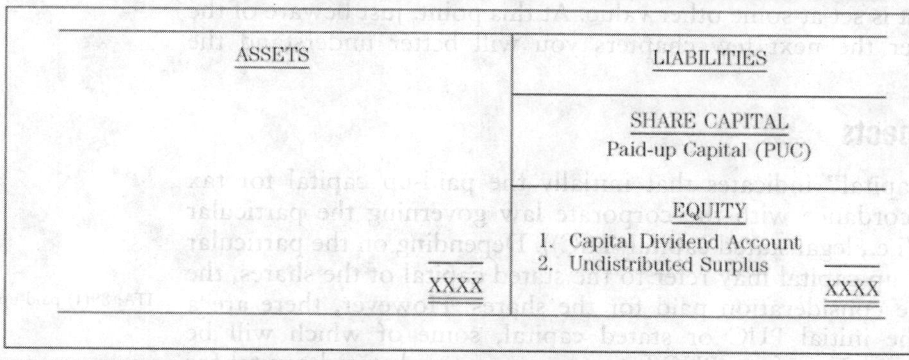

ASSETS
LIABILITIES
SHARE CAPITAL
Paid-up Capital (PUC)
EQUITY
1. Capital Dividend Account
2. Undistributed Surplus
XXXX
XXXX

Equity can be subdivided into two amounts. The capital dividend account (CDA) generally represents the non-taxed portion of net capital gains. This account provides for the integration of capital gains through a private corporation as discussed in a previous chapter. The other amount might be termed "undistributed surplus" because it has no special tax surplus designation. It consists primarily of income generated and not distributed through dividends or other means.

Corporate surpluses can be distributed in a variety of ways. Paid-up capital, discussed below, can be returned as a tax-free capital receipt to shareholders under certain conditions. The capital dividend account of a private corporation can be used to pay tax-free dividends through an election. Finally, most distributions of corporate surplus are made in the form of taxable dividends. ITA: 83(2) Capital dividend

¶15,020 Paid-Up Capital of Shares

¶15,025 The Tax Concept

Paid-up capital (PUC) is an important tax concept. It is the amount which the corporation can return to the shareholder without it being reported as a dividend to the shareholder. The rationale for this tax-free return is that PUC was contributed from the after-tax funds of the shareholder on the initial investment in corporate shares. Therefore, PUC should not be taxed as a dividend on its return to the shareholder. However, on a *disposition* of shares by the shareholder it is the adjusted cost base, not the paid-up capital that is used to determine the gain or loss.

It should be noted that much confusion surrounds the tax term "paid-up capital" because this concept is also used in accounting and in corporate law. In accounting it is called share capital, and it reflects the capital contributed to the corporation. However, in related-party transactions, the amount recorded as share capital may be different than that recorded for tax purposes. In corporate law it is called legal stated capital and usually reflects the value of the property contributed to the corporation in exchange for shares. For example, if you were to buy shares from a corporation for $1,000, then the paid-up capital, share capital, and legal stated capital should all be the same at $1,000. However, assume that you contributed a piece of property that you have owned for some time to the corporation and received only shares in exchange. Also, assume that the fair market value of the property is $1,000 and the cost base to you is $600. If the corporation is a related corporation under accounting standards, the paid-up capital for tax purposes will be $1,000, the share capital for accounting purposes will be $600, and the legal stated capital will be $1,000, unless it is set at some other value. At this point, just beware of the potential for differences. Over the next few chapters you will better understand the differences.

¶15,030 Technical Tax Aspects

The definition of "paid-up capital" indicates that initially the paid-up capital for tax purposes is determined in accordance with the corporate law governing the particular corporation under discussion (i.e., legal stated capital (LSC)). Depending on the particular corporate law, the initial paid-up capital may refer to the stated capital of the shares, the par value of the shares or the consideration paid for the shares. However, there are a number of adjustments to the initial PUC or stated capital, some of which will be examined in subsequent chapters. Therefore, PUC for tax purposes and stated capital for accounting purposes may not be the same. These differences are seldom disclosed in the notes to the financial statements.

ITA: 89(1) paid-up capital

Note that paragraph (*a*) in the definition of PUC defines the paid-up capital of a share in terms of the average paid-up capital of the entire class. As a result, the paid-up capital of a particular share may not be the same amount as that paid for the share on its original issue. Further issues of shares from the same class at different amounts will change the paid-up capital of a particular share after such subsequent issues. Hence, the paid-up capital per share is an average, over time, of issue prices of shares in a particular class.

ITA: 89(1) Definitions

Consider the following example for illustrative purposes.

Joe incorporated Smithco Inc. five years ago and paid $1,000 to the corporation for 1,000 common shares. His ACB of these shares is $1,000 and the PUC at the corporate level is $1,000.

This year Joe needed additional capital for expansion. Bill agreed to invest $100,000 for an additional 1,000 fully-paid common shares to be issued from Smithco Inc. After this transaction, Joe will still have an ACB on his 1,000 shares of $1,000. Bill will have an ACB on his 1,000 common shares of $100,000. At the corporate level the PUC will be $101,000. Since the PUC is allocated equally among the shares of that class it means that Joe's shares have a PUC of $50,500 and Bill's shares have a PUC of $50,500.

¶15,035 The Effect of Corporate Law

Most jurisdictions in Canada now permit only shares without par value. Examples of such corporate laws are the *Canada Business Corporations Act*, the *Ontario Business Corporations Act* and the *Alberta Business Corporations Act*. With respect to corporations governed by such Acts, the PUC is the "stated capital" as determined by the directors of the corporation. Generally, this stated capital will be the fair market value of the consideration for which the shares were issued. However, these statutes provide that, in connection with certain non-arm's length transactions, the corporation may establish a stated capital amount which is less than the consideration for which the shares were issued. This reduced stated capital (i.e., less than the fair market value of the consideration received) will then be the initial amount of PUC for tax purposes. Accordingly, a corporation may, under most jurisdictions, establish shares with a low PUC and a high redemption amount (commonly referred to as "high-low shares"). In a few situations, the corporate law may not permit the creation of such shares and, in such event, it will be necessary for an alternative approach to be considered. The significance of these shares will become more evident when the topic of redemption of shares is discussed later in the chapter.

In jurisdictions which permit both par value and no par value shares to be issued, the PUC with respect to the par value shares will generally be equal to the par value of the shares. When such par value shares are issued for property with a fair market value greater than the par value of the shares such surplus amount (contributed surplus in accounting terms) can be converted to paid-up capital as long as the transaction(s) was (were) not accomplished on a (tax-free) rollover basis. Amounts so converted will have been contributed to the corporation with after-tax or tax-paid property and, hence, should logically be accessible on distribution to shareholders on a tax-free basis. Generally, the PUC with respect to the no par value or stated value shares will be equal to the fair market value of the property transferred to the corporation and for which the corporation issued such shares, except for certain reorganizations with non-arm's length parties, as previously mentioned.

ITA: 84(1)(c.3)

¶15,040 Effect of PUC on a Redemption of Shares

The PUC is computed at the corporate level (not the shareholder level) by reference to all the shares of a particular class. However, the amount of paid-up capital is relevant to any shareholder on a redemption or cancellation of the shares. These events might occur when some of the shares of the corporation are redeemed or when all of the shares are, in essence, redeemed and cancelled on the winding-up of a corporation. On the other hand, the adjusted cost base is calculated only for the shares held by a particular shareholder (i.e., at the shareholder level, not the corporate level) and is relevant only where there is a disposition or deemed disposition of the shares. However, since a redemption or cancellation of shares involves a disposition of the shares held by a shareholder, any deemed dividend arising on the redemption or cancellation must be removed in calculating the resultant capital gain or loss. (Refer to the definition of proceeds of disposition.) That deemed dividend is subject to tax, as a dividend, separately and should not be double-counted in the capital gain or loss.

ITA: 84(2) Distribution on winding-up, etc., 84(3) Redemption, etc.

Share redemption follows a two-step process:

Step 1: There is a deemed dividend if the redemption proceeds exceed the PUC of the shares being redeemed.

Step 2: There is a capital gain or capital loss when the adjusted proceeds (actual proceeds minus the deemed dividend) differ from the ACB of the shares being redeemed.

Refer to ¶15,165.30 for more details.

Consider the previous example of Joe and Bill.

The following shows the adjusted cost base, paid-up capital, and fair market value of their shares immediately after Bill buys his 1,000 common shares. It then shows the tax implications if Joe and Bill each redeem their shares (i.e., the company uses corporate funds to buy the shares from them).

	# of Shares	ACB	PUC	FMV
Joe	1,000	$1,000	$50,500	$100,000
Bill	1,000	$100,000	$50,500	$100,000

	Redemption	Joe	Bill
(1)	Deemed dividend:		
	Proceeds	$100,000	$100,000
	Paid-up capital	(50,500)	(50,500)
	Deemed dividend (A)	$49,500	$49,500
(2)	Capital gain (loss):		
	Proceeds	$100,000	$100,000
	Deemed dividend	(49,500)	(49,500)
	Adjusted proceeds	$50,500	$50,500
	Adjusted cost base	(1,000)	(100,000)
	Capital gain (loss) (B)	$49,500	(49,500)
A + B		$99,000	—

As you can see, Joe will recognize his full "economic gain" of $99,000 as a combination of deemed dividend and capital gain. Bill did not have an economic gain on the disposal, but, because the paid-up capital is allocated equally at the corporate level to each share of that class issued while adjusted cost base is calculated at the individual shareholder level, the nature of the income on redemption is not what you would otherwise expect. In fact, it may not be "fair" in terms of the tax implications of dividends, capital gains, and capital losses. A more detailed discussion on redemption of shares can be found later in this chapter.

¶15,045 PUC Distributions

As will be demonstrated, the Act is very protective about amounts that are added to PUC, because amounts in PUC can be distributed to shareholders without creating a deemed dividend. Therefore, amounts added to PUC must represent the value of property contributed to the corporation with after-tax or tax-paid funds. If an amount added to PUC does not represent tax-paid funds contributed to the corporation, then, usually, a deemed taxable dividend will result, so that the amount added to PUC is tax paid.

Where PUC is distributed to a shareholder, there is a corresponding reduction in the ACB of the shareholder's shares.

ITA: 53(2)(a) [Amounts to be deducted — Share of the capital stock of a corporation]

Summary

Paid-up capital (PUC)	Adjusted cost base (ACB)
Calculated at the corporate level:	Calculated at the shareholder level:
• Based on capital contributed to the corporation;	• Based on amount paid for the shares;
• Averaged among all shareholders of that class based on shares held;	• Unique to each shareholder;
Can be withdrawn from the company free of deemed dividend.	Used to calculate a capital gain/loss on the disposition of the shares.

¶15,050 Capital Dividend Account

The purpose of the capital dividend account is to complete integration of corporate and personal income tax on capital gains and similar receipts. When an individual realizes a capital gain of, say, $400, the individual pays income tax on ½ of the capital gain or $200. The other $200 is not taxed. When a private corporation realizes the same capital gain of $400, the private corporation is taxed (including additional refundable tax and net of any dividend refund) on $200. The other ½ or $200 is added to the private corporation's capital dividend account, to be distributed tax free to the corporation's shareholders. This is done to ensure that the integration concept applies to capital gains.

¶15,055 Components of the Account

This account begins to accumulate amounts only for private corporations. For most private corporations, the period covered would be from the date of incorporation, but this cannot be earlier than January 1, 1972, which is the date when capital gains became taxable in Canada.

¶15,055.10 The Components in Concept

Conceptually, for the purposes of this chapter, this account includes five basic components:

(1) the portion of net capital gains (i.e., capital gains in excess of capital losses) not recognized in computing income for tax purposes, that is, the non-taxable portion of net capital gains, *plus*

(2) capital dividends received from another corporation, *plus*

(3) the pre-2018 non-taxable portion of the economic gain (now ½ of the excess of proceeds over actual original cost) on the disposition of eligible capital property, *plus*

(4) proceeds arising on death from certain life insurance policies received by the corporation net of the cost basis of the policies, *minus*

(5) capital dividends paid.

¶15,055.20 The Major Components Technically

The balance of this account is computed for the entire period (refer to the next section for a discussion of "the period") as the sum of the following abridged amounts described here in simplified terms:

(1) *the untaxed portion of net capital gains which is computed as:*

(a) generally, the excess, if any, of all capital gains (net of capital losses), ITA: 89(1) Definitions

minus:

(b) taxable capital gains (net of allowable capital losses) included in income at the appropriate inclusion rate on a disposition during the period;[1]

(2) *capital dividends received:* capital dividends received from another corporation; ITA: 83(2) Capital dividend

(3) *the untaxed portion of gains on eligible capital property:* ½ of the "economic gain" on a pre-2017 disposition of eligible capital property. The "economic gain" is considered to be, conceptually, the excess, if any, of the full proceeds for eligible capital property disposed over the full cost of all eligible capital property reflected in the CEC account balance. ITA: 89(1) Definitions

(4) *untaxed insurance proceeds:* proceeds received, or in certain circumstances deemed to be received, as a result of death, from certain life insurance policies by the corporation in a period since it last became a private corporation, as a beneficiary of a policy, minus the adjusted cost basis of the policyholder's interest in the policy; ITA: 89(1) Definitions

minus (from the aggregate of the above four items):

(5) capital dividends paid or payable by the corporation. ITA: 89(1) Definitions

Note that, technically, this account does not continue a balance from one year to the next with one year's opening balance being the previous year's closing balance. Each subparagraph accumulates from the beginning of "the period" to the particular time that a calculation of the balance in the account is being made. In this respect, notice that all subparagraphs except (b) require the inclusion of "the amount, *if any*, by which" the aggregate of one item exceeds another item. Thus, it is not possible to have a negative amount for these subparagraphs at a particular point in time. However, at a subsequent point in time the aggregate for one of these subparagraphs may be positive after offsetting aggregate losses or expenditures at that particular time.

[1] Inclusion rates have changed over the years as follows: ½ for gains and losses realized before 1988, ⅔ for gains and losses realized in 1988 and 1989, ¾ for gains and losses realized from 1990 to February 27, 2000, ⅔ for gains and losses realized from February 28, 2000 to October 17, 2000 and ½ thereafter.

¶15,060 "The Period"

As indicated previously, the specific wording of the definition of the "capital dividend account" must be read very carefully (not just the above summary) when actually doing the capital dividend account calculation. The "period" normally starts on the later of the date of incorporation and January 1, 1972.

Example Problem 15-1

Surplus Accumulation Ltd. provides you with the following information:

Dispositions during the fiscal year ended December 31, 2018.

	Cost	Selling costs	Proceeds
Land	$20,000	$1,500	$35,000
Equipment	5,000	100	500
Indefinite life license	6,000		19,000
Securities	3,000	200	2,000

Capital dividends received in "the period"	$10,000
Capital dividends paid in "the period"	5,000

No CCA has been claimed on the indefinite life license.

REQUIRED

Compute the balance in the corporation's capital dividend account as at December 31, 2018.

SOLUTION

Capital dividend account:

Untaxed fraction of net capital gains or losses:

Land			
P of D		$35,000	
ACB	$20,000		
Selling costs	1,500	21,500	
Capital gain		$13,500	
1/2(1) thereof			$6,750

Equipment			
(No capital loss on depreciable property)			Nil
Indefinite life license			
P of D		$19,000	
ACB		$6,000	
Capital loss		$13,000	
½ thereof			$6,500
Securities			
P of D		$2,000	
ACB	$3,000		
Selling costs	200	3,200	
Capital loss		$(1,200)	
½ thereof			(600)
Excess			$12,650
Capital dividends received			10,000
			$22,650
Less: capital dividends paid			(5,000)
Balance — December 31, 2018			$17,650

The following alternative format may be useful to keep track of the transactions, particularly when they occur in different years.

Capital dividend account

Year	Asset	Untaxed fraction of net cap. gains	Capital dividend received	Untaxed life ins. proceeds	Capital dividend paid	Balance
2018	Land	$6,750				
	Equipment	Nil				
	Securities	(600)				
	Licence	6,500				

Capital dividend account

Year	Asset	Untaxed fraction of net cap. gains	Capital dividend received	Untaxed life ins. proceeds	Capital dividend paid	Balance
	Capital dividend received		$10,000			
	Capital dividend paid				$(5,000)	
		$12,650	$10,000		$(5,000)	$17,650

NOTES TO SOLUTION

(1) The one-half rate represents the current untaxed portion of the capital gain which is computed in the definition of capital dividend account as the full capital gain minus the taxable capital gain at the ½ inclusion rate.

¶15,069.99 Practise What You've Learned

Refer to the following sections of the Study Guide to practise what you've learned:

¶15,800 — Review Questions

- Question 4 — Capital dividend account
- Question 5 — Capital dividend account

¶15,825 — Multiple Choice Questions

- Question 1 — Capital dividend

¶15,850 — Exercises

- Exercise 1 — Capital dividend account
- Exercise 9 — Capital dividend account

¶15,100 Use of Corporate Surplus Balances

¶15,110 Income Tax Treatment of Taxable Dividends Received or Deemed To Be Received

¶15,115 Treatment of Taxable Dividends

A dividend, whether paid in cash, in stock, or in kind, or deemed to be a dividend, is treated by a shareholder like a dividend paid in cash. Where the shareholder is a corporation, the dividend is included in income for tax purposes; however, if it is declared by a Canadian corporation, the dividend is deducted in the calculation of taxable income of the recipient corporation. Depending on the circumstances, the dividend may be subject to Part IV tax on portfolio dividends.

Where the shareholder is an individual and the dividend, of whatever type, is from a Canadian corporation, the individual is subject to the gross-up and tax credit system. An "eligible dividend" to which the 38% gross-up and tax credit apply must be designated as eligible by the corporation paying or deemed to have paid the taxable dividend. The corporation must notify the shareholder in writing that all or any part of the dividend is an eligible dividend. A dividend that is not an eligible dividend is subject to the 16% gross-up and tax credit when received or deemed to be received by an individual.

¶15,120 Source of Taxable Dividends

A CCPC, which may have earned business income subject to the general or high rate of tax, may designate an eligible dividend to the extent of its general rate income pool (GRIP). A designation of an eligible dividend in excess of that GRIP balance that exists at the end of a taxation year will result in a 20% tax on the excessive eligible dividend.

ITA: Part III.1 Additional Tax on Excessive Eligible Dividend Designations

Very simply, the GRIP balance comprises:

- the CCPC's GRIP balance at the end of the preceding year (can be nil or negative);
- the after-tax earnings, assuming a corporate tax rate of 27% (or a 73% retention rate), for the year of the corporation that have not benefited from the small business deduction and are not considered to be aggregate investment income eligible for refundable tax, i.e., high-rate business income (losses of this nature reduce the GRIP balance);
- the eligible dividends received by the corporation in the taxation year.

The GRIP balance is reduced by the corporation's eligible dividends (that were not excessive eligible dividends) paid in the taxation year.

Non-CCPCs could have a low rate income pool (LRIP), if the corporation receives a dividend out of the LRIP of a CCPC. A non-CCPC must pay dividends from its LRIP first to the extent of that balance. If it pays an eligible dividend when it has an LRIP, it will be subject to a penalty. A dividend received by an individual from a corporation's LRIP is subject to the 16% gross-up and tax credit.

Refer to ¶12,040 for further discussion of GRIP and LRIP.

¶15,130 Cash or Stock Dividends

Corporate surpluses are used in the process of paying dividends. Dividends may be paid in cash, stock or kind. Where a stock dividend is paid by any corporation, it will be taxed in the same manner as a taxable dividend paid in cash. The definition of "dividend" includes a stock dividend. However, the amount of the dividend will be deemed to be equal to the increase in the corporation's paid-up capital as a result of the stock dividend. This amount is used regardless of the fair market value of the shares received. This same amount will be considered to be the shareholder's cost of the shares received.

ITA: 248(1) dividend, 248(1) amount, 52(3)(a)

¶15,140 Dividends in Kind

It is possible for a corporation to declare a dividend to be paid neither in cash nor in shares but in assets of the corporation. Such dividends are known as dividends in kind or in *specie*. The tax effect of declaring a dividend in kind is equivalent to the corporation selling the assets for fair market value and paying a cash dividend with the proceeds of disposition. Thus, as a result of paying a dividend in kind:

(1) the corporation is deemed to have disposed of the assets at their fair market value, such that any gains or losses are realized;

(2) the shareholders are deemed to have acquired the assets at their fair market value; and

ITA: 52(2)(3)(a)

(3) the corporation is considered to have paid and the shareholders are considered to have received a dividend equal to the fair market value of the assets distributed.

A loss to the corporation on the transfer of the assets to a controlling shareholder is denied.

ITA: 40(3.3) When subsection (3.4) applies, 40(3.4) Loss on certain properties

¶15,150 Deemed Dividends

Generally, anything in a corporation's equity that is not PUC or a capital dividend account balance is taxable retained earnings. The only way those retained earnings can be distributed by the corporation to a shareholder is by a taxable dividend. Therefore, any distribution made by a corporation to a shareholder in excess of PUC and not elected as a capital dividend or declared as a taxable dividend will be deemed to be a dividend that will be taxable. Dividends may be deemed to have been paid in certain situations.

ITA: 84 Deemed dividend

Conceptually, distributions from a corporation to a shareholder can be monitored by the following diagram of the simple equity accounts:

Simple equity		***Distribution***
PUC	$xxxxx	Not taxable as a dividend
Capital dividend account	xxxxx	Not taxable by election of capital dividend
Retained Earnings	xxxxx	Taxable dividend (declared or deemed)

Amounts distributed from PUC or the capital dividend account are not taxable to the shareholders as a dividend. Once a distribution has dipped into the retained earnings pool, the part of the distribution from retained earnings will be a taxable dividend, because the only way that these retained earnings can be distributed is by a taxable dividend.

¶15,155 Deemed Dividend on Increase in PUC

The paid-up capital of a class of shares has considerable tax significance in limiting the amount that a corporation can return to its shareholders without being taxed as a dividend.[2] The Act prevents a corporation from arbitrarily increasing this limit without causing a deemed dividend and ensures that increases in paid-up capital represent contributions of after-tax funds or tax-paid property to the corporation. ITA: 84(1) Deemed dividend, 53(1)(b) [Adjustments to cost base — Deemed dividend]

A deemed dividend may occur where a corporation increases its paid-up capital without a corresponding increase in net assets. This situation might arise on the sale of property to a corporation (other than on a tax-free rollover basis discussed in the next chapter). In that case, the paid-up capital of the shares issued might exceed the fair market value of the property transferred to the corporation net of the value of debt issued by the corporation. The amount of the resultant deemed dividend is added to the adjusted cost base of the shareholders' shares, so that it is not taxed again as a capital gain on the disposition of the shares.

However, no deemed dividend will arise in the following situations, among others:

(1) where the increase in paid-up capital results from the payment of a stock dividend because other tax consequences will result as discussed previously; ITA: 84(1)(a)

(2) where the paid-up capital is increased as a result of an equivalent or greater increase in net assets at fair market value as would be the case on the issue of shares for cash or other assets or on the issue of shares for existing debt; ITA: 84(1)(b)

(3) where the paid-up capital of one class of shares is decreased and the paid-up capital of another class is increased by an amount not greater than the decrease of the first class (i.e., where there has been no net increase in the paid-up capital of the corporation);[3] and ITA: 84(1)(c)

(4) where a corporation converts its contributed surplus that arose on the issuance of shares into paid-up capital except those transactions which involve the tax-free rollover provisions as discussed in Chapters 16 and 17. ITA: 84(1)(c.3)

The following numerical examples summarize these rules for a deemed dividend, showing the conditions for the exception in (2), above: ITA: 84(1) Deemed dividend, 84(1)(b)

---

[2] While the return of capital represented by paid-up capital is not taxed as a dividend, there may still be a capital gain or loss as will be shown subsequently.

[3] Under the tax-free rollover provisions discussed in Chapters 16 and 17, there is usually no subsection 84(1) deemed dividend, because the potential paid-up capital increase is offset by an equal reduction.

	A	B	C
Facts			
Increase in FMV of net assets (cash)	$100	$90	$110
Increase in PUC of shares issued	$100	$100	$100
Results			
Deemed dividend			
Increase in paid-up capital	$100	$100	$100
Minus: net assets increase, if any	(100)	(90)	(110)
Excess, if any (i.e., deemed dividend)	Nil	$10	Nil
Contributed surplus (which can only be distributed by a taxable dividend unless converted to PUC) (see point (4) above)	Nil	Nil	$10

ITA: 84(1) Deemed dividend

¶15,160 Deemed Dividend on Winding-Up

A deemed dividend will also result where a corporation distributes its assets to its shareholders on winding-up or reorganization. This process will be discussed in more detail later in this chapter and will be seen to be very similar to the results of a redemption discussed next.

ITA: 84(2) Distribution on winding-up, etc.

¶15,165 Deemed Dividend on Redemption, Acquisition, or Cancellation of Shares

¶15,165.10 Basic Application

Where a corporation redeems, acquires or cancels its shares, there will be a deemed dividend to the extent of the excess of the amount paid by the corporation on the redemption (redemption price) over the paid-up capital of the shares. The redemption price is normally the fair market value of the shares. In addition to the deemed dividend, there may also be a capital gain or loss on the transaction. However, to remove the element of double taxation, the proceeds for capital gain (loss) purposes are reduced by the amount of the deemed dividend.

ITA: 84(3) Redemption, etc., 54 proceeds of disposition

Example Problem 15-2

Ms. T incorporated a company with an initial capitalization of 10 common shares @ $10 per share.

In the third year of operations, Ms. T acquired an additional 10 common shares @ $20 per share of paid-up capital equal to the fair market value.

Two years later, Ms. T caused the corporation to redeem 5 of her shares at the then fair market value of $50.

During this period, the corporation's business income has been taxed at the low rate on business income.

REQUIRED

Indicate the tax consequences of the above transactions.

SOLUTION

First year: Ms. T's shares have an adjusted cost base and paid-up capital of $10 per share.

Third year: Ms. T's shares have an adjusted cost base of $15 per share:

$10	×	10	shares =	$100
$20	×	10	shares =	200
		20		$300

Ms. T's shares have a paid-up capital per share of $15:

$10	×	10	shares =	$100
$20	×	10	shares =	200
		20		$300

Fifth year:

Step 1: Deemed dividend on redemption

ITA: 84(3) Redemption, etc.

Redemption price ($50 × 5 shares) =	$ 250
Paid-up capital ($15 × 5 shares) =	75
Deemed dividend	$ 175

Step 2: Capital gain (loss)

Proceeds of disposition (redemption amount) (5 shares @ $50)		$ 250
Less: deemed dividend		175
Adjusted proceeds of disposition (equal to PUC)		$ 75
Adjusted cost base ($15 × 5 shares)		75
Capital gain		$ —

ITA: 84(3) Redemption, etc., 54 proceeds of disposition

Reconciliation

Economic gain		
Actual proceeds (5 shares @ $50)		$ 250
Cost (5 shares @ $15)		75
		$ 175
Deemed dividend	$ 175	
Capital gain	—	$ 175

ITA: 84(3) Redemption, etc.

Comments

Assuming this redemption occurs in a province with a provincial personal tax on income rate of 17%, and a provincial dividend tax credit rate on non-eligible dividends of $^{3}/_{11}$ of the 16% gross-up, then the deemed dividend of $175 would bear tax at a top rate of 42% (see Note (1), below), whereas a capital gain would bear a tax rate of 25% (see Note (2), below). Therefore, given a choice, a taxpayer would prefer a capital gain on an outright sale rather than a deemed dividend. For example, if Ms. T wanted to sell one-half of her shares to one of her employees, then it would be to Ms. T's advantage to sell her shares to the employee directly, rather than to redeem her shares and then have the corporation sell treasury shares to the employee.

NOTES TO SOLUTION

(1) $(100\% \times 1.16) \rightarrow 116\% \times (0.50) - 16\% = 42\%$

(2) $(^{1}/_{2} \times 100\%) \rightarrow 50\% \times (0.50) = 25\%$

As demonstrated in the previous example problem, on a redemption of shares, the proceeds of disposition for the calculation of the capital gain or loss will be equal to the PUC used for the calculation of the deemed dividend. This works since the adjusted proceeds for capital gains purposes is equal to the actual proceeds minus the deemed dividend which must mathematically equal the

PUC. The implications of this are that where the PUC and the ACB are different there will either be a capital gain (PUC > ACB) or a capital loss (PUC < ACB).

¶15,165.20 Denied Capital Loss on Redemption

If there is a capital loss on the redemption of shares, then the Act may deny the loss by what is referred to as a "stop-loss" rule. This provision applies if the shareholder and the corporation are "affiliated", as defined in the Act, immediately after the redemption. For example, a shareholder and the redeeming corporation are affiliated if the shareholder and/or his or her spouse or common-law partner control the redeeming corporation. If that is the case then the capital loss will be denied and added to the ACB of any shares that the redeeming shareholder has.

ITA: 40(3.6) Loss on shares, 251.1 Definition of "affiliated persons"

Consider the following example for illustrative purposes.

Mr. A owns all 100 common shares and all 1,000 Class A shares of Aco Inc.

The ACB and PUC of these shares are as follows:

	ACB	PUC
Common	$100	$100
Class A	$1,000	$100

If the Class A shares are redeemed for $2,000 then there will be a deemed dividend of $1,900 and a capital loss of $900. Since Mr. A owns all of the common shares he controls, and is, therefore, affiliated with Aco Inc., so the stop-loss rule would apply to deny the capital loss of $900 and add it to the ACB of Mr. A's common shares.

ITA: 40(3.6) Loss on shares

	ACB	PUC
Common	$1,000	$100
	($100 + $900)	

As a result, the common shares will have an ACB of $1,000 and the PUC will remain the same at $100.

¶15,165.30 Summary

Redemption of Shares

In summary, a redemption of shares involves a set of calculations that can be completed in two steps.

Step 1: Deemed dividend

ITA: 84(3) Redemption, etc.

Redemption amount	$xxx
Less: PUC of shares redeemed	xxx
Deemed dividend on redemption	$xxx

In the context of the simple equity diagram introduced previously, note that the deemed dividend arises because the corporation has distributed an amount that exceeds the PUC layer and, in the absence of a capital dividend account balance, dips into the retained earnings layer.

Step 2: Capital gain (loss)

Since the process of redeeming shares involves, in essence, a disposition by the shareholder, Step 2 computes first the adjusted proceeds of disposition and then any capital gain or loss:

ITA: 84(9) Shares disposed of on redemptions, etc.

ITA: 54 proceeds of disposition

Proceeds of disposition (redemption amount)	$xxx
Less: deemed dividend	xxx
Adjusted proceeds of disposition	$xxx

Adjusted proceeds of disposition	$xxx
Less: adjusted cost base	xxx
Capital gain (loss)	$xxx

Since a disposition includes a share redemption/cancellation, both a deemed dividend and a capital gain/loss may occur at the same time.

The deemed dividend provisions do not apply where a corporation purchases its shares on the open market in the same manner as any member of the public would purchase shares in the open market. Investors in public company shares incur only capital gains or losses on a repurchase of the shares.

ITA: 84(6)(b)

In summary, the following differences between PUC and ACB of share capital should be noted.

PUC	ACB
(1) PUC is utilized in determining the deemed dividend arising from a redemption and/or cancellation of a share.	(1) ACB is utilized in determining the capital gain or capital loss on a disposition.
(2) PUC is calculated at the corporate level and attaches itself to a particular class or series of shares, not to particular shareholders. Therefore, any increase or decrease in PUC affects all shareholders equally.	(2) ACB is calculated at the shareholder level and relates to a particular class or series held by a particular shareholder and may very well be a unique amount for each shareholder. For example, the price paid by each shareholder for his or her shares in an open market purchase will normally differ in each circumstance. However, the PUC will be the same for each shareholder.

PUC and ACB have a number of separate and, in most cases, independent adjustments. PUC adjustments are scattered throughout the reorganization sections of the Act and will be discussed in the next two chapters. ACB adjustments are found in subsections 53(1) and (2) and may or may not affect each taxpayer on an identical basis.

¶15,170 Deemed Dividends and Capital Gains on PUC Reductions

A deemed dividend would occur where a corporation considers it appropriate to return some of the shareholders' capital without redeeming any of the issued shares. As an example of this situation, a corporation may divest itself of a major part of its business and pay the sale proceeds to its shareholders rather than reinvest those proceeds. Where such a payment is made by a private corporation and the paid-up capital of the shares is reduced by an amount equal to the payment, there will be no deemed dividend. The shareholders' adjusted cost base of the shares will also be reduced by the PUC reduction.

ITA: 84(4) Reduction of paid-up capital, 53(2)(2)(ii), 84(1)(c)

If the payment is in excess of the paid-up capital, there will be a deemed dividend.

That portion of the payment, which is deemed to be a dividend, does not reduce the adjusted cost base of the shares, since the amount has already been included in income and taxed.

ITA: 84(4) Reduction of paid-up capital, 84(4.1) Deemed dividend on reduction of paid-up capital

For example, if a private corporation makes a distribution of capital in the amount of $8 per share on shares with a paid-up capital of $10, but reduces the paid-up capital by only $7, there will be a deemed dividend of $1. Hence, if the corporation does not reduce its paid-up capital by the full amount of the distribution, the excess distribution is considered to be from taxable surplus and is taxed as a dividend. The adjusted cost base is reduced by the amount of this paid-up capital reduction, because cost has been reduced by the amount distributed as a return of paid-up capital, that is, $7 in the example. Conceptually, the effects on a "tax-basis" balance sheet might occur as follows:

ITA: 84(4) Reduction of paid-up capital

Tax-Basis Balance Sheet

ASSETS		LIABILITIES	
Cash	↓ $8		
		CAPITAL STOCK	
		Paid-up Capital (PUC)	↓ $7
		RETAINED EARNINGS	
		1. Capital Dividend Account	
		2. Undistributed Surplus (deemed dividend)	↓ $1
	↓ $8		↓ $8

Note that where a corporation reduces its paid-up capital (without making any payments to its shareholders in excess of the actual paid-up capital) there will be no tax consequences unless the shareholder's ACB is less than the reduction. If the PUC reduction results in a negative ACB, there is a capital gain equal to the negative balance (i.e., the amount of the excess of the reduction over ACB).

Consider the following example for illustrative purposes.

In an earlier illustrative example two shareholders, Joe and Bill each owned 1,000 common shares of Smithco Inc. Their share characteristics were as follows.

	# of Shares	**ACB**	**PUC**	**FMV**
Joe	1,000	$1,000	$50,500	$100,000
Bill	1,000	$100,000	$50,500	$100,000

Assume that the company reduces PUC by $100,000

PUC reduction

PUC in corporation	$101,000
PUC in reduction	(100,000)
Deemed dividend (if negative)	—
PUC balance (if positive)	$1,000

Capital Gain	**Joe**	**Bill**
ACB	$ 1,000	$100,000
PUC reduction	(50,000)	(50,000)
Capital gain (if negative)	$(49,000)	
Revised ACB	$ —	$ 50,000

If the paid-up capital of Smithco Inc. is reduced by $100,000 there will not be a deemed dividend to either Joe or Bill since the amount of the reduction does not exceed the amount of the PUC. However, Joe will report a capital gain of $49,000 and the ACB of his 1,000 common shares will be nil. Bill will not report a capital gain, but the ACB of his 1,000 common shares will be reduced to $50,000.

Summary

To summarize the tax principles underlying the concept of a deemed dividend:

(1) a corporation may return its paid-up capital to the shareholders as a tax-free capital receipt with any excess being deemed to be a dividend; and

(2) a corporation may not increase its total paid-up capital beyond an increase in net assets without tax consequences.

¶15,179.99 Practise What You've Learned

Refer to the following sections of the Study Guide to practise what you've learned:

¶15,800 — Review Questions

- Question 1 — Par value shares
- Question 2 — Paid-up capital
- Question 3 — High-low shares
- Question 6 — PUC Distribution

¶15,825 — Multiple Choice Questions

- Question 2 — Redemption of shares
- Question 5 — Paid-up capital

¶15,850 — Exercises

- Exercise 3 — Withdrawing cash from a corporation
- Exercise 4 — Stock dividend
- Exercise 5 — Independent situations — tax consequences

¶15,180 Capital Dividend

All dividends, whether actual or deemed, are taxable dividends unless some action is taken by the corporation prior to payment. The action that can be taken in the case of a private corporation in certain circumstances is to make an election to treat either an actual dividend or a deemed dividend as having been distributed from its capital dividend account. Such a dividend is received tax-free by the shareholder. However, an election in excess of the amount in the capital dividend account will result in a penalty tax under Part III of 3/5 or 60% of the excess.

ITA: 83(2) Capital dividend, 184(2) Tax on excessive elections

There are situations envisaged by the Act in which an excess election is made inadvertently. For example, a corporation may compute the balance in its capital dividend account based on the assumption that a particular transaction resulted in a capital gain, rather than business income. On this basis, the corporation may have elected to distribute a capital dividend. Later, on reassessment, it may be determined that the gain on the transaction was business income and an amount must be removed from the capital dividend account. This could make the dividend paid in excess of the reassessed balance in the capital dividend account. Recognizing this possibility, an election which allows the corporation to avoid the 60% penalty is available. This election allows the corporation to separate the dividend paid into a part that does not exceed the balance in the capital dividend account and a part that can be considered as a taxable dividend. The election must be made not later than 90 days after the day of mailing of the notice of assessment in respect of the 60% penalty.

ITA: 184(3) Election to treat excess as separate dividend

Example Problem 15-3

Hum Along Records Ltd., a Canadian-controlled private corporation, has 5,000 outstanding preferred shares with a redemption and current fair market value of $6,000 and a paid-up capital value of $5,000 in total. The balance in its capital dividend account is $800. The company has decided to redeem the preferred shares at their fair market value and to properly elect a capital dividend on all preferred shares. As a result, a part of the deemed dividend on the redemption of the preferred shares will be a capital dividend.

REQUIRED

What are the tax consequences to Mr. Hal Little who is unrelated to other shareholders and who owns 500 of the preferred shares which cost him $1.00 per share?

SOLUTION

The following would be the results for the 10% shareholder:

Step 1: Deemed Dividend

Redemption amount paid (10% of $6,000)	$600
Less: PUC of shares redeemed (10% of $5,000)	(500)
Deemed dividend on redemption	$100
Capital dividend(1) (10% of $800)	(80)
Taxable deemed dividend	$20

ITA: 84(3) Redemption, etc.

ITA: 83(2) Capital dividend

Step 2: Capital Gain (Loss)

Proceeds of disposition (redemption amount)	$600
Less: deemed dividend	(100)
Adjusted proceeds of disposition	$500
Adjusted proceeds of disposition	$500
Less: adjusted cost base (500 shares × $1.00)	(500)
Capital loss	$(Nil)
Allowable capital loss	$Nil

ITA: 84(3) Redemption, etc., 54 proceeds of disposition

NOTE TO SOLUTION

(1) Since a capital dividend can only be elected on the full amount of a dividend, an election must be made to treat the excess of $20 as a separate taxable dividend.

ITA: 83(2) Capital dividend, 184(3) Election to treat excess as separate dividend

¶15,200 Winding-Up of a Canadian Corporation

What is a winding-up? On the winding-up of a corporation, its assets and liabilities are transferred to the shareholders and the shares are cancelled. The corporation ceases to exist. Where the shareholder is not a corporation, the transfer of the assets and liabilities on wind-up will occur at fair market value (i.e., no rollover is available). A common scenario would involve an individual who is retiring and has decided to sell his or her incorporated business assets and wind-up the corporation. On the wind-up of the corporation, any remaining assets would transfer to the individual shareholder at fair market value.

ITA: 69(5) Idem

A rollover provision is available where a subsidiary Canadian corporation is wound-up into a taxable Canadian corporate parent. This rollover provision is discussed in Chapter 17. If the conditions apply, the tax on the wind-up can be deferred and the assets and liabilities will transfer to the parent at tax cost. It is important to Assess the Situation to distinguish a wind-up eligible for the rollover provision from the taxable winding-up provision discussed here.

ITA: 88(1) Winding-up

¶15,210 Disposition of Net Assets of the Corporation

On the winding-up of a corporation, the assets could be liquidated on the open market with the net proceeds, after paying the liabilities, distributed to the shareholders. Alternatively, the assets and liabilities might be distributed directly to the shareholders. If the second alternative is chosen, all property of the corporation so distributed is deemed to have been distributed at its fair market value immediately before the winding-up. In either case, the disposition may result in income and losses within the corporation on the sale of current assets, such as inventory, in recapture or terminal losses on the disposition of depreciable property and in capital gains or losses on the disposition

ITA: 89(1) Definitions

of capital property. This may result in an income tax liability and, perhaps, an increase in the refundable dividend tax on hand if the company is a private corporation. It may also result in adjustments to the "capital dividend account".

¶15,220 Deemed Dividend on Winding-Up

¶15,225 Timing of Winding-Up

The sale of the assets of a corporation need not be followed immediately by a winding-up. The proceeds from the sale of assets can be reinvested in a new set of assets to carry on a new business or in a portfolio of securities, using the corporation as a holding company. Alternatively, the proceeds from the sale of assets can be distributed to shareholders, maintaining the corporation merely as a shell with nominal assets and shares. In this situation, distributions that did not represent a tax-free reduction of paid-up capital or a tax-free distribution from the capital dividend account will be treated as taxable dividends to the shareholders. A winding-up may not be completed for several years after the sale of the assets of a corporation, because certain clearance certificates must be issued to attest to the fact that creditors' claims, including Canada Revenue Agency (CRA), have been satisfied.

¶15,230 Components of the Winding-Up Distribution

When a distribution on a winding-up does occur, the Act establishes the portion of the amount received by the shareholders in a winding-up that is taxable in their hands. This subsection provides that any amount received in excess of the paid-up capital is deemed to be a dividend. However, as indicated in the previous part of this chapter, this winding-up dividend can be broken into separate amounts abridged to two as follows:

ITA: 84(2) Distribution on winding-up, etc, 89(1) Definitions, 88(2)(b)

(1) a capital dividend to the extent of the balance in the company's capital dividend account if the corporation *elects* on that amount; and

ITA: 83(2) Capital dividend

(2) a taxable dividend to the extent of the balance of the deemed dividend.

In the winding-up, the shareholders dispose of their shares in return for the amounts received from the corporations. For the purpose of computing the capital gain or loss on the disposition of the shares, proceeds of disposition are deemed to be actual proceeds, or amounts received from the corporation, less the amount of the deemed dividend.

ITA: 54 proceeds of disposition

Similar to the redemption of shares discussed earlier, the calculations for the winding-up can be completed in two steps.

Step 1: Deemed Dividend		
Funds or property available for distribution to the shareholder(s)	$xxx	
Less: Paid-up capital	(xxx)	
Deemed dividend on winding-up	$xxx	ITA: 84(2) Distribution on winding-up, etc.
Less: Elected amount of capital dividend	(xxx)	ITA: 88(2)(b)(ii)
Deemed dividend taxable in hands of shareholder	$xxx	

Step 2: Capital Gain or Loss

Funds or property available for distribution to the shareholder(s)	$xxx	
Less: Deemed dividend above	(xxx)	ITA: 54 proceeds of disposition
Adjusted proceeds of disposition (= PUC)	$xxx	
Adjusted cost base of shares	xxx	
Capital gain	$xxx	

The components of the distribution can be illustrated conceptually by Exhibit 15-2.

Exhibit 15-2 Distribution on Winding-Up

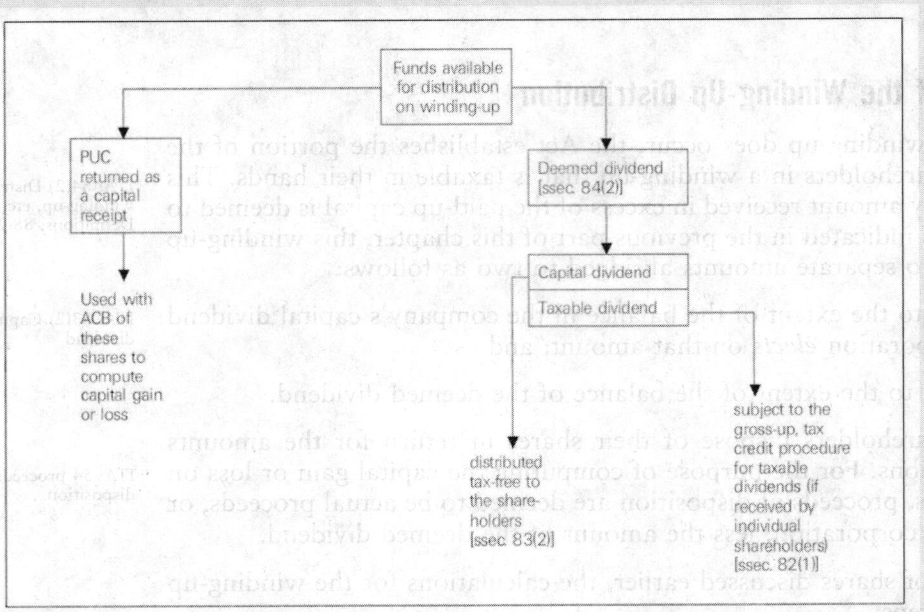

Note the similarity between the redemption/cancellation procedure described previously in the chapter and the winding-up procedure. Both provisions have the same essential purpose on the distribution of funds from a corporation to a shareholder. The provisions must differentiate between the tax-free return of capital and a taxable distribution from retained earnings. The main difference is that a redemption usually pertains to all or part of one class of shares, while a winding-up involves the redemption or cancellation of all shares. Of course, part or all of the remaining winding-up deemed dividend can be treated as an elective non-taxable capital dividend.

ITA: 84(3) Redemption, etc.., 84(2) Distribution on winding-up, etc.

¶15,240 Application of the Winding-Up Rules

Example Problem 15-4

Windemere Limited is a Canadian-controlled private corporation founded 12 years ago by Mr. White who holds all of the shares which he purchased at that time from the company for $1,000. As of December 31, 2018, its tax balance sheet appears as follows:

Windemere Limited

BALANCE SHEET

as of December 31, 2018

Assets		*Liabilities*	
Cash	$ 5,000	Liabilities	Nil
RTDOH (non-eligible)	5,000		
Land at cost (FMV $210,000)	150,000	*Shareholders' Equity*	
Building at UCC (cost $200,000; FMV $250,000)	125,000	Paid-up capital	$ 1,000
		Surplus	284,000
Total	$285,000	Total	$285,000

The surplus accounts include $50,000 in the capital dividend account. The assets are to be sold to a purchaser corporation on January 1, 2019 and the net proceeds are to be distributed to Mr. White on the winding-up.

He would like your advice on how much capital he would have to invest personally after the wind-up. Assume the company pays provincial corporate tax at a rate of 4% on the first $500,000 of active business income and 12% on aggregate investment income.

Assume Mr. White will pay tax on a dividend on wind-up at the highest tax rate of 50% and the company does not have a GRIP balance and does not have a balance in the eligible RDTOH account.

REQUIRED

(A) Assess the situation

(B) Identify the issues

(C) Analyze the issues

(D) Advise/recommend

SOLUTION

(A) Assess the Situation

(1) Draw a diagram identifying all stakeholders and their relationships (e.g., corporate org charts)

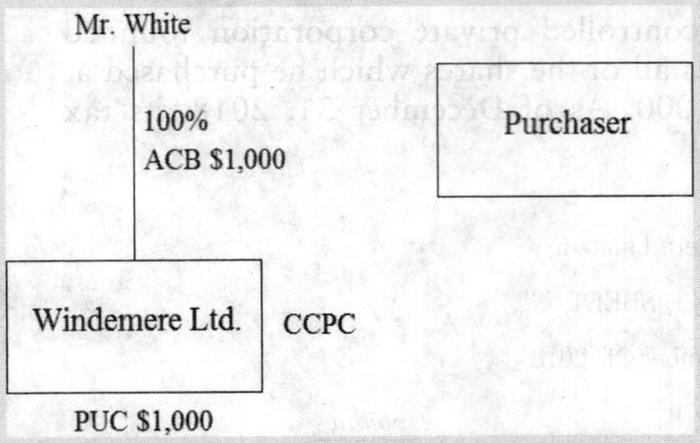

(2) Identify the relationships among the stakeholders (e.g., related, affiliated, associated, connected)

Mr. White owns 100% of the company so they are related and affiliated

(3) Identify the profile of each stakeholder (e.g., tax features, risk profile)

a. Mr. White

- An individual resident in Canada (since Windemere Ltd. is a CCPC)
- Taxed in the highest tax bracket.
- Planning to sell the assets of Windemere on January 1, 2019 and wind-up the company

b. Windemere Ltd.

- CCPC (given)

c. Purchaser

- A corporation

(4) Understand the decision maker and their objectives

Mr. White wants the company to sell its assets and wind-up

(5) Identify the relevant past transactions/events or planned future transactions/events and create a timeline

Mr. White wants the company to sell its assets on January 1, 2019 and then wind-up

(B) Identify the Issues

(1) Identify all of the major tax issues and any non-tax issues

a. What is the tax treatment to Windemere Ltd. of the disposition of the assets to the purchaser?

b. What is the tax treatment of the wind-up of Windemere Ltd. to Mr. White?

(2) Identify missing information or assumptions made

a. Assume that Windemere Ltd. and the purchaser are neither related not affiliated

(C) Analyze the Major Issues

(1) Identify and perform the qualitative analysis of the transactions and plans including an analysis of the applicable provisions of the Act

a. Tax treatment of the sale of assets to the purchaser

- The sale of assets will result in:
  - — Dispositions for tax purposes of the properties
  - — Taxable income in Windemere Ltd. resulting from capital gains on the land and building as well as recapture on the sale of the building
  - — Possible additions to the CDA and non-eligible RDTOH
  - — Liabilities, including income tax, paid
  - — After-tax cash in the corporation available for distribution to Mr. White
  - — Tax treatment of the wind-up of Windemere Ltd.
- If Windemere Ltd. is to be "wound-up" 84(2) applies
  - — While s. 84(2) does apply, the assets have already been sold so there are no assets remaining to be deemed to be disposed of; the only asset is cash.
  - — As a consequence of wind-up, the shares will disappear along with the company. As a result, the wind-up is treated like a redemption since the funds are coming from the company to Mr. White. Therefore, we need to calculate;
    - A deemed dividend [84(2)]
    - A capital gain or loss [84(9)]
  - — We need to consider the use of the capital dividend account.

(2) Identify and complete the supporting quantitative analysis of the transactions and plans using an appropriate analysis format

Sale of Assets

Calculate the tax cost of selling all the assets of the company and the after-tax corporate cash available for distribution

Income generated

	Actual or deemed proceeds[1]	Bus.	Invest.	Capital dividend account	Non-Eligible RDTOH
Opening balance		Nil	Nil	$50,000	$5,000
Cash	$5,000	Nil	Nil		
Land[2]	210,000	Nil	$30,000	30,000	
Building[3]	250,000	$75,000	25,000	25,000	
Income tax[4]	(38,367)	$75,000[5]	$55,000		16,867
Non-Eligible RDTOH[6]	21,867				$21,867
	$448,500			$105,000	

Funds available for distribution to shareholder	$448,500
Less: paid-up capital (return of capital)	(1,000)
Deemed dividend on winding-up	$447,500
Less: capital dividend elected	(105,000)
Deemed taxable dividend (sufficient to clear non-eligible RDTOH)	$342,500

ITA: 83(2) Capital dividend

ITA: 83(2) Capital dividend, 88(2)(b)(i)

ITA: 88(2)(b)(iii)

Taxable capital gain to Mr. White:	
Actual proceeds on winding-up	$448,500
Less: Deemed dividend	(447,500)
Proceeds of disposition	$1,000
Cost	(1,000)
Capital gain	Nil[7]
Taxable capital gain ($^1/_2$ × Nil)	Nil[7]

ITA: 84(2) Distribution on winding-up, etc, 54 proceeds of disposition

After-tax cash to Mr. White:

Cash distribution		$448,500
Tax on non-eligible dividend[1]	42% × $342,500	(143,850)
After-tax cash		$304,650

[1] (1 + 0.16) × 50% – 0.16 = 42%

(3) Identify any risks including missing information, assumptions and uncertain research positions

None identified

(4) Reach a conclusion on each issue

If Mr. White sells the assets for the amounts specified and subsequently winds up the company he will have personal after-tax cash of $304,650.

(5) Evaluate the strengths/weaknesses/risks of your conclusions

No weaknesses identified

(D) Advise/Recommend

(1) Advise the decision maker, integrating your conclusions on each of the issues with their objectives, giving priority to the most important issues.

Mr. White should consider not winding-up and instead retain the corporation and pay out the PUC and CDA. He could then have Windemere Ltd. pay a dividend to generate the dividend refund when he is in a lower tax bracket. Also, he could choose to wind-up the company when he is in a lower tax bracket. Retaining the corporation results in a deferral of the tax on the winding-up dividend. However, he will have ongoing compliance costs associated with retaining the corporation. As well, as seen in earlier chapters, there is a tax cost and no tax deferral benefit to earning investment income in a CCPC.

NOTES TO SOLUTION

(1) It should be noted that in a winding-up of this nature it is possible either to sell the assets to any purchaser for proceeds equal to the fair market value of the assets or to distribute the assets to the shareholders of the corporation. If the latter alternative is taken, proceeds of disposition are deemed to be the fair market value of the assets so distributed.

(2) Proceeds on sale of land	$210,000
Cost	150,000
Capital gain	$60,000
Taxable capital gain (1/2 × $60,000) (Canadian investment income)	$30,000
Capital dividend account (1/2 × $60,000)	$30,000

(3) Proceeds on sale of building	$250,000
Cost	$200,000
Capital gain	$ 50,000
Taxable capital gain (½ × $50,000) (Cdn. investment income)	$ 25,000
UCC	(125,000)
Lesser of Cost and Proceeds	$200,000
Recapture (active business income)	$75,000
Capital dividend account (½ × $50,000)	$25,000

(4) Tax @ (38% – 10% – 18% + 4% = 14%) on $75,000 of recapture	$10,500	
Tax @ (38% – 10% + 10.67% + 12% = 50.67%) on $55,000 of investment income	27,867	
	$38,367	
RDTOH (30⅔% of $55,000)	$16,867	ITA: 129(3)(a)(i)

(5) The $500,000 business limit for the small business deduction must be prorated for the number of days in the taxation year. Since the winding-up may take some time to complete, this solution assumes that the corporation maintains its eligibility for the small business deduction in the year in which the sale of assets occurs. In this case, there would be no need to bonus down to the business limit for the small business deduction, given active business income of $75,000. The CRA's policy of not challenging the reasonableness of bonuses paid by a CCPC to an active shareholder, resident in Canada, from the normal earnings of an active business, may not apply if a bonus is paid from the sale of assets that is not part of normal business. The CRA has indicated that it is a question of fact in a specific situation whether such a bonus from non-normal business income is reasonable.

Interpretation Bulletins: IT-73R6 The Small Business Deduction

(6) Assumes a minimum $57,044 (i.e., $21,867/0.3833) is to be distributed as a taxable dividend to produce a refund. Given the funds available for distribution, net of the capital dividend account, it can be seen, by inspection, that the taxable dividend resulting on the winding-up will exceed the minimum necessary to obtain the full refund.

ITA: 129(1) Dividend refund to private corporation

(7) Had there been a taxable capital gain, the capital gains deduction for qualified small business corporation shares would not apply, because the shares would not meet the small business corporation test (as discussed in Chapter 13) after the assets have been sold for cash.

Summary of the Winding-Up Procedure

The winding-up procedure demonstrated above can be summarized as follows:

(1) dispose of all assets at FMV and determine any resulting income or loss and adjustments to the capital dividend account;

(2) consider a bonus to bring business income down to below the small business limit to minimize corporate tax liability and maximize RRSP room;

(3) pay the liabilities including any tax liability and bonus generated;

(4) calculate the balance for both the eligible and/or non-eligible RDTOH and assume it to be fully refunded;

(5) distribute the net proceeds to the shareholder, determining a deemed dividend as the excess, if any, of such proceeds over the paid-up capital;[4]

(6) elect on an amount not in excess of the capital dividend account. Elect that the remainder is a separate taxable dividend;

ITA: 83(2) Capital dividend, 184(3) Election to treat excess as separate dividend

(7) check to see if the taxable dividend is sufficient to generate the full dividend refund that was assumed under (c); and

(8) compute the shareholder's gain or loss on the disposition of the shares.

¶15,249.99 Practise What You've Learned

Refer to the following sections of the Study Guide to practise what you've learned:

¶15,800 — Review Questions

- Question 7 — Distribution on winding-up
- Question 8 — Subsection 13(21.2)
- Question 9 — Winding-up distribution

¶15,825 — Multiple Choice Questions

- Question 3 — Winding-up consequences
- Question 4 — Winding-up — available for distribution
- Question 6 — Sale of goodwill — tax consequences

[4] For the purposes of corporate law, the full distribution to the shareholders (including PUC) is done by way of a dividend, although only certain elements of the distribution will be taxed as a dividend.

¶15,850 — Exercises

- Exercise 6 — Winding-up
- Exercise 7 — Winding-up
- Exercise 8 — Winding-up

¶15,300 Sale of an Incorporated Business

¶15,310 Assets Versus Shares

The sale of an incorporated business can be handled by two basic methods.

(1) Selling the shares which entitles the buyer to control the corporation holding the net assets of the business. This method results in a standard capital gains computation on the sale of shares.

(2) Selling the assets of the corporation. The proceeds from the sale of assets after taxes are paid would remain in the corporation after such a sale. The shareholder could then re-invest those net proceeds in the corporation or he or she could distribute them, perhaps, by winding up the corporation. This method, ultimately, results in the same procedure as the winding-up procedure demonstrated in the previous part of this chapter.

¶15,315 Allocation of Amounts in Consideration for Disposition of Property

ITA: 68 Allocation of amounts in consideration for property, services or restrictive covenants

If an amount received or receivable from a person can reasonably be regarded as being in part the consideration for:

(1) the disposition of a particular property of a taxpayer,

(2) the provision of particular services by a taxpayer, or

(3) a restrictive covenant,

the consideration must be allocated reasonably among them, irrespective of the form or legal effect of a contract or agreement. The person to whom the property was disposed of is deemed to have acquired it for the same amount. The provision would be applicable to an allocation within a category such as property. As a result, the allocation between land and building could be at issue. This provision appears to allow the CRA to challenge the allocation, even where it was made in an arm's length transaction.

¶15,320 Analysis for the Decision — Assets Versus Shares

Example Problem 15-5

Mr. Nudge owns all of the shares of Strikeout Ltd., a Canadian-controlled private corporation with no GRIP balance, whose wholesaling operations have been successful, but Mr. Nudge has little time to devote to this company. As a result he is considering an offer from a Canadian public company to buy his business as at January 1, 2019. The offer is to buy the shares for $130,000. This value for the shares reflects the fact that the purchaser will not have access to tax-free dividends from the corporation's capital dividend account. Alternatively, the public company is prepared to pay $166,000 for the assets (including an investment in cash which it will need for working capital). Strikeout's fiscal year end is December 31.

Financial information concerning Strikeout Ltd. on December 31, 2018 was as follows:

Assets	Actual cost	UCC	FMV at Dec. 31, 2018
Cash	$4,000		$4,000
Accounts receivable	10,000		7,000
Inventory	30,000		37,000
Land	10,000		20,000
Buildings (Class 1)	35,000	$10,000	39,000
Equipment (Class 8)	25,000	18,000	12,000
Goodwill	Nil		47,000
			$166,000

Liabilities	
Current liabilities	$20,000
Future income taxes	3,000
Depreciation claimed	22,000
Paid-up capital	10,000
Retained earnings	57,000
Reserve for doubtful accounts	2,000

The surplus accounts on December 31, 2018 before the sale were as follows:

Tax-paid retained earnings	$37,000
Capital dividend account	20,000

You should assume the following:

(1) Mr. Nudge's marginal tax rate, federal and provincial, on income from this transaction is 50%.

(2) Cost of the shares in Strikeout Ltd. was $10,000.

(3) Strikeout pays tax at a provincial corporate rate of 4% on active business income up to $500,000, 12% on active business income not eligible for the small business deduction, and aggregate investment income.

(4) The corporation has a nil GRIP balance at the time of the winding-up.

(5) The 16% gross-up is applicable on dividends paid.

REQUIRED

(1) Mr. Nudge requests your advice on whether he should sell his shares or have Strikeout sell its assets. Assume that he would begin winding up the company immediately if assets are sold to the Canadian public company.

(2) What factors should the purchaser have considered in setting the offer price for the shares if the purchaser were: (a) another Canadian-controlled private corporation, (b) a Canadian public corporation, or (c) a non-resident corporation?

(3) Determine a selling price for the shares that results in the same after-tax net cash retained on the sale of assets and winding-up.

(4) Based on an offer of $166,000 for the assets, what is the maximum price the Canadian public company should be willing to pay for the shares of Strikeout Ltd.? Assume that the public company pays tax at a 27% rate, that it uses an after-tax discount rate of 4% and that it does not expect to sell the fixed assets of Strikeout Ltd. for a very long time.

SOLUTION

Part (1): Options

Option 1 — Sale of shares for $130,000

Proceeds	$130,000
Adjusted cost base	10,000
Capital gain	$120,000
Taxable capital gain (½ × $120,000)	$60,000[1]
Tax thereon at 50% of $60,000	$30,000
Net proceeds ($130,000 – $30,000)	$100,000

---

[1] This capital gain would also be eligible for the QSBCS capital gains deduction to a maximum of $424,126 if the tests for a small business corporation are met, as discussed in Chapter 13.

Option 2 — Sale of assets and subsequent winding-up

Calculation of funds available for distribution on winding-up:

		Income generated			
	Actual or deemed proceeds[1]	Bus.	Invest.	Capital dividend account	Non-eligible RDTOH
Opening balance		Nil	Nil	$20,000	Nil
Cash	$4,000	Nil	Nil		
Accounts receivable[1]	7,000	$ (1,000)	Nil		
Inventory	37,000	7,000	Nil		
Land[2]	20,000	Nil	$5,000	5,000	
Building[3]	39,000	25,000	2,000	2,000	
Equipment[4]	12,000	(6,000)	Nil		
Goodwill[5]	47,000		$23,500	23,500	
Current liabilities[6]	(20,000)				
Income tax[8]	(18,954)	$ 25,000[7]	$30,500		$ 9,353
Non-eligible RDTOH[9]	9,353				9,353
	$136,399[10]			$50,500	

ITA: 23(1) Sale of inventory

Calculation of deemed taxable dividend on the winding-up:

Funds available for distribution	$136,399	
Less: paid-up capital	(10,000)	
Deemed dividend on winding-up	$126,399	ITA: 84(2) Distribution on winding-up, etc.
Less: capital dividend elected	(50,500)	ITA: 83(2) Capital dividend, 88(2)(b)(i)
Deemed taxable dividend (sufficient to clear non-eligible RDTOH)	$75,899	

Calculation of taxable capital gain on disposition of shares in the winding-up:

Actual proceeds from distribution	$136,399	
Less: deemed dividend	(126,399)	ITA: 54 proceeds of disposition
Proceeds of disposition (also equal to PUC)	$10,000	
Cost	(10,000)	
Capital gain	Nil	
Taxable capital gain	Nil	

These results can be verified by the use of Exhibit 15-2.

Net cash retained after sale of assets and subsequent winding-up:

Funds distributed on wind-up		$136,399
Tax on incremental income from distribution:		
Deemed taxable dividend (no GRIP)	$75,899	
Gross-up (16% × $75,899)	12,143	
Grossed-up dividend	$88,043	
Taxable capital gain	Nil	
Incremental taxable income	$88,043	
Combined federal and provincial tax @ 50%	$44,021	
Less: approximate combined dividend tax credit (($^8/_{11}$ + $^3/_{11}$) of $12,143)	(12,143)	(31,878)
Net cash retained		$104,521
Sell assets to retain net proceeds of		$104,521

If Mr. Nudge instead sells shares of the company his after-tax proceeds will be $100,000 assuming he doesn't have any capital gains exemption available to shelter the gain:

$130,000 – 0.5 × ½($130,000 – $10,000)

The asset sale results in after-tax proceeds of $104,521. As a result, Mr. Nudge would prefer an asset sale.

NOTES TO PART (1) SOLUTION

(1) The reserve of $2,000 must be added to income whether or not a section 22 election is used. If this election is used the excess of face amount over proceeds of $3,000 would be a business loss such that the net effect on income in this case would be a $1,000 business loss. Under section 22, the purchaser must include the difference ($3,000) between the face amount and the amount paid in income. This inclusion permits the purchaser to deduct a reasonable reserve for doubtful debts on the receivables purchased and to deduct any bad debts as they occur. Note that one of the conditions of this election is that the seller must dispose of all or substantially all of its business assets to a purchaser who must propose to carry on the business. The following are the effects of the election made jointly between the vendor and the purchaser, as discussed in Chapter 4:

ITA: 20(1)(l) Doubtful or impaired debts, 20(1)(p) Bad debts

Vendor			**Purchaser**		
Reserve	$2,000				
Business income		$2,000			
Consideration	$7,000		Accounts receivable	$10,000	
Business loss	3,000		Consideration		$7,000
Accounts receivable		10,000	Income		3,000

If section 22 is not used, the $3,000 loss incurred by the vendor will be a capital loss (deductible only against capital gains) and any gain or loss realized by the purchaser on collection of the receivables will be a capital gain or loss with no reserve or write-off permitted to the purchaser.

(2) Proceeds on sale of land	$20,000
Actual cost	10,000
Full increase in value	$10,000
Taxable capital gain (½ × $10,000) (investment income)	$5,000
Capital dividend account (½ × $10,000)	$5,000

[3] Proceeds on sale of building	$39,000
Actual cost	$35,000
Capital gain	$4,000
Taxable capital gain (½ × ($39,000 – $35,000)) (investment income)	$2,000
Capital dividend account (½ × ($39,000 – $35,000))	2,000
Tax value (UCC)	(10,000)
Lesser of Cost and Proceeds	$35,000
Recapture ($35,000 – $10,000) (business income)	$25,000

[4] Proceeds on sale of equipment	$12,000
Actual cost	25,000
No capital loss on depreciable property	—
UCC	$(18,000)
Lesser of Cost and Proceeds	12,000
Terminal loss (active business income offset)	$(6,000)

[5] Proceeds on sale of goodwill	$47,000
Actual cost	Nil
Capital gain	$47,000
Taxable capital gain (½ of $47,000) (investment income)	$23,500
Capital dividend account (½ of $47,000)	$23,500

ITA: 14 [Eligible capital property]

[6] The future income tax credit is not a liability that must be paid directly. The actual income tax liability resulting from the sale of the corporation's assets is computed below.

(7) The $500,000 business limit for the small business deduction must be prorated for the number of days in the taxation year. Since the winding-up may take some time to complete, this solution assumes that the corporation maintains its eligibility for the small business deduction in the year in which the sale of assets occurs. In this case, there would be no need to bonus down to the business limit for the small business deduction, given active business income of $25,000.

Interpretation Bulletins: IT-73R6 The Small Business Deduction

(8)Tax @ (38% – 10% – 18% + 4% = 14%) on $25,000	$ 3,500
Tax @ (38% – 10% + 10.67% + 12% = 50.67%) on $30,500	15,454
Total Part I tax	$18,954
(9) Refundable portion of Part I tax to non-eligible RDTOH 30⅔% of investment income ($30,500)	$9,353

A distribution of $24,401 (i.e., $9,353/38.33%) in taxable dividends will be required to receive a dividend refund of $9,353 which clears the non-eligible RDTOH account.

(10) There is no reason why Mr. Nudge could not use the net cash within the corporation to invest in securities or in another business if he wishes. In that case, the winding-up would not take place and, as a result, the refund of the non-eligible RDTOH of $9,353 would not be available until dividends are paid by the corporation. On the other hand, Mr. Nudge avoids (postpones) the income taxes on the deemed dividend of $75,899. This example distributes the net proceeds in a winding-up to compare with the after-tax consequences of a sale of shares.

Part (2): Factors to be Considered by the Purchaser

Theoretically, the value of a company's shares to a purchaser should be the present value of the expected future after-tax cash flows accruing to the purchaser when these cash flows are discounted at the purchaser's required rate of return appropriately adjusted for the risk of the situation. Tax considerations may affect the discount rate. Interest on money borrowed to acquire shares is deductible, reduces the after-tax cost of funds and, hence, it affects the discount rate used. The result of using a relatively lower discount rate is a relatively higher present value for the shares.

Tax considerations also affect the present value of the shares primarily through their effect on cash flows. The level of after-tax cash flows accruing to all purchasers will be affected by the amount of capital cost allowance that can be taken on the assets of the company whose shares have been purchased. Since, in the purchase of shares, there is no step-up in the capital cost to fair market value of the assets,[5] the after-tax cash flows arising from capital cost allowance are not affected by the purchase of shares.

[5] Unless an election to step up the cost base of the assets on an acquisition of control is made.

The deductibility of loss carryovers which reduce future taxes and, hence, increase future cash flows may be affected by the purchase of shares. The Act permits a corporation in which there has been an acquisition of control of shares to deduct non-capital losses if the business in which the losses were incurred continues to be carried on after the acquisition of control under restrictive conditions discussed in Chapter 11. However, the Act does not permit the carryover of net capital losses when there has been an acquisition of control of the shares. If such losses cannot be carried over, the future after-tax cash flows are reduced, thereby reducing the value of the shares to the purchaser.

ITA: 111(5) Loss restriction event — non-capital losses and farm losses, 111(4) Loss restriction event — capital losses

(a) Considerations of a Canadian-Controlled Private Corporation as Purchaser

Most of the tax advantages of the small business deduction would continue if the shares of a Canadian-controlled private corporation were acquired by another Canadian-controlled private corporation as long as the corporate group had some eligibility for the small business deduction left (i.e., active business income does not exceed the business limit of $500,000). However, it should be noted that the amount of the small business deduction for a year must be allocated within a group of associated corporations resulting in a potential reduction of the deduction for a particular corporation in the group and, therefore, increased tax and lower after-tax cash flows.

(b) Considerations of a Canadian Public Corporation as Purchaser

The small business deduction would be lost to the acquired corporation on the purchase of control of its shares by a Canadian public corporation. This will reduce future after-tax cash flows and, hence, the value of the shares to the purchaser. Amounts in the acquired company's capital dividend account are no longer available for tax-free distribution after control of the company has been purchased by a Canadian public corporation. As a result, it might be advisable to elect and pay a dividend out of the capital dividend account before the purchase of control and to reduce the selling price of the shares accordingly. While ordinary dividends would still be received by the purchasing corporation without attracting tax, such dividends paid to the shareholders of the purchasing corporation may be subject to tax, thereby reducing the value of the acquiring company's shares. This may increase the cost of funds to the purchaser, thereby increasing the required return. Also, refundable taxes would be lost on the acquisition of control by a Canadian public corporation. This would clearly reduce future cash flows.

(c) Considerations of a Non-Resident Corporation as Purchaser

Again, the small business deduction would be lost to the acquired corporation on the purchase of control of its shares by a non-resident corporation. This will result in additional tax that will reduce the value of the shares. Management fees, royalties, interest, dividends and capital dividend payments paid to a non-resident purchaser will be subject to withholding tax. This will result in a cash outflow earlier than might otherwise be the case, if such tax did not have to be paid immediately, resulting in a reduction of the present value of the shares. The thin capitalization rules (discussed in Chapter 19) may operate to reduce the deductibility of interest on debt, if any, held by the non-resident corporation purchaser. This will reduce future cash flows. A rollover (as discussed in the next chapter) on the winding-up of a wholly owned Canadian corporation would not be available if the purchaser is not another Canadian corporation. If such a winding-up were contemplated it may result in higher taxes being paid earlier resulting in lower cash flows in early years after the acquisition and a lower value for the shares. Finally, the acquisition of shares by a non-resident corporation could be subject to government review. This would result in relatively higher expenses of acquisition and a lower value for the shares.

ITA: 18(4) Limitation on deduction of interest, 88 Winding-up

Part (3): Minimum Share Price Acceptable to Mr. Nudge

The calculation of the net proceeds in Part (1) above can be represented algebraically as:

$$P - 0.50\,[\tfrac{1}{2}\,(P - \$10{,}000)]$$

where P = proceeds of disposition.

To equate the above expression with the net cash retained of $104,754 from the sale of assets and wind-up of the corporation, the following equation in one unknown results:

$$P - 0.50\,[\tfrac{1}{2}\,(P - \$10{,}000)] = \$104{,}521$$

$$\text{Solving for P, } P = \$136{,}028$$

Therefore, Mr. Nudge should be willing to accept a minimum offer of $136,028 for the shares. The purchaser has offered $130,000 for the shares resulting in after-tax proceeds of only $100,000. Thus, Mr. Nudge is better off with the asset sale and would be unlikely to accept a price of only $130,000 for the shares.

A more tax-effective plan for the sale of shares would be to have Strikeout Ltd. elect to pay a tax-free dividend from its capital dividend account balance of $20,000 before the sale of the shares. This may require that the corporation borrow the cash to pay the dividend. The result would be a decrease in the value of the shares, but a saving of the tax on $20,000 which would otherwise be in the proceeds of disposition on the shares and would be taxed as a capital gain. The calculation of the net proceeds needed for the shares to equate the after-tax retention from the sale of assets would be given by the following equation:

$$\$20{,}000 + P - 0.50\,[\tfrac{1}{2}\,(P - \$10{,}000)] = \$104{,}521$$

$$\text{Solving for P, } P = \$109{,}361$$

As the purchaser is unable to use the capital dividend account after the purchase (i.e., the purchaser is a public company), a price of $109,361 to reflect the payment of the capital dividend before the purchase would be acceptable to Mr. Nudge.

Part (4): Maximum Share Price Acceptable to Canadian Public Company

When shares are purchased, the purchaser, in essence, steps into the tax position of the acquired corporation. As a result, there is no step-up of cost values such as ACB and UCC to fair market value.[6] Therefore, the purchaser assumes the eventual tax liability on accrued gains on the assets and loses the opportunity to benefit from the write-off of stepped-up costs. The increased write-offs on the purchase of assets can be thought of as reducing the net cost of the assets to the purchaser. Also, avoiding the assumption of inherent tax liabilities by the purchase of assets at fair market value and establishing their cost at that value can be thought of as decreasing the net cost of assets.

Consider the comparative effects of a purchaser of each asset in this case:

On the purchase of accounts receivable, electing under section 22, income of $3,000 must be recorded, as shown. However, the purchaser can deduct a reserve in respect of those accounts receivable. If shares are purchased, the prior year's reserve of $2,000 must be included, but a new reserve can be deducted. The net result between a purchase of assets and a purchase of shares would be about the same in this case.

ITA: 111(5.3) Loss restriction event — doubtful debts and bad debts

On the purchase of inventory, the cost is established at fair market value of $37,000. If shares are purchased, the purchaser assumes the liability for tax on the $7,000 of income (i.e., $37,000 – $30,000) when the inventory is sold. Since inventory is likely to be sold within the year, the tax would amount to $1,890 (i.e., 27% of $7,000). Purchasing assets avoids this tax cost.

On the purchase of the land, the ACB is established at fair market value of $20,000. If shares are purchased, the purchaser assumes the inherent liability for tax on the $10,000 of capital gain accrued on the land. However, this tax is only incurred on the sale of the land by the purchaser. In this case, since the purchaser does not anticipate a sale in the foreseeable future, the present value of this future tax can be assumed to be negligible.

On the purchase of the building, the UCC and the ACB are established at fair market value of $39,000. If shares are purchased, the purchaser assumes the liability for tax on the $25,000 of recapture and $4,000 of capital gain, if this income is realized on the ultimate disposition of the building. Again, since the purchaser does not anticipate a sale of the building in the foreseeable future, the present value of this future tax can be assumed to be negligible.

ITA: 111(5.1) Loss restriction event — UCC computation

However, on the purchase of the building, the purchaser can benefit from an increase in CCA relative to a purchase of shares which will shield future income from tax. The present value of the tax shield for the purchase of the building in Class 1 (4%) in this case is given by:

[6] Unless an election to step up the cost base of the assets on an acquisition of control is made.

$$\left[\frac{c \times d \times t}{d + r}\right] \times \left[\frac{1 + r/2}{1 + r}\right]$$

= [($39,000 × 0.04 × 0.27)/(0.04 + 0.05)] × [(1 + 0.05/2)/(1 + 0.05)]

= $4,569

where

c = capital cost

d = CCA rate

t = tax rate

r = after-tax discount rate

If shares are purchased, the corporation continues to deduct CCA in Class 1 on a UCC base of $10,000, providing a tax shield with a present value given by:

(c × d × t)/(d + r)

= ($10,000 × 0.04 × 0.27)/(0.04 + 0.05)

= $1,200

The incremental tax saved from CCA on the purchase of assets in present value terms is $3,369 (i.e., $4,569 – $1,200). This can be considered a decrease in the net cost of purchasing assets.

On the purchase of equipment at a fair market value of $12,000 (which is less than UCC of $18,000), the UCC base for future UCC is established at $12,000 and the first year's CCA after the purchase is subject to the half-year rule. However, on the purchase of shares, there is an acquisition of control which causes the UCC after the acquisition of control to be reduced to fair market value of $12,000, but the half-year rule is not applicable to the CCA in this case. As a result, there is a difference between the effect of a purchase of the equipment and a purchase of shares in this case, based on the application of the half-year rule in the calculation of CCA on the purchase of assets. The difference is negligible and will be ignored in the subsequent analysis, since it does not affect the decision.

On the purchase of goodwill at a fair market value of $47,000, the purchaser can add $47,000 to Class 14.1 and can benefit from CCA deductions at a rate of 5%. The present value of the write-off is given by:

= ($47,000 × 0.04 × 0.27)/(0.04 + 0.05) × (1 × 0.05/2)/(1 + 0.05)

= $5,506

If shares are purchased, there is no balance in Class 14.1. Therefore, the $5,506 is a net cost reduction on the purchase of assets.

To summarize these effects, the following is a calculation of the cost of a purchase of assets net of the cost reduction discussed above:

Cost of gross assets, per offer		$166,000
Tax savings — Present value of future		
CCA:		
Building	$4,569	
Goodwill	5,506	(10,075)
After-tax cost of assets		$155,925

If the purchaser acquired shares instead, the after-tax cost of the shares would be:

Price of shares	$130,000
Liabilities assumed	$20,000
Tax savings — Present value of future CCA	
Building	$(1,200)
Tax savings — Present value of tax on accrued gains	
Inventory	$1,890
After-tax cost of shares	$150,690

The purchaser would prefer the share purchase as the after-tax cost is lower.

Next, what the purchaser would pay for the shares to have an after-tax cost of the shares equal to the after-tax cost of assets can be determined. This calculation would be as follows where x in the first column represents the price of the shares that the calculation solves for:

Price of shares	$x =$	$135,235
Liabilities assumed		20,000
Tax savings — Present value of future CCA:		
Building		(1,200)
Tax costs — Present value of tax on accrued gains:		

Inventory	1,890
After-tax cost of shares	$155,925

This price of $135,235 is the maximum amount that the Canadian public purchaser corporation should be willing to pay for the shares in this case.

Summary

The results of the analysis in Parts (3) and (4) can be summarized, in terms of pre-tax costs and equivalent values, as follows:

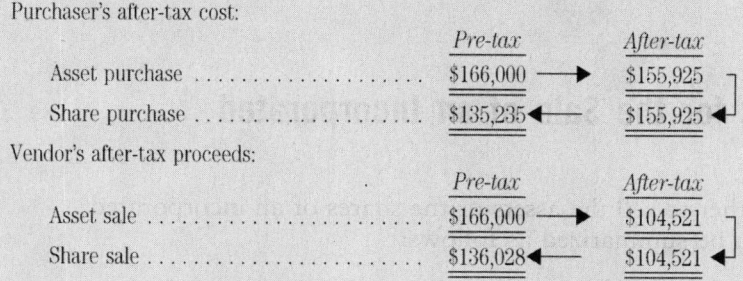

Purchaser's after-tax cost:

	Pre-tax		*After-tax*
Asset purchase	$166,000	→	$155,925
Share purchase	$135,235	←	$155,925

Vendor's after-tax proceeds:

	Pre-tax		*After-tax*
Asset sale	$166,000	→	$104,521
Share sale	$136,028	←	$104,521

This table can be further summarized by the grid as follows:

	Assets	**Shares**
Maximum that purchaser will pay	$166,000	$135,235
Minimum that vendor will accept	$166,000	$136,028

From this grid it can be seen that if the value of the assets is in fact $166,000, then the vendor should be willing to accept no less than $136,028 for the shares and the purchaser should be willing to pay no more than $135,235 for the shares. This establishes that, in this particular case, there is no negotiation range. However, the margin between the maximum the purchaser will pay and the minimum acceptable to the vendor for a share transaction is very small at $793. A negotiation should be possible.

The $130,000 share price will not be acceptable to Mr. Nudge. He will retain less in after-tax proceeds than on a sale of assets.

On the other side, the purchaser will prefer a share purchase because a purchase of shares at $130,000 (the offer given in the problem) results in a lower net tax cost of $150,690 than a purchase of assets with a net after-tax cost of $155,925.

As the vendor will not be willing to accept $130,000 for the shares if both parties agree on the value of the assets at $166,000, they will transact in assets and not shares in this particular case.

If the $20,000 balance in the capital dividend account is paid to Mr. Nudge as a tax-free dividend, then he requires a minimum of only $109,361 (Part (3)) for the shares to be indifferent between a sale of shares and a sale of assets in terms of his after-tax retention. If the minimum that he will accept for the shares is $109,361 and the maximum that the purchaser will pay is $115,235 ($135,235 – $20,000), then there is negotiation range of $5,874 within which a transaction price will make both parties better off from the sale of shares. The lower maximum that the purchaser would be willing to pay for the shares is due to the reduction in their value and the value of the net assets after the capital dividend of $20,000 is paid.

¶15,330 Summary of Steps for the Sale of an Incorporated Business

The analysis of the decision of whether to sell the assets or the shares of an incorporated business as demonstrated above can be summarized as follows:

Vendor's Procedures

Sale of Assets:

(1) Dispose of all assets at FMV and follow winding-up procedures at the end of ¶15,240.

(2) Determine the net after-tax cash retained by the shareholder on sale of assets after the winding-up.

Sale of Shares:

(3) Based on net after-tax cash retained from sale assets, calculate the minimum share price acceptable to shareholder. This can be determined by solving for *P* in the following expression:

$$P - t\,[\tfrac{1}{2}\,(P - ACB) - CGD] = \text{Net after-tax cash}$$

where:

P = proceeds of disposition

t = shareholder tax rate

ACB = adjusted cost base of shares

CGD = capital gain deduction

(4) Consider a payment of a tax-free dividend from the capital dividend account before the sale of the shares. Recalculate the minimum share price using expression above but add the capital dividend account balance to the left hand side and then solve for *P*.

Based on these four steps, the vendor will determine the minimum that he or she will accept for selling the assets or for selling the shares.

Purchaser's Procedures

(5) Determine the after-tax cost of purchasing the assets at FMV. Deduct from the cost of assets the tax savings available from the present value of future CCA from the step up in cost values to FMV.

(6) Determine the price for the shares the purchaser would pay to have the after-tax cost of the shares equal to the after-tax cost of purchasing the assets. The after-tax cost of the shares is calculated by adding the liabilities assumed and tax costs from the present value on accrued gains (e.g., inventory) and deducting the tax savings from the present value of the future CCA from the price of the shares. Thus, the price of the shares can be determined by working backwards from the after-tax cost of the shares.

Based on these two final steps, the purchaser will determine the maximum that he or she will pay for purchasing the assets or for purchasing the shares.

¶15,339.99 Practise What You've Learned

Refer to the following sections of the Study Guide to practise what you've learned:

¶15,800 — Review Questions

- Question 5 — Capital dividend account

CHAPTER 16

Income Deferral: Rollovers on Transfers to a Corporation and Pitfalls

ADVANCED CONTENT IN THIS CHAPTER

- Ⓐ Benefits Conferred on Shareholders and Related Persons ¶16,140
- Ⓐ Dividend Stripping on the Non-Arm's Length Sale of Shares by an Individual ¶16,210
- Ⓐ Capital Gains Stripping on the Sale of Shares by a Corporation ¶16,240

Learning Goals

Know

By the end of this chapter you will know:

- The basic provisions of the *Income Tax Act* that relate to the transfer of property to a corporation on a tax-deferred basis.
- The basic provisions of the *Income Tax Act* that relate to the transfer of shares of a corporation in both non-arm's length and arm's length transactions.

Review Questions
¶16,800 in the Study Guide

Multiple Choice Questions
¶16,825 in the Study Guide

Exercises
¶16,850 in the Study Guide

Understand and Explain

By the end of this chapter you will understand and be able to explain:

- The basic tax consequences of the transfer of property to a corporation by a shareholder on a rollover basis.
- The means that a corporation can use to pay for the property transferred.
- Potential traps or pitfalls on the transfer of shares to a corporation.

Apply

By the end of this chapter you will be able to apply your knowledge and understanding to:

- Calculate the tax consequences of the transfer of property to a corporation on a rollover basis.
- Use the rollover tools to accomplish a taxpayer's objectives.

Assignment Problems
¶16,875 in the Study Guide

Overview

The general rule for the taxation of capital gains and losses is that all dispositions of capital property result in an immediate recognition of a capital gain or loss. This rule also applies to non-arm's length dispositions. However, in some circumstances, particularly in non-arm's length transactions, there is often no real change in the *economic interest* in the property. For example, where an individual transfers property to a wholly owned corporation, there is no real change in the individual's economic interest in the property.

ITA: 69 Inadequate considerations

A "rollover" may provide, in limited circumstances, a deferral of capital gains or losses, as well as other types of income where the economic interest in the property continues. A rollover normally provides for a transfer of property at a value that will be referred to initially as its "tax value". This term is not used in the Act, but is meant to refer to adjusted cost base, undepreciated capital cost or other tax value representing cost.

In return for the property transferred, the transferor should receive a "package" of consideration, the total fair market value of which should be equal to the fair market value of the property transferred. This fair market value exchange is done to avoid adverse tax consequences. On the ultimate disposition of the property by the recipient, the gain or loss that was deferred at the time of the rollover is included in the transferee's income. This chapter will discuss the rollover provisions in the Act pertaining to the transfer of property to a corporation by a shareholder. The chapter will also discuss two major pitfalls that can arise on the transfer of shares. The next chapter will complete the discussion of rollovers involving corporations and their shareholders.

ITA: 85 Transfer of property to corporation by shareholders, 84.1 Non-arm's length sale of shares, 55(2) Deemed proceeds or gain

The following chart will help to locate the major provisions of the Act discussed in this chapter.

PART I — DIVISION B, SUBDIVISION h

CORPORATIONS RESIDENT IN CANADA AND THEIR SHAREHOLDERS

DIVISION

A	Liability for tax
B	**Computation of income**
C	Computation of taxable income
D	Taxable income earned in Canada by non-residents
E	Computation of tax
E.1	Minimum tax
F	Special rules applicable in certain circumstances
G	Deferred and other special income arrangements
H	Exemptions
I	Returns, assessments, payment and appeals
J	Appeals to the Tax Court of Canada and the Federal Court of Appeal

SUBDIVISION

	Basic rules
a	Income or loss from an office or employment
b	Income or loss from a business or property
c	Taxable capital gains and allowable capital losses
d	Other sources of income
e	Deductions in computing income
f	Rules relating to computation of income
g	Amounts not included in computing income
h	**Corporations resident in Canada and their shareholders**
i	Shareholders of corporations not resident in Canada
j	Partnerships and their members
k	Trusts and their beneficiaries

SECTION

82	Taxable dividends
83(1)	Tax-deferred dividends
83(2)-(5)	Capital dividends
84(1)	Deemed dividend
84(2)	Winding-up dividend
84(3)	Redemption dividend
84(4)	PUC reduction dividend
84.1-84.2	**NAL sale of shares**
85	**Transfer of property to a corporation**
85.1	Share-for-share exchange
86	Reorganization of capital
87	Amalgamation
88	Winding-up
89	Definitions

¶16,000 Transfer of Property to a Corporation by a Shareholder

¶16,010 The Basic Concepts of a Rollover

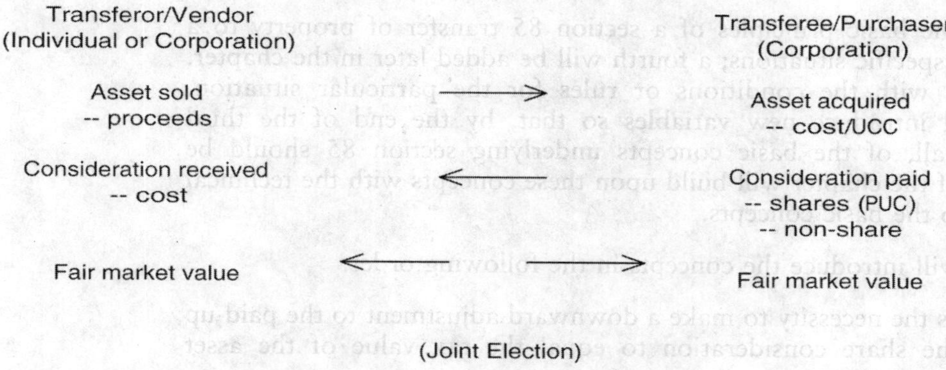

On the transfer of assets to a corporation, there is a disposition at fair market value. An election allows the transferor to choose the proceeds of disposition to defer some or all of the gain.

ITA: 85(1) Transfer of property to corporation by shareholders

Section 85 of the Act permits a tax-free rollover of property to a corporation but only as long as the transferor accepts shares as part of the consideration for the transfer. The basic concept is that the transferor, who is now a shareholder of the transferee corporation, should be in the same economic position that he or she was in before the transfer. Therefore, the adjusted cost base of the shares that he or she receives should be exactly equal to the tax value of the asset transferred. The income inclusion (e.g., capital gain) deferred at the time of the rollover will be triggered if the shares are sold in an arm's length transaction. Similarly, the corporation should retain the tax value of the transferred property. The above is the basic concept behind a pure tax-free rollover.

However, there are additional variables that add complexity to the pure concept:

- First, the transferor is permitted to trigger income inclusions (e.g., capital gains, recapture, etc. depending on the nature of the property) if he or she so desires.
- Second, the consideration can be, not only shares (common and preferred), but also debt or cash (boot).

Terminology

Share consideration: The transferor *must* receive some shares as part of the consideration received for the sale of the asset to the corporation.

Non-share consideration: The transferor *may* receive consideration other than shares such as cash, debt, or the assumption of the transferor's liabilities.

Elected amount: If there is a tax gain, such as a capital gain or recapture, on the asset being transferred, the two parties can elect to designate proceeds that will defer all or part of the income for the transferor.

Boot: This is the common term for non-share consideration such as cash, debt or the assumption of the transferor's liabilities.

Tax value: This is usually the cost, UCC, or ACB. If the proceeds are greater than this value there will be some form of income.

PUC: This is the paid-up capital of the shares issued by the purchasing company as consideration for the assets received.

Demonstration of Concepts

This part will introduce the basic principles of a section 85 transfer of property to a corporation through three specific situations; a fourth will be added later in the chapter. Each situation will begin with the conditions or rules for the particular situation. Subsequent situations will introduce new variables so that, by the end of the third situation, some, but not all, of the basic concepts underlying section 85 should be understood. The balance of the chapter will build upon these concepts with the technical rules to add refinements to the basic concepts.

The first three situations will introduce the concepts in the following order:

- Situation One shows the necessity to make a downward adjustment to the paid-up capital (PUC) of the share consideration to equal the tax value of the asset transferred.
- Situation Two introduces the concept of a transfer price other than the tax value of the transferred asset to trigger income inclusions.
- Situation Three introduces the possibility of accepting non-share consideration (e.g., debt or cash).

A fourth situation, which is introduced later in this chapter, demonstrates the concept that the FMV of the property transferred must equal the FMV of the consideration received, or adverse tax consequences will occur.

Note that the situations described are a conceptual introduction to section 85. The underlying technical rules are discussed later in the chapter. An understanding of these concepts will assist you in applying the complex technical rules that follow. Read these three initial situations carefully. In fact, you may find it helpful to revisit these concepts after you have attempted the technical readings, exercises and assignment problems.

At this point, it is important to understand the concept of "elected amount". The Act allows you to transfer assets to a corporation and "elect" your proceeds of disposition. While you cannot create a loss, you can either elect at the tax value to defer any gain or elect at some higher amount to recognize some or all of the gain on the property transferred. This "elected amount" also becomes the cost of the property to the corporation.

ITA: 85(1) Transfer of property to corporation by shareholders

¶16,015 Situation One

¶16,015.10 Conditions for Transfer

To defer any accrued gain, the assets must be transferred choosing an elected amount equal to their tax value, i.e., adjusted cost base (ACB), undepreciated capital cost (UCC), etc., depending on the type of property, so that there are no tax consequences in respect of the transfer. The consideration received on the transfer in this first situation will be common shares.

¶16,015.20 Facts

Ms. Ava wishes to transfer some land that is capital property to a corporation, Ava Ltd., which she presently controls through the ownership of all the Class A common shares. The land has an ACB of $10,000 and an FMV of $50,000. Ms. Ava will accept as consideration one Class B common share.

The following diagram depicts the facts for Situation One.

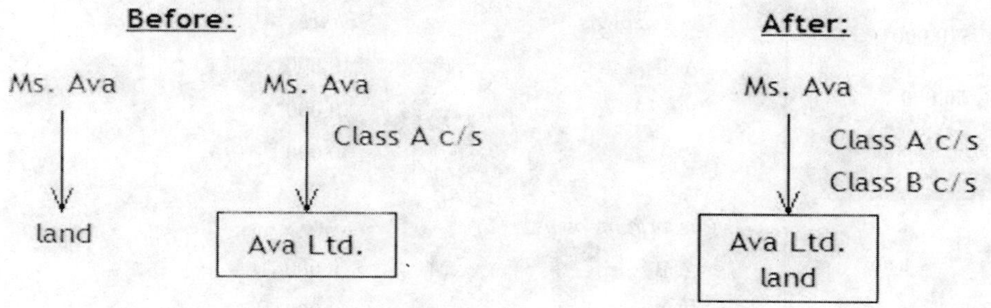

¶16,015.30 Results

Since Ms. Ava does not want any tax consequences from the transfer, Ms. Ava and the corporation should be in the same economic position as if the transfer did not happen.

Land

(1) The proceeds of disposition should be the elected amount of $10,000, which is the ACB of the land so that no gain is triggered.

(2) The cost of the land to Ava Ltd. should also be the elected amount of $10,000, which is Ms. Ava's ACB so that Ava Ltd. is in the same economic position (i.e., there is a potential capital gain of $40,000 upon the disposition of the land by Ava Ltd.).

Consideration — One Class B common share

(1) The ACB of the Class B common share should also be equal to Ms. Ava's $10,000 ACB of the land. She is now in the same economic position as before with a potential capital gain of $40,000 on the one Class B common share. The ACB of the share represents the cost of the land acquired with after-tax or tax-paid funds. It can be recovered on a disposition of the share.

(2) The FMV of the Class B share should be $50,000, equal to the underlying value of the land transferred to Ava Ltd. The result is that Ms. Ava had exchanged land with a fair market value of $50,000 for shares with a fair market value of $50,000.

(3) Logically, the paid-up capital (PUC) of the Class B share should be $10,000, the amount that can be withdrawn tax-free on a redemption of the share, since this $10,000 represents the cost of the land that could be recovered tax-free on its disposition. However, under corporate law, the stated capital (the equivalent of paid-up capital for tax purposes) would normally be equal to the fair market value of the transferred property of $50,000. Therefore, the paid-up capital must be reduced to the ACB of the land of $10,000 in this particular situation. Note that this PUC *reduction* (i.e., $40,000) is exactly equal to the deferred accrued capital gain on the land (i.e., $50,000 – $10,000). Further modifications of the

PUC reduction will be introduced later as additional conditions are added to the following situations.

In summary, the following has occurred.

Before transfer		*After transfer*	
Ms. Ava owned	*Land*	*Ms. Ava owns*	*Class B Shares*
ACB	$10,000	ACB	$10,000
FMV	50,000	PUC	10,000
		FMV	50,000
		Corporation owns	*Land*
		ACB	$10,000
		FMV	50,000

¶16,015.40 Conclusion

This situation demonstrates that if an asset is transferred to a corporation at its tax value and only common share consideration is accepted, there will be no tax consequences to the transferor, Ms. Ava. Her proceeds of disposition and ACB of the consideration are exactly equal to the tax value of the transferred property. At the same time, the corporation assumes the tax value for the ACB of its newly acquired property. The PUC of the common share must also be the tax value of the transferred asset. If this is not the case under corporate law, then the paid-up capital must be reduced for tax purposes.

¶16,020 Situation Two

¶16,020.10 Conditions for Transfer

The assets can now be transferred with proceeds chosen at any elected amount between the tax value (ACB, etc.) and the FMV of the particular asset. This range of elected amounts will permit the taxpayer to trigger the appropriate amount of taxable capital gains or other income (e.g., recapture) to offset loss carryforwards and the allowable capital losses in the transfer year. Again, the consideration received on the transfer in this situation will be common shares.

¶16,020.20 Facts

Ms. Elizabeth wishes to transfer land and a building to a corporation, Elizabeth Ltd., which she presently controls through the ownership of all of the Class A common shares.

Land	— ACB	$10,000
	— FMV	50,000

Building	— cost	95,000
	— UCC	75,000
	— FMV	110,000

Ms. Elizabeth will accept as consideration for the transfer of the land and building, Class B common shares. Ms. Elizabeth has a net capital loss carried forward from the preceding year ½ inclusion rate year) of $10,000 which she wishes to utilize on the transfer.

The following diagram depicts the facts for Situation Two.

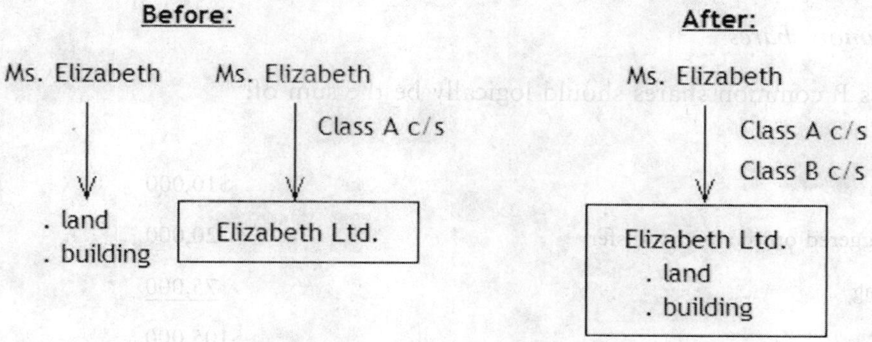

¶16,020.30 Results

Since Ms. Elizabeth wishes to utilize the net capital loss of $10,000 on the transfer, she must first decide on which asset she will trigger the taxable capital gain and what the elected amount will be. If she chooses the building, then at the same time she will trigger recapture as well as a capital gain. Since there is no evidence that she has a business loss for this year or non-capital losses, this course of action is not recommended. In respect of the land, she can choose an elected transfer price between $10,000 and $50,000. If she chooses an elected amount of $30,000, a taxable capital gain of $10,000 will result (i.e., ($30,000 – $10,000) × ½, which will offset the net capital loss).

Therefore, the recommended elected amounts would be:

Land	$30,000
Building	75,000

Land

(1) The proceeds of disposition for Ms. Elizabeth will be $30,000, the elected amount as discussed above.

(2) The cost of the land to Elizabeth Ltd. should also be $30,000, the elected amount, so that the remaining accrued gain of $20,000 (i.e., $50,000 – $30,000) will not be triggered on the transfer, but will be included in Elizabeth Ltd.'s income on the ultimate disposition of the land.

Building

On the assumption that no additional income (i.e., recapture and/or a capital gain) should be triggered, the elected amount chosen should be the tax value or UCC of $75,000.

(1) The proceeds of disposition for Ms. Elizabeth, therefore, will be the elected amount of $75,000, resulting in no recapture or capital gain.

(2) The UCC of the building for Elizabeth Ltd. will also be the elected amount of $75,000 (i.e., the original UCC for Ms. Elizabeth). In addition, Elizabeth Ltd. will assume Ms. Elizabeth's capital cost of the building of $95,000 so that the corporation will be responsible for the potential recapture of $20,000 and capital gain of $15,000.

Consideration — Class B common shares

(1) The ACB of the Class B common shares should logically be the sum of:

(a)	ACB of the land	$10,000
(b)	the capital gain triggered on the land transfer	20,000
(c)	UCC of the building	75,000
		$105,000

Another way of looking at it would be the sum of the elected amounts:

Land	$30,000
Building	75,000
	$105,000

(2) The FMV of the Class B shares should be $160,000, the underlying fair market values of the land and building transferred to Elizabeth Ltd.

(3) The stated value of the Class B shares for accounting and corporate law purposes would be $160,000, that is, the fair market value of the land and building. (Remember that the starting point for determining paid-up capital is the accounting or corporate law stated value.) However, the paid-up capital should be reduced to $105,000, which represents the ACB and UCC of the land and building, respectively, for Elizabeth Ltd. (i.e., $10,000 and $75,000) plus the accrued capital gain recognized and included in income on the transfer of the land (i.e., $20,000). This paid-up capital reduction of $55,000 should be exactly equal to the stated value of the Class B shares ($160,000) minus the elected amount ($105,000) [i.e., FMV ($160,000) minus Elizabeth Ltd.'s tax values ($30,000 + $75,000)]. The PUC after the reduction should reflect the tax-paid cost values of the assets of $105,000 (i.e., ($10,000 + $20,000) + $75,000).

In summary, the following has occurred:

Before transfer

Ms. Elizabeth owned	*Land*	*Building*
ACB/Cost	$10,000	$ 95,000
UCC	n/a	75,000
FMV	50,000	110,000

Ms. Elizabeth had a net capital loss carryforward of $10,000.

After transfer

Ms. Elizabeth owns	*Class B Shares*
ACB	$105,000
PUC	105,000
FMV	160,000

Taxable capital gain of $10,000 offset by net capital losses.

Corporation owns	*Land*	*Building*
ACB/Cost	$30,000	$ 95,000
UCC	n/a	75,000
FMV	50,000	110,000

¶16,020.40 Conclusion

As long as the transferor (Ms. Elizabeth) elects an amount for the transferred asset(s) within the range between tax value (ACB, UCC, etc.) and the FMV, this elected amount will be:

(1) the proceeds of disposition of the transferor (Ms. Elizabeth);

(2) the tax value (i.e., ACB, UCC, etc.) of the transferred asset to the transferee corporation (Elizabeth Ltd.);

(3) the ACB of the common share consideration received by the transferor (Ms. Elizabeth); and

(4) the paid-up capital of the common shares held by the transferor (Ms. Elizabeth) after the paid-up capital reduction.

¶16,025 Situation Three

¶16,025.10 Conditions for Transfer

The asset(s) can be transferred at any amount between the tax value and FMV of the particular asset. However, in this situation, the consideration can be a mixture of common shares and non-share consideration (referred to in practice as "boot") such as cash or debt, including debt attached to the transferred property (assumed debt). The inclusion of non-share consideration, however, imposes a further limitation — namely, that the non-share consideration or boot cannot exceed the elected amount without adverse tax consequences which are discussed below.

¶16,025.20 Facts

Mr. Benjamin wishes to transfer land to a corporation, Benjamin Ltd., which he presently controls through the ownership of all the Class A common shares.

Land	— ACB	$10,000
	— FMV	50,000

The land has an outstanding mortgage of $4,000 attached to it. Mr. Benjamin will accept as consideration for the transfer:

(1) a promissory note of $14,000 from Benjamin Ltd.;

(2) the assumption of the mortgage of $4,000 by Benjamin Ltd.; and

(3) the balance of the FMV of the land in Class B common shares.

Mr. Benjamin has $4,000 of net capital losses which he wishes to utilize on the transfer.

The following diagram depicts the facts for Situation Three.

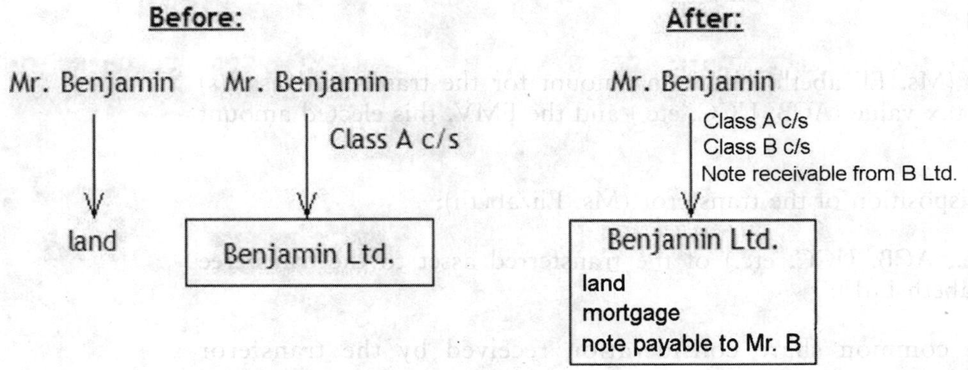

¶16,025.30 Results

Since Mr. Benjamin wishes to utilize the $4,000 of net capital losses, he must elect at an amount which will trigger a capital gain of $8,000, yielding a taxable capital gain of $4,000. Therefore, he should elect at $18,000 ($10,000 ACB plus $8,000 capital gain). Since he has accepted, as part of his consideration, boot of $18,000 (a $14,000 note plus the assumed mortgage of $4,000) he has not violated the condition that the boot cannot exceed the elected amount (i.e., $18,000).

Land

(1) The proceeds of disposition to Mr. Benjamin is the elected amount of $18,000 which will trigger a capital gain of $8,000 to offset the net capital loss of $4,000 (i.e., ½ × $8,000).

(2) The cost of the land to Benjamin Ltd. will be the elected amount of $18,000 so that the corporation will only be liable for the remaining capital gain of $32,000.

Consideration

(1) The ACB of the Class B common shares will be the elected amount minus the FMV of the boot.

Elected amount		$18,000
Boot — note	$14,000	
— mortgage	4,000	18,000
Excess		Nil
ACB of the shares is nil.		

This result is logical since Mr. Benjamin has recovered from the corporation $18,000 of debt consideration equal to the full amount of the ACB of land ($10,000) plus the realized capital gain of $8,000. When the debt is repaid by the corporation, there will be no further tax consequences since the repayment amount reflects the tax-paid cost of the land transferred after the realization of $8,000 of capital gain.

(2) The PUC should logically be nil since Mr. Benjamin has recouped all of his invested cost in the land in the form of boot. If Mr. Benjamin had not accepted boot as part of the consideration package, then the PUC would have been equal to the tax-paid cost of the transferred land (i.e., $18,000) as demonstrated in Situations One and Two. However, in this situation Mr. Benjamin has recovered all of the tax cost of the land (i.e., note of $14,000 and a mortgage of $4,000). Therefore, the stated value of the Class B common shares (i.e., FMV of $32,000) must be reduced by $32,000 to give a paid-up capital of nil.

Another way of arriving at the PUC of nil is:

Stated capital (FMV of land ($50,000) – Boot ($18,000))		$32,000
Minus: elected amount	$18,000	
Less: boot	18,000	Nil
PUC reduction		$32,000
PUC = (FMV ($32,000) – PUC reduction ($32,000))		Nil

Thus the PUC of nil reflects the fact that all of the tax-paid cost of the land has been recovered through boot, leaving no more tax-paid cost to be recovered in the shares on their redemption.

Note how this result differs from Situation Two where only Class B common shares were accepted as consideration. The ACB and the paid-up capital were not reduced to nil in Situation Two, since Ms. Elizabeth had not extracted from the corporation any non-share consideration (i.e., cash or debt).

In summary, the following has occurred:

Before transfer		*After transfer*			
Mr. Benjamin owned	*Land*	*Mr. Benjamin owns*	*Note receivable*	*Corporation owns*	*Land*
ACB	$ 10,000	ACB	$ 14,000	ACB	$ 18,000
FMV	50,000	FMV	14,000	FMV	50,000
Mr. Benjamin owed $4,000 on a mortgage.		*Mr. Benjamin owns*	*Class B Shares*	*Corporation owes to:*	
Mr. Benjamin had a net capital loss carryforward of $4,000 (adjusted).		ACB	Nil	Mr. Benjamin	$ 14,000
		PUC	Nil	Mortgage	4,000
		FMV	$ 32,000		
		Mr. Benjamin no longer owes $4,000 on a mortgage.			
		Taxable capital gain of $4,000 offset by net capital losses.			

¶16,025.40 Conclusion

The elected amount of $18,000 in this situation was used to determine the following values:

(1) proceeds of disposition to Mr. Benjamin of $18,000, triggering a capital gain of $8,000;

(2) an ACB of the Class B common shares of nil, since all of the elected amount was assigned to the boot of $18,000;

(3) a cost of the land to Benjamin Ltd. of $18,000 since the corporation is responsible for the remaining capital gain of $32,000; and

(4) a paid-up capital of the Class B common shares of nil since all of the elected amount has been extracted from Benjamin Ltd. through the boot consideration.

Finally, the non-share consideration or boot did not result in any adverse tax consequences, since the total boot (debt of $14,000 and the assumption of Mr. Benjamin's liability of $4,000) did not exceed the elected amount of $18,000.

¶16,025.50 Boot Consideration in Excess of Elected Amount

If Mr. Benjamin had forgotten the assumed mortgage of $4,000 was part of the non-share/boot consideration and had taken back a promissory note of $18,000 (equal to the elected amount), the following would be the tax consequences.

(1) The elected amount would be bumped up automatically by the $4,000 which is the excess boot over the elected amount (i.e., ($18,000 + $4,000) – $18,000) to arrive at a new elected amount of $22,000.

(2) The proceeds of disposition to Mr. Benjamin would be the *new* elected amount of $22,000, triggering a taxable capital gain of $6,000 (½ × ($22,000 – $10,000)) of which only $4,000 would have been offset by the net capital loss (as adjusted).

(3) The cost of the land to Benjamin Ltd. would be the *new* elected amount of $22,000.

(4) The ACB of the Class B common shares would still be nil, computed as:

New elected amount			
Less:	boot:		$22,000
	(a) note	$18,000	
	(b) mortgage	4,000	22,000
ACB of Class B shares			Nil

(5) The paid-up capital of the Class B common shares would still be nil since the entire elected amount of $22,000 would be recovered through boot.

PUC Reduction		
Stated value of shares[1]		$28,000
Minus: elected amount	$22,000	
Less: boot:	$22,000	Nil
Reduction		$28,000
PUC = ($28,000 – $28,000)		Nil

[1] FMV of land transferred of $50,000 minus the boot or non-share consideration of $22,000 ($4,000 + $18,000).

¶16,025.99 Practise What You've Learned

Refer to the following sections of the Study Guide to practise what you've learned:

¶16,800 — Review Questions

- Question 1 — What is a Rollover?

¶16,030 Basic Technical Rules on the Transfer

¶16,035 Conditions for the Rollover To Apply

In order for the Section 85 rollover to apply there must be:

(1) a transfer of "eligible property", as defined, to a taxable Canadian corporation by a taxpayer, and the taxpayer must receive at least one share of the corporation as consideration for the transfer; and

(2) a joint election filed.

The taxpayer transferring property (i.e., the transferor) can be an individual, a trust, a corporation or a partnership, either resident or non-resident in Canada.

Eligible property includes:

ITA: 85(1.1) Definition of "eligible property"

- Capital property (including depreciable capital property), and
- Inventory (other than real property inventory).

The taxpayer(s) and the corporation must jointly elect to have these rollover provisions apply (form T2057 for transfers from an individual, trust, or corporation or T2058 for transfers from a partnership). The election must be filed on or before the first time for filing a tax return of any person, who was a party to the election, for the year in which the property was transferred.

A late election may be filed within three years of the due date. There is a penalty equal to the lesser of 1/4 of 1% of the deferred gain and $100 for each month that the election is late to a maximum penalty of $8,000. The Minister may accept new elections or amendments to previous elections filed after the three-year deadline in cases where this would be just and equitable.

ITA: 85(1)(a), 85(6) Time for election, 85(7) Late filed election, 85(7.1) Special cases, 85(8) Penalty for late filed election; Information Circulars: IC 76-19R3 Transfer of property to a corporation under section 85

The importance of filing the election with complete and correct information is evident from the case of *Deconinck v. The Queen* (affirmed by the Federal Court of Appeal), in which the taxpayer failed to refer to four of the five properties he intended to transfer in his rollover election. The Federal Court–Trial Division held that section 85 provides a significant advantage to the taxpayer, but to take advantage of that provision, the information provided must be correct. The intention of the taxpayer is not sufficient. As a result, the four properties were not subject to the rollover and were considered to be transferred at their fair market value.

Section 85 is applicable to many transfers of property to a corporation. A common use of the provision includes the transfer of property on the incorporation of a proprietorship, a partnership, or an investment portfolio. Section 85 is commonly used for property transfers between corporations within a corporation group, such as transfers from a parent company to a subsidiary. It is also applicable to the transfer by an individual of shares in one corporation to another corporation to accomplish a business purpose.

Cases: *Serge E. Deconinck v. Her Majesty The Queen*, 88 DTC 6410 (FCTD)*Serge E. Deconinck v. Her Majesty the Queen*, 90 DTC 6617 (FCA)

¶16,039.99 Practise What You've Learned

Refer to the following sections of the Study Guide to practise what you've learned:

¶16,800 — Review Questions

- Question 2 — Section 85 Eligibility

¶16,045 Elected Transfer Price

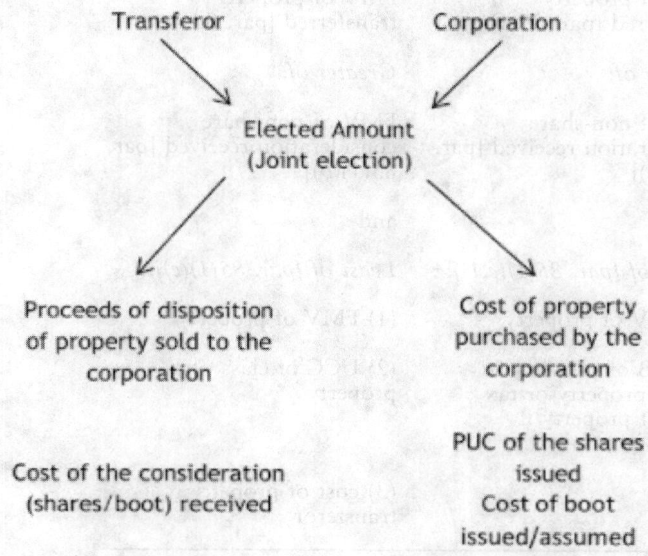

The price at which property is transferred may be elected within a range set out in Exhibit 16-1. This elected transfer price is very important because it is used to solve the following four problems that arise on the transfer:

(1) proceeds of disposition to the transferor;

(2) the cost of the property to the corporation; ITA: 85(1)(a)

(3) the cost of the package of consideration taken by the transferor from the corporation in return for the assets transferred to the corporation; and ITA: 85(1)(f), 85(1)(g), 85(1)(h)

(4) a part of the calculation of paid-up capital for tax purposes of the share consideration received. ITA: 85(2.1) Computing paid-up capital

In order to defer the maximum capital gain or income, the elected transfer price should be the minimum in the range. To ensure that the absolute minimum is selected, it is necessary to make sure that consideration other than shares, e.g., debt, cash, etc. (boot, or non-share consideration) taken from the corporation is no more than the tax value of the property transferred. The tax value of the property is the lesser or least of two or three amounts at the bottom of the appropriate column in Exhibit 16-1. The amount of this non-share consideration taken from the corporation is the only decision variable in establishing the limits on the elected transfer price range. The other items such as fair market value and tax value of the property transferred are fixed, although often not with great precision, at the time of the transfer and cannot be varied on the transfer.

Exhibit 16-1 Restrictions on Elected Transfer Price

	Inventory or capital property other than depreciable property [par. 85(1.1)(a), (f)][1]	Depreciable property [par. 85(1.1)(a)]
Upper Limit	FMV of property transferred [par. 85(1)(*c*)]	FMV of property transferred [par. 85(1)(*c*)]
Lower Limit	*Greater of:*	*Greater of:*
[par. 85(1)(*e*.3)]	FMV of non-share consideration received [par. 85(1)(*b*)]	FMV of non-share consideration received [par. 85(1)(*b*)]
	and	and
	Lesser of [par. 85(1)(c.1)]:[2]	*Least of [par. 85(1)(e)]:*
	(1) FMV of property[3]	(1) FMV of property[3]
	(2) ACB of property if capital property or tax value of property if inventory	(2) UCC of class of property
		(3) cost of property to transferor

[1] Inventory other than real property (i.e., land and buildings) held as inventory.

[2] The tax value of the property transferred.

[3] The fair market value of the property restriction prevents the creation of an artificial loss. Further restricted by subsection 13(21.2) for depreciable capital property, to be discussed subsequently.

¶16,050 Non-Share Consideration or Boot

Although it is not necessary to take non-share consideration (i.e., boot), it will usually be beneficial to take the maximum amount of boot that will still permit the full deferral of the accrued gains on the property. This boot can be withdrawn from the corporation tax free at any time following the transfer.

One of the most common errors in the application of section 85 is to forget to include in non-share consideration the debts of the transferor that are assumed by the corporation. Where the maximum new debt has already been exchanged on the transfer, this omission will cause unwanted income inclusions through an automatic bump in the elected amount for the excess boot (i.e., the assumed debts).

If the fair market value of boot is greater than the fair market value of property transferred to the corporation, then the transfer price will be the latter amount. This will create other problems subsequently discussed in more detail.

¶16,060 Determining the Elected Amount

Therefore, there are three key variables to consider in the determination of the elected amount:

(1) fair market value (FMV) of the property transferred,

(2) tax value of the property transferred, and

(3) non-share consideration (boot) received.

Consider the following three scenarios:

Scenario 1 — Non-share consideration up to tax cost

Consider the case where a property has an FMV of $100, a tax value of $75, and is transferred to a corporation for shares worth $40 and boot of $60. The maximum elected amount is the FMV of $100. The minimum elected amount is $75. If the objective is to fully defer the accrued gain on the property of $25 (i.e., $100 – $75) on the transfer, the elected transfer price should be $75. Taking boot of up to $75 as consideration would not jeopardize the lower limit on the transfer price of $75. Boot is considered to be "hard" consideration. It can be cash or debt that can be repaid in cash, both of which can be received without tax consequences. Taking the maximum of $75 in this case is most beneficial. Taking less than $75 of boot will still permit a full deferral of the accrued gain on the property transferred, but it wastes an opportunity to receive immediate consideration without tax consequences. It represents a tax-free recovery of the cost of the property transferred. That cost was incurred by expending after-tax funds to purchase the asset transferred.

Scenario 2 — Non-share consideration below tax cost

Note that in Scenario 1, if boot of less than $75 were received as consideration, the deficiency below the elected amount would become paid up capital (PUC) of the share consideration received. Like boot, PUC can be distributed tax-free. For instance, if boot of $60 were received on the transfer, the PUC of share consideration would be $15. This PUC could be distributed without any tax consequences in the future. The advantage to receiving boot up to the elected amount is the accessibility of the cash to the transferor.

Scenario 3 — Non-share consideration in excess of tax cost

Consider the case where a property has an FMV of $100, a tax value of $60, and is transferred to a corporation for shares worth $25 and boot of $75. The maximum elected amount is $100. The minimum elected amount is $75 because the non-share consideration exceeds the tax value of the asset transferred.

The taxpayer has extracted from the corporation $75 of boot, which is $15 more than the tax value of the asset transferred (i.e., $60). Since the elected amount is the proceeds of disposition to the transferor, a capital gain of $15 is triggered (i.e., $75 – $60). Under the technical rules of section 85, this result is accomplished by automatically bumping the elected amount by the excess of the boot over the cost amount.

Scenario 4 — Loss properties

Consider the case where property has an FMV of $75, a tax value of $100, and is transferred to a corporation for shares worth $15 and boot of $60. The maximum elected amount is $75. The minimum elected amount is $75. There is no range of elected amounts, but only one amount is both the upper and lower limit. In this case, there is no accrued gain on the property to defer, so a section 85 election would not be used. It would have been possible to receive boot of $75 (i.e., the fair market value of the asset transferred, without adverse tax consequences).

Example Problem 16-1

Mr. Sam Moyer owns the following assets in a business that he wants to incorporate:

	Tax value[1]	Fair market value
Short-term investments	$15,000	$18,000
Inventory	45,000	46,000
Machinery (cost: $54,375)	26,250	38,500
Goodwill	—	30,000
	$86,250	$132,500
Liabilities	10,000	10,000
	$76,250	$122,500

[1] Cost values for tax purposes used to describe the lowest limit of the elected transfer price range in Exhibit 16-1.

As fair market value consideration, he wants $70,000 in new debt, $35,000 in preferred shares and the balance in common shares to total the fair market value of the net assets transferred to the corporation. Also, the corporation will assume the existing debt of the proprietorship.

REQUIRED

Indicate the appropriate elected amounts for each property that should be used to defer any taxation upon the incorporation of the proprietorship.

SOLUTION

				FMV of consideration[2]				
	Tax value	Fair market value	Elected transfer price	Assumed debt[3]	New debt[3]	Preferred shares	Common shares	Income/ TCG
Short-term investments[1]	$15,000	$18,000	$15,000	$10,000	$5,000	$3,000	$ —	Nil
Inventory	45,000	46,000	45,000	—	45,000	1,000	—	Nil
Machinery	26,250	38,500	26,250	—	20,000	18,500	—	Nil
Goodwill	Nil	30,000	1[4]	—	—	12,500	17,500	$0.50
	$86,250	$132,500	$86,251[5]	$10,000	$70,000	$35,000	$17,500	

NOTES TO SOLUTION

(1) Short-term investments should only be transferred to the corporation if they can be considered assets used in the active business of the corporation, i.e., an investment of temporarily surplus cash needed for active business operations. The status of the corporation's shares as qualifying small business corporation shares (QSBCS) is an important consideration.

(2) The order of the allocation of debt and share consideration, as shown in this example, is arbitrarily made in the order that the assets are listed in the facts. This particular method, while not required by the legislation, allows for a systematic allocation, first of the boot, including assumed debt, up to the maximum, if desired, and, then, of the share consideration.

(3) Note that the debt, as non-share consideration, can be set at any level, but the amount taken affects the minimum elected transfer price. It is the only consideration that has an effect on that minimum elected transfer price and must be selected to meet the transferor's objective of, in this case, deferring any taxation on the transfer. In this situation, the maximum new debt consideration or boot (i.e., $76,251) was not taken in order to demonstrate certain effects. However, the transferor might be advised to take debt consideration, including assumed debt, to a total of $86,251 which is equal to the desired minimum elected amount. By not receiving the maximum debt consideration, where financially feasible, the transferor is wasting an opportunity to recover, at the time of the transfer to the corporation, his cost in the property transferred on a tax-free basis. The share consideration, which has no effect on the elected amount, is used to balance the fair market value of the total consideration received, including boot and shares, with the total fair market value of all property transferred to the corporation. Under the rollover, this balancing of fair market value is necessary to avoid the problems which will be discussed later.

Note, however, that preferred shares generally have a fixed value (i.e., redemption value or retraction value), whereas common shares have a floating value which absorbs the fair market value of the property transferred net of the other consideration (i.e., boot and preferred shares).

(4) To have a valid election the minimum elected transfer price must be a nominal amount (i.e., $1.00).

Information Circulars: IC 76-19R3 Transfer of property to a corporation under section 85

(5) The elected amount is used as proceeds of disposition to the transferor, as the cost of the property to the corporation and as adjusted cost base of the consideration received by the transferor from the corporation.

¶16,070 The Corporation's Position

The elected transfer price becomes the corporation's cost of the property. For depreciable property, the corporation steps into the transferor's tax position in all respects on transfer of the assets of the corporation. The Act provides that the capital cost of the property to the corporation will be deemed to equal the capital cost of the property to the transferor. The corporation will be deemed to have claimed capital cost allowance equal to the amount by which the capital cost exceeds the transfer price to determine the undepreciated capital cost of the property to the corporation. After the transfer, the corporation takes capital cost allowance from the undepreciated capital cost and will be liable for recapture up to the transferor's original capital cost.

ITA: 85(1)(a), 85(1)(b), 85(1)(c)

Note that the half-year rule for calculating capital cost allowance in the year of acquisition of an asset does not apply in this election if two conditions apply:

ITA: 85(1) Transfer of property to corporation by shareholders; ITR: 1100(2.2) Property Acquired in the Year

- the transferor was not dealing at arm's length with the corporation at the time of the transfer; and
- the property was owned continuously by the transferor for the period from one year before the end of the taxation year of the corporation in which the asset was acquired to the acquisition date.

For example, a corporation with a December 31, 2017 taxation year end acquiring a property on July 1, 2017, from a non-arm's length person would not be required to use the half-year rule as long as the non-arm's length person owned the property from January 1, 2017 to July 1, 2017 (i.e., the non-arm's length person acquired the property before 2017).

Similarly non-arm's length transfers of depreciable property retain the same capital cost allowance class. For example, a Class 3 asset (building) acquired by a non-arm's length corporation would be placed in Class 3. In an arm's length acquisition, the asset would be placed in Class 1 or Class 1-NRB (non-residential building).

ITR: 1102(1.4)

¶16,080 The Shareholder's Position

For the shareholder, the elected transfer price is allocated to become the cost of the property received (i.e., boot or shares) as consideration in exchange for the property transferred in the following order:

(1) property other than shares (i.e., boot or non-share consideration) up to the fair market value of that property; ITA: 85(1)(f)

(2) preferred shares up to the fair market value of those shares (i.e., the redemption value); and ITA: 85(1)(g)

(3) common shares to the extent that proceeds of disposition (elected amount) exceeds the sum of the fair market value of the non-share consideration and the cost allocated to the preferred shares in (2). ITA: 85(1)(h)

The Act defines a preferred share as a share other than a common share. A preferred share has a fixed redemption/retraction value. A common share is a share the holder of which is not precluded from participating in the assets of the corporation. The value of a common share fluctuates. At the time of the transfer of property to a corporation, the value of the common share consideration is equal to the value of the property transferred to the corporation less any boot and preferred share consideration received. Subsequent to the transfer, the value of the common shares will fluctuate with the value of the corporation's business. The value of the preferred shares is fixed at the redemption/retraction value.

ITA: 248(1) common share, preferred share, 54.2 Certain shares deemed to be capital property

Example Problem 16-2

Reconsider the Example Problem 16-1 in ¶16,060.

REQUIRED

Compute the cost of the consideration taken from the corporation for the net assets transferred.

SOLUTION

Elected transfer price		$86,251
Allocation to cost of non-share consideration:		
Liabilities assumed	$10,000	
New debt	70,000	80,000
Allocation to preferred shares (up to their FMV)		$6,251
Allocation to common shares		Nil

Note that the $86,251 of elected amount represents the tax-paid cost in the assets transferred to the corporation, that is, $86,250 of tax value and $1 elected on goodwill and included in income. The cost of the consideration received for these assets reflects that tax-paid cost. The $10,000 of liabilities are assumed without any tax consequences on the transfer or in the future. The new debt of $70,000 can be repaid without tax consequences in the future. The preferred shares have a cost of $6,251 that can be recovered tax free in the future. The common shares have a cost of nil, because all of the tax-paid cost in the assets transferred to the corporation has been recovered in the debt and preferred shares received.

¶16,080.99 Practise What You've Learned

Refer to the following sections of the Study Guide to practise what you've learned:

¶16,800 — Review Questions

- Question 3 — Elected Amount
- Question 4 — Elected Amount
- Question 5 — Boot
- Question 9 — Half-Year Rule
- Question 10 — Cost of Consideration

¶16,850 — Exercises

- Exercise 1 — Elected Amount, Non-share Consideration

¶16,090 Paid-Up Capital Reduction on Shares Issued as Consideration

¶16,095 The Issue in Concept

A paid-up capital reduction is necessary after the use of a rollover because the paid-up capital has to reflect the tax-paid cost of the assets transferred to the corporation that has not been returned to the transferor in non-share consideration (boot). In a rollover situation, the tax-paid cost of the assets transferred is the elected amount.

Recall the discussion of paid-up capital of shares in the previous chapter. Where shares have no par value or stated value under corporate law, their paid-up capital value normally reflects the fair market value of the property for which the shares were issued. In Example Problem 16-1 (in ¶16,060), this legal stated capital (LSC) was $52,500; $35,000 for the preferred shares; and $17,500 for the common shares. On the issue of the shares, the fair market value of net assets of the corporation increased by a total of $52,500 (i.e., $132,500 – ($10,000 + $70,000)). This value of $52,500 reflects, in part, the un-taxed accrued income on the inventory, machinery and goodwill deferred on the transfer of those assets to the corporation.

Since the adjusted cost base of the preferred shares is $6,251 and that of the common shares is nil, a capital gain would result from an arm's length sale of the shares of either class. This capital gain may be eligible for the QSBC share capital gains deduction while the original income deferred on the transfer would not have been eligible. The individual shareholder can legitimately access his capital gains exemption through incorporating his business.

The purpose behind the PUC reduction calculation in the ITA is illustrated by considering the result if there were no reduction in the legal stated capital as determined under corporate law.

ITA: 85(2.1) Computing paid-up capital

In Example Problem 16-1 (in ¶16,060), if the individual shareholder were to continue to hold the shares received as consideration (rather than sell the shares), without a paid-up capital reduction, the paid-up capital could be distributed on a tax-free basis. The full $52,500 could be removed from the corporation to the shareholder tax-free when tax was never paid on the accrued income because of the section 85 election.

ITA: 84(3) Redemption, etc.

Further, without a paid-up capital reduction, if the shares were redeemed by the corporation for their fair market value, there would be no deemed dividend, because their fair market value is equal to their paid-up capital value. As a result, on the redemption there would be a capital gain that may be eligible for the QSBC share capital gains deduction. This would allow the shareholder to access the capital gains exemption without selling the business to an arm's length person.

¶16,100 The Technical Solution

The QSBC share capital gains deduction has apparently necessitated an anti-avoidance rule which provides for a reduction (often referred to in practice as a "grind") in the paid-up capital of a *particular* class of shares of a corporation after the disposition of property equal to:

ITA: 85(2.1)(a)

$$(A - B) \times C/A$$

where

A = the increase in legal stated capital of all shares of the corporation after the disposition under section 85;

B = the excess, if any, of the corporation's cost of the property (i.e., the elected amount) *over* the fair market value of the non-share consideration (i.e., the boot);

C = the increase in legal stated capital of a particular class of shares on the transfer of property to the corporation.

If the amount (A – B) is negative, it is deemed to be nil.

ITA: 257 Negative amounts

The result of the paid-up capital reduction formula is to reduce the paid-up capital of the shares to the elected amount less any non-share consideration received on the transfer.

¶16,105 Illustration of Application

To better understand the effects of the PUC reduction, consider a capital asset with the following features: ITA: 85(2.1) Computing paid-up capital

Tax value	$10,000
Fair market value	15,000

If this property is sold in an arm's length transaction, there will be either business income or a capital gain, depending on the nature of the asset, in the amount of $5,000. Hence, of the $15,000 of proceeds received, $5,000 is income subject to tax in some form and the other $10,000 is a recovery of the cost (i.e., tax value) of the asset on a tax-free basis, because the asset was purchased with after-tax funds.

Now consider a transfer of the above asset to a corporation using the rollover as follows: ITA: 85(1) Transfer of property to corporation by shareholders

Elected amount (equal to tax value)	$10,000
Fair market value of non-share consideration (boot)	10,000
Fair market value and LSC of share consideration	5,000
Adjusted cost base of share consideration	Nil

ITA: 85(1)(g), 85(1)(h)

If the share consideration received from the corporation is subsequently sold in an arm's length transaction for its current fair market value, a capital gain of $5,000 would result in most circumstances. This capital gain is equal to the gain that had accrued on the asset transferred to the corporation. If the asset was a capital property that would have resulted in a capital gain on its arm's length disposition, the usual capital gain on the disposition of the share consideration would provide the equivalent treatment, that is, taxation of one-half of the gain.

If the asset was inventory that would have resulted in business income on its arm's length disposition, a transfer to a corporation in the manner described would potentially convert the business income into a capital gain on the ultimate sale of the share consideration. The Act allows this as long as the inventory is part of a transfer of substantially all of the assets of an active business. Shares accepted as consideration on a disposition to a corporation are deemed to be capital property of the transferor as long as all or substantially all of the assets, used in an active business by the transferor, are disposed of to the corporation. The definition of a business specifically excludes an adventure in the nature of trade. Thus, the Act provides capital gains treatment for the shares and potential use of the capital gains deduction as long as this condition is met. ITA: 54.2 Certain shares deemed to be capital property, 248(1) business

If the share consideration received from the corporation is instead subsequently redeemed by the corporation, without a PUC reduction, a capital gain will arise on the redemption. If the shares are QSBC shares, the capital gains deduction can be used. Further, if the shares were instead retained by the shareholder, the legal stated capital could be distributed tax free through a PUC distribution. The PUC reduction effectively eliminates these potential benefits. The rule will reduce (or grind) the paid-up capital for tax purposes of the share consideration to nil as follows:

ITA: 85(2.1) Computing paid-up capital

LSC of share consideration before reduction				$5,000
Less: reduction in PUC				
(1) increase in LSC of all shares on the transfer to the corporation		$5,000	(A)	
(2) elected amount	$10,000			
less: boot	10,000			
excess if any		Nil	(B)	
total reduction (A – B)				5,000[1]
Tax PUC of share consideration after reduction				Nil

ITA: 85(2.1) Computing paid-up capital

[1] This PUC reduction equals the untaxed gain (i.e., the deferred gain) on the transfer of the property to the corporation.

Since only one class of shares was assumed to have been received as consideration, there is no need to apply the prorating component of the formula.

PUC of New Shares Received

Note how the tax PUC of the share consideration after the reduction is nil. This PUC value for tax purposes represents the amount of the original cost of the asset transferred (i.e., $10,000) that has not been recovered through boot. Since the boot of $10,000 in this case can be thought of as a full recovery of the original cost of the asset transferred, there is no further amount of that cost to be recovered on a tax-free basis and, hence, the tax PUC value should be nil. Recall that PUC represents an amount that can be returned to a shareholder on a tax-free basis, because it represents a contribution to the capital of the corporation made with after-tax funds. In this case, the "funds" contributed to the corporation consisted of a property with an untaxed, accrued capital gain. This conceptual approach to determining the tax value of the PUC of shares can be used to predict or to check the application of the technical formula.

ITA: 85(2.1) Computing paid-up capital

¶16,110 The Effect of Redeeming the Shares Received

Assume the shares received as consideration are now redeemed for their fair market value of $5,000. The following compares the effects of the PUC reduction on the results of a redemption if the PUC reduction had not been added to the legislation:

ITA: 85(2.1) Computing paid-up capital

	With PUC reduction	Without PUC reduction
Proceeds on redemption	$5,000	$5,000
Less: PUC	Nil	5,000
Deemed dividend	$5,000	Nil
Proceeds on redemption	$5,000	$5,000
Less: deemed dividend	5,000	Nil
Proceeds of disposition	Nil	$5,000
Less: adjusted cost base	Nil	Nil
Capital gain	Nil	$5,000

ITA: 84(3) Redemption, etc.

ITA: 54 Definitions

ITA: 85(1) Transfer of property to corporation by shareholders

Note that a *redemption* of the shares, received as consideration under the rollover transfer, results in a deemed dividend, rather than a capital gain that might have been eligible for the QSBC share capital gains deduction. In other words, the PUC reduction converts what would have been a taxable capital gain into a deemed dividend if the corporation is redeeming the shares.

ITA: 85(2.1) Computing paid-up capital

The foregoing analysis illustrates the effects of the PUC reduction as an anti-avoidance rule which prevents the conversion of an amount that might have been taxed as property income into a potentially tax-free capital gain on the *redemption* of shares received as consideration.

ITA: 85(2.1) Computing paid-up capital

Example Problem 16-3

Reconsider Example Problem 16-1 in ¶16,060.

REQUIRED

Compute the paid-up capital for tax purposes of the preferred and common shares received from the corporation.

SOLUTION

			Preferred shares	Common shares
Reduction in PUC:				
(1) increase in LSC of *all* shares on the transfer to the corporation		$52,500 (A)		
(2) elected amount	$86,251			
less: non-share consideration	80,000			
excess, if any		6,251 (B)		
total reduction (A – B)		$46,249[1]		
(3) increase in LSC of a class of shares issued			$35,000 (C)	$17,500 (C)
Reduction in each class [(A – B) × C/A				
Preferred shares:	$\frac{\$46,249 \times \$35,000}{\$52,500}$		(30,833)	
Common shares:	$\frac{\$46,249 \times \$17,500}{\$52,500}$			(15,416)
PUC (for tax purposes) of each class			$4,167	$2,084

ITA: 85(2.1) Computing paid-up capital

This PUC reduction will have no tax consequences unless and until the shares are *redeemed* by the corporation. Arm's length sales are unaffected by the PUC reduction. On redemption for fair market value of the shares, the following will occur:

	Preferred shares	Common shares
Redemption amount (FMV)	$35,000	$17,500
Less: PUC (tax)	4,167	2,084
Deemed dividend	$30,833	$15,416
Redemption amount	$35,000	$17,500
Less: deemed dividend	30,833	15,416
Proceeds of disposition	$4,167	$2,084

ITA: 84(3) Redemption, etc.

ITA: 54 Definitions

	Preferred shares	Common shares
Proceeds of disposition	$4,167	$2,084
Less: adjusted cost base	6,251	Nil
Capital gain (loss)	$(2,084)	$2,084

ITA: 85(1) Transfer of property to corporation by shareholders

Note that, had the PUC not been reduced, there would not have been a deemed dividend, because redemption proceeds would have been equal to PUC. The result would have been a capital gain on the preferred shares of $28,749 (i.e., $35,000 – $6,251) and on the common shares of $17,500 (i.e., $17,500 – Nil). Therefore, the PUC reduction converts, at least in part, what might have been a taxable capital gain into a taxable deemed dividend.

NOTE TO SOLUTION

(1) Again, this PUC reduction appears to be the untaxed gain (i.e., the deferred gain) on the transfer of property with a fair market value of $132,500 at an elected amount of $86,251 for a deferred gain of $46,249 (i.e., $132,500 – $86,251). The resultant PUC for tax purposes of $6,251 (i.e., $4,167 + $2,084) represents the tax value or cost that has not been recovered through debt consideration, including assumed debt. Of the $86,251 of tax value in the assets originally transferred, $80,000 (i.e., $10,000 + $70,000) has been recovered through boot received on the transfer. The remainder of unrecovered tax value is $6,250 (i.e., $86,250 – $80,000) which differs from the tax value of PUC by the $1 included in income from the required elected amount on the goodwill.

From the foregoing example problem, it can be seen that each of fair market value, the adjusted cost base, and the paid-up capital of the shares can and sometimes will all be different as each is determined independently.

¶16,110.99 Practise What You've Learned

Refer to the following sections of the Study Guide to practise what you've learned:

¶16,800 — Review Questions

- Question 7 — Cost of consideration
- Question 11 — Cost of consideration

¶16,825 — Multiple Choice Questions

- Question 4 — Cost of consideration
- Question 6 — Section 85

¶16,850 — Exercises

- Exercise 2 — Cost of consideration
- Exercise 3 — Elected amount, Cost of consideration
- Exercise 5 — Boot
- Exercise 11 — Elected amount, Cost of consideration

¶16,120 Other Rules Applicable in the Rollover

¶16,125 Depreciable Property

¶16,125.10 Ordering of Dispositions Within a Class

When a transfer involves a number of items of depreciable property of the same prescribed class, the taxpayer must designate the order of disposition. Otherwise the Minister will make the designation. By having separate, sequential dispositions, the undepreciated capital cost will be reduced after each separate disposition for the purpose of determining the minimum transfer price.

ITA: 13(21.2) Loss on certain transfers, 251.1 Definition of "affiliated persons"

¶16,125.30 Limitations on Transferee's Cost Basis for CCA

Where depreciable property with an accrued capital gain (and, perhaps, an undepreciated capital cost equal to or less than capital cost) is transferred to a corporation with which the transferor does not deal at arm's length, there may be a temptation to elect at fair market value on the transfer to trigger the accrued capital gain. The capital gain would be only ½ taxable, and the corporation would be deemed to have acquired depreciable property at full fair market value which would become the base for the future undepreciated capital cost in the corporation. The prospect of such a transfer probably resulted in the introduction of a rule which, conceptually, restricts any step-up of the original capital cost, in respect of a non-arm's length transfer, to the *taxable* capital gain realized.

ITA: 13(7)(e)

Consider the transfer by an individual to a corporation, which he or she controls, of a depreciable capital property, the only asset in the class, with an undepreciated capital cost of $50,000, a capital cost of $55,000 and a fair market value of $95,000. If the individual can offset all of the accrued taxable capital gain with net capital losses, and he or she elects, under the rollover, to transfer the property at $85,000, the following taxable income would result for the individual:

ITA: 85(1) Transfer of property to corporation by shareholders

Recapture ($55,000 – $50,000)	$5,000
Taxable capital gain [½ × ($85,000 – $55,000)]	15,000
Income	$20,000

Where the cost of the property to the corporation (i.e., the elected amount of $85,000) exceeds the capital cost of the property to the transferor (i.e., $55,000) on a non-arm's length transfer of depreciable property, the capital cost of the property to the corporation is deemed to be equal to the aggregate of: ITA: 13(7)(e)(i)

(a)	transferor's original capital cost	$55,000
(b)	taxable capital gain [½ × ($85,000 – $55,000)]	15,000
	Deemed capital cost	$70,000

This deemed capital cost of $70,000 will be the base for future capital cost allowance for the corporation and the limit of recapture on a future disposition. Hence, only an amount that has been fully taxed to the transferor is eligible for the CCA base which will give rise to fully deductible CCA. However, for the purposes of future capital gains, the capital cost will be the $85,000 elected amount which is not affected by the limitation on capital cost for that purpose. ITA: 85(1)(a), 13(7)(e)(i)

¶16,130 Stop Loss Rules

The legislation imposes restrictions on terminal and capital losses arising from property that is transferred to certain non-arm's length persons, referred to as "affiliated persons". Some of the restrictions depend upon the type of the affiliated person (i.e., individual, corporation, etc.); others are common to all affiliated persons. These provisions are often referred to as the "stop-loss" rules.

¶16,130.10 Definition of Affiliated Persons

In order to understand the definition of "affiliated person", a few additional rules should be noted at the outset. Persons are considered to be affiliated with themselves, and a person includes a partnership. The following terms are defined: ITA: 251.1(1) Definition of "affiliated persons", 251.1(3) Definitions

(1) an "affiliated group of persons" refers to a group each member of which is affiliated with every other member; and

(2) "controlled" means controlled, directly or indirectly in any manner whatever, and, hence, includes *de facto* control as defined, discussed in a previous chapter. ITA: 256(5.1) Control in fact

Two individuals are considered to be affiliated only when they are spouses of each other, including common-law partner as defined. ITA: 248(1) common-law partner, 251.1(1)(a)

A corporation is described as being affiliated with three types of persons: ITA: 251.1(1)(b)

(1) a person by whom the corporation is controlled (as defined above);

(2) each member of an affiliated group (as defined above) by which the corporation is controlled; and

(3) the spouse of a person in either of the first two categories above.

Very generally, for example, a corporation affiliated with an individual transferor, as contemplated by section 85, is one that is controlled by the individual or the individual's spouse.

Consider the following example. A, an individual who is not married, controls A Ltd., A and two other individuals, B and C, own an equal number of shares and votes in ABC Ltd. B and C are married to each other. ITA: 85(1)(e), 85(1)(e.1)

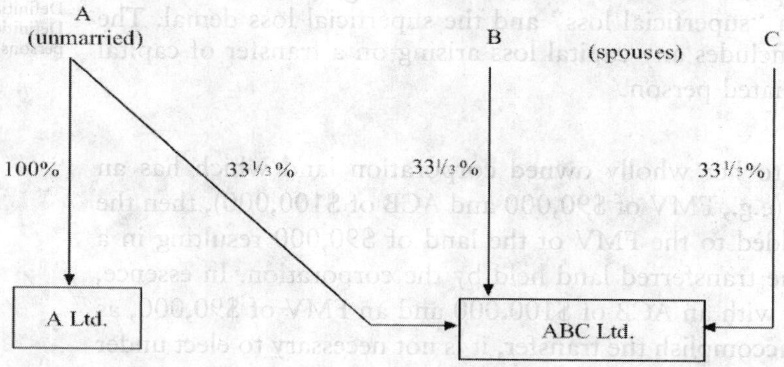

A is not affiliated with any individual, since he is not married. B and C are affiliated, because they are spouses. A Ltd. is affiliated with A since A controls it. ABC Ltd. is affiliated with both B and C, since they are members of an affiliated group that controls (i.e., owns 66⅔% of) ABC Ltd. ABC Ltd. is not affiliated with A unless A has some form of non-voting *de facto* control.

¶16,130.15 Terminal Losses

A terminal loss generally occurs where there is a positive balance in a depreciable capital property class, and the taxpayer no longer owns any property in that class. Although depreciable capital property can be transferred under section 85, depreciable capital property with an unrealized terminal loss cannot. If a transfer of such depreciable property with an unrealized terminal loss is desirable, it should be sold to the corporation at fair market value, taking back debt consideration. ITA: 13(21.2) Loss on certain transfers

A stop-loss rule denies a terminal loss on a transfer of depreciable capital property by an individual, corporation, trust, or partnership to a corporation with which the transferor is affiliated. The amount of the unrealized terminal loss is held as a notional depreciable capital property in the capital cost allowance class from which the property came and the transferor who is subject to these rules will be allowed to claim capital cost allowance on that class. On the occurrence of one of several specified events in the future, involving a disposition or deemed disposition of the property by the transferee corporation, the remaining UCC can be written off as a terminal loss by the transferor. The recipient corporation is allowed to deduct capital cost allowance on a UCC equal to the FMV of the property at the time of the transfer. The recipient corporation will be liable for recapture up to the original capital cost of the property to the transferor.

¶16,130.20 Unrealized Capital Losses

The stop-loss provisions deny the immediate recognition of the capital loss in all situations where the transferee is affiliated with the transferor. However, the subsequent treatment of the capital loss will depend upon the type of non-depreciable asset that is transferred and the type of person transferring the property.

(i) Individual transferors

For individual transferors, the denied capital loss (except for certain share transfers discussed below) is added to the adjusted cost base of the property held by the corporate transferee. For individuals, the capital loss denial is achieved through the interaction of two provisions: the definition of a "superficial loss" and the superficial loss denial. The definition of a "superficial loss" includes any capital loss arising on a transfer of capital property by individuals to an affiliated person.

ITA: 53(1)(f) [Adjustments to cost base — Substituted property], 40(2)(g), 54 Definitions, 251.1 Definition of "affiliated persons"

For example, if Ms. X transfers to her wholly owned corporation land which has an unrealized capital loss of $10,000 (e.g., FMV of $90,000 and ACB of $100,000), then the capital loss of $10,000 will be added to the FMV of the land of $90,000 resulting in a $100,000 adjusted cost base of the transferred land held by the corporation. In essence, the corporation will hold the land with an ACB of $100,000 and an FMV of $90,000, as Ms. X did before the transfer. To accomplish the transfer, it is not necessary to elect under section 85 with its conditions. A simple sale at fair market value for consideration like debt of equal fair market value is all that is necessary in the case of an individual transferor.

(ii) Corporate, trust, and partnership transferors

For corporations, trusts and partnerships, the denied capital loss (except for certain share transfers, discussed below) is subject to stop-loss rules that cause the affected capital loss to be retained by the transferor. Its recognition by the transferor is deferred until the earliest of the following events:

(1) a subsequent disposition of the transferred property to a person not affiliated with the transferor;

(2) a deemed disposition on leaving Canada and changing residence; or

ITA: 40(3.4) Loss on certain properties

(3) an acquisition of control of the corporation.

(iii) All transferors

For all taxpayers, another stop-loss rule denies a capital loss arising from the redemption of shares of a corporation where the corporation is affiliated with the taxpayer immediately after the redemption. The denied capital loss is added to the adjusted cost base of any remaining shares held by the taxpayer in the transferee corporation. For example, if the taxpayer (or another affiliated shareholder) controls the corporation after the redemption, then the loss is denied and the denied loss is added to the adjusted cost base of the remaining shares held by the taxpayer. If the taxpayer does not hold any shares after the transfer, but is still affiliated, the denied loss is lost because the taxpayer does not own any shares to which the denied loss can be added.

If all of the taxpayer's shares are redeemed and, as a result, the taxpayer is no longer affiliated, then the loss is recognized because the taxpayer is no longer affiliated with the corporation.

¶16,135 Summary of Stop-Loss Rules

The loss denial or stop-loss rules discussed above are summarized in Exhibit 16-2.

Exhibit 16-2 Stop-Loss Rules

Transferor is a corporation, trust or partnership	Transferor is an individual
Capital loss on transfer	**Capital loss on transfer**
• to an affiliated purchaser [sec. 251.1]	• to an affiliated purchaser [sec. 251.1]
• capital loss is denied [sec. 40(3.4)]	• capital loss is denied as a superficial loss [sec. 54, par. 40(2)(*g*)]
• capital loss is kept with the transferor until the transferee sells the asset to a non-affiliated person	• denied loss is added to the cost of the asset to the transferee
Terminal loss	**Terminal loss**
• on transfer to an affiliated purchaser [sec. 251.1]	• same as for corporations, trusts or partnerships
• terminal loss is denied [sec. 13(21.2)]	
• terminal loss is kept with the transferor until the transferee sells the asset to a non-affiliated person	
• transferee records the asset with a cost equal to the cost to the transferor and an addition to UCC equal to FMV [par. 13(7)(*e*)]	
Capital loss on redemption	**Capital loss on redemption**
• affiliated [sec. 251.1] immediately after the redemption	• same as for corporations, trusts or partnerships
• capital loss is denied [sec. 40(3.6)]	
• capital loss is added to the ACB of any other shares owned by the transferor; if no other shares owned, but the transferor is still affiliated, then capital loss is lost	

¶16,135.99 Practise What You've Learned

Refer to the following sections of the Study Guide to practise what you've learned:

¶16,800 — Review Questions

- Question 6 — Half-year rule
- Question 8 — Stop-loss rules

¶16,825 — Multiple Choice Questions

- Question 1 — Section 85

¶16,850 — Exercises

- Exercise 7 — Section 85

¶16,137 Section 22 Election

Where there is a potential capital loss on the transfer of accounts receivable to a corporation by an affiliated person, the rollover should not be used. Accounts receivable are capital property, and any capital loss triggered on any transfer (not just a section 85 election) to an affiliated corporation would be denied, as discussed previously. For an individual transferor, this capital loss would be passed on to the corporation through a bump in the adjusted cost base of the accounts receivable. For other transferors, the recognition is deferred in a different manner, as discussed previously. The better alternative is to use an election under section 22 on the transfer of accounts receivable in order to allow a reserve for doubtful debts and bad debt write-off in the corporation.

ITA: 85(1) Transfer of property to corporation by shareholders, 53(1)(f) [Adjustments to cost base — Substituted property]; Forms: T2202 Education and Textbooks Amounts Certificate; Information Circulars: IC 89-3 Policy statement on business equity valuations

One of the main requirements for the deduction of a reserve or a bad debt is that the transaction that gave rise to the debt must have been included previously in the taxpayer's income. If the corporation purchases the receivables and one subsequently goes bad, it cannot meet this test. Section 22 improves this situation in a case where a person has sold all or substantially all the property (including receivables) used in a business to a purchaser who proposes to continue the business. The CRA indicates that where 90% of the assets of the business carried on in Canada are sold, "all or substantially all" of the assets of such business will be considered sold. If the vendor and purchaser jointly execute and file an agreement in the prescribed form, a future reserve for doubtful debts and bad debt write-offs will be permitted to the purchaser.

ITA: 20(1)(l) Doubtful or impaired debts, 20(1)(p)(ii); Interpretation Bulletins: IT-188R Sale of accounts receivable

Consider the following set of facts:

(1) the accounts receivable have a face amount of $6,000;

(2) they have a fair market value of $4,700; and

(3) last year, the allowance for doubtful accounts was $500.

In this case the following entries would be made under the section 22 election:

Proprietor (Vendor)		
Reserve	$ 500	
Income [(par. 12(1)(*d*)]		$ 500
Consideration	4,700	
Loss from business	1,300	
Accounts receivable . . .		6,000
— Note that loss offsets income.		

Corporation (Purchaser)		
Accounts receivable	$6,000	
Consideration		$4,700
Income		1,300
— Can take reserve at year-end.		
— Can write off bad debts.		

If the section 22 election is not made, the vendor will still have to include last year's reserve in income ($500 in this case), but the loss in this case ($1,300) would be a capital loss. This loss would be denied on the transfer to the corporation by an individual as a superficial loss and would be added to the adjusted cost base of the accounts receivable in the corporation. The purchaser will have acquired the accounts receivable as capital property at the transferor's cost (i.e., FMV plus the denied capital loss). If the corporation collects less than adjusted cost base, it will have a capital loss. The purchaser would not be eligible to take a reserve for doubtful accounts or a bad debt write-off for tax purposes on the accounts acquired. ITA: 40(2)(g)

The decision tree in Exhibit 16-3 may be useful in providing an approach to problems dealing with transfer of property to a corporation.

Exhibit 16-3 Subsection 85(1) Decision Tree

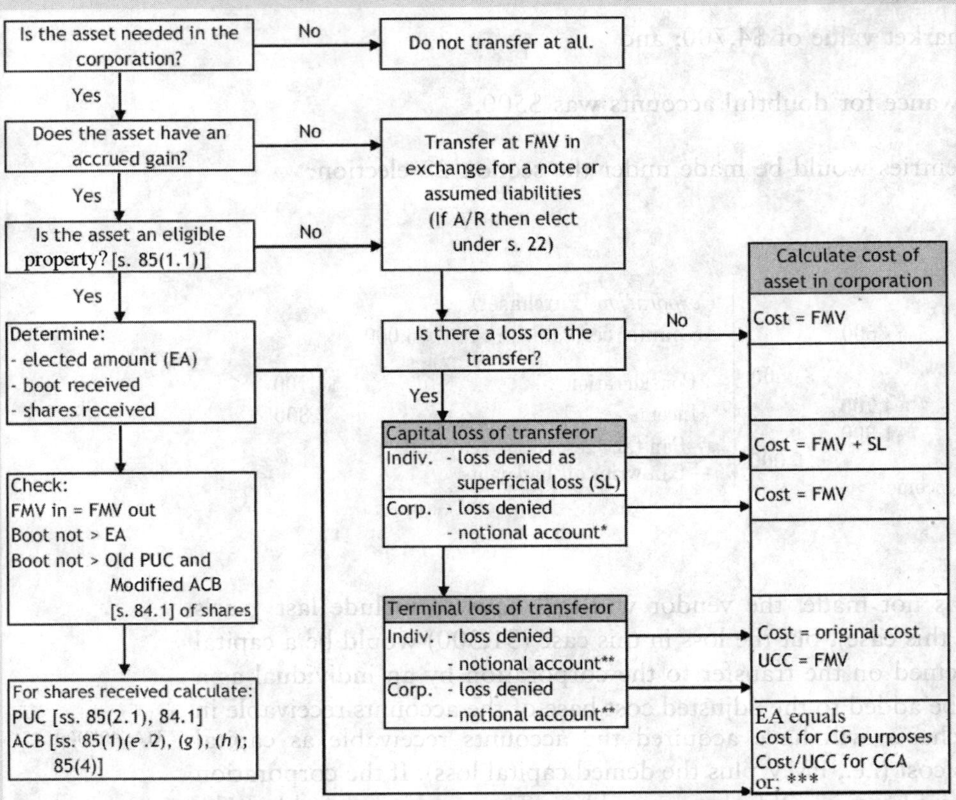

* Loss is held by a corporate transferor until the transferee corporation disposes of the property on which the loss was realized [ss. 40(3.4)].

** Balance of UCC equal to what would have been a terminal loss is held by the transferor until the transferee disposes of the property on which the loss was realized [ss.13(21.2)].

*** Cost/UCC for CCA = original cost + TCG

¶16,137.99 Practise What You've Learned

Refer to the following sections of the Study Guide to practise what you've learned:

¶16,825 — Multiple Choice Questions

- Question 5 — Section 22

¶16,140 Benefits Conferred on Shareholders and Related Persons

Throughout the chapter so far, it has been emphasized that the fair market value of the consideration taken back by the transferor must equal the fair market value of the property transferred. Now the adverse tax consequences of not adhering to this principle will be examined through the following conceptual example.

¶16,145 Conceptual Example

¶16,145.10 Conditions for Transfer

The assets can be transferred at any amount between the tax value and the fair market value of the particular asset. The consideration in this situation will be preferred shares with a specific redemption value or retraction value (shares are redeemed at the option of the corporation and retracted at the option of the shareholder). Remember that common shares, as used in the previous situations, will automatically pick up the FMV of the asset transferred net of any boot or non-share consideration. This is not true for preferred shares unless the retraction or redemption value is fixed exactly equal to the FMV of the property transferred net of any boot. Therefore, as long as the FMV of the property transferred is exactly equal to the FMV of the consideration (i.e., boot plus preferred shares) there will be no negative tax consequences as demonstrated below.

¶16,145.20 Facts

Mr. Philip wishes to transfer land to a corporation, Philip Ltd., which his daughter, Abigail, presently controls through the ownership of all the common shares.

Land — ACB	$30,000
— FMV	150,000

Mr. Philip is considering three different consideration packages:

Package (a)

Promissory note	$30,000
Non-voting preferred shares with a retraction and stated value	120,000
Total consideration	$150,000

Package (b)

Promissory note	$10,000
Non-voting preferred shares with a retraction and stated value	20,000
Total consideration	$30,000

Package (c)

Promissory note	$200,000
Non-voting preferred shares with a nominal retraction and stated value	1
Total consideration	$200,001

Package (a) is on-side and there are no adverse tax consequences.

Package (b) is off side since the FMV of the consideration is less than the FMV of the land.

Package (c) is off side since the FMV of the consideration is greater than the FMV of the land.

Both (b) and (c) result in adverse tax consequences.

Mr. Philip and Philip Ltd. are going to choose an elected amount of $30,000 equal to the ACB of the land.

The following diagram depicts the facts for this example.

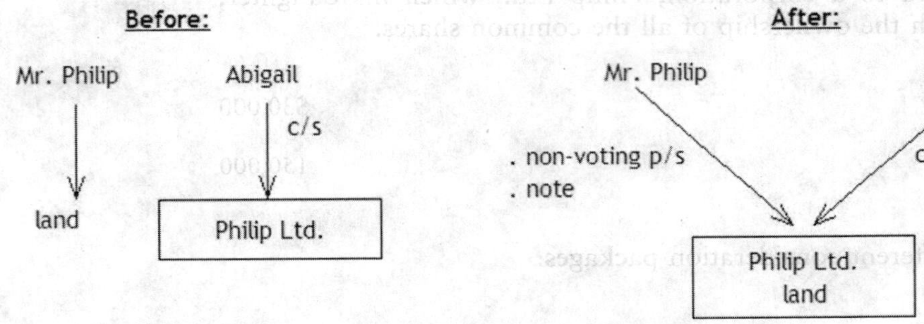

¶16,145.30 Results

Package (a)

The *first* consideration package is on-side and will not have any adverse tax consequences since the FMV of land (i.e., $150,000) equals the FMV of the consideration (i.e., $30,000 of boot plus preferred shares retractable at $120,000). Note that the boot is also on-side since it does not exceed the elected amount of $30,000. The $30,000 of boot, which will be received ultimately tax-free, reflects the tax-paid cost of the land. See Package (c) where the boot is off-side.

In summary, the following has occurred:

Before transfer		*After transfer*			
Mr. Philip owned	*Land*	*Mr. Philip owns*	*Debt*	*Corporation owns*	*Land*
ACB	$ 30,000	ACB	$ 30,000	ACB	$ 30,000
FMV	150,000	FMV	30,000	FMV	150,000
		Mr. Philip owns	*Preferred Shares*	*Corporation owes to:*	
		ACB	Nil	Mr. Philip	$ 30,000
		PUC	Nil		
		FMV	$120,000		

Package (b) Benefit conferred on a related person

A benefit is deemed to have been conferred on a related person:

(a) where the fair market value of the property, immediately before it is transferred to the corporation, exceeds the greater of:

(i) the fair market value immediately after the transfer of all consideration received from the corporation, and

(ii) the elected amount; and

(b) where it is reasonable to regard any part of that excess as a benefit conferred by the taxpayer on a person related to the taxpayer.

The result is that the elected amount or transfer price is increased by that part of the excess that is a benefit, but there is no increase in the cost of the share consideration received. ITA: 85(1)(e.2)

The *second* consideration package is off-side since Mr. Philip has accepted consideration which, in total, is less than the FMV of the land (i.e., ($10,000 + $20,000) compared to $150,000). Mr. Philip is deemed to have conferred a benefit (gift) on his daughter of $120,000 (i.e., the FMV of the land ($150,000) – the FMV of the consideration ($10,000 + $20,000)). Since the daughter is the common shareholder, this $120,000 difference (contributed surplus in accounting terms) will increase the FMV of the common shares. In essence, Mr. Philip has attempted to pass $120,000 of the accumulated growth in the land that should be taxed in his hands to his daughter. The tax consequences of this off-side transaction will be as follows: ITA: 69(1)(b), 69(1)(c)

(1) The original elected amount of $30,000 will be bumped by the amount of the gift (i.e., $120,000) to $150,000 which is exactly equal to the FMV of the land (i.e., $150,000) and a capital gain of $120,000 will be triggered in Mr. Philip's hands since his proceeds of disposition are now $150,000.

(2) The ACB of the land now held by Philip Ltd. will be the new elected amount of $150,000.

(3) Since the ACB of the preferred shares cannot exceed their retraction amount of $20,000 (the fair market value), a downward adjustment must be made from the elected amount. The ACB of the preferred shares of $20,000 is determined as the original elected amount of $30,000 (not the new elected amount of $150,000) minus the $10,000 allocated to the boot. This ACB of $20,000 is now equal to the retraction amount. However, there is an inherent but hidden penalty in

Abigail's common shares, since they retain their original ACB while the value has increased by $120,000 as a result of the gift. Therefore, she will realize a capital gain of $120,000 on the ultimate disposition of her shares upon which her dad has already paid tax. This is analogous to the one-sided adjustments in section 69, discussed in Chapter 8, on non-arm's length transfers that can result in a double-counting of income. To avoid the pitfall of this benefit rule, the transferor should always take as consideration from the corporation a package with a total fair market value equal to the fair market value of the property transferred to the corporation. In the above example, if Mr. Philip owned 100% of the shares of the corporation, there would be no benefit. If he owned some but not all of the common shares, then the benefit would have been prorated between the Mr. Philip and his daughter, with the amount allocated to Abigail comprising the benefit.

(4) The PUC of Mr. Philip's preferred shares, however, will be calculated with the *increased* elected amount of $150,000 as calculated below:

Stated capital[1]		$20,000
Less: elected amount (new)	$150,000	
less: boot	10,000	140,000
PUC reduction		Nil
Therefore PUC		$20,000

[1] Note that under the *Canada Business Corporations Act* (CBCA), normally the stated value of the share consideration must equal the fair market value of the property transferred (i.e., $150,000, the FMV of the land). However, for non-arm's length transactions, the stated value can, at the discretion of the corporate directors, be set at less than the fair market value (i.e., $20,000).

This $20,000 represents the remaining cost of the land transferred (i.e., $30,000) after taking out boot in the form of a promissory note (i.e., $10,000).

In summary, the following has occurred:

Before transfer		*After transfer*			
Mr. Philip owned	*Land*	*Mr. Philip owns*	*Debt*	*Corporation owns*	*Land*
ACB	$ 30,000	ACB	$ 10,000	ACB	$150,000
FMV	150,000	FMV	10,000	FMV	150,000
			Preferred	*Corporation owes to:*	
		Mr. Philip owns	*Shares*	*Mr. Philip*	*$10,000*
		ACB	$ 20,000		
		PUC	20,000		
		FMV	20,000		
		Mr. Philip has a capital gain of $120,000 to include in his income, but no compensating increase in the ACB of his shares.		*The value of the corporation's common shares held by the daughter has increased by $120,000 with no ACB increase for daughter.*	

Package (c) Subsection 15(1) benefit conferred on a shareholder

This benefit rule provides for what is, in essence, a penalty where the fair market value of the property transferred to a corporation is less than the fair market value of the non-share consideration received from the corporation. In these circumstances, the Act encourages a balancing of the fair market value of the total consideration with the fair market value of the property transferred. The excess consideration will result in a benefit conferred on a shareholder that is taxed as income to the transferor.

The *third* consideration package is also off-side since Mr. Philip has accepted consideration which, in total, is more than the FMV of the land (i.e., $150,000 compared to $200,000 boot plus preferred shares with a retraction and stated value of a nominal amount). The tax consequences are as follows:

(1) The boot of $200,000 exceeds the elected amount of $30,000; hence, the elected amount is bumped to $150,000 triggering a capital gain of $120,000. Note that the elected amount can never exceed the FMV of the transferred property (i.e., land with a FMV of $150,000 in this case).

(2) There will be a benefit conferred on Mr. Philip as a shareholder:

FMV of consideration			
Boot	$200,000		
Retraction value of preferred shares	nominal	$200,000	
Less: FMV of land		150,000	
Benefit		$50,000	ITA: 15(1) Benefit conferred on shareholder

This benefit of $50,000 will be added to the cost of the boot consideration received. Since the elected amount of $150,000 becomes the initial cost of boot, the ACB of the boot is increased to $200,000 (i.e., the $150,000 of the elected amount allocated to the boot plus the subsection 15(1) benefit of $50,000).

ITA: 15(1) Benefit conferred on shareholder, 52(1) Cost of certain property the value of which is included in income

(3) The cost to the corporation of the land will be the *new* elected amount of $150,000.

(4) The ACB of the preferred shares will be:

Elected amount (new)	$150,000
Less: boot	200,000
Excess	Nil

(5) The PUC will be reduced to nil as follows:

Stated value		nominal
Less: elected amount (new)	$150,000	
boot	(200,000)	Nil
Reduction		nominal
Therefore PUC = (nominal – nominal)		Nil

All of the tax-paid cost of $200,000 is represented in the value of the boot which will be repaid without further tax cost in the future. Therefore, nothing is left to recover tax free in the PUC of the shares on their redemption. In this situation, after the transfer, there is a total tax-paid cost of $200,000 derived from:

Cost of the original land	$30,000	
Capital gain triggered on the section 85 transfer (i.e., $150,000 – $30,000)	120,000	
Benefit	50,000	ITA: 15(1) Benefit conferred on shareholder
	$200,000	

This tax-paid cost is reflected in the ACB of the boot (i.e., the $200,000 demonstrated above).

In summary, the following has occurred:

Before transfer		*After transfer*			
Mr. Philip owned	*Land*	*Mr. Philip owns*	*Debt*	*Corporation owns*	*Land*
ACB	$ 30,000	ACB	$200,000	ACB	$150,000
FMV	150,000	FMV	200,000	FMV	150,000
		Mr. Philip owns	*Shares*	*Corporation owes to:*	
		ACB	Nil	Mr. Philip	$200,000
		PUC	Nil		
		FMV	Nil		
		Mr. Philip has income from a capital gain of $120,000 and property income of $50,000.			

¶16,145.40 Conclusion

This situation clearly demonstrates that as long as the FMV of the consideration received equals the FMV of the property transferred there will be no adverse tax consequences. Where these two amounts are not equal then income inclusions will be triggered.

¶16,145.99 Practise What You've Learned

Refer to the following sections of the Study Guide to practise what you've learned:

¶16,825 — Multiple Choice Questions

- Question 2 — Boot
- Question 3 — Transfer of depreciable property

¶16,850 — Exercises

- Exercise 4 — Consideration

¶16,170 Fair Market Value

From the foregoing discussion, the importance of the role of fair market value should be apparent. The fair market value of property transferred to a corporation must be established in order to determine the fair market value of both non-share and share consideration to receive from the corporation. The valuation of common shares of a privately-held corporation, in particular, can present problems.

The term "fair market value" is mentioned more than 600 times in the Act. In addition to the requirements of section 85, determinations of fair market value are most commonly required pursuant to the following sections:

- Subsection 52(2) — payment of dividends in kind;
- Section 69 — non-arm's length transactions;
- Section 70 — deemed dispositions on death;
- Subsection 104(4) — deemed disposition of trust property after 21 years;
- Section 160 — certain transfers between spouses.

Historically, the Canada Revenue Agency (CRA) has provided little guidance as to what was required of taxpayers to support valuations required for these sections. Business valuations are generally not filed with the CRA as part of typical transaction documentation. In order to ensure that a subsequent review of fair market values by the CRA does not result in a one-sided adjustment causing double taxation, many taxpayers avail themselves of a price adjustment clause.

A price adjustment clause can ensure that if the CRA determines that a sale price does not reflect fair market value, the price will be adjusted appropriately. Case law indicates that a price adjustment clause will only be recognized if the parties have reasonably, and in good faith, attempted to determine transaction prices that equal fair market values.[1]

Income Tax Folio: S4-F3-C1 Price Adjustment Clauses

An Information Circular provides a detailed listing of specific factors that should be considered and analyzed in business valuations. The Circular discusses the conventional approaches to business valuations, being the assets and the earnings methods, and also deals with such sophisticated areas as options, buy-sell agreements and the concepts of family and group control.

Information Circulars: IC 89-3 Policy statement on business equity valuations

The CRA undertakes sophisticated reviews of fair market value determinations. Undoubtedly, the income tax practitioner must be aware of these requirements in order to ensure compliance with the various sections of the Act as illustrated by section 85 where fair market value determinations are required.

¶16,170.99 Practise What You've Learned

Refer to the following sections of the Study Guide to practise what you've learned:

¶16,800 — Review Questions

- Question 12 — Consideration

¶16,190 Application of Section 85

Example Problem 16-4

Randall operates an unincorporated business having the following balance sheet stated in tax values at its taxation year end:

	Tax value	Fair market value
Cash	$1,000	$1,000
Marketable securities	11,000	15,000
Accounts receivable	5,500	4,700
Inventory	7,000	7,000

[1] *Guilder News Co. (1963) Ltd. et al. v. M.N.R.*, 73 DTC 5048 (F.C.A.).

	Tax value	Fair market value
Prepaid rent	3,000	3,000
Land	42,000	31,000
Buildings (capital cost — $46,000)	28,000	50,000
Equipment (capital cost — $20,000)	8,000	3,000
Goodwill	—	47,000
Total assets	$105,500	$161,700
Liabilities		8,000
		$153,700

The marketable securities represent an investment of surplus funds held for anticipated future expansion and can be considered to pertain to the active business. The accounts receivable figure is shown net of the reserve of $500 deducted at the end of the preceding taxation year.

Randall has just met with you to talk about incorporating his business.

He is a Canadian resident and wishes to transfer all of his business assets and liabilities to a corporation. He wants your advice on how to do this with the minimum amount of personal tax.

Randall has specifically asked you to provide him with a tax-effective plan to achieve his objectives.

He has heard that he will have to receive some shares as consideration, so he wants to know the tax consequences if he sells these shares or has the company buy them back at a later date.

For the next meeting you agree that you will:

REQUIRED

(A) Assess the situation

(B) Identify the issues

(C) Analyze the issues

(D) Advise/recommend

(A) Assess the Situation

(1) Draw a diagram identifying all stakeholders, e.g., corporate org charts

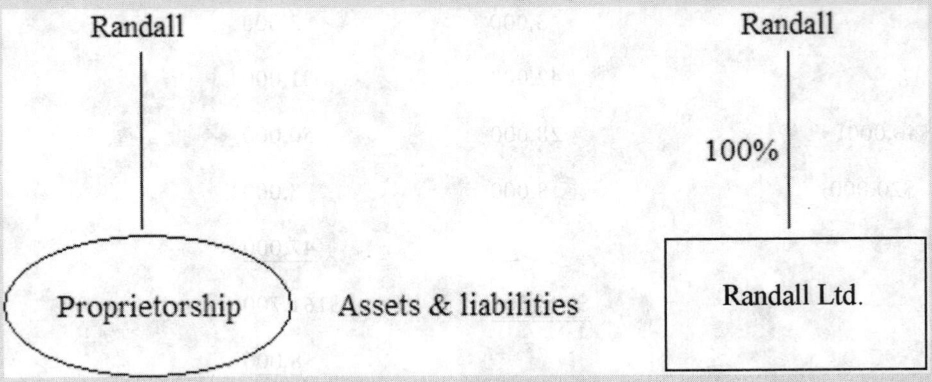

(2) Identify the relationships among the stakeholders, e.g., related, affiliated, associated, connected

Randall and Randall Ltd. are related and affiliated since he owns 100% of the shares

(3) Identify the profile of each stakeholder, e.g., tax features, risk profile

a. Randall
- — An individual resident in Canada
- — Carrying on a business through a proprietorship

b. Randall Ltd.
- — A CCPC since it is a private corporation owned by a Canadian-resident individual
- — It will be carrying on an active business after Randall transfers the proprietorship assets

(4) Understand the decision maker and their objectives

a. Randall wants to incorporate his business

b. He wants advice on how to do this with the minimum amount of tax

c. He wants you to come up with a tax-efficient plan

d. He wants to know the tax consequences if he sells or redeems the shares he receives as consideration

(5) Identify the relevant past transaction/events or planned future transactions/events and create a timeline

a. On a future date, Randall will transfer all of his business assets and liabilities to Randall Ltd.

b. Randall will own common shares of Randall Ltd. after the transfer

(B) Identify the Issues

(1) Identify all of the major tax issues and any non-tax issues

a. Confirm that s. 85(1) can be used to defer the gain on the sale of the assets to the corporation

b. Identify the assets that should not be transferred at all but kept by Randall

c. Identify the assets that should be transferred but where s. 85(1) cannot be used

— Determine any resulting tax liability

— Determine the type/amount of consideration to be received

d. Identify the assets that can be transferred with an election under s. 85(1)

— Determine an elected amount for each asset

— Determine the type/amount of consideration to be received

— Determine the ACB/PUC of shares received

e. Identify characteristics of the shares that give them value and meet the client's objectives

f. Identify tax consequences if the share consideration is sold or redeemed

(2) Identify missing information or assumptions made

None identified

(C) Analyze the Major Issues

(1) Identify and perform the qualitative analysis of the transactions and plans including an analysis of the applicable provisions of the Act

a. Does s. 85(1) apply?

— Randall is a taxpayer

— Randall Ltd. will be a taxable Canadian corporation

— A joint election between Randall and Randall Ltd. must be filed

— Property must be eligible property

— Share consideration must be received

b. Items that should not be transferred at all

Marketable Securities

The marketable securities would not be earning Canadian active business income. It may therefore make sense to keep them out of the corporation to ensure that Randall Ltd. qualifies as a small business corporation [ssec. 248(1)] and a qualified small business corporation [sec. 110.6].

c. Assets transferred without s. 85(1)

Prepaids and cash

Prepaid expenses and cash are not eligible property and cannot be transferred using section 85.

Loss properties

Properties with losses should not be transferred using s. 85(1). Capital property with accrued losses should not be transferred to the corporation under section 85 since there is no gain to defer. These properties can be sold at fair market value in return for boot like any of the above assets. The stop loss rules need to be considered.

Inventory

A transfer of the inventory under the rollover is not recommended, because there is no income to defer on the transfer and the transfer would be subject to all of the section 85 restrictions.

ITA: 85(1) Transfer of property to corporation by shareholders

Land

A transfer of the land under the rollover is not recommended, because there is no gain to defer on the transfer. The capital loss will be denied on the transfer. However, the accrued loss would be preserved in the ACB of $42,000 in the corporation. Where the fair market value is less than the adjusted cost base of capital property (but not depreciable capital property) to be transferred to a corporation by an individual, the capital loss is denied for any transfer to an affiliated person. The denied loss, however, is added to the corporation's adjusted cost base of the transferred asset. This puts the corporation in exactly the same tax position as an individual transferor was in prior to the transfer.

ITA: 40(2)(g), 54 Definitions, 85(1) Transfer of property to corporation by shareholders

Equipment

A transfer of the equipment under the rollover is not permitted because of the unrealized terminal loss on the property. Randall can sell the equipment directly to the corporation and take back debt equal to the fair market value. The terminal loss will be denied and suspended. Randall will continue to claim CCA on the terminal loss until the corporation disposes of the equipment in the future.

ITA: 13(21.2) Loss on certain transfers, 85(1) Transfer of property to corporation by shareholders

Accounts receivable — Section 22

Accounts receivable are capital property; hence, any capital loss arising on the transfer would be denied and, for an individual transferor, added to the adjusted cost base of the transferred accounts receivable. If, however, Randall and the corporation jointly elect under section 22, then:

(1) the loss of $1,300 (i.e., $5,500 tax value net of reserve + $500 reserve taken into income − $4,700 fair market value) is deemed to be a business loss, rather than a capital loss; and

(2) the business loss of Randall must be taken into the corporation's income. This action will permit the corporation to write off any

uncollectible accounts receivable and to set up a reserve in respect of doubtful accounts receivable.

d. Assets transferred with s. 85(1)

Goodwill must be transferred at least at a nominal amount of $1.00 so that it is listed in the election. Since the courts have consistently determined that Nil is not an amount, the CRA would apply the non-arm's length transfer rule to deem the sale at the fair market value which would trigger a taxable capital gain. Note that it is permissible to take $1 in debt, but the instruction was to take debt only to the nearest $100.

ITA: 85(1) Transfer of property to corporation by shareholders, 69 Inadequate considerations

The elected transfer price becomes the proceeds of disposition for each property to the transferor, the cost of each property to the corporation and the adjusted cost base of the consideration received from the corporation by the transferor.

The building would be transferred at tax cost of $28,000 by choosing an elected amount of that amount. This would defer the realization of the recapture and capital gain on the property until the corporation disposes of the property in the future. The corporation acquires the building with a UCC of $28,000 and capital cost of $46,000. The corporation assumes the tax attributes and unrealized recapture and capital gain on the building.

Consider the liabilities assumed by the corporation as part of the consideration other than shares received from the corporation against part of the property transferred, thereby reducing the amount of new debt to be taken. According to the CRA, the most common error made in using the rollover election is to forget that assumed liabilities are part of the boot received. Note that the $8,000 of liabilities could have been assumed by the corporation in return for the assets not transferred under the rollover, instead of in return for the assets transferred under the rollover.

e. Identify characteristics of the shares that give them value and meet the objectives of the client

— Shares should be taken as consideration to bring the total consideration up to the fair market value of the property transferred.

— Preferred shares should be redeemable and retractable.

— Dividend rights/rates should be considered in meeting the client's income earning objectives.

— Voting rights should be considered in meeting the client's control objectives.

f. Identify tax consequences if the share consideration is sold or redeemed

If the share consideration is sold in the future, as long as all or substantially all of the properties used in the active business were transferred to the corporation, the shares are deemed to be capital property and the disposition of the shares results in a capital gain or loss. If the shares are QSBC shares at the time, the capital gains exemption may be available for use to minimize tax. If the shares are redeemed in the future, a deemed dividend and possibly a capital gain/loss could result.

(2) Identify and complete the supporting quantitative analysis of the transactions and plans using an appropriate analysis format

Assets transferred without s. 85(1)

	Tax value	Fair market value	Transfer price	New debt	Income effect
Cash	$1,000	$1,000	$1,000	$1,000	Nil
Accounts receivable	6,000	4,700	4,700	4,700	business loss allowed
Inventory	7,000	7,000	7,000	7,000	Nil
Prepaid rent	3,000	3,000	3,000	3,000	Nil
Land	42,000	31,000	31,000	31,000	capital loss denied
Equipment	8,000	3,000	3,000	3,000	terminal loss denied
Total	$67,000	$49,700	$49,700	$49,700	

ITA: 251.1 Definition of "affiliated persons", 53(1)(f) [Adjustments to cost base — Substituted property]

ITA: 85(1) Transfer of property to corporation by shareholders

Assets transferred under s. 85(1)

	Tax value	Fair market value	Elected transfer price	FMV of consideration: Assumed debt	New debt	Shares	Income/ Effect
Buildings	28,000	50,000	28,000	8,000	20,000	22,000	Nil
Goodwill	Nil	47,000	1	—	—	47,000	$0.50
	$28,000	$97,000	$28,001	$8,000	$20,000	$69,000	

(B) The cost of shares would be:

Elected transfer price of assets (in total)		$28,001
Deduct:		
Debt issued	$20,000	
Liabilities assumed	8,000	28,000
ACB of the common shares		$1

The tax PUC of the shares would be:

ITA: 85(2.1) Computing paid-up capital

ITA: 85(1) Transfer of property to corporation by shareholders

LSC of share consideration before reduction			$69,000
Less: reduction in PUC:			
(i) increase in LSC of all shares on the transfer to the corporation		$69,000 (A)	
(ii) elected amount	$28,001		
less: non-share consideration	28,000		
excess, if any		1 (B)	
	(A – B)	$68,999	
(iii) increase in LSC of a class of shares issued on the transfer		$69,000 (C)	
Reduction: (A – B) × C/A = $68,999 × $69,000/$69,000			$68,999
Tax PUC of share consideration			$1

Tax consequences if share consideration sold or redeemed

Taxable capital gain

Proceeds of disposition	$69,000
ACB of shares	1
Capital gain	$68,999
Taxable capital gain (1/2 × $68,999)	$34,500

(ii) Tax consequence of redemption of all the shares

Redemption amount	$69,000
Less: tax PUC	1
Deemed dividend	$68,999
Redemption amount	$69,000
Less: deemed dividend	$68,999
Proceeds of disposition	$1
Less: adjusted cost base	1
Capital gain/loss	Nil

ITA: 84(3) Redemption, etc.

ITA: 54 Definitions

Note how the net economic effect of $68,999 of deemed dividend on the redemption is the same as the capital gain in (c)(i) above and is equal to the gain on the assets deferred by the rollover on their transfer to the corporation.

ITA: 85(1) Transfer of property to corporation by shareholders

Identify risks including missing information, assumptions and uncertain research positions

Corporate attribution [74.4]/Benefit conferred [85(1)(e.2)]

— No issues as only Randall will own common shares of Randall Ltd. after the asset transfer.

(D) Advise/Recommend

(1) Advise the decision maker, integrating your conclusions on each of the issues with their objectives, giving priority to the most important issues

Randall should transfer the cash, accounts receivable and the prepaid expenses, but not under s. 85 as they are not eligible property. He should elect under s. 22 for the accounts receivable to receive business loss treatment for the doubtful accounts. Inventory, land and equipment also should be transferred but not under s. 85 as there are no gains or income to defer on these assets.

He should transfer the rest of the assets and elect under s. 85 at tax values to defer the capital gain/recapture.

He should have the corporation assume the liabilities as partial consideration for the transfer of assets.

If Randall sells the shares, he will have a capital gain of $69,000 and tax of $17,250 (at 25%). He will receive $51,750 of after-tax proceeds.

If he redeems the shares, he will have a deemed dividend of $68,999 and no capital gain or loss and tax of $28,980 (at 42%). He will receive $40,020 of after-tax proceeds. The sale of the shares is more tax effective but requires him to find a buyer to purchase the shares.

Example Problem 16-4 Extension

If Randall had a net capital loss available for use at the time of the transfer, how could the election under s. 85 be optimized to use the loss?

SOLUTION

An election, at up to $47,000, for the goodwill would have resulted in a taxable capital gain of $23,500. The capital cost to the corporation would be restricted to only $23,500 (i.e., the original capital cost of nil plus the taxable capital gain of $23,500 for purposes of calculating CCA on the Class 14.1 asset). This election would allow boot (debt consideration) of $47,000 that could be repaid by the corporation later without any tax consequences. Furthermore, the corporation would be deemed to have acquired the goodwill at an adjusted cost base of $47,000 for purposes of calculating the capital gain on a future disposition.

If an election were made on the building at fair market value of $50,000 to trigger the accrued capital gain of $4,000, the capital cost to the corporation would be restricted to only $48,000 (i.e., the original capital cost of $46,000 plus the taxable capital gain of $2,000 (½ × ($50,000 – $46,000))). The transferor would also trigger recapture of $18,000 (i.e., capital cost of $46,000 minus UCC of $28,000). The corporation will have an adjusted cost base of $50,000 for calculating the capital gain on a future disposition. The latter election on the building would probably not be beneficial unless the transferor had some non-capital losses to offset the recapture.

ITA: 85(1) Transfer of property to corporation by shareholders; Information Circulars: IC -76-19R3

¶16,190.99 Practise What You've Learned

Refer to the following sections of the Study Guide to practise what you've learned:

¶16,850 — Exercises

- Exercise 6 — Incorporate sole proprietorship
- Exercise 12 — Incorporate sole proprietorship

¶16,200 Transfer of Shares

¶16,210 Dividend Stripping on the Non-Arm's Length Sale of Shares by an Individual

¶16,215 What Is Dividend Stripping

To understand the intent behind the legislation in the ITA designed to prevent dividend stripping, it is helpful to first consider the result ignoring the existence of such legislation. The following example illustrates how without s. 84.1 it would be possible through a non-arm's length transaction to extract surplus from a corporation that would otherwise be subject to tax as a deemed dividend arising on the redemption of the shares of the corporation.

Example

Consider the case of Mr. Sinclair. Mr. Sinclair has $99,000 of remaining capital exemption. He incorporated a company Streamline Limited, about 20 years ago, investing $1,000 in common shares. These shares, all of which are owned by Mr. Sinclair, currently have a fair market value of $200,000. If Mr. Sinclair sold the shares in an arm's length transaction, he would realize a capital gain of $199,000. Perhaps more important, Mr. Sinclair would receive part of the capital gain tax free by offsetting it with the $99,000 of his available QSBC share capital gains exemption.

However, Mr. Sinclair does not want to sell his shares and give up the business, but the prospect of receiving $99,000 of the accrued gain tax-free is attractive, particularly if he can receive it out of surplus sitting in Streamline Limited. If Mr. Sinclair continues to own the shares, the only way that he can receive the surplus represented by the $200,000 value is to receive a taxable dividend of $199,000, which would be subject to a 42% tax rate if he were in the highest tax bracket and the dividend were a LRIP dividend.

To achieve his objective of using his capital gains exemption without losing control of the corporation, Mr. Sinclair decides to set up a holding company, Holdit Ltd., and transfers his shares in Streamline Ltd. to Holdit Ltd. using the provisions of section 85. He chooses to transfer his shares at an elected amount of $100,000 to realize $99,000 of capital gains on the transfer. As consideration for these shares, he can take from Holdit Ltd. up to $100,000 in debt. As long as his non-share consideration does not exceed the elected amount, all of his capital gain will be offset by capital gains exemption. He also needs to receive at least one share of Holdit Ltd., to qualify the transfer under section 85. It should be easy to see that if he takes, for example, cash of $100,000 from Holdit Ltd., he will have received $99,000 of the accrued gain on the shares of Streamline Ltd. tax free. Holdit could borrow the $100,000 for this purpose.

The $100,000 loan could be repaid by having Streamline Ltd., which Holdit Ltd. now owns, pay a dividend to Holdit Ltd. which, in turn, would be used to repay the borrowed funds. This dividend would be received by Holdit Ltd. free of Part I tax and, normally, free of Part IV tax, since Streamline Ltd. is connected with Holdit Ltd. Other variations of this scheme are possible using debt or shares of Holdit Ltd. issued to Mr. Sinclair. The general situation can be diagrammed as shown in Exhibit 16-4.

Exhibit 16-4 Non-Arm's Length Sale of Shares

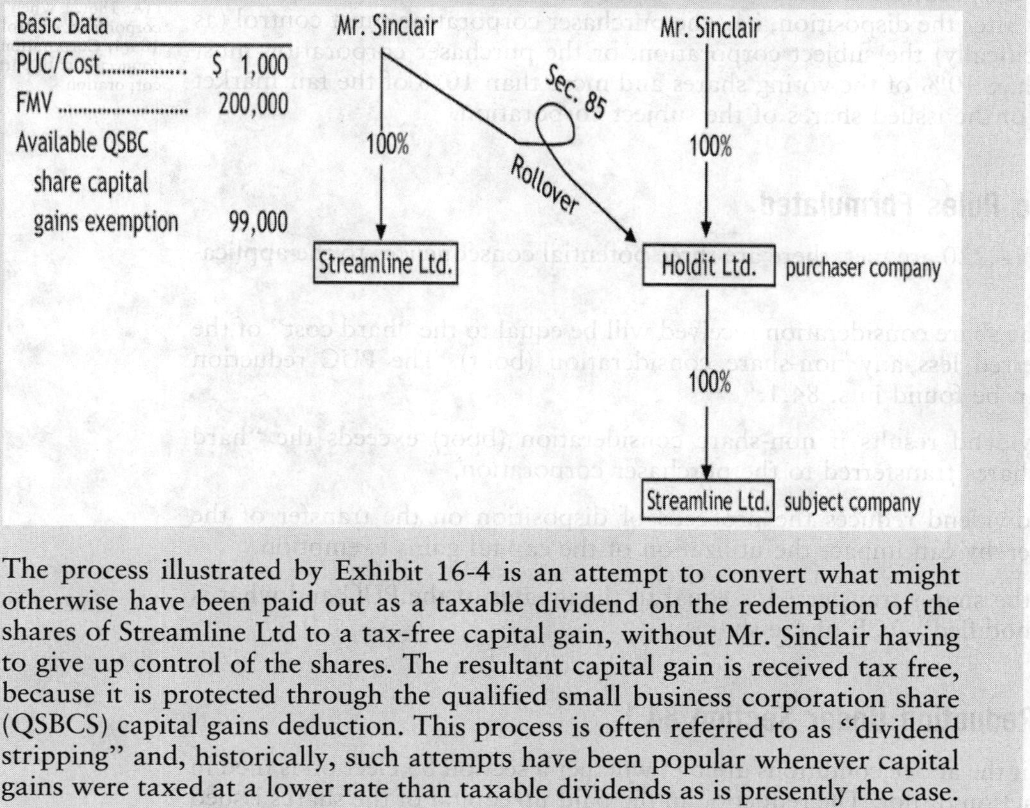

The process illustrated by Exhibit 16-4 is an attempt to convert what might otherwise have been paid out as a taxable dividend on the redemption of the shares of Streamline Ltd to a tax-free capital gain, without Mr. Sinclair having to give up control of the shares. The resultant capital gain is received tax free, because it is protected through the qualified small business corporation share (QSBCS) capital gains deduction. This process is often referred to as "dividend stripping" and, historically, such attempts have been popular whenever capital gains were taxed at a lower rate than taxable dividends as is presently the case.

A provision will be shown to turn capital gains derived by the process described back into taxable deemed dividends under certain conditions. It appears to be the non-arm's length nature of the sale of shares, in which the benefits of owning the shares are effectively maintained, that offends the legislation. Any other type of asset, such as land, buildings or eligible capital property, transferred to a corporation under similar conditions is not affected by this provision.

ITA: 84.1 Non-arm's length sale of shares

¶16,220 Conditions for Section 84.1 To Apply

The following conditions, as set out at the beginning of the provision, must exist in order for section 84.1 to apply:

ITA: 84.1(1) Non-arm's length sale of shares

(1) the disposition must be made by a taxpayer resident in Canada other than a corporation;

(2) the subject shares (the shares being transferred) must be shares of a corporation resident in Canada and must be capital property to the taxpayer;

(3) the disposition must be made to a corporation with which the taxpayer does not deal at arm's length within the standard meaning of the phrase under subsection 251(1);[2] and

(4) the subject corporation must be connected with the purchaser corporation immediately after the disposition, i.e., the purchaser corporation must control (as defined specifically) the subject corporation, or the purchaser corporation must own more than 10% of the voting shares and more than 10% of the fair market value of all of the issued shares of the subject corporation.

ITA: 186(2) When corporation controlled, 186(4) Corporations connected with particular corporation

¶16,225 The Basic Rules Formulated

If the conditions in ¶16,220 are met, there are three potential consequences to the application of section 84.1:

- The PUC of the share consideration received will be equal to the "hard cost" of the shares transferred less any non-share consideration (boot). The PUC reduction calculation can be found in s. 84.1.
- A deemed dividend results if non-share consideration (boot) exceeds the "hard cost" of the shares transferred to the purchaser corporation.
- The deemed dividend reduces the proceeds of disposition on the transfer of the shares and thereby can impact the utilization of the capital gains exemption.

The "hard cost" of the shares transferred is equal to the greater of the PUC and what is referred to as the "modified" ACB of the shares.

ITA: 84.1(2)(a)

¶16,225.10 PUC Reduction Under Section 84.1

Section 84.1 applies if the above conditions are met whether a section 85 election is filed in relation to the transaction or not. The reduction in the paid-up capital of the shares issued by a purchaser company where section 84.1 applies is calculated under the provision using the "hard cost" of the shares transferred. The PUC reduction that applies when property is transferred using section 85 does not apply where section 84.1 applies (see the condition in the preamble of s. 85(2.1)). Remember that the PUC reduction calculation in section 85 results in a PUC for the share consideration that equals the elected amount less any non-share consideration (boot).

ITA: 84.1(1)(a)

The following formula computes a reduction in paid-up capital for all new shares of the corporation issued and, then, allocates a part of the reduction to each class of shares.

[2] The definition of non-arm's length is extended to include groups of persons under certain circumstances [par. 84.1(2)(*b*) and sec. 84.1(2.2)].

PUC reduction:			
(1) Increase, if any, in legal stated capital (LSC) of purchaser corporation			xxx (A)
Less:			
(2) Greater of:			
(a) PUC of shares transferred	xxx		
(b) modified ACB of shares transferred (based on adjusted actual cost ignoring any increase in the ACB as a result of the capital gains exemption)	xxx	xxx	
Less: Fair market value of non-share consideration received (boot)		(xxx)	
Excess, if any			xxx (B)
Total PUC reduction of all shares (A – B)			xxx

PUC reduction of shares of any particular class for which increase in LSC was C:

$$(A - B) \times C/A$$

As noted above, the hard cost of the shares transferred is equal to the greater of the PUC and what is referred to as the "modified" ACB of the shares. ITA: 84.1(2)(a)

If the ACB of the shares includes an amount claimed as the capital gains exemption by that person or a related person, then the modified ACB will be determined by deducting the capital gains exemption claimed from the ACB of the shares otherwise determined.

Recognize that a reduction in paid-up capital has no tax consequences unless and until the shares received as consideration are redeemed by the issuing corporation. ITA: 84.1(1)(a)

Conceptually, the PUC of the shares after the reduction will be equal to their "hard cost" (i.e., the greater of PUC and modified ACB) that has not been recovered by the boot received by the transferor.

¶16,225.20 Deemed Dividend Under Section 84.1

The rules provide for an immediate deemed dividend to the transferor of subject shares depending on the level of boot taken back on the transfer. The following formula computes the deemed dividend. ITA: 84.1(1)(b)

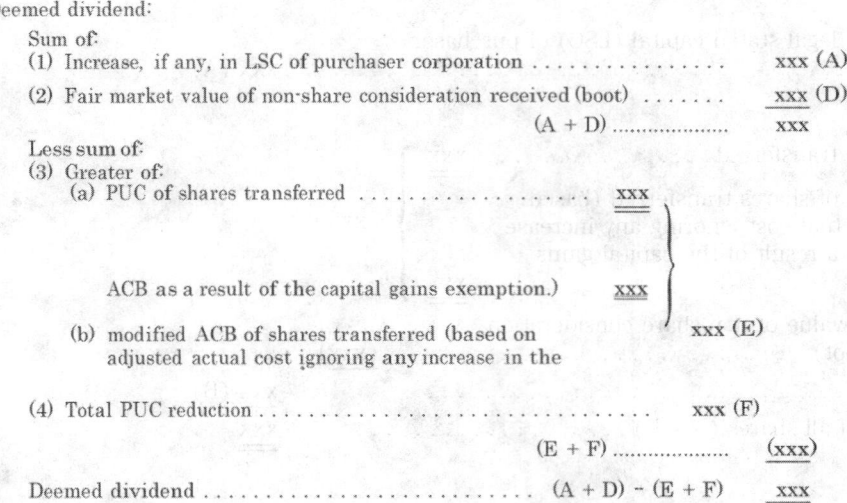

Deemed dividend:			
Sum of:			
(1) Increase, if any, in LSC of purchaser corporation			xxx (A)
(2) Fair market value of non-share consideration received (boot)			xxx (D)
	(A + D)		xxx
Less sum of:			
(3) Greater of:			
(a) PUC of shares transferred	xxx		
ACB as a result of the capital gains exemption.)	xxx		
(b) modified ACB of shares transferred (based on adjusted actual cost ignoring any increase in the		xxx (E)	
(4) Total PUC reduction		xxx (F)	
	(E + F)		(xxx)
Deemed dividend	(A + D) − (E + F)		xxx

Conceptually, the deemed dividend will usually be equal to the boot received by the transferor in excess of the "hard cost" of the shares transferred (i.e., the greater of their PUC and their modified ACB).

¶16,230 Application of Rules

Recall the case of Mr. Sinclair, at ¶16,215, with the following basic data:

Paid-up capital and cost of shares transferred (Streamline)	$1,000
Fair market value of shares transferred	200,000
Elected amount under sec. 85(1)	100,000
Available QSBC share capital gains exemption	99,000

Exhibit 16-5 shows the application of these rules to the situation if Mr. Sinclair takes one of two consideration packages from Holdit Ltd. on the transfer of the above shares. Case A uses non-share consideration in excess of hard cost. It illustrates how the rules are designed to prevent a dividend strip and the importance of limiting non-share consideration to the hard cost of the shares transferred. Case B uses no non-share consideration and illustrates the situation where use of the capital gains exemption is possible in a non-arm's length transaction without resulting in immediate tax consequences.

ITA: 84.1 Non-arm's length sale of shares

Exhibit 16-5 Examples of Section 84.1 Application

Consideration received by individual on transfer of shares			*A*	*B*
Cash, notes or other non-share consideration			$100K	Nil
Common shares (LSC and FMV)			100K	$200K
Total FMV			$200K	$200K
PUC reduction [par. 84.1(1)(a)]				
(1) Increase in LSC of purchaser corporation	(A)		$100K	$200K
Less				
(2) Greater of:				
(a) PUC of shares transferred		$ 1K		
(b) Modified ACB of shares transferred		$ 1K	$ 1K	$ 1K
Less: FMV of non-share consideration received			100K	Nil
Excess, if any	(B)		Nil	$ 1K
PUC reduction	(A − B)		$100K	$199K
PUC after reduction			Nil	$ 1K
Deemed dividend [par. 84.1(1)(b)]				
Sum of:				
(1) Increase in LSC of purchaser corporation	(A)		$100K	$200K
(2) FMV of non-share consideration received	(D)		100K	Nil
	(A + D)		$200K	$200K
Less sum of:				
(3) Greater of:				
(a) PUC of shares transferred		$ 1K		
(b) Modified ACB of shares transferred	(E)	$ 1K	$ 1K	$ 1K
(4) PUC reduction [par. 84.1(1)(*a*)]	(F)		100K	199K
	(E + F)		$101K	$200K
Deemed dividend	(A + D) − (E + F)		$ 99K	Nil

In Case A, note how the PUC of the shares received as consideration is reduced to nil, because all of the hard cost of the old shares (i.e., $1,000) has been recovered through the receipt of boot. Note, also, how the deemed dividend of $99,000 is equal to the excess of boot of $100,000 over the $1,000 of hard cost.

In Case B, since there is no boot consideration, the PUC after the reduction is $1,000, exactly equal to the hard cost, and there is no deemed dividend. Hence, the rules in section 84.1 only permit the immediate tax-free recovery of hard cost.

To generalize, the deemed dividend can be avoided, as in Case B, by limiting the fair market value of non-share consideration to the greater of:

(1) the paid-up capital of the subject shares transferred, and

(2) the modified adjusted cost base of the subject shares transferred.

¶16,235 Impact on the Capital Gain and Use of the Capital Gains Exemption

The deemed dividend under section 84.1 reduces the proceeds of disposition for the subject shares transferred and, therefore, reduces or eliminates the ability to use the capital gains exemption.

ITA: 84.1 Non-arm's length sale of shares, 84.1(1)(b), 54 proceeds of disposition, 84(3) Redemption, etc., 40(2)(g)

Exhibit 16-6 illustrates the effect of the deemed dividend on the proceeds of disposition of the subject shares. Note how the deemed dividend is excluded from the proceeds of disposition. This procedure is similar to the one used in Chapter 15 in determining the proceeds of disposition for capital gains purposes on the redemption of shares. Since the definition of "proceeds of disposition" is of general application within Subdivision c, this exclusion will occur whether or not section 85 is used for the transfer of subject shares to the purchaser corporation.

ITA: 84.1(1)(b)

Exhibit 16-6 Calculation of Capital Gain of Seller (Mr. Sinclair) and ACB of Purchaser Corporation (Holdit Ltd.) Shares

	A	B
Elected amount under sec. 85(1) (proceeds of disposition)	$100K	$100K
Less: sec. 84.1 deemed dividend	99K	Nil
Adjusted proceeds of disposition for transferred shares	$1K	$100K
ACB of transferred shares	1K	1K
Capital gain (capital loss may be denied by par. 40(2)(g))[1]	Nil	$99K
Less: Capital gains exemption utilized	Nil	99K
Effect on taxable income of capital gain	Nil	Nil
Effect on taxable income of deemed dividend	$99K	
ACB of purchaser (Holdit Ltd.) shares after sec. 85(1)[2]		

	A	B
(a) Elected amount ($100K) – Boot ($100K)	Nil	
(b) Elected amount ($100K) – Boot (Nil)		$100K

[1] Loss denial, if any, depends on whether the corporation was controlled by an affiliated person, e.g., the transferor, the transferor's spouse or corporation(s) controlled by the transferor or the spouse. If the loss is denied, it is added to the ACB of the Streamline Ltd. shares held by Holdit Ltd. [par. 53(1)(*i*)].

[2] Note that for the purposes of determining the adjusted cost base of the purchaser corporation's shares, the deemed dividend has no impact. The ACB of the share consideration is determined in paragraph 85(1)(*h*) where a section 85 election has been filed.

In summary, in Case A, the provision deemed the transferor to have received a taxable dividend of $99,000 on the transfer (Exhibit 16-6). Thus, the attempt to strip the $99,000 taxable surplus by converting it into an exempt capital gain, resulted in the same amount of taxable dividend as the amount of surplus that would otherwise have been converted. Note, in particular, that no capital gain resulted from the transfer of the shares to the holding company, although a capital gain was the objective of electing on the transfer at $100,000. In essence, the deemed dividend removed the capital gain by adjusting the proceeds, leaving nothing available against which to use the QSBC share capital gains deduction.

In Case B, where non-share consideration did not exceed $1,000, there was no deemed dividend. The ACB of the holding company shares reflected the elected amount in excess of non-share consideration. This higher ACB would reduce a future capital gain on the disposition of the holding company shares, thereby resulting in a benefit from utilizing the QSBC share capital gains deduction on the original transfer and election at $100,000.

Therefore, if non-share consideration is limited to hard cost in this manner, section 84.1 will not prevent the "crystallization" of an individual's QSBC share capital gains deduction through the transfer of shares to a holding company. Section 84.1 discourages the removal of non-share consideration in excess of the greater of PUC or adjusted cost base of the shares transferred in the non-arm's length transaction.

Conclusions

ITA: 84.1(1)(a)

The impact of section 84.1 can be summarized as follows:

(1) The paid-up capital reduction is for tax purposes only and has effect only if and when the shares of a purchaser corporation are redeemed. The amount of PUC after the reduction will represent the amount of hard cost in the old shares that has not been recovered through boot. ITA: 84.1(1)(b)

(2) The deemed dividend which arises immediately on transfer of the subject shares and which is the penalty inherent in section 84.1 caused by receiving boot in excess of the hard cost in the old shares, can be avoided by limiting the fair market value of non-share consideration to the greater of: ITA: 84(3) Redemption, etc.

(a) paid-up capital of the subject shares transferred; and

(b) modified adjusted cost base (based on actual cost with section 53 adjustments made to it) of the subject shares transferred.

(3) The deemed dividend will reduce the proceeds of disposition used to compute the capital gain on the transfer of the subject company shares and impact the utilization of the capital gains exemption.

Example Problem 16-5

Ms. Annalen owns all of the common shares of Margen Ltd. The shares have a PUC and a cost of $10,000. Their current fair market value is $100,000. She transferred these shares to a holding company, Howal Ltd., receiving as consideration controlling shares of Howal Ltd. having an LSC value of $75,000 and debt with a principal amount of $25,000. She elected under section 85 at $25,000 in order to use $15,000 of her available QSBC share capital gains exemption.

REQUIRED

(1) Indicate conceptually the immediate tax consequences of the transfer.

(2) Provide a technical explanation and computations to support your conclusions in Part (A).

(3) Assume that Ms. Annalen has $90,000 of QSBC share capital gains exemption available and that she sells her shares of Margen Ltd. to Howal Ltd., in which she already owns controlling shares, for their fair market value of $100,000, receiving as consideration $100,000 of debt from Howal Ltd. No subsection 85(1) election is made. Determine the immediate tax consequences of the sale.

(4) Assume, again, that Ms. Annalen has $90,000 of QSBC share capital gains exemption available and that she sells her shares of Margen Ltd. to Howal Ltd., which she controls, for their fair market value of $100,000, receiving as consideration $100,000 of preferred shares of Howal Ltd. No section 85 election is made. The preferred shares are subsequently redeemed for $100,000. Determine the tax consequences of the sale of Margen Ltd. shares and the ultimate redemption of the Howal Ltd. preferred shares.

SOLUTION

Verify that all of the conditions for section 84.1 to apply are met:

(1) the share disposition was made by a taxpayer resident in Canada other than a corporation, Ms. Annalen;

(2) the subject shares, shares of Margen Ltd., are shares of a corporation resident in Canada and are capital property to Ms. Annalen;

(3) Ms. Annalen and Howal Ltd. are not dealing at arm's length, since Ms. Annalen controls Howal Ltd.; and ITA: 186(4)(a)

(4) the subject corporation, Margen Ltd., is connected with the purchaser corporation, Howal Ltd., after the transfer, since Howal Ltd. controls Margen Ltd. ITA: 84.1(1)(a)

---

(1) The following tax consequences should occur on the application of section 84.1:

(a) the PUC of the Howal Ltd. shares should be nil since Ms. Annalen has taken back debt ($25,000) which is greater than the PUC and modified ACB of the Margen Ltd. shares ($10,000);

(b) there will be a deemed dividend of $15,000 because the debt received ($25,000) exceeds the greater of the PUC and modified ACB of the Margen Ltd. shares ($10,000); and

(c) the proceeds of disposition on the transfer of the Margen Ltd. shares will be reduced by the deemed dividend of $15,000. As a result, Ms. Annalen cannot use all of her capital gains exemption.

(2) PUC reduction:

(1) increase in LSC of Howal Ltd.			$75,000 (A)
less			
(2) greater of:			
(a) PUC of Margen Ltd. shares	$10,000		
		$10,000	
(b) Modified ACB of Margen Ltd. shares	$10,000		
Less: FMV of boot		25,000	
Excess, if any			Nil (B)
PUC reduction (A – B)			$75,000
PUC of Howal Ltd. after reduction ($75,000 – $75,000)			Nil

While this PUC reduction occurs on the transfer, because all of the $10,000 hard cost of the Margen Ltd. shares was recovered in the boot received from Howal Ltd., the reduced PUC has no effect unless and until the shares of Howal Ltd. are redeemed. There will also be a deemed dividend immediately, as a result of the transfer, because the $25,000 of boot received exceeds the $10,000 hard cost of the Margen Ltd. shares transferred, computed as follows:

ITA: 84.1(1)(b); 84.1(1)(a)

Deemed dividend:			
Sum of:			
(1) increase in LSC of Howal Ltd. shares			$ 75,000 (A)
(2) FMV of boot			25,000 (D)
(A + D)			$100,000
Less sum of:			
(3) greater of:			
(a) PUC of Margen Ltd. shares	$10,000		
		$10,000 (E)	
(b) Modified ACB of Margen Ltd. shares	$10,000		
(4) PUC reduction		75,000 (F)	
(E + F)			85,000
Deemed dividend (A + D) − (E + F)			$ 15,000

This particular case involves an attempt, which is thwarted by section 84.1, to convert $15,000 of surplus in Margen Ltd., which could otherwise be realized only through a taxable dividend, into an exempt capital gain on the transfer. The result is a deemed taxable dividend of $15,000 and, as is shown below, no capital gain is eligible for the QSBC share exemption. The case, also, involves an increase in PUC from the $10,000 that existed in Margen Ltd. to the $75,000 of LSC shares issued from Howal Ltd. However, the individual only has an entitlement to recover the $10,000 in PUC on a tax-free basis, since that is all that was originally contributed on an after-tax basis. Since the $10,000 was recovered in debt from Howal Ltd. on a tax-free basis, the PUC of the Howal Ltd. shares issued should be reduced to nil for tax purposes, reflecting the fact that no more of the PUC of Margen Ltd. is left to be recovered on a tax-free basis.

ITA: 54 proceeds of disposition

The adjusted cost base of the Howal Ltd. shares held by Ms. Annalen would be computed as follows:

Elected amount	$25,000	ITA: 84.1(1)(a)
Less: non-share consideration (debt)	$25,000	
ACB of Howal Ltd. shares after rollover	Nil	ITA: 84.1(1)(b)

The capital gain or loss on the disposition of the Margen Ltd. shares would be determined as follows:

Elected amount — Proceeds of disposition of Margen Ltd. shares	$25,000	ITA: 84.1(1)(a)
Less: exclusion from proceeds for sec. 84.1 deemed dividend	15,000	
Adjusted proceeds of disposition for Margen Ltd. shares	$10,000	
ACB of Margen Ltd. shares	(10,000)	
Capital gain (capital loss denied by par. 40(2)(*g*))	Nil	

In this case there is no denied superficial loss on the disposition of the transferred shares to add to the ACB of the Howal Ltd. shares owned. There is no capital gain on the disposition of the Margen Ltd. shares and, hence, nothing against which to use the capital gains exemption. ITA: 84.1(1)(a)

(3) The conditions of section 84.1 also apply to this sale of shares at their fair market value. Shares of a corporation resident in Canada (Margen Ltd.), held as capital property by an individual (Ms. Annalen), are sold to a non-arm's length corporation (Howal Ltd., controlled by Ms. Annalen). Since Howal Ltd. will control all of the shares of Margen Ltd. the corporations are connected.

Since no new shares of Howal Ltd. were issued in this transaction, there is no PUC reduction. However, there will be an immediate deemed dividend, because the $100,000 of boot received exceeds the $10,000 of hard cost in the Margen Ltd. shares, computed as follows: ITA: 84(3) Redemption, etc.

Sum of:			
(1) increase in LSC of Howal Ltd. shares			Nil (A)
(2) FMV of boot			$100,000 (D)
(A + D)			$100,000
Less sum of:			
(3) greater of:			
(a) PUC of Margen Ltd. shares	$10,000	$10,000 (E)	
(b) Modified ACB of Margen Ltd. shares	$10,000		
(4) PUC reduction		Nil (F)	
(E + F)			10,000
Deemed dividend (A + D) − (E + F)			$ 90,000

Proceeds of disposition for the Margen Ltd. shares will be reduced, so that there will be no capital gain against which to offset the capital gains deduction, as follows:

ITA: 84(3) Redemption, etc; 54 Definitions

Proceeds of disposition (i.e., debt received)	$100,000
Less: exclusion from proceeds for sec. 84.1 deemed dividend	90,000
Adjusted proceeds of disposition	$10,000
ACB of Margen Ltd. shares	(10,000)
Capital gain	Nil

When the $100,000 of debt is repaid by Howal Ltd. there will be no further tax consequences, since all of the appreciation in the shares has been taxed on their sale to Howal Ltd. as a deemed dividend.

(4) Again the conditions of section 84.1 would be met by this transaction. There would be a PUC reduction computed as follows:

PUC reduction:			
(1) increase in LSC of Howal Ltd.			$100,000 (A)
less			
(2) greater of:			
(a) PUC of Margen Ltd. shares	$10,000	$10,000	
(b) Modified ACB of Margen Ltd. shares	$10,000		
Less: FMV of boot		Nil	
Excess, if any			10,000 (B)
PUC reduction (A – B)			$ 90,000
PUC of Howal Ltd. after reduction ($100,000 – $90,000)			$ 10,000

Note how the PUC of the Howal Ltd. shares is reduced to $10,000 despite there being no boot. The $10,000 of PUC of the Howal Ltd. shares reflects the $10,000 of hard cost of the Margen Ltd. shares transferred.

Since no boot was received, there will be no deemed dividend, as shown by the following:

Deemed dividend:			
Sum of:			
(1) increase in LSC of Howal Ltd. shares			$100,000 (A)
(2) FMV of boot			Nil (D)
(A + D)			$100,000
Less sum of:			
(3) greater of:			
(a) PUC of Margen Ltd. shares	$10,000		
		$10,000 (E)	
(b) Modified ACB of Margen Ltd. shares	$10,000		
(4) PUC reduction		90,000 (F)	
(E + F)			100,000
Deemed dividend (A + D) − (E + F)			Nil

Since there is no deemed dividend, proceeds of disposition for the Margen Ltd. shares are equal to the $100,000 of preferred share consideration received from Howal Ltd. The result is the following:

Proceeds of disposition for Margen Ltd. shares	$100,000
ACB	(10,000)
Capital gain	$90,000
Taxable capital gain (½ × $90,000)	$45,000
Less: QSBC share capital gains deduction	45,000
Effect on taxable income of Ms. Annalen	Nil

On the ultimate redemption of all of the Howal Ltd. preferred shares, the following will result:

(1)	Deemed dividend on redemption:	
	Redemption proceeds	$100,000
	Less: PUC after reduction	10,000
	Deemed dividend	$90,000

(2)	Proceeds of disposition	$100,000
	Less: Deemed dividend	90,000
	Adjusted proceeds of disposition	$10,000
	ACB of Howal Ltd. shares (equal to FMV of property sold for preferred shares)	(100,000)
	Capital loss	$(90,000)

The net economic effect of the redemption is seen to be nil, but in reality the deemed dividend of $90,000 cannot be offset by the capital loss of $90,000.

In this case, the sale of the Margen Ltd. shares for preferred shares of Howal Ltd. resulted in the successful crystallization of the $45,000 QSBC share capital gains deduction (i.e., $1/2 \times$ $90,000 capital gains exemption). The crystallization effect is found in the increased ACB of the Howal Ltd. shares which results in a capital loss on their redemption. That capital loss can be used to offset capital gains from other property, thereby preserving the benefit of the capital gains deduction in the future.

Draft legislative proposals released December 13, 2017, amend the provisions of the *Income Tax Act* dealing with Tax on Split Income (TOSI) and are discussed at ¶13,260. Tax on split income for individuals 18 years and older includes taxable capital gains from the disposition of property that are shares of a private corporation unless the taxable capital gain is on qualified small business corporation (QSBC) shares. As a result, it is important when disposing of shares of a private corporation to consider these provisions. Should shares of a private corporation be transferred to a holding company on a rollover basis using section 85, TOSI will not apply. Further, if the shares are transferred at fair market value or at an elected amount using section 85 that results in a taxable capital gain, TOSI will not be a concern as long as the shares are QSBC shares. This is the case in all of the above examples.

¶16,235.99 Practise What You've Learned

Refer to the following sections of the Study Guide to practise what you've learned:

¶16,800 — Review Questions

- Question 13 — 84.1 Purpose
- Question 14 — 84.1 Boot

¶16,850 — Exercises

- Exercise 8 — 84.1, 85, Redemption
- Exercise 9 — Share sale 84.1
- Exercise 13 — Dividend stripping
- Exercise 15 — Dividend stripping

¶16,240 Capital Gains Stripping on the Sale of Shares by a Corporation

¶16,245 Situation Addressed by Section 55

These rules form a set of anti-avoidance provisions that prevent a Canadian-resident corporate shareholder from converting a capital gain on the disposition of shares held in another corporation into a dividend that would not be taxable under Part I or under Part IV due to the connected corporation exemption. This conversion is referred to as capital gains stripping and is opposite to the dividend stripping prevented by section 84.1. ITA: 55(1)-(6)

A typical set of transactions which would be caught by section 55 is described below.

Facts:

(1) Corp. B is a wholly owned subsidiary of Corp. A.

(2) Corp. A wishes to dispose of the shares of Corp. B to Corp. C but does not wish to trigger a capital gain on the sale.

Avoidance transactions:

(1) Prior to the sale of the Corp. B shares, Corp. A causes Corp. B to declare a large dividend the funds for which are obtained by a short-term bank loan.

(2) The shares of Corp. B are sold to Corp. C.

(3) Corp. C injects enough cash into Corp. B to pay off the bank loan.

The following diagram depicts the facts for this example situation.

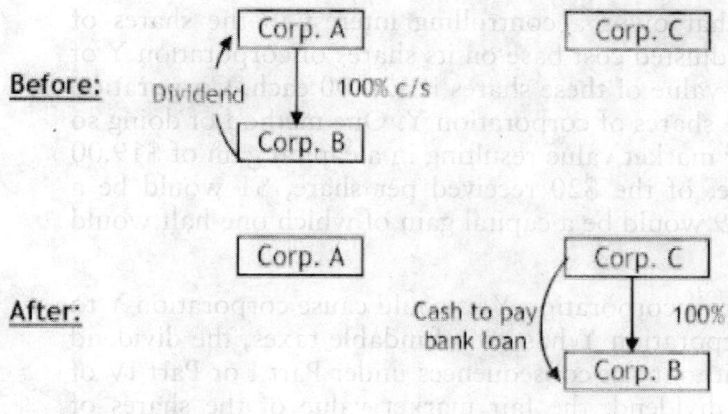

Results of the avoidance transactions:

ITA: 112 Deduction of taxable dividends received by corporation resident in Canada, 186(1) Tax on assessable dividends, 186(4) Corporations connected with particular corporation

(1) The inter-company dividend is not taxed:

(a) under Part I because of the deduction in the calculation of taxable income, or

ITA: 55(3)(a), 248(10) Series of transactions

(b) under Part IV because of the connected corporation rules.

(2) The fair market value of the Corp. B shares will drop by the amount of the dividend and should, with good planning, eliminate the capital gain on the sale of the Corp. B shares.

Effects of section 55:

(1) The offensive dividend is deemed not to be a dividend but a capital gain thereby re-establishing the capital gain which Corp. A tried to avoid.

(2) However, the offensive dividend is reduced by any post-1971 income (referred to as "safe income") and/or dividends subject to Part IV tax (that is not refunded through a dividend payment as part of the series of transactions).

The provision applies to intercorporate dividends where one of the main purposes of the dividend is to reduce a capital gain on the disposition of a share. It also applies to intercorporate dividends resulting in any significant reduction in the fair market value of a share of a corporation or a significant increase in the total cost of property to the dividend recipient. An exception is made where the intercorporate dividend arises from a redemption, acquisition or cancellation of a share by the corporation receiving the dividend in a related party reorganization.

ITA: 55(3)(a), 55(4) Avoidance of subsection (2), 55(5)(e)

As a result, any inter-corporate cash or in-kind dividend can be subject to 55(2). Such dividends must be paid from safe income to avoid the application of 55(2).

The term "related person" is defined generally in the Act, and related persons in the general definition include brothers and sisters. However, as an exception to these general rules, brothers and sisters are deemed not to be related to each other such that the "not related" condition in subsection 55(2) would apply to transactions between corporations which they control. Furthermore, if an attempt is made to escape subsection 55(2) by transactions which cause two or more persons to be related, these persons shall be deemed not to be related to each other.

¶16,250 Illustration of the Effect of Section 55

Consider the case of corporation X that owns a controlling interest in the shares of corporation Y. Corporation X has an adjusted cost base on its shares of corporation Y of $1.00 each and the current fair market value of these shares is $20.00 each. Corporation X wishes to dispose of its interest in the shares of corporation Y. One method of doing so would be to sell the shares for their fair market value resulting in a capital gain of $19.00 per share (i.e., $20 – $1). In that case, of the $20 received per share, $1 would be a tax-free return of cost and the other $19 would be a capital gain of which one-half would be subject to tax.

Alternatively, since corporation X controls corporation Y, it could cause corporation Y to pay a dividend of $19 per share. If corporation Y has no refundable taxes, the dividend would be received by corporation X without tax consequences under Part I or Part IV of the Act. With the payment of a $19 dividend, the fair market value of the shares of corporation Y should fall to $1.00 each. These shares could then be sold to an unrelated purchaser for their fair market value which is now equal to their adjusted cost base of $1.00 with no tax consequences. The result of this alternative would be to convert what would have been a $19 capital gain subject to tax into a $19 dividend not subject to tax in corporation X on the disposition of its shares in corporation Y.

However, to the extent that the $19 dividend cannot reasonably be considered to be attributable to income earned or realized by corporation Y after 1971 and before the dividend was received by corporation X, it will be deemed not to be a dividend received by corporation X. Then the provision will deem the $19 amount received in the transaction to be a capital gain on the shares held by corporation X, which is the same outcome as the original sale of the shares for proceeds of disposition of $20. The following calculation would be made:

ITA: 55(2)(a), 55(2)(b)

Dividend received		$19	
Less: dividend attributable to post-1971 income	Nil		ITA: 55(5)(f)
dividend subject to Part IV tax (not refunded)	Nil	(Nil)	
Deemed capital gain		$19	ITA: 55(2)(b)

Note that 55(2) applies irrespective of the relationship of the purchaser to corporation X.

Now consider another alternative for corporation X to dispose of its shares of corporation Y. Corporation X could transfer its shares in corporation Y to a purchaser corporation, selecting an elected amount of the $1.00 adjusted cost base of the shares transferred. As consideration for this transfer, corporation X could receive shares of the purchaser corporation with a paid-up capital and redemption/retraction value of $20 which represents the fair market value of the shares of corporation Y transferred. The paid-up capital value of the shares received after the reduction would be $1.00. The adjusted cost base of the shares received as consideration by corporation X would be $1.00, the elected amount, since the transaction did not involve boot. If the appropriate number of shares (votes and value test) are received as consideration, corporation X may be connected with the purchaser corporation (i.e., more than 10% of the votes and value of all the outstanding shares).

ITA: 85(1) Transfer of property to corporation by shareholders, 85(2.1) Computing paid-up capital

The purchaser corporation could then redeem its shares held by corporation X for $20 each. This would result in a deemed dividend to the extent that the redemption price of $20 exceeds the paid-up capital of $1.00 of the shares redeemed. This deemed dividend of $19 would not be taxable under Part I or Part IV of the Act. Furthermore, corporation X would be deemed to have disposed of its shares of the purchaser corporation for proceeds of disposition equal to the excess of the redemption price of $20 over the deemed dividend of $19. This would result in proceeds which are equal to the adjusted cost base of the shares of $1.00 such that there is no capital gain on the disposition of the shares.

ITA: 84(3) Redemption, etc.

The following diagram depicts the facts for this situation.

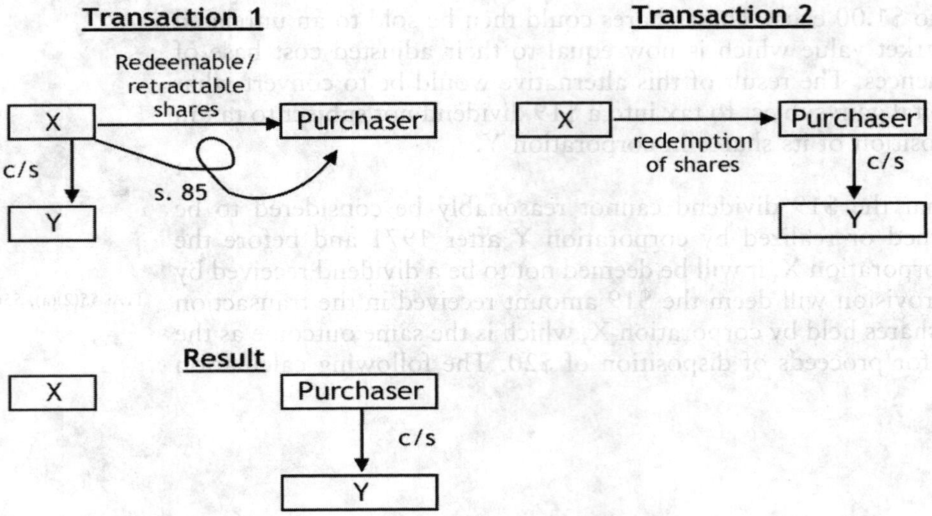

Again, the provision would apply in this case with the same result as that in the previous illustration. Thus, the deemed dividend of $19 would be deemed not to be a dividend and would be part of the proceeds of disposition of the shares in corporation Y. Using the two-step redemption procedure outlined previously, the following would result:

ITA: 55(2) Deemed proceeds or gain

Step 1 — Deemed dividend on redemption

Redemption amount paid		$20	
Less: PUC		1	
Deemed dividend on redemption		$19	ITA: 84(3) Redemption, etc.
Less: part of dividend designated as a separate dividend attributable to post-1971 income	Nil		ITA: 84(3) Redemption, etc.
part of dividend subject to Part IV tax	Nil	Nil	
Part of dividend deemed not to be a dividend		$19	ITA: 84(3) Redemption, etc.

Step 2 — Capital gain or loss on disposition of shares

Redemption amount paid	$20	
Less: designated part of dividend (see above)	Nil	ITA: 84(3) Redemption, etc.
Proceeds of disposition	$20	
Less: adjusted cost base	1	
Capital gain	$19	

Note that in this scenario, if the purchaser were a related person, 55(2) would not apply to the deemed dividend resulting on the redemption of the shares. By structuring the transaction to result in a deemed dividend under 84(3) on the share redemption, 55(2) would only apply if the purchaser were an arm's length person.

¶16,255 Exceptions to the Application of Section 55

It should be emphasized that where section 55 applies to the dividend, it is not applicable to the portion that can reasonably be considered to be attributable to income, referred to as "safe income" earned or realized on a tax basis by corporation Y after the later date of the acquisition of the shares and 1971 and before the dividend was received by corporation X. In this situation, the dividend is not deemed to be proceeds of disposition or a capital gain on the shares disposed of by corporation X. Therefore, it does not offend this legislation to pay a tax-free intercorporate dividend from "post-1971 earnings". The provision automatically separates the total dividend resulting from the transaction into a part that would not be affected by subsection 55(2) because it was attributed to post-1971[3] realized earnings and a part that would be subject to the rules of subsection 55(2). Note that the post-1971 income of a corporation, earned or realized *after* the transaction or series of transactions that gave rise to the dividend in question, cannot be used to reduce the tax liability under subsection 55(2). ITA: 55(5)(f)

Therefore, in the previous numerical examples, if corporation Y had post-1971 income of, for example, $15, the capital gain would have been only $4 in both cases.

If the dividend received by corporation X in the foregoing illustrations had been subject to Part IV tax either because corporation X was not connected with the corporation paying the dividend or because that payer corporation had refundable taxes, then that dividend received would also not be subject to subsection 55(2). However, for this exception to apply, the Part IV tax paid cannot be refunded as a consequence of the payment of a dividend as part of a series of transactions or events.

Finally, a rule provides an exemption for *bona fide* corporate reorganizations including an estate freeze and what is known in practice as a "butterfly" transaction. The latter typically involves the breaking up of a corporation with the assets of the corporation being distributed to holding companies owned by the shareholders of the corporation being broken up. The specifics of these transactions are beyond the scope of this text. ITA: 55(3)(b)

Key signals:

Here are five key factors which may signal an application of section 55:

(1) an intercorporate dividend(s), ordinary or deemed, has occurred;

(2) one of the main purposes was to effect a significant reduction of the potential unrealized capital gain on a share, the fair market value of any share, or increase the cost of property of the dividend recipient;

(3) the dividend is not the result of a share redemption, acquisition or cancellation of shares as part of a related party reorganization;

(4) the dividend is followed by the disposition of shares of a corporation; and

[3] For the CRA's view on the calculation of post-1971 income, see John R. Robertson, "Capital Gain Strips: A Revenue Canada Perspective on the Provisions of Section 55", *1981 Conference Report*, Canadian Tax Foundation, pp. 88-91 and Michael A. Hiltz, "Section 55: An Update," *1984 Corporate Management Tax Conference*, Canadian Tax Foundation, pp. 45-46. For the courts' views on the calculation of "safe income", see the cases of *The Queen v. Nassau Walnut Investments Inc.*, 97 DTC 5051 (F.C.A.), and *The Queen v. Kruco Inc.*, 2003 DTC 5506 (F.C.A.). These cases illustrate a divergence by the courts from the CRA's administrative position.

(5) the dividend is not the result of a share redemption, acquisition or cancellation of shares as part of a series of transactions resulting in a disposition to a related person.

Many standard corporate transactions such as cash dividends within a related group of corporations, dividends paid from an operating company to a holding company to protect assets from creditors, purification for capital gains exemption purposes, loss consolidation transactions, etc. may be impacted by subsection 55(2). It is important for safe income on hand to be tracked and ensure that intercorporate dividends not meeting the related person exception in 55(3)(*a*) do not exceed the balance available.

¶16,255.99 Practise What You've Learned

Refer to the following sections of the Study Guide to practise what you've learned:

¶16,850 — Exercises

- Exercise 10 — Capital gains stripping
- Exercise 14 — Capital gains stripping
- Exercise 16 — Capital gains stripping

CHAPTER 17

Income Deferral: Other Rollovers and Use of Rollovers in Estate Planning

ADVANCED CONTENT IN THIS CHAPTER

Learning Goals

Know

By the end of this chapter you will know:

- The basic provisions of the *Income Tax Act* pertaining to corporate rollovers that are useful in many planning situations.

Understand and Explain

By the end of this chapter you will understand and be able to explain:

- The tax consequences of the various rollovers discussed and their uses in various planning situations.
- The use of rollovers to execute an estate freeze.

Apply

By the end of this chapter you will be able to apply your knowledge and understanding to:

- Determine the tax consequences of a wind-up or an amalgamation.
- Determine the tax consequences of a basic estate freeze.
- Determine whether an estate freeze achieves a client's goals.

Review Questions
¶17,800 in the Study Guide

Multiple Choice Questions
¶17,825 in the Study Guide

Exercises
¶17,850 in the Study Guide

Assignment Problems
¶17,875 in the Study Guide

Overview

This chapter completes the discussion of rollovers which permit the deferral of income on transactions between corporations and their shareholders. The chapter also discusses the application of some of the rules presented in this and previous chapters to the planning technique known as an "estate freeze".

ⒶAccording to the CPA Knowledge Supplement, the topics of business combinations, amalgamations, and the winding up of subsidiaries into their parents are viewed as advanced topics to be covered in detail in the *elective* stage. Therefore, our advanced symbol (Ⓐ) in this chapter identifies material within these subjects that is more complex and non-routine in nature.

The following chart will help to locate the major provisions of the Act discussed in this chapter.

PART I — DIVISION B, SUBDIVISION h

CORPORATIONS RESIDENT IN CANADA AND THEIR SHAREHOLDERS

DIVISION

A	Liability for tax
B	**Computation of income**
C	Computation of taxable income
D	Taxable income earned in Canada by non-residents
E	Computation of tax
E.1	Minimum tax
F	Special rules applicable in certain circumstances
G	Deferred and other special income arrangements
H	Exemptions
I	Returns, assessments, payment and appeals
J	Appeals to the Tax Court of Canada and the Federal Court of Appeal

SUBDIVISION

	Basic rules
a	Income or loss from an office or employment
b	Income or loss from a business or property
c	Taxable capital gains and allowable capital losses
d	Other sources of income
e	Deductions in computing income
f	Rules relating to computation of income
g	Amounts not included in computing income
h	**Corporations resident in Canada and their shareholders**
i	Shareholders of corporations not resident in Canada
j	Partnerships and their members
k	Trusts and their beneficiaries

SECTION

82	Taxable dividends
83(1)	Tax-deferred dividends
83(2)-(5)	Capital dividends
84(1)	Deemed dividend
84(2)	Winding-up dividend
84(3)	Redemption dividend
84(4)	PUC reduction dividend
84.1-84.2	NAL sale of shares
85	Transfer of property to a corporation
85.1	**Share-for-share exchange**
86	**Reorganization of capital**
87	**Amalgamation**
88	**Winding-up**
89	Definitions

¶17,000 Rollovers Involving Corporations and Their Shareholders

¶17,010 Share-for-Share Exchange — Section 85.1

¶17,015 The Concept

The Act permits a tax-free rollover where a shareholder of a corporation exchanges his or her shares for shares of another corporation in an arm's length transaction. The provision is most often used in a business combination or take-over situation where a shareholder of one corporation exchanges his or her shares for shares of the purchasing corporation. While the application of this provision is automatic, this deferral of the potential capital gains or losses is conditional on a set of very specific rules that must be adhered to in order to avoid immediate tax consequences. "Automatic" means that, if the conditions outlined below are met, the rollover applies without any election.

ITA: 85.1 Share for share exchange; Income Tax Folio: S4-F5-C1 Share for Share Exchange

For example, Mr. Zheng owns shares of A Ltd. An unrelated company, B Ltd., wants to acquire his A Ltd. shares in exchange for shares in B Ltd. Where Mr. Zheng exchanges his A Ltd. shares for new shares of B Ltd., the inherent capital gain or loss on the shares of A. Ltd. is deferred. The adjusted cost base to Mr. Zheng, now holding the new shares from B Ltd., is the adjusted cost base of the original A Ltd. shares. Therefore, Mr. Zheng is in the same tax position that existed prior to the exchange.

The facts of this example are depicted in the following diagram.

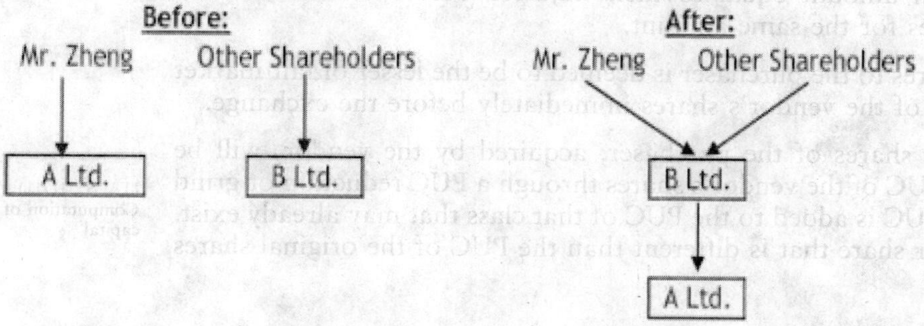

Unlike other rollover provisions, this provision deems that the cost of A Ltd. shares, now held by B Ltd., is the lesser of the fair market value and the paid-up capital of A Ltd. shares prior to the exchange. If the fair market value of the A Ltd. shares has increased above the PUC of those shares, establishing their cost to B Ltd. at their PUC will be disadvantageous to B. Ltd. on the future sale of the A Ltd. shares. Establishing cost to the purchaser at this lesser amount is mandatory and is independent of whether the vendor chose to defer the gain on the exchange of A Ltd. shares. A section 85 election may be considered as a more advantageous alternative to the automatic section 85.1 rollover in such case.

ITA: 85.1 Share for share exchange

¶17,020 The Conditions

The provision envisages a situation where a taxpayer, referred to as the "vendor", exchanges shares in a corporation for shares in another corporation, referred to as the "purchaser".

ITA: 54 capital property, 85.1(5) Foreign share for foreign share exchange, 85.1(6) Where subsection (5) does not apply, 89(1) Canadian corporation

(1) The transferred shares of the vendor must be capital property.

(2) The purchaser must be a Canadian corporation. The provision allows for foreign share-for-share exchanges, but this topic is beyond the scope of this book.

(3) The only consideration, given by the purchaser to the taxpayer/vendor, must be previously unissued shares of any particular class. Therefore, the consideration is restricted to shares of only one class. ITA: 85.1(2)(d)

(4) Immediately prior to the exchange, the vendor and the purchaser must be dealing with each other at arm's length. ITA: 85.1(2)(a)

(5) Immediately after the exchange, the vendor, along with non-arm's length persons, must not:

(a) control the purchaser; or

(b) own more than 50% of the fair market value of all the outstanding shares. ITA: 85.1(2)(b)

(6) The vendor and the purchaser cannot have elected under section 85 in respect of the exchanged shares.

(7) The vendor cannot have recognized any portion of the potential capital gain or loss in respect of the exchanged shares through any other provision.

ITA: 85(1) Transfer of property to corporation by shareholders, 85(2) Transfer of property to corporation from partnership, 85.1(2)(c), 85.1(1)(a)

¶17,025 The Consequences

If the above conditions are met on the exchange, then the vendor is deemed to have disposed of the shares for an amount equal to their adjusted cost base and to have acquired the purchaser's shares for the same amount.

ITA: 85.1(1)(a), 85.1(1)(b)

The cost of the exchanged shares to the purchaser is deemed to be the lesser of fair market value and the paid-up capital of the vendor's shares immediately before the exchange.

Furthermore, the PUC of the shares of the purchaser, acquired by the vendor, will be limited to the amount of the PUC of the vendor's shares through a PUC reduction or grind mechanism. Remember, this PUC is added to the PUC of that class that may already exist. This could result in a PUC per share that is different than the PUC of the original shares held by the vendor.

ITA: 85.1(2.1) Computation of paid-up capital

Vendor	Purchaser
Proceeds — shares sold disposed of for deemed proceeds equal to ACB of those shares.	Cost of shares — cost is equal to the lesser of the FMV and PUC of the vendor's shares sold to the purchaser.
Cost of new shares — new shares deemed to be acquired for cost equal to ACB of the shares sold.	
PUC of new shares — the new shares will have a PUC equal to the PUC of the shares sold. This PUC is added to the PUC of any other shares in that class of the purchaser.	

¶17,030 Other Issues

If any of the above conditions are not met, the vendor will not receive the benefit of a deferral of the capital gain or loss on exchange. As a result, the exchange would take place for proceeds equal to fair market value.

In situations where the paid-up capital of the vendor's shares is less than their cost, section 85 should be considered as an alternative to avoid the deemed cost restriction described above. The elected amount becomes the transferee corporation's cost and the capital gain is thereby deferred. The subsection 85(1) alternative may not be practical if the vendors hold shares in a public corporation and the transfer requires literally hundreds of section 85 elections. The deemed cost restriction under the share-for-share exchange rollover, described above, may not be important if the purchaser is anticipating a subsequent amalgamation or wind-up of a subsidiary, as described later in the chapter.

ITA: 85.1(1)(b), 87 Amalgamations, 88 Winding-up

Finally, the condition that the consideration be only shares of any particular class of shares of the purchaser does not preclude another separate and distinct transaction which includes non-share consideration and/or shares of a different class.

Example Problem 17-1

Nat owns common shares in Nat's Trading Corporation Limited with the following values:

FMV	$950,000
ACB	100,000
PUC	10,000

Elaine's Pubco Ltd., a widely-held Canadian public company, has acquired all of the common shares of Nat's Trading Corporation Limited owned by Nat. In exchange for these common shares, Elaine's Pubco Ltd. has issued its common shares for a total fair market value of $950,000, representing 10% of the fair market value of all of its shares.

Nat would like to defer the realization of the capital gain accrued on his shares.

REQUIRED

What are the tax consequences of applying the share-for-share exchange rollover in this case?

ITA: 85.1 Share for share exchange

SOLUTION

As long as Nat (the vendor) does not include in his income any portion of the gain on the shares he has given up in the exchange, all of the conditions of the rollover appear to apply. The tax consequences of the rollover, which applies automatically, to Nat will be as follows:

ITA: 85.1 Share for share exchange

Proceeds of disposition for Nat's Trading Corporation Limited shares	$100,000
ACB of Nat's Trading Corporation Limited shares	(100,000)
Capital gain	Nil
ACB of Elaine's Pubco Ltd. shares acquired on exchange	$100,000

As a result, the ACB of the shares given up becomes the ACB of the shares acquired in the exchange and the accrued capital gain is deferred.

The ACB of the Nat's Trading Corporation Limited shares to Elaine's Pubco Ltd. (the purchaser) will be equal to $10,000 being the lesser of:

FMV of Nat's Trading Corporation Limited shares before exchange	$950,000
PUC of Nat's Trading Corporation Limited shares before exchange	$10,000

The rules will apply to limit the addition to the PUC of Elaine's Pubco Ltd. on the issue of its shares in the exchange to the amount of the PUC of Nat's Trading Corporation Limited (i.e., $10,000) through a PUC "grind" mechanism. ITA: 85.1(2.1) Computation of paid-up capital

Nat may not receive non-share consideration from Elaine's Pubco Ltd. for his shares. If this restriction on the use of section 85.1 is a concern, then a subsection 85(1) election can be made, as an alternate method of accomplishing a deferral of the accrued gain in the exchange. Thus, Nat and the purchaser corporation could jointly elect to transfer Nat's shares at an elected amount of $100,000. Nat could receive as consideration boot for up to the $100,000 ACB of these shares and shares of Elaine's Pubco Ltd. for the remaining $850,000 (i.e., $950,000 – $100,000) of value. ITA: 85.1(2)(d)

An election under section 85 may not be feasible when the exchange involves vendors' shares that are widely dispersed share holdings held by many diverse shareholders who must elect. In these cases, the automatic nature of section 85.1 is more advantageous. That is not the case in this particular situation. In fact, in this situation, using section 85 may be a good option. Electing under section 85 at $100,000 would allow Elaine Pubco Ltd. to establish the ACB of the shares at $100,000 instead of the $10,000 calculated above under section 85.1.

¶17,030.99 Practise What You've Learned

Refer to the following sections of the Study Guide to practise what you've learned:

¶17,825 — Multiple Choice Questions

- Question 4 — Share-for-share exchange

¶17,850 — Exercises

- Exercise 1 — Share-for-share exchange
- Exercise 6 — Section 85.1

¶17,040 Reorganization of Capital — Section 86

¶17,045 Overview

In the course of a reorganization of capital of a corporation, a class of outstanding shares may be changed into another newly authorized class of shares[1] and, perhaps, there may also be non-share consideration. Such reorganization will be accomplished by way of

[1] There is no statutory definition of the phrase "in the course of a reorganization of capital"; nor have the Canadian courts addressed this issue. Conservative planning for a section 86 reorganization would require a change in the articles of incorporation to authorize completely new shares for the exchange.

amendment to the articles or letters patent of the corporation. Such an amending document is referred to as articles of amendment or supplementary letters patent, respectively. Of course, the governing corporate law must permit the desired changes to be effected.

Such capital reorganizations might involve the exchange of common shares for special (preferred) shares, for example, to allow for an estate freeze discussed later in this chapter or to facilitate the purchase of a business. In such a reorganization the outstanding common shares would be exchanged for newly authorized special shares with, usually, a fixed dividend rate and a provision with respect to the redemption/retraction amount of the share. Newly authorized common shares would be issued and these might be subscribed for by, say, trusts for the children in the case of an estate freeze or by the purchaser where the business is being sold. Other examples of capital reorganizations might involve an exchange of voting shares for a new class of voting shares and another new class of non-voting shares on the reorganization of control of the corporation or a reorganization of an existing class of shares into two new classes, one of which would have a lower unit value in order to facilitate an employee share purchase program.

Generally, the automatic rollover on a capital reorganization provides for a deferral of any accrued gain on the shares held immediately prior to the reorganization as long as the sum of the fair market value of the non-share consideration (boot) and the paid-up capital of the share consideration which are received as part of the reorganization does not exceed the paid-up capital of the existing shares. The PUC of the new shares will normally be equal to the PUC of the old shares less any non-share consideration.

ITA: 86 Exchange of shares by a shareholder in course of reorganization of capital

¶17,050 Conditions

In order for the rollover to apply, the following conditions must be met:

(1) the shares are capital property to the shareholder;

(2) all of the shares of a particular class owned by the shareholder are exchanged; and

(3) property receivable by the shareholder on the exchange includes other shares.

The exchange need not apply to all shareholders who hold a particular class of shares for the rollover to apply. Only one class of shares need be the subject of the exchange. A class of shares also includes a subclass or what is referred to as a "series of shares".

ITA: 248(6) "Class" of shares issued in series

Note that section 86 will not apply if a rollover in section 85 has been used.

ITA: 86(3) Application

¶17,055 A Conceptual View of the Rollover for a Reorganization of Capital

A capital reorganization rollover involves, in essence, the issuance of new shares and the redemption or cancellation of old shares. Therefore, the capital reorganization rollover consists of two transactions and related calculations.

ITA: 86 Exchange of shares by a shareholder in course of reorganization of capital

Section 86 — Overview

Step 1: Issuance of new shares

Calculate:

- PUC of the new shares; and
- ACB of the new shares.

Step 2: Redemption of old shares

Calculate:

- deemed dividend on the redemption of the old shares; and
- capital gain or loss on the disposition of the old shares.

Note:

- To fully defer the unrealized gain on the old shares, i.e., for a full rollover, non-share consideration (boot) exchanged for the old shares should not exceed their PUC.
- To avoid the benefit rule, balance the fair market value of the old shares with the total fair market value of the package of consideration received.

Step 1: Issuance of New Shares

Calculate:

- PUC of the new shares; and
- ACB of the new shares.

On the issuance of new shares under the rollover there is a downward adjustment to the paid-up capital of the new shares in order to avoid the triggering of a deemed dividend. In the end, the PUC of the new shares issued should reflect the PUC in the old shares that has not been recovered in non-share consideration received on the exchange.

ITA: 86 Exchange of shares by a shareholder in course of reorganization of capital, 84(1) Deemed dividend

The cost and, hence, the adjusted cost base of the new shares received in the exchange are computed by first allocating the adjusted cost base of the existing shares to the non-share consideration received, if any, up to its fair market value and, then, allocating the remainder to the new shares. If more than one class of new shares is received, the remaining adjusted cost base allocation must be made to each class in the proportion that the fair market value of the shares of a given class received is to the fair market value of all classes of shares received.

ITA: 86(1)(a), 86(1)(b)

Step 2: Redemption of Old Shares

Calculate:

- deemed dividend on the redemption of the old shares, and
- capital gain or loss on the disposition of the old shares.

In Chapter 15, the redemption proceeds were only cash or debt and usually resulted in a deemed dividend plus a capital gain or loss. The mandatory inclusion of shares in the exchange transaction adds additional complexity.

ITA: 84(3) Redemption, etc.

The proceeds for the redemption of the old shares under the capital reorganization rollover will be the sum of any boot consideration plus the PUC of the newly issued shares.

ITA: 84(5)(d), 86 Exchange of shares by a shareholder in course of reorganization of capital

The proceeds of disposition for capital gains purposes will equal the sum of any boot consideration plus the ACB of the newly issued shares less any deemed dividend on the redemption, under the usual redemption rules.

The rules in section 86 may result in a capital loss being realized. If a capital loss is triggered, the resultant tax treatment depends on whether the corporation, after the exchange, is affiliated with the shareholder. If, for example, the shareholder or the shareholder's spouse still controls the corporation and, hence, the corporation is affiliated with the shareholder, then the capital loss is denied and added to the ACB of the remaining shares, including the exchanged shares owned by the shareholder after the transaction.

ITA: 40(3.6) Loss on shares, 53(1)(f.2) [Adjustments to cost base — Denied loss on transfer of shares to corporation]

The capital loss will only likely occur if the PUC of the old shares was less than the adjusted cost base of those shares and the boot exceeds that PUC.

If, during the reorganization, a benefit is conferred on a related person, then a different calculation of the capital gain or loss must be completed, as discussed later in this chapter.

ITA: 86 Exchange of shares by a shareholder in course of reorganization of capital

Exhibit 17-1 uses a simple numerical example to summarize all of the steps in the calculation that must be done when the rollover is used. Note that a balancing of the fair market value of the shares given up with the fair market value of the total package of consideration received on the exchange is essential. Also, note from the facts that the exchange will not result in the realization of income through a deemed dividend because the total of the non-share consideration does not exceed the PUC of the old shares. Therefore, the consideration in this case allows for a perfect rollover.

ITA: 84(3) Redemption, etc.

Exhibit 17-1 Summary of Calculation Procedure for Section 86

Facts:

Old shares given up		Package of consideration received		
FMV	$150	Boot — FMV	$100	$150
ACB	100			
PUC	100	New shares — FMV	50	
		— LSC	50	

Calculation Procedure:

Step 1: Issuance of New Shares

(1) Reduced PUC:

ITA: 86(2.1)(a)

LSC increase for new shares		$50
Less: PUC of old shares	$100	
Less: boot	100	Nil
PUC reduction		$50
Reduced PUC ($50 – $50)		Nil

(2) Cost of new shares received:

ITA: 86(1)(b)

ACB of old shares		$100	
Less: FMV of non-share consideration		100	
Cost of new shares (allocate if more than one class)		Nil	
Cost of non-share consideration (boot) received (equal to its FMV)		$100	ITA: 86(1)(a)

Step 2: Redemption of Old Shares

(1) Proceeds on redemption of old shares: ITA: 84(5)(d)

Reduced PUC of new shares		Nil	
FMV of non-share consideration (boot)		$100	
Redemption proceeds		$100	
Deemed dividend on redemption:			ITA: 84(3) Redemption, etc.
Redemption proceeds (above)		$100	
PUC of old shares		(100)	
Deemed dividend on redemption		Nil	ITA: 84(3) Redemption, etc.

(2) Proceeds of disposition of old shares for capital gains purposes: ITA: 86(1)(c)

Cost of new shares (above)	Nil		
FMV of boot	$100	$100	
Less: deemed dividend on redemption		Nil	ITA: 84(3) Redemption, etc.
Proceeds of disposition of old shares		$100	
Capital gain (loss) on old shares:			
Proceeds of disposition		$100	
ACB		(100)	
Capital gain (loss) (may be denied, but, if so, add to cost base of new shares)		Nil	ITA: 40(3.6) Loss on shares, 53(1)(f.2) [Adjustments to cost base — Denied loss on transfer of shares to corporation]

Net Economic Effect:

Deemed dividends on redemption	Nil	ITA: 84(3) Redemption, etc.
Capital gain (loss) on sale of old shares	Nil	

Accrued capital gain on new shares:		
Fair market value	$50	
ACB — Cost of new shares	Nil	$50
Net economic effect (equal to accrued gain on old shares)		$50

PUC of new shares will be Nil since all of the original PUC of $100 has been recovered through the boot of $100. ITA: 86(2.1)(a)

Example Problem 17-2

Robert Baker owns a controlling interest in Six Sixty-One Ltd. and, therefore, is not at arm's length with the corporation. His present common shares have a PUC and adjusted cost base of $2,500 and a fair market value of $3,700. The corporation is in the process of reorganizing its capital structure and will exchange these shares for the following package of consideration:

Notes (at fair market value)	$1,000
New preferred shares (fair market value and legal stated capital)	2,700
Total	$3,700

REQUIRED

Determine the tax consequences to Mr. Baker as a result of the capital reorganization.

SOLUTION

Calculation Procedure:

Step 1: Issuance of new shares

(1) Reduced PUC: ITA: 86(2.1)(a)

LSC increase for new preferred shares		$2,700
Less: PUC of old common shares	$2,500	
Less: boot	1,000	1,500

PUC reduction	$1,200
Reduced PUC ($2,700 – $1,200)	$1,500

The primary objective of this calculation is to show that the PUC reduction will avoid the triggering of a deemed dividend. ITA: 84(1) Deemed dividend

(2) Cost of preferred shares received: ITA: 86(1)(b)

Adjusted cost base of old shares	$2,500
Less: fair market value of non-share consideration	1,000
Cost of preferred shares received	$1,500
Cost of the notes received (equal to their fair market value)	$1,000

ITA: 86(1)(a)

Step 2: Redemption of old shares

(1) Proceeds on redemption of old shares: ITA: 84(5)(d)

FMV of boot	$1,000
Reduced PUC — New preferred shares (as determined in (1), above)	1,500
Redemption proceeds	$2,500
Proceeds on redemption — above	$2,500
PUC — Old common shares	2,500
Deemed dividend on redemption	Nil

ITA: 84(3) Redemption, etc.

(2) Proceeds of disposition of old shares for capital gains purposes: ITA: 86(1)(c)

Cost of all new shares (as determined in (2), above)	$1,500
Plus: cost of all non-share considerations	$1,000
Proceeds of disposition of old shares	$2,500
Less: deemed dividend on redemption	Nil
Proceeds of disposition of old shares	$2,500
Proceeds of disposition of old shares	$2,500
ACB — Old shares	2,500
Capital gain/loss	Nil

ITA: 84(3) Redemption, etc.

Net Economic Effect:

Deemed dividend on redemption		Nil
Capital gain (loss) on sale of old shares		Nil
Accrued capital gain on new shares:		
Fair market value	$2,700	
ACB — Cost of new shares	1,500	$1,200
Net economic effect (equal to accrued gain on old shares)		$1,200

ITA: 84(3) Redemption, etc.

Comments

(1) The reduced PUC of the preferred shares of $1,500 reflects the fact that only $1,000 of the original PUC of $2,500 of the old common shares has been recovered through boot consideration. The receipt of boot up to $2,500 is tax free both on the exchange and in the future, if the boot is debt that is repaid later.

(2) Since the reduced PUC of the preferred shares ($1,500) plus the boot ($1,000) is less than or equal to the PUC of the old common shares ($2,500) there can be no deemed dividend.

ITA: 84(1) Deemed dividend

(3) No deemed dividend is triggered on the redemption of the old common shares since the proceeds on redemption (the reduced PUC of $1,500 plus the boot of $1,000) is equal to the PUC of the old common shares.

ITA: 84(3) Redemption, etc.

(4) There is no capital gain or loss since the proceeds of disposition for capital gains purposes (cost of the new shares of $1,500 plus the boot of $1,000) is exactly equal to the ACB of the old common shares of $2,500.

(5) If the new preferred shares are sold immediately, there would be a capital gain of $1,200, exactly equal to the accrued capital gain on the old common shares.

New preferred shares:	P of D ($2,700) – cost ($1,500)	=	$1,200
Old common shares:	FMV ($3,700) – ACB ($2,500)	=	$1,200

Example Problem 17-3

Ms. Oasis owns some of the common shares of Capital Structure Ltd. with an adjusted cost base and paid-up capital of $1,200 and a fair market value of $3,700. In the course of a capital reorganization, Ms. Oasis exchanged all of her shares for the following package of consideration:

Cash	$500
Notes (at fair market value)	1,500
New preferred shares (at fair market value and LSC)	1,000
New common shares (at fair market value and LSC)	700
Total	$3,700

REQUIRED

Determine the tax consequences to Ms. Oasis as a result of the capital reorganization.

SOLUTION

Calculation Procedure:

Step 1: Issuance of new shares

ITA: 86(2.1)(a)

(1) Reduced PUC:

LSC increase for all new shares		$1,700
Less: PUC of old commons	$1,200	
Less: boot ($500 + $1,500)	2,000	Nil
PUC reduction in total		$1,700

Proration of PUC reduction:

(1) Preferred shares: $1,700 × $1,000 / $1,700 = $1,000

(2) Common shares: $1,700 × $700 / $1,700 = $700

	Preferred shares	Common shares
LSC increase by class of share	$1,000	$700
Less: PUC reduction by class of share	1,000	700
Reduced PUC	Nil	Nil

(2) Cost of preferred and common shares received: ITA: 86(1)(b)

Adjusted cost base of old shares	$1,200
Less: fair market value of non-share consideration	2,000
Cost of preferred and common shares received	Nil
Allocation of cost of new shares:	
Preferred shares:	
(FMV of preferred shares / FMV of all shares) × total cost of new shares	
[$1,000 / ($1,000 + $700)] × Nil	Nil
Common shares:	
(FMV of common shares / FMV of all shares) × total cost of new shares	
[$700 / ($1,000 + $700)] × Nil	Nil
Cost of the cash and notes received at FMV	$2,000

ITA: 86(1)(a)

Step 2: Redemption of old shares

(1) Proceeds on redemption: ITA: 84(5)(d)

Boot	— Cash	$500	
	— Notes	1,500	$2,000
Reduced PUC	— New preferreds	Nil	
	— New commons	Nil	Nil
			$2,000

Deemed dividend on redemption:	
Proceeds on redemption	$2,000
PUC of old common shares	1,200
Deemed dividend on redemption	$800

ITA: 84(3) Redemption, etc.

ITA: 84(3) Redemption, etc.

(2) Proceeds of disposition:

Cost of boot	$2,000
Cost of shares	
— Preferred shares	Nil

— Common shares		Nil	
		$2,000	
Less: deemed dividend on redemption		800	ITA: 84(3) Redemption, etc.
Proceeds of disposition of old shares		$1,200	
Capital gain (loss) on old shares:			
Proceeds of disposition of old shares		$1,200	
Less: ACB of old shares		1,200	
Capital gain (loss[1])		Nil	

Net Economic Effect:

In the foregoing case, the "net economic effect" can be aggregated as a conceptual illustration as follows:

Deemed dividend on redemption		$800	ITA: 84(3) Redemption, etc.
Accrued capital gain on new shares:			
Fair market value	$1,700		
ACB (total)	Nil	1,700	
Net economic effect equal to accrued gain on old common shares (i.e., $3,700 – $1,200)		$2,500	

Comments:

The final PUC of Nil for both the new common and preferred shares is logical since all of the PUC of the old common shares ($1,200) has been removed in the form of boot (i.e., cash of $500 and notes of $1,500).

The redemption deemed dividend was caused by taking back a non-share consideration package (i.e., boot comprised of cash of $500 and notes of $1,500) in excess of the PUC of the old shares (i.e., $1,200). The deemed dividend could have been avoided by taking back less boot to reflect the $1,200 of PUC in the old shares that can be received tax free.

ITA: 84(3) Redemption, etc.

NOTES TO SOLUTION

ITA: 40(3.6) Loss on shares, 53(1)(f.2) [Adjustments to cost base — Denied loss on transfer of shares to corporation]

(1) If a capital loss is triggered, the resultant tax treatment depends on whether the corporation, after the exchange, is affiliated with the shareholder.

¶17,060 Benefit Rule

There is a benefit rule provided (similar to the one in section 85) to reduce the effect of a deferral where a reorganization is used to confer a benefit on a related person. The benefit is any part of the excess of the fair market value of the old shares over the cost of the non-share consideration received plus the fair market value of the new shares that can reasonably be regarded as a benefit conferred on a person related to the taxpayer. ITA: 86(2) Idem, 85(1)(e.2)

Where there is a benefit, the proceeds of disposition of the old shares for capital gains purposes are different from the non-benefit situation previously outlined. Proceeds of disposition will be deemed to be the lesser of: ITA: 86(1) Exchange of shares by a shareholder in course of reorganization of capital

(1) the fair market value of the non-share consideration plus the amount of the gift determined by the excess above; and

(2) the fair market value of the old shares.

Where a capital loss is created, the loss is deemed to be nil. The cost of the new shares will be reduced by the fair market value of the non-share consideration plus the benefit. ITA: 86(2)(d), 86(2)(e)

If the non-share consideration is equal to the ACB of the old shares, the amount of the benefit (gift) will be treated as a capital gain to the taxpayer. As the benefit received by the related person will increase the value of their existing shares, the benefit will be taxed again when the related person sells their shares in the future — double tax results.

Example Problem 17-4

Adam owns all of the Class A common shares of BJay Ltd. His son, Stieb, owns all of the Class B common shares and is active in the management of the corporation. Adam is now prepared to pass all of the future growth in the corporation to his son. To do so, Adam will give up all of his Class A common shares which have a fair market value of $500,000, an adjusted cost base of $100,000 and a paid-up capital value of $100,000. In return, he will receive $100,000 in cash and preferred shares with a fair market value of $350,000 and a legal stated capital of $350,000. Stieb will then own all of the only class of common shares outstanding and, thereby, will receive all of the future growth of BJay Ltd.

REQUIRED

What are the income tax consequences under the capital reorganization rollover to Adam on the proposed transaction? ITA: 86 Exchange of shares by a shareholder in course of reorganization of capital

SOLUTION

The benefit rule will apply in this case, because the $500,000 fair market value of Adam's Class A common shares is greater than the sum of the $100,000 of cash and $350,000 fair market value of the preferred shares received on the reorganization. Furthermore, it is reasonable to regard the $50,000 excess as a benefit that Adam desired to have conferred on a related person, his son. ITA: 86(2) Idem

The following are the consequences of the transaction:

Step 1: Issuance of new shares — ITA: 86(2.1)(a)

(1) Reduced PUC:

LSC increase for new shares		$350,000
Less: PUC of old shares	$100,000	
Less: boot	100,000	Nil
PUC reduction		$350,000
Reduced PUC ($350,000 – $350,000)		Nil

(2) Cost of preferred shares received:

ACB of Class A shares		$100,000
Less: cost (equal to FMV) of non-share		
consideration	$100,000	
benefit	50,000	150,000
Cost of preferred shares (excess, if any)		Nil
Cost of non-share consideration (equal to its FMV)		$100,000

ITA: 86(2)(e)

Step 2: Redemption of old shares

(1) Proceeds on redemption of old shares:

Reduced PUC of preferred shares	Nil
FMV of non-share consideration	$100,000
Proceeds on redemption	$100,000
Deemed dividend on redemption:	
Redemption proceeds	$100,000
PUC of Class A shares	(100,000)
Deemed dividend on redemption	Nil

ITA: 84(3) Redemption, etc.

(2) Proceeds of disposition of Class A shares: — ITA: 84(3) Redemption, etc.

Lesser of:

(a) cost (equal to FMV) of non-share consideration $100,000 — ITA: 86(2)(c)

Plus: benefit	50,000	
	$150,000	
(b) FMV of Class A shares	$500,000	
Proceeds of disposition		$150,000
Capital gain (loss) on Class A shares:		
Proceeds of disposition		$150,000
ACB		(100,000)
Capital gain		$50,000

Net Economic Effect:

Deemed dividend on redemption		Nil
Capital gain on sale of Class A shares		$50,000
Accrued gain on preferred shares:		
FMV	$350,000	
ACB	Nil	350,000
Total (equal to the accrued gain on the old shares)		$400,000

ITA: 84(3) Redemption, etc.

The final PUC of the new shares reflects the fact that, of the $100,000 of the PUC of the old shares, all $100,000 has been recovered in boot. Therefore, the final PUC of the new shares is logically nil.

Note the total net economic effect in this case. In addition to the immediate capital gain of $50,000, there is an accrued gain on the new shares of $350,000 to be realized on ultimate disposition. This $400,000 reflects the gain that had accrued on the Class A shares (i.e., $500,000 – $100,000) before the reorganization. However, it should be recognized that Adam has given up shares with a value of $500,000 for a package of consideration worth a total of only $450,000. He has paid tax on $50,000 of capital gain on the Class A shares and he has received consideration with a total cost value of $100,000 in non-share consideration and preferred shares with a paid-up capital of nil in return for the Class A shares which had a cost of $100,000. As a result, he has incurred a tax-paid cost on $50,000 of capital gain that he cannot recover after the reorganization.

Furthermore, the fair market value of the common shares held by the son, Stieb, will increase in value by the $50,000 benefit without any offset in the cost base of the common shares. Therefore, the $50,000 of accrued gain will be taxed on the disposition of the common shares. This potential $50,000 gain to be taxed in the hands of the common shareholder, along with the lost opportunity for Adam to recover the $50,000, is the penalty inherent in subsection 86(2).

To avoid this penalty the fair market value of the total package of consideration received in the reorganization should be equal to the fair market value of the shares given up in the exchange.

¶17,060.99 Practise What You've Learned

Refer to the following sections of the Study Guide to practise what you've learned:

¶17,800 — Review Questions

- Question 1 — Capital Reorganizations
- Question 2 — Capital Reorganizations
- Question 3 — Capital Reorganizations

¶17,8825 — Multiple Choice Questions

- Question 3 — Capital Reorganizations

¶17,850 — Exercises

- Exercise 2 — Capital Reorganizations
- Exercise 3 — Capital Reorganizations
- Exercise 7 — Capital Reorganizations

Ⓐ ¶17,070 Statutory Amalgamations — Section 87

¶17,075 Overview

An amalgamation is a merger of two or more corporations (called "predecessors") into a single entity, which is legally not a new corporation but a continuation of all of the predecessors.

Income Tax Folio: S4-F7-C1 Amalgamations of Canadian Corporations

The ITA provides a rollover provision which applies automatically at both the corporate level and the shareholder level in an amalgamation situation. Note that a statutory amalgamation is distinct from business combination accounting. In a statutory amalgamation, two or more corporations are merged into one with the result being a single legal entity with one charter. In business combination accounting, for which consolidated financial statements are usually prepared, the original companies continue to exist as separate legal entities and are taxed separately.

¶17,080 Conditions

The provision sets out several conditions for the rollover to apply:

ITA: 87(1) Amalgamations

(1) the predecessor corporations must be taxable Canadian corporations;

(2) all of the property and liabilities of the predecessor corporations, except inter-company accounts, must belong to the new corporation by virtue of the amalgamation;

(3) all shareholders of the predecessor corporations, other than predecessor corporate shareholders, must receive shares of the new corporation by virtue of the amalgamation; and

(4) the transfer of property cannot occur as the result of a normal purchase of such property or the distribution on a winding-up of a corporation.

¶17,085 Two Levels of Rollover

The rollover for a statutory amalgamation deals with:

(1) the transfer of capital property from the predecessor corporation to the successor or amalgamated corporation to permit a deferral of accrued capital gains transferred at the corporate level; and

(2) the exchange of shares of a predecessor corporation by its shareholders for shares of the successor corporation to permit a deferral of capital gains at the shareholder level.

¶17,090 Income Tax Consequences

¶17,090.10 General Effects

The amalgamated corporation is treated, for many purposes, as a continuation of the predecessor corporations. The effect would be like placing the balance sheets of two corporations side by side and adding together the similar accounts on each balance sheet based on the tax values such as adjusted cost base or undepreciated capital cost of each asset. The result would be a single balance sheet based on those tax values with no realization of capital gains or losses or recapture.

ITA: 87 Amalgamations

While the new corporation is considered by most Corporations Acts to be a continuation of the predecessor corporations, for tax purposes a new corporation is deemed to have been formed and the predecessor corporations are deemed to have a year end immediately before the amalgamation.[2] Thus, any provision of the tax legislation that counts taxation years will be affected by the amalgamation. As a result, the following could occur:

- one short taxation year will be counted in respect of unpaid amounts subject to treatment under section 78;
- capital cost allowance will be prorated for a short taxation year;

[2] Paragraph 1.15 of Income Tax Folio S4-F7-C1 states that "the effective date of amalgamation is governed by corporate law and is generally the date of issuance of letters patent or the date shown or set forth in the certificate of amalgamation, as the case may be. The time of the amalgamation is the earliest moment on that date in the absence of a particular time specified in the certificate of amalgamation".

- the amount of the business limit ($500,000) allocated for the small business deduction will also be prorated for a short taxation year; and
- non-capital losses carried forward by a predecessor corporation will be deductible in the short taxation year, but that taxation year will count as one of the carryforward years available.

¶17,090.20 Loss Utilization

The new corporation begins its first taxation year on the date of amalgamation. It may choose any year end it wishes, but in this first year it will be liable for instalments of tax based on the instalment bases of the predecessor corporations adjusted for a 12-month equivalent in the case of a short taxation year.

Consider the case of Corporation A with a December 31 year end and Corporation B with a June 30 year end. Assume that an amalgamation took place on October 1, 2018, and that the amalgamated corporation, Amalco, chooses a December 31 year end. This situation can be diagrammed as follows:

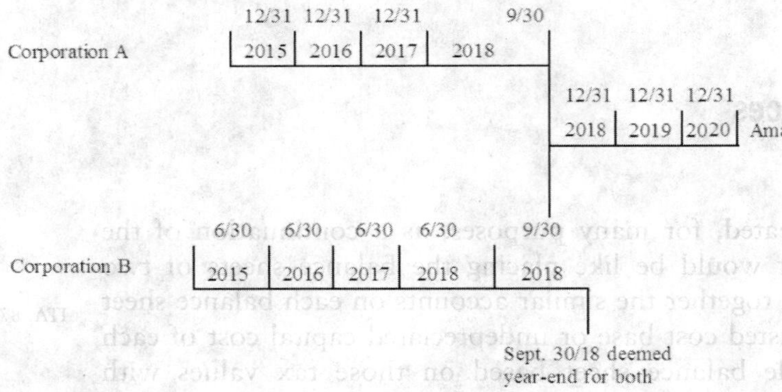

While pre-amalgamation losses can be carried forward for the remainder of their carryforward taxation years, post-amalgamation losses, generally, cannot be carried back. However, there is an exception to this restriction on the carryback of losses for the case of a vertical amalgamation, described below. In that case, the newly amalgamated corporation is deemed to be a continuation of the former parent corporation for the purposes of carrying back the losses. This exception for a vertical amalgamation provides for the same effect that is available in the winding-up of a subsidiary into its parent, discussed subsequently, on the carryback of post-reorganization losses.

ITA: 87(2.1) Non-capital losses, etc., of predecessor corporations, 87(2.11) Vertical amalgamations, 88(1.1) Non-capital losses, etc., of subsidiary

¶17,090.30 Rollover Effects

Exhibit 17-2 summarizes the effect of the major rollover provisions.

ITA: 87 Amalgamations

Exhibit 17-2 Major Rollover Provisions of Section 87

Paragraph	Item	Rollover effect
	Assets and Reserves	
Par. 87(2)(*b*)	Inventory	at cost amount
Par. 87(2)(*d*)	Depreciable capital property	at UCC[1]
Par. 87(2)(*e*)	Non-depreciable capital property	at ACB
Par. 87(2)(*g*)	Reserves	flowed through
	Loss Carryforwards	
Ssec. 87(2.1)	Non-capital losses	flowed through[2]
Ssec. 87(2.1)	Net capital losses	flowed through
Ssec. 87(2.1)	Restricted farm losses	flowed through
Ssec. 87(2.1)	Farm losses	flowed through
	Tax Accounts	
Par. 87(2)(*l*)	SR&ED pool/ITCs	flowed through
Par. 87(2)(*z.1*)	Capital dividend account	flowed through[3]
Par. 87(2)(*aa*)	Refundable dividend tax on hand	flowed through[3]
Par. 87(2)(*vv*)	General rate income pool	flowed through
Par. 87(2)(*ww*)	Low rate income pool	flowed through

[1] The new corporation will be liable for recapture in the same manner that a predecessor corporation would have been liable for such recapture.

[2] The limitations regarding the carrying on of the loss business on a previous acquisition of control of a predecessor corporation will apply after the amalgamation to losses previously subject to those limitations in the predecessor corporation. Note that there is not necessarily an acquisition of control on amalgamation itself (e.g., the relative shareholdings have not changed from those of the predecessor corporations). The deemed year end of a predecessor corporation on amalgamation will be counted as one of the twenty years available for the carryforward of non-capital losses.

[3] These accounts which pertain only to private corporations would be lost if one of the predecessor corporations were a public corporation.

¶17,095 Availability of a "Bump" on Vertical Amalgamation

Where a parent corporation and one or more subsidiary corporations are amalgamated, in what is commonly known as a "vertical amalgamation", an added advantage is available. The new corporation formed on amalgamation can increase its cost of certain capital property acquired by it on the amalgamation. This increase in cost is permitted without triggering any of the unrealized gain on the property at the time of the amalgamation. This "bump" in cost, therefore, places the new corporation in a position to recover more cost on a tax-free basis on the ultimate sale of the assets. The provision refers to the rules in subsection 88(1) which provides the same opportunity for a "bump" on the winding-up of a subsidiary into its parent. A discussion of how the "bump" works and the reasons for its existence is deferred to the winding-up of a subsidiary discussion in the next part of this chapter. Also, a formula for the calculation for the parent of proceeds of disposition for the shares of the subsidiary, which uses the rules in subsection 88(1), will be discussed in ¶17,140.

ITA: 87(11) Vertical amalgamations

¶17,100 Planning Opportunities

Planning opportunities involving the use of an amalgamation might include:

- the utilization of prior year losses that might not be absorbed by the income of a predecessor corporation;
- the utilization of current year losses in one predecessor corporation against the income of another predecessor corporation; or
- the faster utilization of capital cost allowance in a high-rate or rapid write-off class.

Other planning opportunities might involve the following:

- where a parent corporation has been amalgamated with one or more wholly owned subsidiary corporations, i.e., a vertical amalgamation, losses realized subsequent to the amalgamation may be carried back by the amalgamated corporation and applied to the income of the predecessor *parent* corporation;
- an amalgamation might facilitate a change in fiscal year end which would ordinarily require the consent of the Canada Revenue Agency (CRA), although an Information Circular pertaining to the general anti-avoidance rule (GAAR) indicates that if an amalgamation is undertaken with a shell corporation solely to effect a year-end change, the GAAR would be applied (as discussed in a previous chapter).

ITA: 87(2.11) Vertical amalgamations

ITA: 245 [General anti-avoidance rule]; Information Circulars: IC 88-2

¶17,105 Effects of the Rollover at the Shareholder Level

At the shareholder's level, the shareholder is deemed to have disposed of his or her shares for proceeds equal to their adjusted cost base and to have acquired the new shares of the amalgamated corporation at that same adjusted cost base. The conditions for this rollover to apply to the shareholder's position are:

ITA: 87(4) Shares of predecessor corporation

(1) that he or she receive no consideration for his or her shares other than shares of the successor corporation or its Canadian parent corporation (i.e., no "boot" can be received);

(2) that the original shares are capital property to the shareholder; and

(3) the amalgamation does not result in a deemed gift to a person related to the shareholder.

Note that the potential problem of a deemed dividend exists if the paid-up capital of the amalgamated corporation increases on the issue of shares by more than the increase in the fair market value of the net assets transferred to that corporation.

ITA: 84(1) Deemed dividend

¶17,105.99 Practise What You've Learned

Refer to the following sections of the Study Guide to practise what you've learned:

¶17,800 — Review Questions

- Question 4 — Amalgamations
- Question 5 — Deemed Year End
- Question 6 — Deemed Year End

¶17,110 Winding Up a Subsidiary — Section 88

¶17,115 Overview

The process of winding up is a tax concept, which is effected in corporate law by the dissolution of a corporation, and the transfer of the dissolved corporation's assets and liabilities to the shareholders. The corporation ceases to exist as a legal entity on the date shown in the certificate of dissolution. The corporate existence of the subsidiary is terminated and the parent corporation remains intact, holding the assets and liabilities that were previously held by the subsidiary.

ITA: 88(1) Winding-up

The ITA sets out rules for an automatic rollover where a taxable Canadian corporation of which at least 90% of each class of shares is owned by another taxable Canadian corporation, is wound up into its parent corporation under appropriate corporate law. These rules are very similar to those for a statutory amalgamation that could take place between a parent company and its subsidiary (i.e., a "vertical amalgamation"). They generally avoid the recognition of accrued capital gains on the transfer of assets from a subsidiary to its parent in a winding-up.

As a rollover provision, subsection 88(1) should be distinguished from the general winding-up provision in subsection 88(2), which is not a rollover provision. Subsection 88(2) was covered in Chapter 15 and results in a taxable distribution of the properties of a corporation on wind-up when the conditions for the rollover under 88(1) do not apply. For example, if the shareholder of the corporation is an individual, then subsection 88(2) will always apply and the distribution of the assets of the corporation to the individual shareholder will be a taxable event. If the shareholder is a corporation, then, generally, subsection 88(1) applies and a rollover results.

The major difference between the subsection 88(1) winding-up and an amalgamation arises in the area of the parent's utilization of the loss carryforwards of the subsidiary, as discussed below.

Again, there are two components to the rollover. The first deals with the transfer of property to the parent in which the subsidiary is deemed to have disposed of its assets for proceeds of the cost amount to the subsidiary. The second deals with the disposition of the shares of the subsidiary by the parent company that occurs at adjusted cost base but can in rare circumstances result in a gain.

ITA: 88(1)(a) [Winding-up — Proceeds of disposition of subsidiary's property], 248(1) cost amount

¶17,120 Availability of a "Bump" and Other Effects on the Parent

The parent is deemed to have acquired the property at a cost equal to the deemed proceeds of the subsidiary. However, when the adjusted cost base of the subsidiary's shares held by the parent exceeds the tax values of the net assets of the subsidiary transferred on the winding-up, there is a possibility of increasing or "bumping" the adjusted cost base of some non-depreciable capital property received from the subsidiary.

This "bump" or "step-up" in adjusted cost base is calculated as follows:

ITA: 88(1)(d) [Winding-up — Addition to cost of property acquired by parent (the "bump")]

Parent's adjusted cost base of the subsidiary's shares *minus* the sum of:

(1) the cost amount of the subsidiary's assets plus cash net of liabilities and certain reserves; and

(2) dividends (including both taxable and capital dividends) paid to the parent on its shares of the subsidiary.

The "bump" may be allocated to any non-depreciable capital property owned by the subsidiary continuously from the time when the parent acquired control of the subsidiary to the date of the winding-up. However, the amount of the increase cannot raise the adjusted cost base of an asset above its fair market value at the time when the parent acquired control of the subsidiary.

¶17,125 Illustration

Consider the case of a subsidiary with the following balance sheet immediately before the winding-up:

Cash	$5,000	Accounts payable	$5,000
Land	160,000	Paid-up capital	20,000
Depreciable property	60,000	Retained earnings	200,000
	$225,000		$225,000

Other relevant facts include the following:

Parent's adjusted cost base of the subsidiary's shares	$300,000
FMV of the land when the parent acquired control of the subsidiary	200,000
Dividends paid by the subsidiary to the parent	10,000

Note that the only item of non-depreciable capital property is the land. Exhibit 17-3 illustrates the application of the bump to this set of facts. The adjusted cost base of the land will be increased from $160,000 to $200,000. Although a total "bump" of $70,000 was available, there were no other non-depreciable capital assets available to absorb the remaining $30,000 which is lost.

ITA: 88(1)(d) [Winding-up — Addition to cost of property acquired by parent (the "bump")]

Exhibit 17-3 Conceptual Application of Paragraph 88(1)(d)

BEFORE WIND-UP		*AFTER WIND-UP*	
PARENT		PARENT	
Shares of subsidiary at ACB	$300,000	Cost amount of net assets of former subsidiary ...	$220,000
Dividends from subsidiary (recovery of cost)	(10,000)	Addition to ACB of former subsidiary's land	40,000*
Net cost	$290,000	Total cost amount	$260,000
SUBSIDIARY		* Limit of "bump" on land:	
Cost amount of net assets ($225K – 5K)	$220,000	FMV of land at time parent acquired control of subsidiary	$ 200,000
		ACB of land at time of wind-up ...	(160,000)
Potential "bump": $70,000 (i.e., $290,000 – $220,000)		Limit	$ 40,000

The shares of the subsidiary, held as assets in the parent, are replaced by the cost amounts of the subsidiary's net assets. Conceptually, the net cost of the subsidiary's shares to the parent is reduced by dividends, either taxable or capital, received from the subsidiary representing a return of $10,000 of the original investment in the subsidiary. The result is that the parent replaces assets having a net cost of $290,000 with assets having a net cost of $220,000. The "bump" is meant to help the parent recover some of the difference in cost.

The same rule applies for the same reasons, in a vertical amalgamation. While there are differences under corporate law, conceptually, a vertical amalgamation and a winding-up of a subsidiary into its parent have the same effect. Therefore, it is reasonable for the tax treatment to be the same. ITA: 87(1)(a)

In the case of depreciable property, the parent corporation is deemed to have a capital cost for the property equal to that of the subsidiary and, thus, becomes potentially liable for recapture.

¶17,130 Loss Utilization

On the winding-up of a subsidiary into its parent, there is no deemed year end for either corporation, as is the case for an amalgamation. The subsidiary, simply, ceases to exist on completion of the winding-up, since it has no assets and no shares outstanding, and the parent corporation continues with its same year end that it had been using. Consider the case of Parentco with a December 31 year end and Subcorp with a June 30 year end. Assume that a winding-up commences October 1, 2018, when the net assets of Subcorp are transferred to Parentco. Subcorp continues to exist until it is formally dissolved some time later. This situation can be diagrammed as follows:

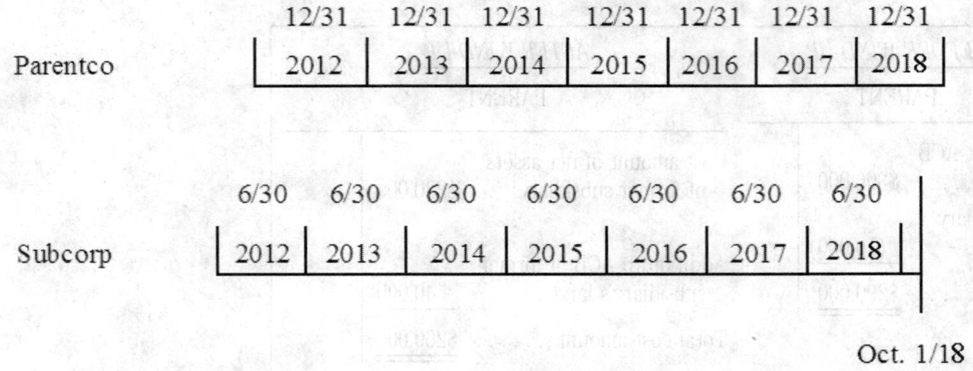

When a subsidiary is wound up into its parent, the deductibility by the parent of the subsidiary's non-capital losses, restricted farm losses, farm losses, limited partnership losses and net capital losses is limited as follows:

ITA: 88(1.1) Non-capital losses, etc., of subsidiary, 88(1.2) Net capital losses of subsidiary

(1) the losses that have not been deducted by the subsidiary are first deductible by the parent in its taxation year following the taxation year in which the winding-up began; and

(2) the losses are only deductible by the parent to the extent that they have not expired. The subsidiary's losses are deemed to be losses of the parent for the year in which the subsidiary's loss year ended for purposes of determining the carryforward period.

When the subsidiary has a taxation year different from that of the parent, the subsidiary's losses will be deemed to have occurred in the parent's taxation year which includes the taxation year end of the subsidiary. The following illustrates this rule schematically:

Losses of the subsidiary for its fiscal year ended become	*Losses of the parent for its fiscal year ended*	*Available for deduction by parent for fiscal years ended December 31*													
		2018	*2019*	*2020*	*2021*	*2022*	*...*	*2032*	*2033*	*2034*	*2035*	*2036*	*2037*	*2038*	*2039*
June 30/18	Dec. 31/18														
June 30/17	Dec. 31/17	X	✓	✓	✓	✓	...	✓	✓	✓	✓	✓	✓	expired	
June 30/16	Dec. 31/16	X	✓	✓	✓	✓	...	✓	✓	✓	✓	✓	expired		
June 30/15	Dec. 31/15	X	✓	✓	✓	✓	...	✓	✓	✓	✓	expired			
June 30/14	Dec. 31/14	X	✓	✓	✓	✓	...	✓	✓	✓	expired				
June 30/13	Dec. 31/13	X	✓	✓	✓	✓	...	✓	✓	expired					
June 30/12	Dec. 31/12	X	✓	✓	✓	✓	...	✓	expired						
June 30/11	Dec. 31/11	X	✓	✓	✓	✓	...	expired							

└► losses not available in year of wind-up

The above assumes that the winding-up commences on October 1, 2018, such that none of the losses would be available to the parent until its 2019 taxation year. This represents an application of the rule that the parent cannot use a subsidiary's losses in the winding-up year. This differs from an amalgamation which provides for a deemed year end and may result in a short year counting as one taxation year for loss carryforwards of the loss corporation. With an amalgamation, losses can be used in the first taxation year end of the amalgamated company.

ITA: 88(1.1) Non-capital losses, etc., of subsidiary

For cases where control of a parent or subsidiary has changed, the Act provides rules restricting the availability of non-capital losses or farm losses that are similar to the restrictions discussed in Chapter 11. An amalgamation or a winding-up within an existing corporate group does not constitute an acquisition of control and, hence, the restrictions on loss carryovers that arise on an acquisition of control do not apply.

ITA: 88(1.1)(e), 111(5) Loss restriction event — non-capital losses and farm losses, 256(7) Acquiring control

¶17,135 Planning Opportunities

The planning opportunities involving the use of a winding-up will generally include the same opportunities as those considered for an amalgamation. A winding-up will usually be preferred from a tax perspective if the timing of loss carryforwards will result in greater deductibility of such losses. It should be recognized, however, that a winding-up is considerably more expensive and time-consuming to implement than an amalgamation. Unlike an amalgamation, the assets and liabilities of the subsidiary must be legally transferred or assumed by the parent to effect a wind-up. Obtaining the consent of third parties may be cumbersome; transfer fees and taxes can be significant; and the preparation and registration of conveyance documents can take time and create additional costs.

¶17,140 Disposition by Parent of Subsidiary's Shares on Winding Up or Vertical Amalgamation

The second component of the rollover deals with the disposition or cancellation of shares by the parent on the winding-up or on a vertical amalgamation. The parent corporation is deemed to have disposed of the shares of the subsidiary for proceeds equal to the greater of:

(1) the lesser of:

(a) the paid-up capital of the shares of the subsidiary, and

(b) the aggregate of the cost amounts of the assets of the subsidiary received, net of any liabilities, and certain tax reserves assumed; and

(2) the adjusted cost base of the shares of the subsidiary held by the parent immediately before the winding-up/amalgamation.

ITA: 88(1)(b) [Winding-up — Disposition of shares of subsidiary]

In the foregoing example, the parent corporation would be deemed to have disposed of the subsidiary for proceeds equal to the greater of:

(a) the lesser of:		
(i) the paid-up capital of the shares of the subsidiary	$20,000	
(ii) the cost amounts of the net assets immediately before the winding-up/amalgamation	$220,000	
the lesser amount		$20,000
(b) the adjusted cost base of the shares of the subsidiary held by the parent		$300,000

Proceeds of disposition would be established at the greater amount (i.e., $300,000). Since this amount is equal to the ACB, no capital gain or loss will result.

As a result of this rule, the parent may realize, in fairly rare circumstances, a gain on the liquidation or amalgamation of its subsidiary, but it may not realize a capital loss because the deemed proceeds of disposition of the shares of the subsidiary cannot be less than their adjusted cost base to the parent. In most situations, the parent will obtain, in effect, a rollover on the disposition of the shares in the subsidiary. A gain would only arise in the unusual circumstance where both the PUC of the shares of the subsidiary and the cost amount of its net assets exceed the ACB of the shares.

As noted above, the same formula applies in the determination of proceeds of disposition to the parent for shares of the subsidiary in a vertical amalgamation. ITA: 87(11)(a)

¶17,140.99 Practise What You've Learned

Refer to the following sections of the Study Guide to practise what you've learned:

¶17,800 — Review Questions

- Question 7 — Wind up of subsidiary

¶17,825 — Multiple Choice Questions

- Question 1 — Amalgamation, wind-up
- Question 2 — Wind-up

¶17,850 — Exercises

- Exercise 4 — Amalgamation, wind-up

¶17,200 Rollovers Involving Shares or Corporate Securities

¶17,210 Convertible Properties — Section 51

Convertible properties are commonly issued in the form of shares, bonds or notes of a corporation. These securities can be exchanged for shares of the corporation under specific conditions at the option of the holder. In essence, the securities held are given up on the conversion in return for share capital. Note how this rollover differs from section 86. This rollover does not require newly authorized shares whereas section 86 appears to require, in the course of a capital reorganization, new shares created by a change in authorized capital through the articles of incorporation. A conversion of shares can be made by shares that are already authorized. ITA: 51 Convertible property

The Act permits a deferral of the inherent gain on the exchanged securities, but only if the following conditions are met: ITA: 51 Convertible property

(1) only shares are issued for the exchanged securities;

(2) the exchanged securities are capital property to the taxpayer; and

(3) the exchanged securities, other than shares, must have a conversion right attached to the particular security.

The provision is not elective but is automatic if the above conditions are met. However, the application of section 51 is denied if section 85 or 86 has been applied to the exchange transaction. ITA: 51(4) Application

When the holder of a convertible property exercises the conversion privilege and as a result acquires the shares of one class of the capital stock of the corporation, the exchange is deemed not to have been a disposition of property. The adjusted cost base of the shares acquired on conversion is deemed to be the adjusted cost base of the convertible security before the exchange. The effect is to defer any capital gain accrued on the convertible security prior to the exchange until such time as the new shares are sold. For example, a taxpayer purchased a $1,000 bond, the terms of which conferred upon the holder the right of conversion into five common shares. The adjusted cost base of the bond is $1,000. If the bond is converted into the five shares when those shares have a value of $225, the taxpayer will not realize the accrued gain on the bond which should have a fair market value of $1,125 (i.e., 5 × $225). Instead the $1,000 cost base of the bond will flow through to the five shares such that each share will have a cost base of $200 (i.e., $1,000/5). If shares of more than one class are received on the conversion, the adjusted cost base of the convertible security before the exchange would be allocated among the classes of shares received on the conversion in proportion to their respective fair market values after the exchange.

A penalty provision applies where a benefit has been conferred on a related person and is similar in effect to the capital reorganization benefit rule. The provision that determines the paid-up capital of the newly issued shares has a formula which is practically identical to that for a capital reorganization, as previously discussed. ITA: 51(2) Idem, 51(3) Computation of paid-up capital, 86(2.1) Computation of paid-up capital

A similar provision covers the case where a bondholder acquires a new bond of the same debtor in exchange for the original bond. There is a similar flow-through of the adjusted cost base of the original bond to the new bond and of any tax-free zone position on the original bond. ITA: 51.1 Conversion of debt obligation

¶17,210.99 Practise What You've Learned

Refer to the following sections of the Study Guide to practise what you've learned:

¶17,800 — Review Questions

- Question 8 — Convertible shares

¶17,850 — Exercises

- Exercise 5 — Convertible property

¶17,220 Interspousal Transfers

An automatic rollover allows the deferral of the recognition of a capital gain or loss on the transfer of property between spouses or to a qualifying trust in favour of one spouse. The taxpayer must elect out of the rollover to allow the recognition of the gain or loss. The rollover applies when capital property is transferred between living spouses (*inter vivos*) either by way of sale at any price or gift. A qualifying trust is one created by the taxpayer under which the spouse is entitled to receive all the income of the trust that arises before the spouse's death and no person except the spouse may receive or obtain the use of any of the trust property before the spouse's death. Also, the spouse or trust must be resident in Canada at the time of the property transfer. The topic of spousal trusts will be discussed more fully in a subsequent chapter.

The Act provides that the property is deemed to have been sold by one spouse and acquired by the other spouse or trust for an amount equal to its adjusted cost base in the case of capital property such as shares. As indicated above, the provision allows an election to transfer such property at its fair market value.

ITA: 73(1) Inter vivos transfers by individuals

A similar rollover applies on a transfer of property to a spouse at death through a will. This rollover, like that between living spouses, is applied automatically, although an election can be made to use the general rules applicable at death to recognize capital gains and losses. For example, a husband may bequeath shares having a cost of $100 and a fair market value at the time of death of $250. If the rollover is used, the shares will be deemed to have been transferred at their adjusted cost base of $100 such that no gain or loss is realized on the transfer. However, if the election is made, the transfer will take place at $250, thereby realizing a capital gain of $150. Again, similar rules apply to depreciable property.

ITA: 70(6) Where transfer or distribution to spouse or spouse trust, 70(6.2) Election, 73(1) Inter vivos transfers by individuals

¶17,250 Summary of Rollovers Covered

The following chart provides a summary of the rollovers in the *Income Tax Act* that have been discussed in this and previous chapters.

Exhibit 17-4 Summary of Rollovers Covered

ITA Ref.	Description	Automatic / Elective	Conditions	Tax Consequences
85	Transfer of property to corporation by shareholder	Elective	(1) Corporate transferee must be a taxable Canadian corporation; (2) Consideration received by the transferor must include shares of the corporation; (3) Property transferred must be capital property, a resource property, or inventory (other than real property); and (4) Taxpayer(s) and the corporation must jointly elect to have rollover provisions apply (T2057).	• Potential deferral of some or all of accrued gains in the transferred property, depending on amount of boot received.

ITA Ref.	Description	Automatic / Elective	Conditions	Tax Consequences
85.1	Share-for-share exchange	Automatic (if conditions met)	(1) Transferred shares of the vendor must be capital property; (2) Purchaser must be a Canadian corporation; (3) Only consideration given by the purchaser to the vendor must be previously unissued shares of any particular class. Consideration is restricted to shares of only one class; (4) Immediately prior to the exchange, the vendor and purchaser must be dealing at arm's length with each other; (5) Immediately after the exchange, the vendor must not (*a*) control the purchaser, or (*b*) own more than 50% of the FMV of all outstanding shares; (6) Vendor and purchaser cannot have elected under section 85; and (7) Vendor cannot have recognized any portion of potential capital gain or loss on exchange.	• Tax-free rollover with deferral of entire capital gain.
86	Reorganization of capital	Automatic (if conditions met)	(1) Shares are capital property to the shareholder; (2) All of the shares of a particular class owned by the shareholder are exchanged; (3) Property receivable by the shareholder on the exchange includes shares; and (4) Section 85 cannot have been used.	• Potential deferral of all or some of accrued gain on the shares, depending on amount of boot received.

ITA Ref.	Description	Automatic / Elective	Conditions	Tax Consequences
87	Statutory amalgamation	Automatic (if conditions met)	(1) Predecessor corporations must be taxable Canadian corporations; (2) All of the property and liabilities of the predecessor corporations must belong to the new corporation; and (3) All shareholders of the predecessor corporations must receive shares of the new corporation.	• Predecessor corporations deemed to have a year end immediately prior to amalgamation. • Potential deferral of some or all accrued capital gains on transfer of capital property at corporate level. • Potential deferral of some or all accrued capital gains on shares at shareholder level. • Availability of "bump" in ACB if vertical amalgamation.
88	Winding up of a subsidiary	Automatic (if conditions met)	(1) A taxable Canadian corporation of which at least 90% of each class of shares is owned by another taxable Canadian corporation is wound up into its parent.	• Potential deferral of some or all accrued gain on transfer of assets to parent. • No deemed year end. • Losses of subsidiary deductible by parent in the taxation year following the year of wind-up. • Availability of "bump" in ACB.
51	Convertible properties	Automatic (if conditions met)	(1) Only shares are issued for the exchanged securities; (2) Exchanged securities are capital property to the taxpayer; and	• Deferral of the accrued gain on the exchanged securities.

ITA Ref.	Description	Automatic / Elective	Conditions	Tax Consequences
			(3) Exchanged securities, other than shares, must have a conversion right attached to particular security.	
73	Interspousal transfers	Automatic (if conditions met)	(1) Transfer of property must be between spouses or to a qualifying trust in favour of one spouse.	• Deferral of entire accrued gain on transfer.

¶17,300 Use of Rollovers in Estate Freezing

¶17,310 Objectives

The primary purpose of estate freezing is to freeze all or part of the value of growing assets at their current fair market value and allow the future growth in these assets to accrue to the next generation of family members. The result will be that this future growth will not be taxed in the hands of the taxpayer on a disposition or at his or her death. In the process of implementing an estate freeze, some of the following secondary objectives may be addressed:

- The taxpayer contemplating an estate freeze will not likely wish to incur any immediate tax cost in implementing the freeze, but may want to establish the amount of the tax liability that will arise on his or her death.
- The taxpayer will often wish to maintain control over the assets the value of which is being frozen even though their future growth in value is being passed to the next generation. At the same time, the taxpayer may wish to retain a source of income from the assets for retirement or living expenses.
- The implementation of an estate freeze may coincide with planning to split income with low tax-rate family members, although great care must be taken to avoid the adverse tax consequences of the attribution rules and the income-splitting tax, discussed in previous chapters (see ¶13,260).
- In the process of implementing an estate freeze, it may be possible to realize capital gains sufficient to use up a taxpayer's capital gains deduction on the disposition of the shares of a small business corporation, as discussed in a previous chapter.
- Through their ownership of common shares, the estate freeze will have the effect of placing the beneficiaries of an estate freeze in a position to generate sufficient future capital gains on those common shares to use their own capital gains deduction.

The focus of the discussion of techniques to accomplish these objectives will be on three principal methods of exchanging growth assets for non-growth assets, which can be termed: holdco freeze, internal freeze, and reverse or asset freeze. The intention is only to provide a conceptual overview without dealing with the details of implementation.

¶17,320 Holdco Freeze

This type of estate freeze uses section 85 as its primary planning device. In this case, a holding company is incorporated and the growing assets are transferred to the corporation, using the rollover to avoid incurring an immediate tax cost. Growing assets subject to the freeze may include: shares of an operating company, assets of an unincorporated business or a portfolio of securities. The estate freeze is implemented by the taxpayer taking, as consideration from the new corporation for the growing assets transferred, debt and preferred shares. The preferred shares can have voting rights attached to them to meet the objective of maintaining control over the assets transferred. Both types of security can provide income to their holder. However, neither type of security, if properly issued with appropriate features, will grow in value as the assets of the corporation grow. In structuring the consideration received from the holding company, care must be taken to avoid the adverse tax consequences of dividend stripping, as discussed previously.

ITA: 85 Transfer of property to corporation by shareholders, 84.1 Non-arm's length sale of shares

The future growth in the assets of the new corporation will be reflected in the value of the common shares of the corporation. These common shares can be subscribed for by the children in the family. Of course, care must be taken not to invoke the corporate or regular attribution rules and the income-splitting tax, as previously discussed (see ¶6,145 and ¶13,390). This problem is of particular concern if a small business corporation is not involved in the estate freeze.

ITA: 248(1) small business corporation

The process of this type of estate freeze can be illustrated schematically by the following diagram:

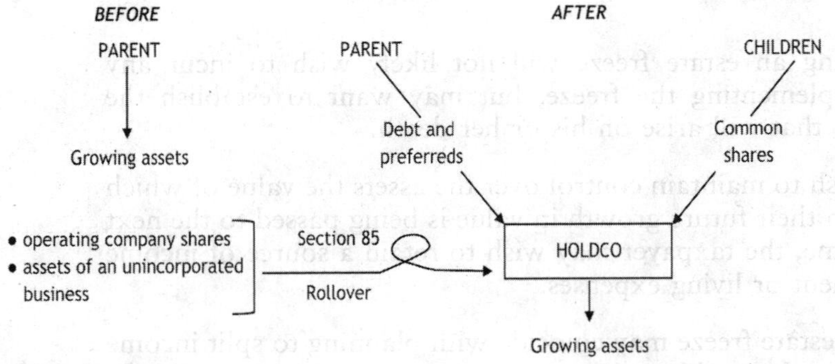

Draft legislative proposals released December 13, 2017 amend the provisions of the Income Tax Act dealing with Tax on Split Income (TOSI) and are discussed in ¶13,260 of the text. TOSI for individuals 18 years and older includes taxable capital gains from the disposition of property that consists of shares of a private corporation unless the taxable capital gain is on qualified small business corporation (QSBC) shares. As a result, it is important when disposing of shares of a private corporation to consider these provisions. In an estate freeze transaction, as long as the operating company shares are transferred to the holding company on a rollover basis using Section 85, TOSI will not apply. Further, if the shares are transferred to the holding company at fair market value or at an elected amount using Section 85 that results in a taxable capital gain, TOSI will not be a concern as long as the shares are QSBC shares.

¶17,330 Internal Freeze

A capital reorganization of an existing corporation is the basis of this type of estate freeze. A taxpayer who owns common shares of a corporation may cause the corporation to undertake a capital reorganization. The taxpayer gives up the common shares in return for debt and newly authorized preferred shares of the corporation, using section 86 to defer any accrued gains on the common shares given up. Again, the preferred shares may have voting rights to maintain control over the corporation. Both the debt and preferred shares can provide the taxpayer with a source of income. The children can subscribe for new common shares to which the future growth in the value of the corporation's assets will accrue.

ITA: 86 Exchange of shares by a shareholder in course of reorganization of capital

This method of estate freeze has several advantages over the holdco freeze.

- First, a new company need not be incorporated, thereby avoiding the costs associated with incorporating and maintaining the additional corporation.
- Second, the rollover provision in section 86 is applied automatically without any need for an election to be made.
- Finally, the dividend stripping rules are not applicable, thereby avoiding a potentially serious problem. However, care must be taken to structure the paid-up capital of the new shares to avoid a deemed dividend problem.

ITA: 84(3) Redemption, etc., 84.1 Non-arm's length sale of shares, 84(1) Deemed dividend

Note that the internal freeze relying on section 86 will not generate a capital gain for purposes of crystallization. [It is possible to generate a capital gain to use the capital gains deduction in an internal freeze by filing a section 85 election. That option is beyond the scope of this textbook and will not be addressed.]

ITA: 86 Exchange of shares by a shareholder in course of reorganization of capital

A final note of warning in respect of both the holdco and the internal freeze is that careful planning is required to ensure that the corporate attribution rules are not triggered. As long as the respective corporations are small business corporations (i.e., meet the 90% active business asset rule), then the corporate attribution rules will not apply.

ITA: 74.4 [Transfers and loans to corporations]

The following diagram provides a conceptual illustration of an internal freeze:

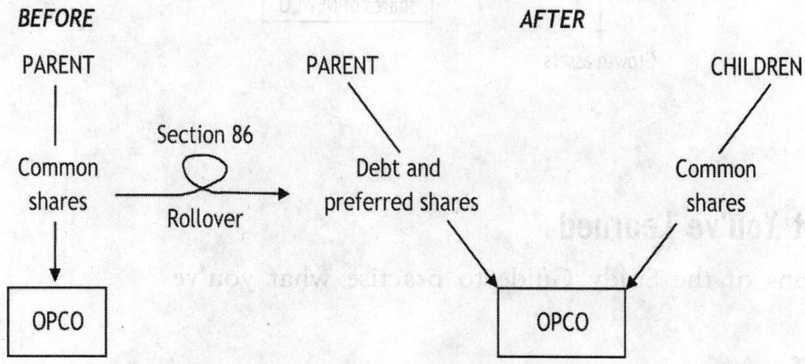

¶17,340 Reverse or Asset Freeze

The basic concept of a reverse freeze is to remove some or all of the *growth* assets of a corporation in which the taxpayer presently owns common shares and replace those growth assets with non-growth assets. The process requires that a new corporation be established with the children subscribing for common shares of that corporation. The taxpayer then causes his or her corporation to transfer the growth assets that it owns to the new corporation. Again, section 85 would be used to accomplish the transfer without incurring an immediate tax cost. Since assets, other than shares of a subject corporation, are being transferred, the dividend stripping provision will not apply. If the preferred shares taken back have voting rights, the taxpayer can maintain control over the assets transferred to the new corporation through the exercise of control over his or her corporation, which owns the voting preferred shares. His or her corporation can also earn income for his or her benefit on the debt and preferred shares it owns. However, the value of the common shares held by the taxpayer in his or her original corporation will not grow in the future if the only assets of that corporation are the non-growth debt and preferred securities of the new corporation. On the other hand, the common shares of the new corporation held by the children will grow in value as the assets transferred to that corporation grow.

ITA: 84.1 Non-arm's length sale of shares

One of the advantages of the reverse freeze technique is that selected growth assets can be transferred, such that the children will only participate in the future growth of the selected assets transferred. Furthermore, if different children are to participate in the future growth of different assets and each child subscribes for the common shares of a different new corporation, selected assets can be transferred to the benefit of each child as desired. Unlike the previous types of freezes, the attribution rules do not apply in the case of a reverse freeze, because the transferor or lender is not an individual.

ITA: 56(4.1) Interest free or low interest loans, 74.1 [Transfers and loans to spouse or common-law partner or minor], 74.2 Gain or loss deemed that of lender or transferor, 74.4(2) Transfers and loans to corporations

The following diagram illustrates conceptually a basic reverse freeze:

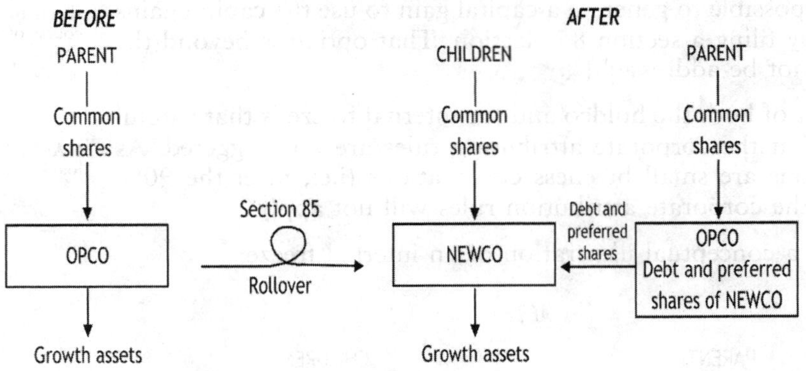

¶17,340.99 Practise What You've Learned

Refer to the following sections of the Study Guide to practise what you've learned:

¶17,800 — Review Questions

- Question 9 — Estate freeze
- Question 10 — Estate freeze

- Question 11 — Asset freeze
- Question 12 — Holdco freeze
- Question 13 — Estate freeze
- Question 14 — Reverse or asset freeze

¶17,825 — Multiple Choice Questions

- Question 5 — Estate freeze
- Question 6 — Estate freeze

CHAPTER 18

Partnerships and Trusts

ADVANCED CONTENT IN THIS CHAPTER

Learning Goals

Know

By the end of this chapter you will know:

- The basic provisions of the *Income Tax Act* that relate to partnerships and trusts.

Understand and Explain

By the end of this chapter you will understand and be able to explain:

- How a partnership and a trust are established.
- How income earned within a partnership is computed.
- How income of a partnership is taxed.

Apply

By the end of this chapter you will be able to apply your knowledge and understanding to:

- Calculate the income of a partner from a partnership.
- Calculate income of a partnership.
- Calculate taxable income and tax payable of a trust.

Review Questions

¶18,800 in the Study Guide

Multiple Choice Questions

¶18,825 in the Study Guide

Exercises

¶18,850 in the Study Guide

Assignment Problems

¶18,875 in the Study Guide

Overview

According to the CPA Knowledge Supplement, the topics of partnerships and trusts are viewed as advanced topics to be covered in detail in the *elective* stage. Therefore, our advanced symbol (Ⓐ) in this chapter identifies material within these subjects that is more complex and non-routine in nature.

This chapter is intended to provide only an overview of the provisions dealing with partnerships. The chapter will deal, in general terms, with the computation of partnership income, the concept of a partnership interest, and some of the rollover provisions affecting partnerships.

The chapter will also introduce some basic concepts in the taxation of trusts and illustrate some of the ways in which trusts are used in tax planning. There are two types of trusts for tax purposes: the personal trust and the commercial trust. This chapter will focus, in general, on the provisions of the Act as they relate to personal trusts. Commercial trusts are used for business and investment purposes. Most Canadian mutual funds are commercial trusts. Certain types of trusts which are provided for specifically in the Act, such as registered pension plans, registered retirement savings plans and deferred profit sharing plans have already been introduced and will not be dealt with here.

The following chart will help locate in the Act the major provisions discussed in this Chapter pertaining to partnerships and trusts.

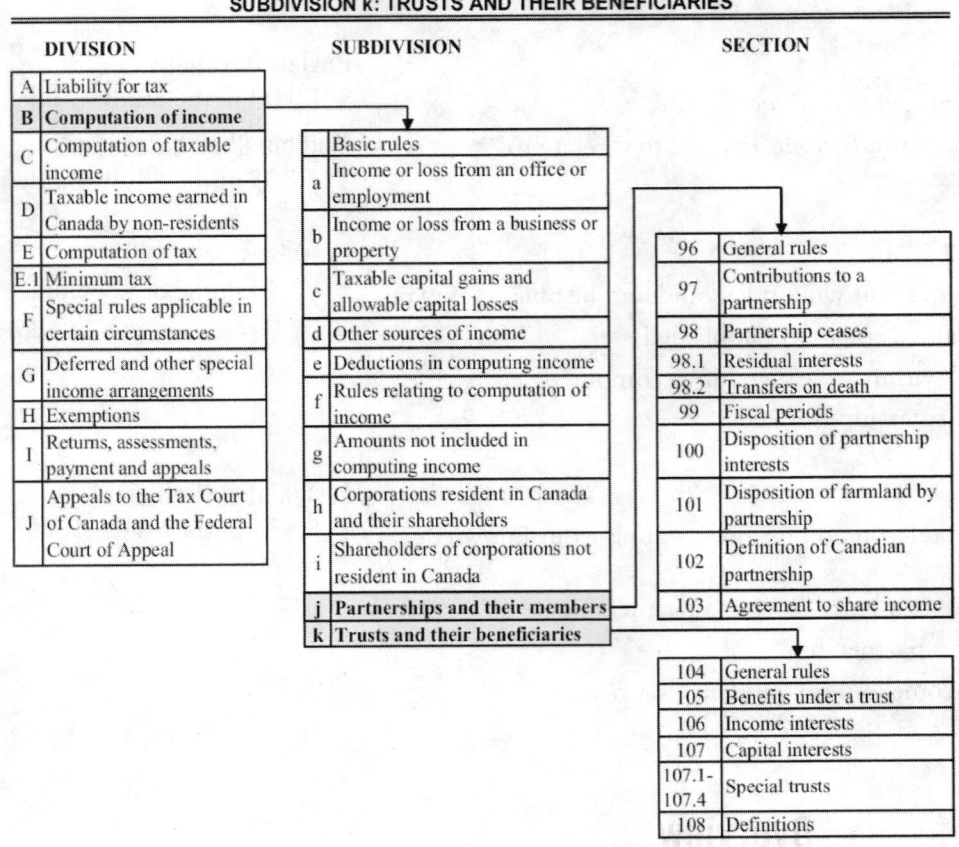

PART I — DIVISION B

SUBDIVISION j: PARTNERSHIPS AND THEIR MEMBERS
SUBDIVISION k: TRUSTS AND THEIR BENEFICIARIES

DIVISION

A	Liability for tax
B	**Computation of income**
C	Computation of taxable income
D	Taxable income earned in Canada by non-residents
E	Computation of tax
E.1	Minimum tax
F	Special rules applicable in certain circumstances
G	Deferred and other special income arrangements
H	Exemptions
I	Returns, assessments, payment and appeals
J	Appeals to the Tax Court of Canada and the Federal Court of Appeal

SUBDIVISION

	Basic rules
a	Income or loss from an office or employment
b	Income or loss from a business or property
c	Taxable capital gains and allowable capital losses
d	Other sources of income
e	Deductions in computing income
f	Rules relating to computation of income
g	Amounts not included in computing income
h	Corporations resident in Canada and their shareholders
i	Shareholders of corporations not resident in Canada
j	**Partnerships and their members**
k	**Trusts and their beneficiaries**

SECTION

96	General rules
97	Contributions to a partnership
98	Partnership ceases
98.1	Residual interests
98.2	Transfers on death
99	Fiscal periods
100	Disposition of partnership interests
101	Disposition of farmland by partnership
102	Definition of Canadian partnership
103	Agreement to share income

104	General rules
105	Benefits under a trust
106	Income interests
107	Capital interests
107.1-107.4	Special trusts
108	Definitions

¶18,000 Partnerships

¶18,010 What Is a Partnership?

¶18,015 Nature of a Partnership

The term "partnership" is not defined in the Act. The Act merely outlines the tax consequences if a partnership exists. In order to determine whether a particular relationship is a partnership, reference must be made to the definitions contained in the various provincial Partnership Acts. Generally, these statutes define a partnership as a legal relationship existing between two or more persons who carry on a business in common for the purpose of profit. Partnerships can be formed by individuals, corporations or a combination of individuals and corporations. In addition, two other factors generally suggest the existence of a partnership:

(1) joint and several liability with respect to debts incurred by the partnership; and

(2) an agreement indicating the method by which profits and losses are to be shared.

The Canada Revenue Agency (CRA) has issued an Interpretation Bulletin which sets out the factors it considers in determining whether a partnership exists.

Income Tax Folio: S4-F16-C1 What is a Partnership?

Partners may set out their interests in partnership property and their rights and duties in relation to the partnership by written agreement. In the absence of a written agreement, the interests of the partners may be implied from all of the surrounding circumstances. If there is no agreement, express or implied, then the Partnership Acts generally provide that all the partners are entitled to share equally in the capital, profits and losses of the partnership.

General Versus Limited Partnership

A partnership with two or more general partners may be referred to as a general partnership. General partners' have unlimited liability for the debts and obligations of the partnership.

A limited partnership has at least one general partner and one or more limited partners. A limited partner is generally a partner whose only interest in the partnership is financial. If a limited partner takes part in the management of the partnership's business then, under provincial partnership law, that partner will lose status as a limited partner. The general partner manages the partnership and is often a corporation with no assets other than an interest in the partnership.

A limited partner's liability is limited under partnership law or a partnership agreement. A limited partnership must be registered under the appropriate provincial or territorial registry system.

Limited Liability Partnerships

A partner in a limited liability partnership (LLP) can be liable for the general debts and obligations of the LLP. However, a partner in an LLP is not liable for the debts of the partnership, or any member of the partnership, arising from negligent acts or omissions committed in the course of the partnership business by another partner or an employee, agent, or representative of the partnership. A partner in an LLP continues to be liable for debts of the partnership arising from negligent acts or omissions committed in the course of the partnership business related to his or her own actions or those he or she supervises. Further, the partnership itself is liable for the negligence of its partners and employees. Thus, all of the assets of the partnership itself remain at risk.

¶18,020 Partnership Versus Joint Venture

A partnership is to be distinguished from a joint venture. The tax consequences of being a partner or co-venturer (a member of a joint venture) are quite different. A partnership is a separate entity. Therefore, unless a rollover provision applies, transfers of property by the partner to the partnership take place at fair market value. On the other hand, a co-venturer generally retains title to any property used in the joint venture. If the co-venturer contributes property to the joint venture, this is not a taxable transaction, as the contribution to a joint venture is not a disposition; there has been no change in ownership. Also, in a partnership, net income is computed at the partnership level. Therefore, capital cost allowance is deducted at the partnership level. Each partner does not have the discretion to deduct capital cost allowance independently of the other partners. In a joint venture, each co-venturer computes net income separately. Therefore, each co-venturer is able to deduct capital cost allowance independently of the other co-venturers.

Whether a particular relationship is a partnership or a joint venture is a question of fact. It is not easy to determine. The fact that an agreement refers to a relationship as a partnership or a joint venture is not determinative of that relationship. The true nature of the relationship must be determined from all the facts.

¶18,020.99 Practise What You've Learned

Refer to the following sections of the Study Guide to practise what you've learned:

¶18,800 — Review Questions

- Question 1 — Partnerships

A Canadian tax case, *Woodlin Developments Ltd. v. M.N.R.*, has stated that the following are indicators of a joint venture:

Cases: *Woodlin Developments Ltd. v. The Minister of National Revenue*, 86 DTC 1116 (TCC)

(1) joint property interest in the subject-matter of the venture;

(2) a right of mutual control and management of the enterprise; and

(3) generally, a limitation of the objective to a single undertaking or a limited number of undertakings.

¶18,030 Partnership Income

¶18,035 General Rules

A partnership is not a person, nor is it deemed to be a person for the purposes of the Act. However, the Act provides that the income of a partner is computed as if the partnership was a separate person resident in Canada. So, for example, deductions such as capital cost allowance are taken at the partnership level.

Each taxable capital gain and allowable capital loss from the disposition of property owned by the partnership and the amount of any income or loss of the partnership from such sources as business or property will be calculated for each fiscal period of the partnership. However, this income under Division B is not taxed at the partnership level but is allocated to the partners according to the terms of the partnership agreement. The partners then include their share of the partnership income in their income for the year. If, in computing income, the partnership deducts amounts under Division C against taxable income or credits from taxes payable, these amounts are added back to the partnership income before they are allocated to the partners. For example, charitable donations are added back to partnership income because, for a corporate partner, a Division C deduction can be made. For an individual partner, a credit from taxes payable can be claimed.

The taxation year of the partnership is the fiscal period of the partnership. The fiscal period of a partnership of which a member is an individual must end on December 31.

¶18,035.10 Nature of Income Retained

The income that flows through to each partner retains its original character or source, thereby enabling the partner to benefit, for example, from the dividend tax credit, the foreign tax credit and the capital gains deduction in respect of qualified farm property or qualified shares of a small business corporation. The income of the partnership will be combined on each partner's tax return with the partner's non-partnership income or losses. For example, non-partnership capital losses of an individual partner may be offset against that partner's share of partnership capital gains, since these gains are allocated to the partner. Similarly, a partner's share of rental income allocated by the partnership may be used to offset rental losses created by capital cost allowance on the partner's own rental property. Each individual or corporate partner reports their partnership income on their own return and pays tax. Taxable income is computed by each partner. The partnership itself does not file a tax return.

¶18,035.20 Reporting Deadlines

The partnership is required to provide an information return to each partner as follows: ITR: 229 Partnership Return

(a) where all of the partners are corporations, five months from the end of the fiscal period;

(b) where all the partners are individuals, March 31st following the December 31st tax year end of the partnership; and

(c) in every other case, the earlier of (a) or (b).

The CRA's administrative policy is to exempt partnerships, where all partners are individuals, from the reporting requirement if:

- revenues plus expenses are not greater than $2 million, and
- assets are not greater than $5 million.

However, it is important for partnerships to file an information return to limit the time period within which the Minister may reassess partnership income to three years from the filing date of the information return. ITR: 152(1.4)

Failure to file a partnership information return (where required by the CRA) on time will result in penalties.

Example Problem 18-1

The following income statement was prepared for the Alpha Beta Partnership, a partnership comprising two individuals that carries on an active business:

Alpha Beta Partnership

INCOME STATEMENT

For the year ended December 31, 2018

Gross revenue			$350,000
Less:			
	Office salaries	$29,000	
	Rent	42,000	
	Office supplies	8,950	
	Amortization on office furniture	3,375	
	Charitable donations	3,000	86,325
			$263,675
Gain on sale of securities		$50,000	
Dividends (actual) received from taxable Canadian public corporations		4,000	54,000
Net income			$317,675

The partners drew a total of $67,000 in "salaries".

REQUIRED

Compute the income to be allocated to the partners for income tax purposes. Assume that the office furniture is included in Class 8 for capital cost allowance purposes. The capital cost allowance available in respect of the office furniture is $2,750, based on an undepreciated capital cost of $13,750.

SOLUTION

Partnership's net income for financial accounting purposes(1)		$317,675
Add: Amortization on office furniture		3,375
	Charitable donations(2)	3,000
	Taxable capital gain (½ × $50,000)	25,000
Deduct: Gain on sale of securities		(50,000)
	Capital cost allowance	(2,750)

Income to be allocated (Division B)	$296,300
	Partnership
Nature of income:	
Taxable capital gain (1/2 × $50,000)	$25,000
Dividends	$4,000
Active business income	267,300
	$296,300

NOTES TO SOLUTION

(1) Salaries paid by a partnership to its members do not constitute a business expense but are a method of distributing partnership income to members of the partnership.

(2) Charitable donations are not deductible in computing Division B income. Instead, they are allocated to the partners and are used as the basis for computing the charitable donations tax credit for an individual partner.

¶18,040 Limited Partners — Limitation on Deduction of Partnership Losses

Generally, business or property losses may be deducted by a limited partner only to the extent of the partner's "at-risk" amount. The at-risk amount represents the taxpayer's investment in the partnership that is at risk of being lost if the partnership business fails. It is calculated as the amount by which the partner's investment in the partnership (ACB) and share of the partnership's profit exceeds amounts such as any amount owing to the partnership by the partner. To the extent that the business or property losses otherwise allocable to the limited partner are restricted in the manner described above, they are added to the limited partner's "limited partnership loss" in respect of the partnership for the year and are carried forward indefinitely. The restricted losses are deductible only to the extent that the partner has an increase in its "at-risk" amount in future years in respect of the partnership that gave rise to the loss. When the limited partner disposes of the partnership interest, any amount remaining in the "limited partnership loss" carryforward balance is added to the adjusted cost base of the partnership interest for purposes of calculating the capital gain or loss on disposition.

ITA: 96(2.1) Limited partnership losses, 96(2.2) At-risk amount

Where a limited partner loses status as a limited partner because of involvement in management of the partnership's business, that partner may nevertheless continue to be a limited partner for purposes of the "at-risk" rules.

The Act excludes from the "at-risk" rules members of limited liability partnerships. A limited liability partnership is a partnership where a partner's liability is limited to liability arising from negligent acts or omissions committed in the course of operating the partnership business that relate to his or her actions or those of employees he or she supervises.

ITA: 96(2.4)(a)

¶18,045 Partnership Allocations: Anti-Avoidance

The partnership agreement will set out how the partners have agreed to allocate any income or loss among themselves. An anti-avoidance provision applies to a situation where the partnership agreement to share income or loss is considered to result in a reduction or postponement of tax that might otherwise have been payable. For example, the income allocated between partners may reflect more of a desire to split income or to allocate losses in an arbitrary way than a desire to reward each partner for his or her respective contribution. An anti-avoidance provision permits the partnership's income sharing arrangement to be set aside for tax purposes. The amounts would then be reallocated to the partners in a manner that is reasonable in the circumstances.

ITA: 103(1) Agreement to share income, etc., so as to reduce or postpone tax otherwise payable, 103(1.1) Agreement to share income, etc., in unreasonable proportions

Where the partners do not deal at arm's length, specific rules are provided to determine a reasonable allocation of profit. Each partner's capital contribution and work performed, together with any other relevant factor, will be considered.

ITA: 103(1.1) Agreement to share income, etc., in unreasonable proportions

¶18,050 Computation of Taxable Income

Charitable gifts made by the partnership are flowed through to a partner according to the partner's share of partnership income. The flowed-through amounts provide a Division C deduction in computing taxable income for partners who are corporations. A partner who is an individual includes his or her share of the donation with their own total charitable gifts for purposes of calculating the personal tax credit.

ITA: 110.1(1)(a) Charitable gifts, 118.1(3) Deduction by individuals for gifts

Taxable capital gains generated by a partnership retain their character as part of the net income of the partnership flowed out to the partners. As a result, these taxable capital gains may provide individual partners with eligibility for the capital gains deduction available for qualified farm property and qualified small business corporation shares and provide partners with an opportunity to utilize personal net capital losses.

Since there is no computation of taxable income at the partnership level, losses carried forward and backward are not deductible by the partnership. Losses of the partnership are allocated to the partners at the end of each fiscal period. Any losses that are not utilized by a partner in the year incurred are carried forward or backward by the partner and deducted by the partner in the computation of that partner's taxable income. However, as already stated, in certain circumstances the ability of a limited partner to deduct an amount may be restricted by the partner's at-risk amount.

ITA: 111 Losses deductible

¶18,055 Personal Tax Credits Generated by the Partnership

Charitable gifts made by the partnership entitle the individual partners to a tax credit. These gifts and the corresponding credits are flowed through to a partner according to the partner's share of partnership income.

ITA: 118.1(8) Gifts made by partnership

Dividend income of the partnership maintains its source characteristics when allocated to the partners. An individual who is a member of a partnership will be entitled to claim a dividend tax credit in respect of the partner's share of any taxable dividend received by the partnership from a taxable Canadian corporation during a fiscal period of a partnership. When dividend income is allocated to a partner who is an individual, the dividend allocated to the partner must be grossed up by the usual rules, when it is included in the partner's income.

ITA: 121 Deduction for taxable dividends, 82(1) Taxable dividends received

Similarly, the partner may deduct from taxes payable any foreign tax credits on foreign income allocated to the partner by the partnership. Partners, other than corporations, may claim a tax credit for political contributions made by a partnership and allocated to each partner. The investment tax credit is treated on a similar basis. However, in certain circumstances, the ability of a limited partner to deduct an amount in respect of the investment tax credit may be restricted by the partner's at-risk amount.

ITA: 126 Foreign tax deduction, 126(3) Employees of international organizations, 127(8.1)–127(8.5)

Example Problem 18-2

Refer to the previous example problem concerning Alpha Beta Partnership. Mrs. Alpha and Mrs. Beta share income equally.

REQUIRED

Compute Mrs. Alpha's taxable income for 2018, assuming she has no other income.

SOLUTION

Income to be allocated (Division B)	$296,300
Dividends (1/2 × $4,000)	$2,000
TCG (1/2 × $25,000)	12,500
ABI (1/2 × $267,300)	133,650
	$148,150
Dividend gross-up (38% of $2,000)	760
Taxable income	$148,910

NOTE TO SOLUTION

Mrs. Alpha will be eligible for a combined federal and provincial dividend tax credit of about $760 (theoretically equal to the gross-up) and a charitable donation credit computed on 1/2 of the partnership's charitable donations in computing her basic federal income tax.

¶18,056 Corporate Partnerships

A corporate partner is allocated income of a partnership in the same manner that an individual is allocated partnership income. The income retains its character as described above.

ITA: 34.2 [Corporate partners — income adjustment]

Where a corporation is a partner and the corporation's year end occurs before the partnership's year end, there would be an opportunity to defer the corporate income earned through the partnership.

For example, if the fiscal year of the partnership ends on December 31 and the corporate partner's taxation year ends on October 31, the corporation includes in its income for its 2017 taxation year its share of the partnership income for the partnership's fiscal year ended December 31, 2016. That would result in partnership income for the period January 1, 2017 to October 31, 2017 being deferred to the corporation's 2018 taxation year. However, the Act provides rules to limit the deferral of tax on the income earned through the partnership in this situation.

ITA: 34.3 [Corporate partners — income shortfall adjustment]

Where the corporation has a "significant interest" (i.e., more than 10%) in the partnership's income, an adjustment, called an "adjusted stub period accrual" (ASPA) is added to the corporate partner's share of partnership income to limit the deferral of tax on partnership income earned in the stub period from January 1, 2017 to October 31, 2017 through an addition to the corporation's income for its 2017 year end. In the corporation's 2018 taxation year, the 2017 ASPA is deducted and a new ASPA is computed and included.

¶18,057 Use of the Small Business Deduction by a Corporate Partner and Non-Arm's Length Corporations

Where the corporate partner is a CCPC, active business income of the partnership will be allocated to the partner and subject to corporate tax. The portion of the income allocated from the partnership and eligible for the small business deduction is determined at the partnership level and is referred to as specified partnership income. Each corporate partner can claim its $500,000 small business deduction on its specified partnership income together with active business income from other sources. The corporation's specified partnership income is equal to the lesser of:

(1) the corporation's active business income allocated from the partnership, and

(2) the partner's *pro rata* share of the $500,000 small business limit (Specified Partnership Income (SPI) limit).

For example, if a partnership earns $2,000,000 of active business income, then a corporation with a 10% interest in the partnership will report $200,000 of active business income from the partnership, but can only use $50,000 (10% × $500,000) of that income in the calculation of the amount eligible for the small business deduction. The remaining $150,000 will be taxed in the corporation at the high corporate tax rate.

ITA: 125(1) Small business deduction, 125(7) Definitions

The Act contains new rules to prevent the multiplication of the small business deduction through the use of a corporation to charge fees to a partnership for services or for the use of property. Prior to the change, a corporation that was not a member of a partnership could charge fees and use the full $500,000 small business deduction limit when calculating tax on the income. The rules now deem a corporation that is non-arm's length with a partner to be a member of the partnership in respect of fees charged for services or use of property. The corporation is referred to as a "designated member" of a partnership. The income from the services or property use will be treated as partnership ABI and the non-arm's length partner must assign all or a portion of their SPI limit to the corporation for the income to be eligible for the small business deduction.

Therefore, in the above example where a corporate partner has an SPI limit of $50,000, it would not be possible for a non-arm's length corporation to charge the partnership fees for services and use the small business deduction. The corporate partner's SPI limit of $50,000 would have to be assigned to the non-arm's length corporation providing services to the partnership for it to be able to use any small business deduction against that income.

ITA: 125(8) Assignment — specified partnership business limit

¶18,057.99 Practise What You've Learned

Refer to the following sections of the Study Guide to practise what you've learned:

¶18,800 — Review Questions

- Question 2 — Limited partnerships
- Question 3 — Income allocations

¶18,825 — Multiple Choice Questions

- Question 1 — Taxable income of a partner

¶18,850 — Exercises

- Exercise 1 — Taxable income of a partner

¶18,060 Partnership Interest

¶18,065 The Concept

As indicated previously, the property of a partnership is owned by the partnership, not the individual partners. Thus, any gains or losses on the disposition of that property are included in the computation of the net income of the partnership. The property owned by the partnership must be distinguished from each partner's interest in the partnership, which is a separate capital property owned by each partner. A taxpayer's "partnership interest" represents his or her total rights and obligations as a partner. It may be bought and sold by the partner. In this respect, a partnership interest is analogous to the share held by a shareholder of a corporation. A person acquires a partnership interest by becoming a member of a partnership and disposes of a partnership interest when he or she withdraws from the partnership.

Generally, a partnership interest is a capital property. As a capital property, a partnership interest has an adjusted cost base. The gain or loss from the disposition of a partnership interest is calculated as the difference between the adjusted cost base of the partnership interest and the partner's proceeds of disposition. The taxable capital gain or allowable capital loss arising on the disposition of the partnership interest is included in a partner's income. The basic computation made on the disposition of a partnership interest is illustrated by Exhibit 18-1.

Exhibit 18-1 Gain or Loss on Disposal of a Partnership Interest

		Case 1		Case 2
Proceeds received by partner for his or her interest		$22,750		$12,750
Less: Adjusted cost base of his or her interest	$16,000		$16,000	
Selling expenses	1,750	17,750	1,750	17,750
Partner's capital gain (loss)		$5,000		$(5,000)
Taxable capital gain (allowable capital loss)		$2,500		$(2,500)

¶18,070 Adjusted Cost Base (ACB)

The adjusted cost base of a partner's partnership interest is basically the partner's net tax-paid investment in the partnership business. As such, the ACB represents an amount that a partner can remove tax-free. Each partner's adjusted cost base is the original cost of the partnership interest with adjustments for earnings, drawings and other similar transactions between a partner and the partnership.

¶18,070.10 Additions to ACB

Generally, items which increase a partner's net investment in the partnership are added to the adjusted cost base of the partnership interest. The following are some of the more common items added to the adjusted cost base:

(1) the partner's share of income of the partnership for each fiscal period, including 100% (instead of 50%) of any gains on the disposition of capital property owned by the partnership; ITA: 53(1)(e)(i)

- The income (including taxable capital gains) will be taxed in the partner's hands and, therefore, represents the amount of tax-paid income that can be withdrawn from the partnership tax-free. The non-taxable portion of capital gains not subject to tax represents an amount that can be withdrawn tax-free.

(2) the partner's share of any capital dividends received on shares of the capital stock of a corporation which were owned by the partnership; ITA: 53(1)(e)(ii), 83(2) Capital dividend

- Capital dividends are not taxable, so they should be able to be withdrawn from the partnership without further tax to the partners. If this was not added to the ACB, then when the funds are withdrawn, a negative ACB would be created with an eventual capital gain higher than it should be.

(3) the partner's share of the net proceeds on death from life insurance policies received by the partnership after 1971; ITA: 53(1)(e)(iii)

- Life insurance proceeds are not taxable, so they should be able to be withdrawn from the partnership without further tax to the partners. If this was not added to the ACB, then when the funds are withdrawn, a negative ACB would be created with an eventual capital gain higher than it should be.

(4) the partner's contributions of capital to the partnership after 1971. ITA: 53(1)(e)(iv)

- Clearly, capital contributions should increase the ACB to allow them to be withdrawn at a later date tax-free.

¶18,070.20 Deductions From ACB

Generally, items that reduce or erode a partner's net investment in the partnership are deducted from the adjusted cost base of the partnership's interest. The following are some of the more common items deducted from the adjusted cost base:

(1) the partner's share of any loss of the partnership for each fiscal period (other than limited partnership losses), including 100% (instead of 50%) of losses on the disposition of capital property owned by the partnership; ITA: 53(2)(c)(i)

- Consistent with the treatment of income explained above, partnership losses are deductible by the partners on their individual or corporate returns, and any tax refunds come to the partners. As a result of receiving this benefit, the losses reduce the ACB.

(2) the partner's share of any charitable gifts or political contributions made by the partnership; ITA: 53(2)(c)(iii)

- The partners, as individuals or corporations, receive the tax benefits of the charitable gifts and political donations allocated to them. This is like them receiving a cash distribution from the partnership and then making the donation themselves. The result is a reduction in the ACB of their partnership interest.

(3) the partner's drawings of his or her share of partnership income or capital; ITA: 53(2)(c)(v)

- As capital contributions increase the partner's ACB, drawings of any kind reduce the ACB.

(4) the amount of any investment tax credit used by the partner in respect of expenditures made by the partnership; ITA: 53(2)(c)(vi)

- The ITC is a credit reported on the partner's tax return, so it is treated in a similar fashion to the charitable and political donations.

¶18,070.30 Summary of ACB Adjustments

Exhibit 18-2 summarizes the most common adjustments to the ACB of a partnership interest.

Exhibit 18-2 Summary — Partner's ACB in a Partnership

Capital	
Add	Capital contributions
Deduct	Capital withdrawals
Income	
Add	Partner's share of the partnership's income (including taxable capital gains)
Deduct	Partner's share of the partnership's losses (including allowable capital losses)
Add	Partner's contributions to finance partnership losses
Deduct	Partner's drawings from partnership income
Add	Untaxed portion of any capital gain
Deduct	Untaxed portion of any capital losses
Add	Partner's share of capital dividends (These dividends are in the partnership, but not in the income, so they need to increase the ACB. Then, their withdrawal will not cause a negative ACB, since the withdrawal is of funds that should be received tax-free.)
Other	
Add	Partner's share of life insurance proceeds received by the partnership (These proceeds are in the partnership, but not in the income, so they need to increase the ACB. Then their withdrawal will not cause a negative ACB, since the withdrawal is of funds that should be received tax-free.)
Deduct	Partner's share of charitable donations or political contributions (Since partnerships do not pay tax, it is the partners who use the charitable donations. This adjustment recognizes that the funds, while not deductible, have been paid out of the partnership.)
Deduct	Partner's share of any investment tax credit earned by the partnership and utilized by the partner.

¶18,070.40 Negative ACB

The adjusted cost base of a partnership interest may be a negative amount. A negative adjusted cost base at the end of a year in respect of all other capital property other than a partnership interest is deemed to be a capital gain at the end of the year in which it arises even when there is no actual disposition of the property at the time. This treatment does not apply where a negative adjusted cost base arises in a partnership interest. As long as there is no actual disposition of his or her interest by the partner, a negative adjusted cost base will not be taxed as a capital gain. However, this special treatment for partnership interests does not apply to a negative adjusted cost base held by limited partners, certain other passive partners, and partners in a professional partnerships.

ITA: 40(3) Deemed gain where amounts to be deducted from adjusted cost base exceed cost plus amounts to be added to adjusted cost base, 40(3.1) Deemed gain for certain partners

The legal form of a professional partnership is a full shield limited liability partnership (LLP). One advantage of this form of partnership is that the personal property of a partner, other than the partnership interest, is protected from liability claims resulting from the negligent acts or omissions of others. For income tax purposes, the LLP is treated like a limited partnership and a negative ACB requires the realization of a capital gain in the year that the negative ACB arises.

Where a taxpayer disposes of only part of his or her partnership interest, the adjusted cost base as calculated at that particular time is apportioned and deducted from the proceeds of disposition in computing the taxpayer's gain or loss.

If the adjusted cost base of the partnership interest is negative at the time of disposition, the negative amount (or, in a partial disposition, an equivalent portion of the negative amount) is added to the gain otherwise determined. Exhibit 18-3 illustrates this treatment.

ITA: 40(1) General rules, 100(2) Gain from disposition of interest in partnership

Exhibit 18-3 Treatment of Negative Adjusted Cost Base

Assumptions: Partner sells a partnership interest for proceeds of disposition of $5,000. The selling expenses total $250. The partner's adjusted cost base of the partnership interest is a negative $1,250.

Proceeds of disposition received	$5,000
Deduct: selling expenses	250
Gain otherwise determined	$4,750
Add: negative adjusted cost base at date of sale	1,250
Partner's capital gain	$6,000
Taxable capital gain (1/2 × $6,000)	$3,000

¶18,070.99 Practise What You've Learned

Refer to the following sections of the Study Guide to practise what you've learned:

¶18,800 — Review Questions

- Question 4 — Partnership Interest ACB
- Question 5 — Partnership Interest ACB

¶18,825 — Multiple Choice Questions

- Question 2 — Partnership Interest ACB

¶18,850 — Exercises

- Exercise 2 — Disposition of a partnership interest
- Exercise 4 — Partnership Income ACB

¶18,080 Reorganization of Partnerships

The provisions which deal with the reorganization of partnerships parallel the tax-free corporate rollover discussed in the preceding chapters. Conceptually, the problems encountered in the partnership scenario are similar in nature to those in the context of a corporation. The major difference is that on a transfer of property to a partnership the consideration received by the transferor must include a "partnership interest" as compared to "share capital". Both types of reorganizations can include non-partnership interest consideration, or "boot", and the amount of boot is restricted to prevent the stripping of accrued gains on the entity's assets.

ITA: 85(1) Transfer of property to corporation by shareholders

¶18,085 Incorporating a Partnership — Transfer of Partnership Property to a Corporation

The partners of the partnership may wish to incorporate the partnership's assets. The eligible assets of the partnership can be transferred to a Canadian corporation for consideration, including shares of the corporation. These shares then become the assets of the partnership. The partnership must be a Canadian partnership to transfer real estate held as capital property (or an interest/option therein) under the provision. This rollover parallels directly the rollover available to a person transferring property to a corporation. A joint election is required by the corporation and all of the members of the partnership.

ITA: 85(1) Transfer of property to corporation by shareholders, 85(2) Transfer of property to corporation from partnership

It may be desirable to subsequently wind up the partnership and have the former partners hold the shares of the corporation directly. This transaction is accomplished on a tax-deferred basis. In order for the rollover to apply, the only partnership assets must be cash or shares received from the corporation as consideration for the transfer of partnership property to the corporation. Also, the partnership must be wound up within 60 days of the transfer. This rollover is automatic and there are no filing requirements.

ITA: 85(3) Where partnership wound up, 85(3)(b), 85(3)(c)

Example Problem 18-3

The partners of ABC Partnership wish to incorporate the partnership's asset. The partnership's asset is land which was purchased about 11 years ago for $12,000. The fair market value of the land is now $48,000 and the land is capital property. On the transfer of the land to the corporation the partnership receives the following from the corporation:

Cash	$12,000
Preferred shares (FMV)	12,000
Common shares (FMV)	24,000
Total	$48,000

One month after the transfer of the land to the corporation, the partnership is wound up. ITA: 85(3) Where partnership wound up

REQUIRED

What is the position of Mr. Aleph who received a ⅔ share of each asset distributed by the partnership on the winding-up? The adjusted cost base of his partnership interest is $12,000.

SOLUTION

Cost of preferred shares: ITA: 85(3)(e)

Lesser of:

(a) fair market value of shares (⅔ × $12,000)	$8,000
(b) ACB of partnership interest less FMV of consideration other than shares ($12,000 – ⅔ × $12,000)	$4,000

Cost of common shares: ITA: 85(3)(f)

ACB of partnership interest		$12,000
Less: FMV of non-share consideration	$8,000	
cost of preferred shares	4,000	12,000
		Nil

Proceeds of disposition of partnership interest: ITA: 85(3)(g)

Deemed cost of preferred shares	$4,000
Deemed cost of common shares	Nil
Other consideration	8,000
Total proceeds	$12,000

Since the proceeds for the partnership interest equal its adjusted cost base, there is no gain or loss on the disposition of the partnership interest. As a general rule, as long as the boot received by the partner does not exceed his or her ACB there will not be a gain.

¶18,090 Transfer of Property to a Partnership

¶18,090.10 Rollover Available

Generally, when a partner transfers property to a partnership, the partner is deemed to dispose of the property for proceeds equal to its fair market value and the partnership is deemed to acquire the property for the same amount. This rule may result in gains or losses where there is no actual change in economic interest in the property. To prevent this inequity, a rollover is provided where a Canadian partnership acquires property from a person who immediately after the transfer is a partner. To qualify, the partnership must be a Canadian partnership immediately after the transfer, and all partners must elect to have the rollover apply. The types of property that can be transferred are limited to capital property (including depreciable capital property), inventory (including land inventory), and certain resource properties.

ITA: 97(1) Contribution of property to partnership, 97(2) Rules if election by partners

A Canadian partnership is defined as a partnership all the members of which are resident in Canada at the particular time.

ITA: 102 Definition of "Canadian partnership"

The partners elect an agreed amount on a form which is filed with the CRA. The agreed amount is the proceeds of disposition of the property to the partner and the cost of the property to the partnership. In essence, the same rules apply for establishing the elected amount range for transfers of property to a partnership as are applicable to transfers of property to a corporation. At the upper limit, the agreed amount at which the property can be transferred is the fair market value of that property. At the lower limit, the agreed amount can be set at the fair market value of consideration, other than a partnership interest, received for the property transferred, if that amount is not less than the lesser of the fair market value and the tax value of the property transferred. Any excess of the agreed amount over the fair market value of the consideration other than a partnership interest received is added to the adjusted cost base of the partnership interest of the partner.

¶18,090.15 Capital Cost of Depreciable Property to the Partnership

On the transfer of depreciable capital property, the partnership generally assumes the position of the transferor with respect to the capital cost of the property for the determination of capital gains and recapture when the partnership eventually disposes of the property.

An adjustment must be made where depreciable property is transferred to the partnership by a non-arm's length person or partnership (the transferor), and the capital cost of the property to the transferor is less than the cost of the property to the partnership. The partnership is deemed to have a capital cost equal to the cost of the property to the transferor plus the person's or partnership's taxable capital gain inclusion. The deemed capital cost is for purposes of computing capital cost allowance, not future capital gains or losses.

ITA: 13(7)(e)

Ⓐ ¶18,090.20 Application of Stop Loss Rules on Property Transfer

Terminal Loss on Depreciable Property

A loss-denial rule applies where there would be a terminal loss on a depreciable property and the transferor is a person (i.e., an individual, a corporation, or a trust), or partnership. Where the transferor or certain affiliated persons hold the property 30 days after the disposition, no loss is recognized on the transfer. Instead, the terminal loss is retained by the transferor as a notional depreciable property in the same CCA class. The recognition of the loss by the transferor will generally be deferred until such time as the depreciable property is transferred to a person who is not an affiliated person.

ITA: 13(21.2) Loss on certain transfers, 251.1 Definition of "affiliated persons"

Capital Loss on Non-Depreciable Property

Where the transferor is a corporation, trust or partnership (but not an individual), a capital loss arising on the transfer of non-depreciable capital property to an affiliated person who still owns the property at the end of 30 days following the transfer is denied. The loss is retained by the transferor and not recognized until the earliest of several events. Where the transferor is an individual who is a majority-interest partner, the superficial loss rule will apply to deny the loss and add it to the cost of the property in the partnership.

ITA: 40(3.3) When subsection (3.4) applies, 40(3.4) Loss on certain properties, 251.1 Definition of "affiliated persons", 40(2)(g)(i), 54 Definitions

Ⓐ ¶18,090.25 Reallocation of Deferred Income

Recognize that, as a result of the rollover, part of the deferred income may, in effect, be transferred to the other partners. Each partner will include his or her proportionate share of the income when the partnership disposes of the property.

ITA: 97(2) Rules if election by partners

Example Problem 18-4

Mr. Black and Mr. Red operate accounting practices as sole practitioners. They wish to form a partnership. Mr. Black will hold a 60% share and Mr. Red a 40% share. The relevant financial data for the separate practices as at December 31 of this year are as follows:

	Mr. Black		Mr. Red	
	Cost	FMV	Cost	FMV
Cash	$94,000	$94,000	$60,000	$60,000
Marketable securities	20,000	10,000	10,000	5,000
Land (capital property)	5,000	50,000	—	—
Accounts receivable	130,000	130,000	40,000	40,000
Furniture and fixtures	80,000	80,000	30,000	34,000
Leasehold improvements	30,000	40,000	20,000	—
Goodwill	20,000	50,000	—	—
	$379,000	$454,000	$160,000	$139,000
Accounts payable		$120,000		$130,000

The tax values of the following assets are:

	Mr. Black	Mr. Red
Furniture and fixtures (UCC)	$70,000	$24,000
Leasehold improvements (UCC)	30,000	—
Goodwill (UCC)	9,000	—

REQUIRED

(1) Compute the values at which the assets should be transferred to defer any immediate tax consequences of the transfer assuming the accounts payable are not transferred to the partnership and no consideration other than a partnership interest is received.

(2) Compute the adjusted cost bases of the partnership interests of Mr. Black and Mr. Red.

(3) Indicate the tax effects of having the partnership assume the accounts payable of Mr. Black and Mr. Red.

(4) Indicate the tax consequences to Mr. Black and Mr. Red of having the partnership dispose of the land next year for proceeds of disposition of $50,000. Assume that the land is capital property to the partnership, and that no consideration, other than a partnership interest, is received by the partners.

SOLUTION

(1)

	Mr. Black	Mr. Red
Cash	$94,000	$60,000
Marketable securities	10,000[(1)]	5,000[(2)]
Land	5,000	—
Accounts receivable	130,000	40,000
Furniture and fixtures	70,000	24,000
Leasehold improvements	30,000	—
Goodwill	9,000	—
	$348,000	$129,000

(2)

Adjusted cost base:		
Transfer value of assets	$348,000	$129,000

(3) If Mr. Black's accounts payable are transferred to the partnership, the transfer value of his net assets would be $228,000 ($348,000 – $120,000) resulting in an adjusted cost base for his partnership interest of $228,000. In Mr. Red's case there will be a gain of $1,000. This results from the requirement that the elected transfer price be no less than the non-partnership interest consideration received (which in this case would be $130,000). Since the proceeds of disposition are $130,000 and the adjusted cost base of the assets is $129,000 there would be a gain of $1,000. Since the proceeds of disposition of the property do not exceed the fair market value of the non-partnership interest consideration received, the adjusted cost base of the partnership interest to Mr. Red would be nil.

(4)

Proceeds of disposition	$50,000
Adjusted cost base	5,000
Capital gain	$45,000
Taxable capital gain (1/2 of $45,000)	$22,500
Income to be allocated	$22,500

	Mr. Black	Mr. Red
Share of income	$13,500	$9,000
Adjusted cost base of partnership interest	$348,000	$129,000
Add: share of capital gain (i.e., income from taxable capital gain + untaxed fraction of capital gain)	27,000	18,000
	$375,000	$147,000

On the transfer of the land to the partnership, Mr. Black deferred the recognition of a $45,000 capital gain. When the partnership disposed of the land, it realized a capital gain of $45,000 and a taxable gain of $22,500. A portion of that capital gain was allocated to each partner as his share of the partnership income for the year. Because a portion of the taxable capital gain was allocated to Mr. Red, as well as Mr. Black, part of the deferred gain ($18,000) and the tax liability on that gain was essentially transferred from Mr. Black to Mr. Red. The partnership agreement could have been structured to require the full amount of this gain to be allocated to Mr. Black to avoid this inequity.

NOTES TO SOLUTION

(1) Under the definition of "superficial loss", Mr. Black will have a superficial loss, since the partnership is a person that is affiliated with him. Accordingly, the loss is deemed to be nil. The amount of the denied loss will be added to the adjusted cost base of the marketable securities to the partnership.

ITA: 54 Definitions, 251.1(1)(e), 53(1)(f) [Adjustments to cost base — Substituted property]

(2) Since Mr. Red is not a majority interest partner he is not denied the loss.

¶18,090.99 Practise What You've Learned

Refer to the following sections of the Study Guide to practise what you've learned:

¶18,800 — Review Questions

- Question 6 — Transfer of Property to a Partnership

¶18,200 Trusts

¶18,210 Nature of a Trust

¶18,215 General

¶18,215.10 Definition of a Trust

Before dealing with the taxation of a trust one must understand what a trust is. The law of trusts is a separate area of law just as the law relating to real estate and the law relating to contracts are separate areas of law.

A trust is not a contract. In a contract, there are mutual covenants (or promises) where one person promises to do something in return for the other person promising to do something. It is enforceable only by the parties and is dependent upon "consideration".[1] A trust is a relationship whereby a person (who is called a trustee) is bound to deal with property over which he or she has control (which is called the trust property) for the benefit of persons (who are called the beneficiaries) any of whom may enforce the obligation.[2]

A trust is created when a person (called the settlor) transfers the title of a property to the trustee who holds it for the benefit of the income and capital beneficiaries. For a trust to exist, there must be three certainties present.

(1) There must be certainty of intention; the settler must have intended to establish a trust.

(2) There must be a certainty of subject matter; there must be a specific property given to the trustee.

(3) There must be certainty of objects; it must be clear who the income and capital beneficiaries are.

One of the fundamental characteristics of a trust is the separation of title-holding and the management of property from its enjoyment. For example, assume that a parent wants to provide an income for a child in order to pay that child's personal living expenses. That parent may also be prepared to transfer income-earning property to the child when he or she has reached a certain age. Until that time, however, the parent does not want the child to control the property. A trust may be used to accomplish all of these objectives. The investments would be transferred to a trustee. The trust agreement would provide for the distribution of income to the child annually and the distribution of the investments to the child when the child reaches a specific age.

The following diagram illustrates the relationship among the settlor, trustees, and beneficiaries.

---

[1] J. Wardlaw, "Inter Vivos Trusts: A Base Primer", *Estates and Trusts Quarterly*, Vol. 5, 1980-81, p. 298.

[2] Underhill and Hayton, *Law Relating to Trusts and Trustees*, 14th ed., 1987, p. 3.

TAXATION OF TRUSTS – OVERVIEW

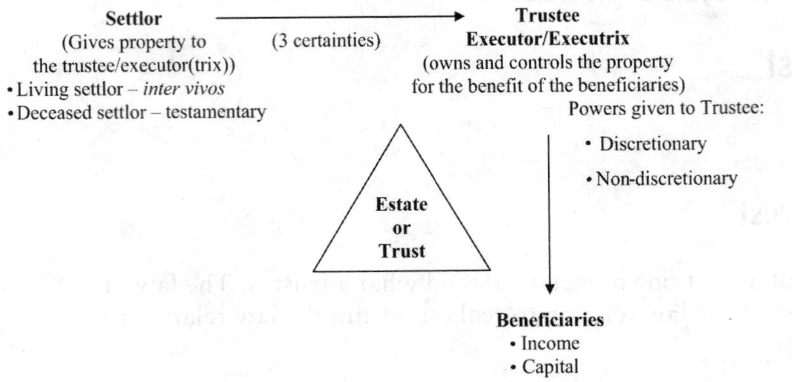

Trusts are particularly useful when the beneficiaries are minors. Generally, with certain limited exceptions, a minor cannot enter into a binding contract. All other contracts are voidable at the option of the minor. This means that they cannot be enforced unless ratified by the minor when he or she reaches the age of majority. As a result, those dealing with minors don't want to transfer property to or contract with them. Instead they would prefer to deal with a trustee who holds property or enters into contracts for the benefit of the minor.

¶18,215.20 Taxation of Trusts

A trust is considered to be a taxpayer separate and distinct from its settlor, trustees or beneficiaries. As a separate taxpayer, the trust is deemed to be an individual. Therefore, the income of the trust is generally computed in the same way as is the income of any individual.

ITA: 104(2) Taxed as individual

¶18,215.30 Residency of Trusts

Determining the residency of a trust is an important tax issue. If the trust is resident in Canada, it will be taxed on its worldwide income. If it is not resident in Canada, it will be taxed in Canada as a non-resident. A non-resident trust can be deemed to be a resident in Canada for specific purposes if the trust has a resident contributor or resident beneficiary.

ITA: 94(3) Liabilities of non-resident trusts and others

On the question of residence of a trust, in the case of *St. Michael Trust Corp. v. Her Majesty the Queen* (also known as *Fundy Settlement* and *Garron*), established, at paragraph 15, the following principle for determining the residence of a trust:

Cases: *St. Michael Trust Corp. v. The Queen*, 2012 DTC 5063 (SCC)

> a trust resides for the purposes of the Act where "its real business is carried on" (*De Beers*, at p. 458), which is where the central management and control of the trust actually takes place.

Cases: *De Beers Consolidated Mines Ltd. v. Howe*, [1906] A.C. 455 (H.L.)

The Supreme Court arrived at this principle by concluding that "there are many similarities between a trust and corporation that would, in our view, justify application of the central management and control test in determining the residence of a trust, just as it is used in determining the residence of a corporation." In the *St. Michael* case, the main beneficiaries of the trusts were found to exercise the central management and control of the trusts in Canada. The corporate trustee, St. Michael Trust Corp., resident in Barbados, had a limited role of providing only administrative services. However, the Court went on to state that:

Cases: *St. Michael Trust Corp. v. The Queen*, 2012 DTC 5063 (SCC)

> this is not to say that the residence of a trust can never be the residence of the trustee. The residence of the trustee will also be the residence of the trust where the trustee carries out the central management and control of the trust, and these duties are performed where the trustee is resident. These, however, were not the facts in this case.

The position of the Supreme Court is reflected in the CRA's Income Tax Folio on trust residency. The CRA indicates that in its view a trust is generally considered to reside where the trustee, executor, administrator, heir or other legal representative who manages the trust or controls the trust's assets resides. The CRA will consider a number of factors in deciding who has management and control of the trust. Where there is more than one trustee, the trust will be considered by the CRA to reside in the jurisdiction in which the trustee who exercises a more substantial portion of management and control resides. Where several trustees exercise equal control and trustees exercising more than 50% of control reside in one jurisdiction, the trust will reside in that jurisdiction.

Income Tax Folio: S6-F1-C1 Residence of a Trust or Estate

¶18,220 Types of Trusts

¶18,220.10 *Inter Vivos* and Testamentary

An *inter vivos* trust is created while the settlor is still alive and it is defined in the Act to be a trust other than a testamentary trust. A testamentary trust arises as the consequence of the death of an individual. A testamentary trust can be "tainted" and, hence, no longer a testamentary trust, if property is contributed to the trust other than as a result of the individual's death. For example, if some other individual contributes property to the trust, the trust loses its testamentary status and becomes an *inter vivos* trust. A trust can also lose its testamentary trust status if it borrows money from a beneficiary or someone not dealing at arm's length with a beneficiary.

ITA: 108(1) Definitions, 108(1) testamentary trust (b)

¶18,220.15 Graduated Rate Estates

When an individual dies, properties that are not jointly owned or transferred directly to a beneficiary will become part of the individual's "estate" until all of the liabilities of the deceased are paid and a clearance certificate is received from the CRA. This estate is treated as a testamentary trust for tax purposes.

ITA: 248(1) graduated rate estate, 159(2) Certificate before distribution

An estate arising on the death of an individual can be designated as a graduated rate estate of the individual for the 36 months following the individual's death. A deceased individual can have only one graduated rate estate and it must be designated as such in the T3 return for the estate's first taxation year. The estate must be a testamentary trust to be a graduated rate estate (i.e., it is important not to taint the trust). A testamentary trust that is created by will (e.g., a spousal testamentary trust) cannot be designated as a graduated rate estate because it is not an "estate" arising on death.

¶18,220.20 Discretionary and Non-Discretionary

Trusts may be discretionary or non-discretionary. In a discretionary trust, the trustee is given the power of choice. The trustee may be given the power to determine the date of the distribution of trust property, whether income is to be paid to a beneficiary, how much is to be paid to a beneficiary and in what proportion among a group of beneficiaries it is to be paid. For example, by using their discretionary powers trustees may, in certain circumstances, allocate income to taxpayers with a lower marginal tax rate. The trustee may also be given the discretion to decide when a trust is to be terminated. The flexibility provided by the discretionary trust has made it a useful tool in tax planning. With a non-discretionary trust, the trustee does not have the power of choice. The trust document sets out certain decisions which the trustees are obliged to implement.

¶18,220.30 Personal Trust and Commercial Trust

A "personal trust" is either a testamentary or an *inter vivos* trust, where no beneficial interest in the trust was acquired for consideration paid to the trust. The term "commercial trust" is not defined in the Act but is generally used to describe a trust that is not a personal trust. A personal trust can distribute property to beneficiaries in settlement or partial settlement of the beneficiary's capital interest on a tax-deferred basis.

ITA: 248(1) personal trust, 122.1 [Specified investment flow-through ("SIFT") trust], 107(2) Distribution by personal trust

¶18,220.40 Spousal Trust

ITA: 73(1) Inter vivos transfers by individuals, 70(6) Where transfer or distribution to spouse or spouse trust

A spousal trust is one which meets certain conditions set out in the Act. The conditions for an *inter vivos* spousal trust are provided in the Act. The conditions for a testamentary spousal trust are also set out in the Act. In either case, under the trust:

(i) the spouse must be entitled to receive all of the income of the trust that arises before the spouse's death; and

(ii) no person except the spouse may, before the spouse's death, receive or otherwise obtain the use of any of the income or capital of the trust.

In addition, for a trust to qualify as a spousal trust, both the settlor and trust must be resident in Canada at the time of transfer. In the case of a testamentary trust there is a further requirement that the property must vest indefeasibly in the trust within 36 months after the death of a taxpayer, or a later period where a written application has been made to the Minister. Vesting indefeasibly refers to an enforceable right to obtain absolute ownership of the property in such a manner that such right cannot be defeated by any future event.

If all of the conditions for a spousal trust have been satisfied, property is transferred to the trust for proceeds equal to its tax cost. For example, non-depreciable capital property may be transferred to the trust at its adjusted cost base, while depreciable capital property may be transferred to a trust at the property's proportionate amount of undepreciated capital cost of the class. The trust is deemed to acquire the property at a cost equal to the tax cost of the property to the transferor. The tax consequences apply automatically. No election need be filed.

An election out of the rollover provisions can be made on the transfer of property to the trust. If this election is made, the general rules apply and the property will be deemed to have been disposed of for proceeds of disposition equal to its fair market value.

ITA: 70(6.2) Election, 73(1) Inter vivos transfers by individuals

Where the spouse beneficiary of the trust dies, there is a deemed disposition of properties of the trust at fair market value on death. That event occurs at the same time that it would have happened if no trust had been established. The taxation year end of the trust is deemed to end on the date of death of the spouse beneficiary. The income for the deemed year end is taxed in the trust unless there is a joint election between the graduated rate estate and the trust to have the income taxed in the spouse beneficiary's terminal return. Where an election is made, the income deemed taxable in the terminal return is deductible in computing the income of trust. The T3 tax return and payment is due 90 days after the calendar year in which the tax year of the trust ends.

ITA: 104(4)(a); 104(13.4) Death of beneficiary — spousal and similar trusts, 104(6)(b)

¶18,220.50 Alter Ego Trust

Alter ego trusts were created to allow an individual to establish a trust for him or herself. The concept is that an individual would transfer property to a trustee who would hold the property for the individual's benefit until the individual asked for the property back or died. The idea was to allow people to organize their financial affairs well in advance of death or disability, and these trusts are often used to avoid probate fees. The trust document would indicate who would receive the property on the individual's death, thus acting as a will. In addition, the trustee would continue to manage the property in the event of the individual's incapacity, thus acting as the individual's power of attorney. The property can be transferred to the trustee without causing a deemed disposition. The rules allow individuals to rollover property to an alter ego trust as long as the following conditions are met:

ITA: 248(1) alter ego trust

(1) the taxpayer was entitled to receive all the income for the trust that arose before the taxpayer's death;

(2) no person, except the taxpayer could, before the taxpayer's death, receive or otherwise obtain the use of any of the income or capital of the trust;

(3) the individual who establishes the trust must have attained 65 years of age; and

(4) the trust is created after 1999.

This type of trust does not avoid the deemed disposition on death. That event occurs at the same time that it would have happened if no trust had been established, on the death of the taxpayer that established the trust.

ITA: 104(4)(a), 248(1) alter ego trust

The taxation year end of the trust is deemed to end on the date of death of the taxpayer. The income for the deemed year end is taxed in the trust unless there is a joint election between the graduated rate estate and the trust to have the income taxed in the individual's terminal return. Where an election is made, the income deemed taxable in the terminal return is deductible in computing the income of the trust. The T3 tax return and payment is due 90 days after the calendar year in which the tax year of the trust ends.

ITA: 104(4)(a), 104(13.4) Death of beneficiary — spousal and similar trusts, 104(6)(b)

¶18,220.60 Joint Spousal or Common-Law Partner Trust

Joint spousal or common-law partner trusts are very similar in purpose and rules to the alter ego trust. The concept is to allow an individual to transfer property to a trust in which he and his spouse or common-law partner are the beneficiaries. The property is managed in the trust until either the property is withdrawn or the individual and the spouse or common-law partner have died and the property is distributed to the beneficiaries. Property can be rolled over to this type of trust as long as the following conditions are met:

ITA: 248(1) joint spousal or common-law partner trust

(1) the taxpayer who created the trust and/or the taxpayer's spouse or common-law partner are entitled to receive all the income of the trust that was earned prior to the later of the death of the taxpayer and the spouse or common-law partner;

(2) that taxpayer who created the trust and/or the taxpayer's spouse or a common-law partner must be the only persons able to receive income or capital of the trust prior to the later of the death of the taxpayer and spouse or the common-law partner;

(3) at the time of the trust's creation, the taxpayer creating the trust was alive and had attained 65 years of age; and

(4) the trust was created after 1999.

This type of trust does not avoid the deemed disposition on death either. The deemed disposition occurs at the same time it would have happened if no trust had been established, on the death of the surviving spouse or common-law partner. ITA: 104(4)(a)

The taxation year end of the trust is deemed to end on the date of death of the surviving spouse or common-law partner. The income for the deemed year end is taxed in the trust unless there is a joint election between the graduated rate estate and the trust to have the income taxed in the spouse beneficiary's terminal return. Where an election is made, the income deemed taxable in the terminal return is deductible in computing the income of trust. The T3 tax return and payment is due 90 days after the calendar year in which the tax year of the trust ends. ITA: 104(4)(a), 104(13.4) Death of beneficiary — spousal and similar trusts

¶18,220.99 Practise What You've Learned

Refer to the following sections of the Study Guide to practise what you've learned:

¶18,800 — Review Questions

- Question 7 — Trusts
- Question 9 — Testamentary and *inter vivos* trusts
- Question 10 — Discretionary trusts

¶18,825 — Multiple Choice Questions

- Question 5 — Trust types

¶18,230 Settlement of a Trust

As a general rule, capital property is transferred to the trust at fair market value. Therefore, if a settlor transfers capital property to a trust with accrued income and gains, these amounts will be taxed in the hands of the settlor. The trust will acquire the assets at a cost equal to their fair market value. As already noted, there are exceptions to the general rule for a qualifying spousal trust, an alter ego trust or a joint spousal or common-law partner trust.

¶18,240 Computation of Income

¶18,245 Income of a Trust

As already discussed, the net income of the trust is computed in generally the same way as is the income of any individual.

¶18,250 Income Payable to Beneficiary

A trust is entitled to deduct in computing its net income, income that is paid or payable to a beneficiary. In this way, the trust is not taxed on such income, but acts as a conduit for its beneficiaries. An amount is considered to be payable to a beneficiary in a taxation year if he or she is entitled in the year to enforce payment thereof.

ITA: 104(6) Deduction in computing income of trust, 104(24) Amount payable

The income deducted from the trust's net income is taxed in the hands of the beneficiary as income from property unless it falls within certain categories specified in the Act. In this case, the income retains its source for the purposes of calculating the taxable income and tax payable of the beneficiary. This special treatment applies to the following sources of income:

ITA: 108(5) Interpretation

(1) taxable dividends from a Canadian corporation (which enables the beneficiary to utilize the dividend tax credit);

ITA: 104(19) Designation in respect of taxable dividends

(2) non-taxable dividends (which are then excluded from the computation of taxable income);

ITA: 104(20) Designation in respect of non-taxable dividends

(3) net taxable capital gains (net capital losses do not flow through to the beneficiary); and

ITA: 104(21) Designation in respect of taxable capital gains

(4) foreign income and its related foreign tax paid (which enables the beneficiary to take full advantage of the foreign tax credit).

ITA: 104(22) Designation in respect of foreign source income

Net taxable capital gains of a trust that are allocated to individual beneficiaries and designated by the trust are eligible for the capital gains deduction available in respect of qualified farm property and qualified shares of a small business corporation. In order to qualify, the trust must be resident in Canada throughout the year. See below for a discussion of the impact of the Tax on Split Income (TOSI) rules in regards to allocations of net taxable capital gains on private corporation shares allocated to individual beneficiaries. As long as the allocated taxable capital gain is for a disposition of shares of a qualified small business corporation, TOSI will not apply.

ITA: 104(21.2) Beneficiaries' taxable capital gain, 104(21.3) Net taxable capital gains of trust determined

A trust is allowed to deduct less than the amount of income paid or payable to a beneficiary in computing its income to enable a trust to utilize its loss carryforwards without having to reduce its current income distributions. A similar rule is provided for taxable capital gains. A trust can only deduct less than the amount paid or payable to the extent of available loss carryforward balances.

ITA: 104(13.1) Amounts deemed not paid

Example Problem 18-5

The income of a trust for the year is $6,000 of dividends from resident Canadian public corporations. The sole beneficiary of the trust is the spouse of the deceased settlor. The trustee paid $5,000 to the beneficiary.

REQUIRED

What is the taxable income of the trust and the spouse?

SOLUTION

Trust

Income from dividends	$6,000
Deduction of amount paid to beneficiary	5,000
Net dividend income	$1,000
Gross-up (38%)	380
Taxable income	$1,380

ITA: 104(6) Deduction in computing income of trust

Spouse

Income (designated)	$5,000
Gross-up (38%)	1,900
Taxable income	$6,900

ITA: 104(19) Designation in respect of taxable dividends

¶18,255 Attribution

As a general rule, where an individual has transferred or loaned property to a trust for the benefit of a non-arm's length person or a niece or nephew under the age of 18, or for the benefit of the spouse, the appropriate attribution rules will operate to include the income from the property in the income of the transferor. These rules are applicable only where the trust income would otherwise be taxed in the hands of a beneficiary. The attribution rules will also apply to any property substituted for the property originally loaned or transferred to the trust. The accumulating income (i.e., income not paid or payable to a beneficiary) will be subject to tax in the trust. It will not be attributed back to the transferor. The income is taxed at the high rate in the *inter vivos* trust.

ITA: 74.3 Transfers or loans to a trust, 74.1 [Transfers and loans to spouse or common-law partner or minor]

Taxable capital gains and allowable capital losses realized by an *inter vivos* spousal trust and allocated out of the trust to be taxed in the hands of the beneficiary spouse will be attributed to the individual who loaned or transferred the property to the spousal trust. For any other *inter vivos* trust, any property income earned in the trust and allocated out to "designated persons" will be subject to attribution.

ITA: 74.2 Gain or loss deemed that of lender or transferor, 74.3 Transfers or loans to a trust, 74.5(5) designated person

The amount to be attributed is determined by the Act. Only the income and capital gains earned by spouses and the income earned by non-arm's length persons and nieces or nephews under 18 ("designated persons") from loaned or transferred property are subject to the attribution rules.

The amount of income of a person, who is a designated person, from property loaned or transferred to a trust to be attributed to the transferor is the lesser of:

ITA: 74.3(1)(a)

(1) the income of that person from the trust; and

(2) the income earned by the trust from loaned or transferred funds multiplied by the fraction where the numerator is the total income of the designated person from the trust and the denominator is the aggregate income from the trust of all designated persons.

The amount of taxable capital gains of a spouse beneficiary of a trust to be attributed is the lesser of: ITA: 74.3(1)(b)

(1) the amount designated by the trust to be a taxable capital gain of the beneficiary spouse; and ITA: 104(21) Designation in respect of taxable capital gains

(2) the net taxable capital gains for the year from the disposition by the trust of the property.

The exceptions to the general attribution rules as discussed in a previous chapter also apply to trusts. ITA: 74.5 Transfers for fair market consideration

Loans of property by an individual to a non-arm's length individual or indebtedness between such individuals are also subject to the attribution rules. Income will be taxed in the hands of the transferor if it may reasonably be considered that one of the main reasons for the loan was to reduce or avoid tax by having the income taxed in the transferee's hands. This rule will also apply where the loan is made to an individual or the indebtedness arises by means of a trust. Note that the attribution rules do not apply to any amount subject to TOSI. ITA: 56(4.1) Interest free or low interest loans

Example Problem 18-6

Assume that this year John Smith makes a non-interest bearing loan of $1,000 to a trust. The trust acquires a $1,000 bond. The trust has four equal beneficiaries: Betty Smith, John's wife, and their three children, one of whom is under 18. The income of the trust for the year prior to claiming any deductions for amounts paid or payable to the beneficiaries is $240 of which $100 is interest from the bond. All income is payable to the beneficiaries.

REQUIRED

How much income is attributed to John Smith in the year?

SOLUTION

There are two designated beneficiaries, Betty Smith and the child who is under 18.

The income attributed to John Smith for each designated beneficiary is determined as follows:

A = income of the designated person from the trust

= $\frac{1}{4}$ × $240 = $60

B = income of all designated persons from the trust

= $120

C = income from the loaned property

= $100

$$A/B \times C = \$60/\$120 \times \$100 = \$50$$

Therefore, the total income attributed to John Smith is $50 × 2 = $100. Each designated beneficiary would include only $10 of the $60 payable to them.

Two aspects of the formula should be noted. First, the income of a designated beneficiary is deemed to be received first from the income derived from property acquired with the loan. Second, the amount of income attributed in respect of the spouse or minor cannot exceed the amount of that person's income from the trust.

¶18,260 Tax on Split Income (TOSI)

ITA: 120.4 Tax on split income [Kiddie tax]

Tax on split income, commonly previously referred to as "kiddie tax", was introduced in 2000 to discourage income splitting with minor children. This tax is levied at the top marginal rate and is imposed on certain income, including income from a trust, of individuals age 17 or under i.e., a specified individual. The types of income which are taxed in this way are:

- Taxable dividends and other shareholder benefits of private Canadian and foreign companies received directly or through a trust or partnership; and
- Income from a partnership or trust where the income is derived by the partnership or trust from the business of providing goods or services to a business carried on by a relative of the specified individual or in which the relative participates.
- Income from a partnership or trust where the income is business or rental income received from third parties and where a relative of the specified individual is actively engaged in earning the income or has an interest in the partnership.
- Taxable capital gains on the disposition of shares of a private corporation. In such case, twice the amount of taxable capital gain is deemed to be a taxable dividend that is not an eligible dividend. The dividend is subject to gross up and the dividend tax credit applies.

Any of the above types of income allocated from a trust to a beneficiary who is a specified individual would be subject to TOSI on the income. Income subject to TOSI is not subject to the attribution rules.

Draft legislation released on December 13, 2017 and applicable to 2018 and later years (discussed in detail in ¶13,360) extends the definition of a specified individual to result in the application of TOSI to split income received by any individual, i.e., the provision is no longer restricted to minor children. Further, the definition of split income has been amended and expanded to include amounts of income allocated from a trust as follows:

- Income derived from one or more related businesses in respect of the individual. See Chapter 13 for the definition of a related business.
- An amount reasonably considered to be attributable to a taxable capital gain from the disposition of shares of a private corporation. Taxable capital gains from the disposition of QSBC shares are excluded.

Starting in 2018, it will be important when distributing income from a trust to any individual beneficiary to consider the source of the income and whether TOSI applies. If the income or taxable capital gain relates to private corporation transactions it will be necessary to consider whether the amount results in split income and consider whether it meets the definition of an excluded amount to determine whether TOSI applies.

¶18,260.99 Practise What You've Learned

Refer to the following sections of the Study Guide to practise what you've learned:

¶18,800 — Review Questions

- Question 8 — Income of a Trust
- Question 11 — Income distributions from a trust

¶18,270 Computation of Tax

¶18,275 Fiscal Years, Filing and Reporting Requirements

The fiscal year end of an *inter vivos* trust is December 31. For an alter-ego, joint spousal, common-law partner or *inter vivos* spousal trust where the beneficiary has died during the year, the trust is deemed to have a tax year end on the date of the death of the beneficiary (the second to die beneficiary in the case of a joint spousal or common-law partner trust). ITA: 249(1)(b), 249(1)(c), 249.1(1)(b)(i.1), 104(13.4)(a)

A testamentary trust also must have a December 31 year end. Only a testamentary trust that is designated as a graduated rate estate can have a non-calendar year end with a fiscal year not exceeding 12 months in length. Therefore, the first fiscal period of a testamentary trust designated as a graduated rate estate can end no later than one year from the death of the settlor. A graduated rate estate must adopt a calendar year end once 36 months following the date of death has passed. ITA: 104(13.4)(a), 150(1)(c) Trusts or estates

For a spousal testamentary trust, the trust is deemed to have a tax year end on the date of the death of the spouse beneficiary. A spousal testamentary trust cannot be designated as a graduated rate estate. Similarly, an alter ego trust has a deemed year end on the date of death of the individual who established the trust and a joint spousal trust has a deemed year end on the date of death of the surviving spouse.

Tax returns must be filed within 90 days of the end of the trust's fiscal period. In the case where a trust year end is deemed to have occurred on the date of the death of the beneficiary as noted above, tax returns must be filed within 90 days of the end of the calendar year end in which the deemed year end falls. ITA: 104(13.4)(c)

A beneficiary includes in income the amount paid or payable by the trust during the year. The beneficiary includes that amount in income in the calendar year in which the trust's taxation year ends. ITA: 104(13) Income of beneficiary

The February 27, 2018 Federal Budget proposes to require reporting for certain trusts to provide additional information on an annual basis, including the identities of all trustees, beneficiaries, settlors of the trust, and each person who has the ability (through the trust terms or a related agreement) to exert control over trustee decisions regarding the appointment of income or capital of the trust (e.g., a protector). The new reporting requirements will apply to express Canadian-resident trusts (i.e., generally, trusts created with the settlor's express intent) and non-resident trusts that are currently required to file a T3 return. The proposed new reporting requirements will apply to returns required to be filed for the 2021 and subsequent taxation years.

¶18,280 Tax Rate

¶18,280.10 General

The Act provides that trusts are to be taxed as individuals. Both *inter vivos* and testamentary trusts are subject to a federal rate of 33%. ITA: 122(1) Tax payable by trust

Only graduated rate estates are subject to marginal rates and only for the first 36 months from the date of death. A graduated rate estate still in existence 36 months after the date of death will be subject to a federal rate of 33% from that point forward. ITA: 117(2) Rates for taxation years after 2015

¶18,285 Tax Credits

No deduction may be made for personal credits in computing the tax payable by a trust for a taxation year. However, trusts are still entitled to claim other credits such as the dividend tax credit and the foreign tax credit. ITA: 122(1.1) Credits available to trusts

¶18,290 Minimum Tax

Trusts are subject to the minimum tax in respect of income that is not paid or payable to beneficiaries.

The $40,000 exemption from the minimum tax is available only to a graduated rate estate.

¶18,290.99 Practise What You've Learned

Refer to the following sections of the Study Guide to practise what you've learned:

¶18,800 — Review Questions

- Question 12 — Trust filing obligations

¶18,825 — Multiple Choice Questions

- Question 3 — Trusts
- Question 4 — Trusts

¶18,850 — Exercises

- Exercise 3 — Taxable income and taxes payable of a trust
- Exercise 5 — Taxable income and taxes payable of a trust and beneficiary
- Exercise 6 — Trust taxation, filings
- Exercise 7 — Trust taxation, attribution

¶18,300 Family Planning Uses of a Trust

The foregoing discussion of trusts would suggest a number of planning opportunities for their use in family situations. While some of these opportunities provide an income tax advantage, others may provide non-tax advantages.

¶18,305 Uses of a Trust for Income Tax Advantages

Income tax can be saved by the following uses of a trust in family planning situations.

(1) Income tax savings — A graduated rate estate, which is taxed on its income with the graduated rates applicable to an individual, may attract less tax on its income than the same income taxed in the hands of an individual beneficiary who is in a high tax bracket. Furthermore, provincial surtaxes on individuals in higher tax brackets can be reduced where the income can be taxed in a graduated rate estate. This would support leaving an inheritance in the graduated rate estate for the first 36 months following the death of the taxpayer (i.e., defer the distribution of the estate to the individual beneficiaries until the 36-month period is over). Savings are only available if the income of the estate is not paid or payable to an individual beneficiary. As a spousal testamentary trust cannot be a graduated rate estate, it would be beneficial to defer the setup of the spousal testamentary trust by keeping the property in the estate for 36 months if possible.

(2) Capital gains deduction utilization — A trust that realizes capital gains on qualifying small business corporation shares (QSBCS) can allocate such gains to the capital beneficiaries who can then use their own capital gains deduction. This sprinkling of the capital gains on such shares results in multiple use of the capital gains deduction.

(3) Family income splitting — Where family income splitting is possible, and TOSI and attribution can be avoided, on a transfer of income-producing and or gains-producing property to a family member, the same income splitting benefits can be achieved with the use of a trust. Note that the amendments to the TOSI provisions noted above greatly restrict the ability to split private corporation income with family members for 2018 and subsequent years.

At the same time, the use of a trust may have additional advantages, as discussed below.

¶18,310 Uses of a Trust for Non-Tax Advantages

Trusts can be used to achieve advantages that are not directly related to income tax considerations in family planning situations.

(1) Control and management — Family members can be provided with a source of income as beneficiaries of a trust without allowing them to control the assets that produce the income. The original owner of the property can maintain control over the assets through the appointment of the trustees. Assets can be managed for the benefit of the beneficiaries where those beneficiaries are not considered to be capable or do not have the time or expertise to manage the assets on their own. Income and capital can be distributed at the appropriate time and in the appropriate manner, according to the objectives of the plan.

(2) Asset protection — Assets held in a trust are generally owned by the trust, as distinct from an individual. These assets held in a trust are, in essence, "creditor proofed" and, generally, not accessible to the creditors of an individual. The assets held in a trust may not be subject to equalization in a marital breakdown situation.

(3) Facilitation of distributions on death — Property held in a trust is not part of an estate subject to a will that must be probated. This may avoid probate fees. Property transferred to a trust prior to death can be transferred in private and not be subject to a public probating of a will or be contested, as a distribution under a will can be.

¶18,310.99 Practise What You've Learned

Refer to the following sections of the Study Guide to practise what you've learned:

¶18,825 — Multiple Choice Questions

- Question 6 — Advantages of using a trust

CHAPTER 19

International Taxation in Canada

ADVANCED CONTENT IN THIS CHAPTER

Learning Goals

Know

By the end of this chapter you will know:

- The basics of Canadian taxation of non-residents.
- The Canadian tax law applicable to cross-border transactions.
- Canadian taxation of residents with foreign investments.

Understand and Explain

By the end of this chapter you will understand and be able to explain:

- The taxation of non-residents with Canadian investments or business dealings.
- The tax treatment of cross-border transactions between Canadian residents and foreign persons.
- The taxation of Canadian residents earning income from foreign investments.
- The basic application of tax treaties.

Apply

By the end of this chapter, you will be able to apply:

- Your knowledge and understanding of the key provisions applicable to non-residents, cross-border transactions, and foreign income earned by Canadian residents.
- Your knowledge and understanding of the impact of a tax treaty on the taxation of various sources of income earned by non-residents in Canada.
- The provisions of the *Income Tax Act* applicable to cross-border loans and transactions.
- Your knowledge and understanding of foreign investment by Canadian residents.

Review Questions
¶19,800 in the Study Guide

Multiple Choice Questions
¶19,825 in the Study Guide

Exercises
¶19,850 in the Study Guide

Assignment Problems
¶19,875 in the Study Guide

Overview

According to the CPA Knowledge Supplement, the topic of non-resident taxation is generally viewed as an advanced topic to be introduced in the core but covered in detail in the *elective* stage. Therefore, our advanced symbol (Ⓐ) in this chapter identifies material within this subject that is more complex and non-routine in nature.

No study of taxation in Canada is complete without at least an overview of international tax matters from a Canadian perspective. Canadians hold significant foreign investments and, conversely, foreign investors hold significant Canadian investments. In addition to direct and indirect investments, there are tax consequences flowing from cross-border employment and business activities. Business has become more global, and knowing the essence of the approaches to international taxation is a necessity. This area is highly complex and some tax practitioners choose to focus solely in this area. This chapter provides an essential overview of how international taxpayers, both Canadian and foreign, and their related transactions are taxed in Canada. An overview is all that can be accomplished due to the sheer magnitude and details of international taxation legislation.

¶19,000 Liability for Canadian Tax

¶19,010 Residents

The concept of residency is discussed in detail in Chapter 2. Residency is the basis under which Canada has jurisdiction to tax income. Citizenship is irrelevant. Persons who are residents of Canada are taxed in Canada on their worldwide income. Foreign tax credits for foreign taxes paid on foreign-source income may be available in computing Canadian income taxes payable.

ITA: 2(1) Tax payable by persons resident in Canada, 126 Foreign tax deduction

¶19,020 Non-Residents

Canadian-source income earned by non-residents is subject to tax in Canada under either Part I or Part XIII of the *Income Tax Act* (the Act). Part I tax generally applies to Canadian income sources considered to be active in nature. Part XIII tax generally applies to passive sources of income, such as investment income, and applies lower tax rates. Where there is greater attachment to location, activities, or properties owned by the non-resident in Canada, the tax liability and filing requirements are more extensive under Part I of the Act.

For non-residents, Canada has jurisdiction to tax income and gains considered to be from a Canadian source. Canadian-source income and gains in general terms include amounts attributable to business or employment activities in Canada and amounts attributable to the disposition of business or real properties located in Canada. The Act provides that a person who is not a resident for a taxation year, but

ITA: 2(3) Tax payable by non-resident persons; Interpretation Bulletins: IT-420R3 Non-residents — Income earned in Canada

(1) was employed in Canada;

(2) carried on a business in Canada; or

(3) disposed of a taxable Canadian property,

any time in the year or a previous year, shall pay tax on their taxable income earned in Canada for the year determined in accordance with Division D of the Act.

Canadian-source income also includes income from passive sources such as dividends or interest paid from Canadian residents to non-resident investors. Canada retains jurisdiction to tax such income amounts through withholding tax provisions in Part XIII, "Tax on Income from Canada of Non-Resident Persons". The main rule provides that:

ITA: 212(1) Tax

> Every non-resident person shall pay an income tax of 25% on every amount that a person resident in Canada pays or credits, or is deemed by Part I to pay or credit, to the non-resident person as, on account or in lieu of payment of, or in satisfaction of, the various forms of passive income as listed.

Taxing income earned in Canada by a non-resident raises the possibility of double taxation, as that income might also be taxable in the country with residence jurisdiction, where the non-resident lives. To eliminate, or to avoid as much double taxation as possible, Canada has bilateral tax treaties with other countries. These treaties (sometimes called conventions), in conjunction with a country's domestic law, generally resolve this problem by including provisions on double taxation and effectively take precedence over certain taxing provisions of the *Income Tax Act*. The provisions usually stipulate that the Canadian tax paid by the non-resident can be claimed in the taxpayer's country of residence as a foreign tax credit. However, not all countries have signed tax agreements with Canada and the possibility of double taxation must not be ignored by non-residents.

¶19,100 Non-Residents

¶19,110 Income Earned in Canada by Non-Residents

A non-resident's income and gains from Canadian sources (with the exception of Canadian-source income subject to withholding tax under Part XIII) are included in the computation of net income and taxable income for Canadian tax purposes as determined under Division D of the Act. Where there is a tax convention between Canada and the non-resident's country of residence, the tax convention may impact the sourcing of the income. Canadian-source income under Canadian domestic tax law may be exempt from Canadian taxation under the treaty. A deduction is available in computing taxable income for income taxable under Canadian domestic law but exempt under the treaty.

ITA: 110(1)(f) Deductions for payments

The normal filing due dates for Canadian corporations and individuals apply for non-residents. Non-resident individuals, similar to Canadian residents, do not need to file if tax is not payable under Part I of the Act, unless the non-resident has disposed of taxable Canadian property (except for dispositions of property exempt from tax under a treaty). See ¶19,130.10.

ITA: 116(6) Definition of "excluded property", 116(6.1) Treaty-exempt property, 150(1.1) Exception, 150(5) Excluded disposition

Canadian-source income subject to withholding tax under Part XIII is not included in income of a non-resident in Division D and, therefore, is not included on a Canadian tax return.

¶19,115 Employment Income

The determination of a non-resident's Canadian employment income is the same as if the person were resident in Canada. The portion of income from an office or employment related to duties performed in Canada is required to be included in Division D income. Income includes employment benefits and deductions for employment expenses can be claimed. The determination of a non-resident individual's status as an employee or an independent contractor (i.e., carrying on business in Canada) is a question of fact and is examined using the tests described in Chapter 3.[1] Where a non-resident is employed in Canada, deductions at source must be withheld from his or her salary as if the individual were a Canadian resident. Whether the employer is a Canadian resident has no impact on this obligation to withhold deductions at source. This requirement ensures that the non-resident pays income taxes in Canada that, at a minimum, is the amount withheld from salary and wages. When the non-resident files a Canadian personal tax return for the year, the withholdings will be applied against taxes payable. Many treaties exempt employment income from taxation where amounts are small or the non-resident is present in Canada for a short period of time (see ¶19,310).

ITA: 115(1)(a), 5 [Income or loss from office or employment], 153(1) Withholding; ITR: 101 Deductions and Remittances, 102 Periodic Payments

[1] This issue was discussed in the case *Wolf v. The Queen*, 2002 DTC 6853 (F.C.A.).

An exemption to the income tax withholding requirement for non-resident employers applies for employers who are resident in a treaty country. The exemption only applies for employees who are resident in a treaty country, are exempt from Canadian tax under the treaty on the employment income, and who work in Canada less than 45 days in the calendar year or are not present in Canada for 90 or more days within a 12-month period during which the salary is paid. The employer will need to obtain certification to be eligible for the waiver.

ITA: 153(1) Withholding, 153(6), 153(7) Certification by Minister; Forms: RC473 Application for Non-Resident Employer Certification

¶19,120 Business Income

The computation of a non-resident's Canadian income from a business is substantially the same as if the taxpayer were resident in Canada. The major question surrounding business income is whether the person is "carrying on business in Canada". Understanding that term is easier if you contrast it with "carrying on business with Canada".

ITA: 9 Income, 20 Deductions permitted in computing income from business or property

Carrying on business in Canada is deemed to include producing, growing, mining, creating, manufacturing, fabricating, improving, packing, preserving, or constructing anything in Canada. It includes the solicitation of orders or offering anything for sale in Canada through an agent or servant. It also includes the disposition of real property inventory situated in Canada. Most of Canada's current tax treaties override Canadian domestic law and provide that business profits are taxable only where they are attributable to a permanent establishment located in Canada.

ITA: 253 Extended meaning of "carrying on business"

The definition of "permanent establishment" in the Canada–U.S. Tax Convention includes a fixed place of business in Canada, including a place of management, office, branch, factory, or workshop. It includes a building site or construction or installation project if it lasts more than 12 months. It includes a person acting on behalf of the non-resident, if such person has, and habitually exercises in Canada, an authority to conclude contracts in Canada in the name of the non-resident. A permanent establishment is deemed not to include a fixed place of business used solely for, or a person engaged solely in,

Tax Treaties: Cda-U.S. TT: Art. V, par. 1, 2, 3, 5

- the use of facilities for storage, display, or delivery of goods of the non-resident,
- the maintenance of goods belonging to the non-resident for the purpose of storage, display, delivery, or for the purpose of processing by another person,
- the purchase of goods or collection of information for the non-resident, or
- advertising, the supply of information, scientific research, or similar activities with a preparatory or auxiliary character for the non-resident.

Tax Treaties: Cda-U.S. TT: Art. V, par. 6

Services of an enterprise can be deemed to be performed through a permanent establishment where services are provided in the state for 183 days or more in a 12-month period.

Tax Treaties: Cda-U.S. TT: Art. V, par. 9

Example Problem 19-1

A U.S. corporation, Tellco Inc., employs three sales employees who live and work in Canada. The sales employees work from home offices. Tellco Inc. does not have an office or other facility in Canada. The employees are paid a monthly salary and quarterly commissions based on sales volume. The employees solicit sales from Canadian customers. The customers order products directly from the U.S. company online or by phone. Goods are shipped directly from the U.S. warehouse to Canadian customers.

REQUIRED

(1) Is Tellco Inc. carrying on business in Canada?

(2) Does Tellco Inc. have a permanent establishment in Canada?

(3) Does Tellco Inc. have a withholding requirement for Canadian employees?

SOLUTION

(1) Tellco is offering product for sale in Canada through a servant (employee) and would be considered to be carrying on business in Canada under domestic law.

ITA: 253 Extended meaning of "carrying on business"

(2) Tellco would be deemed to have a permanent establishment in Canada, if the employees negotiate and habitually conclude contracts in Tellco's name. As long as the sales contracts are concluded in the U.S., Tellco would not have a permanent establishment in Canada. The Convention overrides Canadian domestic law.

Tax Treaties: Cda-U.S. TT: Art. V, par. 5

(3) Source deductions are required for payments of salary, wages, or other remuneration. Remuneration includes commissions paid to an officer or employee. Tellco must withhold and remit prescribed amounts to the Receiver General for the Canadian employees. Assuming that the employees are residents of Canada, Canadian personal tax returns will be filed and the withholdings will reduce the taxes payable on the returns. The exemption from withholdings does not apply to Tellco. Although the company is resident in a treaty country, the employees are residents of Canada and liable for tax on the employment income in Canada.

ITA: 153(1) Withholding; ITR: 100(1), 101 Deductions and Remittances, 102 Periodic Payments, 105(1); Information Circulars: IC 75-6R2 Required Withholding from Amounts Paid to Non-Resident Persons Performing Services in Canada

¶19,123 Regulation 105 Withholding Requirements

Every person paying a fee, commission, or other amount to a non-resident in respect of services rendered in Canada (other than remuneration) is required to withhold and remit a 15% tax. A non-resident carrying on a business that involves providing services in Canada will be impacted by Regulation 105 because the customer will withhold 15% of the fees to be paid to the non-resident to remit to the CRA. A waiver application can be filed by the non-resident with the CRA to claim a treaty exemption where the non-resident will not be liable for tax on the fees received because the non-resident does not have a permanent establishment in Canada. Where a waiver is not requested or accepted by the CRA, the non-resident can obtain a refund of any excess of the tax withheld over any taxes payable on the income from carrying on business included in the Canadian tax return. Regulation 105 ensures the protection of Canada's tax base by placing the tax liability with the Canadian resident payer at the time the payment for services is made. It is easier for the CRA to collect tax from a Canadian resident. Regulation 105 also ensures that a minimum tax of 15% is collected with respect to such income.

¶19,125 Branch Tax

A branch tax is imposed on non-resident corporations carrying on business in Canada through a branch. This tax is charged in addition to any Part I tax and is computed as 25% (unless reduced by a tax treaty) of after-tax Canadian-source income adjusted for an allowance for investment in property in Canada. The branch tax is intended to put the branch in the same position as a Canadian subsidiary which must withhold tax on dividends paid to the foreign parent. The branch tax, in essence, is paid on Canadian-source income of the branch that is not retained and reinvested in Canada, just as a withholding tax is levied on dividends paid from income that is not retained and reinvested in Canada.

ITA: 219 Additional tax; ITR: 808 Allowances in Respect of Investment in Property in Canada; Interpretation Bulletins: IT-137R3 Additional Tax on Certain Corporations Carrying on Business in Canada

This tax is subject to overriding provisions within an income tax treaty. For example, the branch tax rate under the Canada–U.S. Tax Treaty is 5%. The Treaty also exempts the first C$500,000 of branch profits not reinvested in the state from branch tax. Treaties generally exempt non-resident corporations from Canadian tax, including branch tax, unless there is a permanent establishment in Canada.

Tax Treaties: Cda-U.S. TT: Art. X, par. 6

Example Problem 19-2

International Links Inc. is a telecommunications company incorporated in the United States with a December 31 year end. It began operating one small pilot project office in Toronto in fiscal 2017 in addition to its 52 U.S. offices. The corporation is not resident in Canada; however, the Canadian office is considered a permanent establishment under the Canada–U.S. Tax Treaty. The corporation's taxable income from Canadian operations was $280,000 in 2018. The corporation has $50,000 of qualified investment property in Canada at the end of 2018. At the end of fiscal 2017, it had $20,000 of qualified investment property.

REQUIRED

Compute the corporation's branch tax liability for 2018 on the assumption that the Ontario provincial corporate tax rate is 12%. (Ignore surtaxes.)

SOLUTION

5%[(1)] of:

Taxable income earned in Canada	$280,000	ITA: 219(1)(a)
Add:		
Amount claimed in previous year as investment allowance	20,000	ITA: 219(1)(g); ITR: 808(1), 808(2)
Deduct: Tax payable under Part I	(42,000)[(2)]	ITA: 219(1)(h)
Tax payable to a province @ 12%	(33,600)[(3)]	ITA: 219(1)(h)

Allowance in respect of qualified investment property in Canada	(50,000)[4]
	$174,400
Branch tax (5% × $174,400)	$8,720[5]

The $174,400 represents the amount of profit for the year that was repatriated to the U.S., i.e., not reinvested in the Canadian operations. If instead the business was incorporated, the repatriation would have been a dividend subject to withholding tax. Branch tax mirrors the withholding tax on dividends.

NOTES TO SOLUTION

(1) The Canada–U.S. Tax Treaty limits the rate of branch tax to 5%.

(2) $280,000 × (38% – 10% – 13%). This tax rate is the basic federal rate net of the federal abatement and the general rate reduction.

(3) $280,000 × 12%. This tax rate reflects a provincial rate of tax on Canadian business income.

(4) Regulation 808(2) lists the specific components of qualified investment property in Canada. Reference to this regulation will be necessary when determining qualified investment property.

(5) Depending on the cumulative business profits associated with the branch, the branch tax could be eliminated under Article X of the Canada–U.S. Tax Convention.

¶19,130 Disposing of Taxable Canadian Property

Non-residents who dispose of taxable Canadian property are liable for Canadian tax on taxable capital gains less allowable capital losses related to that property.

The definition of taxable Canadian property includes: ITA: 248(1) Definitions

- real or immovable property situated in Canada;
- property used or held in, or inventory of a business carried on in Canada;
- a share of a corporation (other than a mutual fund corporation) that is not listed on a designated stock exchange, an interest in a partnership, or a capital interest in a trust if at any time during the 60 months immediately preceding the disposition, more than 50% of the fair market value of the shares or interest was derived from real or immovable property situated in Canada; and
- a share of a corporation listed on a designated stock exchange (a mutual fund corporation or a unit in a mutual fund trust), if, at any time during the 60 months immediately preceding the disposition, the non-resident and non-arm's length persons owned 25% or more of the issued shares of the capital stock of the

corporation (or trust units) and more than 50% of the fair market value of the shares (or units) was derived from real or immovable property situated in Canada.

Effectively, taxable Canadian property includes properties used in a business operating in Canada or properties tied to real properties located in Canada. The definition coordinates Canada's domestic tax law with many of its tax treaties.

¶19,130.10 Section 116 Certificates

To ensure that non-residents comply with their obligations to report dispositions of taxable Canadian property and that the taxes are paid, the *Income Tax Act* imposes a withholding tax at the time of disposition.

Taxable Canadian Property — Non-Depreciable Capital Property

A non-resident who plans to dispose of taxable Canadian property that is non-depreciable capital property should file a notice with the Minister at any time prior to the disposition, or within 10 days of the disposition, indicating the name and address of the proposed purchaser, a description of the property, the estimated sale price, and the ACB of the property. Where the non-resident vendor does not obtain a certificate of compliance, a "failure to comply" penalty will be assessed.

Forms: T2062 Request by a Non-Resident of Canada for a Certificate of Compliance Related to the Disposition of Taxable Canadian Property; Information Circulars: IC 72-17R6 Procedures concerning the disposition of taxable Canadian property by non-residents of Canada – Section 116

The non-resident must include with the notice a tax payment of 25% of the estimated or actual capital gain on the property. The non-resident can provide acceptable security in lieu of the withholding tax. Once the tax is paid, or the security provided, the non-resident is provided with a certificate to that effect. If the actual proceeds of sale are more than the estimated proceeds in the certificate (i.e., the limit), the purchaser must withhold an amount equal to 25% of the excess. Without a certificate, 25% of the full purchase price must be remitted by the purchaser.

ITA: 116(2) Certificate in respect of proposed disposition, 116(5) Liability of purchaser

Taxable Canadian Property — Depreciable Property and Real Property Inventory

Similar requirements apply to dispositions or proposed dispositions of taxable Canadian property that is depreciable property and real property inventory. The non-resident must include a tax payment of 25% of the capital gain plus estimated tax on recaptured CCA, with the notice filed with the Minister, or furnish acceptable security to receive a certificate of compliance. If the actual proceeds of sale are more than the estimated proceeds in the certificate (i.e., the limit), the purchaser must withhold an amount equal to 50% of the excess. Without a certificate, 50% of the full purchase price must be remitted by the purchaser. Again, the onus is on the purchaser to pay the tax if the vendor does not obtain a certificate.

ITA: 116(5.2) Certificates for dispositions; Forms: T2602A

The purchaser must remit any amount required to be withheld within 30 days after the end of the month in which the property was acquired. The purchaser is liable for the withheld tax and is entitled to recover the tax by deducting it from any amount due to the vendor, or by other means.

ITA: 116(5) Liability of purchaser, 116(5.3) Liability of purchaser in certain cases

The rules put the onus on the purchaser, who is usually a resident of Canada, to ensure that the tax owing on the disposition of taxable Canadian property is collected by the Canadian government.

Excluded Property

Relief from the withholding requirements is available for transactions involving residents of Canada's treaty countries. The withholding requirements do not apply to excluded property. Excluded property includes inventory (other than real property inventory) of a business carried on in Canada, listed shares of a corporation and treaty-protected property. A treaty-protected property is a treaty-exempt property where the purchaser has taken some steps to ensure the treaty-exempt status of the property.

ITA: 116(5.01) Treaty-protected property, 116(6) Definition of "excluded property", 116(6.1) Treaty-exempt property

A purchaser of property from a non-resident vendor need not withhold if:

ITA: 116(5) Liability of purchaser, 116(5.3) Liability of purchaser in certain cases

(1) the purchaser concludes after reasonable inquiry that the vendor is a resident of a country that has a tax treaty with Canada;

(2) the property is treaty-protected (gains/income arising on disposition are exempt from tax under treaty); and

(3) the purchaser sends a notice to the Minister within 30 days of the date of acquisition.

ITA: 116(5.02) Notice by purchaser in respect of an acquisition of property

Example Problem 19-3

Joe Solder is a resident of the United States and owns 25% of the shares of a Canadian-controlled private corporation with operations in Waterloo. The value of the shares is $150,000. He was issued the shares for $300 on incorporation in 1998. Joe's brother, Samuel, owns 75% of the shares of the company. Samuel lives and works in Waterloo. Samuel has offered to purchase Joe's shares at fair market value on April 1, 2018.

REQUIRED

Part A — Assuming the shares are not treaty protected:

(1) If today's date is January 15, 2018, what compliance requirements should be met by Joe?

(2) If today's date is April 20, 2018, and the transaction has already occurred, what compliance requirements should be met by Joe and Samuel?

Part B — Answer the above assuming the shares are treaty protected.

SOLUTION

Part A — Not treaty-protected under Article XIII

Taxable Canadian property includes unlisted shares of a corporation resident in Canada if, at any time during the 60 months immediately preceding the disposition, more than 50% of the fair market value of the shares was derived from real or immovable property situated in Canada. Under the Canada–U.S. Tax Convention, Article XIII, gains on the disposition of shares of a Canadian resident corporation are subject to tax in Canada if the value of the

ITA: 248 Definitions

shares is derived principally from real property situated in Canada. Part A assumes that the gain on the shares is not exempt from tax under Article XIII (i.e., the value of the shares is derived principally from real property situated in Canada).

(1) Anytime before the disposition, or not later than 10 days after the disposition, Joe may complete Form T2062, "Request by a Non-Resident of Canada for a Certificate of Compliance Related to the Disposition of Taxable Canadian Property", to report the disposition and pay 25% of the gain, i.e., 25% of ($150,000 – $300) or provide acceptable security. The Minister will provide a certificate of compliance. If Form T2062 is not filed, a "failure to comply" penalty will be assessed under subsection 162(7).

(2) If Form T2062 is not completed within the above-noted time frame or the purchase price exceeds the estimated purchase price in a certificate requested before the disposition, Samuel will become liable for 25% of the cost of the shares, i.e., 25% of $150,000 (or 25% of $150,000 less the limit fixed in the certificate). He must remit the amount to the Receiver General by May 30, 2018. Samuel can deduct or withhold the amount from any amount paid or credited to Joe or otherwise recover the amount paid.

Joe must file a personal Canadian tax return to report the gain from the disposition of taxable Canadian property by April 30, 2019. His taxes payable will be reduced by any tax paid to the Minister with Form T2062.

ITA: 116(1) Disposition by non-resident person of certain property, 116(3) Notice to Minister; 116(5) Liability of purchaser; 116(5.02) Notice by purchaser in respect of an acquisition of property, 150(1.1) Exception, 150(5) Excluded disposition

Part B — Treaty-protected under Article XIII

Part B assumes that, although the shares meet the definition of taxable Canadian property, the gain is exempt because the value of the shares is derived principally from real property situated in Canada under Article XIII.

The non-resident vendor is not required to complete form T2062 for the disposition. The purchaser must file a notice with the Minister including the date of the transaction, the amount paid, the name and address of the non-resident, and identifying the Canada–U.S. Tax Convention as the treaty providing protection within 30 days of the acquisition (i.e., May 1, 2018) or become liable for 25% of the purchase price. Joe will not need to file a personal Canadian tax return as long as there is no Part I tax payable for the year, and he does not owe tax for a prior tax year.

The certificate and withholding tax requirement applies to property that is transferred by way of a gift, or to a non-arm's length person for consideration that is less than full value. In these cases, the proceeds are based on fair market value. The certificate and withholding tax requirements do not apply to property transferred because of a non-resident's death. Although the certificate requirement does not apply, the deceased non-resident may be liable for Canadian tax because of a deemed disposition of taxable Canadian property at the time of death.

ITA: 116(5.1) Gifts, etc, 70 Death of a taxpayer

¶19,140 Deductions and Credits Allowed a Non-Resident

Certain deductions in determining the non-resident's taxable income for Canadian tax purposes are allowed. Specifically, the non-resident can deduct: employment losses, business losses, business investment losses, loss carryovers under section 111, stock option deductions, amounts exempt from tax under a tax convention, and other types of compensation that are not taxable in Canada. For corporations, the deductions for dividends received by a corporation in determining taxable income and charitable gifts are available.

Where all or substantially all (which is 90% or more) of the non-resident person's income for the year is included in computing the non-resident person's taxable income earned in Canada for the year, such of the other deductions permitted for the purpose of computing taxable income (i.e., other Division C deductions) may be deducted as may reasonably be considered wholly applicable.

ITA: 115(1) Non-resident's taxable income in Canada, 115(1)(f)

¶19,145 Tax Credits Available to Non-Residents

The following non-refundable tax credits may be claimed by all non-residents, irrespective of the type and amount of their Canadian-source income, if they satisfy the conditions of eligibility.

ITA: 118.94 Tax payable by non-residents (credits restricted), 118.1 [Charitable and other gifts], 118.3(1) Credit for mental or physical impairment, 118.5 Tuition credit, 118.81 Tuition tax credit transferred, 118.7 Credit for EI and QPIP premiums and CPP contributions, 118.62 Credit for interest on student loan

- Charitable gifts
- Mental or physical impairment tax credit
- Tuition tax credit
- EI and CPP/QPP tax credits
- Student loan interest

All other credits may be claimed by those non-residents whose Canadian-source income represents at least 90% of their worldwide income. The non-resident may be required to furnish the CRA with evidence to establish that is the case.

¶19,150 Provincial/Territorial Income Tax Obligation

A non-resident will typically be liable to pay provincial or territorial income tax in addition to federal income tax on income earned in a province. The rates of tax vary from province to province (and territory). For these purposes, income earned in a province is the aggregate of the taxpayer's income from an office or employment that is reasonably attributable to the duties performed by him in the province and the taxpayer's income for the year from carrying on business earned in the province.

ITA: 120(1) Income not earned in a province, 120(4) Definitions; ITR: 2602 Non-Residents

If a non-resident's income subject to federal tax is not considered income earned in a province, an additional tax of 48% of the federal tax otherwise payable is added in respect of that income. Note that a non-resident's taxable capital gains from the disposition of taxable Canadian property will not be considered income earned in a province, and, therefore, will be subject to the additional federal tax. The additional federal tax has the effect of making the non-resident's tax on a gain approximately the same as would apply to a resident who has to pay provincial income tax (that is, combined federal plus provincial tax).

¶19,160 Withholding Taxes on Canadian-Source Income — Part XIII Tax

While non-residents are liable for Canadian income taxes under Part I, on income from employment, carrying on business in Canada, and any gain on dispositions of taxable Canadian property, this is not the only possible taxation of a non-resident's Canadian-source income.

Part XIII of the Act, requires a resident who pays or credits certain amounts (such as interest, dividends, royalties, and pensions) to a non-resident to withhold 25% for Canadian tax. Part XIII tax should not be confused with Part I tax. These are two separate taxing provisions. If a non-resident pays Part XIII tax on a particular source of income, then the non-resident does not pay Part I tax on that same source, and *vice versa*. No tax return is required to be filed by the non-resident for income subject to Part XIII tax.

ITA: 212 Tax; Information Circulars: IC 76-12R6 Applicable Rate of Part XIII Tax on Amounts Paid or Credited to Persons in Countries with which Canada has a Tax Convention, IC 77-16R4 Non-Resident Income Tax

Common income types subject to Part XIII withholding tax are as follows:

(1) Management fees;

ITA: 212(1)(a) Management fee

(2) Interest paid or payable to a non-arm's length person (that is not fully exempt interest) and participating debt interest;

ITA: 212(1)(b) Interest, 212(3) Interest — definitions

(3) Estate or trust income;

ITA: 212(1)(c) Estate or trust income

(4) Rents and royalties;

ITA: 212(1)(d) Rents, royalties, etc.

(5) Pension benefits;

ITA: 212(1)(h) Pension benefits

(6) Registered retirement savings plan and registered retirement income fund payments;

ITA: 212(1)(l) Registered retirement savings plan payments, 212(1)(q) Registered retirement income fund payments

(7) Deferred profit sharing plan payments;

ITA: 212(1)(m) Deferred profit sharing plan payments

(8) Annuity payments; and

ITA: 212(1)(o) Other annuity payments

(9) Taxable dividends and capital dividends.

ITA: 212(2) Tax on dividends

An exclusive list can be found in the Act. Many provisions in the section include exemptions for certain types of payments within the above categories. A thorough review of this provision and related provisions may be required to determine applicability of the withholding tax.

ITA: 212 Tax

Generally, the payer is responsible for withholding and remitting the Part XIII tax to the CRA. If the payer does not withhold or remit, he or she may be held liable for the tax not withheld, plus interest (jointly with the non-resident) and penalties.

ITA: 215(6) Liability for tax, 227(8) Penalty, 227(8.1) Joint and several, or solidary, liability, 227(8.3) Interest on amounts not deducted or withheld

The payer resident is required to file an NR4 return (similar to a T4/T4A return) with the CRA. The non-resident then uses this NR4 information slip to report the income in their country of residence and claim any foreign tax credit that the foreign country might grant under its tax system.

Example Problem 19-4

Janet Smith is about to emigrate from Canada. She has $50,000 in her RRSP.

REQUIRED

What are her alternatives in connection with this RRSP?

SOLUTION

Janet could collapse the RRSP prior to leaving Canada. In this case, the RRSP would be included as income in her final Canadian tax return and taxed at her marginal rate. Alternatively, she could collapse the RRSP after having left Canada. In that case, there would be a 25% withholding tax. The income may be subject to tax in the foreign jurisdiction and a foreign tax credit received for the Canadian withholding tax. She should choose the approach that produces the lesser tax.

ITA: 212(1)(l) Registered retirement savings plan payments

The 25% withholding rate in Part XIII can be reduced pursuant to a treaty between Canada and the country of the income recipient. It is the payer's responsibility to withhold at the appropriate rate. Form NR301, "Declaration of Benefits under a Tax Treaty for a Non-resident Taxpayer", has been developed by the CRA to help non-residents establish and assure payers of eligibility for treaty rate reductions. The CRA recommends payers withhold the full 25% if the form has not been provided.

Ⓐ ¶19,165 Rental Income Alternative — Section 216 Elections

As noted above, rental income paid to a non-resident is subject to a 25% Part XIII tax. The Part XIII tax can be punitive to the landlord who might have mortgage payments, property taxes, maintenance, and other types of expenses funded by the gross rental income. The withholding tax can impact cash flow and the ability to pay expenses related to the property. To address this, the non-resident is provided with an option to report net rental income subject to the regular Part I tax rates to recoup all or a portion of the Part XIII tax.

ITA: 216 Alternatives re rents and timber royalties; Interpretation Bulletins: IT-393R2 Election re Tax on Rents and Timber Royalties — Non-Residents

The non-resident may elect to file a Canadian income tax return and report the rental income and expenses. The expenses allowed in this optional tax return are the same as those allowed against rental income of a resident, including capital cost allowance on the property. This return is optional on an annual basis, and must be filed within two years after the end of the applicable taxation year in which the income was earned, showing only net rental income from property in Canada. Where the alternative is chosen, income taxes are payable based on the net rental income. This election does not relieve the Canadian payer from the obligation to withhold the Part XIII tax; however, the 25% withholding tax is considered an instalment on account against those taxes payable, and any excess is refundable. This tax return is separate from any other income tax return the non-resident may otherwise be required to file. No deductions in computing taxable income or any tax credits may be claimed in completing the tax return. Tax is computed using the rates in effect for the year that are applicable to the type of non-resident person filing the return. For example, graduated rates would apply for non-resident individuals. Corporate tax rates would apply for non-resident corporations.

ITA: 216(1) Alternatives re rents and timber royalties; Forms: T1159 Income Tax Return for Electing Under Section 216

While the alternative to file a tax return provides the non-resident with an opportunity to reduce his or her Canadian tax liability, it does not assist with the cash-flow difficulties that the 25% withholding tax requirement might impose. For this reason, the non-resident is given yet another alternative for Canadian rental income.

ITA: 216(4) Optional method of payment

The non-resident may file an undertaking with the CRA, that the elective tax return will be filed within six months of the end of the taxation year. The undertaking must be filed no later than the first day of each year or the date on which the first rental payment is made. The undertaking allows the non-resident's Canadian agent to elect to pay the 25% withholding tax on net rather than gross rental income (before CCA) and reduce the required payments under Part XIII. Filing this elective tax return allows the non-resident to file a Canadian tax return to declare net rental income, including the CCA deduction, and receive a refund of any excess Part XIII tax.

Forms: NR6 Undertaking to File an Income Tax Return by a Non-Resident Receiving Rent from Real or Immovable Property or Receiving a Timber Royalty

Example Problem 19-5

Jack Lajoha is a resident of Spain, but has a rental property in Canada. The gross rents are $1,500 monthly, and are collected by Jack's agent, Tom Kelly. From the rental income, Tom pays his rental agent's fee, the mortgage, property taxes, and maintenance totalling $14,400. Available CCA on the property will be $5,000 for 2018. On average there is about $300 a month net cash available.

REQUIRED

How does Jack Lajoha account for this rental income in Canada?

SOLUTION

Tom Kelly is required to deduct 25% of the gross monthly rental income and remit it to the CRA as withholding tax. The withholding tax of $375 exceeds, on average, the net cash available. Jack will have to send Tom about $75 a month to meet the cash-flow requirements.

Jack may, if he so chooses, file a Canadian tax return (Form T1159) within two years, and receive a refund of the withholding tax over the actual tax required by that return as follows:

Estimated rental income for 2018:

Gross rentals		$18,000
Expenses before CCA	$14,400	
CCA (maximum allowed)	3,600	(18,000)
Net rentals		$ —
If an election is made under subsection 216(1) Net income and taxable income		$ —

Part I tax	$ —
Less: Income tax deducted (25% × $18,000)	4,500
Refund	$4,500

Another alternative would be for Jack to provide an undertaking by January 1, 2018 (Form NR6) to file a tax return within six months of the end of the taxation year. This would allow Tom to elect to remit the withholding tax of $900, based on 25% of the $300 available monthly. Jack would then receive a refund of the amount ($900) on filing the tax return. Jack should file the income tax return under Part I no later than June 30 following the end of the taxation year.

Where the undertaking is given, it is the non-resident's Canadian agent or representative who elects to remit the withholding tax based on the lesser "amount available". If the non-resident does not file the required tax return or does not pay any additional tax required on filing the tax return, the Canadian agent/representative will be liable to pay the difference between the amount actually remitted and 25% of the gross rents.

ITA: 216(4) Optional method of payment

When a non-resident disposes of real property in Canada and CCA was claimed in prior years on a tax return under Part I, a tax return must be filed, and any recapture of CCA resulting from the disposition is included in income.

ITA: 216(5) Disposition by non-resident

Note that Part XIII withholding tax only applies to rental income that is not considered to be income from carrying on a business in Canada. The determination of whether rental income is business or property income is a question of fact tied to the level of services provided by the landlord. Where rental income is income from carrying on business in Canada, the net rental income is taxed under Part I. A certificate request confirming that Part XIII does not apply should be received from the Minister.

ITA: 115(1) Non-resident's taxable income in Canada, 2(3) Tax payable by non-resident persons; ITR: 805 Other Non-Resident Persons, 805.1 Payee Certificate

Ⓐ ¶19,170 Canadian Benefits Alternative — Section 217 Election

Non-residents receiving the following types of income (referred to as "Canadian benefits") are provided with another alternative to the 25% withholding tax requirement:

ITA: 217 Alternative re Canadian benefits

- pension benefits;
- death benefits (and others under section 56);
- retiring allowances;
- supplementary unemployment benefits (SUB plans);
- RRSP benefits;
- DPSP benefits; or
- RRIF benefits.

The non-resident is able to file a Canadian income tax return within six months of the taxation year end and elect that section 217 apply. This should only be done where the tax liability, as calculated under Part I in that return, is less than the 25% Part XIII withholding tax (or the reduced rate under the applicable treaty). Unlike the alternative rental income return under section 216, this section 217 return is not separate from any other return the non-resident is required to file (employment income, business income, disposition of taxable Canadian property).

ITA: 217(2) Part I return, 217(3) Taxable income earned in Canada, 217(6) Special credit

¶19,200 Part-Year Residents

¶19,210 Income, Deductions, and Credits

Persons who are residents of Canada for only a part of the year are subject to specific rules. A person may be a Canadian resident for only part of the year under two situations:

ITA: 114 Individual resident in Canada for only part of year

- when a Canadian resident leaves the country at some point in the year to take up permanent residence in another country (emigration); and
- when a resident of another country leaves that country at some point in the year to become a permanent Canadian resident (immigration).

For income tax purposes, this person is considered a resident of Canada only during the time of permanent residence. The Canadian tax liability, under Part I, is based on worldwide income during the period in the year a person was resident in Canada, and on Canadian-source income for the period when the person was non-resident.

ITA: 2(1) Tax payable by persons resident in Canada, 2(3) Tax payable by non-resident persons

A part-year resident does not include an individual deemed a resident as a sojourner. Such an individual is deemed resident throughout the year.

ITA: 250(1)(a)

When calculating *net* income in Canada for a part-year resident, certain deductions, such as RRSP contributions and spousal and child support payments made during the period of residency in Canada, are allowed under the normal rules. Qualifying child care expenses for the period of residency in Canada are also allowed under the normal rules.

The deductions generally allowed in calculating *taxable* income for a part-year resident are the employee stock option deduction and loss carryforwards. The capital gains deduction (CGD) can be deducted by part-year residents only if they were resident throughout either the preceding or the immediately following taxation year.

ITA: 114(b), 110.6(5) Deemed resident in Canada; Interpretation Bulletins: IT-262R2 Losses of Non-Residents and Part-Year Residents

The income tax rates used to compute the tax payable under Part I by a part-year resident are the same as those for all other Canadian residents. The tax credits allowed to reduce income tax payable are more limited in comparison to those for a person residing in Canada all year.

In the year of immigration or emigration, some of the personal tax credits of the taxpayer are prorated based on the number of days that the individual is resident in Canada. The following credits are prorated:

ITA: 118.91 Part-year residents

- basic personal tax credit, married or common-law status, equivalent-to-spouse credit, and Canada caregiver credit;

ITA: 118(1) Personal credits

- age amount;

ITA: 118(2) Age credit

- disability (mental or physical impairment) for self or transferred from dependant;

ITA: 118.3 Credit for mental or physical impairment

- unused credits transferred from a spouse or common-law partner; and

ITA: 118.8 Transfer of unused credits to spouse or common-law partner

- unused tuition amounts transferred from a child or grandchild.

ITA: 118.9 Transfer to parent or grandparent

All other personal tax credits can be claimed in full for the period in which the individual is resident in Canada.

Example Problem 19-6

Aaron Levy immigrated to Canada during 2018, arriving on August 15. Aaron had earned a salary in Israel of C$65,000 before coming to Canada. On arriving in Canada, he went to work for the City of Winnipeg, where he earned $35,000 in employment income. He also attended the University of Winnipeg on a part-time basis for four months and his tuition fees were $2,900.

REQUIRED

Aaron asks you to help him with his Canadian income taxes.

SOLUTION

Income for Canadian tax purposes:				
	Israeli salary	$0	(not taxable, earned before resident)	
	Canadian salary	35,000		
		$35,000		
Federal and provincial				
(15% + 10% = 25%)		$8,750		
Personal tax credits (federal + provincial):				
25% of the total of:				
	Basic	$4,497	($11,809 × 139/365 days)	ITA: 118(1) Personal credits
	Tuition	2,900	(tuition paid)	ITA: 118.5 Tuition credit
	Employment credit	1,195		ITA: 118.(10)
	CPP	1,559	(4.95% of ($35,000 – $3,500) = $1,559)	ITA: 118.7 Credit for EI and QPIP premiums and CPP contributions
	EI	581	(1.66% of $35,000 = $581)	
		$10,732		
	Credits	$2,683		

Aaron would owe tax of $6,067 for 2018.

¶19,220 Deemed Acquisition on Entering Canada

Taxpayers taking up Canadian residence are deemed to have disposed of each of the properties that they owned before entering Canada, and to have reacquired the properties at their then fair market value. This rule applies to most types of property and not just to capital property, although capital property is the most common application. Consequently, for future dispositions, the gain or loss accrued on property owned before entering Canada will not be considered for Canadian income tax purposes. The deemed acquisition amount becomes the cost base for Canadian tax purposes. ITA: 128.1(1)(b) Deemed disposition, 128.1(1)(c) Deemed acquisition

This rule ensures that immigrants are only subject to Canadian tax on gains made after becoming residents.

Example Problem 19-7

When Aaron Levy immigrated to Canada, he owned 5,000 shares of a public company listed on the New York Stock Exchange. His original purchase price was US$18 a share, and the fair market value of the shares when he entered Canada was US$24 a share. The exchange rate was 1.31.

REQUIRED

What is his adjusted cost base ("ACB") for tax purposes? If Aaron sold the shares in 2018 for $32 per share, what amount would be included in his Division B income for tax purposes? Assume that the exchange rate at the date of sale was 1.32.

SOLUTION

Aaron is deemed to have acquired the shares at US$24, or US$120,000 in total. The exchange rate applicable at the time of entry in Canada is used to convert the U.S. dollars to Canadian dollars. Aaron's ACB upon entering Canada is $157,200. ITA: 128.1(1)(c) Deemed acquisition

On the disposition of the shares, Aaron would include a taxable capital gain in Division B income of:

Proceeds of disposition ($32 × 5,000 × 1.32)	$211,200
Adjusted cost base ($24 × 5,000 × 1.31)	(157,200)
Capital gain	$54,000
Taxable capital gain	$27,000

The deemed disposition/acquisition rule does not apply to the following properties held by an individual:

- taxable Canadian property (see definition in ¶19,130);
- inventory of a business carried on in Canada;
- Class 14.1 property of a business carried on in Canada;
- "excluded rights or interests", which include rights under most pension and deferred income plans including salary deferral arrangements, registered pension plans, retirement compensation arrangements, registered retirement savings plans, rights to receive benefits under the *Canada Pension Plan* and the *Old Age Security Act*, and employee stock options.

ITA: 128.1(1)(b) Deemed disposition; 128.1(10) Definitions

These properties are exempt from the deemed disposition/acquisition rule and the tax cost is not increased when taking up residence. These properties are exempt from the rules because income and gains attributed to ownership of these properties are Canadian source regardless of the owner's residency status.

¶19,230 Deemed Disposition on Leaving Canada

When a taxpayer gives up his or her Canadian residence, the taxpayer is deemed to have disposed of all his or her property at its then fair market value. This rule applies, with certain exceptions, to both capital and non-capital property. By deeming a disposition, Canada is assured that taxes are paid on any income/gains accrued on the property while the taxpayer was a resident of Canada. Depending on the nature of the property, this deemed disposition may result in a taxable capital gain, allowable capital loss, capital cost allowance recapture, terminal loss, or business income or loss. The tax on this deemed disposition is commonly referred to as "departure tax".

ITA: 128.1(4) Emigration; Forms: T1243 Deemed Disposition of Property by an Emigrant of Canada

Because of the potential tax consequences for an individual leaving Canada, it is very important to establish the date on which he or she becomes a non-resident. This is generally the latest of the dates on which:

- the individual leaves Canada;
- the spouse and/or dependants, if any, leave Canada; or
- the individual becomes a resident of another country.

Income Tax Folio: S5-F1-C1 Determining an Individual's Residence Status

Example Problem 19-8

Carol Ann Thomas emigrated from Canada this year. At the time she left, she owned 500 shares of XYZ Ltd., a listed company on a designated Canadian stock exchange. The fair market value of the shares at that time was $20. Her ACB was $8 per share.

REQUIRED

What would Carol Ann report on her Canadian tax return for the year of departure?

SOLUTION

Deemed proceeds ($20 × 500)	$10,000
ACB ($8 × 500)	4,000
Capital gain	$6,000
Taxable capital gain	$3,000

Properties of an individual exempt from the deemed disposition rule are:

(1) real property situated in Canada, Canadian or timber resource properties; ITA: 128.1(4)(b) Deemed disposition

(2) property (including capital property, Class 14.1 property, and inventory) of a business carried on in Canada by the taxpayer through a permanent establishment in Canada at the time of emigration;

(3) "excluded rights or interests", which include rights under most pension and deferred income plans, including salary deferral arrangements, registered pension plans, retirement compensation arrangements, registered retirement savings plans, rights to receive benefits under the *Canada Pension Plan* and the *Old Age Security Act*, and employee stock options; ITA: 128.1(10) Definitions

(4) certain properties if the individual was a short-term resident (resident in Canada for 60 months or less during the 10-year period preceding the cessation of Canadian residence); and

(5) property where the taxpayer elects to unwind the deemed disposition from a previous departure upon returning to Canada. ITA: 128.1(6) Returning former resident

Again, properties exempt from the deemed disposition are generally properties for which future gains and income attributed to ownership of the property are Canadian-source and continue to be taxed in Canada.

An individual can elect that the deemed disposition at fair market value apply to properties described in (1) or (2), above. An emigrant may file this election to use a loss on such properties against gains arising because of the deemed disposition. Losses realized because of the election may only offset the increase in the taxpayer's income from the deemed disposition and cannot be used against other sources of income. ITA: 128.1(4)(d) Individual — elective disposition; Forms: T2061A Election by an Emigrant to Report Deemed Dispositions of Property and any Resulting Capital Gain or

Each property subject to the deemed disposition rule is deemed to have been reacquired by the individual at its fair market value. ITA: 128.1(4)(c) Reacquisition

As these rules may result in a large tax burden because there is no actual disposition or cash generated on the deemed disposition, tax relief is also included in the legislation. Individuals ceasing to be resident can elect to post security with the CRA for the purpose of deferring the payment of the tax that results from the deemed disposition rule. The election must be made and the security provided on or before the balance due date for the year in which emigration takes place. Where the election is made, the payment of the tax can be deferred without interest until the properties are actually sold. Security is not required for tax calculated on the first $100,000 of capital gains (i.e., $50,000 of taxable income) using the highest tax bracket rate.

ITA: 220(4.5) Security for departure tax, 220(4.51) Deemed security; Forms: T1244 Election, Under Subsection 220(4.5) of the Income Tax Act , to Defer the Payment of Tax on Income Relating to the Deemed Disposition of Property

In addition, individuals who cease to be resident in Canada and own property that has a total fair market value of greater than $25,000 (excluding cash, pensions, RRSPs, and personal-use property worth less than $10,000) at the time of their departure are required to file a form to list such property.

Forms: T1161 List of Properties by an Emigrant of Canada

¶19,300 Impact of Canada-Foreign Country Tax Treaties

Canada has entered into bilateral tax conventions or agreements with more than 90 countries for the purpose of avoiding double taxation, preventing tax evasion, facilitating and encouraging business transactions between the countries, determining the distribution of tax revenues to the governments of the contracting countries, and exchanging tax-related information. Canada is a party to the Vienna Convention on the Law of Treaties and, as a result, is required to abide by its provisions under international law. Generally, tax conventions avoid double taxation in two ways: by determining each jurisdiction's right to tax or not to tax a particular type of income, and by requiring the contracting countries to grant tax credits for income tax paid on such income to the other country.

To prevent tax evasion, most of Canada's tax treaties contain an article pertaining to the exchange of information between the contracting countries. The Canada–U.S. Tax Convention goes further in this area than any other existing treaty. Canada and the United States have agreed to provide comprehensive assistance to each other in the enforcement of their respective tax laws.

The terms of any tax convention or agreement are given the force of law in Canada by virtue of legislation passed by the Parliament of Canada to implement them. The implementing statutes establish that in the event of inconsistency between the terms of Canadian income tax law and the terms of the agreement or convention, the terms of the agreement are to prevail.

The Income Tax Conventions Interpretation Act (ITCIA) defines terms and provides clarification for concepts used in income tax conventions with other countries signed by Canada. Some of the provisions in the ITCIA can override a treaty. Terms that are not defined in a Convention, or are defined by reference to the laws of Canada, are to be interpreted using the meaning for purposes of the Act. In addition, they are to be interpreted using an ambulatory rather than a static approach, which means that a term is to be interpreted using the meaning under the current version of the Act rather than the version on the date the convention was entered into.

Tax treaties are not documents possessing the same degree of intricacy that, for example, characterizes the *Income Tax Act*. In interpreting the terms of legislation implementing a tax convention, it may not be proper to apply the strict rules of interpretation that normally apply to taxing statutes. The *OECD Model Tax Convention on Income and*

Capital (OECD Model) and the *United Nations Model Double Taxation Convention Between Developed and Developing Nations* (UN Model) have been used by the Canadian government to develop Canada's tax treaties. The commentary of the provisions of the OECD Model is widely used and accepted as a guide to interpretation of most treaties worldwide. The Canadian courts have identified the OECD Model as an important interpretation tool. In the *Crown Forest Industries Ltd. v. Canada* case, the OECD Model and commentary was considered more than a supplementary source of interpretation and was of "high persuasive value".

Cases: *The Queen v. Crown Forest Industries Limited*, 95 DTC 5389 (SCC)

The tax systems of provincial governments are not bound by tax treaties. Provincial legislation must be reviewed to determine whether treaties or specific articles of the treaties are recognized for provincial tax purposes.

¶19,310 Application of the Treaties

The Canadian taxation of non-residents as covered in this text, has used the domestic law of Canada — the *Income Tax Act* — as its basis. In reality, this income is subject to the treatment provided by the applicable Canadian tax treaty, if any, with the country in which the non-resident resides. In other words, the applicable tax convention has priority over the countries' domestic tax legislation. Where there is a conflict between the Act and the treaty, generally the treaty provision prevails.

The tax conventions between Canada and other countries are relevant for Canadian residents and for non-residents. Canadian residents need to refer to treaties to determine the taxation of their sources of income in the foreign country and relief available from double taxation in Canada. Non-residents need to determine the taxation of their sources of income in Canada and relief available from double taxation in the foreign country. For example, if a Canadian corporation expands its business by establishing a branch in another country, the analysis of the relevant tax convention will be important to determine whether the income from the foreign operation will be taxed in the foreign country. If it will, the analysis will also be important to ensure that relief from double taxation in Canada is available. Furthermore, the opening of a branch in another country could imply the transfer of some employees. These employees, in certain circumstances, will become non-residents of Canada. The convention will be important with respect to determining how their Canadian-source income, if any, will be taxed in Canada.

It is well recognized that tax conventions do not levy income taxes but limit the tax otherwise assessed by the contracting countries. The following citation is found in the analysis by the Supreme Court of Canada in the tax case, *The Queen v. Melford Developments Inc.*: "It is well to remind ourselves in analyzing these statutes and the subtended tax Agreement that the international Agreement does not itself levy taxes but simply authorizes the contracting parties, within the terms of the Agreement, to do so".

Cases: *Her Majesty The Queen v. Melford Developments Inc.*, 82 DTC 6281 (SCC)

When dealing with international transactions, the practice requirement is to first examine the *Income Tax Act* to determine whether an income item is taxable. If it is established to be taxable under the Act, then the appropriate tax convention should be consulted to determine in which country it is taxable and at what tax rate.

The Canada–U.S. Tax Convention contains articles commonly used in Canada's tax treaties. The application of selected articles from the Convention is highlighted as follows:

Article I — Personal Scope: The treaty is only applicable to residents of one or both countries.

Article IV — Residence: This article defines the meaning of the term "resident of a Contracting State" for the purpose of Article I. The article also includes what is commonly referred to as a tiebreaker rule. It determines the residency status of a person where the person is a resident of both Canada and the United States under each country's respective domestic law.

Article V — Permanent Establishment: This article is used in conjunction with Article VII. (See discussion at ¶19,120.)

Article VII — Business Profits: Business profits are taxed only in the country of residence unless the business is carried on through a permanent establishment in the other country. Business profits attributable to the permanent establishment are taxed in the other country. This provision can override Canada's jurisdiction to tax income from carrying on business in accordance with subsection 2(3) of the Act where a U.S. resident is carrying on business but does not have a permanent establishment in Canada.

Article IX — Related Persons: The treaty partners are authorized to adjust the amount of "income, loss or tax payable" for arrangements between a person in one state and a related person in another if the arrangements "differ from those that would be made between unrelated persons". Time frames for adjustments are provided. This article is consistent with the transfer pricing provisions in the Act. ITA: 247 [Transfer pricing adjustment]

Article X — Dividends: The 25% withholding tax rate under the Act is limited to 5% if the beneficial owner is a company owning "at least 10% of the voting stock of the company paying the dividends" and 15% in all other cases. The article also limits branch tax to 5% and exempts the first $500,000 of cumulative income from branch tax. ITA: 212 Part XIII Tax

Article XI — Interest: Withholding tax under the Act is eliminated on cross-border interest payments between Canada and the United States. ITA: 212 Part XIII Tax

Article XIII — Gains: Capital gains of U.S. residents on Canadian property are exempt from Canadian tax unless the property is real property situated in Canada, or a share in a Canadian resident corporation or an interest in a partnership or trust, the value of which is derived principally from real property in Canada. Capital gains of Canadian residents on U.S. property are exempt from U.S. tax unless the property is real property situated in the U.S. or a "real property interest" as defined in section 897(c) of the *Internal Revenue Code*, which includes shares of a U.S. corporation meeting an asset-ratio test.

Article XV — Income from Employment: Wages and other employment remuneration earned by a resident of one country for services performed in the other are not taxable in the other country if

- the remuneration is $10,000 or less (in the currency of the other country), or
- the person is present in the other country for 183 days or less in any 12-month period commencing or ending in the year and the remuneration was not paid by or on behalf of a person resident in the other country or borne by a permanent establishment in the other country.

Article XXVI — Mutual Agreement Procedure: Competent authority procedures and notification time limits are outlined for resolving cases with a result that is not in accordance with provisions of the treaty (e.g., double taxation).

The Canada–U.S. Tax Convention includes a technical explanation for each article and is a useful interpretation tool for applying the convention. It reflects understandings reached during the negotiation of the treaty on the meaning of provisions used in the articles. It is important to recognize that these technical explanations are not legally binding. For other

Canadian tax treaties, no technical explanation is provided and reference to the OECD model and UN model commentaries, or case law is necessary for interpretation purposes.

A reference table in the front of Wolters Kluwer's Canadian Income Tax Act with Regulations summarizes in table format the withholding tax rates under the various Canada-foreign country treaties. A quick glance at that table reveals that the 25% withholding rate required under the Act is often reduced under a treaty. ITA: 212 Part XIII Tax

¶19,400 Cross-Border Transactions and Loans

¶19,410 Transfer Pricing

The phrase "transfer pricing" refers to the pricing used by a Canadian taxpayer for transactions with a non-arm's length non-resident person. Transactions can involve goods, services, and/or intangibles. Transfer pricing legislation is designed to ensure that transfer prices between related persons are set at arm's length prices. Without legislation, it would be easy for taxpayers to arrange transfer prices in a manner that would allocate profits to lower tax jurisdictions. ITA: 247 [Transfer pricing adjustment]; Information Circulars: IC 87-2R International Transfer Pricing

In the Canadian *Income Tax Act*, a transfer price for a transaction includes, "a price, a rental, a royalty, a payment for, or for the use, production or reproduction of, property or as consideration for services". A "transfer pricing adjustment" (either income or capital) will result where a taxpayer or partnership and a non-arm's length non-resident participate in a transaction: ITA: 247(1) Definitions

(1) where the terms and conditions differ from those that would apply in an arm's length transaction, or

(2) that would not have been entered into by arm's length persons and the purpose of the transaction was to obtain a tax benefit.

The "transfer pricing adjustment" is whatever is required in terms of adjusting the price used for the transaction or, in the case of (2), above, changing the nature of the transaction to what would have occurred between arm's length persons.

The OECD Transfer Pricing Guidelines recommend a number of transfer pricing methodologies to be used to determine an arm's length price. The traditional transaction methods (TTMs) include the comparable uncontrolled price (CUP) method, the resale price method (commonly used for distributors) and the cost plus method (commonly used for contract manufacturers and service providers). The transactional profit methods (TPMs) include the profit split method and transactional net margin method. The CRA has expressed preference for the use of TTMs over TPMs and view there to be a natural hierarchy in methods with the CUP method being most reliable.

Where an adjustment is made, a penalty is assessable. The penalty is calculated as 10% of the transfer pricing adjustment. The penalty does not apply if the taxpayer made reasonable efforts to determine and use arm's length prices for the transaction. A taxpayer is deemed to have made reasonable efforts if contemporaneous documentation was prepared and includes the information specified in the Act. The documentation must have been prepared by the person's or partnership's tax filing or information return due date for the year and must be provided within three months of a written request from CRA. The penalty also does not apply if the transfer pricing adjustment is less than the lesser of 10% of the taxpayer's gross revenue for the year and $5 million. ITA: 247(3) Penalty, 247(4) Contemporaneous documentation

Example Problem 19-9

A Canadian importer (Canco) purchases goods from an arm's length U.S. supplier at a price of C$30/unit. The Canadian company's gross annual revenue is $6 million. The Canadian importer incorporates a subsidiary (BCo) in a low tax jurisdiction. The U.S. supplier begins to sell the goods to BCo at the C$30/unit price. The Canadian importer purchases the goods from BCo at a price of C$40/unit. The goods are shipped directly to the Canadian importer's customers.

REQUIRED

(1) Will a transfer pricing adjustment apply to Canco?

(2) Will a penalty apply to Canco?

SOLUTION

(1) Canco and BCo are related persons and therefore deemed non-arm's length for purposes of the Act. The terms of the transactions between Canco and BCo do not appear to be at arm's length. The CRA is likely to adjust the cost of sales of Canco to an amount that reflects an arm's length price and increase taxable income of the Canadian company. The arm's length price is likely the C$30/unit, unless Canco can prove that a comparable uncontrolled price is at a higher amount, i.e., Canco can purchase the same product from an arm's length supplier at the higher price. ITA: 251(1) Arm's length

(2) A penalty will apply if the transfer pricing adjustment is greater than $600,000 (10% of $6,000,000) unless Canco can produce contemporaneous documentation supporting the pricing used within three months of a written request from the CRA.

Where a Canadian company has overpaid for goods, services, or intangibles purchased from a non-arm's length non-resident, the resulting transfer pricing adjustment (overpayment) will be deemed to be a dividend paid immediately before the end of the tax year of the adjustment. The deemed dividend represents the benefit conferred on the non-resident and is subject to Part XIII tax. However, an overpayment to a foreign affiliate (as defined in ITA section 17) of a Canadian company will not be subject to Part XIII tax. ITA: 247(12) Deemed dividends to non-residents, 212(2) Tax on dividends

Where the non-resident person pays an amount to the corporation to repay the Canadian company for the overpayment, the deemed dividend can be reduced by the amount the Minister considers appropriate. Interest applies to the Part XIII tax from the time of the deemed dividend to the time of any repayment of the amount and/or the Part XIII tax is paid. Penalties will not apply for failed withholding tax. ITA: 214(13) Repatriation, 227(8.5) No penalty — certain deemed payments

The normal reassessment period is extended by three years for a reassessment made as a consequence of a transaction involving a taxpayer and a non-arm's length non-resident. ITA: 152(4) Assessment and reassessment

¶19,415 Country-by-Country Reporting

The Organisation for Economic Co-Operation and Development (OECD) and the G20 have been working to address base erosion and profit shifting (BEPS). BEPS are tax planning arrangements undertaken by multinational enterprises (MNEs) to take advantage of domestic and international tax rules to minimize tax.

The Canadian government requires MNEs to complete country-by-country reports and to file the reports with the tax administration of the ultimate parent entity. The reports provide high-level overviews of the global operations of large MNEs for use primarily in transfer pricing reviews and effective risk assessment. The ultimate Canadian resident parent entity of an MNE group (as defined) must file a country-by-country report in prescribed form within 12 months of the end of the reporting fiscal year. The filing requirement only applies if the MNE group has consolidated group revenue of at least 750 million euros. The report will include information on the activities, revenue, profit, tax paid, stated capital, accumulated earnings, number of employees, and tangible assets for each entity in the MNE group.

ITA: 233.8 Country-by-country report — definitions; Forms: RC4649 Country-by-Country Report

If the ultimate parent entity of an MNE group is outside Canada in a country that does not have country-by-country reporting or a qualifying competent authority agreement in effect with Canada, a Canadian entity in the group will be required to report under the rules. Such a corporation is referred to as a constituent entity. An exception applies where the MNE group has designated a corporation in the group to be a surrogate corporation for filing country-by-country reports and that corporation is resident in a country that requires country-by-country reporting and has a qualifying competent authority agreement with Canada.

Once received, the CRA will automatically exchange the report with jurisdictions of subsidiaries in the group that have implemented country-by-country reporting.

Penalties apply if the report is not filed as required.

ITA: 162(7) Failure to comply, 162(10) Failure to furnish foreign-based information

¶19,420 Corporate Debt Owed to a Non-Resident — Inbound Loans

Ⓐ ¶19,425 Thin Capitalization

Interest on loans used to earn income from business or property is deductible in computing taxable income of a Canadian corporation. The tax deductibility of interest creates a preference for debt over equity for non-residents financing Canadian operations, particularly where tax rates are lower in the lending jurisdiction.

ITA: 20(1)(c) Interest, 18(4) Limitation on deduction of interest; Interpretation Bulletins: IT-59R3 Interest on Debts Owing to Specified Non-Residents (Thin Capitalization)

The "thin capitalization rules" are a set of rules designed to discourage non-resident shareholders, who hold significant equity positions in a Canadian corporation from removing profits of that corporation by way of tax deductible interest payments instead of through dividends.

The rules need to be considered any time a Canadian corporation owes an interest-bearing amount to a non-resident. If the non-resident is a "specified non-resident", there is a potential limitation to the interest deduction on the debt. A specified non-resident includes:

(a) a specified non-resident shareholder of the corporation, and

(b) a non-resident who is non-arm's length with a specified shareholder of the corporation.

A specified shareholder is a person who either alone or together with non-arm's length persons owns 25% or more of the votes or value of the corporation. Note that the rule applies even if the non-resident does not hold shares in the Canadian corporation if the non-resident is related to a specified shareholder of the Canadian corporation. In such case, that specified shareholder does not have to be a non-resident.

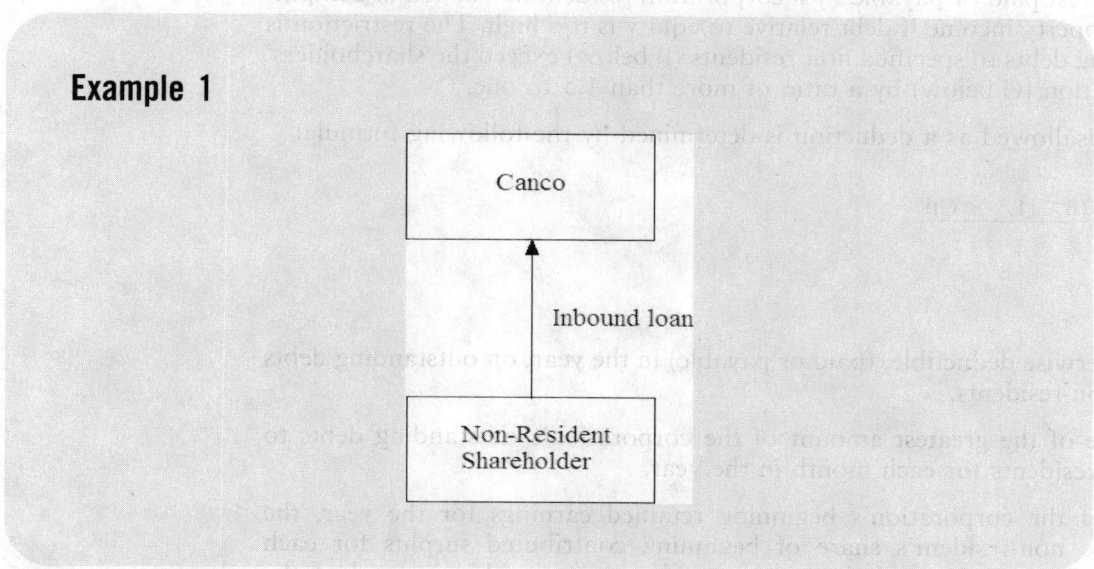

Example 1

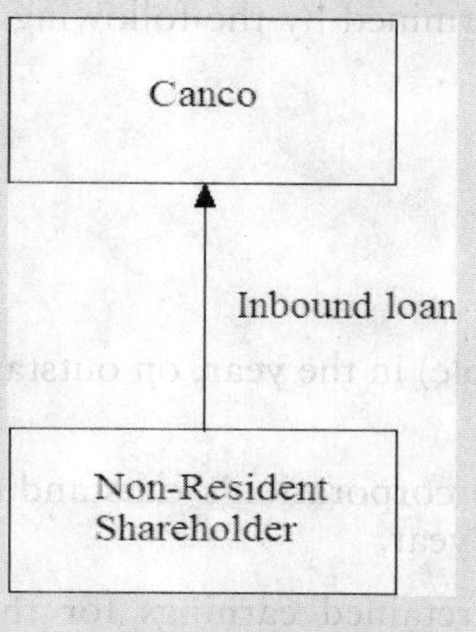

In the above example, assume that the non-resident shareholder holds 25% or more of the shares of Canco. The thin capitalization rules apply to the interest Canco pays on the loan.

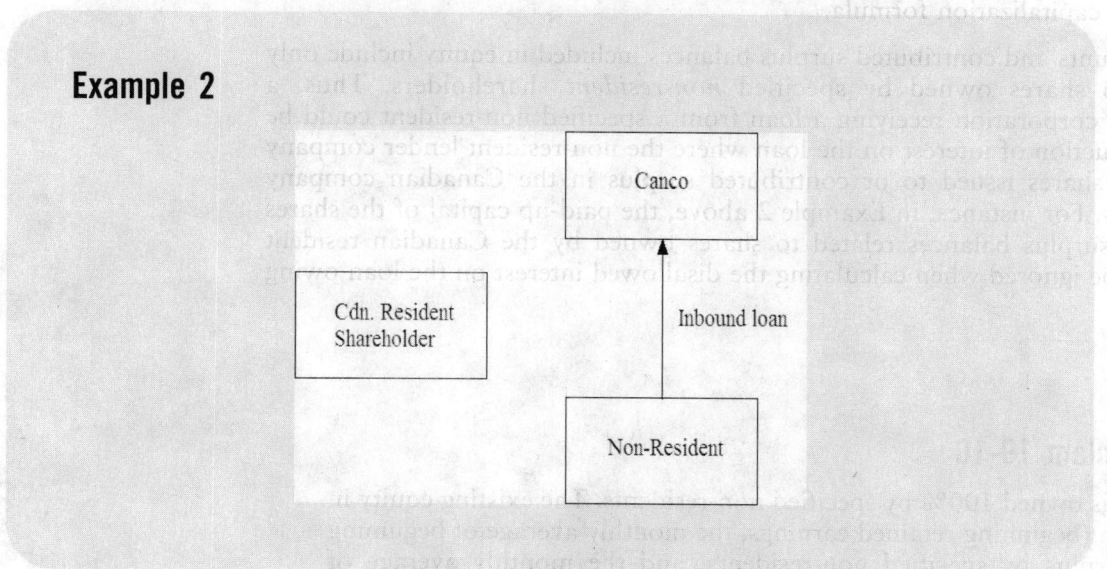

Example 2

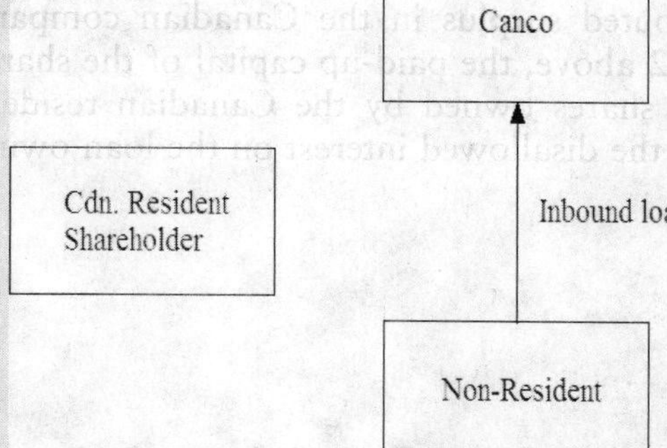

In the above example, assume that the Canadian resident shareholder holds 25% or more of the shares of Canco. It also controls the non-resident corporation that has loaned funds to the Canadian corporation. Assume that the non-resident doesn't own any shares in

Canco. Because the non-resident lender is non-arm's length with a specified shareholder of Canco, the thin capitalization rules apply to the interest Canco pays on the loan. Note that the residency of the shareholder is not relevant (i.e., the Canadian resident shareholder could instead be a non-resident). The thin capitalization rules would still apply.

A formula is used to calculate the interest that is not allowed as a deduction and restricts the deduction for interest paid or payable by a corporation resident in Canada in computing its business or property income if debt relative to equity is too high. The restriction is imposed if outstanding debts to specified non-residents (B below) exceed the shareholders' equity of the corporation (C below) by a ratio of more than 1.5 to one.

The interest that is disallowed as a deduction is determined by the following formula:

$$A \times \frac{(B - (1.5 \times C))}{B}$$

A = Interest otherwise deductible, (paid or payable) in the year, on outstanding debts to specified non-residents.

B = The average of the greatest amount of the corporation's outstanding debts to specified non-residents for each month in the year.

C = The sum of the corporation's beginning retained earnings for the year, the average of the non-resident's share of beginning contributed surplus for each month ending in the year, and the average of beginning paid-up capital of the non-resident's shares for each month ending in the year.

Note that only retained earnings of the Canadian corporation deducting the interest is included in C. As a result, unconsolidated financial statements of the legal entity need to be used for the thin capitalization formula.

Paid-up capital amounts and contributed surplus balances included in equity include only amounts related to shares owned by specified *non-resident* shareholders. Thus, a lower-tier Canadian corporation receiving a loan from a specified non-resident could be restricted in the deduction of interest on the loan where the non-resident lender company does not have any shares issued to or contributed surplus in the Canadian company borrowing the funds. For instance, in Example 2 above, the paid-up capital of the shares or the contributed surplus balances related to shares owned by the Canadian resident shareholder would be ignored when calculating the disallowed interest on the loan owing to the non-resident.

Example Problem 19-10

Canada Corp. is owned 100% by specified non-residents. The existing equity in the corporation (beginning retained earnings, the monthly average of beginning contributed surplus by specified non-residents, and the monthly average of beginning paid-up capital of the specified non-residents' shares) is $200,000. Interest paid in the year on a $1 million debt (average of the greatest amount of debt for each month) due to the specified non-resident shareholders was $125,000 for 2018.

REQUIRED

What is the impact, if any, of the thin capitalization rule on the corporation's 2018 Division B income calculation?

SOLUTION

The maximum interest deduction allowed by Canada Corp. on the debt owing to specified non-residents is limited by the formula provided by subsection 18(4). The denied deductible interest is $87,500, as calculated:

$125,000 interest × ($1,000,000 – 1.5 ($200,000)) / $1,000,000 = $87,500

Therefore, Canada Corp, can deduct $37,500 of interest for the year ($125,000 interest paid – $87,500 non-deductible interest in computing Division B income).

Even short-term increases in debt owing to specified non-residents could result in or increase the non-deductible portion of interest because of the averages used in the formula. Where a thin capitalization problem becomes evident midway through a taxation year, steps can be taken to repay debt, infuse capital, or convert debt to capital to reduce the non-deductible interest.

Subsection 18(4) also applies to debts owed by trusts to specified beneficiaries of a trust and by partnerships of which a Canadian resident corporation is a member. Disallowed interest under the thin capitalization rules is deemed to have been paid as a dividend by the corporation at the end of the tax year for the purposes of Part XIII tax. Penalties for failure to withhold will not apply.

ITA: 214(16) Deemed dividends, 214(17) Deemed interest payments

Ⓐ ¶19,427 Upstream Loans

The upstream loan provisions are designed to tax a loan made by a foreign affiliate of a Canadian company within the corporate group where the lent funds would have been subject to tax had dividends instead been paid to the Canadian parent. The legislation is designed to prevent the avoidance of the Canadian income inclusion and related tax that would arise on dividends paid from hybrid and taxable surplus of foreign affiliates. [See ¶19,530 for a discussion on hybrid and taxable surplus dividends from foreign affiliates.]

ITA: 90(6) Loan from foreign affiliate, 90(15) Definitions

A foreign affiliate is a non-resident corporation in which the Canadian company has an equity percentage of at least 1%, and total equity percentage with related persons of at least 10%.

ITA: 95(1) Definitions for this subdivision

Where a person who meets the definition of a specified debtor receives a loan from a foreign affiliate of a taxpayer resident in Canada, the loan amount defined as the "specified amount" is included in the income of the Canadian taxpayer in the year the loan is received.

A specified debtor is defined to include the taxpayer and a person who is non-arm's length with the taxpayer. It also includes partnerships of which the taxpayer or non-arm's length persons are members. A specified debtor cannot include a controlled foreign affiliate of the taxpayer. A controlled foreign affiliate for purposes of the upstream loan provisions is in general terms a foreign affiliate that is controlled by the taxpayer or controlled by the taxpayer with a group of Canadian residents. A specified debtor also excludes foreign affiliates of the taxpayer meeting specified ownership conditions.

ITA: 90(15) Definitions, 17(5) Anti-avoidance rule — loan through trust

The result is that the provisions will apply where a foreign affiliate of a Canadian corporation makes a loan directly to the Canadian corporation as long as the foreign affiliate is not a controlled foreign affiliate or a foreign affiliate meeting specified ownership conditions.

ITA: 90(15) Definitions; ITR: 5905(13)

Example 1

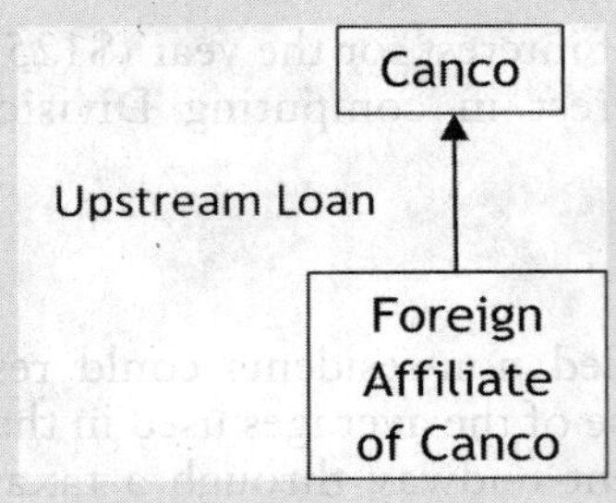

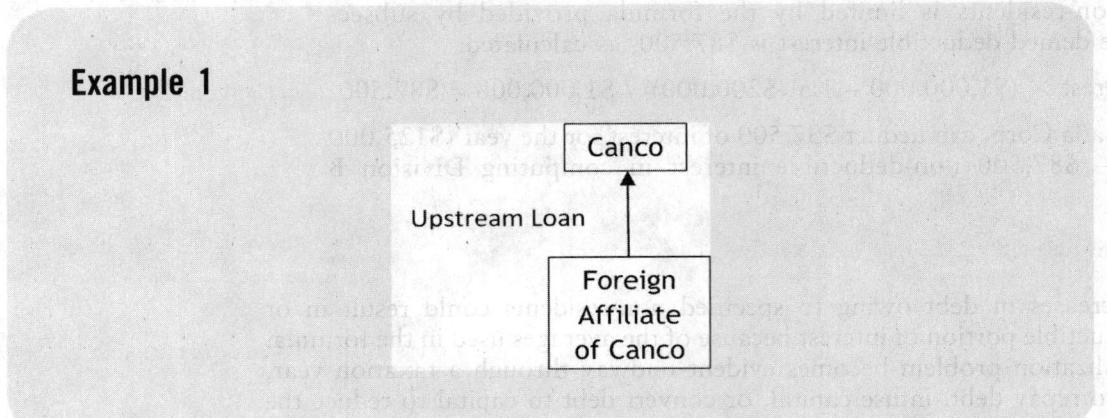

The provisions also apply where the foreign affiliate makes a loan to any person non-arm's length with the Canadian corporation as long as the person is not a controlled foreign affiliate of the Canadian corporation or a foreign affiliate meeting specified ownership conditions.

Example 2

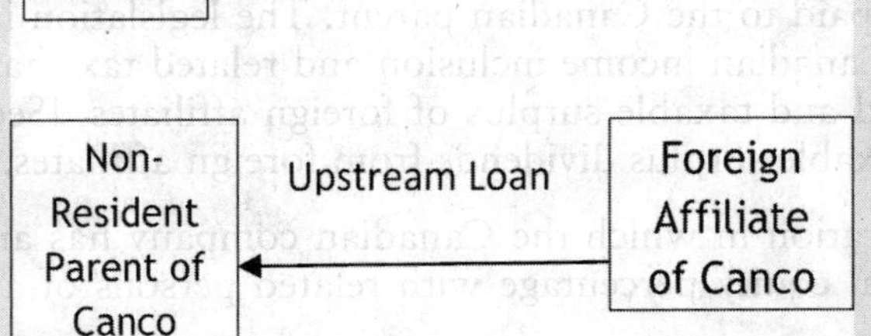

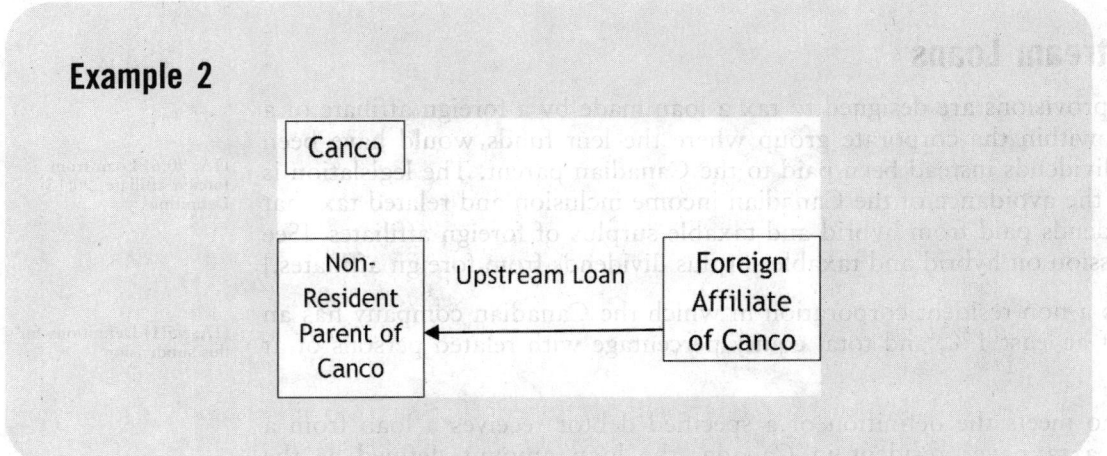

The specified amount included in the income of each Canadian taxpayer with an interest in the foreign affiliate providing the loan is determined based on its surplus entitlement percentage in the foreign affiliate. Where there is only one class of share of the foreign affiliate, the surplus entitlement percentage is the Canadian company's equity interest in the foreign entity. In the above examples, if Canco has a 15% interest in the foreign affiliate, 15% of the loan amount would be included in Canco's income in the year of the loan. Note that in Example 2, even though the loan is entirely outside of Canada, an income inclusion to the Canadian company can result.

The loan is only included in the income of the Canadian taxpayer if it is not repaid within two years of the date the loan was made. Therefore, short-term loans by foreign affiliates are not caught by the rules. Thus, in both of the above examples if the loan is repaid within two years the Canadian company will not have an income inclusion. There is also no income inclusion for debt that arose in the ordinary course of business of the creditor where *bona fide* arrangements for repayment within a reasonable time were made at the time of the loan.

ITA: 90(8) Exceptions to subsection (6)

Where there is an income inclusion to the Canadian company, an offsetting deduction can be made based on the exempt, hybrid, taxable surplus balances, and pre-acquisition surplus (up to the adjusted cost base of the shares) of the foreign affiliate. The deduction represents the amount that would have been deductible under Division C if the loan had been paid as a dividend to the Canadian taxpayer. The deductible amount is treated as a reserve and included in income the next year so that there is an annual inclusion/deduction for the period the loan is outstanding. The reserve is intended to allow taxpayers to make loans instead of paying dividends where there is no intention to avoid Canadian tax.

ITA: 90(9) Corporations: deduction for amounts included under subsection (6) or (12), 113(1) Deduction in respect of dividend received from foreign affiliate, 90(12) Add-back for subsection (9) deduction

When repayments of the loan included in the income of the Canadian taxpayer are made, a deduction is available in proportion to the specified amount that was originally included in the income relative to the full amount of the loan. The reserve deduction is not allowed for the portion of the specified amount repaid.

ITA: 90(14) Repayment of loan, 90(13) No double deduction

¶19,430 Corporate Debt Owed by a Non-Resident — Outbound Loans

¶19,435 Cross-Border Shareholder Loans/Balances

In a domestic context, the shareholder loan provisions (per ¶13,080) of the ITA prevent Canadian shareholders of closely held corporations from removing funds from the corporation tax-free through loans instead of through the receipt of dividends taxable under Part I of the Act. Loans caught under the provisions are included in the income of the shareholder as property income.

ITA: 15(2) Shareholder debt

The shareholder loan provisions also apply in a cross-border context to prevent a Canadian corporation from loaning funds to a related non-resident instead of paying a dividend that would be subject to withholding tax under Part XIII. The shareholder loan provisions will result in the loan being deemed to be a dividend for purposes of Part XIII withholding tax. The provision applies where the loan is made to a non-resident shareholder or a non-resident person who is non-arm's length (connected) with a shareholder.[2]

ITA: 214(3)(a)

[2] Other than a foreign affiliate of the corporation (or of a Canadian resident who is non-arm's length with the corporation).

Example 1

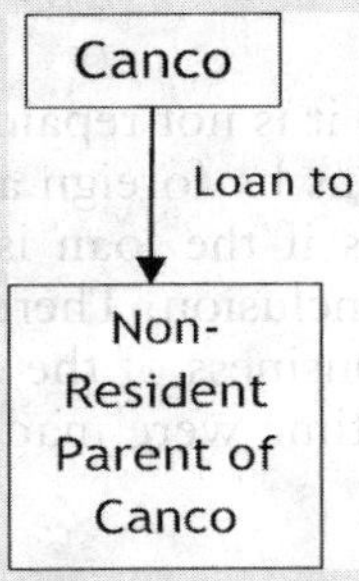

Example 2

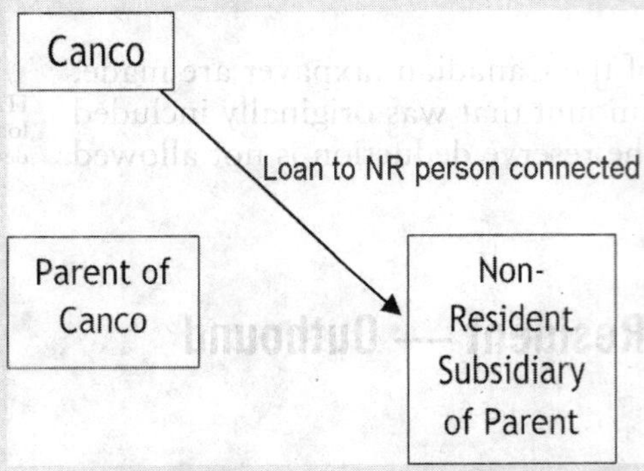

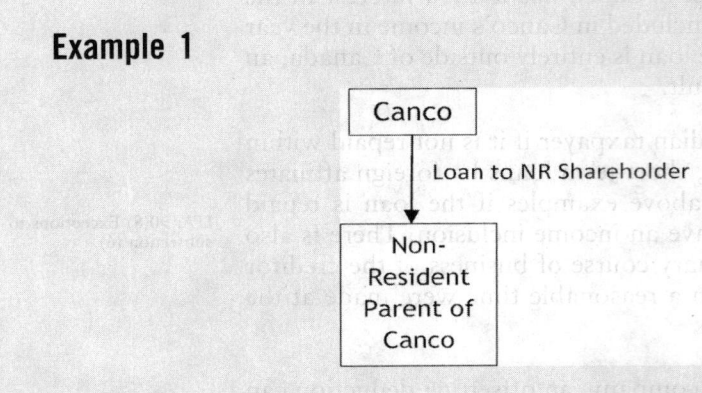

The loan will be deemed to have been paid to the non-resident as a dividend if the balance is not repaid within one year of the end of the taxation year in which the loan was made. Withholding tax will apply to the dividend at the reduced rate (if any) under the applicable treaty. The dividend is deemed to have been paid at the time the loan was made. Administratively, the CRA will calculate the interest on the Part XIII tax from the 15th day of the 13th month following the taxation year of the loan. A refund of the withholding tax may be received upon written application to the CRA within two years after the calendar year in which a repayment of the loan balance is made.

ITA: 227(6.1) Repayment of non-resident shareholder loan

Where a loan is repaid within one year of the end of the taxation year in which the loan is made, the loan balance will not be deemed to be a dividend. However, if the interest rate charged on the loan for the period outstanding is less than the prescribed interest rate, an interest benefit computed at the prescribed rate less interest paid on the loan (by 30 days of the end of the applicable taxation year) will instead be deemed to be a dividend paid to the non-resident and will be subject to Part XIII tax. Similarly, if a refund of Part XIII tax applicable to the loan balance is received because the loan balance was repaid, an interest

ITA: 15(9) Deemed benefit to shareholder by corporation, 80.4(2) Idem, 214(3)(a), 227(6.1) Repayment of non-resident shareholder loan benefit (if any) will be computed on the loan balance for the period the loan was outstanding. Part XIII tax will apply to the interest benefit deemed to be a dividend.

Note that the tax treatment of the shareholder loan in the cross-border context is similar to the tax treatment of a shareholder loan to a Canadian resident individual. For a loan to a Canadian shareholder, if the loan is repaid within one year from the end of the taxation year, there is no income inclusion for the loan balance but the shareholder instead has an income inclusion for an interest benefit (if any) on the loan.

The shareholder loan provisions do not apply to a pertinent loan or indebtedness (PLOI). A PLOI is a loan that was made or debt incurred by a corporation resident in Canada (a CRIC) that is controlled by either the non-resident receiving the loan or by a non-resident who is non-arm's length with the person receiving the loan. For the loan to be treated as a PLOI, the CRIC and the non-resident corporation controlling the CRIC must file an election by the filing due date of the CRIC for the year of the loan. If the election is filed, the loan is not subject to 15(2) and is not deemed to be a dividend. Instead, there is a deemed interest income inclusion for the loan/debt (see ¶19,440). In the above Example 1, the non-resident parent of Canco and Canco could file an election to avoid subsection 15(2). In above Example 2, Canco and the non-resident parent of Canco (who is non-arm's length with the borrower) could file a PLOI election to avoid 15(2).

ITA: 15(2.11) Pertinent loan or indebtedness, 15(2) Shareholder debt, 17.1(1) Deemed interest income — sections 15 and 212.3

Example Problem 19-11

Canco, a Canadian subsidiary of a U.S. parent company (USCo) loans $300,000 of excess cash to USCo in its December 31, 2018 taxation year end and does not charge interest.

REQUIRED

Does subsection 15(2) apply to the loan transaction?

SOLUTION

The $300,000 loan to USCo, a non-resident shareholder, will be deemed a dividend unless the amount is repaid by USCo by December 31, 2019. A 5% withholding tax (the reduced amount under the Canada–U.S. Tax Convention) is owing by Canco on the deemed dividend plus interest computed from January 15, 2020. If USCo repays the $300,000 loan balance in the future, Canco can apply no later than two years after the end of the calendar year of the repayment to receive a refund of the withholding tax.

ITA: 15(2) Shareholder debt, 214(3)(a), 227(6.1) Repayment of non-resident shareholder loan

If the balance is repaid and Part XIII tax refunded, an interest benefit, equal to the prescribed rate applied to the loan for the period it was outstanding, will be deemed to be a dividend subject to Part XIII tax.

If USCo and Canco elect to treat the loan as a PLOI, the loan will not be subject to 15(2) implications. Instead, imputed interest must be computed on the loan balance and included in the Canadian company's income.

ITA: 15(2.11) Pertinent loan or indebtedness, 17.1(1) Deemed interest income — sections 15 and 212.3

¶19,440 Low-Interest Cross-Border Loans/Balances

In addition to potential Part XIII tax implications, loans from Canadian residents to non-residents can also result in a deemed interest income inclusion for the Canadian company. ITA: 17(1) Amount owing by non-resident

To prevent Canadian corporations from avoiding Canadian income taxes by providing capital to non-residents at low or no interest, the Act requires a minimum amount of interest (deemed interest) income to be recognized. This provision only applies to debt that has been outstanding for more than one year.

Where the Canadian resident corporation's income inclusion related to the amount owing from the non-resident is less than a reasonable rate of interest on the balance, the Canadian corporation is required to report interest income using the prescribed rate, less the amount already included in income. Whether interest is computed at a reasonable rate is a question of fact, and has to be measured in market terms after giving consideration to the risk inherent in the loan (i.e., quality of any security or lack thereof).

Example Problem 19-12

Harold Chui is the sole shareholder of CCPC Ltd. and of USCO Inc. CCPC Ltd. has advanced USCO Inc. $100,000 to assist in financing its relatively new operations in Port Huron, Michigan. USCO Inc. does not pay any interest to CCPC Ltd. on this indebtedness, which has been outstanding for more than a year.

REQUIRED

Is this loan of any consequence to CCPC Ltd.'s Canadian taxes?

SOLUTION

Yes, CCPC Ltd. is required to report deemed interest on the $100,000 at the prescribed rate. Assuming a prescribed rate of 2%, CCPC Ltd. will have to report deemed interest income of $2,000 annually. Note that USCO Inc. does not have to be related to CCPC Ltd. for subsection 17(1) to apply. ITA: 17 Amount owing by non-resident

The deemed interest rules do not apply to a loan by a Canadian resident corporation to:

(1) a controlled foreign affiliate if the loan is used for the purpose of earning active business income; ITA: 17(8) Exception

(2) a loan to an unrelated person arising from the sale of goods or services under arm's length terms or conditions; or ITA: 17(9) Exception

(3) a loan if Part XIII withholding tax has been paid on the loan amount as is the case where the shareholder loan provisions discussed in ¶19,435 apply. However, where a refund of the Part XIII withholding tax is received when the loan balance is repaid, the deemed interest rules will apply during the period the loan balance was outstanding. ITA: 17(7) Exception, 227(6.1) Repayment of non-resident shareholder loan, 17(1) Amount owing by non-resident

An anti-avoidance provision prevents the Canadian resident corporation from circumventing the income inclusion resulting from the deemed interest rules by making an indirect loan to a non-resident.[3] The provision applies where a loan or transfer of property (or anticipated loan or transfer of property)[4] by a Canadian resident corporation results in an amount owing between non-residents. In such a case, the non-resident receiving the loan is deemed to owe the amount to the Canadian resident corporation for purposes of determining the income inclusion under the deemed interest rules. The anti-avoidance rule does not apply where:

ITA: 17(2) Anti-avoidance rule — indirect loan, 17(1) Amount owing by non-resident

(1) both non-residents are controlled foreign affiliates of the corporation resident in Canada. For purposes of this exception, a controlled foreign affiliate is controlled by Canadian residents; or

ITA: 17(3)(a), 17(15) Definitions

(2) the non-residents are not related and the terms or conditions of the loan between them are arm's length.

ITA: 17(3)(b)

Example Problem 19-13

CCPC Ltd., per Example Problem 19-12, attempts to circumvent the income inclusion under the deemed interest rules by investing the $100,000 in share capital of another corporation, Bermuda Inc., owned by Harold Chui, instead of making a direct loan to USCO Inc. Bermuda Inc. loans the funds interest-free to USCO Inc. The loan is outstanding for more than a year.

ITA: 17(1) Amount owing by non-resident

REQUIRED

What are the income tax consequences of this plan? Assume a prescribed interest rate of 2%.

SOLUTION

The investment in shares of Bermuda Inc. would be considered a non-exempt transfer of property by CCPC Ltd. The anti-avoidance provision would deem USCO Inc. to owe the $100,000 to CCPC Ltd. CCPC Ltd. would report interest income of $2,000. USCO Inc. is not a controlled foreign affiliate of CCPC Ltd., and USCO Inc. and Bermuda Inc. are related persons so neither of the exceptions would apply.

ITA: 17(2) Anti-avoidance rule — indirect loan, 17(3) Exception to anti-avoidance rule — indirect loan

If the loan or debt is owing to a Canadian-resident corporation that is a CRIC and an election is filed to treat the loan/debt as a PLOI, the deemed interest rule under subsection 17(1) does not apply. Instead, the interest inclusion is computed at the greater of:

ITA: 17.1(1) Deemed interest income — sections 15 and 212.3, 15(2.11) Pertinent loan or indebtedness, 212.3(11) Pertinent loan or indebtedness; ITR: 4301(b.1)

(1) the amount of interest computed on the balance using a high prescribed rate of interest (4% higher than the prescribed rate under 17(1)), and

(2) interest payable on a balance owing by the CRIC that can reasonably be considered to have been used to fund the loan.

[3] Similar anti-avoidance provisions apply for loans through and to partnerships and through trusts.

[4] Other than an exempt loan or transfer defined in subsection 17(15).

Any interest received by the CRIC on the loan reduces the amount included in the CRIC's income.

If the interest payable on a debt obligation of a CRIC used to fund a loan or debt to a non-resident is higher than the income inclusion that is computed using the high prescribed rate, the interest deduction will be entirely offset. This mechanism eliminates any interest deduction benefit gained by a foreign-owned Canadian entity borrowing to fund loans to a non-resident.

Example Problem 19-11 Revisited

Canco, a Canadian subsidiary of a U.S. parent company (USCo), with a December year end, loans $300,000 of excess cash to USCo on December 1, 2018 and does not charge interest. Canco's combined corporate tax rate is 27%.

REQUIRED

(1) Will Canco have a deemed interest income inclusion for the loan if the loan is not elected to be a PLOI? Will 15(2) apply? Assume the loan is repaid on December 15, 2019.

(2) Will Canco have a deemed interest inclusion for the loan if the loan is elected to be a PLOI? Assume the loan is repaid January 15, 2020. Will 15(2) apply?

SOLUTION

(1) If the loan is not elected to be treated as a PLOI, there will be an income inclusion for Canco for interest computed at the prescribed rate of 1% from the time the loan was made until December 15, 2019 because the debt has been outstanding more than a year. There will also be a deemed dividend subject to Part XIII tax equal to the interest benefit computed at the prescribed rate of 1% for the period the loan was outstanding. Subsection 15(2) will not apply because the loan is repaid within one year of the end of the taxation year end in which the loan was made.

ITA: 17(1) Amount owing by non-resident, 15(9) Deemed benefit to shareholder by corporation, 214(3)(a)

Canco will therefore incur the following:

	Interest Income Inclusion 17(1)	Part I Tax at 27%	Deemed Dividend	Part XIII Tax at 5%
2018	$ 247[(1)]	$ 67	$ 247[(1)]	$ 12
2019	$2,868[(2)]	$774	$2,868[(2)]	$143
Total		$841		$155

NOTES TO SOLUTION

(1) 2018 — 30/365 × 1% × $300,000

(2) 2019 — 349/365 × 1% × $300,000

(2) Subsection 15(2) would apply to the loan because it is not repaid within one year of the end of the taxation year end in which the loan is made. This would result in a deemed dividend subject to Part XIII tax of $15,000 owing by Canco for 2018. However, 15(2) does not apply where the loan is elected to be treated as a PLOI. If the loan is elected to be treated as a PLOI, instead there will be an income inclusion for Canco for interest computed at a prescribed rate of 5% from the time the loan was made until repaid January 15, 2020. There will still be a deemed dividend subject to Part XIII tax on the interest benefit computed at the prescribed rate of 1% for the period the loan was outstanding.

ITA: 17.1(1) Deemed interest income — sections 15 and 212.3, 15(2.11) Pertinent loan or indebtedness, 15(9) Deemed benefit to shareholder by corporation, 214(3)(a)

Canco will therefore incur the following:

	Interest Income Inclusion 17.1(1)	Part I Tax at 27%	Deemed Dividend	Part XIII Tax at 5%
2018	$ 1,233[(1)]	$ 333	$ 247[(4)]	$ 12
2019	$15,000[(2)]	$4,050	$3,000[(5)]	$150
2020	$ 616[(3)]	$ 166	$ 123[(6)]	$ 6
Total		$4,549		$168

NOTES TO SOLUTION

(1) 2018 — 30/365 × 5% × $300,000

(2) 2019 — 5% × $300,000

(3) 2020 — 15/365 × 5% × $300,000

(4) 2018 — 30/365 × 1% × $300,000

(5) 2019 — 1% × $300,000

(6) 2020 — 15/365 × 1% × $300,000

Note that the cost to the Canadian company will be lower with the PLOI election (tax of $4,549 + $168 = $4,717 vs. $15,000 of Part XIII withholding tax).

Note also that the repayment of the loan before December 31, 2019 in (1) above results in a significantly lower overall tax liability of $841 + $155 = $996 vs. $4,717.

Ⓐ ¶19,450 Foreign Affiliate Dumping

The foreign affiliate dumping provisions were added to the ITA to address erosion of the Canadian tax base by Canadian subsidiaries of foreign-based multinational groups. Without the dumping provisions, erosion of the tax base can arise due to interest deductions in Canada on funds borrowed by the Canadian entity to invest in a foreign affiliate in combination with the exempt treatment of dividends received by Canadian companies from foreign affiliates. The provisions are far-reaching and should be considered any time a Canadian corporation controlled by a non-resident has financial transactions with non-resident corporations.

ITA: 212.3 [Foreign affiliate dumping], 212.3(2) Foreign affiliate dumping — consequences

The dumping provision applies where a corporation resident in Canada (CRIC) controlled by a non-resident corporation invests in a company that is a foreign affiliate of the CRIC or of a Canadian corporation that is non-arm's length with a CRIC. The CRIC is deemed to have paid a dividend to the foreign parent company equal to the fair market value of the following amounts if they can reasonably be considered to relate to the investment in the foreign affiliate:

(1) Any property (other than shares of the CRIC) transferred by the CRIC,

(2) Any obligation assumed or incurred by the CRIC,

(3) Any benefit otherwise conferred by the CRIC, or

(4) Any property transferred to the CRIC to reduce an amount owing to the CRIC.

The consequence of the deemed dividend is that the CRIC will incur a Part XIII withholding tax liability related to the amount. In computing the paid-up capital of the shares of the CRIC, there is also a deduction for any increase in the paid-up capital of the CRIC's shares that relate to the investment. The paid-up capital grind can impact the ability of the CRIC to repatriate funds tax free to the non-resident parent and can also impact the deductibility of interest on inbound loans subject to the thin capitalization rules. However, in specified circumstances the paid-up capital can be reinstated.

ITA: 212(2) Tax on dividends, 212.3(9) Paid-up capital reinstatement

An exception to the deemed dividend and paid-up capital reduction applies where it is possible to demonstrate that:

(1) the investment in the foreign affiliate by the CRIC is a strategic acquisition of a business that is more closely connected to its business than to that of a non-resident member of the multi-national group;

ITA: 212.3(16) Exception — more closely connected business activities

(2) officers of the CRIC (or of a non-arm's length Canadian resident corporation), who are residents and work principally in Canada exercised the principal decision-making authority in respect to making the investment; and

(3) the officers in (2) will have and exercise the ongoing principal decision-making authority in respect of the investment, the majority of the officers will be resident and work principally in Canada and the performance evaluation and compensation of the officers will be based on the results of the operations of the foreign affiliate more so than will be for officers of a non-resident corporation.

This "more closely connected" exception recognizes that not all investments by a CRIC in a foreign affiliate are made for tax planning purposes and provides an exception where the investment in the foreign affiliate occurred for business reasons.

The above exception does not apply where the investment is a preferred share investment in the foreign affiliate.

ITA: 212.3(19) Preferred shares, 212.3(7) Reduction of deemed dividend

The deemed dividend resulting from the debt dumping rules may be reduced by an amount of paid-up capital of the CRIC's shares if an election is filed. This election effectively allows the CRIC the choice of reducing paid-up capital instead of being taxed on a deemed dividend. However, once paid-up capital is eliminated future transfers of property by the CRIC will result in deemed dividends.

An investment in the foreign affiliate can include:

ITA: 212.3(10) Investment in subject corporation, 212.3(18) Exception — corporate reorganizations

(1) An acquisition of shares by the CRIC.

(2) A contribution of capital or benefit conferred by the CRIC.

(3) A transaction resulting in an amount owing to the CRIC other than an amount arising in the ordinary course of business of the CRIC that is repaid within 180 days.

(4) A non-arm's length acquisition of a debt obligation of the foreign affiliate.

An investment in a foreign affiliate does not include a pertinent loan or indebtedness (PLOI). For a debt to meet the definition of PLOI, a joint election between the CRIC and its parent must be filed. If the election is filed, the debt dumping rules do not apply. Instead, such a loan results in an imputed interest income inclusion to the CRIC at a rate 4% higher than the prescribed rate of interest. As noted earlier, if the loan is a PLOI, the income inclusion to the Canadian company is computed under section 17.1 rather than section 17 using the higher prescribed rate.

ITA: 212.3(11) Pertinent loan or indebtedness, 17.1 Deemed interest income — sections 15 and 212.3

Example 1

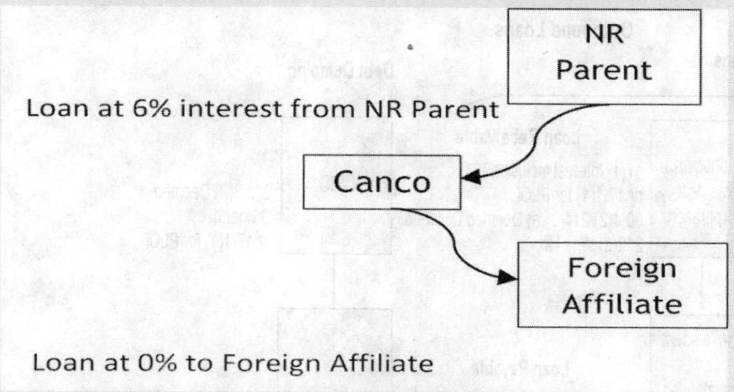

The interest deducted on the loan from the non-resident parent company to Canco is subject to the thin capitalization rules under subsection 18(4). The loan to the foreign affiliate will be subject to the debt dumping rules. It will result in a deemed dividend to the NR parent company subject to Part XIII withholding tax unless an election is made to treat the loan to the foreign affiliate as a PLOI. There will also be a subsection 17(1) interest income inclusion to Canco computed using the prescribed rate of 1% for the period the loan to the foreign affiliate is outstanding.

Where the election is made to treat the loan as a PLOI, there will be an interest income inclusion to Canco computed as the greater of:

- the income inclusion calculated using a prescribed rate of 5% on the loan owing from the foreign affiliate for the period it is outstanding, and
- the interest payable on the loan to the parent company, i.e., 6%.

Overall, the interest income inclusion will offset the interest deduction by Canco, eliminating the tax benefit gained through funding the loan to the foreign affiliate through a Canadian company.

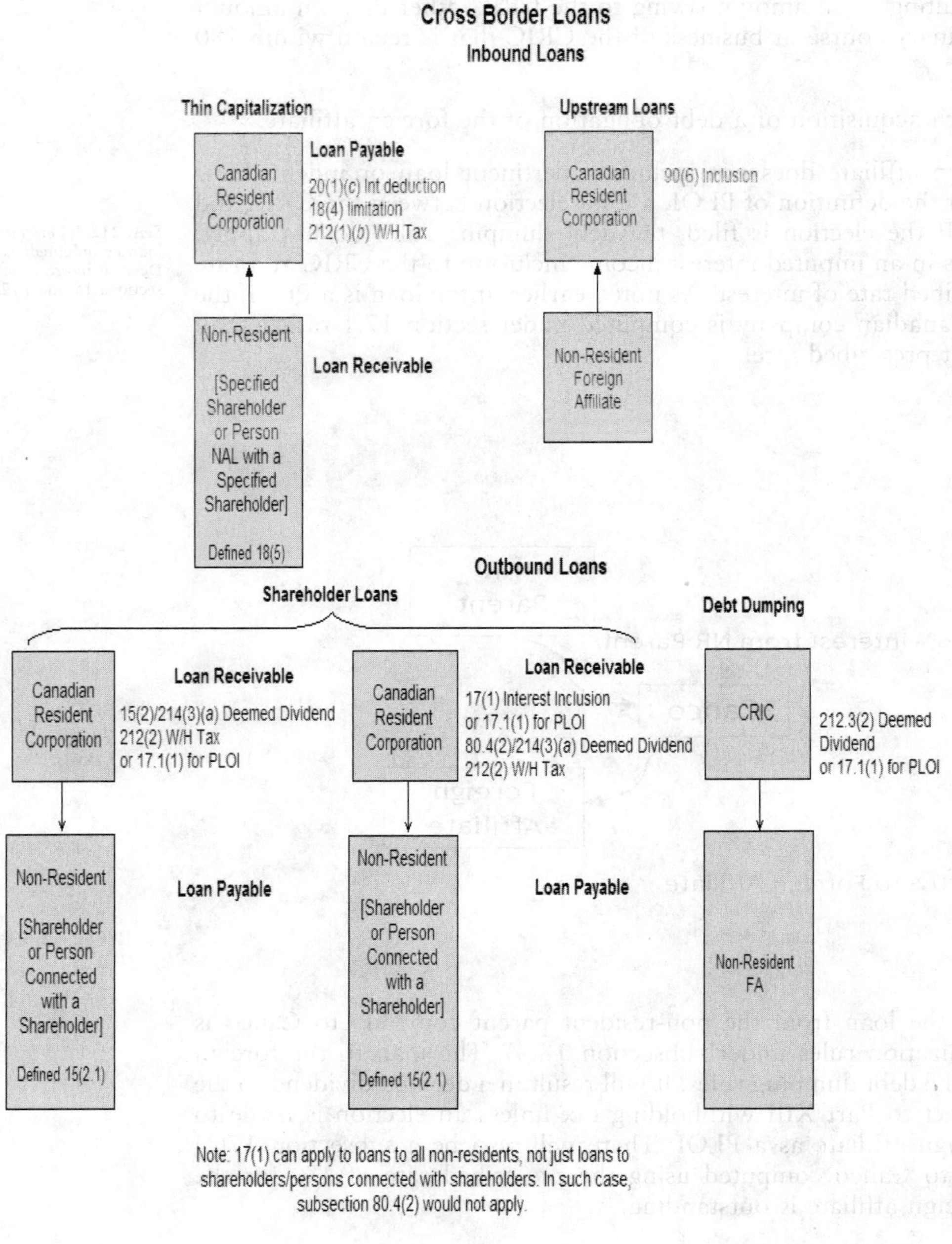

¶19,500 Taxation of Canadian Residents With Foreign Investments

The Canadian tax treatment of investment by a Canadian resident in a foreign country depends on the nature of the investment. The tax treatment of investment in active business activities in a foreign jurisdiction differs from the tax treatment of investment in passive activities.

¶19,510 Active Business Income Earned in a Foreign Jurisdiction

¶19,515 Unincorporated Foreign Branch Operations

Canadian residents are taxable on worldwide income. Consequently, a Canadian resident earning business income in a foreign jurisdiction through an unincorporated branch includes the income in Canadian taxable income computed under Part I of the *Income Tax Act*. If the income is also subject to tax in the foreign jurisdiction after considering the applicable tax treaty, if any, a foreign tax credit (business income tax deduction, described at ¶11,335) can be used to reduce the Canadian Part I tax liability. Any unused tax deduction can be carried back three years and carried forward ten years.

ITA: 126(2) Idem

¶19,520 Individuals Receiving Dividends From Foreign Corporations

A Canadian resident individual earning business income in a foreign jurisdiction through an incorporated entity will not pay tax on the income as it is earned. When dividends are paid from the foreign entity, the dividend is included in income. To prevent double taxation, a foreign tax credit (non-business income tax deduction, described at ¶10,475) for the foreign tax withheld from the dividend and remitted to the foreign taxing authority can reduce Canadian Part I tax. Only tax withheld at a rate of 15% or less can be used to reduce the Part I tax. An individual may deduct any withholding tax in excess of 15% against income from property in computing Division B income. The inability to claim a full foreign tax credit for withholding taxes above 15% reflects the Canadian government's unwillingness to relinquish tax jurisdiction to a foreign country for income subject to withholding tax rates higher than 15%. This can result in double taxation. Canada's tax treaty with the United States addresses this issue of double taxation by resourcing property income to allow a credit in the United States for Canadian tax paid on the income in excess of 15%.

ITA: 12(1)(k) Foreign corporations, trusts and investment entities, 90(1) Dividend from non-resident corporation, 126(1) Foreign tax deduction, 20(11) Foreign taxes on income from property exceeding 15%; Tax Treaties: Cda-U.S. TT: Art. XXIV, par. 5; Income Tax Folio: SS-F2-C1

Alternatively, the individual has the option to claim a deduction for all of the tax withheld on a dividend in computing Division B income instead of using a foreign tax credit to reduce Part I tax. A taxpayer would choose this option in a situation where a foreign tax credit cannot be claimed, for example, where foreign withholding tax applies to income that is considered to be Canadian-source.

ITA: 20(12) Foreign non-business income tax, 126(7) non-business income tax

Note that foreign tax credits are not provided for the underlying foreign corporate tax paid by the foreign corporation on the business income from which the dividend was paid. This lack of cross-border integration results in double taxation.

¶19,525 Corporations Receiving Dividends From Non-Foreign Affiliates

A Canadian resident corporation earning business income in a foreign jurisdiction through an incorporated entity, again, will not pay tax on the income as it is earned. When dividends are paid from the foreign entity to the Canadian corporation, the tax treatment of the dividend depends on whether the dividend is received from a foreign affiliate of the Canadian corporation. A foreign affiliate is a non-resident corporation in which a Canadian resident owns not less than 1% of the shares and not less than 10% of the shares with related persons.

ITA: 95(1) Definitions for this subdivision, 12(1)(k) Foreign corporations, trusts and investment entities, 90(1) Dividend from non-resident corporation, 126(1) Foreign tax deduction

If the foreign entity is not a foreign affiliate of the Canadian corporation, the dividend will be included in income and a full foreign tax credit for the foreign tax withheld can be claimed. Again, no credit is provided for the underlying corporate tax paid to the foreign jurisdiction on the business income earned by the corporation from which the dividend was paid, resulting in double taxation. The corporation has the option to claim a deduction for the tax withheld against income from business or property in computing Division B income instead of using a foreign tax credit to reduce Part I tax.

ITA: 126(7) Definitions, 20(12) Foreign non-business income tax

Example Problem 19-14

Jane Snow, a Canadian resident, received $20,000 in dividend income in 2018 from a 5% investment she owns in her boyfriend's company in Tanzania. Withholding tax of 25% applied to the dividend. Jane also earned Canadian employment income of $60,000 in 2018.

REQUIRED

(1) Compute the tax liability Jane paid on her 2018 income.

(2) What option exists regarding the tax treatment of the withholding tax?

(3) What would change if the share investment had been held by Jane's Canadian corporation?

SOLUTION

(1)

Employment income	$60,000
Property income	$20,000
Subsection 20(11) deduction (withholding tax in excess of 15% of dividend)	$(2,000)
Taxable income	$78,000

Federal tax:

15% of $45,605	$6,841
20.5% of $32,395	$6,641
	$13,482

Tax credits:

Personal (15% of $11,809)	$(1,771)
Employment (15% of $1,195)	$(179)
CPP (15% of $2,594)	$(389)
EI (15% of $858)	$(129)
Part I tax payable	$11,014
Foreign tax credit	$(2,824)
Federal tax payable	$8,190

Foreign tax credit calculation:

Lesser of:

(a) Non-business income tax paid to a foreign country = $3,000 ($20,000 × 15% limit)

(b) [Net non-business foreign income included under Division B/Total income included under Division B] × tax otherwise payable under Part I

($20,000/$78,000) × $11,014 = $2,824

(2) Jane could claim a deduction for the full amount of the withholding tax of $5,000 under subsection 20(12). However, this alternative would only make sense where a full foreign tax credit was not available, i.e., she would save tax of only $615 (20.5% of 3,000) through a deduction compared to $2,824 available as a foreign tax credit.

(3) If the dividend was received by a Canadian corporation, the dividend would be included in the computation of Division B income. A Division C deduction would not be available because the dividend is from a corporation that is not a foreign affiliate of the Canadian corporation. Taxable income would be subject to a federal corporate tax rate of 38.67% (38% – 10% + 10 ⅔%). A foreign tax credit would be available under subsection 126(1) of the lesser of:

ITA: 12(1)(k) Foreign corporations, trusts and investment entities

(a) Non-business income tax paid to a foreign country = $5,000

(b) [Net non-business foreign income included under Division B/Income included under Division B] × tax otherwise payable under Part I

($20,000/$20,000) × $7,733 = $7,733

¶19,530 Corporations Receiving Dividends From Foreign Affiliates

If the corporation paying the dividend is a foreign affiliate of the Canadian resident corporation, the tax treatment of the dividend depends on whether the dividend is paid out of exempt surplus, hybrid surplus, taxable surplus, or pre-acquisition surplus as defined by Regulation. The dividend will be included in income and offsetting Division C deductions will be claimed depending on the classification of the income from which the dividend is determined to have been paid.

ITA: 12(1)(k) Foreign corporations, trusts and investment entities, 90(1) Dividend from non-resident corporation, 113(1) Deduction in respect of dividend received from foreign affiliate; ITR: 5907(1)

Exempt surplus

Exempt surplus dividends are fully deductible under Division C. The exemption for dividends paid from exempt surplus results in the income being taxed at foreign country rates. Canada has relinquished its jurisdiction to tax this type of income. Exempt surplus includes:

ITA: 113(1) Deduction in respect of dividend received from foreign affiliate, 95(1) excluded property; ITR: 5907(1)

(1) Active business income earned in countries with which Canada has a tax convention or a comprehensive tax information exchange agreement (TIEA), i.e., designated treaty countries,

(2) Capital gains on the disposition of property used or held by the foreign affiliate principally for the purpose of gaining or producing income from an active business carried on by it in a designated treaty country,

(3) 50% of capital gains (representing the non-taxable portion) on properties used or held principally to gain or produce active business income but **not** in a designated treaty country.

Thus, dividends paid from the non-taxable portion of gains are not taxed in Canada. This treatment is consistent with the tax treatment of the non-taxable portion of gains realized on the disposition of properties held directly by Canadian residents.

Hybrid surplus

Hybrid surplus includes capital gains on the disposition of shares of foreign affiliates and partnership interests. 100% of capital gains on the disposition of shares of foreign affiliates is included in hybrid surplus where the shares are excluded property (see ¶19,530.10). When a hybrid surplus dividend is paid, half of the dividend (representing the non-taxable portion of gains) is fully deductible. Therefore, consistent with the treatment of capital gains in Canada, the non-taxable portion of the gain is received tax free by the Canadian company when a dividend is paid from hybrid surplus. The Division C deduction for the other half of the dividend relates to 50% of the underlying tax paid by the foreign entity on the gain and 50% of the foreign withholding tax on the dividend. The "relevant tax factor" is used to convert the tax to a deduction. Therefore, the other half of the gain is taxed at Canadian tax rates when paid as a dividend from hybrid surplus to the extent that it has not been taxed in the foreign country.

ITA: 113(1)(a.1); ITR: 5907(1) hybrid surplus

Taxable surplus

Taxable surplus earned by a foreign affiliate includes:

(1) active business income earned by the entity in a country with which Canada does not have a tax convention or TIEA; ITR: 5907(1)

(2) foreign accrual property income (FAPI), including taxable capital gains on the disposition of shares of a foreign affiliate that are not excluded property, see ¶19,530.10; and ITA: 95(1) Definitions for this subdivision

(3) 50% of capital gains (representing the taxable portion of the gains) on properties used or held principally to gain or produce active business income in a country that is **not** a designated treaty country.

The Division C deduction for dividends paid from taxable surplus relates to both the underlying tax paid by the foreign entity on the earnings from which the dividend is paid and the foreign withholding tax paid on the dividend. Instead of providing a credit against Part I tax for these amounts, the deduction converts the underlying tax and withholding tax using the "relevant tax factor" to a deduction against income. The deduction represents the portion of the income that has been taxed in the foreign country. The end result is that the dividend is taxed at Canadian rates and double taxation is prevented through a deduction related to the underlying tax and withholding tax paid to the foreign jurisdiction.

ITA: 95(1) Definitions for this subdivision, 113(1)(b), 113(1)(c)

Ordering

Where a foreign corporation has exempt, taxable, and hybrid surplus balances, dividends are considered to be paid in the order of exempt surplus, hybrid surplus, taxable surplus, and pre-acquisition surplus. Pre-acquisition surplus dividends represent a return of investment and are fully deductible and thus non-taxable. Pre-acquisition surplus dividends are deducted from the adjusted cost base of shares of a foreign affiliate. If the dividend exceeds the adjusted cost base, a capital gain results.

ITA: 113(1)(d), 40(3) Deemed gain where amounts to be deducted from adjusted cost base exceed cost plus amounts to be added to adjusted cost base; ITR: 5901(1)

A taxpayer can elect to have dividends paid from exempt, hybrid, and taxable surplus to instead be paid from pre-acquisition surplus. A capital gain arising from such an election will automatically be treated as a dividend from exempt surplus, hybrid surplus, and taxable surplus in that order. This prevents the election being used to convert hybrid or taxable surplus to a capital gain. The election must be filed by the filing due date for the tax year the dividend is paid.

ITA: 40(3) Deemed gain where amounts to be deducted from adjusted cost base exceed cost plus amounts to be added to adjusted cost base, 93(1) Election re disposition of share of foreign affiliate, 93(1.1) Application of subsection (1.11), 93(1.11) Deemed election; ITR: 5901(2)(b)

A Canadian-resident corporation earning a dividend from a foreign affiliate cannot claim a foreign tax credit for the foreign withholding tax on the dividend. ITA: 126(1) Foreign tax deduction

The surplus distribution rules for the following types of income earned by a foreign affiliate can be summarized as follows: ITA: 95(1) non-qualifying country, non-qualifying business

- Active business income earned by a corporation in a foreign jurisdiction is exempt from tax in Canada in the case of business income earned in a designated treaty country.
- The non-taxable portion of capital gains and the taxable portion of capital gains on dispositions of property used in an active business in a designated treaty country by a foreign affiliate are exempt from tax in Canada.

- Canadian tax is paid on the taxable portion of gains on the disposition of shares of a foreign affiliate but is deferred until dividends are paid to Canada (unless included in FAPI).
- Canadian tax is paid on active business income earned in non-treaty, non-TIEA countries but is deferred until dividends are paid to Canada.

Example Problem 19-15

Canco, a Canadian resident corporation, holds a 50% common share interest in two foreign subsidiaries. Both subsidiaries were incorporated in 2005. Canco was issued the common shares at the time of incorporation of the subsidiaries. Subsidiary A is located in the United States and is a furniture manufacturer earning 100% business income. Subsidiary B is located in Guatemala and produces textiles used by Subsidiary A. In its December 31, 2018 taxation year end, Subsidiary A paid a dividend of C$60,000 to Canco. Subsidiary A withheld tax at 5% from the dividend. Subsidiary A pays tax at a rate of 18% on its earnings.

In the same year, Subsidiary B paid a dividend of C$50,000 to Canco. Subsidiary B withheld tax at 10% from the dividend. Subsidiary B pays tax at a rate of 5% on its earnings. Subsidiary B had a taxable surplus balance of C$500,000 on December 31, 2017.

REQUIRED

How will the dividends be treated for tax purposes by Canco? Assume that only active business income has been earned by both subsidiaries since incorporation and both subsidiaries have been profitable each year since incorporation. Unrelated, non-resident persons own the other 50% of shares of each company.

SOLUTION

Subsidiary A and Subsidiary B are foreign affiliates of Canco because Canco owns not less than 10% of the shares of each company. The dividends received by Canco will be included in income. Dividends from Subsidiary A will be considered to have been paid from exempt surplus because the dividend is paid from active business income earned in a country with which Canada has a tax convention. The dividend will be fully deductible. A foreign tax credit will not be available for the 5% withholding tax paid to the U.S. government.

ITA: 90(1) Dividend from non-resident corporation, 113(1)(a)

Dividends from Subsidiary B will be considered to have been paid from taxable surplus because the dividend is paid from active business income earned in a country with which Canada does not have a tax convention or TIEA. The deduction for the underlying tax will be computed as follows:

The "underlying foreign tax" related to the taxable surplus balance is $26,316 computed as $500,000/0.95 – $500,000 = $26,316.[(1)]

ITR: 5907 Interpretation

The "underlying foreign tax applicable" to the $100,000 whole dividend paid by Subsidiary B from taxable surplus is:

ITR: 5907 Interpretation

$26,316 × $100,000/$500,000 = $5,263

The foreign tax applicable to the $50,000 dividend received by Canco is:

$5,263 × $50,000/$100,000 = $2,632 ITR: 5900(d)

The Division C deduction for the underlying tax paid by Subsidiary B on the taxable surplus from which the $50,000 dividend is paid is computed as the lesser of: ITA: 113(1)(b)

(1) $2,632 × (1/(38% – 13%) – 1) = $7,896, and

(2) $50,000

The Division C deduction for the withholding tax paid by Subsidiary B on the $50,000 dividend is the lesser of: ITA: 113(1)(c)

(1) $50,000 × 10% × (1/(38% – 13%)) = $20,000 (withholding tax × the relevant tax factor)

(2) $50,000 – $7,896 = $42,104 (taxable surplus dividend less: par. 113(1)(*b*) deduction)

Overall Canco will pay tax on the following:

Dividends	$110,000
Par. 113(1)(*a*)	$(60,000)
Par. 113(1)(*b*) deduction for underlying tax	$(7,896)
Par. 113(1)(*c*) deduction for withholding tax	$(20,000)
	$22,104
Tax at 25%	$5,526

Note that the result is the same as if the income earned by Subsidiary B from which the dividend was paid was taxed at Canadian rates and a foreign tax credit was provided for the underlying tax paid on that income and withholding taxes paid on the dividend as follows:

Income of Subsidiary B before tax ($50,000/.95)	$52,632
Tax at Canadian rate (25%)	$13,158
Foreign tax credit for underlying tax ($52,632 × 5%)	$(2,632)
Foreign tax credit for withholding tax	$(5,000)
Net tax payable	$5,526

NOTE TO SOLUTION

(1) The taxable surplus balance of $500,000 is net of the underlying foreign tax paid on the company's earnings.

¶19,530.10 Main Components of Surplus Balances

Exempt Surplus	Taxable Surplus	Hybrid Surplus
Active business income in a designated treaty country (treaty or TEIA)	Active business income in a non-treaty/non-TEIA country	Capital gains on dispositions of shares of foreign affiliates that are excluded property*
Capital gains on dispositions of property used in an active business carried on in a designated treaty country	Taxable capital gains on dispositions of property used in an active business carried on in a non-treaty/non-TEIA country	
Non-taxable portion of capital gains on dispositions of properties (not included in hybrid surplus)	Taxable capital gains on dispositions of all other properties (not included in exempt or hybrid surplus)	
	FAPI (including taxable capital gains on dispositions of shares of a foreign affiliate that are not excluded property)*	
Dividends received from exempt surplus of a foreign affiliate	Dividends received from taxable surplus of a foreign affiliate	Dividends received from hybrid surplus of a foreign affiliate

*Excluded property includes property of the foreign affiliate that is used or held principally for the purpose of gaining or producing income from an active business carried on by it. It also includes the capital stock of another foreign affiliate of the taxpayer where all or substantially all of the fair market value of the property of the foreign affiliate is attributable to property that is excluded property. ITA: 95(1) excluded property

Dividends paid by the foreign affiliate reduce the relative surplus balance from which it is paid (i.e., exempt surplus dividends reduce exempt surplus). Surplus balances are cumulative in nature. When a dividend is paid, the cumulative surplus balances at the end of the preceding taxation year end are used to determine the nature of the dividend. Where the whole dividend is paid from more than one type of surplus account, each dividend received by the shareholder will be treated as coming from each surplus account on a *pro rata* basis. For example, if the foreign affiliate pays a $100,000 dividend on its shares and 50% of the dividend is from exempt surplus and 50% is from taxable surplus, a 10% shareholder is treated as having received a $5,000 dividend from exempt surplus and a $5,000 dividend from taxable surplus. ITR: 5900(1)

If a dividend is paid after 90 days from the end of the preceding tax year and under the ordering rule all or a portion of the dividend would be treated as pre-acquisition surplus, a 90-day rule deems the pre-acquisition surplus dividend to have been paid immediately following the end of the taxation year. As a result, the surplus balances at the end of the ITR: 5900(2) year in which the dividend was paid will be considered in regards to the tax treatment of the dividend.

Paid-up capital distributions from foreign affiliates

Where a taxpayer (individual or corporate) receives a *pro rata* distribution in respect of shares of a foreign affiliate (other than on liquidation, dissolution, or on a redemption, acquisition, or cancellation of shares) it is deemed to be a dividend paid on the shares. If, however, the distribution is a reduction of paid-up capital, a qualifying return of capital (QROC) election can be made to exempt the distribution from treatment as a dividend for tax purposes. The QROC amount reduces the adjusted cost base of the shares. In some cases, the adjusted cost base reduction could result in a negative balance treated as a capital gain.

ITA: 90(3) Qualifying return of capital, 53(2)(b) [Amounts to be deducted — Share of non-resident corporation]

A capital gain arising from a QROC election will be subject to an automatic election that treats the capital gain as a dividend from exempt surplus, hybrid surplus, and taxable surplus in that order. This prevents the election being used to convert low-taxed hybrid or taxable surplus into a capital gain.

ITA: 93(1.1) Application of subsection (1.11)

Taxation of Canadian Residents with Foreign Investments
Active Business Income Earned in the Foreign Country.

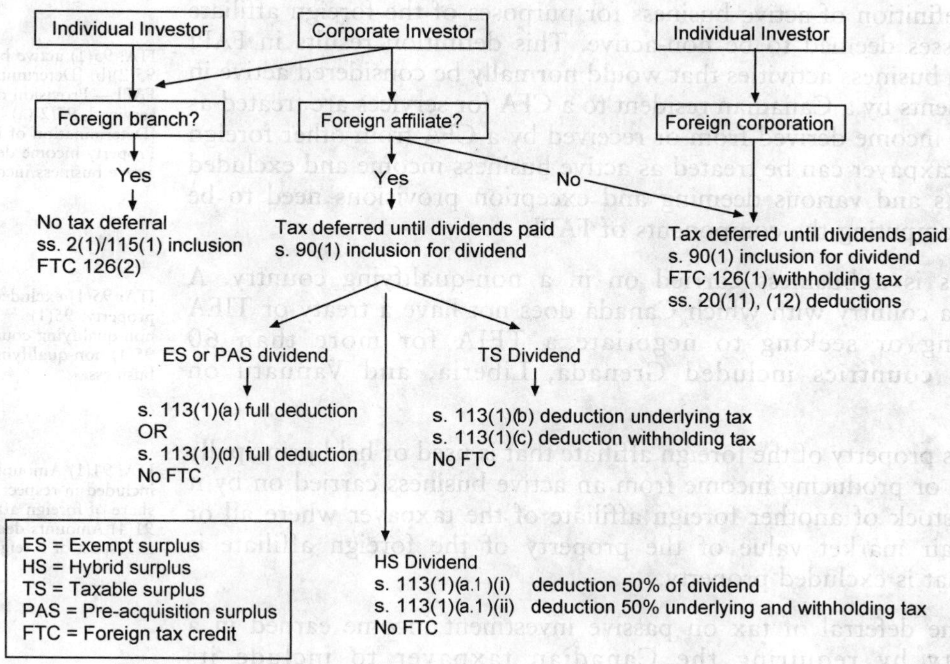

¶19,540 Passive Income Earned in a Foreign Jurisdiction

❹ ¶19,545 Controlled Foreign Affiliates (CFAs)

The foreign accrual property income (FAPI) rules are designed to prevent a Canadian resident taxpayer from avoiding Canadian tax by earning passive investment income in a foreign jurisdiction. Where a Canadian resident individual or corporation holds an interest in a CFA, the participating percentage of the FAPI income earned by the CFA must be included in the Canadian resident's Division B income each year and is subject to Part I tax. FAPI income, in general terms, represents passive investment income earned by the CFA.

ITA: 95(1) Definitions for this subdivision, 91(1) Amounts to be included in respect of share of foreign affiliate

Included in FAPI is:

(1) Income (less losses) from property (including an investment business and adventure in the nature of trade),

(2) Income (less losses) for the year from a business other than an active business,

(3) Income (less losses) for the year from a non-qualifying business, and

(4) Income or taxable capital gains (less losses and allowable capital losses) from the disposition of property that is not excluded property.

The definitions relevant to the computation of FAPI are included in Subdivision i. An investment business includes a business the principal purpose of which is to derive income from property, etc., with exceptions for specific types of businesses (e.g., traders of securities) who employ more than five full-time employees. Note that where structures have been set up to pool assets and employees, the five full-time employees test must be passed at the contributing party level, not at the pooled level.

ITA: 95(1) investment business

Subdivision i includes a definition of active business for purposes of the foreign affiliate rules and excludes businesses deemed to be non-active. This definition results in FAPI inclusions for income from business activities that would normally be considered active in nature. For example, payments by a Canadian resident to a CFA for services are treated as FAPI. Also, some property income derived from or received by a CFA from other foreign affiliates of the Canadian taxpayer can be treated as active business income and excluded from FAPI. The definitions and various deeming and exception provisions need to be reviewed carefully when computing the components of FAPI.

ITA: 95(1) active business, 95(2)(b) [Determination of FAPI — Provision of services], 95(2)(a) [Determination of FAPI — Property income deemed active business income]

A non-qualifying business is a business carried on in a non-qualifying country. A non-qualifying country is a country with which Canada does not have a treaty or TIEA but has been negotiating or seeking to negotiate a TEIA for more than 60 months. Non-qualifying countries included Grenada, Liberia, and Vanuatu on December 31, 2017.

ITA: 95(1) excluded property, 95(1) non-qualifying country, 95(1) non-qualifying business

Excluded property includes property of the foreign affiliate that is used or held principally for the purpose of gaining or producing income from an active business carried on by it and shares of the capital stock of another foreign affiliate of the taxpayer where all or substantially all of the fair market value of the property of the foreign affiliate is attributable to property that is excluded property.

ITA: 91(1) Amounts to be included in respect of share of foreign affiliate, 91(4) Amounts deductible in respect of foreign taxes

The FAPI rules prevent the deferral of tax on passive investment income earned in a controlled foreign entity by requiring the Canadian taxpayer to include its participating percentage of FAPI in income each year. A deduction is available for the underlying foreign tax paid by the foreign entity on the FAPI. The income inclusion, net of

ITA: 92(1) Adjusted cost base of share of foreign affiliate

the deduction, is added to the adjusted cost base of the share investment to prevent double taxation on the disposition of the shares of the CFA.

When the FAPI is fully paid to the investor as a dividend, the previous FAPI inclusions/deductions related to the investment are reversed to eliminate double taxation. When a dividend is paid by the CFA out of FAPI, the dividend is included in income. An offsetting deduction limited to the amount of the dividend income inclusion is available for the amount of previous FAPI inclusions (net of the deductions for underlying tax). If the investor is an individual, a foreign tax credit is provided for the foreign withholding tax on the dividend. If the investor is a corporation, the taxable surplus dividend deduction precedes the FAPI deduction. A foreign tax credit is not available.

ITA: 12(1)(k) Foreign corporations, trusts and investment entities, 90(1) Dividend from non-resident corporation, 95(1) Definitions for this subdivision, 126(1) Foreign tax deduction, 113(1)(b), 113(1)(c)

A CFA is a foreign affiliate of the Canadian resident that is controlled by the Canadian resident alone or together with

(1) persons (foreign or Canadian) who are non-arm's length with the Canadian resident;

(2) up to four Canadian residents (relevant Canadian shareholders) arm's length with the Canadian resident taxpayer;

(3) persons (foreign or Canadian) non-arm's length with relevant Canadian shareholders, or

(4) any combination of (1) to (3).

Example Problem 19-16

Up until the end of 2017, Fred Murphy held stock and mutual fund investments in an investment account with a Canadian bank. In 2017, he earned $32,000 in interest and dividends on the investments. Fred is a resident of Canada and earns income exceeding the highest tax bracket. Fred's brother Joe lives in Florida. Joe incorporated a U.S. entity on January 1, 2018. Fred and Joe each contributed $400,000 and each received 50% of the common shares of the corporation. Fred sold his investments in Canada to make the contribution. The $800,000 of cash was invested by the U.S. entity in a rental condominium in Florida. Joe manages the property and will collect a $100,000 salary from the corporation in 2018. The condo is marketed in Canada and the United States and rented to vacationers throughout the year. Profit from the rental is expected to be $80,000 for 2018. U.S. tax at a rate of 20% will apply to the profit.

REQUIRED

(1) What are the Canadian tax implications of the investment to Fred in 2018?

(2) What are the Canadian tax implications of the investment to Fred in 2019 when the company pays a $64,000 dividend to the shareholders? Withholding tax of 15% will apply to the dividend paid to Fred.

SOLUTION

(1) For 2018, the income earned by the corporation will meet the definition of FAPI. FAPI includes income from property. Income from property includes income from an investment business. An investment business is a business, the principal purpose of which is to derive income from property including rents. The U.S. entity does not employ more than five full-time employees.

ITA: 95(1) Definitions for this subdivision

The U.S. corporation will be a foreign affiliate of Fred because Fred will own not less than 1% of the shares of the corporation and not less than 10% of the shares with related persons. The U.S. corporation is a controlled foreign affiliate because the corporation is a foreign affiliate of Fred that is controlled by Fred and Joe, who is non-arm's length with Fred. As a result, Fred must include 50% of the FAPI in his income for each year. His income inclusion for 2018, will be as follows:

ITA: 95(1) Definitions for this subdivision

ITA: 91(1) Amounts to be included in respect of share of foreign affiliate

ITA: 91(4) Amounts deductible in respect of foreign taxes

Income Inclusion for FAPI 50% of $80,000	$40,000
Deduction for underlying tax	
Lesser of:	
(i) Foreign accrual tax × RTF = $8,000 (20% of $40,000) × 1.9 = $15,200	
(ii) FAPI inclusion $40,000	$(15,200)
2018 Net Inclusion	$24,800

$24,800 will be added to the adjusted cost base (ACB) of the shares held by Fred.

Note that, at the highest personal tax rate of 50%, Fred would pay $12,400 of tax on the net income inclusion. This amount is approximately equal to the personal tax that Fred would pay on his share of the $80,000 of profit of the corporation at the highest personal rate less a foreign tax credit for $8,000 of underlying tax paid by the corporation on Fred's share of income (i.e., 50% × $40,000 – $8,000 = $12,000). The $400 difference is because a relevant tax factor of 1.9 converts the underlying tax to an equivalent Canadian tax using a tax rate of 52.63%.

(2) Fred will receive a dividend of $32,000 in 2019, which will be included in income. He will receive a deduction to reverse the 2018 income inclusion as follows:

ITA: 90(1) Dividend from non-resident corporation

Lesser of:

(a) Dividend from a CFA = $32,000

(b) Net amounts added to the ACB of the share before the dividend was received = $24,800

ITA: 91(5) Amounts deductible in respect of dividends received; Forms: T1134B Information Return Relating to Controlled Foreign Affiliates (2003 and later taxation years), T1135 Foreign Income Verification Statement

The ACB of Fred's shares will be reduced by $24,800 back to the original balance. He will also receive a foreign tax credit for the $4,800 of withholding tax paid on the dividend.

Note that once the income of the corporation is paid as a dividend, the FAPI inclusion is reversed. Overall, the same amount of income has been taxed as though a dividend were paid in the year the income was earned. Instead, the rental income (passive investment income) earned by the foreign corporation and not paid out as dividends until a later year, is taxed in the year it is earned. The FAPI regime prevents a tax deferral on the rental income earned by the CFA.

Note that Fred will also be required to prepare an information form to report the investment in shares of the foreign corporation because the cost amount of the shares exceeds $100,000.

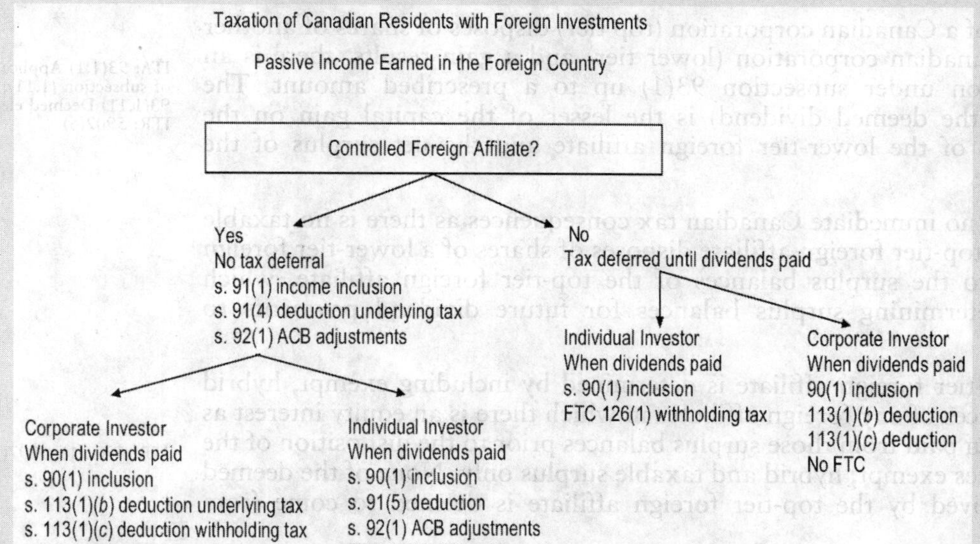

FAPI is taxable surplus for the purpose of subsection 113(1) deductions.

ITR: 5907 taxable earnings

¶19,600 Dispositions of Foreign Affiliates

Ⓐ ¶19,610 Dispositions of Top-Tier Foreign Affiliates

Where a Canadian corporation disposes of the shares of a foreign affiliate, it is possible for all or a portion of the gain on the disposition to be treated as a dividend if an election is filed. The amount designated in the election is deemed to be a dividend and reduces the proceeds of disposition, thereby reducing or eliminating the gain. The dividend is treated in the same manner as a dividend payment from a foreign affiliate and will be considered to be paid out of exempt, hybrid, taxable and pre-acquisition surplus applying the ordering rule.

ITA: 93(1)(a); ITR: 5901(1), 5902 Election in Respect of Capital Gains

The surplus balances of the foreign affiliate being disposed of by the Canadian corporation are deemed to include exempt, hybrid and taxable surplus balances of any lower-tier foreign affiliates as though dividends had been paid from those surplus balances prior to the disposition. This will determine the designated amount available for the election. If all or a portion of the dividend arising from the election is from exempt surplus, the result is a reduction in the gain and taxable capital gain subject to tax in Canada. The election eliminates the need for dividends to be paid from the foreign affiliate prior to the sale of the shares to minimize tax on their disposition.

ITR: 5902(1)

Where a portion of the deemed dividend arising from the election is a pre-acquisition surplus dividend, the adjusted cost base of the shares is reduced. Normally a negative adjusted cost base will result in a capital gain for tax purposes. However, where there is an election under subsection 93(1) such a capital gain is eliminated.

ITA: 40(3) Deemed gain where amounts to be deducted from adjusted cost base exceed cost plus amounts to be added to adjusted cost base, 93(1)(b)

Ⓐ ¶19,620 Dispositions of Lower-Tier Foreign Affiliates

Where a foreign affiliate of a Canadian corporation (top tier) disposes of shares of another foreign affiliate of the Canadian corporation (lower tier) and a gain results, there is an automatic deemed election under subsection 93(1) up to a prescribed amount. The prescribed amount (i.e., the deemed dividend) is the lesser of the capital gain on the disposition of the shares of the lower-tier foreign affiliate and the net surplus of the lower-tier foreign affiliate.

ITA: 93(1.1) Application of subsection (1.11), 93(1.11) Deemed election; ITR: 5902(6)

The deemed election has no immediate Canadian tax consequences as there is no taxable event in Canada where a top-tier foreign affiliate disposes of shares of a lower-tier foreign affiliate. The impact is to the surplus balances of the top-tier foreign affiliate, which becomes relevant for determining surplus balances for future dividend payments to Canadian corporations.

Net surplus of the lower-tier foreign affiliate is determined by including exempt, hybrid and taxable surplus balances of any foreign affiliates in which there is an equity interest as though dividends had been paid from those surplus balances prior to the disposition of the shares. Net surplus includes exempt, hybrid and taxable surplus only. None of the deemed dividend considered received by the top-tier foreign affiliate is deemed to come from pre-acquisition surplus.

ITR: 5902(1), 5907(1)

The deemed dividend will result in adjustments to the respective surplus accounts of the top-tier foreign affiliate, e.g., the exempt surplus portion of the deemed dividend will be added to exempt surplus of the foreign affiliate. The deemed dividend will also reduce the proceeds of disposition and, therefore, the capital gain on the disposition of the shares of the lower-tiered foreign affiliate. The capital gain will again impact the calculation of the surplus balances of the top-tier foreign affiliate. Hybrid or taxable surplus of the top-tier foreign affiliate will be adjusted depending on whether the shares of the lower-tier foreign affiliate being disposed of are excluded property.

¶19,700 Information Reporting

In the mid-1990s, the Canadian government became concerned with the likelihood of Canadian residents owning foreign property and (presumably) not reporting any income on those properties. Taxpayers must disclose on the annual T1 income tax return whether they hold foreign property with a total cost of more than C$100,000.

Where the question is answered affirmatively, a form must be filed with the tax return (or partnership information return). The form requires reporting of the types of property, the cost of the property, and where the property is located. It is the cost of the property that is determinative of the filing requirement. The current value of the property is not relevant. Additionally, and importantly, some foreign property holdings are not included. The two most common exclusions are property held in the course of carrying on an active business and personal-use property (such as a vacation home). Excluded property is not included in the base $100,000 requirement, so for many Canadian tax filers, the reporting is not required. The normal reassessment period is extended by three years if the taxpayer has failed to file form T1135 when required or has failed to report the information required on the form and also failed to report income from the specified foreign property required to be reported. Simplified reporting requirements are available for taxpayers whose foreign property cost less than $250,000.

ITA: 233.3 [Reporting for ownership of specified foreign property], 152(4)(b.2); Forms: T1135 Foreign Income Verification Statement

The form is not the only information return required with respect to foreign properties. Other forms are detailed in the following table.

Other Foreign Property Information Returns Required under the *Income Tax Act*

T106	Non-arm's length transactions with non-residents (Transfer Pricing)
T1141	Transfers or loans to a non-resident trust
T1134A	Non-controlled foreign affiliates
T1134B	Controlled foreign affiliates
T1142	Distributions from and indebtedness to a non-resident trust

Failure to file an information return can result in a penalty of $500 a month (24-month maximum). The February 27, 2018 Federal Budget proposes to change the T1134 reporting deadline from 15 months to 6 months after the end of the taxpayer's taxation year.

ITA: 162(10) Failure to furnish foreign-based information

¶19,750 Offshore Tax Informant Program

The Offshore Tax Informant Program (OTIP) is in place to combat international tax evasion. The program allows the CRA to make financial awards to individuals (Canadian or non-Canadian) who provide information related to major international tax non-compliance that leads to the collection of taxes owing. To be eligible under the OTIP, individuals must provide the CRA with specific and credible details of major international tax non-compliance that lead to additional taxes being assessed and collected. When program requirements are met, the CRA may enter into a contract with the individual that could lead to an award if the potential additional assessment of federal tax, excluding interest and penalties, is more than $100,000. The award is between 5% and 15% of the tax collected.

CHAPTER 20

Goods and Services Tax (GST)/Harmonized Sales Tax (HST)

Learning Goals

Know, Understand and Explain

By the end of this chapter you will know, understand and be able to explain:

- The basic provisions of the *Excise Tax Act* (ETA).
- The general structure of GST/HST.
- The GST/HST implications for various goods and services.
- Who must be registered for GST/HST.
- The GST/HST implications of the two types of supplies: Taxable, which includes zero-rated, and exempt.

Multiple Choice Questions

¶2,825, MCQ 6, in the Study Guide

Exercises

¶4,850, Exercise 14, in the Study Guide

Apply

By the end of this chapter you will know, understand and be able to apply your knowledge and understanding to:

- Calculate the net GST/HST remittable (receivable) by a person.
- Calculate the Employee GST/HST Rebate.

¶20,000 Goods and Services Tax (GST)/ Harmonized Sales Tax (HST)

¶20,010 Overview

According to the CPA Knowledge Supplement, the topic of GST and HST is a level B at the entry level and a level A at the elective level. The intent of the discussion of GST/HST in this chapter is to give you a basic working knowledge of the rules. The rules related to GST/HST can be found in the *Excise Tax Act* (ETA). This book does not attempt to cover all the technical areas that are associated with the GST/HST. The rules related to GST/HST are complex, and it requires significant education to fully understand the implications of every transaction. You are encouraged to do further research as needed in this important area of taxation, which affects virtually every business organization in Canada. The implementation of GST/HST has resulted in substantial work for tax and other accounting professionals.

After working through this chapter, ¶20,000, you will be able to:

- Understand the general structure of GST/HST.

¶20,020 History of GST/HST

The GST was implemented on January 1, 1991 to replace the federal sales tax system, which was riddled with inequities and inconsistent administrative practice, and which often led to distortions in business practices in the Canadian economy. The GST rate, originally introduced at 7%, is now 5%.

The HST is a harmonization of the GST and a provincial sales tax and is adopted at the discretion of the provinces. In return for aligning provincial sales tax rules with GST rules the provinces receive the benefit of having the federal government administer the tax. HST was first implemented on April 1, 1997, in the provinces of Nova Scotia, New Brunswick, and Newfoundland and Labrador at the rate of 15%, subsequently reduced to 13% when the federal GST portion was reduced from 7% to 5%. Prince Edward Island was the last Maritime province to harmonize with the HST system, at the rate of 14% on April 1, 2013.

Since then, deteriorating economic conditions have forced the Maritime provinces to raise the provincial portion of the HST, bringing the rate back up to 15%.

Effective July 1, 2010, Ontario and British Columbia adopted the HST. The HST rate in Ontario is 13%, consisting of an 8% provincial component and a 5% federal GST component, while the HST rate in British Columbia was 12%, consisting of a 7% provincial component and the 5% federal GST component. However, effective April 1, 2013, British Columbia returned to the PST system with a 7% rate in addition to the 5% GST rate. The following is a breakdown of the GST/HST and PST provinces and territories:

Province	**GST**	**PST**	**HST**
British Columbia	5%	7%	-
Alberta	5%	-	-
Saskatchewan	5%	6%	-
Manitoba	5%	8%	-
Ontario	-	-	13%
Newfoundland and Labrador	-	-	15%
New Brunswick	-	-	15%
Nova Scotia	-	-	15%
Prince Edward Island	-	-	15%
Yukon	5%	-	-
Northwest Territories	5%	-	-
Nunavut	5%	-	-

Quebec is not a participating province as such, but Quebec has harmonized the Quebec Sales Tax (QST) with the GST. For all practical purposes, the QST is Quebec's provincial portion of the GST/HST, although it remains administered under a separate provincial legislation.

The HST is administered by the CRA, as is the GST (except in Quebec, which administers both the GST and QST on its territory). Registrants account for GST/HST on a single form. Quebec-based registrants have the option of filing the GST/QST on a single return with the Agence du revenu du Québec (ARQ). QST registrants in other provinces must file their GST/HST with the CRA and their QST return with the ARQ.

¶20,030 Basic Concepts

The GST/HST is a tax on the consumption of goods and services in Canada. It also applies to most supplies of intangible property (e.g., intellectual property) and most real property. The tax is collected by businesses (referred to as "registrants") who make taxable supplies in Canada. GST/HST is collected by registrants throughout the production and distribution chain. Any person who is engaged in a "commercial activity" is required to register and collect GST/HST. This includes persons who carry on business in Canada. "Business" is defined quite broadly in the legislation and generally does not require a profit motive (except for individuals that are registrants). For example, charities and non-profit organizations are required to register if they engage in commercial activities, even if these entities are not subject to income tax.

Goods that are imported into Canada may be subject to GST or HST at the time of importation, and persons who acquire services or intangible personal property outside of Canada may be required to self-assess GST/HST.

The GST/HST is considered an end-user tax, which means the cost of GST is borne by the final consumer. Thus, while businesses are charged GST/HST on their purchases, they are entitled to a credit for this tax (referred to as an "input tax credit"). Input tax credits are available to the extent purchases are used in commercial activities. Businesses are required to remit to the government the difference between the amount of GST/HST collected or collectible and the amount of any input tax credit entitlement. For example, in a province that has 13% HST the flow through would look similar to this:

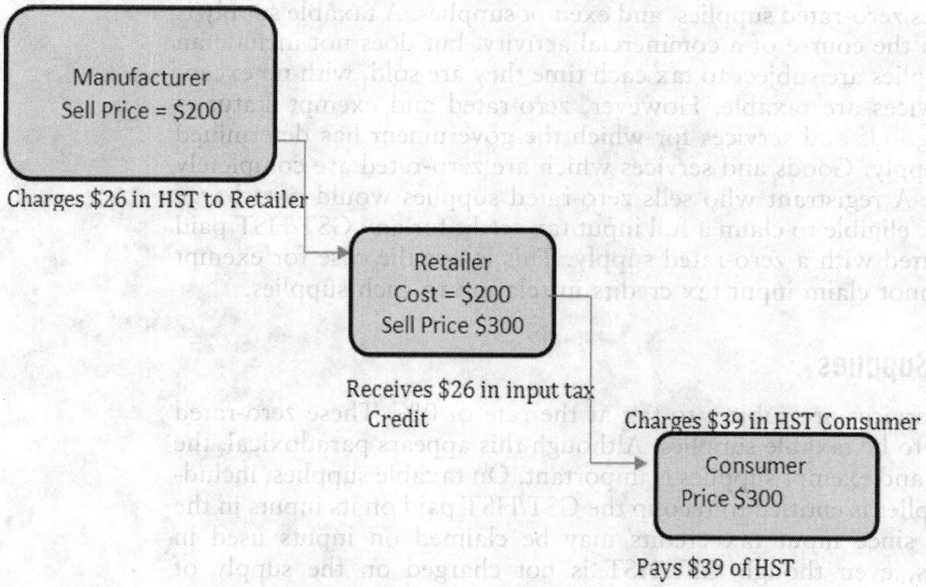

Total HST paid on this product would be $39 ($300 × 13%), which is born by the end consumer.

Supplies of goods and services are divided into two categories:

- Taxable supplies, which includes zero-rated supplies:
  - Taxable supplies are subject to GST at the rate of 5%, or HST at the appropriate provincial rate outlined above,
  - zero-rated supplies, considered taxable supplies but subject to a 0% rate.

- Exempt supplies, which do not attract GST, nor are the registrants able to claim an input tax credit. Making exempt supplies is not considered a "commercial activity".

The next two sections will expand on the concepts of "supply" and "input tax credits".

¶20,030.10 Supplies

The concept of "supply" is essential to an understanding of GST/HST. While in many cases the term will be synonymous with "sale", it has a much broader scope for GST/HST purposes.

The provision of a supply includes, among other things:

- sales or rentals of goods;
- rendering of services;
- leases, sales, or other transfers of real property;
- licensing of copyrights or patents; and
- barter and exchange transactions and gifts.

Once it is determined that there is a supply, a further determination must be made as to the type of supply. As discussed above, there are two types of supplies under the GST/HST: taxable, which includes zero-rated supplies, and exempt supplies. A taxable supply is defined as a supply made in the course of a commercial activity, but does not include an exempt supply. Taxable supplies are subject to tax each time they are sold, with no exceptions. Most goods and services are taxable. However, zero-rated and exempt status is extended to a short list of goods and services for which the government has determined that GST/HST should not apply. Goods and services which are zero-rated are completely free of any tax component. A registrant who sells zero-rated supplies would not charge GST/HST, but would still be eligible to claim a full input tax credit for any GST/HST paid on the taxable costs associated with a zero-rated supply. This is not the case for exempt supplies, since suppliers cannot claim input tax credits in relation to such supplies.

¶20,030.20 Zero-rated Supplies

A short list of goods and services are subject to tax at the rate of 0%. These zero-rated supplies are still considered to be taxable supplies. Although this appears paradoxical, the distinction between taxable and exempt supplies is important. On taxable supplies, including zero-rated ones, the supplier is entitled to recoup the GST/HST paid on its inputs in the form of input tax credits, since input tax credits may be claimed on inputs used in commercial activities. Thus, even though GST/HST is not charged on the supply of zero-rated goods and services, the entitlement to input tax credits ensures that these supplies are effectively tax-free. The following are some examples of goods and services that are zero-rated:

- prescription drugs;
- medical devices;
- basic groceries; and
- exported goods and services.

Zero-rated supplies are listed in Schedule VI of the ETA.

¶20,030.30 Exempt Supplies

Like suppliers of zero-rated supplies, suppliers of exempt goods and services are not required to collect GST/HST on these supplies. However, unlike zero-rated supplies, relief from GST/HST is not available on inputs used in the supply of exempt goods and services. The GST/HST paid by the supplier on purchases attributable to those exempt supplies is buried in the cost of the goods or services. For income tax purposes, however, the GST/HST paid on such inputs represents part of the cost of the inputs, and, hence, is deductible, except for interest and penalties incurred in respect of GST which are not deductible.

For example, when a bank purchases inputs to be used in the supply of financial services (which are exempt supplies), the bank is not entitled to recover the GST/HST incurred in respect of those inputs. Consequently, even though the bank does not charge GST/HST on the supply of those exempt financial services, the GST/HST incurred on the bank's purchases is buried in the cost of those financial services.[1] The bank will be able to deduct the GST/HST paid on these purchases for income tax purposes as part of the cost of the purchases.

The following are some examples of exempt goods and services:

- health care, child care, and personal care services;
- educational services;
- financial services; and
- sales of used residential housing and rentals of residential premises.

Exempt supplies are listed in Schedule V of the ETA.

¶20,040 Point-of-Sale Rebates

Point-of-sale rebates are intended to provide consumers with targeted sales tax relief of the provincial portion of the HST on purchases of certain designated items. Generally, purchasers of these items automatically have their rebate paid or credited to them at the point of sale by the registrant supplier, and only pay the 5% federal GST component. If the rebate is not paid or credited at the time of sale, the purchaser may claim a rebate from the CRA within four years of the day the tax became payable. The rebates generally apply to designated items purchased from retailers located in the HST provinces, as well as to items imported into an HST province from outside of Canada and items brought into the HST province from a non-HST province.

The point-of-sale rebates are granted under the authority of provincial legislation, rather than under the *Excise Tax Act*, and the items eligible for rebate vary to some degree across the provinces. They may be available, for example, on books in various forms, on children's clothing and footwear, on children's car seats, etc.

¶20,050 Input Tax Credits (ITCs)

An integral part of the GST/HST system is the entitlement to claim input tax credits on business purchases. This ensures that only the end user pays the GST/HST on taxable

[1] It is worth noting that because financial institutions are involved in a wide range of activities, some of which fall outside the definition of financial service and are thus taxable (and in respect of which input tax credits can be claimed), the rules relating to the supply of services by these institutions are quite complex. Uncertainties in terms of interpretation and application continue to arise.

supplies. In order to qualify for an input tax credit ("ITC"), the goods and services must have been purchased for use in a commercial activity. As the GST/HST is designed to be a tax on consumption to be borne by the end user, there are certain restrictions on the claiming of ITCs. These restrictions generally mirror the restrictions on claiming expenses under the ITA.

Input tax credits claimed by a registrant during a reporting period are subtracted from the tax collected on goods and services during the period to arrive at the net tax payable.

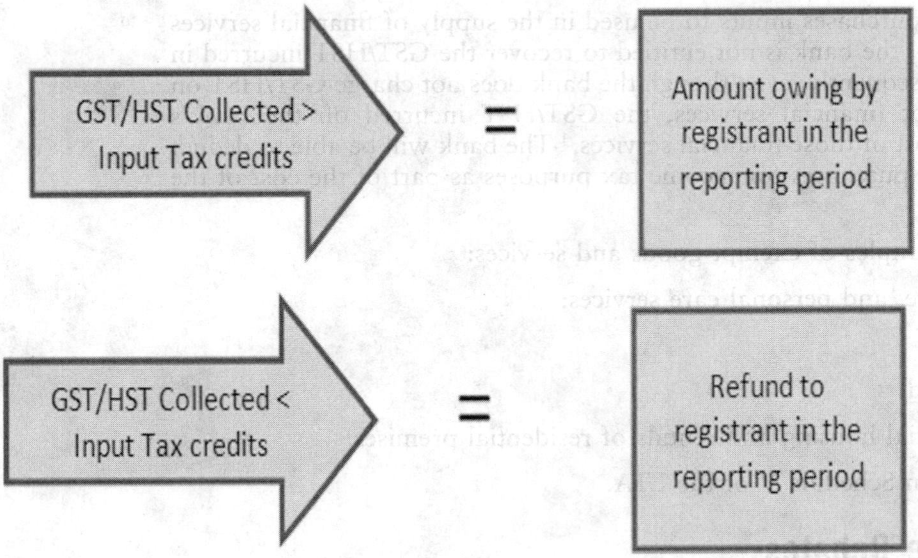

Where ITCs exceed tax payable, the registrant is entitled to a refund. An important concept related to ITCs is that purchases and sales need not be matched in order to claim an ITC. The credit can be claimed when the purchase is paid for or becomes due. A more detailed discussion on ITCs is provided later in this chapter under ¶20,300.

GST/HST registrants are entitled to claim ITCs at the rate of 5% where only federal GST was paid or payable and the purchases are for use in a commercial activity. Registrants can recover all of the HST paid or payable on purchases made in an HST province where those purchases are for use in a commercial activity. The rate of recovery is not dependent on where the registrant is located. However, temporary ITC restrictions apply in certain cases for large businesses in respect of the provincial portion of the HST in Ontario and Prince Edward Island, which are similar to those in place under the QST regime in Quebec. "Large businesses" are defined as those making taxable supplies worth more than $10 million annually, and certain financial institutions.

The "recapture of input tax credit" restrictions discussed above are progressively being eliminated. They will be fully eliminated in Ontario as of July 1, 2018. PEI begins to eliminate them as of April 1, 2018 (25% reduction). Quebec began a similar reduction (25%) of its restriction on January 1, 2018.

Registrants are required to maintain certain documentation to support ITCs. These requirements are discussed later in this chapter.

¶20,090 Pause and Reflect — Summary of Learning Goals

After working through this section, you should be able to:

- Explain the difference between a taxable supply, zero-rated supply, and exempt supply;
- Explain the GST/HST implications on imported supplies.

¶20,100 Liability for Goods and Services Tax (GST)/ Harmonized Sales Tax (HST)

While the legal liability for payment of GST/HST rests with the purchaser, the responsibility for collecting and remitting the tax generally lies with the supplier. The GST is charged in a province where the province either has no provincial sales tax or has decided not to harmonize the provincial and federal sales taxes. The HST combines the provincial retail sales tax and federal goods and services tax into a single rate value-added tax, and is charged on goods and services in the province. The rules relating to the collection and remittance of GST/HST will be examined in the context of the residency of the supplier, since the rules are somewhat different for resident and non-resident suppliers.

A taxable supply is defined as a supply made in the course of a commercial activity. The term includes both supplies taxed at the general rate of 5% (or at the applicable HST rate) and those that are zero-rated. (A zero-rated supply is defined as a supply included in Schedule VI of the *Excise Tax Act*.) For a person to be subject to GST/HST, the supply must be:

(1) made in Canada, and

(2) made by another person who is engaged in a commercial activity.

The definition of a commercial activity does not include activities engaged in by a business that involve the making of an exempt supply (which, in turn, is defined as a supply included in Schedule V of the *Excise Tax Act*). Rules have been introduced to determine when a supply is made in Canada and within the scope of GST/HST.

A relieving provision provides that if, at the time consideration is paid or becomes due for a supply, the supplier is a small supplier (who is not registered or required to be registered), no GST/HST is payable. However, this relieving provision does not apply to the sale of real property. Small suppliers are discussed in greater detail later in this chapter.

ETA: 166 Supply by small supplier not a registrant

¶20,100.10 Supplies in Canada

Supplies are subject to GST/HST if they are made in Canada, and imported goods and services may also be subject to GST/HST. Goods are deemed to be made in Canada as set out in the list below.

ETA: 142(1) [General rule — in Canada]

(1) Sale of goods: A sale of goods is deemed to be made in Canada if the goods are delivered or made available to the recipient in Canada.

(2) Leased goods: The supply is deemed to be made in Canada if possession or use of the goods is given or made available to the recipient in Canada.

(3) Real property: In the case of a supply of real property or a service in relation to real property, the supply is deemed to be made in Canada if the real property is situated in Canada.

(4) Supply of any other services: In the case of a supply of any other service, if the service is to be performed in whole or in part in Canada, the supply of the service is deemed to be made in Canada.

(5) Intangible personal property: The supply of intangible personal property is deemed to be made in Canada if the property may be used in whole or in part in Canada. If the intangible personal property is in respect of real property situated in Canada, of goods ordinarily situated in Canada, or of a service to be performed in Canada, the supply is also deemed to be made in Canada. ETA: 142(1)(c)(ii)

For supplies of intangible personal property, the determination of whether a supply is made in Canada can be more difficult. Intangible personal property is not defined in the ETA. However, the term "property" is defined to include "any property, whether real or personal, movable or immovable, tangible or intangible ...". The main categories of property under the ETA are real property, tangible personal property (generally referred to as goods), and intangible personal property. Intangible personal property includes a property that has no intrinsic or marketable value but merely evidence of value and is enforceable by law, such as contractual rights, stock certificates, intellectual property, etc. Intellectual property includes patents, trademarks, industrial designs, etc. ETA: 123(1) [Definitions]

¶20,100.20 Supplies in an HST Province

Once it is determined that a supply is made in Canada, it must be determined whether the supply is made in an HST province to ensure the correct rate of GST/HST is charged, i.e., GST of 5% or HST at the appropriate provincial rate. The sale of tangible personal property (or goods) takes place in the province in which the vendor delivers it or makes it available to the purchaser. Schedule IX of the ETA and the *New Harmonized Value-Added Tax System Regulations* set out the rules for determining the place of supply for the application of the HST in all participating provinces, and include rules for goods, services, intangibles, real property, etc.

When a taxable supply (other than a zero-rated supply) is made in Canada and is treated as made in a participating province under the HST place of supply rules, the supplier must collect HST at the appropriate rate for that province. Otherwise, the supplier must collect only 5% GST. The place of supply rules provided for in the ITA and Regulations generally align the place of supply with the place of consumption for supplies of services and intangible personal property. This is intended to remove competitive disadvantages for businesses that sell from HST participating provinces.

¶20,100.30 Supplies by Non-Residents

As a general rule, a supply of goods or services made in Canada by a non-resident is deemed to be made in Canada if: ETA: 143(1) [Supply by non-resident]

- the supply is made in the course of a business carried on in Canada;
- the non-resident is registered for GST/HST purposes at the time the supply is made; or
- the supply is a supply of an admission in respect of a place of amusement, a seminar, an activity, or an event, and the non-resident supplies admissions directly to consumers.

Unless any of the above situations apply, supplies by a non-resident are outside the scope of GST/HST. As a general rule, a supply made in Canada (and/or in an HST province) will only be subject to GST/HST if it is made by a registrant. Such supplies may, in certain circumstances, be subject to tax in the hands of the recipient under the imported supplies rules discussed below.

¶20,100.40 Imports

As the GST/HST is a tax on consumption in Canada, it also applies to imports. The ETA imposes GST (or the federal component of the HST) on the value of imported goods. The GST is payable by the person who is liable under the *Customs Act* to pay duty on the imported goods or who would be so liable if the goods were subject to duty. The value of the goods is based on the value for customs purposes, plus duties and excise taxes (excluding GST/HST). No tax is payable on zero-rated goods, such as basic groceries and medical devices, or goods that qualify as non-taxable importations under Schedule VII of the ETA.

ETA: 212 Imposition of goods and services tax, 212.1 Meaning of "commercial goods", 213 Exception , 215(1) [Value of goods]

Generally, the provincial component of the HST applies to importations of taxable non-commercial goods imported by a resident of a participating province. The provincial component of the HST is not payable by registrants on imports of commercial goods that are destined for a participating province. The goods will be subject to self-assessment if they are not consumed, used, or supplied exclusively (90% or more) in commercial activities. "Commercial goods" include goods that are imported for sale or for any commercial, industrial, occupational, institutional, or other similar use.

ETA: 212.1 Meaning of "commercial goods", 220.07 Imported commercial goods

Self-assessment of GST/HST is required by recipients of "imported taxable supplies". Imported taxable supplies are defined to include intangible personal property (i.e., intellectual property) and services that are supplied outside Canada to a Canadian resident for use in Canada. GST/HST does not apply where the imported taxable supply is for use in Canada exclusively (90% or more, and 100% in the case of financial institutions) in a commercial activity.

ETA: 217 Definitions, 218 Imposition of goods and services tax, 220.08 Tax in participating province

Example

An Ontario resident purchases furniture in Alberta for $2,000, paying 5% GST or $100. Ontario's HST rate is 13%. On return to Ontario, the Ontario resident would be required to self-assess tax on the furniture. The self-assessed tax would be equal to $160 ($2,000 × (13%-5%)).

Where a person carries on business through permanent establishments located in and outside of Canada, self-assessment of the GST/HST is required in respect of taxable imports of services and intangibles from one branch to another.

ETA: 220 Definitions

The duty-free limits that apply to Canadian individuals on non-commercial importations are as follows:

- For absences of less than 24 hours, there are no duty or tax exemptions.
- For absences of 24 hours to 48 hours, the travellers' exemption is $200.
- For absences of 48 hours or more, the travellers' exemption is $800.

An imported taxable supply taken into one of the HST provinces may be subject to 5% GST as an imported taxable supply, and the HST provincial component as property or services taken into an HST province.

¶20,120 Registration Requirements for Residents

A person who makes a taxable supply in the course of a commercial activity in Canada (discussed below) is required to register for GST/HST purposes. Persons registered or required to be registered under the legislation are referred to as registrants. The rights and obligations of registrants under the ETA are discussed later in this chapter. It should be noted that as agents of the Crown, registrants are required to collect and remit GST/HST as required under the ETA.

ETA: 240(1) [Registration required], 123(1) [Definitions]

If the Minister has reason to believe that a non-registered person is required to be registered for GST/HST purposes, the Minister may send a notice in writing (a notice of intent) to the person that the Minister proposes to register the person. If the person does not register or does not satisfy the Minister that registration is not required, the Minister may register the person 60 days after the day the notice of intent was sent.

ETA: 241(1.3) Notice of intent, 241(1.5) Registration by Minister

The definition of "person" for the purposes of GST/HST is broadly based to include an individual, partnership, corporation, trust or estate, or a body that is a society, union, club, association, commission, or other organization of any kind. Therefore, virtually any kind of organized unit or individual can be considered to be a person and can be required to register.

ETA: 123(1) [Definitions]

Unlike the ITA, the ETA treats partnerships as persons for purposes of the GST/HST. Therefore, the partnership is considered to be a person for registration purposes and is liable for GST/HST collected on taxable supplies, rather than the individual partners. Similarly, the partnership is eligible for an input tax credit for its purchases attributable to commercial activities.

¶20,120.10 Definition of Commercial Activity

Central to determining if a person is required to register is the issue of whether the person is engaged in commercial activities. This topic will be discussed in greater detail below. For the purposes of the discussion of the registration requirements, it should be noted that a commercial activity is defined as:

ETA: 123(1) [Definitions]

- a business that is carried on;
- an adventure or concern in the nature of trade; and
- the supply of real property.

Business is defined broadly to include a profession, calling, trade, manufacture, or undertaking of any kind whatever, regardless of whether the activity engaged in is for profit. This test is broader than the business test under the ITA as there does not need to be a profit motive present for an activity to be considered a business for GST/HST purposes (except with respect to individuals).

The GST/HST is a tax on consumption or value added, and not on income. Many activities engaged in by non-profit organizations, charities, and governments may constitute a business for GST/HST purposes. These entities engage in activities that add value to the economy in competition with profit-motivated businesses. For example, a non-profit organization will be considered to be engaged in a commercial activity for GST/HST purposes if it supplies taxable goods or services for consideration. Therefore, subject to the exceptions discussed below, any entity that engages in an activity of a commercial nature, regardless of whether the activity is engaged in primarily for profit, will be considered to be engaged in a commercial activity. Consequently, the entity will be required to register for GST/HST purposes.

An adventure or concern in the nature of trade, which is not defined but has the common law meaning discussed in ¶ 4,110.20, also constitutes a commercial activity. This concept is discussed in more detail below in ¶20,200. The supply of real property also constitutes a commercial activity unless the supply is exempt. Most sales and leases of non-residential property constitute a commercial activity.

¶20,120.20 Exclusions from Commercial Activity

The definition of commercial activity contains certain exclusions of which readers should be aware.

(1) Activities that involve the making of exempt supplies do not constitute commercial activities.

Example

The supply of medical services by a physician is exempt and, therefore, not a commercial activity. Consequently, physicians providing only exempt medical services are not able to register for GST/HST purposes and cannot claim input tax credits in respect of GST/HST paid on inputs. However, the GST/HST component of these expenses can be deducted for income tax purposes.

(2) Commercial activity does not include any activity engaged in by an individual (a personal trust or a partnership comprising individuals) without a reasonable expectation of profit. Hobbies and recreational pastimes of individuals would not be considered to be commercial activities and registration would be neither required nor permitted. The phrase "reasonable expectation of profit" is discussed in Chapter 4.

¶20,130 Exceptions From the Registration Requirements

The registration requirements contain an exception for small suppliers. The rules for determining whether a person qualifies as a small supplier are set out in the ETA. Basically, this includes persons whose revenues from taxable supplies do not exceed $30,000[2] in the four preceding calendar quarters. This calculation is based on the supplier's total worldwide sales including any supply made outside Canada by its "associates".

ETA: 148 Small suppliers, 240(1) [Registration required]

Unregistered small suppliers are not required to collect GST/HST on taxable supplies. Persons who qualify as small suppliers and who are engaged in a commercial activity may register on a voluntary basis. Registration would permit these persons to claim input tax credits, and it may be advantageous if taxable supplies are made to registrants. Since registrants are able to claim input tax credits on their purchases, they

[2] $50,000 in the case of public service bodies, which include non-profit organizations, charities, municipalities, school authorities, hospital authorities, public colleges, and universities.

will likely prefer to deal with other registrants. Purchases from non-registrants may contain indirect GST/HST because non-registrants are unable to recover GST/HST paid on purchases through the input tax credit mechanism.

¶20,140 Registration and Collection Requirements for Non-Residents

The place of supply rules discussed earlier in this section must be read in conjunction with the registration requirements to determine when non-residents are required to register and collect GST/HST.

¶20,140.10 Meaning of Non-Resident

For purposes of the GST/HST, non-residents are defined as "not resident in Canada". In the absence of a definition of "resident", reference should be made to the dictionary meaning of the term and to the interpretation of the term under the ITA, as discussed earlier in this chapter.

ETA: 132 Person resident in Canada

The ETA does contain deeming rules that provide that a corporation is deemed to be resident in Canada if it is incorporated in Canada, similar to the rules under the ITA. In addition, a corporation originally incorporated in a foreign jurisdiction that continues (a special form of incorporation) in Canada and not elsewhere is deemed to be resident in Canada.

In the case of a partnership or unincorporated society, club, association, or organization, or a branch thereof, the entity is deemed to be resident in Canada if a majority of its members, having management and control, are resident in Canada at the time of registration. A labour union is deemed to be resident in Canada if it carries on its activities in Canada and has a local union or branch in Canada at that time.

An individual is deemed to be resident in Canada if the individual is deemed under any of paragraphs 250(1)(*b*) to (*f*) of the ITA to be resident in Canada at that time.

Where a non-resident person has a permanent establishment in Canada, the person is deemed to be resident in Canada in respect of the activities carried on through that particular establishment. For GST/HST purposes, a permanent establishment is defined as a fixed place of business, including:

- a place of management,
- branch,
- office,
- factory,
- workshop,
- mine, oil or gas well, quarry, timberland, or other place of extraction of mineral resources through which supplies are made, or
- fixed place of business of another person (other than a broker, general commission agent, or other independent agent) making supplies on behalf of the person in the ordinary course of business.

Because the definition of permanent establishment under the ETA differs from that generally found in Canada's income tax treaties, there may be situations where the existence of a permanent establishment is different for income tax and GST/HST purposes.

¶20,150 Mandatory Registration

According to the registration requirements, non-resident persons who do not carry on any business in Canada are not required to register. While the test for residents is based on engaging in a commercial activity, the test for non-residents is based on the narrower concept of carrying on business. In basic terms, the difference for a non-resident is that registration is not required if the activities undertaken in Canada are not of a regular and continuous nature. The distinction between commercial activity and carrying on business is discussed in more detail ¶20,200 below.

ETA: 240(1) [Registration required]

A non-resident who directly supplies admissions to a place of amusement, a seminar, an activity or an event must register before making any such supplies in Canada.

ETA: 240(2) Non-resident performers, etc.

The small supplier exemption, for suppliers with less than $30,000 in sales per year, is also available to non-residents, other than those who supply admissions as described above.

ETA: 148(3) Application

For individuals, an individual is deemed to be a resident of Canada at any time if they meet certain conditions of the ITA. A deemed resident (other than a sojourner) for income tax purposes is also a resident for GST/HST purposes.

ITA: 250(1)(b), 250(1)(f)

¶20,160 Voluntary Registration

Voluntary registration is available to non-residents, provided certain requirements are met. The non-resident person must, in the ordinary course of carrying on business outside Canada:

(1) regularly solicit orders for the supply of goods for export to, or delivery in, Canada; or

(2) have entered into an agreement for the supply of:

- services to be performed in Canada,
- intangibles to be used in Canada or that relate to real property in Canada,
- goods ordinarily situated in Canada, or
- services performed in Canada.

Voluntary registration is also available to certain foreign banks and other corporations, as outlined in the legislation.

¶20,190 Pause and Reflect — Summary of Learning Goals

After working through this section, ¶20,100, you should be able to:

- Explain when a person must register for GST.

¶20,200 Commercial Activity

Overview

As noted earlier in the chapter, the issue of whether a person is engaged in a commercial activity is central to the determination of whether the person is required to register and collect GST/HST. Commercial activity means any business that is carried on (except to the extent to which the business involves the making of exempt supplies), an adventure or concern in the nature of trade (except to the extent to which the adventure or concern involves the making of exempt supplies), or the making of a supply of real property (other than an exempt supply).

¶20,210 Carrying on Business

To some extent, the concept of carrying on business under the ITA has been adopted for GST/HST purposes. Generally, if an entity is carrying on business for income tax purposes, it is also considered to be carrying on business for GST/HST purposes. However, some entities not considered to be carrying on business for income tax purposes may still be considered to be carrying on business for GST/HST purposes, as the comparable provisions under the ETA are generally broader in scope than those under the ITA. ETA: 123(1) [Definitions]

The term "business" is defined to include a profession, calling, trade, manufacture, or undertaking of any kind whatever. However, unlike the definition of carrying on business in the ITA, it is generally not necessary to establish that the business has a reasonable expectation of profit. Therefore, an entity engaged in activities with continuous, repetitious effort is generally considered to be a business for GST/HST purposes, whether the activity or undertaking is engaged in for profit. The definition specifically excludes an office or employment. ETA: 123(1) [Definitions]

Because of the absence of the profit test, a number of organizations established on a not-for-profit basis are considered to be carrying on business for GST/HST purposes and, thus, to be engaged in commercial activities. For example, where a hospital operates a parking lot, this is considered to be a commercial activity and the hospital may be required to collect GST/HST in certain circumstances on that supply. Therefore, even if an activity is considered ancillary to achieving a not-for-profit purpose for income tax purposes, and, therefore, outside the definition of carrying on business for purposes of the ITA, it is still considered to be a business for purposes of the GST/HST.

Another distinction from the ITA is the inclusion of leasing activities in the definition of business. Any activity that is engaged in on a regular and continuous basis that involves the supply of property by way of lease, licence, or similar arrangement is considered to be a business. Thus, rents received from the rental of an automobile, for example, are regarded as being earned from a business for GST/HST purposes, regardless of the effort required by the owner of the automobile to earn the rental income. This can be contrasted with the treatment under the ITA, where the activity may not be considered to be a business, but rather, may be regarded as income from property. This distinction for income tax purposes is discussed in Chapter 6. ETA: 123(1) [Definitions]

¶20,210.10 Exclusions From the Definition of Commercial Activity

There are two key activities which are specifically excluded from the definition of commercial activity. As a result, supplies made in the course of these activities will not be considered to be taxable supplies. The supplier of these goods and services is not required to collect GST/HST on these supplies and, in turn, is not entitled to claim input tax credits. They include: ETA: 123(1) [Definitions]

- that part of a business or adventure or concern in the nature of trade that involves the making of an exempt supply; or
- a business or adventure or concern in the nature of trade carried on by an individual, a personal trust, or a partnership consisting solely of individuals without a reasonable expectation of profit.

Exempt supplies include, for example, health care services, educational services, and legal aid services. While the making of exempt supplies is excluded from the definition of a commercial activity, the making of zero-rated supplies is not excluded. Thus, any person who sells zero-rated groceries or exports goods in the course of a business or an adventure or concern in the nature of trade is considered to be engaged in a commercial activity and is entitled to claim input tax credits in respect of GST/HST paid on purchases. Zero-rated supplies are set out in Schedule VI of the ETA. If a supply is not considered to be made in the course of a commercial activity because it falls within one of these exclusions, or if the supply is not made in the course of a business or an adventure or concern in the nature of trade or is not a supply of real property, the supply will not be a taxable supply and no GST/HST will apply. Although no input tax credit may be claimed for GST/HST paid in respect of these supplies, this GST/HST is deductible for income tax purposes. ETA: Schedule V

¶20,210.20 Value for Tax

GST/HST is imposed on the value of consideration for a supply. Consideration is the price paid for property or services and is, generally, expressed in monetary terms. ETA: 165(1) [Imposition of goods and services tax]

Goods or services are often sold on terms that allow for a discount for prompt payment, or for a penalty in the case of a late payment. The value on which GST/HST is imposed is not affected by the discount or penalty. In either case, GST/HST applies to the amount of consideration shown on the invoice (i.e., the full sale price). If, however, the invoice is for an amount that is net of a cash discount, GST/HST applies on the net amount. ETA: 161 Early or late payments

¶20,210.30 When GST/HST Is Payable

GST/HST is generally payable by a recipient of a taxable supply at the time the consideration for the supply is paid to the supplier or the time the consideration becomes due, whichever is earlier. Where partial payments are made in respect of a supply, GST/HST must be paid on each payment. GST/HST generally becomes due when it is invoiced. Specifically, the consideration becomes due on the earliest of: ETA: 152(1) [When consideration due], 168(1) [General rule], 168(2) Partial consideration

(1) the day on which the invoice for the amount is issued;

(2) the date on the invoice;

(3) the day on which the invoice would have been issued, if not for an undue delay; and

(4) the day on which the amount becomes due under an agreement in writing.

Where property is supplied by way of lease, licence, or similar agreement, the consideration is deemed to become due on the day the recipient is required to pay the consideration under the agreement.

ETA: 152(2) Consideration under leases, etc.

Notwithstanding the general rule, there are a number of special cases. For example, where the supply involves goods, liability occurs on the earlier of the date determined under the general rule and the end of the month following the month in which ownership or possession of the goods is transferred to the purchaser. In the case of a deposit, GST/HST is not payable on the deposit until the time the supplier applies the deposit against the consideration for the supply. For real property, GST/HST is generally payable on the earliest of transfer of possession or transfer of ownership, with some particularities regarding supplies of residential condominiums.

ETA: 168(1) [General rule], 168(3) Supply completed, 168(9) Deposits; 168(5) Sale of real property

¶20,210.40 Automobile Operating Cost Benefits Paid by Employer

Recall from Chapter 3 that an employer provides a taxable benefit when the employee's operating costs for an employer-provided automobile are paid by the employer. The value of the benefit is determined by one of two methods. The employee may use a per kilometre method or elect to value the benefit as 50% of the standby charge in respect of the employer-provided car. Likewise, where the employee uses his or her own car but the operating costs are paid by the employer, an operating cost benefit is required to be determined under the ITA. In either case, the registrant employer is required to remit GST equal to a prescribed percentage of 3%[3] of the benefit, however computed. The prescribed percentage is less than 5% to recognize that the benefit includes exempt supplies such as insurance and licence fees.

ETA: 173(1)(d)(vi)(A), 6(1)(k) Automobile operating expense benefit, 6(1)(l) Where standby charge does not apply

¶20,290 Pause and Reflect — Summary of Learning Goals

After working through this section, ¶20, 200, you should be able to:

- Explain what a commercial activity is,
- Outline the exemptions to a commercial activity, and
- Explain when GST is payable.

¶20,300 Input Tax Credits (ITCs)

Overview

Although businesses may be required to collect GST/HST, they also receive a credit for GST/HST on all business-related expenses. The GST/HST on business-related expenses generates input tax credits (ITCs) that can be deducted from GST/HST collected by the business to reduce the amount required to be remitted to the government or to generate a net amount that may be received by the business in the form of a GST/HST refund. The detailed rules are discussed below.

¶20,310 General Rules

ITCs are available to registrants for GST/HST paid on goods and services that are purchased for use in a commercial activity. For persons other than financial institutions,

[3] The prescribed percentage varies where HST applies or where the employer is considered a "large business" for recapture of input tax credits purposes.

the general rule is that if the use of the input is exclusively in a "commercial activity", which is defined in the ETA to mean "all or substantially all" (and which is interpreted to mean 90% or more), a full credit may be claimed. Conversely, if a business input will not be used at all in respect of a commercial activity, no credit will be allowed. Under this latter rule, if the extent of use in a commercial activity is less than 10%, no credit may be claimed. For example, if an input is to be used 90% or more in the course of making an exempt supply, no credit may be claimed. It is important to note that the test for eligibility is the intended use of the input at the time of purchase. Apart from the change-of-use rules for capital real property discussed in Chapter 8, a registrant is not required to adjust the input tax credit for subsequent changes of use. Registrants are entitled to claim the credit in the reporting period in which the GST/HST is paid or, if earlier, when it becomes payable.

ETA: 169(1) [General rule for credits], 123(1) [Definitions]

There are circumstances where a purchase will be used in respect of a combination of taxable and exempt supplies. In these cases, except for certain capital goods which are discussed later in this chapter, registrants are required to apportion the input tax credit between the taxable (including zero-rated) and exempt activity.

Example

Consider the case of a hospital that purchases an industrial dishwasher for use in its kitchen. The dishwasher will be used to clean dishes from both patients and cafeteria patrons. Because meals provided to patients are exempt and cafeteria sales are taxable, the hospital will be required to apportion the ITC between the taxable and exempt activities.

For apportionment purposes, inputs acquired for use in a business or other activity (referred to as an "endeavour" in the *Excise Tax Act*) are considered to be for use in commercial activities. They qualify for input tax credits only to the extent that they are for use in making taxable supplies (including zero-rated supplies) for consideration (which in this context does not include nominal consideration). On the other hand, to the extent inputs are for use in making exempt supplies for consideration, they are treated as being for use in non-commercial activities (and thus not eligible for input tax credits). Inputs that are not for use in making supplies of any kind are also regarded as being for use in non-commercial activities. The legislation does not prescribe allocation methods to be used in apportioning input tax credits. Provided the allocation basis is fair and reasonable and is used on a consistent basis throughout the fiscal year, the allocation will likely not be challenged by the CRA.

ETA: 141.01 Meaning of "endeavour"

¶20,310.10 Restrictions

Certain purchases made by a registrant may have a personal consumption element or are for goods and services that are available to employees. As a result, there are certain circumstances where input tax credits are not allowed, in full or in part. In many circumstances, the GST/HST restrictions parallel the restrictions contained in the ITA in respect of business deductions. The more significant restrictions include the following.

Club Memberships

Input tax credits are not allowed in respect of membership fees or dues in any club whose main purpose is to provide dining, recreational, or sporting facilities. Common examples of these clubs include business persons' clubs, golf clubs, and fitness clubs. However, if meal and entertainment expenses are incurred at the club in respect of a commercial activity, input tax credits are allowed, subject to the recapture rule discussed below.

ETA: 170(1)(a)

Home Office Expenses

Input tax credits are not allowed in respect of expenses incurred by an individual in respect of a home office unless the office is the individual's principal place of business or a place that is both used exclusively for the purpose of earning income from a business and used on a regular and continuous basis for meeting clients, customers, or patients. This provision is consistent with the ITA, which denies a deduction in such circumstances.

ETA: 170(1)(a.1), 18(12) Work space in home

Reasonableness

Another concept is borrowed from the ITA, namely, that of reasonableness. In claiming an input tax credit, the nature or cost of the property or services purchased by the registrant must be reasonable in the circumstances, having regard to the nature of the commercial activities of the registrant. In addition, the amount of the input tax credit must be calculated on consideration that is reasonable in the circumstances.

Automobile Allowances

Where an employer has paid an automobile allowance to an employee for travel in respect of the employer's business and the employee is not required to include the allowance in income because the allowance is a reasonable one, the employer is permitted to claim an ITC on that amount. As is the case for ITA purposes, such allowances may be deemed not reasonable if not based on a per kilometre basis.

ETA: 174 Travel and other allowances

¶20,330 Application of the Rules

Example Problem 20-1

You are the auditor for Corporate Welfare Limited and you have been given an income statement prepared for financial accounting purposes showing a loss for its fiscal year ended December 31, 2018 of $112,000. Your audit uncovers the following:

(a) appraisal expense contains cost of determining asset values for insurance purposes		$4,000
(b) wages expense contains amounts (matched by employees) relating to money purchase (defined contribution) registered pension plan contributions, made during the first 120 days of 2019 but allocated by the accountant to 2018, in respect of current services on behalf of the following executives (employment compensation for the year shown in brackets):		
President (Mr. C.S. Bloom, 100% owner; $200,000)	$15,710	
Vice-President ($95,000)	6,000	
Accountant ($80,000)	5,000	
Plant Supervisor ($65,000)	4,000	30,710
(c) cost of landscaping written off		10,000
(d) legal expenses for		
(i) defence of a suit, brought by a customer, for failure to deliver merchandise on time	$2,500	
(ii) articles of amendment to revise company's articles of incorporation	3,500	
(iii) cost of disputing income tax	4,000	10,000
(e) revenues included a dividend received from a Canadian subsidiary		80,000
(f) interest expense included amortization of bond discount on bonds maturing in 2018		12,000
(g) miscellaneous expense contained donations for the year to		
(i) duly registered charities	$4,000	
(ii) the Conlibdem political party (a registered party)	7,000	11,000
(h) insurance expense contained whole life insurance premium paid on the life of Mr. C.S. Bloom (proceeds payable to the company; not group life)		10,000
(i) salaries expense contained a dividend payable to Mr. Bloom		8,000
(j) bad debts expense including $4,000 in respect of a loan to a shareholder of a supplier totalled		10,000
(k) salaries expense included a bonus paid to Mr. Bloom		15,000

(l) convention expenses over three days of Mr. Bloom and his family ($2,000 thereof represents costs relating to Mrs. Bloom and their two children, who attended for social purposes only; $500 of the remaining amount relates to the cost of meals consumed by Mr. Bloom)	5,000
(m) administration expense contains an embezzlement loss caused by a minor employee of the company	10,000
(n) (i) management bonuses included in wages expense but not paid in 2018	50,000
(ii) bonuses accrued at the end of 2017 which were not, and will not be, paid in 2018	35,000
(o) property taxes paid in 2018 include an amount paid for the company's fishing lodge	1,000
(p) the company as a lessor agreed to pay and expensed $15,000 on June 30, 2018 to cancel a lease that could have been in force until December 31, 2023 with renewal periods, but in 2018 actually paid only	10,000
(q) the company paid damages for failing to deliver goods on time under an action for breach of contract brought by one of its suppliers and the amount was expensed in the financial accounts	12,000
(r) cost of constructing a cement ramp to facilitate wheelchair access to the company's premises, capitalized by the accountant	6,000

Required

Outline the proper GST/HST treatment by the corporation of the items presented.

Solution

(1) General

Since the corporation is carrying on business, it is engaged in a commercial activity. Therefore, the corporation is required to register and collect GST/HST on its supplies, i.e., sales of goods or services, which are "taxable supplies." As a registrant, the corporation is entitled to a full input tax credit in respect of GST/HST paid or payable on goods and services that it purchases exclusively for use in its commercial activity. If GST/HST collected or collectible on its sales exceeds its ITCs, the corporation must remit the difference. On the other hand, if ITCs exceed GST/HST collected or collectible, a refund of the excess is available.

ETA: 123(1) [Definitions], 169(1) [General rule for credits]

(2) Items Listed

(a) The appraisal expenses incurred for insurance appraisal purposes are for the provision of an exempt supply of a financial service which does not give rise to an ITC since no GST/HST was payable. ETA: Schedule V, PartVII

(b) Employer contributions to a registered pension plan involve a payment for an exempt supply on which GST/HST is not charged. As a result, no ITC is available. ETA: 123(1) [Definitions]

(c) Landscaping costs involve a payment for taxable supplies of goods or services resulting in the availability of an ITC.

(d) Payments for legal services give rise to an ITC since the services are taxable supplies.

(e) Dividends received involve an exempt supply of a financial service onwhich no GST/HST is collected. ETA: Schedule V, PartVII

(f) The payment of interest is a financial service which is an exempt supply.

(g) No GST/HST is charged on a donation which involves a transfer of money. As a result, no ITC is available. ETA: 123(1) [Definitions], 164 Donation — value of consideration

(h) Insurance premiums are for an exempt supply of a financial service and no ITC is available since no GST/HST was paid.

(i) The payment of a dividend is an exempt supply of a financial service.

(j) A loan is a financial instrument which is an exempt supply, on which no GST/HST is charged. Hence, the write-off of this bad debt has no GST/HST effect.

(k) Amounts paid to employees as remuneration are not supplies, since these amounts are excluded from the definition of services. As a result, remuneration is not subject to GST/HST. ETA: 123(1) [Definitions]

(l) Initially, an ITC is available on the full amount of GST/HST paid in respect of meals and entertainment. However, 50% of the ITC in respect of such expenditures is recaptured in the first period of the next fiscal year. As well, temporary input tax credit restrictions may apply in Ontario and Prince Edward Island. ETA: 236 Food, beverages and entertainment

(m) Embezzlement losses involve a transfer of money for which there are no GST/HST implication.

(n) Bonuses are employment remuneration excluded from the definition of service and, hence, are not subject to GST/HST.

(o) Property tax involves an exempt supply on which no GST/HST is charged.

(p) A lease cancellation fee paid by a lessor is subject to GST/HST. The payer is deemed to have paid GST/HST equal to 5/105 (or the appropriate factor, depending on the applicable rate of HST in the province) of the payment and, hence, an ITC is available.

(q) The payer of damages is deemed to have paid or the recipient deemed to have received GST/HST equal to 5/105 (or the appropriate factor, depending on the applicable rate of HST in the province) of the damages. As a result, the corporation is entitled to an ITC. ETA: 182 Forfeiture, extinguished debt, etc

(r) Construction and repair costs involve a payment for taxable supplies for goods or services resulting in the availability of an ITC.

¶20,390 Pause and Reflect — Summary of Learning Goals

After working through this section, ¶20,300, you should be able to:

- Explain what goods and services are eligible to claim an ITC, and
- Describe the GST/HST implication for various types of goods and services.

¶20,400 Capital Personal Property and the Input Tax Credit System Under GST/HST

In determining the net remittance for a reporting period, the total ITC for the period is deducted from the tax collected or collectible for that period. Where the total ITC for the period exceeds the tax collected or collectible, the registrant will be entitled to a refund.

An important feature of the ITC mechanism is that purchases and sales need not be matched in order to claim an ITC. The credit can be claimed for the period in which the tax is paid or becomes payable. Similarly, for purchases of capital property, there is no requirement for amortization. Under the general input tax credit rules, a registrant may claim an ITC for the tax paid on the purchase of property or a service which was acquired for use in commercial activities. However, special rules have been developed for capital property, as the useful life of capital property generally often extends for several years and the use of the property may change over that period. Under the ETA, capital property is divided into two main groups — capital personal property and capital real property — and different rules apply to each group.

For GST/HST purposes, capital property is defined to include any property that is capital property for income tax purposes, other than property included in Class 12 (e.g., small tools or utensils costing less than $500, video tape, computer software, etc.), Class 14 (e.g., patents, franchises, concessions, or licences for a limited period, etc.), Class 14.1 (e.g., qualifying goodwill), or Class 44 (e.g., a patent or right to use patented information) of the capital cost allowance classes. This definition for GST/HST purposes applies regardless of whether or not the registrant is a taxpayer under the ITA.

Separate rules apply to passenger vehicles and aircraft that are acquired by an individual or a partnership, and certain input tax credit restrictions apply to all passenger vehicles.

¶20,410 Passenger Vehicles and Aircraft

Restrictions on claiming ITCs apply to passenger vehicles owned by all registrants, with special additional rules applying to passenger vehicles owned by registrants that are individuals or partnerships. Many of these rules are based on the rules for passenger ITA: 248(1) Definitions vehicles under the ITA. The definition of passenger vehicle under the ETA has the meaning assigned under the ITA.

¶20,420 Passenger Vehicles Owned by Registrants Other Than Individuals and Partnerships

Following the rules for deductibility under the ITA, the ETA refers to specific paragraphs of the ITA. As a result, no input tax credit may be claimed on the portion of the cost of a vehicle that exceeds $30,000 excluding GST/HST and/or provincial sales tax. Similarly, an input tax credit may not be claimed in respect of an improvement to the vehicle to the extent the accumulated cost of the vehicle, including the improvement, exceeds $30,000.

ETA: 201 Value of passenger vehicle , 202(1) [Improvement to passenger vehicle] , 13(7)(g), 13(7)(h)

As with other capital personal property (i.e., capital property other than capital real property), a full input tax credit may be claimed for the first $30,000 of the cost of passenger vehicles where the primary-use test is met. If the use in a commercial activity is 50% or less, no input tax credit may be claimed.

On the actual disposition of a passenger vehicle, the sale is subject to GST/HST only where the vehicle was used primarily in a commercial activity prior to that time.

ETA: 203(1) Sale of a passenger vehicle

¶20,430 Passenger Vehicles and Aircraft Owned by Registrants Who Are Individuals or Partnerships

Registrants who are individuals (e.g., sole proprietorships) or partnerships are entitled to claim a full input tax credit in respect of the acquisition of a passenger vehicle only if the vehicle is used exclusively (i.e., 90% or more) in a commercial activity. Similarly, a full input tax credit may be claimed in respect of any improvement of the vehicle only if the vehicle was used exclusively in a commercial activity since its acquisition and will continue to be so used immediately after the improvement. As with other registrants, no input tax credit may be claimed on the portion of the cost of a vehicle (or improvements thereto) that exceeds $30,000, exclusive of provincial sales tax and GST/HST.

ETA: 202(2) Input tax credit on passenger vehicle or aircraft , 202(3) Improvement to passenger vehicle or aircraft

If the vehicle or aircraft is used less than exclusively in a commercial activity, a full input tax credit may not be claimed in respect of the acquisition or improvement. However, the individual or partnership is entitled to claim an input tax credit equal to 5/105 (or the applicable HST factor, depending on the particular province) of the capital cost allowance claimed for income tax purposes, to the extent the vehicle or aircraft is used in a commercial activity. For example, if an individual purchases a car in Ontario for $16,000 (including GST/HST) for use 60% in a commercial activity, the individual would be able to claim an input tax credit equal to $166 (i.e., ½ X 30% of $16,000 X 60% X 13/113) in the first year. An input tax credit may also be claimed in subsequent years based on capital cost allowance claims.

ETA: 202(4) Non-exclusive use of passenger vehicle or aircraft

On the actual disposition of a passenger vehicle or aircraft, GST/HST applies only if the vehicle or aircraft was used exclusively in a commercial activity since its acquisition.

ETA: 203(3) Sale of passenger vehicle, etc.

Where an individual or partnership sells a passenger vehicle that was used exclusively in a commercial activity immediately before the sale, the individual or partnership is entitled to claim an input tax credit. The input tax credit is calculated in the same manner as other registrants (see the paragraph above) on all or a portion of the cost on acquisition and any improvements that exceeded $30,000 and that were previously denied.

ETA: 203(1) Sale of a passenger vehicle

¶20,500 GST and Property Income

Interest and Dividends

Interest and dividends are exempt from GST/HST. A number of provisions and definitions in the ETA must be reviewed to explain the basis for this exemption. First, financial services rendered to residents in Canada are exempt from GST/HST. A "financial service" is defined to include a broad range of transactions and services. For example, the payment or receipt of interest, dividends, or any other amount in respect of a "financial instrument" is included in the definition of financial service. A "financial instrument" is defined to include a debt security, an equity security, an insurance policy, etc. A "debt security" is defined in the same subsection to mean a right to be paid money and includes a deposit of money. An "equity security" is defined to mean a share of the capital stock of a corporation or any interest in or right to such a share. Consequently, payments of interest and dividends in respect of financial instruments are exempt from GST/HST. It is important to note that the definition of financial service contains several exclusions. For example, paragraph (r) of the definition excludes the provision of a professional service by an accountant, actuary, lawyer, or notary in the course of a professional practice. Consequently, these services are subject to GST/HST in the normal manner. ETA: Part VII of Sch.V

"Soft Costs"

GST/HST applies to sales and rentals of real property unless the supply is specifically exempt under Part I of Schedule V of the ETA (such as sales of used residential housing and long-term residential rents). The GST/HST affects real estate developers and builders in the same manner that it affects other businesses that make taxable supplies. To the extent property and services are purchased for use in commercial activities, input tax credits in respect of the GST/HST paid on those purchases may be claimed. For example, when a builder incurs GST/HST in respect of legal and accounting fees during the period of construction, renovation, or alteration of a building or in respect of the ownership of the related land, the tax may be recovered as an input tax credit.

Certain other soft costs incurred by builders are classified as exempt supplies under the ETA, and hence not subject to GST/HST. These would include, for example, interest, insurance, and property taxes. As discussed above, interest is exempt as a financial service. Similarly, insurance premiums are exempt as financial services. Property taxes are exempt. ETA: Part VII of Sch.V

Since sales of used residential properties are exempt from GST/HST, special rules have been incorporated into the ETA to deal with "substantial renovations" of used residential properties. These rules are intended to ensure that persons in the business of renovating homes for resale are treated in the same manner as builders of new homes. The term "substantial renovation" is defined to mean: ETA: Part VI, Sch. V

> . . . the renovation or alteration of the whole or that part of a building, . . . in which one or more residential units are located to such an extent that all or substantially all of the building or part, as the case may be, other than the foundation, external walls, interior supporting walls, floors, roof, staircases and, in the case of that part of a building . . . the common areas and other appurtenances, that existed immediately before the renovation or alteration was begun has been removed or replaced if, after completion of the renovation or alteration, the building or part, as the case maybe, is, or forms part of, a residential complex.

Since the sale of a substantially renovated home is treated as the sale of new residential property, GST/HST is charged on the sale and the builder is able to claim input tax credits on purchases of property and services. Consequently, any GST/HST paid on soft costs would be recoverable.

Where a residential property is renovated and the renovation is not considered to be substantial, the sale of the property is exempt as a sale of used residential property.

¶20,510 Refundable Goods and Services Tax/Harmonized Sales Tax (GST/HST) Credit

A refundable GST/HST credit is designed to offset all or part of the GST/HST for families and individuals with lower incomes. Application for the credit is made with the taxpayer's income tax return, but the credit is received separately in quarterly instalments. The payments based on the taxpayer's 2017 income tax return are made in July and October 2018 and in January and April 2019. Eligibility for the credit and the amount paid in each quarter reflect changes in the family the next year. For payments based on 2017 income, the amount is the sum of:

ITA: 122.5 [GST/HST credit], 122.5(3) Deemed payment on account of tax

(1) $284 for an eligible individual, other than a trust, who is, at the end of the year, resident in Canada and married, a parent, or over 18 years of age;

ITA: 122.5(1) Definitions, 122.5(2) Persons not eligible individuals, qualified relations or qualified dependants

(2) $284 for a qualified relation (as discussed below) or for a qualified dependant (as discussed below) in respect of whom the individual is entitled to deduct an amount under equivalent-to-married status;

ITA: 118(1)(b) Wholly dependent person

(3) $149 for each other qualified dependant of the individual; and

(4) where the individual has no qualified relation for the year:

(a) $149 if the individual has one or more qualified dependants for the year,

(b) if the individual has no qualified dependants for the year, the lesser of:

(i) $149, and

(ii) 2% of the excess, if any, of the individual's Division B income for the year over the base (i.e., $9,209 in 2018).

A qualified relation is a cohabiting spouse or common-law partner. However, the credit cannot be double counted (i.e., the individual or the spouse or common-law partner may make the claim but not both). A qualified dependant is also defined as, in essence, a person who is claimed as a dependant or a child of the individual who resides with the individual at the end of the year. Two credits cannot be claimed in respect of the same person as an eligible individual and as a qualified dependant.

ITA: 122.5(1) Definitions, 122.5(2) Persons not eligible individuals, qualified relations or qualified dependants, 122.6 Definitions, 118 Personal credits

The credit is reduced by 5% of combined incomes, as set out in the definition of "adjusted income" over a $36,976 threshold for 2018. The refundability feature arises from the wording in the provision, which deems the amount of the credit to have been paid as tax like the refundable child tax credit.

ITA: 122.5(1) Definitions, 122.5(3) Deemed payment on account of tax

Example Problem 20-2

Woody Carver is divorced and has custody of his two children, ages 8 and 13. Woody had net income of $40,000 for 2017.

Required

Compute the refundable goods and services tax credit, beginning in July 2018, assuming no changes in his family situation.

Solution

Credit ($284 + $284 + ($149 X 1))		$717
Add the GST/HST credit supplement for single parents		149
		$866
Deduct: Income	$ 40,000	
Threshold	(36,976)	
Excess	$ 3,024	
5% of the excess		(151)
GST/HST credit		$715

This credit will be paid in four instalments of $179 in July and October 2018 and January and April 2019

¶20,600 Obligations of the Registrant Under the *Excise Tax Act*

¶20,610 Collection and Remittance of Tax

A registrant who makes a taxable supply in Canada is required, as an agent of the Crown, to collect any tax payable by the recipient in respect of the supply.

ETA: 221(1) [Collection of tax], 222(2) Withdrawal from trust

Any GST/HST collected by a person is deemed to be held in trust for the Crown until it is remitted. Input tax credits that may be claimed by the person may be deducted from the amount held in trust when the GST/HST return for the period is filed.

¶20,620 Disclosure of Tax

Registrants are required to provide certain information regarding the GST/HST content of taxable supplies made by them. Registrants may either:

(1) indicate on the invoice or receipt issued, or on the written agreement entered into, the consideration paid or payable and the amount of GST/HST payable in respect of that supply; or

(2) indicate on the documentation that the amount paid or payable by the recipient includes the GST/HST payable in respect of that supply.

The *Disclosure of Tax (GST/HST) Regulations* (P.C. 1990-2747) prescribe a third method of fulfilling the disclosure requirements. Where a registrant includes GST/HST in the price but does not indicate on the invoice or receipt the amount of GST/HST payable, or that GST/HST is included in the price, the registrant must provide a clearly visible notice at the place of supply (the business establishment) that GST/HST is included in the price of purchases. As with the second disclosure method noted above, the purchaser is able to compute the GST/HST content in purchases of taxable supplies by multiplying the tax-included price by $^5/_{105}$ (or the applicable HST factor for HST purposes).

The ETA requires that a registrant provide, if requested by another registrant receiving a supply from that registrant, particulars of the transaction that may be necessary to substantiate an input tax credit claim. ETA: 223(2) Particulars

¶20,630 Returns and Reporting Periods

Registrants are required to file returns for each reporting period by the dates specified. The net tax for a reporting period must generally be remitted by the date on which the return is filed, as discussed in the next section. The reporting period of a registrant may be either the fiscal month, quarter, or year. If a registrant's reporting period is the fiscal month, a return must be filed for each month. If the fiscal quarter is used as the reporting period, a return must be filed for each quarter. If the fiscal year is used as the reporting period, only one return must be filed for the year, although quarterly instalments must be filed, as discussed below. Conditions for these options are discussed below. ETA: 238(1) [Filing required]

The "fiscal year" of a person is defined as either the person's taxation year, or the period elected to be the person's fiscal year. "Taxation year" is defined in the same subsection as the person's taxation year for purposes of the ITA. Where the taxation year of a person is not the calendar year, the person may elect to have fiscal years that are calendar years, effective on the first day of any calendar year. "Fiscal month" and "fiscal quarter" are determined in accordance with the ETA. ETA: 123(1) [Definitions], 238(1) [Filing required], 244(1) [Election for fiscal year], 243(1) [Determination of fiscal quarters], 243(2) Determination of fiscal months

In general, larger businesses that are registered for GST/HST purposes are required to adopt monthly reporting periods, and thus must file GST/HST returns on a monthly basis. A registrant's reporting period is automatically the fiscal month if the registrant's yearly revenues from taxable (including zero-rated) supplies exceeds $6 million. Revenue in these circumstances is determined by reference to the registrant's threshold amount for the fiscal year and the fiscal quarter. The threshold amount for a fiscal year and fiscal quarter refers to taxable (including zero-rated) supplies made during the preceding fiscal year or preceding fiscal quarters ending in the current year. Thus, monthly returns are required where revenue is greater than $6 million in the preceding fiscal year or in the previous quarters ending in the current fiscal year. ETA: 245(2) Reporting period of registrant

Quarterly and annual reporting periods are available for smaller businesses, depending on the level of sales. Quarterly reporting is required where revenue is $6 million or less in the preceding fiscal year and in the preceding quarters ending in the current fiscal year. An election for quarterly reporting is also available in certain circumstances. ETA: 245(2) Reporting period of registrant, 247(1) [Election for fiscal quarters], 248 Election for fiscal years

Annual reporting rather than quarterly is available where revenue in the preceding year does not exceed $1.5 million. If revenue from taxable supplies is more than $1.5 million during the current fiscal year, the registrant is required to report more frequently beginning with the first fiscal quarter in the next fiscal year.

The above reporting period requirements are summarized by the following.

GST/HST Returns — Reporting periods & remittances

Annual taxable sales and revenues	Reporting period	Optional reporting periods
$1,500,000 or less	Annual	Monthly, quarterly
$1,500,001 – $6,000,000	Quarterly	Monthly
$6,000,001 or more	Monthly	Nil

Returns for monthly and quarterly filers must be filed within one month following the end of the registrant's reporting period. Persons filing on an annual basis are required to file their annual return within three months following the end of their reporting period.

Any registrant can opt to file on a monthly basis if desired. For example, exporters may wish to file on a monthly basis in order to obtain GST/HST refunds on a more frequent basis (since exports are zero-rated). However, once a registrant has decided on the frequency of filing its GST/HST return, it must proceed on that basis for the entire fiscal year.

ETA: 246(1) [Election for fiscal months]

A registrant can apply to the Minister of National Revenue to have one or more reporting periods designated for the purpose of not having to file returns. Reporting periods eligible for designation are essentially those in which the total of the GST/HST collected (received) or collectible (receivable) for the period, plus any other amounts that are remittable for the period, does not exceed $1,000. Input tax credits or other allowable deductions are ignored for purposes of this calculation. If more than one period is to be designated, the $1,000 threshold is determined on a cumulative basis.

ETA: 238.1 Definitions

Returns are generally filed on a legal-entity basis. However, where a corporation has divisions with separate accounting systems, an election can be made to file on a divisional basis. In these cases, the divisions must be identifiable by virtue of their activities or locations, and separate records must be maintained.

ETA: 239(1) [Authority for separate returns]

¶20,640 Remittance of Tax

In filing a return for a period, registrants are required to calculate "the net tax" for the period and to remit that tax. Where the net tax for a reporting period is a negative amount, a refund may be claimed. Net tax is determined by adding the total amount of GST/HST that was collected (received) or became collectible (receivable) during the period plus any amount that is required to be added for that period, and then subtracting the total amount of input tax credits claimed for the period and any amount that may be deducted for the period. For example, assume $50,000 of GST/HST has been collected, $10,000 is collectible but not yet collected, and another $5,000 must be added because a bad debt that was previously written off and deducted from net tax is recovered. Further, an input tax credit of $45,000 may be claimed and $6,000 may be deducted to reflect a refund made to a purchaser of excess GST/HST that was previously collected. The net tax

ETA: 228(1) [Calculation of net tax], 228(2) Remittance, 228(3) Net tax refund, 225(1) [Net tax]

in this example is calculated as [($50,000 + $10,000 + $5,000) – ($45,000 + $6,000)] = $14,000. Where net tax is owed for a reporting period, that amount must be remitted to the Receiver General by the date on which the return is due.

In determining net tax, where an amount was previously included in calculating the amount of GST/HST that was collected or collectible for a period, it must not be included in a return for a subsequent period. Similarly, where an amount was previously claimed as an input tax credit, it may not be claimed again in a later period. These two subsections are intended to prevent double-counting.

ETA: 225(2) Restriction, 225(3) Restriction

There is a four-year time limit on claiming input tax credits. For most registrants, an input tax credit is not available unless it is claimed in a return filed within four years from the time the return in which the claim could have originally been made was required to be filed. For example, if a registrant who files GST/HST returns on a monthly basis purchased goods to be used in commercial activities on February 1, 2014, an input tax credit could have been claimed in a return filed for that period (i.e., for the month of February), which is due March 31, 2014. If the input tax credit was not claimed at that time, the registrant has until March 31, 2018 to claim the credit before entitlement to the credit would be lost.

ETA: 225(4) Limitation

Large registrants (those with more than $6 million in annual taxable supplies) that have more than 10% exempt sales, as well as listed financial institutions, face a two-year limit for carrying input tax credits. An input tax credit for a particular reporting period is not available to these registrants unless it is claimed in a return filed for a reporting period that ends within two years after the period in which the ITC could have first been claimed.

Where annual reporting has been elected, quarterly instalments of tax are required. The instalments are payable to the Receiver General within one month after the end of each fiscal quarter. The amount of each instalment is equal to one-quarter of the registrant's previous year's net tax. Where the instalment base for a reporting period is less than $3,000, the instalment base for that period is deemed to be nil.

ETA: 237 Instalments, 248 Election for fiscal years

Under the instalment base formula, a registrant is able to base instalments for the current year on an estimate of the net tax for the year, on a similar basis to income tax instalments. This is advantageous for registrants who anticipate that less tax will be payable in the current year than had been payable in the preceding year.

¶20,650 Books and Records

Registrants are required to maintain documentation to support input tax credits, as prescribed by regulation. These requirements, which are contained in the *Input Tax Credit (GST/HST) Information Regulations* (P.C. 1990-2755), are not restricted in terms of form or physical characteristics. Supporting documentation may include invoices, receipts, credit card receipts, debit notes, books or ledgers of account, written contracts or agreements, computer records, and other validly issued or signed documents.

ETA: 169(4) Required documentation

Depending on the value of the purchase, the information requirements vary. The relevant information and thresholds at which requirements change are summarized below.

(1) Purchases under $30:

- the vendor's name or trading name,
- sufficient information to identify when the GST/HST was paid or became payable, and

- the total consideration paid or payable for the supply.

(2) Purchases of $30 or more and less than $150:

- the above, plus
- the vendor's GST/HST registration number, and
- the total amount of GST/HST charged on the supply or, if prices are on a tax-included basis, a statement to this effect (however, if one document is used in respect of both taxable and exempt supplies, the tax status of each supply must be indicated).

(3) Purchases of $150 or more:

- the above, plus
- the purchaser's name or trading name,
- sufficient information to ascertain the terms of sale (e.g., cash or credit sale), and
- a description sufficient to identify the supply.

To a large extent, documents already being used to support expense deductions under the ITA may be used to support input tax credit claims. The retention period is also generally six years. Supporting documentation is not required for items such as reasonable *per diem* reimbursements, or other cases where the Minister is satisfied that sufficient records are otherwise available. ETA: 169(5) Exemption

Registrants are required to issue an appropriate document containing the requisite information if requested by a purchaser who is also a registrant. ETA: 223(2) Particulars

Similar to the requirements under the *Income Tax Act*, adequate books and records must be kept. The following persons are required to maintain records and books of account for the CRA's audit purposes:

- persons who carry on business or engage in a commercial activity in Canada;
- persons who are required to file a GST/HST return; or
- persons who make an application for a refund or rebate.

The records must be adequate to determine the amount of the person's liability under the ETA or the amount of any refund or rebate to which the person is entitled. The records must be kept in either English or French at the person's place of business in Canada, unless otherwise permitted by the Minister. As under the *Income Tax Act*, the retention period is generally six years. Chapter 15.2 of the GST/HST Memoranda Series sets out the CRA's administrative policy in respect of computerized records.

¶20,660 Powers and Obligations of the CRA in Respect of the *Excise Tax Act*

While the Department of Finance has the responsibility for tax policy, the CRA is responsible for the administration and enforcement of the ETA. The duties of the Minister of National Revenue and his or her employees are set out in section 275 of the ETA. The Commissioner, the CRA's chief executive officer, is empowered to exercise all the powers and perform all of the duties of the Minister under the ETA. On imported goods, the GST/HST is administered and enforced by the Canada Border Services Agency (CBSA).

¶20,660.10 Assessments and Reassessments

The CRA is given broad powers to assess persons for tax remittable or payable, and for interest and penalties. Reassessments and additional assessments may also be made. The CRA may also assess or reassess rebate applications. Assessments must be made within the following time limits:

ETA: 296(1) [Assessments], 297(1) [Assessment of rebate], 298 Period for assessment

(1) at any time, if the person has committed fraud or made any misrepresentation that is attributable to the person's neglect, carelessness or wilful default;

(2) within four years after the later of the day on which the return for a period was filed or the day on which it was required to be filed; or

(3) at any time if the person has filed a waiver.

The Minister of National Revenue has authority, on an *ex parte* application to the court, to obtain judicial authorization to assess and take action to recover an amount determined by the Minister to be remittable by a registrant at the time the application is heard. This gives the Minister the power to take action to recover tax before the normal due date for the registrant's remittance. Where the court is satisfied that any delay in issuing the assessment would jeopardize the collection of GST/HST and consequently grants the authorization, the CRA will be permitted to issue the assessment and take immediate collection action.

ETA: 322.1 Definitions

¶20,660.20 Refunds and Interest

If the net tax for a reporting period is a negative amount, a refund may be claimed in the return for that period. The Minister is required to pay the refund with all due dispatch. Interest on unpaid refunds begins accruing 30 days after the tax return claiming the particular refund has been filed, provided that all required returns have been filed up to that time. Interest is payable at the prescribed rate.[4] In assessing net tax, the Minister is required to apply the amount of any net tax overpayment against any GST/HST liability of the person for any other reporting period, and refund that part of the overpayment that was not so applied.

ETA: 228(3) Net tax refund, 229(1) [Payment of net tax refund], 229(2) Restriction, 229(3) Interest on refund, 296(3) Application or payment of credit

Interest at the same prescribed rate used for late or deficient remittances and instalments is paid on overpayments of net tax 30 days from the later of:

ETA: 297 Assessment of rebate

(1) the day on which the return for the period was filed; and

(2) the day on which the return was required to be filed.

Interest on rebate claims is payable, provided that a rebate application has been filed; interest accrues from the 30th or 60th day after filing, depending on the nature of the rebate.

---

[4] Subsection 229(2) provides that a net tax refund will not be paid to a person at any time until the person files all returns, of which the Minister of National Revenue has knowledge, that the person is required to file up to that time under the ETA (both GST/HST and non-GST/HST portions), the *Air Travellers Security Charge Act*, the *Excise Act, 2001*, and the *Income Tax Act*. Subsection 229(2.1) provides that a net tax refund is not required to be paid to a registrant unless the Minister is satisfied that all information relating to the identification, contact information, and business description of the registrant that was required to be given on the application for registration has been provided and is accurate.

Interest is compounded daily.[5] Any refund interest received is taxable under the ITA as interest income in the year received.

¶20,670 Rights of the Registrant

¶20,670.10 Objections and Appeals

Where a person is unable to resolve a dispute with the CRA after receiving a notice of assessment, a notice of objection may be filed within 90 days of the mailing of the notice of assessment. As noted in Chapter 14, taxpayers often file a notice of objection as protection if the 90-day period is about to expire, even if a favourable resolution appears likely.

ETA: 301(1.1) Objection to assessment

If, in response to the notice of objection, the Minister confirms the assessment or reassesses, the person may appeal to the Tax Court of Canada. The appeal must be made within 90 days after notice is sent that the Minister has confirmed the assessment or has reassessed.

ETA: 302 Appeal to Tax Court

As described in Chapter 14, a person seeking to appeal to the Tax Court of Canada may choose to have the appeal heard under the more formal general procedure or under the informal procedure. The various time limits described earlier also apply to appeals that relate to GST/HST.

A decision of the Tax Court of Canada may be appealed to the Federal Court of Appeal and from there to the Supreme Court of Canada.

It should be noted that an assessment must be paid (or arrangements made) even if the taxpayer appeals a decision. Appealing an assessment does not stop the collection process.

¶20,670.20 Amended Returns and GST/HST Adjustments

The CRA has indicated that if a change needs to be made to any return that has already been filed, another return should not be filed. The procedure to follow depends on the type of change that is required, as outlined below.

Generally, if there are unclaimed input tax credits, the unclaimed amount should be added to the next GST/HST return.

If the amount of GST/HST collected or collectible needs to be increased or a change is needed in respect of any other line in the return, the change can be made through the CRA's online service, My Business Account, or a letter can be sent to the appropriate tax centre. The letter should indicate the person's business number, the GST/HST reporting period to be amended, and the corrected amounts for each line number on the GST/HST return. If a correction is required in respect of recaptured input tax credits (in certain cases large businesses are subject to temporary restricted input tax credits), the request cannot be made online, and a letter should be sent to the appropriate tax centre.

The letter must be signed and include the name and telephone number of a person that the CRA can contact.

---

[5] The interest rates are as follows:

- on amounts payable to the Minister, 5%, and
- on amounts payable by the Minister, 1% for corporate taxpayers and 3% for non-corporate taxpayers.

[See Interest Rates (*Excise Tax Act*) Regulations, SOR/2006-230.]

The legislation outlines the procedure for refunding GST/HST to purchasers in certain circumstances. The ETA permits an adjustment, refund, or credit of the GST/HST in two situations. First, where an excess amount of GST/HST has been charged or collected, and secondly, where consideration for a supply is reduced after the GST/HST has been charged or collected and the supplier adjusts, refunds, or credits the GST/HST charged on the original consideration. Any such adjustment, refund, or credit must be made within two years after the end of the supplier's reporting period in which the tax was collected or charged, or within four years in the case of a price reduction. To document the tax adjustment, the supplier may issue a credit note or the recipient may issue a debit note.

ETA: 232 Refund or adjustment of tax

¶20,680 Simplified Method and Quick Method

Special simplified accounting methods exist to help small businesses minimize paperwork and to reduce accounting and bookkeeping costs. These simplified accounting procedures are the Quick Method and the Simplified Method. The rules for these methods are authorized in the ETA and are contained in the *Streamlined Accounting (GST/HST) Regulations* (P.C. 1990-2748).

ETA: 227(1) [Election for streamlined accounting]

The simplified method is available to small businesses with annual taxable supplies of $1 million or less and taxable purchases (excluding zero-rated purchases) of $4 million or less (based on the preceding fiscal year). These businesses are permitted to calculate their input tax credits by simply multiplying the total amount of their GST/HST-taxable purchases (including GST/HST, provincial sales taxes, and gratuities) by a factor of 5/105 (or the applicable HST factor for HST purposes). This factor also applies in the case of reimbursements for taxable expenses incurred by employees and partners.

The quick method is available to small businesses with annual taxable supplies of $400,000 or less, with some exceptions (e.g., accountants, lawyers, financial consultants). Under the quick method, the amount of GST/HST to remit is calculated as a percentage of taxable supplies for the period, including GST/HST but not provincial sales tax.

The special quick method for public service bodies is a simplified accounting option whereby GST is charged at the 5% rate (or the applicable HST rate) on taxable supplies, but in calculating the amount of GST/HST that is to be remitted, the amount of GST/HST-included supplies for the reporting period is multiplied by the remittance rate, or rates, that apply in the particular situation. Certain supplies of goods and services are not included in the special quick method calculation.

ETA: 225.1 Meaning of "specified supply"

As well, the legislation sets out a streamlined accounting method by which certain charities calculate their net tax.

¶20,700 GST/HST Rebate on Employee Deductions

Employees who are able to deduct GST/HST-paid employment expenses can obtain a refund of the GST/HST component of these expenses in a similar manner to their employers who are registrants. Although the employee refund mechanism is quite different from the input tax credit system, the effect of this refund is quite similar.

As a general rule, employees do not have GST/HST registration numbers and, hence, are not eligible for input tax credits. However, employees who have deductible expenses for income tax purposes may have paid GST/HST on some of those expenses and should be eligible for some sort of refund mechanism. Therefore, in order to refund employees of registrants, other than financial institutions, who have paid GST/HST on non-reimbursed

ETA: 253(1) [Employees and partners]

expenses, a GST/HST "rebate" system, as opposed to a GST/HST "input tax credit" system has been established. The following description is based on a provision of the ETA.

The GST/HST rebate system is based on amounts which are deductible from employment income. These deductible amounts will include the GST/HST component. In the calendar year following the year in which the deduction is made, the employee is eligible to file a rebate application in prescribed form. The employee has four years from the end of the taxation year in which the expense was claimed for income tax purposes to apply for the rebate. The amount of GST/HST rebate that is received is then required to be included in income in the year that it is received. This employment inclusion has the effect of offsetting the GST/HST component of the expense deducted in a preceding year. The reason for this effect is that a rebate received in respect of an expense that has been deducted lowers the net cost and, hence, should lower the net deduction.

The goods and services tax rebate is not considered to be a reimbursement received by the taxpayer. As a result, the employee is allowed to deduct, in the year of payment, GST/HST along with the expenses to which it attaches. In view of the required inclusion of the rebate, the rule in subsection 8(11) of the ITA is needed to allow the deduction of GST/HST which is ultimately offset by the inclusion.

ITA: 6(8) GST rebates re costs of property or service, 8(11) Goods and services tax

The employee GST/HST rebate is calculated as — for example, where the provincial HST rate is 8% and is added to the federal rate of 5% — 13/113 times the amounts deducted for income tax purposes. An employee is not entitled to a GST/HST rebate for expenses in respect of which the employee has received an allowance unless the employer certifies that it did not consider the allowance to be a reasonable allowance and therefore must be included in income. If the allowance was considered to be a reasonable allowance by the employer, it would have claimed the input tax credit under a provision of the ETA. The certification precludes recovery of the GST/HST by both the employer and the employee.

ETA: 174 Travel and other allowances

In the year in which the employee actually receives the rebate, there is an offsetting adjustment under the ITA for the GST/HST component, if any, of the deductible expenses. The Act includes in employment income the GST/HST component of the deductible employment expenses, other than capital cost allowance, for the preceding year. The GST/HST component of the capital cost allowance, which is buried in the cost of the asset, is deemed to be government assistance and, thereby, reduces the capital cost of the asset eligible for CCA.

ITA: 6(8)(d), 6(8)(c), 13(7.1) Deemed capital cost of certain property

Example Problem 20-3

Ms. Tang uses her own car in the performance of her employment duties away from her employer's place of business and is required by her employment contract to pay for her travel expenses. She is not reimbursed for any of her travel expenses, but she does receive a kilometre allowance. Her employer will certify that it did not consider the allowance to be reasonable at the time it was

Ms. Tang uses her own car in the performance of her employment duties away from her employer's place of business and is required by her employment contract to pay for her travel expenses. She is not reimbursed for any of her travel expenses, but she does receive a kilometre allowance. Her employer will certify that it did not consider the allowance to be reasonable at the time it was paid. The example is based on the assumption that her automobile was purchased in early 2017 and was subject to HST at the rate of 13%.

The following information pertains to Ms. Tang's 2017 employment income as correctly prepared by her accountant. The amount of the expenses indicated reflects all pertinent income tax restrictions (e.g., the limit on capital cost of the automobile, 50% for meals, and a proration of employment kilometres to total kilometres. The deductible expenses, where appropriate, include HST, as indicated below). The deductible expenses, where appropriate, include HST, as indicated below.

Inclusions:		
Salary[1]	$85,000	
Car allowance[1]	3,000	
Premiums paid by Treeline Ltd. for non-group disability insurance[2]	400	
Imputed interest on a car loan[2]	2,160	$ 90,560
Deductions:		
Travel expenses:		
Transportation, including HST of $390	$ 3,390	
Accommodation, including HST of $520	4,520	
Meals, including HST of $325	2,825	(10,735)
Automobile expenses:		
Operating costs, including HST of $195	$ 1,695	
Interest[2]	3,120	
Insurance and licence[2]	800	
Capital cost allowance[3]	2,000	(7,615)
Professional fees, including HST of $85[4]		(735)
Employment income		$ 71,475

Notes

(1) Salary and car allowance are not subject to GST/HST since the definition of property in the ETA excludes money. ETA: 123(1) [Definitions]

(2) Insurance, licence, and interest are exempt supplies. ETA: Schedule V

(3) Capital cost allowance is not subject to GST/HST. However, there is a GST/HST component in the capital cost allowance claimed.

(4) Membership fees in professional organizations of which an employee must be a member to maintain a professional status recognized by statute are exempt supplies. However, an election is available to these organizations under this provision to deem these fees to be taxable supplies. This election would normally be made where the majority of the members can obtain a refund under either the input tax credit system or rebate system. In addition, the professional organization will also be able to claim an input tax credit on its acquisition of taxable supplies. ETA: Schedule V, Part VI

Required

(1) Calculate the amount of GST/HST rebate which Ms. Tang is entitled to receive in 2017.

(2) Indicate the income tax consequences of the GST/HST rebate.

Solution

(1) Ms. Tang can apply for a GST/HST rebate in 2018 based on her deductible expenses in 2017. This would normally be done on the filing of her 2017 income tax return. The amount of the rebate would be calculated as: ETA: 253(1) [Employees and partners]

13/113 of the sum of:

(a) Deductible expenses, including HST	
Transportation	$ 3,390
Accommodation	4,520
Meals	2,825
Automobile operating expenses	1,695
Professional fees	735
	$13,165
(b) Capital cost allowance	2,000
	$15,165
(c) Less: any expenses for which a reasonable allowance was received	Nil
	$15,165
13/113 thereof	$1,745

(2) On the assumption that Ms. Tang receives the GST/HST rebate in 2018, she would make the following income tax adjustments in 2018:

Par. 6(8)(c) employment income inclusion

$13,165/$15,165 X $1,745 = $1,515

Par. 6(8)(d) capital cost reduction

$2,000/$15,165 X $1,745 = $230

¶20,900 Pause and Reflect — Summary of Learning Goals for this Chapter

After working through all the sections of the chapter, you should be able to:

- Explain the GST/HST implications for various goods and services;
- Explain who must be registered for GST/HST;
- Determine the tax filing requirements for various registrants;
- Explain the GST/HST implications of the three types of supplies: Taxable, zero-rated and exempt;
- Calculate the net GST/HST remittable (receivable) by a person; and
- Calculate the Employee GST/HST Rebate.

¶20,900.99 Practise What You've Learned

Refer to the following sections of the Study Guide to practise what you've learned:

Note: the GST exercises are located in various study guide chapters and are listed below

¶2,825 — Multiple Choice

- Question 6 — HST remittance

¶4,850 — Exercises

- Exercise 14 — Schedule 1 reconciliation — HST

Topical Index